HARPER COLLINS
ITALIAN
DICTIONARY

HARPER COLLINS
ITALIAN
DICTIONARY
ITALIAN·ENGLISH ENGLISH·ITALIAN

HarperResource
An Imprint of HarperCollins*Publishers*

ISBN 0-06-273752-X

The HarperCollins website address is
www.harpercollins.com

The HarperCollins UK website address is
www.fireandwater.com

Harper*Resource*   A Division of HarperCollins*Publishers*
10 East 53rd Street, New York, N.Y. 10022

first published 1990
second edition 2000

First Harper*Resource* printing: 2000

Typeset by Morton Word Processing Ltd, Scarborough
Printed in the United States of America

Harper*Resource* and colophons are trademarks of
HarperCollins*Publishers*

INDICE

CONTENTS

I marchi registrati

Note on trademarks

INTRODUZIONE

Vi ringraziamo di aver scelto il Dizionario inglese Collins e ci auguriamo che esso si riveli uno strumento utile e piacevole da usare nello studio, in vacanza e sul lavoro.

In questa introduzione troverete alcuni suggerimenti per aiutarvi a trarre il massimo beneficio dal vostro nuovo dizionario, ricco non solo per il suo ampio lemmario ma anche per il gran numero di informazioni contenute in ciascuna voce. Ciò vi consentirà di imparare a capire ed esprimervi correttamente in un inglese attuale.

All'inizio del dizionario troverete l'elenco delle abbreviazioni usate nel testo e l'illustrazione della pronuncia espressa con i simboli fonetici. In fondo troverete un utile elenco delle forme dei verbi irregolari italiani e inglesi.

COME USARE IL DIZIONARIO COLLINS

Per imparare ad usare in modo efficace il dizionario è importante comprendere la funzione delle differenziazioni tipografiche, dei simboli e delle abbreviazioni usati nel testo. Vi forniamo pertanto qui di seguito alcuni chiarimenti in merito a tali convenzioni.

I lemmi

Sono le parole in **neretto** elencate in ordine alfabetico. Il primo e l'ultimo lemma di ciascuna pagina appaiono al margine superiore.

Dove opportuno, informazioni sull'ambito d'uso o il livello di formalità di certe parole vengono fornite tra parentesi in corsivo e spesso in forma abbreviata dopo la trascrizione fonetica (es. (*COMM*), (*inf*)).

In certi casi più parole con radice comune sono raggruppate sotto lo stesso lemma. Tali parole appaiono in neretto ma in un carattere leggermente ridotto (es. **acceptance**).

Esempi d'uso del lemma sono a loro volta in neretto ma in un carattere diverso dal lemma (es. **to be cold**).

La trascrizione fonetica

La trascrizione fonetica che illustra la corretta pronuncia del lemma è in parentesi quadra e segue immediatamente il lemma (es. **knead** [ni:d]). L'elenco dei simboli fonetici è alle pagine xiii-xiv.

Le traduzioni

Le traduzioni sono in carattere tondo e se si riferiscono a diversi significati del lemma sono separate da un punto e virgola. Spesso diverse traduzioni di un lemma sono introdotte da una o più parole in corsivo in parentesi tonda: la loro funzione è di chiarire a quale significato del lemma si riferisce la traduzione. Possono essere sinonimi, indicazioni di ambito d'uso o di registro del lemma (es. **party** (*POL*) (*team*) (*celebration*), **laid back** (*inf*) etc.).

Le "parole chiave"

Un trattamento particolare è stato riservato a quelle parole che, per frequenza d'uso o complessità, necessitano una strutturazione più chiara ed esauriente (es. **da, di, avere** in italiano, **at, to, be, this** in inglese). Il simbolo ♦ e dei numeri sono usati per guidarvi attraverso le varie distinzioni grammaticali e di significato e, dove necessario, ulteriori informazioni sono fornite in corsivo tra parentesi.

Informazioni grammaticali

Le parti del discorso (noun, adjective ecc.) sono espresse da abbreviazioni convenzionali in corsivo (*n, adj* ecc) e seguono la trascrizione fonetica del lemma.

Eventuali ulteriori informazioni grammaticali, come ad esempio le forme di un verbo irregolare o il plurale irregolare di un sostantivo, precedono tra la parentesi la parte del discorso (es. **fall** (*pt* **fell**, *pp* **fallen**) *n*; **man** (*pl* **men**) *n*).

INTRODUCTION

We are delighted you have decided to buy the Collins Italian Dictionary and hope you will enjoy and benefit from using it at school, at home, on holiday or at work.

This introduction gives you a few tips on how to get the most out of your dictionary — not simply from its comprehensive wordlist but also from the information provided in each entry. This will help you to read and understand modern Italian, as well as communicate and express yourself in the language.

The Collins Italian Dictionary begins by listing the abbreviations used in the text and illustrating the sounds shown by the phonetic symbols. You will find Italian verb tables and English irregular verbs at the back.

USING YOUR COLLINS DICTIONARY

A wealth of information is presented in the dictionary, using various type-faces, sizes of type, symbols, abbreviations and brackets. The conventions and symbols used are explained in the following sections.

Headwords

The words you look up in a dictionary — "headwords" — are listed alpha-betically. They are printed in **bold type** for rapid identification. The two headwords appearing at the top of each page indicate the first and last word dealt with on the page in question.

Information about the usage or form of certain headwords is given in brackets after the phonetic spelling. This usually appears in abbreviated form and in italics (e.g. (*fam*), (*COMM*)).

Where appropriate, words related to headwords are grouped in the same entry (**illustrare, illustrazione**) in a slightly smaller bold type than the headword.

Common expressions in which the headword appears are shown in a different bold roman type (e.g. **aver freddo**).

Phonetic spellings

Where the phonetic spelling of headwords (indicating their pronuncia-tion) is given, it will appear in square brackets immediately after the head-word (e.g. **calza** ['kaltsa]). A list of these symbols is given on pages xiii-xiv.

Translations

Headword translations are given in ordinary type and, where more than one meaning or usage exists, these are separated by a semi-colon. You will often find other words in italics in brackets before the translations. These offer suggested contexts in which the headword might appear (e.g. **duro** (*pietra*) or (*lavoro*)) or provide synonyms (e.g. **duro** (*ostinato*)).

"Key" words

Special status is given to certain Italian and English words which are considered as "key" words in each language. They may, for example, occur very frequently or have several types of usage (e.g. **da, di, avere**). A combination of lozenges ♦ and numbers helps you to distinguish different parts of speech and different meanings. Further helpful information is provided in brackets and in italics.

Grammatical information

Parts of speech are given in abbreviated form in italics after the phonetic spellings of headwords (e.g. *vt, av, cong*).

Genders of Italian nouns are indicated as follows: *sm* for a masculine and *sf* for a feminine noun. Feminine and irregular plural forms of nouns are also shown (**dottore, essa; droga, ghe**).

Feminine adjective endings are given as are plural forms (**opaco, a, chi, che**).

ABBREVIAZIONI

ABBREVIATIONS

abbreviazione	abbr	abbreviation
aggettivo	adj	adjective
amministrazione	ADMIN	administration
avverbio	adv	adverb
aeronautica, viaggi aerei	AER	flying, air travel
aggettivo	ag	adjective
agricoltura	AGR	agriculture
amministrazione	AMM	administration
anatomia	ANAT	anatomy
architettura	ARCHIT	architecture
articolo determinativo	art def	definite article
articolo indeterminativo	art indef	indefinite article
attributivo	attrib	attributive
ausiliare	aus, aux	auxiliary
l'automobile	AUT	the motor car and motoring
avverbio	av	adverb
aeronautica, viaggi aerei	AVIAT	flying, air travel
biologia	BIOL	biology
botanica	BOT	botany
inglese della Gran Bretagna	BRIT	British English
consonante	c	consonant
chimica	CHIM, CHEM	chemistry
commercio, finanza, banca	COMM	commerce, finance, banking
comparativo	compar	comparative
informatica	COMPUT	computers
congiunzione	cong, conj	conjunction
edilizia	CONSTR	building
sostantivo usato come aggettivo, non può essere usato né come attributo, né dopo il sostantivo qualificato	cpd	compound element: noun used as adjective and which cannot follow the noun it qualifies
cucina	CUC, CULIN	cookery
davanti a	dav	before
articolo determinativo	def art	definite article
determinativo: articolo, aggettivo dimostrativo o indefinito etc	det	determiner: article, demonstrative etc
diminutivo	dimin	diminutive
diritto	DIR	law
economia	ECON	economics
edilizia	EDIL	building
elettricità, elettronica	ELETTR, ELEC	electricity, electronics electronics
esclamazione	escl, excl	exclamation
femminile	f	feminine
familiare (! da evitare)	fam(!)	colloquial usage (! particularly offensive)
ferrovia	FERR	railways
figurato	fig	figurative use
fisiologia	FISIOL	physiology
fotografia	FOT	photography

Italiano	Abbr.	English
verbo inglese la cui particella è inseparabile dal verbo	fus	(phrasal verb) where the particle cannot be separated from main verb
nella maggior parte dei sensi; generalmente	gen	in most or all senses; generally
geografia, geologia	GEO	geography, geology
geometria	GEOM	geometry
impersonale	impers	impersonal
articolo indeterminativo	indef art	indefinite article
familiare (!da evitare)	inf(!)	colloquial usage (!particularly offensive)
infinitivo	infin	infinitive
informatica	INFORM	computers
insegnamento, sistema scolastico e universitario	INS	schooling, schools and universities
invariabile	inv	invariable
irregolare	irreg	irregular
grammatica, linguistica	LING	grammar, linguistics
maschile	m	masculine
matematica	MAT(H)	mathematics
termine medico, medicina	MED	medical term, medicine
il tempo, meteorologia	METEOR	the weather, meteorology
maschile o femminile	m/f	either masculine or feminine depending on sex
esercito, linguaggio militare	MIL	military matters
musica	MUS	music
sostantivo	n	noun
nautica	NAUT	sailing, navigation
numerale (aggettivo, sostantivo)	num	numeral adjective or noun
	o.s.	oneself
peggiorativo	peg, pej	derogatory, pejorative
fotografia	PHOT	photography
fisiologia	PHYSIOL	physiology
plurale	pl	plural
politica	POL	politics
participio passato	pp	past participle
preposizione	prep	preposition
pronome	pron	pronoun
psicologia, psichiatria	PSIC, PSYCH	psychology, psychiatry
tempo passato	pt	past tense
qualcosa	qc	
qualcuno	qn	
religione, liturgia	REL	religions, church service
sostantivo	s	noun
	sb	somebody
insegnamento, sistema scolastico e universitario	SCOL	schooling, schools and universities
singolare	sg	singular

ABBREVIAZIONI

ABBREVIATIONS

soggetto (grammaticale)	**sog**	(grammatical) subject
	sth	something
congiuntivo	**sub**	subjunctive
soggetto (grammaticale)	**subj**	(grammatical) subject
superlativo	**superl**	superlative
termine tecnico, tecnologia	**TECN, TECH**	technical term, technology
telecomunicazioni	**TEL**	telecommunications
tipografia	**TIP**	typography, printing
televisione	**TV**	television
tipografia	**TYP**	typography, printing
inglese degli Stati Uniti	**US**	American English
vocale	**V**	vowel
verbo	**vb**	verb
verbo o gruppo verbale con funzione intransitiva	**vi**	verb or phrasal verb used intransitively
verbo riflessivo	**vr**	reflexive verb
verbo o gruppo verbale con funzione transitiva	**vt**	verb or phrasal verb used transitively
zoologia	**ZOOL**	zoology
marchio registrato	®	registered trademark
introduce un'equivalenza culturale	≈	introduces a cultural equivalent

TRASCRIZIONE FONETICA

PHONETIC TRANSCRIPTION

CONSONANTS CONSONANTI

VOWELS VOCALI

NB The pairing of some vowel sounds only indicates approximate equivalence/La messa in equivalenza di certi suoni indica solo una rassomiglianza approssimativa.

NB **p, b, t, d, k, g** are not aspirated in Italian/sono seguiti da un'aspirazione in inglese.

puppy	p	*p*adre
baby	b	*b*am*b*ino
tent	t	*t*u*tt*o
daddy	d	*d*a*d*o
cork ki*ss*	k	*c*ane *ch*e
*ch*ord		
gag guess	g	*g*ola *gh*iro
so ri*ce* ki*ss*	s	*s*ano
cou*s*in bu*zz*	z	*s*vago e*s*ame
*sh*eep *s*ugar	ʃ	*sc*ena
plea*s*ure bei*ge*	ʒ	
*ch*ur*ch*	tʃ	pe*ce* lan*ci*are
*j*udge *g*eneral	dʒ	*gi*ro *gi*oco
*f*arm ra*ff*le	f	a*f*a *f*aro
*v*ery re*v*	v	*v*ero *b*ravo
*th*in ma*th*s	θ	
*th*at o*th*er	ð	
*l*ittle bal*l*	l	*l*etto a*l*a
	ʎ	g*l*i
*r*at b*r*at	r	*r*ete a*r*co
mummy co*mb*	m	*r*a*m*o *m*adre
no ra*n*	n	*n*o fuma*n*te
	ɲ	*gn*omo
si*ng*i*ng* ba*nk*	ŋ	
*h*at re*h*eat	h	
*y*et	j	bu*i*o *pi*acere
*w*all be*w*ail	w	*u*omo g*u*aio
lo*ch*	x	

*hee*l *bea*d	iː i	v*i*no *i*dea
*hi*t p*i*ty	ɪ	
	e	st*e*lla *e*dera
s*e*t t*e*nt	ɛ	*e*poca ecc*e*tto
*a*pple b*a*t	æ a	m*a*mma
		*a*more
*a*fter c*a*r c*a*lm	ɑː	
f*u*n c*ou*sin	ʌ	
*o*ver *a*bove	ə	
*u*rn f*e*rn w*o*rk	əː	
w*a*sh p*o*t	ɔ	r*o*sa *o*cchio
b*o*rn c*o*rk	ɔː	
	o	p*o*nte *o*gnuno
	ø	f*ö*hn
f*u*ll s*oo*t	u	*u*tile z*u*cca
b*oo*n l*ew*d	uː	

DIPHTHONGS DITTONGHI

	ɪə	b*ee*r t*ie*r
	ɛə	t*ea*r f*ai*r th*e*re
	eɪ	d*a*te pl*ai*ce
		d*ay*
	aɪ	l*i*fe b*uy* cr*y*
	au	*ow*l f*ou*l n*ow*
	əu	l*ow* n*o*
	ɔɪ	b*oi*l b*oy* *oi*ly
	uə	p*oo*r t*ou*r

MISCELLANEOUS

VARIE

* per l'inglese: la "r" finale viene pronunciata se seguita da una vocale.

' precedes the stressed syllable/precede la sillaba accentata.

ITALIAN PRONUNCIATION

VOWELS

Where the vowel **e** or the vowel **o** appears in a stressed syllable it can be either open [ɛ], [ɔ] or closed [e], [o]. As the open or closed pronunciation of these vowels is subject to regional variation, the distinction is of little importance to the user of this dictionary. Phonetic transcription for headwords containing these vowels will therefore only appear where other pronunciation difficulties are present.

CONSONANTS

c before "e" or "i" is pronounced *tch*.

ch is pronounced like the "*k*" in "kit".

g before "e" or "i" is pronounced like the "*j*" in "jet".

gh is pronounced like the "*g*" in "get".

gl before "e" or "i" is normally pronounced like the "*lli*" in "million", and in a few cases only like the "*gl*" in "glove".

gn is pronounced like the "*ny*" in "canyon".

sc before "e" or "i" is pronounced *sh*.

z is pronounced like the "*ts*" in "stetson", or like the "*d's*" in "bird's-eye".

Headwords containing the above consonants and consonantal groups have been given full phonetic transcription in this dictionary.

NB All double written consonants in Italian are fully sounded: eg. the *tt* in "tutto" is pronounced as in "ha*t t*rick".

ITALIANO - INGLESE

ITALIAN - ENGLISH

A, a

A *abbr* (= *autostrada*) ≈ M (= *motorway*)

PAROLA CHIAVE
---

a (*a+il* = **al**, *a+lo* = **allo**, *a+l'* = **all'**, *a+la* = **alla**, *a+i* = **ai**, *a+gli* = **agli**, *a+le* = **alle**) *prep*
1 (*stato in luogo*) at; (: *in*) in; **essere alla stazione** to be at the station; **essere ~ casa/ ~ scuola/~ Roma** to be at home/at school/in Rome; **è ~ 10 km da qui** it's 10 km from here, it's 10 km away
2 (*moto a luogo*) to; **andare ~ casa/~ scuola** to go home/to school
3 (*tempo*) at; (*epoca, stagione*) in; **alle cinque** at five (o'clock); **~ mezzanotte/Natale** at midnight/Christmas; **al mattino** in the morning; **~ maggio/primavera** in May/spring; **~ cinquant'anni** at fifty (years of age); **~ domani!** see you tomorrow!
4 (*complemento di termine*) to; **dare qc ~ qn** to give sth to sb
5 (*mezzo, modo*) with, by; **~ piedi/cavallo** on foot/horseback; **fatto ~ mano** made by hand, handmade; **una barca ~ motore** a motorboat; **~ uno ~ uno** one by one; **all'italiana** the Italian way, in the Italian fashion
6 (*rapporto*) a, per; (: *con prezzi*) at; **prendo 500.000 lire al mese** I get 500,000 lire a o per month; **pagato ~ ore** paid by the hour; **vendere qc ~ 2500 lire il chilo** to sell sth at 2,500 lire a o per kilo

---

abbacchi'ato, a [abbak'kjato] *ag* downhearted, in low spirits
abbagli'ante [abbaʎ'ʎante] *ag* dazzling; **~i** *smpl* (AUT): **accendere gli ~i** to put one's headlights on full (BRIT) o high (US) beam
abbagli'are [abbaʎ'ʎare] *vt* to dazzle; (*illudere*) to delude; **ab'baglio** *sm* blunder; **prendere un abbaglio** to blunder, make a blunder
abbai'are *vi* to bark
abba'ino *sm* dormer window; (*soffitta*) attic room
abbando'nare *vt* to leave, abandon, desert; (*trascurare*) to neglect; (*rinunciare a*) to abandon, give up; **~rsi** *vr* to let o.s. go; **~rsi a** (*ricordi, vizio*) to give o.s. up to; **abban'dono** *sm* abandonment; neglect; (SPORT) withdrawal; (*fig*) abandon; **in abbandono** (*edificio, giardino*) neglected

abbas'sare *vt* to lower; (*radio*) to turn down; **~rsi** *vr* (*chinarsi*) to stoop; (*livello, sole*) to go down; (*fig: umiliarsi*) to demean o.s.; **~ i fari** (AUT) to dip o dim (US) one's lights
ab'basso *escl*: **~ il re!** down with the king!
abbas'tanza [abbas'tantsa] *av* (*a sufficienza*) enough; (*alquanto*) quite, rather, fairly; **non è ~ furbo** he's not shrewd enough; **un vino ~ dolce** quite a sweet wine; **averne ~ di qn/qc** to have had enough of sb/sth
ab'battere *vt* (*muro, casa*) to pull down; (*ostacolo*) to knock down; (*albero*) to fell; (: *sog: vento*) to bring down; (*bestie da macello*) to slaughter; (*cane, cavallo*) to destroy, put down; (*selvaggina, aereo*) to shoot down; (: *sog: malattia, disgrazia*) to lay low; **~rsi** *vr* (*avvilirsi*) to lose heart; **abbat'tuto, a** *ag* (*fig*) depressed
abba'zia [abbat'tsia] *sf* abbey
abbece'dario [abbetʃe'darjo] *sm* primer
abbel'lire *vt* (*ornare*) to embellish
abbeve'rare *vt* to water; **~rsi** *vr* to drink
'abbia *etc vb vedi* **avere**
abbicì [abbit'tʃi] *sm inv* alphabet; (*sillabario*) primer; (*fig*) rudiments *pl*
abbi'enti *smpl*: **gli ~** the well-to-do
abbiglia'mento [abbiʎʎa'mento] *sm* dress *no pl*; (*indumenti*) clothes *pl*; (*industria*) clothing industry
abbigli'are [abbiʎ'ʎare] *vt* to dress up
abbi'nare *vt*: **~ (a)** to combine (with)
abbindo'lare *vt* (*fig*) to cheat, trick
abbocca'mento *sm* talks *pl*, meeting
abboc'care *vi* (*pesce*) to bite; (*tubi*) to join; **~ (all'amo)** (*fig*) to swallow the bait
abboc'cato, a *ag* (*vino*) sweetish
abbona'mento *sm* subscription; (*alle ferrovie etc*) season ticket; **fare l'~** to take out a subscription (o season ticket)
abbo'narsi *vr*: **~ a un giornale** to take out a subscription to a newspaper; **~ al teatro/alle ferrovie** to take out a season ticket for the theatre/the train; **abbo'nato, a** *sm/f* subscriber; season-ticket holder
abbon'dante *ag* abundant, plentiful; (*giacca*) roomy
abbon'danza [abbon'dantsa] *sf* abundance; plenty
abbon'dare *vi* to abound, be plentiful; **~ in** *o* **di** to be full of, abound in

abbor'dabile ag (persona) approachable; (prezzo) reasonable

abbor'dare vt (nave) to board; (persona) to approach; (argomento) to tackle

abbotto'nare vt to button up, do up

abboz'zare [abbot'tsare] vt to sketch, outline; (SCULTURA) to rough-hew; ~ un sorriso to give a hint of a smile; **ab'bozzo** sm sketch, outline; (DIR) draft

abbracci'are [abbrat'tʃare] vt to embrace; (persona) to hug, embrace; (professione) to take up; (contenere) to include; ~rsi vr to hug o embrace (one another); **ab'braccio** sm hug, embrace

abbrevi'are vt to shorten; (parola) to abbreviate

abbreviazi'one [abbrevjat'tsjone] sf abbreviation

abbron'zante [abbron'dzante] ag tanning, sun cpd

abbron'zare [abbron'dzare] vt (pelle) to tan; (metalli) to bronze; ~rsi vr to tan, get a tan; **abbronza'tura** sf tan, suntan

abbrusto'lire vt (pane) to toast; (caffè) to roast

abbru'tire vt to exhaust; to degrade

abbu'ono sm (COMM) allowance, discount; (SPORT) handicap

abdi'care vi to abdicate; ~ a to give up, renounce

aberrazi'one [aberrat'tsjone] sf aberration

a'bete sm fir (tree); ~ rosso spruce

abi'etto, a ag despicable, abject

'abile ag (idoneo): ~ (a qc/a fare qc) fit (for sth/to do sth); (capace) able; (astuto) clever; (accorto) skilful; ~ al servizio militare fit for military service; **abilità** sf inv ability; cleverness; skill

abili'tato, a ag qualified; (TEL) which has an outside line; **abilitazi'one** sf qualification

a'bisso sm abyss, gulf

abi'tacolo sm (AER) cockpit; (AUT) inside; (: di camion) cab

abi'tante sm/f inhabitant

abi'tare vt to live in, dwell in ♦ vi: ~ in campagna/a Roma to live in the country/in Rome; **abi'tato, a** ag inhabited; lived in ♦ sm (anche: centro abitato) built-up area; **abitazi'one** sf residence; house

'abito sm dress no pl; (da uomo) suit; (da donna) dress; (abitudine, disposizione, REL) habit; ~i smpl (vestiti) clothes; in ~ da sera in evening dress

abitu'ale ag usual, habitual; (cliente) regular

abitu'are vt: ~ qn a to get sb used o accustomed to; ~rsi a to get used to, accustom o.s. to

abitudi'nario, a ag of fixed habits ♦ sm/f regular customer

abi'tudine sf habit; aver l'~ di fare qc to be in the habit of doing sth; d'~ usually; per ~ from o out of habit

abo'lire vt to abolish; (DIR) to repeal

abomi'nevole ag abominable

abo'rigeno [abo'ridʒeno] sm aborigine

abor'rire vt to abhor, detest

abor'tire vi (MED) to miscarry, have a miscarriage; (: deliberatamente) to have an abortion; (fig) to miscarry, fail; **a'borto** sm miscarriage; abortion

abrasi'one sf abrasion; **abra'sivo, a** ag, sm abrasive

abro'gare vt to repeal, abrogate

A'bruzzo sm: l'~, gli ~i the Abruzzi

'abside sf apse

a'bulico, a, ci, che ag lacking in will power

abu'sare vi: ~ di to abuse, misuse; (alcool) to take to excess; (approfittare, violare) to take advantage of; **a'buso** sm abuse, misuse; excessive use

a.C. av abbr (= avanti Cristo) B.C.

a'cacia, cie [a'katʃa] sf (BOT) acacia

'acca sf letter H; **non capire un'~** not to understand a thing

acca'demia sf (società) learned society; (scuola: d'arte, militare) academy; **acca'demico, a, ci, che** ag academic ♦ sm academician

acca'dere vb impers to happen, occur; **acca'duto** sm: raccontare l'accaduto to describe what has happened

accalappi'are vt to catch

accal'carsi vr: ~ (in) to crowd (into)

accal'darsi vr to grow hot

accalo'rarsi vr (fig) to get excited

accampa'mento sm camp

accam'pare vt to encamp; (fig) to put forward, advance; ~rsi vr to camp

accani'mento sm fury; (tenacia) tenacity, perseverance

acca'nirsi vr (infierire) to rage; (ostinarsi) to persist; **acca'nito, a** ag (odio, gelosia) fierce, bitter; (lavoratore) assiduous, dogged; (fumatore) inveterate

ac'canto av near, nearby; ~ a prep near, beside, close to

accanto'nare vt (problema) to shelve; (somma) to set aside

accapar'rare vt (COMM) to corner, buy up; ~rsi qc (fig: simpatia, voti) to secure sth (for o.s.)

accapigli'arsi [akkapiʎ'ʎarsi] vr to come to blows; (fig) to quarrel

accappa'toio sm bathrobe

accappo'nare vi: far ~ la pelle a qn to bring sb out in goose pimples

accarez'zare [akkaret'tsare] vt to caress,

stroke, fondle; (*fig*) to toy with
acca'sarsi *vr* to set up house; to get married
accasci'arsi [akkaʃ'ʃarsi] *vr* to collapse; (*fig*) to lose heart
accat'tone, a *sm/f* beggar
accaval'lare *vt* (*gambe*) to cross; **~rsi** *vr* (*sovrapporsi*) to overlap; (*addensarsi*) to gather
acce'care [attʃe'kare] *vt* to blind ♦ *vi* to go blind
ac'cedere [at'tʃedere] *vi*: **~ a** to enter; (*richiesta*) to grant, accede to
accele'rare [attʃele'rare] *vt* to speed up ♦ *vi* (*AUT*) to accelerate; **~ il passo** to quicken one's pace; **accele'rato** *sm* (*FERR*) slow train; **accelera'tore** *sm* (*AUT*) accelerator; **accelerazi'one** *sf* acceleration
ac'cendere [at'tʃendere] *vt* (*fuoco, sigaretta*) to light; (*luce, televisione*) to put on, switch on, turn on; (*AUT: motore*) to switch on; (*COMM: conto*) to open; (*fig: suscitare*) to inflame, stir up; **~rsi** *vr* (*luce*) to come o go on; (*legna*) to catch fire, ignite; **accen'dino** *sm*, **accendi'sigaro** *sm* (cigarette) lighter
accen'nare [attʃen'nare] *vt* (*MUS*) to pick out the notes of; to hum ♦ *vi*: **~ a** (*fig: alludere a*) to hint at; (: *far atto di*) to make as if; **~ un saluto** (*con la mano*) to make as if to wave; (*col capo*) to half nod; **accenna a piovere** it looks as if it's going to rain
ac'cenno [at'tʃenno] *sm* (*cenno*) sign; nod; (*allusione*) hint
accensi'one [attʃen'sjone] *sf* (*vedi accendere*) lighting; switching on; opening; (*AUT*) ignition
accen'tare [attʃen'tare] *vt* (*parlando*) to stress; (*scrivendo*) to accent
ac'cento [at'tʃento] *sm* accent; (*FONETICA, fig*) stress; (*inflessione*) tone of voice)
accen'trare [attʃen'trare] *vt* to centralize
accentu'are [attʃentu'are] *vt* to stress, emphasize; **~rsi** *vr* to become more noticeable
accerchi'are [attʃer'kjare] *vt* to surround, encircle
accerta'mento [attʃerta'mento] *sm* check; assessment
accer'tare [attʃer'tare] *vt* to ascertain; (*verificare*) to check; (*reddito*) to assess; **~rsi** *vr*: **~rsi (di)** to make sure (of)
ac'ceso, a [at'tʃeso] *pp di* **accendere** ♦ *ag* lit; on; open; (*colore*) bright
acces'sibile [attʃes'sibile] *ag* (*luogo*) accessible; (*persona*) approachable; (*prezzo*) reasonable
ac'cesso [at'tʃesso] *sm* (*anche INFORM*) access; (*MED*) attack, fit; (*impulso violento*) fit, outburst
acces'sorio, a [attʃes'sɔrjo] *ag* secondary, of

secondary importance; **~i** *smpl* accessories
ac'cetta [at'tʃetta] *sf* hatchet
accet'tabile [attʃet'tabile] *ag* acceptable
accet'tare [attʃet'tare] *vt* to accept; **~ di fare qc** to agree to do sth; **accettazi'one** *sf* acceptance; (*locale di servizio pubblico*) reception; **accettazione bagagli** (*AER*) check-in (desk)
ac'cetto, a [at'tʃetto] *ag*: (**ben**) **~** welcome; (*persona*) well-liked
accezi'one [attʃet'tsjone] *sf* meaning
acchiap'pare [akkjap'pare] *vt* to catch
acci'acco, chi [at'tʃakko] *sm* ailment
acciaie'ria [attʃaje'ria] *sf* steelworks *sg*
acci'aio [at'tʃajo] *sm* steel
acciden'tale [attʃiden'tale] *ag* accidental
acciden'tato, a [attʃiden'tato] *ag* (*terreno etc*) uneven
acci'dente [attʃi'dɛnte] *sm* (*caso imprevisto*) accident; (*disgrazia*) mishap; **non si capisce un ~** it's as clear as mud; **~i!** (*fam: per rabbia*) damn (it)!; (: *per meraviglia*) good heavens!
accigli'ato, a [attʃiʎ'ʎato] *ag* frowning
ac'cingersi [at'tʃindʒersi] *vr*: **~ a fare qc** to be about to do sth
acciuf'fare [attʃuf'fare] *vt* to seize, catch
acci'uga, ghe [at'tʃuga] *sf* anchovy
accla'mare *vt* (*applaudire*) to applaud; (*eleggere*) to acclaim; **acclamazi'one** *sf* applause; acclamation
acclima'tare *vt* to acclimatize; **~rsi** *vr* to become acclimatized
ac'cludere *vt* to enclose; **ac'cluso, a** *pp di* **accludere** ♦ *ag* enclosed
accocco'larsi *vr* to crouch
accogli'ente [akkoʎ'ʎɛnte] *ag* welcoming, friendly; **accogli'enza** *sf* reception; welcome
ac'cogliere [ak'koʎʎere] *vt* (*ricevere*) to receive; (*dare il benvenuto*) to welcome; (*approvare*) to agree to, accept; (*contenere*) to hold, accommodate
accol'lato, a *ag* (*vestito*) high-necked
accoltel'lare *vt* to knife, stab
ac'colto, a *pp di* **accogliere**
accoman'dita *sf* (*DIR*) limited partnership
accomia'tare *vt* to dismiss; **~rsi** *vr*: **~rsi (da)** to take one's leave (of)
accomoda'mento *sm* agreement, settlement
accomo'dante *ag* accommodating
accomo'dare *vt* (*aggiustare*) to repair, mend; (*riordinare*) to tidy; (*conciliare*) to settle; **~rsi** *vr* (*sedersi*) to sit down; **s'accomodi!** (*venga avanti*) come in!; (*si sieda*) take a seat!
accompagna'mento [akkompaɲɲa'mento] *sm* (*MUS*) accompaniment
accompa'gnare [akkompaɲ'ɲare] *vt* to

accompany, come o go with; (*MUS*) to accompany; (*unire*) to couple; ~ **la porta** to close the door gently

accompagna'tore, trice *sm/f* companion; ~ **turistico** courier

accomu'nare *vt* to pool, share; (*avvicinare*) to unite

acconcia'tura [akkontʃaˈtura] *sf* hairstyle

accondi'scendere [akkondiʃˈʃɛndere] *vi*: ~ **a** to agree o consent to; **accondi'sceso, a** *pp di* **accondiscendere**

acconsen'tire *vi*: ~ (**a**) to agree o consent (to)

acconten'tare *vt* to satisfy; ~**rsi di** to be satisfied with, content o.s. with

ac'conto *sm* part payment; **pagare una somma in** ~ to pay a sum of money as a deposit

accoppi'are *vt* to couple, pair off; (*BIOL*) to mate; ~**rsi** *vr* to pair off; to mate

acco'rato, a *ag* heartfelt

accorci'are [akkorˈtʃare] *vt* to shorten; ~**rsi** *vr* to become shorter

accor'dare *vt* to reconcile; (*colori*) to match; (*MUS*) to tune; (*DIR*) to grant; (*LING*): ~ **qc con qc** to make sth agree with sth; ~**rsi** *vr* to agree, come to an agreement; (*colori*) to match

ac'cordo *sm* agreement; (*armonia*) harmony; (*MUS*) chord; **essere d'~** to agree; **andare d'~** to get on well together; **d'~!** all right!, agreed!

ac'corgersi [akˈkɔrdʒersi] *vr*: ~ **di** to notice; (*fig*) to realize; **accorgi'mento** *sm* shrewdness *no pl*; (*espediente*) trick, device

ac'correre *vi* to run up

ac'corso, a *pp di* **accorrere**

ac'corto, a *pp di* **accorgersi** ♦ *ag* shrewd; **stare** ~ to be on one's guard

accos'tare *vt* (*avvicinare*): ~ **qc a** to bring sth near to, put sth near to; (*avvicinarsi a*) to approach; (*socchiudere*: *imposte*) to half-close; (: *porta*) to leave ajar ♦ *vi* (*NAUT*) to come alongside; ~**rsi a** to draw near, approach; (*fig*) to support

accovacci'arsi [akkovatˈtʃarsi] *vr* to crouch

accoz'zaglia [akkotˈtsaʎʎa] (*peg*) *sf* (*di idee, oggetti*) jumble, hotchpotch

accredi'tare *vt* (*notizia*) to confirm the truth of; (*COMM*) to credit; (*diplomatico*) to accredit; ~**rsi** *vr* (*fig*) to gain credit

ac'crescere [akˈkreʃʃere] *vt* to increase; ~**rsi** *vr* to increase, grow; **accresci'tivo, a** *ag, sm* (*LING*) augmentative; **accresci'uto, a** *pp di* **accrescere**

accucci'arsi [akkutˈtʃarsi] *vr* (*cane*) to lie down

accu'dire *vt* (*anche*: *vi*: ~ **a**) to attend to

accumu'lare *vt* to accumulate

accumula'tore *sm* (*ELETTR*) accumulator

accura'tezza [akkuraˈtettsa] *sf* care; accuracy

accu'rato, a *ag* (*diligente*) careful; (*preciso*) accurate

ac'cusa *sf* accusation; (*DIR*) charge; **la pubblica** ~ the prosecution

accu'sare *vt*: ~ **qn di qc** to accuse sb of sth; (*DIR*) to charge sb with sth; ~ **ricevuta di** (*COMM*) to acknowledge receipt of

accu'sato, a *sm/f* accused; defendant

accusa'tore, 'trice *sm/f* accuser ♦ *sm* (*DIR*) prosecutor

a'cerbo, a [aˈtʃɛrbo] *ag* bitter; (*frutta*) sour, unripe; (*persona*) immature

'acero [ˈatʃero] *sm* maple

a'cerrimo, a [aˈtʃɛrrimo] *ag* very fierce

a'ceto [aˈtʃeto] *sm* vinegar

ace'tone [atʃeˈtone] *sm* nail varnish remover

A.C.I. [ˈatʃi] *sigla m* = **Automobile Club d'Italia**

'acido, a [ˈatʃido] *ag* (*sapore*) acid, sour; (*CHIM*) acid ♦ *sm* (*CHIM*) acid

'acino [ˈatʃino] *sm* berry; ~ **d'uva** grape

'acne *sf* acne

'acqua *sf* water; (*pioggia*) rain; ~**e** *sfpl* (*di mare, fiume etc*) waters; **fare** ~ (*NAUT*) to leak, take in water; ~ **in bocca!** mum's the word!; ~ **corrente** running water; ~ **dolce** fresh water; ~ **minerale** mineral water; ~ **potabile** drinking water; ~ **salata** salt water; ~ **tonica** tonic water

acqua'forte (*pl* **acque'forti**) *sf* etching

a'cquaio *sm* sink

acqua'ragia [akkwaˈradʒa] *sf* turpentine

a'cquario *sm* aquarium; (*dello zodiaco*): **A~** Aquarius

acqua'santa *sf* holy water

ac'quatico, a, ci, che *ag* aquatic; (*SPORT, SCIENZA*) water *cpd*

acqua'vite *sf* brandy

acquaz'zone [akkwatˈtsone] *sm* cloudburst, heavy shower

acque'dotto *sm* aqueduct; waterworks *pl*, water system

'acqueo, a *ag*: **vapore** ~ water vapour

acque'rello *sm* watercolour

acqui'rente *sm/f* purchaser, buyer

acqui'sire *vt* to acquire

acquis'tare *vt* to purchase, buy; (*fig*) to gain; **a'cquisto** *sm* purchase; **fare acquisti** to go shopping

acqui'trino *sm* bog, marsh

acquo'lina *sf*: **far venire l'~ in bocca a qn** to make sb's mouth water

a'cquoso, a *ag* watery

'acre *ag* acrid, pungent; (*fig*) harsh, biting

a'crobata, i, e *sm/f* acrobat

acu'ire *vt* to sharpen

a'culeo *sm* (*ZOOL*) sting; (*BOT*) prickle

a'**cume** *sm* acumen, perspicacity

a'**custica** *sf* (*scienza*) acoustics *sg*; (*di una sala*) acoustics *pl*

a'**cuto, a** *ag* (*appuntito*) sharp, pointed; (*suono, voce*) shrill, piercing; (*MAT, LING, MED*) acute; (*MUS*) high-pitched; (*fig: dolore, desiderio*) intense; (: *perspicace*) acute, keen

ad (*before V*) *prep* = a

adagi'**are** [ada'dʒare] *vt* to lay *o* set down carefully; ~**rsi** *vr* to lie down, stretch out

a'**dagio** [a'dadʒo] *av* slowly ♦ *sm* (*MUS*) adagio; (*proverbio*) adage, saying

adatta'**mento** *sm* adaptation

adat'**tare** *vt* to adapt; (*sistemare*) to fit; ~**rsi** (**a**) (*ambiente, tempi*) to adapt (to); (*essere adatto*) to be suitable (for)

a'**datto, a** *ag*: ~ (**a**) suitable (for), right (for)

addebi'**tare** *vt*: ~ **qc a qn** to debit sb with sth

ad'**debito** *sm* (*COMM*) debit

adden'**sare** *vt* to thicken; ~**rsi** *vr* to thicken; (*nuvole*) to gather

adden'**tare** *vt* to bite into

adden'**trarsi** *vr*: ~ **in** to penetrate, go into

ad'**dentro** *av*: **essere molto ~ in qc** to be well-versed in sth

addestra'**mento** *sm* training

addes'**trare** *vt* to train; ~**rsi** *vr* to train; ~**rsi in qc** to practise (*BRIT*) *o* practice (*US*) sth

ad'**detto, a** *ag*: ~ **a** (*persona*) assigned to; (*oggetto*) intended for ♦ *sm* employee; (*funzionario*) attaché; ~ **commerciale/stampa** commercial/press attaché; **gli ~i ai lavori** authorized personnel; (*fig*) those in the know

addì *av* (*AMM*): ~ **3 luglio 1998** on the 3rd of July 1998 (*BRIT*), on July 3rd 1998 (*US*)

addi'**accio** [ad'djattʃo] *sm* (*MIL*) bivouac; **dormire all'~** to sleep in the open

addi'**etro** *av* (*indietro*) behind; (*nel passato, prima*) before, ago

ad'**dio** *sm, escl* goodbye, farewell

addirit'**tura** *av* (*veramente*) really, absolutely; (*perfino*) even; (*direttamente*) directly, right away

ad'**dirsi** *vr*: ~ **a** to suit, be suitable for

addi'**tare** *vt* to point out; (*fig*) to expose

addi'**tivo** *sm* additive

addizio'**nare** [addittsjo'nare] *vt* (*MAT*) to add (up); **addizi'one** *sf* addition

addob'**bare** *vt* to decorate; **ad'dobbo** *sm* decoration

addol'**cire** [addol'tʃire] *vt* (*caffè etc*) to sweeten; (*acqua, fig: carattere*) to soften; ~**rsi** *vr* (*fig*) to mellow, soften

addolo'**rare** *vt* to pain, grieve; ~**rsi** (**per**) to be distressed (by)

ad'**dome** *sm* abdomen

addomesti'**care** *vt* to tame

addormen'**tare** *vt* to put to sleep; ~**rsi** *vr* to fall asleep, go to sleep

addos'**sare** *vt* (*appoggiare*): ~ **qc a qc** to lean sth against sth; (*fig*): ~ **la colpa a qn** to lay the blame on sb; ~**rsi qc** (*responsabilità etc*) to shoulder sth

ad'**dosso** *av* on; **mettersi ~ il cappotto** to put one's coat on; ~ **a** (*sopra*) on; (*molto vicino*) right next to; **stare ~ a qn** (*fig*) to breathe down sb's neck; **dare ~ a qn** (*fig*) to attack sb

ad'**dotto, a** *pp di* **addurre**

ad'**durre** *vt* (*DIR*) to produce; (*citare*) to cite

adegu'**are** *vt*: ~ **qc a** to adjust *o* relate sth to; ~**rsi** *vr* to adapt; **adegu'ato, a** *ag* adequate; (*conveniente*) suitable; (*equo*) fair

a'**dempiere** *vt* to fulfil, carry out

adem'**pire** *vt* = **adempiere**

ade'**rente** *ag* adhesive; (*vestito*) close-fitting ♦ *sm/f* follower; **ade'renza** *sf* adhesion; **aderenze** *sfpl* connections, contacts

ade'**rire** *vi* (*stare attaccato*) to adhere, stick; ~ **a** to adhere to, stick to; (*fig: società, partito*) to join; (: *opinione*) to support; (*richiesta*) to agree to

ades'**care** *vt* to lure, entice

adesi'**one** *sf* adhesion; (*fig*) agreement, acceptance; **ade'sivo, a** *ag, sm* adhesive

a'**desso** *av* (*ora*) now; (*or ora, poco fa*) just now; (*tra poco*) any moment now

adia'**cente** [adja'tʃɛnte] *ag* adjacent

adi'**bire** *vt* (*usare*): ~ **qc a** to turn sth into

adi'**rarsi** *vr*: ~ (**con** *o* **contro qn per qc**) to get angry (with sb over sth)

a'**dire** *vt* (*DIR*): ~ **le vie legali** to take legal proceedings

'**adito** *sm*: **dare ~ a** to give rise to

adocchi'**are** [adok'kjare] *vt* (*scorgere*) to catch sight of; (*occhieggiare*) to eye

adole'**scente** [adoleʃ'ʃɛnte] *ag, sm/f* adolescent; **adole'scenza** *sf* adolescence

adope'**rare** *vt* to use; ~**rsi** *vr* to strive; ~**rsi per qn/qc** to do one's best for sb/sth

ado'**rare** *vt* to adore; (*REL*) to adore, worship

adot'**tare** *vt* to adopt; (*decisione, provvedimenti*) to pass; **adot'tivo, a** *ag* (*genitori*) adoptive; (*figlio, patria*) adopted; **adozi'one** *sf* adoption

adri'**atico, a, ci, che** *ag* Adriatic ♦ *sm*: **l'A~, il mare A~** the Adriatic, the Adriatic Sea

adu'**lare** *vt* to adulate, flatter

adulte'**rare** *vt* to adulterate

adul'**terio** *sm* adultery

a'**dulto, a** *ag* adult; (*fig*) mature ♦ *sm* adult, grown-up

adu'**nanza** [adu'nantsa] *sf* assembly, meeting

adu'**nare** *vt* to assemble, gather; ~**rsi** *vr* to assemble, gather; **adu'nata** *sf* (*MIL*) parade, muster

a'**dunco, a, chi, che** *ag* hooked

a'ereo, a ag air cpd; (radice) aerial ♦ sm aerial; (aeroplano) plane; **~ a reazione** jet (plane); **~ da caccia** fighter (plane); **~ di linea** airliner; **ae'robica** sf aerobics sg; **aerodi'namica** sf aerodynamics sg; **aerodi'namico, a, ci, che** ag aerodynamic; (affusolato) streamlined; **aero'nautica** sf (scienza) aeronautics sg; **aeronautica militare** air force; **aero'plano** sm (aero)plane (BRIT), (air)plane (US)

aero'porto sm airport

aero'sol sm inv aerosol

'afa sf sultriness

af'fabile ag affable

affaccen'dato, a [affatt∫en'dato] ag (persona) busy

affacci'arsi [affat't∫arsi] vr: **~ (a)** to appear (at)

affa'mato, a ag starving; (fig): **~ (di)** eager (for)

affan'nare vt to leave breathless; (fig) to worry; **~rsi** vr: **~rsi per qn/qc** to worry about sb/sth; **af'fanno** sm breathlessness; (fig) anxiety, worry; **affan'noso, a** ag (respiro) difficult; (fig) troubled, anxious

af'fare sm (faccenda) matter, affair; (COMM) piece of business, (business) deal; (occasione) bargain; (DIR) case; (fam: cosa) thing; **~i** smpl (COMM) business sg; **Ministro degli A~i esteri** Foreign Secretary (BRIT), Secretary of State (US); **affa'rista, i** sm profiteer, unscrupulous businessman

affasci'nante [affa∫∫i'nante] ag fascinating

affasci'nare [affa∫∫i'nare] vt to bewitch; (fig) to charm, fascinate

affati'care vt to tire; **~rsi** vr (durar fatica) to tire o.s. out

af'fatto av completely; **non ... ~** not ... at all; **niente ~** not at all

affer'mare vt (dichiarare) to maintain, affirm; **~rsi** vr to assert o.s., make one's name known; **affermazi'one** sf affirmation, assertion; (successo) achievement

affer'rare vt to seize, grasp; (fig: idea) to grasp; **~rsi** vr: **~rsi a** to cling to

affet'tare vt (tagliare a fette) to slice; (ostentare) to affect; **affet'tato, a** ag sliced; affected ♦ sm sliced cold meat

affet'tivo, a ag emotional, affective

af'fetto sm affection; **affettu'oso, a** ag affectionate

affezio'narsi [affettsjo'narsi] vr: **~ a** to grow fond of

affian'care vt to place side by side; (MIL) to flank; (fig) to support; **~ qc a qc** to place sth next to o beside sth; **~rsi a qn** to stand beside sb

affia'tato, a ag: **essere molto ~i** to get on very well

affibbi'are vt (fig: dare) to give

affi'dabile ag reliable

affida'mento sm (DIR: di bambino) custody; (fiducia): **fare ~ su qn** to rely on sb; **non dà nessun ~** he's not to be trusted

affi'dare vt: **~ qc o qn a qn** to entrust sth o sb to sb; **~rsi** vr: **~rsi a** to place one's trust in

affievo'lirsi vr to grow weak

af'figgere [af'fidd3ere] vt to stick up, post up

affi'lare vt to sharpen

affili'arsi vr: **~ a** to become affiliated to

affi'nare vt to sharpen

affinché [affin'ke] cong in order that, so that

af'fine ag similar; **affinità** sf inv affinity

affio'rare vi to emerge

affissi'one sf billposting

af'fisso, a pp di affiggere ♦ sm bill, poster; (LING) affix

affit'tare vt (dare in affitto) to let, rent (out); (prendere in affitto) to rent; **af'fitto** sm rent; (contratto) lease

af'fliggere [af'flidd3ere] vt to torment; **~rsi** vr to grieve; **af'flitto, a** pp di affliggere; **afflizi'one** sf distress, torment

afflosci'arsi [afflo∫'∫arsi] vr to go limp

afflu'ente sm tributary; **afflu'enza** sf flow; (di persone) crowd

afflu'ire vi to flow; (fig: merci, persone) to pour in; **af'flusso** sm influx

affo'gare vt, vi to drown; **~rsi** vr to drown; (deliberatamente) to drown o.s.

affol'lare vt to crowd; **~rsi** vr to crowd; **affol'lato, a** ag crowded

affon'dare vt to sink

affran'care vt to free, liberate; (AMM) to redeem; (lettera) to stamp; (: meccanicamente) to frank (BRIT), meter (US); **~rsi** vr to free o.s.; **affranca'tura** sf (di francobollo) stamping; franking (BRIT), metering (US); (tassa di spedizione) postage

af'franto, a ag (esausto) worn out; (abbattuto) overcome

af'fresco, schi sm fresco

affret'tare vt to quicken, speed up; **~rsi** vr to hurry; **~rsi a fare qc** to hurry o hasten to do sth

affron'tare vt (pericolo etc) to face; (nemico) to confront; **~rsi** vr (reciproco) to come to blows

af'fronto sm affront, insult

affumi'care vt to fill with smoke; to blacken with smoke; (alimenti) to smoke

affuso'lato, a ag tapering

a'foso, a ag sultry, close

'Africa sf: **l'~** Africa; **afri'cano, a** ag, sm/f African

afrodi'siaco, a, ci, che ag, sm aphrodisiac

a'genda [a'd3enda] sf diary

a'gente [a'd3ente] sm agent; **~ di cambio**

stockbroker; ~ **di polizia** police officer;
agen'zia sf agency; (succursale) branch;
agenzia di collocamento employment agency;
agenzia immobiliare estate agent's (office)
(BRIT), real estate office (US); **agenzia
pubblicitaria/viaggi** advertising/travel agency
agevo'lare [adʒevo'lare] vt to facilitate,
make easy
a'gevole [a'dʒevole] ag easy; (strada)
smooth
agganci'are [aggan'tʃare] vt to hook up;
(FERR) to couple
ag'geggio [ad'dʒeddʒo] sm gadget,
contraption
agget'tivo [addʒet'tivo] sm adjective
agghiacci'ante [aggjat'tʃante] ag chilling
agghin'darsi [aggin'darsi] vr to deck o.s.
out
aggior'nare [addʒor'nare] vt (opera,
manuale) to bring up-to-date; (seduta etc) to
postpone; ~**rsi** vr to bring (o keep) o.s. up-
to-date; **aggior'nato, a** ag up-to-date
aggi'rare [addʒi'rare] vt to go round; (fig:
ingannare) to trick; ~**rsi** vr to wander about;
il prezzo s'aggira sul milione the price is
around the million mark
aggiudi'care [addʒudi'kare] vt to award;
(all'asta) to knock down; ~**rsi qc** to win sth
aggi'ungere [ad'dʒundʒere] vt to add;
aggi'unta sf addition; **aggi'unto, a** pp di
aggiungere ♦ ag assistant cpd ♦ sm assistant
aggius'tare [addʒus'tare] vt (accomodare) to
mend, repair; (riassettare) to adjust; (fig: lite)
to settle; ~**rsi** vr (arrangiarsi) to make do;
(con senso reciproco) to come to an
agreement
agglome'rato sm (di rocce) conglomerate;
(di legno) chipboard; ~ **urbano** built-up area
aggrap'parsi vr: ~ **a** to cling to
aggra'vare vt (aumentare) to increase;
(appesantire: anche fig) to weigh down, make
heavy; (pena) to make worse; ~**rsi** vr to
worsen, become worse
aggrazi'ato, a [aggrat'tsjato] ag graceful
aggre'dire vt to attack, assault
aggre'gare vt: ~ **qn a qc** to admit sb to sth;
~**rsi** vr to join; ~**rsi a** to join, become a
member of
aggressi'one sf aggression; (atto) attack,
assault
aggres'sivo, a ag aggressive
aggrot'tare vt: ~ **le sopracciglia** to frown
aggrovigli'are [aggroviʎ'ʎare] vt to tangle;
~**rsi** vr (fig) to become complicated
agguan'tare vt to catch, seize
aggu'ato sm trap; (imboscata) ambush;
tendere un ~ a qn to set a trap for sb
agguer'rito, a ag fierce
agi'ato, a [a'dʒato] ag (vita) easy; (persona)

well-off, well-to-do
'agile ['adʒile] ag agile, nimble; **agilità** sf
agility, nimbleness
'agio ['adʒo] sm ease, comfort; **mettersi a
proprio ~** to make o.s. at home o comfortable
a'gire [a'dʒire] vi to act; (esercitare un'azione)
to take effect; (TECN) to work, function;
~ **contro qn** (DIR) to take action against sb
agi'tare [adʒi'tare] vt (bottiglia) to shake;
(mano, fazzoletto) to wave; (fig: turbare) to
disturb; (: incitare) to stir (up); (: dibattere)
to discuss; ~**rsi** vr (mare) to be rough;
(malato, dormitore) to toss and turn;
(bambino) to fidget; (emozionarsi) to get
upset; (POL) to agitate; **agi'tato, a** ag
rough; restless; fidgety; upset, perturbed;
agitazi'one sf agitation; (POL) unrest,
agitation; **mettere in agitazione qn** to upset o
distress sb
'agli ['aʎʎi] prep + det vedi **a**
'aglio ['aʎʎo] sm garlic
a'gnello [aɲ'ɲɛllo] sm lamb
'ago (pl **'aghi**) sm needle
ago'nia sf agony
ago'nistico, a, ci, che ag athletic; (fig)
competitive
agoniz'zare [agonid'dzare] vi to be dying
agopun'tura sf acupuncture
a'gosto sm August
a'graria sf agriculture
a'grario, a ag agrarian, agricultural; (riforma)
land cpd
a'gricolo, a ag agricultural, farm cpd;
agricol'tore sm farmer; **agricol'tura** sf
agriculture, farming
agri'foglio [agri'fɔʎʎo] sm holly
agrimen'sore sm land surveyor
agritu'rismo sm farm holidays pl
'agro, a ag sour, sharp; ~**dolce** ag
bittersweet; (salsa) sweet and sour
a'grume sm (spesso al pl: pianta) citrus;
(: frutto) citrus fruit
aguz'zare [agut'tsare] vt to sharpen; ~ **gli
orecchi** to prick up one's ears
a'guzzo, a [a'guttso] ag sharp
'ai prep + det vedi **a**
'Aia sf: **l'~** the Hague
'aia sf threshing floor
AIDS sigla f o m AIDS
ai'rone sm heron
aiu'ola sf flower bed
aiu'tante sm/f assistant ♦ sm (MIL) adjutant;
(NAUT) master-at-arms; ~ **di campo** aide-de-
camp
aiu'tare vt to help; ~ **qn (a fare)** to help sb
(to do)
ai'uto sm help, assistance, aid; (aiutante)
assistant; **venire in ~ di qn** to come to sb's
aid; ~ **chirurgo** assistant surgeon

aiz'zare [ait'tsare] *vt* to incite; ~ **i cani contro qn** to set the dogs on sb

al *prep + det vedi* **a**

'ala (*pl* **'ali**) *sf* wing; **fare** ~ to fall back, make way; ~ **destra/sinistra** (*SPORT*) right/left wing

'alacre *ag* quick, brisk

a'lano *sm* Great Dane

a'lare *ag* wing *cpd*

'alba *sf* dawn

Alba'nia *sf*: **l'~** Albania

'albatro *sm* albatross

albeggi'are [albed'dʒare] *vi, vb impers* to dawn

alberghi'ero, a [alber'gjɛro] *ag* hotel *cpd*

al'bergo, ghi *sm* hotel; ~ **della gioventù** youth hostel

'albero *sm* tree; (*NAUT*) mast; (*TECN*) shaft; ~ **genealogico** family tree; ~ **a gomiti** crankshaft; ~ **di Natale** Christmas tree; ~ **maestro** mainmast; ~ **di trasmissione** transmission shaft

albi'cocca, che *sf* apricot; **albi'cocco, chi** *sm* apricot tree

'albo *sm* (*registro*) register, roll; (*AMM*) notice board

'album *sm* album; ~ **da disegno** sketch book

al'bume *sm* albumen

'alce ['altʃe] *sm* elk

al'colico, a, ci, che *ag* alcoholic ♦ *sm* alcoholic drink

alcoliz'zato, a [alcolid'dzato] *sm/f* alcoholic

'alcool *sm* alcohol; **alco'olico** *etc* = **alcolico** *etc*

al'cuno, a (*det: dav sm:* **alcun** +*C, V,* **alcuno** +*s impura, gn, pn, ps, x, z; dav sf:* **alcuna** +*C,* **alcun'** +*V*) *det* (*nessuno*): **non ... ~** no, not any; ~**i, e** *det pl* some, a few; **non c'è ~a fretta** there's no hurry, there isn't any hurry; **senza alcun riguardo** without any consideration ♦ *pron pl:* ~**i, e** some, a few

aldilà *sm:* **l'~** the after-life

alfa'beto *sm* alphabet

alfi'ere *sm* standard-bearer; (*MIL*) ensign; (*SCACCHI*) bishop

'alga, ghe *sf* seaweed *no pl*, alga

'algebra ['aldʒebra] *sf* algebra

Alge'ria [aldʒe'ria] *sf:* **l'~** Algeria

ali'ante *sm* (*AER*) glider

'alibi *sm inv* alibi

a'lice [a'litʃe] *sf* anchovy

alie'nare *vt* (*DIR*) to alienate, transfer; (*rendere ostile*) to alienate; ~**rsi qn** to alienate sb; **alie'nato, a** *ag* alienated; transferred; (*fuor di senno*) insane ♦ *sm* lunatic, insane person; **alienazi'one** *sf* alienation; transfer; insanity

ali'eno, a *ag* (*avverso*): ~ (**da**) opposed (to), averse (to) ♦ *sm/f* alien

alimen'tare *vt* to feed; (*TECN*) to feed; to supply; (*fig*) to sustain ♦ *ag* food *cpd*; ~**i** *smpl* foodstuffs; (*anche: negozio di* ~**i**) grocer's shop; **alimentazi'one** *sf* feeding; supplying; sustaining; (*gli alimenti*) diet

ali'mento *sm* food; ~**i** *smpl* (*cibo*) food *sg*; (*DIR*) alimony

a'liquota *sf* share; (*d'imposta*) rate

alis'cafo *sm* hydrofoil

'alito *sm* breath

all. *abbr* (= *allegato*) encl.

'alla *prep + det vedi* **a**

allacci'are [allat'tʃare] *vt* (*scarpe*) to tie, lace (up); (*cintura*) to do up, fasten; (*luce, gas*) to connect; (*amicizia*) to form

alla'gare *vt* to flood; ~**rsi** *vr* to flood

allar'gare *vt* to widen; (*vestito*) to let out; (*aprire*) to open; (*fig: dilatare*) to extend

allar'mare *vt* to alarm

al'larme *sm* alarm; ~ **aereo** air-raid warning

allar'mismo *sm* scaremongering

allat'tare *vt* to feed

'alle *prep + det vedi* **a**

alle'anza [alle'antsa] *sf* alliance

alle'arsi *vr* to form an alliance; **alle'ato, a** *ag* allied ♦ *sm/f* ally

alle'gare *vt* (*accludere*) to enclose; (*DIR: citare*) to cite, adduce; (*denti*) to set on edge; **alle'gato, a** *ag* enclosed ♦ *sm* enclosure; **in allegato** enclosed

allegge'rire [alleddʒe'rire] *vt* to lighten, make lighter; (*fig: lavoro, tasse*) to reduce

alle'gria *sf* gaiety, cheerfulness

al'legro, a *ag* cheerful, merry; (*un po' brillo*) merry, tipsy; (*vivace: colore*) bright ♦ *sm* (*MUS*) allegro

allena'mento *sm* training

alle'nare *vt* to train; ~**rsi** *vr* to train; **allena'tore** *sm* (*SPORT*) trainer, coach

allen'tare *vt* to slacken; (*disciplina*) to relax; ~**rsi** *vr* to become slack; (*ingranaggio*) to work loose

aller'gia, 'gie [aller'dʒia] *sf* allergy; **al'lergico, a, ci, che** *ag* allergic

alles'tire *vt* (*cena*) to prepare; (*esercito, nave*) to equip, fit out; (*spettacolo*) to stage

allet'tare *vt* to lure, entice

alleva'mento *sm* breeding, rearing; (*luogo*) stock farm

alle'vare *vt* (*animale*) to breed, rear; (*bambino*) to bring up

allevi'are *vt* to alleviate

alli'bito, a *ag* astounded

allibra'tore *sm* bookmaker

allie'tare *vt* to cheer up, gladden

alli'evo *sm* pupil; (*apprendista*) apprentice; (*MIL*) cadet

alliga'tore *sm* alligator

alline'are *vt* (*persone, cose*) to line up; (*TIP*) to align; (*fig: economia, salari*) to adjust, align; **~rsi** *vr* to line up; (*fig: a idee*): **~rsi a** to come into line with

'allo *prep* + *det vedi* **a**

al'locco, a, chi, che *sm* tawny owl ♦ *sm/f* oaf

allocuzi'one [allokut'tsjone] *sf* address, solemn speech

al'lodola *sf* (sky)lark

alloggi'are [allod'dʒare] *vt* to accommodate ♦ *vi* to live; **al'loggio** *sm* lodging, accommodation (*BRIT*), accommodations (*US*)

allontana'mento *sm* removal; dismissal

allonta'nare *vt* to send away, send off; (*impiegato*) to dismiss; (*pericolo*) to avert, remove; (*estraniare*) to alienate; **~rsi** *vr*: **~** (*da*) to go away (from); (*estraniarsi*) to become estranged (from)

al'lora *av* (*in quel momento*) then ♦ *cong* (*in questo caso*) well then; (*dunque*) well then, so; **la gente d'~** people then *o* in those days; **da ~ in poi** from then on

allor'ché [allor'ke] *cong* (*formale*) when, as soon as

al'loro *sm* laurel

'alluce ['allutʃe] *sm* big toe

alluci'nante [allutʃi'nante] *ag* awful; (*fam*) amazing

allucinazi'one [allutʃinat'tsjone] *sf* hallucination

al'ludere *vi*: **~ a** to allude to, hint at

allu'minio *sm* aluminium (*BRIT*), aluminum (*US*)

allun'gare *vt* to lengthen; (*distendere*) to prolong, extend; (*diluire*) to water down; **~rsi** *vr* to lengthen; (*ragazzo*) to stretch, grow taller; (*sdraiarsi*) to lie down, stretch out

allusi'one *sf* hint, allusion

al'luso, a *pp di* **alludere**

alluvi'one *sf* flood

al'meno *av* at least ♦ *cong*: (**se**) **~** if only; (**se**) **~ piovesse!** if only it would rain!

a'logeno, a [a'lɔdʒeno] *ag*: **lampada ~a** halogen lamp

a'lone *sm* halo

'Alpi *sfpl*: **le ~** the Alps

alpi'nismo *sm* mountaineering, climbing; **alpi'nista, i, e** *sm/f* mountaineer, climber

al'pino, a *ag* Alpine; mountain *cpd*

al'quanto *av* rather, a little; **~, a** *det a* certain amount of, some ♦ *pron* a certain amount, some; **~i, e** *det pl, pron pl* several, quite a few

alt *escl* halt!, stop!

alta'lena *sf* (*a funi*) swing; (*in bilico, anche fig*) seesaw

al'tare *sm* altar

alte'rare *vt* to alter, change; (*cibo*) to adulterate; (*registro*) to falsify; (*persona*) to irritate; **~rsi** *vr* to alter; (*cibo*) to go bad;

(*persona*) to lose one's temper

al'terco, chi *sm* altercation, wrangle

alter'nare *vt* to alternate; **~rsi** *vr* to alternate; **alterna'tiva** *sf* alternative; **alterna'tivo, a** *ag* alternative; **alter'nato, a** *ag* alternate; (*ELETTR*) alternating; **alterna'tore** *sm* alternator

al'terno, a *ag* alternate; **a giorni ~i** on alternate days, every other day

al'tezza [al'tettsa] *sf* height; width, breadth; depth; pitch; (*GEO*) latitude; (*titolo*) highness; (*fig: nobiltà*) greatness; **essere all'~ di** to be on a level with; (*fig*) to be up to *o* equal to; **altez'zoso, a** *ag* haughty

al'ticcio, a, ci, ce [al'tittʃo] *ag* tipsy

altipi'ano *sm* = **altopiano**

alti'tudine *sf* altitude

'alto, a *ag* high; (*persona*) tall; (*tessuto*) wide, broad; (*sonno, acque*) deep; (*suono*) high(-pitched); (*GEO*) upper; (: *settentrionale*) northern ♦ *sm* top (part) ♦ *av* high; (*parlare*) aloud, loudly; **il palazzo è ~ 20 metri** the building is 20 metres high; **ad ~a voce** aloud; **a notte ~a** in the dead of night; **in ~** up, upwards; at the top; **dall'~ in o al basso** up and down; **degli ~i e bassi** (*fig*) ups and downs; **~a fedeltà** high fidelity, hi-fi; **~a finanza** high finance; **~a moda** haute couture; **~a società** high society

alto'forno *sm* blast furnace

altolo'cato, a *ag* of high rank

altopar'lante *sm* loudspeaker

altopi'ano (*pl* **altipi'ani**) *sm* plateau, upland plain

altret'tanto, a *ag, pron* as much; (*pl*) as many ♦ *av* equally; **tanti auguri! — grazie, ~** all the best! — thank you, the same to you

'altri *pron inv* (*qualcuno*) somebody; (: *in espressioni negative*) anybody; (*un'altra persona*) another (person)

altri'menti *av* otherwise

'altro, a *det* **1** (*diverso*) other, different; **questa è un'~a cosa** that's another *o* a different thing

2 (*supplementare*) other; **prendi un ~ cioccolatino** have another chocolate; **hai avuto ~e notizie?** have you had any more *o* any other news?

3 (*nel tempo*): **l'~ giorno** the other day; **l'altr'anno** last year; **l'~ ieri** the day before yesterday; **domani l'~** the day after tomorrow; **quest'~ mese** next month

4: **d'~a parte** on the other hand

♦ *pron* **1** (*persona, cosa diversa o supplementare*): **un ~, un'~a** another (one); **lo farà un ~** someone else will do it; **~i, e** others; **gli ~i** (*la gente*) others, other people; **l'uno e l'~** both (of them); **aiutarsi l'un l'~** to help one another; **da un giorno all'~** from day to day; (*nel giro di 24 ore*) from one day to the next; (*da un momento all'altro*) any day now **2** (*sostantivo: solo maschile*) something else; (: *in espressioni interrogative*) anything else; **non ho ~ da dire** I have nothing else o I don't have anything else to say; **più che ~** above all; **se non ~** at least; **tra l'~** among other things; **ci mancherebbe ~!** that's all we need!; **non faccio ~ che lavorare** I do nothing but work; **contento? — ~ che!** are you pleased? — and how!; *vedi* **senza; noialtri; voialtri; tutto**

al'tronde *av*: **d'~** on the other hand
al'trove *av* elsewhere, somewhere else
al'trui *ag inv* other people's ♦ *sm*: **l'~** other people's belongings *pl*
altru'ista, i, e *ag* altruistic
al'tura *sf* (*rialto*) height, high ground; (*alto mare*) open sea; **pesca d'~** deep-sea fishing
a'lunno, a *sm/f* pupil
alve'are *sm* hive
'alveo *sm* riverbed
al'zare [al'tsare] *vt* to raise, lift; (*issare*) to hoist; (*costruire*) to build, erect; **~rsi** *vr* to rise; (*dal letto*) to get up; (*crescere*) to grow tall (o taller); **~ le spalle** to shrug one's shoulders; **~rsi in piedi** to stand up, get to one's feet; **al'zata** *sf* lifting, raising; **un'alzata di spalle** a shrug
a'mabile *ag* lovable; (*vino*) sweet
a'maca, che *sf* hammock
amalga'mare *vt* to amalgamate
a'mante *ag*: **~ di** (*musica etc*) fond of ♦ *sm/f* lover/mistress
a'mare *vt* to love; (*amico, musica, sport*) to like
amareggi'ato, a [amared'dʒato] *ag* upset, saddened
ama'rena *sf* sour black cherry
ama'rezza [ama'rettsa] *sf* bitterness
a'maro, a *ag* bitter ♦ *sm* bitterness; (*liquore*) bitters *pl*
ambasci'ata [ambaʃ'ʃata] *sf* embassy; (*messaggio*) message; **ambascia'tore, 'trice** *sm/f* ambassador/ambassadress
ambe'due *ag inv*: **~ i ragazzi** both boys ♦ *pron inv* both
ambien'tare *vt* to acclimatize; (*romanzo, film*) to set; **~rsi** *vr* to get used to one's surroundings
ambi'ente *sm* environment; (*fig: insieme di persone*) milieu; (*stanza*) room
am'biguo, a *ag* ambiguous
am'bire *vt* (*anche: vi: ~ a*) to aspire to
'ambito *sm* sphere, field
ambizi'one [ambit'tsjone] *sf* ambition;

ambizi'oso, a *ag* ambitious
'ambo *ag inv* both ♦ (*al gioco*) double
'ambra *sf* amber; **~ grigia** ambergris
ambu'lante *ag* itinerant ♦ *sm* peddler
ambu'lanza [ambu'lantsa] *sf* ambulance
ambula'torio *sm* (*studio medico*) surgery
a'meno, a *ag* pleasant; (*strano*) funny
A'merica *sf*: **l'~** America; **l'~ latina** Latin America; **ameri'cano, a** *ag, sm/f* American
ami'anto *sm* asbestos
a'mica *sf vedi* **amico**
ami'chevole [ami'kevole] *ag* friendly
ami'cizia [ami'tʃittsja] *sf* friendship; **~e** *sfpl* (*amici*) friends
a'mico, a, ci, che *sm/f* friend; (*fidanzato*) boyfriend/girlfriend; **~ del cuore** o **intimo** bosom friend
'amido *sm* starch
ammac'care *vt* (*pentola*) to dent; (*persona*) to bruise; **~rsi** *vr* to bruise
ammaes'trare *vt* (*animale*) to train
ammai'nare *vt* to lower, haul down
amma'larsi *vr* to fall ill; **amma'lato, a** *ag* ill, sick ♦ *sm/f* sick person; (*paziente*) patient
ammali'are *vt* (*fig*) to enchant, charm
am'manco, chi *sm* deficit
amma'nettare *vt* to handcuff
ammas'sare *vt* (*ammucchiare*) to amass; (*raccogliere*) to gather together; **~rsi** *vr* to pile up; to gather; **am'masso** *sm* mass; (*mucchio*) pile, heap; (*ECON*) stockpile
ammat'tire *vi* to go mad
ammaz'zare [ammat'tsare] *vt* to kill; **~rsi** *vr* (*uccidersi*) to kill o.s.; (*rimanere ucciso*) to be killed; **~rsi di lavoro** to work o.s. to death
am'menda *sf* amends *pl*; (*DIR, SPORT*) fine
am'messo, a *pp di* **ammettere** ♦ *cong*: **~ che** supposing that
am'mettere *vt* to admit; (*riconoscere: fatto*) to acknowledge, admit; (*permettere*) to allow, accept; (*supporre*) to suppose
ammez'zato [ammed'dzato] *sm* (*anche: piano ~*) mezzanine, entresol
ammic'care *vi*: **~ (a)** to wink (at)
amminis'trare *vt* to run, manage; (*REL, DIR*) to administer; **amministra'tivo, a** *ag* administrative; **amministra'tore** *sm* administrator; (*di condominio*) flats manager; **amministratore delegato** managing director; **amministrazi'one** *sf* management; administration
ammiragli'ato [ammiraʎ'ʎato] *sm* admiralty
ammi'raglio [ammi'raʎʎo] *sm* admiral
ammi'rare *vt* to admire; **ammira'tore, 'trice** *sm/f* admirer; **ammirazi'one** *sf* admiration
ammissi'one *sf* admission
ammobili'ato, a *ag* furnished
am'modo *av* properly ♦ *ag inv* respectable,

nice

am'mollo *sm*: **lasciare in ~** to leave to soak

ammo'niaca *sf* ammonia

ammoni'mento *sm* warning; admonishment

ammo'nire *vt* (*avvertire*) to warn; (*rimproverare*) to admonish; (*DIR*) to caution

ammon'tare *vi*: **~ a** to amount to ♦ *sm* (*total*) amount

ammorbi'dente *sm* fabric conditioner

ammorbi'dire *vt* to soften

ammortiz'zare [ammortid'dzare] *vt* (*ECON*) to pay off, amortize; (: *spese d'impianto*) to write off; (*AUT, TECN*) to absorb, deaden; **ammortizza'tore** *sm* (*AUT, TECN*) shock-absorber

ammucchi'are [ammuk'kjare] *vt* to pile up, accumulate

ammuf'fire *vi* to go mouldy (*BRIT*) o moldy (*US*)

ammutina'mento *sm* mutiny

ammuto'lire *vi* to be struck dumb

amnis'tia *sf* amnesty

'amo *sm* (*PESCA*) hook; (*fig*) bait

a'modo *av* = **ammodo**

a'more *sm* love; **~i** *smpl* love affairs; **il tuo bambino è un ~** your baby's a darling; **fare l'~ o all'~** to make love; **per ~ o per forza** by hook or by crook; **amor proprio** self-esteem, pride; **amo'revole** *ag* loving, affectionate

a'morfo, a *ag* amorphous; (*fig: persona*) lifeless

amo'roso, a *ag* (*affettuoso*) loving, affectionate; (*d'amore: sguardo*) amorous; (: *poesia, relazione*) love *cpd*

ampi'ezza [am'pjettsa] *sf* width, breadth, spaciousness; (*fig: importanza*) scale, size

'ampio, a *ag* wide, broad; (*spazioso*) spacious; (*abbondante: vestito*) loose; (: *gonna*) full; (: *spiegazione*) ample, full

am'plesso *sm* intercourse

ampli'are *vt* (*ingrandire*) to enlarge; (*allargare*) to widen

amplifi'care *vt* to amplify; **amplifica'tore** *sm* (*TECN, MUS*) amplifier

am'polla *sf* (*vasetto*) cruet

ampu'tare *vt* (*MED*) to amputate

amu'leto *sm* lucky charm

anabbagli'ante [anabbaʎ'ʎante] *ag* (*AUT*) dipped (*BRIT*), dimmed (*US*); **~i** *smpl* dipped (*BRIT*) o dimmed (*US*) headlights

a'nagrafe *sf* (*registro*) register of births, marriages and deaths; (*ufficio*) registry office (*BRIT*), office of vital statistics (*US*)

anal'colico, a, ci, che *ag* non-alcoholic ♦ *sm* soft drink

analfa'beta, i, e *ag, sm/f* illiterate

anal'gesico, a, ci, che [anal'dʒeziko] *ag, sm* analgesic

a'nalisi *sf inv* analysis; (*MED*: *esame*) test; **~ grammaticale** parsing; **ana'lista, i, e** *sm/f* analyst; (*PSIC*) (psycho)analyst

analiz'zare [analid'dzare] *vt* to analyse; (*MED*) to test

analo'gia, 'gie [analo'dʒia] *sf* analogy

a'nalogo, a, ghi, ghe *ag* analogous

'ananas *sm inv* pineapple

anar'chia [anar'kia] *sf* anarchy; **a'narchico, a, ci, che** *ag* anarchic(al) ♦ *sm/f* anarchist

'ANAS *sigla f* (= *Azienda Nazionale Autonoma delle Strade*) national roads department

anato'mia *sf* anatomy; **ana'tomico, a, ci, che** *ag* anatomical; (*sedile*) contoured

'anatra *sf* duck

'anca, che *sf* (*ANAT*) hip

'anche ['anke] *cong* (*inoltre, pure*) also, too; (*perfino*) even; **vengo anch'io** I'm coming too; **~ se** even if

an'cora¹ *av* still; (*di nuovo*) again; (*di più*) some more; (*persino*): **~ più forte** even stronger; **non ~** not yet; **~ una volta** once more, once again; **~ un po'** a little more; (*di tempo*) a little longer

'ancora² *sf* anchor; **gettare/levare l'~** to cast/weigh anchor; **anco'raggio** *sm* anchorage; **anco'rare** *vt* to anchor; **ancorarsi** *vr* to anchor

anda'mento *sm* progress, movement; course; state

an'dante *ag* (*corrente*) current; (*di poco pregio*) cheap, second-rate ♦ *sm* (*MUS*) andante

an'dare *sm*: **a lungo ~** in the long run ♦ *vi* to go; (*essere adatto*): **~ a** to suit; (*piacere*): **il suo comportamento non mi va** I don't like the way he behaves; **ti va di ~ al cinema?** do you feel like going to the cinema?; **andarsene** to go away; **questa camicia va lavata** this shirt needs a wash o should be washed; **~ a cavallo** to ride; **~ in macchina/aereo** to go by car/plane; **~ a fare qc** to go and do sth; **~ a pescare/sciare** to go fishing/skiing; **~ a male** to go bad; **come va?** (*lavoro, progetto*) how are things?; **come va?** — **bene, grazie!** how are you? — fine, thanks!; **va fatto entro oggi** it's got to be done today; **ne va della nostra vita** our lives are at stake; **an'data** *sf* going; (*viaggio*) outward journey; **biglietto di sola andata** single (*BRIT*) o one-way ticket; **biglietto di andata e ritorno** return (*BRIT*) o round-trip (*US*) ticket; **anda'tura** *sf* (*modo di andare*) walk, gait; (*SPORT*) pace; (*NAUT*) tack

an'dazzo [an'dattso] (*peg*) *sm*: **prendere un brutto ~** to take a turn for the worse

andirivi'eni *sm inv* coming and going

'andito *sm* corridor, passage

an'drone *sm* entrance hall

a'neddoto *sm* anecdote

ane'lare vi: ~ a to long for, yearn for

a'nelito sm (fig): ~ di longing o yearning for

a'nello sm ring; (di catena) link

a'nemico, a, ci, che ag anaemic

a'nemone sm anemone

aneste'sia sf anaesthesia; anes'tetico, a, ci, che ag, sm anaesthetic

anfite'atro sm amphitheatre

an'fratto sm ravine

an'gelico, a, ci, che [an'dʒɛliko] ag angelic(al)

'angelo ['andʒelo] sm angel; ~ custode guardian angel

anghe'ria [ange'ria] sf vexation

an'gina [an'dʒina] sf tonsillitis; ~ pectoris angina

angli'cano, a ag Anglican

angli'cismo [angli'tʃizmo] sm anglicism

anglo'sassone ag Anglo-Saxon

ango'lare ag angular

angolazi'one [angolat'tsjone] sf (FOT etc, fig) angle

'angolo sm corner; (MAT) angle

an'goscia, sce [an'gɔʃʃa] sf deep anxiety, anguish no pl; angosci'oso, a ag (d'angoscia) anguished; (che dà angoscia) distressing, painful

angu'illa sf eel

an'guria sf watermelon

an'gustia sf (ansia) anguish, distress; (povertà) poverty, want

angusti'are vt to distress; ~rsi vr: ~rsi (per) to worry (about)

an'gusto, a ag (stretto) narrow

'anice ['anitʃe] sm (CUC) aniseed; (BOT) anise

a'nidride sf (CHIM): ~ carbonica/solforosa carbon/sulphur dioxide

'anima sf soul; (abitante) inhabitant; non c'era ~ viva there wasn't a living soul

ani'male sm, ag animal; ~ domestico pet

ani'mare vt to give life to, liven up; (incoraggiare) to encourage; ~rsi vr to become animated, come to life; ani'mato, a ag animate; (vivace) lively, animated; (: strada) busy; anima'tore, 'trice sm/f guiding spirit; (CINEMA) animator; (di festa) life and soul; animazi'one sf liveliness; (di strada) bustle; (CINEMA) animation; animazione teatrale amateur dramatics

'animo sm (mente) mind; (cuore) heart; (coraggio) courage; (disposizione) character, disposition; avere in ~ di fare qc to intend o have a mind to do sth; perdersi d'~ to lose heart

'anitra sf = anatra

anna'cquare vt to water down, dilute

annaffi'are vt to water; annaffia'toio sm watering can

an'nali smpl annals

annas'pare vi to flounder

an'nata sf year; (importo annuo) annual amount; vino d'~ vintage wine

annebbi'are vt (fig) to cloud; ~rsi vr to become foggy; (vista) to become dim

annega'mento sm drowning

anne'gare vt, vi to drown; ~rsi vr (accidentalmente) to drown; (deliberatamente) to drown o.s.

anne'rire vt to blacken ♦ vi to become black

an'nesso, a pp di annettere ♦ ag attached; (POL) annexed; ... e tutti gli ~i e connessi ... and so on and so forth

an'nettere vt (POL) to annex; (accludere) to attach

annichi'lire [anniki'lire] vt = annichilare

anni'darsi vr to nest

annien'tare vt to annihilate, destroy

anniver'sario sm anniversary

'anno sm year; ha 8 ~i he's 8 (years old)

anno'dare vt to knot, tie; (fig: rapporto) to form

annoi'are vt to bore; (seccare) to annoy; ~rsi vr to be bored; to be annoyed

an'noso, a ag (problema etc) age-old

anno'tare vt (registrare) to note, note down; (commentare) to annotate; annotazi'one sf note; annotation

annove'rare vt to number

annu'ale ag annual

annu'ario sm yearbook

annu'ire vi to nod; (acconsentire) to agree

annul'lare vt to annihilate, destroy; (contratto, francobollo) to cancel; (matrimonio) to annul; (sentenza) to quash; (risultati) to declare void

annunci'are [annun'tʃare] vt to announce; (dar segni rivelatori) to herald; annuncia'tore, 'trice sm/f (RADIO, TV) announcer; l'Annunciazi'one sf the Annunciation

an'nuncio [an'nuntʃo] sm announcement; (fig) sign; ~ pubblicitario advertisement; ~i economici classified advertisements, small ads

'annuo, a ag annual, yearly

annu'sare vt to sniff, smell; ~ tabacco to take snuff

'ano sm anus

anoma'lia sf anomaly

a'nomalo, a ag anomalous

a'nonimo, a ag anonymous ♦ sm (autore) anonymous writer (o painter etc); società ~a (COMM) joint stock company

anores'sia sf anorexia

anor'male ag abnormal ♦ sm/f subnormal person

ANSA sigla f (= Agenzia Nazionale Stampa Associata) press agency

'ansa *sf* (*manico*) handle; (*di fiume*) bend, loop

'ansia *sf* anxiety

ansietà *sf* = ansia

ansi'mare *vi* to pant

ansi'oso, a *ag* anxious

'anta *sf* (*di finestra*) shutter; (*di armadio*) door

antago'nismo *sm* antagonism

an'tartico, a, ci, che *ag* Antarctic ♦ *sm*: l'A~ the Antarctic

An'tartide *sf*: l'~ Antarctica

antece'dente [antetʃe'dɛnte] *ag* preceding, previous

ante'fatto *sm* previous events *pl*; previous history

antegu'erra *sm* pre-war period

ante'nato *sm* ancestor, forefather

an'tenna *sf* (*RADIO, TV*) aerial; (*ZOOL*) antenna, feeler; (*NAUT*) yard; ~ **parabolica** satellite dish

ante'prima *sf* preview

anteri'ore *ag* (*ruota, zampa*) front; (*fatti*) previous, preceding

antia'ereo, a *ag* anti-aircraft

antia'tomico, a, ci, che *ag* anti-nuclear; **rifugio ~** fallout shelter

antibi'otico, a, ci, che *ag, sm* antibiotic

anti'camera *sf* anteroom; **fare ~** to wait (for an audience)

antichità [antiki'ta] *sf inv* antiquity; (*oggetto*) antique

antici'pare [antitʃi'pare] *vt* (*consegna, visita*) to bring forward, anticipate; (*somma di denaro*) to pay in advance; (*notizia*) to disclose ♦ *vi* to be ahead of time; **anticipazi'one** *sf* anticipation; (*di notizia*) advance information; (*somma di denaro*) advance; **an'ticipo** *sm* anticipation; (*di denaro*) advance; **in anticipo** early, in advance

an'tico, a, chi, che *ag* (*quadro, mobili*) antique; (*dell'antichità*) ancient; **all'~a** old-fashioned

anticoncezio'nale [antikontʃettsjo'nale] *sm* contraceptive

anticonfor'mista, i, e *ag, sm/f* non-conformist

anti'corpo *sm* antibody

antidepres'sivo *sm* antidepressant

an'tidoto *sm* antidote

anti'furto *sm* anti-theft device

anti'gelo [anti'dʒɛlo] *ag inv*: (*liquido*) ~ (*per motore*) antifreeze; (*per cristalli*) de-icer

An'tille *sfpl*: le ~ the West Indies

antin'cendio [antin'tʃɛndjo] *ag inv* fire *cpd*

antio'rario [antio'rarjo] *ag*: **in senso ~** anticlockwise

anti'pasto *sm* hors d'œuvre

antipa'tia *sf* antipathy, dislike; **anti'patico, a, ci, che** *ag* unpleasant, disagreeable

antiquari'ato *sm* antique trade; **un oggetto d'~** an antique

anti'quario *sm* antique dealer

anti'quato, a *ag* antiquated, old-fashioned

antise'mita, i, e *ag* anti-Semitic

anti'settico, a, ci, che *ag, sm* antiseptic

antista'minico, a, ci, che *ag, sm* antihistamine

antolo'gia, 'gie [antolo'dʒia] *sf* anthology

anu'lare *ag* ring *cpd* ♦ *sm* third finger

'anzi ['antsi] *av* (*invece*) on the contrary; (*o meglio*) or rather, or better still

anzianità [antsjani'ta] *sf* old age; (*AMM*) seniority

anzi'ano, a [an'tsjano] *ag* old; (*AMM*) senior ♦ *sm/f* old person; senior member

anziché [antsi'ke] *cong* rather than

anzi'tutto [antsi'tutto] *av* first of all

apa'tia *sf* apathy, indifference

a'patico, a, ci, che *ag* apathetic

'ape *sf* bee

aperi'tivo *sm* apéritif

a'perto, a *pp di* aprire ♦ *ag* open; **all'~** in the open (air)

aper'tura *sf* opening; (*ampiezza*) width; (*FOT*) aperture; ~ **alare** wing span

'apice ['apitʃe] *sm* apex; (*fig*) height

ap'nea *sf*: **immergersi in ~** to dive without breathing apparatus

a'postolo *sm* apostle

a'postrofo *sm* apostrophe

appa'gare *vt* to satisfy

ap'palto *sm* (*COMM*) contract; **dare/prendere in ~ un lavoro** to let out/undertake a job on contract

appan'nare *vt* (*vetro*) to mist; (*vista*) to dim; **~rsi** *vr* to mist over; to grow dim

appa'rato *sm* equipment, machinery; (*ANAT*) apparatus; ~ **scenico** (*TEATRO*) props *pl*

apparecchi'are [apparek'kjare] *vt* to prepare; (*tavola*) to set ♦ *vi* to set the table; **apparecchia'tura** *sf* equipment; (*macchina*) machine, device

appa'recchio [appa'rekkjo] *sm* piece of apparatus, device; (*aeroplano*) aircraft *inv*; ~ **televisivo/telefonico** television set/telephone

appa'rente *ag* apparent; **appa'renza** *sf* appearance; **in** o **all'apparenza** apparently

appa'rire *vi* to appear; (*sembrare*) to seem, appear; **appari'scente** *ag* (*colore*) garish, gaudy; (*bellezza*) striking

ap'parso, a *pp di* apparire

apparta'mento *sm* flat (*BRIT*), apartment (*US*)

appar'tarsi *vr* to withdraw; **appar'tato, a** *ag* (*luogo*) secluded

apparte'nere *vi*: ~ **a** to belong to

appassio'nare *vt* to thrill; (*commuovere*) to move; **~rsi a qc** to take a great interest in sth;

appassio'nato, a *ag* passionate; (*entusiasta*): **appassionato (di)** keen (on)

appas'sire *vi* to wither

appel'larsi *vr* (*ricorrere*): **~ a** to appeal to; (*DIR*): **~ contro** to appeal against; **ap'pello** *sm* roll-call; (*implorazione*, *DIR*) appeal; **fare appello a** to appeal to

ap'pena *av* (*a stento*) hardly, scarcely; (*solamente*, *da poco*) just ♦ *cong* as soon as; **(non) ~ furono arrivati ...** as soon as they had arrived ...; **~ ... che** *o* **quando** no sooner ... than

ap'pendere *vt* to hang (up)

appen'dice [appen'ditʃe] *sf* appendix; **romanzo d'~** popular serial

appendi'cite [appendi'tʃite] *sf* appendicitis

Appen'nini *smpl*: **gli ~** the Apennines

appesan'tire *vt* to make heavy; **~rsi** *vr* to grow stout

ap'peso, a *pp di* **appendere**

appe'tito *sm* appetite; **appeti'toso, a** *ag* appetizing; (*fig*) attractive, desirable

appia'nare *vt* to level; (*fig*) to smooth away, iron out

appiat'tire *vt* to flatten; **~rsi** *vr* to become flatter; (*farsi piatto*) to flatten o.s.; **~rsi al suolo** to lie flat on the ground

appic'care *vt*: **~ il fuoco a** to set fire to, set on fire

appicci'care [appittʃi'kare] *vt* to stick; **~rsi** *vr* to stick; (*fig*: *persona*) to cling

appi'eno *av* fully

appigli'arsi [appiλ'λarsi] *vr*: **~ a** (*afferrarsi*) to take hold of; (*fig*) to cling to; **ap'piglio** *sm* hold; (*fig*) pretext

appiso'larsi *vr* to doze off

applau'dire *vt*, *vi* to applaud; **ap'plauso** *sm* applause

appli'care *vt* to apply; (*regolamento*) to enforce; **~rsi** *vr* to apply o.s.; **applicazi'one** *sf* application; enforcement

appoggi'are [appod'dʒare] *vt* (*mettere contro*): **~ qc a qc** to lean o rest sth against sth; (*fig*: *sostenere*) to support; **~rsi** *vr*: **~rsi a** to lean against; (*fig*) to rely upon; **ap'poggio** *sm* support

appollai'arsi *vr* (*anche fig*) to perch

ap'porre *vt* to affix

appor'tare *vt* to bring

apposita'mente *av* specially; (*apposta*) on purpose

ap'posito, a *ag* appropriate

ap'posta *av* on purpose, deliberately

appos'tarsi *vr* to lie in wait

ap'prendere *vt* (*imparare*) to learn

appren'dista, i, e *sm/f* apprentice

apprensi'one *sf* apprehension; **appren'sivo, a** *ag* apprehensive

ap'presso *av* (*accanto*, *vicino*) close by, near;

(*dietro*) behind; (*dopo*, *più tardi*) after, later ♦ *ag inv* (*dopo*): **il giorno ~** the next day; **~ a** (*vicino a*) near, close to

appres'tare *vt* to prepare, get ready; **~rsi** *vr*: **~rsi a fare qc** to prepare *o* get ready to do sth

ap'pretto *sm* starch

apprezza'mento [apprettsa'mento] *sm* appreciation; (*giudizio*) opinion

apprez'zare [appret'tsare] *vt* to appreciate

ap'proccio [ap'prɔttʃo] *sm* approach

appro'dare *vi* (*NAUT*) to land; (*fig*): **non ~ a nulla** to come to nothing; **ap'prodo** *sm* landing; (*luogo*) landing-place

approfit'tare *vi*: **~ di** to make the most of; (*peg*) to take advantage of

approfon'dire *vt* to deepen; (*fig*) to study in depth

appropri'ato, a *ag* appropriate

approssi'marsi *vr*: **~ a** to approach

approssima'tivo, a *ag* approximate, rough; (*impreciso*) inexact, imprecise

appro'vare *vt* (*condotta*, *azione*) to approve of; (*candidato*) to pass; (*progetto di legge*) to approve; **approvazi'one** *sf* approval

approvvigio'nare [approvvidʒo'nare] *vt* to supply

appunta'mento *sm* appointment; (*amoroso*) date; **darsi ~** to arrange to meet (one another)

appun'tato *sm* (*CARABINIERI*) corporal

ap'punto *sm* note; (*rimprovero*) reproach ♦ *av* (*proprio*) exactly, just; **per l'~!, ~!** exactly!

appu'rare *vt* to check, verify

apribot'tiglie [apribot'tiλλe] *sm inv* bottle opener

a'prile *sm* April

a'prire *vt* to open; (*via*, *cadavere*) to open up; (*gas*, *luce*, *acqua*) to turn on ♦ *vi* to open; **~rsi** *vr* to open; **~rsi a qn** to confide in sb, open one's heart to sb

apris'catole *sm inv* tin (*BRIT*) *o* can opener

a'quario *sm* = **acquario**

'aquila *sf* (*ZOOL*) eagle; (*fig*) genius

aqui'lone *sm* (*giocattolo*) kite; (*vento*) North wind

A'rabia Sau'dita *sf*: **l'~** Saudi Arabia

'arabo, a *ag*, *sm/f* Arab ♦ *sm* (*LING*) Arabic

a'rachide [a'rakide] *sf* peanut

ara'gosta *sf* crayfish; lobster

a'rancia, ce [a'rantʃa] *sf* orange; **aranci'ata** *sf* orangeade; **a'rancio** *sm* (*BOT*) orange tree; (*colore*) orange ♦ *ag inv* (*colore*) orange; **aranci'one** *ag inv*: **(color) arancione** bright orange

a'rare *vt* to plough (*BRIT*), plow (*US*)

a'ratro *sm* plough (*BRIT*), plow (*US*)

a'razzo [a'rattso] *sm* tapestry

arbi'trare *vt* (*SPORT*) to referee; to umpire;

(DIR) to arbitrate

arbi'trario, a ag arbitrary

ar'bitrio sm will; (abuso, sopruso) arbitrary act

'arbitro sm arbiter, judge; (DIR) arbitrator; (SPORT) referee; (: TENNIS, CRICKET) umpire

ar'busto sm shrub

'arca, che sf (sarcofago) sarcophagus; **l'~ di Noè** Noah's Ark

ar'cangelo [ar'kandʒelo] sm archangel

ar'cata sf (ARCHIT, ANAT) arch; (ordine di archi) arcade

archeolo'gia [arkeolo'dʒia] sf arch(a)eology; **arche'ologo, a, gi, ghe** sm/f arch(a)eologist

ar'chetto [ar'ketto] sm (MUS) bow

architet'tare [arkitet'tare] vt (fig: ideare) to devise; (: macchinare) to plan, concoct

archi'tetto [arki'tetto] sm architect; **architet'tura** sf architecture

ar'chivio [ar'kivjo] sm archives pl; (INFORM) file

arci'ere [ar'tʃere] sm archer

arci'cigno, a [ar'tʃiɲɲo] ag grim, severe

arci'vescovo [artʃi'veskovo] sm archbishop

'arco sm (arma, MUS) bow; (ARCHIT) arch; (MAT) arc

arcoba'leno sm rainbow

arcu'ato, a ag curved, bent

ar'dente ag burning; (fig) burning, ardent

'ardere vt, vi to burn

ar'desia sf slate

ar'dire vi to dare ♦ sm daring; **ar'dito, a** ag brave, daring, bold; (sfacciato) bold

ar'dore sm burning heat; (fig) ardour, fervour

'arduo, a ag arduous, difficult

'area sf area; (EDIL) land, ground

a'rena sf arena; (per corride) bullring; (sabbia) sand

are'narsi vr to run aground

areo'plano sm = **aeroplano**

'argano sm winch

argente'ria [ardʒente'ria] sf silverware, silver

Argen'tina [ardʒen'tina] sf: **l'~** Argentina; **argen'tino, a** ag, sm/f Argentinian

ar'gento [ar'dʒento] sm silver; **~ vivo** quicksilver

ar'gilla [ar'dʒilla] sf clay

'argine ['ardʒine] sm embankment, bank; (diga) dyke, dike

argo'mento sm argument; (motivo) motive; (materia, tema) subject

argu'ire vt to deduce

ar'guto, a ag sharp, quick-witted; **ar'guzia** sf wit; (battuta) witty remark

'aria sf air; (espressione, aspetto) air, look; (MUS: melodia) tune; (: di opera) aria; **mandare all'~ qc** to ruin o upset sth; **all'~ aperta** in the open (air)

'arido, a ag arid

arieggi'are [arjed'dʒare] vt (cambiare aria) to air; (imitare) to imitate

ari'ete sm ram; (MIL) battering ram; (dello zodiaco): **A~** Aries

a'ringa, ghe sf herring inv

'arista sf (CUC) chine of pork

aristo'cratico, a, ci, che ag aristocratic

arit'metica sf arithmetic

arlec'chino [arlek'kino] sm harlequin

'arma, i sf weapon, arm; (parte dell'esercito) arm; **chiamare alle ~i** to call up (BRIT), draft (US); **sotto le ~i** in the army (o forces); **alle ~i!** to arms!; **~ da fuoco** firearm

ar'madio sm cupboard; (per abiti) wardrobe; **~ a muro** built-in cupboard

armamen'tario sm equipment

arma'mento sm (MIL) armament; (: materiale) arms pl, weapons pl; (NAUT) fitting out; manning

ar'mare vt to arm; (arma da fuoco) to cock; (NAUT: nave) to rig, fit out; to man; (EDIL: volta, galleria) to prop up, shore up; **~rsi** vr to arm o.s.; (MIL) to take up arms; **ar'mata** sf (MIL) army; (NAUT) fleet; **arma'tore** sm shipowner; **arma'tura** sf (struttura di sostegno) framework; (impalcatura) scaffolding; (STORIA) armour no pl, suit of armour

armeggi'are [armed'dʒare] vi: **~ (intorno a qc)** to mess about (with sth)

armis'tizio [armis'tittsjo] sm armistice

armo'nia sf harmony; **ar'monica, che** sf (MUS) harmonica; **~ a bocca** mouth organ; **ar'monico, a, ci, che** ag harmonic; (fig) harmonious; **armoni'oso, a** ag harmonious

armoniz'zare [armonid'dzare] vt to harmonize; (colori, abiti) to match ♦ vi to be in harmony; to match

ar'nese sm tool, implement; (oggetto indeterminato) thing, contraption; **male in ~** (malvestito) badly dressed; (di salute malferma) in poor health; (di condizioni economiche) down-at-heel

'arnia sf hive

a'roma, i sm aroma; fragrance; **~i** smpl (CUC) herbs and spices; **aromatera'pia** sf aromatherapy; **aro'matico, a, ci, che** ag aromatic; (cibo) spicy

'arpa sf (MUS) harp

ar'peggio [ar'peddʒo] sm (MUS) arpeggio

ar'pia sf (anche fig) harpy

arpi'one sm (gancio) hook; (cardine) hinge; (PESCA) harpoon

arrabat'tarsi vr to do all one can, strive

arrabbi'are vi (cane) to be affected with rabies; **~rsi** vr (essere preso dall'ira) to get angry, fly into a rage; **arrabbi'ato, a** ag rabid, with rabies; furious, angry

arraf'fare vt to snatch, seize; (*sottrarre*) to pinch

arrampi'carsi vr to climb (up)

arran'care vi to limp, hobble

arran'giare [arran'dʒare] vt to arrange; **~rsi** vr to manage, do the best one can

arre'care vt to bring; (*causare*) to cause

arreda'mento sm (*studio*) interior design; (*mobili etc*) furnishings pl

arre'dare vt to furnish; **arreda'tore, 'trice** sm/f interior designer; **ar'redo** sm fittings pl, furnishings pl

ar'rendersi vr to surrender

arres'tare vt (*fermare*) to stop, halt; (*catturare*) to arrest; **~rsi** vr (*fermarsi*) to stop; **ar'resto** sm (*cessazione*) stopping; (*fermata*) stop; (*cattura*, MED) arrest; **subire un arresto** to come to a stop o standstill; **mettere agli arresti** to place under arrest; **arresti domiciliari** house arrest sg

arre'trare vt, vi to withdraw; **arre'trato, a** ag (*lavoro*) behind schedule; (*paese, bambino*) backward; (*numero di giornale*) back cpd; **arretrati** smpl arrears

arric'chire [arrik'kire] vt to enrich; **~rsi** vr to become rich

arricci'are [arrit'tʃare] vt to curl

ar'ringa, ghe sf harangue; (*DIR*) address by counsel

arrischi'are [arris'kjare] vt to risk; **~rsi** vr to venture, dare; **arrischi'ato, a** ag risky; (*temerario*) reckless, rash

arri'vare vi to arrive; (*accadere*) to happen, occur; **~ a** (*livello, grado etc*) to reach; **lui arriva a Roma alle 7** he gets to o arrives at Rome at 7; **non ci arrivo** I can't reach it; (*fig: non capisco*) I can't understand it

arrive'derci [arrive'dertʃi] escl goodbye!

arrive'derla escl (*forma di cortesia*) goodbye!

arri'vista, i, e sm/f go-getter

ar'rivo sm arrival; (*SPORT*) finish, finishing line

arro'gante ag arrogant

arro'lare vb = **arruolare**

arros'sire vi (*per vergogna, timidezza*) to blush, flush; (*per gioia, rabbia*) to flush

arros'tire vt to roast; (*pane*) to toast; (*ai ferri*) to grill

ar'rosto sm, ag inv roast

arro'tare vt to sharpen; (*investire con un veicolo*) to run over

arroto'lare vt to roll up

arroton'dare vt (*forma, oggetto*) to round; (*stipendio*) to add to; (*somma*) to round off

arrovel'larsi vr to rack one's brains

arruf'fare vt to ruffle; (*fili*) to tangle; (*fig: questione*) to confuse

arrugi'nire [arruddʒi'nire] vt to rust; **~rsi** vr to rust; (*fig*) to become rusty

arruo'lare vt (*MIL*) to enlist; **~rsi** vr to enlist, join up

arse'nale sm (*MIL*) arsenal; (*cantiere navale*) dockyard

'arso, a pp di **ardere ♦** ag (*bruciato*) burnt; (*arido*) dry; **ar'sura** sf (*calore opprimente*) burning heat; (*siccità*) drought

'arte sf art; (*abilità*) skill

arte'fatto, a ag (*cibo*) adulterated; (*fig: modi*) artificial

ar'tefice [ar'tefitʃe] sm/f craftsman/woman; (*autore*) author

ar'teria sf artery

'artico, a, ci, che ag Arctic

artico'lare ag (*ANAT*) of the joints, articular **♦** vt to articulate; (*suddividere*) to divide, split up; **articolazi'one** sf articulation; (*ANAT, TECN*) joint

ar'ticolo sm article; **~ di fondo** (*STAMPA*) leader, leading article

'Artide sm: **l'~** the Arctic

artifici'ale [artifi'tʃale] ag artificial

arti'ficio [arti'fitʃo] sm (*espediente*) trick, artifice; (*ricerca di effetto*) artificiality

artigia'nato [artidʒa'nato] sm craftsmanship; craftsmen pl

artigi'ano, a [arti'dʒano] sm/f craftsman/woman

artiglie'ria [artiʎʎe'ria] sf artillery

ar'tiglio [ar'tiʎʎo] sm claw; (*di rapaci*) talon

ar'tista, i, e sm/f artist; **ar'tistico, a, ci, che** ag artistic

'arto sm (*ANAT*) limb

ar'trite sf (*MED*) arthritis

ar'trosi sf osteoarthritis

ar'zillo, a [ar'dzillo] ag lively, sprightly

a'scella [aʃ'ʃella] sf (*ANAT*) armpit

ascen'dente [aʃʃen'dente] sm ancestor; (*fig*) ascendancy; (*ASTR*) ascendant

ascensi'one [aʃʃen'sjone] sf (*ALPINISMO*) ascent; (*REL*): **l'A~** the Ascension

ascen'sore [aʃʃen'sore] sm lift

a'scesa [aʃ'ʃesa] sf ascent; (*al trono*) accession

a'scesso [aʃ'ʃesso] sm (*MED*) abscess

'ascia ['aʃʃa] (*pl* **asce**) sf axe

asciugaca'pelli [aʃʃugaka'pelli] sm hair-drier

asciuga'mano [aʃʃuga'mano] sm towel

asciu'gare [aʃʃu'gare] vt to dry; **~rsi** vr to dry o.s.; (*diventare asciutto*) to dry

asci'utto, a [aʃ'ʃutto] ag dry; (*fig: magro*) lean; (: *burbero*) curt; **restare a bocca ~a** (*fig*) to be disappointed

ascol'tare vt to listen to; **ascolta'tore, 'trice** sm/f listener; **as'colto** sm: **essere o stare in ascolto** to be listening; **dare o prestare ascolto (a)** to pay attention (to)

as'falto sm asphalt

asfissi'are vt to suffocate

'Asia sf: **l'~** Asia; **asi'atico, a, ci, che** ag, sm/f Asiatic, Asian a'silo *sm* refuge, sanctuary; ~ (d'infanzia) nursery(-school); ~ nido crèche; ~ politico political asylum

'asino *sm* donkey, ass

'asma *sf* asthma

'asola *sf* buttonhole

as'parago, gi *sm* asparagus *no pl*

aspet'tare *vt* to wait for; *(anche* COMM*)* to await; *(aspettarsi)* to expect ♦ *vi* to wait; ~rsi *vr* to expect; ~ un bambino to be expecting (a baby); questo non me l'aspettavo I wasn't expecting this; aspetta'tiva *sf* wait; expectation; inferiore all'aspettativa worse than expected; essere in aspettativa *(AMM)* to be on leave of absence

as'petto *sm (apparenza)* aspect, appearance, look; *(punto di vista)* point of view; di bell'~ good-looking

aspi'rante *ag (attore etc)* aspiring ♦ *sm/f* candidate, applicant

aspira'polvere *sm inv* vacuum cleaner

aspi'rare *vt (respirare)* to breathe in, inhale; *(sog: apparecchi)* to suck (up) ♦ *vi*: ~ a to aspire to; aspira'tore *sm* extractor fan

aspi'rina *sf* aspirin

aspor'tare *vt (anche* MED*)* to remove, take away

'aspro, a *ag (sapore)* sour, tart; *(odore)* acrid, pungent; *(voce, clima, fig)* harsh; *(superficie)* rough; *(paesaggio)* rugged

assaggi'are [assad'dʒare] *vt* to taste

assag'gini [assad'dʒini] *smpl* (CUC) selection of first courses

as'sai *av (molto)* a lot, much; (: *con ag)* very; *(a sufficienza)* enough ♦ *ag inv (quantità)* a lot of, much; *(numero)* a lot of, many; ~ contento very pleased

assa'lire *vt* to attack, assail

as'salto *sm* attack, assault

assapo'rare *vt* to savour

assassi'nare *vt* to murder; to assassinate; *(fig)* to ruin; assas'sinio *sm* murder; assassination; assas'sino, a *ag* murderous ♦ *sm/f* murderer; assassin

'asse *sm (TECN)* axle; *(MAT)* axis ♦ *sf* board; ~ *sf* da stiro ironing board

assedi'are *vt* to besiege; as'sedio *sm* siege

asse'gnare [assen'ɲare] *vt* to assign, allot; *(premio)* to award

as'segno [as'seɲɲo] *sm* allowance; *(anche:* ~ bancario) cheque (BRIT), check (US); contro ~ cash on delivery; ~ circolare bank draft; ~ sbarrato crossed cheque; ~ di viaggio traveller's cheque; ~ a vuoto dud cheque; ~i familiari ≈ child benefit *no pl*

assem'blea *sf* assembly

assen'nato, a *ag* sensible

as'senso *sm* assent, consent

as'sente *ag* absent; *(fig)* faraway, vacant;

as'senza *sf* absence

asses'sore *sm (*POL*)* councillor

asses'tare *vt (mettere in ordine)* to put in order, arrange; ~rsi *vr* to settle in; ~ un colpo a qn to deal sb a blow

asse'tato, a *ag* thirsty, parched

as'setto *sm* order, arrangement; *(*NAUT, AER*)* trim; in ~ di guerra on a war footing

assicu'rare *vt (accertare)* to ensure; *(infondere certezza)* to assure; *(fermare, legare)* to make fast, secure; *(fare un contratto di assicurazione)* to insure; ~rsi *vr (accertarsi)*: ~rsi (di) to make sure (of); *(contro il furto etc)*: ~rsi (contro) to insure o.s. (against); assicu'rata *sf (anche: lettera assicurata)* registered letter; assicu'rato, a *ag* insured; assicurazi'one *sf* assurance; insurance

assidera'mento *sm* exposure

as'siduo, a *ag (costante)* assiduous; *(frequentatore etc)* regular

assi'eme *av (insieme)* together; ~ a (together) with

assil'lare *vt* to pester, torment

as'sillo *sm (fig)* worrying thought

as'sise *sfpl (*DIR*)* assizes; Corte *sf* d'A~ Court of Assizes, ≈ Crown Court (BRIT)

assis'tente *sm/f* assistant; ~ sociale social worker; ~ di volo (AER) steward/stewardess

assis'tenza [assis'tɛntsa] *sf* assistance; ~ ospedaliera free hospital treatment; ~ sanitaria health service; ~ sociale welfare services *pl*

as'sistere *vt (aiutare)* to assist, help; *(curare)* to treat ♦ *vi*: ~ (a qc) *(essere presente)* to be present (at sth), to attend (sth)

'asso *sm* ace; piantare qn in ~ to leave sb in the lurch

associ'are [asso'tʃare] *vt* to associate; ~rsi *vr* to enter into partnership; ~rsi a to become a member of, join; *(dolori, gioie)* to share in; ~ qn alle carceri to take sb to prison

associazi'one [assotʃat'tsjone] *sf* association; *(*COMM*)* association, society; ~ a delinquere (DIR) criminal association

asso'dato, a *ag* well-founded

assogget'tare [assoddʒet'tare] *vt* to subject, subjugate

asso'lato, a *ag* sunny

assol'dare *vt* to recruit

as'solto, a *pp di* assolvere

assoluta'mente *av* absolutely

asso'luto, a *ag* absolute

assoluzi'one [assolut'tsjone] *sf (*DIR*)* acquittal; *(*REL*)* absolution

as'solvere *vt (*DIR*)* to acquit; *(*REL*)* to absolve; *(adempiere)* to carry out, perform

assomigli'are [assomiʎ'ʎare] *vi*: ~ a to resemble, look like

asson'nato, a *ag* sleepy

asso'pirsi vr to doze off

assor'bente ag absorbent ♦ sm: ~ **igienico** sanitary towel; ~ **interno** tampon

assor'bire vt to absorb

assor'dare vt to deafen

assorti'mento sm assortment

assor'tito, a ag assorted; matched, matching

as'sorto, a ag absorbed, engrossed

assottigli'are [assottiʎ'ʎare] vt to make thin, to thin; (aguzzare) to sharpen; (ridurre) to reduce; **~rsi** vr to grow thin; (fig: ridursi) to be reduced

assue'fare vt to accustom; **~rsi a** to get used to, accustom o.s. to

as'sumere vt (impiegato) to take on, engage; (responsabilità) to assume, take upon o.s.; (contegno, espressione) to assume, put on; (droga) to consume; **as'sunto, a** pp di **assumere** ♦ sm (tesi) proposition

assurdità sf inv absurdity; **dire delle ~** to talk nonsense

as'surdo, a ag absurd

'asta sf pole; (vendita) auction

astan'teria sf casualty department

as'temio, a ag teetotal ♦ sm/f teetotaller

aste'nersi vr: ~ **(da)** to abstain (from), refrain (from); (POL) to abstain (from)

aste'risco, schi sm asterisk

'astice ['astitʃe] sm lobster

asti'nenza [asti'nɛntsa] sf abstinence; **essere in crisi di ~** to suffer from withdrawal symptoms

'astio sm rancour, resentment

as'tratto, a ag abstract

'astro sm star

'astro... prefisso: **astrolo'gia** [astrolo'dʒia] sf astrology; **as'trologo, a, ghi, ghe** sm/f astrologer; **astro'nauta, i, e** sm/f astronaut; **astro'nave** sf space ship; **astrono'mia** sf astronomy; **astro'nomico, a, ci, che** ag astronomic(al)

as'tuccio [as'tuttʃo] sm case, box, holder

as'tuto, a ag astute, cunning, shrewd; **as'tuzia** sf astuteness, shrewdness; (azione) trick

A'tene sf Athens

ate'neo sm university

'ateo, a ag, sm/f atheist

at'lante sm atlas

at'lantico, a, ci, che ag Atlantic ♦ sm: **l'A~, l'Oceano A~** the Atlantic, the Atlantic Ocean

at'leta, i, e sm/f athlete; **at'letica** sf athletics sg; **atletica leggera** track and field events pl; **atletica pesante** weightlifting and wrestling

atmos'fera sf atmosphere

a'tomico, a, ci, che ag atomic; (nucleare) atomic, atom cpd, nuclear

'atomo sm atom

'atrio sm entrance hall, lobby

a'troce [a'trotʃe] ag (che provoca orrore) dreadful; (terribile) atrocious

attacca'mento sm (fig) attachment, affection

attacca'panni sm hook, peg; (mobile) hall stand

attac'care vt (unire) to attach; (cucendo) to sew on; (far aderire) to stick (on); (appendere) to hang (up); (assalire: anche fig) to attack; (iniziare) to begin, start; (fig: contagiare) to pass on ♦ vi to stick, adhere; **~rsi** vr to stick, adhere; (trasmettersi per contagio) to be contagious; (afferrarsi): **~rsi (a)** to cling (to); (fig: affezionarsi): **~rsi (a)** to become attached (to); ~ **discorso** to start a conversation; **at'tacco, chi** sm (azione offensiva: anche fig) attack; (MED) attack, fit; (SCI) binding; (ELETTR) socket

atteggia'mento [atteddʒa'mento] sm attitude

atteggi'arsi [atted'dʒarsi] vr: ~ **a** to pose as

attem'pato, a ag elderly

at'tendere vt to wait for, await ♦ vi: ~ **a** to attend to

atten'dibile ag (storia) credible; (testimone) reliable

atte'nersi vr: ~ **a** to keep o stick to

atten'tare vi: ~ **a** to make an attempt on; **atten'tato** sm attack; **attentato alla vita di qn** attempt on sb's life

at'tento, a ag attentive; (accurato) careful, thorough; **stare ~ a qc** to pay attention to sth; **~!** be careful!

attenu'ante sf (DIR) extenuating circumstance

attenu'are vt to attenuate; (dolore, rumore) to lessen, deaden; (pena, tasse) to alleviate; **~rsi** vr to ease, abate

attenzi'one [atten'tsjone] sf attention; **~!** watch out!, be careful!

atter'raggio [atter'raddʒo] sm landing

atter'rare vt to bring down ♦ vi to land

atter'rire vt to terrify

at'tesa sf waiting; (tempo trascorso aspettando) wait; **essere in ~ di qc** to be waiting for sth

at'teso, a pp di **attendere**

attes'tato sm certificate

'attico, ci sm attic

at'tiguo, a ag adjacent, adjoining

attil'lato, a ag (vestito) close-fitting

'attimo sm moment; **in un ~** in a moment

atti'nente ag: ~ **a** relating to, concerning

atti'rare vt to attract

atti'tudine sf (disposizione) aptitude; (atteggiamento) attitude

atti'vare *vt* to activate; (*far funzionare*) to set going, start

attività *sf inv* activity; (*COMM*) assets *pl*

at'tivo, a *ag* active; (*COMM*) profit-making, credit *cpd* ♦ *sm* (*COMM*) assets *pl*; **in ~** in credit

attiz'zare [attit'tsare] *vt* (*fuoco*) to poke

'atto *sm* act; (*azione, gesto*) action, act, deed; (*DIR: documento*) deed, document; **~i** *smpl* (*di congressi etc*) proceedings; **mettere in ~** to put into action; **fare ~ di fare qc** to make as if to do sth

at'tonito, a *ag* dumbfounded, astonished

attorcigli'are [attortʃiʎ'ʎare] *vt* to twist; **~rsi** *vr* to twist

at'tore, 'trice *sm/f* actor/actress

at'torno *av* round, around, about; **~ a** round, around, about

at'tracco, chi *sm* (*NAUT*) docking *no pl*; berth

attra'ente *ag* attractive

at'trarre *vt* to attract; **attrat'tiva** *sf* (*fig: fascino*) attraction, charm; **at'tratto, a** *pp di* **attrarre**

attraversa'mento *sm*: **~ pedonale** pedestrian crossing

attraver'sare *vt* to cross; (*città, bosco, fig: periodo*) to go through; (*sog: fiume*) to run through

attra'verso *prep* through; (*da una parte all'altra*) across

attrazi'one [attrat'tsjone] *sf* attraction

attrez'zare [attret'tsare] *vt* to equip; (*NAUT*) to rig; **attrezza'tura** *sf* equipment *no pl*; rigging; **at'trezzo** *sm* tool, instrument; (*SPORT*) piece of equipment

attribu'ire *vt*: **~ qc a qn** (*assegnare*) to give o award sth to sb; (*quadro etc*) to attribute sth to sb; **attri'buto** *sm* attribute

at'trice [at'tritʃe] *sf vedi* **attore**

at'trito *sm* (*anche fig*) friction

attu'ale *ag* (*presente*) present; (*di attualità*) topical; (*che è in atto*) actual; **attualità** *sf inv* topicality; (*avvenimento*) current event; **attual'mente** *av* at the moment, at present

attu'are *vt* to carry out; **~rsi** *vr* to be realized

attu'tire *vt* to deaden, reduce

au'dace [au'datʃe] *ag* audacious, daring, bold; (*provocante*) provocative; (*sfacciato*) impudent, bold; **au'dacia** *sf* audacity, daring; boldness; provocativeness; impudence

audiovi'sivo, a *ag* audiovisual

audizi'one [audit'tsjone] *sf* hearing; (*MUS*) audition

'auge ['audʒe] *sf*: **in ~** popular

augu'rare *vt* to wish; **~rsi qc** to hope for sth

au'gurio *sm* (*presagio*) omen; (*voto di benessere etc*) (good) wish; **essere di buon/**

cattivo ~ to be of good omen/be ominous; **fare gli ~i a qn** to give sb one's best wishes; **tanti ~i!** all the best!

'aula *sf* (*scolastica*) classroom; (*universitaria*) lecture theatre; (*di edificio pubblico*) hall

aumen'tare *vt, vi* to increase; **au'mento** *sm* increase

au'reola *sf* halo

au'rora *sf* dawn

ausili'are *ag, sm, sm/f* auxiliary

aus'picio [aus'pitʃo] *sm* omen; (*protezione*) patronage; **sotto gli ~i di** under the auspices of

aus'tero, a *ag* austere

Aus'tralia *sf*: **l'~** Australia; **australi'ano, a** *ag, sm/f* Australian

'Austria *sf*: **l'~** Austria; **aus'triaco, a, ci, che** *ag, sm/f* Austrian

au'tentico, a, ci, che *ag* authentic, genuine

au'tista, i *sm* driver

'auto *sf inv* car

autoade'sivo, a *ag* self-adhesive ♦ *sm* sticker

autobiogra'fia *sf* autobiography

auto'botte *sf* tanker

'autobus *sm inv* bus

auto'carro *sm* lorry (*BRIT*), truck

autocorri'era *sf* coach, bus

au'tografo, a *ag, sm* autograph

auto'grill ® *sm inv* motorway restaurant

autogrù *sf inv* breakdown van

auto'linea *sf* bus company

au'toma, i *sm* automaton

auto'matico, a, ci, che *ag* automatic ♦ *sm* (*bottone*) snap fastener; (*fucile*) automatic

automazi'one [automat'tsjone] *sf* automation

auto'mezzo [auto'mɛddzo] *sm* motor vehicle

auto'mobile *sf* (motor) car

automobi'lista, i, e *sm/f* motorist

autono'leggio *sm* car hire

autono'mia *sf* autonomy; (*di volo*) range

au'tonomo, a *ag* autonomous, independent

autop'sia *sf* post-mortem, autopsy

auto'radio *sf inv* (*apparecchio*) car radio; (*autoveicolo*) radio car

au'tore, 'trice *sm/f* author

auto'revole *ag* authoritative; (*persona*) influential

autori'messa *sf* garage

autorità *sf inv* authority

autoriz'zare [autorid'dzare] *vt* (*permettere*) to authorize; (*giustificare*) to allow, sanction; **autorizzazi'one** *sf* authorization

autoscu'ola *sf* driving school

autos'top *sm* hitchhiking; **autostop'pista,**

i, e *sm/f* hitchhiker

autos'trada *sf* motorway (*BRIT*), highway (*US*)

auto'treno *sm* articulated lorry (*BRIT*), semi (trailer) (*US*)

autove'icolo *sm* motor vehicle

auto'velox ® *sm inv* (police) speed camera

autovet'tura *sf* (motor) car

au'tunno *sm* autumn

avam'braccio [avam'brattʃo] (*pl(f)* **-cia**) *sm* forearm

avangu'ardia *sf* vanguard

a'vanti *av* (*stato in luogo*) in front; (*moto: andare, venire*) forward; (*tempo: prima*) before ♦ *prep* (*luogo*): ~ **a** before, in front of; (*tempo*): ~ **Cristo** before Christ ♦ *escl* (*entrate*) come (*o* go) in!; (*MIL*) forward!; (*coraggio*) come on! ♦ *sm inv* (*SPORT*) forward; ~ **e indietro** backwards and forwards; **andare** ~ to go forward; (*continuare*) to go on; (*precedere*) to go (on) ahead; (*orologio*) to be fast; **essere** ~ **negli studi** to be well advanced with one's studies

avanza'mento [avantsa'mento] *sm* progress; promotion

avan'zare [avan'tsare] *vt* (*spostare in avanti*) to move forward, advance; (*domanda*) to put forward; (*promuovere*) to promote; (*essere creditore*): ~ **qc da qn** to be owed sth by sb ♦ *vi* (*andare avanti*) to move forward, advance; (*progredire*) to make progress; (*essere d'avanzo*) to be left, remain; **avan'zata** *sf* (*MIL*) advance; **a'vanzo** *sm* (*residuo*) remains *pl*, left-overs *pl*; (*MAT*) remainder; (*COMM*) surplus; **averne d'avanzo di qc** to have more than enough of sth; **avanzo di galera** jailbird

ava'ria *sf* (*guasto*) damage; (: *meccanico*) breakdown

a'varo, a *ag* avaricious, miserly ♦ *sm* miser

a'vena *sf* oats *pl*

PAROLA CHIAVE
---

a'vere *sm* (*COMM*) credit; **gli ~i** (*ricchezze*) wealth *sg*

♦ *vt* **1** (*possedere*) to have; **ha due bambini/una bella casa** she has (got) two children/a lovely house; **ha i capelli lunghi** he has (got) long hair; **non ho da mangiare/bere** I've (got) nothing to eat/drink, I don't have anything to eat/drink

2 (*indossare*) to wear, have on; **aveva una maglietta rossa** he was wearing *o* he had on a red tee-shirt; **ha gli occhiali** he wears *o* has glasses

3 (*ricevere*) to get; **hai avuto l'assegno?** did you get *o* have you had the cheque?

4 (*età, dimensione*) to be; **ha 9 anni** he is 9 (years old); **la stanza ha 3 metri di lunghezza** the room is 3 metres in length; *vedi* **fame**; **paura** *etc*

5 (*tempo*): **quanti ne abbiamo oggi?** what's the date today?; **ne hai per molto?** will you be long?

6 (*fraseologia*): **avercela con qn** to be angry with sb; **cos'hai?** what's wrong *o* what's the matter (with you)?; **non ha niente a che vedere** *o* **fare con me** it's got nothing to do with me

♦ *vb aus* **1** to have; **aver bevuto/mangiato** to have drunk/eaten

2 (+*da* +*infinito*): ~ **da fare qc** to have to do sth; **non hai che da chiederlo** you only have to ask him

---

'avi *smpl* ancestors, forefathers

aviazi'one [avjat'tsjone] *sf* aviation; (*MIL*) air force

avidità *sf* eagerness; greed

'avido, a *ag* eager; (*peg*) greedy

avo'cado *sm* avocado

a'vorio *sm* ivory

Avv. *abbr* = **avvocato**

avvalla'mento *sm* sinking *no pl*; (*effetto*) depression

avvalo'rare *vt* to confirm

avvam'pare *vi* (*incendio*) to flare up

avvantaggi'are [avvantad'dʒare] *vt* to favour; ~**rsi** *vr*: ~**rsi negli affari/sui concorrenti** to get ahead in business/of one's competitors

avvele'nare *vt* to poison

avve'nente *ag* attractive, charming

avveni'mento *sm* event

avve'nire *vi, vb impers* to happen, occur ♦ *sm* future

avven'tarsi *vr*: ~ **su** *o* **contro qn/qc** to hurl o.s. *o* rush at sb/sth

avven'tato, a *ag* rash, reckless

avven'tizio, a [avven'tittsjo] *ag* (*impiegato*) temporary; (*guadagno*) casual

av'vento *sm* advent, coming; (*REL*): **l'A~** Advent

avven'tore *sm* (*regular*) customer

avven'tura *sf* adventure; (*amorosa*) affair

avventu'rarsi *vr* to venture

avventu'roso, a *ag* adventurous

avve'rarsi *vr* to come true

av'verbio *sm* adverb

avver'sario, a *ag* opposing ♦ *sm* opponent, adversary

av'verso, a *ag* (*contrario*) contrary; (*sfavorevole*) unfavourable

avver'tenza [avver'tentsa] *sf* (*ammonimento*) warning; (*cautela*) care; (*premessa*) foreword; ~**e** *sfpl* (*istruzioni per l'uso*) instructions

avverti'mento *sm* warning

avver'tire *vt* (*avvisare*) to warn; (*rendere consapevole*) to inform, notify; (*percepire*) to feel

av'vezzo, a [av'vettso] *ag*: ~ **a** used to

avvia'mento *sm* (*atto*) starting; (*effetto*) start; (*AUT*) starting; (: *dispositivo*) starter; (*COMM*) goodwill

avvi'are *vt* (*mettere sul cammino*) to direct; (*impresa, trattative*) to begin, start; (*motore*) to start; **~rsi** *vr* to set off, set out

avvicen'darsi [avvitʃen'darsi] *vr* to alternate

avvici'nare [avvitʃi'nare] *vt* to bring near; (*trattare con: persona*) to approach; **~rsi** *vr*: **~rsi (a qn/qc)** to approach (sb/sth), draw near (to sb/sth)

avvi'lire *vt* (*umiliare*) to humiliate; (*degradare*) to disgrace; (*scoraggiare*) to dishearten, discourage; **~rsi** *vr* (*abbattersi*) to lose heart

avvilup'pare *vt* (*avvolgere*) to wrap up

avvinaz'zato, a [avvinat'tsato] *ag* drunk

avvin'cente *ag* captivating

av'vincere [av'vintʃere] *vt* to charm, enthral

avvinghi'are [avvin'gjare] *vt* to clasp; **~rsi** *vr*: **~rsi a** to cling to

avvi'sare *vt* (*far sapere*) to inform; (*mettere in guardia*) to warn; **av'viso** *sm* warning; (*annuncio*) announcement; (: *affisso*) notice; (*inserzione pubblicitaria*) advertisement; **a mio avviso** in my opinion; **avviso di chiamata** (*TEL*) call waiting service

avvis'tare *vt* to sight

avvi'tare *vt* to screw down (*o* in)

avviz'zire [avvit'tsire] *vi* to wither

avvo'cato, 'essa *sm/f* (*DIR*) barrister (*BRIT*), lawyer; (*fig*) defender, advocate

av'volgere [av'voldʒere] *vt* to roll up; (*avviluppare*) to wrap up; **~rsi** *vr* (*avvilupparsi*) to wrap o.s. up; **avvol'gibile** *sm* roller blind (*BRIT*), blind

avvol'toio *sm* vulture

azi'enda [ad'dzjenda] *sf* business, firm, concern; **~ agricola** farm

azio'nare [attsjo'nare] *vt* to activate

azio'ne [at'tsjone] *sf* action; (*COMM*) share; **azio'nista, i, e** *sm/f* (*COMM*) shareholder

a'zoto [ad'dzɔto] *sm* nitrogen

azzan'nare [attsan'nare] *vt* to sink one's teeth into

azzar'darsi [addzar'darsi] *vr*: **~ a fare** to dare (to) do; **azzar'dato, a** *ag* (*impresa*) risky; (*risposta*) rash

az'zardo [ad'dzardo] *sm* risk

azzec'care [attsek'kare] *vt* (*risposta etc*) to get right

azzuf'farsi [attsuf'farsi] *vr* to come to blows

az'zurro, a [ad'dzurro] *ag* blue ♦ *sm* (*colore*) blue; **gli ~i** (*SPORT*) the Italian national team

B, b

bab'beo *sm* simpleton

'babbo *sm* (*fam*) dad, daddy; **B~ Natale** Father Christmas

bab'buccia, ce [bab'buttʃa] *sf* slipper; (*per neonati*) bootee

ba'bordo *sm* (*NAUT*) port side

ba'cato, a *ag* worm-eaten, rotten

'bacca, che *sf* berry

baccalà *sm* dried salted cod; (*fig: peg*) dummy

bac'cano *sm* din, clamour

bac'cello [bat'tʃello] *sm* pod

bac'chetta [bak'ketta] *sf* (*verga*) stick, rod; (*di direttore d'orchestra*) baton; (*di tamburo*) drumstick; **~ magica** magic wand

baci'are [ba'tʃare] *vt* to kiss; **~rsi** *vr* to kiss (one another)

baci'nella [batʃi'nella] *sf* basin

ba'cino [ba'tʃino] *sm* basin; (*MINERALOGIA*) field, bed; (*ANAT*) pelvis; (*NAUT*) dock

'bacio [ba'tʃo] *sm* kiss

'baco, chi *sm* worm; **~ da seta** silkworm

ba'dare *vi* (*fare attenzione*) to take care, be careful; (*occuparsi di*): **~ a** to look after, take care of; (*dar ascolto*): **~ a** to pay attention to; **bada ai fatti tuoi!** mind your own business!

ba'dia *sf* abbey

ba'dile *sm* shovel

'baffi *smpl* moustache *sg*; (*di animale*) whiskers; **ridere sotto i ~** to laugh up one's sleeve; **leccarsi i ~** to lick one's lips

ba'gagli [ba'gaʎʎi] *smpl* luggage *sg*; **fare i ~** to pack

bagagli'aio [bagaʎ'ʎajo] *sm* luggage van (*BRIT*) *o* car (*US*); (*AUT*) boot (*BRIT*), trunk (*US*)

bagli'ore [baʎ'ʎore] *sm* flash, dazzling light; **un ~ di speranza** a ray of hope

ba'gnante [baɲ'ɲante] *sm/f* bather

ba'gnare [baɲ'ɲare] *vt* to wet; (*inzuppare*) to soak; (*innaffiare*) to water; (*sog: fiume*) to flow through; (: *mare*) to wash, bathe; **~rsi** *vr* to get wet; (*al mare*) to go swimming *o* bathing; (*in vasca*) to have a bath

ba'gnato, a [baɲ'ɲato] *ag* wet

ba'gnino [baɲ'ɲino] *sm* lifeguard

'bagno [baɲ'ɲo] *sm* bath; (*locale*) bathroom; **~i** *smpl* (*stabilimento*) baths; **fare il ~** to have a bath; (*nel mare*) to go swimming *o* bathing; **fare il ~ a qn** to give sb a bath; **mettere a ~** to soak; **~ schiuma** bubble bath

bagnoma'ria [baɲɲoma'ria] *sm*: **cuocere a ~** to cook in a double saucepan

'baia *sf* bay

baio'netta *sf* bayonet

balbet'tare *vi* to stutter, stammer; (*bimbo*)

to babble ♦ *vt* to stammer out
balbuzi'ente [balbut'tsjɛnte] *ag* stuttering, stammering
bal'cone *sm* balcony
baldac'chino [baldak'kino] *sm* canopy
bal'danza [bal'dantsa] *sf* self-confidence
'baldo, a *ag* bold, daring
bal'doria *sf*: **fare ~** to have a riotous time
ba'lena *sf* whale
bale'nare *vb impers*: **balena** there's lightning
♦ *vi* to flash; **mi balenò un'idea** an idea flashed through my mind; **ba'leno** *sm* flash of lightning; **in un baleno** in a flash
ba'lestra *sf* crossbow
ba'lia *sf*: **in ~ di** at the mercy of
'balla *sf* (*di merci*) bale; (*fandonia*) (tall) story
bal'lare *vt, vi* to dance; **bal'lata** *sf* ballad
balle'rina *sf* dancer; ballet dancer; (*scarpa*) ballet shoe
balle'rino *sm* dancer; ballet dancer
bal'letto *sm* ballet
'ballo *sm* dance; (*azione*) dancing *no pl*; **essere in ~** (*fig: persona*) to be involved; (*: cosa*) to be at stake
ballot'taggio [ballot'taddʒo] *sm* (*POL*) second ballot
balne'are *ag* seaside *cpd*; (*stagione*) bathing
balneazi'one *sf* bathing; **è vietata la ~** bathing strictly prohibited
ba'locco, chi *sm* toy
ba'lordo, a *ag* stupid, senseless
'balsamo *sm* (*aroma*) balsam; (*lenimento, fig*) balm
balu'ardo *sm* bulwark
'balza ['baltsa] *sf* (*dirupo*) crag; (*di stoffa*) frill
bal'zare [bal'tsare] *vi* to bounce; (*lanciarsi*) to jump, leap; **'balzo** *sm* bounce; jump, leap; (*del terreno*) crag
bam'bagia [bam'badʒa] *sf* (*ovatta*) cotton wool (*BRIT*), absorbent cotton (*US*); (*cascame*) cotton waste
bam'bina *ag, sf vedi* **bambino**
bambi'naia *sf* nanny, nurse(maid)
bam'bino, a *sm/f* child
bam'boccio [bam'bɔttʃo] *sm* plump child; (*pupazzo*) rag doll
'bambola *sf* doll
bambù *sm* bamboo
ba'nale *ag* banal, commonplace
ba'nana *sf* banana; **ba'nano** *sm* banana tree
'banca, che *sf* bank; **~ dei dati** data bank
banca'rella *sf* stall
ban'cario, a *ag* banking, bank *cpd* ♦ *sm* bank clerk
banca'rotta *sf* bankruptcy; **fare ~** to go bankrupt
ban'chetto [ban'ketto] *sm* banquet
banchi'ere [ban'kjɛre] *sm* banker

ban'china [ban'kina] *sf* (*di porto*) quay; (*per pedoni, ciclisti*) path; (*di stazione*) platform; **~ cedevole** (*AUT*) soft verge (*BRIT*) o shoulder (*US*)
'banco, chi *sm* bench; (*di negozio*) counter; (*di mercato*) stall; (*di officina*) (work-)bench; (*GEO, banca*) bank; **~ di corallo** coral reef; **~ degli imputati** dock; **~ dei pegni** pawnshop; **~ di nebbia** bank of fog; **~ di prova** (*fig*) testing ground; **~ dei testimoni** witness box
'Bancomat ® *sm inv* automated banking; (*tessera*) cash card
banco'nota *sf* banknote
'banda *sf* band; (*di stoffa*) band, stripe; (*lato, parte*) side; **~ perforata** punch tape
banderu'ola *sf* (*METEOR*) weathercock
bandi'era *sf* flag, banner
ban'dire *vt* to proclaim; (*esiliare*) to exile; (*fig*) to dispense with
ban'dito *sm* outlaw, bandit
bandi'tore *sm* (*di aste*) auctioneer
'bando *sm* proclamation; (*esilio*) exile, banishment; **~ alle chiacchiere!** that's enough talk!
'bandolo *sm*: **il ~ della matassa** (*fig*) the key to the problem
bar *sm inv* bar
'bara *sf* coffin
ba'racca, che *sf* shed, hut; (*peg*) hovel; **mandare avanti la ~** to keep things going
bara'onda *sf* hubbub, bustle
ba'rare *vi* to cheat
'baratro *sm* abyss
barat'tare *vt*: **~ qc con** to barter sth for, swap sth for; **ba'ratto** *sm* barter
ba'rattolo *sm* (*di latta*) tin; (*di vetro*) jar; (*di coccio*) pot
'barba *sf* beard; **farsi la ~** to shave; **farla in ~ a qn** (*fig*) to do sth to sb's face; **che ~!** what a bore!
barbabi'etola *sf* beetroot (*BRIT*), beet (*US*); **~ da zucchero** sugar beet
bar'barico, a, ci, che *ag* barbarian; barbaric
'barbaro, a *ag* barbarous; **~i** *smpl* barbarians
barbi'ere *sm* barber
bar'bone *sm* (*cane*) poodle; (*vagabondo*) tramp
bar'buto, a *ag* bearded
'barca, che *sf* boat; **~ a remi** rowing boat; **~ a vela** sail(ing) boat; **barcai'olo** *sm* boatman
barcol'lare *vi* to stagger
bar'cone *sm* (*per ponti di barche*) pontoon
ba'rella *sf* (*lettiga*) stretcher
ba'rile *sm* barrel, cask
ba'rista, i, e *sm/f* barman/maid; (*proprietario*) bar owner
ba'ritono *sm* baritone

bar'lume *sm* glimmer, gleam

ba'rocco, a, chi, che *ag, sm* baroque

ba'rometro *sm* barometer

ba'rone *sm* baron; **baro'nessa** *sf* baroness

'barra *sf* bar; (*NAUT*) helm; (*linea grafica*) line, stroke

barri'care *vt* to barricade; **barri'cata** *sf* barricade

barri'era *sf* barrier; (*GEO*) reef

ba'ruffa *sf* scuffle

barzel'letta [bardzel'letta] *sf* joke, funny story

ba'sare *vt* to base, found; **~rsi** *vr*: **~rsi su** (*sog: fatti, prove*) to be based o founded on; (*: persona*) to base one's arguments on

'basco, a, schi, sche *ag* Basque ♦ *sm* (*copricapo*) beret

'base *sf* base; (*fig: fondamento*) basis; (*POL*) rank and file; **di ~** basic; **in ~ a** on the basis of, according to; **a ~ di caffè** coffee-based

ba'setta *sf* sideburn

ba'silica, che *sf* basilica

ba'silico *sm* basil

bassi'fondi *smpl*: **i ~** the slums

'basso, a *ag* low; (*di statura*) short; (*meridionale*) southern ♦ *sm* bottom, lower part; (*MUS*) bass; **la ~a Italia** southern Italy

bassorili'evo *sm* bas-relief

'basta *escl* (that's) enough!, that will do!

bas'tardo, a *ag* (*animale, pianta*) hybrid, crossbreed; (*persona*) illegitimate, bastard (*peg*) ♦ *sm/f* illegitimate child, bastard (*peg*)

bas'tare *vi, vb impers* to be enough, be sufficient; **~ a qn** to be enough for sb; **basta chiedere** o **che chieda a un vigile** you have only to o need only ask a policeman

basti'mento *sm* ship, vessel

basto'nare *vt* to beat, thrash

baston'cino [baston'tʃino] *sm* (*SCI*) ski pole; **~i di pesce** fish fingers

bas'tone *sm* stick; **~ da passeggio** walking stick

bat'taglia [bat'taʎʎa] *sf* battle; fight

bat'taglio [bat'taʎʎo] *sm* (*di campana*) clapper; (*di porta*) knocker

battagli'one [battaʎʎone] *sm* battalion

bat'tello *sm* boat

bat'tente *sm* (*imposta: di porta*) wing, flap; (*: di finestra*) shutter; (*batacchio: di porta*) knocker; (*: di orologio*) hammer; **chiudere i ~i** (*fig*) to shut up shop

'battere *vt* to beat; (*grano*) to thresh; (*percorrere*) to scour ♦ *vi* (*bussare*) to knock; (*urtare*): **~ contro** to hit o strike against; (*pioggia, sole*) to beat down; (*cuore*) to beat; (*TENNIS*) to serve; **~rsi** *vr* to fight; **~ le mani** to clap; **~ i piedi** to stamp one's feet; **~ a macchina** to type; **~ bandiera italiana** to fly the Italian flag; **~ in testa** (*AUT*) to knock;

in un batter d'occhio in the twinkling of an eye

bat'teri *smpl* bacteria

batte'ria *sf* battery; (*MUS*) drums *pl*

bat'tesimo *sm* (*rito*) baptism; christening

battez'zare [batted'dzare] *vt* to baptize; to christen

batticu'ore *sm* palpitations *pl*

batti'mano *sm* applause

batti'panni *sm inv* carpet-beater

battis'tero *sm* baptistry

battis'trada *sm inv* (*di pneumatico*) tread; (*di gara*) pacemaker

battitap'peto *sm* vacuum cleaner

'battito *sm* beat, throb; **~ cardiaco** heartbeat

bat'tuta *sf* blow; (*di macchina da scrivere*) stroke; (*MUS*) bar; beat; (*TEATRO*) cue; (*frase spiritosa*) witty remark; (*di caccia*) beating; (*POLIZIA*) combing, scouring; (*TENNIS*) service

ba'ule *sm* trunk; (*AUT*) boot (*BRIT*), trunk (*US*)

'bava *sf* (*di animale*) slaver, slobber; (*di lumaca*) slime; (*di vento*) breath

bava'glino [bavaʎ'ʎino] *sm* bib

ba'vaglio [ba'vaʎʎo] *sm* gag

'bavero *sm* collar

Bavi'era *sf* Bavaria

ba'zar [bad'dzar] *sm inv* bazaar

baz'zecola [bad'dzekola] *sf* trifle

bazzi'care [battsi'kare] *vt* to frequent ♦ *vi*: **~ in/con** to frequent

be'ato, a *ag* blessed; (*fig*) happy; **~ te!** lucky you!

bebè *sm inv* baby

bec'caccia, ce [bek'kattʃa] *sf* woodcock

bec'care *vt* to peck; (*fig: raffreddore*) to catch; **~rsi qc** to catch sth

bec'cata *sf* peck

beccheggi'are [bekked'dʒare] *vi* to pitch

bec'chino [bek'kino] *sm* gravedigger

'becco, chi *sm* beak, bill; (*di caffettiera etc*) spout; lip

Be'fana *sf* old woman who, according to legend, brings children their presents at the Epiphany; (*Epifania*) Epiphany; (*donna brutta*): **b~** hag, witch

'beffa *sf* practical joke; **farsi ~e di qn** to make a fool of sb; **bef'fardo, a** *ag* scornful, mocking; **bef'fare** *vt* (*anche: beffarsi di*) to make a fool of, mock

'bega, ghe *sf* quarrel

'begli ['beʎʎi] *ag vedi* **bello**

'bei *ag vedi* **bello**

bel *ag vedi* **bello**

be'lare *vi* to bleat

'belga, gi, ghe *ag, sm/f* Belgian

'Belgio ['beldʒo] *sm*: **il ~** Belgium

bel'lezza [bel'lettsa] *sf* beauty

'bella *sf* (*SPORT*) decider; *vedi anche* **bello**

PAROLA CHIAVE

'bello, a (*ag*: dav *sm* **bel** +C, **bell'** +V, **bello** +*s impura, gn, pn, ps, x, z, pl* **bei** +C, **begli** +*s impura etc o* V) *ag* 1 (*oggetto, donna, paesaggio*) beautiful, lovely; (*uomo*) handsome; (*tempo*) beautiful, fine, lovely; **le belle arti** fine arts

2 (*quantità*): **una ~a cifra** a considerable sum of money; **un bel niente** absolutely nothing 3 (*rafforzativo*): **è una truffa ~a e buona!** it's a real fraud!; **è bell'e finito** it's already finished
♦ *sm* 1 (*bellezza*) beauty; (*tempo*) fine weather

2: **adesso viene il ~** now comes the best bit; **sul più ~** at the crucial point; **cosa fai di ~?** are you doing anything interesting? ♦ *av*: **fa ~** the weather is fine, it's fine

'belva *sf* wild animal
belve'dere *sm inv* panoramic viewpoint
benché [ben'ke] *cong* although
'benda *sf* bandage; (*per gli occhi*) blindfold; **ben'dare** *vt* to bandage; to blindfold
'bene *av* well; (*completamente, affatto*): **è ben difficile** it's very difficult ♦ *ag inv*: **gente ~** well-to-do people ♦ *sm* good; **~i** *smpl* (*averi*) property *sg*, estate *sg*; **io sto ~/poco ~** I'm well/not very well; **va ~** all right; **volere un ~ dell'anima a qn** to love sb very much; **un uomo per ~** a respectable man; **fare ~** to do the right thing; **fare ~ a** (*salute*) to be good for; **fare del ~ a qn** to do sb a good turn; **~i di consumo** consumer goods
bene'detto, a *pp di* benedire ♦ *ag* blessed, holy
bene'dire *vt* to bless; to consecrate; **benedizi'one** *sf* blessing
benedu'cato, a *ag* well-mannered
benefi'cenza [benefi'tʃɛntsa] *sf* charity
bene'ficio [bene'fitʃo] *sm* benefit; **con ~ d'inventario** (*fig*) with reservations
be'nefico, a, ci, che *ag* beneficial; charitable
beneme'renza [beneme'rɛntsa] *sf* merit
bene'merito, a *ag* meritorious
be'nessere *sm* well-being
benes'tante *ag* well-to-do
benes'tare *sm* consent, approval
be'nevolo, a *ag* benevolent
be'nigno, a [be'niɲɲo] *ag* kind, kindly; (*critica etc*) favourable; (*MED*) benign
benin'teso *av* of course
bensì *cong* but (rather)
benve'nuto, a *ag, sm* welcome; **dare il ~ a qn** to welcome sb
ben'zina [ben'dzina] *sf* petrol (*BRIT*), gas (*US*); **fare ~** to get petrol (*BRIT*) o gas (*US*); **~ verde** unleaded (petrol); **benzi'naio** *sm*

petrol (*BRIT*) o gas (*US*) pump attendant
'bere *vt* to drink; **darla a ~ a qn** (*fig*) to fool sb
ber'lina *sf* (*AUT*) saloon (car) (*BRIT*), sedan (*US*)
Ber'lino *sf* Berlin
ber'noccolo *sm* bump; (*inclinazione*) flair
ber'retto *sm* cap
bersagli'are [bersaʎ'ʎare] *vt* to shoot at; (*colpire ripetutamente, fig*) to bombard
ber'saglio [ber'saʎʎo] *sm* target
bes'temmia *sf* curse; (*REL*) blasphemy
bestemmi'are *vi* to curse, swear; to blaspheme ♦ *vt* to curse, swear at; to blaspheme
'bestia *sf* animal; **andare in ~** (*fig*) to fly into a rage; **besti'ale** *ag* beastly; animal *cpd*; (*fam*): **fa un freddo bestiale** it's bitterly cold; **besti'ame** *sm* livestock; (*bovino*) cattle *pl*
'bettola (*peg*) *sf* dive
be'tulla *sf* birch
be'vanda *sf* drink, beverage
bevi'tore, 'trice *sm/f* drinker
be'vuta *sf* drink
be'vuto, a *pp di* bere
bi'ada *sf* fodder
bianche'ria [bjanke'ria] *sf* linen; **~ intima** underwear; **~ da donna** ladies' underwear, lingerie
bi'anco, a, chi, che *ag* white; (*non scritto*) blank ♦ *sm* white; (*intonaco*) whitewash ♦ *sm/f* white, white man/woman; **in ~** (*foglio, assegno*) blank; (*notte*) sleepless; **in ~ e nero** (*TV, FOT*) black and white; **mangiare in ~** to follow a bland diet; **pesce in ~** boiled fish; **andare in ~** (*non riuscire*) to fail; **~ dell'uovo** egg-white
biasi'mare *vt* to disapprove of, censure; **bi'asimo** *sm* disapproval, censure
'bibbia *sf* (*anche fig*) bible
bibe'ron *sm inv* feeding bottle
'bibita *sf* (soft) drink
biblio'teca, che *sf* library; (*mobile*) bookcase; **bibliote'cario, a** *sm/f* librarian
bicarbo'nato *sm*: **~ (di sodio)** bicarbonate (of soda)
bicchi'ere [bik'kjɛre] *sm* glass
bici'cletta [bitʃi'kletta] *sf* bicycle; **andare in ~** to cycle
bidé *sm inv* bidet
bi'dello, a *sm/f* (*INS*) janitor
bi'done *sm* drum, can; (*anche*: **~ dell'immondizia**) (dust)bin; (*fam: truffa*) swindle; **fare un ~ a qn** (*fam*) to let sb down; to cheat sb
bien'nale *ag* biennial
bi'ennio *sm* period of two years
bi'etola *sf* beet
bifor'carsi *vr* to fork; **biforcazi'one** *sf* fork
bighello'nare [bigello'nare] *vi* to loaf (about)

bigiotte'ria [bidʒotte'ria] *sf* costume jewellery; (*negozio*) jeweller's (*selling only costume jewellery*)

bigli'ardo [biʎ'ʎardo] *sm* = biliardo

bigliet'taio, a *sm/f* (*in treno*) ticket inspector; (*in autobus*) conductor

bigliette'ria [biʎʎette'ria] *sf* (*di stazione*) ticket office; booking office; (*di teatro*) box office

bigli'etto [biʎ'ʎetto] *sm* (*per viaggi, spettacoli etc*) ticket; (*cartoncino*) card; (*anche: ~ di banca*) (bank)note; **~ d'auguri/da visita** greetings/visiting card; **~ d'andata e ritorno** return (ticket), round-trip ticket (*US*)

bignè [biɲ'ɲe] *sm inv* cream puff

bigo'dino *sm* roller, curler

bi'gotto, a *ag* over-pious ♦ *sm/f* church fiend

bi'lancia, ce [bi'lantʃa] *sf* (*pesa*) scales *pl*; (: *di precisione*) balance; (*dello zodiaco*): **B~** Libra; **~ commerciale/dei pagamenti** balance of trade/payments; **bilanci'are** *vt* (*pesare*) to weigh; (: *fig*) to weigh up; (*pareggiare*) to balance

bi'lancio [bi'lantʃo] *sm* (*COMM*) balance (-sheet); (*statale*) budget; **fare il ~ di** (*fig*) to assess; **~ consuntivo** (final) balance; **~ preventivo** budget

'bile *sf* bile; (*fig*) rage, anger

bili'ardo *sm* billiards *sg*; billiard table

bi'lico, chi *sm*: **essere in ~** to be balanced; **tenere qn in ~** (*fig*) to keep sb in suspense

bi'lingue *ag* bilingual

bili'one *sm* (*mille milioni*) thousand million; (*milione di milioni*) billion (*BRIT*), trillion (*US*)

'bimbo, a *sm/f* little boy/girl

bimen'sile *ag* fortnightly

bimes'trale *ag* two-monthly, bimonthly

bi'nario, a *ag* (*sistema*) binary ♦ *sm* (railway) track o line; (*piattaforma*) platform; **~ morto** dead-end track

bi'nocolo *sm* binoculars *pl*

bio... *prefisso*: **bio'chimica** [bio'kimika] *sf* biochemistry; **biodegra'dabile** *ag* biodegradable; **biogra'fia** *sf* biography; **biolo'gia** *sf* biology; **bio'logico, a, ci, che** *ag* biological

bi'ondo, a *ag* blond, fair

bir'bante *sm* rogue, rascal

biri'chino, a [biri'kino] *ag* mischievous ♦ *sm/f* scamp, little rascal

bi'rillo *sm* skittle (*BRIT*), pin (*US*); **~i** *smpl* (*gioco*) skittles *sg* (*BRIT*), bowling (*US*)

'biro ® *sf inv* biro ®

'birra *sf* beer; **a tutta ~** (*fig*) at top speed; **birra chiara** ≈ lager; **birra scura** ≈ stout; **birre'ria** *sf* ≈ bierkeller

bis *escl, sm inv* encore

bis'betico, a, ci, che *ag* ill-tempered, crabby

bisbigli'are [bisbiʎ'ʎare] *vt, vi* to whisper

'bisca, sche *sf* gambling-house

'biscia, sce ['biʃʃa] *sf* snake; **~ d'acqua** grass snake

bis'cotto *sm* biscuit

bises'tile *ag*: **anno ~** leap year

bis'lungo, a, ghi, ghe *ag* oblong

bis'nonno, a *sm/f* great grandfather/grandmother

biso'gnare [bizoɲ'ɲare] *vb impers*: **bisogna che tu parta/lo faccia** you'll have to go/do it; **bisogna parlargli** we'll (*o* I'll) have to talk to him

bi'sogno [bi'zoɲɲo] *sm* need; **~i** *smpl*: **fare i propri ~i** to relieve o.s.; **avere ~ di qc/di fare qc** to need sth/to do sth; **al ~, in caso di ~** if need be; **biso'gnoso, a** *ag* needy, poor; **bisognoso di** in need of, needing

bis'tecca, che *sf* steak, beefsteak

bisticci'are [bistit'tʃare] *vi* to quarrel, bicker; **~rsi** *vr* to quarrel, bicker; **bis'ticcio** *sm* quarrel, squabble; (*gioco di parole*) pun

'bisturi *sm* scalpel

bi'sunto, a *ag* very greasy

'bitter *sm inv* bitters *pl*

bi'vacco, chi *sm* bivouac

'bivio *sm* fork; (*fig*) dilemma

'bizza ['biddza] *sf* tantrum; **fare le ~e** (*bambino*) to be naughty

biz'zarro, a [bid'dzarro] *ag* bizarre, strange

biz'zeffe [bid'dzeffe]: **a ~** *av* in plenty, galore

blan'dire *vt* to soothe; to flatter

'blando, a *ag* mild, gentle

bla'sone *sm* coat of arms

blate'rare *vi* to chatter

blin'dato, a *ag* armoured

bloc'care *vt* to block; (*isolare*) to isolate, cut off; (*porto*) to blockade; (*prezzi, beni*) to freeze; (*meccanismo*) to jam; **~rsi** *vr* (*motore*) to stall; (*freni, porta*) to jam, stick; (*ascensore*) to stop, get stuck

bloc'chetto [blok'ketto] *sm* notebook; (*di biglietti*) book

'blocco, chi *sm* block; (*MIL*) blockade; (*dei fitti*) restriction; (*quadernotto*) pad; (*fig: unione*) coalition; (*il bloccare*) blocking; isolating, cutting-off; blockading; freezing; jamming; **in ~** (*nell'insieme*) as a whole; (*COMM*) in bulk; **~ cardiaco** cardiac arrest

blu *ag inv, sm* dark blue

'blusa *sf* (*camiciotto*) smock; (*camicetta*) blouse

'boa *sm inv* (*ZOOL*) boa constrictor; (*sciarpa*) feather boa ♦ *sf* buoy

bo'ato *sm* rumble, roar

bo'bina *sf* reel, spool; (*di pellicola*) spool; (*di film*) reel; (*ELETTR*) coil

'bocca, che *sf* mouth; **in ~ al lupo!** good

luck!

boc'caccia, ce [bok'kattʃa] sf (malalingua) gossip; **fare le ~ce** to pull faces

boc'cale sm jug; **~ da birra** tankard

boc'cetta [bot'tʃetta] sf small bottle

boccheggi'are [bokked'dʒare] vi to gasp

boc'chino [bok'kino] sm (di sigaretta, sigaro: cannella) cigarette-holder; cigar-holder; (di pipa, strumenti musicali) mouthpiece

'boccia, ce ['bottʃa] sf bottle; (da vino) decanter, carafe; (palla) bowl; **gioco delle ~ce** bowls sg

bocci'are [bot'tʃare] vt (proposta, progetto) to reject; (INS) to fail; (BOCCE) to hit; **boccia'tura** sf failure

bocci'olo [bot'tʃɔlo] sm bud

boc'cone sm mouthful, morsel

boc'coni av face downwards

'boia sm inv executioner; hangman

boi'ata sf botch

boicot'tare vt to boycott

'bolide sm meteor; **come un ~** like a flash, at top speed

'bolla sf bubble; (MED) blister; **~ papale** papal bull; **~ di consegna** (COMM) delivery note

bol'lare vt to stamp; (fig) to brand

bol'lente ag boiling; boiling hot

bol'letta sf bill; (ricevuta) receipt; **essere in ~** to be hard up

bol'lettino sm bulletin; (COMM) note; **~ meteorologico** weather report; **~ di spedizione** consignment note

bol'lire vt, vi to boil; **bol'lito** sm (CUC) boiled meat

bolli'tore sm (CUC) kettle; (per riscaldamento) boiler

'bollo sm stamp; **~ per patente** driving licence tax

'bomba sf bomb; **~ atomica** atom bomb

bombarda'mento sm bombardment; bombing

bombar'dare vt to bombard; (da aereo) to bomb

bombardi'ere sm bomber

bom'betta sf bowler (hat)

'bombola sf cylinder

bo'naccia, ce [bo'nattʃa] sf dead calm

bo'nario, a ag good-natured, kind

bo'nifica, che sf reclamation; reclaimed land

bo'nifico, ci sm (riduzione, abbuono) discount; (versamento a terzi) credit transfer

bontà sf goodness; (cortesia) kindness; **aver la ~ di fare qc** to be good o kind enough to do sth

borbot'tare vi to mumble

'borchia ['borkja] sf stud

borda'tura sf (SARTORIA) border, trim

bor'deaux [bor'dɔ] ag inv, sm inv maroon

'bordo sm (NAUT) ship's side; (orlo) edge; (striscia di guarnizione) border, trim; **a ~ di** (nave, aereo) aboard, on board; (macchina) in

bor'gata sf (in campagna) hamlet

bor'ghese [bor'geze] ag (spesso peg) middle-class; bourgeois; **abito ~** civilian dress; **borghe'sia** sf middle classes pl; bourgeoisie

'borgo, ghi sm (paesino) village; (quartiere) district; (sobborgo) suburb

'boria sf self-conceit, arrogance

boro'talco sm talcum powder

bor'raccia, ce [bor'rattʃa] sf canteen, water-bottle

'borsa sf bag; (anche: ~ da signora) handbag; (ECON): **la B~ (valori)** the Stock Exchange; **~ nera** black market; **~ della spesa** shopping bag; **~ di studio** grant; **borsai'olo** sm pickpocket; **borsel'lino** sm purse; **bor'setta** sf handbag; **bor'sista, i, e** sm/f (ECON) speculator; (INS) grant-holder

bos'caglia [bos'kaʎʎa] sf woodlands pl

boscai'olo sm woodcutter; forester

'bosco, schi sm wood; **bos'coso, a** ag wooded

'bossolo sm cartridge-case

bo'tanica sf botany

bo'tanico, a, ci, che ag botanical ♦ sm botanist

'botola sf trap door

'botta sf blow; (rumore) bang

'botte sf barrel, cask

bot'tega, ghe sf shop; (officina) workshop; **botte'gaio, a** sm/f shopkeeper; **botte'ghino** sm ticket office; (del lotto) public lottery office

bot'tiglia [bot'tiʎʎa] sf bottle; **bottiglie'ria** sf wine shop

bot'tino sm (di guerra) booty; (di rapina, furto) loot

'botto sm bang; crash; **di ~** suddenly

bot'tone sm button; **attaccare ~ a qn** (fig) to buttonhole sb

bo'vino, a ag bovine; **~i** smpl cattle

boxe [bɔks] sf boxing

'bozza ['bɔttsa] sf draft; sketch; (TIP) proof; **boz'zetto** sm sketch

'bozzolo ['bɔttsolo] sm cocoon

BR sigla fpl = **Brigate Rosse**

brac'care vt to hunt

brac'cetto [brat'tʃetto] sm: **a ~** arm in arm

bracci'ale [brat'tʃale] sm bracelet; (distintivo) armband; **braccia'letto** sm bracelet, bangle

bracci'ante [brat'tʃante] sm (AGR) day labourer

bracci'ata [brat'tʃata] sf (nel nuoto) stroke

'braccio ['brattʃo] (pl(f) **braccia**) sm (ANAT) arm; (pl(m) **bracci**: di gru, fiume) arm; (: di edificio) wing; **~ di mare** sound; **bracci'olo**

sm (*appoggio*) arm

'bracco, chi *sm* hound

bracconi'ere *sm* poacher

'brace ['bratʃe] *sf* embers *pl*; **braci'ere** *sm* brazier

braci'ola [bra'tʃɔla] *sf* (*CUC*) chop

bra'mare *vt*: ~ **qc/di fare** to long for sth/to do

'branca, che *sf* branch

'branchia ['brankja] *sf* (*ZOOL*) gill

'branco, chi *sm* (*di cani, lupi*) pack; (*di pecore*) flock; (*peg: di persone*) gang, pack

branco'lare *vi* to grope, feel one's way

'branda *sf* camp bed

bran'dello *sm* scrap, shred; **a ~i** in tatters, in rags

bran'dire *vt* to brandish

'brano *sm* piece; (*di libro*) passage

bra'sato *sm* braised beef

Bra'sile *sm*: **il ~** Brazil; **brasili'ano, a** *ag*, *sm/f* Brazilian

'bravo, a *ag* (*abile*) clever, capable, skilful; (*buono*) good, honest; (: *bambino*) good; (*coraggioso*) brave; **~!** well done!; (*a teatro*) bravo!

bra'vura *sf* cleverness, skill

'breccia, ce ['brettʃa] *sf* breach

bre'tella *sf* (*AUT*) link; **~e** *sfpl* (*di calzoni*) braces

'breve *ag* brief, short; **in ~** in short

brevet'tare *vt* to patent

bre'vetto *sm* patent; **~ di pilotaggio** pilot's licence (*BRIT*) o license (*US*)

'brezza ['breddza] *sf* breeze

'bricco, chi *sm* jug; **~ del caffè** coffeepot

bric'cone, a *sm/f* rogue, rascal

'briciola ['britʃola] *sf* crumb

'briciolo ['britʃolo] *sm* (*specie fig*) bit

'briga, ghe *sf* (*fastidio*) trouble, bother; **pigliarsi la ~ di fare qc** to take the trouble to do sth

brigadi'ere *sm* (*dei carabinieri etc*) ≈ sergeant

bri'gante *sm* bandit

bri'gata *sf* (*MIL*) brigade; (*gruppo*) group, party; **B~e Rosse** (*POL*) Red Brigades

'briglia ['briʎʎa] *sf* rein; **a ~ sciolta** at full gallop; (*fig*) at full speed

bril'lante *ag* bright; (*anche fig*) brilliant; (*che luccica*) shining ♦ *sm* diamond

bril'lare *vi* to shine; (*mina*) to blow up ♦ *vt* (*mina*) to set off

'brillo, a *ag* merry, tipsy

'brina *sf* hoarfrost

brin'dare *vi*: ~ **a qn/qc** to drink to o toast sb/sth

'brindisi *sm inv* toast

'brio *sm* liveliness, go

bri'oche [bri'ɔʃ] *sf inv* brioche

bri'oso, a *ag* lively

bri'tannico, a, ci, che *ag* British

'brivido *sm* shiver; (*di ribrezzo*) shudder; (*fig*) thrill

brizzo'lato, a [brittso'lato] *ag* (*persona*) going grey; (*barba, capelli*) greying

'brocca, che *sf* jug

broc'cato *sm* brocade

'broccolo *sm* broccoli *sg*

'brodo *sm* broth; (*per cucinare*) stock; **~ ristretto** consommé

brogli'accio [broʎ'ʎattʃo] *sm* scribbling pad

'broglio ['brɔʎʎo] *sm*: **~ elettorale** gerrymandering

bron'chite [bron'kite] *sf* (*MED*) bronchitis

'broncio ['brontʃo] *sm* sulky expression; **tenere il ~** to sulk

'bronco, chi *sm* bronchial tube

bronto'lare *vi* to grumble; (*tuono, stomaco*) to rumble

'bronzo ['brondzo] *sm* bronze

'browser ['brauzer] *sm inv* (*INFORM*) browser

bru'care *vt* to browse on, nibble at

brucia'pelo [brutʃa'pelo]: **a ~** *av* point-blank

bruci'are [bru'tʃare] *vt* to burn; (*scottare*) to scald ♦ *vi* to burn; **brucia'tore** *sm* burner; **brucia'tura** (*atto*) burning *no pl*; (*segno*) burn; (*scottatura*) scald; **bruci'ore** *sm* burning o smarting sensation; **bruciore di stomaco** heartburn

'bruco, chi *sm* caterpillar; grub

brughi'era [bru'gjera] *sf* heath, moor

bruli'care *vi* to swarm

'brullo, a *ag* bare, bleak

'bruma *sf* mist

'bruno, a *ag* brown, dark; (*persona*) dark (-haired)

'brusco, a, schi, sche *ag* (*sapore*) sharp; (*modi, persona*) brusque, abrupt; (*movimento*) abrupt, sudden

bru'sio *sm* buzz, buzzing

bru'tale *ag* brutal

'bruto, a *ag* (*forza*) brute *cpd* ♦ *sm* brute

brut'tezza [brut'tettsa] *sf* ugliness

'brutto, a *ag* ugly; (*cattivo*) bad; (*malattia, strada, affare*) nasty, bad; **~ tempo** bad weather; **brut'tura** *sf* (*cosa brutta*) ugly thing; (*sudiciume*) filth; (*azione meschina*) mean action

Bru'xelles [bry'sɛl] *sf* Brussels

bub'bone *sm* swelling

'buca, che *sf* hole; (*avvallamento*) hollow; **~ delle lettere** letterbox

buca'neve *sm inv* snowdrop

bu'care *vt* (*forare*) to make a hole (o holes) in; (*pungere*) to pierce; (*biglietto*) to punch; **~rsi** *vr* (*di eroina*) to mainline; **~ una gomma** to have a puncture

bu'cato *sm* (*operazione*) washing; (*panni*)

wash, washing

'**buccia, ce** ['buttʃa] sf skin, peel

bucherel'lare [bukerel'lare] vt to riddle with holes

'**buco, chi** sm hole

bu'dello sm (ANAT: pl(f) ~a) bowel, gut; (fig: tubo) tube; (vicolo) alley

bu'dino sm pudding

'**bue** sm ox; **carne di ~** beef

'**bufalo** sm buffalo

bu'fera sf storm

'**buffo, a** ag funny; (TEATRO) comic

buf'fone sm buffoon; (peg) clown

bu'gia, 'gie [bu'dʒia] sf lie; **dire una ~** to tell a lie; **bugi'ardo, a** ag lying, deceitful ♦ sm/f liar

bugi'gattolo [budʒi'gattolo] sm poky little room

'**buio, a** ag dark ♦ sm dark, darkness

'**bulbo** sm (BOT) bulb; **~ oculare** eyeball

Bulga'ria sf: **la ~** Bulgaria

bul'lone sm bolt

buona'notte escl good night! ♦ sf: **dare la ~ a** to say good night to

buona'sera escl good evening!

buongi'orno [bwon'dʒorno] escl good morning (o afternoon)!

buongus'taio, a sm/f gourmet

buon'gusto sm good taste

bu'ono, a (ag: dav sm **buon** +C o V, **buono** +s impura, gn, pn, ps, x, z; dav sf **buon'** +V) ag 1 (gen) good; **un buon pranzo/ristorante** a good lunch/restaurant; **(stai) ~!** behave!
2 (benevolo): **~ (con)** good (to), kind (to)
3 (giusto, valido) right; **al momento ~** at the right moment
4 (adatto): **~ a/da** fit for/to; **essere ~ a nulla** to be no good o use at anything
5 (auguri): **buon anno!** happy New Year!; **buon appetito!** enjoy your meal!; **buon compleanno!** happy birthday!; **buon divertimento!** have a nice time!; **~a fortuna!** good luck!; **buon riposo!** sleep well!; **buon viaggio!** bon voyage!, have a good trip!
6: **a buon mercato** cheap; **di buon'ora** early; **buon senso** common sense; **alla ~a** ag simple ♦ av in a simple way, without any fuss
♦ sm 1 (bontà) goodness, good
2 (COMM) voucher, coupon; **~ di cassa** cash voucher; **~ di consegna** delivery note; **~ del Tesoro** Treasury bill

buontem'pone, a sm/f jovial person

burat'tino sm puppet

'**burbero, a** ag surly, gruff

'**burla** sf prank, trick; **bur'lare** vt: **burlare qc/ qn, burlarsi di qc/qn** to make fun of sth/sb

burocra'zia [burokrat'tsia] sf bureaucracy

bur'rasca, sche sf storm

'**burro** sm butter

bur'rone sm ravine

bus'care vt (anche: ~rsi: raffreddore) to get, catch; **buscarle** (fam) to get a hiding

bus'sare vi to knock

'**bussola** sf compass

'**busta** sf (da lettera) envelope; (astuccio) case; **in ~ aperta/chiusa** in an unsealed/sealed envelope; **~ paga** pay packet

busta'rella sf bribe, backhander

'**busto** sm bust; (indumento) corset, girdle; **a mezzo ~** (foto) half-length

buttafu'ori sm inv bouncer

but'tare vt to throw; (anche: ~ via) to throw away; **~ giù** (scritto) to scribble down; (cibo) to gulp down; (edificio) to pull down, demolish; (pasta, verdura) to put into boiling water

C, c

ca'bina sf (di nave) cabin; (da spiaggia) beach hut; (di autocarro, treno) cab; (di aereo) cockpit; (di ascensore) cage; **~ telefonica** call o (tele)phone box; **cabi'nato** sm cabin cruiser

ca'cao sm cocoa

'**caccia** ['kattʃa] sf hunting; (con fucile) shooting; (inseguimento) chase; (cacciagione) game ♦ sm inv (aereo) fighter; (nave) destroyer; **~ grossa** big-game hunting; **~ all'uomo** manhunt

cacciabombardi'ere [kattʃabombar'djɛre] sm fighter-bomber

cacciagi'one [kattʃa'dʒone] sf game

cacci'are [kat'tʃare] vt to hunt; (mandar via) to chase away; (ficcare) to shove, stick ♦ vi to hunt; **~rsi** vr: **dove s'è cacciata la mia borsa?** where has my bag got to?; **~rsi nei guai** to get into trouble; **~ fuori qc** to whip o pull sth out; **~ un urlo** to let out a yell; **caccia'tore** sm hunter; **cacciatore di frodo** poacher

caccia'vite [kattʃa'vite] sm inv screwdriver

'**cactus** sm inv cactus

ca'davere sm (dead) body, corpse

ca'dente ag falling; (casa) tumbledown

ca'denza [ka'dɛntsa] sf cadence; (ritmo) rhythm; (MUS) cadenza

ca'dere vi to fall; (denti, capelli) to fall out; (tetto) to fall in; **questa gonna cade bene** this skirt hangs well; **lasciar ~** (anche fig) to drop; **~ dal sonno** to be falling asleep on one's feet; **~ dalle nuvole** (fig) to be taken aback

ca'detto, a ag younger; (squadra) junior cpd ♦ sm cadet

ca'duta sf fall; **la ~ dei capelli** hair loss

caffè *sm inv* coffee; (*locale*) café; **~ macchiato** coffee with a dash of milk; **~ macinato** ground coffee

caffel'latte *sm inv* white coffee

caffetti'era *sf* coffeepot

cagio'nare [kadʒo'nare] *vt* to cause

cagio'nevole [kadʒo'nevole] *ag* delicate, weak

cagli'are [kaʎ'ʎare] *vi* to curdle

'cagna ['kaɲɲa] *sf* (*ZOOL, peg*) bitch

ca'gnesco, a, schi, sche [kaɲ'ɲesko] *ag* (*fig*): **guardare qn in ~** to scowl at sb

cala'brone *sm* hornet

cala'maio *sm* inkpot; inkwell

cala'maro *sm* squid

cala'mita *sf* magnet

calamità *sf inv* calamity, disaster

ca'lare *vt* (*far discendere*) to lower; (*MAGLIA*) to decrease ♦ *vi* (*discendere*) to go (o come) down; (*tramontare*) to set, go down; **~ di peso** to lose weight

'calca *sf* throng, press

cal'cagno [kal'kaɲɲo] *sm* heel

cal'care *sm* limestone ♦ *vt* (*premere coi piedi*) to tread, press down; (*premere con forza*) to press down; (*mettere in rilievo*) to stress; **~ la mano** to overdo it, exaggerate

'calce ['kaltʃe] *sm*: **in ~** at the foot of the page ♦ *sf* lime; **~ viva** quicklime

calces'truzzo [kaltʃes'truttso] *sm* concrete

calci'are [kal'tʃare] *vt, vi* to kick; **calcia'tore** *sm* footballer

'calcio ['kaltʃo] *sm* (*pedata*) kick; (*sport*) football, soccer; (*di pistola, fucile*) butt; (*CHIM*) calcium; **~ d'angolo** (*SPORT*) corner (kick); **~ di punizione** (*SPORT*) free kick

'calco, chi *sm* (*ARTE*) casting, moulding; cast, mould

calco'lare *vt* to calculate, work out, reckon; (*ponderare*) to weigh (up); **calcola'tore, 'trice** *ag* calculating ♦ *sm* calculator; (*fig*) calculating person; **calcolatore elettronico** computer; **calcola'trice** *sf* calculator

'calcolo *sm* (*anche MAT*) calculation; (*infinitesimale etc*) calculus; (*MED*) stone; **fare i propri ~i** (*fig*) to weigh the pros and cons; **per ~** out of self-interest

cal'daia *sf* boiler

caldeggi'are |kalded'dʒare| *vt* to support

'caldo, a *ag* warm; (*molto ~*) hot; (*fig: appassionato*) keen; hearty ♦ *sm* heat; **ho ~** I'm warm; I'm hot; **fa ~** it's warm; it's hot

calen'dario *sm* calendar

'calibro *sm* (*di arma*) calibre, bore; (*TECN*) callipers *pl*; (*fig*) calibre; **di grosso ~** (*fig*) prominent

'calice ['kalitʃe] *sm* goblet; (*REL*) chalice

ca'ligine [ka'lidʒine] *sf* fog; (*mista con fumo*) smog

'callo *sm* callus; (*ai piedi*) corn

'calma *sf* calm

cal'mante *sm* tranquillizer

cal'mare *vt* to calm; (*lenire*) to soothe; **~rsi** *vr* to grow calm, calm down; (*vento*) to abate; (*dolori*) to ease

calmi'ere *sm* controlled price

'calmo, a *ag* calm, quiet

'calo *sm* (*COMM: di prezzi*) fall; (*: di volume*) shrinkage; (*: di peso*) loss

ca'lore *sm* warmth; heat; **in ~** (*ZOOL*) on heat

calo'ria *sf* calorie

calo'roso, a *ag* warm

calpes'tare *vt* to tread on, trample on; **"è vietato ~ l'erba"** "keep off the grass"

ca'lunnia *sf* slander; (*scritta*) libel

cal'vario *sm* (*fig*) affliction, cross

cal'vizie [kal'vittsje] *sf* baldness

'calvo, a *ag* bald

'calza ['kaltsa] *sf* (*da donna*) stocking; (*da uomo*) sock; **fare la ~** to knit; **~e di nailon** nylons, (nylon) stockings

cal'zare [kal'tsare] *vt* (*scarpe, guanti: mettersi*) to put on; (*: portare*) to wear ♦ *vi* to fit; **calza'tura** *sf* footwear

calzet'tone [kaltset'tone] *sm* heavy knee-length sock

cal'zino [kal'tsino] *sm* sock

calzo'laio [kaltso'lajo] *sm* shoemaker; (*che ripara scarpe*) cobbler; **calzole'ria** *sf* (*negozio*) shoe shop

calzon'cini [kaltson'tʃini] *smpl* shorts

cal'zone [kal'tsone] *sm* trouser leg; (*CUC*) savoury turnover made with pizza dough; **~i** *smpl* (*pantaloni*) trousers (*BRIT*), pants (*US*)

cambi'ale *sf* bill (of exchange); (*pagherò cambiario*) promissory note

cambia'mento *sm* change

cambi'are *vt* to change; (*modificare*) to alter, change; (*barattare*): **~ (qc con qn/qc)** to exchange (sth with sb/for sth) ♦ *vi* to change, alter; **~rsi** *vr* (*d'abito*) to change; **~ casa** to move (house); **~ idea** to change one's mind; **~ treno** to change trains

'cambio *sm* change; (*modifica*) alteration, change; (*scambio, COMM*) exchange; (*corso dei cambi*) rate (of exchange); (*TECN, AUT*) gears *pl*; **in ~ di** in exchange for; **dare il ~ a qn** to take over from sb

'camera *sf* room; (*anche: ~ da letto*) bedroom; (*POL*) chamber, house; **~ ardente** mortuary chapel; **~ d'aria** inner tube; (*di pallone*) bladder; **C~ di Commercio** Chamber of Commerce; **C~ dei Deputati** Chamber of Deputies, ≈ House of Commons (*BRIT*), ≈ House of Representatives (*US*); **~ a gas** gas chamber; **~ a un letto/a due letti/matrimoniale** single/twin-bedded/double room; **~ oscura** (*FOT*) dark room

came'rata, i, e *sm/f* companion, mate ♦ *sf* dormitory

cameri'era *sf* (*domestica*) maid; (*che serve a tavola*) waitress; (*che fa le camere*) chambermaid

cameri'ere *sm* (man)servant; (*di ristorante*) waiter

came'rino *sm* (*TEATRO*) dressing room

'camice ['kamitʃe] *sm* (*REL*) alb; (*per medici etc*) white coat

cami'cetta [kami'tʃetta] *sf* blouse

ca'micia, cie [ka'mitʃa] *sf* (*da uomo*) shirt; (*da donna*) blouse; ~ **di forza** straitjacket

cami'netto *sm* hearth, fireplace

ca'mino *sm* chimney; (*focolare*) fireplace, hearth

'camion *sm inv* lorry (*BRIT*), truck (*US*); **camion'cino** *sm* van

cam'mello *sm* (*ZOOL*) camel; (*tessuto*) camel hair

cammi'nare *vi* to walk; (*funzionare*) to work, go; **cammi'nata** *sf* walk

cam'mino *sm* walk; (*sentiero*) path; (*itinerario, direzione, tragitto*) way; **mettersi in** ~ to set o start off

camo'milla *sf* camomile; (*infuso*) camomile tea

ca'morra *sf* camorra; racket

ca'moscio [ka'moʃʃo] *sm* chamois; **di** ~ (*scarpe, borsa*) suede *cpd*

cam'pagna [kam'paɲɲa] *sf* country, countryside; (*POL, COMM, MIL*) campaign; **in** ~ in the country; **andare in** ~ to go to the country; **fare una** ~ to campaign; **campa'gnola** *sf* (*AUT*) cross-country vehicle; **campa'gnolo, a** *ag* country *cpd*

cam'pale *ag* field *cpd*; (*fig*): **una giornata** ~ a hard day

cam'pana *sf* bell; (*anche*: ~ **di vetro**) bell jar; **campa'nella** *sf* small bell; (*di tenda*) curtain ring; **campa'nello** *sm* (*all'uscio, da tavola*) bell

campa'nile *sm* bell tower, belfry; **campani'lismo** *sm* parochialism

cam'pare *vi* to live; (*tirare avanti*) to get by, manage

cam'pato, a *ag*: ~ **in aria** unfounded

campeggi'are [kamped'dʒare] *vi* to camp; (*risaltare*) to stand out; **campeggia'tore, 'trice** *sm/f* camper; **cam'peggio** *sm* camping; (*terreno*) camp site; **fare (del) campeggio** to go camping

cam'pestre *ag* country *cpd*, rural

campio'nario, a *ag*: **fiera** ~**a** trade fair ♦ *sm* collection of samples

campio'nato *sm* championship

campi'one, 'essa *sm/f* (*SPORT*) champion ♦ *sm* (*COMM*) sample

'campo *sm* field; (*MIL*) field; (*: accampa-*

mento) camp; (*spazio delimitato: sportivo etc*) ground; field; (*di quadro*) background; **i** ~**i** (*campagna*) the countryside; ~ **da aviazione** airfield; ~ **di battaglia** (*MIL, fig*) battlefield; ~ **di golf** golf course; ~ **da tennis** tennis court; ~ **visivo** field of vision

campo'santo (*pl* **campisanti**) *sm* cemetery

camuf'fare *vt* to disguise

'Canada *sm*: **il** ~ Canada; **cana'dese** *ag*, *sm/f* Canadian ♦ *sf* (*anche*: **tenda canadese**) ridge tent

ca'naglia [ka'naʎʎa] *sf* rabble, mob; (*persona*) scoundrel, rogue

ca'nale *sm* (*anche fig*) channel; (*artificiale*) canal

'canapa *sf* hemp; ~ **indiana** (*droga*) cannabis

cana'rino *sm* canary

cancel'lare [kantʃel'lare] *vt* (*con la gomma*) to rub out, erase; (*con la penna*) to strike out; (*annullare*) to annul, cancel; (*disdire*) to cancel

cancelle'ria [kantʃelle'ria] *sf* chancery; (*materiale per scrivere*) stationery

cancelli'ere [kantʃel'ljere] *sm* chancellor; (*di tribunale*) clerk of the court

can'cello [kan'tʃello] *sm* gate

can'crena *sf* gangrene

'cancro *sm* (*MED*) cancer; (*dello zodiaco*): **C~** Cancer

candeg'gina [kanded'dʒina] *sf* bleach

can'dela *sf* candle; ~ (**di accensione**) (*AUT*) spark(ing) plug

cande'labro *sm* candelabra

candeli'ere *sm* candlestick

candi'dato, a *sm/f* candidate; (*aspirante a una carica*) applicant

'candido, a *ag* white as snow; (*puro*) pure; (*sincero*) sincere, candid

can'dito, a *ag* candied

can'dore *sm* brilliant white; purity; sincerity; candour

'cane *sm* dog; (*di pistola, fucile*) cock; **fa un freddo** ~ it's bitterly cold; **non c'era un** ~ there wasn't a soul; ~ **da caccia/guardia** hunting/guard dog; ~ **lupo** alsatian

ca'nestro *sm* basket

'canfora *sf* camphor

cangi'ante [kan'dʒante] *ag* iridescent

can'guro *sm* kangaroo

ca'nile *sm* kennel; (*di allevamento*) kennels *pl*; ~ **municipale** dog pound

ca'nino, a *ag, sm* canine

'canna *sf* (*pianta*) reed; (*: indica, da zucchero*) cane; (*bastone*) stick, cane; (*di fucile*) barrel; (*di organo*) pipe; (*fam: droga*) joint; ~ **da pesca** (fishing) rod; ~ **da zucchero** sugar cane

can'nella *sf* (*CUC*) cinnamon

cannel'loni *smpl* pasta tubes stuffed with sauce and baked

cannocchi'ale [kannok'kjale] *sm* telescope

can'none *sm* (*MIL*) gun; (: *STORIA*) cannon; (*tubo*) pipe, tube; (*piega*) box pleat; (*fig*) ace

can'nuccia, ce [kan'nuttʃa] *sf* (drinking) straw

ca'noa *sf* canoe

'canone *sm* canon, criterion; (*mensile, annuo*) rent; fee

ca'nonico, ci *sm* (*REL*) canon

ca'noro, a *ag* (*uccello*) singing, song *cpd*

canot'taggio [kanot'taddʒo] *sm* rowing

canotti'era *sf* vest

ca'notto *sm* small boat, dinghy; canoe

cano'vaccio [kano'vattʃo] *sm* (*tela*) canvas; (*strofinaccio*) duster; (*trama*) plot

can'tante *sm/f* singer

can'tare *vt, vi* to sing; **cantau'tore, 'trice** *sm/f* singer-composer

canti'ere *sm* (*EDIL*) (building) site; (*anche*: ~ *navale*) shipyard

canti'lena *sf* (*filastrocca*) lullaby; (*fig*) sing-song voice

can'tina *sf* cellar; (*bottega*) wine shop

'canto *sm* song; (*arte*) singing; (*REL*) chant, chanting; (*poesia*) poem, lyric; (*parte di una poesia*) canto; (*parte, lato*): **da un ~** on the one hand; **d'altro ~** on the other hand

canto'nata *sf* corner; **prendere una ~** (*fig*) to blunder

can'tone *sm* (in Svizzera) canton

can'tuccio [kan'tuttʃo] *sm* corner, nook

canzo'nare [kantso'nare] *vt* to tease

can'zone [kan'tsone] *sf* song; (*POESIA*) canzone; **canzoni'ere** *sm* (*MUS*) songbook; (*LETTERATURA*) collection of poems

'caos *sm inv* chaos; **ca'otico, a, ci, che** *ag* chaotic

C.A.P. *sigla m* = **codice di avviamento postale**

ca'pace [ka'patʃe] *ag* able, capable; (*ampio, vasto*) large, capacious; **sei ~ di farlo?** can you o are you able to do it?; **capacità** *sf inv* ability; (*DIR, di recipiente*) capacity; **capaci'tarsi** *vr* to understand

ca'panna *sf* hut

capan'none *sm* (*AGR*) barn; (*fabbricato industriale*) (factory) shed

ca'parbio, a *ag* stubborn

ca'parra *sf* deposit, down payment

ca'pello *sm* hair; ~**i** *smpl* (*capigliatura*) hair *sg*

capez'zale [kapet'tsale] *sm* bolster; (*fig*) bedside

ca'pezzolo [ka'pettsolo] *sm* nipple

capi'enza [ka'pjentsa] *sf* capacity

capiglia'tura [kapiʎʎa'tura] *sf* hair

ca'pire *vt* to understand

capi'tale *ag* (*mortale*) capital; (*fondamentale*) main, chief ♦ *sf* (*città*) capital ♦ *sm* (*ECON*) capital; **capita'lismo** *sm* capitalism

capitane'ria *sf*: ~ **di porto** port authorities *pl*

capi'tano *sm* captain

capi'tare *vi* (*giungere casualmente*) to happen to go, find o.s.; (*accadere*) to happen; (*presentarsi: cosa*) to turn up, present itself ♦ *vb impers* to happen; **mi è capitato un guaio** I've had a spot of trouble

capi'tello *sm* (*ARCHIT*) capital

ca'pitolo *sm* chapter

capi'tombolo *sm* headlong fall, tumble

'capo *sm* head; (*persona*) head, leader; (: *in ufficio*) head, boss; (: *in tribù*) chief; (*di oggetti*) head; top; end; (*GEO*) cape; **andare a ~** to start a new paragraph; **da ~** over again; ~ **di bestiame** head *inv* of cattle; ~ **di vestiario** item of clothing

'capo... *prefisso*: **capocu'oco, chi** *sm* head cook; **Capo'danno** *sm* New Year; **capo'fitto: a capofitto** *av* headfirst, headlong; **capo'giro** *sm* dizziness *no pl*; **capola'voro, i** *sm* masterpiece; **capo'linea** (*pl* **capi'linea**) *sm* terminus; **capo'lino** *sm*: **fare capolino** to peep out (o in *etc*); **capolu'ogo** (*pl* **-ghi** o **capilu'oghi**) *sm* chief town, administrative centre

capo'rale *sm* (*MIL*) lance corporal (*BRIT*), private first class (*US*)

'capo... *prefisso*: **capostazi'one** (*pl* **capi-stazi'one**) *sm* station master; **capo'treno** (*pl* **capi'treno** o **capo'treni**) *sm* guard

capo'volgere [kapo'voldʒere] *vt* to overturn; (*fig*) to reverse; ~**rsi** *vr* to overturn; (*barca*) to capsize; (*fig*) to be reversed; **capo'volto, a** *pp di* **capovolgere**

'cappa *sf* (*mantello*) cape, cloak; (*del camino*) hood

cap'pella *sf* (*REL*) chapel; **cappel'lano** *sm* chaplain

cap'pello *sm* hat

'cappero *sm* caper

cap'pone *sm* capon

cap'potto *sm* (over)coat

cappuc'cino [kapput'tʃino] *sm* (*frate*) Capuchin monk; (*bevanda*) cappuccino, frothy white coffee

cap'puccio [kap'puttʃo] *sm* (*copricapo*) hood; (*della biro*) cap

'capra *sf* (she-)goat; **ca'pretto** *sm* kid

ca'priccio [ka'prittʃo] *sm* caprice, whim; (*bizza*) tantrum; **fare i ~i** to be very naughty; **capricci'oso, a** *ag* capricious, whimsical; naughty

Capri'corno *sm* Capricorn

capri'ola *sf* somersault

capri'olo *sm* roe deer

'capro *sm*: ~ **espiatorio** scapegoat

'capsula *sf* capsule; (*di arma, per bottiglie*) cap

cap'tare *vt* (*RADIO, TV*) to pick up; (*cattivarsi*)

to ˈgain, win

caraˈbina sf rifle

carabiniˈere sm member of Italian military police force

caˈraffa sf carafe

caraˈmella sf sweet

caˈrattere sm character; (caratteristica) characteristic, trait; **avere un buon ~** to be good-natured; **caratteˈristica, che** sf characteristic, trait, peculiarity; **caratteˈristico, a, ci, che** ag characteristic; **caratterizˈzare** vt to characterize

carˈbone sm coal

carbuˈrante sm (motor) fuel

carburaˈtore sm carburettor

carˈcassa sf carcass; (fig: peg: macchina etc) (old) wreck

carceˈrato, a [kartʃeˈrato] sm/f prisoner

ˈcarcere [ˈkartʃere] sm prison; (pena) imprisonment

carciˈofo [karˈtʃɔfo] sm artichoke

carˈdiaco, a, ci, che ag cardiac, heart cpd

cardiˈnale ag, sm cardinal

ˈcardine sm hinge

ˈcardo sm thistle

caˈrenza [kaˈrɛntsa] sf lack, scarcity; (vitaminica) deficiency

caresˈtia sf famine; (penuria) scarcity, dearth

caˈrezza [kaˈrettsa] sf caress; **carezˈzare** vt to caress, stroke

ˈcarica, che sf (mansione ufficiale) office, position; (MIL, TECN, ELETTR) charge; **ha una forte ~ di simpatia** he's very likeable; vedi anche **carico**

cariˈcare vt to load; (orologio) to wind up; (batteria, MIL) to charge

ˈcarico, a, chi, che ag (che porta un peso): **~ di** loaded o laden with; (fucile) loaded; (orologio) wound up; (batteria) charged; (colore) deep; (caffè, tè) strong ♦ sm (il caricare) loading; (ciò che si carica) load; (fig: peso) burden, weight; **persona a ~** dependent; **essere a ~ di qn** (spese etc) to be charged to sb

ˈcarie sf (dentaria) decay

caˈrino, a ag (grazioso) lovely, pretty, nice; (riferito a uomo, anche simpatico) nice

caˈrità sf charity; **per ~!** (escl di rifiuto) good heavens, no!

carnagiˈone [karnaˈdʒone] sf complexion

carˈnale ag (amore) carnal

ˈcarne sf flesh; (bovina, ovina etc) meat; **~ di manzo/maiale/pecora** beef/pork/mutton; **~ tritata** mince (BRIT), hamburger meat (US), minced (BRIT) o ground (US) meat

carˈnefice [karˈnefitʃe] sm executioner; (alla forca) hangman

carneˈvale sm carnival

carˈnoso, a ag fleshy

ˈcaro, a ag (amato) dear; (costoso) dear, expensive

caˈrogna [kaˈroɲɲa] sf carrion; (fig: fam) swine

caˈrota sf carrot

caroˈvana sf caravan

caroˈvita sm high cost of living

carpentiˈere sm carpenter

carˈpire vt: **~ qc a qn** (segreto etc) to get sth out of sb

carˈponi av on all fours

carˈrabile ag suitable for vehicles; **"passo ~"** "keep clear"

carˈraio, a ag: **passo ~** driveway

carreggiˈata [karredˈdʒata] sf carriageway (BRIT), (road)way

carˈrello sm trolley; (AER) undercarriage; (CINEMA) dolly; (di macchina da scrivere) carriage

carriˈera sf career; **fare ~** to get on; **a gran ~** at full speed

carriˈola sf wheelbarrow

ˈcarro sm cart, wagon; **~ armato** tank; **~ attrezzi** breakdown van

carˈrozza [karˈrɔttsa] sf carriage, coach

carrozzeˈria [karrottseˈria] sf body, coachwork (BRIT); (officina) coachbuilder's workshop (BRIT), body shop

carrozˈzina [karrotˈtsina] sf pram (BRIT), baby carriage (US)

ˈcarta sf paper; (al ristorante) menu; (GEO) map; plan; (documento, da gioco) card; (costituzione) charter; **~e** sfpl (documenti) papers, documents; **alla ~** (al ristorante) à la carte; **~ assegni** bank card; **~ assorbente** blotting paper; **~ bollata** o **da bollo** official stamped paper; **~ di credito** credit card; **~ (geografica)** map; **~ d'identità** identity card; **~ igienica** toilet paper; **~ d'imbarco** (AER, NAUT) boarding card; **~ da lettere** writing paper; **~ libera** (AMM) unstamped paper; **~ da parati** wallpaper; **~ stradale** road map; **~ verde** (AUT) green card; **~ vetrata** sandpaper; **~ da visita** visiting card

cartacarˈbone (pl cartecarˈbone) sf carbon paper

carˈtaccia, ce [karˈtattʃa] sf waste paper

cartaˈpecora sf parchment

cartaˈpesta sf papier-mâché

carˈteggio [karˈteddʒo] sm correspondence

carˈtella sf (scheda) card; (custodia: di cartone) folder; (: di uomo d'affari etc) briefcase; (: di scolaro) schoolbag, satchel; **~ clinica** (MED) case sheet

carˈtello sm sign; (pubblicitario) poster; (stradale) sign, signpost; (ECON) cartel; (in dimostrazioni) placard; **cartelˈlone** sm (pubblicitario) advertising poster; (della tombola) scoring frame; (TEATRO) playbill;

tenere il **cartellone** (*spettacolo*) to have a long run
carti'era *sf* paper mill
car'tina *sf* (*AUT, GEO*) map
car'toccio [kar'tɔttʃo] *sm* paper bag
cartole'ria *sf* stationer's (shop)
carto'lina *sf* postcard; **~ postale** ready-stamped postcard
car'tone *sm* cardboard; (*ARTE*) cartoon; **~i animati** *smpl* (*CINEMA*) cartoons
car'tuccia, ce [kar'tuttʃa] *sf* cartridge
'casa *sf* house; (*in senso astratto*) home; (*COMM*) firm, house; **essere a ~** to be at home; **vado a ~ mia/tua** I'm going home/to your house; **~ di cura** nursing home; **~ dello studente** student hostel; **~e popolari** ≈ council houses (*o* flats) (*BRIT*), ≈ public housing units (*US*); **vino della ~** house wine
ca'sacca, che *sf* military coat; (*di fantino*) blouse
casa'linga, ghe *sf* housewife
casa'lingo, a, ghi, ghe *ag* household, domestic; (*fatto a casa*) home-made; (*semplice*) homely; (*amante della casa*) home-loving; **~ghi** *smpl* household articles; **cucina ~a** plain home cooking
cas'care *vi* to fall; **cas'cata** *sf* fall; (*d'acqua*) cascade, waterfall
ca'scina [kaʃʃina] *sf* farmstead
'casco, schi *sm* helmet; (*del parrucchiere*) hair-drier; (*di banane*) bunch
casei'ficio [kazei'fitʃo] *sm* creamery
ca'sella *sf* pigeon-hole; **~ postale** post office box
casel'lario *sm* filing cabinet; **~ giudiziale** court records *pl*
ca'sello *sm* (*di autostrada*) toll-house
ca'serma *sf* barracks *pl*
ca'sino (*fam*) *sm* brothel; (*confusione*) row, racket
casinò *sm inv* casino
'caso *sm* chance; (*fatto, vicenda*) event, incident; (*possibilità*) possibility; (*MED, LING*) case; **a ~** at random; **per ~** by chance, by accident; **in ogni ~, in tutti i ~i** in any case, at any rate; **al ~** should the opportunity arise; **nel ~ che** in case; **~ mai** if by chance; **~ limite** borderline case
caso'lare *sm* cottage
'cassa *sf* case, crate, box; (*bara*) coffin; (*mobile*) chest; (*involucro: di orologio etc*) case; (*macchina*) cash register, till; (*luogo di pagamento*) checkout (counter); (*fondo*) fund; (*istituto bancario*) bank; **~ automatica prelievi** cash dispenser; **~ continua** night safe; **~ integrazione: mettere in ~ integrazione** ≈ to lay off; **~ mutua** *o* **malattia** health insurance scheme; **~ di risparmio** savings bank; **~ toracica** (*ANAT*) chest

cassa'forte (*pl* **casse'forti**) *sf* safe
cassa'panca (*pl* **cassa'panche** *o* **casse'panche**) *sf* settle
casse'rola *sf* = **casseruola**
casseru'ola *sf* saucepan
cas'setta *sf* box; (*per registratore*) cassette; (*CINEMA, TEATRO*) box-office takings *pl*; **film di ~** box-office draw; **~ di sicurezza** strongbox; **~ delle lettere** letterbox
cas'setto *sm* drawer; **casset'tone** *sm* chest of drawers
cassi'ere, a *sm/f* cashier; (*di banca*) teller
casso'netto *sm* wheelie-bin
'casta *sf* caste
cas'tagna [kas'taɲɲa] *sf* chestnut
cas'tagno [kas'taɲɲo] *sm* chestnut (tree)
cas'tano, a *ag* chestnut (brown)
cas'tello *sm* castle; (*TECN*) scaffolding
casti'gare *vt* to punish; **cas'tigo, ghi** *sm* punishment
castità *sf* chastity
cas'toro *sm* beaver
cas'trare *vt* to castrate; to geld; to doctor (*BRIT*), fix (*US*)
casu'ale *ag* chance *cpd*; (*INFORM*) random *cpd*
cata'comba *sf* catacomb
ca'talogo, ghi *sm* catalogue
catarifran'gente [katarifran'dʒɛnte] *sm* (*AUT*) reflector
ca'tarro *sm* catarrh
ca'tasta *sf* stack, pile
ca'tasto *sm* land register; land registry office
ca'tastrofe *sf* catastrophe, disaster
catego'ria *sf* category
ca'tena *sf* chain; **~ di montaggio** assembly line; **~e da neve** (*AUT*) snow chains; **cate'naccio** *sm* bolt
cate'ratta *sf* cataract; (*chiusa*) sluice-gate
cati'nella *sf*: **piovere a ~e** to pour
ca'tino *sm* basin
ca'trame *sm* tar
'cattedra *sf* teacher's desk; (*di docente*) chair
catte'drale *sf* cathedral
catti'veria *sf* malice, spite; naughtiness; (*atto*) spiteful act; (*parole*) malicious *o* spiteful remark
cattività *sf* captivity
cat'tivo, a *ag* bad; (*malvagio*) bad, wicked; (*turbolento: bambino*) bad, naughty; (*: mare*) rough; (*odore, sapore*) nasty, bad
cat'tolico, a, ci, che *ag, sm/f* (Roman) Catholic
cat'tura *sf* capture
cattu'rare *vt* to capture
caucciù [kaut'tʃu] *sm* rubber
'causa *sf* cause; (*DIR*) lawsuit, case, action; **a ~ di, per ~ di** because of; **fare** *o* **muovere ~ a qn** to take legal action against sb

cau'sare vt to cause
cau'tela sf caution, prudence
caute'lare vt to protect; ~**rsi** vr: ~**rsi (da)** to take precautions (against)
'cauto, a ag cautious, prudent
cauzi'one [kaut'tsjone] sf security; (DIR) bail
cav. abbr = **cavaliere**
'cava sf quarry
caval'care vt (cavallo) to ride; (muro) to sit astride; (sog: ponte) to span; **caval'cata** sf ride; (gruppo di persone) riding party
cavalca'via sm inv flyover
cavalci'oni [kaval'tʃoni]: **a ~ di** prep astride
cavali'ere sm rider; (feudale, titolo) knight; (soldato) cavalryman; (al ballo) partner; **cavalle'resco, a, schi, sche** ag chivalrous; **cavalle'ria** sf (di persona) chivalry; (milizia a cavallo) cavalry
cavalle'rizzo, a [kavalle'rittso] sm/f riding instructor; circus rider
caval'letta sf grasshopper
caval'letto sm (FOT) tripod; (da pittore) easel
ca'vallo sm horse; (SCACCHI) knight; (AUT: anche: ~ vapore) horsepower; (dei pantaloni) crotch; **a ~** on horseback; **a ~ di** astride, straddling; **~ di battaglia** (fig) hobby-horse; **~ da corsa** racehorse
ca'vare vt (togliere) to draw out, extract, take out; (: giacca, scarpe) to take off; (: fame, sete, voglia) to satisfy; **cavarsela** to manage, get on all right; (scamparla) to get away with it
cava'tappi sm inv corkscrew
ca'verna sf cave
'cavia sf guinea pig
cavi'ale sm caviar
ca'viglia [ka'viʎʎa] sf ankle
ca'villo sm quibble
'cavo, a ag hollow ♦ sm (ANAT) cavity; (corda, ELETTR, TEL) cable
cavolfi'ore sm cauliflower
'cavolo sm cabbage; (fam): **non m'importa un ~** I don't give a dar?n; **~ di Bruxelles** Brussels sprout
cazzu'ola [kat'tswola] sf trowel
c/c abbr = **conto corrente**
CD sm inv CD
CD-ROM [tʃidi'rom] sm inv CD-ROM
C.E. [tʃe] sigla f (= Comunità Europea) EC
ce [tʃe] pron, av vedi **ci**
'cece [tʃetʃe] sm chickpea
cecità [tʃetʃi'ta] sf blindness
'ceco, a ['tʃɛko] ag, sm/f Czech; **la Repubblica ~a** the Czech Republic
Cecoslo'vacchia [tʃekoslo'vakkja] sf: **la ~** Czechoslovakia
'cedere ['tʃɛdere] vt (concedere: posto) to give up; (DIR) to transfer, make over ♦ vi (cadere) to give way, subside; **~ (a)** to surrender (to),

yield (to), give in (to); **ce'devole** ag (terreno) soft; (fig) yielding
'cedola ['tʃɛdola] sf (COMM) coupon; voucher
'cedro ['tʃɛdro] sm cedar; (albero da frutto, frutto) citron
'ceffo ['tʃɛffo] (peg) sm ugly mug
cef'fone [tʃef'fone] sm slap, smack
ce'lare [tʃe'lare] vt to conceal; ~**rsi** to hide
cele'brare [tʃele'brare] vt to celebrate; **celebrazi'one** sf celebration
'celebre ['tʃelebre] ag famous, celebrated; **celebrità** sf inv fame; (persona) celebrity
'celere ['tʃelere] ag fast, swift; (corso) crash cpd
ce'leste [tʃe'lɛste] ag celestial; heavenly; (colore) sky-blue
'celibe ['tʃɛlibe] ag single, unmarried
'cella ['tʃɛlla] sf cell
'cellula ['tʃɛllula] sf (BIOL, ELETTR, POL) cell; **cellu'lare** sm cellphone
cellu'lite [tʃellu'lite] sf cellulite
cemen'tare [tʃemen'tare] vt (anche fig) to cement
ce'mento [tʃe'mento] sm cement; **~ armato** reinforced concrete
'cena ['tʃena] sf dinner; (leggera) supper
ce'nare [tʃe'nare] vi to dine, have dinner
'cencio ['tʃentʃo] sm piece of cloth, rag; (per spolverare) duster
'cenere ['tʃenere] sf ash
'cenno ['tʃenno] sm (segno) sign, signal; (gesto) gesture; (col capo) nod; (con la mano) wave; (allusione) hint, mention; (breve esposizione) short account; **far ~ di sì/no** to nod (one's head)/shake one's head
censi'mento [tʃensi'mento] sm census
cen'sura [tʃen'sura] sf censorship; censor's office; (fig) censure
cente'nario, a [tʃente'narjo] ag (che ha cento anni) hundred-year-old; (che ricorre ogni cento anni) centennial, centenary cpd ♦ sm/f centenarian ♦ sm centenary
cen'tesimo, a [tʃen'tezimo] ag, sm hundredth
cen'tigrado, a [tʃen'tigrado] ag centigrade; **20 gradi ~i** 20 degrees centigrade
cen'timetro [tʃen'timetro] sm centimetre
centi'naio [tʃenti'najo] (pl(f) -**aia**) sm: **un ~ (di)** a hundred; about a hundred
'cento ['tʃento] num a hundred, one hundred
cen'trale [tʃen'trale] ag central ♦ sf: **~ telefonica** (telephone) exchange; **~ elettrica** electric power station; **centrali'nista** sm/f operator; **centra'lino** sm (telephone) exchange; (di albergo etc) switchboard
cen'trare [tʃen'trare] vt to hit the centre of; (TECN) to centre
cen'trifuga [tʃen'trifuga] sf spin-drier
'centro ['tʃentro] sm centre; **~ civico** civic

centre; ~ **commerciale** shopping centre; (*città*) commercial centre

'**ceppo** ['tʃeppo] *sm* (*di albero*) stump; (*pezzo di legno*) log

'**cera** ['tʃera] *sf* wax; (*aspetto*) appearance

ce'**ramica, che** [tʃe'ramika] *sf* ceramic; (*ARTE*) ceramics *sg*

cerbi'**atto** [tʃer'bjatto] *sm* (*ZOOL*) fawn

'**cerca** ['tʃerka] *sf*: **in o alla ~ di** in search of

cer'**care** [tʃer'kare] *vt* to look for, search for ♦ *vi*: ~ **di fare qc** to try to do sth

'**cerchia** ['tʃerkja] *sf* circle

'**cerchio** ['tʃerkjo] *sm* circle; (*giocattolo, di botte*) hoop

cere'**ale** [tʃere'ale] *sm* cereal

ceri'**monia** [tʃeri'mɔnja] *sf* ceremony

ce'**rino** [tʃe'rino] *sm* wax match

'**cernia** ['tʃernja] *sf* (*ZOOL*) stone bass

cerni'**era** [tʃer'njera] *sf* hinge; ~ **lampo** zip (fastener) (*BRIT*), zipper (*US*)

'**cernita** ['tʃernita] *sf* selection

'**cero** ['tʃero] *sm* (*church*) candle

ce'**rotto** [tʃe'rɔtto] *sm* sticking plaster

certa'**mente** [tʃerta'mente] *av* certainly

cer'**tezza** [tʃer'tettsa] *sf* certainty

certifi'**cato** *sm* certificate; ~ **medico/di nascita** medical/birth certificate

'**certo, a** ['tʃerto] *ag* (*sicuro*): ~ **(di/che)** certain *o* sure (of/that)
♦ *det* **1** (*tale*) certain; **un ~ signor Smith** a (certain) Mr Smith
2 (*qualche: con valore intensivo*) some; **dopo un ~ tempo** after some time; **un fatto di una ~a importanza** a matter of some importance; **di una ~a età** past one's prime, not so young
♦ *pron*: ~**i, e** *pl* some
♦ *av* (*certamente*) certainly; (*senz'altro*) of course; **di ~** certainly; **no (di) ~!, ~ che no!** certainly not!; **sì ~** yes indeed, certainly

cer'**vello, i** [tʃer'vello] (*ANAT*: *pl(f)* **-a**) *sm* brain

'**cervo, a** ['tʃervo] *sm/f* stag/doe ♦ *sm* deer; ~ **volante** stag beetle

ce'**sello** [tʃe'zello] *sm* chisel

ce'**soie** [tʃe'zoje] *sfpl* shears

ces'**puglio** [tʃes'puʎʎo] *sm* bush

ces'**sare** [tʃes'sare] *vi, vt* to stop, cease; ~ **di fare qc** to stop doing sth

'**cesso** ['tʃesso] (*fam*) *sm* (*gabinetto*) bog

'**cesta** ['tʃesta] *sf* (large) basket

ces'**tino** [tʃes'tino] *sm* basket; (*per la carta straccia*) wastepaper basket; ~ **da viaggio** (*FERR*) packed lunch (*o* dinner)

'**cesto** ['tʃesto] *sm* basket

'**ceto** ['tʃeto] *sm* (social) class

cetrio'**lino** [tʃetrio'lino] *sm* gherkin

cetri'**olo** [tʃetri'ɔlo] *sm* cucumber

CFC *sm inv* (= clorofluorocarburo) CFC

cfr. *abbr* (= confronta) cf

CGIL *sigla f* (= *Confederazione Generale Italiana del Lavoro*) trades union organization

che [ke] *pron* **1** (*relativo: persona: soggetto*) who; (: *oggetto*) whom, that; (: *cosa, animale*) which, that; **il ragazzo ~ è venuto** the boy who came; **l'uomo ~ io vedo** the man (whom) I see; **il libro ~ è sul tavolo** the book which *o* that is on the table; **il libro ~ vedi** the book (which *o* that) you see; **la sera ~ ti ho visto** the evening I saw you
2 (*interrogativo, esclamativo*) what; ~ **(cosa) fai?** what are you doing?; **a ~ (cosa) pensi?** what are you thinking about?; **non sa ~ (cosa) fare** he doesn't know what to do; **ma ~ dici!** what are you saying!
3 (*indefinito*): **quell'uomo ha un ~ di losco** there's something suspicious about that man; **un certo non so ~** an indefinable something
♦ *det* **1** (*interrogativo: tra tanti*) what; (: *tra pochi*) which; ~ **tipo di film preferisci?** what sort of film do you prefer?; ~ **vestito ti vuoi mettere?** what (*o* which) dress do you want to put on?
2 (*esclamativo: seguito da aggettivo*) how; (: *seguito da sostantivo*) what; ~ **buono!** how delicious!; ~ **bel vestito!** what a lovely dress!
♦ *cong* **1** (*con proposizioni subordinate*) that; **credo ~ verrà** I think he'll come; **voglio ~ tu studi** I want you to study; **so ~ tu c'eri** I know (that) you were there; **non ~: non ~ sia sbagliato, ma ...** not that it's wrong, but ...
2 (*finale*) so that; **vieni qua, ~ ti veda** come here, so (that) I can see you
3 (*temporale*): **arrivai ~ eri già partito** you had already left when I arrived; **sono anni ~ non lo vedo** I haven't seen him for years
4 (*in frasi imperative, concessive*): ~ **venga pure!** let him come by all means!; ~ **tu sia benedetto!** may God bless you!
5 (*comparativo: con più, meno*) than; *vedi anche* **più; meno; così** *etc*

cheti'**chella** [keti'kella]: **alla ~** *av* stealthily, unobtrusively

chi [ki] *pron* **1** (*interrogativo: soggetto*) who; (: *oggetto*) who, whom; ~ **è?** who is it?; **di ~ è questo libro?** whose book is this?, whose is this book?; **con ~ parli?** who are you talking to?; **a ~ pensi?** who are you thinking about?; ~ **di voi?** which of you?; **non so a ~ rivolgermi** I don't know who to ask
2 (*relativo*) whoever, anyone who; **dillo a**

~ **vuoi** tell whoever you like
3 (*indefinito*): ~ ... ~ ... some ... others ...;
~ **dice una cosa,** ~ **dice un'altra** some say one thing, others say another

chiacchie'rare [kjakkje'rare] *vi* to chat; (*discorrere futilmente*) to chatter; (*far pettegolezzi*) to gossip; **chiacchie'rata** *sf* chat; **chi'acchiere** *sfpl*: **fare due o quattro chiacchiere** to have a chat; **chiacchie'rone, a** *ag* talkative, chatty; gossipy ♦ *sm/f* chatterbox; gossip

chia'mare [kja'mare] *vt* to call; (*rivolgersi a qn*) to call (in), send for; **~rsi** *vr* (*aver nome*) to be called; **mi chiamo Paolo** my name is Paolo, I'm called Paolo; ~ **alle armi** to call up; ~ **in giudizio** to summon; **chia'mata** *sf* (*TEL*) call; (*MIL*) call-up

chia'rezza [kja'rettsa] *sf* clearness; clarity

chia'rire [kja'rire] *vt* to make clear; (*fig: spiegare*) to clear up, explain; **~rsi** *vr* to become clear

chi'aro, a ['kjaro] *ag* clear; (*luminoso*) clear, bright; (*colore*) pale, light

chiaroveg'gente [kjaroved'dʒente] *sm/f* clairvoyant

chi'asso ['kjasso] *sm* uproar, row; **chias'soso, a** *ag* noisy, rowdy; (*vistoso*) showy, gaudy

chi'ave ['kjave] *sf* key ♦ *ag inv* key *cpd*; ~ **d'accensione** (*AUT*) ignition key; ~ **inglese** monkey wrench; ~ **di volta** keystone; **chiavis'tello** *sm* bolt

chi'azza ['kjattsa] *sf* stain; splash

'chicco, chi ['kikko] *sm* grain; (*di caffè*) bean; ~ **d'uva** grape

chi'edere ['kjedere] *vt* (*per sapere*) to ask; (*per avere*) to ask for ♦ *vi*: ~ **di qn** to ask after sb; (*al telefono*) to ask for o want sb; ~ **qc a qn** to ask sb for sth; ~ **a qn** to ask sb for sth

chi'erico, ci ['kjεriko] *sm* cleric; altar boy

chi'esa ['kjεza] *sf* church

chi'esto, a *pp di* **chiedere**

'chiglia ['kiʎʎa] *sf* keel

'chilo [kilo] *sm* kilo; **chilo'grammo** *sm* kilogram(me); **chilome'traggio** *sm* ≈ mileage; **~metraggio illimitato** unlimited mileage; **chi'lometro** *sm* kilometre

'chimica ['kimika] *sf* chemistry

'chimico, a, ci, che ['kimiko] *ag* chemical ♦ *sm/f* chemist

'china ['kina] *sf* (*pendio*) slope, descent; (*inchiostro*) Indian ink

chi'nare [ki'nare] *vt* to lower, bend; **~rsi** *vr* to stoop, bend

chi'nino [ki'nino] *sm* quinine

chi'occiola ['kjɔttʃola] *sf* snail; **scala a ~** spiral staircase

chi'odo ['kjɔdo] *sm* nail; (*fig*) obsession

chi'oma ['kjɔma] *sf* (*capelli*) head of hair

chi'osco, schi ['kjɔsko] *sm* kiosk, stall

chi'ostro ['kjɔstro] *sm* cloister

chiro'mante [kiro'mante] *sm/f* palmist

chirur'gia [kirur'dʒia] *sf* surgery; ~ **estetica** cosmetic surgery; **chi'rurgo, ghi o gi** *sm* surgeon

chissà [kis'sa] *av* who knows, I wonder

chi'tarra [ki'tarra] *sf* guitar

chi'udere ['kjudere] *vt* to close, shut; (*luce, acqua*) to put off, turn off; (*definitivamente: fabbrica*) to close down, shut down; (*strada*) to close; (*recingere*) to enclose; (*porre termine a*) to end ♦ *vi* to close, shut; to close down, shut down; to end; **~rsi** *vr* to shut, close; (*ritirarsi: anche fig*) to shut o.s. away; (*ferita*) to close up

chi'unque [ki'unkwe] *pron* (*relativo*) whoever; (*indefinito*) anyone, anybody; ~ **sia** whoever it is

chi'uso, a ['kjuso] *pp di* **chiudere** ♦ *sf* (*di corso d'acqua*) sluice, lock; (*recinto*) enclosure; (*di discorso etc*) conclusion, ending; **chiu'sura** *sf* (*vedi* **chiudere**) closing; shutting; closing o shutting down; enclosing; putting o turning off; ending; (*dispositivo*) catch; fastening; fastener

---

PAROLA CHIAVE

ci [tʃi] (*dav lo, la, li, le, ne diventa* **ce**) *pron*
1 (*personale: complemento oggetto*) us; (: *a noi: complemento di termine*) (to) us; (: *riflessivo*) ourselves; (: *reciproco*) each other, one another; (*impersonale*): ~ **si veste** we get dressed; ~ **ha visti** he's seen us; **non ~ ha dato niente** he gave us nothing; ~ **vestiamo** we get dressed; ~ **amiamo** we love one another o each other
2 (*dimostrativo: di ciò, su ciò, in ciò etc*) about (o on o of) it; **non so cosa far~** I don't know what to do about it; **che c'entro io?** what have I got to do with it?
♦ *av* (*qui*) here; (*lì*) there; (*moto attraverso luogo*): ~ **passa sopra un ponte** a bridge passes over it; **non ~ passa più nessuno** nobody comes this way any more; **esser~** *vedi* **essere**

---

cia'batta [tʃa'batta] *sf* slipper; (*pane*) ciabatta

ci'alda ['tʃalda] *sf* (*CUC*) wafer

ciam'bella [tʃam'bεlla] *sf* (*CUC*) ring-shaped cake; (*salvagente*) rubber ring

ci'ao ['tʃao] *escl* (*all'arrivo*) hello!; (*alla partenza*) cheerio! (*BRIT*), bye!

cias'cuno, a [tʃas'kuno] (*det: dav sm*: **ciascun** +C, V, **ciascuno** +*s impura, gn, pn, ps, x, z*; *dav sf*: **ciascuna** +C, **ciascun'** +V) *det* every, each; (*ogni*) every ♦ *pron* each (one); (*tutti*) everyone, everybody

ci'barie [tʃi'barje] *sfpl* foodstuffs

'cibo ['tʃibo] *sm* food

ci'cala [tʃi'kala] *sf* cicada

cica'trice [tʃika'tritʃe] *sf* scar

'cicca ['tʃikka] *sf* cigarette end

'ciccia ['tʃittʃa] *(fam) sf* fat

cice'rone [tʃitʃe'rone] *sm* guide

ci'clismo [tʃi'klizmo] *sm* cycling; **ci'clista, i, e** *sm/f* cyclist

'ciclo ['tʃiklo] *sm* cycle; *(di malattia)* course

ciclomo'tore [tʃiklomo'tore] *sm* moped

ci'clone [tʃi'klone] *sm* cyclone

ci'cogna [tʃi'koɲɲa] *sf* stork

ci'coria [tʃi'kɔrja] *sf* chicory

ci'eco, a, chi, che ['tʃɛko] *ag* blind ♦ *sm/f* blind man/woman

ci'elo ['tʃɛlo] *sm* sky; *(REL)* heaven

'cifra ['tʃifra] *sf (numero)* figure; numeral; *(somma di denaro)* sum, figure; *(monogramma)* monogram, initials *pl*; *(codice)* code, cipher

'ciglio, i ['tʃiʎʎo] *(delle palpebre: pl(f) ciglia) sm (margine)* edge, verge; *(eye)lash; (eye)lid; (sopracciglio)* eyebrow

'cigno ['tʃiɲɲo] *sm* swan

cigo'lare [tʃigo'lare] *vi* to squeak, creak

'Cile ['tʃile] *sm*: **il ~** Chile

ci'lecca [tʃi'lekka] *sf*: **far ~** to fail

cili'egia, gie o ge [tʃi'ljedʒa] *sf* cherry; **cili'egio** *sm* cherry tree

cilin'drata [tʃilin'drata] *sf (AUT)* (cubic) capacity; **una macchina di grossa ~** a big-engined car

ci'lindro [tʃi'lindro] *sm* cylinder; *(cappello)* top hat

'cima ['tʃima] *sf (sommità)* top; *(di monte)* top, summit; *(estremità)* end; **in ~ a** at the top of; **da ~ a fondo** from top to bottom; *(fig)* from beginning to end

'cimice ['tʃimitʃe] *sf (ZOOL)* bug; *(puntina)* drawing pin *(BRIT)*, thumbtack *(US)*

cimini'era [tʃimi'njɛra] *sf* chimney; *(di nave)* funnel

cimi'tero [tʃimi'tɛro] *sm* cemetery

'Cina ['tʃina] *sf*: **la ~** China

cin'cin [tʃin'tʃin] *escl* cheers!

cin cin [tʃin'tʃin] *escl* = **cincin**

'cinema ['tʃinema] *sm inv* cinema; **cine'presa** *sf* cine-camera

ci'nese [tʃi'nese] *ag, sm/f, sm* Chinese *inv*

'cingere ['tʃindʒere] *vt (attorniare)* to surround, encircle

'cinghia ['tʃingja] *sf* strap; *(cintura, TECN)* belt

cinghi'ale [tʃin'gjale] *sm* wild boar

cinguet'tare [tʃingwet'tare] *vi* to twitter

'cinico, a, ci, che ['tʃiniko] *ag* cynical ♦ *sm/f* cynic; **ci'nismo** *sm* cynicism

cin'quanta [tʃin'kwanta] *num* fifty; **cinquan'tesimo, a** *num* fiftieth

cinquan'tina [tʃinkwan'tina] *sf (serie)*: **una ~ (di)** about fifty; *(età)*: **essere sulla ~** to be about fifty

'cinque ['tʃinkwe] *num* five; **avere ~ anni** to be five (years old); **il ~ dicembre 1998** the fifth of December 1998; **alle ~ (ora)** at five (o'clock)

cinque'cento [tʃinkwe'tʃento] *num* five hundred ♦ *sm*: **il C~** the sixteenth century

'cinto, a ['tʃinto] *pp di* **cingere**

cin'tura [tʃin'tura] *sf* belt; **~ di salvataggio** lifebelt *(BRIT)*, life preserver *(US)*; **~ di sicurezza** *(AUT, AER)* safety o seat belt

ciò [tʃɔ] *pron* this; that; **~ che** what; **~ nonostante** o **nondimeno** nevertheless, in spite of that

ci'occa, che ['tʃɔkka] *sf (di capelli)* lock

ciocco'lata [tʃokko'lata] *sf* chocolate; *(bevanda)* (hot) chocolate; **cioccola'tino** *sm* chocolate; **ciocco'lato** *sm* chocolate

cioè [tʃo'ɛ] *av* that is (to say)

ciondo'lare [tʃondo'lare] *vi* to dangle; *(fig)* to loaf (about); **ci'ondolo** *sm* pendant

ci'otola ['tʃɔtola] *sf* bowl

ci'ottolo ['tʃɔttolo] *sm* pebble; *(di strada)* cobble(stone)

ci'polla [tʃi'polla] *sf* onion; *(di tulipano etc)* bulb

ci'presso [tʃi'presso] *sm* cypress (tree)

'cipria ['tʃiprja] *sf (face)* powder

'Cipro ['tʃipro] *sm* Cyprus

'circa ['tʃirka] *av* about, roughly ♦ *prep* about, concerning; **a mezzogiorno ~** about midday

'circo, chi ['tʃirko] *sm* circus

circo'lare [tʃirko'lare] *vi* to circulate; *(AUT)* to drive (along), move (along) ♦ *ag* circular ♦ *sf (AMM)* circular; *(di autobus)* circle (line); **circolazi'one** *sf* circulation; *(AUT)*: **la circolazione** (the) traffic

'circolo ['tʃirkolo] *sm* circle

circon'dare [tʃirkon'dare] *vt* to surround

circonfe'renza [tʃirkonfe'rentsa] *sf* circumference

circonvallazi'one [tʃirkonvallat'tsjone] *sf* ring road *(BRIT)*, beltway *(US)*; *(per evitare una città)* by-pass

circos'critto, a [tʃirkos'kritto] *pp di* **circoscrivere**

circos'crivere [tʃirkos'krivere] *vt* to circumscribe; *(fig)* to limit, restrict; **circoscrizi'one** *sf (AMM)* district, area; **circoscrizione elettorale** constituency

circos'petto, a [tʃirkos'petto] *ag* circumspect, cautious

circos'tante [tʃirkos'tante] *ag* surrounding, neighbouring

circos'tanza [tʃirkos'tantsa] *sf* circumstance; *(occasione)* occasion

cir'cuito [tʃir'kuito] *sm* circuit

CISL sigla f (= Confederazione Italiana Sindacati Lavoratori) trades union organization

'**ciste** ['tʃiste] sf = **cisti**

cis'**terna** [tʃis'tɛrna] sf tank, cistern

'**cisti** ['tʃisti] sf cyst

C.I.T. [tʃit] sigla f = **Compagnia Italiana Turismo**

ci'**tare** [tʃi'tare] vt (DIR) to summon; (autore) to quote; (a esempio, modello) to cite; **citazi'one** sf summons sg; quotation; (di persona) mention

ci'**tofono** [tʃi'tɔfono] sm entry phone; (in uffici) intercom

cit**tà** [tʃit'ta] sf inv town; (importante) city; ~ **universitaria** university campus

cittadi'**nanza** [tʃittadi'nantsa] sf citizens pl; (DIR) citizenship

citta'**dino, a** [tʃitta'dino] ag town cpd; city cpd ♦ sm/f (di uno Stato) citizen; (abitante di città) townsman, city dweller

ci'**uco, a, chi, che** ['tʃuko] sm/f ass

ci'**uffo** ['tʃuffo] sm tuft

ci'**vetta** [tʃi'vetta] sf (ZOOL) owl; (fig: donna) coquette, flirt ♦ ag inv: **auto/nave** ~ decoy car/ship

'**civico, a, ci, che** ['tʃiviko] ag civic; (museo) municipal, town cpd; city cpd

ci'**vile** [tʃi'vile] ag civil; (non militare) civilian; (nazione) civilized ♦ sm civilian

civilizzazi'one [tʃiviliddzat'tsjone] sf civilization

civil**tà** [tʃivil'ta] sf civilization; (cortesia) civility

'**clacson** sm inv (AUT) horn

cla'**more** sm (frastuono) din, uproar, clamour; (fig) outcry; **clamo'roso, a** ag noisy; (fig) sensational

clandes'**tino, a** ag clandestine; (POL) underground, clandestine ♦ sm/f stowaway

clari'**netto** sm clarinet

'**classe** sf class; **di** ~ (fig) with class; of excellent quality

'**classico, a, ci, che** ag classical; (tradizionale: moda) classic(al) ♦ sm classic; classical author

clas'**sifica** sf classification; (SPORT) placings pl

classifi'**care** vt to classify; (candidato, compito) to grade; ~**rsi** vr to be placed

'**clausola** sf (DIR) clause

'**clava** sf club

clavi'**cembalo** [klavi'tʃembalo] sm harpsichord

cla'**vicola** sf (ANAT) collar bone

cle'**mente** ag merciful; (clima) mild; **cle'menza** sf mercy, clemency; mildness

'**clero** sm clergy

clic'**care** vi (INFORM): ~ **su** to click on

cli'**ente** sm/f customer, client; **clien'tela** sf customers pl, clientèle

'**clima, i** sm climate; **cli'matico, a, ci, che** ag climatic; **stazione climatica** health resort; **climatizzatore** sm air conditioning system; **climatizzazi'one** sf (TECN) air conditioning

'**clinica, che** sf (scienza) clinical medicine; (casa di cura) clinic, nursing home; (settore d'ospedale) clinic

'**clinico, a, ci, che** ag clinical ♦ sm (medico) clinician

clo'**aca, che** sf sewer

'**cloro** sm chlorine

cloro'**formio** sm chloroform

club sm inv club

c.m. abbr = **corrente mese**

coabi'**tare** vi to live together

coagu'**lare** vt to coagulate ♦ vi to coagulate; (latte) to curdle; ~**rsi** vr to coagulate; to curdle

coalizi'**one** [koalit'tsjone] sf coalition

co'**atto, a** ag (DIR) compulsory, forced

'**COBAS** sigla mpl (= Comitati di base) independent trades unions

Coca-Cola ® sf Coca-Cola ®

coca'**ina** sf cocaine

cocci'**nella** [kottʃi'nɛlla] sf ladybird (BRIT), ladybug (US)

'**coccio** ['kɔttʃo] sm earthenware; (vaso) earthenware pot; ~**i** smpl (frammenti) fragments (of pottery)

cocci'**uto, a** [kot'tʃuto] ag stubborn, pigheaded

'**cocco, chi** sm (pianta) coconut palm; (frutto): **noce di** ~ coconut ♦ sm/f (fam) darling

cocco'**drillo** sm crocodile

cocco'**lare** vt to cuddle, fondle

co'**cente** [ko'tʃente] ag (anche fig) burning

co'**comero** sm watermelon

co'**cuzzolo** [ko'kuttsolo] sm top; (di capo, cappello) crown

'**coda** sf tail; (fila di persone, auto) queue (BRIT), line (US); (di abiti) train; **con la** ~ **dell'occhio** out of the corner of one's eye; **mettersi in** ~ to queue (up) (BRIT), line up (US); to join the queue (BRIT) o line (US); ~ **di cavallo** (acconciatura) ponytail

co'**dardo, a** ag cowardly ♦ sm/f coward

'**codice** ['koditʃe] sm code; ~ **di avviamento postale** postcode (BRIT), zip code (US); ~ **fiscale** tax code; ~ **della strada** highway code

coe'**rente** ag coherent; **coe'renza** sf coherence

coe'**taneo, a** ag, sm/f contemporary

'**cofano** sm (AUT) bonnet (BRIT), hood (US); (forziere) chest

'**cogli** ['kɔʎʎi] prep + det = **con** + **gli**; vedi **con**

'**cogliere** ['kɔʎʎere] vt (fiore, frutto) to pick, gather; (sorprendere) to catch, surprise;

(*bersaglio*) to hit; (*fig: momento opportuno etc*) to grasp, seize, take; (: *capire*) to grasp; ~ **qn in flagrante** o **in fallo** to catch sb red-handed

co'gnato, a [koɲˈɲato] *sm/f* brother-/sister-in-law

co'gnome [koɲˈɲome] *sm* surname

'coi *prep* + *det* = **con** + **i**; *vedi* **con**

coinci'denza [kointʃiˈdentsa] *sf* coincidence; (*FERR, AER, di autobus*) connection

coin'cidere [koinˈtʃidere] *vi* to coincide; **coin'ciso, a** *pp di* **coincidere**

coin'volgere [koinˈvɔldʒere] *vt*: ~ **in** to involve in; **coin'volto, a** *pp di* **coinvolgere**

col *prep* + *det* = **con** + **il**; *vedi* **con**

cola'brodo *sm inv* strainer

cola'pasta *sm inv* colander

co'lare *vt* (*liquido*) to strain; (*pasta*) to drain; (*oro fuso*) to pour ♦ *vi* (*sudore*) to drip; (*botte*) to leak; (*cera*) to melt; ~ **a picco** *vt, vi* (*nave*) to sink

co'lata (*di lava*) flow; (*FONDERIA*) casting

colazi'one [kolatˈtsjone] *sf* (*anche: prima* ~) breakfast; (*anche: seconda* ~) lunch; **fare** ~ to have breakfast (o lunch)

co'lei *pron vedi* **colui**

co'lera *sm* (*MED*) cholera

'colica *sf* (*MED*) colic

'colla *sf* glue; (*di farina*) paste

collabo'rare *vi* to collaborate; ~ **a** to collaborate on; (*giornale*) to contribute to; **collabora'tore, 'trice** *sm/f* collaborator; contributor

col'lana *sf* necklace; (*collezione*) collection, series

col'lant [kɔˈlã] *sm inv* tights *pl*

col'lare *sm* collar

col'lasso *sm* (*MED*) collapse

collau'dare *vt* to test, try out; **col'laudo** *sm* testing *no pl*; test

'colle *sm* hill

col'lega, ghi, ghe *sm/f* colleague

collega'mento *sm* connection; (*MIL*) liaison

colle'gare *vt* to connect, join, link; **~rsi** *vr* (*RADIO, TV*) to link up; **~rsi con** (*TEL*) to get through to

col'legio [kolˈlɛdʒo] *sm* college; (*convitto*) boarding school; ~ **elettorale** (*POL*) constituency

'collera *sf* anger

col'lerico, a, ci, che *ag* quick- tempered, irascible

col'letta *sf* collection

collettività *sf* community

collet'tivo, a *ag* collective; (*interesse*) general, everybody's; (*biglietto, visita etc*) group *cpd* ♦ *sm* (*POL*) (political) group

col'letto *sm* collar

collezio'nare [kollettsjoˈnare] *vt* to collect

collezi'one [kolletˈtsjone] *sf* collection

colli'mare *vi* to correspond, coincide

col'lina *sf* hill

col'lirio *sm* eyewash

collisi'one *sf* collision

'collo *sm* neck; (*di abito*) neck, collar; (*pacco*) parcel; ~ **del piede** instep

colloca'mento *sm* (*impiego*) employment; (*disposizione*) placing, arrangement

collo'care *vt* (*libri, mobili*) to place; (*COMM: merce*) to find a market for

col'loquio *sm* conversation, talk; (*ufficiale, per un lavoro*) interview; (*INS*) preliminary oral exam

col'mare *vt*: ~ **di** (*anche fig*) to fill with; (*dare in abbondanza*) to load o overwhelm with; **'colmo, a** *ag*: **colmo (di)** full (of) ♦ *sm* summit, top; (*fig*) height; **al colmo della disperazione** in the depths of despair; **è il colmo!** it's the last straw!

co'lombo, a *sm/f* dove; pigeon

co'lonia *sf* colony; (*per bambini*) holiday camp; (**acqua di**) ~ (eau de) cologne; **coloni'ale** *ag* colonial ♦ *sm/f* colonist, settler

co'lonna *sf* column; ~ **vertebrale** spine, spinal column

colon'nello *sm* colonel

co'lono *sm* (*coltivatore*) tenant farmer

colo'rante *sm* colouring

colo'rare *vt* to colour; (*disegno*) to colour in

co'lore *sm* colour; **a** ~**i** in colour, colour *cpd*; **farne di tutti i** ~**i** to get up to all sorts of mischief

colo'rito, a *ag* coloured; (*viso*) rosy, pink; (*linguaggio*) colourful ♦ *sm* (*tinta*) colour; (*carnagione*) complexion

co'loro *pron vedi* **colui**

co'losso *sm* colossus

'colpa *sf* fault; (*biasimo*) blame; (*colpevolezza*) guilt; (*azione colpevole*) offence; (*peccato*) sin; **di chi è la** ~? whose fault is it?; **è** ~ **sua** it's his fault; **per** ~ **di** through, owing to; **col'pevole** *ag* guilty

col'pire *vt* to hit, strike; (*fig*) to strike; **rimanere colpito da qc** to be amazed o struck by sth

'colpo *sm* (*urto*) knock; (: *affettivo*) blow, shock; (: *aggressivo*) blow; (*di pistola*) shot; (*MED*) stroke; (*rapina*) raid; **di** ~ suddenly; **fare** ~ to make a strong impression; ~ **di grazia** coup de grâce; ~ **di scena** (*TEATRO*) coup de théâtre; (*fig*) dramatic turn of events; ~ **di sole** sunstroke; ~ **di Stato** coup d'état; ~ **di telefono** phone call; ~ **di testa** (sudden) impulse o whim; ~ **di vento** gust (of wind)

coltel'lata *sf* stab

col'tello *sm* knife; ~ **a serramanico** clasp knife

colti'vare *vt* to cultivate; (*verdura*) to grow,

cultivate; **coltiva'tore** *sm* farmer;
coltivazi'one *sf* cultivation; growing
'colto, a *pp di* **cogliere** ♦ *ag* (*istruito*)
cultured, educated
'coltre *sf* blanket
col'tura *sf* cultivation
co'lui (*f* **co'lei,** *pl* **co'loro**) *pron* the one; ~ **che
parla** the one o the man o the person who is
speaking; **colei che amo** the one o the
woman o the person (whom) I love
'coma *sm inv* coma
comanda'mento *sm* (*REL*) commandment
coman'dante *sm* (*MIL*) commander,
commandant; (*di reggimento*) commanding
officer; (*NAUT, AER*) captain
coman'dare *vi* to be in command ♦ *vt* to
command; (*imporre*) to order, command;
~ **a qn di fare** to order sb to do; **co'mando**
sm (*ingiunzione*) order, command; (*autorità*)
command; (*TECN*) control
co'mare *sf* (*madrina*) godmother
combaci'are [komba't∫are] *vi* to meet; (*fig:
coincidere*) to coincide
com'battere *vt, vi* to fight; **combat-
ti'mento** *sm* fight; fighting *no pl*; (*di pugilato*) match
combi'nare *vt* to combine; (*organizzare*) to
arrange; (*fam: fare*) to make, cause; **com-
binazi'one** *sf* combination; (*caso fortuito*)
coincidence; **per combinazione** by chance
combus'tibile *ag* combustible ♦ *sm* fuel
com'butta (*peg*) *sf:* **in ~** in league

⎡ PAROLA CHIAVE ⎤

'come *av* **1** (*alla maniera di*) like; **ti comporti
~ lui** you behave like him o like he does;
bianco ~ la neve (as) white as snow; ~ **se** as
if, as though
2 (*in qualità di*) as a; **lavora ~ autista** he
works as a driver
3 (*interrogativo*) how; ~ **ti chiami?** what's
your name?; ~ **sta?** how are you?; **com'è il
tuo amico?** what is your friend like?; ~**?**
(*prego?*) pardon?, sorry?; ~ **mai?** how come?;
~ **mai non ci hai avvertiti?** why on earth
didn't you warn us?
4 (*esclamativo*): ~ **sei bravo!** how clever you
are!; ~ **mi dispiace!** I'm terribly sorry!
♦ *cong* **1** (*in che modo*) how; **mi ha spiegato
~ l'ha conosciuto** he told me how he met him
2 (*correlativo*) as; (*con comparativi di
maggioranza*) than; **non è bravo ~ pensavo**
he isn't as clever as I thought; **è meglio di
~ pensassi** it's better than I thought
3 (*appena che, quando*) as soon as; ~ **arrivò,
iniziò a lavorare** as soon as he arrived, he set
to work; *vedi* **così; tanto**

'comico, a, ci, che *ag* (*TEATRO*) comic;
(*buffo*) comical ♦ *sm* (*attore*) comedian,
comic actor
co'mignolo [ko'miɲɲolo] *sm* chimney
top
cominci'are [komin't∫are] *vt, vi* to begin,
start; ~ **a fare/col fare** to begin to do/by
doing
comi'tato *sm* committee
comi'tiva *sf* party, group
co'mizio [ko'mittsjo] *sm* (*POL*) meeting,
assembly
com'mando *sm inv* commando (squad)
com'media *sf* comedy; (*opera teatrale*) play;
(*: che fa ridere*) comedy; (*fig*) playacting *no
pl*; **commedi'ante** (*peg*) *sm/f* third-rate
actor/actress; (*fig*) sham
commemo'rare *vt* to commemorate
commenda'tore *sm* official title awarded for
services to one's country
commen'tare *vt* to comment on; (*testo*) to
annotate; (*RADIO, TV*) to give a commentary
on; **commenta'tore, 'trice** *sm/f*
commentator; **com'mento** *sm* comment;
(*a un testo, RADIO, TV*) commentary
commerci'ale [kommer't∫ale] *ag*
commercial, trading; (*peg*) commercial
commerci'ante [kommer't∫ante] *sm/f*
trader, dealer; (*negoziante*) shopkeeper
commerci'are [kommer't∫are] *vt, vi:* ~ **in** to
deal o trade in
com'mercio [kom'mert∫o] *sm* trade,
commerce; **essere in ~** (*prodotto*) to be on
the market o on sale; **essere nel ~** (*persona*)
to be in business; ~ **elettronico** e-commerce
com'messa *sf* (*COMM*) order
com'messo, a *pp di* **commettere** ♦ *sm/f*
shop assistant (*BRIT*), sales clerk (*US*) ♦ *sm*
(*impiegato*) clerk; ~ **viaggiatore** commercial
traveller
commes'tibile *ag* edible; ~**i** *smpl* foodstuffs
com'mettere *vt* to commit
com'miato *sm* leave-taking
commi'nare *vt* (*DIR*) to threaten; to inflict
commissari'ato *sm* (*AMM*) commissioner-
ship; (*: sede*) commissioner's office; (*: di
polizia*) police station
commis'sario *sm* commissioner; (*di
pubblica sicurezza*) ≈ (police) superintendent
(*BRIT*), ≈ (police) captain (*US*); (*SPORT*)
steward; (*membro di commissione*) member of
a committee o board
commissio'nario *sm* (*COMM*) agent, broker
commissi'one *sf* (*incarico*) errand;
(*comitato, percentuale*) commission; (*COMM:
ordinazione*) order
commit'tente *sm/f* (*COMM*) purchaser,
customer
com'mosso, a *pp di* **commuovere**
commo'vente *ag* moving

commozi'one [kommot'tsjone] *sf* emotion, deep feeling; **~ cerebrale** (*MED*) concussion

commu'overe *vt* to move, affect; **~rsi** *vr* to be moved

commu'tare *vt* (*pena*) to commute; (*ELETTR*) to change *o* switch over

comò *sm inv* chest of drawers

como'dino *sm* bedside table

comodità *sf inv* comfort; convenience

'comodo, a *ag* comfortable; (*facile*) easy; (*conveniente*) convenient; (*utile*) useful, handy ♦ *sm* comfort; convenience; **con ~** at one's convenience *o* leisure; **fare il proprio ~** to do as one pleases; **far ~** to be useful *o* handy

compae'sano, a *sm/f* fellow countryman; person from the same town

com'pagine [kom'padʒine] *sf* (*squadra*) team

compa'gnia [kompaɲˈɲia] *sf* company; (*gruppo*) gathering

com'pagno, a [kom'paɲɲo] *sm/f* (*di classe, gioco*) companion; (*POL*) comrade

compa'rare *vt* to compare

compara'tivo, a *ag*, *sm* comparative

compa'rire *vi* to appear; **com'parsa** *sf* appearance; (*TEATRO*) walk-on; (*CINEMA*) extra; **comparso, a** *pp di* comparire

compartecipazi'one [kompartetʃi-pat'tsjone] *sf* sharing; (*quota*) share; **~ agli utili** profit-sharing

comparti'mento *sm* compartment; (*AMM*) district

compas'sato, a *ag* (*persona*) composed

compassi'one *sf* compassion, pity; **avere ~ di qn** to feel sorry for sb, to pity sb

com'passo *sm* (pair of) compasses *pl*; callipers *pl*

compa'tibile *ag* (*scusabile*) excusable; (*conciliabile, INFORM*) compatible

compa'tire *vt* (*aver compassione di*) to sympathize with, feel sorry for; (*scusare*) to make allowances for

com'patto, a *ag* compact; (*roccia*) solid; (*folla*) dense; (*fig: gruppo, partito*) united

com'pendio *sm* summary; (*libro*) compendium

compen'sare *vt* (*equilibrare*) to compensate for, make up for; (*rimunerare*) to pay *o* remunerate sb for; (*risarcire*) to pay compensation to sb for; (*fig: fatiche, dolori*) to reward sb for; **com'penso** *sm* compensation; payment, remuneration; reward; **in compenso** (*d'altra parte*) on the other hand

'compera *sf* (*acquisto*) purchase; **fare le ~e** to do the shopping

compe'rare *vt* = comprare

compe'tente *ag* competent; (*mancia*) apt,

suitable; **compe'tenza** *sf* competence; **competenze** *sfpl* (*onorari*) fees

com'petere *vi* to compete, vie; (*DIR: spettare*): **~ a** to lie within the competence of; **competizi'one** *sf* competition

compia'cente [kompja'tʃɛnte] *ag* courteous, obliging; **compia'cenza** *sf* courtesy

compia'cere [kompja'tʃere] *vi*: **~ a** to gratify, please ♦ *vt* to please; **~rsi** *vr* (*provare soddisfazione*): **~rsi di** *o* **per qc** to be delighted at sth; (*rallegrarsi*): **~rsi con qn** to congratulate sb; (*degnarsi*): **~rsi di fare** to be so good as to do; **compiaci'uto, a** *pp di* compiacere

compi'angere [kom'pjandʒere] *vt* to sympathize with, feel sorry for; **compi-'anto, a** *pp di* compiangere

'compiere *vt* (*concludere*) to finish, complete; (*adempiere*) to carry out, fulfil; **~rsi** *vr* (*avverarsi*) to be fulfilled, come true; **~ gli anni** to have one's birthday

compi'lare *vt* (*modulo*) to fill in; (*dizionario, elenco*) to compile

com'pire *vt* = compiere

compi'tare *vt* to spell out

'compito *sm* (*incarico*) task, duty; (*dovere*) duty; (*INS*) exercise; (*: a casa*) piece of homework; **fare i ~i** to do one's homework

com'pito, a *ag* well-mannered, polite

comple'anno *sm* birthday

complemen'tare *ag* complementary; (*INS: materia*) subsidiary

comple'mento *sm* complement; (*MIL*) reserve (troops); **~ oggetto** (*LING*) direct object

complessità *sf* complexity

comples'sivo, a *ag* (*globale*) comprehensive, overall; (*totale: cifra*) total

com'plesso, a *ag* complex ♦ *sm* (*PSIC, EDIL*) complex; (*MUS: corale*) ensemble; (*: orchestrina*) band; (*: di musica pop*) group; **in** *o* **nel ~** on the whole

comple'tare *vt* to complete

com'pleto, a *ag* complete; (*teatro, autobus*) full ♦ *sm* suit; **al ~** full; (*tutti presenti*) all present

compli'care *vt* to complicate; **~rsi** *vr* to become complicated; **complicazi'one** *sf* complication

'complice ['kɔmplitʃe] *sm/f* accomplice

complimen'tarsi *vr*: **~ con** to congratulate

compli'mento *sm* compliment; **~i** *smpl* (*cortesia eccessiva*) ceremony *sg*; (*ossequi*) regards, compliments; **~i!** congratulations!; **senza ~i!** don't stand on ceremony!; make yourself at home!; help yourself!

complot'tare *vi* to plot, conspire

com'plotto *sm* plot, conspiracy

compo'nente *sm/f* member ♦ *sm* component

componi'mento *sm* (*DIR*) settlement; (*INS*) composition; (*poetico, teatrale*) work

com'porre *vt* (*musica, testo*) to compose; (*mettere in ordine*) to arrange; (*DIR: lite*) to settle; (*TIP*) to set; (*TEL*) to dial

comporta'mento *sm* behaviour

compor'tare *vt* (*implicare*) to involve; **~rsi** *vr* to behave

composi'tore, 'trice *sm/f* composer; (*TIP*) compositor, typesetter

composizi'one [kompozit'tsjone] *sf* composition; (*DIR*) settlement

com'posta *sf* (*CUC*) stewed fruit *no pl*; (*AGR*) compost; *vedi anche* **composto**

compos'tezza [kompos'tettsa] *sf* composure; decorum

com'posto, a *pp di* **comporre** ♦ *ag* (*persona*) composed, self-possessed; (: *decoroso*) dignified; (*formato da più elementi*) compound *cpd* ♦ *sm* compound

com'prare *vt* to buy; **compra'tore, 'trice** *sm/f* buyer, purchaser

com'prendere *vt* (*contenere*) to comprise, consist of; (*capire*) to understand

comprensi'one *sf* understanding

compren'sivo, a *ag* (*prezzo*): **~ di** inclusive of; (*indulgente*) understanding

com'preso, a *pp di* **comprendere** ♦ *ag* (*incluso*) included

com'pressa *sf* (*MED*: *garza*) compress; (: *pastiglia*) tablet; *vedi anche* **compresso**

compressi'one *sf* compression

com'presso, a *pp di* **comprimere** ♦ *ag* (*vedi* **comprimere**) pressed; compressed; repressed

com'primere *vt* (*premere*) to press; (*FISICA*) to compress; (*fig*) to repress

compro'messo, a *pp di* **compromettere** ♦ *sm* compromise

compro'mettere *vt* to compromise

compro'vare *vt* to confirm

com'punto, a *ag* contrite

compu'tare *vt* to calculate

com'puter *sm inv* computer

computiste'ria *sf* accounting, book-keeping

'computo *sm* calculation

comu'nale *ag* municipal, town *cpd*, ≈ borough *cpd*

co'mune *ag* common; (*consueto*) common, everyday; (*di livello medio*) average; (*ordinario*) ordinary ♦ *sm* (*AMM*) town council; (: *sede*) town hall ♦ *sf* (*di persone*) commune; **fuori del ~** out of the ordinary; **avere in ~** to have in common, share; **mettere in ~** to share

comuni'care *vt* (*notizia*) to pass on, convey; (*malattia*) to pass on; (*ansia etc*) to communicate; (*trasmettere: calore etc*) to transmit, communicate; (*REL*) to administer communion to ♦ *vi* to communicate; **~rsi** *vr* (*propagarsi*): **~rsi a** to spread to; (*REL*) to receive communion

comuni'cato *sm* communiqué; **~ stampa** press release

comunicazi'one [komunikat'tsjone] *sf* communication; (*annuncio*) announcement; (*TEL*): **~ (telefonica)** (telephone) call; **dare la ~ a qn** to put sb through; **ottenere la ~** to get through

comuni'one *sf* communion; **~ di beni** (*DIR*) joint ownership of property

comu'nismo *sm* communism; **comu'nista, i, e** *ag, sm/f* communist

comunità *sf inv* community; **C~ Europea** European Community

co'munque *cong* however, no matter how ♦ *av* (*in ogni modo*) in any case; (*tuttavia*) however, nevertheless

con *prep* with; **partire col treno** to leave by train; **~ mio grande stupore** to my great astonishment; **~ tutto ciò** for all that

co'nato *sm*: **~ di vomito** retching

'conca, che *sf* (*GEO*) valley

con'cedere [kon'tʃedere] *vt* (*accordare*) to grant; (*ammettere*) to admit, concede; **~rsi qc** to treat o.s. to sth, to allow o.s. sth

concentra'mento [kontʃentra'mento] *sm* concentration

concen'trare [kontʃen'trare] *vt* to concentrate; **~rsi** *vr* to concentrate; **concentrazi'one** *sf* concentration

conce'pire [kontʃe'pire] *vt* (*bambino*) to conceive; (*progetto, idea*) to conceive (of); (*metodo, piano*) to devise

con'cernere [kon'tʃɛrnere] *vt* to concern

concer'tare [kontʃer'tare] *vt* (*MUS*) to harmonize; (*ordire*) to devise, plan; **~rsi** *vr* to agree

con'certo [kon'tʃerto] *sm* (*MUS*) concert; (: *componimento*) concerto

concessio'nario [kontʃessjo'narjo] *sm* (*COMM*) agent, dealer

con'cesso, a [kon'tʃesso] *pp di* **concedere**

con'cetto [kon'tʃetto] *sm* (*pensiero, idea*) concept; (*opinione*) opinion

concezi'one [kontʃet'tsjone] *sf* conception

con'chiglia [kon'kiʎʎa] *sf* shell

'concia ['kontʃa] *sf* (*di pelle*) tanning; (*di tabacco*) curing; (*sostanza*) tannin

conci'are [kon'tʃare] *vt* (*pelli*) to tan; (*tabacco*) to cure; (*fig: ridurre in cattivo stato*) to beat up; **~rsi** *vr* (*sporcarsi*) to get in a mess; (*vestirsi male*) to dress badly

concili'are [kontʃi'ljare] *vt* to reconcile; (*contravvenzione*) to pay on the spot; (*sonno*) to be conducive to, induce; **~rsi qc** to gain o win sth (for o.s.); **~rsi qn** to win sb over; **~rsi**

con to be reconciled with; **conciliazi'one** *sf* reconciliation; (*DIR*) settlement

con'cilio [kon'tʃiljo] *sm* (*REL*) council

con'cime [kon'tʃime] *sm* manure; (*chimico*) fertilizer

con'ciso, a [kon'tʃizo] *ag* concise, succinct

conci'tato, a [kontʃi'tato] *ag* excited, emotional

concitta'dino, a [kontʃitta'dino] *sm/f* fellow citizen

con'cludere *vt* to conclude; (*portare a compimento*) to conclude, finish, bring to an end; (*operare positivamente*) to achieve ♦ *vi* (*essere convincente*) to be conclusive; **~rsi** *vr* to come to an end, close; **conclusi'one** *sf* conclusion; (*risultato*) result; **conclu'sivo, a** *ag* conclusive; (*finale*) final; **con'cluso, a** *pp di* **concludere**

concor'danza [konkor'dantsa] *sf* (*anche LING*) agreement

concor'dare *vt* (*tregua, prezzo*) to agree on; (*LING*) to make agree ♦ *vi* to agree; **concor'dato** *sm* agreement; (*REL*) concordat

con'corde *ag* (*d'accordo*) in agreement; (*simultaneo*) simultaneous

concor'rente *sm/f* competitor; (*INS*) candidate; **concor'renza** *sf* competition

con'correre *vi*: ~ **(in)** (*MAT*) to converge o meet (in); ~ **(a)** (*competere*) to compete (for); (: *INS: a una cattedra*) to apply (for); (*partecipare: a un'impresa*) to take part (in), contribute (to); **con'corso, a** *pp di* **concorrere** ♦ *sm* competition; (*INS*) competitive examination; **concorso di colpa** (*DIR*) contributory negligence

con'creto, a *ag* concrete

concussi'one *sf* (*DIR*) extortion

con'danna *sf* sentence; conviction; condemnation

condan'nare *vt* (*DIR*): ~ **a** to sentence to; ~ **per** to convict of; (*disapprovare*) to condemn; **condan'nato, a** *sm/f* convict

conden'sare *vt* to condense; **~rsi** *vr* to condense; **condensazi'one** *sf* condensation

condi'mento *sm* seasoning; dressing

con'dire *vt* to season; (*insalata*) to dress

condi'videre *vt* to share; **condi'viso, a** *pp di* **condividere**

condizio'nale [kondittsjo'nale] *ag* conditional ♦ *sm* (*LING*) conditional ♦ *sf* (*DIR*) suspended sentence

condizio'nare [kondittsjo'nare] *vt* to condition; **ad aria condizionata** air-conditioned; **condiziona'tore** *sm* air conditioner

condizi'one [kondit'tsjone] *sf* condition; **~i** *sfpl* (*di pagamento etc*) terms, conditions; **a ~ che** on condition that, provided that

condogli'anze [kondoʎˈʎantse] *sfpl*

condolences

condo'minio *sm* joint ownership; (*edificio*) jointly-owned building

condo'nare *vt* (*DIR*) to remit; **con'dono** *sm* remission; **condono fiscale** conditional amnesty for people evading tax

con'dotta *sf* (*modo di comportarsi*) conduct, behaviour; (*di un affare etc*) handling; (*di acqua*) piping; (*incarico sanitario*) country medical practice controlled by a local authority

con'dotto, a *pp di* **condurre** ♦ *ag*: **medico ~** local authority doctor (*in country district*) ♦ *sm* (*canale, tubo*) pipe, conduit; (*ANAT*) duct

condu'cente [kondu'tʃente] *sm* driver

con'durre *vt* to conduct; (*azienda*) to manage; (*accompagnare: bambino*) to take; (*automobile*) to drive; (*trasportare: acqua, gas*) to convey, conduct; (*fig*) to lead ♦ *vi* to lead; **condursi** *vr* to behave, conduct o.s.

condut'tore *ag*: **filo ~** (*REL*) thread ♦ *sm* (*di mezzi pubblici*) driver; (*FISICA*) conductor

con'farsi *vr*: ~ **a** to suit, agree with

confederazi'one [konfederat'tsjone] *sf* confederation

confe'renza [konfe'rentsa] *sf* (*discorso*) lecture; (*riunione*) conference; ~ **stampa** press conference; **conferenzi'ere, a** *sm/f* lecturer

confe'rire *vt*: ~ **qc a qn** to give sth to sb, bestow sth on sb ♦ *vi* to confer

con'ferma *sf* confirmation

confer'mare *vt* to confirm

confes'sare *vt* to confess; **~rsi** *vr* to confess; **andare a ~rsi** (*REL*) to go to confession; **confessio'nale** *ag, sm* confessional; **confessi'one** *sf* confession; (*setta religiosa*) denomination; **confes'sore** *sm* confessor

con'fetto *sm* sugared almond; (*MED*) pill

confezio'nare [konfettsjo'nare] *vt* (*vestito*) to make (up); (*merci, pacchi*) to package

confezi'one [konfet'tsjone] *sf* (*di abiti: da uomo*) tailoring; (: *da donna*) dressmaking; (*imballaggio*) packaging; ~ **regalo** gift pack; **~i per signora** ladies' wear; **~i da uomo** menswear

confic'care *vt*: ~ **qc in** to hammer o drive sth into; **~rsi** *vr* to stick

confi'dare *vi*: ~ **in** to confide in, rely on ♦ *vt* to confide; **~rsi con qn** to confide in sb; **confi'dente** *sm/f* (*persona amica*) confidant/confidante; (*informatore*) informer; **confi'denza** *sf* (*familiarità*) intimacy, familiarity; (*fiducia*) trust, confidence; (*rivelazione*) confidence; **confidenzi'ale** *ag* familiar, friendly; (*segreto*) confidential

configu'rarsi *vr*: ~ **a** to assume the shape o form of

confi'nare *vi*: ~ **con** to border on ♦ *vt* (*POL*) to intern; (*fig*) to confine; **~rsi** *vr* (*isolarsi*):

~rsi in to shut o.s. up in

Confin'dustria *sigla f* (= *Confederazione Generale dell'Industria Italiana*) employers' association, ≈ CBI (*BRIT*)

con'fine *sm* boundary; (*di paese*) border, frontier

con'fino *sm* internment

confis'care *vt* to confiscate

con'flitto *sm* conflict

conflu'enza [konflu'ɛntsa] *sf* (*di fiumi*) confluence; (*di strade*) junction

conflu'ire *vi* (*fiumi*) to flow into each other, meet; (*strade*) to meet

con'fondere *vt* to mix up, confuse; (*imbarazzare*) to embarrass; **~rsi** *vr* (*mescolarsi*) to mingle; (*turbarsi*) to be confused; (*sbagliare*) to get mixed up

confor'mare *vt* (*adeguare*): **~ a** to adapt o conform to; **~rsi** *vr*: **~rsi (a)** to conform (to)

confor'tare *vt* to comfort, console; **confor'tevole** *ag* (*consolante*) comforting; (*comodo*) comfortable; **con'forto** *sm* comfort, consolation

confron'tare *vt* to compare

con'fronto *sm* comparison; **in o a ~ di** in comparison with, compared to; **nei miei** (*o* **tuoi** *etc*) **~i** towards me (*o you etc*)

confusi'one *sf* confusion; (*chiasso*) racket, noise; (*imbarazzo*) embarrassment

con'fuso, a *pp di* **confondere** ♦ *ag* (*vedi confondere*) confused; embarrassed

confu'tare *vt* to refute

conge'dare [kondʒe'dare] *vt* to dismiss; (*MIL*) to demobilize; **~rsi** *vr* to take one's leave; **con'gedo** *sm* (*anche MIL*) leave; **prendere congedo da qn** to take one's leave of sb; **congedo assoluto** (*MIL*) discharge

conge'gnare [kondʒen'nare] *vt* to construct, put together; **con'gegno** *sm* device, mechanism

conge'lare [kondʒe'lare] *vt* to freeze; **~rsi** *vr* to freeze; **congela'tore** *sm* freezer

congestio'nare [kondʒestjo'nare] *vt* to congest

congesti'one [kondʒes'tjone] *sf* congestion

conget'tura [kondʒet'tura] *sf* conjecture

con'giungere [kon'dʒundʒere] *vt* to join (together); **~rsi** *vr* to join (together)

congiunti'vite [kondʒunti'vite] *sf* conjunctivitis

congiun'tivo [kondʒun'tivo] *sm* (*LING*) subjunctive

congi'unto, a [kon'dʒunto] *pp di* **congiungere** ♦ *ag* (*unito*) joined ♦ *sm/f* relative

congiun'tura [kondʒun'tura] *sf* (*giuntura*) junction, join; (*ANAT*) joint; (*circostanza*) juncture; (*ECON*) economic situation

congiunzi'one [kondʒun'tsjone] *sf* (*LING*) conjunction

congi'ura [kon'dʒura] *sf* conspiracy; **congiu'rare** *vi* to conspire

conglome'rato *sm* (*GEO*) conglomerate; (*fig*) conglomeration; (*EDIL*) concrete

congratu'larsi *vr*: **~ con qn per qc** to congratulate sb on sth

congratulazi'oni [kongratulat'tsjoni] *sfpl* congratulations

con'grega, ghe *sf* band, bunch

con'gresso *sm* congress

congu'aglio [kon'gwaʎʎo] *sm* balancing, adjusting; (*somma di denaro*) balance

coni'are *vt* to mint, coin; (*fig*) to coin.

co'niglio [ko'niʎʎo] *sm* rabbit

coniu'gare *vt* (*LING*) to conjugate; **~rsi** *vr* to get married; **coniu'gato, a** *ag* (*sposato*) married; **coniugazi'one** *sf* (*LING*) conjugation

'coniuge ['kɔnjudʒe] *sm/f* spouse

connazio'nale [konnattsjo'nale] *sm/f* fellow-countryman/woman

connessi'one *sf* connection

con'nesso, a *pp di* **connettere**

con'nettere *vt* to connect, join ♦ *vi* (*fig*) to think straight

conni'vente *ag* conniving

conno'tati *smpl* distinguishing marks

'cono *sm* cone; **~ gelato** ice-cream cone

cono'scente [konoʃ'ʃente] *sm/f* acquaintance

cono'scenza [konoʃ'ʃentsa] *sf* (*il sapere*) knowledge *no pl*; (*persona*) acquaintance; (*facoltà sensoriale*) consciousness *no pl*; **perdere ~** to lose consciousness

co'noscere [ko'noʃʃere] *vt* to know; **ci siamo conosciuti a Firenze** we (first) met in Florence; **conosci'tore, 'trice** *sm/f* connoisseur; **conosci'uto, a** *pp di* **conoscere** ♦ *ag* well-known

con'quista *sf* conquest

conquis'tare *vt* to conquer; (*fig*) to gain, win

consa'crare *vt* (*REL*) to consecrate; (: *sacerdote*) to ordain; (*dedicare*) to dedicate; (*fig*: *uso etc*) to sanction; **~rsi a** to dedicate o.s. to

consangu'ineo, a *sm/f* blood relation

consa'pevole *ag*: **~ di** aware o conscious of; **consapevo'lezza** *sf* awareness, consciousness

'conscio, a, sci, sce ['kɔnʃo] *ag*: **~ di** aware o conscious of

consecu'tivo, a *ag* consecutive; (*successivo*: *giorno*) following, next

con'segna [kon'seɲɲa] *sf* delivery; (*merce consegnata*) consignment; (*custodia*) care, custody; (*MIL*: *ordine*) orders *pl*; (: *punizione*) confinement to barracks; **pagamento alla ~** cash on delivery; **dare qc in ~ a qn** to entrust sth to sb

conse'gnare [konseɲ'ɲare] vt to deliver; (affidare) to entrust, hand over; (MIL) to confine to barracks

consegu'enza [konse'gwɛntsa] sf consequence; **per o di ~** consequently

consegu'ire vt to achieve ♦ vi to follow

con'senso sm approval, consent

consen'tire vi: **~ a** to consent o agree to ♦ vt to allow, permit

con'serva sf (CUC) preserve; **~ di frutta** jam; **~ di pomodoro** tomato purée

conser'vare vt (CUC) to preserve; (custodire) to keep; (: dalla distruzione etc) to preserve, conserve; **~rsi** vr to keep

conserva'tore, 'trice sm/f (POL) conservative

conservazi'one [konservat'tsjone] sf preservation; conservation

conside'rare vt to consider; (reputare) to consider, regard; **considerazi'one** sf consideration; (stima) regard, esteem; **prendere in considerazione** to take into consideration; **conside'revole** ag considerable

consigli'are [konsiʎ'ʎare] vt (persona) to advise; (metodo, azione) to recommend, advise, suggest; **~rsi** vr: **~rsi con qn** to ask sb for advice; **consigli'ere, a** sm/f adviser ♦ sm: **consigliere d'amministrazione** board member; **consigliere comunale** town councillor; **con'siglio** sm (suggerimento) advice no pl, piece of advice; (assemblea) council; **consiglio d'amministrazione** board; **il Consiglio dei Ministri** (POL) ≈ the Cabinet; **Consiglio d'Europa** Council of Europe

consis'tente ag thick; solid; (fig) sound, valid; **consis'tenza** sf consistency, thickness; solidity; validity

con'sistere vi: **~ in** to consist of; **consis'tito, a** pp di **consistere**

conso'lare ag consular ♦ vt (confortare) to console, comfort; (rallegrare) to cheer up; **~rsi** vr to be comforted; to cheer up

conso'lato sm consulate

consolazi'one [konsolat'tsjone] sf consolation, comfort

'console[1] sm consul

con'sole[2] [kon'sɔl] sf (quadro di comando) console

conso'nante sf consonant

'consono, a ag: **~ a** consistent with, consonant with

con'sorte sm/f consort

con'sorzio [kon'sɔrtsjo] sm consortium

con'stare vi: **~ di** to consist of ♦ vb impers: **mi consta che** it has come to my knowledge that, it appears that

consta'tare vt to establish, verify;

constatazi'one sf observation; **constatazione amichevole** jointly-agreed statement for insurance purposes

consu'eto, a ag habitual, usual; **consue'tudine** sf habit, custom; (usanza) custom

consu'lente sm/f consultant; **consu'lenza** sf consultancy

consul'tare vt to consult; **~rsi** vr: **~rsi con qn** to seek the advice of sb; **consultazi'one** sf consultation; **consultazioni** sfpl (POL) talks, consultations

consul'torio sm: **~ familiare** family planning clinic

consu'mare vt (logorare: abiti, scarpe) to wear out; (usare) to consume, use up; (mangiare, bere) to consume; (DIR) to consummate; **~rsi** vr to wear out; to be used up; (anche fig) to be consumed; (combustibile) to burn out; **consuma'tore** sm consumer; **consumazi'one** sf (bibita) drink; (spuntino) snack; (DIR) consummation; **consu'mismo** sm consumerism; **con'sumo** sm consumption; wear; use

consun'tivo sm (ECON) final balance

con'tabile ag accounts cpd, accounting ♦ sm/f accountant; **contabilità** sf (attività, tecnica) accounting, accountancy; (insieme dei libri etc) books pl, accounts pl; (ufficio) accounts department

contachi'lometri [kontaki'lɔmetri] sm inv ≈ mileometer

conta'dino, a sm/f countryman/woman; farm worker; (peg) peasant

contagi'are [konta'dʒare] vt to infect

con'tagio [kon'tadʒo] sm infection; (per contatto diretto) contagion; (epidemia) epidemic; **contagi'oso, a** ag infectious; contagious

conta'gocce [konta'gottʃe] sm inv (MED) dropper

contami'nare vt to contaminate

con'tante sm cash; **pagare in ~i** to pay cash

con'tare vt to count; (considerare) to consider ♦ vi to count, be of importance; **~ su qn** to count o rely on sb; **~ di fare qc** to intend to do sth; **conta'tore** sm meter

contat'tare vt to contact

con'tatto sm contact

'conte sm count

conteggi'are [konted'dʒare] vt to charge, put on the bill; **con'teggio** sm calculation

con'tegno [kon'teɲɲo] sm (comportamento) behaviour; (atteggiamento) attitude; **darsi un ~** to act nonchalant; to pull o.s. together

contem'plare vt to contemplate, gaze at; (DIR) to make provision for

contemporanea'mente av simultaneously; at the same time

contempo'raneo, a *ag, sm/f* contemporary

conten'dente *sm/f* opponent, adversary

con'tendere *vi* (*competere*) to compete; (*litigare*) to quarrel ♦ *vt*: ~ **qc a qn** to contend with o be in competition with sb for sth

conte'nere *vt* to contain; **conteni'tore** *sm* container

conten'tare *vt* to please, satisfy; **~rsi di** to be satisfied with, content o.s. with

conten'tezza [konten'tettsa] *sf* contentment

con'tento, a *ag* pleased, glad; ~ **di** pleased with

conte'nuto *sm* contents *pl*; (*argomento*) content

con'tesa *sf* dispute, argument

con'teso, a *pp di* **contendere**

con'tessa *sf* countess

contes'tare *vt* (*DIR*) to notify; (*fig*) to dispute; **contestazi'one** *sf* (*DIR*) notification; dispute; (*protesta*) protest

con'testo *sm* context

con'tiguo, a *ag*: ~ **(a)** adjacent (to)

continen'tale *ag, sm/f* continental

conti'nente *ag* continent ♦ *sm* (*GEO*) continent; (: *terra ferma*) mainland

contin'gente [kontin'dʒɛnte] *ag* contingent ♦ *sm* (*COMM*) quota; (*MIL*) contingent; **contin'genza** *sf* circumstance; (*ECON*): (**indennità di) contingenza** cost-of-living allowance

continu'are *vt* to continue (with), go on with ♦ *vi* to continue, go on; ~ **a fare qc** to go on o continue doing sth; **continuazi'one** *sf* continuation

continuità *sf* continuity

con'tinuo, a *ag* (*numerazione*) continuous; (*pioggia*) continual, constant; (*ELETTR*): **corrente ~a** direct current; **di ~** continually

'conto *sm* (*calcolo*) calculation; (*COMM, ECON*) account; (*di ristorante, albergo*) bill; (*fig*: *stima*) consideration, esteem; **fare i ~i con qn** to settle one's account with sb; **fare ~ su qn/ qc** to count o rely on sb; **rendere ~ a qn di qc** to be accountable to sb for sth; **tener ~ di qn/qc** to take sb/sth into account; **per ~ di** on behalf of; **per ~ mio** as far as I'm concerned; **a ~i fatti, in fin dei ~i** all things considered; **~ corrente** current account; **~ alla rovescia** countdown

con'torcere [kon'tortʃere] *vt* to twist; **~rsi** *vr* to twist, writhe

contor'nare *vt* to surround

con'torno *sm* (*linea*) outline, contour; (*ornamento*) border; (*CUC*) vegetables *pl*

con'torto, a *pp di* **contorcere**

contrabbandi'ere, a *sm/f* smuggler

contrab'bando *sm* smuggling, contraband;

merce di ~ contraband, smuggled goods *pl*

contrab'basso *sm* (*MUS*) (double) bass

contraccambi'are *vt* (*favore etc*) to return

contraccet'tivo, a [kontrattʃet'tivo] *ag, sm* contraceptive

contrac'colpo *sm* rebound; (*di arma da fuoco*) recoil; (*fig*) repercussion

con'trada *sf* street; district

contrad'detto, a *pp di* **contraddire**

contrad'dire *vt* to contradict; **contraddit'torio, a** *ag* contradictory; (*sentimenti*) conflicting ♦ *sm* (*DIR*) cross-examination; **contraddizi'one** *sf* contradiction

contraf'fare *vt* (*persona*) to mimic; (*alterare: voce*) to disguise; (*firma*) to forge, counterfeit; **contraf'fatto, a** *pp di* **contraffare** ♦ *ag* counterfeit; **contraffazi'one** *sf* mimicking *no pl*; disguising *no pl*; forging *no pl*; (*cosa contraffatta*) forgery

contrap'peso *sm* counterbalance, counterweight

contrap'porre *vt*: ~ **qc a qc** to counter sth with sth; (*paragonare*) to compare sth with sth; **contrap'posto, a** *pp di* **contrapporre**

contraria'mente *av*: ~ **a** contrary to

contrari'are *vt* (*contrastare*) to thwart, oppose; (*irritare*) to annoy, bother; **~rsi** *vr* to get annoyed

contrarietà *sf* adversity; (*fig*) aversion

con'trario, a *ag* opposite; (*sfavorevole*) unfavourable ♦ *sm* opposite; **essere ~ a qc** (*persona*) to be against sth; **in caso ~** otherwise; **avere qc in ~** to have some objection; **al ~** on the contrary

con'trarre *vt* to contract; **contrarsi** *vr* to contract

contrasse'gnare [kontrassen'ɲare] *vt* to mark; **contras'segno** *sm* (*distintivo*) distinguishing mark; **spedire in contrassegno** to send C.O.D.

contras'tare *vt* (*avversare*) to oppose; (*impedire*) to bar; (*negare: diritto*) to contest, dispute ♦ *vi*: ~ **(con)** (*essere in disaccordo*) to contrast (with); (*lottare*) to struggle (with); **con'trasto** *sm* contrast; (*conflitto*) conflict; (*litigio*) dispute

contrat'tacco *sm* counterattack

contrat'tare *vt, vi* to negotiate

contrat'tempo *sm* hitch

con'tratto, a *pp di* **contrarre** ♦ *sm* contract; **contrattu'ale** *ag* contractual

contravvenzi'one [kontravven'tsjone] *sf* contravention; (*ammenda*) fine

contrazi'one [kontrat'tsjone] *sf* contraction; (*di prezzi etc*) reduction

contribu'ente *sm/f* taxpayer; ratepayer (*BRIT*), property tax payer (*US*)

contribu'ire *vi* to contribute; **contri'buto** *sm* contribution; (*tassa*) tax

'contro *prep* against; **~ di me/lui** against me/him; **pastiglie ~ la tosse** throat lozenges; **~ pagamento** (*COMM*) on payment ♦ *prefisso:* **contro'battere** *vt* (*fig: a parole*) to answer back; (: *confutare*) to refute; **controfi'gura** *sf* (*CINEMA*) double; **controfir'mare** *vt* to countersign

control'lare *vt* (*accertare*) to check; (*sorvegliare*) to watch, control; (*tenere nel proprio potere, fig: dominare*) to control; **con'trollo** *sm* check; watch; control; **controllo delle nascite** birth control; **control'lore** *sm* (*FERR, AUTOBUS*) (ticket) inspector

controprodu'cente [kontroprodu'tʃɛnte] *ag* counterproductive

contro'senso *sm* (*contraddizione*) contradiction in terms; (*assurdità*) nonsense

controspio'naggio [kontrospio'naddʒo] *sm* counterespionage

contro'versia *sf* controversy; (*DIR*) dispute

contro'verso, a *ag* controversial

contro'voglia [kontro'vɔʎʎa] *av* unwillingly

contu'macia [kontu'matʃa] *sf* (*DIR*) default

contusi'one *sf* (*MED*) bruise

convale'scente [konvaleʃ'ʃɛnte] *ag, sm/f* convalescent; **convale'scenza** *sf* convalescence

convali'dare *vt* (*AMM*) to validate; (*fig: sospetto, dubbio*) to confirm

con'vegno [kon'veɲɲo] *sm* (*incontro*) meeting; (*congresso*) convention, congress; (*luogo*) meeting place

conve'nevoli *smpl* civilities

conveni'ente *ag* suitable; (*vantaggioso*) profitable; (: *prezzo*) cheap; **conveni'enza** *sf* suitability; advantage; cheapness; **le convenienze** *sfpl* social conventions

conve'nire *vi* (*riunirsi*) to gather, assemble; (*concordare*) to agree; (*tornare utile*) to be worthwhile ♦ *vb impers:* **conviene fare questo** it is advisable to do this; **conviene andarsene** we should go; **ne convengo** I agree

con'vento *sm* (*di frati*) monastery; (*di suore*) convent

convenzio'nale [konventsjo'nale] *ag* conventional

convenzi'one [konven'tsjone] *sf* (*DIR*) agreement; (*nella società*) convention; **le ~i** *sfpl* social conventions

conver'sare *vi* to have a conversation, converse

conversazi'one [konversat'tsjone] *sf* conversation; **fare ~** to chat, have a chat

conversi'one *sf* conversion; **~ ad U** (*AUT*) U-turn

conver'tire *vt* (*trasformare*) to change; (*POL,*

REL) to convert; **~rsi** *vr:* **~rsi (a)** to be converted (to)

con'vesso, a *ag* convex

con'vincere [kon'vintʃere] *vt* to convince; **~ qn di qc** to convince sb of sth; **~ qn a fare qc** to persuade sb to do sth; **con'vinto, a** *pp di* **convincere**; **convinzi'one** *sf* conviction, firm belief

convis'suto, a *pp di* **convivere**

con'vivere *vi* to live together

convo'care *vt* to call, convene; (*DIR*) to summon; **convocazi'one** *sf* meeting; summons *sg*

convogli'are [konvoʎ'ʎare] *vt* to convey; (*dirigere*) to direct, send; **con'voglio** *sm* (*di veicoli*) convoy; (*FERR*) train

convulsi'one *sf* convulsion

con'vulso, a *ag* (*pianto*) violent, convulsive; (*attività*) feverish

coope'rare *vi:* **~ (a)** to cooperate (in); **coope'rativa** *sf* cooperative; **cooperazi'one** *sf* cooperation

coordi'nare *vt* to coordinate; **coordi'nate** *sfpl* (*MAT, GEO*) coordinates; **coordi'nati** *smpl* (*MODA*) coordinates

co'perchio [ko'perkjo] *sm* cover; (*di pentola*) lid

co'perta *sf* cover; (*di lana*) blanket; (*da viaggio*) rug; (*NAUT*) deck

coper'tina *sf* (*STAMPA*) cover, jacket

co'perto, a *pp di* **coprire** ♦ *ag* covered; (*cielo*) overcast ♦ *sm* place setting; (*posto a tavola*) place; (*al ristorante*) cover charge; **~ di** covered in *o* with

coper'tone *sm* (*AUT*) rubber tyre

coper'tura *sf* (*anche ECON, MIL*) cover; (*di edificio*) roofing

'copia *sf* copy; **brutta/bella ~** rough/final copy

copi'are *vt* to copy; **copia'trice** *sf* copier, copying machine

copi'one *sm* (*CINEMA, TEATRO*) script

'coppa *sf* (*bicchiere*) goblet; (*per frutta, gelato*) dish; (*trofeo*) cup, trophy; **~ dell'olio** oil sump (*BRIT*) *o* pan (*US*)

'coppia *sf* (*di persone*) couple; (*di animali, SPORT*) pair

coprifu'oco, chi *sm* curfew

copri'letto *sm* bedspread

co'prire *vt* to cover; (*occupare: carica, posto*) to hold; **~rsi** *vr* (*cielo*) to cloud over; (*vestirsi*) to wrap up, cover up; (*ECON*) to cover o.s.; **~rsi di** (*macchie, muffa*) to become covered in

co'raggio [ko'raddʒo] *sm* courage, bravery; **~!** (*forza!*) come on!; (*animo!*) cheer up!; **coraggi'oso, a** *ag* courageous, brave

co'rallo *sm* coral

co'rano *sm* (*REL*) Koran

co'razza [ko'rattsa] *sf* armour; (*di animali*) carapace, shell; (*MIL*) armour(-plating);

coraz'zata *sf* battleship

corbelle'ria *sf* stupid remark; **~e** *sfpl* nonsense *no pl*

'corda *sf* cord; (*fune*) rope; (*spago, MUS*) string; **dare ~ a qn** to let sb have his (o her) way; **tenere sulla ~ qn** to keep sb on tenterhooks; **tagliare la ~** to slip away, sneak off; **~e vocali** vocal cords

cordi'ale *ag* cordial, warm ♦ *sm* (*bevanda*) cordial

cor'doglio [kor'dɔʎʎo] *sm* grief; (*lutto*) mourning

cor'done *sm* cord, string; (*linea: di polizia*) cordon; **~ ombelicale** umbilical cord

Co'rea *sf*: **la ~** Korea

coreogra'fia *sf* choreography

cori'andolo *sm* (*BOT*) coriander; **~i** *smpl* confetti *sg*

cori'carsi *vr* to go to bed

'corna *sfpl vedi* **corno**

cor'nacchia [kor'nakkja] *sf* crow

corna'musa *sf* bagpipes *pl*

cor'netta *sf* (*MUS*) cornet; (*TEL*) receiver

cor'netto *sm* (*CUC*) croissant; (*gelato*) cone

cor'nice [kor'nitʃe] *sf* frame; (*fig*) setting, background

cornici'one [korni'tʃone] *sm* (*di edificio*) ledge; (*ARCHIT*) cornice

'corno (*pl*(*f*) **-a**) *sm* (*ZOOL*) horn; (*pl*(*m*) **-i**: *MUS*) horn; **fare le ~a a qn** to be unfaithful to sb

Corno'vaglia [korno'vaʎʎa] *sf*: **la ~** Cornwall

cor'nuto, a *ag* (*con corna*) horned; (*fam!: marito*) cuckolded ♦ *sm* (*fam!*) cuckold; (: *insulto*) bastard (!)

'coro *sm* chorus; (*REL*) choir

co'rona *sf* crown; (*di fiori*) wreath; **coro'nare** *vt* to crown

'corpo *sm* body; (*militare, diplomatico*) corps *inv*; **prendere ~** to take shape; **a ~ a ~** hand-to-hand; **~ di ballo** corps de ballet; **~ insegnante** teaching staff

corpo'rale *ag* bodily; (*punizione*) corporal

corpora'tura *sf* build, physique

corporazi'one [korporat'tsjone] *sf* corporation

corpu'lento, a *ag* stout

corre'dare *vt*: **~ di** to provide o furnish with; **cor'redo** *sm* equipment; (*di sposa*) trousseau

cor'reggere [kor'reddʒere] *vt* to correct; (*compiti*) to correct, mark

cor'rente *ag* (*acqua: di fiume*) flowing; (: *di rubinetto*) running; (*moneta, prezzo*) current; (*comune*) everyday ♦ *sm*: **essere al ~ (di)** to be well-informed (about); **mettere al ~ (di)** to inform (of) ♦ *sf* (*d'acqua*) current, stream; (*spiffero*) draught; (*ELETTR, METEOR*) current; (*fig*) trend, tendency; **la vostra lettera del 5**

~ mese (*COMM*) your letter of the 5th of this month; **corrente'mente** *av* commonly; **parlare una lingua correntemente** to speak a language fluently

'correre *vi* to run; (*precipitarsi*) to rush; (*partecipare a una gara*) to race, run; (*fig: diffondersi*) to go round ♦ *vt* (*SPORT: gara*) to compete in; (*rischio*) to run; (*pericolo*) to face; **~ dietro a qn** to run after sb; **corre voce che ...** it is rumoured that ...

cor'retto, a *pp di* **correggere** ♦ *ag* (*comportamento*) correct, proper; **caffè ~ al cognac** coffee laced with brandy

correzi'one [korret'tsjone] *sf* correction; marking; **~ di bozze** proofreading

corri'doio *sm* corridor

corri'dore *sm* (*SPORT*) runner; (: *su veicolo*) racer

corri'era *sf* coach (*BRIT*), bus

corri'ere *sm* (*diplomatico, di guerra, postale*) courier; (*COMM*) carrier

corrispet'tivo *sm* (*somma*) amount due

corrispon'dente *ag* corresponding ♦ *sm/f* correspondent

corrispon'denza [korrispon'dentsa] *sf* correspondence

corris'pondere *vi* (*equivalere*): **~ (a)** to correspond (to) ♦ *vt* (*stipendio*) to pay; (*fig: amore*) to return; **corris'posto, a** *pp di* **corrispondere**

corrobo'rare *vt* to strengthen, fortify; (*fig*) to corroborate, bear out

cor'rodere *vt* to corrode; **~rsi** *vr* to corrode

cor'rompere *vt* to corrupt; (*comprare*) to bribe

corrosi'one *sf* corrosion

cor'roso, a *pp di* **corrodere**

cor'rotto, a *pp di* **corrompere** ♦ *ag* corrupt

corrucci'arsi [korrut'tʃarsi] *vr* to grow angry o vexed

corru'gare *vt* to wrinkle; **~ la fronte** to knit one's brows

corruzi'one [korrut'tsjone] *sf* corruption; bribery

'corsa *sf* running *no pl*; (*gara*) race; (*di autobus, taxi*) journey, trip; **fare una ~** to run, dash; (*SPORT*) to run a race

cor'sia *sf* (*AUT, SPORT*) lane; (*di ospedale*) ward

cor'sivo *sm* cursive (writing); (*TIP*) italics *pl*

'corso, a *pp di* **correre** ♦ *sm* course; (*strada cittadina*) main street; (*di unità monetaria*) circulation; (*di titoli, valori*) rate, price; **in ~** in progress, under way; (*annata*) current; **~ d'acqua** river, stream; (*artificiale*) waterway; **~ d'aggiornamento** refresher course; **~ serale** evening class

'corte *sf* (court)yard; (*DIR, regale*) court; **fare la ~ a qn** to court sb; **~ marziale** court-martial

cor'teccia, ce [kor'tettʃa] *sf* bark

corteggi'are [korted'dʒare] vt to court
cor'teo sm procession
cor'tese ag courteous; **corte'sia** sf courtesy;
  per cortesia ... excuse me, please ...
cortigi'ana [korti'dʒana] sf courtesan
cortigi'ano, a [korti'dʒano] sm/f courtier
cor'tile sm (court)yard
cor'tina sf curtain; (anche fig) screen
'corto, a ag short; **essere a ~ di qc** to be
  short of sth; **~ circuito** short-circuit
'corvo sm raven
'cosa sf thing; (faccenda) affair, matter,
  business no pl; (che) ~? what?; (che) cos'è?
  what is it?; **a ~ pensi?** what are you thinking
  about?
'coscia, sce ['kɔʃʃa] sf thigh; **~ di pollo** (CUC)
  chicken leg
cosci'ente [koʃ'ʃente] ag conscious; **~ di**
  conscious o aware of; **cosci'enza** sf
  conscience; (consapevolezza) consciousness;
  coscienzi'oso, a ag conscientious
cosci'otto [koʃ'ʃɔtto] sm (CUC) leg
cos'critto sm (MIL) conscript

PAROLA CHIAVE
---

così av 1 (in questo modo) like this, (in) this
  way; (in tal modo) so; **le cose stanno ~** this is
  the way things stand; **non ho detto ~!** I didn't
  say that!; **come stai? — (e) ~** how are you? —
  so-so; **e ~ via** and so on; **per ~ dire** so to
  speak
  2 (tanto) so; **~ lontano** so far away; **un**
  ragazzo ~ intelligente such an intelligent boy
  ♦ ag inv (tale): **non ho mai visto un film ~**
  I've never seen such a film
  ♦ cong 1 (perciò) so, therefore
  2: **~ ... come** as ... as; **non è ~ bravo come te**
  he's not as good as you; **~ ... che** so ... that

---

cosid'detto, a ag so-called
cos'metico, a, ci, che ag, sm cosmetic
cos'pargere [kos'pardʒere] vt: **~ di** to
  sprinkle with; **cos'parso, a** pp di cospargere
cos'petto sm: **al ~ di** in front of; in the
  presence of
cos'picuo, a ag considerable, large
cospi'rare vi to conspire; **cospirazi'one** sf
  conspiracy
'costa sf (tra terra e mare) coast(line);
  (litorale) shore; (ANAT) rib; **la C~ Azzurra** the
  French Riviera
cos'tante ag constant; (persona) steadfast
  ♦ sf constant
cos'tare vi, vt to cost; **~ caro** to be
  expensive, cost a lot
cos'tata sf (CUC) large chop
cos'tato sm (ANAT) ribs pl
costeggi'are [kosted'dʒare] vt to be close
  to; to run alongside

cos'tei pron vedi costui
costi'era sf stretch of coast
costi'ero, a ag coastal, coast cpd
costitu'ire vt (comitato, gruppo) to set up,
  form; (sog: elementi, parti: comporre) to make
  up, constitute; (rappresentare) to constitute;
  (DIR) to appoint; **~rsi alla polizia** to give o.s.
  up to the police
costituzio'nale [kostituttsjo'nale] ag
  constitutional
costituzi'one [kostitut'tsjone] sf setting up;
  building up; constitution
'costo sm cost; **a ogni o qualunque ~, a tutti i**
  ~i at all costs
'costola sf (ANAT) rib
cos'toro pron pl vedi costui
cos'toso, a ag expensive, costly
cos'tretto, a pp di costringere
cos'tringere [kos'trindʒere] vt: **~ qn a fare**
  qc to force sb to do sth; **costrizi'one** sf
  coercion
costru'ire vt to construct, build;
  costruzi'one sf construction, building
cos'tui (f cos'tei, pl cos'toro) pron (soggetto)
  he/she; (pl) they; (complemento) him/her; pl
  them; **si può sapere chi è ~?** (peg) just who is
  that fellow?
cos'tume sm (uso) custom; (foggia di vestire,
  indumento) costume; **~i** smpl (condotta
  morale) morals, morality sg; **~ da bagno**
  bathing o swimming costume (BRIT),
  swimsuit; (da uomo) bathing o swimming
  trunks pl
co'tenna sf bacon rind
co'togna [ko'toɲɲa] sf quince
coto'letta sf (di maiale, montone) chop; (di
  vitello, agnello) cutlet
co'tone sm cotton; **~ idrofilo** cotton wool
  (BRIT), absorbent cotton (US)
'cotta sf (fam: innamoramento) crush
'cottimo sm: **lavorare a ~** to do piecework
'cotto, a pp di cuocere ♦ ag cooked; (fam:
  innamorato) head-over-heels in love; **ben ~**
  (carne) well done
cot'tura sf cooking; (in forno) baking; (in
  umido) stewing
co'vare vt to hatch; (fig: malattia) to be
  sickening for; (: odio, rancore) to nurse ♦ vi
  (fuoco, fig) to smoulder
'covo sm den
co'vone sm sheaf
'cozza ['kɔttsa] sf mussel
coz'zare [kot'tsare] vi: **~ contro** to bang into,
  collide with
C.P. abbr (= casella postale) P.O. Box
crack [kræk] sm inv (droga) crack
'crampo sm cramp
'cranio sm skull
cra'tere sm crater

cra'vatta *sf* tie

cre'anza [kre'antsa] *sf* manners *pl*

cre'are *vt* to create; **cre'ato** *sm* creation; **crea'tore, 'trice** *ag* creative ♦ *sm* creator; **crea'tura** *sf* creature; (*bimbo*) baby, infant; **creazi'one** *sf* creation; (*fondazione*) foundation, establishment

cre'dente *sm/f* (REL) believer

cre'denza [kre'dentsa] *sf* belief; (*armadio*) sideboard

credenzi'ali [kreden'tsjali] *sfpl* credentials

'credere *vt* to believe ♦ *vi*: ~ **in**, ~ **a** to believe in; ~ **qn onesto** to believe sb (to be) honest; ~ **che** to believe o think that; **~rsi furbo** to think one is clever

'credito *sm* (*anche* COMM) credit; (*reputazione*) esteem, repute; **comprare a** ~ to buy on credit

'credo *sm inv* creed

'crema *sf* cream; (*con uova, zucchero etc*) custard; ~ **solare** sun cream

cre'mare *vt* to cremate

Crem'lino *sm*: **il** ~ the Kremlin

'crepa *sf* crack

cre'paccio [kre'pattʃo] *sm* large crack, fissure; (*di ghiacciaio*) crevasse

crepacu'ore *sm* broken heart

cre'pare *vi* (*fam*: *morire*) to snuff it, kick the bucket; ~ **dalle risa** to split one's sides laughing

crepi'tare *vi* (*fuoco*) to crackle; (*pioggia*) to patter

cre'puscolo *sm* twilight, dusk

'crescere ['kreʃʃere] *vi* to grow ♦ *vt* (*figli*) to raise; **'crescita** *sf* growth; **cresci'uto, a** *pp di* **crescere**

'cresima *sf* (REL) confirmation

'crespo, a *ag* (*capelli*) frizzy; (*tessuto*) puckered ♦ *sm* crêpe

'cresta *sf* crest; (*di polli, uccelli*) crest, comb

'creta *sf* chalk; clay

cre'tino, a *ag* stupid ♦ *sm/f* idiot, fool

cric *sm inv* (TECN) jack

'cricca, che *sf* clique

cri'ceto [kri'tʃeto] *sm* hamster

crimi'nale *ag, sm/f* criminal

'crimine *sm* (DIR) crime

'crine *sm* horsehair; **crini'era** *sf* mane

crisan'temo *sm* chrysanthemum

'crisi *sf inv* crisis; (MED) attack, fit; ~ **di nervi** attack o fit of nerves

cristalliz'zare [kristalid'dzare] *vi* to crystallize; (*fig*) to become fossilized; **~rsi** *vr* to crystallize; to become fossilized

cris'tallo *sm* crystal

cristia'nesimo *sm* Christianity

cristi'ano, a *ag, sm/f* Christian

'Cristo *sm* Christ

cri'terio *sm* criterion; (*buon senso*)

(common) sense

'critica, che *sf* criticism; **la** ~ (*attività*) criticism; (*persone*) the critics *pl*; *vedi anche* **critico**

criti'care *vt* to criticize

'critico, a, ci, che *ag* critical ♦ *sm* critic

Croa'zia [kroa'ttsja] *sf* Croatia

croc'cante *ag* crisp, crunchy

'croce ['krotʃe] *sf* cross; **in** ~ (*di traverso*) crosswise; (*fig*) on tenterhooks; **la C~ Rossa** the Red Cross

croce'figgere *etc* [krotʃe'fiddʒere] = **croci-figgere** *etc*

croce'via *sm inv* crossroads *sg*

croci'ata [kro'tʃata] *sf* crusade

cro'cicchio [kro'tʃikkjo] *sm* crossroads *sg*

croci'era [kro'tʃera] *sf* (*viaggio*) cruise; (ARCHIT) transept

croci'figgere [krotʃi'fiddʒere] *vt* to crucify; **crocifissi'one** *sf* crucifixion; **croci'fisso, a** *pp di* **crocifiggere**

crogi'olo [kro'dʒɔlo] *sm* (*fig*) melting pot

crol'lare *vi* to collapse; **'crollo** *sm* collapse; (*di prezzi*) slump, sudden fall

cro'mato, a *ag* chromium-plated

'cromo *sm* chrome, chromium

'cronaca, che *sf* (STAMPA) news *sg*; (: *rubrica*) column; (TV, RADIO) commentary; **fatto o episodio di** ~ news item; ~ **nera** crime news *sg*; crime column

'cronico, a, ci, che *ag* chronic

cro'nista, i *sm* (STAMPA) reporter

cronolo'gia [kronolo'dʒia] *sf* chronology

cro'nometro *sm* chronometer; (*a scatto*) stopwatch

'crosta *sf* crust

cros'tacei [kros'tatʃei] *smpl* shellfish

cros'tata *sf* (CUC) tart

cros'tino *sm* (CUC) croûton; (: *da antipasto*) canapé

'cruccio ['kruttʃo] *sm* worry, torment

cruci'verba *sm inv* crossword (puzzle)

cru'dele *ag* cruel; **crudeltà** *sf* cruelty

'crudo, a *ag* (*non cotto*) raw; (*aspro*) harsh, severe

cru'miro (*peg*) *sm* blackleg (BRIT), scab

'crusca *sf* bran

crus'cotto *sm* (AUT) dashboard

CSI *sigla f inv* (= *Comunità Stati Indipendenti*) CIS

'Cuba *sf* Cuba

cu'betto *sm*: ~ **di ghiaccio** ice cube

'cubico, a, ci, che *ag* cubic

'cubo, a *ag* cubic ♦ *sm* cube; **elevare al** ~ (MAT) to cube

cuc'cagna [kuk'kaɲɲa] *sf*: **paese della** ~ land of plenty; **albero della** ~ greasy pole (*fig*)

cuc'cetta [kut'tʃetta] *sf* (FERR) couchette; (NAUT) berth

cucchiai'ata [kukja'jata] *sf* spoonful
cucchia'ino [kukkja'ino] *sm* teaspoon;
coffee spoon
cucchi'aio [kuk'kjajo] *sm* spoon
'cuccia, ce ['kuttʃa] *sf* dog's bed; **a ~!** down!
'cucciolo ['kuttʃolo] *sm* cub; (*di cane*) puppy
cu'cina [ku'tʃina] *sf* (*locale*) kitchen; (*arte
culinaria*) cooking, cookery; (*le vivande*) food,
cooking; (*apparecchio*) cooker; **~ componibile**
fitted kitchen; **cuci'nare** *vt* to cook
cu'cire [ku'tʃire] *vt* to sew, stitch; **cuci'trice**
sf stapler; **cuci'tura** *sf* sewing, stitching;
(*costura*) seam
cucù *sm inv* = **cuculo**
cu'culo *sm* cuckoo
'cuffia *sf* bonnet, cap; (*da infermiera*) cap;
(*da bagno*) (bathing) cap; (*per ascoltare*)
headphones *pl*, headset
cu'gino, a [ku'dʒino] *sm/f* cousin

'cui *pron* **1** (*nei complementi indiretti: persona*)
whom; (: *oggetto, animale*) which; **la
persona/le persone a ~ accennavi** the person/
people you were referring to o to whom you
were referring; **i libri di ~ parlavo** the books I
was talking about o about which I was
talking; **il quartiere in ~ abito** the district
where I live; **la ragione per ~** the reason why
2 (*inserito tra articolo e sostantivo*) whose; **la
donna i ~ figli sono scomparsi** the woman
whose children have disappeared; **il signore,
dal ~ figlio ho avuto il libro** the man from
whose son I got the book

culi'naria *sf* cookery
'culla *sf* cradle
cul'lare *vt* to rock
culmi'nare *vi*: **~ con** to culminate in
'culmine *sm* top, summit
'culo (*fam!*) *sm* arse (*Brit!*), ass (*US!*); (*fig:
fortuna*): **aver ~** to have the luck of the devil
'culto *sm* (*religione*) religion; (*adorazione*)
worship, adoration; (*venerazione: anche fig*)
cult
cul'tura *sf* culture; education, learning;
cultu'rale *ag* cultural
cumula'tivo, a *ag* cumulative; (*prezzo*)
inclusive; (*biglietto*) group *cpd*
'cumulo *sm* (*mucchio*) pile, heap; (*METEOR*)
cumulus
'cuneo *sm* wedge
cu'netta *sf* (*avvallamento*) dip; (*di scolo*)
gutter
cu'oca *sf vedi* **cuoco**
cu'ocere ['kwɔtʃere] *vt* (*alimenti*) to cook;
(*mattoni etc*) to fire ♦ *vi* to cook; **~ al forno**
(*pane*) to bake; (*arrosto*) to roast; **cu'oco, a,
chi, che** *sm/f* cook; (*di ristorante*) chef

cu'oio *sm* leather; **~ capelluto** scalp
cu'ore *sm* heart; **~i** *smpl* (*CARTE*) hearts; **avere
buon ~** to be kind-hearted; **stare a ~ a qn** to
be important to sb
cupi'digia [kupi'didʒa] *sf* greed,
covetousness
'cupo, a *ag* dark; (*suono*) dull; (*fig*) gloomy,
dismal
'cupola *sf* dome; cupola
'cura *sf* care; (*MED: trattamento*) (course of)
treatment; **aver ~ di** (*occuparsi di*) to look
after; **a ~ di** (*libro*) edited by; **~ dimagrante**
diet
cu'rare *vt* (*malato, malattia*) to treat; (: *guarire*) to cure; (*aver cura di*) to take care of;
(*testo*) to edit; **~rsi** *vr* to take care of o.s.;
(*MED*) to follow a course of treatment; **~rsi di**
to pay attention to
cu'rato *sm* parish priest; (*protestante*) vicar,
minister
cura'tore, 'trice *sm/f* (*DIR*) trustee; (*di
antologia etc*) editor
curio'sare *vi* to look round, wander round;
(*tra libri*) to browse; **~ nei negozi** to look o
wander round the shops
curiosità *sf inv* curiosity; (*cosa rara*) curio,
curiosity
curi'oso, a *ag* curious; **essere ~ di** to be
curious about
cur'sore *sm* (*INFORM*) cursor
'curva *sf* curve; (*stradale*) bend, curve
cur'vare *vt* to bend ♦ *vi* (*veicolo*) to take a
bend; (*strada*) to bend, curve; **~rsi** *vr* to
bend; (*legno*) to warp
'curvo, a *ag* curved; (*piegato*) bent
cusci'netto [kuʃʃi'netto] *sm* pad; (*TECN*)
bearing ♦ *ag inv*: **stato ~** buffer state; **~ a
sfere** ball bearing
cu'scino [kuʃ'ʃino] *sm* cushion; (*guanciale*)
pillow
'cuspide *sf* (*ARCHIT*) spire
cus'tode *sm/f* keeper, custodian
cus'todia *sf* care; (*DIR*) custody; (*astuccio*)
case, holder
custo'dire *vt* (*conservare*) to keep; (*assistere*)
to look after, take care of; (*fare la guardia*) to
guard
'cute *sf* (*ANAT*) skin
C.V. *abbr* (= *cavallo vapore*) h.p.

D, d

da (*da+il* = **dal**, *da+lo* = **dallo**, *da+l'* = **dall'**,
da+la = **dalla**, *da+i* = **dai**, *da+gli* = **dagli**,
da+le = **dalle**) *prep* **1** (*agente*) by; **dipinto
~ un grande artista** painted by a great artist

2 (*causa*) with; **tremare dalla paura** to tremble with fear

3 (*stato in luogo*) at; **abito ~ lui** I'm living at his house o with him; **sono dal giornalaio/ ~ Francesco** I'm at the newsagent's/ Francesco's (house)

4 (*moto a luogo*) to; (*moto per luogo*) through; **vado ~ Pietro/dal giornalaio** I'm going to Pietro's (house)/to the newsagent's; **sono passati dalla finestra** they came in through the window

5 (*provenienza, allontanamento*) from; **arrivare/partire ~ Milano** to arrive/depart from Milan; **scendere dal treno/dalla macchina** to get off the train/out of the car; **si trova a 5 km ~ qui** it's 5 km from here

6 (*tempo: durata*) for; (*: a partire da: nel passato*) since; (*: nel futuro*) from; **vivo qui ~ un anno** I've been living here for a year; **è dalle 3 che ti aspetto** I've been waiting for you since 3 (o'clock); **~ oggi in poi** from today onwards; **~ bambino** as a child, when I (o he *etc*) was a child

7 (*modo, maniera*) like; **comportarsi ~ uomo** to behave like a man; **l'ho fatto ~ me** I did it (by) myself

8 (*descrittivo*): **una macchina ~ corsa** a racing car; **una ragazza dai capelli biondi** a girl with blonde hair; **un vestito ~ 100.000 lire** a 100,000 lire dress

da 'capo *av* = **daccapo**

dac'capo *av* (*di nuovo*) (once) again; (*dal principio*) all over again, from the beginning

'dado *sm* (*da gioco*) dice o die; (*CUC*) stock (*BRIT*) o bouillon (*US*) cube; (*TECN*) (screw)nut; **giocare a ~i** to play dice

daf'fare *sm* work, toil

'dagli ['daʎʎi] *prep + det vedi* **da**

'dai *prep + det vedi* **da**

'daino *sm* (*fallow*) deer *inv*; (*pelle*) buckskin

dal *prep + det vedi* **da**

dall' *prep + det vedi* **da**

'dalla *prep + det vedi* **da**

'dalle *prep + det vedi* **da**

'dallo *prep + det vedi* **da**

dal'tonico, a, ci, che *ag* colour-blind

'dama *sf* lady; (*nei balli*) partner; (*gioco*) draughts *sg* (*BRIT*), checkers *sg* (*US*)

damigi'ana [dami'dʒana] *sf* demijohn

da'naro *sm* = **denaro**

da'nese *ag* Danish ♦ *sm/f* Dane ♦ *sm* (*LING*) Danish

Dani'marca *sf*: **la ~** Denmark

dan'nare *vt* (*REL*) to damn; **~rsi** *vr* (*fig: tormentarsi*) to be worried to death; **far ~ qn** to drive sb mad; **dannazi'one** *sf* damnation

danneggi'are [danned'dʒare] *vt* to damage; (*rovinare*) to spoil; (*nuocere*) to harm

'danno *sm* damage; (*a persona*) harm, injury; **~i** *smpl* (*DIR*) damages; **dan'noso, a** *ag*: **dannoso (a, per)** harmful (to), bad (for)

Da'nubio *sm*: **il ~** the Danube

'danza ['dantsa] *sf*: **la ~** dancing; **una ~** a dance

dan'zare [dan'tsare] *vt, vi* to dance

dapper'tutto *av* everywhere

dap'poco *ag inv* inept, worthless

dap'prima *av* at first

'dare *sm* (*COMM*) debit ♦ *vt* to give; (*produrre: frutti, suono*) to produce ♦ *vi* (*guardare*): **~ su** to look (out) onto; **~rsi** *vr*: **~rsi a** to dedicate o.s. to; **~rsi al commercio** to go into business; **~rsi al bere** to take to drink; **~ da mangiare a qn** to give sb sth to eat; **~ per certo qc** to consider sth certain; **~ per morto qn** to give sb up for dead; **~rsi per vinto** to give in

'darsena *sf* dock; dockyard

'data *sf* date; **~ di nascita** date of birth; **~ limite d'utilizzo** o **di consumo** best-before date

da'tare *vt* to date ♦ *vi*: **~ da** to date from

'dato, a *ag* (*stabilito*) given ♦ *sm* datum; **~i** *smpl* data *pl*; **~ che** given that; **un ~ di fatto** a fact

da'tore, trice *sm/f*: **~ di lavoro** employer

'dattero *sm* date

dattilogra'fare *vt* to type; **dattilogra'fia** *sf* typing; **datti'lografo, a** *sm/f* typist

da'vanti *av* in front; (*dirimpetto*) opposite ♦ *ag inv* front ♦ *sm* front; **~ a** in front of; facing, opposite; (*in presenza di*) before, in front of

davan'zale [davan'tsale] *sm* windowsill

d'a'vanzo [da'vantso] *av* more than enough

dav'vero *av* really, indeed

'dazio ['dattsjo] *sm* (*somma*) duty; (*luogo*) customs *pl*

DC *sigla f* = **Democrazia Cristiana**

d. C. *ad abbr* (= *dopo Cristo*) A.D.

'dea *sf* goddess

'debito, a *ag* due, proper ♦ *sm* debt; (*COMM: dare*) debit; **a tempo ~** at the right time; **debi'tore, 'trice** *sm/f* debtor

'debole *ag* weak, feeble; (*suono*) faint; (*luce*) dim ♦ *sm* weakness; **debo'lezza** *sf* weakness

debut'tare *vi* to make one's début; **de'butto** *sm* début

deca'denza [deka'dentsa] *sf* decline; (*DIR*) loss, forfeiture

decaffei'nato, a *ag* decaffeinated

decan'tare *vt* to praise, sing the praises of

decap'pot'tabile *ag, sf* convertible

dece'duto, a [detʃe'duto] *ag* deceased

de'cennio [de'tʃennjo] *sm* decade

de'cente [de'tʃɛnte] *ag* decent, respectable, proper; (*accettabile*) satisfactory, decent

de'cesso [de'tʃɛsso] sm death
de'cidere [de'tʃidere] vt: ~ qc to decide on
  sth; (questione, lite) to settle sth; ~ di fare/che
  to decide to do/that; ~ di qc (sog: cosa) to
  determine sth; ~rsi (a fare) to decide (to do),
  make up one's mind (to do)
deci'frare [detʃi'frare] vt to decode; (fig) to
  decipher, make out
deci'male [detʃi'male] ag decimal
'decimo, a ['dɛtʃimo] num tenth
de'cina [de'tʃina] sf ten; (circa dieci): una
  ~ (di) about ten
decisi'one [detʃi'zjone] sf decision; prendere
  una ~ to make a decision
de'ciso, a [de'tʃizo] pp di decidere
declas'sare vt to downgrade; to lower in
  status
decli'nare vi (pendio) to slope down; (fig:
  diminuire) to decline ♦ vt to decline
declinazi'one sf (LING) declension
de'clino sm decline
decodifica'tore sm (TEL) decoder
decol'lare vi (AER) to take off; de'collo sm
  take-off
decolo'rare vt to bleach
decom'porre vt to decompose; decomporsi
  vr to decompose; decom'posto, a pp di
  decomporre
deconge'lare [dekondʒe'lare] vt to defrost
deco'rare vt to decorate; decora'tore,
  'trice sm/f (interior) decorator;
  decorazi'one sf decoration
de'coro sm decorum; deco'roso, a ag
  decorous, dignified
de'correre vi to pass, elapse; (avere effetto)
  to run, have effect; de'corso, a pp di
  decorrere ♦ sm (evoluzione: anche MED)
  course
de'crepito, a ag decrepit
de'crescere [de'kreʃʃere] vi (diminuire) to
  decrease, diminish; (acque) to subside, go
  down; (prezzi) to go down; decresci'uto, a
  pp di decrescere
de'creto sm decree; ~ legge decree with the
  force of law
'dedalo sm maze, labyrinth
'dedica, che sf dedication
dedi'care vt to dedicate
'dedito, a ag: ~ a (studio etc) dedicated o
  devoted to; (vizio) addicted to
de'dotto, a pp di dedurre
de'durre vt (concludere) to deduce;
  (defalcare) to deduct; deduzi'one sf
  deduction
defal'care vt to deduct
defe'rente ag respectful, deferential
defe'rire vt: ~ a (DIR) to refer to
defezi'one [defet'tsjone] sf defection,
  desertion

defici'ente [defi'tʃɛnte] ag (mancante): ~ di
  deficient in; (insufficiente) insufficient ♦ sm/f
  mental defective; (peg: cretino) idiot
'deficit ['dɛfitʃit] sm inv (ECON) deficit
defi'nire vt to define; (risolvere) to settle;
  defini'tivo, a ag definitive, final;
  definizi'one sf definition; settlement
deflet'tore sm (AUT) quarter-light
de'flusso sm (della marea) ebb
defor'mare vt (alterare) to put out of shape;
  (corpo) to deform; (pensiero, fatto) to distort;
  ~rsi vr to lose its shape
de'forme ag deformed; disfigured;
  deformità sf inv deformity
defrau'dare vt: ~ qn di qc to defraud sb of
  sth, cheat sb out of sth
de'funto, a ag late cpd ♦ sm/f deceased
degene'rare [dedʒene'rare] vi to
  degenerate; de'genere ag degenerate
de'gente [de'dʒɛnte] sm/f (in ospedale) in-
  patient
'degli ['deʎʎi] prep + det vedi di
de'gnarsi [deɲ'ɲarsi] vr: ~ di fare to deign o
  condescend to do
'degno, a ['deɲɲo] ag dignified; ~ di worthy of; ~ di
  lode praiseworthy
degra'dare vt (MIL) to demote; (privare della
  dignità) to degrade; ~rsi vr to demean o.s.
degustazi'one [degustat'tsjone] sf
  sampling, tasting
'dei prep + det vedi di
del prep + det vedi di
dela'tore, 'trice sm/f police informer
'delega, ghe sf (procura) proxy
dele'gare vt to delegate; dele'gato sm
  delegate
dele'terio, a ag damaging; (per salute etc)
  harmful
del'fino sm (ZOOL) dolphin; (STORIA)
  dauphin; (fig) probable successor
delibe'rare vt to come to a decision on ♦ vi
  (DIR): ~ (su qc) to rule (on sth)
delica'tezza [delika'tettsa] sf delicacy;
  frailty; thoughtfulness; tactfulness
deli'cato, a ag delicate; (salute) delicate,
  frail; (fig: gentile) thoughtful, considerate;
  (: che dimostra tatto) tactful
deline'are vt to outline; ~rsi vr to be
  outlined; (fig) to emerge
delin'quente sm/f criminal, delinquent;
  ~ abituale regular offender, habitual offender;
  delin'quenza sf criminality, delinquency;
  delinquenza minorile juvenile delinquency
deli'rare vi to be delirious, rave; (fig) to rave
de'lirio sm delirium; (ragionamento insensato)
  raving; (fig): andare/mandare in ~ to go/send
  into a frenzy
de'litto sm crime
de'lizia [de'littsja] sf delight; delizi'oso, a

ag delightful; (*cibi*) delicious

dell' *prep + det vedi* **di**

'della *prep + det vedi* **di**

'delle *prep + det vedi* **di**

'dello *prep + det vedi* **di**

delta'plano *sm* hang-glider; **volo col ~** hang-gliding

de'ludere *vt* to disappoint; **delusi'one** *sf* disappointment; **de'luso, a** *pp di* **deludere**

de'manio *sm* state property

de'menza [de'mɛntsa] *sf* dementia; (*stupidità*) foolishness

demo'cratico, a, ci, che *ag* democratic

democra'zia [demokrat'tsia] *sf* democracy

democristi'ano, a *ag, sm/f* Christian Democrat

demo'lire *vt* to demolish

'demone *sm* demon

de'monio *sm* demon, devil; **il D~** the Devil

de'naro *sm* money

denomi'nare *vt* to name; **denomina-zi'one** *sf* name; denomination; **denominazione d'origine controllata** *label guaranteeing the quality and origin of a wine*

densità *sf inv* density

'denso, a *ag* thick, dense

den'tale *ag* dental

'dente *sm* tooth; (*di forchetta*) prong; **al ~** (*CUC: pasta*) al dente; **~i del giudizio** wisdom teeth; **denti'era** *sf* (set of) false teeth *pl*

denti'fricio [denti'fritʃo] *sm* toothpaste

den'tista, i, e *sm/f* dentist

'dentro *av* inside; (*in casa*) indoors; (*fig*: *nell'intimo*) inwardly ♦ *prep*: **~ (a)** in; **piegato in ~** folded over; **qui/là ~** in here/there; **~ di sé** (*pensare, brontolare*) to oneself

de'nuncia, ce o **cie** [de'nuntʃa] *sf* denunciation; declaration; **~ dei redditi** (income) tax return

denunci'are [denun'tʃare] *vt* to denounce; (*dichiarare*) to declare

de'nunzia *etc* [de'nuntsja] = **denuncia** *etc*

denutrizi'one [denutrit'tsjone] *sf* malnutrition

deodo'rante *sm* deodorant

depe'rire *vi* to waste away

depila'torio, a *ag* hair-removing *cpd*, depilatory

dépli'ant [depli'ɑ̃] *sm inv* leaflet; (*opuscolo*) brochure

deplo'revole *ag* deplorable

de'porre *vt* (*depositare*) to put down; (*rimuovere: da una carica*) to remove; (: *re*) to depose; (*DIR*) to testify

depor'tare *vt* to deport

deposi'tare *vt* (*gen, GEO, ECON*) to deposit; (*lasciare*) to leave; (*merci*) to store

de'posito *sm* deposit; (*luogo*) warehouse; depot; (: *MIL*) depot; **~ bagagli** left-luggage office

deposizi'one [depozit'tsjone] *sf* deposition; (*da una carica*) removal

de'posto, a *pp di* **deporre**

depra'vato, a *ag* depraved ♦ *sm/f* degenerate

depre'dare *vt* to rob, plunder

depressi'one *sf* depression

de'presso, a *pp di* **deprimere** ♦ *ag* depressed

deprez'zare [depret'tsare] *vt* (*ECON*) to depreciate

de'primere *vt* to depress

depu'rare *vt* to purify

depu'tato *sm* (*POL*) deputy, ≈ Member of Parliament (*BRIT*), ≈ Member of Congress (*US*)

deragli'are [deraʎ'ʎare] *vi* to be derailed; **far ~** to derail

dere'litto, a *ag* derelict

dere'tano (*fam*) *sm* bottom, buttocks *pl*

de'ridere *vt* to mock, deride; **de'riso, a** *pp di* **deridere**

de'riva *sf* (*NAUT, AER*) drift; **andare alla ~** (*anche fig*) to drift

deri'vare *vi*: **~ da** to derive from ♦ *vt* to derive; (*corso d'acqua*) to divert; **derivazi'one** *sf* derivation; diversion

derma'tologo, a, gi, ghe *sm/f* dermatologist

der'rate *sfpl*: **~ alimentari** foodstuffs

deru'bare *vt* to rob

des'critto, a *pp di* **descrivere**

des'crivere *vt* to describe; **descrizi'one** *sf* description

de'serto, a *ag* deserted ♦ *sm* (*GEO*) desert; **isola ~a** desert island

deside'rare *vt* to want, wish for; (*sessualmente*) to desire; **~ fare/che qn faccia** to want o wish to do/sb to do; **desidera fare una passeggiata?** would you like to go for a walk?

desi'derio *sm* wish; (*più intenso, carnale*) desire

deside'roso, a *ag*: **~ di** longing o eager for

desi'nenza [dezi'nɛntsa] *sf* (*LING*) ending, inflexion

de'sistere *vi*: **~ da** to give up, desist from; **desis'tito, a** *pp di* **desistere**

deso'lato, a *ag* (*paesaggio*) desolate; (*persona: spiacente*) sorry

des'tare *vt* to wake (up); (*fig*) to awaken, arouse; **~rsi** *vr* to wake (up)

desti'nare *vt* to destine; (*assegnare*) to appoint, assign; (*indirizzare*) to address; **~ qc a qn** to intend to give sth to sb, intend sb to have sth; **destina'tario, a** *sm/f* (*di lettera*) addressee

destinazi'one [destinat'tsjone] *sf* destination; (*uso*) purpose

des'tino *sm* destiny, fate

destitu'ire *vt* to dismiss, remove

'desto, a *ag* (wide) awake

'destra *sf* (*mano*) right hand; (*parte*) right (side); (*POL*): **la ~** the Right; **a ~** (*essere*) on the right; (*andare*) to the right

destreggi'arsi [destred'dʒarsi] *vr* to manoeuvre (*BRIT*), maneuver (*US*)

des'trezza [des'trettsa] *sf* skill, dexterity

'destro, a *ag* right, right-hand

dete'nere *vt* (*incarico, primato*) to hold; (*proprietà*) to have, possess; (*in prigione*) to detain, hold; **dete'nuto, a** *sm/f* prisoner; **detenzi'one** *sf* holding; possession; detention

deter'gente [deter'dʒɛnte] *ag* detergent; (*crema, latte*) cleansing ♦ *sm* detergent

deterio'rare *vt* to damage; **~rsi** *vr* to deteriorate

determi'nare *vt* to determine; **determinazi'one** *sf* determination; (*decisione*) decision

deter'sivo *sm* detergent

detes'tare *vt* to detest, hate

de'trarre *vt*: **~ (da)** to deduct (from), take away (from); **de'tratto, a** *pp di* **detrarre**; **detrazi'one** *sf* deduction; **detrazione d'imposta** tax allowance

de'trito *sm* (*GEO*) detritus

'detta *sf*: **a ~ di** according to

dettagli'are [dettaʎ'ʎare] *vt* to detail, give full details of

det'taglio [det'taʎʎo] *sm* detail; (*COMM*): **il ~** retail; **al ~** (*COMM*) retail; separately

det'tare *vt* to dictate; **~ legge** (*fig*) to lay down the law; **det'tato** *sm* dictation; **detta'tura** *sf* dictation

'detto, a *pp di* **dire** ♦ *ag* (*soprannominato*) called, known as; (*già nominato*) above-mentioned ♦ *sm* saying; **~ fatto** no sooner said than done

detur'pare *vt* to disfigure; (*moralmente*) to sully

devas'tare *vt* to devastate; (*fig*) to ravage

devi'are *vi*: **~ (da)** to turn off (from) ♦ *vt* to divert; **deviazi'one** *sf* (*anche AUT*) diversion

devo'luto, a *pp di* **devolvere**

devoluzi'one [devolut'tsjone] *sf* (*DIR*) devolution, transfer

de'volvere *vt* (*DIR*) to transfer, devolve

de'voto, a *ag* (*REL*) devout, pious; (*affezionato*) devoted

devozi'one [devot'tsjone] *sf* devoutness; (*anche REL*) devotion

---

PAROLA CHIAVE

---

di (*di+il* = **del**, *di+lo* = **dello**, *di+l'* = **dell'**, *di+la* = **della**, *di+i* = **dei**, *di+gli* = **degli**, *di+le* = **delle**) *prep* **1** (*possesso, specificazione*) of;

(*composto da, scritto da*) by; **la macchina ~ Paolo/mio fratello** Paolo's/my brother's car; **un amico ~ mio fratello** a friend of my brother's, one of my brother's friends; **un quadro ~ Botticelli** a painting by Botticelli

2 (*caratterizzazione, misura*) of; **una casa ~ mattoni** a brick house, a house made of bricks; **un orologio d'oro** a gold watch; **un bimbo ~ 3 anni** a child of 3, a 3-year-old child

3 (*causa, mezzo, modo*) with; **tremare ~ paura** to tremble with fear; **morire ~ cancro** to die of cancer; **spalmare ~ burro** to spread with butter

4 (*argomento*) about, of; **discutere ~ sport** to talk about sport

5 (*luogo: provenienza*) from; out of; **essere ~ Roma** to be from Rome; **uscire ~ casa** to come out of o leave the house

6 (*tempo*) in; **d'estate/d'inverno** in (the) summer/winter; **~ notte** by night, at night; **~ mattina/sera** in the morning/evening; **~ lunedì** on Mondays

♦ *det* (*una certa quantità di*) some; (: *negativo*) any; (: *interrogativo*) any, some; **del pane** (some) bread; **delle caramelle** (some) sweets; **degli amici miei** some friends of mine; **vuoi del vino?** do you want some o any wine?

---

dia'bete *sm* diabetes *sg*

di'acono *sm* (*REL*) deacon

dia'dema, i *sm* diadem; (*di donna*) tiara

dia'framma, i *sm* (*divisione*) screen; (*ANAT, FOT, contraccettivo*) diaphragm

di'agnosi [di'aɲɲozi] *sf* diagnosis *sg*

diago'nale *ag, sf* diagonal

dia'gramma, i *sm* diagram

dia'letto *sm* dialect

di'alisi *sf* dialysis *sg*

di'alogo, ghi *sm* dialogue

dia'mante *sm* diamond

di'ametro *sm* diameter

di'amine *escl*: **che ~ ...?** what on earth ...?

diaposi'tiva *sf* transparency, slide

di'ario *sm* diary

diar'rea *sf* diarrhoea

di'avolo *sm* devil

di'battere *vt* to debate, discuss; **~rsi** *vr* to struggle; **di'battito** *sm* debate, discussion

dicas'tero *sm* ministry

di'cembre [di'tʃɛmbre] *sm* December

dice'ria [ditʃe'ria] *sf* rumour, piece of gossip

dichia'rare [dikja'rare] *vt* to declare; **dichiarazi'one** *sf* declaration

dician'nove [ditʃan'nɔve] *num* nineteen

dicias'sette [ditʃas'sette] *num* seventeen

dici'otto [di'tʃɔtto] *num* eighteen

dici'tura [ditʃi'tura] *sf* words *pl*, wording

di'eci ['djɛtʃi] *num* ten; **die'cina** *sf* = **decina**

'diesel ['dizəl] *sm inv* diesel engine

di'eta *sf* diet; **essere a ~** to be on a diet
di'etro *av* behind; (*in fondo*) at the back ♦ *prep* behind; (*tempo: dopo*) after ♦ *sm* back, rear ♦ *ag inv* back *cpd*: **le zampe di ~** the hind legs; **~ richiesta** on demand; (*scritta*) on application
di'fatti *cong* in fact, as a matter of fact
di'fendere *vt* to defend; **difen'sivo, a** *ag* defensive ♦ *sf*: **stare sulla difensiva** (*anche fig*) to be on the defensive; **difen'sore, a** *sm/f* defender; **avvocato difensore** counsel for the defence; **di'fesa** *sf* defence; **di'feso, a** *pp di* **difendere**
difet'tare *vi* to be defective; **~ di** to be lacking in, lack; **difet'tivo, a** *ag* defective
di'fetto *sm* (*mancanza*): **~ di** lack of; shortage of; (*di fabbricazione*) fault, flaw, defect; (*morale*) fault, failing, defect; (*fisico*) defect; **far ~** to be lacking; **in ~** at fault; in the wrong; **difet'toso, a** *ag* defective, faulty
diffa'mare *vt* to slander; to libel
diffe'rente *ag* different
diffe'renza [diffe'rɛntsa] *sf* difference; **a ~ di** unlike
differenzi'are [differen'tsjare] *vt* to differentiate; **~rsi da** to differentiate o.s. from; to differ from
diffe'rire *vt* to postpone, defer ♦ *vi* to be different
dif'ficile [dif'fitʃile] *ag* difficult; (*persona*) hard to please, difficult (to please); (*poco probabile*): **è ~ che sia libero** it is unlikely that he'll be free ♦ *sm* difficult part; difficulty; **difficoltà** *sf inv* difficulty
dif'fida *sf* (*DIR*) warning, notice
diffi'dare *vi*: **~ di** to be suspicious o distrustful of ♦ *vt* (*DIR*) to warn; **~ qn dal fare qc** to warn sb not to do sth, caution sb against doing sth; **diffi'dente** *ag* suspicious, distrustful; **diffi'denza** *sf* suspicion, distrust
dif'fondere *vt* (*luce, calore*) to diffuse; (*notizie*) to spread, circulate; **~rsi** *vr* to spread; **diffusi'one** *sf* diffusion; spread; (*anche di giornale*) circulation; (*FISICA*) scattering; **dif'fuso, a** *pp di* **diffondere** ♦ *ag* (*malattia, fenomeno*) widespread
difi'lato *av* (*direttamente*) straight, directly; (*subito*) straight away
difte'rite *sf* (*MED*) diphtheria
'diga, dighe *sf* dam; (*portuale*) breakwater
dige'rente [didʒe'rɛnte] *ag* (*apparato*) digestive
dige'rire [didʒe'rire] *vt* to digest; **digesti'one** *sf* digestion; **diges'tivo, a** *ag* digestive ♦ *sm* (*after-dinner*) liqueur
digi'tale [didʒi'tale] *ag* digital; (*delle dita*) finger *cpd*, digital ♦ *sf* (*BOT*) foxglove
digi'tare [didʒi'tare] *vt, vi* (*INFORM*) to key (in)

digiu'nare [didʒu'nare] *vi* to starve o.s.; (*REL*) to fast; **digi'uno, a** *ag*: **essere digiuno** not to have eaten ♦ *sm* fast; **a digiuno** on an empty stomach
dignità [diɲɲi'ta] *sf inv* dignity; **digni'toso, a** *ag* dignified
'DIGOS ['digos] *sigla f* (= *Divisione Investigazioni Generali e Operazioni Speciali*) police department dealing with political security
digri'gnare [digriɲ'ɲare] *vt*: **~ i denti** to grind one's teeth
dila'gare *vi* to flood; (*fig*) to spread
dilani'are *vt* (*preda*) to tear to pieces
dilapi'dare *vt* to squander, waste
dila'tare *vt* to dilate; (*gas*) to cause to expand; (*passaggio, cavità*) to open (up); **~rsi** *vr* to dilate; (*FISICA*) to expand
dilazio'nare [dilattsjo'nare] *vt* to delay, defer; **dilazi'one** *sf* delay; (*COMM: di pagamento etc*) extension; (*rinvio*) postponement
dilegu'are *vi* to vanish, disappear; **~rsi** *vr* to vanish, disappear
di'lemma, i *sm* dilemma
dilet'tante *sm/f* dilettante; (*anche SPORT*) amateur
dilet'tare *vt* to give pleasure to, delight; **~rsi** *vr*: **~rsi di** to take pleasure in, enjoy
di'letto, a *ag* dear, beloved ♦ *sm* pleasure, delight
dili'gente [dili'dʒɛnte] *ag* (*scrupoloso*) diligent; (*accurato*) careful, accurate; **dili'genza** *sf* diligence; care; (*carrozza*) stagecoach
dilu'ire *vt* to dilute
dilun'garsi *vr* (*fig*): **~ su** to talk at length on o about
diluvi'are *vb impers* to pour (down)
di'luvio *sm* downpour; (*inondazione, fig*) flood
dima'grire *vi* to get thinner, lose weight
dime'nare *vt* to wave, shake; **~rsi** *vr* to toss and turn; (*fig*) to struggle; **~ la coda** (*sog: cane*) to wag its tail
dimensi'one *sf* dimension; (*grandezza*) size
dimenti'canza [dimenti'kantsa] *sf* forgetfulness; (*errore*) oversight, slip; **per ~** inadvertently
dimenti'care *vt* to forget; **~rsi di qc** to forget sth
di'messo, a *pp di* **dimettere** ♦ *ag* (*voce*) subdued; (*uomo, abito*) modest, humble
dimesti'chezza [dimesti'kettsa] *sf* familiarity
di'mettere *vt*: **~ qn da** to dismiss sb from; (*dall'ospedale*) to discharge sb from; **~rsi (da)** to resign (from)
dimez'zare [dimed'dzare] *vt* to halve
diminu'ire *vt* to reduce, diminish; (*prezzi*) to

bring down, reduce ♦ vi to decrease, diminish; (rumore) to die down, die away; (prezzi) to fall, go down; **diminuzi'one** sf decreasing, diminishing

dimissi'oni sfpl resignation sg; **dare** o **presentare le ~** to resign, hand in one's resignation

di'mora sf residence

dimo'rare vi to reside

dimos'trare vt to demonstrate, show; (provare) to prove, demonstrate; **~rsi** vr: **~rsi molto abile** to show o.s. o prove to be very clever; **dimostra 30 anni** he looks about 30 (years old); **dimostrazi'one** sf demonstration; proof

di'namica sf dynamics sg

di'namico, a, ci, che ag dynamic

dina'mite sf dynamite

'dinamo sf inv dynamo

di'nanzi [di'nantsi]: **~ a** prep in front of

dini'ego, ghi sm refusal; denial

dinocco'lato, a ag lanky

din'torno av round, (round) about; **~i** smpl outskirts; **nei ~i di** in the vicinity o neighbourhood of

'dio (pl **'dei**) sm god; **D~** God; **gli dei** the gods; **D~ mio!** my goodness!, my God!

di'ocesi [di'ɔtʃezi] sf inv diocese

dipa'nare vt (lana) to wind into a ball; (fig) to disentangle, sort out

diparti'mento sm department

dipen'dente ag dependent ♦ sm/f employee; **dipen'denza** sf dependence; **essere alle dipendenze di qn** to be employed by sb o in sb's employ

di'pendere vi: **~ da** to depend on; (finanziariamente) to be dependent on; (derivare) to come from, be due to; **di'peso, a** pp di **dipendere**

di'pingere [di'pindʒere] vt to paint; **di'pinto, a** pp di **dipingere** ♦ sm painting

di'ploma, i sm diploma

diplo'mare vt to award a diploma to, graduate (US); **~rsi** vr to obtain a diploma, graduate (US)

diplo'matico, a, ci, che ag diplomatic ♦ sm diplomat

diploma'zia [diplomat'tsia] sf diplomacy

di'porto: imbarcazione da ~ sf pleasure craft

dira'dare vt to thin (out); (visite) to reduce, make less frequent; **~rsi** vr to disperse; (nebbia) to clear (up)

dira'mare vt to issue ♦ vi (strade) to branch; **~rsi** vr to branch

'dire vt to say; (segreto, fatto) to tell; **~ qc a qn** to tell sb sth; **~ a qn di fare qc** to tell sb to do sth; **~ di sì/no** to say yes/no; **si dice che ...** they say that ...; **si direbbe che ...** it looks (o sounds) as though ...; **dica, signora?** (in un

negozio) yes, Madam, can I help you?

di'retto, a pp di **dirigere** ♦ ag direct ♦ sm (FERR) through train

diret'tore, 'trice sm/f (di azienda) director; manager/ess; (di scuola elementare) head (teacher) (BRIT), principal (US); **~ d'orchestra** conductor; **~ vendite** sales director o manager

direzi'one [diret'tsjone] sf board of directors; management; (senso di movimento) direction; **in ~ di** in the direction of, towards

diri'gente [diri'dʒente] sm/f executive; (POL) leader ♦ ag: **classe ~** ruling class

di'rigere [di'ridʒere] vt to direct; (impresa) to run, manage; (MUS) to conduct; **~rsi** vr: **~rsi verso** o **a** to make o head for

dirim'petto av opposite; **~ a** opposite, facing

di'ritto, a ag straight; (onesto) straight, upright ♦ av straight, directly; **andare ~** to go straight on ♦ sm right side; (TENNIS) forehand; (MAGLIA) plain stitch; (prerogativa) right; (leggi, scienza): **il ~** law; **~i** smpl (tasse) duty sg; **stare ~** to stand up straight; **aver ~ a** qc to be entitled to sth; **~i d'autore** royalties

dirit'tura sf (SPORT) straight; (fig) rectitude

diroc'cato, a ag tumbledown, in ruins

dirot'tare vt (nave, aereo) to change the course of; (aereo: sotto minaccia) to hijack; (traffico) to divert ♦ vi (nave, aereo) to change course; **dirotta'tore, 'trice** sm/f hijacker

di'rotto, a ag (pioggia) torrential; (pianto) unrestrained; **piovere a ~** to pour; **piangere a ~** to cry one's heart out

di'rupo sm crag, precipice

disabi'tato, a ag uninhabited

disabitu'arsi vr: **~ a** to get out of the habit of

disac'cordo sm disagreement

disadat'tato, a ag (PSIC) maladjusted

disa'dorno, a ag plain, unadorned

disagi'ato, a [diza'dʒato] ag poor, needy; (vita) hard

di'sagio [di'zadʒo] sm discomfort; (disturbo) inconvenience; (fig: imbarazzo) embarrass- ment; **essere a ~** to be ill at ease

disappro'vare vt to disapprove of; **disapprovazi'one** sf disapproval

disap'punto sm disappointment

disar'mare vt, vi to disarm; **di'sarmo** sm (MIL) disarmament

di'sastro sm disaster

disat'tento, a ag inattentive; **disattenzi'one** sf carelessness, lack of attention

disa'vanzo [diza'vantso] sm (ECON) deficit

disavven'tura sf misadventure, mishap

dis'brigo, ghi sm (prompt) clearing up o settlement

dis'capito *sm*: **a ~ di** to the detriment of

dis'carica, che *sf (di rifiuti)* rubbish tip o dump

discen'dente [diʃʃen'dɛnte] *ag* descending ♦ *sm/f* descendant

di'scendere [diʃʃendere] *vt* to go (o come) down ♦ *vi* to go (o come) down; *(strada)* to go down; *(smontare)* to get off; **~ da** *(famiglia)* to be descended from; **~ dalla macchina/dal treno** to get out of the car/out of o off the train; **~ da cavallo** to dismount, get off one's horse

di'scepolo, a [diʃʃepolo] *sm/f* disciple

di'scernere [diʃʃernere] *vt* to discern

di'scesa [diʃʃesa] *sf* descent; *(pendio)* slope; **in ~** *(strada)* downhill *cpd*, sloping; **~ libera** *(SCI)* downhill (race)

di'sceso, a [diʃʃeso] *pp di* **discendere**

disci'ogliere [diʃʃɔʎʎere] *vt* to dissolve; *(fondere)* to melt; **~rsi** *vr* to dissolve; to melt; **disci'olto, a** *pp di* **disciogliere**

disci'plina [diʃʃi'plina] *sf* discipline; **discipli'nare** *ag* disciplinary ♦ *vt* to discipline

'disco, schi *sm* disc; *(SPORT)* discus; *(fonografico)* record; *(INFORM)* disk; **~ orario** *(AUT)* parking disc; **~ rigido** *(INFORM)* hard disk; **~ volante** flying saucer

discol'pare *vt* to clear of blame

disco'noscere [disko'noʃʃere] *vt (figlio)* to disown; *(meriti)* to ignore, disregard; **disconosci'uto, a** *pp di* **disconoscere**

dis'corde *ag* conflicting, clashing; **dis'cordia** *sf* discord; *(dissidio)* disagreement, clash

dis'correre *vi*: **~ (di)** to talk (about)

dis'corso, a *pp di* **discorrere** ♦ *sm* speech; *(conversazione)* conversation, talk

dis'costo, a *ag* faraway, distant ♦ *av* far away; **~ da** far from

disco'teca, che *sf (raccolta)* record library; *(locale)* disco

discre'panza [diskre'pantsa] *sf* disagreement

dis'creto, a *ag* discreet; *(abbastanza buono)* reasonable, fair; **discrezi'one** *sf* discretion; *(giudizio)* judgment, discernment; **a discrezione di** at the discretion of

discriminazi'one [diskriminat'tsjone] *sf* discrimination

discussi'one *sf* discussion; *(litigio)* argument; **fuori ~** out of the question

dis'cusso, a *pp di* **discutere**

dis'cutere *vt* to discuss, debate; *(contestare)* to question ♦ *vi (conversare)*: **~ (di)** to discuss; *(litigare)* to argue

disde'gnare [disdeɲ'ɲare] *vt* to scorn

dis'detta *sf (di prenotazione etc)* cancellation; *(sfortuna)* bad luck

dis'detto, a *pp di* **disdire**

dis'dire *vt (prenotazione)* to cancel; *(DIR)*: **~ un contratto d'affitto** to give notice (to quit)

dise'gnare [diseɲ'ɲare] *vt* to draw; *(progettare)* to design; *(fig)* to outline

disegna'tore, 'trice *sm/f* designer

di'segno [di'seɲɲo] *sm* drawing; design; outline; **~ di legge** *(DIR)* bill

diser'bante *sm* weed-killer

diser'tare *vt, vi* to desert; **diser'tore** *sm (MIL)* deserter

dis'fare *vt* to undo; *(valigie)* to unpack; *(meccanismo)* to take to pieces; *(neve)* to melt; **~rsi** *vr* to come undone; *(neve)* to melt; **~ il letto** to strip the bed; **~rsi di qn** *(liberarsi)* to get rid of sb; **dis'fatta** *sf (sconfitta)* rout; **dis'fatto, a** *pp di* **disfare**

dis'gelo [diz'dʒelo] *sm* thaw

dis'grazia |diz'grattsja| *sf (sventura)* misfortune; *(incidente)* accident, mishap; **disgrazi'ato, a** *ag* unfortunate ♦ *sm/f* wretch

disgre'gare *vt* to break up; **~rsi** *vr* to break up

disgu'ido *sm* hitch; **~ postale** error in postal delivery

disgus'tare *vt* to disgust; **~rsi** *vr*: **~rsi di** to be disgusted by

dis'gusto *sm* disgust; **disgus'toso, a** *ag* disgusting

disidra'tare *vt* to dehydrate

disil'ludere *vt* to disillusion, disenchant

disimpa'rare *vt* to forget

disinfet'tante *ag, sm* disinfectant

disinfet'tare *vt* to disinfect

disini'bito, a *ag* uninhibited

disinte'grare *vt, vi* to disintegrate

disinteres'sarsi *vr*: **~ di** to take no interest in

disinte'resse *sm* indifference; *(generosità)* unselfishness

disintossi'care *vt (alcolizzato, drogato)* to treat for alcoholism (o drug addiction); **~ l'organismo** to clear out one's system

disin'volto, a *ag* casual, free and easy; **disinvol'tura** *sf* casualness, ease

disles'sia *sf* dyslexia

dislo'care *vt* to station, position

dismi'sura *sf* excess; **a ~** to excess, excessively

disobbe'dire *etc* = **disubbidire** *etc*

disoccu'pato, a *ag* unemployed ♦ *sm/f* unemployed person; **disoccupazi'one** *sf* unemployment

diso'nesto, a *ag* dishonest

diso'nore *sm* dishonour, disgrace

di'sopra *av (con contatto)* on top; *(senza contatto)* above; *(al piano superiore)* upstairs

♦ *ag inv* (*superiore*) upper ♦ *sm inv* top, upper part

disordi'nato, a *ag* untidy; (*privo di misura*) irregular, wild

di'sordine *sm* (*confusione*) disorder, confusion; (*sregolatezza*) debauchery

disorien'tare *vt* to disorientate; **~rsi** *vr* (*fig*) to get confused, lose one's bearings

di'sotto *av* below, underneath; (*in fondo*) at the bottom; (*al piano inferiore*) downstairs ♦ *ag inv* (*inferiore*) lower; bottom *cpd* ♦ *sm inv* (*parte inferiore*) lower part; bottom

dis'paccio [dis'pattʃo] *sm* dispatch

'dispari *ag inv* odd, uneven

dis'parte: in ~ *av* (*da lato*) aside, apart; **tenersi o starsene in ~** to keep to o.s., hold o.s. aloof

dispendi'oso, a *ag* expensive

dis'pensa *sf* pantry, larder; (*mobile*) sideboard; (*DIR*) exemption; (*REL*) dispensation; (*fascicolo*) number, issue

dispen'sare *vt* (*elemosine, favori*) to distribute; (*esonerare*) to exempt

dispe'rare *vi*: **~ (di)** to despair (of); **~rsi** *vr* to despair; **dispe'rato, a** *ag* (*persona*) in despair; (*caso, tentativo*) desperate; **disperazi'one** *sf* despair

dis'perdere *vt* (*disseminare*) to disperse; (*MIL*) to scatter, rout; (*fig: consumare*) to waste, squander; **~rsi** *vr* to disperse; to scatter; **dis'perso, a** *pp di* **disperdere** ♦ *sm/f* missing person

dis'petto *sm* spite *no pl*, spitefulness *no pl*; **fare un ~ a qn** to play a (nasty) trick on sb; **~ di** in spite of; **dispet'toso, a** *ag* spiteful

dispia'cere [dispja'tʃere] *sm* (*rammarico*) regret, sorrow; (*dolore*) grief; **~i** *smpl* (*preoccupazioni*) troubles, worries ♦ *vi*: **~ a** to displease ♦ *vb impers*: **mi dispiace (che)** I am sorry (that); **se non le dispiace, me ne vado adesso** if you don't mind, I'll go now; **dispiaci'uto, a** *pp di* **dispiacere** ♦ *ag* sorry

dispo'nibile *ag* available; **disponibilità** *sf inv* (*di biglietti, camere*) availability; (*gentilezza*) helpfulness; (*spec pl: FIN*) liquid assets *pl*

dis'porre *vt* (*sistemare*) to arrange; (*preparare*) to prepare; (*DIR*) to order; (*persuadere*): **~ qn a** to incline o dispose sb towards ♦ *vi* (*decidere*) to decide; (*usufruire*): **~ di** to use, have at one's disposal; (*essere dotato*): **~ di** to have; **disporsi** *vr* (*ordinarsi*) to place o.s., arrange o.s.

disposi'tivo *sm* (*meccanismo*) device

disposizi'one [dispozit'tsjone] *sf* arrangement, layout; (*stato d'animo*) mood; (*tendenza*) bent, inclination; (*comando*) order; (*DIR*) provision, regulation; **a ~ di qn** at sb's disposal

dis'posto, a *pp di* **disporre**

disprez'zare [dispret'tsare] *vt* to despise

dis'prezzo [dis'prettso] *sm* contempt

'disputa *sf* dispute, quarrel

dispu'tare *vt* (*contendere*) to dispute, contest; (*gara*) to take part in ♦ *vi* to quarrel; **~ di** to discuss; **~rsi qc** to fight for sth

dissan'guare *vt* (*fig: persona*) to bleed white; (: *patrimonio*) to suck dry; **~rsi** *vr* (*MED*) to lose blood; (*fig: rovinarsi*) to ruin o.s.

dissec'care *vt* to dry up; **~rsi** *vr* to dry up

dissemi'nare *vt* to scatter; (*fig: notizie*) to spread

dis'senso *sm* dissent; (*disapprovazione*) disapproval

dissente'ria *sf* dysentery

dissen'tire *vi*: **~ (da)** to disagree (with)

dissertazi'one [dissertat'tsjone] *sf* dissertation

disser'vizio [disser'vittsjo] *sm* inefficiency

disses'tare *vt* (*ECON*) to ruin; **dis'sesto** *sm* (financial) ruin

disse'tante *ag* refreshing

dis'sidio *sm* disagreement

dis'simile *ag* different, dissimilar

dissimu'lare *vt* (*fingere*) to dissemble; (*nascondere*) to conceal

dissi'pare *vt* to dissipate; (*scialacquare*) to squander, waste

dis'solto, a *pp di* **dissolvere**

disso'luto, a *pp di* **dissolvere** ♦ *ag* dissolute, licentious

dis'solvere *vt* to dissolve; (*neve*) to melt; (*fumo*) to disperse; **~rsi** *vr* to dissolve; to melt; to disappear

dissu'adere *vt*: **~ qn da** to dissuade sb from; **dissu'aso, a** *pp di* **dissuadere**

distac'care *vt* to detach, separate; (*SPORT*) to leave behind; **~rsi** *vr* to be detached; (*fig*) to stand out; **~rsi da** (*fig: allontanarsi*) to grow away from

dis'tacco, chi *sm* (*separazione*) separation; (*fig: indifferenza*) detachment; (*SPORT*): **vincere con un ~ di ...** to win by a distance of ...

dis'tante *av* far away ♦ *ag*: **~ (da)** distant (from), far away (from)

dis'tanza [dis'tantsa] *sf* distance

distanzi'are [distan'tsjare] *vt* to space out, place at intervals; (*SPORT*) to outdistance; (*fig: superare*) to outstrip, surpass

dis'tare *vi*: **distiamo pochi chilometri da Roma** we are only a few kilometres (away) from Rome

dis'tendere *vt* (*coperta*) to spread out; (*gambe*) to stretch (out); (*mettere a giacere*) to lay; (*rilassare: muscoli, nervi*) to relax; **~rsi** *vr* (*rilassarsi*) to relax; (*sdraiarsi*) to lie down;

distensi'one sf stretching; relaxation; (POL) détente

dis'tesa sf expanse, stretch

dis'teso, a pp di **distendere**

distil'lare vt to distil

distille'ria sf distillery

dis'tinguere vt to distinguish

dis'tinta sf (nota) note; (elenco) list

distin'tivo, a ag distinctive; distinguishing ♦ sm badge

dis'tinto, a pp di **distinguere** ♦ ag (dignitoso ed elegante) distinguished; **~i saluti** (in lettera) yours faithfully

distinzi'one [distin'tsjone] sf distinction

dis'togliere [dis'tɔʎʎere] vt: **~ da** to take away from; (fig) to dissuade from; **dis'tolto, a** pp di **distogliere**

distorsi'one sf (MED) sprain; (FISICA, OTTICA) distortion

dis'trarre vt to distract; (divertire) to entertain, amuse; **distrarsi** vr (non fare attenzione) to be distracted, let one's mind wander; (svagarsi) to amuse o enjoy o.s.; **dis'tratto, a** pp di **distrarre** ♦ ag absent-minded; (disattento) inattentive; **distra-zi'one** sf absent-mindedness; inattention; (svago) distraction, entertainment

dis'tretto sm district

distribu'ire vt to distribute; (CARTE) to deal (out); (posta) to deliver; (lavoro) to allocate, assign; (ripartire) to share out; **distribu'tore** sm (di benzina) petrol (BRIT) o gas (US) pump; (AUT, ELETTR) distributor; (automatico) vending machine; **distribuzi'one** sf distribution; delivery

distri'care vt to disentangle, unravel

dis'truggere [dis'truddʒere] vt to destroy; **dis'trutto, a** pp di **distruggere**; **distru-zi'one** sf destruction

distur'bare vt to disturb, trouble; (sonno, lezioni) to disturb, interrupt; **~rsi** vr to put o.s. out

dis'turbo sm trouble, bother, inconvenience; (indisposizione) (slight) disorder, ailment; **~i** smpl (RADIO, TV) static sg

disubbidi'ente ag disobedient; **disub-bidi'enza** sf disobedience

disubbi'dire vi: **~ (a qn)** to disobey (sb)

disugu'ale ag unequal; (diverso) different; (irregolare) uneven

disu'mano, a ag inhuman

di'suso sm: **andare** o **cadere in ~** to fall into disuse

'dita fpl di **dito**

di'tale sm thimble

'dito (pl(f) **'dita**) sm finger; (misura) finger, finger's breadth; **~ (del piede)** toe

'ditta sf firm, business

ditta'tore sm dictator

ditta'tura sf dictatorship

dit'tongo, ghi sm diphthong

di'urno, a ag day cpd, daytime cpd

'diva sf vedi **divo**

diva'gare vi to digress

divam'pare vi to flare up, blaze up

di'vano sm sofa; divan

divari'care vt to open wide

di'vario sm difference

dive'nire vi = **diventare**

diven'tare vi to become; **~ famoso/ professore** to become famous/a teacher

dive'nuto, a pp di **divenire**

di'verbio sm altercation

di'vergere [di'verdʒere] vi to diverge

diversifi'care vt to diversify, vary; to differentiate

diversi'one sf diversion

diversità sf inv difference, diversity; (varietà) variety

diver'sivo sm diversion, distraction

di'verso, a ag (differente): **~ (da)** different (from); **~i, e** det pl several, various; (COMM) sundry ♦ pron pl several (people), many (people)

diver'tente ag amusing

diverti'mento sm amusement, pleasure; (passatempo) pastime, recreation

diver'tire vt to amuse, entertain; **~rsi** vr to amuse o enjoy o.s.

divi'dendo sm dividend

di'videre vt (anche MAT) to divide; (distribuire, ripartire) to divide (up), split (up); **~rsi** vr (separarsi) to separate; (strade) to fork

divi'eto sm prohibition; **"~ di sosta"** (AUT) "no parking"

divinco'larsi vr to wriggle, writhe

divinità sf inv divinity

di'vino, a ag divine

di'visa sf (MIL etc) uniform; (COMM) foreign currency

divisi'one sf division

di'viso, a pp di **dividere**

'divo, a sm/f star

divo'rare vt to devour

divorzi'are [divor'tsjare] vi: **~ (da qn)** to divorce (sb); **divorzi'ato, a** sm/f divorcee

di'vorzio [di'vɔrtsjo] sm divorce

divul'gare vt to divulge, disclose; (rendere comprensibile) to popularize; **~rsi** vr to spread

dizio'nario [ditsjo'narjo] sm dictionary

dizi'one [dit'tsjone] sf diction; pronunciation

do sm (MUS) C; (: solfeggiando) do(h)

DOC [dɔk] abbr (= denominazione di origine controllata) label guaranteeing the quality of wine

'doccia, ce ['dottʃa] sf (bagno) shower; **fare la ~** to have a shower

do'cente [do'tʃɛnte] *ag* teaching ♦ *sm/f* teacher; (*di università*) lecturer

'docile ['dɔtʃile] *ag* docile

documen'tare *vt* to document; **~rsi** *vr*: **~rsi (su)** to gather information o material (about)

documen'tario *sm* documentary

docu'mento *sm* document; **~i** *smpl* (*d'identità etc*) papers

'dodici ['dɔditʃi] *num* twelve

do'gana *sf* (*ufficio*) customs *pl*; (*tassa*) (customs) duty; **passare la ~** to go through customs; **doga'nale** *ag* customs *cpd*; **dogani'ere** *sm* customs officer

'doglie ['dɔʎʎe] *sfpl* (*MED*) labour *sg*, labour pains

'dolce ['doltʃe] *ag* sweet; (*carattere, persona*) gentle, mild; (*fig: mite: clima*) mild; (*non ripido: pendio*) gentle ♦ *sm* (*sapore dolce*) sweetness, sweet taste; (*CUC: portata*) sweet, dessert; (: *torta*) cake; **dol'cezza** *sf* sweetness; softness; mildness; gentleness; **dolcifi'cante** *sm* sweetener; **dolci'umi** *smpl* sweets

do'lente *ag* sorrowful, sad

do'lere *vi* to be sore, hurt, ache; **~rsi** *vr* to complain; (*essere spiacente*): **~rsi di** to be sorry for; **mi duole la testa** my head aches, I've got a headache

'dollaro *sm* dollar

'dolo *sm* (*DIR*) malice

Dolo'miti *sfpl*: **le ~** the Dolomites

do'lore *sm* (*fisico*) pain; (*morale*) sorrow, grief; **dolo'roso, a** *ag* painful; sorrowful, sad

do'loso, a *ag* (*DIR*) malicious

do'manda *sf* (*interrogazione*) question; (*richiesta*) demand; (: *cortese*) request; (*DIR: richiesta scritta*) application; (*ECON*): **la ~** demand; **fare una ~ a qn** to ask sb a question; **fare ~ (per un lavoro)** to apply (for a job)

doman'dare *vt* (*per avere*) to ask for; (*per sapere*) to ask; (*esigere*) to demand; **~rsi** *vr* to wonder; to ask o.s.; **~ qc a qn** to ask sb for sth; to ask sb sth

do'mani *av* tomorrow ♦ *sm*: **il ~** (*il futuro*) the future; (*il giorno successivo*) the next day; **~ l'altro** the day after tomorrow

do'mare *vt* to tame

domat'tina *av* tomorrow morning

do'menica, che *sf* Sunday; **di ~** on Sundays; **domeni'cale** *ag* Sunday *cpd*

do'mestica, che *sf vedi* **domestico**

do'mestico, a, ci, che *ag* domestic ♦ *sm/f* servant, domestic

domi'cilio [domi'tʃiljo] *sm* (*DIR*) domicile, place of residence

domi'nare *vt* to dominate; (*fig: sentimenti*) to control, master ♦ *vi* to be in the dominant position; **~rsi** *vr* (*controllarsi*) to control o.s.;

~ su (*fig*) to surpass, outclass; **dominazi'one** *sf* domination

do'minio *sm* dominion; (*fig: campo*) field, domain

do'nare *vt* to give, present; (*per beneficenza etc*) to donate ♦ *vi* (*fig*): **~ a** to suit, become; **~ sangue** to give blood; **dona'tore, 'trice** *sm/f* donor; **donatore di sangue/di organi** blood/organ donor

dondo'lare *vt* (*cullare*) to rock; **~rsi** *vr* to swing, sway; **'dondolo** *sm*: **sedia/cavallo a dondolo** rocking chair/horse

'donna *sf* woman; **~ di casa** housewife; home-loving woman; **~ di servizio** maid

donnai'olo *sm* ladykiller

'donnola *sf* weasel

'dono *sm* gift

'dopo *av* (*tempo*) afterwards; (: *più tardi*) later; (*luogo*) after, next ♦ *prep* after ♦ *cong* (*temporale*): **~ aver studiato** after having studied; **~ mangiato va a dormire** after having eaten o after a meal he goes for a sleep ♦ *ag inv*: **il giorno ~** the following day; **un anno ~** a year later; **~ di me/lui** after me/him

dopo'barba *sm inv* after-shave

dopodo'mani *av* the day after tomorrow

dopogu'erra *sm* postwar years *pl*

dopo'pranzo [dopo'prandzo] *av* after lunch (o dinner)

doposcì [dopoʃ'ʃi] *sm inv* après-ski outfit

doposcu'ola *sm inv* school club offering extra tuition and recreational facilities

dopo'sole *sm inv* aftersun (lotion)

dopo'tutto *av* (*tutto considerato*) after all

doppi'aggio [dop'pjaddʒo] *sm* (*CINEMA*) dubbing

doppi'are *vt* (*NAUT*) to round; (*SPORT*) to lap; (*CINEMA*) to dub

'doppio, a *ag* double; (*fig: falso*) double-dealing, deceitful ♦ *sm* (*quantità*): **il ~ di** twice as much (o many as), double the amount (o number) of; (*SPORT*) doubles *pl* ♦ *av* double

doppi'one *sm* duplicate (copy)

doppio'petto *sm* double-breasted jacket

do'rare *vt* to gild; (*CUC*) to brown; **do'rato, a** *ag* golden; (*ricoperto d'oro*) gilt, gilded; **dora'tura** *sf* gilding

dormicchi'are [dormik'kjare] *vi* to doze

dormigli'one, a [dormiʎ'ʎone] *sm/f* sleepyhead

dor'mire *vt, vi* to sleep; **andare a ~** to go to bed; **dor'mita** *sf*: **farsi una dormita** to have a good sleep

dormi'torio *sm* dormitory

dormi'veglia [dormi'veʎʎa] *sm* drowsiness

'dorso *sm* back; (*di montagna*) ridge, crest; (*di libro*) spine; **a ~ di cavallo** on horseback

do'sare *vt* to measure out; (*MED*) to dose

'dose *sf* quantity, amount; (*MED*) dose

'dosso *sm* (*rilievo*) rise; (*di strada*) bump; (*dorso*): **levarsi di ~ i vestiti** to take one's clothes off

do'tare *vt*: **~ di** to provide *o* supply with; **dotazi'one** *sf* (*insieme di beni*) endowment; (*di macchine etc*) equipment

'dote *sf* (*di sposa*) dowry; (*assegnata a un ente*) endowment; (*fig*) gift, talent

Dott. *abbr* (= dottore) Dr.

'dotto, a *ag* (*colto*) learned ♦ *sm* (*sapiente*) scholar; (*ANAT*) duct

dotto'rato *sm* degree; **~ di ricerca** doctorate, doctor's degree

dot'tore, essa *sm/f* doctor

dot'trina *sf* doctrine

Dott.ssa *abbr* (= dottoressa) Dr.

'dove *av* (*gen*) where; (*in cui*) where, in which; (*dovunque*) wherever ♦ *cong* (*mentre, laddove*) whereas; **~ sei?/vai?** where are you?/are you going?; **dimmi dov'è** tell me where it is; **di ~ sei?** where are you from?; **per ~ si passa?** which way should we go?; **la città ~ abito** the town where *o* in which I live; **siediti ~ vuoi** sit wherever you like

do'vere *sm* (*obbligo*) duty ♦ *vt* (*essere debitore*): **~ qc (a qn)** to owe (sb) sth ♦ *vi* (*seguito dall'infinito*): **obbligo**) to have to; **rivolgersi a chi di ~** to apply to the appropriate authority *o* person; **lui deve farlo** he has to do it, he must do it; **è dovuto partire** he had to leave; **ha dovuto pagare** he had to pay; (: *intenzione*): **devo partire domani** I'm (due) to leave tomorrow; (: *probabilità*): **dev'essere tardi** it must be late; **come si deve** (*lavorare, comportarsi*) properly; **una persona come si deve** a respectable person

dove'roso, a *ag* (right and) proper

do'vunque *av* (*in qualunque luogo*) wherever; (*dappertutto*) everywhere; **~ io vada** wherever I go

do'vuto, a *ag* (*causato*): **~ a** due to

doz'zina [dod'dzina] *sf* dozen; **una ~ di uova** a dozen eggs

dozzi'nale [doddzi'nale] *ag* cheap, second-rate

dra'gare *vt* to dredge

'drago, ghi *sm* dragon

'dramma, i *sm* drama; **dram'matico, a, ci, che** *ag* dramatic; **drammatiz'zare** *vt* to dramatize; **dramma'turgo, ghi** *sm* playwright, dramatist

drappeggi'are [draped'dʒare] *vt* to drape

drap'pello *sm* (*MIL*) squad; (*gruppo*) band, group

'drastico, a, ci, che *ag* drastic

dre'naggio [dre'naddʒo] *sm* drainage

dre'nare *vt* to drain

'dritto, a *ag, av* = **diritto**

driz'zare [drit'tsare] *vt* (*far tornare dritto*) to straighten; (*innalzare: antenna, muro*) to erect; **~rsi** *vr*: **~rsi (in piedi)** to stand up; **~ le orecchie** to prick up one's ears

'droga, ghe *sf* (*sostanza aromatica*) spice; (*stupefacente*) drug; **dro'gare** *vt* to season, spice; to drug, dope; **drogarsi** *vr* to take drugs; **dro'gato, a** *sm/f* drug addict

droghe'ria [droge'ria] *sf* grocer's shop (*BRIT*), grocery (store) (*US*)

'dubbio, a *ag* (*incerto*) doubtful, dubious; (*ambiguo*) dubious ♦ *sm* (*incertezza*) doubt; **avere il ~ che** to be afraid that, suspect that; **mettere in ~ qc** to question sth; **dubbi'oso, a** *ag* doubtful, dubious

dubi'tare *vi*: **~ di** to doubt; (*risultato*) to be doubtful of

Dub'lino *sf* Dublin

'duca, chi *sm* duke

du'chessa [du'kessa] *sf* duchess

'due *num* two

due'cento [due'tʃento] *num* two hundred ♦ *sm*: **il D~** the thirteenth century

due'pezzi [due'pettsi] *sm* (*costume da bagno*) two-piece swimsuit; (*abito femminile*) two-piece suit

du'etto *sm* duet

'dunque *cong* (*perciò*) so, therefore; (*riprendendo il discorso*) well (then) ♦ *sm inv*: **venire al ~** to come to the point

du'omo *sm* cathedral

'duplex *sm inv* (*TEL*) party line

dupli'cato *sm* duplicate

'duplice ['duplitʃe] *ag* double, twofold; **in ~ copia** in duplicate

du'rante *prep* during

du'rare *vi* to last; **~ fatica a** to have difficulty in; **du'rata** *sf* length (of time); duration; **dura'turo, a** *ag* lasting

du'rezza [du'rettsa] *sf* hardness; stubbornness; harshness; toughness

'duro, a *ag* (*pietra, lavoro, materasso, problema*) hard; (*persona: ostinato*) stubborn, obstinate; (: *severo*) harsh, hard; (*voce*) harsh; (*carne*) tough ♦ *sm* hardness; (*difficoltà*) hard part; (*persona*) tough guy; **tener ~** to stand firm, hold out; **~ d'orecchi** hard of hearing

du'rone *sm* hard skin

E, e

e (*dav V spesso* **ed**) *cong* and; **~ lui?** what about him?; **~ compralo!** well buy it then!

è *vb vedi* **essere**

E. *abbr* (= est) E

'ebano *sm* ebony

eb'bene cong well (then)

eb'brezza [eb'brettsa] sf intoxication

'ebbro, a ag drunk; **~ di** (gioia etc) beside o.s. o wild with

'ebete ag stupid, idiotic

ebolli'zione [ebollit'tsjone] sf boiling; **punto di ~** boiling point

e'braico, a, ci, che ag Hebrew, Hebraic ♦ sm (LING) Hebrew

e'breo, a ag Jewish ♦ sm/f Jew/Jewess

'Ebridi sfpl: **le (isole) ~** the Hebrides

ecc av abbr (= eccetera) etc

ecce'denza [ettʃe'dɛntsa] sf excess, surplus

ec'cedere [et'tʃedere] vt to exceed ♦ vi to go too far; **~ nel bere/mangiare** to indulge in drink/food to excess

eccel'lente [ettʃel'lɛnte] ag excellent; **eccel'lenza** sf excellence; (titolo) Excellency

ec'cellere [et'tʃɛllere] vi: **~ (in)** to excel (at); **ec'celso, a** pp di **eccellere**

ec'centrico, a, ci, che [et'tʃɛntriko] ag eccentric

ecces'sivo, a [ettʃes'sivo] ag excessive

ec'cesso [et'tʃɛsso] sm excess; **all'~** (gentile, generoso) to excess, excessively; **~ di velocità** (AUT) speeding

ec'cetera [et'tʃetera] av et cetera, and so on

ec'cetto [et'tʃɛtto] prep except, with the exception of; **~ che** except, other than; **~ che (non)** unless

eccet'tuare [ettʃettu'are] vt to except

eccezio'nale [ettʃetsjo'nale] ag exceptional

eccezi'one [ettʃet'tsjone] sf exception, (DIR) objection; **a ~ di** with the exception of, except for; **d'~** exceptional

ec'cidio [et'tʃidio] sm massacre

ecci'tare [ettʃi'tare] vt (curiosità, interesse) to excite, arouse; (folla) to incite; **~rsi** vr to get excited; (sessualmente) to become aroused; **eccitazi'one** sf excitement

'ecco av (per dimostrare): **~ il treno!** here's o here comes the train!; (dav pron): **~mi!** here I am!; **~ne uno!** here's one (of them)!; (dav pp): **~ fatto!** there, that's it done!

echeggi'are [eked'dʒare] vi to echo

e'clissi sf eclipse

'eco (pl(m) **'echi**) sm o f echo

ecogra'fia sf (MED) scan

ecolo'gia [ekolo'dʒia] sf ecology

eco'nomia sf economy; (scienza) economics sg; (risparmio: azione) saving; **fare ~** to economize, make economies; **eco'nomico, a, ci, che** ag economic; (poco costoso) economical; **econo'mista, i** sm economist; **economiz'zare** vt, vi to save; **e'conomo, a** ag thrifty ♦ sm/f (INS) bursar

E'CU [e'ku] sm inv (= Unità monetaria europea) ECU n

ed cong vedi **e**

'edera sf ivy

e'dicola sf newspaper kiosk o stand (US)

edifi'care vt to build; (fig: teoria, azienda) to establish; (indurre al bene) to edify

edi'ficio [edi'fitʃo] sm building

e'dile ag building cpd; **edi'lizia** sf building, building trade; **edi'lizio, a** ag building cpd

Edim'burgo sf Edinburgh

edi'tore, 'trice ag publishing cpd ♦ sm/f publisher; (curatore) editor; **edito'ria** sf publishing; **editori'ale** ag publishing cpd ♦ sm editorial, leader

edizi'one [edit'tsjone] sf edition; (tiratura) printing

edu'care vt to educate; (gusto, mente) to train; **~ qn a fare** to train sb to do; **edu'cato, a** ag polite, well-mannered; **educazi'one** sf education; (familiare) upbringing; (comportamento) (good) manners pl; **educazione fisica** (INS) physical training o education

effemi'nato, a ag effeminate

effet'tivo, a ag (reale) real, actual; (impiegato, professore) permanent; (MIL) regular ♦ sm (MIL) strength; (di patrimonio etc) sum total

ef'fetto sm effect; (COMM: cambiale) bill; (fig: impressione) impression; **in ~i** in fact, actually; **~ serra** greenhouse effect; **effettu'are** vt to effect, carry out

effi'cace [effi'katʃe] ag effective

effici'ente [effi'tʃɛnte] ag efficient; **effici'enza** sf efficiency

ef'fimero, a ag ephemeral

E'geo [e'dʒeo] sm: **l'~, il mare ~** the Aegean (Sea)

E'gitto [e'dʒitto] sm: **l'~** Egypt

egizi'ano, a [edʒit'tsjano] ag, sm/f Egyptian

'egli ['eʎʎi] pron he; **~ stesso** he himself

ego'ismo sm selfishness, egoism; **ego'ista, i, e** ag selfish, egoistic ♦ sm/f egoist

egr. abbr = **egregio**

e'gregio, a, gi, gie [e'grɛdʒo] ag (nelle lettere): **E~ Signore** Dear Sir

eguagli'anza etc [egwaʎ'ʎantsa] = **uguaglianza** etc

E.I. abbr = **Esercito Italiano**

elabo'rare vt (progetto) to work out, elaborate; (dati) to process; **elabora'tore** sm (INFORM): **elaboratore elettronico** computer; **elaborazi'one** sf elaboration; **elaborazione dei dati** data processing

elasticiz'zato, a [elastitʃid'dzato] ag stretch cpd

e'lastico, a, ci, che ag elastic; (fig: andatura) springy; (: decisione, vedute) flexible ♦ sm (di gomma) rubber band; (per il cucito) elastic no pl

ele'fante sm elephant

ele'gante ag elegant

e'leggere [e'lɛddʒere] vt to elect

elemen'tare ag elementary; **le (scuole) ~i** sfpl primary (BRIT) o grade (US) school

ele'mento sm element; (parte componente) element, component, part; **~i** smpl (della scienza etc) elements, rudiments

ele'mosina sf charity, alms pl; **chiedere l'~** to beg

elen'care vt to list

e'lenco, chi sm list; **~ telefonico** telephone directory

e'letto, a pp di **eleggere** ♦ sm/f (nominato) elected member; **eletto'rale** ag electoral, election cpd; **eletto'rato** sm electorate; **elet'tore, 'trice** sm/f voter, elector

elet'trauto sm inv workshop for car electrical repairs; (tecnico) car electrician

elettri'cista, i [elettri'tʃista] sm electrician

elettricità [elettritʃi'ta] sf electricity

e'lettrico, a, ci, che ag electric(al)

elettriz'zare [elettrid'dzare] vt to electrify

e'lettro... prefisso: **elettrocardio'gramma, i** sm electrocardiogram; **elettrodo'mestico, a, ci, che** ag: **apparecchi elettrodomestici** domestic (electrical) appliances; **elet'trone** sm electron; **elet'tronica** sf electronics sg; **elet'tronico, a, ci, che** ag electronic

ele'vare vt to raise; (edificio) to erect; (multa) to impose

elezi'one [elet'tsjone] sf election; **~i** sfpl (POL) election(s)

'elica, che sf propeller

eli'cottero sm helicopter

elimi'nare vt to eliminate; **elimina'toria** sf eliminating round

'elio sm helium

elisoc'corso sm helicopter ambulance

'ella pron she; (forma di cortesia) you; **~ stessa** she herself; you yourself

el'metto sm helmet

e'logio [e'lɔdʒo] sm (discorso, scritto) eulogy; (lode) praise (di solito no pl)

elo'quente ag eloquent

e'ludere vt to evade; **elu'sivo, a** ag evasive

ema'nare vt to send out, give off; (fig: leggi, decreti) to issue ♦ vi: **~ da** to come from

emanci'pare [emantʃi'pare] vt to emancipate; **~rsi** vr (fig) to become liberated o emancipated

embri'one sm embryo

emenda'mento sm amendment

emen'dare vt to amend

emer'genza [emer'dʒentsa] sf emergency; **in caso di ~** in an emergency

e'mergere [e'merdʒere] vi to emerge; (sommergibile) to surface; (fig: distinguersi) to stand out; **e'merso, a** pp di **emergere**

e'messo, a pp di **emettere**

e'mettere vt (suono, luce) to give out, emit; (onde radio) to send out; (assegno, francobollo, ordine) to issue

emi'crania sf migraine

emi'grare vi to emigrate; **emigrazi'one** sf emigration

emi'nente ag eminent, distinguished

emis'fero sm hemisphere; **~ boreale/australe** northern/southern hemisphere

emissi'one sf (vedi emettere) emission; sending out; issue; (RADIO) broadcast

emit'tente ag (banca) issuing; (RADIO) broadcasting, transmitting ♦ sf (RADIO) transmitter

emorra'gia, 'gie [emorra'dʒia] sf haemorrhage

emor'roidi sfpl haemorrhoids pl (BRIT), hemorrhoids pl (US)

emo'tivo, a ag emotional

emozio'nante [emottsjo'nante] ag exciting, thrilling

emozio'nare [emottsjo'nare] vt (appassionare) to thrill, excite; (commuovere) to move; (innervosire) to upset; **~rsi** vr to be excited; to be moved; to be upset

emozi'one [emot'tsjone] sf emotion; (agitazione) excitement

'empio, a ag (sacrilego) impious; (spietato) cruel, pitiless; (malvagio) wicked, evil

emulsi'one sf emulsion

enciclope'dia [entʃiklope'dia] sf encyclopaedia

endove'noso, a ag (MED) intravenous

'ENEL ['enel] sigla m (= Ente Nazionale per l'Energia Elettrica) national electricity company

ener'gia, 'gie [ener'dʒia] sf (FISICA) energy; (fig) energy, strength, vigour; **~ eolica** wind power; **~ solare** solar energy, solar power; e'nergico, a, ci, che ag energetic, vigorous

'enfasi sf emphasis; (peg) bombast, pomposity; **en'fatico, a, ci, che** ag emphatic; pompous

en'nesimo, a ag (MAT, fig) nth; **per l'~a volta** for the umpteenth time

e'norme ag enormous, huge; **enormità** sf inv enormity, huge size; (assurdità) absurdity; **non dire enormità!** don't talk nonsense!

'ente sm (istituzione) body, board, corporation; (FILOSOFIA) being

en'trambi, e pron pl both (of them) ♦ ag pl: **~ i ragazzi** both boys, both of the boys

en'trare vi to go (o come) in; **~ in** (luogo) to enter, go (o come) into; (trovar posto, poter stare) to fit into; (essere ammesso a: club etc) to join, become a member of; **~ in automobile** to get into the car; **far ~ qn** (visitatore etc) to show sb in; **questo non c'entra** (fig) that's got nothing to do with it; **en'trata** sf entrance, entry; **entrate** sfpl

(COMM) receipts, takings; (ECON) income sg

'entro prep (temporale) within

entusias'mare vt to excite, fill with enthusiasm; **~rsi (per qc/qn)** to become enthusiastic (about sth/sb); **entusi'asmo** sm enthusiasm; **entusi'asta, i, e** ag enthusiastic ♦ sm/f enthusiast; **entusi'astico, a, ci, che** ag enthusiastic

enunci'are [enun'tfare] vt (teoria) to set out

epa'tite sf hepatitis

'epico, a, ci, che ag epic

epide'mia sf epidemic

epi'dermide sf skin, epidermis

Epifa'nia sf Epiphany

epiles'sia sf epilepsy

e'pilogo, ghi sm conclusion

epi'sodio sm episode

e'piteto sm epithet

'epoca, che sf (periodo storico) age, era; (tempo) time; (GEO) age

ep'pure cong and yet, nevertheless

equa'tore sm equator

equazi'one [ekwat'tsjone] sf (MAT) equation

e'questre ag equestrian

equi'latero, a ag equilateral

equili'brare vt to balance; **equi'librio** sm balance, equilibrium; **perdere l'~** to lose one's balance

e'quino, a ag horse cpd, equine

equipaggi'are [ekwipad'dʒare] vt (di persone) to man; (di mezzi) to equip; **equi'paggio** sm crew

equipa'rare vt to make equal

equità sf equity, fairness

equitazi'one [ekwitat'tsjone] sf (horse-)riding

equiva'lente ag, sm equivalent; **equiva'lenza** sf equivalence

equivo'care vi to misunderstand; **e'quivoco, a, ci, che** ag equivocal, ambiguous; (sospetto) dubious ♦ sm misunderstanding; **a scanso di equivoci** to avoid any misunderstanding; **giocare sull'equivoco** to equivocate

'equo, a ag fair, just

'era sf era

'erba sf grass; (aromatica, medicinale) herb; **in ~** (fig) budding; **er'baccia, ce** sf weed

e'rede sm/f heir; **eredità** sf (DIR) inheritance; (BIOL) heredity; **lasciare qc in eredità a qn** to leave o bequeath sth to sb; **eredi'tare** vt to inherit; **eredi'tario, a** ag hereditary

ere'mita, i sm hermit

ere'sia sf heresy; **e'retico, a, ci, che** ag heretical ♦ sm/f heretic

e'retto, a pp di **erigere** ♦ ag erect, upright; **erezi'one** sf (FISIOL) erection

er'gastolo sm (DIR: pena) life imprisonment

'erica sf heather

e'rigere [e'ridʒere] vt to erect, raise; (fig: fondare) to found

ERM sigla (= Meccanismo dei tassi di cambio) ERM n

ermel'lino sm ermine

er'metico, a, ci, che ag hermetic

'ernia sf (MED) hernia

e'roe sm hero

ero'gare vt (somme) to distribute; (gas, servizi) to supply

e'roico, a, ci, che ag heroic

ero'ina sf heroine; (droga) heroin

ero'ismo sm heroism

erosi'one sf erosion

e'rotico, a, ci, che ag erotic

er'rare vi (vagare) to wander, roam; (sbagliare) to be mistaken

er'rore sm error, mistake; (morale) error; **per ~** by mistake

'erta sf steep slope; **stare all'~** to be on the alert

erut'tare vt (sog: vulcano) to throw out, belch

eruzi'one [erut'tsjone] sf eruption

esacer'bare [ezatʃer'bare] vt to exacerbate

esage'rare [ezadʒe'rare] vt to exaggerate ♦ vi to exaggerate; (eccedere) to go too far; **esagerazi'one** sf exaggeration

e'sagono sm hexagon

esal'tare vt to exalt; (entusiasmare) to excite, stir; **esal'tato, a** sm/f fanatic

e'same sm examination; (INS) exam, examination; **fare o dare un ~** to sit o take an exam; **~ del sangue** blood test

esami'nare vt to examine

e'sanime ag lifeless

esaspe'rare vt to exasperate; to exacerbate; **~rsi** vr to become annoyed o exasperated; **esasperazi'one** sf exasperation

esatta'mente av exactly; accurately, precisely

esat'tezza [ezat'tettsa] sf exactitude, accuracy, precision

e'satto, a pp di **esigere** ♦ ag (calcolo, ora) correct, right, exact; (preciso) accurate, precise; (puntuale) punctual

esat'tore sm (di imposte etc) collector

esau'dire vt to grant, fulfil

esauri'ente ag exhaustive

esauri'mento sm exhaustion; **~ nervoso** nervous breakdown

esau'rire vt (stancare) to exhaust, wear out; (provviste, miniera) to exhaust; **~rsi** vr to exhaust o.s., wear o.s. out; (provviste) to run out; **esau'rito, a** ag exhausted; (merci) sold out; **registrare il tutto esaurito** (TEATRO) to have a full house; **e'sausto, a** ag exhausted

'esca (pl **'esche**) sf bait

escande'scenza [eskandeʃ'ʃentsa] sf: **dare**

in **~e** to lose one's temper, fly into a rage

'esce etc ['ɛʃe] vb vedi **uscire**

eschi'mese [eski'mese] ag, sm/f Eskimo

escla'mare vi to exclaim, cry out; **esclamazi'one** sf exclamation

es'cludere vt to exclude

esclu'siva sf (DIR, COMM) exclusive o sole rights pl

esclu'sivo, a ag exclusive

es'cluso, a pp di **escludere**

'esco etc vb vedi **uscire**

escogi'tare [eskodʒi'tare] vt to devise, think up

escursi'one sf (gita) excursion, trip; (: a piedi) hike, walk; (METEOR) range

ese'crare vt to loathe, abhor

esecu'tivo, a ag, sm executive

esecu'tore, 'trice sm/f (MUS) performer; (DIR) executor

esecuzi'one [ezekut'tsjone] sf execution, carrying out; (MUS) performance; **~ capitale** execution

esegu'ire vt to carry out, execute; (MUS) to perform, execute

e'sempio sm example; **per ~** for example, for instance; **fare un ~** to give an example; **esem'plare** ag exemplary ♦ sm example; (copia) copy; **esemplifi'care** vt to exemplify

esen'tare vt: **~ qn/qc da** to exempt sb/sth from

e'sente ag: **~ da** (dispensato da) exempt from; (privo di) free from; **esenzi'one** sf exemption

e'sequie sfpl funeral rites; funeral service sg

eser'cente [ezer'tʃɛnte] sm/f trader, dealer; shopkeeper

eserci'tare [ezertʃi'tare] vt (professione) to practise (BRIT), practice (US); (allenare: corpo, mente) to exercise, train; (diritto) to exercise; (influenza, pressione) to exert; **~rsi** vr to practise; **~rsi alla lotta** to practise fighting; **esercitazi'one** sf (scolastica, militare) exercise

e'sercito [e'zɛrtʃito] sm army

eser'cizio [ezer'tʃittsjo] sm practice; exercising; (fisico, di matematica) exercise; (ECON) financial year; (azienda) business, concern; **in ~** (medico etc) practising

esi'bire vt to exhibit, display; (documenti) to produce, present; **~rsi** vr (attore) to perform; (fig) to show off; **esibizi'one** sf exhibition; (di documento) presentation; (spettacolo) show, performance

esi'gente [ezi'dʒɛnte] ag demanding; **esi'genza** sf demand, requirement

e'sigere [e'zidʒere] vt (pretendere) to demand; (richiedere) to demand, require; (imposte) to collect

e'siguo, a ag small, slight

'esile ag (persona) slender, slim; (stelo) thin; (voce) faint

esili'are vt to exile; **e'silio** sm exile

e'simere vt: **~ qn/qc da** to exempt sb/sth from; **~rsi** vr: **~rsi da** to get out of

esis'tenza [ezis'tɛntsa] sf existence

e'sistere vi to exist

esis'tito, a pp di **esistere**

esi'tare vi to hesitate; **esitazi'one** sf hesitation

'esito sm result, outcome

'esodo sm exodus

esone'rare vt to exempt

e'sordio sm début

esor'tare vt: **~ qn a fare** to urge sb to do

e'sotico, a, ci, che ag exotic

es'pandere vt to expand; (confini) to extend; (influenza) to extend, spread; **~rsi** vr to expand; **espansi'one** sf expansion; **espan'sivo, a** ag expansive, communicative

espatri'are vi to leave one's country

espedi'ente sm expedient

es'pellere vt to expel

esperi'enza [espe'rjɛntsa] sf experience

esperi'mento sm experiment

es'perto, a ag, sm expert

espi'are vt to atone for

espi'rare vt, vi to breathe out

espli'care vt (attività) to carry out, perform

es'plicito, a [es'plitʃito] ag explicit

es'plodere vi (anche fig) to explode ♦ vt to fire

esplo'rare vt to explore; **esplora'tore** sm explorer; **giovane esploratore** (boy) scout

esplosi'one sf explosion; **esplo'sivo, a** ag, sm explosive; **es'ploso, a** pp di **esplodere**

espo'nente sm/f (rappresentante) representative

es'porre vt (merci) to display; (quadro) to exhibit, show; (fatti, idee) to explain, set out; (porre in pericolo, FOT) to expose

espor'tare vt to export; **esportazi'one** sf exportation; export

esposizi'one [espozit'tsjone] sf displaying; exhibiting; setting out; (anche FOT) exposure; (mostra) exhibition; (narrazione) explanation, exposition

es'posto, a pp di **esporre** ♦ ag: **~ a nord** facing north ♦ sm (AMM) statement, account; (: petizione) petition

espressi'one sf expression

espres'sivo, a ag expressive

es'presso, a pp di **esprimere** ♦ ag express ♦ sm (lettera) express letter; (anche: treno ~) express train; (anche: caffè ~) espresso

es'primere vt to express

espulsi'one sf expulsion; **es'pulso, a** pp di **espellere**

'essa (pl **'esse**) pron f vedi **esso**

es'senza [es'sɛntsa] *sf* essence; **essenzi'ale** *ag* essential; **l'essenziale** the main *o* most important thing

---
PAROLA CHIAVE

'essere *sm* being; **~ umano** human being
♦ *vb copulativo* **1** (*con attributo, sostantivo*) to be; **sei giovane/simpatico** you are *o* you're young/nice; **è medico** he is *o* he's a doctor
2 (+*di*: *appartenere*) to be; **di chi è la penna?** whose pen is it?; **è di Carla** it is *o* it's Carla's, it belongs to Carla
3 (+*di*: *provenire*) to be; **è di Venezia** he is *o* he's from Venice
4 (*data, ora*): **è il 15 agosto/lunedì** it is *o* it's the 15th of August/Monday; **che ora è?, che ore sono?** what time is it?; **è l'una** it is *o* it's one o'clock; **sono le due** it is *o* it's two o'clock
5 (*costare*): **quant'è?** how much is it?; **sono 20.000 lire** it's 20,000 lire
♦ *vb aus* **1** (*attivo*): **~ arrivato/venuto** to have arrived/come; **è gia partita** she has already left
2 (*passivo*) to be; **~ fatto da** to be made by; **è stata uccisa** she has been killed
3 (*riflessivo*): **si sono lavati** they washed, they got washed
4 (+*da* +*infinito*): **è da farsi subito** it must be *o* it has to be done immediately
♦ *vi* **1** (*esistere, trovarsi*) to be; **sono a casa** I'm at home; **~ in piedi/seduto** to be standing/sitting
2: **esserci**: **c'è** there is; **ci sono** there are; **che c'è?** what's the matter?, what is it?; **ci sono!** (*fig: ho capito*) I get it!; *vedi anche* **ci**
♦ *vb impers*: **è tardi/Pasqua** it's late/Easter; **è possibile che venga** he may come; **è così** that's the way it is

'esso, a *pron* it; (*riferito a persona: soggetto*) he/she; (: *complemento*) him/her; **~i, e** *pron pl* they; (*complemento*) them

est *sm* east

'estasi *sf* ecstasy

es'tate *sf* summer

es'tendere *vt* to extend; **~rsi** *vr* (*diffondersi*) to spread; (*territorio, confini*) to extend; **estensi'one** *sf* extension; (*di superficie*) expanse; (*di voce*) range

esteri'ore *ag* outward, external

ester'nare *vt* to express

es'terno, a *ag* (*porta, muro*) outer, outside; (*scala*) outside; (*alunno, impressione*) external ♦ *sm* outside, exterior ♦ *sm/f* (*allievo*) day pupil; **per uso ~** for external use only

'estero, a *ag* foreign ♦ *sm*: **all'~** abroad

es'teso, a *pp di* **estendere** ♦ *ag* extensive, large; **scrivere per ~** to write in full

es'tetico, a, ci, che *ag* aesthetic ♦ *sf* (*disciplina*) aesthetics *sg*; (*bellezza*) attractiveness; **este'tista, i, e** *sm/f* beautician

'estimo *sm* valuation; (*disciplina*) surveying

es'tinguere *vt* to extinguish, put out; (*debito*) to pay off; **~rsi** *vr* to go out; (*specie*) to become extinct; **es'tinto, a** *pp di* **estinguere**; **estin'tore** *sm* (*fire*) extinguisher; **estinzi'one** *sf* putting out; (*di specie*) extinction

estir'pare *vt* (*pianta*) to uproot, pull up; (*fig: vizio*) to eradicate

es'tivo, a *ag* summer *cpd*

es'torcere [es'tɔrtʃere] *vt*: **~ qc (a qn)** to extort sth (from sb); **es'torto, a** *pp di* **estorcere**

estradizi'one [estradit'tsjone] *sf* extradition

es'traneo, a *ag* foreign ♦ *sm/f* stranger; **rimanere ~ a qc** to take no part in sth

es'trarre *vt* to extract; (*minerali*) to mine; (*sorteggiare*) to draw; **es'tratto, a** *pp di* **estrarre** ♦ *sm* extract; (*di documento*) abstract; **estratto conto** statement of account; **estratto di carne** (*CUC*) meat extract; **estratto di nascita** birth certificate; **estrazi'one** *sf* extraction; mining; drawing *no pl*; draw

estremità *sf inv* extremity, end ♦ *sfpl* (*ANAT*) extremities

es'tremo, a *ag* extreme; (*ultimo*: *ora, tentativo*) final, last ♦ *sm* extreme; (*di pazienza, forze*) limit, end; **~i** *smpl* (*AMM: dati essenziali*) details, particulars; **l'~ Oriente** the Far East

'estro *sm* (*capriccio*) whim, fancy; (*ispirazione creativa*) inspiration; **es'troso, a** *ag* whimsical, capricious; inspired

estro'verso, a *ag, sm* extrovert

'esule *sm/f* exile

età *sf inv* age; **all'~ di 8 anni** at the age of 8, at 8 years of age; **ha la mia ~** he (*o* she) is the same age as me *o* as I am; **raggiungere la maggiore ~** to come of age; **essere in ~ minore** to be under age

'etere *sm* ether; **e'tereo, a** *ag* ethereal

eternità *sf* eternity

e'terno, a *ag* eternal

etero'geneo, a [etero'dʒɛneo] *ag* heterogeneous

'etica *sf* ethics *sg*; *vedi anche* **etico**

eti'chetta [eti'ketta] *sf* label; (*cerimoniale*): **l'~** etiquette

'etico, a, ci, che *ag* ethical

etimolo'gia, 'gie [etimolo'dʒia] *sf* etymology

Eti'opia *sf*: **l'~** Ethiopia

'Etna *sm*: **l'~** Etna

'etnico, a, ci, che *ag* ethnic

e'trusco, a, schi, sche *ag, sm/f* Etruscan

'ettaro *sm* hectare (= 10,000 m^2)

'etto sm abbr = ettogrammo

etto'grammo sm hectogram(me) (= 100 grams)

Eucaris'tia sf: l'~ the Eucharist

'euro sm inv (divisa) euro

eurocity [euro'siti] sm international express train

Euro'landia sf Euroland

Eu'ropa sf: l'~ Europe; euro'peo, a ag, sm/f European

evacu'are vt to evacuate

e'vadere vi (fuggire): ~ da to escape from ♦ vt (sbrigare) to deal with, dispatch; (tasse) to evade

evan'gelico, a, ci, che [evan'dʒɛliko] ag evangelical

evapo'rare vi to evaporate; evaporazi'one sf evaporation

evasi'one sf (vedi evadere) escape; dispatch; ~ fiscale tax evasion

eva'sivo, a ag evasive

e'vaso, a pp di evadere ♦ sm escapee

eveni'enza [eve'njentsa] sf: pronto(a) per ogni ~ ready for any eventuality

e'vento sm event

eventu'ale ag possible

eventual'mente av if necessary

evi'dente ag evident, obvious; evi'denza sf obviousness; mettere in evidenza to point out, highlight; evidenzi'are vt to emphasize; (con evidenziatore) to highlight; evidenzia'tore sm highlighter

evi'tare vt to avoid; ~ di fare to avoid doing; ~ qc a qn to spare sb sth

'evo sm age, epoch

evo'care vt to evoke

evo'luto, a pp di evolvere ♦ ag (civiltà) (highly) developed, advanced; (persona) independent

evoluzi'one [evolut'tsjone] sf evolution

e'volversi vr to evolve

ev'viva escl hurrah!; ~ il re! long live the king!, hurrah for the king!

ex prefisso ex, former

'extra ag inv first-rate; top-quality ♦ sm inv extra; extracomuni'tario, a ag from outside the EC ♦ sm/f non-EC citizen; extraconiu'gale ag extramarital

F, f

fa vb vedi fare ♦ sm inv (MUS) F; (: solfeggiando la scala) fa ♦ av: 10 anni ~ 10 years ago

fabbi'sogno [fabbi'zoɲɲo] sm needs pl, requirements pl

'fabbrica sf factory; fabbri'cante sm manufacturer, maker; fabbri'care vt to build; (produrre) to manufacture, make; (fig)

to fabricate, invent

'fabbro sm (black)smith

fac'cenda [fat'tʃɛnda] sf matter, affair; (cosa da fare) task, chore

fac'chino [fak'kino] sm porter

'faccia, ce ['fattʃa] sf face; (di moneta, medaglia) side; ~ a ~ face to face

facci'ata [fat'tʃata] sf façade; (di pagina) side

'faccio ['fattʃo] vb vedi fare

'facile ['fatʃile] ag easy; (disposto): ~ a inclined to, prone to; (probabile): è ~ che piova it's likely to rain; facilità sf easiness; (disposizione, dono) aptitude; facili'tare vt to make easier

facoltà sf inv faculty; (autorità) power

facolta'tivo, a ag optional; (fermata d'autobus) request cpd

fac'simile sm facsimile

'faggio ['faddʒo] sm beech

fagi'ano [fa'dʒano] sm pheasant

fagio'lino [fadʒo'lino] sm French (BRIT) o string bean

fagi'olo [fa'dʒɔlo] sm bean

fa'gotto sm bundle; (MUS) bassoon; far ~ (fig) to pack up and go

'fai vb vedi fare

'falce ['faltʃe] sf scythe; falci'are vt to cut; (fig) to mow down

'falco, chi sm hawk

fal'cone sm falcon

'falda sf layer, stratum; (di cappello) brim; (di cappotto) tails pl; (di monte) lower slope; (di tetto) pitch

fale'gname [falen'ɲame] sm joiner

fal'lace [fal'latʃe] ag misleading

falli'mento sm failure; bankruptcy

fal'lire vi (non riuscire): ~ (in) to fail (in); (DIR) to go bankrupt ♦ vt (colpo, bersaglio) to miss; fal'lito, a ag unsuccessful; bankrupt ♦ sm/f bankrupt

'fallo sm error, mistake; (imperfezione) defect, flaw; (SPORT) foul; fault; senza ~ without fail

falò sm inv bonfire

fal'sare vt to distort, misrepresent; fal'sario sm forger; counterfeiter; falsifi'care vt to forge; (monete) to forge, counterfeit

'falso, a ag false; (errato) wrong; (falsificato) forged; fake; (: oro, gioielli) imitation cpd ♦ sm forgery; giurare il ~ to commit perjury

'fama sf fame; (reputazione) reputation, name

'fame sf hunger; aver ~ to be hungry; fa'melico, a, ci, che ag ravenous

fa'miglia [fa'miʎʎa] sf family

famili'are ag (della famiglia) family cpd; (ben noto) familiar; (rapporti, atmosfera) friendly; (LING) informal, colloquial ♦ sm/f relative, relation; familiarità sf familiarity; friendliness; informality

fa'moso, a ag famous, well-known

fa'nale *sm* (*AUT*) light, lamp (*BRIT*); (*luce stradale, NAUT*) light; (*di faro*) beacon

fa'natico, a, ci, che *ag* fanatical; (*del teatro, calcio etc*): ~ **di** o **per** mad o crazy about ♦ *sm/f* fanatic; (*tifoso*) fan

fanci'ullo, a [fan'tʃullo] *sm/f* child

fan'donia *sf* tall story; ~**e** *sfpl* (*assurdità*) nonsense *sg*

fan'fara *sf* (*musica*) fanfare

'fango, ghi *sm* mud; **fan'goso, a** *ag* muddy

'fanno *vb vedi* **fare**

fannul'lone, a *sm/f* idler, loafer

fantasci'enza [fantaʃʃɛntsa] *sf* science fiction

fanta'sia *sf* fantasy, imagination; (*capriccio*) whim, caprice ♦ *ag inv*: **vestito** ~ patterned dress

fan'tasma, i *sm* ghost, phantom

fan'tastico, a, ci, che *ag* fantastic; (*potenza, ingegno*) imaginative

'fante *sm* infantryman; (*CARTE*) jack, knave (*BRIT*); **fante'ria** *sf* infantry

fan'toccio [fan'tɔttʃo] *sm* puppet

fara'butto *sm* crook

fard *sm inv* blusher

far'dello *sm* bundle; (*fig*) burden

PAROLA CHIAVE

'fare *sm* **1** (*modo di fare*): **con** ~ **distratto** absent-mindedly; **ha un** ~ **simpatico** he has a pleasant manner

2: **sul far del giorno/della notte** at daybreak/nightfall

♦ *vt* **1** (*fabbricare, creare*) to make; (: *casa*) to build; (: *assegno*) to make out; ~ **un pasto/una promessa/un film** to make a meal/a promise/a film; ~ **rumore** to make a noise

2 (*effettuare: lavoro, attività, studi*) to do; (: *sport*) to play; **cosa fa?** (*adesso*) what are you doing?; (*di professione*) what do you do?; ~ **psicologia/italiano** (*INS*) to do psychology/Italian; ~ **un viaggio** to go on a trip o journey; ~ **una passeggiata** to go for a walk; ~ **la spesa** to do the shopping

3 (*funzione*) to be; (*TEATRO*) to play, be; ~ **il medico** to be a doctor; ~ **il malato** (*fingere*) to act the invalid

4 (*suscitare: sentimenti*): ~ **paura a qn** to frighten sb; (**non**) **fa niente** (*non importa*) it doesn't matter

5 (*ammontare*): **3 più 3 fa 6** 3 and 3 are o make 6; **fanno 6.000 lire** that's 6,000 lire; **Roma fa 2.000.000 di abitanti** Rome has 2,000,000 inhabitants; **che ora fai?** what time do you make it?

6 (+ *infinito*): **far** ~ **qc a qn** (*obbligare*) to make sb do sth; (*permettere*) to let sb do sth; **fammi vedere** let me see; **far partire il motore**

to start (up) the engine; **far riparare la macchina/costruire una casa** to get o have the car repaired/a house built

7: ~**rsi**: ~**rsi una gonna** to make o.s. a skirt; ~**rsi un nome** to make a name for o.s.; ~**rsi la permanente** to get a perm; ~**rsi tagliare i capelli** to get one's hair cut; ~**rsi operare** to have an operation

8 (*fraseologia*): **farcela** to succeed, manage; **non ce la faccio più** I can't go on; **ce la faremo** we'll make it; **me l'hanno fatta!** (*imbrogliare*) I've been done!; **lo facevo più giovane** I thought he was younger; **fare sì/no con la testa** to nod/shake one's head

♦ *vi* **1** (*agire*) to act, do; **fate come volete** do as you like; ~ **presto** to be quick; ~ **da** to act as; **non c'è niente da** ~ it's no use; **saperci** ~ **con qn/qc** to know how to deal with sb/sth; **faccia pure!** go ahead!

2 (*dire*) to say; "**davvero?**" **fece** "really?" he said

3: ~ **per** (*essere adatto*) to be suitable for; ~ **per** ~ **qc** to be about to do sth; **fece per andarsene** he made as if to leave

4: ~**rsi**: **si fa così** you do it like this, this is the way it's done; **non si fa così!** (*rimprovero*) that's no way to behave!; **la festa non si fa** the party is off

5: ~ **a gara con qn** to compete o vie with sb; ~ **a pugni** to come to blows; ~ **in tempo a** ~ to be in time to do

♦ *vb impers*: **fa bel tempo** the weather is fine; **fa caldo/freddo** it's hot/cold; **fa notte** it's getting dark

♦ *vr*: ~**rsi 1** (*diventare*) to become; ~**rsi prete** to become a priest; ~**rsi grande/vecchio** to grow tall/old

2 (*spostarsi*): ~**rsi avanti/indietro** to move forward/back

3 (*fam: drogarsi*) to be a junkie

---

far'falla *sf* butterfly

fa'rina *sf* flour

farma'cia, 'cie [farma'tʃia] *sf* pharmacy; (*negozio*) chemist's (shop) (*BRIT*), pharmacy; **farma'cista, i, e** *sm/f* chemist (*BRIT*), pharmacist

'farmaco, ci o **chi** *sm* drug, medicine

'faro *sm* (*NAUT*) lighthouse; (*AER*) beacon; (*AUT*) headlight

'farsa *sf* farce

'fascia, sce ['faʃʃa] *sf* band, strip; (*MED*) bandage; (*di sindaco, ufficiale*) sash; (*parte di territorio*) strip, belt; (*di contribuenti etc*) group, band; **essere in** ~**sce** (*anche fig*) to be in one's infancy; ~ **oraria** time band

fasci'are [faʃʃare] *vt* to bind; (*MED*) to bandage

fa'scicolo [faʃʃikolo] *sm* (*di documenti*) file,

dossier; (*di rivista*) issue, number; (*opuscolo*) booklet, pamphlet

'fascino ['faʃʃino] *sm* charm, fascination

'fascio ['faʃʃo] *sm* bundle, sheaf; (*di fiori*) bunch; (*di luce*) beam; (*POL*): **il F~** the Fascist Party

fa'scismo [faʃ'ʃizmo] *sm* fascism

'fase *sf* phase; (*TECN*) stroke; **fuori ~** (*motore*) rough

fas'tidio *sm* bother, trouble; **dare ~ a qn** to bother o annoy sb; **sento ~ allo stomaco** my stomach's upset; **avere ~i con la polizia** to have trouble o bother with the police; **fastidi'oso, a** *ag* annoying, tiresome

'fasto *sm* pomp, splendour

'fata *sf* fairy

fa'tale *ag* fatal; (*inevitabile*) inevitable; (*fig*) irresistible; **fatalità** *sf inv* inevitability; (*avversità*) misfortune; (*fato*) fate, destiny

fa'tica, che *sf* hard work, toil; (*sforzo*) effort; (*di metalli*) fatigue; **a ~** with difficulty; **fare ~ a fare qc** to have a job doing sth; **fati'care** *vi* to toil; **faticare a fare qc** to have difficulty doing sth; **fati'coso, a** *ag* tiring, exhausting; (*lavoro*) laborious

'fato *sm* fate, destiny

'fatto, a *pp di* **fare** ♦ *ag*: **un uomo ~** a grown man; **~ a mano/in casa** hand-/home-made ♦ *sm* fact; (*azione*) deed; (*avvenimento*) event, occurrence; (*di romanzo, film*) action, story; **cogliere qn sul ~** to catch sb red-handed; **il ~ sta** o **è che** the fact remains o is that; **in ~ di** as for, as far as ... is concerned

fat'tore *sm* (*AGR*) farm manager; (*MAT*, *elemento costitutivo*) factor

fatto'ria *sf* farm; farmhouse

fatto'rino *sm* errand-boy; (*di ufficio*) office-boy; (*d'albergo*) porter

fat'tura *sf* (*COMM*) invoice; (*di abito*) tailoring; (*malia*) spell

fattu'rare *vt* (*COMM*) to invoice

fattu'rato *sm* (*COMM*) turnover

'fatuo, a *ag* vain, fatuous

'fauna *sf* fauna

fau'tore, trice *sm/f* advocate, supporter

fa'villa *sf* spark

'favola *sf* (*fiaba*) fairy tale; (*d'intento morale*) fable; (*fandonia*) yarn; **favo'loso, a** *ag* fabulous; (*incredibile*) incredible

fa'vore *sm* favour; **per ~** please; **fare un ~ a qn** to do sb a favour; **favo'revole** *ag* favourable

favo'rire *vt* to favour; (*il commercio, l'industria, le arti*) to promote, encourage; **vuole ~?** won't you help yourself?; **favorisca in salotto** please come into the sitting room; **favo'rito, a** *ag, sm/f* favourite

fazzo'letto [fattso'letto] *sm* handkerchief; (*per la testa*) (head)scarf; **~ di carta** tissue

feb'braio *sm* February

'febbre *sf* fever; **aver la ~** to have a high temperature; **~ da fieno** hay fever; **feb'brile** *ag* (*anche fig*) feverish

'feccia, ce ['fettʃa] *sf* dregs *pl*

'fecola *sf* potato flour

fecondazi'one [fekondat'tsjone] *sf* fertilization; **~ artificiale** artificial insemination

fe'condo, a *ag* fertile

'fede *sf* (*credenza*) belief, faith; (*REL*) faith; (*fiducia*) faith, trust; (*fedeltà*) loyalty; (*anello*) wedding ring; (*attestato*) certificate; **aver ~ in qn** to have faith in sb; **in buona/cattiva ~** in good/bad faith; "**in ~**" (*DIR*) "in witness whereof"; **fe'dele** *ag*: **fedele (a)** faithful (to) ♦ *sm/f* follower; **i fedeli** (*REL*) the faithful; **fedeltà** *sf* faithfulness; (*coniugale*) fidelity; **alta fedeltà** (*RADIO*) high fidelity

'federa *sf* pillowslip, pillowcase

fede'rale *ag* federal

'fegato *sm* liver; (*fig*) guts *pl*, nerve

'felce ['feltʃe] *sf* fern

fe'lice [fe'litʃe] *ag* happy; (*fortunato*) lucky; **felicità** *sf* happiness

felici'tarsi [felitʃi'tarsi] *vr* (*congratularsi*): **~ con qn per qc** to congratulate sb on sth

fe'lino, a *ag, sm* feline

'felpa *sf* sweatshirt

'feltro *sm* felt

'femmina *sf* (*ZOOL, TECN*) female; (*figlia*) girl, daughter; (*spesso peg*) woman; **femmi'nile** *ag* feminine; (*sesso*) female; (*lavoro, giornale, moda*) woman's ♦ *sm* (*LING*) feminine; **femmi'nismo** *sm* feminism

'fendere *vt* to cut through; **fendi'nebbia** *sm inv* (*AUT*) fog lamp

fe'nomeno *sm* phenomenon

'feretro *sm* coffin

feri'ale *ag*: **giorno ~** weekday

'ferie *sfpl* holidays (*BRIT*), vacation *sg* (*US*); **andare in ~** to go on holiday o vacation

fe'rire *vt* to injure; (*deliberatamente: MIL etc*) to wound; (*colpire*) to hurt; **fe'rita** *sf* injury, wound; **fe'rito, a** *sm/f* wounded o injured man/woman

'ferma *sf* (*MIL*) (period of) service; (*CACCIA*): **cane da ~** pointer

fer'maglio [fer'maʎʎo] *sm* clasp; (*per documenti*) clip

fer'mare *vt* to stop, halt; (*POLIZIA*) to detain, hold ♦ *vi* to stop; **~rsi** *vr* to stop, halt; **~rsi a fare qc** to stop to do sth

fer'mata *sf* stop; **~ dell'autobus** bus stop

fer'mento *sm* (*anche fig*) ferment; (*lievito*) yeast

fer'mezza [fer'mettsa] *sf* (*fig*) firmness, steadfastness

'fermo, a *ag* still, motionless; (*veicolo*) stationary; (*orologio*) not working; (*saldo*:

anche fig) firm; (voce, mano) steady ♦ escl stop!; keep still! ♦ sm (chiusura) catch, lock; (DIR): ~ **di polizia** police detention

'fermo 'posta av, sm inv poste restante (BRIT), general delivery (US)

fe'roce [fe'rotʃe] ag (animale) fierce, ferocious; (persona) cruel, fierce; (fame, dolore) raging; **le bestie ~i** wild animals

ferra'gosto sm (festa) feast of the Assumption; (periodo) August holidays pl

ferra'menta sfpl: **negozio di ~** ironmonger's (BRIT), hardware shop o store (US)

fer'rato, a ag (FERR): **strada ~a** railway (BRIT) o railroad (US) line; (fig): **essere ~ in** to be well up in

'ferro sm iron; **una bistecca ai ~i** a grilled steak; ~ **battuto** wrought iron; ~ **da calza** knitting needle; ~ **di cavallo** horseshoe; ~ **da stiro** iron

ferro'via sf railway (BRIT), railroad (US); ferrovi'ario, a ag railway cpd (BRIT), railroad cpd (US); ferrovi'ere sm railwayman (BRIT), railroad man (US)

'fertile ag fertile; fertiliz'zante sm fertilizer

'fervido, a ag fervent

fer'vore sm fervour, ardour

'fesso, a pp di fendere ♦ ag (fam: sciocco) crazy, cracked

fes'sura sf crack, split; (per gettone, moneta) slot

'festa sf (religiosa) feast; (pubblica) holiday; (compleanno) birthday; (onomastico) name day; (ricevimento) celebration, party; **far ~** to have a holiday; to live it up; **far ~ a qn** to give sb a warm welcome

festeggi'are [fested'dʒare] vt to celebrate; (persona) to have a celebration for

fes'tino sm party; (con balli) ball

fes'tivo, a ag (atmosfera) festive; **giorno ~** holiday

fes'toso, a ag merry, joyful

fe'ticcio [fe'tittʃo] sm fetish

'feto sm foetus (BRIT), fetus (US)

'fetta sf slice

fettuc'cine [fettut'tʃine] sfpl (CUC) ribbon-shaped pasta

FF.SS. abbr = Ferrovie dello Stato

fi'aba sf fairy tale

fi'acca sf weariness; (svogliatezza) listlessness

fiac'care vt to weaken

fi'acco, a, chi, che ag (stanco) tired, weary; (svogliato) listless; (debole) weak; (mercato) slack

fi'accola sf torch

fi'ala sf phial

fi'amma sf flame

fiam'mante ag (colore) flaming; **nuovo ~** brand new

fiam'mifero sm match

fiam'mingo, a, ghi, ghe ag Flemish ♦ sm/f Fleming ♦ sm (LING) Flemish; **i F~ghi** the Flemish

fiancheggi'are [fjanked'dʒare] vt to border; (fig) to support, back (up); (MIL) to flank

fi'anco, chi sm side; (MIL) flank; **di ~** sideways, from the side; **a ~ a ~** side by side

fi'asco, schi sm flask; (fig) fiasco; **fare ~** to fail

fi'ato sm breath; (resistenza) stamina; **avere il ~ grosso** to be out of breath; **prendere ~** to catch one's breath; **~i** smpl (MUS) wind instruments; **strumento a ~** wind instrument

'fibbia sf buckle

'fibra sf fibre; (fig) constitution

fic'care vt to push, thrust, drive; **~rsi** vr (andare a finire) to get to

'fico, chi sm (pianta) fig tree; (frutto) fig; ~ **d'India** prickly pear; ~ **secco** dried fig

fidanza'mento [fidantsa'mento] sm engagement

fidan'zarsi [fidan'tsarsi] vr to get engaged; fidan'zato, a sm/f fiancé/fiancée

fi'darsi vr: ~ **di** to trust; fi'dato, a ag reliable, trustworthy

'fido, a ag faithful, loyal ♦ sm (COMM) credit

fi'ducia [fi'dutʃa] sf confidence, trust; **incarico di ~** position of trust, responsible position; **persona di ~** reliable person

fi'ele sm (fig) bitterness

fie'nile sm barn; hayloft

fi'eno sm hay

fi'era sf fair

fie'rezza [fje'rettsa] sf pride

fi'ero, a ag proud; (audace) bold

'fifa (fam) sf: **aver ~** to have the jitters

'figlia ['fiʎʎa] sf daughter

figli'astro, a [fiʎ'ʎastro] sm/f stepson/daughter

'figlio ['fiʎʎo] sm son; (senza distinzione di sesso) child; ~ **di papà** spoilt, wealthy young man; ~ **unico** only child; figli'occio, a, ci, ce sm/f godchild, godson/daughter

fi'gura sf figure; (forma, aspetto esterno) form, shape; (illustrazione) picture, illustration; **far ~** to look smart; **fare una brutta ~** to make a bad impression

figu'rare vi to appear ♦ vt: **~rsi qc** to imagine sth; **~rsi** vr: **figurati!** imagine that!; **ti do noia? — ma figurati!** am I disturbing you? — not at all!

figura'tivo, a ag figurative

figu'rina sf figurine; (cartoncino) picture card

'fila sf row, line; (coda) queue; (serie) series, string; **di ~** in succession; **fare la ~** to queue; **in ~ indiana** in single file

filantro'pia sf philanthropy

fi'lare vt to spin ♦ vi (baco, ragno) to spin; (formaggio fuso) to go stringy; (discorso) to hang together; (*fam: amoreggiare*) to go steady; (*muoversi a forte velocità*) to go at full speed; **~ diritto** (*fig*) to toe the line; **~ via** to dash off

filas'trocca, che *sf* nursery rhyme

filate'lia *sf* philately, stamp collecting

fi'lato, a *ag* spun ♦ *sm* yarn; **3 giorni ~i** 3 days running *o* on end

fi'letto *sm* (*di vite*) thread; (*di carne*) fillet

fili'ale *ag* filial ♦ *sf* (*di impresa*) branch

fili'grana *sf* (*in oreficeria*) filigree; (*su carta*) watermark

film *sm inv* film; **fil'mare** *vt* to film

'**filo** *sm* (*anche fig*) thread; (*filato*) yarn; (*metallico*) wire; (*di lama, rasoio*) edge; **per ~ e per segno** in detail; **~ d'erba** blade of grass; **~ interdentale** dental floss; **~ di perle** string of pearls; **~ spinato** barbed wire; **con un ~ di voce** in a whisper

'**filobus** *sm inv* trolley bus

filon'cino [filon'tʃino] *sm* ≈ French stick

fi'lone *sm* (*di minerali*) seam, vein; (*pane*) ≈ Vienna loaf; (*fig*) trend

filoso'fia *sf* philosophy; **fi'losofo, a** *sm/f* philosopher

fil'trare *vt, vi* to filter

'**filtro** *sm* filter; **~ dell'olio** (*AUT*) oil filter

fin *av, prep* = **fino**

fi'nale *ag* final ♦ *sm* (*di opera*) end, ending; (: *MUS*) finale ♦ *sf* (*SPORT*) final; **finalità** *sf* (*scopo*) aim, purpose; **final'mente** *av* finally, at last

fi'nanza [fi'nantsa] *sf* finance; **~e** *sfpl* (*di individuo, Stato*) finances; **finanzi'ario, a** *ag* financial; **finanzi'ere** *sm* financier; (*doganale*) customs officer; (*della tributaria*) inland revenue official

finché [fin'ke] *cong* (*per tutto il tempo che*) as long as; (*fino al momento in cui*) until; **aspetta ~ io (non) sia ritornato** wait until I get back

'**fine** *ag* (*lamina, carta*) thin; (*capelli, polvere*) fine; (*vista, udito*) keen, sharp; (*persona: raffinata*) refined, distinguished; (*osservazione*) subtle ♦ *sf* end ♦ *sm* aim, purpose; (*esito*) result, outcome; **secondo ~** ulterior motive; **in o alla ~** in the end, finally; **~ settimana** *sm o f inv* weekend

fi'nestra *sf* window; **fines'trino** *sm* (*di treno, auto*) window

'**fingere** ['findʒere] *vt* to feign; (*supporre*) to imagine, suppose; **~rsi** *vr*: **~rsi ubriaco/pazzo** to pretend to be drunk/mad; **~ di fare** to pretend to do

fini'mondo *sm* pandemonium

fi'nire *vt* to finish ♦ *vi* to finish, end; **~ di fare** (*compiere*) to finish doing; (*smettere*) to stop doing; **~ in galera** to end up *o* finish up in prison; **fini'tura** *sf* finish

finlan'dese *ag, sm* (*LING*) Finnish ♦ *sm/f* Finn

Fin'landia *sf*: **la ~** Finland

'**fino, a** *ag* (*capelli, seta*) fine; (*oro*) pure; (*fig: acuto*) shrewd ♦ *av* (*spesso troncato in* **fin**: *pure, anche*) even ♦ *prep* (*spesso troncato in* **fin**: *tempo*): **fin quando?** till when?; (: *luogo*): **fin qui** as far as here; **~ a** (*tempo*) until, till; (*luogo*) as far as, (up) to; **fin da domani** from tomorrow onwards; **fin da ieri** since yesterday; **fin dalla nascita** from *o* since birth

fi'nocchio [fi'nɔkkjo] *sm* fennel; (*fam: peg: omosessuale*) queer

fi'nora *av* up till now

'**finta** *sf* pretence, sham; (*SPORT*) feint; **far ~ (di fare)** to pretend (to do)

'**finto, a** *pp di* **fingere** ♦ *ag* false; artificial

finzi'one [fin'tsjone] *sf* pretence, sham

fi'occo, chi *sm* (*di nastro*) bow; (*di stoffa, lana*) flock; (*di neve*) flake; (*NAUT*) jib; **coi ~chi** (*fig*) first-rate; **~chi di granoturco** cornflakes

fi'ocina ['fjɔtʃina] *sf* harpoon

fi'oco, a, chi, che *ag* faint, dim

fi'onda *sf* catapult

fio'raio, a *sm/f* florist

fi'ore *sm* flower; **~i** *smpl* (*CARTE*) clubs; **a fior d'acqua** on the surface of the water; **avere i nervi a fior di pelle** to be on edge

fioren'tino, a *ag* Florentine

fio'retto *sm* (*SCHERMA*) foil

fio'rire *vi* (*rosa*) to flower; (*albero*) to blossom; (*fig*) to flourish

Fi'renze [fi'rentse] *sf* Florence

'**firma** *sf* signature

fir'mare *vt* to sign; **un abito firmato** a designer suit

fisar'monica, che *sf* accordion

fis'cale *ag* fiscal, tax *cpd*; **medico ~** doctor employed by Social Security to verify cases of sick leave

fischi'are [fis'kjare] *vi* to whistle ♦ *vt* to whistle; (*attore*) to boo, hiss

'**fischio** ['fiskjo] *sm* whistle

'**fisco** *sm* tax authorities *pl*, ≈ Inland Revenue (*BRIT*), ≈ Internal Revenue Service (*US*)

'**fisica** *sf* physics *sg*

'**fisico, a, ci, che** *ag* physical ♦ *sm/f* physicist ♦ *sm* physique

fisiolo'gia [fizjolo'dʒia] *sf* physiology

fisiono'mia *sf* face, physiognomy

fisiotera'pia *sf* physiotherapy

fis'sare *vt* to fix, fasten; (*guardare intensamente*) to stare at; (*data, condizioni*) to fix, establish, set; (*prenotare*) to book; **~rsi su** (*sog: sguardo, attenzione*) to focus on; (*fig: idea*) to become obsessed with; **fissazi'one** *sf* (*PSIC*) fixation

'**fisso, a** *ag* fixed; (*stipendio, impiego*) regular ♦ *av*: **guardare ~ qc/qn** to stare at sth/sb

'fitta sf sharp pain; vedi anche **fitto**

fit'tizio, a ag fictitious, imaginary

'fitto, a ag thick, dense; (pioggia) heavy ♦ sm depths pl, middle; (affitto, pigione) rent

fi'ume sm river

fiu'tare vt to smell, sniff; (sog: animale) to scent; (fig: inganno) to get wind of, smell; ~ **tabacco/cocaina** to take snuff/cocaine; **fi'uto** sm (sense of) smell; (fig) nose

fla'gello [fla'dʒɛllo] sm scourge

fla'grante ag: **cogliere qn in** ~ to catch sb red-handed

fla'nella sf flannel

flash [flaʃ] sm inv (FOT) flash; (giornalistico) newsflash

'flauto sm flute

'flebile ag faint, feeble

'flemma sf (calma) coolness, phlegm

fles'sibile ag pliable; (fig: che si adatta) flexible

'flesso, a pp di **flettere**

flessu'oso, a ag supple, lithe

'flettere vt to bend

'flipper sm inv pinball machine

F.lli abbr (= fratelli) Bros.

'flora sf flora

'florido, a ag flourishing; (fig) glowing with health

'floscio, a, sci, sce ['flɔʃʃo] ag (cappello) floppy, soft; (muscoli) flabby

'flotta sf fleet

'fluido, a ag, sm fluid

flu'ire vi to flow

flu'oro sm fluorine

fluo'ruro sm fluoride

'flusso sm flow; (FISICA, MED) flux; ~ **e riflusso** ebb and flow

fluttu'are vi (mare) to rise and fall; (ECON) to fluctuate

fluvi'ale ag river cpd, fluvial

'foca, che sf (ZOOL) seal

fo'caccia, ce [fo'kattʃa] sf kind of pizza; (dolce) bun

'foce ['fotʃe] sf (GEO) mouth

foco'laio sm (MED) centre of infection; (fig) hotbed

foco'lare sm hearth, fireside; (TECN) furnace

'fodera sf (di vestito) lining; (di libro, poltrona) cover; **fode'rare** vt to line; to cover

'fodero sm (di spada) scabbard; (di pugnale) sheath; (di pistola) holster

'foga sf enthusiasm, ardour

'foggia, ge ['fɔddʒa] sf (maniera) style; (aspetto) form, shape

'foglia ['fɔʎʎa] sf leaf; ~ **d'argento/d'oro** silver/gold leaf; **fogli'ame** sm foliage, leaves pl

'foglio ['fɔʎʎo] sm (di carta) sheet (of paper); (di metallo) sheet; ~ **rosa** (AUT) provisional licence; ~ **di via** (DIR) expulsion order; ~ **volante** pamphlet

'fogna ['fɔɲɲa] sf drain, sewer; **fogna'tura** sf drainage, sewerage

föhn [føːn] sm inv hair dryer

folgo'rare vt (sog: fulmine) to strike down; (: alta tensione) to electrocute

'folla sf crowd, throng

'folle ag mad, insane; (TECN) idle; **in** ~ (AUT) in neutral

fol'lia sf folly, foolishness; foolish act; (pazzia) madness, lunacy

'folto, a ag thick

fomen'tare vt to stir up, foment

fon sm inv hair dryer

fondamen'tale ag fundamental, basic

fonda'mento sm foundation; ~**a** sfpl (EDIL) foundations

fon'dare vt to found; (fig: dar base): ~ **qc su** to base sth on; **fondazi'one** sf foundation

'fondere vt (neve) to melt; (metallo) to fuse, melt; (fig: colori) to merge, blend; (: imprese, gruppi) to merge ♦ vi to melt; ~**rsi** vr to melt; (fig: partiti, correnti) to unite, merge; **fonde'ria** sf foundry

'fondo, a ag deep ♦ sm (di recipiente, pozzo) bottom; (di stanza) back; (quantità di liquido che resta, deposito) dregs pl; (sfondo) background; (unità immobiliare) property, estate; (somma di denaro) fund; (SPORT) long-distance race; ~**i** smpl (denaro) funds; **a notte ~a** at dead of night; **in** ~ **a** at the bottom of; at the back of; (strada) at the end of; **andare a** ~ (nave) to sink; **conoscere a** ~ to know inside out; **dar** ~ **a** (fig: provviste, soldi) to use up; **in** ~ (fig) after all, all things considered; **andare fino in** ~ **a** (fig) to examine thoroughly; **a** ~ **perduto** (COMM) without security; ~**i di caffè** coffee grounds; ~**i di magazzino** old o unsold stock sg

fo'netica sf phonetics sg

fon'tana sf fountain

'fonte sf spring, source; (fig) source ♦ sm: ~ **battesimale** (REL) font

fon'tina sm sweet full-fat hard cheese from Val d'Aosta

fo'raggio [fo'raddʒo] sm fodder, forage

fo'rare vt to pierce, make a hole in; (pallone) to burst; (biglietto) to punch; ~ **una gomma** to burst a tyre (BRIT) o tire (US)

'forbici ['fɔrbitʃi] sfpl scissors

'forca, che sf (AGR) fork, pitchfork; (patibolo) gallows sg

for'cella [for'tʃɛlla] sf (TECN) fork; (di monte) pass

for'chetta [for'ketta] sf fork

for'cina [for'tʃina] sf hairpin

'forcipe ['fɔrtʃipe] sm forceps pl

fo'resta sf forest

foresti'ero, a ag foreign ♦ sm/f foreigner

'forfora sf dandruff

forgi'are vt to forge

'forma sf form; (aspetto esteriore) form,
shape; (DIR: procedura) procedure; (per
calzature) last; (stampo da cucina) mould; ~e
sfpl (del corpo) figure, shape; le ~e
(convenzioni) appearances; essere in ~ to be
in good shape

formag'gino [formad'dʒino] sm processed
cheese

for'maggio [for'maddʒo] sm cheese

for'male ag formal; formalità sf inv
formality

for'mare vt to form, shape, make; (numero
di telefono) to dial; (fig: carattere) to form,
mould; ~rsi vr to form, take shape; for'mato
sm format, size; formazi'one sf formation;
(fig: educazione) training

for'mica, che sf ant; formi'caio sm anthill

formico'lare vi (anche fig): ~ di to be
swarming with; mi formicola la gamba I've
got pins and needles in my leg; formico'lio
sm pins and needles pl; swarming

formi'dabile ag powerful, formidable;
(straordinario) remarkable

'formula sf formula; ~ di cortesia courtesy
form

formu'lare vt to formulate; to express

for'nace [for'natʃe] sf (per laterizi etc) kiln;
(per metalli) furnace; ~ a microonde
microwave oven

for'naio sm baker

for'nello sm (elettrico, a gas) ring; (di pipa)
bowl

for'nire vt: ~ qn di qc, ~ qc a qn to provide o
supply sb with sth, to supply sth to sb

'forno sm (di cucina) oven; (panetteria)
bakery; (TECN: per calce etc) kiln; (: per
metalli) furnace; ~ a microonde microwave
oven

'foro sm (buco) hole; (STORIA) forum;
(tribunale) (law) court

'forse av perhaps, maybe; (circa) about;
essere in ~ to be in doubt

forsen'nato, a ag mad, insane

'forte ag strong; (suono) loud; (spesa)
considerable, great; (passione, dolore) great,
deep ♦ av strongly; (velocemente) fast; (a
voce alta) loud(ly); (violentemente) hard ♦ sm
(edificio) fort; (specialità) forte, strong point;
essere ~ in qc to be good at sth

for'tezza [for'tettsa] sf (morale) strength;
(luogo fortificato) fortress

for'tuito, a ag fortuitous, chance

for'tuna sf (destino) fortune, luck; (buona
sorte) success, fortune; (eredità, averi)
fortune; per ~ luckily, fortunately; di ~

makeshift, improvised; atterraggio di ~
emergency landing; fortu'nato, a ag lucky,
fortunate; (coronato da successo) successful

'forza ['fɔrtsa] sf strength; (potere) power;
(FISICA) force; ~e sfpl (fisiche) strength sg;
(MIL) forces ♦ escl come on!; per ~ against
one's will; (naturalmente) of course; a viva ~
by force; a ~ di by dint of; ~ maggiore
circumstances beyond one's control; la
~ pubblica the police pl; le ~e armate the
armed forces; ~e dell'ordine the forces of law
and order

for'zare [for'tsare] vt to force; ~ qn a fare to
force sb to do; for'zato, a ag forced ♦ sm
(DIR) prisoner sentenced to hard labour

fos'chia [fos'kia] sf mist, haze

'fosco, a, schi, sche ag dark, gloomy

'fosforo sm phosphorous

'fossa sf pit; (di cimitero) grave; ~ biologica
septic tank

fos'sato sm ditch; (di fortezza) moat

fos'setta sf dimple

'fossile ag, sm fossil

'fosso sm ditch; (MIL) trench

'foto sf photo ♦ prefisso: foto'copia sf
photocopy; fotocopi'are vt to photocopy;
fotogra'fare vt to photograph; fotogra'fia
sf (procedimento) photography; (immagine)
photograph; fare una fotografia to take a
photograph; una fotografia a colori/in bianco
e nero a colour/black and white photograph;
fo'tografo, a sm/f photographer;
fotoro'manzo sm romantic picture story;
foto'tessera sf passport-size photo

fra prep = tra

fracas'sare vt to shatter, smash; ~rsi vr to
shatter, smash; (veicolo) to crash; fra'casso
sm smash; crash; (baccano) din, racket

'fradicio, a, ci, ce ['fraditʃo] ag (molto
bagnato) soaking (wet); ubriaco ~ blind
drunk

'fragile ['fradʒile] ag fragile; (fig: salute)
delicate

'fragola sf strawberry

fra'gore sm roar; (di tuono) rumble

frago'roso, a ag deafening

fra'grante ag fragrant

frain'tendere vt to misunderstand;
frain'teso, a pp di fraintendere

fram'mento sm fragment

'frana sf landslide; (fig: persona): essere una ~
to be useless; fra'nare vi to slip, slide down

fran'cese [fran'tʃeze] ag French ♦ sm/f
Frenchman/woman ♦ sm (LING) French; i F~i
the French

fran'chezza [fran'kettsa] sf frankness,
openness

'Francia ['frantʃa] sf: la ~ France

'franco, a, chi, che ag (COMM) free;

(*sincero*) frank, open, sincere ♦ *sm* (*moneta*) franc; **farla ~a** (*fig*) to get off scot-free; **~ di dogana** duty-free; **prezzo ~ fabbrica** ex-works price; **~ tiratore** *sm* sniper

franco'bollo *sm* (postage) stamp

fran'gente [fran'dʒɛnte] *sm* (*onda*) breaker; (*scoglio emergente*) reef; (*circostanza*) situation, circumstance

'frangia, ge ['frandʒa] *sf* fringe

frantu'mare *vt* to break into pieces, shatter; **~rsi** *vr* to break into pieces, shatter

frap'pé *sm* milk shake

'frasca, sche *sf* (leafy) branch

'frase *sf* (*LING*) sentence; (*locuzione, espressione, MUS*) phrase; **~ fatta** set phrase

'frassino *sm* ash (tree)

frastagli'ato, a [frastaʎ'ʎato] *ag* (*costa*) indented, jagged

frastor'nare *vt* to daze; to befuddle

frastu'ono *sm* hubbub, din

'frate *sm* friar, monk

fratel'lanza [fratel'lantsa] *sf* brotherhood; (*associazione*) fraternity

fratel'lastro *sm* stepbrother

fra'tello *sm* brother; **~i** *smpl* brothers; (*nel senso di fratelli e sorelle*) brothers and sisters

fra'terno, a *ag* fraternal, brotherly

frat'tanto *av* in the meantime, meanwhile

frat'tempo *sm*: **nel ~** in the meantime, meanwhile

frat'tura *sf* fracture; (*fig*) split, break

frazi'one [frat'tsjone] *sf* fraction; (*di comune*) small town

'freccia, ce ['frettʃa] *sf* arrow; **~ di direzione** (*AUT*) indicator

fred'dare *vt* to shoot dead

fred'dezza [fred'dettsa] *sf* coldness

'freddo, a *ag, sm* cold; **fa ~** it's cold; **aver ~** to be cold; **a ~** (*fig*) deliberately; **freddo'loso, a** *ag* sensitive to the cold

fred'dura *sf* pun

fre'gare *vt* to rub; (*fam: truffare*) to take in, cheat; (: *rubare*) to swipe, pinch; **fregarsene** (*fam!*): **chi se ne frega?** who gives a damn (about it)?

fre'gata *sf* rub; (*fam*) swindle; (*NAUT*) frigate

'fregio ['fredʒo] *sm* (*ARCHIT*) frieze; (*ornamento*) decoration

'fremere *vi*: **~ di** to tremble o quiver with; **'fremito** *sm* tremor, quiver

fre'nare *vt* (*veicolo*) to slow down; (*cavallo*) to rein in; (*lacrime*) to restrain, hold back ♦ *vi* to brake; **~rsi** *vr* (*fig*) to restrain o.s., control o.s.; **fre'nata** *sf*: **fare una frenata** to brake

frene'sia *sf* frenzy

'freno *sm* brake; (*morso*) bit; **~ a disco** disc brake; **~ a mano** handbrake; **tenere a ~** to restrain

frequen'tare *vt* (*scuola, corso*) to attend;

(*locale, bar*) to go to, frequent; (*persone*) to see (often)

fre'quente *ag* frequent; **di ~** frequently; **fre'quenza** *sf* frequency; (*INS*) attendance

fres'chezza [fres'kettsa] *sf* freshness

'fresco, a, schi, sche *ag* fresh; (*temperatura*) cool; (*notizia*) recent, fresh ♦ *sm*: **godere il ~** to enjoy the cool air; **stare ~** (*fig*) to be in for it; **mettere al ~** to put in a cool place

'fretta *sf* hurry, haste; **in ~** in a hurry; **in ~ e furia** in a mad rush; **aver ~** to be in a hurry; **fretto'loso, a** *ag* (*persona*) in a hurry; (*lavoro etc*) hurried, rushed

fri'abile *ag* (*terreno*) friable; (*pasta*) crumbly

'friggere ['friddʒere] *vt* to fry ♦ *vi* (*olio etc*) to sizzle

'frigido, a ['fridʒido] *ag* (*MED*) frigid

'frigo *sm* fridge

frigo'rifero, a *ag* refrigerating ♦ *sm* refrigerator

fringu'ello *sm* chaffinch

frit'tata *sf* omelette; **fare una ~** (*fig*) to make a mess of things

frit'tella *sf* (*CUC*) fritter

'fritto, a *pp di* **friggere** ♦ *ag* fried ♦ *sm* fried food; **~ misto** mixed fry

frit'tura *sf* (*CUC*): **~ di pesce** mixed fried fish

'frivolo, a *ag* frivolous

frizi'one [frit'tsjone] *sf* friction; (*di pelle*) rub, rub-down; (*AUT*) clutch

friz'zante [frid'dzante] *ag* (*anche fig*) sparkling

fro'dare *vt* to defraud, cheat

'frode *sf* fraud; **~ fiscale** tax evasion

'frollo, a *ag* (*carne*) tender; (: *di selvaggina*) high; **pasta ~a** short(crust) pastry

'fronda *sf* (leafy) branch; (*di partito politico*) internal opposition

fron'tale *ag* frontal; (*scontro*) head-on

'fronte *sf* (*ANAT*) forehead; (*di edificio*) front, façade ♦ *sm* (*MIL, POL, METEOR*) front; **a ~, di ~** facing, opposite; **di ~ a** (*posizione*) opposite, facing, in front of; (*a paragone di*) compared with

fronteggi'are [fronted'dʒare] *vt* (*avversari, difficoltà*) to face, stand up to; (*spese*) to cope with

fronti'era *sf* border, frontier

'fronzolo ['frondzolo] *sm* frill

'frottola *sf* fib; **~e** *sfpl* (*assurdità*) nonsense *sg*

fru'gare *vi* to rummage ♦ *vt* to search

frul'lare *vt* (*CUC*) to whisk ♦ *vi* (*uccelli*) to flutter; **frul'lato** *sm* milk shake; fruit drink; **frulla'tore** *sm* electric mixer; **frul'lino** *sm* whisk

fru'mento *sm* wheat

fru'scio [fruʃ'ʃio] *sm* rustle; rustling; (*di acque*) murmur '**frusta** *sf* whip; (*CUC*) whisk

frus'tare *vt* to whip

frus'tino *sm* riding crop

frus'trare *vt* to frustrate

'**frutta** *sf* fruit; (*portata*) dessert; **~ candita/secca** candied/dried fruit

frut'tare *vi* to bear dividends, give a return

frut'teto *sm* orchard

frutti'vendolo, a *sm/f* greengrocer (*BRIT*), produce dealer (*US*)

'**frutto** *sm* fruit; (*fig: risultato*) result(s); (*ECON: interesse*) interest; (: *reddito*) income; **~i di mare** seafood *sg*

FS *abbr* = **Ferrovie dello Stato**

fu *vb vedi* **essere** ♦ *ag inv*: **il ~ Paolo Bianchi** the late Paolo Bianchi

fuci'lare [futʃi'lare] *vt* to shoot; **fuci'lata** *sf* rifle shot

fu'cile [fu'tʃile] *sm* rifle, gun; (*da caccia*) shotgun, gun

fu'cina [fu'tʃina] *sf* forge

'**fuga** *sf* escape, flight; (*di gas, liquidi*) leak; (*MUS*) fugue; **~ di cervelli** brain drain

fu'gace [fu'gatʃe] *ag* fleeting, transient

fug'gevole [fud'dʒevole] *ag* fleeting

fuggi'asco, a, schi, sche [fud'dʒasko] *ag, sm/f* fugitive

fuggi'fuggi [fuddʒi'fuddʒi] *sm* scramble, stampede

fug'gire [fud'dʒire] *vi* to flee, run away; (*fig: passar veloce*) to fly ♦ *vt* to avoid; **fuggi'tivo, a** *sm/f* fugitive, runaway

ful'gore *sm* brilliance, splendour

fu'liggine [fu'liddʒine] *sf* soot

fulmi'nare *vt* (*sog: fulmine*) to strike; (: *elettricità*) to electrocute; (*con arma da fuoco*) to shoot dead; (*fig: con lo sguardo*) to look daggers at

fulmine *sm* thunderbolt; lightning *no pl*

fu'mare *vi* to smoke; (*emettere vapore*) to steam ♦ *vt* to smoke; **fu'mata** *sf* (*segnale*) smoke signal; **farsi una fumata** to have a smoke; **fuma'tore, 'trice** *sm/f* smoker

fu'metto *sm* comic strip; **giornale** *sm* **a ~i** comic

'**fumo** *sm* smoke; (*vapore*) steam; (*il fumare tabacco*) smoking; **~i** *smpl* (*industriali etc*) fumes; **i ~i dell'alcool** the after-effects of drink; **vendere ~** to deceive, cheat; **~ passivo** passive smoking; **fu'moso, a** *ag* smoky; (*fig*) muddled

fu'nambolo, a *sm/f* tightrope walker

'**fune** *sf* rope, cord; (*più grossa*) cable

'**funebre** *ag* (*rito*) funeral; (*aspetto*) gloomy, funereal

fune'rale *sm* funeral

'**fungere** ['fundʒere] *vi*: **~ da** to act as

'**fungo, ghi** *sm* fungus; (*commestibile*) mushroom; **~ velenoso** toadstool

funico'lare *sf* funicular railway

funi'via *sf* cable railway

funzio'nare [funtsjo'nare] *vi* to work, function; (*fungere*): **~ da** to act as

funzio'nario [funtsjo'narjo] *sm* official

funzi'one [fun'tsjone] *sf* function; (*carica*) post, position; (*REL*) service; **in ~** (*meccanismo*) in operation; **in ~ di** (*come*) as; **fare la ~ di qn** (*farne le veci*) to take sb's place

fu'oco, chi *sm* fire; (*fornello*) ring; (*FOT, FISICA*) focus; **dare ~ a qc** to set fire to sth; **far ~** (*sparare*) to fire; **~ d'artificio** firework

fuorché [fwor'ke] *cong, prep* except

fu'ori *av* outside; (*all'aperto*) outdoors, outside; (*fuori di casa, SPORT*) out; (*esclamativo*) get out! ♦ *prep*: **~ (di)** out of, outside ♦ *sm* outside; **lasciar ~ qc/qn** to leave sth/sb out; **far ~ qn** (*fam*) to kill sb, do sb in; **essere ~ di sé** to be beside o.s.; **~ luogo** (*inopportuno*) out of place, uncalled for; **~ mano** out of the way, remote; **~ pericolo** out of danger; **~ uso** old-fashioned; obsolete

fu'ori... *prefisso*: **fuori'bordo** *sm inv* speedboat (with outboard motor); outboard motor; **fuori'classe** *sm/f inv* (undisputed) champion; **fuorigi'oco** *sm* offside; **fuori'legge** *sm/f inv* outlaw; **fuori'serie** *ag inv* (*auto etc*) custom-built ♦ *sf* custom-built car; **fuori'strada** *sm* (*AUT*) cross-country vehicle; **fuor(i)u'scito, a** *sm/f* exile; **fuorvi'are** *vt* to mislead; (*fig*) to lead astray ♦ *vi* to go astray

'**furbo, a** *ag* clever, smart; (*peg*) cunning

fu'rente *ag*: **~ (contro)** furious (with)

fur'fante *sm* rascal, scoundrel

fur'gone *sm* van

'**furia** *sf* (*ira*) fury, rage; (*fig: impeto*) fury, violence; (*fretta*) rush; **a ~ di** by dint of; **andare su tutte le ~e** to get into a towering rage; **furi'bondo, a** *ag* furious

furi'oso, a *ag* furious

fu'rore *sm* fury; (*esaltazione*) frenzy; **far ~** to be all the rage

fur'tivo, a *ag* furtive

'**furto** *sm* theft; **~ con scasso** burglary

'**fusa** *sfpl*: **fare le ~** to purr

fu'sibile *sm* (*ELETTR*) fuse

fusi'one *sf* (*di metalli*) fusion, melting; (*colata*) casting; (*COMM*) merger; (*fig*) merging

'**fuso, a** *pp di* **fondere** ♦ *sm* (*FILATURA*) spindle; **~ orario** time zone

fus'tagno [fus'taɲɲo] *sm* corduroy

fus'tino *sm* (*di detersivo*) tub

'**fusto** *sm* stem; (*ANAT, di albero*) trunk; (*recipiente*) drum, can

fu'turo, a *ag, sm* future

G, g

gab'bare vt to take in, dupe; **~rsi** vr: **~rsi di qn** to make fun of sb

'gabbia sf cage; (da imballaggio) crate; **~ dell'ascensore** lift (BRIT) o elevator (US) shaft; **~ toracica** (ANAT) rib cage

gabbi'ano sm (sea)gull

gabi'netto sm (MED etc) consulting room; (POL) ministry; (WC) toilet, lavatory; (INS: di fisica etc) laboratory

'gaffe [gaf] sf inv blunder

gagli'ardo, a [gaʎˈʎardo] ag strong, vigorous

'gaio, a ag cheerful, gay

'gala (sfarzo) pomp; (festa) gala

ga'lante ag gallant, courteous; (avventura) amorous; **galante'ria** sf gallantry

galantu'omo (pl **galantu'omini**) sm gentleman

ga'lassia sf galaxy

gala'teo sm (good) manners pl

gale'otto sm (rematore) galley slave; (carcerato) convict

ga'lera sf (NAUT) galley; (prigione) prison

'galla sf: **a ~** afloat; **venire a ~** to surface, come to the surface; (fig: verità) to come out

galleggi'ante [galledˈdʒante] ag floating ♦ sm (di pescatore, lenza, TECN) float

galleggi'are [galledˈdʒare] vi to float

galle'ria sf (traforo) tunnel; (ARCHIT, d'arte) gallery; (TEATRO) circle; (strada coperta con negozi) arcade

'Galles sm: **il ~** Wales; **gal'lese** ag, sm (LING) Welsh ♦ sm/f Welshman/woman

gal'letta sf cracker

gal'lina sf hen

'gallo sm cock

gal'lone sm piece of braid; (MIL) stripe; (unità di misura) gallon

galop'pare vi to gallop

ga'loppo sm gallop; **al** o **di ~** at a gallop

'gamba sf leg; (asta: di lettera) stem; **in ~** (in buona salute) well; (bravo, sveglio) bright, smart; **prendere qc sotto ~** (fig) to treat sth too lightly

gambe'retto sm shrimp

'gambero sm (di acqua dolce) crayfish; (di mare) prawn

'gambo sm stem; (di frutta) stalk

'gamma sf (MUS) scale; (di colori, fig) range

ga'nascia, sce [gaˈnaʃʃa] sf jaw; **~sce del freno** (AUT) brake shoes

'gancio [ˈgantʃo] sm hook

'gangheri [ˈgangeri] smpl: **uscire dai ~** (fig) to fly into a temper

'gara sf competition; (SPORT) competition; contest; match; (: corsa) race; **fare a ~** to compete, vie

ga'rage [gaˈraʒ] sm inv garage

garan'tire vt to guarantee; (debito) to stand surety for; (dare per certo) to assure

garan'zia [garanˈtsia] sf guarantee; (pegno) security

gar'bato, a ag courteous, polite

'garbo sm (buone maniere) politeness, courtesy; (di vestito etc) grace, style

gareggi'are [garedˈdʒare] vi to compete

gar'garismo sm gargle; **fare i ~i** to gargle

ga'rofano sm carnation; **chiodo di ~** clove

'garza [ˈgardza] sf (per bende) gauze

gar'zone [garˈdzone] sm (di negozio) boy

gas sm inv gas; **a tutto ~** at full speed; **dare ~** (AUT) to accelerate

ga'solio sm diesel (oil)

ga's(s)ato, a ag (bibita) aerated, fizzy

gas'sosa sf fizzy drink

gas'soso, a ag gaseous; gassy

gastrono'mia sf gastronomy

gat'tino sm kitten

'gatto, a sm/f cat, tomcat/she-cat; **~ selvatico** wildcat; **~ delle nevi** (AUT, SCI) snowcat

gatto'pardo sm: **~ africano** serval; **~ americano** ocelot

'gaudio sm joy, happiness

ga'vetta sf (MIL) mess tin; **venire dalla ~** (MIL, fig) to rise from the ranks

'gazza [ˈgaddza] sf magpie

gaz'zella [gadˈdzɛlla] sf gazelle

gaz'zetta [gadˈdzetta] sf news sheet; **G~ Ufficiale** official publication containing details of new laws

gel [dʒɛl] sm inv gel

ge'lare [dʒeˈlare] vt, vi, vb impers to freeze; **ge'lata** sf frost

gelate'ria [dʒelateˈria] sf ice-cream shop

gela'tina [dʒelaˈtina] sf gelatine; **~ esplosiva** dynamite; **~ di frutta** fruit jelly

ge'lato, a [dʒeˈlato] ag frozen ♦ sm ice cream

'gelido, a [ˈdʒɛlido] ag icy, ice-cold

'gelo [ˈdʒɛlo] sm (temperatura) intense cold; (brina) frost; (fig) chill; **ge'lone** sm chilblain

gelo'sia [dʒeloˈsia] sf jealousy

ge'loso, a [dʒeˈloso] ag jealous

'gelso [ˈdʒɛlso] sm mulberry (tree)

gelso'mino [dʒelsoˈmino] sm jasmine

ge'mello, a [dʒeˈmɛllo] ag, sm/f twin; **~i** smpl (di camicia) cufflinks; (dello zodiaco): **G~i** Gemini sg

'gemere [ˈdʒɛmere] vi to moan, groan; (cigolare) to creak; **'gemito** sm moan, groan

'gemma [ˈdʒɛmma] sf (BOT) bud; (pietra preziosa) gem

gene'rale [dʒeneˈrale] ag, sm general; **in ~**

(*per sommi capi*) in general terms; (*di solito*) usually, in general; **generalità** *sfpl* (*dati d'identità*) particulars; **generaliz'zare** *vt, vi* to generalize; **general'mente** *av* generally

gene'rare [dʒene'rare] *vt* (*dar vita*) to give birth to; (*produrre*) to produce; (*causare*) to arouse; (*TECN*) to produce, generate; **genera'tore** *sm* (*TECN*) generator; **generazi'one** *sf* generation

'genere ['dʒenere] *sm* kind, type, sort; (*BIOL*) genus; (*merce*) article, product; (*LING*) gender; (*ARTE, LETTERATURA*) genre; **in ~** generally, as a rule; **il ~ umano** mankind; **~i alimentari** foodstuffs

ge'nerico, a, ci, che [dʒe'nɛriko] *ag* generic; (*vago*) vague, imprecise

'genero ['dʒenero] *sm* son-in-law

generosità [dʒenerosi'ta] *sf* generosity

gene'roso, a [dʒene'roso] *ag* generous

ge'netica [dʒe'netika] *sf* genetics *sg*

ge'netico, a, ci, che [dʒe'netiko] *ag* genetic

gen'giva [dʒen'dʒiva] *sf* (*ANAT*) gum

geni'ale [dʒen'jale] *ag* (*persona*) of genius; (*idea*) ingenious, brilliant

'genio ['dʒenjo] *sm* genius; **andare a ~ a qn** to be to sb's liking, appeal to sb

geni'tale [dʒeni'tale] *ag* genital; **~i** *smpl* genitals

geni'tore [dʒeni'tore] *sm* parent, father *o* mother; **i miei ~i** my parents, my father and mother

gen'naio [dʒen'najo] *sm* January

'Genova ['dʒenova] *sf* Genoa

gen'taglia [dʒen'taʎʎa] (*peg*) *sf* rabble

'gente ['dʒɛnte] *sf* people *pl*

gen'tile [dʒen'tile] *ag* (*persona, atto*) kind; (*: garbato*) courteous, polite; (*nelle lettere*): **G~ Signore** Dear Sir; (*: sulla busta*): **G~ Signor Fernando Villa** Mr Fernando Villa; **genti'lezza** *sf* kindness; courtesy, politeness; **per gentilezza** (*per favore*) please

gentilu'omo [dʒentil'lwɔmo] (*pl* **gentilu'omini**) *sm* gentleman

genu'ino, a [dʒenu'ino] *ag* (*prodotto*) natural; (*persona, sentimento*) genuine, sincere

geogra'fia [dʒeogra'fia] *sf* geography

geolo'gia [dʒeolo'dʒia] *sf* geology

ge'ometra, i, e [dʒe'ɔmetra] *sm/f* (*professionista*) surveyor

geome'tria [dʒeome'tria] *sf* geometry; **geo'metrico, a, ci, che** *ag* geometric(al)

gerar'chia [dʒerar'kia] *sf* hierarchy

ge'rente [dʒe'rɛnte] *sm/f* manager/manageress

'gergo, ghi ['dʒergo] *sm* jargon; slang

geria'tria [dʒerja'tria] *sf* geriatrics *sg*

Ger'mania [dʒer'manja] *sf*: **la ~** Germany;

la **~ occidentale/orientale** West/East Germany

'germe ['dʒɛrme] *sm* germ; (*fig*) seed

germogli'are [dʒermoʎ'ʎare] *vi* to sprout; to germinate; **ger'moglio** *sm* shoot; bud

gero'glifico, ci [dʒero'glifiko] *sm* hieroglyphic

'gesso ['dʒɛsso] *sm* chalk; (*SCULTURA, MED, EDIL*) plaster; (*statua*) plaster figure; (*minerale*) gypsum

gesti'one [dʒes'tjone] *sf* management

ges'tire [dʒes'tire] *vt* to run, manage

'gesto ['dʒɛsto] *sm* gesture

ges'tore [dʒes'tore] *sm* manager

Gesù [dʒe'zu] *sm* Jesus

gesu'ita, i [dʒezu'ita] *sm* Jesuit

get'tare [dʒet'tare] *vt* to throw; (*anche:* **~ via**) to throw away *o* out; (*SCULTURA*) to cast; (*EDIL*) to lay; (*acqua*) to spout; (*grido*) to utter; **~rsi** *vr*: **~rsi in** (*sog: fiume*) to flow into; **~ uno sguardo su** to take a quick look at; **get'tata** *sf* (*di cemento, gesso, metalli*) cast; (*diga*) jetty

'getto ['dʒetto] *sm* (*di gas, liquido, AER*) jet; **a ~ continuo** uninterruptedly; **di ~** (*fig*) straight off, in one go

get'tone [dʒet'tone] *sm* token; (*per giochi*) counter; (*: roulette etc*) chip; **~ telefonico** telephone token

ghiacci'aio [gjat'tʃajo] *sm* glacier

ghiacci'are [gjat'tʃare] *vt* to freeze; (*fig*): **~ qn** to make sb's blood run cold ♦ *vi* to freeze, ice over; **ghiacci'ato, a** *ag* frozen; (*bevanda*) ice-cold

ghi'accio ['gjattʃo] *sm* ice

ghiacci'olo [gjat'tʃɔlo] *sm* icicle; (*tipo di gelato*) ice lolly (*BRIT*), Popsicle ® (*US*)

ghi'aia ['gjaja] *sf* gravel

ghi'anda ['gjanda] *sf* (*BOT*) acorn

ghi'andola ['gjandola] *sf* gland

ghigliot'tina [giʎʎot'tina] *sf* guillotine

ghi'gnare [giɲ'ɲare] *vi* to sneer

ghi'otto, a ['gjotto] *ag* greedy; (*cibo*) delicious, appetizing; **ghiot'tone, a** *sm/f* glutton

ghiri'goro [giri'gɔro] *sm* scribble, squiggle

ghir'landa [gir'landa] *sf* garland, wreath

'ghiro ['giro] *sm* dormouse

'ghisa ['giza] *sf* cast iron

già [dʒa] *av* already; (*ex, in precedenza*) formerly ♦ *escl* of course!, yes indeed!

gi'acca, che ['dʒakka] *sf* jacket; **~ a vento** windcheater (*BRIT*), windbreaker (*US*)

giacché [dʒak'ke] *cong* since, as

giac'chetta [dʒak'ketta] *sf* (light) jacket

gia'cenza [dʒa'tʃɛntsa] *sf*: **merce in ~** goods in stock; **~e di magazzino** unsold stock

gia'cere [dʒa'tʃere] *vi* to lie; **giaci'mento** *sm* deposit

gia'cinto [dʒa'tʃinto] *sm* hyacinth

gi'ada ['dʒada] sf jade

giaggi'olo [dʒad'dʒɔlo] sm iris

giagu'aro [dʒa'gwaro] sm jaguar

gi'allo ['dʒallo] ag yellow; (carnagione) sallow
♦ sm yellow; (anche: romanzo ~) detective
novel; (anche: film ~) detective film;
~ dell'uovo yolk

giam'mai [dʒam'mai] av never

Giap'pone [dʒap'pone] sm Japan;
giappo'nese ag, sm/f, sm Japanese inv

gi'ara ['dʒara] sf jar

giardi'naggio [dʒardi'naddʒo] sm
gardening

giardini'era [dʒardi'njera] sf (misto di
sottaceti) mixed pickles pl

giardini'ere, a [dʒardi'njere] sm/f gardener

giar'dino [dʒar'dino] sm garden; ~ d'infanzia
nursery school; ~ pubblico public gardens pl,
(public) park; ~ zoologico zoo

giarretti'era [dʒarret'tjera] sf garter

giavel'lotto [dʒavel'lɔtto] sm javelin

gi'gante, 'essa [dʒi'gante] sm/f giant ♦ ag
giant, gigantic; (COMM) giant-size;
gigan'tesco, a, schi, sche ag gigantic

'giglio ['dʒiʎʎo] sm lily

gilè [dʒi'lɛ] sm inv waistcoat

gin [dʒin] sm inv gin

gine'cologo, a, gi, ghe [dʒine'kɔlogo]
sm/f gynaecologist

gi'nepro [dʒi'nepro] sm juniper

gi'nestra [dʒi'nestra] sf (BOT) broom

Gi'nevra [dʒi'nevra] sf Geneva

gingil'larsi [dʒindʒil'larsi] vr to fritter away
one's time; (giocare): ~ con to fiddle with

gin'gillo [dʒin'dʒillo] sm plaything

gin'nasio [dʒin'nazjo] sm the 4th and 5th
year of secondary school in Italy

gin'nasta, i, e [dʒin'nasta] sm/f gymnast;
gin'nastica sf gymnastics sg; (esercizio fisico)
keep-fit exercises; (INS) physical education

gi'nocchio [dʒi'nɔkkjo] (pl(m) gi'nocchi o
pl(f) gi'nocchia) sm knee; stare in ~ to kneel,
be on one's knees; mettersi in ~ to kneel
(down); ginocchi'oni av on one's knees

gio'care [dʒo'kare] vt to play; (scommettere)
to stake, wager, bet; (ingannare) to take in
♦ vi to play; (a roulette etc) to gamble; (fig)
to play a part, be important; ~ a (gioco,
sport) to play; (cavalli) to bet on; ~rsi la
carriera to put one's career at risk;
gioca'tore, 'trice sm/f player; gambler

gio'cattolo [dʒo'kattolo] sm toy

gio'chetto [dʒo'ketto] sm (tranello) trick;
(fig): è un ~ it's child's play

gi'oco, chi ['dʒɔko] sm game; (divertimento,
TECN) play; (al casinò) gambling; (CARTE)
hand; (insieme di pezzi etc necessari per un
gioco) set; per ~ for fun; fare il doppio ~ con
qn to double-cross sb; ~ d'azzardo game of

chance; ~ degli scacchi chess set; i Giochi
Olimpici the Olympic Games

giocoli'ere [dʒoko'ljere] sm juggler

gio'coso, a [dʒo'koso] ag playful, jesting

gi'ogo, ghi ['dʒɔgo] sm yoke

gi'oia ['dʒɔja] sf joy, delight; (pietra preziosa)
jewel, precious stone

gioielle'ria [dʒojelle'ria] sf jeweller's craft;
jeweller's (shop)

gioielli'ere, a [dʒojel'ljere] sm/f jeweller

gioi'ello [dʒo'jello] sm jewel, piece of
jewellery; i miei ~i my jewels o jewellery

gioi'oso, a [dʒo'joso] ag joyful

Gior'dania [dʒor'danja] sf: la ~ Jordan

giorna'laio, a [dʒorna'lajo] sm/f newsagent
(BRIT), newsdealer (US)

gior'nale [dʒor'nale] sm (news) paper;
(diario) journal, diary; (COMM) journal; ~ di
bordo log; ~ radio radio news sg

giornali'ero, a [dʒorna'ljero] ag daily; (che
varia: umore) changeable ♦ sm day labourer

giorna'lismo [dʒorna'lizmo] sm journalism

giorna'lista, i, e [dʒorna'lista] sm/f
journalist

gior'nata [dʒor'nata] sf day; ~ lavorativa
working day

gi'orno ['dʒorno] sm day; (opposto alla notte)
day, daytime; (luce del ~) daylight; al ~ per
day; di ~ by day; al ~ d'oggi nowadays

gi'ostra ['dʒɔstra] sf (per bimbi) merry-go-
round; (torneo storico) joust

gi'ovane [dʒo'vane] ag young; (aspetto)
youthful ♦ sm/f youth/girl, young man/
woman; i ~i young people; giova'nile ag
youthful; (scritti) early; (errore) of youth;
giova'notto sm young man

gio'vare [dʒo'vare] vi: ~ a (essere utile) to be
useful to; (far bene) to be good for ♦ vb
impers (essere bene, utile) to be useful; ~rsi di
qc to make use of sth

giovedì [dʒove'di] sm inv Thursday; di o il ~
on Thursdays

gioventù [dʒoven'tu] sf (periodo) youth; (i
giovani) young people pl, youth

giovi'ale [dʒo'vjale] ag jovial, jolly

giovi'nezza [dʒovi'nettsa] sf youth

gira'dischi [dʒira'diski] sm inv record player

gi'raffa [dʒi'raffa] sf giraffe

gi'randola [dʒi'randola] sf (fuoco d'artificio)
Catherine wheel; (giocattolo) toy windmill;
(banderuola) weather vane, weathercock

gi'rare [dʒi'rare] vt (far ruotare) to turn;
(percorrere, visitare) to go round; (CINEMA) to
shoot; to make; (COMM) to endorse ♦ vi to
turn; (più veloce) to spin; (andare in giro) to
wander, go around; ~rsi vr to turn; ~ attorno
a to go round; to revolve round; far ~ la
testa a qn to make sb dizzy; (fig) to turn sb's
head

girar'rosto [dʒirar'rɔsto] *sm* (*CUC*) spit

gira'sole [dʒira'sole] *sm* sunflower

gi'rata [dʒi'rata] *sf* (*passeggiata*) stroll; (*con veicolo*) drive; (*COMM*) endorsement

gira'volta [dʒira'vɔlta] *sf* twirl, turn; (*curva*) sharp bend; (*fig*) about-turn

gi'revole [dʒi'revole] *ag* revolving, turning

gi'rino [dʒi'rino] *sm* tadpole

'giro [dʒiro] *sm* (*circuito, cerchio*) circle; (*di chiave, manovella*) turn; (*viaggio*) tour, excursion; (*passeggiata*) stroll, walk; (*in macchina*) drive; (*in bicicletta*) ride; (*SPORT: della pista*) lap; (*di denaro*) circulation; (*CARTE*) hand; (*TECN*) revolution; **prendere in ~ qn** (*fig*) to pull sb's leg; **fare un ~** to go for a walk (*o a drive o a ride*); **andare in ~** to go about, walk around; **a stretto ~ di posta** by return of post; **nel ~ di un mese** in a month's time; **essere nel ~** (*fig*) to belong to a circle (of friends); **~ d'affari** (*COMM*) turnover; **~ di parole** circumlocution; **~ di prova** (*AUT*) test drive; **~ turistico** sightseeing tour; **giro'collo** *sm*: **a girocollo** crew-neck *cpd*

gironzo'lare [dʒirondzo'lare] *vi* to stroll about

'gita ['dʒita] *sf* excursion, trip; **fare una ~** to go for a trip, go on an outing

gi'tano, a [dʒi'tano] *sm/f* gipsy

giù [dʒu] *av* down; (*dabbasso*) downstairs; **in ~** downwards, down; **~ di lì** (*pressappoco*) thereabouts; **bambini dai 6 anni in ~** children aged 6 and under; **~ per: cadere ~ per le scale** to fall down the stairs; **essere ~** (*fig: di salute*) to be run down; (: *di spirito*) to be depressed

giub'botto [dʒub'bɔtto] *sm* jerkin; **~ antiproiettile** bulletproof vest

gi'ubilo ['dʒubilo] *sm* rejoicing

giudi'care [dʒudi'kare] *vt* to judge; (*accusato*) to try; (*lite*) to arbitrate in; **~ qn/ qc bello** to consider sb/sth (to be) beautiful

gi'udice ['dʒuditʃe] *sm* judge; **~ conciliatore** justice of the peace; **~ istruttore** examining (*BRIT*) o committing (*US*) magistrate; **~ popolare** member of a jury

giu'dizio [dʒu'dittsjo] *sm* judgment; (*opinione*) opinion; (*DIR*) judgment, sentence; (: *processo*) trial; (: *verdetto*) verdict; **aver ~** to be wise o prudent; **citare in ~** to summons; **giudizi'oso, a** *ag* prudent, judicious

gi'ugno ['dʒuɲɲo] *sm* June

giul'lare [dʒul'lare] *sm* jester

giu'menta [dʒu'menta] *sf* mare

gi'unco, chi ['dʒunko] *sm* rush

gi'ungere ['dʒundʒere] *vi* to arrive ♦ *vt* (*mani etc*) to join; **~ a** to arrive at, reach

gi'ungla ['dʒungla] *sf* jungle

gi'unta ['dʒunta] *sf* addition; (*organo esecutivo, amministrativo*) council, board; **per**

~ into the bargain, in addition; **~ militare** military junta

gi'unto, a ['dʒunto] *pp di* **giungere** ♦ *sm* (*TECN*) coupling, joint; **giun'tura** *sf* joint

giuo'care [dʒwo'kare] *etc* = **giocare** *etc*

giura'mento [dʒura'mento] *sm* oath; **~ falso** perjury

giu'rare [dʒu'rare] *vt* to swear ♦ *vi* to swear, take an oath; **giu'rato, a** *ag*: **nemico giurato** sworn enemy ♦ *sm/f* juror, juryman/woman

giu'ria [dʒu'ria] *sf* jury

giu'ridico, a, ci, che [dʒu'ridiko] *ag* legal

giustifi'care [dʒustifi'kare] *vt* to justify; **giustificazi'one** *sf* justification; (*INS*) (note of) excuse

gius'tizia [dʒus'tittsja] *sf* justice; **giustizi'are** *vt* to execute, put to death; **giustizi'ere** *sm* executioner

gi'usto, a ['dʒusto] *ag* (*equo*) fair, just; (*vero*) true, correct; (*adatto*) right, suitable; (*preciso*) exact, correct ♦ *av* (*esattamente*) exactly, precisely; (*per l'appunto, appena*) just; **arrivare ~** to arrive just in time; **ho ~ bisogno di te** you're just the person I need

glaci'ale [gla'tʃale] *ag* glacial

gli [ʎi] (*dav V, s impura, gn, pn, ps, x, z*) *det mpl* the ♦ *pron* (*a lui*) to him; (*a esso*) to it; (*in coppia con lo, la, li, le, ne: a lui, a lei, a loro etc*): **gliele do** I'm giving them to him (*o her o them*); *vedi anche* **il**

gli'ela ['ʎela] *etc vedi* **gli**

glo'bale *ag* overall

'globo *sm* globe

'globulo *sm* (*ANAT*): **~ rosso/bianco** red/white corpuscle

'gloria *sf* glory; **glori'oso, a** *ag* glorious

glos'sario *sm* glossary

'gnocchi ['ɲɔkki] *smpl* (*CUC*) small dumplings made of semolina pasta or potato

'gobba *sf* (*ANAT*) hump; (*protuberanza*) bump

'gobbo, a *ag* hunchbacked; (*ricurvo*) round-shouldered ♦ *sm/f* hunchback

'goccia, ce ['gottʃa] *sf* drop; **goccio'lare** *vi, vt* to drip

go'dere *vi* (*compiacersi*): **~ (di)** to be delighted (at), rejoice (at); (*trarre vantaggio*): **~ di** to enjoy, benefit from ♦ *vt* to enjoy; **~rsi la vita** to enjoy life; **~sela** to have a good time, enjoy o.s.; **godi'mento** *sm* enjoyment

'goffo, a *ag* clumsy, awkward

'gola *sf* (*ANAT*) throat; (*golosità*) gluttony, greed; (*di camino*) flue; (*di monte*) gorge; **fare ~** (*anche fig*) to tempt

golf *sm inv* (*SPORT*) golf; (*maglia*) cardigan

'golfo *sm* gulf

go'loso, a *ag* greedy

'gomito *sm* elbow; (*di strada etc*) sharp bend

go'mitolo *sm* ball

'gomma *sf* rubber; (*per cancellare*) rubber,

eraser; (*di veicolo*) tyre (*BRIT*), tire (*US*);
~ americana o **da masticare** chewing gum;
~ a terra flat tyre (*BRIT*) o tire (*US*);
gommapi'uma ® *sf* foam rubber;
gom'mone *sm* rubber dinghy
'gondola *sf* gondola; **gondoli'ere** *sm*
gondolier
gonfa'lone *sm* banner
gonfi'are *vt* (*pallone*) to blow up, inflate;
(*dilatare, ingrossare*) to swell; (*fig: notizia*) to
exaggerate; **~rsi** *vr* to swell; (*fiume*) to rise;
'gonfio, a *ag* swollen; (*stomaco*) bloated;
(*vela*) full; **gonfi'ore** *sm* swelling
gongo'lare *vi* to look pleased with o.s.; **~ di
gioia** to be overjoyed
'gonna *sf* skirt; **~ pantalone** culottes *pl*
'gonzo ['gondzo] *sm* simpleton, fool
gorgheggi'are [gorged'dʒare] *vi* to warble;
to trill
'gorgo, ghi *sm* whirlpool
gorgogli'are [gorgoʎ'ʎare] *vi* to gurgle
go'rilla *sm inv* gorilla; (*guardia del corpo*)
bodyguard
'gotta *sf* gout
gover'nante *sm/f* ruler ♦ *sf* (*di bambini*)
governess; (*donna di servizio*) housekeeper
gover'nare *vt* (*stato*) to govern, rule;
(*pilotare, guidare*) to steer; (*bestiame*) to
tend, look after; **governa'tivo, a** *ag*
government *cpd*; **governa'tore** *sm* governor
go'verno *sm* government
gozzovigli'are [gottsoviʎ'ʎare] *vi* to make
merry, carouse
gracchi'are [grak'kjare] *vi* to caw
graci'dare [gratʃi'dare] *vi* to croak
'gracile ['gratʃile] *ag* frail, delicate
gra'dasso *sm* boaster
gradazi'one [gradat'tsjone] *sf* (*sfumatura*)
gradation; **~ alcolica** alcoholic content,
strength
gra'devole *ag* pleasant, agreeable
gradi'mento *sm* pleasure, satisfaction; **è di
suo ~?** is it to your liking?
gradi'nata *sf* flight of steps; (*in teatro,
stadio*) tiers *pl*
gra'dino *sm* step; (*ALPINISMO*) foothold
gra'dire *vt* (*accettare con piacere*) to accept;
(*desiderare*) to wish, like; **gradisce una tazza
di tè?** would you like a cup of tea?; **gra'dito, a** *ag* pleasing; welcome
'grado *sm* (*MAT, FISICA etc*) degree; (*stadio*)
degree, level; (*MIL, sociale*) rank; **essere in
~ di fare** to be in a position to do
gradu'ale *ag* gradual
gradu'are *vt* to grade; **gradu'ato, a** *ag*
(*esercizi*) graded; (*scala, termometro*)
graduated ♦ *sm* (*MIL*) non-commissioned
officer
'graffa *sf* (*gancio*) clip; (*segno grafico*) brace

graffi'are *vt* to scratch
'graffio *sm* scratch
gra'fia *sf* spelling; (*scrittura*) handwriting
'grafica *sf* graphic arts *pl*
'grafico, a, ci, che *ag* graphic ♦ *sm* graph;
(*persona*) graphic designer
gra'migna [gra'miɲɲa] *sf* weed; couch grass
gram'matica, che *sf* grammar;
grammati'cale *ag* grammatical
'grammo *sm* gram(me)
gran *ag vedi* **grande**
'grana *sf* (*granello, di minerali, corpi spezzati*)
grain; (*fam: seccatura*) trouble; (: *soldi*) cash
♦ *sm inv* Parmesan (cheese)
gra'naio *sm* granary, barn
gra'nata *sf* (*proiettile*) grenade
Gran Bre'tagna [-bre'taɲɲa] *sf*: **la ~** Great
Britain
'granchio ['grankjo] *sm* crab; (*fig*) blunder;
prendere un ~ (*fig*) to blunder
grandango'lare *sm* wide-angle lens *sg*
'grande (*qualche volta* **gran** +*C*, **grand'** +*V*) *ag*
(*grosso, largo, vasto*) big, large; (*alto*) tall;
(*lungo*) long; (*in sensi astratti*) great ♦ *sm/f*
(*persona adulta*) adult, grown-up; (*chi ha
ingegno e potenza*) great man/woman; **fare le
cose in ~** to do things in style; **una gran bella
donna** a very beautiful woman; **non è una
gran cosa** o **un gran che** it's nothing special;
non ne so gran che I don't know very much
about it
grandeggi'are [granded'dʒare] *vi* (*emergere
per grandezza*): **~ su** to tower over; (*darsi
arie*) to put on airs
gran'dezza [gran'dettsa] *sf* (*dimensione*)
size; magnitude; (*fig*) greatness; **in ~ naturale**
lifesize
grandi'nare *vb impers* to hail
'grandine *sf* hail
gran'duca, chi *sm* grand duke
gra'nello *sm* (*di cereali, uva*) seed; (*di frutta*)
pip; (*di sabbia, sale etc*) grain
gra'nita *sf* kind of water ice
gra'nito *sm* granite
'grano *sm* (*in quasi tutti i sensi*) grain;
(*frumento*) wheat; (*di rosario, collana*) bead;
~ di pepe peppercorn
gran'turco *sm* maize
'grappa *sf* rough, strong brandy
'grappolo *sm* bunch, cluster
gras'setto *sm* (*TIP*) bold (type)
'grasso, a *ag* fat; (*cibo*) fatty; (*pelle*) greasy;
(*terreno*) rich; (*fig: guadagno, annata*)
plentiful ♦ *sm* (*di persona, animale*) fat;
(*sostanza che unge*) grease; **gras'soccio, a,
ci, ce** *ag* plump
'grata *sf* grating
gra'ticola *sf* grill
gra'tifica, che *sf* bonus

'**gratis** av free, for nothing
grati'**tudine** sf gratitude
'**grato, a** ag grateful; (gradito) pleasant, agreeable
gratta'**capo** sm worry, headache
grattaci'**elo** [gratta'tʃɛlo] sm skyscraper
grat'**tare** vt (pelle) to scratch; (raschiare) to scrape; (pane, formaggio, carote) to grate; (fam: rubare) to pinch ♦ vi (stridere) to grate; (AUT) to grind; ~**rsi** vr to scratch o.s.; **gratta e vinci** ≈ scratch card
grat'**tugia, gie** [grat'tudʒa] sf grater; grattugi'**are** vt to grate; **pane grattugiato** breadcrumbs pl
gra'**tuito, a** ag free; (fig) gratuitous
gra'**vare** vt to burden ♦ vi: ~ **su** to weigh on
'**grave** ag (danno, pericolo, peccato etc) grave, serious; (responsabilità) heavy, grave; (contegno) grave, solemn; (voce, suono) deep, low-pitched; (LING): **accento** ~ grave accent; **un malato** ~ a person who is seriously ill
gravi'**danza** [gravi'dantsa] sf pregnancy
'**gravido, a** ag pregnant
gravità sf seriousness; (anche FISICA) gravity
gra'**voso, a** ag heavy, onerous
'**grazia** ['grattsja] sf grace; (favore) favour; (DIR) pardon; grazi'**are** vt (DIR) to pardon
'**grazie** ['grattsje] escl thank you!; ~ **mille!** o **tante!** o **infinite!** thank you very much!; ~ **a** thanks to
grazi'**oso, a** [gra'tsjoso] ag charming, delightful; (gentile) gracious
'**Grecia** ['grɛtʃa] sf: **la** ~ Greece; '**greco, a, ci, che** ag, sm/f, sm Greek
'**gregge** ['greddʒe] (pl(f) -**i**) sm flock
'**greggio, gi** ['greddʒo] sm (anche: petrolio ~) crude (oil)
grembi'**ule** sm apron; (sopravveste) overall
'**grembo** sm lap; (ventre della madre) womb
gre'**mito, a** ag: ~ (**di**) packed o crowded (with)
'**gretto, a** ag mean, stingy; (fig) narrow-minded
'**greve** ag heavy
'**grezzo, a** ['greddzo] ag raw, unrefined; (diamante) rough, uncut; (tessuto) unbleached
gri'**dare** vi (per chiamare) to shout, cry (out); (strillare) to scream, yell ♦ vt to shout (out), yell (out); ~ **aiuto** to cry o shout for help
'**grido** (pl(m) -**i** o pl(f) -**a**) sm shout, cry; scream, yell; (di animale) cry; **di** ~ famous
'**grigio, a, gi, gie** ['gridʒo] ag, sm grey
'**griglia** ['griʎʎa] sf (per arrostire) grill; (ELETTR) grid; (inferriata) grating; **alla** ~ (CUC) grilled; grigli'**ata** sf (CUC) grill
gril'**letto** sm trigger
'**grillo** sm (ZOOL) cricket; (fig) whim

grimal'**dello** sm picklock
'**grinta** sf grim expression; (SPORT) fighting spirit
'**grinza** ['grintsa] sf crease, wrinkle; (ruga) wrinkle; **non fare una** ~ (fig: ragionamento) to be faultless; **grin'zoso, a** ag creased; wrinkled
gris'**sino** sm bread-stick
'**gronda** sf eaves pl
gron'**daia** sf gutter
gron'**dare** vi to pour; (essere bagnato): ~ **di** to be dripping with ♦ vt to drip with
'**groppa** sf (di animale) back, rump; (fam: dell'uomo) back, shoulders pl
'**groppo** sm tangle; **avere un** ~ **alla gola** (fig) to have a lump in one's throat
gros'**sezza** [gros'settsa] sf size; thickness
gros'**sista, i, e** sm/f (COMM) wholesaler
'**grosso, a** ag big, large; (di spessore) thick; (grossolano: anche fig) coarse; (grave, insopportabile) serious, great; (tempo, mare) rough ♦ sm: **il** ~ **di** the bulk of; **un pezzo** ~ (fig) a VIP, a bigwig; **farla** ~**a** to do something very stupid; **dirle** ~**e** to tell tall stories; **sbagliarsi di** ~ to be completely wrong
grosso'**lano, a** ag rough, coarse; (fig) coarse, crude; (: errore) stupid
grosso'**modo** av roughly
'**grotta** sf cave; grotto
grot'**tesco, a, schi, sche** ag grotesque
grovi'**era** sm o f gruyère (cheese)
gro'**viglio** [gro'viʎʎo] sm tangle; (fig) muddle
gru sf inv crane
'**gruccia, ce** ['gruttʃa] sf (per camminare) crutch; (per abiti) coat-hanger
gru'**gnire** [grup'ɲire] vi to grunt; **gru'gni-to** sm grunt
gru'**gno** ['gruɲɲo] sm snout; (fam: faccia) mug
'**grullo, a** ag silly, stupid
'**grumo** sm (di sangue) clot; (di farina etc) lump
'**gruppo** sm group; ~ **sanguigno** blood group
gruvi'**era** sm o f = **groviera**
guada'**gnare** [gwadaɲ'ɲare] vt (ottenere) to gain; (soldi, stipendio) to earn; (vincere) to win; (raggiungere) to reach
gua'**dagno** [gwa'daɲɲo] sm earnings pl; (COMM) profit; (vantaggio, utile) advantage, gain; ~ **lordo/netto** gross/net earnings pl
gu'**ado** sm ford; **passare a** ~ to ford
gu'**ai** escl: ~ **a te** (o **lui** etc)! woe betide you (o him etc)!
gua'**ina** sf (fodero) sheath; (indumento per donna) girdle
gu'**aio** sm trouble, mishap; (inconveniente) trouble, snag

gua'ire *vi* to whine, yelp
gu'ancia, ce ['gwantʃa] *sf* cheek
guanci'ale [gwan'tʃale] *sm* pillow
gu'anto *sm* glove
gu'arda... *prefisso:* **~'boschi** *sm inv*
forester; **~'caccia** *sm inv* gamekeeper;
~'coste *sm inv* coastguard; (*nave*)
coastguard patrol vessel; **~'linee** *sm inv*
(*SPORT*) linesman
guar'dare *vt* (*con lo sguardo: osservare*) to
look at; (*film, televisione*) to watch;
(*custodire*) to look after, take care of ♦ *vi* to
look; (*badare*): **~ a** to pay attention to;
(*luoghi: esser orientato*): **~ a** to face; **~rsi** *vr*
to look at o.s.; **~rsi da** (*astenersi*) to refrain
from; (*stare in guardia*) to beware of; **~rsi
dal fare** to take care not to do; **guarda di
non sbagliare** try not to make a mistake; **~
a vista qn** to keep a close watch on sb
guarda'roba *sm inv* wardrobe; (*locale*)
cloakroom; **guardarobi'ere, a** *sm/f*
cloakroom attendant
gu'ardia *sf* (*individuo, corpo*) guard;
(*sorveglianza*) watch; **fare la ~ a qc/qn** to
guard sth/sb; **stare in ~** (*fig*) to be on one's
guard; **di ~** (*medico*) on call; **~ carceraria**
(*prison*) warder; **~ del corpo** bodyguard; **~ di
finanza** (*corpo*) customs *pl*; (*persona*) customs
officer; **~ medica** emergency doctor service
guardi'ano, a *sm/f* (*di carcere*) warder; (*di
villa etc*) caretaker; (*di museo*) custodian; (*di
zoo*) keeper; **~ notturno** night watchman
guar'dingo, a, ghi, ghe *ag* wary,
cautious
guardi'ola *sf* porter's lodge; (*MIL*) look-out
tower
guard'rail ['ga:dreil] *sm inv* crash barrier
guarigi'one [gwari'dʒone] *sf* recovery
gua'rire *vt* (*persona, malattia*) to cure;
(*ferita*) to heal ♦ *vi* to recover, be cured; to
heal (up)
guarnigi'one [gwarni'dʒone] *sf* garrison
guar'nire *vt* (*ornare: abiti*) to trim; (*CUC*) to
garnish; **guarnizi'one** *sf* trimming; garnish;
(*TECN*) gasket
guasta'feste *sm/f inv* spoilsport
guas'tare *vt* to spoil, ruin; (*meccanismo*) to
break; **~rsi** *vr* (*cibo*) to go bad; (*meccanismo*)
to break down; (*tempo*) to change for the
worse
gu'asto, a *ag* (*non funzionante*) broken;
(*: telefono etc*) out of order; (*andato a male*)
bad, rotten; (*: dente*) decayed, bad; (*fig:
corrotto*) depraved ♦ *sm* breakdown; (*avaria*)
failure; **~ al motore** engine failure
gu'ercio, a, ci, ce ['gwertʃo] *ag* cross-eyed
gu'erra *sf* war; (*tecnica: atomica, chimica etc*)
warfare; **fare la ~ (a)** to wage war (against);
~ mondiale world war; **guerri'ero, a** *ag*

warlike ♦ *sm* warrior; **guer'riglia** *sf* guerrilla
warfare; **guerrigli'ero** *sm* guerrilla
'gufo *sm* owl
gu'ida *sf* guidebook; (*comando, direzione*)
guidance, direction; (*AUT*) driving; (*tappeto,
di tenda, cassetto*) runner; **~ a destra/sinistra**
(*AUT*) right-/left-hand drive; **~ telefonica**
telephone directory; **~ turistica** tourist guide
gui'dare *vt* to guide; (*squadra, rivolta*) to
lead; (*auto*) to drive; (*aereo, nave*) to pilot;
sai ~? can you drive?; **guida'tore, trice**
sm/f (*conducente*) driver
guin'zaglio [gwin'tsaʎʎo] *sm* leash, lead
gu'isa *sf:* **a ~ di** like, in the manner of
guiz'zare [gwit'tsare] *vi* to dart; to flicker; to
leap
'guscio ['guʃʃo] *sm* shell
gus'tare *vt* (*cibi*) to taste; (: *assaporare con
piacere*) to enjoy, savour; (*fig*) to enjoy,
appreciate ♦ *vi*: **~ a** to please; **non mi gusta
affatto** I don't like it at all
'gusto *sm* taste; (*sapore*) flavour; (*godimento*)
enjoyment; **al ~ di fragola** strawberry-
flavoured; **mangiare di ~** to eat heartily;
prenderci ~: ci ha preso ~ he's acquired a
taste for it, he's got to like it; **gus'toso, a**
ag tasty; (*fig*) agreeable

H, h

h *abbr* = **ora; altezza**
ha *etc* [a] *vb vedi* **avere**
ha'cker [hæ'kə*] *sm inv* hacker
hall [hɔl] *sf inv* hall, foyer
'handicap ['handikap] *sm inv* handicap;
handicap'pato, a *ag* handicapped ♦ *sm/f*
handicapped person, disabled person
'hanno ['anno] *vb vedi* **avere**
'hascisc ['haʃiʃ] *sm* hashish
'herpes ['ɛrpes] *sm* (*MED*) herpes *sg*; **~ zoster**
shingles *sg*
ho [ɔ] *vb vedi* **avere**
'hobby ['hɔbi] *sm inv* hobby
'hockey ['hɔki] *sm* hockey; **~ su ghiaccio** ice
hockey
'hostess ['houstis] *sf inv* air hostess (*BRIT*) o
stewardess
ho'tel *sm inv* hotel

I, i

i *det mpl* the
i'ato *sm* hiatus
ibernazi'one [ibernat'tsjone] *sf* hibernation
'ibrido, a *ag, sm* hybrid
Id'dio *sm* God
i'dea *sf* idea; (*opinione*) opinion, view; (*ideale*)

ideal; **dare l'~ di** to seem, look like; **~ fissa** obsession; **neanche** o **neppure per ~!** certainly not!

ide'ale *ag, sm* ideal

ide'are *vt* (*immaginare*) to think up, conceive; (*progettare*) to plan

i'dentico, a, ci, che *ag* identical

identifi'care *vt* to identify; **identificazi'one** *sf* identification

identità *sf inv* identity

ideolo'gia, 'gie [ideolo'dʒia] *sf* ideology

idi'oma, i *sm* idiom, language; **idio'matico, a, ci, che** *ag* idiomatic; **frase idiomatica** idiom

idi'ota, i, e *ag* idiotic ♦ *sm/f* idiot

idola'trare *vt* to worship; (*fig*) to idolize

'idolo *sm* idol

idoneità *sf* suitability

i'doneo, a *ag*: **~ a** suitable for, fit for; (MIL) fit for; (*qualificato*) qualified for

i'drante *sm* hydrant

idra'tante *ag* moisturizing ♦ *sm* moisturizer

i'draulica *sf* hydraulics *sg*

i'draulico, a, ci, che *ag* hydraulic ♦ *sm* plumber

idroe'lettrico, a, ci, che *ag* hydroelectric

i'drofilo, a *ag vedi* **cotone**

i'drogeno [i'drɔdʒeno] *sm* hydrogen

idros'calo *sm* seaplane base

idrovo'lante *sm* seaplane

i'ena *sf* hyena

i'eri *av, sm* yesterday; **il giornale di ~** yesterday's paper; **~ l'altro** the day before yesterday; **~ sera** yesterday evening

igi'ene [i'dʒɛne] *sf* hygiene; **~ pubblica** public health; **igi'enico, a, ci, che** *ag* hygienic; (*salubre*) healthy

i'gnaro, a [iɲ'naro] *ag*: **~ di** unaware of, ignorant of

i'gnobile [iɲ'nɔbile] *ag* despicable, vile

igno'rante [iɲɲo'rante] *ag* ignorant

igno'rare [iɲɲo'rare] *vt* (*non sapere, conoscere*) to be ignorant o unaware of, not to know; (*fingere di non vedere, sentire*) to ignore

i'gnoto, a [iɲ'nɔto] *ag* unknown

PAROLA CHIAVE

il (*pl* (*m*) **i**; *diventa* **lo** (*pl* **gli**) *davanti a s impura, gn, pn, ps, x, z;* f la (*pl* **le**)) *det m*

1 the; **~ libro/lo studente/l'acqua** the book/the student/the water; **gli scolari** the pupils

2 (*astrazione*): **~ coraggio/l'amore/la giovinezza** courage/love/youth

3 (*tempo*): **~ mattino/la sera** in the morning/evening; **~ venerdì** *etc* (*abitualmente*) on Fridays *etc*; (*quel giorno*) on (the) Friday *etc*; **la settimana prossima** next week

4 (*distributivo*) a, an; **2.500 lire ~ chilo/paio**

2,500 lire a o per kilo/pair

5 (*partitivo*) some, any; **hai messo lo zucchero?** have you added sugar?; **hai comprato ~ latte?** did you buy (some o any) milk?

6 (*possesso*): **aprire gli occhi** to open one's eyes; **rompersi la gamba** to break one's leg; **avere i capelli neri/~ naso rosso** to have dark hair/a red nose

7 (*con nomi propri*): **~ Petrarca** Petrarch; **~ Presidente Clinton** President Clinton; **dov'è la Francesca?** where's Francesca?

8 (*con nomi geografici*): **~ Tevere** the Tiber; **l'Italia** Italy; **~ Regno Unito** the United Kingdom; **l'Everest** Everest

---

'ilare *ag* cheerful; **ilarità** *sf* hilarity, mirth

illazi'one [illat'tsjone] *sf* inference, deduction

ille'gale *ag* illegal

illeg'gibile [illed'dʒibile] *ag* illegible

ille'gittimo, a [ille'dʒittimo] *ag* illegitimate

il'leso, a *ag* unhurt, unharmed

illi'bato, a *ag*: **donna ~a** virgin

illimi'tato, a *ag* boundless; unlimited

ill.mo *abbr* = **illustrissimo**

il'ludere *vt* to deceive, delude; **~rsi** *vr* to deceive o.s., delude o.s.

illumi'nare *vt* to light up, illuminate; (*fig*) to enlighten; **~rsi** *vr* to light up; **~ a giorno** to floodlight; **illuminazi'one** *sf* lighting; illumination; floodlighting; (*fig*) flash of inspiration

illusi'one *sf* illusion; **farsi delle ~i** to delude o.s.

illusio'nismo *sm* conjuring

il'luso, a *pp di* **illudere**

illus'trare *vt* to illustrate; **illustra'tivo, a** *ag* illustrative; **illustrazi'one** *sf* illustration

il'lustre *ag* eminent, renowned; **illus'trissimo, a** *ag* (*negli indirizzi*) very revered

imbacuc'care *vt* to wrap up; **~rsi** *vr* to wrap up

imbal'laggio [imbal'laddʒo] *sm* packing *no pl*

imbal'lare *vt* to pack; (AUT) to race; **~rsi** *vr* (AUT) to race

imbalsa'mare *vt* to embalm

imbambo'lato, a *ag* (*sguardo*) vacant, blank

imban'dire *vt*: **~ un pranzo** to prepare a lavish meal

imbaraz'zare [imbarat'tsare] *vt* (*mettere a disagio*) to embarrass; (*ostacolare: movimenti*) to hamper

imba'razzo [imba'rattso] *sm* (*disagio*) embarrassment; (*perplessità*) puzzlement, bewilderment; **~ di stomaco** indigestion

imbarca'dero *sm* landing stage

imbar'care vt (passeggeri) to embark; (merci) to load; **~rsi** vr: **~rsi su** to board; **~rsi per l'America** to sail for America; **~rsi in** (fig: affare etc) to embark on

imbarcazi'one [imbarkat'tsjone] sf (small) boat, (small) craft inv; **~ di salvataggio** lifeboat

im'barco, chi sm embarkation; loading; boarding; (banchina) landing stage

imbas'tire vt (cucire) to tack; (fig: abbozzare) to sketch, outline

im'battersi vr: **~ in** (incontrare) to bump o run into

imbat'tibile ag unbeatable, invincible

imbavagli'are [imbavaʎ'ʎare] vt to gag

imbec'cata sf (TEATRO) prompt

imbe'cille [imbe'tʃille] ag idiotic ♦ sm/f idiot; (MED) imbecile

imbel'lire vt to adorn, embellish ♦ vi to grow more beautiful

im'berbe ag beardless

im'bevere vt to soak; **~rsi** vr: **~rsi di** to soak up, absorb

imbian'care vt to whiten; (muro) to whitewash ♦ vi to become o turn white

imbian'chino [imbjan'kino] sm (house) painter, painter and decorator

imboc'care vt (bambino) to feed; (entrare: strada) to enter, turn into

imbocca'tura sf mouth; (di strada, porto) entrance; (MUS, del morso) mouthpiece

im'bocco, chi sm entrance

imbos'care vt to hide; **~rsi** vr (MIL) to evade military service

imbos'cata sf ambush

imbottigli'are [imbottiʎ'ʎare] vt to bottle; (NAUT) to blockade; (MIL) to hem in; **~rsi** vr to be stuck in a traffic jam

imbot'tire vt to stuff; (giacca) to pad; **imbot'tita** sf quilt; **imbot'tito, a** ag stuffed; (giacca) padded; **panino imbottito** filled roll; **imbotti'tura** sf stuffing; padding

imbrat'tare vt to dirty, smear, daub

imbrigli'are [imbriʎ'ʎare] vt to bridle

imbroc'care vt (fig) to guess correctly

imbrogli'are [imbroʎ'ʎare] vt to mix up; (fig: raggirare) to deceive, cheat; (: confondere) to confuse, mix up; **~rsi** vr to get tangled; (fig) to become confused; **im'broglio** sm (groviglio) tangle; (situazione confusa) mess; (truffa) swindle, trick; **imbrogli'one, a** sm/f cheat, swindler

imbronci'ato, a ag sulky

imbru'nire vi, vb impers to grow dark; **all'~** at dusk

imbrut'tire vt to make ugly ♦ vi to become ugly

imbu'care vt to post

imbur'rare vt to butter

im'buto sm funnel

imi'tare vt to imitate; (riprodurre) to copy; (assomigliare) to look like; **imitazi'one** sf imitation

immaco'lato, a ag spotless; immaculate

immagazzi'nare [immagaddzi'nare] vt to store

immagi'nare [immadʒi'nare] vt to imagine; (supporre) to suppose; (inventare) to invent; **s'immagini!** don't mention it!, not at all!; **immagi'nario, a** ag imaginary; **immagi- nazi'one** sf imagination; (cosa immaginata) fancy

im'magine [im'madʒine] sf image; (rappresentazione grafica, mentale) picture

imman'cabile ag certain; unfailing

im'mane ag (smisurato) enormous; (spaventoso) terrible

immangi'abile [imman'dʒabile] ag inedible

immatrico'lare vt to register; **~rsi** vr (INS) to matriculate, enrol; **immatricolazi'one** sf registration; matriculation, enrolment

imma'turo, a ag (frutto) unripe; (persona) immature; (prematuro) premature

immedesi'marsi vr: **~ in** to identify with

immediata'mente av immediately, at once

immedi'ato, a ag immediate

im'memore ag: **~ di** forgetful of

im'menso, a ag immense

im'mergere [im'merdʒere] vt to immerse, plunge; **~rsi** vr to plunge; (sommergibile) to dive, submerge; (dedicarsi a): **~rsi in** to immerse o.s. in

immeri'tato, a ag undeserved

immeri'tevole ag undeserving, unworthy

immersi'one sf immersion; (di sommergibile) submersion, dive; (di palombaro) dive

im'merso, a pp di **immergere**

im'mettere vt: **~ (in)** to introduce (into); **~ dati in un computer** to enter data on a computer

immi'grato, a sm/f immigrant; **immigra- zi'one** sf immigration

immi'nente ag imminent

immischi'are [immis'kjare] vt: **~ qn in** to involve sb in; **~rsi** vr to interfere o meddle in

immissi'one sf (di aria, gas) intake; **~ di dati** (INFORM) data entry

im'mobile ag motionless, still; **~i** smpl (anche: beni **~i**) real estate sg; **immobili'are** ag (DIR) property cpd; **immobilità** sf stillness; immobility

immo'desto, a ag immodest

immo'lare vt to sacrifice, immolate

immon'dizia [immon'dittsja] sf dirt, filth; (spesso al pl: spazzatura, rifiuti) rubbish no pl, refuse no pl

im'mondo, a ag filthy, foul

immo'rale ag immoral

immor'tale ag immortal

im'mune ag (esente) exempt; (MED, DIR) immune; **immunità** sf immunity; **immunità parlamentare** parliamentary privilege

immu'tabile ag immutable; unchanging

impacchet'tare [impakket'tare] vt to pack up

impacci'are [impat'tʃare] vt to hinder, hamper; **impacci'ato, a** ag awkward, clumsy; (imbarazzato) embarrassed; **im'paccio** sm obstacle; (imbarazzo) embarrassment; (situazione imbarazzante) awkward situation

im'pacco, chi sm (MED) compress

impadro'nirsi vr: ~ **di** to seize, take possession of; (fig: apprendere a fondo) to master

impa'gabile ag priceless

impagi'nare [impadʒi'nare] vt (TIP) to paginate, page (up)

impagli'are [impaʎ'ʎare] vt to stuff (with straw)

impa'lato, a ag (fig) stiff as a board

impalca'tura sf scaffolding

impalli'dire vi to turn pale; (fig) to fade

impa'nare vt (CUC) to dip in breadcrumbs

impanta'narsi vr to sink (in the mud); (fig) to get bogged down

impappi'narsi vr to stammer, falter

impa'rare vt to learn

imparen'tarsi vr: ~ **con** to marry into

'impari ag inv (disuguale) unequal; (dispari) odd

impar'tire vt to bestow, give

imparzi'ale [impar'tsjale] ag impartial, unbiased

impas'sibile ag impassive

impas'tare vt (pasta) to knead

im'pasto sm (l'impastare: di pane) kneading; (: di cemento) mixing; (pasta) dough; (anche fig) mixture

im'patto sm impact

impau'rire vt to scare, frighten ♦ vi (anche: ~rsi) to become scared o frightened

im'pavido, a ag intrepid, fearless

impazi'ente [impat'tsjɛnte] ag impatient; **impazi'enza** sf impatience

impaz'zata [impat'tsata] sf: **all'~** (precipitosamente) at breakneck speed

impaz'zire [impat'tsire] vi to go mad; ~ **per qn/qc** to be crazy about sb/sth

impec'cabile ag impeccable

impedi'mento sm obstacle, hindrance

impe'dire vt (vietare): ~ **a qn di fare** to prevent sb from doing; (ostruire) to obstruct; (impacciare) to hamper, hinder

impe'gnare [impeɲ'ɲare] vt (dare in pegno) to pawn; (onore etc) to pledge; (prenotare) to book, reserve; (obbligare) to oblige; (occupare) to keep busy; (MIL: nemico) to engage; ~**rsi** vr (vincolarsi): ~**rsi a fare** to undertake to do; (mettersi risolutamente): ~**rsi in qc** to devote o.s. to sth; ~**rsi con qn** (accordarsi) to come to an agreement with sb; **impegna'tivo, a** ag binding; (lavoro) demanding, exacting; **impe'gnato, a** ag (occupato) busy; (fig: romanzo, autore) committed, engagé

im'pegno [im'peɲɲo] sm (obbligo) obligation; (promessa) promise, pledge; (zelo) diligence, zeal; (compito, d'autore) commitment

impel'lente ag pressing, urgent

impene'trabile ag impenetrable

impen'narsi vr (cavallo) to rear up; (AER) to nose up; (fig) to bridle

impen'sato, a ag unforeseen, unexpected

impensie'rire vt to worry; ~**rsi** vr to worry

impe'rare vi (anche fig) to reign, rule

impera'tivo, a ag, sm imperative

impera'tore, 'trice sm/f emperor/empress

imperdo'nabile ag unforgivable, unpardonable

imper'fetto, a ag imperfect ♦ sm (LING) imperfect (tense); **imperfezi'one** sf imperfection

imperi'ale ag imperial

imperi'oso, a ag (persona) imperious; (motivo, esigenza) urgent, pressing

impe'rizia [impe'rittsja] sf lack of experience

imperma'lirsi vr to take offence

imperme'abile ag waterproof ♦ sm raincoat

imperni'are vt: ~ **qc su** to hinge sth on; (fig) to base sth on; ~**rsi** vr (fig): ~**rsi su** to be based on

im'pero sm empire; (forza, autorità) rule, control

imperscru'tabile ag inscrutable

imperso'nale ag impersonal

imperso'nare vt to personify; (TEATRO) to play, act (the part of)

imperter'rito, a ag fearless, undaunted; impassive

imperti'nente ag impertinent

imperver'sare vi to rage

'impeto sm (moto, forza) force, impetus; (assalto) onslaught; (fig: impulso) impulse; (: slancio) transport; **con ~** energetically, vehemently

impet'tito, a ag stiff, erect

impetu'oso, a ag (vento) strong, raging; (persona) impetuous

impian'tare vt (motore) to install; (azienda, discussione) to establish, start

impi'anto sm (installazione) installation; (apparecchiature) plant; (sistema) system;

~ **elettrico** wiring; ~ **sportivo** sports complex; ~**i di risalita** (SCI) ski lifts

impiastricci'are [impjastrit'tʃare] vt = **impiastrare**

impi'astro sm poultice

impic'care vt to hang; ~**rsi** vr to hang o.s.

impicci'are [impit'tʃare] vt to hinder, hamper; ~**rsi** vr to meddle, interfere; **im'piccio** sm (ostacolo) hindrance; (seccatura) trouble, bother; (affare imbrogliato) mess; **essere d'impiccio** to be in the way

impie'gare vt (usare) to use, employ; (spendere: denaro, tempo) to spend; (investire) to invest; **impie'gato, a** sm/f employee

impi'ego, ghi sm (uso) use; (occupazione) employment; (posto di lavoro) (regular) job, post; (ECON) investment

impieto'sire vt to move to pity; ~**rsi** vr to be moved to pity

impie'trire vt (fig) to petrify

impigli'are [impiʎ'ʎare] vt to catch, entangle; ~**rsi** vr to get caught up o entangled

impi'grire vt to make lazy ♦ vi (anche: ~rsi) to grow lazy

impli'care vt to imply; (coinvolgere) to involve; **implicazi'one** sf implication

im'plicito, a [im'plitʃito] ag implicit

implo'rare vt to implore; (pietà etc) to beg for

impolve'rare vt to cover with dust; ~**rsi** vr to get dusty

impo'nente ag imposing, impressive

impo'nibile ag taxable ♦ sm taxable income

impopo'lare ag unpopular

im'porre vt to impose; (costringere) to force, make; (far valere) to impose, enforce; **imporsi** vr (persona) to assert o.s.; (cosa: rendersi necessario) to become necessary; (aver successo: moda, attore) to become popular; ~ **a qn di fare** to force sb to do, make sb do

impor'tante ag important; **impor'tanza** sf importance; **dare importanza a qc** to attach importance to sth; **darsi importanza** to give o.s. airs

impor'tare vt (introdurre dall'estero) to import ♦ vi to matter, be important ♦ vb impers (essere necessario) to be necessary; (interessare) to matter; **non importa!** it doesn't matter!; **non me ne importa!** I don't care!; **importazi'one** sf importation; (merci importate) imports pl

im'porto sm (totale) amount

importu'nare vt to bother

impor'tuno, a ag irksome, annoying

imposizi'one [impozit'tsjone] sf imposition; order, command; (onere, imposta) tax

imposses'sarsi vr: ~ **di** to seize, take possession of

impos'sibile ag impossible; **fare l'~** to do one's utmost, do all one can; **impossibilità** sf impossibility; **essere nell'impossibilità di fare qc** to be unable to do sth

im'posta sf (di finestra) shutter; (tassa) tax; ~ **sul reddito** income tax; ~ **sul valore aggiunto** value added tax (BRIT), sales tax (US)

impos'tare vt (imbucare) to post; (preparare) to plan, set out; (avviare) to begin, start off; (voce) to pitch

im'posto, a pp di **imporre**

impo'tente ag weak, powerless; (anche MED) impotent

impove'rire vt to impoverish ♦ vi (anche: ~rsi) to become poor

imprati'cabile ag (strada) impassable; (campo da gioco) unplayable

imprati'chirsi [imprati'kirsi] vr: ~ **in qc** to practise (BRIT) o practice (US) sth

impre'gnare [impreɲ'ɲare] vt: ~ (**di**) (imbevere) to soak o impregnate (with); (riempire: anche fig) to fill (with)

imprendi'tore sm (industriale) entrepreneur; (appaltatore) contractor; **piccolo** ~ small businessman

im'presa sf (iniziativa) enterprise; (azione) exploit; (azienda) firm, concern

impre'sario sm (TEATRO) manager, impresario; ~ **di pompe funebri** funeral director

imprescin'dibile [impreʃʃin'dibile] ag not to be ignored

impressio'nante ag impressive; upsetting

impressio'nare vt to impress; (turbare) to upset; (FOT) to expose; ~**rsi** vr to be easily upset

impressi'one sf impression; (fig: sensazione) sensation, feeling; (stampa) printing; **fare** ~ (colpire) to impress; (turbare) to frighten, upset; **fare buona/cattiva ~ a** to make a good/bad impression on

im'presso, a pp di **imprimere**

impres'tare vt: ~ **qc a qn** to lend sth to sb

impreve'dibile ag unforeseeable; (persona) unpredictable

imprevi'dente ag lacking in foresight

impre'visto, a ag unexpected, unforeseen ♦ sm unforeseen event; **salvo ~i** unless anything unexpected happens

imprigio'nare [imprid3o'nare] vt to imprison

im'primere vt (anche fig) to impress, stamp; (comunicare: movimento) to transmit, give

impro'babile ag improbable, unlikely

im'pronta sf imprint, impression, sign; (di piede, mano) print; (fig) mark, stamp; ~ **digitale** fingerprint

impro'perio *sm* insult
im'proprio, a *ag* improper; **arma ~a** offensive weapon
improvvisa'mente *av* suddenly; unexpectedly
improvvi'sare *vt* to improvise; **~rsi** *vr*: **~rsi cuoco** to (decide to) act as cook; **improvvi'sata** *sf* (pleasant) surprise
improv'viso, a *ag* (*imprevisto*) unexpected; (*subitaneo*) sudden; **all'~** unexpectedly; suddenly
impru'dente *ag* unwise, rash
impu'dente *ag* impudent
impu'dico, a, chi, che *ag* immodest
impu'gnare [impuɲ'ɲare] *vt* to grasp, grip; (*DIR*) to contest
impul'sivo, a *ag* impulsive
im'pulso *sm* impulse
impun'tarsi *vr* to stop dead, refuse to budge; (*fig*) to be obstinate
impu'tare *vt* (*ascrivere*): **~ qc a** to attribute sth to; (*DIR: accusare*): **~ qn di** to charge sb with, accuse sb of; **impu'tato, a** *sm/f* (*DIR*) accused, defendant; **imputazi'one** *sf* (*DIR*) charge
imputri'dire *vi* to rot

PAROLA CHIAVE

in (*in+il* = **nel**, *in+lo* = **nello**, *in+l'* = **nell'**, *in+la* = **nella**, *in+i* = **nei**, *in+gli* = **negli**, *in+le* = **nelle**) *prep* **1** (*stato in luogo*) in; **vivere ~ Italia/città** to live in Italy/town; **essere ~ casa/ufficio** to be at home/the office; **se fossi ~ te** if I were you
2 (*moto a luogo*) to; (: *dentro*) into; **andare ~ Germania/città** to go to Germany/town; **andare ~ ufficio** to go to the office; **entrare ~ macchina/casa** to get into the car/go into the house
3 (*tempo*) in; **nel 1989** in 1989; **~ giugno/estate** in June/summer
4 (*modo, maniera*) in; **~ silenzio** in silence; **~ abito da sera** in evening dress; **~ guerra** at war; **~ vacanza** on holiday; **Maria Bianchi ~ Rossi** Maria Rossi née Bianchi
5 (*mezzo*) by; **viaggiare ~ autobus/treno** to travel by bus/train
6 (*materia*) made of; **~ marmo** made of marble, marble *cpd*; **una collana ~ oro** a gold necklace
7 (*misura*) in; **siamo ~ quattro** there are four of us; **~ tutto** in all
8 (*fine*): **dare ~ dono** to give as a gift; **spende tutto ~ alcool** he spends all his money on drink; **~ onore di** in honour of

---

inabi'tabile *ag* uninhabitable
inacces'sibile [inattʃes'sibile] *ag* (*luogo*) inaccessible; (*persona*) unapproachable

inaccet'tabile [inattʃet'tabile] *ag* unacceptable
ina'datto, a *ag*: **~ (a)** unsuitable *o* unfit (for)
inadegu'ato, a *ag* inadequate
inadempi'enza [inadem'pjɛntsa] *sf*: **~ (a)** non-fulfilment (of)
inaffer'rabile *ag* elusive; (*concetto, senso*) difficult to grasp
inalbe'rarsi *vr* (*fig*) to flare up, fly off the handle
inalte'rabile *ag* unchangeable; (*colore*) fast, permanent; (*affetto*) constant
inalte'rato, a *ag* unchanged
inami'dato, a *ag* starched
inani'mato, a *ag* inanimate; (*senza vita: corpo*) lifeless
inappa'gabile *ag* insatiable
inappel'labile *ag* (*decisione*) final, irrevocable; (*DIR*) final, not open to appeal
inappe'tenza [inappe'tɛntsa] *sf* (*MED*) lack of appetite
inappun'tabile *ag* irreproachable
inar'care *vt* (*schiena*) to arch; (*sopracciglia*) to raise; **~rsi** *vr* to arch
inari'dire *vt* to make arid, dry up ♦ *vi* (*anche*: **~rsi**) to dry up, become arid
inaspet'tato, a *ag* unexpected
inas'prire *vt* (*disciplina*) to tighten up, make harsher; (*carattere*) to embitter; **~rsi** *vr* to become harsher; to become bitter; to become worse
inattac'cabile *ag* (*anche fig*) unassailable; (*alibi*) cast-iron
inatten'dibile *ag* unreliable
inat'teso, a *ag* unexpected
inattu'abile *ag* impracticable
inau'dito, a *ag* unheard of
inaugu'rare *vt* to inaugurate, open; (*monumento*) to unveil
inavver'tenza [inavver'tɛntsa] *sf* carelessness, inadvertence
incagli'are [inkaʎ'ʎare] *vi* (*NAUT: anche*: **~rsi**) to run aground
incal'lito, a *ag* calloused; (*fig*) hardened, inveterate; (: *insensibile*) hard
incal'zare [inkal'tsare] *vt* to follow *o* pursue closely; (*fig*) to press ♦ *vi* (*urgere*) to be pressing; (*essere imminente*) to be imminent
incammi'nare *vt* (*fig: avviare*) to start up; **~rsi** *vr* to set off
incande'scente [inkandeʃ'ʃɛnte] *ag* incandescent, white-hot
incan'tare *vt* to enchant, bewitch; **~rsi** *vr* (*rimanere intontito*) to be spellbound; to be in a daze; (*meccanismo: bloccarsi*) to jam; **incanta'tore, 'trice** *ag* enchanting, bewitching ♦ *sm/f* enchanter/enchantress; **incan'tesimo** *sm* spell, charm; **incan'tevole** *ag* charming, enchanting

in'canto sm spell, charm, enchantment; (*asta*) auction; **come per ~** as if by magic; **mettere all'~** to put up for auction

inca'pace [inka'patʃe] ag incapable; **incapacità** sf inability; (*DIR*) incapacity

incapo'nirsi vr to be stubborn, be determined

incap'pare vi: **~ in qc/qn** (*anche fig*) to run into sth/sb

incapricci'arsi [inkaprit'tʃarsi] vr: **~ di** to take a fancy to o for

incapsu'lare vt (*dente*) to crown

incarce'rare [inkartʃe'rare] vt to imprison

incari'care vt: **~ qn di fare** to give sb the responsibility of doing; **~rsi di** to take care o charge of; **incari'cato, a** ag: **incaricato (di)** in charge (of), responsible (for) ♦ sm/f delegate, representative; **professore incaricato** teacher with a temporary appointment

in'carico, chi sm task, job

incar'nare vt to embody; **~rsi** vr to be embodied; (*REL*) to become incarnate

incarta'mento sm dossier, file

incar'tare vt to wrap (in paper)

incas'sare vt (*merce*) to pack (in cases); (*gemma: incastonare*) to set; (*ECON: riscuotere*) to collect; (*PUGILATO: colpi*) to take, stand up to; **in'casso** sm cashing, encashment; (*introito*) takings pl

incasto'nare vt to set; **incastona'tura** sf setting

incas'trare vt to fit in, insert; (*fig: intrappolare*) to catch; **~rsi** vr (*combaciare*) to fit together; (*restare bloccato*) to become stuck; **in'castro** sm slot, groove; (*punto di unione*) joint

incate'nare vt to chain up

incatra'mare vt to tar

incatti'vire vt to make wicked; **~rsi** vr to turn nasty

in'cauto, a ag imprudent, rash

inca'vare vt to hollow out; **in'cavo** sm hollow; (*solco*) groove

incendi'are [intʃen'djare] vt to set fire to; **~rsi** vr to catch fire, burst into flames

incendi'ario, a [intʃen'djarjo] ag incendiary ♦ sm/f arsonist

in'cendio [in'tʃendjo] sm fire

incene'rire [intʃene'rire] vt to burn to ashes, incinerate; (*cadavere*) to cremate; **~rsi** vr to be burnt to ashes

in'censo [in'tʃenso] sm incense

incensu'rato, a [intʃensu'rato] ag (*DIR*): **essere ~** to have a clean record

incen'tivo [intʃen'tivo] sm incentive

incep'pare [intʃep'pare] vt to obstruct, hamper; **~rsi** vr to jam

ince'rata [intʃe'rata] sf (*tela*) tarpaulin; (*impermeabile*) oilskins pl

incer'tezza [intʃer'tettsa] sf uncertainty

in'certo, a [in'tʃerto] ag uncertain; (*irresoluto*) undecided, hesitating ♦ sm uncertainty

in'cetta [in'tʃetta] sf buying up; **fare ~ di qc** to buy up sth

inchi'esta [in'kjesta] sf investigation, inquiry

inchi'nare [inki'nare] vt to bow; **~rsi** vr to bend down; (*per riverenza*) to bow; (: *donna*) to curtsy; **in'chino** sm bow; curtsy

inchio'dare [inkjo'dare] vt to nail (down); **~ la macchina** (*AUT*) to jam on the brakes

inchi'ostro [in'kjɔstro] sm ink; **~ simpatico** invisible ink

inciam'pare [intʃam'pare] vi to trip, stumble

inci'ampo [in'tʃampo] sm obstacle; **essere d'~ a qn** (*fig*) to be in sb's way

inci'dente [intʃi'dɛnte] sm accident; **~ d'auto** car accident

inci'denza [intʃi'dɛntsa] sf incidence; **avere una forte ~ su qc** to affect sth greatly

in'cidere [in'tʃidere] vi: **~ su** to bear upon, affect ♦ vt (*tagliare incavando*) to cut into; (*ARTE*) to engrave; to etch; (*canzone*) to record

in'cinta [in'tʃinta] ag f pregnant

incipri'are [intʃi'prjare] vt to powder

in'circa [in'tʃirka] av: **all'~** more or less, very nearly

incisi'one [intʃi'zjone] sf cut; (*disegno*) engraving; etching; (*registrazione*) recording; (*MED*) incision

in'ciso, a [in'tʃizo] pp di **incidere** ♦ sm: **per ~** incidentally, by the way

inci'tare [intʃi'tare] vt to incite

inci'vile [intʃi'vile] ag uncivilized; (*villano*) impolite

incl. abbr (= *incluso*) encl.

incli'nare vt to tilt; **~rsi** vr (*barca*) to list; (*aereo*) to bank; **incli'nato, a** ag sloping; **inclinazi'one** sf slope; (*fig*) inclination, tendency; **in'cline** ag: **incline a** inclined to

in'cludere vt to include; (*accludere*) to enclose; **in'cluso, a** pp di **includere** ♦ ag included; enclosed

incoe'rente ag incoherent; (*contraddittorio*) inconsistent

in'cognita [in'koɲɲita] sf (*MAT, fig*) unknown quantity

in'cognito, a [in'koɲɲito] ag unknown ♦ sm: **in ~** incognito

incol'lare vt to glue, gum; (*unire con colla*) to stick together

incolon'nare vt to draw up in columns

inco'lore ag colourless

incol'pare vt: **~ qn di** to charge sb with

in'colto, a ag (*terreno*) uncultivated; (*trascurato: capelli*) neglected; (*persona*) uneducated in'colume *ag* safe and sound, unhurt

incom'benza [inkom'bentsa] *sf* duty, task

in'combere *vi* (*sovrastare minacciando*): ~ su to threaten, hang over

incominci'are [inkomin'tʃare] *vi, vt* to begin, start

in'comodo *sm* inconvenience

incompe'tente *ag* incompetent

incompi'uto, a *ag* unfinished, incomplete

incom'pleto, a *ag* incomplete

incompren'sibile *ag* incomprehensible

incom'preso, a *ag* not understood; misunderstood

inconce'pibile [inkontʃe'pibile] *ag* inconceivable

inconcili'abile [inkontʃi'ljabile] *ag* irreconcilable

inconclu'dente *ag* inconclusive; (*persona*) ineffectual

incondizio'nato, a [inkondittsjo'nato] *ag* unconditional

inconfu'tabile *ag* irrefutable

incongru'ente *ag* inconsistent

inconsa'pevole *ag*: ~ di unaware of, ignorant of

in'conscio, a, sci, sce [in'kɔnʃo] *ag* unconscious ♦ *sm* (*PSIC*): l'~ the unconscious

inconsis'tente *ag* insubstantial; unfounded

inconsu'eto, a *ag* unusual

incon'sulto, a *ag* rash

incon'trare *vt* to meet; (*difficoltà*) to meet with; ~rsi *vr* to meet

incontras'tabile *ag* incontrovertible, indisputable

in'contro *av*: ~ a (*verso*) towards ♦ *sm* meeting; (*SPORT*) match; meeting; ~ di calcio football match

inconveni'ente *sm* drawback, snag

incoraggia'mento [inkoraddʒa'mento] *sm* encouragement

incoraggi'are [inkorad'dʒare] *vt* to encourage

incornici'are [inkorni'tʃare] *vt* to frame

incoro'nare *vt* to crown; incoronazi'one *sf* coronation

incorpo'rare *vt* to incorporate; (*fig: annettere*) to annex

in'correre *vi*: ~ in to meet with, run into

incosci'ente [inkoʃʃente] *ag* (*inconscio*) unconscious; (*irresponsabile*) reckless, thoughtless; incosci'enza *sf* unconsciousness; recklessness, thoughtlessness

incre'dibile *ag* incredible, unbelievable

in'credulo, a *ag* incredulous, disbelieving

incremen'tare *vt* to increase; (*dar sviluppo a*) to promote

incre'mento *sm* (*sviluppo*) development; (*aumento numerico*) increase, growth

incresci'oso, a [inkreʃ'ʃoso] *ag* (*incidente etc*) regrettable

incres'parsi *vr* (*acqua*) to ripple; (*capelli*) to go frizzy; (*pelle, tessuto*) to wrinkle

incrimi'nare *vt* (*DIR*) to charge

incri'nare *vt* to crack; (*fig: rapporti, amicizia*) to cause to deteriorate; ~rsi *vr* to crack; to deteriorate; incrina'tura *sf* crack; (*fig*) rift

incroci'are [inkro'tʃare] *vt* to cross; (*incontrare*) to meet ♦ *vi* (*NAUT, AER*) to cruise; ~rsi *vr* (*strade*) to cross, intersect; (*persone, veicoli*) to pass each other; ~ le braccia/le gambe to fold one's arms/cross one's legs; incrocia'tore *sm* cruiser

in'crocio [in'krotʃo] *sm* (*anche FERR*) crossing; (*di strade*) crossroads

incros'tare *vt* to encrust

incuba'trice [inkuba'tritʃe] *sf* incubator

'incubo *sm* nightmare

in'cudine *sf* anvil

incu'rante *ag*: ~ (di) heedless (of), careless (of)

incurio'sire *vt* to make curious; ~rsi *vr* to become curious

incursi'one *sf* raid

incur'vare *vt* to bend, curve; ~rsi *vr* to bend, curve

in'cusso, a *pp di* incutere

incusto'dito, a *ag* unguarded, unattended

in'cutere *vt*: ~ timore/rispetto a qn to strike fear into sb/command sb's respect

'indaco *sm* indigo

indaffa'rato, a *ag* busy

inda'gare *vt* to investigate

in'dagine [in'dadʒine] *sf* investigation, inquiry; (*ricerca*) research, study

indebi'tarsi *vr* to run o get into debt

in'debito, a *ag* undue; undeserved

indebo'lire *vt, vi* (*anche: ~rsi*) to weaken

inde'cente [inde'tʃente] *ag* indecent; inde'cenza *sf* indecency

inde'ciso, a [inde'tʃizo] *ag* indecisive; (*irresoluto*) undecided

inde'fesso, a *ag* untiring, indefatigable

indefi'nito, a *ag* (*anche LING*) indefinite; (*impreciso, non determinato*) undefined

in'degno, a [in'deɲɲo] *ag* (*atto*) shameful; (*persona*) unworthy

indelica'tezza [indelika'tettsa] *sf* tactlessness

indemoni'ato, a *ag* possessed (by the devil)

in'denne *ag* unhurt, uninjured; indennità *sf inv* (*rimborso: di spese*) allowance; (*: di perdita*) compensation, indemnity; indennità di contingenza cost-of-living allowance; indennità di trasferta travel expenses *pl*

indenniz'zare [indennid'dzare] *vt* to compensate; inden'nizzo *sm* (*somma*) compensation, indemnity

indero'gabile *ag* binding

'**India** *sf*: **l'~** India; **indi'ano, a** *ag* Indian
♦ *sm/f* (*d'India*) Indian; (*d'America*) Native
American, (American) Indian

indiavo'lato, a *ag* possessed (by the devil);
(*vivace, violento*) wild

indi'care *vt* (*mostrare*) to show, indicate;
(: *col dito*) to point to, point out; (*consigliare*)
to suggest, recommend; **indica'tivo, a** *ag*
indicative ♦ *sm* (*LING*) indicative (mood);
indica'tore *sm* (*elenco*) guide; directory;
(*TECN*) gauge; indicator; **indicatore di velocità**
(*AUT*) speedometer; **indicatore della benzina**
fuel gauge; **indicazi'one** *sf* indication;
(*informazione*) piece of information

'**indice** ['inditʃe] *sm* index; (*fig*) sign; (*dito*)
index finger, forefinger; **~ di gradimento**
(*RADIO, TV*) popularity rating

indi'cibile [indi'tʃibile] *ag* inexpressible

indietreggi'are [indietred'dʒare] *vi* to draw
back, retreat

indi'etro *av* back; (*guardare*) behind, back;
(*andare, cadere*: *anche*: **all'~**) backwards;
rimanere ~ to be left behind; **essere ~** (*col
lavoro*) to be behind; (*orologio*) to be slow;
rimandare qc ~ to send sth back

indi'feso, a *ag* (*città etc*) undefended;
(*persona*) defenceless

indiffe'rente *ag* indifferent; **indiffe'renza**
sf indifference

in'digeno, a [in'didʒeno] *ag* indigenous,
native ♦ *sm/f* native

indi'gente [indi'dʒɛnte] *ag* poverty-stricken,
destitute; **indi'genza** *sf* extreme poverty

indigesti'one [indidʒes'tjone] *sf* indigestion

indi'gesto, a [indi'dʒɛsto] *ag* indigestible

indi'gnare [indiɲ'ɲare] *vt* to fill with
indignation; **~rsi** *vr* to get indignant

indimenti'cabile *ag* unforgettable

indipen'dente *ag* independent;
indipen'denza *sf* independence

in'dire *vt* (*concorso*) to announce; (*elezioni*)
to call

indi'retto, a *ag* indirect

indiriz'zare [indirit'tsare] *vt* (*dirigere*) to
direct; (*mandare*) to send; (*lettera*) to
address

indi'rizzo [indi'rittso] *sm* address; (*direzione*)
direction; (*avvio*) trend, course

indis'creto, a *ag* indiscreet

indis'cusso, a *ag* unquestioned

indispen'sabile *ag* indispensable, essential

indispet'tire *vt* to irritate, annoy ♦ *vi*
(*anche*: **~rsi**) to get irritated o annoyed

in'divia *sf* endive

individu'ale *ag* individual; **individualità** *sf*
individuality

individu'are *vt* (*dar forma distinta a*) to
characterize; (*determinare*) to locate;

(*riconoscere*) to single out

indi'viduo *sm* individual

indizi'ato, a *ag* suspected ♦ *sm/f* suspect

in'dizio [in'dittsjo] *sm* (*segno*) sign,
indication; (*POLIZIA*) clue; (*DIR*) piece of
evidence

'**indole** *sf* nature, character

indolen'zito, a [indolen'tsito] *ag* stiff,
aching; (*intorpidito*) numb

indo'lore *ag* painless

indo'mani *sm*: **l'~** the next day, the
following day

Indo'nesia *sf*: **l'~** Indonesia

indos'sare *vt* (*mettere indosso*) to put on;
(*avere indosso*) to have on; **indossa'tore,
'trice** *sm/f* model

in'dotto, a *pp di* **indurre**

indottri'nare *vt* to indoctrinate

indovi'nare *vt* (*scoprire*) to guess;
(*immaginare*) to imagine, guess; (*il futuro*) to
foretell; **indovi'nato, a** *ag* successful;
(*scelta*) inspired; **indovi'nello** *sm* riddle;
indo'vino, a *sm/f* fortuneteller

indubbia'mente *av* undoubtedly

in'dubbio, a *ag* certain, undoubted

indugi'are [indu'dʒare] *vi* to take one's time,
delay

in'dugio [in'dudʒo] *sm* (*ritardo*) delay; **senza
~** without delay

indul'gente [indul'dʒɛnte] *ag* indulgent;
(*giudice*) lenient; **indul'genza** *sf* indulgence;
leniency

in'dulgere [in'duldʒere] *vi*: **~ a** (*accondiscendere*) to comply with; (*abbandonarsi*) to
indulge in; **in'dulto, a** *pp di* **indulgere** ♦ *sm*
(*DIR*) pardon

indu'mento *sm* article of clothing, garment;
~i *smpl* (*vestiti*) clothes

indu'rire *vt* to harden ♦ *vi* (*anche*: **~rsi**) to
harden, become hard

in'durre *vt*: **~ qn a fare qc** to induce o
persuade sb to do sth; **~ qn in errore** to
mislead sb

in'dustria *sf* industry; **industri'ale** *ag*
industrial ♦ *sm* industrialist

industri'arsi *vr* to do one's best, try hard

industri'oso, a *ag* industrious, hard-
working

induzi'one [indut'tsjone] *sf* induction

inebe'tito, a *ag* dazed, stunned

inebri'are *vt* (*anche fig*) to intoxicate; **~rsi** *vr*
to become intoxicated

inecce'pibile [inettʃe'pibile] *ag*
unexceptionable

i'nedia *sf* starvation

i'nedito, a *ag* unpublished

ineffi'cace [ineffi'katʃe] *ag* ineffective

ineffici'ente [ineffi'tʃɛnte] *ag* inefficient

inegu'ale *ag* unequal; (*irregolare*) uneven

ine'rente *ag*: ~ a concerning, regarding

i'nerme *ag* unarmed; defenceless

inerpi'carsi *vr*: ~ (su) to clamber (up)

i'nerte *ag* inert; (*inattivo*) indolent, sluggish; i'nerzia *sf* inertia; indolence, sluggishness

ine'satto, a *ag* (*impreciso*) inexact; (*erroneo*) incorrect; (AMM: *non riscosso*) uncollected

inesis'tente *ag* non-existent

inesperi'enza [inespe'rjɛntsa] *sf* inexperience

ines'perto, a *ag* inexperienced

i'netto, a *ag* (*incapace*) inept; (*che non ha attitudine*): ~ (a) unsuited (to)

ine'vaso, a *ag* (*ordine, corrispondenza*) outstanding

inevi'tabile *ag* inevitable

i'nezia [i'nɛttsja] *sf* trifle, thing of no importance

infagot'tare *vt* to bundle up, wrap up; ~rsi *vr* to wrap up

infal'libile *ag* infallible

infa'mante *ag* defamatory

in'fame *ag* infamous; (*fig: cosa, compito*) awful, dreadful

infan'gare *vt* to cover with mud; (*fig: reputazione*) to sully

infan'tile *ag* child *cpd*; childlike; (*adulto, azione*) childish; letteratura ~ children's books *pl*

in'fanzia [in'fantsja] *sf* childhood; (*bambini*) children *pl*; prima ~ babyhood, infancy

infari'nare *vt* to cover with (o sprinkle with o dip in) flour; infarina'tura *sf* (*fig*) smattering

in'farto *sm* (MED) heart attack

infasti'dire *vt* to annoy, irritate; ~rsi *vr* to get annoyed o irritated

infati'cabile *ag* tireless, untiring

in'fatti *cong* as a matter of fact, in fact, actually

infatu'arsi *vr*: ~ di to become infatuated with, fall for; infatuazi'one *sf* infatuation

in'fausto, a *ag* unpropitious, unfavourable

infe'condo, a *ag* infertile

infe'dele *ag* unfaithful; infedeltà *sf* infidelity

infe'lice [infe'litʃe] *ag* unhappy; (*sfortunato*) unlucky, unfortunate; (*inopportuno*) inopportune, ill-timed; (*mal riuscito: lavoro*) bad, poor; infelicità *sf* unhappiness

inferi'ore *ag* lower; (*per intelligenza, qualità*) inferior ♦ *sm/f* inferior; ~ a (*numero, quantità*) less o smaller than; (*meno buono*) inferior to; ~ alla media below average; inferiorità *sf* inferiority

inferme'ria *sf* infirmary; (*di scuola, nave*) sick bay

infermi'ere, a *sm/f* nurse

infermità *sf inv* illness; infirmity

in'fermo, a *ag* (*ammalato*) ill; (*debole*) infirm

infer'nale *ag* infernal; (*proposito, complotto*) diabolical

in'ferno *sm* hell

inferri'ata *sf* grating

infervo'rarsi *vr* to get excited, get carried away

infes'tare *vt* to infest

infet'tare *vt* to infect; ~rsi *vr* to become infected; infet'tivo, a *ag* infectious; in'fetto, a *ag* infected; (*acque*) polluted, contaminated; infezi'one *sf* infection

infiac'chire [infjak'kire] *vt* to weaken ♦ *vi* (*anche*: ~rsi) to grow weak

infiam'mabile *ag* inflammable

infiam'mare *vt* to set alight; (*fig, MED*) to inflame; ~rsi *vr* to catch fire; (MED) to become inflamed; infiammazi'one *sf* (MED) inflammation

in'fido, a *ag* unreliable, treacherous

infie'rire *vi*: ~ su (*fisicamente*) to attack furiously; (*verbalmente*) to rage at

in'figgere [in'fiddʒere] *vt*: ~ qc in to thrust o drive sth into

infi'lare *vt* (*ago*) to thread; (*mettere: chiave*) to insert; (: *anello, vestito*) to slip o put on; (*strada*) to turn into, take; ~rsi *vr*: ~rsi in to slip into; (*indossare*) to slip on; ~ l'uscio to slip in; to slip out

infil'trarsi *vr* to penetrate, seep through; (MIL) to infiltrate; infiltrazi'one *sf* infiltration

infil'zare [infil'tsare] *vt* (*infilare*) to string together; (*trafiggere*) to pierce

'infimo, a *ag* lowest

in'fine *av* finally; (*insomma*) in short

infinità *sf* infinity; (*in quantità*): un'~ di an infinite number of

infi'nito, a *ag* infinite; (LING) infinitive ♦ *sm* infinity; (LING) infinitive; all'~ (*senza fine*) endlessly

infinocchi'are [infinok'kjare] (*fam*) *vt* to hoodwink

infischi'arsi [infis'kjarsi] *vr*: ~ di not to care about

in'fisso, a *pp di* infiggere ♦ *sm* fixture; (*di porta, finestra*) frame

infit'tire *vt, vi* (*anche*: ~rsi) to thicken

inflazi'one [inflat'tsjone] *sf* inflation

in'fliggere [in'fliddʒere] *vt* to inflict; in'flitto, a *pp di* infliggere

influ'ente *ag* influential; influ'enza *sf* influence; (MED) influenza, flu

influ'ire *vi*: ~ su to influence

in'flusso *sm* influence

infol'tire *vt, vi* to thicken

infon'dato, a *ag* unfounded, groundless

in'fondere *vt*: ~ qc in qn to instil sth in sb

infor'care *vt* to fork (up); (*bicicletta, cavallo*) to get on; (*occhiali*) to put on

infor'mare *vt* to inform, tell; **~rsi** *vr*: **~rsi (di o su)** to inquire (about)

infor'matica *sf* computer science

informa'tivo, a *ag* informative

informa'tore *sm* informer

informazi'one [informat'tsjone] *sf* piece of information; **prendere ~i sul conto di qn** to get information about sb; **chiedere un'~** to ask for (some) information

in'forme *ag* shapeless

informico'larsi *vr* = **informicolirsi**

informico'lirsi *vr* to have pins and needles

infor'tunio *sm* accident; **~ sul lavoro** industrial accident, accident at work

infos'sarsi *vr* (*terreno*) to sink; (*guance*) to become hollow; **infos'sato, a** *ag* hollow; (*occhi*) deep-set; (: *per malattia*) sunken

in'frangere [in'frandʒere] *vt* to smash; (*fig: legge, patti*) to break; **~rsi** *vr* to smash, break; **infran'gibile** *ag* unbreakable; **in'franto, a** *pp di* **infrangere** ♦ *ag* broken

infrazi'one [infrat'tsjone] *sf*: **~ a** breaking of, violation of

infred'datura *sf* slight cold

infred'dolito, a *ag* cold, chilled

infruttu'oso, a *ag* fruitless

infu'ori *av* out; **all'~** outwards; **all'~ di** (*eccetto*) except, with the exception of

infuri'are *vi* to rage; **~rsi** *vr* to fly into a rage

infusi'one *sf* infusion

in'fuso, a *pp di* **infondere** ♦ *sm* infusion

Ing. *abbr* = **ingegnere**

ingabbi'are *vt* to cage

ingaggi'are [ingad'dʒare] *vt* (*assumere con compenso*) to take on, hire; (*SPORT*) to sign on; (*MIL*) to engage; **in'gaggio** *sm* hiring; signing on

ingan'nare *vt* to deceive; (*fisco*) to cheat; (*eludere*) to dodge, elude; (*fig: tempo*) to while away ♦ *vi* (*apparenza*) to be deceptive; **~rsi** *vr* to be mistaken, be wrong; **ingan'nevole** *ag* deceptive

in'ganno *sm* deceit, deception; (*azione*) trick; (*menzogna, frode*) cheat, swindle; (*illusione*) illusion

ingarbugli'are [ingarbuʎ'ʎare] *vt* to tangle; (*fig*) to confuse, muddle; **~rsi** *vr* to become confused o muddled

inge'gnarsi [indʒeɲ'ɲarsi] *vr* to do one's best, try hard; **~ per vivere** to live by one's wits

inge'gnere [indʒeɲ'ɲere] *sm* engineer; **~ civile/navale** civil/naval engineer; **ingegne'ria** *sf* engineering; **~ genetica** genetic engineering

in'gegno [in'dʒeɲɲo] *sm* (*intelligenza*) intelligence, brains *pl*; (*capacità creativa*) ingenuity; (*disposizione*) talent; **inge'gno- so, a** *ag* ingenious, clever

ingelo'sire [indʒelo'zire] *vt* to make jealous ♦ *vi* (*anche: ~rsi*) to become jealous

in'gente [in'dʒɛnte] *ag* huge, enormous

ingenuità [indʒenui'ta] *sf* ingenuousness

in'genuo, a [in'dʒɛnuo] *ag* ingenuous, naïve

inge'rire [indʒe'rire] *vt* to ingest

inges'sare [indʒes'sare] *vt* (*MED*) to put in plaster; **ingessa'tura** *sf* plaster

Inghil'terra [ingil'terra] *sf*: **l'~** England

inghiot'tire [ingjot'tire] *vt* to swallow

ingial'lire [indʒal'lire] *vi* to go yellow

ingigan'tire [indʒigan'tire] *vt* to enlarge, magnify ♦ *vi* to become gigantic o enormous

inginocchi'arsi [indʒinok'kjarsi] *vr* to kneel (down)

ingiù [in'dʒu] *av* down, downwards

ingiunzi'one [indʒun'tsjone] *sf* injunction

ingi'uria [in'dʒurja] *sf* insult; (*fig: danno*) damage; **ingiuri'are** *vt* to insult, abuse; **ingiuri'oso, a** *ag* insulting, abusive

ingius'tizia [indʒus'tittsja] *sf* injustice

ingi'usto, a [in'dʒusto] *ag* unjust, unfair

in'glese *ag* English ♦ *sm/f* Englishman/woman ♦ *sm* (*LING*) English; **gli I~i** the English; **andarsene o filare all'~** to take French leave

ingoi'are *vt* to gulp (down); (*fig*) to swallow (up)

ingol'fare *vt* (*motore*) to flood; **~rsi** *vr* to flood

ingom'brante *ag* cumbersome

ingom'brare *vt* (*strada*) to block; (*stanza*) to clutter up; **in'gombro, a** *ag* (*strada, passaggio*) blocked ♦ *sm* obstacle; **essere d'ingombro** to be in the way

in'gordo, a *ag*: **~ di** greedy for; (*fig*) greedy o avid for

in'gorgo, ghi *sm* blockage, obstruction; (*anche: ~ stradale*) traffic jam

ingoz'zare [ingot'tsare] *vt* (*animali*) to fatten; (*fig: persona*) to stuff; **~rsi** *vr*: **~rsi (di)** to stuff o.s. (with)

ingra'naggio [ingra'naddʒo] *sm* (*TECN*) gear; (*di orologio*) mechanism; **gli ~i della burocrazia** the bureaucratic machinery

ingra'nare *vi* to mesh, engage ♦ *vt* to engage; **~ la marcia** to get into gear

ingrandi'mento *sm* enlargement; extension

ingran'dire *vt* (*anche FOT*) to enlarge; (*estendere*) to extend; (*OTTICA, fig*) to magnify ♦ *vi* (*anche: ~rsi*) to become larger o bigger; (*aumentare*) to grow, increase; (*espandersi*) to expand

ingras'sare *vt* to make fat; (*animali*) to fatten; (*lubrificare*) to oil, lubricate ♦ *vi* (*anche: ~rsi*) to get fat, put on weight

in'grato, a *ag* ungrateful; (*lavoro*) thankless, unrewarding

ingredi'ente sm ingredient

in'gresso sm (porta) entrance; (atrio) hall; (l'entrare) entrance, entry; (facoltà di entrare) admission; **"~ libero"** "admission free"

ingros'sare vt to increase; (folla, livello) to swell ♦ vi (anche: ~rsi) to increase; to swell

in'grosso av: **all'~** (COMM) wholesale; (all'incirca) roughly, about

ingua'ribile ag incurable

'inguine sm (ANAT) groin

ini'bire vt to forbid, prohibit; (PSIC) to inhibit; **inibizi'one** sf prohibition; inhibition

iniet'tare vt to inject; **~rsi** vr: **~rsi di sangue** (occhi) to become bloodshot; **iniezi'one** sf injection

inimi'carsi vr: **~ con qn** to fall out with sb

ininter'rotto, a ag unbroken; uninterrupted

iniquità sf inv iniquity; (atto) wicked action

inizi'ale [init'tsjale] ag, sf initial

inizi'are [init'tsjare] vi, vt to begin, start; **~ qn a** to initiate sb into; (pittura etc) to introduce sb to; **~ a fare qc** to start doing sth

inizia'tiva [initttsja'tiva] sf initiative; **~ privata** private enterprise

i'nizio [i'nittsjo] sm beginning; **all'~** at the beginning, at the start; **dare ~ a qc** to start sth, get sth going

innaffi'are etc = **annaffiare** etc

innal'zare [innal'tsare] vt (sollevare, alzare) to raise; (rizzare) to erect; **~rsi** vr to rise

innamo'rarsi vr: **~ (di qn)** to fall in love (with sb); **innamo'rato, a** ag (che nutre amore): **innamorato (di)** in love (with); (appassionato): **innamorato di** very fond of ♦ sm/f lover; sweetheart

in'nanzi [in'nantsi] av (stato in luogo) in front, ahead; (moto a luogo) forward, on; (tempo: prima) before ♦ prep (prima) before; **~ a** in front of; **innanzi'tutto** av first of all

in'nato, a ag innate

innatu'rale ag unnatural

inne'gabile ag undeniable

innervo'sire vt: **~ qn** to get on sb's nerves; **~rsi** vr to get irritated o upset

innes'care vt to prime

innes'tare vt (BOT, MED) to graft; (TECN) to engage; (inserire: presa) to insert; **in'nesto** sm graft; grafting no pl; (TECN) clutch; (ELETTR) connection

'inno sm hymn; **~ nazionale** national anthem

inno'cente [inno'tʃɛnte] ag innocent; **inno'cenza** sf innocence

in'nocuo, a ag innocuous, harmless

innova'tivo, a ag innovative

innume'revole ag innumerable

ino'doro, a ag odourless

inol'trare vt (AMM) to pass on, forward; **~rsi** vr (addentrarsi) to advance, go forward

i'noltre av besides, moreover

inon'dare vt to flood; **inondazi'one** sf flooding no pl; flood

inope'roso, a ag inactive, idle

inoppor'tuno, a ag untimely, ill-timed; inappropriate; (momento) inopportune

inorgo'glire [inorgoʎ'ʎire] vt to make proud ♦ vi (anche: ~rsi) to become proud; **~rsi di qc** to pride o.s. on sth

inorri'dire vt to horrify ♦ vi to be horrified

inospi'tale ag inhospitable

inosser'vato, a ag (non notato) unobserved; (non rispettato) not observed, not kept

inossi'dabile ag stainless

inqua'drare vt (foto, immagine) to frame; (fig) to situate, set

inqui'etare vt (turbare) to disturb, worry; **~rsi** vr to worry, become anxious; (impazientirsi) to get upset

inqui'eto, a ag restless; (preoccupato) worried, anxious; **inquie'tudine** sf anxiety, worry

inqui'lino, a sm/f tenant

inquina'mento sm pollution

inqui'nare vt to pollute

inqui'sire vt, vi to investigate; **inquisi'tore, 'trice** ag (sguardo) inquiring; **inquisizi'one** sf (STORIA) inquisition

insabbi'are vt (fig: pratica) to shelve; **~rsi** vr (arenarsi: barca) to run aground; (fig: pratica) to be shelved

insac'cati smpl (CUC) sausages

insa'lata sf salad; **~ mista** mixed salad; **insalati'era** sf salad bowl

insa'lubre ag unhealthy

insa'nabile ag (piaga) which cannot be healed; (situazione) irremediable; (odio) implacable

insangui'nare vt to stain with blood

insa'puta sf: **all'~ di qn** without sb knowing

insce'nare [inʃe'nare] vt (TEATRO) to stage, put on; (fig) to stage

insedi'are vt to install; **~rsi** vr to take up office; (popolo, colonia) to settle

in'segna [in'seɲɲa] sf sign; (emblema) sign, emblem; (bandiera) flag, banner; **~e** sfpl (decorazioni) insignia pl

insegna'mento [inseɲɲa'mento] sm teaching

inse'gnante [inseɲ'ɲante] ag teaching ♦ sm/f teacher

inse'gnare [inseɲ'ɲare] vt, vi to teach; **~ a qn qc** to teach sb sth; **~ a qn a fare qc** to teach sb (how) to do sth

insegui'mento sm pursuit, chase

insegu'ire vt to pursue, chase

inselvati'chire [inselvati'kire] vi (anche: ~rsi) to grow wild

insena'tura sf inlet, creek

insen'sato, a *ag* senseless, stupid

insen'sibile *ag* (*nervo*) insensible; (*persona*) indifferent

inse'rire *vt* to insert; (ELETTR) to connect; (*allegare*) to enclose; (*annuncio*) to put in, place; ~**rsi** *vr* (*fig*): ~**rsi in** to become part of; **in'serto** *sm* (*pubblicazione*) insert

inservi'ente *sm/f* attendant

inserzi'one [inser'tsjone] *sf* insertion; (*avviso*) advertisement; **fare un'~ sul giornale** to put an advertisement in the paper

insetti'cida, i [insetti'tʃida] *sm* insecticide

in'setto *sm* insect

insi'curo, a *ag* insecure

in'sidia *sf* snare, trap; (*pericolo*) hidden danger; **insidi'are** *vt*: ~ **la vita di qn** to make an attempt on sb's life

insi'eme *av* together ♦ *prep*: ~ **a o con** together with ♦ *sm* whole; (MAT, *servizio, assortimento*) set; (MODA) ensemble, outfit; **tutti ~** all together; **tutto ~** all together; (*in una volta*) at one go; **nell'~** on the whole; **d'~** (*veduta etc*) overall

in'signe [in'siɲɲe] *ag* (*persona*) famous, distinguished; (*città, monumento*) notable

insignifi'cante [insiɲɲifi'kante] *ag* insignificant

insi'gnire [insiɲ'ɲire] *vt*: ~ **qn di** to honour o decorate sb with

insin'cero, a [insin'tʃero] *ag* insincere

insinda'cabile *ag* unquestionable

insinu'are *vt* (*introdurre*): ~ **qc in** to slip o slide sth into; (*fig*) to insinuate, imply; ~**rsi** *vr*: ~**rsi in** to seep into; (*fig*) to creep into; to worm one's way into

in'sipido, a *ag* insipid

insis'tente *ag* insistent; persistent

in'sistere *vi*: ~ **su qc** to insist on sth; ~ **in qc/a fare** (*perseverare*) to persist in sth/in doing; **insis'tito, a** *pp di* **insistere**

insoddis'fatto, a *ag* dissatisfied

insoffe'rente *ag* intolerant

insolazi'one [insolat'tsjone] *sf* (MED) sunstroke

inso'lente *ag* insolent; **insolen'tire** *vi* to grow insolent ♦ *vt* to insult, be rude to

in'solito, a *ag* unusual, out of the ordinary

inso'luto, a *ag* (*non risolto*) unsolved

in'somma *av* (*in conclusione*) in short; (*dunque*) well ♦ *escl* for heaven's sake!

in'sonne *ag* sleepless; **in'sonnia** *sf* insomnia, sleeplessness

insonno'lito, a *ag* sleepy, drowsy

insoppor'tabile *ag* unbearable

in'sorgere [in'sordʒere] *vi* (*ribellarsi*) to rise up, rebel; (*apparire*) to come up, arise

in'sorto, a *pp di* **insorgere** ♦ *sm/f* rebel, insurgent

insospet'tire *vt* to make suspicious ♦ *vi*

(*anche*: ~**rsi**) to become suspicious

inspi'rare *vt* to breathe in, inhale

in'stabile *ag* (*carico, indole*) unstable; (*tempo*) unsettled; (*equilibrio*) unsteady

instal'lare *vt* to install; ~**rsi** *vr* (*sistemarsi*): ~**rsi in** to settle in; **installazi'one** *sf* installation

instan'cabile *ag* untiring, indefatigable

instau'rare *vt* to introduce, institute

instra'dare *vt*: ~ (**verso**) to direct (towards)

insuc'cesso [insut'tʃesso] *sm* failure, flop

insudici'are [insudi'tʃare] *vt* to dirty; ~**rsi** *vr* to get dirty

insuffici'ente [insuffi'tʃente] *ag* insufficient; (*compito, allievo*) inadequate; **insuffici'enza** *sf* insufficiency; inadequacy; (INS) fail

insu'lare *ag* insular

insu'lina *sf* insulin

in'sulso, a *ag* (*sciocco*) inane, silly; (*persona*) dull, insipid

insul'tare *vt* to insult, affront

in'sulto *sm* insult, affront

insussis'tente *ag* non-existent

intac'care *vt* (*fare tacche*) to cut into; (*corrodere*) to corrode; (*fig: cominciare ad usare: risparmi*) to break into; (: *ledere*) to damage

intagli'are [intaʎ'ʎare] *vt* to carve; **in'taglio** *sm* carving

intan'gibile [intan'dʒibile] *ag* untouchable; inviolable

in'tanto *av* (*nel frattempo*) meanwhile, in the meantime; (*per cominciare*) just to begin with; ~ **che** while

in'tarsio *sm* inlaying *no pl*, marquetry *no pl*; inlay

inta'sare *vt* to choke (up), block (up); (AUT) to obstruct, block; ~**rsi** *vr* to become choked o blocked

intas'care *vt* to pocket

in'tatto, a *ag* intact; (*puro*) unsullied

intavo'lare *vt* to start, enter into

inte'grale *ag* complete; (*pane, farina*) wholemeal (BRIT), whole-wheat (US); (MAT): **calcolo ~** integral calculus

inte'grante *ag*: **parte ~** integral part

inte'grare *vt* to complete; (MAT) to integrate; ~**rsi** *vr* (*persona*) to become integrated

integrità *sf* integrity

'integro, a *ag* (*intatto, intero*) complete, whole; (*retto*) upright

intelaia'tura *sf* frame; (*fig*) structure, framework

intel'letto *sm* intellect; **intellettu'ale** *ag, sm/f* intellectual

intelli'gente [intelli'dʒente] *ag* intelligent; **intelli'genza** *sf* intelligence

intem'perie *sfpl* bad weather *sg*

intempes'tivo, a *ag* untimely
inten'dente *sm*: ~ **di Finanza** inland (*BRIT*) o internal (*US*) revenue officer; **inten'denza** *sf*: **intendenza di Finanza** inland (*BRIT*) o internal (*US*) revenue office
in'tendere *vt* (*avere intenzione*): ~ **fare qc** to intend o mean to do sth; (*comprendere*) to understand; (*udire*) to hear; (*significare*) to mean; **~rsi** *vr* (*conoscere*): **~rsi di** to know a lot about, be a connoisseur of; (*accordarsi*) to get on (well); **intendersela con qn** (*avere una relazione amorosa*) to have an affair with sb; **intendi'mento** *sm* (*intelligenza*) understanding; (*proposito*) intention; **intendi'tore, 'trice** *sm/f* connoisseur, expert
intene'rire *vt* (*fig*) to move (to pity); **~rsi** *vr* (*fig*) to be moved
inten'sivo, a *ag* intensive
in'tenso, a *ag* intense
in'tento, a *ag* (*teso, assorto*): ~ (a) intent (on), absorbed (in) ♦ *sm* aim, purpose
intenzio'nale [intentsjo'nale] *ag* intentional
intenzi'one [inten'tsjone] *sf* intention; (*DIR*) intent; **avere ~ di fare qc** to intend to do sth, have the intention of doing sth
interat'tivo, a *ag* interactive
interca'lare *sm* pet phrase, stock phrase ♦ *vt* to insert
interca'pedine *sf* gap, cavity
intercet'tare [intertʃet'tare] *vt* to intercept
intercity [ɪntəsˈɪtɪ] *sm inv* (*FERR*) ≈ intercity (train)
inter'detto, a *pp di* **interdire** ♦ *ag* forbidden, prohibited; (*sconcertato*) dumbfounded ♦ *sm* (*REL*) interdict
inter'dire *vt* to forbid, prohibit, ban; (*REL*) to interdict; (*DIR*) to deprive of civil rights; **interdizi'one** *sf* prohibition, ban
interessa'mento *sm* interest
interes'sante *ag* interesting; **essere in stato ~** to be expecting (a baby)
interes'sare *vt* to interest; (*concernere*) to concern, be of interest to; (*far intervenire*): ~ **qn a** to draw sb's attention to ♦ *vi*: ~ **a** to interest, matter to; **~rsi** *vr* (*mostrare interesse*): **~rsi a** to take an interest in, be interested in; (*occuparsi*): **~rsi di** to take care of
inte'resse *sm* (*anche COMM*) interest
inter'faccia, ce [inter'fattʃa] *sf* (*INFORM*) interface
interfe'renza [interfe'rentsa] *sf* interference
interfe'rire *vi* to interfere
interiezi'one [interjet'tsjone] *sf* exclamation, interjection
interi'ora *sfpl* entrails
interi'ore *ag* interior, inner, inside, internal; (*fig*) inner
inter'ludio *sm* (*MUS*) interlude

inter'medio, a *ag* intermediate
inter'mezzo [inter'meddzo] *sm* (*intervallo*) interval; (*breve spettacolo*) intermezzo
inter'nare *vt* (*arrestare*) to intern; (*MED*) to commit (to a mental institution)
'Internet ['internet] *sf* Internet; **in ~** on the Internet
internazio'nale [internattsjo'nale] *ag* international
in'terno, a *ag* (*di dentro*) internal, interior, inner; (: *mare*) inland; (*nazionale*) domestic; (*allievo*) boarding ♦ *sm* inside, interior; (*di paese*) interior; (*fodera*) lining; (*di appartamento*) flat (number); (*TEL*) extension ♦ *sm/f* (*INS*) boarder; **~i** *smpl* (*CINEMA*) interior shots; **all'~** inside; **Ministero degli I~i** Ministry of the Interior, ≈ Home Office (*BRIT*), ≈ Department of the Interior (*US*)
in'tero, a *ag* (*integro, intatto*) whole, entire; (*completo, totale*) complete; (*numero*) whole; (*non ridotto: biglietto*) full; (*latte*) full-cream
interpel'lare *vt* to consult
inter'porre *vt* (*ostacolo*): ~ **qc a qc** to put sth in the way of sth; (*influenza*) to use; **interporsi** *vr* to intervene; **interporsi fra** (*mettersi in mezzo*) to come between; **inter'posto, a** *pp di* **interporre**
interpre'tare *vt* to interpret; **in'terprete** *sm/f* interpreter; (*TEATRO*) actor/actress, performer; (*MUS*) performer
interregio'nale [interredʒo'nale] *sm* long distance train (*stopping frequently*)
interro'gare *vt* to question; (*INS*) to test; **interroga'tivo, a** *ag* (*occhi, sguardo*) questioning, inquiring; (*LING*) interrogative ♦ *sm* question; (*fig*) mystery; **interro'gatorio, a** *ag* interrogatory, questioning ♦ *sm* (*DIR*) questioning *no pl*; **interro-gazi'one** *sf* questioning *no pl*; (*INS*) oral test
inter'rompere *vt* to interrupt; (*studi, trattative*) to break off, interrupt; **~rsi** *vr* to break off, stop; **inter'rotto, a** *pp di* **interrompere**
interrut'tore *sm* switch
interruzi'one [interrut'tsjone] *sf* interruption; break
interse'care *vt* to intersect; **~rsi** *vr* to intersect
inter'stizio [inter'stittsjo] *sm* interstice, crack
interur'bana *sf* trunk o long-distance call
interur'bano, a *ag* inter-city; (*TEL: chiamata*) trunk *cpd*, long-distance; (: *telefono*) long-distance
inter'vallo *sm* interval; (*spazio*) space, gap
interve'nire *vi* (*partecipare*): ~ **a** to take part in; (*intromettersi: anche POL*) to intervene; (*MED: operare*) to operate; **inter'vento** *sm* participation; (*intromissione*) intervention; (*MED*) operation; **fare un intervento nel corso**

di (*dibattito, programma*) to take part in
inter'vista *sf* interview; **intervis'tare** *vt* to interview
in'tesa *sf* understanding; (*accordo*) agreement, understanding
in'teso, a *pp di* **intendere ♦** *ag* agreed; **siamo ~i?** OK?
intes'tare *vt* (*lettera*) to address; (*proprietà*): **~ a** to register in the name of; **~ un assegno a qn** to make out a cheque to sb; **intestazi'one** *sf* heading; (*su carta da lettere*) letterhead
intes'tino *sm* (ANAT) intestine
inti'mare *vt* to order, command
intimidazi'one [intimidat'tsjone] *sf* intimidation
intimi'dire *vt* to intimidate ♦ *vi* (*anche*: ~rsi) to grow shy
intimità *sf* intimacy; privacy; (*familiarità*) familiarity
'intimo, a *ag* intimate; (*affetti, vita*) private; (*fig: profondo*) inmost ♦ *sm* (*persona*) intimate *o* close friend; (*dell'animo*) bottom, depths *pl*; **parti ~e** (ANAT) private parts
intimo'rire *vt* to frighten; ~rsi *vr* to become frightened
in'tingolo *sm* sauce; (*pietanza*) stew
intiriz'zire [intirid'dzire] *vt* to numb ♦ *vi* (*anche*: ~rsi) to go numb
intito'lare *vt* to give a title to; (*dedicare*) to dedicate
intolle'rabile *ag* intolerable
intolle'rante *ag* intolerant
in'tonaco, ci *o* **chi** *sm* plaster
into'nare *vt* (*canto*) to start to sing; (*armonizzare*) to match; ~**rsi** *vr* (*colori*) to go together; ~**rsi a** (*carnagione*) to suit; (*abito*) to go with, match
inton'tire *vt* to stun, daze ♦ *vi* (*anche*: ~rsi) to be stunned *o* dazed
in'toppo *sm* stumbling block, obstacle
in'torno *av* around; **~ a** (*attorno a*) around; (*riguardo, circa*) about
intorpi'dire *vt* to numb; (*fig*) to make sluggish ♦ *vi* (*anche*: ~rsi) to grow numb; (*fig*) to become sluggish
intossi'care *vt* to poison; **intossicazi'one** *sf* poisoning
intralci'are [intral'tʃare] *vt* to hamper, hold up
'intranet ['intranet] *sf* intranet
intransi'tivo, a *ag, sm* intransitive
intrapren'dente *ag* enterprising, go-ahead
intra'prendere *vt* to undertake
intrat'tabile *ag* intractable
intratte'nere *vt* to entertain; to engage in conversation; ~**rsi** *vr* to linger; ~**rsi su qc** to dwell on sth
intrave'dere *vt* to catch a glimpse of; (*fig*)

to foresee
intrecci'are [intret'tʃare] *vt* (*capelli*) to plait, braid; (*intessere: anche fig*) to weave, interweave, intertwine; ~**rsi** *vr* to intertwine, become interwoven; ~ **le mani** to clasp one's hands; **in'treccio** *sm* (*fig: trama*) plot, story
intri'gare *vi* to manoeuvre (BRIT), maneuver (US), scheme; **in'trigo, ghi** *sm* plot, intrigue
in'trinseco, a, ci, che *ag* intrinsic
in'triso, a *ag*: **~ (di)** soaked (in)
intro'durre *vt* to introduce; (*chiave etc*): **~ qc in** to insert sth into; (*persone: far entrare*) to show in; **introdursi** *vr* (*moda, tecniche*) to be introduced; **introdursi in** (*persona: penetrare*) to enter; (: *entrare furtivamente*) to steal *o* slip into; **introduzi'one** *sf* introduction
in'troito *sm* income, revenue
intro'mettersi *vr* to interfere, meddle; (*interporsi*) to intervene
in'truglio [in'truʎʎo] *sm* concoction
in'truso, a *sm/f* intruder
intu'ire *vt* to perceive by intuition; (*rendersi conto*) to realize; **in'tuito** *sm* intuition; (*perspicacia*) perspicacity; **intuizi'one** *sf* intuition
inu'mano, a *ag* inhuman
inumi'dire *vt* to dampen, moisten; ~**rsi** *vr* to become damp *o* wet
i'nutile *ag* useless; (*superfluo*) pointless, unnecessary; **inutilità** *sf* uselessness; pointlessness
inutil'mente *av* unnecessarily; (*senza risultato*) in vain
inva'dente *ag* (*fig*) interfering, nosey
in'vadere *vt* to invade; (*affollare*) to swarm into, overrun; (*sog: acque*) to flood
inva'ghirsi [inva'girsi] *vr*: **~ di** to take a fancy to
invalidità *sf* infirmity; disability; (DIR) invalidity
in'valido, a *ag* (*infermo*) infirm, invalid; (*al lavoro*) disabled; (DIR: *nullo*) invalid ♦ *sm/f* invalid; disabled person
in'vano *av* in vain
invasi'one *sf* invasion
in'vaso, a *pp di* **invadere**
inva'sore, invadi'trice [invadi'tritʃe] *ag* invading ♦ *sm* invader
invecchi'are [invek'kjare] *vi* (*persona*) to grow old; (*vino, popolazione*) to age; (*moda*) to become dated ♦ *vt* to age; (*far apparire più vecchio*) to make look older
in'vece [in'vetʃe] *av* instead; (*al contrario*) on the contrary; **~ di** instead of
inve'ire *vi*: **~ contro** to rail against
inven'tare *vt* to invent; (*pericoli, pettegolezzi*) to make up, invent
inven'tario *sm* inventory; (COMM)

stocktaking *no pl*

inven'tivo, a *ag* inventive ♦ *sf* inventiveness

inven'tore *sm* inventor

invenzi'one [inven'tsjone] *sf* invention; (*bugia*) lie, story

inver'nale *ag* winter *cpd*; (*simile all'inverno*) wintry

in'verno *sm* winter

invero'simile *ag* unlikely

inversi'one *sf* inversion; reversal; "**divieto d'~**" (*AUT*) "no U-turns"

in'verso, a *ag* opposite; (*MAT*) inverse ♦ *sm* contrary, opposite; **in senso ~** in the opposite direction; **in ordine ~** in reverse order

inver'tire *vt* to invert, reverse; **~ la marcia** (*AUT*) to do a U-turn; **inver'tito, a** *sm/f* homosexual

investi'gare *vt, vi* to investigate; **investiga'tore, trice** *sm/f* investigator, detective; **investigazi'one** *sf* investigation, inquiry

investi'mento *sm* (*ECON*) investment

inves'tire *vt* (*denaro*) to invest; (*sog: veicolo: pedone*) to knock down; (: *altro veicolo*) to crash into; (*apostrofare*) to assail; (*incaricare*): **~ qn di** to invest sb with

invi'are *vt* to send; **invi'ato, a** *sm/f* envoy; (*STAMPA*) correspondent

in'vidia *sf* envy; **invidi'are** *vt*: **invidiare qn (per qc)** to envy sb (for sth); **invidiare qc a qn** to envy sb sth; **invidi'oso, a** *ag* envious

in'vio, 'vii *sm* sending; (*insieme di merci*) consignment

invipe'rito, a *ag* furious

invischi'are [invis'kjare] *vt* (*fig*): **~ qn in** to involve sb in; **~rsi** *vr*: **~rsi (con qn/in qc)** to get mixed up o involved (with sb/in sth)

invi'sibile *ag* invisible

invi'tare *vt* to invite; **~ qn a fare** to invite sb to do; **invi'tato, a** *sm/f* guest; **in'vito** *sm* invitation

invo'care *vt* (*chiedere: aiuto, pace*) to cry out for; (*appellarsi: la legge, Dio*) to appeal to, invoke

invogli'are [invoʎ'ʎare] *vt*: **~ qn a fare** to tempt sb to do, induce sb to do

involon'tario, a *ag* (*errore*) unintentional; (*gesto*) involuntary

invol'tino *sm* (*CUC*) roulade

in'volto *sm* (*pacco*) parcel; (*fagotto*) bundle

in'volucro *sm* cover, wrapping

involuzi'one [involut'tsjone] *sf* (*di stile*) convolutedness; (*regresso*): **subire un'~** to regress

inzacche'rare [intsakke'rare] *vt* to spatter with mud

in'zup'pare [intsup'pare] *vt* to soak; **~rsi** *vr* to get soaked

'io *pron* I ♦ *sm inv*: **l'~** the ego, the self;

~ stesso(a) I myself

i'odio *sm* iodine

l'onio *sm*: **lo ~, il mar ~** the Ionian (Sea)

ipermer'cato *sm* hypermarket

ipertensi'one *sf* high blood pressure, hypertension

iper'testo *sm* hypertext

ip'nosi *sf* hypnosis; **ipno'tismo** *sm* hypnotism; **ipnotiz'zare** *vt* to hypnotize

ipocri'sia *sf* hypocrisy

i'pocrita, i, e *ag* hypocritical ♦ *sm/f* hypocrite

ipo'teca, che *sf* mortgage; **ipote'care** *vt* to mortgage

i'potesi *sf inv* hypothesis; **ipo'tetico, a, ci, che** *ag* hypothetical

'ippica *sf* horseracing

'ippico, a, ci, che *ag* horse *cpd*

ippocas'tano *sm* horse chestnut

ip'podromo *sm* racecourse

ippo'potamo *sm* hippopotamus

'ira *sf* anger, wrath

l'ran *sm*: **l'~** Iran

l'raq *sm*: **l'~** Iraq

'iride *sf* (*arcobaleno*) rainbow; (*ANAT, BOT*) iris

Ir'landa *sf*: **l'~** Ireland; **l'~ del Nord** Northern Ireland, Ulster; **la Repubblica d'~** Eire, the Republic of Ireland; **irlan'dese** *ag* Irish ♦ *sm/f* Irishman/woman; **gli Irlandesi** the Irish

iro'nia *sf* irony; **i'ronico, a, ci, che** *ag* ironic(al)

irradi'are *vt* to radiate; (*sog: raggi di luce: illuminare*) to shine on ♦ *vi* (*diffondersi: anche: ~rsi*) to radiate

irragio'nevole [irradʒo'nevole] *ag* irrational; unreasonable

irrazio'nale [irrattsjo'nale] *ag* irrational

irre'ale *ag* unreal

irrecupe'rabile *ag* irretrievable; (*fig: persona*) irredeemable

irrecu'sabile *ag* (*offerta*) not to be refused; (*prova*) irrefutable

irrego'lare *ag* irregular; (*terreno*) uneven

irremo'vibile *ag* (*fig*) unshakeable, unyielding

irrepa'rabile *ag* irreparable; (*fig*) inevitable

irrepe'ribile *ag* nowhere to be found

irrequi'eto, a *ag* restless

irresis'tibile *ag* irresistible

irrespon'sabile *ag* irresponsible

irridu'cibile [irridu'tʃibile] *ag* irreducible; (*fig*) indomitable

irri'gare *vt* (*annaffiare*) to irrigate; (*sog: fiume etc*) to flow through; **irrigazi'one** *sf* irrigation

irrigi'dire [irridʒi'dire] *vt* to stiffen; **~rsi** *vr* to stiffen

irri'sorio, a *ag* derisory

irri'tare *vt* (*mettere di malumore*) to irritate,

annoy; (*MED*) to irritate; **~rsi** *vr (stizzirsi)* to become irritated o annoyed; (*MED*) to become irritated; **irritazi'one** *sf* irritation; annoyance

ir'rompere *vi*: ~ **in** to burst into

irro'rare *vt* to sprinkle; (*AGR*) to spray

irru'ente *ag (fig)* impetuous, violent

irruzi'one [irrut'tsjone] *sf*: **fare** ~ **in** to burst into; (*sog: polizia*) to raid

'irto, a *ag* bristly; ~ **di** bristling with

is'critto, a *pp di* **iscrivere ♦** *sm/f* member; **per** o **in** ~ in writing

is'crivere *vt* to register, enter; (*persona*): ~ **(a)** to register (in), enrol (in); **~rsi** *vr*: **~rsi (a)** *(club, partito)* to join; *(università)* to register o enrol (at); *(esame, concorso)* to register o enter (for); **iscrizi'one** *sf (epigrafe etc)* inscription; *(a scuola, società)* enrolment, registration; *(registrazione)* registration

Is'lam *sm*: **l'~** Islam

Is'landa *sf*: **l'~** Iceland

'isola *sf* island; ~ **pedonale** *(AUT)* pedestrian precinct

isola'mento *sm* isolation; *(TECN)* insulation

iso'lante *ag* insulating ♦ *sm* insulator

iso'lare *vt* to isolate; *(TECN)* to insulate; (: *acusticamente*) to soundproof; **iso'lato, a** *ag* isolated; insulated ♦ *sm (gruppo di edifici)* block

ispetto'rato *sm* inspectorate

ispet'tore *sm* inspector

ispezio'nare [ispettsjo'nare] *vt* to inspect; **ispezi'one** *sf* inspection

'ispido, a *ag* bristly, shaggy

ispi'rare *vt* to inspire; **~rsi** *vr*: **~rsi a** to draw one's inspiration from

Isra'ele *sm*: **l'~** Israel; **israeli'ano, a** *ag, sm/f* Israeli

is'sare *vt* to hoist

istan'taneo, a *ag* instantaneous ♦ *sf (FOT)* snapshot

is'tante *sm* instant, moment; **all'~, sull'~** instantly, immediately

is'tanza [is'tantsa] *sf* petition, request

is'terico, a, ci, che *ag* hysterical

iste'rismo *sm* hysteria

isti'gare *vt* to incite; **istigazi'one** *sf* incitement; **istigazione a delinquere** *(DIR)* incitement to crime

is'tinto *sm* instinct

istitu'ire *vt (fondare)* to institute, found; *(porre: confronto)* to establish; *(intraprendere: inchiesta)* to set up

isti'tuto *sm* institute; *(di università)* department; *(ente, DIR)* institution; ~ **di bellezza** beauty salon

istituzi'one [istitut'tsjone] *sf* institution

'istmo *sm (GEO)* isthmus

'istrice ['istritʃe] *sm* porcupine

istri'one *(peg)* *sm* ham actor

istru'ire *vt (insegnare)* to teach; *(ammaestrare)* to train; *(informare)* to instruct, inform; *(DIR)* to prepare; **istrut'tore, 'trice** *sm/f* instructor ♦ *ag*: **giudice istruttore** *vedi* **giudice**; **istrut'toria** *sf (DIR)* (preliminary) investigation and hearing; **istruzi'one** *sf* education; training; *(direttiva)* instruction

l'talia *sf*: **l'~** Italy

itali'ano, a *ag* Italian ♦ *sm/f* Italian ♦ *sm* *(LING)* Italian; **gli l~i** the Italians

itine'rario *sm* itinerary

itte'rizia [itte'rittsja] *sf (MED)* jaundice

'ittico, a, ci, che *ag* fish *cpd*; fishing *cpd*

Iugos'lavia *etc* = **Jugoslavia** *etc*

i'uta *sf* jute

I.V.A. ['iva] *sigla f (= imposta sul valore aggiunto)* VAT

J, j

jazz [dʒaz] *sm* jazz

jeans [dʒinz] *smpl* jeans

Jugos'lavia [jugoz'lavja] *sf*: **la ~** Yugoslavia; **la ex-~** former Yugoslavia; **jugos'lavo, a** *ag, sm/f* Yugoslav(ian)

'juta ['juta] *sf* = **iuta**

K, k

K *abbr (INFORM)* K

k *abbr (= kilo)* k

karatè *sm* karate

Kg *abbr (= chilogrammo)* kg

'killer *sm inv* gunman, hired gun

'kiwi ['kiwi] *sm inv* kiwi fruit

km *abbr (= chilometro)* km

'krapfen *sm inv (CUC)* doughnut

L, l

l' *det vedi* **la; lo; il**

la¹ *(dav V* **l'**) *det f* the ♦ *pron (oggetto: persona)* her; (: *cosa*) it; (: *forma di cortesia*) you; *vedi anche* **il**

la² *sm inv (MUS)* A; (: *solfeggiando*) la

là *av* there; **di** ~ *(da quel luogo)* from there; *(in quel luogo)* in there; *(dall'altra parte)* over there; **di** ~ **di** beyond; **per di** ~ that way; **più in** ~ further on; *(tempo)* later on; **fatti in** ~ move up; ~ **dentro/sopra/sotto** in/up (o on)/ under there; *vedi anche* **quello**

'labbro *(pl(f)*: **labbra**: *solo nel senso ANAT)* *sm* lip

labi'rinto *sm* labyrinth, maze

labora'torio *sm* (*di ricerca*) laboratory; (*di arti, mestieri*) workshop; ~ **linguistico** language laboratory

labori'oso, a *ag* (*faticoso*) laborious; (*attivo*) hard-working

labu'rista, i, e *ag* Labour (*BRIT*) *cpd* ♦ *sm/f* Labour Party member (*BRIT*)

'lacca, che *sf* lacquer

'laccio ['lattʃo] *sm* noose; (*legaccio, tirante*) lasso; (*di scarpa*) lace; ~ **emostatico** tourniquet

lace'rare [latʃe'rare] *vt* to tear to shreds, lacerate; ~**rsi** *vr* to tear; **'lacero, a** *ag* (*logoro*) torn, tattered; (*MED*) lacerated

'lacrima *sf* tear; **in ~e** in tears; **lacri'mare** *vi* to water; **lacri'mogeno, a** *ag*: **gas lacri-mogeno** tear gas

la'cuna *sf* (*fig*) gap

'ladro *sm* thief; **ladro'cinio** *sm* theft, larceny

laggiù [lad'dʒu] *av* down there; (*di là*) over there

la'gnarsi [laɲ'ɲarsi] *vr*: ~ (**di**) to complain (about)

'lago, ghi *sm* lake

la'guna *sf* lagoon

'laico, a, ci, che *ag* (*apostolato*) lay; (*vita*) secular; (*scuola*) non-denominational ♦ *sm/f* layman/woman

'lama *sm inv* (*ZOOL*) llama; (*REL*) lama ♦ *sf* blade

lam'bire *vt* to lick; to lap

lamen'tare *vt* to lament; ~**rsi** *vr* (*emettere lamenti*) to moan, groan; (*rammaricarsi*): ~**rsi (di)** to complain (about); **lamen'tela** *sf* complaining *no pl*; **lamen'tevole** *ag* (*voce*) complaining, plaintive; (*destino*) pitiful; **la'mento** *sm* moan, groan; wail; **lamen'toso, a** *ag* plaintive

la'metta *sf* razor blade

lami'era *sf* sheet metal

'lamina *sf* (*lastra sottile*) thin sheet (*o layer o plate*); ~ **d'oro** gold leaf; gold foil; **lami'nare** *vt* to laminate; **lami'nato, a** *ag* laminated; (*tessuto*) lamé ♦ *sm* laminate

'lampada *sf* lamp; ~ **a gas** gas lamp; ~ **da tavolo** table lamp

lampa'dario *sm* chandelier

lampa'dina *sf* light bulb; ~ **tascabile** pocket torch (*BRIT*) o flashlight (*US*)

lam'pante *ag* (*fig: evidente*) crystal clear, evident

lampeggi'are [lamped'dʒare] *vi* (*luce, fari*) to flash ♦ *vb impers*: **lampeggia** there's lightning; **lampeggia'tore** *sm* (*AUT*) indicator

lampi'one *sm* street light o lamp (*BRIT*)

'lampo *sm* (*METEOR*) flash of lightning; (*di luce, fig*) flash; ~**i** *smpl* lightning *no pl* ♦ *ag inv*: **cerniera ~** zip (fastener) (*BRIT*), zipper

(*US*); **guerra ~** blitzkrieg

lam'pone *sm* raspberry

'lana *sf* wool; ~ **d'acciaio** steel wool; **pura ~ vergine** pure new wool; ~ **di vetro** glass wool

lan'cetta [lan'tʃetta] *sf* (*indice*) pointer, needle; (*di orologio*) hand

'lancia ['lantʃa] *sf* (*arma*) lance; (: **picca**) spear; (*di pompa antincendio*) nozzle; (*imbarcazione*) launch

lanciafi'amme [lantʃa'fjamme] *sm inv* flamethrower

lanci'are [lan'tʃare] *vt* to throw, hurl, fling; (*SPORT*) to throw; (*far partire: automobile*) to get up to full speed; (*bombe*) to drop; (*razzo, prodotto, moda*) to launch; ~**rsi** *vr*: ~**rsi contro/su** to throw o hurl o fling o.s. against/on; ~**rsi in** (*fig*) to embark on

lanci'nante [lantʃi'nante] *ag* (*dolore*) shooting, throbbing; (*grido*) piercing

'lancio ['lantʃo] *sm* throwing *no pl*; throw; dropping *no pl*; drop; launching *no pl*; launch; ~ **del peso** putting the shot

'landa *sf* (*GEO*) moor

'languido, a *ag* (*fiacco*) languid, weak; (*tenero, malinconico*) languishing

langu'ore *sm* weakness, languor

lani'ficio [lani'fitʃo] *sm* woollen mill

la'noso, a *ag* woolly

lan'terna *sf* lantern; (*faro*) lighthouse

la'nugine [la'nudʒine] *sf* down

lapi'dario, a *ag* (*fig*) terse

'lapide *sf* (*di sepolcro*) tombstone; (*commemorativa*) plaque

'lapis *sm inv* pencil

Lap'ponia *sf* Lapland

'lapsus *sm inv* slip

'laptop ['læptɔp] *sm inv* laptop (computer)

'lardo *sm* bacon fat, lard

lar'ghezza [lar'gettsa] *sf* width; breadth; looseness; generosity; ~ **di vedute** broad-mindedness

'largo, a, ghi, ghe *ag* wide; broad; (*maniche*) wide; (*abito: troppo ampio*) loose; (*fig*) generous ♦ *sm* width; breadth; (*mare aperto*): **il ~** the open sea ♦ *sf*: **stare o tenersi alla ~a (da qn/qc)** to keep one's distance (from sb/sth), keep away (from sb/sth); ~ **due metri** two metres wide; ~ **di spalle** broad-shouldered; **di ~ghe vedute** broad-minded; **su ~a scala** on a large scale; **di manica ~a** generous, open-handed; **al ~ di Genova** off the coast of) Genoa; **farsi ~ tra la folla** to push one's way through the crowd

'larice ['laritʃe] *sm* (*BOT*) larch

larin'gite [larin'dʒite] *sf* laryngitis

'larva *sf* larva; (*fig*) shadow

la'sagne [la'zaɲɲe] *sfpl* lasagna *sg*

lasci'are [laʃ'ʃare] *vt* to leave; (*abbandonare*)

to leave, abandon, give up; (cessare di tenere) to let go of ♦ vb aus: ~ **fare qn** to let sb do; ~ **andare** o **correre** o **perdere** to let things go their own way; ~ **stare qc/qn** to leave sth/sb alone; **~rsi** vr (persone) to part; (coppia) to split up; **~rsi andare** o let o.s. go

'lascito ['laʃʃito] sm (DIR) legacy

'laser ['lazer] ag, sm inv: **(raggio) ~** laser (beam)

lassa'tivo, a ag, sm laxative

'lasso sm: ~ **di tempo** interval, lapse of time

lassù av up there

'lastra sf (di pietra) slab; (di metallo, FOT) plate; (di ghiaccio, vetro) sheet; (radiografica) X-ray (plate)

lastri'cato sm paving

late'rale ag lateral, side cpd; (uscita, ingresso etc) side cpd ♦ sm (CALCIO) half-back

late'rizio [late'rittsjo] sm (perforated) brick

lati'fondo sm large estate

la'tino, a ag, sm Latin; **~-ameri'cano, a** ag Latin-American

lati'tante sm/f fugitive (from justice)

lati'tudine sf latitude

'lato, a ag (fig) wide, broad ♦ sm side; (fig) aspect, point of view; **in senso ~** broadly speaking

la'trare vi to bark

la'trina sf public lavatory

'latta sf tin (plate); (recipiente) tin, can

lat'taio, a sm/f milkman/woman; dairyman/woman

lat'tante ag unweaned

'latte sm milk; **~ detergente** cleansing milk o lotion; **~ in polvere** dried o powdered milk; **~ scremato** skimmed milk; **latte'ria** sf dairy; **latti'cini** smpl dairy products

lat'tina sf (di birra etc) can

lat'tuga, ghe sf lettuce

'laurea sf degree; **laurearsi** vr to graduate; **laure'ato, a** ag, sm/f graduate

'lauro sm laurel

'lauto, a ag (pranzo, mancia) lavish

'lava sf lava

la'vabo sm washbasin

la'vaggio [la'vaddʒo] sm washing no pl; **~ del cervello** brainwashing no pl

la'vagna [la'vaɲɲa] sf (GEO) slate; (di scuola) blackboard

la'vanda sf (anche MED) wash; (BOT) lavender; **lavan'daia** sf washerwoman; **lavande'ria** sf laundry; **lavanderia automatica** launderette; **lavanderia a secco** dry-cleaner's; **lavan'dino** sm sink

lavapi'atti sm/f dishwasher

la'vare vt to wash; **~rsi** vr to wash, have a wash; **~ a secco** to dry-clean; **~rsi le mani/i denti** to wash one's hands/clean one's teeth

lava'secco sm o f inv drycleaner's

lavasto'viglie [lavasto'viʎʎe] sm o f inv (macchina) dishwasher

lava'trice [lava'tritʃe] sf washing machine

lava'tura sf washing no pl; **~ di piatti** dishwater

lavo'rante sm/f worker

lavo'rare vi to work; (fig: bar, studio etc) to do good business ♦ vt to work; **~rsi qn** (persuaderlo) to work on sb; **~ a** to work on; **~ a maglia** to knit; **lavora'tivo, a** ag working; **lavora'tore, 'trice** sm/f worker ♦ ag working; **lavorazi'one** sf (gen) working; (di legno, pietra) carving; (di film) making; (di prodotto) manufacture; (modo di esecuzione) workmanship; **lavo'rio** sm intense activity

la'voro sm work; (occupazione) job, work no pl; (opera) piece of work, job; (ECON) labour; **~i forzati** hard labour sg; **~i pubblici** public works

le det fpl the ♦ pron (oggetto) them; (: a lei, a essa) (to) her; (: forma di cortesia) (to) you; vedi anche **il**

le'ale ag loyal; (sincero) sincere; (onesto) fair; **lealtà** sf loyalty; sincerity; fairness

'lebbra sf leprosy

'lecca 'lecca sm inv lollipop

leccapi'edi (peg) sm/f inv toady, bootlicker

lec'care vt to lick; (sog: gatto: latte etc) to lick o lap up; (fig) to flatter; **~rsi i baffi** to lick one's lips

'leccio ['lettʃo] sm holm oak, ilex

leccor'nia sf titbit, delicacy

'lecito, a ['lɛtʃito] ag permitted, allowed

'ledere vt to damage, injure

'lega, ghe sf league; (di metalli) alloy

le'gaccio [le'gattʃo] sm string, lace

le'gale ag legal ♦ sm lawyer; **legaliz'zare** vt to authenticate; (regolarizzare) to legalize

le'game sm (corda, fig: affettivo) tie, bond; (nesso logico) link, connection

le'gare vt (prigioniero, capelli, cane) to tie (up); (libro) to bind; (CHIM) to alloy; (fig: collegare) to bind, join ♦ vi (far lega) to unite; (fig) to get on well

le'gato sm (REL) legate; (DIR) legacy, bequest

lega'tura sf (di libro) binding; (MUS) ligature

le'genda [le'dʒɛnda] sf (di carta geografica etc) = **leggenda**

'legge ['leddʒe] sf law

leg'genda [led'dʒɛnda] sf (narrazione) legend; (di carta geografica etc) key, legend

'leggere ['lɛddʒere] vt, vi to read

legge'rezza [leddʒe'rettsa] sf lightness; thoughtlessness; fickleness

leg'gero, a [led'dʒɛro] ag light; (agile, snello) nimble, agile, light; (tè, caffè) weak; (fig: non grave, piccolo) slight; (: spensierato) thoughtless; (: incostante) fickle; free and easy; **alla ~a** thoughtlessly

leggi'adro, a [led'dʒadro] *ag* pretty, lovely; (*movimenti*) graceful

leg'gio, 'gii [led'dʒio] *sm* lectern; (*MUS*) music stand

legisla'tura [ledʒizla'tura] *sf* legislature

legislazi'one [ledʒizlat'tsjone] *sf* legislation

le'gittimo, a [le'dʒittimo] *ag* legitimate; (*fig: giustificato, lecito*) justified, legitimate; **~a difesa** (*DIR*) self-defence

'legna ['leɲɲa] *sf* firewood; **le'gname** *sm* wood, timber

'legno ['leɲɲo] *sm* wood; (*pezzo di ~*) piece of wood; **di ~** wooden; **~ compensato** plywood; **le'gnoso, a** *ag* wooden; woody; (*carne*) tough

le'gumi *smpl* (*BOT*) pulses

'lei *pron* (*soggetto*) she; (*oggetto: per dare rilievo, con preposizione*) her; (*forma di cortesia: anche: L~*) you ♦ *sm*: **dare del ~ a qn** to address sb as "lei"; **~ stessa** she herself; you yourself

'lembo *sm* (*di abito, strada*) edge; (*striscia sottile: di terra*) strip

'lemma, i *sm* headword

'lemme 'lemme *av* (very) very slowly

'lena *sf* (*fig*) energy, stamina

le'nire *vt* to soothe

lenta'mente *av* slowly

'lente *sf* (*OTTICA*) lens *sg*; **~ d'ingrandimento** magnifying glass; **~i a contatto** *o* **corneali** contact lenses

len'tezza [len'tettsa] *sf* slowness

len'ticchia [len'tikkja] *sf* (*BOT*) lentil

len'tiggine [len'tiddʒine] *sf* freckle

'lento, a *ag* slow; (*molle: fune*) slack; (*non stretto: vite, abito*) loose ♦ *sm* (*ballo*) slow dance

'lenza ['lɛntsa] *sf* fishing-line

lenzu'olo [len'tswɔlo] *sm* sheet; **~a** *sfpl* pair of sheets

le'one *sm* lion; (*dello zodiaco*): **L~** Leo

lepo'rino, a *ag*: **labbro ~** harelip

'lepre *sf* hare

'lercio, a, ci, cie ['lɛrtʃo] *ag* filthy

'lesbica, che ['lɛzbika] *sf* lesbian

lesi'nare *vt* to be stingy with ♦ *vi*: **~ (su)** to skimp (on), be stingy (with)

lesi'one *sf* (*MED*) lesion; (*DIR*) injury, damage; (*EDIL*) crack

'leso, a *pp di* **ledere** ♦ *ag* (*offeso*) injured; **parte ~a** (*DIR*) injured party

les'sare *vt* (*CUC*) to boil

'lessico, ci *sm* vocabulary; lexicon

'lesso, a *ag* boiled ♦ *sm* boiled meat

'lesto, a *ag* quick; (*agile*) nimble; **~ di mano** (*per rubare*) light-fingered; (*per picchiare*) free with one's fists

le'tale *ag* lethal; fatal

leta'maio *sm* dunghill

le'tame *sm* manure, dung

le'targo, ghi *sm* lethargy; (*ZOOL*) hibernation

le'tizia [le'tittsja] *sf* joy, happiness

'lettera *sf* letter; **~e** *sfpl* (*letteratura*) literature *sg*; (*studi umanistici*) arts (subjects); **alla ~** literally; **in ~e** in words, in full; **lette'rale** *ag* literal

lette'rario, a *ag* literary

lette'rato, a *ag* well-read, scholarly

lettera'tura *sf* literature

let'tiga, ghe *sf* (*barella*) stretcher

let'tino *sm* cot (*BRIT*), crib (*US*)

'letto, a *pp di* **leggere** ♦ *sm* bed; **andare a ~** to go to bed; **~ a castello** bunk beds *pl*; **~ a una piazza/a due piazze** *o* **matrimoniale** single/double bed

let'tore, 'trice *sm/f* reader; (*INS*) (foreign language) assistant (*BRIT*), (foreign) teaching assistant (*US*) ♦ *sm* (*TECN*): **~ ottico** optical character reader

let'tura *sf* reading

leuce'mia [leutʃe'mia] *sf* leukaemia

'leva *sf* lever; (*MIL*) conscription; **far ~ su qn** to work on sb; **~ del cambio** (*AUT*) gear lever

le'vante *sm* east; (*vento*) East wind; **il L~** the Levant

le'vare *vt* (*occhi, braccio*) to raise; (*sollevare, togliere: tassa, divieto*) to lift; (*indumenti*) to take off, remove; (*rimuovere*) to take away; (*: dal di sopra*) to take off; (*: dal di dentro*) to take out; **~rsi** *vr* to get up; (*sole*) to rise; **le'vata** *sf* (*di posta*) collection

leva'toio, a *ag*: **ponte ~** drawbridge

leva'tura *sf* intelligence, mental capacity

levi'gare *vt* to smooth; (*con carta vetrata*) to sand

levri'ere *sm* greyhound

lezi'one [let'tsjone] *sf* lesson; (*UNIV*) lecture; **fare ~** to teach; to lecture; **dare una ~ a qn** to teach sb a lesson

lezi'oso, a [let'tsjoso] *ag* affected; simpering

'lezzo ['leddzo] *sm* stench, stink

li *pron pl* (*oggetto*) them

lì *av* there; **di** *o* **da ~** from there; **per di ~** that way; **di ~ a pochi giorni** a few days later; **~ per ~** there and then; at first; **essere ~ (~)** **per fare** to be on the point of doing, be about to do; **~ dentro** in there; **~ sotto** under there; **~ sopra** on there; up there; *vedi anche* **quello**

liba'nese *ag, sm/f* Lebanese *inv*

Li'bano *sm*: **il ~** the Lebanon

'libbra *sf* (*peso*) pound

li'beccio [li'bettʃo] *sm* south-west wind

li'bello *sm* libel

li'bellula *sf* dragonfly

libe'rale *ag, sm/f* liberal

liberaliz'zare [liberalid'dzare] *vt* to liberalize

libe'rare *vt* (*rendere libero: prigioniero*) to release; (: *popolo*) to free, liberate; (*sgombrare: passaggio*) to clear; (: *stanza*) to vacate; (*produrre: energia*) to release; **~rsi** *vr*: **~rsi di qc/qn** to get rid of sth/sb; **libera'tore, 'trice** *ag* liberating ♦ *sm/f* liberator; **liberazi'one** *sf* liberation, freeing; release; rescuing

'libero, a *ag* free; (*strada*) clear; (*non occupato: posto etc*) vacant; not taken; empty; not engaged; **~ di fare qc** free to do sth; **~ da** free from; **~ arbitrio** free will; **~ professionista** self-employed professional person; **~ scambio** free trade; **libertà** *sf inv* freedom; (*tempo disponibile*) free time ♦ *sfpl* (*licenza*) liberties; **in libertà provvisoria/ vigilata** released without bail/on probation

'Libia *sf*: **la ~** Libya; **'libico, a, ci, che** *ag, sm/f* Libyan

li'bidine *sf* lust

li'braio *sm* bookseller

li'brarsi *vr* to hover

libre'ria *sf* (*bottega*) bookshop; (*stanza*) library; (*mobile*) bookcase

li'bretto *sm* booklet; (*taccuino*) notebook; (*MUS*) libretto; **~ degli assegni** cheque book; **~ di circolazione** (*AUT*) logbook; **~ di risparmio** (*savings*) bank-book, passbook; **~ universitario** student's report book

'libro *sm* book; **~ di cassa** cash book; **~ mastro** ledger; **~ paga** payroll; **~ di testo** textbook

li'cenza [li'tʃentsa] *sf* (*permesso*) permission, leave; (*di pesca, caccia, circolazione*) permit, licence; (*MIL*) leave; (*INS*) school leaving certificate; (*libertà*) liberty; licence; licentiousness; **andare in ~** (*MIL*) to go on leave

licenzia'mento [litʃentsja'mento] *sm* dismissal

licenzi'are [litʃen'tsjare] *vt* (*impiegato*) to dismiss; (*COMM: per eccesso di personale*) to make redundant; (*INS*) to award a certificate to; **~rsi** *vr* (*impiegato*) to resign, hand in one's notice; (*INS*) to obtain one's school-leaving certificate

li'ceo [li'tʃeo] *sm* (*INS*) secondary (*BRIT*) o high (*US*) school (*for 14- to 19-year-olds*)

'lido *sm* beach, shore

li'eto, a *ag* happy, glad; **"molto ~"** (*nelle presentazioni*) "pleased to meet you"

li'eve *ag* light; (*di poco conto*) slight; (*sommesso: voce*) faint, soft

lievi'tare *vi* (*anche fig*) to rise ♦ *vt* to leaven

li'evito *sm* yeast; **~ di birra** brewer's yeast

'ligio, a, gi, gie ['lidʒo] *ag* faithful, loyal

'lilla *sm inv* lilac

'lillà *sm inv* lilac

'lima *sf* file

limacci'oso, a [limat'tʃoso] *ag* slimy; muddy

li'mare *vt* to file (down); (*fig*) to polish

'limbo *sm* (*REL*) limbo

li'metta *sf* nail file

limi'tare *vt* to limit, restrict; (*circoscrivere*) to bound, surround; **limita'tivo, a** *ag* limiting, restricting; **limi'tato, a** *ag* limited, restricted

'limite *sm* limit; (*confine*) border, boundary; **~ di velocità** speed limit

li'mitrofo, a *ag* neighbouring

limo'nata *sf* lemonade (*BRIT*), (lemon) soda (*US*); lemon squash (*BRIT*), lemonade (*US*)

li'mone *sm* (*pianta*) lemon tree; (*frutto*) lemon

'limpido, a *ag* clear; (*acqua*) limpid, clear

'lince ['lintʃe] *sf* lynx

linci'are *vt* to lynch

'lindo, a *ag* tidy, spick and span; (*biancheria*) clean

'linea *sf* line; (*di mezzi pubblici di trasporto: itinerario*) route; (: *servizio*) service; **a grandi ~e** in outline; **mantenere la ~** to look after one's figure; **aereo di ~** airliner; **nave di ~** liner; **volo di ~** scheduled flight; **~ aerea** airline; **~ di partenza/d'arrivo** (*SPORT*) starting/finishing line; **~ di tiro** line of fire

linea'menti *smpl* features; (*fig*) outlines

line'are *ag* linear; (*fig*) coherent, logical

line'etta *sf* (*trattino*) dash; (*d'unione*) hyphen

lin'gotto *sm* ingot, bar

'lingua *sf* (*ANAT, CUC*) tongue; (*idioma*) language; **mostrare la ~** to stick out one's tongue; **di ~ italiana** Italian-speaking; **~ madre** mother tongue; **una ~ di terra** a spit of land

lingu'aggio [lin'gwaddʒo] *sm* language

lingu'etta *sf* (*di strumento*) reed; (*di scarpa, TECN*) tongue; (*di busta*) flap

lingu'istica *sf* linguistics *sg*

'lino *sm* (*pianta*) flax; (*tessuto*) linen

li'noleum *sm inv* linoleum, lino

liposuzi'one [liposut'tsjone] *sf* liposuction

lique'fare *vt* (*render liquido*) to liquefy; (*fondere*) to melt; **~rsi** *vr* to liquefy; to melt

liqui'dare *vt* (*società, beni; persona: uccidere*) to liquidate; (*persona: sbarazzarsene*) to get rid of; (*conto, problema*) to settle; (*COMM: merce*) to sell off, clear; **liquidazi'one** *sf* liquidation; settlement; clearance sale

liquidità *sf* liquidity

'liquido, a *ag, sm* liquid; **~ per freni** brake fluid

liqui'rizia [likwi'rittsja] *sf* liquorice

li'quore *sm* liqueur

'lira *sf* (*unità monetaria*) lira; (*MUS*) lyre; **~ sterlina** pound sterling

'lirica, che *sf* (*poesia*) lyric poetry;

(*componimento poetico*) lyric; (*MUS*) opera

'**lirico, a, ci, che** *ag* lyric(al); (*MUS*) lyric; **cantante/teatro** ~ opera singer/house

'**lisca, sche** *sf* (*di pesce*) fishbone

lisci'are [liʃʃare] *vt* to smooth; (*fig*) to flatter

'**liscio, a, sci, sce** ['liʃʃo] *ag* smooth; (*capelli*) straight; (*mobile*) plain; (*bevanda alcolica*) neat; (*fig*) straightforward, simple ♦ *av*: **andare** ~ to go smoothly; **passarla** ~**a** to get away with it

'**liso, a** *ag* worn out, threadbare

'**lista** *sf* (*elenco*) list; ~ **elettorale** electoral roll; ~ **delle vivande** menu; ~ **delle spese** shopping list

lis'tino *sm* list; ~ **dei cambi** (foreign) exchange rate; ~ **dei prezzi** price list

Lit. *abbr* = **lire italiane**

'**lite** *sf* (*elenco*) list; (*DIR*) lawsuit

liti'gare *vi* to quarrel; (*DIR*) to litigate

li'tigio [li'tidʒo] *sm* quarrel; **litigi'oso, a** *ag* quarrelsome; (*DIR*) litigious

litogra'fia *sf* (*sistema*) lithography; (*stampa*) lithograph

lito'rale *ag* coastal, coast *cpd* ♦ *sm* coast

'**litro** *sm* litre

livel'lare *vt* to level, make level; ~**rsi** *vr* to become level; (*fig*) to level out, balance out

li'vello *sm* level; (*fig*) level, standard; **ad alto** ~ (*fig*) high-level; ~ **del mare** sea level

'**livido, a** *ag* livid; (*per percosse*) bruised, black and blue; (*cielo*) leaden ♦ *sm* bruise

li'vore *sm* malice, spite

Li'vorno *sf* Livorno, Leghorn

li'vrea *sf* livery

'**lizza** ['littsa] *sf* lists *pl*; **scendere in** ~ (*anche fig*) to enter the lists

lo (*dav s impura, gn, pn, ps, x, z; dav V l'*) *det m* the ♦ *pron* (*oggetto: persona*) him; (: *cosa*) it; ~ **sapevo** I knew it; ~ **so** I know; **sii buono, anche se lui non** ~ **è** be good, even if he isn't; *vedi anche* **il**

lo'cale *ag* local ♦ *sm* room; (*luogo pubblico*) premises *pl*; ~ **notturno** nightclub; **località** *sf inv* locality; **localiz'zare** *vt* (*circoscrivere*) to confine, localize; (*accertare*) to locate, place

lo'canda *sf* inn; **locandi'ere, a** *sm/f* innkeeper

loca'tario, a *sm/f* tenant

loca'tore, 'trice *sm/f* landlord/lady

locazi'one [lokat'tsjone] *sf* (*da parte del locatario*) renting *no pl*; (*da parte del locatore*) renting out *no pl*, letting *no pl*; (**contratto di**) ~ lease; (**canone di**) ~ rent; **dare in** ~ to rent out, let

locomo'tiva *sf* locomotive

locomo'tore *sm* electric locomotive

locomozi'one [lokomot'tsjone] *sf* locomotion; **mezzi di** ~ vehicles, means of transport

lo'custa *sf* locust

locuzi'one [lokut'tsjone] *sf* phrase, expression

lo'dare *vt* to praise

'**lode** *sf* praise; (*INS*): **laurearsi con 110 e** ~ ≈ to graduate with a first-class honours degree (*BRIT*), graduate summa cum laude (*US*)

'**loden** *sm inv* (*stoffa*) loden; (*cappotto*) loden overcoat

lo'devole *ag* praiseworthy

loga'ritmo *sm* logarithm

'**loggia, ge** ['lɔddʒa] *sf* (*ARCHIT*) loggia; (*circolo massonico*) lodge; **loggi'one** *sm* (*di teatro*): **il loggione** the gods *sg*

'**logica** *sf* logic

'**logico, a, ci, che** ['lɔdʒiko] *ag* logical

logo'rare *vt* to wear out; (*sciupare*) to waste; ~**rsi** *vr* to wear out; (*fig*) to wear o.s. out

logo'rio *sm* wear and tear; (*fig*) strain

lo'goro, a *ag* (*stoffa*) worn out, threadbare; (*persona*) worn out

lom'baggine [lom'baddʒine] *sf* lumbago

Lombar'dia *sf*: **la** ~ Lombardy

lom'bata *sf* (*taglio di carne*) loin

'**lombo** *sm* (*ANAT*) loin

lom'brico, chi *sm* earthworm

londi'nese *ag* London *cpd* ♦ *sm/f* Londoner

'**Londra** *sf* London

lon'gevo, a [lon'dʒevo] *ag* long-lived

longi'tudine [londʒi'tudine] *sf* longitude

lonta'nanza [lonta'nantsa] *sf* distance; absence

lon'tano, a *ag* (*distante*) distant, faraway; (*assente*) absent; (*vago*: *sospetto*) slight, remote; (*tempo*: *remoto*) far-off, distant; (*parente*) distant, remote ♦ *av* far; **è** ~**a la casa?** is it far to the house?, is the house far from here?; **è** ~ **un chilometro** it's a kilometre away *o* a kilometre from here; **più** ~ farther; **da** *o* **di** ~ from a distance; ~ **da** a long way from; **alla** ~**a** slightly, vaguely

'**lontra** *sf* otter

lo'quace [lo'kwatʃe] *ag* talkative, loquacious; (*fig*: *gesto etc*) eloquent

'**lordo, a** *ag* dirty, filthy; (*peso, stipendio*) gross

'**loro** *pron pl* (*oggetto, con preposizione*) them; (*complemento di termine*) to them; (*soggetto*) they; (*forma di cortesia*: *anche*: L~) you; to you; **il(la)** ~, **i(le)** ~ *det* their; (*forma di cortesia*: *anche*: L~) your ♦ *pron* theirs; (*forma di cortesia*: *anche*: L~) yours; ~ **stessi(e)** they themselves; you yourselves

'**losco, a, schi, sche** *ag* (*fig*) shady, suspicious

'**lotta** *sf* struggle, fight; (*SPORT*) wrestling; ~ **libera** all-in wrestling; **lot'tare** *vi* to fight, struggle; to wrestle; **lotta'tore, trice** *sm/f* wrestler

lotte'ria *sf* lottery; (*di gara ippica*) sweepstake

'lotto *sm* (*gioco*) (state) lottery; (*parte*) lot; (*EDIL*) site

lozi'one [lot'tsjone] *sf* lotion

lubrifi'cante *sm* lubricant

lubrifi'care *vt* to lubricate

luc'chetto [luk'ketto] *sm* padlock

lucci'care [luttʃi'kare] *vi* to sparkle, glitter, twinkle

'luccio ['luttʃo] *sm* (*ZOOL*) pike

'lucciola ['luttʃola] *sf* (*ZOOL*) firefly; glowworm

'luce ['lutʃe] *sf* light; (*finestra*) window; **alla ~ di** by the light of; **fare ~ su qc** (*fig*) to shed o throw light on sth; **~ del sole/della luna** sun/moonlight; **lu'cente** *ag* shining

lucer'nario [lutʃer'narjo] *sm* skylight

lu'certola [lu'tʃertola] *sf* lizard

luci'dare [lutʃi'dare] *vt* to polish

lucida'trice [lutʃida'tritʃe] *sf* floor polisher

'lucido, a ['lutʃido] *ag* shining, bright; (*lucidato*) polished; (*fig*) lucid ♦ *sm* shine, lustre; (*per scarpe etc*) polish; (*disegno*) tracing

'lucro *sm* profit, gain; **lu'croso, a** *ag* lucrative, profitable

'luglio ['luʎʎo] *sm* July

'lugubre *ag* gloomy

'lui *pronome* (*soggetto*) he; (*oggetto: per dare rilievo, con preposizione*) him; **~ stesso** he himself

lu'maca, che *sf* slug; (*chiocciola*) snail

'lume *sm* light; (*lampada*) lamp; (*fig*): **chiedere ~i a qn** to ask sb for advice; **a ~ di naso** (*fig*) by rule of thumb

lumi'naria *sf* (*per feste*) illuminations *pl*

lumi'noso, a *ag* (*che emette luce*) luminous; (*cielo, colore, stanza*) bright; (*sorgente*) of light, light *cpd*; (*fig: sorriso*) bright, radiant

'luna *sf* moon; **~ nuova/piena** new/full moon; **~ di miele** honeymoon

'luna park *sm inv* amusement park, funfair

lu'nare *ag* lunar, moon *cpd*

lu'nario *sm* almanac; **sbarcare il ~** to make ends meet

lu'natico, a, ci, che *ag* whimsical, temperamental

lunedì *sm inv* Monday; **di** o **il ~** on Mondays

lun'gaggine [lun'gaddʒine] *sf* slowness; **~i della burocrazia** red tape

lun'ghezza [lun'gettsa] *sf* length; **~ d'onda** (*FISICA*) wavelength

'lungi ['lundʒi] *sm*: **~ da** *prep* far from

'lungo, a, ghi, ghe *ag* long; (*lento: persona*) slow; (*diluito: caffè, brodo*) weak, watery, thin ♦ *sm* length ♦ *prep* along; **~ 3 metri** 3 metres long; **a ~ for** a long time; **a ~ andare** in the long run; **di gran ~a** (*molto*) by far; **andare in** o **per le lunghe** to drag on;

saperla ~a to know what's what; **in ~ e in largo** far and wide, all over; **~ il corso dei secoli** throughout the centuries

lungo'mare *sm* promenade

lu'notto *sm* (*AUT*) rear o back window; **~ termico** heated rear window

lu'ogo, ghi *sm* place; (*posto: di incidente etc*) scene, site; (*punto, passo di libro*) passage; **in ~ di** instead of; **in primo ~** in the first place; **aver ~** to take place; **dar ~ a** to give rise to; **~ comune** commonplace; **~ di nascita** birthplace; (*AMM*) place of birth; **~ di provenienza** place of origin

luogote'nente *sm* (*MIL*) lieutenant

lu'para *sf* sawn-off shotgun

'lupo, a *sm/f* wolf

'luppolo *sm* (*BOT*) hop

'lurido, a *ag* filthy

lu'singa, ghe *sf* (*spesso al pl*) flattery *no pl*

lusin'gare *vt* to flatter; **lusinghi'ero, a** *ag* flattering, gratifying

lus'sare *vt* (*MED*) to dislocate

Lussem'burgo *sm* (*stato*): **il ~** Luxembourg ♦ *sf* (*città*) Luxembourg

'lusso *sm* luxury; **di ~** luxury *cpd*; **lussu'oso, a** *ag* luxurious

lussureggi'ante [lussured'dʒante] *ag* luxuriant

lus'suria *sf* lust

lus'trare *vt* to polish, shine

lustras'carpe *sm/f inv* shoeshine

lus'trino *sm* sequin

'lustro, a *ag* shiny; (*pelo*) glossy ♦ *sm* shine, gloss; (*fig*) prestige, glory; (*quinquennio*) five-year period

'lutto *sm* mourning; **essere in/portare il ~** to be in/wear mourning; **luttu'oso, a** *ag* mournful, sad

M, m

ma *cong* but; **~ insomma!** for goodness sake!; **~ no!** of course not!

'macabro, a *ag* gruesome, macabre

macché [mak'ke] *escl* not at all!, certainly not!

macche'roni [makke'roni] *smpl* macaroni *sg*

'macchia ['makkja] *sf* stain, spot; (*chiazza di diverso colore*) spot; splash, patch; (*tipo di boscaglia*) scrub; **alla ~** (*fig*) in hiding; **macchi'are** *vt* (*sporcare*) to stain, mark; **macchiarsi** *vr* (*persona*) to get o.s. dirty; (*stoffa*) to stain; to get stained o marked

'macchina ['makkina] *sf* machine; (*motore, locomotiva*) engine; (*automobile*) car; (*fig: meccanismo*) machinery; **andare in ~** (*AUT*) to go by car; (*STAMPA*) to go to press; **~ da cucire** sewing machine; **~ fotografica** camera;

~ **da presa** cine o movie camera; ~ **da scrivere** typewriter; ~ **a vapore** steam engine

macchi'nare [makki'nare] vt to plot

macchi'nario [makki'narjo] sm machinery

macchi'netta [makki'netta] (fam) sf (caffettiera) percolator; (accendino) lighter

macchi'nista, i [makki'nista] sm (di treno) engine-driver; (di nave) engineer

macchi'noso, a [makki'noso] ag complex, complicated

mace'donia [matʃe'dɔnja] sf fruit salad

macel'laio [matʃel'lajo] sm butcher

macel'lare [matʃel'lare] vt to slaughter, butcher; **macelle'ria** sf butcher's (shop); **ma'cello** sm (mattatoio) slaughterhouse, abattoir (BRIT); (fig) slaughter, massacre; (: disastro) shambles sg

mace'rare [matʃe'rare] vt to macerate; (CUC) to marinate; ~**rsi** vr (fig): ~**rsi in** to be consumed with

ma'cerie [ma'tʃerje] sfpl rubble sg, debris sg

ma'cigno [ma'tʃiɲɲo] sm (masso) rock, boulder

'macina ['matʃina] sf (pietra) millstone; (macchina) grinder; **macinacaffè** sm inv coffee grinder; **macina'pepe** sm inv peppermill

maci'nare [matʃi'nare] vt to grind; (carne) to mince (BRIT), grind (US); **maci'nato** sm meal, flour; (carne) minced (BRIT) o ground (US) meat

maci'nino [matʃi'nino] sm coffee grinder; peppermill

'madido, a ag: ~ (**di**) wet o moist (with)

Ma'donna sf (REL) Our Lady

mador'nale ag enormous, huge

'madre sf mother; (matrice di bolletta) counterfoil ♦ ag inv mother cpd; **ragazza** ~ unmarried mother; **scena** ~ (TEATRO) principal scene; (fig) terrible scene

madre'lingua sf mother tongue, native language

madre'perla sf mother-of-pearl

ma'drina sf godmother

maestà sf inv majesty; **maes'toso, a** ag majestic

ma'estra sf vedi maestro

maes'trale sm north-west wind, mistral

maes'tranze [maes'trantse] sfpl workforce sg

maes'tria sf mastery, skill

ma'estro, a sm/f (INS: anche: ~ di scuola o elementare) primary (BRIT) o grade school (US) teacher; (esperto) expert ♦ sm (artigiano, fig: guida) master; (MUS) maestro ♦ ag (principale) main; (di grande abilità) masterly, skilful; ~**a d'asilo** nursery teacher; ~ **di cerimonie** master of ceremonies

'mafia sf Mafia; **mafi'oso** sm member of the Mafia

'maga sf sorceress

ma'gagna [ma'gaɲɲa] sf defect, flaw, blemish; (noia, guaio) problem

ma'gari escl (esprime desiderio): ~ **fosse vero!** if only it were true!; **ti piacerebbe andare in Scozia? — ~!** would you like to go to Scotland? — and how! ♦ av (anche) even; (forse) perhaps

magaz'zino [magad'dzino] sm warehouse; **grande** ~ department store

'maggio ['maddʒo] sm May

maggio'rana [maddʒo'rana] sf (BOT) (sweet) marjoram

maggio'ranza [maddʒo'rantsa] sf majority

maggio'rare [maddʒo'rare] vt to increase, raise

maggior'domo [maddʒor'dɔmo] sm butler

maggi'ore [mad'dʒore] ag (comparativo: più grande) bigger, larger; taller; greater; (: più vecchio: sorella, fratello) older, elder; (: di grado superiore) senior; (: più importante, MIL, MUS) major; (superlativo) biggest, largest; tallest; greatest; oldest, eldest ♦ sm/f (di grado) superior; (di età) elder; (MIL) major; (: AER) squadron leader; **la maggior parte** the majority; **andare per la** ~ (cantante etc) to be very popular; **maggio'renne** ag of age ♦ sm/f person who has come of age; **maggior'mente** av much more; (con senso superlativo) most

ma'gia [ma'dʒia] sf magic; **'magico, a, ci, che** ag magic; (fig) fascinating, charming, magical

'magio ['madʒo] sm (REL): **i re Magi** the Magi, the Three Wise Men

magis'tero [madʒis'tero] sm: **facoltà di M~** ≈ teachers' training college; **magis'trale** ag primary (BRIT) o grade school (US) teachers', primary (BRIT) o grade school (US) teaching cpd; skilful

magis'trato [madʒis'trato] sm magistrate; **magistra'tura** sf magistrature; (magistrati): **la magistratura** the Bench

'maglia ['maʎʎa] sf stitch; (lavoro ai ferri) knitting no pl; (tessuto, SPORT) jersey; (maglione) jersey, sweater; (di catena) link; (di rete) mesh; ~ **diritta/rovescia** plain/purl; **maglie'ria** sf knitwear; (negozio) knitwear shop; **magli'etta** sf (canottiera) vest; (tipo camicia) T-shirt; **magli'ficio** sm knitwear factory

'maglio ['maʎʎo] sm mallet; (macchina) power hammer

magli'one sm sweater, jumper

ma'gnanimo, a [maɲ'ɲanimo, a] ag magnanimous

ma'gnete [maɲ'ɲete] sm magnet; **ma'gnetico, a, ci, che** ag magnetic

magne'tofono [maɲɲe'tɔfono] *sm* tape recorder

ma'gnifico, a, ci, che [maɲ'ɲifiko] *ag* magnificent, splendid; (*ospite*) generous

'magno, a ['maɲɲo] *ag*: **aula ~a** main hall

ma'gnolia [maɲ'nɔlja] *sf* magnolia

'mago, ghi *sm* (*stregone*) magician, wizard; (*illusionista*) magician

ma'grezza [ma'grettsa] *sf* thinness

'magro, a *ag* (very) thin, skinny; (*carne*) lean; (*formaggio*) low-fat; (*fig: scarso, misero*) meagre, poor; (: *meschino: scusa*) poor, lame; **mangiare di ~** not to eat meat

'mai *av* (*nessuna volta*) never; (*talvolta*) ever; **non ... ~** never; **~ più** never again; **come ~?** why (*o* how) on earth?; **chi/dove/quando ~?** whoever/wherever/whenever?

mai'ale *sm* (*ZOOL*) pig; (*carne*) pork

maio'nese *sf* mayonnaise

'mais *sm inv* maize

mai'uscola *sf* capital letter

mai'uscolo, a *ag* (*lettera*) capital; (*fig*) enormous, huge

mal *av*, *sm vedi* **male**

malac'corto, a *ag* rash, careless

mala'fede *sf* bad faith

mala'lingua (*pl* **male'lingue**) *sf* gossip(monger)

mala'mente *av* badly; dangerously

malan'dato, a *ag* (*persona: di salute*) in poor health; (: *di condizioni finanziarie*) badly off; (*trascurato*) shabby

ma'lanno *sm* (*disgrazia*) misfortune; (*malattia*) ailment

mala'pena *sf*: **a ~** hardly, scarcely

ma'laria *sf* (*MED*) malaria

mala'sorte *sf* bad luck

mala'ticcio, a [mala'tittʃo] *ag* sickly

ma'lato, a *ag* ill, sick; (*gamba*) bad; (*pianta*) diseased ♦ *sm/f* sick person; (*in ospedale*) patient; **malat'tia** *sf* (*infettiva etc*) illness, disease; (*cattiva salute*) illness, sickness; (*di pianta*) disease

malau'gurio *sm* bad *o* ill omen

mala'vita *sf* underworld

mala'voglia [mala'vɔʎʎa] *sf*: **di ~** unwillingly, reluctantly

mal'concio, a, ci, ce [mal'kontʃo] *ag* in a sorry state

malcon'tento *sm* discontent

malcos'tume *sm* immorality

mal'destro, a *ag* (*inabile*) inexpert, inexperienced; (*goffo*) awkward

maldi'cenza [maldi'tʃentsa] *sf* malicious gossip

maldis'posto, a *ag*: **~ (verso)** ill-disposed (towards)

'male *av* badly ♦ *sm* (*ciò che è ingiusto, disonesto*) evil; (*danno, svantaggio*) harm;

(*sventura*) misfortune; (*dolore fisico, morale*) pain, ache; **di ~ in peggio** from bad to worse; **sentirsi ~** to feel ill; **far ~** (*dolere*) to hurt; **far ~ alla salute** to be bad for one's health; **far del ~ a qn** to hurt *o* harm sb; **restare** *o* **rimanere ~** to be sorry; to be disappointed; to be hurt; **andare a ~** to go bad; **come va? — non c'è ~** how are you? — not bad; **mal di cuore** heart trouble; **~ di dente** toothache; **mal di mare** seasickness; **avere mal di gola/testa** to have a sore throat/a headache; **aver ~ ai piedi** to have sore feet

male'detto, a *pp di* **maledire** ♦ *ag* cursed, damned; (*fig: fam*) damned, blasted

male'dire *vt* to curse; **maledizi'one** *sf* curse; **maledizione!** damn it!

maledu'cato, a *ag* rude, ill-mannered

male'fatta *sf* misdeed

male'ficio [male'fitʃo] *sm* witchcraft

ma'lefico, a, ci, che *ag* (*influsso, azione*) evil

ma'lessere *sm* indisposition, slight illness; (*fig*) uneasiness

ma'levolo, a *ag* malevolent

malfa'mato, a *ag* notorious

mal'fatto, a *ag* (*persona*) deformed; (*oggetto*) badly made; (*lavoro*) badly done

malfat'tore, 'trice *sm/f* wrongdoer

mal'fermo, a *ag* unsteady, shaky; (*salute*) poor, delicate

malformazi'one [malformat'tsjone] *sf* malformation

malgo'verno *sm* maladministration

mal'grado *prep* in spite of, despite ♦ *cong* although; **mio (o tuo etc) ~** against my (*o* your *etc*) will

mali'gnare [maliɲ'ɲare] *vi*: **~ su** to malign, speak ill of

ma'ligno, a [ma'liɲɲo] *ag* (*malvagio*) malicious, malignant; (*MED*) malignant

malinco'nia *sf* melancholy, gloom; **malin'conico, a, ci, che** *ag* melancholy

malincu'ore: a ~ reluctantly, unwillingly

malintenzio'nato, a [malintentsjo'nato] *ag* ill-intentioned

malin'teso, a *ag* misunderstood; (*riguardo, senso del dovere*) mistaken, wrong ♦ *sm* misunderstanding

ma'lizia [ma'littsja] *sf* (*malignità*) malice; (*furbizia*) cunning; (*espediente*) trick; **malizi'oso, a** *ag* malicious; cunning; (*vivace, birichino*) mischievous

mal'loppo *sm* (*involto*) bundle; (*fam: refurtiva*) loot

malme'nare *vt* to beat up

mal'messo, a *ag* shabby

malnu'trito, a *ag* undernourished

ma'locchio [ma'lɔkkjo] *sm* evil eye

ma'lora *sf*: **andare in ~** to go to the dogs

ma'lore *sm* (sudden) illness

mal'sano, a *ag* unhealthy

malsi'curo, a *ag* unsafe

'Malta *sf* Malta

'malta *sf* (EDIL) mortar

mal'tempo *sm* bad weather

'malto *sm* malt

maltrat'tare *vt* to ill-treat

malu'more *sm* bad mood; (*irritabilità*) bad temper; (*discordia*) ill feeling; **di ~** in a bad mood

mal'vagio, a, gi, gie [mal'vadʒo] *ag* wicked, evil

malversazi'one [malversat'tsjone] *sf* (DIR) embezzlement

mal'visto, a *ag*: **~ (da)** disliked (by), unpopular (with)

malvi'vente *sm* criminal

malvolenti'eri *av* unwillingly, reluctantly

'mamma *sf* mummy, mum; **~ mia!** my goodness!

mam'mella *sf* (ANAT) breast; (*di vacca, capra etc*) udder

mam'mifero *sm* mammal

'mammola *sf* (BOT) violet

ma'nata *sf* (*colpo*) slap; (*quantità*) handful

'manca *sf* left (hand); **a destra e a ~** left, right and centre, on all sides

man'canza [man'kantsa] *sf* lack; (*carenza*) shortage, scarcity; (*fallo*) fault; (*imperfezione*) failing, shortcoming; **per ~ di tempo** through lack of time; **in ~ di meglio** for lack of anything better

man'care *vi* (*essere insufficiente*) to be lacking; (*venir meno*) to fail; (*sbagliare*) to be wrong, make a mistake; (*non esserci*) to be missing, not to be there; (*essere lontano*): **~ (da)** to be away (from) ♦ *vt* to miss; **~ di** to lack; **~ a** (*promessa*) to fail to keep; **tu mi manchi** I miss you; **mancò poco che morisse** he very nearly died; **mancano ancora 10 sterline** we're still £10 short; **manca un quarto alle 6** it's a quarter to 6; **man'cato, a** *ag* (*tentativo*) unsuccessful; (*artista*) failed

'mancia, ce ['mantʃa] *sf* tip; **~ competente** reward

manci'ata [man'tʃata] *sf* handful

man'cino, a [man'tʃino] *ag* (*braccio*) left; (*persona*) left-handed; (*fig*) underhand

'manco *av* (*nemmeno*): **~ per sogno** o **per idea!** not on your life!

man'dante *sm/f* (*di delitto*) instigator

manda'rancio [manda'rantʃo] *sm* clementine

man'dare *vt* to send; (*far funzionare*: *macchina*) to drive; (*emettere*) to send out; (*: grido*) to give, utter, let out; **~ a chiamare qn** to send for sb; **~ avanti** (*fig*: *famiglia*) to provide for; (*: fabbrica*) to run, look after;

~ giù to send down; (*anche fig*) to swallow; **~ via** to send away; (*licenziare*) to fire

manda'rino *sm* mandarin (orange); (*cinese*) mandarin

man'data *sf* (*quantità*) lot, batch; (*di chiave*) turn; **chiudere a doppia ~** to double-lock

man'dato *sm* (*incarico*) commission; (DIR: *provvedimento*) warrant; (*di deputato etc*) mandate; (*ordine di pagamento*) postal o money order; **~ d'arresto** warrant for arrest

man'dibola *sf* mandible, jaw

'mandorla *sf* almond; **'mandorlo** *sm* almond tree

'mandria *sf* herd

maneggi'are [maned'dʒare] *vt* (*creta, cera*) to mould, work, fashion; (*arnesi, utensili*) to handle; (: *adoperare*) to use; (*fig*: *persone, denaro*) to handle, deal with; **ma'neggio** *sm* moulding; handling; use; (*intrigo*) plot, scheme; (*per cavalli*) riding school

ma'nesco, a, schi, sche *ag* free with one's fists

ma'nette *sfpl* handcuffs

manga'nello *sm* club

manga'nese *sm* manganese

mange'reccio, a, ci, ce [mandʒe'rettʃo] *ag* edible

mangi'are [man'dʒare] *vt* to eat; (*intaccare*) to eat into o away; (CARTE, SCACCHI etc) to take ♦ *vi* to eat ♦ *sm* eating; (*cibo*) food; (*cucina*) cooking; **~rsi le parole** to mumble; **~rsi le unghie** to bite one's nails; **man-gia'toia** *sf* feeding-trough

man'gime [man'dʒime] *sm* fodder

'mango, ghi *sm* mango

ma'nia *sf* (PSIC) mania; (*fig*) obsession, craze; **ma'niaco, a, ci, che** *ag* suffering from a mania; **maniaco (di)** obsessed (by), crazy (about)

'manica *sf* sleeve; (*fig*: *gruppo*) gang, bunch; (GEO): **la M~, il Canale della M~** the (English) Channel; **essere di ~ larga/stretta** to be easy-going/strict; **~ a vento** (AER) wind sock

mani'chino [mani'kino] *sm* (*di sarto, vetrina*) dummy

'manico, ci *sm* handle; (MUS) neck

mani'comio *sm* mental hospital; (*fig*) madhouse

mani'cotto *sm* muff; (TECN) coupling; sleeve

mani'cure *sm o f inv* manicure ♦ *sf inv* manicurist

mani'era *sf* way, manner; (*stile*) style, manner; **~e** *sfpl* (*comportamento*) manners; **in ~ che** so that; **in ~ da** so as to; **in tutte le ~e** at all costs

manie'rato, a *ag* affected

manifat'tura *sf* (*lavorazione*) manufacture; (*stabilimento*) factory

manifes'tare *vt* to show, display;

(*esprimere*) to express; (*rivelare*) to reveal, disclose ♦ *vi* to demonstrate; **~rsi** *vr* to show o.s.; **~rsi amico** to prove o.s. (to be) a friend; **manifestazi'one** *sf* show, display; expression; (*sintomo*) sign, symptom; (*dimostrazione pubblica*) demonstration; (*cerimonia*) event

mani'festo, a *ag* obvious, evident ♦ *sm* poster, bill; (*scritto ideologico*) manifesto

ma'niglia [ma'niʎʎa] *sf* handle; (*sostegno: negli autobus etc*) strap

manipo'lare *vt* to manipulate; (*alterare: vino*) to adulterate; **manipolazi'one** *sf* manipulation; adulteration

'manna *sf* (*REL*) manna; (*fig*) godsend

man'naia *sf* (*del boia*) (executioner's) axe; (*per carni*) cleaver

man'naro: lupo ~ *sm* werewolf

'mano, i *sf* hand; (*strato: di vernice etc*) coat; **di prima ~** (*notizia*) first-hand; **di seconda ~** second-hand; **man ~** little by little, gradually; **man ~ che** as; **darsi o stringersi la ~** to shake hands; **mettere le ~i avanti** (*fig*) to safeguard o.s.; **restare a ~i vuote** to be left empty-handed; **venire alle ~i** to come to blows; **a ~** by hand; **~i in alto!** hands up!

mano'dopera *sf* labour

mano'messo, a *pp di* **manomettere**

ma'nometro *sm* gauge, manometer

mano'mettere *vt* (*alterare*) to tamper with; (*aprire indebitamente*) to break open illegally

ma'nopola *sf* (*dell'armatura*) gauntlet; (*guanto*) mitt; (*di impugnatura*) hand-grip; (*pomello*) knob

manos'critto, a *ag* handwritten ♦ *sm* manuscript

mano'vale *sm* labourer

mano'vella *sf* handle; (*TECN*) crank

ma'novra *sf* manoeuvre (*BRIT*), maneuver (*US*); (*FERR*) shunting; **mano'vrare** *vt* (*veicolo*) to manoeuvre (*BRIT*), maneuver (*US*); (*macchina, congegno*) to operate; (*fig: persona*) to manipulate ♦ *vi* to manoeuvre

manro'vescio [manro'veʃʃo] *sm* slap (*with back of hand*)

man'sarda *sf* attic

mansi'one *sf* task, duty, job

mansu'eto, a *ag* gentle, docile

man'tello *sm* cloak; (*fig: di neve etc*) blanket, mantle; (*ZOOL*) coat

mante'nere *vt* to maintain; (*adempiere: promesse*) to keep, abide by; (*provvedere a*) to support, maintain; **~rsi** *vr*: **~rsi calmo/ giovane** to stay calm/young; **manteni'mento** *sm* maintenance

'mantice ['mantitʃe] *sm* bellows *pl*

'manto *sm* cloak; **~ stradale** road surface

manu'ale *ag* manual ♦ *sm* (*testo*) manual, handbook

ma'nubrio *sm* handle; (*di bicicletta etc*) handlebars *pl*; (*SPORT*) dumbbell

manu'fatto *sm* manufactured article

manutenzi'one [manuten'tsjone] *sf* maintenance, upkeep; (*d'impianti*) maintenance, servicing

'manzo ['mandzo] *sm* (*ZOOL*) steer; (*carne*) beef

'mappa *sf* (*GEO*) map; **mappa'mondo** *sm* map of the world; (*globo girevole*) globe

mara'tona *sf* marathon

'marca, che *sf* (*COMM: di prodotti*) brand; (*contrassegno, scontrino*) ticket, check; **prodotto di ~** (*di buona qualità*) high-class product; **~ da bollo** official stamp

mar'care *vt* (*munire di contrassegno*) to mark; (*a fuoco*) to brand; (*SPORT: gol*) to score; (*: avversario*) to mark; (*accentuare*) to stress; **~ visita** (*MIL*) to report sick

'Marche ['marke] *sfpl*: **le ~** the Marches (*region of central Italy*)

mar'chese, a [mar'keze] *sm/f* marquis o marquess/marchioness

marchi'are [mar'kjare] *vt* to brand; **'marchio** *sm* (*di bestiame, COMM, fig*) brand; **marchio depositato** registered trademark; **marchio di fabbrica** trademark

'marcia, ce ['martʃa] *sf* (*anche MUS, MIL*) march; (*funzionamento*) running; (*il camminare*) walking; (*AUT*) gear; **mettere in ~** to start; **mettersi in ~** to get moving; **far ~ indietro** (*AUT*) to reverse; (*fig*) to back-pedal

marciapi'ede [martʃa'pjɛde] *sm* (*di strada*) pavement (*BRIT*), sidewalk (*US*); (*FERR*) platform

marci'are [mar'tʃare] *vi* to march; (*andare: treno, macchina*) to go; (*funzionare*) to run, work

'marcio, a, ci, ce ['martʃo] *ag* (*frutta, legno*) rotten, bad; (*MED*) festering; (*fig*) corrupt, rotten

mar'cire [mar'tʃire] *vi* (*andare a male*) to go bad, rot; (*suppurare*) to fester; (*fig*) to rot, waste away

'marco, chi *sm* (*unità monetaria*) mark

'mare *sm sea*; **in ~** at sea; **andare al ~** (*in vacanza etc*) to go to the seaside; **il M~ del Nord** the North Sea

ma'rea *sf* tide; **alta/bassa ~** high/low tide

mareggi'ata [mared'dʒata] *sf* heavy sea

mare'moto *sm* seaquake

maresci'allo [mareʃ'ʃallo] *sm* (*MIL*) marshal; (*: sottufficiale*) warrant officer

marga'rina *sf* margarine

marghe'rita [marge'rita] *sf* (ox-eye) daisy, marguerite; (*di stampante*) daisy wheel

'margine ['mardʒine] *sm* margin; (*di bosco, via*) edge, border

ma'rina sf navy; (costa) coast; (quadro) seascape; ~ **militare/mercantile** navy/merchant navy (BRIT) o marine (US)

mari'naio sm sailor

mari'nare vt (CUC) to marinate; ~ **la scuola** to play truant; **mari'nata** sf marinade

ma'rino, a ag sea cpd, marine

mario'netta sf puppet

mari'tare vt to marry; ~**rsi** vr: ~**rsi a** o **con qn** to marry sb, get married to sb

ma'rito sm husband

ma'rittimo, a ag maritime, sea cpd

mar'maglia [mar'maʎʎa] sf mob, riff-raff

marmel'lata sf jam; (di agrumi) marmalade

mar'mitta sf (recipiente) pot; (AUT) silencer; ~ **catalitica** catalytic converter

'marmo sm marble

mar'mocchio [mar'mɔkkjo] (fam) sm tot, kid

mar'motta sf (ZOOL) marmot

Ma'rocco sm: **il** ~ Morocco

mar'rone ag inv brown ♦ sm (BOT) chestnut

mar'sala sm inv (vino) Marsala

mar'sina sf tails pl, tail coat

mar'supio sm pouch; (per denaro) bum bag; (per neonato) sling

marte'dì sm inv Tuesday; **di** o **il** ~ **on** Tuesdays; ~ **grasso** Shrove Tuesday

martel'lare vt to hammer ♦ vi (pulsare) to throb; (: cuore) to thump

mar'tello sm hammer; (di uscio) knocker

marti'netto sm (TECN) jack

'martire sm/f martyr; **mar'tirio** sm martyrdom; (fig) agony, torture

'martora sf marten

martori'are vt to torment, torture

mar'xista, i, e ag, sm/f Marxist

marza'pane [martsa'pane] sm marzipan

'marzo ['martso] sm March

mascal'zone [maskal'tsone] sm rascal, scoundrel

ma'scella [maʃ'ʃella] sf (ANAT) jaw

'maschera ['maskera] sf mask; (travestimento) disguise; (: per un ballo etc) fancy dress; (TEATRO, CINEMA) usher/usherette; (personaggio del teatro) stock character; **masche'rare** vt to mask; (travestire) to disguise; to dress up; (fig: celare) to hide, conceal; (MIL) to camouflage; ~**rsi da** to disguise o.s. as; to dress up as; (fig) to masquerade as

mas'chile [mas'kile] ag masculine; (sesso, popolazione) male; (abiti) men's; (per ragazzi: scuola) boys'

'maschio, a ['maskjo] ag (BIOL) male; (virile) manly ♦ sm (anche ZOOL, TECN) male; (uomo) man; (ragazzo) boy; (figlio) son

masco'lino, a ag masculine

'massa sf mass; (di errori etc): **una** ~ **di** heaps of, masses of; (di gente) mass, multitude; (ELETTR) earth; **in** ~ (COMM) in bulk; (tutti insieme) en masse; **adunata in** ~ mass meeting; **di** ~ (cultura, manifestazione) mass cpd

mas'sacro sm massacre, slaughter; (fig) mess, disaster

mas'saggio [mas'saddʒo] sm massage

mas'saia sf housewife

masse'rizie [masse'rittsje] sfpl (household) furnishings

mas'siccio, a, ci, ce [mas'sittʃo] ag (oro, legno) solid; (palazzo) massive; (corporatura) stout ♦ sm (GEO) massif

'massima sf (sentenza, regola) maxim; (METEOR) maximum temperature; **in linea di** ~ generally speaking; vedi anche **massimo**

massi'male sm maximum

'massimo, a ag, sm maximum; **al** ~ at (the) most

'masso sm rock, boulder

mas'sone sm freemason; **massone'ria** sf freemasonry

mas'tello sm tub

masti'care vt to chew

'mastice ['mastitʃe] sm mastic; (per vetri) putty

mas'tino sm mastiff

ma'tassa sf skein

mate'matica sf mathematics sg

mate'matico, a, ci, che ag mathematical ♦ sm/f mathematician

materas'sino sm mat; (gonfiabile) air bed

mate'rasso sm mattress; ~ **a molle** spring o interior-sprung mattress

ma'teria sf (FISICA) matter; (TECN, COMM) material, matter no pl; (disciplina) subject; (argomento) subject matter, material; ~**e prime** raw materials; **in** ~ **di** (per quanto concerne) on the subject of

materi'ale ag material; (fig: grossolano) rough, rude ♦ sm material; (insieme di strumenti etc) equipment no pl, materials pl

maternità sf motherhood, maternity; (reparto) maternity ward

ma'terno, a ag (amore, cura etc) maternal, motherly; (nonno) maternal; (lingua, terra) mother cpd

ma'tita sf pencil

ma'trice [ma'tritʃe] sf matrix; (COMM) counterfoil; (fig: origine) background

ma'tricola sf (registro) register; (numero) registration number; (nell'università) freshman, fresher

ma'trigna [ma'triɲɲa] sf stepmother

matrimoni'ale ag matrimonial, marriage cpd

matri'monio sm marriage, matrimony; (durata) marriage, married life;

(*cerimonia*) wedding

ma'trona *sf* (*fig*) matronly woman

mat'tina *sf* morning; matti'nata *sf* morning; (*spettacolo*) matinée, afternoon performance; mattini'ero, a *ag*: essere mattiniero to be an early riser

mat'tino *sm* morning

'matto, a *ag* mad, crazy; (*fig*: *falso*) false, imitation ♦ *sm/f* madman/woman; avere una voglia ~a di qc to be dying for sth

mat'tone *sm* brick; (*fig*): questo libro/film è un ~ this book/film is heavy going

matto'nella *sf* tile

matu'rare *vi* (*anche*: ~rsi) (*frutta, grano*) to ripen; (*ascesso*) to come to a head; (*fig*: *persona, idea, ECON*) to mature ♦ *vt* to ripen; to (make) mature

maturità *sf* maturity; (*di frutta*) ripeness, maturity; (*INS*) school-leaving examination, ≈ GCE A-levels (*BRIT*)

ma'turo, a *ag* mature; (*frutto*) ripe, mature

maxiprocesso *n* criminal trial involving large numbers of co-accused

'mazza ['mattsa] *sf* (*bastone*) club; (*martello*) sledge-hammer; (*SPORT*: *da golf*) club; (: *da baseball, cricket*) bat

maz'zata [mat'tsata] *sf* (*anche fig*) heavy blow

'mazzo ['mattso] *sm* (*di fiori, chiavi etc*) bunch; (*di carte da gioco*) pack

me *pron me*; ~ stesso(a) myself; sei bravo quanto ~ you are as clever as I (am) *o* as me

me'andro *sm* meander

mec'canica, che *sf* mechanics *sg*; (*attività tecnologica*) mechanical engineering; (*meccanismo*) mechanism

mec'canico, a, ci, che *ag* mechanical ♦ *sm* mechanic

mecca'nismo *sm* mechanism

me'daglia [me'daʎʎa] *sf* medal; medagli'one *sm* (*ARCHIT*) medallion; (*gioiello*) locket

me'desimo, a *ag* same; (*in persona*): io ~ I myself

'media *sf* average; (*MAT*) mean; (*INS*: *voto*) end-of-term average; in ~ on average; *vedi anche* medio

medi'ano, a *ag* median; (*valore*) mean ♦ *sm* (*CALCIO*) half-back

medi'ante *prep* by means of

medi'are *vt* (*fare da mediatore*) to act as mediator in; (*MAT*) to average

media'tore, 'trice *sm/f* mediator; (*COMM*) middle man, agent

medica'mento *sm* medicine, drug

medi'care *vt* to treat; (*ferita*) to dress; medicazi'one *sf* treatment, medication; dressing

medi'cina [medi'tʃina] *sf* medicine; ~ legale forensic medicine; medici'nale *ag* medicinal ♦ *sm* drug, medicine

'medico, a, ci, che *ag* medical ♦ *sm* doctor; ~ generico general practitioner, GP

medie'vale *ag* medieval

'medio, a *ag* average; (*punto, ceto*) middle; (*altezza, statura*) medium ♦ *sm* (*dito*) middle finger; licenza ~a leaving certificate awarded at the end of 3 years of secondary education; scuola ~a first 3 years of secondary school

medi'ocre *ag* mediocre, poor

medioe'vale *ag* = medievale

medio'evo *sm* Middle Ages *pl*

medi'tare *vt* to ponder over, meditate on; (*progettare*) to plan, think out ♦ *vi* to meditate

mediter'raneo, a *ag* Mediterranean; il (mare) M~ the Mediterranean (Sea)

me'dusa *sf* (*ZOOL*) jellyfish

me'gafono *sm* megaphone

'meglio ['mɛʎʎo] *av, ag inv* better; (*con senso superlativo*) best ♦ *sm* (*la cosa migliore*): il ~ the best (thing); faresti ~ ad andartene you had better leave; alla ~ as best one can; andar di bene in ~ to get better and better; fare del proprio ~ to do one's best; per il ~ for the best; aver la ~ su qn to get the better of sb

'mela *sf* apple; ~ cotogna quince

mela'grana *sf* pomegranate

melan'zana [melan'dzana] *sf* aubergine (*BRIT*), eggplant (*US*)

me'lenso, a *ag* dull, stupid

mel'lifluo, a (*peg*) *ag* sugary, honeyed

'melma *sf* mud, mire

'melo *sm* apple tree

melo'dia *sf* melody

me'lone *sm* (*musk*)melon

'membro *sm* member; (*pl*(*f*) ~a: *arto*) limb

memo'randum *sm inv* memorandum

me'moria *sf* memory; ~e *sfpl* (*opera autobiografica*) memoirs; a ~ (*imparare, sapere*) by heart; a ~ d'uomo within living memory; memori'ale *sm* (*raccolta di memorie*) memoirs *pl*; (*DIR*) memorial

mena'dito: a ~ *av* perfectly, thoroughly; sapere qc a ~ to have sth at one's fingertips

me'nare *vt* to lead; (*picchiare*) to hit, beat; (*dare: colpi*) to deal; ~ la coda (*cane*) to wag its tail

mendi'cante *sm/f* beggar

mendi'care *vt* to beg for ♦ *vi* to beg

PAROLA CHIAVE

'meno *av* 1 (*in minore misura*) less; dovresti mangiare ~ you should eat less, you shouldn't eat so much

2 (*comparativo*): ~ ... di not as ... as, less ... than; sono ~ alto di te I'm not as tall as you

(are), I'm less tall than you (are); ~ ... **che** not as ... as, less ... than; ~ **che mai** less than ever; **è ~ intelligente che ricco** he's more rich than intelligent; **fumo più mangio** the less I smoke the more I eat

3 (*superlativo*) least; **il ~ dotato degli studenti** the least gifted of the students; **è quello che compro ~ spesso** it's the one I buy least often

4 (*MAT*) minus; **8 ~ 5** 8 minus 5, 8 take away 5; **sono le 8 ~ un quarto** it's a quarter to 8; **~ 5 gradi** 5 degrees below zero, minus 5 degrees; **mille lire in ~ a** thousand lire less 5 (*fraseologia*): **quanto ~ poteva telefonare** he could at least have phoned; **non so se accettare o ~ I** don't know whether to accept or not; **fare a ~ di qc/qn** to do without sth/ sb; **non potevo fare a ~ di ridere I** couldn't help laughing; **~ male!** thank goodness!; **~ male che sei arrivato** it's a good job that you've come

♦ *ag inv* (*tempo, denaro*) less; (*errori, persone*) fewer; **ha fatto ~ errori di tutti** he made fewer mistakes than anyone, he made the fewest mistakes of all

♦ *sm inv* **1**: **il ~** (*il minimo*) the least; **parlare del più e del ~** to talk about this and that **2** (*MAT*) minus

♦ *prep* (*eccetto*) except (for), apart from; **a ~ che, a ~ di** unless; **a ~ che non piova** unless it rains; **non posso, a ~ di prendere ferie I** can't, unless I take some leave

meno'mare *vt* (*danneggiare*) to maim, disable

meno'pausa *sf* menopause

'mensa *sf* (*locale*) canteen; (: *MIL*) mess; (: *nelle università*) refectory

men'sile *ag* monthly ♦ *sm* (*periodico*) monthly (magazine); (*stipendio*) monthly salary

'mensola *sf* bracket; (*ripiano*) shelf; (*ARCHIT*) corbel

'menta *sf* mint; (*anche:* ~ *piperita*) peppermint; (*bibita*) peppermint cordial; (*caramella*) mint, peppermint

men'tale *ag* mental; **mentalità** *sf inv* mentality

'mente *sf* mind; **imparare/sapere qc a ~** to learn/know sth by heart; **avere in ~ qc** to have sth in mind; **passare di ~ a qn** to slip sb's mind

men'tire *vi* to lie

'mento *sm* chin

men'tolo *sm* menthol

'mentre *cong* (*temporale*) while; (*avversativo*) whereas

menù *sm inv* menu; ~ **turistico** set menu

menzio'nare [mentsjo'nare] *vt* to mention

menzi'one [men'tsjone] *sf* mention; **fare**

~ **di** to mention

men'zogna [men'tsɔɲɲa] *sf* lie

mera'viglia [mera'viʎʎa] *sf* amazement, wonder; (*persona, cosa*) marvel, wonder; **a ~** perfectly, wonderfully; **meravigli'are** *vt* to amaze, astonish; **meravigliarsi (di)** to marvel (at); (*stupirsi*) to be amazed (at), be astonished (at); **meravigli'oso, a** *ag* wonderful, marvellous

mer'cante *sm* merchant; **~ d'arte** art dealer; **mercanteggi'are** *vt* (*onore, voto*) to sell ♦ *vi* to bargain, haggle; **mercan'tile** *ag* commercial, mercantile; (*nave, marina*) merchant *cpd* ♦ *sm* (*nave*) merchantman; **mercan'zia** *sf* merchandise, goods *pl*

mer'cato *sm* market; **~ dei cambi** exchange market; **~ nero** black market

'merce ['mɛrtʃe] *sf* goods *pl*, merchandise; **~ deperibile** perishable goods *pl*

mercé [mer'tʃe] *sf* mercy

merce'nario, a [mertʃe'narjo] *ag, sm* mercenary

merce'ria [mertʃe'ria] *sf* (*articoli*) haberdashery (*BRIT*), notions *pl* (*US*); (*bottega*) haberdasher's shop (*BRIT*), notions store (*US*)

mercoledì *sm inv* Wednesday; **di o il ~ on** Wednesdays; **~ delle Ceneri** Ash Wednesday

mer'curio *sm* mercury

'merda (*fam!*) *sf* shit (*!*)

me'renda *sf* afternoon snack

meridi'ana *sf* (*orologio*) sundial

meridi'ano, a *ag* meridian; midday *cpd*, noonday ♦ *sm* meridian

meridio'nale *ag* southern ♦ *sm/f* southerner

meridi'one *sm* south

me'ringa, ghe *sf* (*CUC*) meringue

meri'tare *vt* to deserve, merit ♦ *vb impers*: **merita andare** it's worth going

meri'tevole *ag* worthy

'merito *sm* merit; (*valore*) worth; **in ~ a** as regards, with regard to; **dare ~ a qn di** to give sb credit for; **finire a pari ~** to finish joint first (*o second etc*); to tie; **meri'torio, a** *ag* praiseworthy

mer'letto *sm* lace

'merlo *sm* (*ZOOL*) blackbird; (*ARCHIT*) battlement

mer'luzzo [mer'luttso] *sm* (*ZOOL*) cod

mes'chino, a [mes'kino] *ag* wretched; (*scarso*) scanty, poor; (*persona: gretta*) mean; (: *limitata*) narrow-minded, petty

mesco'lanza [mesko'lantsa] *sf* mixture

mesco'lare *vt* to mix; (*vini, colori*) to blend; (*mettere in disordine*) to mix up, muddle up; (*carte*) to shuffle; **~rsi** *vr* to mix; to blend; to get mixed up; (*fig*): **~rsi in** to get mixed up in, meddle in

'mese *sm* month

'**messa** *sf* (*REL*) mass; (*il mettere*): **~ in moto** starting; **~ in piega** set; **~ a punto** (*TECN*) adjustment; (*AUT*) tuning; (*fig*) clarification; **~ in scena** = **messinscena**

messag'gero [messad'dʒero] *sm* messenger

mes'saggio [mes'saddʒo] *sm* message

mes'sale *sm* (*REL*) missal

'**messe** *sf* harvest

Mes'sia *sm inv* (*REL*): **il ~** the Messiah

'**Messico** *sm*: **il ~** Mexico

messin'scena [messin'ʃena] *sf* (*TEATRO*) production

'**messo, a** *pp di* **mettere** ♦ *sm* messenger

mesti'ere *sm* (*professione*),job; (: *manuale*) trade; (: *artigianale*) craft; (*fig*: *abilità nel lavoro*) skill, technique; **essere del ~** to know the tricks of the trade

'**mesto, a** *ag* sad, melancholy

'**mestolo** *sm* (*CUC*) ladle

mestruazi'one [mestruat'tsjone] *sf* menstruation

'**meta** *sf* destination; (*fig*) aim, goal

metà *sf inv* half; (*punto di mezzo*) middle; **dividere qc a** *o* **per ~** to divide sth in half, halve sth; **fare a ~ (di qc con qn)** to go halves (with sb in sth); **a ~ prezzo** at half price; **a ~ strada** halfway

me'tafora *sf* metaphor

me'tallico, a, ci, che *ag* (*di metallo*) metal *cpd*; (*splendore, rumore etc*) metallic

me'tallo *sm* metal

metalmec'canico, a, ci, che *ag* engineering *cpd* ♦ *sm* engineering worker

me'tano *sm* methane

meteorolo'gia [meteorolo'dʒia] *sf* meteorology; **meteoro'logico, a, ci, che** *ag* meteorological, weather *cpd*

me'ticcio, a, ci, ce [me'tittʃo] *sm/f* half-caste, half-breed

me'todico, a, ci, che *ag* methodical

'**metodo** *sm* method

'**metrica** *sf* metrics *sg*; '**metrico, a, ci, che** *ag* metric; (*POESIA*) metrical

'**metro** *sm* metre; (*nastro*) tape measure; (*asta*) (metre) rule

metropoli'tana *sf* underground, subway

metropoli'tana, a *ag* metropolitan

'**mettere** *vt* to put; (*abito*) to put on; (: *portare*) to wear; (*installare*: *telefono*) to put in; (*fig*: *provocare*): **~ fame/allegria a qn** to make sb hungry/happy; (*supporre*): **mettiamo che ...** let's suppose *o* say that ...; **~rsi** *vr* (*persona*) to put o.s.; (*oggetto*) to go; (*disporsi*: *faccenda*) to turn out; **~rsi a sedere** to sit down; **~rsi a letto** to get into bed; (*per malattia*) to take to one's bed; **~rsi il cappello** to put on one's hat; **~rsi a** (*cominciare*) to begin, to start to; **~rsi al lavoro** to set to work; **~rsi con qn** (*in società*) to team up with

sb; (*in coppia*) to start going out with sb; **~rci**: **~rci molta cura/molto tempo** to take a lot of care/a lot of time; **ci ho messo 3 ore per venire** it's taken me 3 hours to get here; **~rcela tutta** to do one's best; **~ a tacere qn/qc** to keep sb/sth quiet; **~ su casa** to set up house; **~ su un negozio** to start a shop; **~ via** to put away

'**mezza** ['meddza] *sf*: **la ~** half-past twelve (*in the afternoon*); *vedi anche* **mezzo**

mez'zadro [med'dzadro] *sm* (*AGR*) sharecropper

mezza'luna [meddza'luna] *sf* half-moon; (*dell'islamismo*) crescent; (*coltello*) (semicircular) chopping knife

mezza'nino [meddza'nino] *sm* mezzanine (floor)

mez'zano, a [med'dzano] *ag* (*medio*) average, medium; (*figlio*) middle *cpd* ♦ *sm/f* (*ruffiano*) pimp

mezza'notte [meddza'nɔtte] *sf* midnight

'**mezzo, a** ['meddzo] *ag* half; **un ~ litro/panino** half a litre/roll ♦ *av* half-; **~ morto** half-dead ♦ *sm* (*metà*) half; (*parte centrale*: *di strada etc*) middle; (*per raggiungere un fine*) means *sg*; (*veicolo*) vehicle; (*nell'indicare l'ora*): **le nove e ~** half past nine; **mezzogiorno e ~** half past twelve; **~i** *smpl* (*possibilità economiche*) means; **di ~a età** middle-aged; **un soprabito di ~a stagione** a spring (*o* autumn) coat; **di ~** middle, in the middle; **andarci di ~** (*patir danno*) to suffer; **levarsi** *o* **togliersi di ~** to get out of the way; **in ~ a** in the middle of; **per** *o* **a ~ di** by means of; **~i di comunicazione di massa** mass media *pl*; **~i pubblici** public transport *sg*; **~i di trasporto** means of transport

mezzogi'orno [meddzo'dʒorno] *sm* midday, noon; **a ~** at 12 (o'clock) *o* midday *o* noon; **il ~ d'Italia** southern Italy

mez'z'ora [med'dzora] *sf* half-hour, half an hour

mi (*dav lo, la, li, le, ne diventa* **me**) *pron* (*oggetto*) me; (*complemento di termine*) to me; (*riflessivo*) myself ♦ *sm* (*MUS*) E; (: *solfeggiando la scala*) mi

'**mia** *vedi* **mio**

miago'lare *vi* to miaow, mew

'**mica** *av* (*fam*): **non ... ~** not ... at all; **non sono ~ stanco** I'm not a bit tired; **non sarà ~ partito?** he wouldn't have left, would he?; **~ male** not bad

'**miccia, ce** ['mittʃa] *sf* fuse

micidi'ale [mitʃi'djale] *ag* fatal; (*dannosissimo*) deadly

mi'crofono *sm* microphone

micros'copio *sm* microscope

mi'dollo (*pl(f)* **~a**) *sm* (*ANAT*) marrow; **~ osseo** bone marrow '**mie** *vedi* **mio**

mi'ei *vedi* **mio**

mi'ele *sm* honey

mi'etere *vt* (*AGR*) to reap, harvest; (*fig: vite*) to take, claim

'**miglia** ['miʎʎa] *sfpl di* **miglio**

migli'aio [miʎ'ʎajo] (*pl*(*f*) ~**a**) *sm* thousand; **un ~ (di)** about a thousand; **a ~a** by the thousand, in thousands

'**miglio** ['miʎʎo] *sm* (*BOT*) millet; (*pl*(*f*) ~**a**: *unità di misura*) mile; **~ marino** *o* **nautico** nautical mile

migliora'mento [miʎʎora'mento] *sm* improvement

miglio'rare [miʎʎo'rare] *vt, vi* to improve

migli'ore [miʎ'ʎore] *ag* (*comparativo*) better; (*superlativo*) best ♦ *sm*: **il ~** the best (thing) ♦ *sm*/*f*: **il(la) ~** the best (person); **il miglior vino di questa regione** the best wine in this area

'**mignolo** ['miɲɲolo] *sm* (*ANAT*) little finger, pinkie; (: *dito del piede*) little toe

mi'grare *vi* to migrate

'**mila** *pl di* **mille**

Mi'lano *sf* Milan

miliar'dario, a *sm*/*f* millionaire

mili'ardo *sm* thousand million, billion (*US*)

mili'are *ag*: **pietra ~** milestone

mili'one *sm* million; **due ~i di lire** two million lire

mili'tante *ag, sm*/*f* militant

mili'tare *vi* (*MIL*) to be a soldier, serve; (*fig: in un partito*) to be a militant ♦ *ag* military ♦ *sm* serviceman; **fare il ~** to do one's military service

'**milite** *sm* soldier

millanta'tore, 'trice *sm*/*f* boaster

'**mille** (*pl* **mila**) *num* **a** *o* one thousand; **dieci mila** ten thousand

mille'foglie [mille'fɔʎʎe] *sm inv* (*CUC*) cream *o* vanilla slice

mil'lennio *sm* millennium

millepi'edi *sm inv* centipede

mil'lesimo, a *ag, sm* thousandth

milli'grammo *sm* milligram(me)

mil'limetro *sm* millimetre

'**milza** ['miltsa] *sf* (*ANAT*) spleen

mimetiz'zare [mimetid'dzare] *vt* to camouflage; **~rsi** *vr* to camouflage o.s.

'**mimica** *sf* (*arte*) mime

'**mimo** *sm* (*attore, componimento*) mime

mi'mosa *sf* mimosa

'**mina** *sf* (*esplosiva*) mine; (*di matita*) lead

mi'naccia, ce [mi'nattʃa] *sf* threat; **minacci'are** *vt* to threaten; **minacciare qn di morte** to threaten to kill sb; **minacciare di fare qc** to threaten to do sth; **minacci'oso, a** *ag* threatening

mi'nare *vt* (*MIL*) to mine; (*fig*) to undermine

mina'tore *sm* miner

mina'torio, a *ag* threatening

mine'rale *ag, sm* mineral

mine'rario, a *ag* (*delle miniere*) mining; (*dei minerali*) ore *cpd*

mi'nestra *sf* soup; **~ in brodo/di verdure** noodle/vegetable soup; **mines'trone** *sm* thick vegetable and pasta soup

mingher'lino, a [minger'lino] *ag* thin, slender

'**mini** *ag inv* mini ♦ *sf inv* miniskirt

minia'tura *sf* miniature

mini'era *sf* mine

mini'gonna *sf* miniskirt

'**minimo, a** *ag* minimum, least, slightest; (*piccolissimo*) very small, slight; (*il più basso*) lowest, minimum ♦ *sm* minimum; **al ~** at least; **girare al ~** (*AUT*) to idle

minis'tero *sm* (*POL, REL*) ministry; (*governo*) government; **M~ delle Finanze** Ministry of Finance, ≈ Treasury

mi'nistro *sm* (*POL, REL*) minister

mino'ranza [mino'rantsa] *sf* minority

mino'rato, a *ag* handicapped ♦ *sm*/*f* physically (*o* mentally) handicapped person

mi'nore *ag* (*comparativo*) less; (*più piccolo*) smaller; (*numero*) lower; (*inferiore*) lower, inferior; (*meno importante*) minor; (*più giovane*) younger; (*superlativo*) least; smallest; lowest; youngest ♦ *sm*/*f* = **minorenne**

mino'renne *ag* under age ♦ *sm*/*f* minor, person under age

mi'nuscolo, a *ag* (*scrittura, carattere*) small; (*piccolissimo*) tiny ♦ *sf* small letter

mi'nuta *sf* rough copy, draft

mi'nuto, a *ag* tiny, minute; (*pioggia*) fine; (*corporatura*) delicate, fine ♦ *sm* (*unità di misura*) minute; **al ~** (*COMM*) retail

'**mio** (*f* '**mia**, *pl* **mi'ei, 'mie**) *det*: **il ~, la mia** etc my ♦ *pron*: **il ~, la mia** etc mine; **i miei** my family; **un ~ amico** a friend of mine

'**miope** *ag* short-sighted

'**mira** *sf* (*anche fig*) aim; **prendere la ~** to take aim; **prendere di ~ qn** (*fig*) to pick on sb

mi'rabile *ag* admirable, wonderful

mi'racolo *sm* miracle

mi'raggio [mi'raddʒo] *sm* mirage

mi'rare *vi*: **~ a** to aim at

mi'rino *sm* (*TECN*) sight; (*FOT*) viewer, viewfinder

mir'tillo *sm* bilberry (*BRIT*), blueberry (*US*), whortleberry

mi'scela [miʃ'ʃela] *sf* mixture; (*di caffè*) blend

miscel'lanea [miʃʃel'lanea] *sf* miscellany

'**mischia** ['miskja] *sf* scuffle; (*RUGBY*) scrum, scrummage

mischi'are [mis'kjare] *vt* to mix, blend; **~rsi** *vr* to mix, blend

mis'cuglio [misˈkuʎʎo] *sm* mixture, hotchpotch, jumble

mise'rabile *ag* (*infelice*) miserable, wretched; (*povero*) poverty-stricken; (*di scarso valore*) miserable

mi'seria *sf* extreme poverty; (*infelicità*) misery; **~e** *sfpl* (*del mondo etc*) misfortunes, troubles; **porca ~!** (*fam*) blast!, damn!

miseri'cordia *sf* mercy, pity

'misero, a *ag* miserable, wretched; (*povero*) poverty-stricken; (*insufficiente*) miserable

mis'fatto *sm* misdeed, crime

mi'sogino [miˈzɔdʒino] *sm* misogynist

'missile *sm* missile

missio'nario, a *ag*, *sm/f* missionary

missi'one *sf* mission

misteri'oso, a *ag* mysterious

mis'tero *sm* mystery

'misto, a *ag* mixed; (*scuola*) mixed, coeducational ♦ *sm* mixture

mis'tura *sf* mixture

mi'sura *sf* measure; (*misurazione, dimensione*) measurement; (*taglia*) size; (*provvedimento*) measure, step; (*moderazione*) moderation; (*MUS*) time; (: *divisione*) bar; (*fig: limite*) bounds *pl*, limit; **nella ~ in cui** inasmuch as, insofar as; **(fatto) su ~** made to measure

misu'rare *vt* (*ambiente, stoffa*) to measure; (*terreno*) to survey; (*abito*) to try on; (*pesare*) to weigh; (*fig: parole etc*) to weigh up; (: *spese, cibo*) to limit ♦ *vi* to measure; **~rsi** *vr*: **~rsi con qn** to have a confrontation with sb; to compete with sb; **misu'rato, a** *ag* (*ponderato*) measured; (*moderato*) moderate

'mite *ag* mild

miti'gare *vt* to mitigate, lessen; (*lenire*) to soothe, relieve; **~rsi** *vr* (*odio*) to subside; (*tempo*) to become milder

'mito *sm* myth; **mitolo'gia, 'gie** *sf* mythology

'mitra *sf* (*REL*) mitre ♦ *sm inv* (*arma*) sub-machine gun

mitraglia'trice [mitraʎʎaˈtritʃe] *sf* machine gun

mit'tente *sm/f* sender

'mobile *ag* mobile; (*parte di macchina*) moving; (*DIR: bene*) movable, personal ♦ *sm* (*arredamento*) piece of furniture; **~i** *smpl* (*mobilia*) furniture *sg*

mo'bilia *sf* furniture

mobili'are *ag* (*DIR*) personal, movable

mo'bilio *sm* = **mobilia**

mobili'tare *vt* to mobilize

mocas'sino *sm* moccasin

mocci'oso, a [motˈtʃoso, a] *sm/f* (*peg*) snotty(-nosed) kid

'moccolo *sm* (*di candela*) candle-end; (*fam: bestemmia*) oath; (: *moccio*) snot; **reggere il ~** to play gooseberry (*BRIT*), act as chaperon

'moda *sf* fashion; **alla ~, di ~** fashionable, in fashion

modalità *sf inv* formality

mo'della *sf* model

model'lare *vt* (*creta*) to model, shape; **~rsi** *vr*: **~rsi su** to model o.s. on

mo'dello *sm* model; (*stampo*) mould ♦ *ag inv* model *cpd*

'modem *sm inv* modem

mode'rare *vt* to moderate; **~rsi** *vr* to restrain o.s.; **mode'rato, a** *ag* moderate

modera'tore, 'trice *sm/f* moderator

mo'derno, a *ag* modern

mo'destia *sf* modesty

mo'desto, a *ag* modest

'modico, a, ci, che *ag* reasonable, moderate

mo'difica, che *sf* modification

modifi'care *vt* to modify, alter; **~rsi** *vr* to alter, change

mo'dista *sf* milliner

'modo *sm* way, manner; (*mezzo*) means, way; (*occasione*) opportunity; (*LING*) mood; (*MUS*) mode; **~i** *smpl* (*comportamento*) manners; **a suo ~, a ~ suo** in his own way; **ad o in ogni ~** anyway; **di o in ~ che** so that; **in ~ da** so as to; **in tutti i ~i** at all costs; (*comunque sia*) anyway; (*in ogni caso*) in any case; **in qualche ~** somehow or other; **~ di dire** turn of phrase; **per ~ di dire** so to speak

modu'lare *vt* to modulate; **modulazi'one** *sf* modulation; **modulazione di frequenza** frequency modulation

'modulo *sm* (*modello*) form; (*ARCHIT, lunare, di comando*) module

'mogano *sm* mahogany

'mogio, a, gi, gie [ˈmɔdʒo] *ag* down in the dumps, dejected

'moglie [ˈmoʎʎe] *sf* wife

mo'ine *sfpl* cajolery *sg*; (*leziosità*) affectation *sg*

'mola *sf* millstone; (*utensile abrasivo*) grindstone

mo'lare *sm* (*dente*) molar

'mole *sf* mass; (*dimensioni*) size; (*edificio grandioso*) massive structure

moles'tare *vt* to bother, annoy; **mo'lestia** *sf* annoyance, bother; **recar molestia a qn** to bother sb; **mo'lesto, a** *ag* annoying

'molla *sf* spring; **~e** *sfpl* (*per camino*) tongs

mol'lare *vt* to release, let go; (*NAUT*) to ease; (*fig: ceffone*) to give ♦ *vi* (*cedere*) to give in

'molle *ag* soft; (*muscoli*) flabby

mol'letta *sf* (*per capelli*) hairgrip; (*per panni stesi*) clothes peg

'mollica, che *sf* crumb, soft part

mol'lusco, schi *sm* mollusc

'molo *sm* mole, breakwater; jetty

mol'teplice [molˈteplitʃe] *ag* (*formato di più*

elementi) complex; **~i** pl (svariati: interessi, attività) numerous, various

moltipli'care vt to multiply; **~rsi** vr to multiply; to increase in number; **moltiplicazi'one** sf multiplication

'molto, a det (quantità) a lot of, much; (numero) a lot of, many; **~ pane/carbone** a lot of bread/coal; **~a gente** a lot of people, many people; **~i libri** a lot of books, many books; **non ho ~ tempo** I haven't got much time; **per ~ (tempo)** for a long time

♦ av **1** a lot, (very) much; **viaggia ~** he travels a lot; **non viaggia ~** he doesn't travel much o a lot

2 (intensivo: con aggettivi, avverbi) very; (: con participio passato) (very) much; **~ buono** very good; **~ migliore**, **~ meglio** much o a lot better

♦ pron much, a lot; **~i, e** pron pl many, a lot; **~i pensano che ...** many (people) think ...

momen'taneo, a ag momentary, fleeting

mo'mento sm moment; **da un ~ all'altro** at any moment; (all'improvviso) suddenly; **al ~ di fare** just as I was (o you were o he was etc) doing; **per il ~** for the time being; **dal ~ che** ever since; (dato che) since; **a ~i** (da un ~ all'altro) any time o moment now; (quasi) nearly

'monaca, che sf nun

'Monaco sf Monaco; **~ (di Baviera)** Munich

'monaco, ci sm monk

mo'narca, chi sm monarch; **monar'chia** sf monarchy

monas'tero sm (di monaci) monastery; (di monache) convent; **mo'nastico, a, ci, che** ag monastic

'monco, a, chi, che ag maimed; (fig) incomplete

mon'dano, a ag (anche fig) worldly; (dell'alta società) society cpd; fashionable

mon'dare vt (frutta, patate) to peel; (piselli) to shell; (pulire) to clean

mondi'ale ag (campionato, popolazione) world cpd; (influenza) world-wide

'mondo sm world; (grande quantità): **un ~ di** lots of, a host of; **il bel ~** high society

mo'nello, a sm/f street urchin; (ragazzo vivace) scamp, imp

mo'neta sf coin; (ECON: valuta) currency; (denaro spicciolo) (small) change; **~ estera** foreign currency; **~ legale** legal tender; **mone'tario, a** ag monetary

mongo'loide ag, sm/f (MED) mongol

'monito sm warning

'monitor sm inv (TECN, TV) monitor

monolo'cale sm studio flat

mono'polio sm monopoly

mo'notono, a ag monotonous

monsi'gnore [monsiɲ'ɲore] sm (REL: titolo) Your (o His) Grace

mon'sone sm monsoon

monta'carichi [monta'kariki] sm inv hoist, goods lift

mon'taggio [mon'taddʒo] sm (TECN) assembly; (CINEMA) editing

mon'tagna [mon'taɲɲa] sf mountain; (zona montuosa): **la ~** the mountains pl; **andare in ~** to go to the mountains; **~e russe** roller coaster sg, big dipper sg (BRIT); **monta'gnoso, a** ag mountainous

monta'naro, a ag mountain cpd ♦ sm/f mountain dweller

mon'tano, a ag mountain cpd; alpine

mon'tare vt to go (o come) up; (cavallo) to ride; (apparecchiatura) to set up, assemble; (CUC) to whip; (ZOOL) to cover; (incastonare) to mount, set; (CINEMA) to edit; (FOT) to mount ♦ vi to go (o come) up; (a cavallo): **~ bene/male** to ride well/badly; (aumentare di livello, volume) to rise; **~rsi** vr to become big-headed; **~ qc** to exaggerate sth; **~ qn o la testa a qn** to turn sb's head; **~ in bicicletta/ macchina/treno** to get on a bicycle/into a car/on a train; **~ a cavallo** to get on o mount a horse

monta'tura sf assembling no pl; (di occhiali) frames pl; (di gioiello) mounting, setting; (fig): **~ pubblicitaria** publicity stunt

'monte sm mountain; **a ~** upstream; **mandare a ~ qc** to upset sth, cause sth to fail; **il M~ Bianco** Mont Blanc; **~ di pietà** pawnshop

mon'tone sm (ZOOL) ram; **carne di ~** mutton

montu'oso, a ag mountainous

monu'mento sm monument

mo'quette [mɔ'kɛt] sf inv fitted carpet

'mora sf (del rovo) blackberry; (del gelso) mulberry; (DIR) delay; (: somma) arrears pl

mo'rale ag moral ♦ sf (scienza) ethics sg, moral philosophy; (complesso di norme) moral standards pl, morality; (condotta) morals pl; (insegnamento morale) moral ♦ sm morale; **essere giù di ~** to be feeling down; **moralità** sf morality; (condotta) morals pl

'morbido, a ag soft; (pelle) soft, smooth

mor'billo sm (MED) measles sg

'morbo sm disease

mor'boso, a ag (fig) morbid

mor'dace [mor'datʃe] ag biting, cutting

mor'dente sm (fig: di satira, critica) bite; (: di persona) drive

'mordere vt to bite; (addentare) to bite into

mori'bondo, a ag dying, moribund

morige'rato, a [moridʒe'rato] ag of good morals

mo'rire vi to die; (abitudine, civiltà) to die

out; **~ di fame** to die of hunger; (*fig*) to be starving; **~ di noia/paura** to be bored/scared to death; **fa un caldo da ~** it's terribly hot

mormo'rare *vi* to murmur; (*brontolare*) to grumble

'moro, a *ag* dark(-haired); dark (-complexioned); **i M~i** *smpl* (*STORIA*) the Moors

mo'roso, a *ag* in arrears ♦ *sm/f* (*fam: innamorato*) sweetheart

'morsa *sf* (*TECN*) vice; (*fig: stretta*) grip

morsi'care *vt* to nibble (at), gnaw (at); (*sog: insetto*) to bite

'morso, a *pp di* **mordere** ♦ *sm* bite; (*di insetto*) sting; (*parte della briglia*) bit; **~i della fame** pangs of hunger

mor'taio *sm* mortar

mor'tale *ag, sm* mortal; **mortalità** *sf* mortality, death rate

'morte *sf* death

mortifi'care *vt* to mortify

'morto, a *pp di* **morire** ♦ *ag* dead ♦ *sm/f* dead man/woman; **i ~i** the dead; **fare il ~** (*nell'acqua*) to float on one's back; **il Mar M~** the Dead Sea

mor'torio *sm* (*anche fig*) funeral

mo'saico, ci *sm* mosaic

'Mosca *sf* Moscow

'mosca, sche *sf* fly; **~ cieca** blind-man's-buff

mos'cato *sm* muscatel (wine)

mosce'rino [moʃʃe'rino] *sm* midge, gnat

mos'chea [mos'kea] *sf* mosque

mos'chetto [mos'ketto] *sm* musket

'moscio, a, sci, sce ['mɔʃʃo] *ag* (*fig*) lifeless

mos'cone *sm* (*ZOOL*) bluebottle; (*barca*) pedalo; (: *a remi*) kind of pedalo with oars

'mossa *sf* movement; (*nel gioco*) move

'mosso, a *pp di* **muovere** ♦ *ag* (*mare*) rough; (*capelli*) wavy; (*FOT*) blurred

mos'tarda *sf* mustard

'mostra *sf* exhibition, show; (*ostentazione*) show; **in ~** on show; **far ~ di** (*fingere*) to pretend; **far ~ di sé** to show off

mos'trare *vt* to show; **~rsi** *vr* to appear

'mostro *sm* monster; **mostru'oso, a** *ag* monstrous

mo'tel *sm inv* motel

moti'vare *vt* (*causare*) to cause; (*giustificare*) to justify, account for; **motivazi'one** *sf* justification; motive; (*PSIC*) motivation

mo'tivo *sm* (*causa*) reason, cause; (*movente*) motive; (*letterario*) (central) theme; (*disegno*) motif, design, pattern; (*MUS*) motif; **per quale ~?** why?, for what reason?

'moto *sm* (*anche FISICA*) motion; (*movimento, gesto*) movement; (*esercizio fisico*) exercise; (*sommossa*) rising, revolt; (*commozione*) feeling, impulse ♦ *sf inv* (*motocicletta*)

motorbike; **mettere in ~** to set in motion; (*AUT*) to start up

motoci'cletta [mototʃi'kletta] *sf* motor-cycle; **motoci'clismo** *sm* motorcycling, motorcycle racing; **motoci'clista, i, e** *sm/f* motorcyclist

mo'tore, 'trice *ag* motor; (*TECN*) driving ♦ *sm* engine, motor; **a ~** motor *cpd*, power-driven; **~ a combustione interna/a reazione** internal combustion/jet engine; **moto'rino** *sm* moped; **motorino di avviamento** (*AUT*) starter; **motoriz'zato, a** *ag* (*truppe*) motorized; (*persona*) having a car o transport

motos'cafo *sm* motorboat

'motto *sm* (*battuta scherzosa*) witty remark; (*frase emblematica*) motto, maxim

'mouse ['maus] *sm inv* (*INFORM*) mouse

mo'vente *sm* motive

movimen'tare *vt* to liven up

movi'mento *sm* movement; (*fig*) activity, hustle and bustle; (*MUS*) tempo, movement

mozi'one [mot'tsjone] *sf* (*POL*) motion

moz'zare [mot'tsare] *vt* to cut off; (*coda*) to dock; **~ il fiato o il respiro a qn** (*fig*) to take sb's breath away

mozza'rella [mottsa'rɛlla] *sf* mozzarella

mozzi'cone [mottsi'kone] *sm* stub, butt, end; (*anche: ~ di sigaretta*) cigarette end

'mozzo ['mottso] *sm* (*NAUT*) ship's boy

'mucca, che *sf* cow

'mucchio ['mukkjo] *sm* pile, heap; (*fig*): **un ~ di** lots of, heaps of

'muco, chi *sm* mucus

'muffa *sf* mould, mildew

mug'gire [mud'dʒire] *vi* (*vacca*) to low, moo; (*toro*) to bellow; (*fig*) to roar; **mug'gito** *sm* low, moo; bellow; roar

'mughetto [mu'getto] *sm* lily of the valley

mu'gnaio, a [muɲ'najo] *sm/f* miller

mugo'lare *vi* (*cane*) to whimper, whine; (*fig: persona*) to moan

muli'nare *vi* to whirl, spin (round and round)

muli'nello *sm* (*moto vorticoso*) eddy, whirl; (*di canna da pesca*) reel

mu'lino *sm* mill; **~ a vento** windmill

'mulo *sm* mule

'multa *sf* fine; **mul'tare** *vt* to fine

'multiplo, a *ag, sm* multiple

multiproprietà *sf inv* time-share

'mummia *sf* mummy

'mungere ['mundʒere] *vt* (*anche fig*) to milk

munici'pale [munitʃi'pale] *ag* municipal; town *cpd*

muni'cipio [muni'tʃipjo] *sm* town council, corporation; (*edificio*) town hall

mu'nire *vt*: **~ qc/qn di** to equip sth/sb with

munizi'oni [munit'tsjoni] *sfpl* (*MIL*) ammunition *sg*

'munto, a *pp di* **mungere**

mu'overe *vt* to move; (*ruota, macchina*) to drive; (*sollevare: questione, obiezione*) to raise, bring up; (: *accusa*) to make, bring forward; **~rsi** *vr* to move; **muoviti!** hurry up!, get a move on!

'mura *sfpl vedi* **muro**

mu'raglia [mu'raʎʎa] *sf* (high) wall

mu'rale *ag* wall *cpd*; mural

mu'rare *vt* (*persona, porta*) to wall up

mura'tore *sm* mason; bricklayer

'muro *sm* wall; **~a** *sfpl* (*cinta cittadina*) walls; **a ~** wall *cpd*; (*armadio etc*) built-in; **~ del suono** sound barrier; **mettere al ~** (*fucilare*) to shoot *o* execute (by firing squad)

'muschio ['muskjo] *sm* (ZOOL) musk; (BOT) moss

musco'lare *ag* muscular, muscle *cpd*

'muscolo *sm* (ANAT) muscle

mu'seo *sm* museum

museru'ola *sf* muzzle

'musica *sf* music; **~ da ballo/camera** dance/chamber music; **musi'cale** *ag* musical; **musi'cista, i, e** *sm/f* musician

'muso *sm* muzzle; (*di auto, aereo*) nose; **tenere il ~** to sulk; **mu'sone, a** *sm/f* sulky person

'muta *sf* (*di animali*) moulting; (*di serpenti*) sloughing; (*per immersioni subacquee*) diving suit; (*gruppo di cani*) pack

muta'mento *sm* change

mu'tande *sfpl* (*da uomo*) (under)pants

mutan'dine *sfpl* (*da donna, bambino*) pants (BRIT), briefs

mu'tare *vt, vi* to change, alter; **mutazi'one** *sf* change, alteration; (BIOL) mutation; **mu'tevole** *ag* changeable

muti'lare *vt* to mutilate, maim; (*fig*) to mutilate, deface; **muti'lato, a** *sm/f* disabled person (*through loss of limbs*)

mu'tismo *sm* (MED) mutism; (*atteggiamento*) (stubborn) silence

'muto, a *ag* (MED) dumb; (*emozione, dolore,* CINEMA) silent; (LING) silent, mute; (*carta geografica*) blank; **~ per lo stupore** *etc* speechless with amazement *etc*

'mutua *sf* (*anche: cassa ~*) health insurance scheme

mutu'are *vt* (*fig*) to borrow

mutu'ato, a *sm/f* member of a health insurance scheme

'mutuo, a *ag* (*reciproco*) mutual ♦ *sm* (ECON) (long-term) loan

N, n

N. *abbr* (= *nord*) N

'nacchere ['nakkere] *sfpl* castanets

'nafta *sf* naphtha; (*per motori diesel*) diesel oil

nafta'lina *sf* (CHIM) naphthalene; (*tarmicida*) mothballs *pl*

'naia *sf* (MIL) slang term for national service

'nailon *sm* nylon

'nanna *sf* (*linguaggio infantile*): **andare a ~** to go to beddy-byes

'nano, a *ag, sm/f* dwarf

napole'tano, a *ag, sm/f* Neapolitan

'Napoli *sf* Naples

'nappa *sf* tassel

nar'ciso [nar'tʃizo] *sm* narcissus

nar'cosi *sf* narcosis

nar'cotico, ci *sm* narcotic

na'rice [na'ritʃe] *sf* nostril

nar'rare *vt* to tell the story of, recount; **narra'tiva** *sf* (*branca letteraria*) fiction; **narra'tivo, a** *ag* narrative; **narra'tore, 'trice** *sm/f* narrator; **narrazi'one** *sf* narration; (*racconto*) story, tale

na'sale *ag* nasal

'nascere ['naʃʃere] *vi* (*bambino*) to be born; (*pianta*) to come *o* spring up; (*fiume*) to rise, have its source; (*sole*) to rise; (*dente*) to come through; (*fig: derivare, conseguire*): **~ da** to arise from, be born out of; **è nata nel 1952** she was born in 1952; **'nascita** *sf* birth

nas'condere *vt* to hide, conceal; **~rsi** *vr* to hide; **nascon'diglio** *sm* hiding place; **nascon'dino** *sm* (*gioco*) hide-and-seek; **nas'costo, a** *pp di* **nascondere** ♦ *ag* hidden; **di nascosto** secretly

na'sello *sm* (ZOOL) hake

'naso *sm* nose

'nastro *sm* ribbon; (*magnetico, isolante,* SPORT) tape; **~ adesivo** adhesive tape; **~ trasportatore** conveyor belt

nas'turzio [nas'turtsjo] *sm* nasturtium

na'tale *ag* of one's birth ♦ *sm* (REL): **N~** Christmas; (*giorno della nascita*) birthday; **natalità** *sf* birth rate; **nata'lizio, a** *ag* (*del Natale*) Christmas *cpd*

na'tante *sm* craft *inv*, boat

'natica, che *sf* (ANAT) buttock

na'tio, a, 'tii, 'tie *ag* native

Nativi'tà *sf* (REL) Nativity

na'tivo, a *ag, sm/f* native

'nato, a *pp di* **nascere** ♦ *ag*: **un attore ~** a born actor; **~a Pieri** née Pieri

na'tura *sf* nature; **pagare in ~** to pay in kind; **~ morta** still life

natu'rale *ag* natural; **natura'lezza** *sf* naturalness; **natura'lista, i, e** *sm/f* naturalist

naturaliz'zare [naturalid'dzare] *vt* to naturalize

natural'mente *av* naturally; (*certamente, sì*) of course

naufra'gare *vi* (*nave*) to be wrecked; (*persona*) to be shipwrecked; (*fig*) to fall through; **nau'fragio** *sm* shipwreck; (*fig*) ruin, failure; **'naufrago, ghi** *sm* castaway, shipwreck victim

'nausea *sf* nausea; **nausea'bondo, a** *ag* nauseating, sickening; **nause'are** *vt* to nauseate, make (feel) sick

'nautica *sf* (art of) navigation

'nautico, a ci, che *ag* nautical

na'vale *ag* naval

na'vata *sf* (*anche*: ~ *centrale*) nave; (*anche*: ~ *laterale*) aisle

'nave *sf* ship, vessel; ~ **cisterna** tanker; ~ **da guerra** warship; ~ **passeggeri** passenger ship

na'vetta *sf* shuttle; (*servizio di collegamento*) shuttle (service)

navi'cella [navi'tʃɛlla] *sf* (*di aerostato*) gondola; ~ **spaziale** spaceship

navi'gare *vi* to sail; ~ **in Internet** to surf the Net; **navigazi'one** *sf* navigation

na'viglio [na'viʎʎo] *sm* (*canale artificiale*) canal; ~ **da pesca** fishing fleet

nazio'nale [nattsjo'nale] *ag* national ♦ *sf* (*SPORT*) national team; **naziona'lismo** *sm* nationalism; **nazionalità** *sf inv* nationality

nazi'one [nat'tsjone] *sf* nation

PAROLA CHIAVE

---

ne *pron* **1** (*di lui, lei, loro*) of him/her/them; about him/her/them; ~ **riconosco la voce** I recognize his (o her) voice

2 (*di questa, quella cosa*) of it; about it; ~ **voglio ancora** I want some more (of it o them); **non parliamone più!** let's not talk about it any more!

3 (*con valore partitivo*): **hai dei libri? — sì,** ~ **ho** have you any books? — yes, I have (some); **hai del pane? — no, non** ~ **ho** have you any bread? — no, I haven't any; **quanti anni hai? —** ~ **ho 17** how old are you? — I'm 17

♦ *av* (*moto da luogo: da lì*) from there; ~ **vengo ora** I've just come from there

---

né *cong*: ~ ... ~ neither ... nor; ~ **l'uno** ~ **l'altro lo vuole** neither of them wants it; **non parla** ~ **l'italiano** ~ **il tedesco** he speaks neither Italian nor German, he doesn't speak either Italian or German; **non piove** ~ **nevica** it isn't raining or snowing

ne'anche [ne'anke] *av, cong* not even; **non** ... ~ not even; ~ **se volesse potrebbe venire** he couldn't come even if he wanted to; **non l'ho visto —** ~ **io** I didn't see him — neither did I o I didn't either; ~ **per idea** o **sogno!** not on your life!

'nebbia *sf* fog; (*foschia*) mist; **nebbi'oso, a** *ag* foggy; misty

nebu'loso, a *ag* (*atmosfera*) hazy; (*fig*) hazy, vague

necessaria'mente [netʃessarja'mente] *av* necessarily

neces'sario, a [netʃes'sarjo] *ag* necessary

necessità [netʃessi'ta] *sf inv* necessity; (*povertà*) need, poverty; **necessi'tare** *vt* to require ♦ *vi* (*aver bisogno*): **necessitare di** to need

necro'logio [nekro'lɔdʒo] *sm* obituary notice

ne'fando, a *ag* infamous, wicked

ne'fasto, a *ag* inauspicious, ill-omened

ne'gare *vt* to deny; (*rifiutare*) to deny, refuse; ~ **di aver fatto/che** to deny having done/that; **nega'tivo, a** *ag, sf, sm* negative; **nega-zi'one** *sf* negation

ne'gletto, a *ag* (*trascurato*) neglected

'negli ['neʎʎi] *prep* +*det vedi* in

negli'gente [negli'dʒɛnte] *ag* negligent, careless; **negli'genza** *sf* negligence, carelessness

negozi'ante [negot'tsjante] *sm/f* trader, dealer; (*bottegaio*) shopkeeper (*BRIT*), storekeeper (*US*)

negozi'are [negot'tsjare] *vt* to negotiate ♦ *vi*: ~ **in** to trade o deal in; **negozi'ato** *sm* negotiation

ne'gozio [ne'gɔttsjo] *sm* (*locale*) shop (*BRIT*), store (*US*)

'negro, a *ag, sm/f* Negro

'nei *prep* +*det vedi* in

nel *prep* +*det vedi* in

nell' *prep* +*det vedi* in

'nella *prep* +*det vedi* in

'nelle *prep* +*det vedi* in

'nello *prep* +*det vedi* in

'nembo *sm* (*METEOR*) nimbus

ne'mico, a ci, che *ag* hostile; (*MIL*) enemy *cpd* ♦ *sm/f* enemy; **essere** ~ **di** to be strongly averse o opposed to

nem'meno *av, cong* = **neanche**

'nenia *sf* dirge; (*motivo monotono*) monotonous tune

'neo *sm* mole; (*fig*) (slight) flaw

neo... *prefisso* neo...

'neon *sm* (*CHIM*) neon

neo'nato, a *ag* newborn ♦ *sm/f* newborn baby

neozelan'dese [neoddzelan'dese] *ag* New Zealand *cpd* ♦ *sm/f* New Zealander

nep'pure *av, cong* = **neanche**

'nerbo *sm* lash; (*fig*) strength, backbone; **nerbo'ruto, a** *ag* muscular; robust

ne'retto *sm* (*TIP*) bold type

'nero, a *ag* black; (*scuro*) dark ♦ *sm* black; **il Mar N~** the Black Sea

nerva'tura *sf* (*ANAT*) nervous system; (*BOT*) veining; (*ARCHIT, TECN*) rib

'nervo *sm* (*ANAT*) nerve; (*BOT*) vein; **avere i ~i** to be on edge; **dare sui ~i a qn** to get on sb's nerves; **ner'voso, a** *ag* nervous; (*irritabile*) irritable ♦ *sm* (*fam*): **far venire il nervoso a qn** to get on sb's nerves

'**nespola** *sf* (*BOT*) medlar; (*fig*) blow, punch;
'**nespolo** *sm* medlar tree

'**nesso** *sm* connection, link

PAROLA CHIAVE

nes'suno, a (*det*: *dav sm* **nessun** +*C, V*,
nessuno +*s impura, gn, pn, ps, x, z*; *dav sf*
nessuna +*C*, **nessun'** +*V*) *det* **1** (*non uno*) no,
espressione negativa +any; **non c'è nessun
libro** there isn't any book, there is no book;
nessun altro no one else, nobody else;
nessun'altra cosa nothing else; **in nessun
luogo** nowhere
2 (*qualche*) any; **hai ~a obiezione?** do you
have any objections?
♦ *pron* **1** (*non uno*) no one, nobody,
espressione negativa +any(one); (: *cosa*)
none, *espressione negativa* +any; **~ è venuto,
non è venuto** ~ nobody came
2 (*qualcuno*) anyone, anybody; **ha telefonato
~?** did anyone phone?

---

net'tare[1] *vt* to clean
'nettare[2] *sm* nectar
net'tezza [net'tettsa] *sf* cleanness,
cleanliness; **~ urbana** cleansing department
'**netto, a** *ag* (*pulito*) clean; (*chiaro*) clear,
clear-cut; (*deciso*) definite; (*ECON*) net
nettur'bino *sm* dustman (*BRIT*), garbage
collector (*US*)
neu'rosi *sf* = **nevrosi**
neu'trale *ag* neutral; **neutralità** *sf*
neutrality; **neutraliz'zare** *vt* to neutralize
'**neutro, a** *ag* neutral; (*LING*) neuter ♦ *sm*
(*LING*) neuter
ne'vaio *sm* snowfield
'**neve** *sf* snow; **nevi'care** *vb impers* to snow;
nevi'cata *sf* snowfall
ne'vischio [ne'viskjo] *sm* sleet
ne'voso, a *ag* snowy; snow-covered
nevral'gia [nevral'dʒia] *sf* neuralgia
nevras'tenico, a, ci, che *ag* (*MED*)
neurasthenic; (*fig*) hot-tempered
ne'vrosi *sf* neurosis
'**nibbio** *sm* (*ZOOL*) kite
'**nicchia** ['nikkja] *sf* niche; (*naturale*) cavity,
hollow
nicchi'are [nik'kjare] *vi* to shilly-shally,
hesitate
'**nichel** ['nikel] *sm* nickel
nico'tina *sf* nicotine
'**nido** *sm* nest; **a ~ d'ape** (*tessuto etc*)
honeycomb *cpd*

PAROLA CHIAVE

ni'ente *pron* **1** (*nessuna cosa*) nothing; **~ può
fermarlo** nothing can stop him; **~ di ~**

absolutely nothing; **nient'altro** nothing else;
nient'altro che nothing but, just, only;
~ affatto not at all, not in the least; **come se
~ fosse** as if nothing had happened; **cose da
~** trivial matters; **per ~** (*gratis, invano*) for
nothing
2 (*qualcosa*): **hai bisogno di ~?** do you need
anything?
3: **non ... ~** nothing, *espressione negativa*
+ anything; **non ho visto ~** I saw nothing, I
didn't see anything; **non ho ~ da dire** I have
nothing o haven't anything to say
♦ *sm* nothing; **un bel ~** absolutely nothing;
basta un ~ per farla piangere the slightest
thing is enough to make her cry
♦ *av* (*in nessuna misura*): **non ... ~** not ... at
all; **non è (per) ~ buono** it isn't good at all

---

nientedi'meno *av* actually, even ♦ *escl*
really!, I say!
niente'meno *av, escl* = **nientedimeno**
'**Nilo** *sm*: **il ~** the Nile
'**ninfa** *sf* nymph
nin'fea *sf* water lily
ninna-'nanna *sf* lullaby
'**ninnolo** *sm* (*gingillo*) knick-knack
ni'pote *sm/f* (*di zii*) nephew/niece; (*di nonni*)
grandson/daughter, grandchild
'**nitido, a** *ag* clear; (*specchio*) bright
ni'trato *sm* nitrate
'**nitrico, a, ci, che** *ag* nitric
ni'trire *vi* to neigh
ni'trito *sm* (*di cavallo*) neighing *no pl*; neigh;
(*CHIM*) nitrite
nitroglice'rina [nitrogliʧe'rina] *sf* nitro-
glycerine
no *av* (*risposta*) no; **vieni o ~?** are you coming
or not?; **perché ~?** why not?; **lo conosciamo?
— tu ~ ma io sì** do we know him? — you
don't but I do; **verrai, ~?** you'll come, won't
you?
'**nobile** *ag* noble ♦ *sm/f* noble, nobleman/
woman; **nobili'are** *ag* noble; **nobiltà** *sf*
nobility; (*di azione*) nobleness
'**nocca, che** *sf* (*ANAT*) knuckle
nocci'ola [not'ʧɔla] *ag inv* (*colore*) hazel,
light brown ♦ *sf* hazelnut
noccio'lina [nottʃo'lina] *sf*: **~ americana**
peanut
'**nocciolo**[1] ['nɔttʃolo] *sm* (*di frutto*) stone;
(*fig*) heart, core
noc'ciolo[2] [not'ʧɔlo] *sm* (*albero*) hazel
'**noce** ['noʧe] *sm* (*albero*) walnut tree ♦ *sf*
(*frutto*) walnut; **~ moscata** nutmeg
no'civo, a [no'ʧivo] *ag* harmful, noxious
'**nodo** *sm* (*di cravatta, legname, NAUT*) knot;
(*AUT, FERR*) junction; (*MED, ASTR, BOT*) node;
(*fig: legame*) bond, tie; (: *punto centrale*)
heart, crux; **avere un ~ alla gola** to have a

lump in one's throat; **no'doso, a** *ag* (*tronco*) gnarled

'noi *pron* (*soggetto*) we; (*oggetto: per dare rilievo, con preposizione*) us; **~ stessi(e)** we ourselves; (*oggetto*) ourselves

'noia *sf* boredom; (*disturbo, impaccio*) bother *no pl*, trouble *no pl*; **avere qn/qc a ~** not to like sb/sth; **mi è venuto a ~** I'm tired of it; **dare ~ a** to annoy; **avere delle ~e con qn** to have trouble with sb

noi'altri *pron* we

noi'oso, a *ag* boring; (*fastidioso*) annoying, troublesome

noleggi'are [noled'dʒare] *vt* (*prendere a noleggio*) to hire (BRIT), rent; (*dare a noleggio*) to hire out (BRIT), rent (out); (*aereo, nave*) to charter; **no'leggio** *sm* hire (BRIT), rental; charter

'nolo *sm* hire (BRIT), rental; charter; (*per trasporto merci*) freight; **prendere/dare a ~ qc** to hire/hire out sth

'nomade *ag* nomadic ♦ *sm/f* nomad

'nome *sm* name; (LING) noun; **in/a ~ di** in the name of; **di o per ~** (*chiamato*) called, named; **conoscere qn di ~** to know sb by name; **~ d'arte** stage name; **~ di battesimo** Christian name; **~ di famiglia** surname

no'mea *sf* notoriety

no'mignolo [no'miɲɲolo] *sm* nickname

'nomina *sf* appointment

nomi'nale *ag* nominal; (LING) noun *cpd*

nomi'nare *vt* to name; (*eleggere*) to appoint; (*citare*) to mention

nomina'tivo, a *ag* (LING) nominative; (ECON) registered ♦ *sm* (LING: *anche:* **caso ~**) nominative (case); (AMM) name

non *av* not ♦ *prefisso* non-; *vedi* **affatto; appena** *etc*

nonché [non'ke] *cong* (*tanto più, tanto meno*) let alone; (*e inoltre*) as well as

noncu'rante *ag:* **~ (di)** careless (of), indifferent (to); **noncu'ranza** *sf* carelessness, indifference

nondi'meno *cong* (*tuttavia*) however; (*nonostante*) nevertheless

'nonno, a *sm/f* grandfather/mother; (*in senso più familiare*) grandma/grandpa; **~i** *smpl* grandparents

non'nulla *sm inv:* **un ~** nothing, a trifle

'nono, a *ag, sm* ninth

nonos'tante *prep* in spite of, notwithstanding ♦ *cong* although, even though

nontiscordardimé *sm inv* (BOT) forget-me-not

nord *sm* North ♦ *ag inv* north; northern; **il Mare del N~** the North Sea; **nor'dest** *sm* north-east; **'nordico, a, ci, che** *ag* nordic, northern European; **nor'dovest** *sm*

north-west

'norma *sf* (*principio*) norm; (*regola*) regulation, rule; (*consuetudine*) custom, rule; **a ~ di legge** according to law, as laid down by law

nor'male *ag* normal; standard *cpd*; **normalità** *sf* normality; **normaliz'zare** *vt* to normalize, bring back to normal

normal'mente *av* normally

norve'gese [norve'dʒese] *ag, sm/f, sm* Norwegian

Nor'vegia [nor'vedʒa] *sf:* **la ~** Norway

nostal'gia [nostal'dʒia] *sf* (*di casa, paese*) homesickness; (*del passato*) nostalgia; **nos'talgico, a, ci, che** *ag* homesick; nostalgic

nos'trano, a *ag* local; national; home-produced

'nostro, a *det:* **il(la) ~(a)** *etc* our ♦ *pron:* **il(la) ~(a)** *etc* ours ♦ *sm:* **il ~** our money; our belongings; **i ~i** our family; our own people; **è dei ~i** he's one of us

'nota *sf* (*segno*) mark; (*comunicazione scritta, MUS*) note; (*fattura*) bill; (*elenco*) list; **degno di ~** noteworthy, worthy of note

no'tabile *ag* notable ♦ *sm* prominent citizen

no'taio *sm* notary

no'tare *vt* (*segnare: errori*) to mark; (*registrare*) to note (down), write down; (*rilevare, osservare*) to note, notice; **farsi ~** to get o.s. noticed

no'tevole *ag* (*talento*) notable, remarkable; (*peso*) considerable

no'tifica, che *sf* notification

notifi'care *vt* (DIR): **~ qc a qn** to notify sb of sth, give sb notice of sth

no'tizia [no'tittsja] *sf* (*piece of*) news *sg*; (*informazione*) piece of information; **~e** *sfpl* (*informazioni*) news *sg*; information *sg*; **notizi'ario** *sm* (RADIO, TV, STAMPA) news *sg*

'noto, a *ag* (*well-*)known

notorietà *sf* fame; notoriety

no'torio, a *ag* well-known; (*peg*) notorious

not'tambulo, a *sm/f* night-bird (*fig*)

not'tata *sf* night

'notte *sf* night; **di ~** at night; (*durante la notte*) in the night, during the night; **~ bianca** sleepless night; **notte'tempo** *av* at night; during the night

not'turno, a *ag* nocturnal; (*servizio, guardiano*) night *cpd*

no'vanta *num* ninety; **novan'tesimo, a** *num* ninetieth; **novan'tina** *sf:* **una novantina (di)** about ninety

'nove *num* nine

nove'cento [nove'tʃɛnto] *num* nine hundred ♦ *sm:* **il N~** the twentieth century

no'vella *sf* (LETTERATURA) short story

novel'lino, a *ag* (*pivello*) green,

inexperienced

no'vello, a [no'vɛllo] ag (piante, patate) new; (insalata, verdura) early; (sposo) newly-married

no'vembre sm November

novi'lunio sm (ASTR) new moon

novità sf inv novelty; (innovazione) innovation; (cosa originale, insolita) something new; (notizia) (piece of) news sg; **le ~ della moda** the latest fashions

no'vizio, a [no'vittsjo] sm/f (REL) novice; (tirocinante) beginner, apprentice

nozi'one [not'tsjone] sf notion, idea; **~i** sfpl (rudimenti) basic knowledge sg, rudiments

'nozze ['nɔttse] sfpl wedding sg, marriage sg; **~ d'argento/d'oro** silver/golden wedding sg

ns. abbr (COMM) = **nostro**

'nube sf cloud; **nubi'fragio** sm cloudburst

'nubile ag (donna) unmarried, single

'nuca sf nape of the neck

nucle'are ag nuclear

'nucleo sm nucleus; (gruppo) team, unit, group; (MIL, POLIZIA) squad; **il ~ familiare** the family unit

nu'dista, i, e sm/f nudist

'nudo, a ag (persona) bare, naked, nude; (membra) bare, naked; (montagna) bare ♦ sm (ARTE) nude

'nugolo sm: **un ~ di** a whole host of

'nulla pron, av = **niente** ♦ sm: **il ~** nothing

nulla'osta sm inv authorization

nullità sf inv nullity; (persona) nonentity

'nullo, a ag useless, worthless; (DIR) null (and void); (SPORT) **incontro ~** draw

nume'rale ag, sm numeral

nume'rare vt to number; **numerazi'one** sf numbering; (araba, decimale) notation

nu'merico, a, ci, che ag numerical

'numero sm number; (romano, arabo) numeral; (di spettacolo) act, turn; **~ civico** house number; **~ di telefono** telephone number; **nume'roso, a** ag numerous, many; (con sostantivo sg) large

'nunzio ['nuntsjo] sm (REL) nuncio

nu'ocere ['nwɔtʃere] vi: **~ a** to harm, damage; **nuoci'uto, a** pp di **nuocere**

nu'ora sf daughter-in-law

nuo'tare vi to swim; (galleggiare: oggetti) to float; **nuota'tore, 'trice** sm/f swimmer; **nu'oto** sm swimming

nu'ova sf (notizia) (piece of) news sg; vedi anche **nuovo**

nuova'mente av again

Nu'ova Ze'landa [-dze'landa] sf: **la ~** New Zealand

nu'ovo, a ag new; **di ~** again; **~ fiammante** o **di zecca** brand-new

nutri'ente ag nutritious, nourishing

nutri'mento sm food, nourishment

nu'trire vt to feed; (fig: sentimenti) to harbour, nurse; **nutri'tivo, a** ag nutritional; (alimento) nutritious; **nutrizi'one** sf nutrition

'nuvola sf cloud; **nuvo'loso, a** ag cloudy

nuzi'ale [nut'tsjale] ag nuptial; wedding cpd

O, o

o (dav V spesso **od**) cong or; **~ ... ~** either ... or; **~ l'uno ~ l'altro** either (of them)

O. abbr (= ovest) W

'oasi sf inv oasis

obbedi'ente etc = **ubbidiente** etc

obbli'gare vt (costringere): **~ qn a fare** to force o oblige sb to do; (DIR) to bind; **~rsi** vr: **~rsi a fare** to undertake to do; **obbli'gato, a** ag (costretto, grato) obliged; (percorso, tappa) set, fixed; **obbliga'torio, a** ag compulsory, obligatory; **obbligazi'one** sf (COMM) bond, debenture; **'obbligo, ghi** sm obligation; (dovere) duty; **avere l'obbligo di fare** to be obliged to do; **essere d'obbligo** (discorso, applauso) to be called for

ob'brobrio sm disgrace; (fig) eyesore

o'beso, a ag obese

obiet'tare vt: **~ che** to object that; **~ su qc** to object to sth, raise objections concerning sth

obiet'tivo, a ag objective ♦ sm (OTTICA, FOT) lens sg, objective; (MIL, fig) objective

obiet'tore sm objector; **~ di coscienza** conscientious objector

obiezi'one [objet'tsjone] sf objection

obi'torio sm morgue, mortuary

o'bliquo, a ag oblique; (inclinato) slanting; (fig) devious, underhand

oblite'rare vt (biglietto) to stamp; (francobollo) to cancel

oblò sm inv porthole

o'blungo, a, ghi, ghe ag oblong

'oboe sm (MUS) oboe

'oca (pl **'oche**) sf goose

occasi'one sf (caso favorevole) opportunity; (causa, motivo, circostanza) occasion; (COMM) bargain; **d'~** (a buon prezzo) bargain cpd; (usato) secondhand

occhi'aia [ok'kjaja] sf eye socket; **avere le ~e** to have shadows under one's eyes

occhi'ali [ok'kjali] smpl glasses, spectacles; **~ da sole** sunglasses; **~ da vista** (prescription) glasses

occhi'ata [ok'kjata] sf look, glance; **dare un'~ a** to have a look at

occhi'ello [ok'kjɛllo] sm buttonhole; (asola) eyelet

'occhio ['ɔkkjo] sm eye; **~!** careful!, watch out!; **a ~ nudo** with the naked eye; **a quattr'~i** privately, tête-à-tête; **dare all'~** o **nell'~ a qn**

to catch sb's eye; **fare l'~ a qc** to get used to sth; **tenere d'~ qn** to keep an eye on sb; **vedere di buon/mal ~ qc** to look favourably/ unfavourably on sth

occhio'lino [okkjo'lino] *sm*: **fare l'~ a qn** to wink at sb

occiden'tale [ottʃiden'tale] *ag* western ♦ *sm/f* Westerner

occi'dente [ottʃi'dɛnte] *sm* west; (*POL*): **l'O~** the West; **a ~** in the west

oc'cipite [ot'tʃipite] *sm* back of the head, occiput

oc'cludere *vt* to block; **occlusi'one** *sf* blockage, obstruction; **oc'cluso, a** *pp di* **occludere**

occor'rente *ag* necessary ♦ *sm* all that is necessary

occor'renza [okkor'rɛntsa] *sf* necessity, need; **all'~** in case of need

oc'correre *vi* to be needed, be required ♦ *vb impers*: **occorre farlo** it must be done; **occorre che tu parta** you must leave, you'll have to leave; **mi occorrono i soldi** I need the money; **oc'corso, a** *pp di* **occorrere**

occul'tare *vt* to hide, conceal

oc'culto, a *ag* hidden, concealed; (*scienze, forze*) occult

occu'pare *vt* to occupy; (*manodopera*) to employ; (*ingombrare*) to occupy, take up; **~rsi** *vr* to occupy o.s., keep o.s. busy; (*impiegarsi*) to get a job; **~rsi di** (*interessarsi*) to take an interest in; (*prendersi cura di*) to look after, take care of; **occu'pato, a** *ag* (*MIL, POL*) occupied; (*persona: affaccendato*) busy; (*posto, sedia*) taken; (*toilette, TEL*) engaged; **occupazi'one** *sf* occupation; (*impiego, lavoro*) job; (*ECON*) employment

o'ceano [o'tʃɛano] *sm* ocean

'ocra *sf* ochre

ocu'lare *ag* ocular, eye *cpd*; **testimone ~** eye witness

ocu'lato, a *ag* (*attento*) cautious, prudent; (*accorto*) shrewd

ocu'lista, i, e *sm/f* eye specialist, oculist

'ode *sf* ode

odi'are *vt* to hate, detest

odi'erno, a *ag* today's, of today; (*attuale*) present

'odio *sm* hatred; **avere in ~ qc/qn** to hate o detest sth/sb; **odi'oso, a** *ag* hateful, odious

odo'rare *vt* (*annusare*) to smell; (*profumare*) to perfume, scent ♦ *vi*: **~ (di)** to smell (of); **odo'rato** *sm* sense of smell

o'dore *sm* smell; **gli ~i** *smpl* (*CUC*) (aromatic) herbs; **odo'roso, a** *ag* sweet-smelling

of'fendere *vt* to offend; (*violare*) to break, violate; (*insultare*) to insult; (*ferire*) to hurt; **~rsi** *vr* (*con senso reciproco*) to insult one another; (*risentirsi*): **~rsi (di)** to take offence

(at), be offended (by); **offen'sivo, a** *ag, sf* offensive

offe'rente *sm* (*in aste*): **al maggior ~** to the highest bidder

of'ferta *sf* offer; (*donazione, anche REL*) offering; (*in gara d'appalto*) tender; (*in aste*) bid; (*ECON*) supply; **"~e d'impiego"** "situations vacant"; **fare un'~a** to make an offer; to tender; to bid

of'ferto, a *pp di* **offrire**

of'fesa *sf* insult, affront; (*MIL*) attack; (*DIR*) offence; *vedi anche* **offeso**

of'feso, a *pp di* **offendere** ♦ *ag* offended; (*fisicamente*) hurt, injured ♦ *sm/f* offended party; **essere ~ con qn** to be annoyed with sb; **parte ~a** (*DIR*) plaintiff

offi'cina [offi'tʃina] *sf* workshop

of'frire *vt* to offer; **~rsi** *vr* (*proporsi*) to offer (o.s.), volunteer; (*occasione*) to present itself; (*esporsi*): **~rsi a** to expose o.s. to; **ti offro da bere** I'll buy you a drink

offus'care *vt* to obscure, darken; (*fig: intelletto*) to dim, cloud; (: *fama*) to obscure, overshadow; **~rsi** *vr* to grow dark; to cloud, grow dim; to be obscured

ogget'tivo, a [oddʒet'tivo] *ag* objective

og'getto [od'dʒetto] *sm* object; (*materia, argomento*) subject (matter); **~i smarriti** lost property *sg*

'oggi ['ɔddʒi] *av, sm* today; **~ a otto** a week today; **oggigi'orno** *av* nowadays

OGM *sigla m* (= *organismo geneticamente modificato*) GMO

'ogni ['oɲɲi] *det* every, each; (*tutti*) all; (*con valore distributivo*) every; **~ uomo è mortale** all men are mortal; **viene ~ due giorni** he comes every two days; **~ cosa** everything; **ad ~ costo** at all costs, at any price; **in ~ luogo** everywhere; **~ tanto** every so often; **~ volta che** every time that

Ognis'santi [oɲɲis'santi] *sm* All Saints' Day

o'gnuno [oɲ'ɲuno] *pron* everyone, everybody

'ohi *escl* oh!; (*esprimendo dolore*) ow!

ohimè *escl* oh dear!

O'landa *sf*: **l'~** Holland; **olan'dese** *ag* Dutch ♦ *sm* (*LING*) Dutch ♦ *sm/f* Dutchman/woman; **gli Olandesi** the Dutch

oleo'dotto *sm* oil pipeline

ole'oso, a *ag* oily; (*che contiene olio*) oil-yielding

ol'fatto *sm* sense of smell

oli'are *vt* to oil

oli'era *sf* oil cruet

olim'piadi *sfpl* Olympic games; **o'limpico, a, ci, che** *ag* Olympic

'olio *sm* oil; **sott'~** (*CUC*) in oil; **~ di fegato di merluzzo** cod liver oil; **~ d'oliva** olive oil; **~ di semi** vegetable oil

o'liva *sf* olive; oli'vastro, a *ag* olive(-coloured); (*carnagione*) sallow; oli'veto *sm* olive grove; o'livo *sm* olive tree

'olmo *sm* elm

oltraggi'are [oltrad'dʒare] *vt* to outrage; to offend gravely

ol'traggio [ol'traddʒo] *sm* outrage; offence, insult; ~ al pudore (*DIR*) indecent behaviour; oltraggi'oso, a *ag* offensive

ol'tralpe *av* beyond the Alps

ol'tranza [ol'trantsa] *sf*: a ~ to the last, to the bitter end

'oltre *av* (*più in là*) further; (*di più: aspettare*) longer, more ♦ *prep* (*di là da*) beyond, over, on the other side of; (*più di*) more than, over; (*in aggiunta a*) besides; (*eccetto*): ~ a except, apart from; oltre'mare *av* overseas; oltre'modo *av* extremely; oltrepas'sare *vt* to go beyond, exceed

o'maggio [o'maddʒo] *sm* (*dono*) gift; (*segno di rispetto*) homage, tribute; ~i *smpl* (*complimenti*) respects; rendere ~ a to pay homage o tribute to; in ~ (*copia, biglietto*) complimentary

ombe'lico, chi *sm* navel

'ombra *sf* (*zona non assolata, fantasma*) shade; (*sagoma scura*) shadow; sedere all'~ to sit in the shade; restare nell'~ (*fig*) to remain in obscurity

om'brello *sm* umbrella; ombrel'lone *sm* beach umbrella

om'bretto *sm* eyeshadow

om'broso, a *ag* shady, shaded; (*cavallo*) nervous, skittish; (*persona*) touchy, easily offended

ome'lia *sf* (*REL*) homily, sermon

omeopa'tia *sf* homoeopathy

omertà *sf* conspiracy of silence

o'messo, a *pp di* omettere

o'mettere *vt* to omit, leave out; ~ di fare to omit o fail to do

omi'cida, i, e [omi'tʃida] *ag* homicidal, murderous ♦ *sm/f* murderer/eress

omi'cidio [omi'tʃidjo] *sm* murder; ~ colposo culpable homicide

omissi'one *sf* omission; ~ di soccorso (*DIR*) failure to stop and give assistance

omogeneiz'zato [omodʒeneid'dzato] *sm* baby food

omo'geneo, a [omo'dʒɛneo] *ag* homogeneous

omolo'gare *vt* to approve, recognize; to ratify

o'monimo, a *sm/f* namesake ♦ *sm* (*LING*) homonym

omosessu'ale *ag, sm/f* homosexual

'oncia, ce [ˈontʃa] *sf* ounce

'onda *sf* wave; mettere o mandare in ~ (*RADIO, TV*) to broadcast; andare in ~ (*RADIO, TV*) to go on the air; ~e corte/medie/lunghe short/medium/long wave; on'data *sf* wave, billow; (*fig*) wave, surge; a ondate in waves; ondata di caldo heatwave

ondeggi'are [onded'dʒare] *vi* (*acqua*) to ripple; (*muoversi sulle onde: barca*) to rock, roll; (*fig: muoversi come le onde, barcollare*) to sway; (: *essere incerto*) to waver

'onere *sm* burden; ~i fiscali taxes; one'roso, a *ag* (*fig*) heavy, onerous

onestà *sf* honesty

o'nesto, a *ag* (*probo, retto*) honest; (*giusto*) fair; (*casto*) chaste, virtuous

'onice [ˈɔnitʃe] *sf* onyx

onnipo'tente *ag* omnipotent

ono'mastico, ci *sm* name-day

ono'ranze [ono'rantse] *sfpl* honours; ~ funebri funeral (service)

ono'rare *vt* to honour; (*far onore a*) to do credit to; ~rsi *vr*: ~rsi di to feel honoured at, be proud of

ono'rario, a *ag* honorary ♦ *sm* fee

o'nore *sm* honour; in ~ di in honour of; fare gli ~i di casa to play host (o hostess); fare ~ a to honour; (*pranzo*) to do justice to; (*famiglia*) to be a credit to; farsi ~ to distinguish o.s.; ono'revole *ag* honourable ♦ *sm/f* (*POL*) ≈ Member of Parliament (*BRIT*); ≈ Congressman/woman (*US*); onorifi'cenza *sf* honour; decoration; ono'rifico, a, ci, che *ag* honorary

'onta *sf* shame, disgrace

on'tano *sm* (*BOT*) alder

'O.N.U. [ˈɔnu] *sigla f* (= *Organizzazione delle Nazioni Unite*) UN, UNO

o'paco, a, chi, che *ag* (*vetro*) opaque; (*metallo*) dull, matt

o'pale *sm o f* opal

'opera *sf* work; (*azione rilevante*) action, deed, work; (*MUS*) work; opus; (: *melodramma*) opera; (: *teatro*) opera house; (*ente*) institution, organization; ~ d'arte work of art; ~ lirica (grand) opera; ~e pubbliche public works

ope'raio, a *ag* working-class; workers' ♦ *sm/f* worker; classe ~a working class

ope'rare *vt* to carry out, make; (*MED*) to operate on ♦ *vi* to operate, work; (*rimedio*) to act, work; (*MED*) to operate; ~rsi *vr* (*MED*) to have an operation; ~rsi d'appendicite to have one's appendix out; opera'tivo, a *ag* operative, operating; opera'tore, 'trice *sm/f* operator; (*TV, CINEMA*) cameraman; operatore economico agent, broker; operatore turistico tour operator; opera'torio, a *ag* (*MED*) operating; operazi'one *sf* operation

ope'retta *sf* (*MUS*) operetta, light opera

ope'roso, a *ag* busy, active, hard-working

opini'one *sf* opinion; ~ pubblica

public opinion

'oppio sm opium

oppo'nente ag opposing ♦ sm/f opponent

op'porre vt to oppose; **opporsi** vr: **opporsi (a qc)** to oppose (sth); to object (to sth); **~ resistenza/un rifiuto** to offer resistance/ refuse

opportu'nista, i, e sm/f opportunist

opportunità sf inv opportunity; (convenienza) opportuneness, timeliness

oppor'tuno, a ag timely, opportune

opposi'tore, 'trice sm/f opposer, opponent

opposizi'one [oppozit'tsjone] sf opposition; (DIR) objection

op'posto, a pp di **opporre** ♦ ag opposite; (opinioni) conflicting ♦ sm opposite, contrary; **all'~** on the contrary

oppressi'one sf oppression

oppres'sivo, a ag oppressive

op'presso, a pp di **opprimere**

oppres'sore sm oppressor

op'primere vt (premere, gravare) to weigh down; (estenuare: sog: caldo) to suffocate, oppress; (tiranneggiare: popolo) to oppress

op'pure cong or (else)

op'tare vi: **~ per** to opt for

o'puscolo sm booklet, pamphlet

opzi'one [op'tsjone] sf option

'ora¹ sf (60 minuti) hour; (momento) time; **che ~ è?, che ~e sono?** what time is it?; **non veder l'~ di fare** to long to do, look forward to doing; **di buon'~** early; **alla buon'~!** at last!; **~ di cena** dinner time; **~ legale** o **estiva** summer time (BRIT), daylight saving time (US); **~ locale** local time; **~ di pranzo** lunchtime; **~ di punta** (AUT) rush hour

ora² av (adesso) now; (poco fa): **è uscito proprio ~** he's just gone out; (tra poco) presently, in a minute; (correlativo): **~ ... ~** now ... now; **d'~ in avanti** o **poi** from now on; **or ~** just now, a moment ago; **5 anni or sono** 5 years ago; **~ come ~** right now, at present

o'racolo sm oracle

'orafo sm goldsmith

o'rale ag, sm oral

ora'mai av = ormai

o'rario, a ag hourly; (fuso, segnale) time cpd; (velocità) per hour ♦ sm timetable, schedule; (di ufficio, visite etc) hours pl, time(s pl); **in ~** on time

o'rata sf (ZOOL) sea bream

ora'tore, 'trice sm/f speaker; orator

ora'toria sf (arte) oratory

ora'torio, a ag oratorical ♦ sm (REL) oratory; (MUS) oratorio

ora'zione [orat'tsjone] sf (REL) prayer; (discorso) speech, oration

or'bene cong so, well (then)

'orbita sf (ASTR, FISICA) orbit; (ANAT) (eye-)socket

or'chestra [or'kestra] sf orchestra; **orches'trare** vt to orchestrate; (fig) to mount, stage-manage

orchi'dea [orki'dεa] sf orchid

'orco, chi sm ogre

'orda sf horde

or'digno [or'diɲno] sm (esplosivo) explosive device

ordi'nale ag, sm ordinal

ordina'mento sm order, arrangement; (regolamento) regulations pl, rules pl; **~ scolastico/giuridico** education/legal system

ordi'nanza [ordi'nantsa] sf (DIR, MIL) order; (persona: MIL) orderly, batman; **d'~** (MIL) regulation cpd

ordi'nare vt (mettere in ordine) to arrange, organize; (COMM) to order; (prescrivere: medicina) to prescribe; (comandare): **~ a qn di fare qc** to order o command sb to do sth; (REL) to ordain

ordi'nario, a ag (comune) ordinary; everyday; standard; (grossolano) coarse, common ♦ sm ordinary; (INS: di università) full professor

ordi'nato, a ag tidy, orderly

ordinazi'one [ordinat'tsjone] sf (COMM) order; (REL) ordination; **eseguire qc su ~** to make sth to order

'ordine sm order; (carattere): **d'~ pratico** of a practical nature; **all'~** (COMM: assegno) to order; **di prim'~** first-class; **fino a nuovo ~** until further notice; **essere in ~** (documenti) to be in order; (stanza, persona) to be tidy; **mettere in ~** to put in order, tidy (up); **~ del giorno** (di seduta) agenda; (MIL) order of the day; **~ di pagamento** (COMM) order for payment; **l'~ pubblico** law and order; **~i (sacri)** (REL) holy orders

or'dire vt (fig) to plot, scheme; **or'dito** sm (di tessuto) warp

orec'chino [orek'kino] sm earring

o'recchio [o'rekkjo] (pl(f) o'recchie) sm (ANAT) ear

orecchi'oni [orek'kjoni] smpl (MED) mumps sg

o'refice [o'refitʃe] sm goldsmith; jeweller; **orefice'ria** sf (arte) goldsmith's art; (negozio) jeweller's (shop)

'orfano, a ag orphan(ed) ♦ sm/f orphan; **~ di padre/madre** fatherless/motherless; **orfano'trofio** sm orphanage

orga'netto sm barrel organ; (fam: armonica a bocca) mouth organ; (: fisarmonica) accordion

or'ganico, a, ci, che ag organic ♦ sm personnel, staff

organi'gramma, i *sm* organization chart

orga'nismo *sm* (*BIOL*) organism; (*corpo umano*) body; (*AMM*) body, organism

organiz'zare [organid'dzare] *vt* to organize; **~rsi** *vr* to get organized; **organizza'tore, 'trice** *ag* organizing ♦ *sm/f* organizer; **organizzazi'one** *sf* organization

'organo *sm* organ; (*di congegno*) part; (*portavoce*) spokesman, mouthpiece

or'gasmo *sm* (*FISIOL*) orgasm; (*fig*) agitation, anxiety

'orgia, ge ['ɔrdʒa] *sf* orgy

or'goglio [or'gɔʎʎo] *sm* pride; **orgogli'oso, a** *ag* proud

orien'tale *ag* oriental; eastern; east

orienta'mento *sm* positioning; orientation; direction; **senso di ~** sense of direction; **perdere l'~** to lose one's bearings; **~ professionale** careers guidance

orien'tare *vt* (*situare*) to position; (*fig*) to direct, orientate; **~rsi** *vr* to find one's bearings; (*fig: tendere*) to tend, lean; (: *indirizzarsi*): **~rsi verso** to take up, go in for

ori'ente *sm* east; **l'O~** the East, the Orient; **a ~** in the east

o'rigano *sm* oregano

origi'nale [oridʒi'nale] *ag* original; (*bizzarro*) eccentric ♦ *sm* original; **originalità** *sf* originality; eccentricity

origi'nare [oridʒi'nare] *vt* to bring about, produce ♦ *vi:* **~ da** to arise *o* spring from

origi'nario, a [oridʒi'narjo] *ag* original; **essere ~ di** to be a native of; (*provenire da*) to originate from; to be native to

o'rigine [o'ridʒine] *sf* origin; **all'~** originally; **d'~ inglese** of English origin; **dare ~ a** to give rise to

origli'are [oriʎ'ʎare] *vi:* **~ (a)** to eavesdrop (on)

o'rina *sf* urine

ori'nare *vi* to urinate ♦ *vt* to pass; **orina'toio** *sm* (public) urinal

ori'undo, a *ag:* **essere ~ di Milano** *etc* to be of Milanese *etc* extraction *o* origin ♦ *sm/f* person of foreign extraction *o* origin

orizzon'tale [oriddzon'tale] *ag* horizontal

oriz'zonte [orid'dzonte] *sm* horizon

or'lare *vt* to hem

'orlo *sm* edge, border; (*di recipiente*) rim, brim; (*di vestito etc*) hem

'orma *sf* (*di persona*) footprint; (*di animale*) track; (*impronta, traccia*) mark, trace

or'mai *av* by now, by this time; (*adesso*) now; (*quasi*) almost, nearly

ormeggi'are [ormed'dʒare] *vt* (*NAUT*) to moor; **or'meggio** *sm* (*atto*) mooring *no pl*; (*luogo*) moorings *pl*

or'mone *sm* hormone

ornamen'tale *ag* ornamental, decorative

orna'mento *sm* ornament, decoration

or'nare *vt* to adorn, decorate; **~rsi** *vr:* **~rsi (di)** to deck o.s. (out) (with); **or'nato, a** *ag* ornate

ornitolo'gia [ornitolo'dʒia] *sf* ornithology

'oro *sm* gold; **d'~, in ~** gold *cpd*; **d'~** (*colore, occasione*) golden; (*persona*) marvellous

orologe'ria [orolodʒe'ria] *sf* watchmaking *no pl*; watchmaker's (shop); clockmaker's (shop); **bomba a ~** time bomb

orologi'aio [orolo'dʒajo] *sm* watchmaker; clockmaker

oro'logio [oro'lɔdʒo] *sm* clock; (*da tasca, da polso*) watch; **~ da polso** wristwatch; **~ al quarzo** quartz watch

o'roscopo *sm* horoscope

or'rendo, a *ag* (*spaventoso*) horrible, awful; (*bruttissimo*) hideous

or'ribile *ag* horrible

'orrido, a *ag* fearful, horrid

orripi'lante *ag* hair-raising, horrifying

or'rore *sm* horror; **avere in ~ qn/qc** to loathe *o* detest sb/sth; **mi fanno ~** I loathe *o* detest them

orsacchi'otto [orsak'kjɔtto] *sm* teddy bear

'orso *sm* bear; **~ bruno/bianco** brown/polar bear

or'taggio [or'taddʒo] *sm* vegetable

or'tensia *sf* hydrangea

or'tica, che *sf* (*stinging*) nettle

orti'caria *sf* nettle rash

'orto *sm* vegetable garden, kitchen garden; (*AGR*) market garden (*BRIT*), truck farm (*US*)

orto'dosso, a *ag* orthodox

ortogra'fia *sf* spelling

orto'lano, a *sm/f* (*venditore*) greengrocer (*BRIT*), produce dealer (*US*)

ortope'dia *sf* orthopaedics *sg*; **orto'pedico, a, ci, che** *ag* orthopaedic ♦ *sm* orthopaedic specialist

orzai'olo [ordza'jɔlo] *sm* (*MED*) stye

or'zata [or'dzata] *sf* barley water

'orzo ['ordzo] *sm* barley

o'sare *vt, vi* to dare; **~ fare** to dare (to) *o* do

oscenità [oʃʃeni'ta] *sf inv* obscenity

o'sceno, a [oʃ'ʃɛno] *ag* obscene; (*ripugnante*) ghastly

oscil'lare [oʃʃil'lare] *vi* (*pendolo*) to swing; (*dondolare: al vento etc*) to rock; (*variare*) to fluctuate; (*TECN*) to oscillate; (*fig*): **~ fra** to waver *o* hesitate between; **oscillazi'one** *sf* oscillation; (*di prezzi, temperatura*) fluctuation

oscura'mento *sm* darkening; obscuring; (*in tempo di guerra*) blackout

oscu'rare *vt* to darken, obscure; (*fig*) to obscure; **~rsi** *vr* (*cielo*) to darken, cloud over; (*persona*): **si oscurò in volto** his face clouded over

os'curo, a *ag* dark; (*fig*) obscure; humble,

lowly ♦ *sm*: **all'~** in the dark; **tenere qn
all'~ di qc** to keep sb in the dark about sth
ospe'dale *sm* hospital; **ospedali'ero, a** *ag*
hospital *cpd*
ospi'tale *ag* hospitable; **ospitalità** *sf*
hospitality
ospi'tare *vt* to give hospitality to; (*sog:
albergo*) to accommodate
'**ospite** *sm/f* (*persona che ospita*) host/hostess;
(*persona ospitata*) guest
os'pizio [os'pittsjo] *sm* (*per vecchi etc*) home
'**ossa** *sfpl vedi* **osso**
ossa'tura *sf* (*ANAT*) skeletal structure, frame;
(*TECN, fig*) framework
'**osseo, a** *ag* bony; (*tessuto etc*) bone *cpd*
os'sequio *sm* deference, respect; **~i** *smpl*
(*saluto*) respects, regards; **ossequi'oso, a**
ag obsequious
osser'vanza [osser'vantsa] *sf* observance
osser'vare *vt* to observe, watch; (*esaminare*)
to examine; (*notare, rilevare*) to notice,
observe; (*DIR: la legge*) to observe, respect;
(*mantenere: silenzio*) to keep, observe; **far
~ qc a qn** to point sth out to sb; **osserva'tore, 'trice** *ag* observant, perceptive
♦ *sm/f* observer; **osserva'torio** *sm* (*ASTR*)
observatory; (*MIL*) observation post; **osser-
vazi'one** *sf* observation; (*di legge etc*) observance; (*considerazione critica*) observation,
remark; (*rimprovero*) reproof; **in osservazione**
under observation
ossessio'nare *vt* to obsess, haunt;
(*tormentare*) to torment, harass
ossessi'one *sf* obsession
os'sesso, a *ag* (*spiritato*) possessed
os'sia *cong* that is, to be precise
ossi'buchi [ossi'buki] *smpl di* **ossobuco**
ossi'dare *vt* to oxidize; **~rsi** *vr* to oxidize
'**ossido** *sm* oxide; **~ di carbonio** carbon
monoxide
ossige'nare [ossidʒe'nare] *vt* to oxygenate;
(*decolorare*) to bleach; **acqua ossigenata**
hydrogen peroxide
os'sigeno *sm* oxygen
'**osso** (*pl(f)* **ossa** *nel senso ANAT*) *sm* bone; **d'~**
(*bottone etc*) of bone, bone *cpd*
osso'buco (*pl* **ossi'buchi**) *sm* (*CUC*)
marrowbone; (: *piatto*) stew made with
knuckle of veal in tomato sauce
os'suto, a *ag* bony
ostaco'lare *vt* to block, obstruct
os'tacolo *sm* obstacle; (*EQUITAZIONE*) hurdle,
jump
os'taggio [os'taddʒo] *sm* hostage
'**oste, os'tessa** *sm/f* innkeeper
osteggi'are [osted'dʒare] *vt* to oppose, be
opposed to
os'tello *sm*: **~ della gioventù** youth hostel
osten'tare *vt* to make a show of, flaunt;

ostentazi'one *sf* ostentation, show
oste'ria *sf* inn
os'tessa *sf vedi* **oste**
os'tetrica *sf* midwife; **os'tetrico, a, ci, che**
ag obstetric ♦ *sm* obstetrician
'**ostia** *sf* (*REL*) host; (*per medicinali*) wafer
'**ostico, a, ci, che** *ag* (*fig*) harsh; hard,
difficult; unpleasant
os'tile *ag* hostile; **ostilità** *sf inv* hostility
♦ *sfpl* (*MIL*) hostilities
osti'narsi *vr* to insist, dig one's heels in; **~ a
fare** to persist (obstinately) in doing;
osti'nato, a *ag* (*caparbio*) obstinate;
(*tenace*) persistent, determined;
ostinazi'one *sf* obstinacy; persistence
'**ostrica, che** *sf* oyster
ostru'ire *vt* to obstruct, block; **ostruzi'one**
sf obstruction, blockage
'**otre** *sm* (*recipiente*) goatskin
ottago'nale *ag* octagonal
ot'tagono *sm* octagon
ot'tanta *num* eighty; **ottan'tesimo, a** *num*
eightieth; **ottan'tina** *sf*: **una ottantina (di)**
about eighty
ot'tava *sf* octave
ot'tavo, a *num* eighth
ottempe'rare *vi*: **~ a** to comply with, obey
otte'nere *vt* to obtain, get; (*risultato*) to
achieve, obtain
'**ottica** *sf* (*scienza*) optics *sg*; (*FOT: lenti, prismi
etc*) optics *pl*
'**ottico, a, ci, che** *ag* (*della vista: nervo*)
optic; (*dell'ottica*) optical ♦ *sm* optician
ottima'mente *av* excellently, very well
otti'mismo *sm* optimism; **otti'mista, i, e**
sm/f optimist
'**ottimo, a** *ag* excellent, very good
'**otto** *num* eight
ot'tobre *sm* October
otto'cento [otto'tʃento] *num* eight hundred
♦ *sm*: **l'O~** the nineteenth century
ot'tone *sm* brass; **gli ~i** (*MUS*) the brass
ottu'rare *vt* to close (up); (*dente*) to fill;
ottura'tore *sm* (*FOT*) shutter; (*nelle armi*)
breechblock; **otturazi'one** *sf* closing (up);
(*dentaria*) filling
ot'tuso, a *ag* (*MAT, fig*) obtuse; (*suono*) dull
o'vaia *sf* (*ANAT*) ovary
o'vale *ag, sm* oval
o'vatta *sf* cotton wool; (*per imbottire*)
padding, wadding; **ovat'tare** *vt* (*fig:
smorzare*) to muffle
ovazi'one [ovat'tsjone] *sf* ovation
over'dose ['ouvədous] *sf inv* overdose
'**ovest** *sm* west
'**ovile** *sm* pen, enclosure
o'vino, a *ag* sheep *cpd*, ovine
ovulazi'one [ovulat'tsjone] *sf* ovulation
'**ovulo** *sm* (*FISIOL*) ovum

o'vunque *av* = dovunque

ov'vero *cong* (*ossia*) that is, to be precise; (*oppure*) or (else)

ovvi'are *vi*: ~ a to obviate

'ovvio, a *ag* obvious

ozi'are [ot'tsjare] *vi* to laze, idle

'ozio ['ɔttsjo] *sm* idleness; (*tempo libero*) leisure; ore d'~ leisure time; stare in ~ to be idle; ozi'oso, a *ag* idle

o'zono [o'dzɔno] *sm* ozone

P, p

P *abbr* (= *parcheggio*) P; (*AUT*: = *principiante*) L

pa'cato, a *ag* quiet, calm

'pacca *sf* pat

pac'chetto [pak'ketto] *sm* packet; ~ azionario (*COMM*) shareholding

pacchi'ano, a [pak'kjano] *ag* vulgar

'pacco, chi *sm* parcel; (*involto*) bundle

'pace ['patʃe] *sf* peace; darsi ~ to resign o.s.; fare la ~ con to make it up with

pacifi'care [patʃifi'kare] *vt* (*riconciliare*) to reconcile, make peace between; (*mettere in pace*) to pacify

pa'cifico, a, ci, che [pa'tʃiːfiko] *ag* (*persona*) peaceable; (*vita*) peaceful; (*fig*: *indiscusso*) indisputable; (: *ovvio*) obvious, clear ♦ *sm*: il P~, l'Oceano P~ the Pacific (Ocean)

paci'fista, i, e [patʃi'fista] *sm/f* pacifist

pa'della *sf* frying pan; (*per infermi*) bedpan

padigli'one [padiʎ'ʎone] *sm* pavilion

'Padova *sf* Padua

'padre *sm* father; ~i *smpl* (*antenati*) forefathers

pa'drino *sm* godfather

padro'nanza [padro'nantsa] *sf* command, mastery

pa'drone, a *sm/f* master/mistress; (*proprietario*) owner; (*datore di lavoro*) employer; essere ~ di sé to be in control of o.s.; ~ di casa (*ospite*) host/hostess; (*per gli inquilini*) landlord/lady; padroneggi'are *vt* (*fig*: *sentimenti*) to master, control; (: *materia*) to master, know thoroughly; padroneggiarsi *vr* to control o.s.

pae'saggio [pae'zaddʒo] *sm* landscape

pae'sano, a *ag* country *cpd* ♦ *sm/f* villager; countryman/woman

pa'ese *sm* (*nazione*) country, nation; (*terra*) country, land; (*villaggio*) village; (small) town; ~ di provenienza country of origin; i P~i Bassi the Netherlands

paf'futo, a *ag* chubby, plump

'paga, ghe *sf* pay, wages *pl*

paga'mento *sm* payment

pa'gano, a *ag*, *sm/f* pagan

pa'gare *vt* to pay; (*acquisto*, *fig*: *colpa*) to pay for; (*contraccambiare*) to repay, pay back ♦ *vi* to pay; quanto l'hai pagato? how much did you pay for it?; ~ con carta di credito to pay by credit card; ~ in contanti to pay cash

pa'gella [pa'dʒella] *sf* (*INS*) report card

'paggio ['paddʒo] *sm* page(boy)

paghe'rò [page'rɔ] *sm inv* acknowledgement of a debt, IOU

'pagina ['padʒina] *sf* page; ~e gialle Yellow Pages

'paglia ['paʎʎa] *sf* straw

pagliac'cetto [paʎʎat'tʃetto] *sm* (*per bambini*) rompers *pl*

pagli'accio [paʎ'ʎattʃo] *sm* clown

pagli'etta [paʎ'ʎetta] *sf* (*cappello per uomo*) (straw) boater; (*per tegami etc*) steel wool

pa'gnotta [paɲ'ɲɔtta] *sf* round loaf

'paio (*pl*(*f*) 'paia) *sm* pair; un ~ di (*alcuni*) a couple of

pai'olo *sm* (copper) pot

'pala *sf* shovel; (*di remo*, *ventilatore*, *elica*) blade; (*di ruota*) paddle

pa'lato *sm* palate

pa'lazzo [pa'lattso] *sm* (*reggia*) palace; (*edificio*) building; ~ di giustizia courthouse; ~ dello sport sports stadium

'palco, chi *sm* (*TEATRO*) box; (*tavolato*) platform, stand; (*ripiano*) layer

palco'scenico, ci [palkoʃ'ʃɛniko] *sm* (*TEATRO*) stage

pale'sare *vt* to reveal, disclose; ~rsi *vr* to reveal o show o.s.

pa'lese *ag* clear, evident

Pales'tina *sf*: la ~ Palestine

pa'lestra *sf* gymnasium; (*esercizio atletico*) exercise, training; (*fig*) training ground, school

pa'letta *sf* spade; (*per il focolare*) shovel; (*del capostazione*) signalling disc

pa'letto *sm* stake, peg; (*spranga*) bolt

'palio *sm* (*gara*): il P~ horse race run at Siena; mettere qc in ~ to offer sth as a prize

'palla *sf* ball; (*pallottola*) bullet; ~ canestro *sm* basketball; ~ nuoto *sm* water polo; ~ ovale rugby ball; ~ volo *sm* volleyball

palleggi'are [palled'dʒare] *vi* (*CALCIO*) to practise with the ball; (*TENNIS*) to knock up

pallia'tivo *sm* palliative; (*fig*) stopgap measure

'pallido, a *ag* pale

pal'lina *sf* (*bilia*) marble

pallon'cino [pallon'tʃino] *sm* balloon; (*lampioncino*) Chinese lantern

pal'lone *sm* (*palla*) ball; (*CALCIO*) football; (*aerostato*) balloon; gioco del ~ football

pal'lore *sm* pallor, paleness

pal'lottola *sf* pellet; (*proiettile*) bullet

'**palma** sf (ANAT) = palmo; (BOT, simbolo) palm; ~ **da datteri** date palm

'**palmo** sm (ANAT) palm; **restare con un ~ di naso** to be badly disappointed

'**palo** sm (legno appuntito) stake; (sostegno) pole; **fare da o il ~ il** (fig) to act as look-out

palom'**baro** sm diver

pa'**lombo** sm (pesce) dogfish

pal'**pare** vt to feel, finger

'**palpebra** sf eyelid

palpi'**tare** vi (cuore, polso) to beat; (: più forte) to pound, throb; (fremere) to quiver; '**palpito** sm (del cuore) beat; (fig: d'amore etc) throb

pal**tò** sm inv overcoat

pa'**lude** sf marsh, swamp; palu'**doso, a** ag marshy, swampy

pa'**lustre** ag marsh cpd, swamp cpd

'**pampino** sm vine leaf

'**panca, che** sf bench

pancar**rè** sm sliced square bread

pan'**cetta** [pan'tʃetta] sf (CUC) bacon

pan'**chetto** [pan'ketto] sm stool; footstool

pan'**china** [pan'kina] sf garden seat; (di giardino pubblico) (park) bench

'**pancia, ce** ['pantʃa] sf belly, stomach; **mettere o fare ~** to be getting a paunch; **avere mal di ~** to have stomachache o a sore stomach

panci'**otto** [pan'tʃɔtto] sm waistcoat

'**pancreas** sm inv pancreas

'**panda** sm inv panda

pande'**monio** sm pandemonium

'**pane** sm bread; (pagnotta) loaf (of bread); (forma): **un ~ di burro** a pat of butter; **guadagnarsi il ~** to earn one's living; ~ **a cassetta** sliced bread; ~ **di Spagna** sponge cake; ~ **integrale** wholemeal bread; ~ **tostato** toast

panette'**ria** sf (forno) bakery; (negozio) baker's (shop), bakery

panetti'**ere, a** sm/f baker

panet'**tone** sm a kind of spiced brioche with sultanas, eaten at Christmas

'**panfilo** sm yacht

pangrat'**tato** sm breadcrumbs pl

'**panico, a, ci, che** ag, sm panic

pani'**ere** sm basket

pani'**ficio** [pani'fitʃo] sm (forno) bakery; (negozio) baker's (shop), bakery

pa'**nino** sm roll; ~ **caldo** toasted sandwich; ~ **imbottito** filled roll; sandwich; panino'**teca** sf sandwich bar

'**panna** sf (CUC) cream; (TECN) = **panne**; ~ **da cucina** cooking cream; ~ **montata** whipped cream

'**panne** sf inv: **essere in ~** (AUT) to have broken down

pan'**nello** sm panel; ~ **solare** solar panel

'**panno** sm cloth; ~**i** smpl (abiti) clothes; **mettiti nei miei ~i** (fig) put yourself in my shoes

pan'**nocchia** [pan'nɔkkja] sf (di mais etc) ear

panno'**lino** sm (per bambini) nappy (BRIT), diaper (US)

pano'**rama, i** sm panorama; pano'**ramico, a, ci, che** ag panoramic; **strada panoramica** scenic route

panta'**loni** smpl trousers (BRIT), pants (US), pair sg of trousers o pants

pan'**tano** sm bog

pan'**tera** sf panther

pan'**tofola** sf slipper

panto'**mima** sf pantomime

pan'**zana** [pan'tsana] sf fib, tall story

pao'**nazzo, a** [pao'nattso] ag purple

'**papa, i** sm pope

pa**pà** sm inv dad(dy)

pa'**pale** ag papal

pa'**pato** sm papacy

pa'**pavero** sm poppy

'**papera** sf (fig) slip of the tongue, blunder; vedi anche **papero**

'**papero, a** sm/f (ZOOL) gosling

pa'**piro** sm papyrus

'**pappa** sf baby cereal

pappa'**gallo** sm parrot; (fig: uomo) Romeo, wolf

pappa'**gorgia, ge** [pappa'gɔrdʒa] sf double chin

pap'**pare** vt (fam: anche: ~rsi) to gobble up

'**para** sf: **suole di ~** crepe soles

pa'**rabola** sf (MAT) parabola; (REL) parable

para'**brezza** [para'breddza] sm inv (AUT) windscreen (BRIT), windshield (US)

paraca'**dute** sm inv parachute

para'**carro** sm kerbstone (BRIT), curbstone (US)

para'**diso** sm paradise

parados'**sale** ag paradoxical

para'**dosso** sm paradox

para'**fango, ghi** sm mudguard

paraf'**fina** sf paraffin, paraffin wax

para'**fulmine** sm lightning conductor

pa'**raggi** [pa'raddʒi] smpl: **nei ~** in the vicinity, in the neighbourhood

parago'**nare** vt: ~ **con/a** to compare with/to

para'**gone** sm comparison; (esempio analogo) analogy, parallel; **reggere al ~** to stand comparison

pa'**ragrafo** sm paragraph

pa'**ralisi** sf paralysis; para'**litico, a, ci, che** ag, sm/f paralytic

paraliz'**zare** [paralid'dzare] vt to paralyse

paral'**lela** sf parallel (line); ~**e** sfpl (attrezzo ginnico) parallel bars

paral'**lelo, a** ag parallel ♦ sm (GEO) parallel; (comparazione): **fare un ~ tra** to draw a parallel between

para'lume sm lampshade

pa'rametro sm parameter

para'noia sf paranoia; **para'noico, a, ci, che** ag, sm/f paranoid

para'occhi [para'ɔkki] smpl blinkers

para'petto sm balustrade

para'piglia [para'piʎʎa] sm commotion, uproar

pa'rare vt (addobbare) to adorn, deck; (proteggere) to shield, protect; (scansare: colpo) to parry; (CALCIO) to save ♦ vi: **dove vuole andare a ~?** what are you driving at?; **~rsi** vr (presentarsi) to appear, present o.s.

para'sole sm inv parasol, sunshade

paras'sita, i sm parasite

pa'rata sf (SPORT) save; (MIL) review, parade

para'tia sf (di nave) bulkhead

para'urti sm inv (AUT) bumper

para'vento sm folding screen; **fare da ~ a qn** (fig) to shield sb

par'cella [par'tʃella] sf account, fee (of lawyer etc)

parcheggi'are [parked'dʒare] vt to park; **par'cheggio** sm parking no pl; (luogo) car park; (singolo posto) parking space

par'chimetro [par'kimetro] sm parking meter

'parco¹, chi sm park; (spazio per deposito) depot; (complesso di veicoli) fleet

'parco², a, chi, che ag: **~ (in)** (sobrio) moderate (in); (avaro) sparing (with)

pa'recchio, a [pa'rekkjo] det quite a lot of; (tempo) quite a lot of, a long; **~i, e** det pl quite a lot of, several ♦ pron quite a lot, quite a bit; (tempo) quite a while, a long time; **~i, e** pron pl quite a lot, several ♦ av (con ag) quite, rather; (con vb) quite a lot, quite a bit

pareggi'are [pared'dʒare] vt to make equal; (terreno) to level, make level; (bilancio, conti) to balance ♦ vi (SPORT) to draw; **pa'reggio** sm (ECON) balance; (SPORT) draw

pa'rente sm/f relative, relation

paren'tela sf (vincolo di sangue, fig) relationship

pa'rentesi sf (segno grafico) bracket, parenthesis; (frase incisa) parenthesis; (digressione) parenthesis, digression

pa'rere sm (opinione) opinion; (consiglio) advice, opinion; **a mio ~** in my opinion ♦ vi to seem, appear ♦ vb impers: **pare che** it seems o appears that, they say that; **mi pare che** it seems to me that; **mi pare di sì** I think so; **fai come ti pare** do as you like; **che ti pare del mio libro?** what do you think of my book?

pa'rete sf wall

'pari ag inv (uguale) equal, same; (in giochi) equal; drawn, tied; (MAT) even ♦ sm inv (POL: di Gran Bretagna) peer ♦ sm/f inv peer, equal;

copiato **~ ~** copied word for word; **alla ~** on the same level; **ragazza alla ~** au pair girl; **mettersi alla ~ con** to place o.s. on the same level as; **mettersi in ~ con** to catch up with; **andare di ~ passo con qn** to keep pace with sb

Pa'rigi [pa'ridʒi] sf Paris

pa'riglia [pa'riʎʎa] sf pair; **rendere la ~ to** give tit for tat

parità sf parity, equality; (SPORT) draw, tie

parlamen'tare ag parliamentary ♦ sm/f ≈ Member of Parliament (BRIT), ≈ Congressman/woman (US) ♦ vi to negotiate, parley

parla'mento sm parliament

parlan'tina (fam) sf talkativeness; **avere ~ to** have the gift of the gab

par'lare vi to speak, talk; (confidare cose segrete) to talk ♦ vt to speak; **~ (a qn) di** to speak o talk (to sb) about; **parla'torio** sm (di carcere etc) visiting room; (REL) parlour

parmigi'ano [parmi'dʒano] sm (grana) Parmesan (cheese)

paro'dia sf parody

pa'rola sf word; (facoltà) speech; **~e** sfpl (chiacchiere) talk sg; **chiedere la ~ to** ask permission to speak; **prendere la ~ to** take the floor; **~ d'onore** word of honour; **~ d'ordine** (MIL) password; **~e incrociate** crossword (puzzle) sg; **paro'laccia, ce** sf bad word, swearword

par'rocchia [par'rɔkkja] sf parish; parish church

'parroco, ci sm parish priest

par'rucca, che sf wig

parrucchi'ere, a [parruk'kjere] sm/f hairdresser ♦ sm barber

parsi'monia sf frugality, thrift

'parso, a pp di parere

'parte sf part; (lato) side; (quota spettante a ciascuno) share; (direzione) direction; (POL) party; faction; (DIR) party; **a ~** ag separate ♦ av separately; **scherzi a ~** joking aside; **a ~ ciò** apart from that; **da ~** (in disparte) to one side, aside; **d'altra ~** on the other hand; **da ~ di** (per conto di) on behalf of; **da ~ mia** as far as I'm concerned, as for me; **da ~ a ~** right through; **da ogni ~** on all sides, everywhere; (moto a luogo) from all sides; **da nessuna ~** nowhere; **da questa ~** (in questa direzione) this way; **prendere ~ a qc** to take part in sth; **mettere da ~** to put aside; **mettere qn a ~ di** to inform sb of

parteci'pare [partetʃi'pare] vi: **~ a** to take part in, participate in; (utili etc) to share in; (spese etc) to contribute to; (dolore, successo di qn) to share (in); **partecipazi'one** sf participation; sharing; (ECON) interest; **partecipazione agli utili** profit-sharing; **partecipazioni di nozze** wedding announcement *card*; **par'tecipe** *ag* participating; **essere partecipe di** to take part in, participate in; to share (in); (*consapevole*) to be aware of

parteggi'are [parted'dʒare] *vi*: ~ **per** to side with, be on the side of

par'tenza [par'tentsa] *sf* departure; (*SPORT*) start; **essere in ~** to be about to leave, be leaving

parti'cella [parti'tʃɛlla] *sf* particle

parti'cipio [parti'tʃipjo] *sm* participle

partico'lare *ag* (*specifico*) particular; (*proprio*) personal, private; (*speciale*) special, particular; (*caratteristico*) distinctive, characteristic; (*fuori dal comune*) peculiar ♦ *sm* detail, particular; **in ~** in particular, particularly; **particolarità** *sf inv* particularity; detail; characteristic, feature

partigi'ano, a [parti'dʒano] *ag* partisan ♦ *sm* (*MIL*) partisan

par'tire *vi* to go, leave; (*allontanarsi*) to go (*o* drive *etc*) away *o* off; (*petardo, colpo*) to go off; (*fig: avere inizio, SPORT*) to start; **sono partita da Roma alle 7** I left Rome at 7; **il volo parte da Ciampino** the flight leaves from Ciampino; **a ~ da** from

par'tita *sf* (*COMM*) lot, consignment; (*ECON: registrazione*) entry, item; (*CARTE, SPORT: gioco*) game; (*: competizione*) match, game; **~ di caccia** hunting party; **~ IVA** VAT registration number

par'tito *sm* (*POL*) party; (*decisione*) decision, resolution; (*persona da maritare*) match

parti'tura *sf* (*MUS*) score

'parto *sm* (*MED*) delivery, (child)birth; labour; **parto'rire** *vt* to give birth to; (*fig*) to produce

parzi'ale [par'tsjale] *ag* (*limitato*) partial; (*non obiettivo*) biased, partial

'pascere ['paʃʃere] *vt* (*brucare*) to graze on; (*far pascolare*) to graze, pasture; **pasci'uto, a** *pp di* **pascere**

pasco'lare *vt, vi* to graze

'pascolo *sm* pasture

'Pasqua *sf* Easter; **pas'quale** *ag* Easter *cpd*; **Pas'quetta** *sf* Easter Monday

pas'sabile *ag* fairly good, passable

pas'saggio [pas'saddʒo] *sm* passing *no pl*, passage; (*traversata*) crossing *no pl*, passage; (*luogo, prezzo della traversata, brano di libro etc*) passage; (*su veicolo altrui*) lift (*BRIT*), ride; (*SPORT*) pass; **di ~** (*persona*) passing through; **~ pedonale/a livello** pedestrian/level (*BRIT*) *o* grade (*US*) crossing

passamon'tagna [passamon'taɲɲa] *sm inv* balaclava

pas'sante *sm/f* passer-by ♦ *sm* loop

passa'porto *sm* passport

pas'sare *vi* (*andare*) to go; (*veicolo, pedone*) to pass (by), go by; (*fare una breve sosta*:

postino etc) to come, call; (*: amico: per fare una visita*) to call *o* drop in; (*sole, aria, luce*) to get through; (*trascorrere: giorni, tempo*) to pass, go by; (*fig: proposta di legge*) to be passed; (*: dolore*) to pass, go away; (*CARTE*) to pass ♦ *vt* (*attraversare*) to cross; (*trasmettere: messaggio*): **~ qc a qn** to pass sth on to sb; (*dare*): **~ qc a qn** to pass sth to sb, give sb sth; (*trascorrere: tempo*) to spend; (*superare: esame*) to pass; (*triturare: verdura*) to strain; (*approvare*) to pass, approve; (*oltrepassare, sorpassare: anche fig*) to go beyond, pass; (*fig: subire*) to go through; **~ da ... a** to pass from ... to; **~ di padre in figlio** to be handed down *o* to pass from father to son; **~ per** (*anche fig*) to go through; **~ per stupido/un genio** to be taken for a fool/a genius; **~ sopra** (*anche fig*) to pass over; **~ attraverso** (*anche fig*) to go through; **~ alla storia** to pass into history; **~ a un esame** to go up (to the next class) after an exam; **~ inosservato** to go unnoticed; **~ di moda** to go out of fashion; **le passo il Signor X** (*al telefono*) here is Mr X; **I'm putting you through to Mr X; lasciar ~ qn/qc** to let sb/sth through; **come te la passi?** how are you getting on *o* along?

pas'sata *sf*: **dare una ~ di vernice a qc** to give sth a coat of paint; **dare una ~ al giornale** to have a look at the paper, skim through the paper

passa'tempo *sm* pastime, hobby

pas'sato, a *ag* past; (*sfiorito*) faded ♦ *sm* past; (*LING*) past (tense); **~ prossimo** (*LING*) present perfect; **~ remoto** (*LING*) past historic; **~ di verdura** (*CUC*) vegetable purée

passa'verdura *sm inv* vegetable mill

passeg'gero, a [passed'dʒero] *ag* passing ♦ *sm/f* passenger

passeggi'are [passed'dʒare] *vi* to go for a walk; (*in veicolo*) to go for a drive; **passeggi'ata** *sf* walk; drive; (*luogo*) promenade; **fare una passeggiata** to go for a walk (*o* drive); **passeg'gino** *sm* pushchair (*BRIT*), stroller (*US*); **pas'seggio** *sm* walk, stroll; (*luogo*) promenade

passe'rella *sf* footbridge; (*di nave, aereo*) gangway; (*pedana*) catwalk

'passero *sm* sparrow

pas'sibile *ag*: **~ di** liable to

passi'one *sf* passion

pas'sivo, a *ag* passive ♦ *sm* (*LING*) passive; (*ECON*) debit; (*: complesso dei debiti*) liabilities *pl*

'passo *sm* step; (*andatura*) pace; (*rumore*) (foot)step; (*orma*) footprint; (*fig: brano*) passage; (*valico*) pass; **a ~ d'uomo** at walking pace; **~ (a)** ~ step by step; **fare due** *o* **quattro ~i** to go for a walk *o* a stroll; **di**

questo ~ at this rate; **"~ carraio"** "vehicle entrance — keep clear"

'pasta sf (CUC) dough; (: impasto per dolce) pastry; (: anche: ~ alimentare) pasta; (massa molle di materia) paste; (fig: indole) nature; **~e** sfpl (pasticcini) pastries; **~ in brodo** noodle soup

pastasci'utta [pastaʃʃutta] sf pasta

pas'tella sf batter

pas'tello sm pastel

pas'ticca, che sf = pastiglia

pasticce'ria [pastittʃe'ria] sf (pasticcini) pastries pl, cakes pl; (negozio) cake shop; (arte) confectionery

pasticci'are [pastit'tʃare] vt to mess up, make a mess of ♦ vi to make a mess

pasticci'ere, a [pastit'tʃere] sm/f pastrycook; confectioner

pas'ticcio [pas'tittʃo] sm (CUC) pie; (lavoro disordinato, imbroglio) mess; **trovarsi nei ~i** to get into trouble

pasti'ficio [pasti'fitʃo] sm pasta factory

pas'tiglia [pas'tiʎʎa] sf pastille, lozenge

pas'tina sf small pasta shapes used in soup

'pasto sm meal

pas'tore sm shepherd; (REL) pastor, minister; (anche: cane ~) sheepdog; **~ tedesco** (ZOOL) Alsatian, German shepherd

pastoriz'zare [pastorid'dzare] vt to pasteurize

pas'toso, a ag doughy; pasty; (fig: voce, colore) mellow, soft

pas'trano sm greatcoat

pa'tata sf potato; **~e fritte** chips (BRIT), French fries; **pata'tine** sfpl (potato) crisps; **~ fritte** chips

pata'trac sm (crollo: anche fig) crash

paté sm inv pâté

pa'tella sf (ZOOL) limpet

pa'tema, i sm anxiety, worry

pa'tente sf licence; (anche: ~ di guida) driving licence (BRIT), driver's license (US)

paternità sf paternity, fatherhood

pa'terno, a ag (affetto, consigli) fatherly; (casa, autorità) paternal

pa'tetico, a, ci, che ag pathetic; (commovente) moving, touching

pa'tibolo sm gallows sg, scaffold

pa'tina sf (su rame etc) patina; (sulla lingua) fur, coating

pa'tire vt, vi to suffer

pa'tito, a sm/f enthusiast, fan, lover

patolo'gia [patolo'dʒia] sf pathology; **pato'logico, a, ci, che** ag pathological

'patria sf homeland

patri'arca, chi sm patriarch

pa'trigno [pa'triɲɲo] sm stepfather

patri'monio sm estate, property; (fig) heritage

patri'ota, i, e sm/f patriot; **patri'ottico, a, ci, che** ag patriotic; **patriot'tismo** sm patriotism

patroci'nare [patrotʃi'nare] vt (DIR: difendere) to defend; (sostenere) to sponsor, support; **patro'cinio** sm defence; support, sponsorship

patro'nato sm patronage; (istituzione benefica) charitable institution o society

pa'trono sm (REL) patron saint; (socio di patronato) patron; (DIR) counsel

'patta sf flap; (dei pantaloni) fly

patteggia'mento [patteddʒa'mento] sm (DIR) plea bargaining

patteggi'are [patted'dʒare] vt, vi to negotiate; (DIR) to plea-bargain

patti'naggio [patti'naddʒo] sm skating

patti'nare vi to skate; **~ sul ghiaccio** to ice-skate; **pattina'tore, 'trice** sm/f skater; **'pattino¹** sm skate; (di slitta) runner; (AER) skid; (TECN) sliding block; **pattini** (da ghiaccio) (ice) skates; **pattini in linea** Rollerblades ®; **pattini a rotelle** roller skates; **pat'tino²** sm (barca) kind of pedalo with oars

'patto sm (accordo) pact, agreement; (condizione) term, condition; **a ~ che** on condition that

pat'tuglia [pat'tuʎʎa] sf (MIL) patrol

pattu'ire vt to reach an agreement on

pattumi'era [pattu'mjera] sf (dust)bin (BRIT), ashcan (US)

pa'ura sf fear; **aver ~ di/di fare/che** to be frightened o afraid of/of doing/that; **far ~ a** to frighten; **per ~ di/che** for fear of/that; **pau'roso, a** ag (che fa paura) frightening; (che ha paura) fearful, timorous

'pausa sf (sosta) break; (nel parlare, MUS) pause

pavi'mento sm floor

pa'vone sm peacock; **pavoneggi'arsi** vr to strut about, show off

pazien'tare [pattsjen'tare] vi to be patient

pazi'ente [pat'tsjɛnte] ag, sm/f patient; **pazi'enza** sf patience

paz'zesco, a, schi, sche [pat'tsesko] ag mad, crazy

paz'zia [pat'tsia] sf (MED) madness, insanity; (azione) folly; (di azione, decisione) madness, folly

'pazzo, a ['pattso] ag (MED) mad, insane; (strano) wild, mad ♦ sm/f madman/woman; **~ di** (gioia, amore etc) mad o crazy with; **~ per qc/qn** mad o crazy about sth/sb

PCI sigla m = **Partito Comunista Italiano**

'pecca, che sf defect, flaw, fault

peccami'noso, a ag sinful

pec'care vi to sin; (fig) to err

pec'cato sm sin; **è un ~ che** it's a pity that; **che ~!** what a shame o pity!

pecca'tore, 'trice sm/f sinner

'**pece** ['petʃe] sf pitch
Pe'chino [pe'kino] sf Beijing
'**pecora** sf sheep; **peco'raio** sm shepherd; **peco'rino** sm sheep's milk cheese
peculi'are ag: **~ di** peculiar to
pe'daggio [pe'daddʒo] sm toll
pedago'gia [pedago'dʒia] sf pedagogy, educational methods pl
peda'lare vi to pedal; (andare in bicicletta) to cycle
pe'dale sm pedal
pe'dana sf footboard; (SPORT: nel salto) springboard; (: nella scherma) piste
pe'dante ag pedantic ♦ sm/f pedant
pe'data sf (impronta) footprint; (colpo) kick; **prendere a ~e** qn/qc to kick sb/sth
pede'rasta, i sm pederast; homosexual
pedi'atra, i, e sm/f paediatrician; **pedia'tria** sf paediatrics sg
pedi'cure sm/f inv chiropodist
pe'dina sf (della dama) draughtsman (BRIT), draftsman (US); (fig) pawn
pedi'nare vt to shadow, tail
pedo'nale ag pedestrian
pe'done, a sm/f pedestrian ♦ sm (SCACCHI) pawn
'**peggio** ['peddʒo] av, ag inv worse ♦ sm o f: **il o la ~** the worst; **alla ~** at worst, if the worst comes to the worst; **peggio'rare** vt to make worse, worsen ♦ vi to grow worse, worsen; **peggiora'tivo, a** ag pejorative; **peggi'ore** ag (comparativo) worse; (superlativo) worst ♦ sm/f: **il(la) peggiore** the worst (person)
'**pegno** ['peɲɲo] sm (DIR) security, pledge; (nei giochi di società) forfeit; (fig) pledge, token; **dare in ~ qc** to pawn sth
pe'lare vt (spennare) to pluck; (spellare) to skin; (sbucciare) to peel; (fig) to make pay through the nose; **~rsi** vr to go bald
pe'lato, a ag: **pomodori ~i** tinned tomatoes
pel'lame sm skins pl, hides pl
'**pelle** sf skin; (di animale) skin, hide; (cuoio) leather; **avere la ~ d'oca** to have goose pimples o goose flesh
pellegri'naggio [pellegri'naddʒo] sm pilgrimage
pelle'grino, a sm/f pilgrim
pelle'rossa (pl **pelli'rosse**) sm/f Red Indian
pellette'ria sf leather goods pl; (negozio) leather goods shop
pelli'cano sm pelican
pellicce'ria [pellittʃe'ria] sf (negozio) furrier's (shop)
pel'liccia, ce [pel'littʃa] sf (mantello di animale) coat, fur; (indumento) fur coat
pel'licola sf (membrana sottile) film, layer; (FOT, CINEMA) film
'**pelo** sm hair; (pelame) coat, hair; (pelliccia) fur; (di tappeto) pile; (di liquido) surface; **per

un ~**: **per un ~ non ho perduto il treno** I very nearly missed the train; **c'è mancato un ~ che affogasse** he escaped drowning by the skin of his teeth; **pe'loso, a** ag hairy
'**peltro** sm pewter
pe'luria sf down
'**pena** sf (DIR) sentence; (punizione) punishment; (sofferenza) sadness no pl, sorrow; (fatica) trouble no pl, effort; (difficoltà) difficulty; **far ~** to be pitiful; **mi fai ~** I feel sorry for you; **prendersi o darsi la ~ di fare** to go to the trouble of doing; **~ di morte** death sentence; **~ pecuniaria** fine; **pe'nale** ag penal; **penalità** sf inv penalty; **penaliz'zare** vt (SPORT) to penalize
pe'nare vi (patire) to suffer; (faticare) to struggle
pen'dente ag hanging; leaning ♦ sm (ciondolo) pendant; (orecchino) drop earring; **pen'denza** sf slope, slant; (grado d'inclinazione) gradient; (ECON) outstanding account
'**pendere** vi (essere appeso): **~ da** to hang from; (essere inclinato) to lean; (fig: incombere): **~ su** to hang over
pen'dice [pen'ditʃe] sf: **alle ~i del monte** at the foot of the mountain
pen'dio, dii sm slope, slant; (luogo in pendenza) slope
'**pendola** sf pendulum clock
pendo'lare sm/f commuter
pendo'lino sm high-speed train
'**pendolo** sm (peso) pendulum; (anche: **orologio a ~**) pendulum clock
'**pene** sm penis
pene'trante ag piercing, penetrating
pene'trare vi to come o get in ♦ vt to penetrate; **~ in** to enter; (sog: proiettile) to penetrate; (: acqua, aria) to go o come into
penicil'lina [penitʃil'lina] sf penicillin
pe'nisola sf peninsula
peni'tenza [peni'tentsa] sf penitence; (punizione) penance
penitenzi'ario [peniten'tsjarjo] sm prison
'**penna** sf (di uccello) feather; (per scrivere) pen; **~e** sfpl (CUC) quills (type of pasta); **~ stilografica/a sfera** fountain/ballpoint pen
penna'rello sm felt(-tip) pen
pennel'lare vi to paint
pen'nello sm brush; (per dipingere) (paint)brush; **a ~** (perfettamente) to perfection, perfectly; **~ per la barba** shaving brush
pen'nino sm nib
pen'none sm (NAUT) yard; (stendardo) banner, standard
pe'nombra sf half-light, dim light
pe'noso, a ag painful, distressing; (faticoso) tiring, laborious

pen'sare vi to think ♦ vt to think; (inventare, escogitare) to think out; ~ a to think of; (amico, vacanze) to think of o about; (problema) to think about; ~ di fare qc to think of doing sth; **ci penso io** I'll see to o take care of it

pensi'ero sm thought; (modo di pensare, dottrina) thinking no pl; (preoccupazione) worry, care, trouble; **stare in ~ per qn** to be worried about sb; **pensie'roso, a** ag thoughtful

'pensile ag hanging

pensi'lina sf (per autobus) bus shelter

pensio'nante sm/f (presso una famiglia) lodger; (di albergo) guest

pensio'nato, a sm/f pensioner

pensi'one sf (al prestatore di lavoro) pension; (vitto e alloggio) board and lodging; (albergo) boarding house; **andare in ~** to retire; **mezza ~** half board; ~ **completa** full board

pen'soso, a ag thoughtful, pensive, lost in thought

pentapar'tito sm five-party government

Pente'coste sf Pentecost, Whit Sunday (BRIT)

penti'mento sm repentance, contrition

pen'tirsi vr: ~ **di** to repent of; (rammaricarsi) to regret, be sorry for

'pentola sf pot; ~ **a pressione** pressure cooker

pe'nultimo, a ag last but one (BRIT), next to last, penultimate

pe'nuria sf shortage

penzo'lare [pendzo'lare] vi to dangle, hang loosely; **penzo'loni** av dangling, hanging down; **stare penzoloni** to dangle, hang down

'pepe sm pepper; ~ **macinato/in grani** ground/whole pepper

pepero'nata sf (CUC) stewed peppers, tomatoes and onions

pepe'rone sm pepper, capsicum; (piccante) chili

pe'pita sf nugget

PAROLA CHIAVE

per prep 1 (moto attraverso luogo) through; **i ladri sono passati ~ la finestra** the thieves got in (o out) through the window; **l'ho cercato ~ tutta la casa** I've searched the whole house o all over the house for it

2 (moto a luogo) for, to; **partire ~ la Germania/il mare** to leave for Germany/the sea; **il treno ~ Roma** the Rome train, the train for o to Rome

3 (stato in luogo): **seduto/sdraiato ~ terra** sitting/lying on the ground

4 (tempo) for; ~ **anni/lungo tempo** for years/a long time; ~ **tutta l'estate** throughout the summer, all summer long; **lo rividi**

~ **Natale** I saw him again at Christmas; **lo faccio ~ lunedì** I'll do it for Monday

5 (mezzo, maniera) by; ~ **lettera/via aerea/ ferrovia** by letter/airmail/rail; **prendere qn ~ un braccio** to take sb by the arm

6 (causa, scopo) for; **assente ~ malattia** absent because of o through o owing to illness; **ottimo ~ il mal di gola** excellent for sore throats

7 (limitazione) for; **è troppo difficile ~ lui** it's too difficult for him; ~ **quel che mi riguarda** as far as I'm concerned; ~ **poco che sia** however little it may be; ~ **questa volta ti perdono** I'll forgive you this time

8 (prezzo, misura) for; (distributivo) a, per; **venduto ~ 3 milioni** sold for 3 million; **1000 lire ~ persona** 1000 lire a o per person; **uno ~ volta** one at a time; **uno ~ uno** one by one; **5 ~ cento** 5 per cent; **3 ~ 4 fa 12** 3 times 4 equals 12; **dividere/moltiplicare 12 ~ 4** to divide/multiply 12 by 4

9 (in qualità di) as; (al posto di) for; **avere qn ~ professore** to have sb as a teacher; **ti ho preso ~ Mario** I mistook you for Mario, I thought you were Mario; **dare ~ morto qn** to give sb up for dead

10 (seguito da vb: finale): ~ **fare qc** (so as) to do sth, in order to do sth; (: causale): ~ **aver fatto qc** for having done sthg; (: consecutivo): **è abbastanza grande ~ andarci da solo** he's big enough to go on his own

---

'pera sf pear

pe'raltro av moreover, what's more

per'bene ag inv respectable, decent ♦ av (con cura) properly, well

percentu'ale [pertʃentu'ale] sf percentage

perce'pire [pertʃe'pire] vt (sentire) to perceive; (ricevere) to receive; **percezi'one** sf perception

---

PAROLA CHIAVE

perché [per'ke] av why; ~ **no?** why not?; ~ **non vuoi andarci?** why don't you want to go?; **spiegami ~ l'hai fatto** tell me why you did it

♦ cong 1 (causale) because; **non posso uscire ~ ho da fare** I can't go out because o as I've a lot to do

2 (finale) in order that, so that; **te lo do ~ tu lo legga** I'm giving it to you so (that) you can read it

3 (consecutivo): **è troppo forte ~ si possa batterlo** he's too strong to be beaten

♦ sm inv reason; **il ~ di** the reason for

---

perciò [per'tʃɔ] cong so, for this (o that) reason

per'correre vt (luogo) to go all over;

(: *paese*) to travel up and down, go all over; (*distanza*) to cover

per'corso, a *pp di* **percorrere** ♦ *sm* (*tragitto*) journey; (*tratto*) route

per'cossa *sf* blow

per'cosso, a *pp di* **percuotere**

percu'otere *vt* to hit, strike

percussi'one *sf* percussion; **strumenti a ~** (MUS) percussion instruments

'perdere *vt* to lose; (*lasciarsi sfuggire*) to miss; (*sprecare: tempo, denaro*) to waste ♦ *vi* to lose; (*serbatoio etc*) to leak; **~rsi** *vr* (*smarrirsi*) to get lost; (*svanire*) to disappear, vanish; **saper ~** to be a good loser; **lascia ~!** forget it!, never mind!

perdigi'orno [perdi'dʒorno] *sm/f inv* idler, waster

'perdita *sf* loss; (*spreco*) waste; (*fuoriuscita*) leak; **siamo in ~** (COMM) we are running at a loss; **a ~ d'occhio** as far as the eye can see

perdo'nare *vt* to pardon, forgive; (*scusare*) to excuse, pardon

per'dono *sm* forgiveness; (DIR) pardon

perdu'rare *vi* to go on, last

perduta'mente *av* desperately, passionately

per'duto, a *pp di* **perdere**

peregri'nare *vi* to wander, roam

pe'renne *ag* eternal, perpetual, perennial; (BOT) perennial

peren'torio, a *ag* peremptory; (*definitivo*) final

per'fetto, a *ag* perfect ♦ *sm* (LING) perfect (tense)

perfezio'nare [perfettsjo'nare] *vt* to improve, perfect; **~rsi** *vr* to improve

perfezi'one [perfet'tsjone] *sf* perfection

'perfido, a *ag* perfidious, treacherous

per'fino *av* even

perfo'rare *vt* to perforate; to punch a hole (o holes) in; (*banda, schede*) to punch; (*trivellare*) to drill; **perfora'trice** *sf* (TECN) boring o drilling machine; (INFORM) card punch; **perforazi'one** *sf* perforation; punching; drilling; (INFORM) punch; (MED) perforation

perga'mena *sf* parchment

'pergola *sf* (*per rampicanti*) pergola

perico'lante *ag* precarious

pe'ricolo *sm* danger; **mettere in ~** to endanger, put in danger; **perico'loso, a** *ag* dangerous

perife'ria *sf* (*di città*) outskirts *pl*

pe'rifrasi *sf* circumlocution

pe'rimetro *sm* perimeter

peri'odico, a, ci, che *ag* periodic(al); (MAT) recurring ♦ *sm* periodical

pe'riodo *sm* period

peripe'zie [peripet'tsie] *sfpl* ups and downs, vicissitudes

pe'rire *vi* to perish, die

pe'rito, a *ag* expert, skilled ♦ *sm/f* expert; (*agronomo, navale*) surveyor; **un ~ chimico** a qualified chemist

pe'rizia [pe'rittsja] *sf* (*abilità*) ability; (*giudizio tecnico*) expert opinion; expert's report

'perla *sf* pearl; **per'lina** *sf* bead

perlus'trare *vt* to patrol

perma'loso, a *ag* touchy

perma'nente *ag* permanent ♦ *sf* permanent wave, perm; **perma'nenza** *sf* permanence; (*soggiorno*) stay

perma'nere *vi* to remain

perme'are *vt* to permeate

per'messo, a *pp di* **permettere** ♦ *sm* (*autorizzazione*) permission, leave; (*dato a militare, impiegato*) leave; (*licenza*) licence, permit; (MIL: *foglio*) pass; **~?, è ~?** (*posso entrare?*) may I come in?; (*posso passare?*) excuse me; **~ di lavoro/pesca** work/fishing permit; **~ di soggiorno** residence permit

per'mettere *vt* to allow, permit; **~ a qn qc/ di fare** to allow sb sth/to do; **~rsi qc/di fare** to allow o.s. sth/to do; (*avere la possibilità*) to afford sth/to do

per'nacchia [per'nakkja] (*fam*) *sf*: **fare una ~** to blow a raspberry

per'nice [per'nitʃe] *sf* partridge

'perno *sm* pivot

pernot'tare *vi* to spend the night, stay overnight

'pero *sm* pear tree

però *cong* (*ma*) but; (*tuttavia*) however, nevertheless

pero'rare *vt* (DIR, *fig*): **~ la causa di qn** to plead sb's case

perpendico'lare *ag, sf* perpendicular

perpe'trare *vt* to perpetrate

perpetu'are *vt* to perpetuate

per'petuo, a *ag* perpetual

per'plesso, a *ag* perplexed; uncertain, undecided

perqui'sire *vt* to search; **perquisizi'one** *sf* (police) search

persecu'tore *sm* persecutor

persecuzi'one [persekut'tsjone] *sf* persecution

persegu'ire *vt* to pursue

persegui'tare *vt* to persecute

perseve'rante *ag* persevering

perseve'rare *vi* to persevere

'Persia *sf*: **la ~** Persia

persi'ana *sf* shutter; **~ avvolgibile** roller shutter

persi'ano, a *ag, sm/f* Persian

'persico, a, ci, che *ag*: **il golfo P~** the Persian Gulf

per'sino *av* = **perfino**

persis'tente *ag* persistent

per'sistere vi to persist; **~ a fare** to persist in doing; **persis'tito, a** pp di persistere

'perso, a pp di perdere

per'sona sf person; (qualcuno): **una ~** someone, somebody, espressione interrogativa +anyone o anybody; **~e** sfpl people; **non c'è ~ che** ... there's nobody who ..., there isn't anybody who ...

perso'naggio [perso'naddʒo] sm (persona ragguardevole) personality, figure; (tipo) character, individual; (LETTERATURA) character

perso'nale ag personal ♦ sm staff; personnel; (figura fisica) build

personalità sf inv personality

personifi'care vt to personify; to embody

perspi'cace [perspi'katʃe] ag shrewd, discerning

persu'adere vt: **~ qn (di qc/a fare)** to persuade sb (of sth/to do); **persuasi'one** sf persuasion; **persua'sivo, a** ag persuasive; **persu'aso, a** pp di persuadere

per'tanto cong (quindi) so, therefore

'pertica, che sf pole

perti'nente ag: **~ (a)** relevant (to), pertinent (to)

per'tosse sf whooping cough

per'tugio [per'tudʒo] sm hole, opening

perturbazi'one [perturbat'tsjone] sf disruption; perturbation; **~ atmosferica** atmospheric disturbance

per'vadere vt to pervade; **per'vaso, a** pp di pervadere

perve'nire vi: **~ a** to reach, arrive at, come to; (venire in possesso): **gli pervenne una fortuna** he inherited a fortune; **far ~ qc a** to have sth sent to; **perve'nuto, a** pp di pervenire

per'verso, a ag depraved, perverse

p. es. abbr (= per esempio) e.g.

'pesa sf weighing no pl; weighbridge

pe'sante ag heavy

pe'sare vt to weigh ♦ vi (avere un peso) to weigh; (essere pesante) to be heavy; (fig) to carry weight; **~ su** (fig) to lie heavy on; to influence; to hang over

'pesca (pl pesche: frutto) sf peach; (il pescare) fishing; **andare a ~** to go fishing; **~ di beneficenza** (lotteria) lucky dip; **~ con la lenza** angling

pes'care vt (pesce) to fish for; to catch; (qc nell'acqua) to fish out; (fig: trovare) to get hold of, find; **andare a ~** to go fishing

pesca'tore sm fisherman; angler

'pesce ['peʃʃe] sm fish gen inv; **P~i** (dello zodiaco) Pisces; **~ d'aprile!** April Fool!; **~ spada** swordfish; **pesce'cane** sm shark

pesche'reccio [peske'rettʃo] sm fishing boat

pesche'ria [peske'ria] sf fishmonger's (shop) (BRIT), fish store (US)

pesci'vendolo, a [peʃʃi'vendolo] sm/f fishmonger (BRIT), fish merchant (US)

'pesco, schi sm peach tree

pes'coso, a ag abounding in fish

'peso sm weight; (SPORT) shot; **rubare sul ~** to give short weight; **essere di ~ a qn** (fig) to be a burden to sb; **~ lordo/netto** gross/net weight; **~ piuma/mosca/gallo/medio/ massimo** (PUGILATO) feather/fly/bantam/ middle/heavyweight

pessi'mismo sm pessimism; **pessi'mista, i, e** ag pessimistic ♦ sm/f pessimist

'pessimo, a ag very bad, awful

pes'tare vt to tread on, trample on; (sale, pepe) to grind; (uva, aglio) to crush; (fig: picchiare): **~ qn** to beat sb up

'peste sf plague; (persona) nuisance, pest

pes'tello sm pestle

pesti'lenza [pesti'lɛntsa] sf pestilence; (fetore) stench

'pesto, a ag: **c'è buio ~** it's pitch-dark; **occhio ~** black eye ♦ sm (CUC) sauce made with basil, garlic, cheese and oil

'petalo sm (BOT) petal

pe'tardo sm firecracker, banger (BRIT)

petizi'one [petit'tsjone] sf petition

'peto (fam!) sm fart (!)

petrol'chimica [petrol'kimika] sf petrochemical industry

petroli'era sf (nave) oil tanker

petro'lifero, a ag oil-bearing; oil cpd

pe'trolio sm oil, petroleum; (per lampada, fornello) paraffin

pettego'lare vi to gossip

pettego'lezzo [pettego'leddzo] sm gossip no pl; **fare ~i** to gossip

pet'tegolo, a ag gossipy ♦ sm/f gossip

petti'nare vt to comb (the hair of); **~rsi** vr to comb one's hair; **pettina'tura** sf (acconciatura) hairstyle

'pettine sm comb; (ZOOL) scallop

petti'rosso sm robin

'petto sm chest; (seno) breast, bust; (CUC: di carne bovina) brisket; (: di pollo etc) breast; **a doppio ~** (abito) double-breasted; **petto'ruto, a** ag broad-chested; full-breasted

petu'lante ag insolent

pe'tunia sf (BOT) petunia

'pezza ['pɛttsa] sf piece of cloth; (toppa) patch; (cencio) rag, cloth

pez'zato, a [pet'tsato] ag piebald

pez'zente [pet'tsɛnte] sm/f beggar

'pezzo ['pɛttso] sm (gen) piece; (brandello, frammento) piece, bit; (di macchina, arnese etc) part; (STAMPA) article; (di tempo): **aspettare un ~** to wait quite a while o some time; **in** o **a ~i** in pieces; **andare in ~i** to break into pieces; **un bel ~ d'uomo** a fine figure of a man; **abito a due ~i** two-piece suit; **~ di cronaca** (STAMPA) report; **~ grosso** (fig) bigwig; **~ di ricambio** spare part

pia'cente [pja'tʃɛnte] ag attractive

pia'cere [pja'tʃere] vi to please; **una ragazza che piace** a likeable girl; an attractive girl; **~ a: mi piace** I like it; **quei ragazzi non mi piacciono** I don't like those boys; **gli piacerebbe andare al cinema** he would like to go to the cinema ♦ sm pleasure; (favore) favour; **"~!"** (nelle presentazioni) "pleased to meet you!"; **con ~** certainly, with pleasure; **per ~!** please; **fare un ~ a qn** to do sb a favour; **piaci'uto, a** pp di **piacere**

pia'cevole ag pleasant, agreeable; **piaci'uto, a** pp di **piacere**

pi'aga, ghe sf (lesione) sore; (ferita: anche fig) wound; (fig: flagello) scourge, curse; (: persona) pest, nuisance

piagnis'teo [pjaɲɲis'teo] sm whining, whimpering

piagnuco'lare [pjaɲɲuko'lare] vi to whimper

pi'alla sf (arnese) plane; **pial'lare** vt to plane

pi'ana sf stretch of level ground; (più estesa) plain

pianeggi'ante [pjaned'dʒante] ag flat, level

piane'rottolo sm landing

pia'neta sm (ASTR) planet

pi'angere ['pjandʒere] vi to cry, weep; (occhi) to water ♦ vt to cry, weep; (lamentare) to bewail, lament; **~ la morte di qn** to mourn sb's death

pianifi'care vt to plan; **pianificazi'one** sf planning

pia'nista, i, e sm/f pianist

pi'ano, a ag (piatto) flat, level; (MAT) plane; (chiaro) clear, plain ♦ av (adagio) slowly; (a bassa voce) softly; (con cautela) slowly, carefully ♦ sm (MAT) plane; (GEO) plain; (livello) level, plane; (di edificio) floor; (programma) plan; (MUS) piano; **pian ~** slowly; (poco a poco) little by little; **in primo/secondo ~** in the foreground/background; **di primo ~** (fig) prominent, high-ranking

piano'forte sm piano, pianoforte

pi'anta sf (BOT) plant; (ANAT: anche: **~ del piede**) sole (of the foot); (grafico) plan; (topografica) map; **in ~ stabile** on the permanent staff; **piantagi'one** sf plantation; **pian'tare** vt to plant; (conficcare) to drive or hammer in; (tenda) to put up, pitch; (fig: lasciare) to leave, desert; **~rsi** vr: **~rsi davanti a qn** to plant o.s. in front of sb; **piantala!** (fam) cut it out!

pianter'reno sm ground floor

pian'tina sf (carta) map

pi'anto, a pp di **piangere** ♦ sm tears pl, crying

pian'tone sm (vigilante) sentry, guard;

(soldato) orderly; (AUT) steering column

pia'nura sf plain

pi'astra sf plate; (di pietra) slab; (di fornello) hotplate; **~ di registrazione** tape deck; **panino alla ~** ≈ toasted sandwich

pias'trella sf tile

pias'trina sf (MIL) identity disc

piatta'forma sf (anche fig) platform

piat'tino sm saucer

pi'atto, a ag flat; (fig: scialbo) dull ♦ sm (recipiente, vivanda) dish; (portata) course; (parte piana) flat (part); **~i** smpl (MUS) cymbals; **~ fondo** soup dish; **~ forte** main course; **~ del giorno** dish of the day, plat du jour; **~ del giradischi** turntable

pi'azza ['pjattsa] sf square; (COMM) market; **far ~ pulita** to make a clean sweep; **~ d'armi** (MIL) parade ground; **piaz'zale** sm (large) square

piaz'zare [pjat'tsare] vt to place; (COMM) to market, sell; **~rsi** vr (SPORT) to be placed

piaz'zista, i [pjat'tsista] sm (COMM) commercial traveller

piaz'zola [pjat'tsɔla] sf (AUT) lay-by

'picca, che sf pike; **~che** sfpl (CARTE) spades

pic'cante ag hot, pungent; (fig) racy; biting

pic'carsi vr: **~ di fare** to pride o.s. on one's ability to do; **~ per qc** to take offence at sth

pic'chetto [pik'ketto] sm (MIL, di scioperanti) picket; (di tenda) peg

picchi'are [pik'kjare] vt (persona: colpire) to hit, strike; (: prendere a botte) to beat (up); (battere) to beat; (sbattere) to bang ♦ vi (bussare) to knock; (: con forza) to bang; (colpire) to hit, strike; (sole) to beat down; **picchi'ata** sf (AER) dive

picchiet'tare [pikkjet'tare] vt (punteggiare) to spot, dot; (colpire) to tap

'picchio ['pikkjo] sm woodpecker

pic'cino, a [pit'tʃino] ag tiny, very small

piccio'naia [pittʃo'naja] sf pigeon-loft; (TEATRO): **la ~** the gods sg

picci'one [pit'tʃone] sm pigeon

'picco, chi sm peak; **a ~** vertically

'piccolo, a ag small; (oggetto, mano, di età: bambino) small, little (dav sostantivo); (di breve durata: viaggio) short; (fig) mean, petty ♦ sm/f child, little one; **~i** smpl (di animale) young pl; **in ~** in miniature

pic'cone sm pick(-axe)

pic'cozza [pik'kɔttsa] sf ice-axe

pic'nic sm inv picnic

pi'docchio [pi'dɔkkjo] sm louse

pi'ede sm foot; (di mobile) leg; **in ~i** standing; **a ~i** on foot; **a ~i nudi** barefoot; **su due ~i** (fig) at once; **prendere ~** (fig) to gain ground, catch on; **sul ~ di guerra** (MIL) ready for action; **~ di porco** crowbar

piedes'tallo sm pedestal

piedipi'atti *sm inv* (*peg*) cop

pi'ega, ghe *sf* (*piegatura, GEO*) fold; (*di gonna*) pleat; (*di pantaloni*) crease; (*grinza*) wrinkle, crease; **prendere una brutta ~** (*fig*) to take a turn for the worse

pie'gare *vt* to fold; (*braccia, gambe, testa*) to bend ♦ *vi* to bend; **~rsi** *vr* to bend; (*fig*): **~rsi (a)** to yield (to), submit (to); **pieghet'tare** *vt* to pleat; **pie'ghevole** *ag* pliable, flexible; (*porta*) folding

Pie'monte *sm*: **il ~** Piedmont

pi'ena *sf* (*di fiume*) flood, spate

pi'eno, a *ag* full; (*muro, mattone*) solid ♦ *sm* (*colmo*) height, peak; (*carico*) full load; **~ di** full of; **in ~ giorno** in broad daylight; **fare il ~ (di benzina)** to fill up (with petrol)

pietà *sf* pity; (*REL*) piety; **senza ~** pitiless, merciless; **avere ~ di** (*compassione*) to pity, feel sorry for; (*misericordia*) to have pity o mercy on

pie'tanza [pje'tantsa] *sf* dish, course

pie'toso, a *ag* (*compassionevole*) pitying, compassionate; (*che desta pietà*) pitiful

pi'etra *sf* stone; **~ preziosa** precious stone, gem; **pie'traia** *sf* (*terreno*) stony ground; **pietrifi'care** *vt* to petrify; (*fig*) to transfix, paralyse

'piffero *sm* (*MUS*) pipe

pigi'ama, i [pi'dʒama] *sm* pyjamas *pl*

'pigia 'pigia ['pidʒa'pidʒa] *sm* crowd, press

pigi'are [pi'dʒare] *vt* to press

pigi'one [pi'dʒone] *sf* rent

pigli'are [piʎ'ʎare] *vt* to take, grab; (*afferrare*) to catch

'piglio ['piʎʎo] *sm* look, expression

pig'meo, a *sm/f* pygmy

'pigna ['piɲɲa] *sf* pine cone

pi'gnolo, a [piɲ'ɲɔlo] *ag* pernickety

pigno'rare [piɲɲo'rare] *vt* to distrain

pigo'lare *vi* to cheep, chirp

pi'grizia [pi'grittsja] *sf* laziness

'pigro, a *ag* lazy

'pila *sf* (*catasta, di ponte*) pile; (*ELETTR*) battery; (*torcia*) torch (*BRIT*), flashlight

pi'lastro *sm* pillar

'pile ['pail] *sm inv* fleece

'pillola *sf* pill; **prendere la ~** to be on the pill

pi'lone *sm* (*di ponte*) pier; (*di linea elettrica*) pylon

pi'lota, i, e *sm/f* pilot; (*AUT*) driver ♦ *ag inv* pilot *cpd*; **~ automatico** automatic pilot; **pilo'tare** *vt* to pilot; to drive

pinaco'teca, che *sf* art gallery

pi'neta *sf* pinewood

ping-'pong [piŋ'pɔŋ] *sm* table tennis

'pingue *ag* fat, corpulent

pingu'ino *sm* (*ZOOL*) penguin

'pinna *sf* (*di pesce*) fin; (*di cetaceo, per nuotare*) flipper

'pino *sm* pine (tree); **pi'nolo** *sm* pine kernel

'pinza ['pintsa] *sf* pliers *pl*; (*MED*) forceps *pl*; (*ZOOL*) pincer

pinzette [pin'tsette] *sfpl* tweezers

'pio, a, 'pii, 'pie *ag* pious; (*opere, istituzione*) charitable, charity *cpd*

pi'oggia, ge ['pjɔddʒa] *sf* rain; **~ acida** acid rain

pi'olo *sm* peg; (*di scala*) rung

piom'bare *vi* to fall heavily; (*gettarsi con impeto*): **~ su** to fall upon, assail ♦ *vt* (*dente*) to fill; **piomba'tura** *sf* (*di dente*) filling

piom'bino *sm* (*sigillo*) (lead) seal; (*del filo a piombo*) plummet; (*PESCA*) sinker

pi'ombo *sm* (*CHIM*) lead; **a ~** (*cadere*) straight down; **senza ~** (*benzina*) unleaded

pioni'ere, a *sm/f* pioneer

pi'oppo *sm* poplar

pi'overe *vb impers* to rain ♦ *vi* (*fig: scendere dall'alto*) to rain down; (*lettere, regali*) to pour into; **piovig'ginare** *vb impers* to drizzle; **pio'voso, a** *ag* rainy

pi'ovra *sf* octopus

'pipa *sf* pipe

pipì (*fam*) *sf*: **fare ~** to have a wee (wee)

pipis'trello *sm* (*ZOOL*) bat

pi'ramide *sf* pyramid

pi'rata, i *sm* pirate; **~ della strada** hit-and-run driver

Pire'nei *smpl*: **i ~** the Pyrenees

'pirico, a, ci, che *ag*: **polvere ~a** gunpowder

pi'rofila, a *ag* heat-resistant; **pi'rofila** *sf* heat-resistant dish

pi'roga, ghe *sf* dug-out canoe

pi'romane *sm/f* pyromaniac; arsonist

pi'roscafo *sm* steamer, steamship

pisci'are [piʃ'ʃare] (*fam!*) *vi* to piss (!), pee (!)

pi'scina [piʃ'ʃina] *sf* (*swimming*) pool; (*stabilimento*) (swimming) baths *pl*

pi'sello *sm* pea

piso'lino *sm* nap

'pista *sf* (*traccia*) track, trail; (*di stadio*) track; (*di pattinaggio*) rink; (*da sci*) run; (*AER*) runway; (*di circo*) ring; **~ da ballo** dance floor

pis'tacchio [pis'takkjo] *sm* pistachio (tree); pistachio (nut)

pis'tola *sf* pistol, gun

pis'tone *sm* piston

pi'tone *sm* python

pit'tore, 'trice *sm/f* painter; **pitto'resco, a, schi, sche** *ag* picturesque

pit'tura *sf* painting; **pittu'rare** *vt* to paint

PAROLA CHIAVE

più *av* **1** (*in maggiore quantità*) more; **~ del solito** more than usual; **in ~, di ~** more; **ne voglio di ~** I want some more; **ci sono 3**

persone in o **di ~** there are 3 more o extra people; **~ o meno** more or less; **per di ~** (*inoltre*) what's more, moreover

2 (*comparativo*) more, *aggettivo corto* +...er; **~ ... di/che** more ... than; **lavoro ~ di te/Paola** I work harder than you/Paola; **è ~ intelligente che ricco** he's more intelligent than rich

3 (*superlativo*) most, *aggettivo corto* +...est; **il ~ grande/intelligente** the biggest/most intelligent; **è quello che compro ~ spesso** that's the one I buy most often; **al ~ presto** as soon as possible; **al ~ tardi** at the latest

4 (*negazione*): **non ... ~** no more, no longer; **non ho ~ soldi** I've got no more money, I don't have any more money; **non lavoro ~** I'm no longer working, I don't work any more; **a ~ non posso** (*gridare*) at the top of one's voice; (*correre*) as fast as one can

5 (MAT) plus; **4 ~ 5 fa 9** 4 plus 5 equals 9; **~ 5 gradi** 5 degrees above freezing, plus 5
♦ *prep* plus
♦ *ag inv* **1**: **~ ... (di)** more ... (than); **~ denaro/tempo** more money/time; **~ persone di quante ci aspettassimo** more people than we expected
2 (*numerosi, diversi*) several; **l'aspettai per ~ giorni** I waited for it for several days
♦ *sm* **1** (*la maggior parte*): **il ~ è fatto** most of it is done
2 (MAT) plus (sign)
3: **i ~** the majority

piuccchepper'fetto [pjukkepper'fetto] *sm* (LING) pluperfect, past perfect

pi'uma *sf* feather; **piu'maggio** *sm* plumage, feathers *pl*; **piu'mino** *sm* (*eider*)down; (*per letto*) eiderdown; (: *tipo danese*) duvet, continental quilt; (*giacca*) quilted jacket (*with goose-feather padding*); (*per cipria*) powder puff; (*per spolverare*) feather duster

piut'tosto *av* rather; **~ che** (*anziché*) rather than

pi'vello, a *sm/f* greenhorn

'pizza ['pittsa] *sf* pizza; **pizze'ria** *sf* place where pizzas are made, sold or eaten

pizzi'cagnolo, a [pittsi'kaɲɲolo] *sm/f* specialist grocer

pizzi'care [pittsi'kare] *vt* (*stringere*) to nip, pinch; (*pungere*) to sting; to bite; (MUS) to pluck ♦ *vi* (*prudere*) to itch, be itchy; (*cibo*) to be hot o spicy

pizziche'ria [pittsike'ria] *sf* delicatessen (shop)

'pizzico, chi ['pittsiko] *sm* (*pizzicotto*) pinch, nip; (*piccola quantità*) pinch, dash; (*d'insetto*) sting; bite

pizzi'cotto [pittsi'kɔtto] *sm* pinch, nip

'pizzo ['pittso] *sm* (*merletto*) lace; (*barbetta*) goatee beard

pla'care *vt* to placate, soothe; **~rsi** *vr* to calm down

'placca, che *sf* plate; (*con iscrizione*) plaque; (*anche: ~ dentaria*) (dental) plaque; **plac'care** *vt* to plate; **placcato in oro/argento** gold-/silver-plated

'placido, a ['platʃido] *ag* placid, calm

plagi'are [pla'dʒare] *vt* (*copiare*) to plagiarize; **'plagio** *sm* plagiarism

pla'nare *vi* (AER) to glide

'plancia, ce ['plantʃa] *sf* (NAUT) bridge

plane'tario, a *ag* planetary ♦ *sm* (*locale*) planetarium

'plasma *sm* plasma

plas'mare *vt* to mould, shape

'plastica, che *sf* (*arte*) plastic arts *pl*; (MED) plastic surgery; (*sostanza*) plastic

'plastico, a, ci, che *ag* plastic ♦ *sm* (*rappresentazione*) relief model; (*esplosivo*): **bomba al ~** plastic bomb

plasti'lina ® *sf* plasticine ®

'platano *sm* plane tree

pla'tea *sf* (TEATRO) stalls *pl*

'platino *sm* platinum

pla'tonico, a, ci, che *ag* platonic

plau'sibile *ag* plausible

'plauso *sm* (*fig*) approval

ple'baglia [ple'baʎʎa] (*peg*) *sf* rabble, mob

'plebe *sf* common people; **ple'beo, a** *ag* plebeian; (*volgare*) coarse, common

ple'nario, a *ag* plenary

pleni'lunio *sm* full moon

'plettro *sm* plectrum

pleu'rite *sf* pleurisy

'plico, chi *sm* (*pacco*) parcel; **in ~ a parte** (COMM) under separate cover

plo'tone *sm* (MIL) platoon; **~ d'esecuzione** firing squad

'plumbeo, a *ag* leaden

plu'rale *ag, sm* plural; **pluralità** *sf* plurality; (*maggioranza*) majority

plus'va'lore *sm* (ECON) surplus

pneu'matico, a, ci, che *ag* inflatable; pneumatic ♦ *sm* (AUT) tyre (BRIT), tire (US)

po' *av, sm vedi* **poco**

PAROLA CHIAVE

'poco, a, chi, che *ag* (*quantità*) little, not much; (*numero*) few, not many; **~ pane/ denaro/spazio** little o not much bread/ money/space; **~che persone/idee** few o not many people/ideas; **ci vediamo tra ~** (*sottinteso: tempo*) see you soon
♦ *av* **1** (*in piccola quantità*) little, not much; (*numero limitato*) few, not many; **guadagna ~** he doesn't earn much, he earns little
2 (*con ag, av*) (a) little, not very; **sta ~ bene** he isn't very well; **è ~ più vecchia di lui** she's a little o slightly older than him

3 (*tempo*): ~ **dopo/prima** shortly afterwards/before; **il film dura** ~ the film doesn't last very long; **ci vediamo molto** ~ we don't see each other very often, we hardly ever see each other

4: **un po'** a little, a bit; **è un po' corto** it's a little o a bit short; **arriverà fra un po'** he'll arrive shortly o in a little while

5: **a dir** ~ to say the least; **a ~ a ~** little by little; **per ~ non cadevo** I nearly fell; **è una cosa da ~** it's nothing, it's of no importance; **una persona da ~** a worthless person

♦ *pron* (a) little; **~chi, che** *pron pl* (*persone*) few (people); (*cose*) few

♦ *sm* **1** little; **vive del ~ che ha** he lives on the little he has

2: **un po'** a little; **un po' di zucchero** a little sugar; **un bel po' di denaro** quite a lot of money; **un po' per ciascuno** a bit each

---

po'dere *sm* (*AGR*) farm
pode'roso, a *ag* powerful
podestà *sm inv* (*nel fascismo*) podesta, mayor
'podio *sm* dais, platform; (*MUS*) podium
po'dismo *sm* (*SPORT*) track events *pl*
po'ema, i *sm* poem
poe'sia *sf* (*arte*) poetry; (*componimento*) poem
po'eta, 'essa *sm/f* poet/poetess; po'etico, a, ci, che *ag* poetic(al)
poggi'are [pod'dʒare] *vt* to lean, rest; (*posare*) to lay, place; poggia'testa *sm inv* (*AUT*) headrest
'poggio ['pɔddʒo] *sm* hillock, knoll
poggi'olo [pod'dʒɔlo] *sm* balcony
'poi *av* then; (*alla fine*) finally, at last; e ~ (*inoltre*) and besides; questa ~ (è bella)! (*ironico*) that's a good one!
poiché [poi'ke] *cong* since, as
'poker *sm* poker
po'lacco, a, chi, che *ag* Polish ♦ *sm/f* Pole
po'lare *ag* polar
po'lemica, che *sf* controversy
po'lemico, a, ci, che *ag* polemic(al), controversial
po'lenta *sf* (*CUC*) sort of thick porridge made with maize flour
poliambula'torio *sm* health centre
poli'clinico, ci *sm* general hospital, polyclinic
poli'estere *sm* polyester
'polio(mie'lite) *sf* polio(myelitis)
'polipo *sm* polyp
polisti'rolo *sm* polystyrene
poli'tecnico, ci *sm* postgraduate technical college
po'litica, che *sf* politics *sg*; (*linea di condotta*) policy; *vedi anche* politico
politiciz'zare [politit∫id'dzare] *vt*

to politicize
po'litico, a, ci, che *ag* political ♦ *sm/f* politician
poli'zia [polit'tsia] *sf* police; ~ giudiziaria ≈ Criminal Investigation Department (*BRIT*), ≈ Federal Bureau of Investigation (*US*); ~ stradale traffic police; polizi'esco, a, schi, sche *ag* police *cpd*; (*film, romanzo*) detective *cpd*; polizi'otto *sm* policeman; cane poliziotto police dog; donna poliziotto policewoman
'polizza ['pɔlittsa] *sf* (*COMM*) bill; ~ di assicurazione insurance policy; ~ di carico bill of lading
pol'laio *sm* henhouse
pol'lame *sm* poultry
pol'lastro *sm* (*ZOOL*) cockerel
'pollice ['pɔllit∫e] *sm* thumb
'polline *sm* pollen
'pollo *sm* chicken
pol'mone *sm* lung; ~ d'acciaio (*MED*) iron lung; polmo'nite *sf* pneumonia
'polo *sm* (*GEO, FISICA*) pole; (*gioco*) polo; il ~ sud/nord the South/North Pole
Po'lonia *sf*: la ~ Poland
'polpa *sf* flesh, pulp; (*carne*) lean meat
pol'paccio [pol'patt∫o] *sm* (*ANAT*) calf
polpas'trello *sm* fingertip
pol'petta *sf* (*CUC*) meatball; polpet'tone *sm* (*CUC*) meatloaf
'polpo *sm* octopus
pol'poso, a *ag* fleshy
pol'sino *sm* cuff
'polso *sm* (*ANAT*) wrist; (*pulsazione*) pulse; (*fig: forza*) drive, vigour
pol'tiglia [pol'ti∆∆a] *sf* (*composto*) mash, mush; (*di fango e neve*) slush
pol'trire *vi* to laze about
pol'trona *sf* armchair; (*TEATRO: posto*) seat in the front stalls (*BRIT*) o orchestra (*US*)
pol'trone *ag* lazy, slothful
'polvere *sf* dust; (*anche: ~ da sparo*) (gun)powder; (*sostanza ridotta minutissima*) powder, dust; latte in ~ dried o powdered milk; caffè in ~ instant coffee; sapone in ~ soap powder; polveri'era *sf* (*MIL*) (gun)powder magazine; polveriz'zare *vt* to pulverize; (*nebulizzare*) to atomize; (*fig*) to crush, pulverize; to smash; polve'rone *sm* thick cloud of dust; polve'roso, a *ag* dusty
po'mata *sf* ointment, cream
po'mello *sm* knob
pomeridi'ano, a *ag* afternoon *cpd*; nelle ore ~e in the afternoon
pome'riggio [pome'riddʒo] *sm* afternoon
'pomice ['pɔmit∫e] *sf* pumice
'pomo *sm* (*mela*) apple; (*ornamentale*) knob; (*di sella*) pommel; ~ d'Adamo (*ANAT*) Adam's apple

pomo'doro sm tomato

'pompa sf pump; (sfarzo) pomp (and ceremony); **~e funebri** funeral parlour sg (BRIT), undertaker's sg; **pom'pare** vt to pump; (trarre) to pump out; (gonfiare d'aria) to pump up

pom'pelmo sm grapefruit

pompi'ere sm fireman

pom'poso, a ag pompous

ponde'rare vt to ponder over, consider carefully

ponde'roso, a ag (anche fig) weighty

po'nente sm west

'ponte sm bridge; (di nave) deck; (: anche: ~ di comando) bridge; (impalcatura) scaffold; **fare il ~** (fig) to take the extra day off (between 2 public holidays); **governo ~** interim government; **~ aereo** airlift; **~ sospeso** suspension bridge

pon'tefice [pon'tefitʃe] sm (REL) pontiff

pontifi'care vi (anche fig) to pontificate

ponti'ficio, a, ci, cie [ponti'fitʃo] ag papal

popo'lano, a ag popular, of the people

popo'lare ag popular; (quartiere, clientela) working-class ♦ vt (rendere abitato) to populate; **~rsi** vr to fill with people, get crowded; **popolarità** sf popularity; **popolazi'one** sf population

'popolo sm people; **popo'loso, a** ag densely populated

'poppa sf (di nave) stern; (seno) breast

pop'pare vt to suck

poppa'toio sm (feeding) bottle

porcel'lana [portʃel'lana] sf porcelain, china; piece of china

porcel'lino, a [portʃel'lino] sm/f piglet

porche'ria [porke'ria] sf filth, muck; (fig: oscenità) obscenity; (: azione disonesta) dirty trick; (: cosa mal fatta) rubbish

por'cile [por'tʃile] sm pigsty

por'cino, a [por'tʃino] ag of pigs, pork cpd ♦ sm (fungo) type of edible mushroom

'porco, ci sm pig; (carne) pork

porcos'pino sm porcupine

'porgere ['pɔrdʒere] vt to hand, give; (tendere) to hold out

pornogra'fia sf pornography; **porno'grafico, a, ci, che** ag pornographic

'poro sm pore; **po'roso, a** ag porous

'porpora sf purple

'porre vt (mettere) to put; (collocare) to place; (posare) to lay (down), put (down); (fig: supporre): **poniamo (il caso) che ...** let's suppose that ...; **porsi** vr (mettersi): **porsi a sedere/in cammino** to sit down/set off; **~ una domanda a qn** to ask sb a question, put a question to sb

'porro sm (BOT) leek; (MED) wart

'porta sf door; (SPORT) goal; **~e** sfpl (di città)

gates; **a ~e chiuse** (DIR) in camera

'porta... prefisso: **portaba'gagli** sm inv (facchino) porter; (AUT, FERR) luggage rack; **porta'cenere** sm inv ashtray; **portachi'avi** sm inv keyring; **porta'cipria** sm inv powder compact; **porta'erei** sf inv (nave) aircraft carrier; **portafi'nestra** (pl portefi'nestre) sf French window; **porta'foglio** sm wallet; (POL, BORSA) portfolio; **portafor'tuna** sm inv lucky charm; mascot; **portagi'oie** sm inv jewellery box

porta'lettere sm/f inv postman/woman (BRIT), mailman/woman (US)

porta'mento sm carriage, bearing

portamo'nete sm inv purse

por'tante ag (muro etc) supporting, load-bearing

portan'tina sf sedan chair; (per ammalati) stretcher

por'tare vt (sostenere, sorreggere: peso, bambino, pacco) to carry; (indossare: abito, occhiali) to wear; (: capelli lunghi) to have; (avere: nome, titolo) to have, bear; (recare): **~ qc a qn** to take (o bring) sth to sb; (fig: sentimenti) to bear; **~rsi** vr (recarsi) to go; **~ avanti** (discorso, idea) to pursue; **~ via** to take away; (rubare) to take; **~ i bambini a spasso** to take the children for a walk; **~ fortuna** to bring good luck

portasiga'rette sm inv cigarette case

por'tata sf (vivanda) course; (AUT) carrying (o loading) capacity; (di arma) range; (volume d'acqua) (rate of) flow; (fig: limite) scope, capability; (: importanza) impact, import; **alla ~ di tutti** (conoscenza) within everybody's capabilities; (prezzo) within everybody's means; **a/fuori ~ (di)** within/out of reach (of); **a ~ di mano** within (arm's) reach

por'tatile ag portable

por'tato, a ag (incline): **~ a** inclined o apt to

porta'tore, 'trice sm/f (anche COMM) bearer; (MED) carrier

portau'ovo sm inv eggcup

porta'voce [porta'votʃe] sm/f inv spokesman/woman

por'tento sm wonder, marvel

porticci'olo [portit'tʃolo] sm marina

'portico, ci sm portico

porti'era sf (AUT) door

porti'ere sm (portinaio) concierge, caretaker; (di hotel) porter; (nel calcio) goalkeeper

porti'naio, a sm/f concierge, caretaker

portine'ria sf caretaker's lodge

'porto pp di **porgere** ♦ sm (NAUT) harbour, port ♦ sm inv port (wine); **~ d'armi** (documento) gun licence

Porto'gallo sm: **il ~** Portugal; **porto'ghese** ag, sm/f, sm Portuguese inv

por'tone sm main entrance, main door
portu'ale ag harbour cpd, port cpd ♦ sm dock worker
porzi'one [por'tsjone] sf portion, share; (di cibo) portion, helping
'**posa** sf (~ FOT) exposure; (atteggiamento, di modello) pose
posa'cenere [posa'tʃenere] sm inv ashtray
po'sare vt to put (down), lay (down) ♦ vi (ponte, edificio, teoria): ~ **su** to rest on; (FOT, atteggiarsi) to pose; ~**rsi** vr (aereo) to land; (uccello) to alight; (sguardo) to settle
po'sata sf piece of cutlery; ~**e** sfpl (servizio) cutlery sg
po'sato, a ag serious
pos'critto sm postscript
posi'tivo, a ag positive
posizi'one [pozit'tsjone] sf position; **prendere** ~ (fig) to take a stand; **luci di** ~ (AUT) sidelights
posolo'gia, 'gie [pozolo'dʒia] sf dosage, directions pl for use
pos'porre vt to place after; (differire) to postpone, defer; **pos'posto, a** pp di **posporre**
posse'dere vt to own, possess; (qualità, virtù) to have, possess; **possedi'mento** sm possession
posses'sivo, a ag possessive
pos'sesso sm ownership no pl; possession
posses'sore sm owner
pos'sibile ag possible ♦ sm: **fare tutto il** ~ to do everything possible; **nei limiti del** ~ as far as possible; **al più tardi** ~ as late as possible; **possibilità** sf inv possibility ♦ sfpl (mezzi) means; **aver la possibilità di fare** to be in a position to do; to have the opportunity to do
possi'dente sm/f landowner
'**posta** sf (servizio) post, postal service; (corrispondenza) post, mail; (ufficio postale) post office; (nei giochi d'azzardo) stake; ~**e** sfpl (amministrazione) post office; ~ **aerea** airmail; ~ **elettronica** E-mail, e-mail, electronic mail; **ministro delle P~e e Telecomunicazioni** Postmaster General; **posta'giro** sm post office cheque, postal giro (BRIT); **pos'tale** ag postal, post office cpd
post'bellico, a, ci, che ag postwar
posteggi'are [posted'dʒare] vt, vi to park; **posteggia'tore, trice** sm/f car park attendant; **pos'teggio** sm car park (BRIT), parking lot (US); (di taxi) rank (BRIT), stand (US)
postelegra'fonico, a, ci, che ag postal and telecommunications cpd
'**poster** sm inv poster
posteri'ore ag (dietro) back; (dopo) later ♦ sm (fam: sedere) behind
pos'ticcio, a, ci, ce [pos'tittʃo] ag false

♦ sm hairpiece
postici'pare [postitʃi'pare] vt to defer, postpone
pos'tilla sf marginal note
pos'tino sm postman (BRIT), mailman (US)
'**posto, a** pp di **porre** ♦ sm (sito, posizione) place; (impiego) job; (spazio libero) room, space; (di parcheggio) space; (sedile: al teatro, in treno etc) seat; (MIL) post; **a** ~ (in ordine) in place, tidy; (fig) settled; (: persona) reliable; **al** ~ **di** in place of; **sul** ~ on the spot; **mettere a** ~ to tidy (up), put in order; (faccende) to straighten out; ~ **di blocco** roadblock; ~ **di polizia** police station
pos'tribolo sm brothel
'**postumo, a** ag posthumous; (tardivo) belated; ~**i** smpl (conseguenze) after-effects, consequences
po'tabile ag drinkable; **acqua** ~ drinking water
po'tare vt to prune
po'tassio sm potassium
po'tente ag (nazione) strong, powerful; (veleno, farmaco) potent, strong; **po'tenza** sf power; (forza) strength
potenzi'ale [poten'tsjale] ag, sm potential

PAROLA CHIAVE

---

po'tere sm power; **al** ~ (partito etc) in power; ~ **d'acquisto** purchasing power
♦ vb aus **1** (essere in grado di) can, be able to; **non ha potuto ripararlo** he couldn't o he wasn't able to repair it; **non è potuto venire** he couldn't o he wasn't able to come; **spiacente di non poter aiutare** sorry not to be able to help
2 (avere il permesso) can, may, be allowed to; **posso entrare?** can o may I come in?; **si può sapere dove sei stato?** where on earth have you been?
3 (eventualità) may, might, could; **potrebbe essere vero** it might o could be true; **può aver avuto un incidente** he may o might o could have had an accident; **può darsi** perhaps; **può darsi** o **essere che non venga** he may o might not come
4 (augurio): **potessi almeno parlargli!** if only I could speak to him!
5 (suggerimento): **potresti almeno scusarti!** you could at least apologise!
♦ vt can, be able to; **può molto per noi** he can do a lot for us; **non ne posso più** (per stanchezza) I'm exhausted; (per rabbia) I can't take any more

---

potestà sf (potere) power; (DIR) authority
'**povero, a** ag poor; (disadorno) plain, bare ♦ sm/f poor man/woman; **i** ~**i** the poor; ~ **di** lacking in, having little; **povertà** sf poverty

'**pozza** ['pottsa] *sf* pool

poz'zanghera [pot'tsangera] *sf* puddle

'**pozzo** ['pottso] *sm* well; (*cava: di carbone*) pit; (*di miniera*) shaft; ~ **petrolifero** oil well

pran'zare [pran'dzare] *vi* to dine, have dinner; to lunch, have lunch

'**pranzo** ['prandzo] *sm* dinner; (*a mezzo-giorno*) lunch

'**prassi** *sf* usual procedure

'pratica, che *sf* practice; (*esperienza*) experience; (*conoscenza*) knowledge, familiarity; (*tirocinio*) training, practice; (AMM: *affare*) matter, case; (: *incartamento*) file, dossier; **in ~** (*praticamente*) in practice; **mettere in ~** to put into practice

prati'cabile *ag* (*progetto*) practicable, feasible; (*luogo*) passable, practicable

prati'cante *sm/f* apprentice, trainee; (REL) (*regular*) churchgoer

prati'care *vt* to practise; (SPORT: *tennis etc*) to play; (: *nuoto, scherma etc*) to go in for; (*eseguire: apertura, buco*) to make; ~ **uno sconto** to give a discount

'pratico, a, ci, che *ag* practical; ~ **di** (*esperto*) experienced *o* skilled in; (*familiare*) familiar with

'**prato** *sm* meadow; (*di giardino*) lawn

preav'viso *sm* notice; **telefonata con ~** personal *o* person to person call

pre'cario, a *ag* precarious; (INS) temporary

precauzi'one [prekaut'tsjone] *sf* caution, care; (*misura*) precaution

prece'dente [pretʃe'dɛnte] *ag* previous ♦ *sm* precedent; **il discorso/film ~** the previous *o* preceding speech/film; **senza ~i** unprecedented; **~i penali** criminal record *sg*; **prece-'denza** *sf* priority, precedence; (AUT) right of way

pre'cedere [pre'tʃedere] *vt* to precede, go (*o* come) before

pre'cetto [pre'tʃetto] *sm* precept; (MIL) call-up notice

precet'tore [pretʃet'tore] *sm* (*private*) tutor

precipi'tare [pretʃipi'tare] *vi* (*cadere*) to fall headlong; (*fig: situazione*) to get out of control ♦ *vt* (*gettare dall'alto in basso*) to hurl, fling; (*fig: affrettare*) to rush; **~rsi** *vr* (*gettarsi*) to hurl *o* fling o.s.; (*affrettarsi*) to rush; **precipitazi'one** *sf* (METEOR) precipitation; (*fig*) haste; **precipi'toso, a** *ag* (*caduta, fuga*) headlong; (*fig: avventato*) rash, reckless; (: *affrettato*) hasty, rushed

preci'pizio [pretʃi'pittsjo] *sm* precipice; **a ~** (*fig: correre*) headlong

preci'sare [pretʃi'zare] *vt* to state, specify; (*spiegare*) to explain (in detail)

precisi'one [pretʃi'zjone] *sf* precision; accuracy

pre'ciso, a [pre'tʃizo] *ag* (*esatto*) precise;

(*accurato*) accurate, precise; (*deciso: idee*) precise, definite; (*uguale*): **2 vestiti ~i** 2 dresses exactly the same; **sono le 9 ~e** it's exactly 9 o'clock

pre'cludere *vt* to block, obstruct; **pre'cluso, a** *pp di* **precludere**

pre'coce [pre'kɔtʃe] *ag* early; (*bambino*) precocious; (*vecchiaia*) premature

precon'cetto [prekon'tʃetto] *sm* preconceived idea, prejudice

precur'sore *sm* forerunner, precursor

'**preda** *sf* (*bottino*) booty; (*animale, fig*) prey; **essere ~ di** to fall prey to; **essere in ~ a** to be prey to; **preda'tore** *sm* predator

predeces'sore, a [predetʃes'sore] *sm/f* predecessor

predesti'nare *vt* to predestine

pre'detto, a *pp di* **predire**

'**predica, che** *sf* sermon; (*fig*) lecture, talking-to

predi'care *vt, vi* to preach

predi'cato *sm* (LING) predicate

predi'letto, a *pp di* **prediligere** ♦ *ag, sm/f* favourite

predilezi'one [predilet'tsjone] *sf* fondness, partiality; **avere una ~ per qc/qn** to be partial to sth/fond of sb

predi'ligere [predi'lidʒere] *vt* to prefer, have a preference for

pre'dire *vt* to foretell, predict

predis'porre *vt* to get ready, prepare; ~ **qn a qc** to predispose sb to sth; **predis'posto, a** *pp di* **predisporre**

predizi'one [predit'tsjone] *sf* prediction

predomi'nare *vi* to predominate; **predo'minio** *sm* predominance; supremacy

prefabbri'cato, a *ag* (EDIL) prefabricated

prefazi'one [prefat'tsjone] *sf* preface, foreword

prefe'renza [prefe'rɛntsa] *sf* preference; **preferenzi'ale** *ag* preferential; **corsia ~** bus and taxi lane

prefe'rire *vt* to prefer, like better; ~ **il caffè al tè** to prefer coffee to tea, like coffee better than tea; **prefe'rito, a** *ag* favourite

pre'fetto *sm* prefect; **prefet'tura** *sf* prefecture

pre'figgersi [pre'fiddʒersi] *vr*: ~ **uno scopo** to set o.s. a goal

pre'fisso, a *pp di* **prefiggere** ♦ *sm* (LING) prefix; (TEL) dialling (BRIT) *o* dial (US) code

pre'gare *vi* to pray ♦ *vt* (REL) to pray to; (*implorare*) to beg; (*chiedere*): ~ **qn di fare** to ask sb to do; **farsi ~** to need coaxing *o* persuading

pre'gevole [pre'dʒevole] *ag* valuable

preghi'era [pre'gjɛra] *sf* (REL) prayer; (*domanda*) request

pregi'ato, a [pre'dʒato] *ag* (*di valore*)

valuable; **vino ~** vintage wine

'**pregio** ['prɛdʒo] *sm* (*stima*) esteem, regard; (*qualità*) (good) quality, merit; (*valore*) value, worth

pregiudi'care [predʒudi'kare] *vt* to prejudice, harm, be detrimental to; **pregiudi'cato, a** *sm/f* (*DIR*) previous offender

pregiu'dizio [predʒu'dittsjo] *sm* (*idea errata*) prejudice; (*danno*) harm *no pl*

'**pregno, a** ['preɲɲo] *ag* (*saturo*): **~ di** full of, saturated with

'**prego** *escl* (*a chi ringrazia*) don't mention it!; (*invitando qn ad accomodarsi*) please sit down!; (*invitando qn ad andare prima*) after you!

pregus'tare *vt* to look forward to

preis'torico, a, ci, che *ag* prehistoric

pre'lato *sm* prelate

prele'vare *vt* (*denaro*) to withdraw; (*campione*) to take; (*sog: polizia*) to take, capture

preli'evo *sm* (*di denaro*) withdrawal; (*MED*): **fare un ~ (di)** to take a sample (of)

prelimi'nare *ag* preliminary; **~i** *smpl* preliminary talks; preliminaries

pre'ludio *sm* prelude

pré-ma'man [prema'mɑ̃] *sm inv* maternity dress

prema'turo, a *ag* premature.

premeditazi'one [premeditat'tsjone] *sf* (*DIR*) premeditation; **con ~** *ag* premeditated ♦ *av* with intent

'**premere** *vt* to press ♦ *vi*: **~ su** to press down on; (*fig*) to put pressure on; **~ a** (*fig: importare*) to matter to

pre'messa *sf* introductory statement, introduction

pre'messo, a *pp di* **premettere**

pre'mettere *vt* to put before; (*dire prima*) to start by saying, state first

premi'are *vt* to give a prize to; (*fig: merito, onestà*) to reward

'**premio** *sm* prize; (*ricompensa*) reward; (*COMM*) premium; (*AMM: indennità*) bonus

premu'nirsi *vr*: **~ di** to provide o.s. with; **~ contro** to protect o.s. from, guard o.s. against

pre'mura *sf* (*fretta*) haste, hurry; (*riguardo*) attention, care; **premu'roso, a** *ag* thoughtful, considerate

prena'tale *ag* antenatal

'**prendere** *vt* to take; (*andare a prendere*) to get, fetch; (*ottenere*) to get; (*guadagnare*) to get, earn; (*catturare: ladro, pesce*) to catch; (*collaboratore, dipendente*) to take on; (*passeggero*) to pick up; (*chiedere: somma, prezzo*) to charge, ask; (*trattare: persona*) to handle ♦ *vi* (*colla, cemento*) to set; (*pianta*)

to take; (*fuoco: nel camino*) to catch; (*voltare*): **~ a destra** to turn (to the) right; **~rsi** *vr* (*azzuffarsi*): **~rsi a pugni** to come to blows; **prendi qualcosa?** (*da bere, da mangiare*) would you like something to eat (*o* drink)?; **prendo un caffè** I'll have a coffee; **~ qn/qc per** (*scambiare*) to take sb/sth for; **~ fuoco** to catch fire; **~ parte a** to take part in; **~rsi cura di qn/qc** to look after sb/sth; **prendersela** (*adirarsi*) to get annoyed; (*preoccuparsi*) to get upset, worry

prendi'sole *sm inv* sundress

preno'tare *vt* to book, reserve; **prenotazi'one** *sf* booking, reservation

preoccu'pare *vt* to worry; to preoccupy; **~rsi** *vr*: **~rsi di qn/qc** to worry about sb/sth; **~rsi per qn** to be anxious for sb; **preoccupazi'one** *sf* worry, anxiety

prepa'rare *vt* to prepare; (*esame, concorso*) to prepare for; **~rsi** *vr* (*vestirsi*) to get ready; **~rsi a qc/a fare** to get ready *o* prepare (o.s.) for sth/to do; **~ da mangiare** to prepare a meal; **prepa'rativi** *smpl* preparations; **prepa'rato** *sm* (*prodotto*) preparation; **preparazi'one** *sf* preparation

preposizi'one [prepozit'tsjone] *sf* (*LING*) preposition

prepo'tente *ag* (*persona*) domineering, arrogant; (*bisogno, desiderio*) overwhelming, pressing ♦ *sm/f* bully; **prepo'tenza** *sf* arrogance; arrogant behaviour

'**presa** *sf* taking *no pl*; catching *no pl*; (*di città*) capture; (*indurimento: di cemento*) setting; (*appiglio, SPORT*) hold; (*di acqua, gas*) (supply) point; (*ELETTR*): **~ (di corrente)** socket; (: *al muro*) point; (*piccola quantità: di sale etc*) pinch; (*CARTE*) trick; **far ~ (colla)** to set; **far ~ sul pubblico** to catch the public's imagination; **~ d'aria** air inlet; **essere alle ~e con** (*fig*) to be struggling with

pre'sagio [pre'zadʒo] *sm* omen

presa'gire [preza'dʒire] *vt* to foresee

'**presbite** *ag* long-sighted

presbi'terio *sm* presbytery

pre'scindere [preʃ'ʃindere] *vi*: **~ da** to leave out of consideration; **a ~ da** apart from

pres'critto, a *pp di* **prescrivere**

pres'crivere *vt* to prescribe; **prescrizi'one** *sf* (*MED, DIR*) prescription; (*norma*) rule, regulation

presen'tare *vt* to present; (*far conoscere*): **~ qn (a)** to introduce sb (to); (*AMM: inoltrare*) to submit; **~rsi** *vr* (*recarsi, farsi vedere*) to present o.s., appear; (*farsi conoscere*) to introduce o.s.; (*occasione*) to arise; **~rsi come candidato** (*POL*) to stand as a candidate; **~rsi bene/male** to have a good/poor appearance; **presentazi'one** *sf* presentation; introduction

pre'sente *ag* present; (*questo*) this ♦ *sm*

present; **i ~i** those present; **aver ~ qc/qn** to remember sth/sb

presenti'mento *sm* premonition

pre'senza [pre'zentsa] *sf* presence; (*aspetto esteriore*) appearance; **~ di spirito** presence of mind

pre'sepe, pre'sepio *sm* crib

preser'vare *vt* to protect; to save; **preserva'tivo** *sm* sheath, condom

'preside *sm/f* (*INS*) head (teacher) (*BRIT*), principal (*US*); (*di facoltà universitaria*) dean

presi'dente *sm* (*POL*) president; (*di assemblea, COMM*) chairman; **~ del consiglio** prime minister; **presiden'tessa** *sf* president; president's wife; chairwoman; **presi'denza** *sf* presidency; office of president; chairmanship

presidi'are *vt* to garrison; **pre'sidio** *sm* garrison

presi'edere *vt* to preside over ♦ *vi*: **~ a** to direct, be in charge of

'preso, a *pp di* prendere

'pressa *sf* (*TECN*) press

pressap'poco *av* about, roughly

pres'sare *vt* to press

pressi'one *sf* pressure; **far ~ su qn** to put pressure on sb; **~ sanguigna** blood pressure

'presso *av* (*vicino*) nearby, close at hand ♦ *prep* (*vicino a*) near; (*accanto a*) beside, next to; (*in casa di*): **~ qn** at sb's home; (*nelle lettere*) care of, c/o; (*alle dipendenze di*): **lavora ~ di noi** he works for *o* with us ♦ *smpl*: **nei ~i di** near, in the vicinity of

pressuriz'zare [pressurid'dzare] *vt* to pressurize

presta'nome (*peg*) *sm/f inv* figurehead

pres'tante *ag* good-looking

pres'tare *vt*: **~** (*qc a qn*) to lend (sb sth *o* sth to sb); **~rsi** *vr* (*offrirsi*): **~rsi a fare** to offer to do; (*essere adatto*): **~rsi a** to lend itself to, be suitable for; **~ aiuto** to lend a hand; **~ attenzione** to pay attention; **~ fede a qc/qn** to give credence to sth/sb; **~ orecchio** to listen; **prestazi'one** *sf* (*TECN, SPORT*) performance; **prestazioni** *sfpl* (*di persona: servizi*) services

prestigia'tore, 'trice [prestidʒa'tore] *sm/f* conjurer

pres'tigio [pres'tidʒo] *sm* (*fama*) prestige; (*illusione*): **gioco di ~** conjuring trick

'prestito *sm* lending *no pl*; loan; **dar in ~ to** lend; **prendere in ~** to borrow

'presto *av* (*tra poco*) soon; (*in fretta*) quickly; (*di buon'ora*) early; **a ~** see you soon; **fare ~ a fare qc** to hurry up and do sth; (*non costare fatica*) to have no trouble doing sth; **si fa ~ a criticare** it's easy to criticize

pre'sumere *vt* to presume, assume; **pre'sunto, a** *pp di* presumere

presuntu'oso, a *ag* presumptuous

presunzi'one [prezun'tsjone] *sf* presumption

presup'porre *vt* to suppose; to presuppose

'prete *sm* priest

preten'dente *sm/f* pretender ♦ *sm* (*corteggiatore*) suitor

pre'tendere *vt* (*esigere*) to demand, require; (*sostenere*): **~ che** to claim that; **pretende di aver sempre ragione** he thinks he's always right

pretenzi'oso, a [preten'tsjoso] *ag* pretentious

pre'tesa *sf* (*esigenza*) claim, demand; (*presunzione, sfarzo*) pretentiousness; **senza ~e** unpretentious

pre'teso, a *pp di* pretendere

pre'testo *sm* pretext, excuse

pre'tore *sm* magistrate; **pre'tura** *sf* magistracy; (*sede*) magistrate's court

preva'lente *ag* prevailing; **preva'lenza** *sf* predominance

preva'lere *vi* to prevail; **pre'valso, a** *pp di* prevalere

preve'dere *vt* (*indovinare*) to foresee; (*presagire*) to foretell; (*considerare*) to make provision for

pre'vendita *sf* advance booking

preve'nire *vt* (*anticipare*) to forestall; to anticipate; (*evitare*) to avoid, prevent

preven'tivo, a *ag* preventive ♦ *sm* (*COMM*) estimate

prevenzi'one [preven'tsjone] *sf* prevention; (*preconcetto*) prejudice

previ'dente *ag* showing foresight; prudent; **previ'denza** *sf* foresight; **istituto di previdenza** provident institution; **previdenza sociale** social security (*BRIT*), welfare (*US*)

previsi'one *sf* forecast, prediction; **~i meteorologiche** *o* **del tempo** weather forecast *sg*

pre'visto, a *pp di* prevedere ♦ *sm*: **più/meno del ~** more/less than expected

prezi'oso, a [pret'tsjoso] *ag* precious; invaluable ♦ *sm* jewel; valuable

prez'zemolo [pret'tsemolo] *sm* parsley

'prezzo ['prettso] *sm* price; **~ d'acquisto/di vendita** buying/selling price

prigi'one [pri'dʒone] *sf* prison; **prigio'nia** *sf* imprisonment; **prigioni'ero, a** *ag* captive ♦ *sm/f* prisoner

'prima *sf* (*TEATRO*) first night; (*CINEMA*) première; (*AUT*) first gear; *vedi anche* **primo** ♦ *av* before; (*in anticipo*) in advance, beforehand; (*per l'addietro*) at one time, formerly; (*più presto*) sooner, earlier; (*in primo luogo*) first ♦ *cong*: **~ di fare/che parta** before doing/he leaves; **~ di** before; **~ o poi** sooner or later

pri'mario, a *ag* primary; (*principale*) chief, leading, primary ♦ *sm* (*MED*) chief physician

pri'mato *sm* supremacy; (*SPORT*) record

prima'vera *sf* spring; **primave'rile** *ag* spring *cpd*

primeggi'are [primed'dʒare] *vi* to excel, be one of the best

primi'tivo, a *ag* primitive; original

pri'mizie [pri'mittsje] *sfpl* early produce *sg*

'primo, a *ag* first; (*fig*) initial; basic; prime ♦ *sm/f* first (one) ♦ *sm* (*CUC*) first course; (*in date*): **il ~ luglio** the first of July; **le ~e ore del mattino** the early hours of the morning; **ai ~i di maggio** at the beginning of May; **viaggiare in ~a** to travel first-class; **in ~ luogo** first of all, in the first place; **di prim'ordine** o **~a qualità** first-class, first-rate; **in un ~ tempo** at first; **~a donna** leading lady; (*di opera lirica*) prima donna

primo'genito, a [primo'dʒenito] *ag, sm/f* firstborn

primordi'ale *ag* primordial

'primula *sf* primrose

princi'pale [printʃi'pale] *ag* main, principal ♦ *sm* manager, boss

princi'pato [printʃi'pato] *sm* principality

'principe ['printʃipe] *sm* prince; **~ ereditario** crown prince; **princi'pessa** *sf* princess

principi'ante [printʃi'pjante] *sm/f* beginner

prin'cipio [prin'tʃipjo] *sm* (*inizio*) beginning, start; (*origine*) origin, cause; (*concetto, norma*) principle; **al** o **in ~** at first; **per ~** on principle

pri'ore *sm* (*REL*) prior

priorità *sf* priority

'prisma, i *sm* prism

pri'vare *vt*: **~ qn di** to deprive sb of; **~rsi di** to go o do without

pri'vato, a *ag* private ♦ *sm/f* private citizen; **in ~** in private

privazi'one [privat'tsjone] *sf* privation, hardship

privilegi'are [privile'dʒare] *vt* to grant a privilege to

privi'legio [privi'ledʒo] *sm* privilege

'privo, a *ag*: **~ di** without, lacking

pro *prep* for, on behalf of ♦ *sm inv* (*utilità*) advantage, benefit; **a che ~?** what's the use?; **il ~ e il contro** the pros and cons

pro'babile *ag* probable, likely; **probabilità** *sf inv* probability

pro'blema, i *sm* problem

pro'boscide [pro'bɔʃʃide] *sf* (*di elefante*) trunk

procacci'are [prokat'tʃare] *vt* to get, obtain

pro'cedere [pro'tʃedere] *vi* to proceed; (*:comportarsi*) to behave; (*iniziare*): **~ a** to start; **~ contro** (*DIR*) to start legal proceedings against; **procedi'mento** *sm* (*modo di*

condurre) procedure; (*di avvenimenti*) course; (*TECN*) process; **procedimento penale** (*DIR*) criminal proceedings; **proce'dura** *sf* (*DIR*) procedure

proces'sare [protʃes'sare] *vt* (*DIR*) to try

processi'one [protʃes'sjone] *sf* procession

pro'cesso [pro'tʃesso] *sm* (*DIR*) trial; proceedings *pl*; (*metodo*) process

pro'cinto [pro'tʃinto] *sm*: **in ~ di fare** about to do, on the point of doing

pro'clama, i *sm* proclamation

procla'mare *vt* to proclaim

procre'are *vt* to procreate

pro'cura *sf* (*DIR*) proxy; power of attorney; (*ufficio*) attorney's office

procu'rare *vt*: **~ qc a qn** (*fornire*) to get o obtain sth for sb; (*causare: noie etc*) to bring o give sb sth

procura'tore, 'trice *sm/f* (*DIR*) ≈ solicitor; (*: chi ha la procura*) attorney; proxy; **~ generale** (*in corte d'appello*) public prosecutor; (*in corte di cassazione*) Attorney General; **~ della Repubblica** (*in corte d'assise, tribunale*) public prosecutor

prodi'gare *vt* to be lavish with; **~rsi per qn** to do all one can for sb

pro'digio [pro'didʒo] *sm* marvel, wonder; (*persona*) prodigy; **prodigi'oso, a** *ag* prodigious; phenomenal

'prodigo, a, ghi, ghe *ag* lavish, extravagant

pro'dotto, a *pp di* **produrre** ♦ *sm* product; **~i agricoli** farm produce *sg*

pro'durre *vt* to produce; **produttività** *sf* productivity; **produt'tivo, a** *ag* productive; **produt'tore, 'trice** *sm/f* producer; **produzi'one** *sf* production; (*rendimento*) output

pro'emio *sm* introduction, preface

Prof. *abbr* (= *professore*) Prof

profa'nare *vt* to desecrate

pro'fano, a *ag* (*mondano*) secular; profane; (*sacrilego*) profane

profe'rire *vt* to utter

profes'sare *vt* to profess; (*medicina etc*) to practise

professio'nale *ag* professional

professi'one *sf* profession; **professio'nista, i, e** *sm/f* professional

profes'sore, 'essa *sm/f* (*INS*) teacher; (*: di università*) lecturer; (*: titolare di cattedra*) professor

pro'feta, i *sm* prophet; **profe'zia** *sf* prophecy

pro'ficuo, a *ag* useful, profitable

profi'larsi *vr* to stand out, be silhouetted; to loom up

profi'lattico *sm* condom

pro'filo *sm* profile; (*breve descrizione*) sketch,

outline; **di ~** in profile

pro'fitto sm advantage, profit, benefit; (fig: progresso) progress; (COMM) profit

profondità sf inv depth

pro'fondo, a ag deep; (rancore, meditazione) profound ♦ sm depth(s pl), bottom; **~ 8 metri** 8 metres deep

'profugo, a, ghi, ghe sm/f refugee

profu'mare vt to perfume ♦ vi to be fragrant; **~rsi** vr to put on perfume o scent

profume'ria sf perfumery; (negozio) perfume shop

pro'fumo sm (prodotto) perfume, scent; (fragranza) scent, fragrance

profusi'one sf profusion; **a ~** in plenty

proget'tare [prodʒet'tare] vt to plan; (edificio) to plan, design; **pro'getto** sm plan; (idea) plan, project; **progetto di legge** bill

pro'gramma, i sm programme; (TV, RADIO) programmes pl; (INS) syllabus, curriculum; (INFORM) program; **program'mare** vt (TV, RADIO) to put on; (INFORM) to program; (ECON) to plan; **programma'tore, 'trice** sm/f (INFORM) computer programmer

progre'dire vi to progress, make progress

progres'sivo, a ag progressive

pro'gresso sm progress no pl; **fare ~i** to make progress

proi'bire vt to forbid, prohibit; **proibi'tivo, a** ag prohibitive; **proibizi'one** sf prohibition

proiet'tare vt (gen, GEOM, CINEMA) to project; (: presentare) to show, screen; (luce, ombra) to throw, cast; **proiet'tile** sm projectile, bullet (o shell etc); **proiet'tore** sm (CINEMA) projector; (AUT) headlamp; (MIL) searchlight; **proiezi'one** sf (CINEMA) projection; showing

'prole sf children pl, offspring

prole'tario, a ag, sm proletarian

prolife'rare vi (di fig) to proliferate

pro'lisso, a ag verbose

'prologo, ghi sm prologue

pro'lunga, ghe sf (di cavo etc) extension

prolun'gare vt (discorso, attesa) to prolong; (linea, termine) to extend

prome'moria sm inv memorandum

pro'messa sf promise

pro'messo, a pp di **promettere**

pro'mettere vt to promise ♦ vi to be o look promising; **~ a qn di fare** to promise sb that one will do

promi'nente ag prominent

promiscuità sf promiscuousness

promon'torio sm promontory, headland

pro'mosso, a pp di **promuovere**

promo'tore, trice sm/f promoter, organizer

promozi'one |promot'tsjone] sf promotion

promul'gare vt to promulgate

promu'overe vt to promote

proni'pote sm/f (di nonni) great-grandchild, great-grandson/granddaughter; (di zii) great-nephew/niece; **~i** smpl (discendenti) descendants

pro'nome sm (LING) pronoun

pro'nostico, ci sm forecast, prediction

pron'tezza [pron'tettsa] sf readiness; quickness, promptness

'pronto, a ag ready; (rapido) fast, quick, prompt; **~!** (TEL) hello!; **~ all'ira** quick-tempered; **~ soccorso** first aid

prontu'ario sm manual, handbook

pro'nuncia [pro'nuntʃa] sf pronunciation

pronunci'are [pronun'tʃare] vt (parola, sentenza) to pronounce; (dire) to utter; (discorso) to deliver; **~rsi** vr to declare one's opinion; **pronunci'ato, a** ag (spiccato) pronounced, marked; (sporgente) prominent

pro'nunzia etc [pro'nuntsja] = **pronuncia** etc

propa'ganda sf propaganda

propa'gare vt (notizia, malattia) to spread; (REL, BIOL) to propagate; **~rsi** vr to spread; (BIOL) to propagate; (FISICA) to be propagated

pro'pendere vi: **~ per** to favour, lean towards; **propensi'one** sf inclination, propensity; **pro'penso, a** pp di **propendere**

propi'nare vt to administer

pro'pizio, a [pro'pittsjo] ag favourable

pro'porre vt (suggerire): **~ qc (a qn)** to suggest sth (to sb); (candidato) to put forward; (legge, brindisi) to propose; **~ di fare** to suggest o propose doing; **proporsi di fare** to propose o intend to do; **proporsi una meta** to set o.s. a goal

proporzio'nale [proportsjo'nale] ag proportional

proporzio'nare [proportsjo'nare] vt: **~ qc a** to proportion o adjust sth to

proporzi'one [propor'tsjone] sf proportion; **in ~ a** in proportion to

pro'posito sm (intenzione) intention, aim; (argomento) subject, matter; **a ~ di** regarding, with regard to; **di ~** (apposta) deliberately, on purpose; **a ~** by the way; **capitare a ~** (cosa, persona) to turn up at the right time

proposizi'one [propozit'tsjone] sf (LING) clause; (: periodo) sentence

pro'posta sf proposal; (suggerimento) suggestion; **~ di legge** bill

pro'posto, a pp di **proporre**

proprietà sf inv (ciò che si possiede) property gen no pl, estate; (caratteristica) property; (correttezza) correctness; **proprie'tario, a** sm/f owner; (di albergo etc) proprietor, owner; (per l'inquilino) landlord/lady

'proprio, a ag (possessivo) own; (: impersonale) one's; (esatto) exact, correct, proper; (senso, significato) literal; (LING: nome) proper; (*particolare*): ~ **di** characteristic of, peculiar to ♦ *av* (*precisamente*) just, exactly; (*davvero*) really; (*affatto*): **non ... ~** not ... at all; **l'ha visto con i (suoi) ~i occhi** he saw it with his own eyes

'**prora** *sf* (NAUT) bow(s *pl*), prow

'**proroga, ghe** *sf* extension; postponement; **proro'gare** *vt* to extend; (*differire*) to postpone, defer

pro'**rompere** *vi* to burst out; **pro'rotto, a** *pp di* **prorompere**

'**prosa** *sf* prose; **pro'saico, a, ci, che** *ag* (*fig*) prosaic, mundane

pro'**sciogliere** [proʃˈʃɔʎʎere] *vt* to release; (DIR) to acquit; **prosci'olto, a** *pp di* **prosciogliere**

prosciu'**gare** [proʃʃuˈgare] *vt* (*terreni*) to drain, reclaim; ~**rsi** *vr* to dry up

prosci'**utto** [proʃˈʃutto] *sm* ham; ~ **cotto/crudo** cooked/cured ham

prosegui'**mento** *sm* continuation; **buon ~!** all the best!; (*a chi viaggia*) enjoy the rest of your journey!

prosegu'**ire** *vt* to carry on with, continue ♦ *vi* to carry on, go on

prospe'**rare** *vi* to thrive; **prosperità** *sf* prosperity; '**prospero, a** *ag* (*fiorente*) flourishing, thriving, prosperous; **prospe'roso, a** *ag* (*robusto*) hale and hearty; (: *ragazza*) buxom

prospet'**tare** *vt* (*esporre*) to point out, show; ~**rsi** *vr* to look, appear

prospet'**tiva** *sf* (ARTE) perspective; (*veduta*) view; (*fig: previsione, possibilità*) prospect

pros'**petto** *sm* (DISEGNO) elevation; (*veduta*) view, prospect; (*facciata*) façade, front; (*tabella*) table; (*sommario*) summary

prospici'**ente** [prospiˈtʃɛnte] *ag*: ~ **qc** facing o overlooking sth

prossimità *sf* nearness, proximity; **in ~ di** near (to), close to

'**prossimo, a** *ag* (*vicino*): ~ **a** near (to), close to; (*che viene subito dopo*) next; (*parente*) close ♦ *sm* neighbour, fellow man

prosti'**tuta** *sf* prostitute; **prostituzi'one** *sf* prostitution

pros'**trare** *vt* (*fig*) to exhaust, wear out; ~**rsi** *vr* (*fig*) to humble o.s.

protago'**nista, i, e** *sm/f* protagonist

pro'**teggere** [proˈtɛddʒere] *vt* to protect

proteggi'**slip** [protɛddʒiˈzlip] *sm inv* panty liner

prote'**ina** *sf* protein

pro'**tendere** *vt* to stretch out; **pro'teso, a** *pp di* **protendere**

pro'**testa** *sf* protest

protes'**tante** *ag, sm/f* Protestant

protes'**tare** *vt, vi* to protest; ~**rsi** *vr*: ~**rsi innocente** *etc* to protest one's innocence o

that one is innocent *etc*

protet'**tivo, a** *ag* protective

pro'**tetto, a** *pp di* **proteggere**

protet'**tore, 'trice** *sm/f* protector; (*sostenitore*) patron

protezi'**one** [protetˈtsjone] *sf* protection; (*patrocinio*) patronage

protocol'**lare** *vt* to register ♦ *ag* formal; of protocol; **proto'collo** *sm* protocol; (*registro*) register of documents

pro'**totipo** *sm* prototype

pro'**trarre** *vt* (*prolungare*) to prolong; **pro'tratto, a** *pp di* **protrarre**

protube'**ranza** [protubeˈrantsa] *sf* protuberance, bulge

'**prova** *sf* (*esperimento, cimento*) test, trial; (*tentativo*) attempt, try; (MAT, *testimonianza, documento etc*) proof; (DIR) evidence *no pl*, proof; (INS) exam, test; (TEATRO) rehearsal; (*di abito*) fitting; **a ~ di** (*in testimonianza di*) as proof of; **a ~ di fuoco** fireproof; **fino a ~ contraria** until it is proved otherwise; **mettere alla ~** to put to the test; **giro di ~** test o trial run; **~ generale** (TEATRO) dress rehearsal

pro'**vare** *vt* (*sperimentare*) to test; (*tentare*) to try, attempt; (*assaggiare*) to try, taste; (*sperimentare in sé*) to experience; (*sentire*) to feel; (*cimentare*) to put to the test; (*dimostrare*) to prove; (*abito*) to try on; ~ **a fare** to try o attempt to do

proveni'**enza** [proveˈnjɛntsa] *sf* origin, source

prove'**nire** *vi*: ~ **da** to come from

pro'**venti** *smpl* revenue *sg*

prove'**nuto, a** *pp di* **provenire**

pro'**verbio** *sm* proverb

pro'**vetta** *sf* test tube; **bambino in ~** test-tube baby

pro'**vetto, a** *ag* skilled, experienced

pro'**vincia, ce** o **cie** [proˈvintʃa] *sf* province; **provinci'ale** *ag* provincial; (**strada**) **provinciale** main road (BRIT), highway (US)

pro'**vino** *sm* (CINEMA) screen test; (*campione*) specimen

provo'**cante** *ag* (*attraente*) provocative

provo'**care** *vt* (*causare*) to cause, bring about; (*eccitare: riso, pietà*) to arouse; (*irritare, sfidare*) to provoke; **provoca'torio, a** *ag* provocative; **provocazi'one** *sf* provocation

provve'**dere** *vi* (*disporre*): ~ **(a)** to provide (for); (*prendere un provvedimento*) to take steps, act; **provvedi'mento** *sm* measure; (*di previdenza*) precaution

provvi'**denza** [provviˈdentsa] *sf*: **la ~** providence; **provvidenzi'ale** *ag* providential

provvigi'**one** [provviˈdʒone] *sf* (COMM) commission

provvi'**sorio, a** *ag* temporary

prov'vista sf provision, supply

'prua sf (NAUT) = prora

pru'dente ag cautious, prudent; (assennato) sensible, wise; **pru'denza** sf prudence, caution; wisdom

'prudere vi to itch, be itchy

'prugna ['pruɲɲa] sf plum; **~ secca** prune

prurigi'noso, a [prurid'ʒinoso] ag itchy

pru'rito sm itchiness no pl; itch

P.S. abbr (= postscriptum) P.S.; (POLIZIA) = **Pubblica Sicurezza**

pseu'donimo sm pseudonym

PSI sigla m = **Partito Socialista Italiano**

psica'nalista, i, e sm/f psychoanalyst

'psiche ['psike] sf (PSIC) psyche

psichi'atra, i, e [psi'kjatra] sm/f psychiatrist; **psichi'atrico, a, ci, che** ag psychiatric

'psichico, a, ci, che ['psikiko] ag psychological

psicolo'gia [psikolo'dʒia] sf psychology; **psico'logico, a, ci, che** ag psychological; **psi'cologo, a, gi, ghe** sm/f psychologist

psico'patico, a, ci, che ag psychopathic ♦ sm/f psychopath

P.T. abbr = **Posta e Telegrafi**

pubbli'care vt to publish

pubblicazi'one [pubblikat'tsjone] sf publication; **~i (matrimoniali)** sfpl (marriage) banns

pubbli'cista, i, e [pubbli'tʃista] sm/f (STAMPA) occasional contributor

pubblicità [pubblitʃi'ta] sf (diffusione) publicity; (attività) advertising; (annunci nei giornali) advertisements pl; **pubblici'tario, a** ag advertising cpd; (trovata, film) publicity cpd

'pubblico, a, ci, che ag public; (statale: scuola etc) state cpd ♦ sm public; (spettatori) audience; **in ~** in public; **~ funzionario** civil servant; **P~ Ministero** Public Prosecutor's Office; **la P~a Sicurezza** the police

'pube sm (ANAT) pubis

pubertà sf puberty

'pudico, a, ci, che ag modest

pu'dore sm modesty

puericul'tura sf paediatric nursing; infant care

pue'rile ag childish

pugi'lato [pudʒi'lato] sm boxing

'pugile ['pudʒile] sm boxer

pugna'lare [puɲɲa'lare] vt to stab

pu'gnale [puɲ'ɲale] sm dagger

'pugno ['puɲɲo] sm fist; (colpo) punch; (quantità) fistful

'pulce ['pultʃe] sf flea

pul'cino [pul'tʃino] sm chick

pu'ledro, a sm/f colt/filly

pu'leggia, ge [pu'leddʒa] sf pulley

pu'lire vt to clean; (lucidare) to polish; **pu'lita** sf quick clean; **pu'lito, a** ag (anche fig) clean; (ordinato) neat, tidy; **puli'tura** sf cleaning; **pulitura a secco** dry cleaning; **puli'zia** sf cleaning; cleanness; **fare le pulizie** to do the cleaning o the housework

'pullman sm inv coach

pul'lover sm inv pullover, jumper

pullu'lare vi to swarm, teem

pul'mino sm minibus

'pulpito sm pulpit

pul'sante sm (push-)button

pul'sare vi to pulsate, beat; **pulsazi'one** sf beat

pul'viscolo sm fine dust

'puma sm inv puma

pun'gente [pun'dʒente] ag prickly; stinging; (anche fig) biting

'pungere ['pundʒere] vt to prick; (sog: insetto, ortica) to sting; (: freddo) to bite

pungigli'one [pundʒiʎ'ʎone] sm sting

pu'nire vt to punish; **punizi'one** sf punishment; (SPORT) penalty

'punta sf point; (parte terminale) tip, end; (di monte) peak; (di costa) promontory; (minima parte) touch, trace; **in ~ di piedi** on tip-toe; **ore di ~** peak hours; **uomo di ~** front-rank o leading man

pun'tare vt (piedi a terra, gomiti sul tavolo) to plant; (dirigere: pistola) to point; (scommettere) to bet ♦ vi (mirare): **~ a** to aim at; **~ su** (dirigersi) to head o make for; (fig: contare) to count o rely on

pun'tata sf (gita) short trip; (scommessa) bet; (parte di opera) instalment; **romanzo a ~e** serial

punteggia'tura [punteddʒa'tura] sf (LING) punctuation

pun'teggio [pun'teddʒo] sm score

puntel'lare vt to support

pun'tello sm prop, support

puntigli'oso, a [puntiʎ'ʎoso] ag punctilious

pun'tina sf: **~ da disegno** drawing pin

pun'tino sm dot; **fare qc a ~** to do sth properly

'punto, a pp di **pungere** ♦ sm (segno, macchiolina) dot; (LING) full stop; (MAT, momento, di punteggio, fig: argomento) point; (posto) spot; (a scuola) mark; (nel cucire, nella maglia, MED) stitch ♦ av: **non ... ~** not at all; **due ~i** sm (LING) colon; **sul ~ di fare** (just) about to do; **fare il ~** (NAUT) to take a bearing; (fig): **fare il ~ della situazione** to take stock of the situation; to sum up the situation; **alle 6 in ~** at 6 o'clock sharp o on the dot; **essere a buon ~** to have reached a satisfactory stage; **mettere a ~** to adjust; (motore) to tune; (cannocchiale) to focus; (fig) to settle; **di ~ in bianco** point-blank;

~ **cardinale** point of the compass, cardinal point; ~ **debole** weak point; ~ **esclamativo/ interrogativo** exclamation/question mark; ~ **di riferimento** landmark; (*fig*) point of reference; ~ **di vendita** retail outlet; ~ **e virgola** semicolon; ~ **di vista** (*fig*) point of view; ~**i di sospensione** suspension points

puntu'ale *ag* punctual; **puntualità** *sf* punctuality

pun'tura *sf* (*di ago*) prick; (*di insetto*) sting, bite; (*MED*) puncture; (: *iniezione*) injection; (*dolore*) sharp pain

punzecchi'are [puntsek'kjare] *vt* to prick; (*fig*) to tease

'pupa *sf* doll

pu'pazzo [pu'pattso] *sm* puppet

pu'pilla *sf* (*ANAT*) pupil

pu'pillo, a *sm/f* (*DIR*) ward; (*prediletto*) favourite, pet

purché [pur'ke] *cong* provided that, on condition that

'pure *cong* (*tuttavia*) and yet, nevertheless; (*anche se*) even if ♦ *av* (*anche*) too, also; **pur di** (*al fine di*) just to; **faccia ~!** go ahead!, please do!

purè *sm* (*CUC*) purée; (: *di patate*) mashed potatoes

pu'rea *sf* = **purè**

pu'rezza [pu'rettsa] *sf* purity

'purga, ghe *sf* (*MED*) purging *no pl*; purge; (*POL*) purge

pur'gante *sm* (*MED*) purgative, purge

pur'gare *vt* (*MED, POL*) to purge; (*pulire*) to clean

purga'torio *sm* purgatory

purifi'care *vt* to purify; (*metallo*) to refine

puri'tano, a *ag, sm/f* puritan

'puro, a *ag* pure; (*acqua*) clear, limpid; (*vino*) undiluted; **puro'sangue** *sm/f inv* thoroughbred

pur'troppo *av* unfortunately

'pustola *sf* pimple

puti'ferio *sm* rumpus, row

putre'fare *vi* to putrefy, rot; **putre'fatto, a** *pp di* **putrefare**

'putrido, a *ag* putrid, rotten

put'tana (*fam!*) *sf* whore (!)

'puzza ['puttsa] *sf* = **puzzo**

puz'zare [put'tsare] *vi* to stink

'puzzo ['puttso] *sm* stink, foul smell

'puzzola ['puttsola] *sf* polecat

puzzo'lente [puttso'lɛnte] *ag* stinking

Q, q

qua *av* here; **in ~** (*verso questa parte*) this way; **da un anno in ~** for a year now; **da quando in ~?** since when?; **per di ~** (*passare*) this way; **al**

di ~ di (*fiume, strada*) on this side of; ~ **dentro/fuori** *etc* in/out here *etc*; *vedi anche* **questo**

qua'derno *sm* notebook; (*per scuola*) exercise book

qua'drante *sm* quadrant; (*di orologio*) face

qua'drare *vi* (*bilancio*) to balance, tally; (*descrizione*) to correspond ♦ *vt* (*MAT*) to square; **non mi quadra** I don't like it; **qua'drato, a** *ag* square; (*fig: equilibrato*) level-headed, sensible; (: *peg*) square ♦ *sm* (*MAT*) square; (*PUGILATO*) ring; **5 al quadrato** 5 squared

qua'dretto *sm*: **a ~i** (*tessuto*) checked; (*foglio*) squared

quadri'foglio [kwadri'fɔʎʎo] *sm* four-leaf clover

'quadro *sm* (*pittura*) painting, picture; (*quadrato*) square; (*tabella*) table, chart; (*TECN*) board, panel; (*TEATRO*) scene; (*fig: scena, spettacolo*) sight; (: *descrizione*) outline, description; ~**i** *smpl* (*POL*) party organizers; (*MIL*) cadres; (*COMM*) managerial staff; (*CARTE*) diamonds

'quadruplo, a *ag, sm* quadruple

quaggiù [kwad'dʒu] *av* down here

'quaglia ['kwaʎʎa] *sf* quail

'qualche ['kwalke] *det* **1** some, a few; (*in interrogative*) any; **ho comprato ~ libro** I've bought some *o* a few books; ~ **volta** sometimes; **hai ~ sigaretta?** have you any cigarettes?

2 (*uno*): **c'è ~ medico?** is there a doctor?; **in ~ modo** somehow

3 (*un certo, parecchio*) some; **un personaggio di ~ rilievo** a figure of some importance

4: ~ **cosa** = **qualcosa**

qualche'duno [kwalke'duno] *pron* = **qualcuno**

qual'cosa *pron* something; (*in espressioni interrogative*) anything; **qualcos'altro** something else; anything else; ~ **di nuovo** something new; anything new; ~ **da mangiare** something to eat; anything to eat; **c'è ~ che non va?** is there something *o* anything wrong?

qual'cuno *pron* (*persona*) someone, somebody; (: *in espressioni interrogative*) anyone, anybody; (*alcuni*) some; ~ **è favorevole a noi** some are on our side; **qualcun altro** someone *o* somebody else; anyone *o* anybody else

'quale (*spesso troncato in qual*) *det* **1** (*interrogativo*) what; (: *scegliendo tra due o più cose* *o persone*) which; ~ **uomo/denaro?** what man/money?; which man/money?; **~i sono i tuoi programmi?** what are your plans?; **~ stanza preferisci?** which room do you prefer?

2 (*relativo: come*): **il risultato fu ~ ci si aspettava** the result was as expected

3 (*esclamativo*) what; **~ disgrazia!** what bad luck!

♦ *pron* **1** (*interrogativo*) which; **~ dei due scegli?** which of the two do you want?

2 (*relativo*): **il(la) ~** (*persona: soggetto*) who; (: *oggetto, con preposizione*) whom; (*cosa*) which; (*possessivo*) whose; **suo padre, il ~ è avvocato,** ... his father, who is a lawyer, ...; **il signore con il ~ parlavo** the gentleman to whom I was speaking; **l'albergo al ~ ci siamo fermati** the hotel where we stayed *o* which we stayed at; **la signora della ~ ammiriamo la bellezza** the lady whose beauty we admire

3 (*relativo: in elenchi*) such as, like; **piante ~i l'edera** plants like *o* such as ivy; **~ sindaco di questa città** as mayor of this town

---

qua'lifica, che *sf* qualification; (*titolo*) title

qualifi'care *vt* to qualify; (*definire*): **~ qn/qc come** to describe sb/sth as; **~rsi** *vr* (*anche SPORT*) to qualify; **qualifica'tivo, a** *ag* qualifying; **qualificazi'one** *sf*: **gara di qualificazione** (*SPORT*) qualifying event

qualità *sf inv* quality; **in ~ di** in one's capacity as

qua'lora *cong* in case, if

qual'siasi *det inv* = **qualunque**

qua'lunque *det inv* any; (*quale che sia*) whatever; (*discriminativo*) whichever; (*posposto: mediocre*) poor, indifferent; ordinary; **mettiti un vestito ~** put on any old dress; **~ cosa** anything; **~ cosa accada** whatever happens; **a ~ costo** at any cost, whatever the cost; **l'uomo ~** the man in the street; **~ persona** anyone, anybody

'quando *cong, av* when; **~ sarò ricco** when I'm rich; **da ~** (*dacché*) since; (*interrogativo*): **da ~ sei qui?** how long have you been here?; **quand'anche** even if

quantità *sf inv* quantity; (*gran numero*): **una ~ di** a great deal of; a lot of; **in grande ~** in large quantities; **quantita'tivo** *sm* (*COMM*) amount, quantity

---

'quanto, a *det* **1** (*interrogativo: quantità*) how much; (: *numero*) how many; **~ pane/ denaro?** how much bread/money?; **~i libri/ ragazzi?** how many books/boys?; **~ tempo?** how long?; **~i anni hai?** how old are you?

2 (*esclamativo*): **~e storie!** what a lot of nonsense!; **~ tempo sprecato!** what a waste

of time!

3 (*relativo: quantità*) as much ... as; (: *numero*) as many ... as; **ho ~ denaro mi occorre** I have as much money as I need; **prendi ~i libri vuoi** take as many books as you like

♦ *pron* **1** (*interrogativo: quantità*) how much; (: *numero*) how many; (: *tempo*) how long; **~ mi dai?** how much will you give me?; **~i me ne hai portati?** how many did you bring me?; **da ~ sei qui?** how long have you been here?; **~i ne abbiamo oggi?** what's the date today?

2 (*relativo: quantità*) as much as; (: *numero*) as many as; **farò ~ posso** I'll do as much as I can; **possono venire ~i sono stati invitati** all those who have been invited can come

♦ *av* **1** (*interrogativo: con ag, av*) how; (: *con vb*) how much; **~ stanco ti sembrava?** how tired did he seem to you?; **~ corre la tua moto?** how fast can your motorbike go?; **~ costa?** how much does it cost?; **quant'è?** how much is it?

2 (*esclamativo: con ag, av*) how; (: *con vb*) how much; **~ sono felice!** how happy I am!; **sapessi ~ abbiamo camminato!** if you knew how far we've walked!; **studierò ~ posso** I'll study as much as *o* all I can; **~ prima** as soon as possible

3: **in ~** (*in qualità di*) as; (*perché, per il fatto che*) as, since; **(in) ~ a** (*per ciò che riguarda*) as for, as regards

4: **per ~** (*nonostante, anche se*) however; **per ~ si sforzi, non ce la farà** try as he may, he won't manage it; **per ~ sia brava, fa degli errori** however good she may be, she makes mistakes; **per ~ io sappia** as far as I know

---

quan'tunque *cong* although, though

qua'ranta *num* forty

quaran'tena *sf* quarantine

quaran'tesimo, a *num* fortieth

quaran'tina *sf*: **una ~ (di)** about forty

qua'resima *sf*: **la ~** Lent

'quarta *sf* (*AUT*) fourth (gear); *vedi anche* **quarto**

quar'tetto *sm* quartet(te)

quarti'ere *sm* district, area; (*MIL*) quarters *pl*; **~ generale** headquarters *pl*

'quarto, a *ag* fourth ♦ *sm* fourth; (*quarta parte*) quarter; **le 6 e un ~** a quarter past six; **~ d'ora** quarter of an hour; **~i di finale** quarter final

'quarzo ['kwartso] *sm* quartz

'quasi *av* almost, nearly ♦ *cong* (*anche: ~ che*) as if; (*non*) ... **~ mai** hardly ever; **~ me ne andrei** I've half a mind to leave

quassù *av* up here

'quatto, a *ag* crouched, squatting; (*silenzioso*) silent; **~ ~** very quietly; stealthily

quat'tordici [kwat'tordit∫i] *num* fourteen

quat'trini *smpl* money *sg*, cash *sg*
'quattro *num* four; in ~ e quatt'otto in less than no time; quattro'cento *num* four hundred ♦ *sm*: il Quattrocento the fifteenth century; quattro'mila *num* four thousand

---PAROLA CHIAVE---

'quello, a (*dav sm* quel +C, quell' +V, quello +s *impura, gn, pn, ps, x, z; pl* quei +C, quegli +V o s *impura, gn, pn, ps, x, z; dav sf* quella +C, quell' +V; *pl* quelle) *det* that; those *pl*; ~a casa that house; quegli uomini those men; voglio ~a camicia (lì o là) I want that shirt ♦ *pron* 1 (*dimostrativo*) that (one); those (ones) *pl*; (*ciò*) that; conosci ~a? do you know that woman?; prendo ~ bianco I'll take the white one; chi è ~? who's that?; prendi ~ (lì o là) take that one (there)
2 (*relativo*): ~(a) che (*persona*) the one (who); (*cosa*) the one (which), the one (that); ~i(e) che (*persone*) those who; (*cose*) those which; è lui ~ che non voleva venire he's the one who didn't want to come; ho fatto ~ che potevo I did what I could

'quercia, ce ['kwertʃa] *sf* oak (tree); (*legno*) oak
que'rela *sf* (*DIR*) (legal) action; quere'lare *vt* to bring an action against
que'sito *sm* question, query; problem
questio'nario *sm* questionnaire
questi'one *sf* problem, question; (*controversia*) issue; (*litigio*) quarrel; in ~ in question; è ~ di tempo it's a matter o question of time

---PAROLA CHIAVE---

'questo, a *det* 1 (*dimostrativo*) this; these *pl*; ~ libro (qui o qua) this book; io prendo ~ cappotto, tu quello I'll take this coat, you take that one; quest'oggi today; ~a sera this evening
2 (*enfatico*): non fatemi più prendere di ~e paure don't frighten me like that again ♦ *pron* (*dimostrativo*) this (one); these (ones) *pl*; (*ciò*) this; prendo ~ (qui o qua) I'll take this one; preferisci ~i o quelli? do you prefer these (ones) or those (ones)?; ~ intendevo io this is what I meant; vengono Paolo e Luca: ~ da Roma, quello di Palermo Paolo and Luca are coming: the former from Palermo, the latter from Rome

ques'tore *sm* ≈ chief constable (*BRIT*), ≈ police commissioner (*US*)
'questua *sf* collection (of alms)
ques'tura *sf* police headquarters *pl*
qui *av* here; da o di ~ from here; di ~ in avanti from now on; di ~ a poco/una settimana in a little while/a week's time; ~ dentro/sopra/vicino in/up/near here; *vedi anche* questo
quie'tanza [kwje'tantsa] *sf* receipt
quie'tare *vt* to calm, soothe
qui'ete *sf* quiet, quietness; calmness; stillness; peace
qui'eto, a *ag* quiet; (*notte*) calm, still; (*mare*) calm
'quindi *av* then ♦ *cong* therefore, so
'quindici ['kwinditʃi] *num* fifteen; ~ giorni a fortnight (*BRIT*), two weeks
quindi'cina [kwindi'tʃina] *sf* (*serie*): una ~ (di) about fifteen; fra una ~ di giorni in a fortnight
quin'quennio *sm* period of five years
quin'tale *sm* quintal (*100 kg*)
'quinte *sfpl* (*TEATRO*) wings
'quinto, a *num* fifth
'quota *sf* (*parte*) quota, share; (*AER*) height, altitude; (*IPPICA*) odds *pl*; prendere/perdere ~ (*AER*) to gain/lose height o altitude; ~ d'iscrizione enrolment fee; (*a club*) membership fee
quo'tare *vt* (*BORSA*) to quote; quotazi'one *sf* quotation
quotidi'ano, a *ag* daily; (*banale*) everyday ♦ *sm* (*giornale*) daily (paper)
quozi'ente [kwot'tsjɛnte] *sm* (*MAT*) quotient; ~ d'intelligenza intelligence quotient, IQ

R, r

ra'barbaro *sm* rhubarb
'rabbia *sf* (*ira*) anger, rage; (*accanimento, furia*) fury; (*MED: idrofobia*) rabies *sg*
rab'bino *sm* rabbi
rabbi'oso, a *ag* angry, furious; (*facile all'ira*) quick-tempered; (*forze, acqua etc*) furious, raging; (*MED*) rabid, mad
rabbo'nire *vt* to calm down; ~rsi *vr* to calm down
rabbrivi'dire *vi* to shudder, shiver
rabbui'arsi *vr* to grow dark
raccapez'zarsi [rakkapet'tsarsi] *vr*: non ~ to be at a loss
raccapricci'ante [rakkaprit'tʃante] *ag* horrifying
raccatta'palle *sm inv* (*SPORT*) ballboy
raccat'tare *vt* to pick up
rac'chetta [rak'ketta] *sf* (*per tennis*) racket; (*per ping-pong*) bat; ~ da neve snowshoe; ~ da sci ski stick
racchi'udere [rak'kjudere] *vt* to contain; racchi'uso, a *pp di* racchiudere
rac'cogliere [rak'kɔʎʎere] *vt* to collect; (*raccattare*) to pick up; (*frutti, fiori*) to pick, pluck; (*AGR*) to harvest; (*approvazione, voti*) to win; ~rsi *vr* to gather; (*fig*) to gather one's

thoughts; to meditate; **raccogli'mento** sm meditation; **raccogli'tore** sm (cartella) folder, binder; **raccoglitore ad anelli** ring binder

rac'colta sf collecting no pl; collection; (AGR) harvesting no pl, gathering no pl; harvest, crop; (adunata) gathering

rac'colto, a pp di **raccogliere ♦** ag (persona: pensoso) thoughtful; (luogo: appartato) secluded, quiet ♦ sm (AGR) crop, harvest

raccoman'dare vt to recommend; (affidare) to entrust; (esortare): ~ **a qn di non fare** to tell o warn sb not to do; **~rsi** vr: **~rsi a qn** to commend o.s. to sb; **mi raccomando!** don't forget!; **raccoman'data** sf (anche: lettera raccomandata) recorded-delivery letter; **raccomandazi'one** sf reccommendation

raccon'tare vt: ~ **(a qn)** (dire) to tell (sb); (narrare) to relate (to sb), tell (sb) about; **rac'conto** sm telling no pl, relating no pl; (fatto raccontato) story, tale

raccorci'are [rakkor'tʃare] vt to shorten

rac'cordo sm (TECN: giunto) connection, joint; (AUT: di autostrada) slip road (BRIT), entrance (o exit) ramp (US); ~ **anulare** (AUT) ring road (BRIT), beltway (US)

ra'chitico, a, ci, che [ra'kitiko] ag suffering from rickets; (fig) scraggy, scrawny

racimo'lare [ratʃimo'lare] vt (fig) to scrape together, glean

'rada sf (natural) harbour

'radar sm radar

raddol'cire [raddol'tʃire] vt (persona, carattere) to soften; **~rsi** vr (tempo) to grow milder; (persona) to soften, mellow

raddoppi'are vt, vi to double

raddriz'zare [raddrit'tsare] vt to straighten; (fig: correggere) to put straight, correct

'radere vt (barba) to shave off; (mento) to shave; (fig: rasentare) to graze; to skim; **~rsi** vr to shave (o.s.); ~ **al suolo** to raze to the ground

radi'are vt to strike off

radia'tore sm radiator

radiazi'one [radjat'tsjone] sf (FISICA) radiation; (cancellazione) striking off

radi'cale ag radical ♦ sm (LING) root

ra'dicchio [ra'dikkjo] sm chicory

ra'dice [ra'ditʃe] sf root

'radio sf inv radio ♦ sm (CHIM) radium; **radioat'tivo, a** ag radioactive; **radiodiffusi'one** sf (radio) broadcasting; **radiogra'fare** vt to X-ray; **radiogra'fia** sf radiography; (foto) X-ray photograph

radi'oso, a ag radiant

'rado, a ag (capelli) sparse, thin; (visite) infrequent; **di** ~ rarely

radu'nare vt to gather, assemble; **~rsi** vr to gather, assemble; **ra'duno** sm meeting

ra'dura sf clearing

raffazzo'nato [raffattso'nato] ag patched up

raf'fermo, a ag stale

'raffica, che sf (METEOR) gust (of wind); (di colpi: scarica) burst of gunfire

raffigu'rare vt to represent

raffi'nare vt to refine; **raffina'tezza** sf refinement; **raffi'nato, a** ag refined; **raffine'ria** sf refinery

raffor'zare [raffor'tsare] vt to reinforce

raffredda'mento sm cooling

raffred'dare vt to cool; (fig) to dampen, have a cooling effect on; **~rsi** vr to grow cool o cold; (prendere un raffreddore) to catch a cold; (fig) to cool (off)

raffred'dato, a ag (MED): **essere ~** to have a cold

raffred'dore sm (MED) cold

raf'fronto sm comparison

'rafia sf (fibra) raffia

ra'gazzo, a [ra'gattso] sm/f boy/girl; (fam: fidanzato) boyfriend/girlfriend

raggi'ante [rad'dʒante] ag radiant, shining

'raggio ['raddʒo] sm (di sole etc) ray; (MAT, distanza) radius; (di ruota etc) spoke; ~ **d'azione** range; **~i X** X-rays

raggi'rare [raddʒi'rare] vt to take in, trick; **rag'giro** sm trick

raggi'ungere [rad'dʒundʒere] vt to reach; (persona: riprendere) to catch up (with); (bersaglio) to hit; (fig: meta) to achieve; **raggi'unto, a** pp di **raggiungere**

raggomito'larsi vr to curl up

raggranel'lare vt to scrape together

raggrup'pare vt to group (together)

raggu'aglio [rag'gwaʎʎo] sm (informazione) piece of information

ragguar'devole ag (degno di riguardo) distinguished, notable; (notevole: somma) considerable

ragiona'mento [radʒona'mento] sm reasoning no pl; arguing no pl; argument

ragio'nare [radʒo'nare] vi to reason; ~ **di** (discorrere) to talk about

ragi'one [ra'dʒone] sf reason; (dimostrazione, prova) argument, reason; (diritto) right; **aver** ~ to be right; **aver ~ di qn** to get the better of sb; **dare ~ a qn** to agree with sb; to prove sb right; **perdere la ~** to become insane; (fig) to take leave of one's senses; **in ~ di** at the rate of; to the amount of; according to; **a o con** ~ rightly, justly; ~ **sociale** (COMM) corporate name; **a ragion veduta** after due consideration

ragione'ria [radʒone'ria] sf accountancy; accounts department

ragio'nevole [radʒo'nevole] ag reasonable

ragioni'ere, a [radʒo'njere] sm/f accountant

ragli'are [raʎˈʎare] vi to bray

ragna'tela [raɲɲaˈtela] sf cobweb, spider's web

'ragno [ˈraɲɲo] sm spider

ragù sm inv (CUC) meat sauce; stew

RAI-TV [raitiˈvu] sigla f = **Radio televisione italiana**

rallegra'menti smpl congratulations

ralle'grare vt to cheer up; **~rsi** vr to cheer up; (provare allegrezza) to rejoice; **~rsi con qn** to congratulate sb

rallen'tare vt to slow down; (fig) to lessen, slacken ♦ vi to slow down

raman'zina [ramanˈdzina] sf lecture, telling-off

'rame sm (CHIM) copper

rammari'carsi vr: **~ (di)** (rincrescersi) to be sorry (about), regret; (lamentarsi) to complain (about); **ram'marico, chi** sm regret

rammen'dare vt to mend; (calza) to darn; **ram'mendo** sm mending no pl; darning no pl; mend; darn

rammen'tare vt to remember, recall; (richiamare alla memoria): **~ qc a qn** to remind sb of sth; **~rsi** vr: **~rsi (di qc)** to remember (sth)

rammol'lire vt to soften ♦ vi (anche: ~rsi) to go soft

'ramo sm branch

ramo'scello [ramoʃˈʃɛllo] sm twig

'rampa sf flight (of stairs); **~ di lancio** launching pad

rampi'cante ag (BOT) climbing

ram'pone sm harpoon; (ALPINISMO) crampon

'rana sf frog

'rancido, a [ˈrantʃido] ag rancid

ran'core sm rancour, resentment

ran'dagio, a, gi, gie o **ge** [ranˈdadʒo] ag (gatto, cane) stray

ran'dello sm club, cudgel

'rango, ghi sm (condizione sociale, MIL: riga) rank

rannicchi'arsi [rannikˈkjarsi] vr to crouch, huddle

rannuvo'larsi vr to cloud over, become overcast

ra'nocchio [raˈnɔkkjo] sm (edible) frog

'rantolo sm wheeze; (di agonizzanti) death rattle

'rapa sf (BOT) turnip

ra'pace [raˈpatʃe] ag (animale) predatory; (fig) rapacious, grasping ♦ sm bird of prey

ra'pare vt (capelli) to crop, cut very short

'rapida sf (di fiume) rapid; vedi anche **rapido**

rapida'mente av quickly, rapidly

rapidità sf speed

'rapido, a ag fast; (esame, occhiata) quick, rapid ♦ sm (FERR) express (train)

rapi'mento sm kidnapping; (fig) rapture

ra'pina sf robbery; **~ a mano armata** armed robbery; **rapi'nare** vt to rob; **rapina'tore, 'trice** sm/f robber

ra'pire vt (cose) to steal; (persone) to kidnap; (fig) to enrapture, delight; **rapi'tore, 'trice** sm/f kidnapper

rappor'tare vt (confrontare) to compare; (riprodurre) to reproduce

rap'porto sm (resoconto) report; (legame) relationship; (MAT, TECN) ratio; **~i** smpl (fra persone, paesi) relations; **~i sessuali** sexual intercourse sg

rap'prendersi vr to coagulate, clot; (latte) to curdle

rappre'saglia [rappreˈsaʎʎa] sf reprisal, retaliation

rappresen'tante sm/f representative; **rappresen'tanza** sf delegation, deputation; (COMM: ufficio, sede) agency

rappresen'tare vt to represent; (TEATRO) to perform; **rappresentazi'one** sf representation; performing no pl; (spettacolo) performance

rap'preso, a pp di **rapprendere**

rapso'dia sf rhapsody

rara'mente av seldom, rarely

rare'fatto, a ag rarefied

'raro, a ag rare

ra'sare vt (barba etc) to shave off; (siepi, erba) to trim, cut; **~rsi** vr to shave (o.s.)

raschi'are [rasˈkjare] vt to scrape; (macchia, fango) to scrape off ♦ vi to clear one's throat

rasen'tare vt (andar rasente) to keep close to; (sfiorare) to skim along (o over); (fig) to border on

ra'sente prep: **~ (a)** close to, very near

'raso, a pp di **radere** ♦ ag (barba) shaved; (capelli) cropped; (con misure di capacità) level; (pieno: bicchiere) full to the brim ♦ sm (tessuto) satin; **~ terra** close to the ground; **un cucchiaio ~** a level spoonful

ra'soio sm razor; **~ elettrico** electric shaver o razor

ras'segna [rasˈseɲɲa] sf (MIL) inspection, review; (esame) inspection; (resoconto) review, survey; (pubblicazione letteraria etc) review; (mostra) exhibition, show; **passare in ~** (MIL, fig) to review

rasse'gnare [rasseɲˈɲare] vt: **~ le dimissioni** to resign, hand in one's resignation; **~rsi** vr (accettare): **~rsi (a qc/a fare)** to resign o.s. (to sth/to doing); **rassegnazi'one** sf resignation

rassere'narsi vr (tempo) to clear up

rasset'tare vt to tidy, put in order; (aggiustare) to repair, mend

rassicu'rare vt to reassure

rasso'dare vt to harden, stiffen

rassomigli'anza [rassomiʎˈʎantsa] sf

resemblance

rassomigli'are [rassomiʎ'ʎare] *vi*: ~ **a** to resemble, look like

rastrel'lare *vt* to rake; (*fig: perlustrare*) to comb

rastrelli'era *sf* rack; (*per piatti*) dish rack

ras'trello *sm* rake

'rata *sf* (*quota*) instalment; **pagare a ~e** to pay by instalments *o* on hire purchase (*BRIT*)

ratifi'care *vt* (*DIR*) to ratify

'ratto *sm* (*DIR*) abduction; (*ZOOL*) rat

rattop'pare *vt* to patch; (*ZOOL*) rat

rattop'pare *vt* to patch; **rat'toppo** *sm* patching *no pl*; patch

rattrap'pirsi *vr* to get stiff

rattris'tare *vt* to sadden; **~rsi** *vr* to become sad

'rauco, a, chi, che *ag* hoarse

rava'nello *sm* radish

ravi'oli *smpl* ravioli *sg*

ravve'dersi *vr* to mend one's ways

ravvici'nare [ravvitʃi'nare] *vt* (*avvicinare*): ~ **qc a** to bring sth nearer to; (: *due tubi*) to bring closer together; (*riconciliare*) to reconcile, bring together

ravvi'sare *vt* to recognize

ravvi'vare *vt* to revive; (*fig*) to brighten up, enliven; **~rsi** *vr* to revive; to brighten up

razio'cinio [ratsjo'tʃinjo] *sm* reasoning *no pl*; reason; (*buon senso*) common sense

razio'nale [rattsjo'nale] *ag* rational

razio'nare [rattsjo'nare] *vt* to ration

razi'one [rat'tsjone] *sf* ration; (*porzione*) portion, share

'razza ['rattsa] *sf* race; (*ZOOL*) breed; (*discendenza, stirpe*) stock, race; (*sorta*) sort, kind

raz'zia [rat'tsia] *sf* raid, foray

razzi'ale [rat'tsjale] *ag* racial

raz'zismo [rat'tsizmo] *sm* racism, racialism

raz'zista, i, e [rat'tsista] *ag, sm/f* racist, racialist

'razzo ['raddzo] *sm* rocket

razzo'lare [rattso'lare] *vi* (*galline*) to scratch about

re *sm inv* king; (*MUS*) D; (: *solfeggiando*) re

rea'gire [rea'dʒire] *vi* to react

re'ale *ag* real; (*di, da re*) royal ♦ *sm*: **il ~** reality; **rea'lismo** *sm* realism; **rea'lista, i, e** *sm/f* realist; (*POL*) royalist

realiz'zare [realid'dzare] *vt* (*progetto etc*) to realize, carry out; (*sogno, desiderio*) to realize, fulfil; (*scopo*) to achieve; (*COMM: titoli etc*) to realize; (*CALCIO etc*) to score; **~rsi** *vr* to be realized; **realizzazi'one** *sf* realization; fulfilment; achievement

real'mente *av* really, actually

real'tà *sf inv* reality

re'ato *sm* offence

reat'tore *sm* (*FISICA*) reactor; (*AER: aereo*) jet;

(: *motore*) jet engine

reazio'nario, a [reattsjo'narjo] *ag* (*POL*) reactionary

reazi'one [reat'tsjone] *sf* reaction

recapi'tare *vt* to deliver

re'capito *sm* (*indirizzo*) address; (*consegna*) delivery

re'care *vt* (*portare*) to bring; (*avere su di sé*) to carry, bear; (*cagionare*) to cause, bring; **~rsi** *vr* to go

re'cedere [re'tʃedere] *vi* to withdraw

recensi'one [retʃen'sjone] *sf* review; **recen'sire** *vt* to review

re'cente [re'tʃente] *ag* recent; **di ~** recently; **recente'mente** *av* recently

recessi'one [retʃes'sjone] *sf* (*ECON*) recession

re'cidere [re'tʃidere] *vt* to cut off, chop off

reci'divo, a [retʃi'divo] *sm/f* (*DIR*) second (*o* habitual) offender, recidivist

re'cinto [re'tʃinto] *sm* enclosure; (*ciò che recinge*) fence; surrounding wall

recipi'ente [retʃi'pjente] *sm* container

re'ciproco, a, ci, che [re'tʃiproko] *ag* reciprocal

re'ciso, a [re'tʃizo] *pp di* **recidere**

'recita ['retʃita] *sf* performance

reci'tare [retʃi'tare] *vt* (*poesia, lezione*) to recite; (*dramma*) to perform; (*ruolo*) to play *o* act (the part of); **recitazi'one** *sf* recitation; (*di attore*) acting

recla'mare *vi* to complain ♦ *vt* (*richiedere*) to demand

ré'clame [re'klam] *sf inv* advertising *no pl*; advertisement, advert (*BRIT*), ad (*fam*)

re'clamo *sm* complaint

reclusi'one *sf* (*DIR*) imprisonment

'recluta *sf* recruit; **reclu'tare** *vt* to recruit

re'condito, a *ag* secluded; (*fig*) secret, hidden

recriminazi'one [rekriminat'tsjone] *sf* recrimination

recrude'scenza [rekrudeʃ'ʃentsa] *sf* fresh outbreak

recupe'rare *vt* = **ricuperare**

redar'guire *vt* to rebuke

re'datto, a *pp di* **redigere**; **redat'tore, 'trice** *sm/f* (*STAMPA*) editor; (: *di articolo*) writer; (*di dizionario etc*) compiler; **redattore capo** chief editor; **redazi'one** *sf* editing; writing; (*sede*) editorial office(s); (*personale*) editorial staff; (*versione*) version

reddi'tizio, a [reddi'tittsjo] *ag* profitable

'reddito *sm* income; (*dello Stato*) revenue; (*di un capitale*) yield

re'dento, a *pp di* **redimere**

redenzi'one [reden'tsjone] *sf* redemption

re'digere [re'didʒere] *vt* to write; (*contratto*) to draw up

'redini *sfpl* reins

'**reduce** |'redutʃe| *ag*: **~ da** returning from, back from ♦ *sm/f* survivor
refe'rendum *sm inv* referendum
refe'renza |refe'rɛntsa| *sf* reference
re'ferto *sm* medical report
refet'torio *sm* refectory
refrat'tario, a *ag* refractory
refrige'rare |refridʒe'rare| *vt* to refrigerate; (*rinfrescare*) to cool, refresh
rega'lare *vt* to give (as a present), make a present of
re'gale *ag* regal
re'galo *sm* gift, present
re'gata *sf* regatta
reg'gente |red'dʒɛnte| *sm/f* regent
'**reggere** |'reddʒere| *vt* (*tenere*) to hold; (*sostenere*) to support, bear, hold up; (*portare*) to carry, bear; (*resistere*) to withstand; (*dirigere: impresa*) to manage, run; (*governare*) to rule, govern; (*LING*) to take, be followed by ♦ *vi* (*resistere*): **~ a** to stand up to, hold out against; (*sopportare*): **~ a** to stand; (*durare*) to last; (*fig: teoria etc*) to hold water; **~rsi** *vr* (*stare ritto*) to stand
'**reggia, ge** |'reddʒa| *sf* royal palace
reggi'calze |reddʒi'kaltse| *sm inv* suspender belt
reggi'mento |reddʒi'mento| *sm* (*MIL*) regiment
reggi'petto |reddʒi'pɛtto| *sm* bra
reggi'seno |reddʒi'seno| *sm* bra
re'gia, 'gie |re'dʒia| *sf* (*TV, CINEMA etc*) direction
re'gime |re'dʒime| *sm* (*POL*) regime; (*DIR: aureo, patrimoniale etc*) system; (*MED*) diet; (*TECN*) (engine) speed
re'gina |re'dʒina| *sf* queen
'**regio, a, gi, gie** |'redʒo| *ag* royal
regio'nale |redʒo'nale| *ag* regional ♦ *sm* local train (*stopping frequently*)
regi'one |re'dʒone| *sf* region; (*territorio*) region, district, area
re'gista, i, e |re'dʒista| *sm/f* (*TV, CINEMA etc*) director
regis'trare |redʒis'trare| *vt* (*AMM*) to register; (*COMM*) to enter; (*notare*) to note, take note of; (*canzone, conversazione, sog: strumento di misura*) to record; (*mettere a punto*) to adjust, regulate; (*bagagli*) to check in; **registra'tore** *sm* (*strumento*) recorder, register; (*magnetofono*) tape recorder; **registratore di cassa** cash register; **registrazi'one** *sf* recording; (*AMM*) registration; (*COMM*) entry; (*di bagagli*) check-in
re'gistro |re'dʒistro| *sm* (*libro, MUS, TECH*) register; ledger; logbook; (*DIR*) registry
re'gnare |reɲ'ɲare| *vi* to reign, rule
'**regno** |'reɲɲo| *sm* kingdom; (*periodo*) reign; (*fig*) realm; **il ~ animale/vegetale** the animal/

vegetable kingdom; **il R~ Unito** the United Kingdom
'**regola** *sf* rule; **a ~ d'arte** duly; perfectly; **in ~** in order
rego'labile *ag* adjustable
regola'mento *sm* (*complesso di norme*) regulations *pl*; (*di debito*) settlement; **~ di conti** (*fig*) settling of scores
rego'lare *ag* regular; (*in regola: domanda*) in order, lawful ♦ *vt* to regulate, control; (*apparecchio*) to adjust, regulate; (*questione, conto, debito*) to settle; **~rsi** *vr* (*moderarsi*): **~rsi nel bere/nello spendere** to control one's drinking/spending; (*comportarsi*) to behave, act; **regolarità** *sf inv* regularity
'**regolo** *sm* ruler; **~ calcolatore** slide rule
reinte'grare *vt* (*energie*) to recover; (*in una carica*) to reinstate
rela'tivo, a *ag* relative
relazi'one |relat'tsjone| *sf* (*fra cose, persone*) relation(ship); (*resoconto*) report, account; **~i** *sfpl* (*conoscenze*) connections
rele'gare *vt* to banish; (*fig*) to relegate
religi'one |reli'dʒone| *sf* religion; **religi'oso, a** *ag* religious ♦ *sm/f* monk/nun
re'liquia *sf* relic
re'litto *sm* wreck; (*fig*) down-and-out
re'mare *vi* to row
remini'scenze |reminiʃ'ʃɛntse| *sfpl* reminiscences
remissi'one *sf* remission
remis'sivo, a *ag* submissive, compliant
'**remo** *sm* oar
re'moto, a *ag* remote
'**rendere** *vt* (*ridare*) to return, give back; (: *saluto etc*) to return; (*produrre*) to yield, bring in; (*esprimere, tradurre*) to render; **~ qc possibile** to make sth possible; **~rsi utile** to make o.s. useful; **~rsi conto di qc** to realize sth
rendi'conto *sm* (*rapporto*) report, account; (*AMM, COMM*) statement of account
rendi'mento *sm* (*reddito*) yield; (*di manodopera, TECN*) efficiency; (*capacità di produrre*) output; (*di studenti*) performance
'**rendita** *sf* (*di individuo*) private o unearned income; (*COMM*) revenue; **~ annua** annuity
'**rene** *sm* kidney
'**reni** *sfpl* back *sg*
reni'tente *ag* reluctant, unwilling; **~ ai consigli di qn** unwilling to follow sb's advice; **essere ~ alla leva** (*MIL*) to fail to report for military service
'**renna** *sf* reindeer *inv*
'**Reno** *sm*: **il ~** the Rhine
'**reo, a** *sm/f* (*DIR*) offender
re'parto *sm* department, section; (*MIL*) detachment
repel'lente *ag* repulsive

repen'taglio [repen'taʎʎo] *sm*: **mettere a ~** to jeopardize, risk

repen'tino, a *ag* sudden, unexpected

repe'rire *vt* to find, trace

re'perto *sm* (ARCHEOLOGIA) find; (MED) report; (DIR: *anche*: ~ **giudiziario**) exhibit

reper'torio *sm* (TEATRO) repertory; (*elenco*) index, (alphabetical) list

'replica, che *sf* repetition; reply, answer; (*obiezione*) objection; (TEATRO, CINEMA) repeat performance; (*copia*) replica

repli'care *vt* (*ripetere*) to repeat; (*rispondere*) to answer, reply

repressi'one *sf* repression

re'presso, a *pp di* **reprimere**

re'primere *vt* to suppress, repress

re'pubblica, che *sf* republic; **repubbli'cano, a** *ag, sm/f* republican

repu'tare *vt* to consider, judge

reputazi'one [reputat'tsjone] *sf* reputation

'requie *sf*: **senza ~** unceasingly

requi'sire *vt* to requisition

requi'sito *sm* requirement

'resa *sf* (*l'arrendersi*) surrender; (*restituzione, rendimento*) return; **~ dei conti** rendering of accounts; (*fig*) day of reckoning

resi'dente *ag* resident; **resi'denza** *sf* residence; **residenzi'ale** *ag* residential

re'siduo, a *ag* residual, remaining ♦ *sm* remainder; (CHIM) residue

'resina *sf* resin

resis'tente *ag* (*che resiste*): **~ a** resistant to; (*forte*) strong; (*duraturo*) long-lasting, durable; **~ al caldo** heat-resistant; **resis'tenza** *sf* resistance; (*di persona: fisica*) stamina, endurance; (: *mentale*) endurance, resistance

re'sistere *vi* to resist; **~ a** (*assalto, tentazioni*) to resist; (*dolore, sog: pianta*) to withstand; (*non patir danno*) to be resistant to; **resis'tito, a** *pp di* **resistere**

'reso, a *pp di* **rendere**

reso'conto *sm* report, account

res'pingere [res'pindʒere] *vt* to drive back, repel; (*rifiutare*) to reject; (INS: *bocciare*) to fail; **res'pinto, a** *pp di* **respingere**

respi'rare *vi* to breathe; (*fig*) to get one's breath; to breathe again ♦ *vt* to breathe (in), inhale; **respira'tore** *sm* respirator; **respirazi'one** *sf* breathing; **respirazione artificiale** artificial respiration; **res'piro** *sm* breathing *no pl*; (*singolo atto*) breath; (*fig*) respite, rest; **mandare un respiro di sollievo** to give a sigh of relief

respon'sabile *ag* responsible ♦ *sm/f* person responsible; (*capo*) person in charge; **~ di** responsible for; (DIR) liable for; **responsabilità** *sf inv* responsibility; (*legale*) liability

res'ponso *sm* answer

'ressa *sf* crowd, throng

res'tare *vi* (*rimanere*) to remain, stay; (*avanzare*) to be left, remain; **~ orfano/cieco** to become o be left an orphan/become blind; **~ d'accordo** to agree; **non resta più niente** there's nothing left; **restano pochi giorni** there are only a few days left

restau'rare *vt* to restore; **restaurazi'one** *sf* (POL) restoration; **res'tauro** *sm* (*di edifici etc*) restoration

res'tio, a, 'tii, 'tie *ag*: **~ a** reluctant to

restitu'ire *vt* to return, give back; (*energie, forze*) to restore

'resto *sm* remainder, rest; (*denaro*) change; (MAT) remainder; **~i** *smpl* (*di cibo*) leftovers; (*di città*) remains; **del ~** moreover, besides; **~i mortali** (mortal) remains

res'tringere [res'trindʒere] *vt* to reduce; (*vestito*) to take in; (*stoffa*) to shrink; (*fig*) to restrict, limit; **~rsi** *vr* (*strada*) to narrow; (*stoffa*) to shrink; **restrizi'one** *sf* restriction

'rete *sf* net; (*fig*) trap, snare; (*di recinzione*) wire netting; (AUT, FERR, *di spionaggio etc*) network; **segnare una ~** (CALCIO) to score a goal; **~ del letto** (sprung) bed base

reti'cente [reti'tʃɛnte] *ag* reticent

retico'lato *sm* grid; (*rete*) wire netting; (*di filo spinato*) barbed wire (fence)

'retina *sf* (ANAT) retina

re'torica *sf* rhetoric

re'torico, a, ci, che *ag* rhetorical

retribu'ire *vt* to pay; **retribuzi'one** *sf* payment

'retro *sm inv* back ♦ *av* (*dietro*): **vedi ~** see over(leaf)

retro'cedere [retro'tʃedere] *vi* to withdraw ♦ *vt* (CALCIO) to relegate; (MIL) to degrade

re'trogrado, a *ag* (*fig*) reactionary, backward-looking

retro'marcia [retro'martʃa] *sf* (AUT) reverse; (: *dispositivo*) reverse gear

retro'scena [retroʃ'ʃena] *sm inv* (TEATRO) backstage; **i ~** (*fig*) the behind-the-scenes activities

retrospet'tivo, a *ag* retrospective

retrovi'sore *sm* (AUT) (rear-view) mirror

'retta *sf* (MAT) straight line; (*di convitto*) charge for bed and board; (*fig: ascolto*): **dar ~ a** to listen to, pay attention to

rettango'lare *ag* rectangular

ret'tangolo, a *ag* right-angled ♦ *sm* rectangle

ret'tifica, che *sf* rectification, correction

rettifi'care *vt* (*curva*) to straighten; (*fig*) to rectify, correct

'rettile *sm* reptile

retti'lineo, a *ag* rectilinear

retti'tudine *sf* rectitude, uprightness

'retto, a *pp di* **reggere** ♦ *ag* straight; (MAT):

angolo ~ right angle; (*onesto*) honest, upright; (*giusto, esatto*) correct, proper, right
ret'tore *sm* (*REL*) rector; (*di università*) ≈ chancellor
reuma'tismo *sm* rheumatism
reve'rendo, a *ag*: **il ~ padre Belli** the Reverend Father Belli
rever'sibile *ag* reversible
revisio'nare *vt* (*conti*) to audit; (*TECN*) to overhaul, service; (*DIR: processo*) to review
revisi'one *sf* auditing *no pl*; audit; servicing *no pl*; overhaul; review; revision
revi'sore *sm*: ~ **di conti/bozze** auditor/proofreader
'revoca *sf* revocation
revo'care *vt* to revoke
re'volver *sm inv* revolver
riabili'tare *vt* to rehabilitate
riagganci'are [riaggan'tʃare] *vt* (*TEL*) to hang up
rial'zare [rial'tsare] *vt* to raise, lift; (*alzare di più*) to heighten, raise; (*aumentare: prezzi*) to increase, raise ♦ *vi* (*prezzi*) to rise, increase; **ri'alzo** *sm* (*di prezzi*) increase, rise; (*sporgenza*) rise
rianimazi'one [rianimat'tsjone] *sf* (*MED*) resuscitation; **centro di ~** intensive care unit
riap'pendere *vt* to rehang; (*TEL*) to hang up
ria'prire *vt* to reopen, open again; ~**rsi** *vr* to reopen, open again
ri'armo *sm* (*MIL*) rearmament
rias'setto *sm* (*di stanza etc*) rearrangement; (*ordinamento*) reorganization
rias'sumere *vt* (*riprendere*) to resume; (*impiegare di nuovo*) to re-employ; (*sintetizzare*) to summarize; **rias'sunto, a** *pp di* **riassumere** ♦ *sm* summary
ria'vere *vt* to have again; (*avere indietro*) to get back; (*riacquistare*) to recover; ~**rsi** *vr* to recover
riba'dire *vt* (*fig*) to confirm
ri'balta *sf* flap; (*TEATRO: proscenio*) front of the stage; (*fig*) limelight; **luci della ~** footlights *pl*
ribal'tabile *ag* (*sedile*) tip-up
ribal'tare *vt, vi* (*anche:* ~**rsi**) to turn over, tip over
ribas'sare *vt* to lower, bring down ♦ *vi* to come down, fall; **ri'basso** *sm* reduction, fall
ri'battere *vt* to return, hit back; (*confutare*) to refute; ~ **che** to retort that
ribel'larsi *vr*: ~ (**a**) to rebel (against); **ri'belle** *ag* (*soldati*) rebel; (*ragazzo*) rebellious ♦ *sm/f* rebel; **ribelli'one** *sf* rebellion
'ribes *sm inv* currant; ~ **nero** blackcurrant; ~ **rosso** redcurrant
ribol'lire *vi* (*fermentare*) to ferment; (*fare bolle*) to bubble, boil; (*fig*) to seethe

ri'brezzo [ri'breddzo] *sm* disgust, loathing; **far ~ a** to disgust
ribut'tante *ag* disgusting, revolting
rica'dere *vi* to fall again; (*scendere a terra, fig: nel peccato etc*) to fall back; (*vestiti, capelli etc*) to hang (down); (*riversarsi: fatiche, colpe*): ~ **su** to fall on; **rica'duta** *sf* (*MED*) relapse
rical'care *vt* (*disegni*) to trace; (*fig*) to follow faithfully
rica'mare *vt* to embroider
ricambi'are *vt* to change again; (*contraccambiare*) to repay, return; **ri'cambio** *sm* exchange, return; (*FISIOL*) metabolism; **ricambi** *smpl* (*TECN*) spare parts
ri'camo *sm* embroidery
ricapito'lare *vt* to recapitulate, sum up
ricari'care *vt* (*arma, macchina fotografica*) to reload; (*pipa*) to refill; (*orologio*) to rewind; (*batteria*) to recharge
ricat'tare *vt* to blackmail; **ricatta'tore, 'trice** *sm/f* blackmailer; **ri'catto** *sm* blackmail
rica'vare *vt* (*estrarre*) to draw out, extract; (*ottenere*) to obtain, gain; **ri'cavo** *sm* proceeds *pl*
ric'chezza [rik'kettsa] *sf* wealth; (*fig*) richness; ~**e** *sfpl* (*beni*) wealth *sg*, riches
'riccio, a ['rittʃo] *ag* curly ♦ *sm* (*ZOOL*) hedgehog; (*: anche:* ~ **di mare**) sea urchin; **'ricciolo** *sm* curl; **ricci'uto, a** *ag* curly
'ricco, a, chi, che *ag* rich; (*persona, paese*) rich, wealthy ♦ *sm/f* rich man/woman; **i ~chi** the rich; ~ **di** full of; rich in
ri'cerca, che [ri'tʃerka] *sf* search; (*indagine*) investigation, inquiry; (*studio*): **la ~** research; **una ~** piece of research
ricer'care [ritʃer'kare] *vt* (*motivi, cause*) to look for, try to determine; (*successo, piacere*) to pursue; (*onore, gloria*) to seek; **ricer'cato, a** *ag* (*apprezzato*) much sought-after; (*affettato*) studied, affected ♦ *sm/f* (*POLIZIA*) wanted man/woman
ri'cetta [ri'tʃetta] *sf* (*MED*) prescription; (*CUC*) recipe
ricettazi'one [ritʃettat'tsjone] *sf* (*DIR*) receiving (stolen goods)
ri'cevere [ri'tʃevere] *vt* to receive; (*stipendio, lettera*) to get, receive; (*accogliere: ospite*) to welcome; (*vedere: cliente, rappresentante etc*) to see; **ricevi'mento** *sm* receiving *no pl*; (*festa*) reception; **ricevi'tore** *sm* (*TECN*) receiver; **ricevito'ria** *sf* lottery o pools office; **rice'vuta** *sf* receipt; **ricevuta fiscale** receipt for tax purposes; **ricezi'one** *sf* (*RADIO, TV*) reception
richia'mare [rikja'mare] *vt* (*chiamare indietro, ritelefonare*) to call back; (*ambasciatore, truppe*) to recall; (*rimproverare*) to reprimand; (*attirare*) to

attract, draw; **~rsi a** (*riferirsi a*) to refer to;
richi'amo *sm* call; recall; reprimand;
attraction
richi'edere [ri'kjɛdere] *vt* to ask again for;
(*chiedere indietro*): **~ qc** to ask for sth back;
(*chiedere: per sapere*) to ask; (: *per avere*) to
ask for; (AMM: *documenti*) to apply for;
(*esigere*) to need, require; **richi'esta** *sf*
(*domanda*) request; (AMM) application,
request; (*esigenza*) demand, request; **a
richiesta** on request; **richi'esto, a** *pp di*
richiedere
rici'clare [ritʃi'klare] *vt* to recycle
'ricino [ˈritʃino] *sm*: **olio di ~** castor oil
ricogni'zione [rikoɲɲi'tsjone] *sf* (MIL)
reconnaissance; (DIR) recognition,
acknowledgement
ricominci'are [rikomin'tʃare] *vt*, *vi* to start
again, begin again
ricom'pensa *sf* reward
ricompen'sare *vt* to reward
riconcili'are [rikontʃi'ljare] *vt* to reconcile;
~rsi *vr* to be reconciled; **riconciliazi'one** *sf*
reconciliation
ricono'scente [rikonoʃ'ʃɛnte] *ag* grateful;
ricono'scenza *sf* gratitude
rico'noscere [riko'noʃʃere] *vt* to recognize;
(DIR: *figlio, debito*) to acknowledge;
(*ammettere: errore*) to admit, acknowledge;
riconosci'mento *sm* recognition;
acknowledgement; (*identificazione*)
identification; **riconosci'uto, a** *pp di*
riconoscere
ricopi'are *vt* to copy
rico'prire *vt* (*coprire*) to cover; (*occupare:
carica*) to hold
ricor'dare *vt* to remember, recall; (*richiamare
alla memoria*): **~ qc a qn** to remind sb of sth;
~rsi *vr*: **~rsi (di)** to remember; **~rsi di qc/di
aver fatto** to remember sth/having done
ri'cordo *sm* memory; (*regalo*) keepsake,
souvenir; (*di viaggio*) souvenir; **~i** *smpl*
(*memorie*) memoirs
ricor'rente *ag* recurrent, recurring;
ricor'renza *sf* recurrence; (*festività*)
anniversary
ri'correre *vi* (*ripetersi*) to recur; **~ a**
(*rivolgersi*) to turn to; (: DIR) to appeal to;
(*servirsi di*) to have recourse to; **ri'corso, a**
pp di ricorrere ♦ *sm* recurrence; (DIR) appeal;
far ricorso a = ricorrere a
ricostitu'ente *ag* (MED): **cura ~** tonic
ricostru'ire *vt* (*casa*) to rebuild; (*fatti*) to
reconstruct; **ricostruzi'one** *sf* rebuilding *no
pl*; reconstruction
ri'cotta *sf* soft white unsalted cheese made
from sheep's milk
ricove'rare *vt* to give shelter to; **~ qn in
ospedale** to admit sb to hospital

ri'covero *sm* shelter, refuge; (MIL) shelter;
(MED) admission (to hospital)
ricre'are *vt* to recreate; (*fig: distrarre*) to
amuse
ricreazi'one [rikreat'tsjone] *sf* recreation,
entertainment; (INS) break
ri'credersi *vr* to change one's mind
ricupe'rare *vt* (*rientrare in possesso di*) to
recover, get back; (*tempo perduto*) to make
up for; (NAUT) to salvage; (: *naufraghi*) to
rescue; (*delinquente*) to rehabilitate; **~ lo
svantaggio** (SPORT) to close the gap
ridacchi'are [ridak'kjare] *vi* to snigger
ri'dare *vt* to return, give back
'ridere *vi* to laugh; (*deridere, beffare*): **~ di** to
laugh at, make fun of
ri'detto, a *pp di* ridire
ri'dicolo, a *ag* ridiculous, absurd
ridimensio'nare *vt* to reorganize; (*fig*) to
see in the right perspective
ri'dire *vt* to repeat; (*criticare*) to find fault
with; to object to; **trova sempre qualcosa da
~** he always manages to find fault
ridon'dante *ag* redundant
ri'dotto, a *pp di* ridurre ♦ *ag* (*biglietto*)
reduced; (*formato*) small
ri'durre *vt* (*anche* CHIM, MAT) to reduce;
(*prezzo, spese*) to cut, reduce; (*accorciare:
opera letteraria*) to abridge; (: RADIO, TV) to
adapt; **ridursi** *vr* (*diminuirsi*) to be reduced,
shrink; **ridursi a** to be reduced to; **ridursi pelle
e ossa** to be reduced to skin and bone;
ridut'tore *sm* (ELEC) adaptor; **riduzi'one** *sf*
reduction; abridgement; adaptation
riem'pire *vt* to fill (up); (*modulo*) to fill in *o*
out; **~rsi** *vr* to fill (up); **~ qc di** to fill sth (up)
with
rien'tranza [rien'trantsa] *sf* recess;
indentation
rien'trare *vi* (*entrare di nuovo*) to go (*o*
come) back in; (*tornare*) to return; (*fare una
rientranza*) to go in, curve inwards; to be
indented; (*riguardare*): **~ in** to be included
among, form part of; **ri'entro** *sm* (*ritorno*)
return; (*di astronave*) re-entry
riepilo'gare *vt* to summarize ♦ *vi* to
recapitulate
ri'fare *vt* to do again; (*ricostruire*) to make
again; (*nodo*) to tie again, do up again;
(*imitare*) to imitate, copy; **~rsi** *vr* (*risarcirsi*):
~rsi di to make up for; (*vendicarsi*): **~rsi di qc
su qn** to get one's own back on sb for sth;
(*riferirsi*): **~rsi a** to go back to; to follow; **~ il
letto** to make the bed; **~rsi una vita** to make
a new life for o.s.; **ri'fatto, a** *pp di* rifare
riferi'mento *sm* reference; **in** *o* **con ~ a** with
reference to
rife'rire *vt* (*riportare*) to report ♦ *vi* to do a
report; **~rsi** *vr*: **~rsi a** to refer to

rifi'nire vt to finish off, put the finishing touches to; **rifini'tura** sf finishing touch; **rifiniture** sfpl (di mobile, auto) finish sg

rifiu'tare vt to refuse; ~ **di fare** to refuse to do; **rifi'uto** sm refusal; **rifiuti** smpl (spazzatura) rubbish sg, refuse sg

riflessi'one sf (FISICA, meditazione) reflection; (il pensare) thought, reflection; (osservazione) remark

rifles'sivo, a ag (persona) thoughtful, reflective; (LING) reflexive

ri'flesso, a pp di **riflettere** ♦ sm (di luce, allo specchio) reflection; (FISIOL) reflex; **di o per** ~ indirectly

ri'flettere vt to reflect ♦ vi to think; **~rsi** vr to be reflected; ~ **su** to think over

riflet'tore sm reflector; (proiettore) floodlight; searchlight

ri'flusso sm flowing back; (della marea) ebb; **un'epoca di** ~ an era of nostalgia

ri'fondere vt to refund, repay

ri'forma sf reform; **la R~** (REL) the Reformation

rifor'mare vt to re-form; (REL, POL) to reform; (MIL: recluta) to declare unfit for service; (: soldato) to invalid out, discharge; **riforma'torio** sm (DIR) community home (BRIT), reformatory (US)

riforni'mento sm supplying, providing; restocking; **~i** smpl (provviste) supplies, provisions

rifor'nire vt (provvedere): ~ **di** to supply o provide with; (fornire di nuovo: casa etc) to restock

rifrazi'one [rifrat'tsjone] sf refraction

rifug'gire [rifud'dʒire] vi to escape again; (fig): ~ **da** to shun

rifugi'arsi [rifu'dʒarsi] vr to take refuge; **rifugi'ato, a** sm/f refugee

ri'fugio [ri'fudʒo] sm refuge, shelter; (in montagna) shelter; ~ **antiaereo** air-raid shelter

'riga, ghe sf line; (striscia) stripe; (di persone, cose) line, row; (regolo) ruler; (scrinatura) parting; **mettersi in** ~ to line up; **a ~ghe** (foglio) lined; (vestito) striped

ri'gagnolo [ri'gaɲɲolo] sm rivulet

ri'gare vt (foglio) to rule ♦ vi: ~ **diritto** (fig) to toe the line

rigatti'ere sm junk dealer

riget'tare [ridʒet'tare] vt (gettare indietro) to throw back; (fig: respingere) to reject; (vomitare) to bring o throw up; **ri'getto** sm (anche MED) rejection

rigidità [ridʒidi'ta] sf rigidity; stiffness; severity, rigours pl; strictness

'rigido, a ['ridʒido] ag rigid, stiff; (membra etc: indurite) stiff; (METEOR) harsh, severe; (fig) strict

rigi'rare [ridʒi'rare] vt to turn; **~rsi** vr to turn

round; (nel letto) to turn over; ~ **qc tra le mani** to turn sth over in one's hands; ~ **il discorso** to change the subject

'rigo, ghi sm line; (MUS) staff, stave

rigogli'oso, a [rigoʎ'ʎoso] ag (pianta) luxuriant; (fig: commercio, sviluppo) thriving

ri'gonfio, a ag swollen

ri'gore sm (METEOR) harshness, rigours pl; (fig) severity, strictness; (anche: calcio di ~) penalty; **di** ~ compulsory; **a rigor di termini** strictly speaking; **rigo'roso, a** ag (severo: persona, ordine) strict; (preciso) rigorous

rigover'nare vt to wash (up)

riguar'dare vt to look at again; (considerare) to regard, consider; (concernere) to regard, concern; **~rsi** vr (aver cura di sé) to look after o.s.

rigu'ardo sm (attenzione) care; (considerazione) regard, respect; ~ **a** concerning, with regard to; **non aver ~i nell'agire/nel parlare** to act/speak freely

rilasci'are [rilaʃ'ʃare] vt (rimettere in libertà) to release; (AMM: documenti) to issue; **ri'lascio** sm release; issue

rilas'sare vt to relax; **~rsi** vr to relax; (fig: disciplina) to become slack

rile'gare vt (libro) to bind; **rilega'tura** sf binding

ri'leggere [ri'leddʒere] vt to reread, read again; (rivedere) to read over

ri'lento: a ~ av slowly

rileva'mento sm (topografico, statistico) survey; (NAUT) bearing

rile'vante ag considerable; important

rile'vare vt (ricavare) to find; (notare) to notice; (mettere in evidenza) to point out; (venire a conoscere: notizia) to learn; (raccogliere: dati) to gather, collect; (TOPOGRAFIA) to survey; (MIL) to relieve; (COMM) to take over

rili'evo sm (ARTE, GEO) relief; (fig: rilevanza) importance; (TOPOGRAFIA) survey; **dar** ~ **a** o **mettere in** ~ **qc** (fig) to bring sth out, highlight sth

rilut'tante ag reluctant; **rilut'tanza** sf reluctance

'rima sf rhyme; (verso) verse

riman'dare vt to send again; (restituire, rinviare) to send back, return; (differire): ~ **qc (a)** to postpone sth o put sth off (till); (fare riferimento): ~ **qn a** to refer sb to; **essere rimandato** (INS) to have to repeat one's exams

ri'mando sm (rinvio) return; (dilazione) postponement; (riferimento) cross-reference

rima'nente ag remaining ♦ sm rest, remainder; **i ~i** (persone) the rest of them, the others; **rima'nenza** sf rest, remainder; **rimanenze** sfpl (COMM) unsold stock sg

rima'nere vi (restare) to remain, stay; (avanzare) to be left, remain; (restare stupito) to be amazed; (restare, mancare): **rimangono poche settimane a Pasqua** there are only a few weeks left till Easter; **rimane da vedere se** it remains to be seen whether; (diventare): **~ vedovo** to be left a widower; (trovarsi): **~ sorpreso** to be surprised

ri'mare vt, vi to rhyme

rimargi'nare [rimardʒi'nare] vt, vi (anche: ~rsi) to heal

ri'masto, a pp di **rimanere**

rima'sugli [rima'suʎʎi] smpl leftovers

rimbal'zare [rimbal'tsare] vi to bounce back, rebound; (proiettile) to ricochet; **rim'balzo** sm rebound; ricochet

rimbam'bito, a ag senile, in one's dotage

rimboc'care vt (coperta) to tuck in; (maniche, pantaloni) to turn o roll up

rimbom'bare vi to resound

rimbor'sare vt to pay back, repay; **rim'borso** sm repayment

rimedi'are vi: **~ a** to remedy ♦ vt (fam: procurarsi) to get o scrape together

ri'medio sm (medicina) medicine; (cura, fig) remedy, cure

rimesco'lare vt to mix well, stir well; (carte) to shuffle; **sentirsi ~ il sangue** (per paura) to feel one's blood run cold; (per rabbia) to feel one's blood boil

ri'messa sf (locale: per veicoli) garage; (: per aerei) hangar; (COMM: di merce) consignment; (: di denaro) remittance; (TENNIS) return; (CALCIO: anche: ~ in gioco) throw-in

ri'messo, a pp di **rimettere**

ri'mettere vt (mettere di nuovo) to put back; (indossare di nuovo): **~ qc** to put sth back on, put sth on again; (affidare) to entrust; (: decisione) to refer; (condonare) to remit; (COMM: merci) to deliver; (: denaro) to remit; (vomitare) to bring up; (perdere: anche: rimetterci) to lose; **~rsi al bello** (tempo) to clear up; **~rsi in salute** to get better, recover one's health

'rimmel ® sm inv mascara

rimoder'nare vt to modernize

rimon'tare vt (meccanismo) to reassemble; (: tenda) to put up again ♦ vi (salire di nuovo): **~ in** (macchina, treno) to get back into; (SPORT) to close the gap

rimorchi'are [rimor'kjare] vt to tow; (fig: ragazza) to pick up; **rimorchia'tore** sm (NAUT) tug(boat)

ri'morchio [ri'mɔrkjo] sm tow; (veicolo) trailer

ri'morso sm remorse

rimozi'one [rimot'tsjone] sf removal; (da un impiego) dismissal; (PSIC) repression

rim'pasto sm (POL) reshuffle

rimpatri'are vi to return home ♦ vt to repatriate; **rim'patrio** sm repatriation

rimpi'angere [rim'pjandʒere] vt to regret; (persona) to miss; **rimpi'anto, a** pp di **rimpiangere** ♦ sm regret

rimpiat'tino sm hide-and-seek

rimpiaz'zare [rimpjat'tsare] vt to replace

rimpiccio'lire [rimpittʃo'lire] vt to make smaller ♦ vi (anche: ~rsi) to become smaller

rimpin'zare [rimpin'tsare] vt: **~ di** to cram o stuff with

rimprove'rare vt to rebuke, reprimand; **rim'provero** sm rebuke, reprimand

rimugi'nare [rimudʒi'nare] vt (fig) to turn over in one's mind

rimunerazi'one [rimunerat'tsjone] sf remuneration; (premio) reward

rimu'overe vt to remove; (destituire) to dismiss

Rinasci'mento [rinaʃʃi'mento] sm: **il ~** the Renaissance

ri'nascita [ri'naʃʃita] sf rebirth, revival

rinca'rare vt to increase the price of ♦ vi to go up, become more expensive

rinca'sare vi to go home

rinchi'udere [rin'kjudere] vt to shut (o lock) up; **~rsi** vr: **~rsi in** to shut o.s. up in; **~rsi in se stesso** to withdraw into o.s.; **rinchi'uso, a** pp di **rinchiudere**

rin'correre vt to chase, run after; **rin'corsa** sf short run; **rin'corso, a** pp di **rincorrere**

rin'crescere [rin'kreʃʃere] vb impers: **mi rincresce che/di non poter fare** I'm sorry that/I can't do, I regret that/being unable to do; **rincresci'mento** sm regret; **rincresci'uto, a** pp di **rincrescere**

rincu'lare vi (arma) to recoil

rinfacci'are [rinfat'tʃare] vt (fig): **~ qc a qn** to throw sth in sb's face

rinfor'zare [rinfor'tsare] vt to reinforce, strengthen ♦ vi (anche: ~rsi) to grow stronger; **rin'forzo** sm: **mettere un rinforzo a** to strengthen; **di rinforzo** (asse, sbarra) strengthening; (esercito) supporting; (personale) extra, additional; **rinforzi** smpl (MIL) reinforcements

rinfran'care vt to encourage, reassure

rinfres'care vt (atmosfera, temperatura) to cool (down); (abito, pareti) to freshen up ♦ vi (tempo) to grow cooler; **~rsi** vr (ristorarsi) to refresh o.s.; (lavarsi) to freshen up; **rin'fresco, schi** sm (festa) party; **rinfreschi** smpl refreshments

rin'fusa sf: **alla ~** in confusion, higgledy-piggledy

ringhi'are [rin'gjare] vi to growl, snarl

ringhi'era [rin'gjera] sf railing; (delle scale) banister(s pl)

ringiova'nire [rindʒova'nire] vt (sog: vestito,

acconciatura etc): ~ **qn** to make sb look younger; (: *vacanze etc*) to rejuvenate ♦ *vi* (*anche*: ~**rsi**) to become (o look) younger

ringrazia'mento [ringrattsja'mento] *sm* thanks *pl*

ringrazi'are [ringrat'tsjare] *vt* to thank; ~ **qn di qc** to thank sb for sth

rinne'gare *vt* (*fede*) to renounce; (*figlio*) to disown, repudiate; **rinne'gato, a** *sm/f* renegade

rinnova'mento *sm* renewal; (*economico*) revival

rinno'vare *vt* to renew; (*ripetere*) to repeat, renew; **rin'novo** *sm* (*di contratto*) renewal; "chiuso per rinnovo dei locali" "closed for alterations"

rinoce'ronte [rinotʃe'ronte] *sm* rhinoceros

rino'mato, a *ag* renowned, celebrated

rinsal'dare *vt* to strengthen

rintoc'care *vi* (*campana*) to toll; (*orologio*) to strike

rintracci'are [rintrat'tʃare] *vt* to track down

rintro'nare *vi* to boom, roar ♦ *vt* (*assordare*) to deafen; (*stordire*) to stun

ri'nuncia [ri'nuntʃa] *etc* = **rinunzia** *etc*

ri'nunzia [ri'nuntsja] *sf* renunciation

rinunzi'are [rinun'tsjare] *vi*: ~ **a** to give up, renounce

rinve'nire *vt* to find, recover; (*scoprire*) to discover, find out ♦ *vi* (*riprendere i sensi*) to come round; (*fiori*) to revive

rinvi'are *vt* (*rimandare indietro*) to send back, return; (*differire*): ~ **qc (a)** to postpone sth o put sth off (till); to adjourn sth (till); (*fare un rimando*): ~ **qn a** to refer sb to

rinvigo'rire *vt* to strengthen

rin'vio, 'vii *sm* (*rimando*) return; (*differimento*) postponement; (: *di seduta*) adjournment; (*in un testo*) cross-reference

ri'one *sm* district, quarter

riordi'nare *vt* (*rimettere in ordine*) to tidy; (*riorganizzare*) to reorganize

riorganiz'zare [riorganid'dzare] *vt* to reorganize

ripa'gare *vt* to repay

ripa'rare *vt* (*proteggere*) to protect, defend; (*correggere: male, torto*) to make up for; (: *errore*) to put right; (*aggiustare*) to repair ♦ *vi* (*mettere rimedio*): ~ **a** to make up for; ~**rsi** *vr* (*rifugiarsi*) to take refuge o shelter; **riparazi'one** *sf* (*di un torto*) reparation; (*di guasto, scarpe*) repairing *no pl*; repair; (*risarcimento*) compensation

ri'paro *sm* (*protezione*) shelter, protection; (*rimedio*) remedy

ripar'tire *vt* (*dividere*) to divide up; (*distribuire*) to share out ♦ *vi* to set off again; to leave again

ripas'sare *vi* to come (o go) back ♦ *vt* (*scritto, lezione*) to go over (again); **ri'passo** *sm* revision (*BRIT*), review (*US*)

ripen'sare *vi* to think; (*cambiare pensiero*) to change one's mind; (*tornare col pensiero*): ~ **a** to recall

ripercu'otersi *vr*: ~ **su** (*fig*) to have repercussions on

ripercussi'one *sf* (*fig*): **avere una ~** o **delle ~i su** to have repercussions on

ripes'care *vt* (*pesce*) to catch again; (*persona, cosa*) to fish out; (*fig: ritrovare*) to dig out

ri'petere *vt* to repeat; (*ripassare*) to go over; **ripetizi'one** *sf* repetition; (*di lezione*) revision; **ripetizioni** *sfpl* (*INS*) private tutoring o coaching *sg*

ripi'ano *sm* (*di mobile*) shelf

ri'picca *sf*: **per ~** out of spite

'ripido, a *ag* steep

ripie'gare *vt* to refold; (*piegare più volte*) to fold (up) ♦ *vi* (*MIL*) to retreat, fall back; (*fig: accontentarsi*): ~ **su** to make do with; ~**rsi** *vr* to bend; **ripi'ego, ghi** *sm* expedient

ripi'eno, a *ag* full; (*CUC*) stuffed; (: *panino*) filled ♦ *sm* (*CUC*) stuffing

ri'porre *vt* (*porre al suo posto*) to put back, replace; (*mettere via*) to put away; (*fiducia, speranza*): ~ **qc in qn** to place o put sth in sb

ripor'tare *vt* (*portare indietro*) to bring (o take) back; (*riferire*) to report; (*citare*) to quote; (*vittoria*) to gain; (*successo*) to have; (*MAT*) to carry; ~**rsi a** (*anche fig*) to go back to; (*riferirsi a*) to refer to; ~ **danni** to suffer damage

ripo'sare *vt, vi* to rest; ~**rsi** *vr* to rest; **ri'poso** *sm* rest; (*MIL*): **riposo!** at ease!; **a riposo** (*in pensione*) retired; **giorno di riposo** day off

ripos'tiglio [ripos'tiʎʎo] *sm* lumber-room

ri'posto, a *pp di* **riporre**

ri'prendere *vt* (*prigioniero, fortezza*) to recapture; (*prendere indietro*) to take back; (*ricominciare: lavoro*) to resume; (*andare a prendere*) to fetch, come back for; (*riassumere: impiegati*) to take on again, re-employ; (*rimproverare*) to tell off; (*restringere: abito*) to take in; (*CINEMA*) to shoot; ~**rsi** *vr* to recover; (*correggersi*) to correct o.s.; **ri'presa** *sf* recapture; resumption; (*economica, da malattia, emozione*) recovery; (*AUT*) acceleration *no pl*; (*TEATRO, CINEMA*) rerun; (*CINEMA: presa*) shooting *no pl*; shot; (*SPORT*) second half; (: *PUGILATO*) round; **a più riprese** on several occasions, several times; **ripreso, a** *pp di* **riprendere**

ripristi'nare *vt* to restore

ripro'durre *vt* to reproduce; **riprodursi** *vr* (*BIOL*) to reproduce; (*riformarsi*) to form again; **riproduzi'one** *sf* reproduction;

riproduzione vietata all rights reserved

ripudi'are vt to repudiate, disown

ripu'gnante [ripuɲ'ɲante] ag disgusting, repulsive

ripu'gnare [ripuɲ'ɲare] vi: ~ **a qn** to repel o disgust sb

ripu'lire vt to clean up; (sog: ladri) to clean out; (perfezionare) to polish, refine

ri'quadro sm square; (ARCHIT) panel

ri'saia sf paddy field

risa'lire vi (ritornare in su) to go back up; ~ **a** (ritornare con la mente) to go back to; (datare da) to date back to, go back to

risal'tare vi (fig: distinguersi) to stand out; (ARCHIT) to project, jut out; **ri'salto** sm prominence; (sporgenza) projection; **mettere** o **porre in risalto qc** to make sth stand out

risa'nare vt (guarire) to heal, cure; (palude) to reclaim; (economia) to improve; (bilancio) to reorganize

risa'puto, a ag: **è ~ che ...** everyone knows that ..., it is common knowledge that ...

risarci'mento [risartʃi'mento] sm: ~ **(di)** compensation (for)

risar'cire [risar'tʃire] vt (cose) to pay compensation for; (persona): ~ **qn di qc** to compensate sb for sth

ri'sata sf laugh

riscalda'mento sm heating; ~ **centrale** central heating

riscal'dare vt (scaldare) to heat; (: mani, persona) to warm; (minestra) to reheat; ~**rsi** vr to warm up

riscat'tare vt (prigioniero) to ransom, pay a ransom for; (DIR) to redeem; ~**rsi** vr (da disonore) to redeem o.s.; **ris'catto** sm ransom; redemption

rischia'rare [riskja'rare] vt (illuminare) to light up; (colore) to make lighter; ~**rsi** vr (tempo) to clear up; (cielo) to clear; (fig: volto) to brighten up; ~**rsi la voce** to clear one's throat

rischi'are [ris'kjare] vt to risk ♦ vi: ~ **di fare qc** to risk o run the risk of doing sth

'rischio ['riskjo] sm risk; **rischi'oso, a** ag risky, dangerous

riscia'cquare [riʃʃa'kware] vt to rinse

riscon'trare vt (rilevare) to find; **ris'contro** sm confirmation; (lettera di risposta) reply

ris'cossa sf (riconquista) recovery, reconquest; vedi anche **riscosso**

riscossi'one sf collection

ris'cosso, a pp di **riscuotere**

ris'cuotere vt (ritirare: somma) to collect; (: stipendio) to draw, collect; (assegno) to cash; (fig: successo etc) to win, earn; ~**rsi** vr: ~**rsi (da)** to shake o.s. (out of), rouse o.s. (from)

risenti'mento sm resentment

risen'tire vt to hear again; (provare) to feel ♦ vi: ~ **di** to feel (o show) the effects of; ~**rsi** vr: ~**rsi di** o **per** to take offence at, resent; **risen'tito, a** ag resentful

ri'serbo sm reserve

ri'serva sf reserve; (di caccia, pesca) preserve; (restrizione, di indigeni) reservation; **di ~** (provviste etc) in reserve

riser'vare vt (tenere in serbo) to keep, put aside; (prenotare) to book, reserve; ~**rsi** vr: ~**rsi di fare qc** to intend to do sth; **riser-va'tezza** sf reserve; **riser'vato, a** ag (prenotato, fig: persona) reserved; (confidenziale) confidential

risi'edere vi: ~ **a** o **in** to reside in

'risma sf (di carta) ream; (fig) kind, sort

'riso (pl(f) ~**a**: il ridere) sm: **il ~ laughter**; (pianta) rice ♦ pp di **ridere**

riso'lino sm snigger

ri'solto, a pp di **risolvere**

risolu'tezza [risolu'tettsa] sf determination

riso'luto, a ag determined, resolute

risoluzi'one [risolut'tsjone] sf solving no pl; (MAT) solution; (decisione, di immagine) resolution

ri'solvere vt (difficoltà, controversia) to resolve; (problema) to solve; (decidere): ~ **di fare** to resolve to do; ~**rsi** vr (decidersi): ~**rsi a fare** to make up one's mind to do; (andare a finire) to end up, turn out; ~**rsi in nulla** to come to nothing

riso'nanza [riso'nantsa] sf resonance; **aver vasta ~** (fig: fatto etc) to be known far and wide

riso'nare vt, vi = **risuonare**

ri'sorgere [ri'sordʒere] vi to rise again; **risorgi'mento** sm revival; **il Risorgimento** (STORIA) the Risorgimento

ri'sorsa sf expedient, resort; ~**e** sfpl (naturali, finanziarie etc) resources; **persona piena di ~e** resourceful person

ri'sorto, a pp di **risorgere**

ri'sotto sm (CUC) risotto

risparmi'are vt to save; (non uccidere) to spare ♦ vi to save; ~ **qc a qn** to spare sb sth

ris'parmio sm saving no pl; (denaro) savings pl

rispec'chiare [rispek'kjare] vt to reflect

rispet'tabile ag respectable

rispet'tare vt to respect; **farsi ~** to command respect

rispet'tivo, a ag respective

ris'petto sm respect; ~**i** smpl (saluti) respects, regards; ~ **a** (in paragone a) compared to; (in relazione a) as regards, as for; **rispet'toso, a** ag respectful

ris'plendere vi to shine

ris'pondere vi to answer, reply; (freni) to respond; ~ **a** (domanda) to answer, reply to;

(*persona*) to answer; (*invito*) to reply to; (*provocazione, sog: veicolo, apparecchio*) to respond to; (*corrispondere a*) to correspond to; (: *speranze, bisogno*) to answer; ~ **di** to answer for; **ris'posta** *sf* answer, reply; **in risposta a** in reply to; **risposto, a** *pp di* **rispondere**

'**rissa** *sf* brawl

ristabi'lire *vt* to re-establish, restore; (*persona: sog: riposo etc*) to restore to health; ~**rsi** *vr* to recover

rista'gnare [ristaɲ'ɲare] *vi* (*acqua*) to become stagnant; (*sangue*) to cease flowing; (*fig: industria*) to stagnate; **ris'tagno** *sm* stagnation

ris'tampa *sf* reprinting *no pl*; reprint

risto'rante *sm* restaurant

risto'rarsi *vr* to have something to eat and drink; (*riposarsi*) to rest, have a rest; **ris'toro** *sm* (*bevanda, cibo*) refreshment; **servizio di ristoro** (FERR) refreshments *pl*

ristret'tezza [ristret'tettsa] *sf* (*strettezza*) narrowness; (*fig: scarsezza*) scarcity, lack; (: *meschinità*) meanness; ~**e** *sfpl* (*povertà*) financial straits

ris'tretto, a *pp di* **restringere** ♦ *ag* (*racchiuso*) enclosed, hemmed in; (*angusto*) narrow; (*limitato*): ~ (**a**) restricted o limited (to); (CUC: *brodo*) thick; (: *caffè*) extra strong

risucchi'are [risuk'kjare] *vt* to suck in

risul'tare *vi* (*dimostrarsi*) to prove (to be), turn out (to be); (*riuscire*): ~ **vincitore** to emerge as the winner; ~ **da** (*provenire*) to result from, be the result of; **mi risulta che ...** I understand that ...; **non mi risulta** not as far as I know; **risul'tato** *sm* result

risuo'nare *vi* (*rimbombare*) to resound

risurrezi'one [risurret'tsjone] *sf* (REL) resurrection

risusci'tare [risuʃʃi'tare] *vt* to resuscitate, restore to life; (*fig*) to revive, bring back ♦ *vi* to rise (from the dead)

ris'veglio [riz'veʎʎo] *sm* waking up; (*fig*) revival

ris'volto *sm* (*di giacca*) lapel; (*di pantaloni*) turn-up; (*di manica*) cuff; (*di tasca*) flap; (*di libro*) inside flap; (*fig*) implication

ritagli'are [ritaʎ'ʎare] *vt* (*tagliar via*) to cut out; **ri'taglio** *sm* (*di giornale*) cutting, clipping; (*di stoffa etc*) scrap; **nei ritagli di tempo** in one's spare time

ritar'dare *vi* (*persona, treno*) to be late; (*orologio*) to be slow ♦ *vt* (*rallentare*) to slow down; (*impedire*) to delay, hold up; (*differire*) to postpone, delay; **ritarda'tario, a** *sm/f* latecomer

ri'tardo *sm* delay; (*di persona aspettata*) lateness *no pl*; (*fig: mentale*) backwardness; **in ~** late

ri'tegno [ri'teɲɲo] *sm* restraint

rite'nere *vt* (*trattenere*) to hold back; (: *somma*) to deduct; (*giudicare*) to consider, believe; **rite'nuta** *sf* (*sul salario*) deduction

riti'rare *vt* to withdraw; (POL: *richiamare*) to recall; (*andare a prendere: pacco etc*) to collect, pick up; ~**rsi** *vr* to withdraw; (*da un'attività*) to retire; (*stoffa*) to shrink; (*marea*) to recede; **riti'rata** *sf* (MIL) retreat; (*latrina*) lavatory; **ri'tiro** *sm* withdrawal; recall; collection; (*luogo appartato*) retreat

'**ritmo** *sm* rhythm; (*fig*) rate; (: *della vita*) pace, tempo

'**rito** *sm* rite; **di ~** usual, customary

ritoc'care *vt* (*disegno, fotografia*) to touch up; (*testo*) to alter; **ri'tocco, chi** *sm* touching up *no pl*; alteration

ritor'nare *vi* to return, go (o come) back; (*ripresentarsi*) to recur; (*ridiventare*): ~ **ricco** to become rich again ♦ *vt* (*restituire*) to return, give back

ritor'nello *sm* refrain

ri'torno *sm* return; **essere di ~** to be back; **avere un ~ di fiamma** (AUT) to backfire; (*fig: persona*) to be back in love again

ritorsi'one *sf* retaliation

ri'trarre *vt* (*trarre indietro, via*) to withdraw; (*distogliere: sguardo*) to turn away; (*rappresentare*) to portray, depict; (*ricavare*) to get, obtain

ritrat'tare *vt* (*disdire*) to retract, take back; (*trattare nuovamente*) to deal with again

ri'tratto, a *pp di* **ritrarre** ♦ *sm* portrait

ri'troso, a *ag* (*restio*): ~ (**a**) reluctant (to); (*schivo*) shy; **andare a ~** to go backwards

ritro'vare *vt* to find; (*salute*) to regain; (*persona*) to find; to meet again; ~**rsi** *vr* (*essere, capitare*) to find o.s.; (*raccapezzarsi*) to find one's way; (*con senso reciproco*) to meet (again); **ri'trovo** *sm* meeting place; **ritrovo notturno** night club

'**ritto, a** *ag* (*in piedi*) standing, on one's feet; (*levato in alto*) erect, raised; (: *capelli*) standing on end; (*posto verticalmente*) upright

ritu'ale *ag, sm* ritual

riuni'one *sf* (*adunanza*) meeting; (*riconciliazione*) reunion

riu'nire *vt* (*ricongiungere*) to join (together); (*riconciliare*) to reunite, bring together (again); ~**rsi** *vr* (*adunarsi*) to meet; (*tornare insieme*) to be reunited

riu'scire [rjuʃ'ʃire] *vi* (*uscire di nuovo*) to go out again, go back out; (*aver esito: fatti, azioni*) to go, turn out; (*aver successo*) to succeed, be successful; (*essere, apparire*) to be, prove; (*raggiungere il fine*) to manage, succeed; ~ **a fare qc** to manage to do o succeed in doing o be able to do sth;

riu'scita sf (esito) result, outcome; (buon esito) success

'riva sf (di fiume) bank; (di lago, mare) shore

ri'vale sm/f rival; **rivalità** sf rivalry

ri'valsa sf (rivincita) revenge

rivalu'tare vt (ECON) to revalue

rivan'gare vt (ricordi etc) to dig up (again)

rive'dere vt to see again; (ripassare) to revise; (verificare) to check

rive'lare vt to reveal; (divulgare) to reveal, disclose; (dare indizio) to reveal, show; **~rsi** vr (manifestarsi) to be revealed; **~rsi onesto** etc to prove to be honest etc; **rivela'tore** sm (TECN) detector; (FOT) developer; **rivelazi'one** sf revelation

rivendi'care vt to claim, demand

ri'vendita sf (bottega) retailer's (shop)

rivendi'tore, 'trice sm/f retailer; **~ autorizzato** (COMM) authorized dealer

ri'verbero sm (di luce, calore) reflection; (di suono) reverberation

rive'renza [rive'rɛntsa] sf reverence; (inchino) bow; curtsey

rive'rire vt (rispettare) to revere; (salutare) to pay one's respects to

river'sare vt (anche fig) to pour; **~rsi** vr (fig: persone) to pour out

rivesti'mento sm covering; coating

rives'tire vt to dress again; (ricoprire) to cover; to coat; (fig: carica) to hold; **~rsi** vr to get dressed again; to change (one's clothes)

rivi'era sf coast; **la ~ ligure** the Italian Riviera

ri'vincita [ri'vintʃita] sf (SPORT) return match; (fig) revenge

rivis'suto, a pp di rivivere

ri'vista sf review; (periodico) magazine, review; (TEATRO) revue; variety show

ri'vivere vi (riacquistare forza) to come alive again; (tornare in uso) to be revived ♦ vt to relive

ri'volgere [ri'vɔldʒere] vt (attenzione, sguardo) to turn, direct; (parole) to address; **~rsi** vr to turn round; (fig: dirigersi per informazioni): **~rsi a** to go and see, go and speak to; (: ufficio) to enquire at

ri'volta sf revolt, rebellion

rivol'tare vt to turn over; (con l'interno all'esterno) to turn inside out; (disgustare: stomaco) to upset, turn; **~rsi** vr (ribellarsi): **~rsi (a)** to rebel (against)

rivol'tella sf revolver

ri'volto, a pp di rivolgere

rivoluzio'nare [rivoluttsjo'nare] vt to revolutionize

rivoluzio'nario, a [rivoluttsjo'narjo] ag, sm/f revolutionary

rivoluzi'one [rivolut'tsjone] sf revolution

riz'zare [rit'tsare] vt to raise, erect; **~rsi** vr to stand up; (capelli) to stand on end

'roba sf stuff, things pl; (possessi, beni) belongings pl, things pl, possessions pl; **~ da mangiare** things pl to eat, food; **~ da matti** sheer madness o lunacy

'robot sm inv robot

ro'busto, a ag robust, sturdy; (solido: catena) strong

'rocca, che sf fortress

rocca'forte sf stronghold

roc'chetto [rok'ketto] sm reel, spool

'roccia, ce ['rɔttʃa] sf rock; **fare ~** (SPORT) to go rock climbing; **roc'cioso, a** ag rocky

ro'daggio [ro'daddʒo] sm running (BRIT) o breaking (US) in; **in ~** running (BRIT) o breaking (US) in

'Rodano sm: **il ~** the Rhone

'rodere vt to gnaw (at); (distruggere poco a poco) to eat into

rodi'tore sm (ZOOL) rodent

rodo'dendro sm rhododendron

'rogna ['rɔɲɲa] sf (MED) scabies sg; (fig) bother, nuisance

ro'gnone [roɲ'ɲone] sm (CUC) kidney

'rogo, ghi sm (per cadaveri) (funeral) pyre; (supplizio): **il ~** the stake

rol'lio sm roll(ing)

'Roma sf Rome

Roma'nia sf: **la ~** Romania

ro'manico, a, ci, che ag Romanesque

ro'mano, a ag, sm/f Roman

romanti'cismo [romanti'tʃizmo] sm romanticism

ro'mantico, a, ci, che ag romantic

ro'manza [ro'mandza] sf (MUS, LETTERATURA) romance

roman'zesco, a, schi, sche [roman-'dzesko] ag (stile, personaggi) fictional; (fig) storybook cpd

romanzi'ere [roman'dzjere] sm novelist

ro'manzo, a [ro'mandzo] ag (LING) romance cpd ♦ sm novel; **~ d'appendice** serial (story)

rom'bare vi to rumble, thunder, roar

'rombo sm rumble, thunder, roar; (MAT) rhombus; (ZOOL) turbot; brill

ro'meno, a ag, sm/f, sm = **rumeno, a**

'rompere vt to break; (fidanzamento) to break off ♦ vi to break; **~rsi** vr to break; **mi rompe le scatole** (fam) he (o she) is a pain in the neck; **~rsi un braccio** to break an arm; **rompi'capo** sm worry, headache; (indovinello) puzzle; (in enigmistica) brainteaser; **rompighi'accio** sm (NAUT) icebreaker; **rompis'catole** (fam) sm/f inv pest, pain in the neck

'ronda sf (MIL) rounds pl, patrol

ron'della sf (TECN) washer

'rondine sf (ZOOL) swallow

ron'done sm (ZOOL) swift

ron'zare [ron'dzare] vi to buzz, hum

ron'zino [ron'dzino] *sm* (*peg: cavallo*) nag
ron'zio [ron'dzio] *sm* buzzing
'rosa *sf* rose ♦ *ag inv, sm* pink; **ro'saio** *sm*
(*pianta*) rosebush, rose tree; (*giardino*) rose
garden; **ro'sato, a** *ag* pink, rosy ♦ *sm* (*vino*)
rosé (wine); **ro'seo, a** *ag* (*anche fig*) rosy
rosicchi'are [rosik'kjare] *vt* to gnaw (at);
(*mangiucchiare*) to nibble (at)
rosma'rino *sm* rosemary
'roso, a *pp di* **rodere**
roso'lare *vt* (*CUC*) to brown
roso'lia *sf* (*MED*) German measles *sg*, rubella
ro'sone *sm* rosette; (*vetrata*) rose window
'rospo *sm* (*ZOOL*) toad
ros'setto *sm* (*per labbra*) lipstick
'rosso, a *ag, sm, sm/f* red; **il mar R~** the Red
Sea; **~ d'uovo** egg yolk; **ros'sore** *sm* flush,
blush
rosticce'ria [rostittʃe'ria] *sf* shop selling roast
meat and other cooked food
ro'tabile *ag* (*percorribile*): **strada ~** roadway;
(*FERR*): **materiale ~** rolling stock
ro'taia *sf* rut, track; (*FERR*) rail
ro'tare *vt, vi* to rotate; **rotazi'one** *sf* rotation
rote'are *vt, vi* to whirl; **~ gli occhi** to roll
one's eyes
ro'tella *sf* small wheel; (*di mobile*) castor
roto'lare *vt, vi* to roll; **~rsi** *vr* to roll (about)
'rotolo *sm* roll; **andare a ~i** (*fig*) to go to rack
and ruin
ro'tonda *sf* rotunda
ro'tondo, a *ag* round
'rotta *sf* (*AER, NAUT*) course, route; (*MIL*) rout;
a ~ di collo at breakneck speed; **essere in
~ con qn** to be on bad terms with sb
rot'tame *sm* fragment, scrap, broken bit; **~i**
smpl (*di nave, aereo etc*) wreckage *sg*
'rotto, a *pp di* **rompere** ♦ *ag* broken;
(*calzoni*) torn, split; **per il ~ della cuffia** by the
skin of one's teeth
rot'tura *sf* breaking *no pl*; break; breaking
off; (*MED*) fracture, break
rou'lotte [ru'lɔt] *sf* caravan
ro'vente *ag* red-hot
'rovere *sm* oak
rovesci'are [roveʃ'ʃare] *vt* (*versare in giù*) to
pour; (: *accidentalmente*) to spill; (*capovolgere*) to turn upside down; (*gettare a terra*)
to knock down; (: *fig: governo*) to overthrow;
(*piegare all'indietro: testa*) to throw back; **~rsi**
vr (*sedia, macchina*) to overturn; (*barca*) to
capsize; (*liquido*) to spill; (*fig: situazione*) to
be reversed
ro'vescio, sci [ro'veʃʃo] *sm* other side,
wrong side; (*della mano*) back; (*di moneta*)
reverse; (*pioggia*) sudden downpour; (*fig*)
setback; (*MAGLIA: anche: punto ~*) purl
(stitch); (*TENNIS*) backhand (stroke); **a ~**
upside-down; inside-out; **capire qc a ~** to

misunderstand sth
ro'vina *sf* ruin; **andare in ~** (*andare a pezzi*)
to collapse; (*fig*) to go to rack and ruin
rovi'nare *vi* to collapse, fall down ♦ *vt*
(*danneggiare, fig*) to ruin; **rovi'noso, a** *ag*
disastrous; damaging; violent
rovis'tare *vt* (*casa*) to ransack; (*tasche*) to
rummage in (o through)
'rovo *sm* (*BOT*) blackberry bush, bramble bush
'rozzo, a [ˈroddzo] *ag* rough, coarse
'ruba *sf*: **andare a ~** to sell like hot cakes
ru'bare *vt* to steal; **~ qc a qn** to steal sth from
sb
rubi'netto *sm* tap, faucet (*US*)
ru'bino *sm* ruby
ru'brica, che *sf* (*STAMPA*) column;
(*quadernetto*) index book; address book
'rude *ag* tough, rough
'rudere *sm* (*rovina*) ruins *pl*
rudimen'tale *ag* rudimentary, basic
rudi'menti *smpl* rudiments; basic principles;
basic knowledge *sg*
ruffi'ano *sm* pimp
'ruga, ghe *sf* wrinkle
'ruggine [ˈruddʒine] *sf* rust
rug'gire [rud'dʒire] *vi* to roar
rugi'ada [ru'dʒada] *sf* dew
ru'goso, a *ag* wrinkled
rul'lare *vi* (*tamburo, nave*) to roll; (*aereo*) to
taxi
rul'lino *sm* (*FOT*) spool; (: *pellicola*) film
'rullo *sm* (*di tamburi*) roll; (*arnese cilindrico,
TIP*) roller; **~ compressore** steam roller; **~ di
pellicola** roll of film
rum *sm* rum
ru'meno, a *ag, sm/f, sm* Romanian
rumi'nare *vt* (*ZOOL*) to ruminate
ru'more *sm*: **un ~** a noise, a sound; (*fig*) a
rumour; **il ~** noise; **rumo'roso, a** *ag* noisy
ru'olo *sm* (*TEATRO, fig*) role, part; (*elenco*)
register, list; **di ~** permanent, on the
permanent staff
ru'ota *sf* wheel; **~ anteriore/posteriore** front/
back wheel; **~ di scorta** spare wheel
ruo'tare *vt, vi* = **rotare**
'rupe *sf* cliff
ru'rale *ag* rural, country *cpd*
ru'scello [ruʃ'ʃɛllo] *sm* stream
'ruspa *sf* excavator
rus'sare *vi* to snore
'Russia *sf*: **la ~** Russia; **'russo, a** *ag, sm/f, sm*
Russian
'rustico, a, ci, che *ag* rustic; (*fig*) rough,
unrefined
rut'tare *vi* to belch; **'rutto** *sm* belch
'ruvido, a *ag* rough, coarse
ruzzo'lare [ruttso'lare] *vi* to tumble down;
ruzzo'loni *av*: **cadere ruzzoloni** to tumble
down

S, s

S. *abbr* (= *sud*) S

sa *vb vedi* **sapere**

'sabato *sm* Saturday; **di** *o* **il ~ on** Saturdays

'sabbia *sf* sand; **~e mobili** quicksand(s); **sabbi'oso, a** *ag* sandy

sabo'taggio [sabo'taddʒo] *sm* sabotage

sabo'tare *vt* to sabotage

'sacca, che *sf* bag; (*bisaccia*) haversack; **~ da viaggio** travelling bag

sacca'rina *sf* saccharin(e)

sac'cente [sat'tʃɛnte] *sm/f* know-all (*BRIT*), know-it-all (*US*)

saccheggi'are [sakked'dʒare] *vt* to sack, plunder; **sac'cheggio** *sm* sack(ing)

sac'chetto [sak'ketto] *sm* (small) bag; (small) sack

'sacco, chi *sm* bag; (*per carbone etc*) sack; (*ANAT, BIOL*) sac; (*tela*) sacking; (*saccheggio*) sack(ing); (*fig: grande quantità*): **un ~ di** lots of, heaps of; **~ a pelo** sleeping bag; **~ per i rifiuti** bin bag

sacer'dote [satʃer'dɔte] *sm* priest; **sacer'dozio** *sm* priesthood

sacra'mento *sm* sacrament

sacrifi'care *vt* to sacrifice; **~rsi** *vr* to sacrifice o.s.; (*privarsi di qc*) to make sacrifices

sacri'ficio [sakri'fitʃo] *sm* sacrifice

sacri'legio [sakri'ledʒo] *sm* sacrilege

'sacro, a *ag* sacred

'sadico, a, ci, che *ag* sadistic ♦ *sm/f* sadist

sa'etta *sf* arrow; (*fulmine: anche fig*) thunderbolt; flash of lightning

sa'fari *sm inv* safari

sa'gace [sa'gatʃe] *ag* shrewd, sagacious

sag'gezza [sad'dʒettsa] *sf* wisdom

saggi'are [sad'dʒare] *vt* (*metalli*) to assay; (*fig*) to test

'saggio, a, gi, ge ['saddʒo] *ag* wise ♦ *sm* (*persona*) sage; (*esperimento*) test; (*fig: prova*) proof; (*campione*) sample; (*scritto*) essay

Sagit'tario [sadʒit'tarjo] *sm* Sagittarius

'sagoma *sf* (*profilo*) outline, profile; (*forma*) form, shape; (*TECN*) template; (*bersaglio*) target; (*fig: persona*) character

'sagra *sf* festival

sagres'tano *sm* sacristan; sexton

sagres'tia *sf* sacristy

Sa'hara [sa'ara] *sm*: **il (deserto del) ~** the Sahara (Desert)

'sai *vb vedi* **sapere**

'sala *sf* hall; (*stanza*) room; **~ d'aspetto** waiting room; **~ da ballo** ballroom; **~ per concerti** concert hall; **~ da gioco** gaming

room; **~ operatoria** operating theatre; **~ da pranzo** dining room

sa'lame *sm* salami *no pl*, salami sausage

sala'moia *sf* (*CUC*) brine

sa'lare *vt* to salt

sa'lario *sm* pay, wages *pl*

sa'lato, a *ag* (*sapore*) salty; (*CUC*) salted, salt *cpd*; (*fig: prezzo*) steep, stiff

sal'dare *vt* (*congiungere*) to join, bind; (*parti metalliche*) to solder; (*: con saldatura autogena*) to weld; (*conto*) to settle, pay; **salda'tura** *sf* soldering; welding; (*punto saldato*) soldered joint; weld

sal'dezza [sal'dettsa] *sf* firmness; strength

'saldo, a *ag* (*resistente, forte*) strong, firm; (*fermo*) firm, steady, stable; (*fig*) firm, steadfast ♦ *sm* (*svendita*) sale; (*di conto*) settlement; (*ECON*) balance

'sale *sm* salt; (*fig*): **ha poco ~ in zucca** he doesn't have much sense; **~ fino/grosso** table/cooking salt

'salice ['salitʃe] *sm* willow; **~ piangente** weeping willow

sali'ente *ag* (*fig*) salient, main

sali'era *sf* salt cellar

sa'lina *sf* saltworks *sg*

sa'lino, a *ag* saline

sa'lire *vi* to go (*o* come) up; (*aereo etc*) to climb, go up; (*passeggero*) to get on; (*sentiero, prezzi, livello*) to go up, rise ♦ *vt* (*scale, gradini*) to go (*o* come) up; **~ su** to climb (up); **~ sul treno/sull'autobus** to board the train/the bus; **~ in macchina** to get into the car; **sa'lita** *sf* climb, ascent; (*erta*) hill, slope; **in salita** *ag, av* uphill

sa'liva *sf* saliva

'salma *sf* corpse

'salmo *sm* psalm

sal'mone *sm* salmon

sa'lone *sm* (*stanza*) sitting room, lounge; (*in albergo*) lounge; (*su nave*) lounge, saloon; (*mostra*) show, exhibition; **~ di bellezza** beauty salon

sa'lotto *sm* lounge, sitting room; (*mobilio*) lounge suite

sal'pare *vi* (*NAUT*) to set sail; (*anche*: **~ l'ancora**) to weigh anchor

'salsa *sf* (*CUC*) sauce; **~ di pomodoro** tomato sauce

sal'siccia, ce [sal'sittʃa] *sf* pork sausage

sal'tare *vi* to jump, leap; (*esplodere*) to blow up, explode; (*: valvola*) to blow; (*venir via*) to pop off; (*non aver luogo: corso etc*) to be cancelled ♦ *vt* to jump (over), leap (over); (*fig: pranzo, capitolo*) to skip, miss (out); (*CUC*) to sauté; **far ~** to blow up; to burst open; **~ fuori** (*fig: apparire all'improvviso*) to turn up

saltel'lare *vi* to skip; to hop

saltim'banco *sm* acrobat

'salto *sm* jump; (*SPORT*) jumping; fare un ~ to jump, leap; fare un ~ da qn to pop over to sb's (place); ~ in alto/lungo high/long jump; ~ con l'asta pole vaulting; ~ mortale somersault

saltu'ario, a *ag* occasional, irregular

sa'lubre *ag* healthy, salubrious

salume'ria *sf* delicatessen

sa'lumi *smpl* salted pork meats

salu'tare *ag* healthy; (*fig*) salutary, beneficial ♦ *vt* (*incontrandosi*) to greet; (*congedandosi*) to say goodbye to; (*MIL*) to salute

sa'lute *sf* health; ~! (*a chi starnutisce*) bless you!; (*nei brindisi*) cheers!; bere alla ~ di qn to drink (to) sb's health

sa'luto *sm* (*gesto*) wave; (*parola*) greeting; (*MIL*) salute; ~i *smpl* (*formula di cortesia*) greetings; cari ~i best regards; vogliate gradire i nostri più distinti ~i Yours faithfully

salvacon'dotto *sm* (*MIL*) safe-conduct

salva'gente [salva'dʒɛnte] *sm* (*NAUT*) lifebuoy; (*ciambella*) life belt; (*giubbotto*) lifejacket; (*stradale*) traffic island

salvaguar'dare *vt* to safeguard

sal'vare *vt* to save; (*trarre da un pericolo*) to rescue; (*proteggere*) to protect; ~rsi *vr* to save o.s.; to escape; salva'taggio *sm* rescue; salva'tore, 'trice *sm/f* saviour

'salve (*fam*) *escl* hi!

sal'vezza [sal'vettsa] *sf* salvation; (*sicurezza*) safety

'salvia *sf* (*BOT*) sage

salvi'etta *sf* napkin; ~ umidificata baby wipe

'salvo, a *ag* safe, unhurt, unharmed; (*fuori pericolo*) safe, out of danger ♦ *sm*: in ~ safe ♦ *prep* (*eccetto*) except; mettere qc in ~ to put sth in a safe place; ~ che (*a meno che*) unless; (*eccetto che*) except (that); ~ imprevisti barring accidents

sam'buco *sm* elder (tree)

san *ag vedi* santo

sa'nare *vt* to heal, cure; (*economia*) to put right

san'cire [san'tʃire] *vt* to sanction

'sandalo *sm* (*BOT*) sandalwood; (*calzatura*) sandal

'sangue *sm* blood; farsi cattivo ~ to fret, get in a state; ~ freddo (*fig*) sang-froid, calm; a ~ freddo in cold blood; sangu'igno, a *ag* blood (*cpd*); (*colore*) blood-red; sangui'nare *vi* to bleed; sangui'noso, a *ag* bloody; sangui'suga *sf* leech

sanità *sf* health; (*salubrità*) healthiness; Ministero della S~ Department of Health; ~ mentale sanity

sani'tario, a *ag* health *cpd*; (*condizioni*) sanitary ♦ *sm* (*AMM*) doctor; (*impianti*) ~i *smpl* bathroom o sanitary fittings

'sanno *vb vedi* sapere

'sano, a *ag* healthy; (*denti, costituzione*) healthy, sound; (*integro*) whole, unbroken; (*fig: politica, consigli*) sound; ~ di mente sane; di ~a pianta completely, entirely; ~ e salvo safe and sound

sant' *ag vedi* santo

santifi'care *vt* to sanctify; (*feste*) to observe

santità *sf* sanctity; holiness; Sua/Vostra ~ (*titolo di Papa*) His/Your Holiness

'santo, a *ag* holy; (*fig*) saintly; (*seguito da nome proprio*) saint ♦ *sm/f* saint; la S~a Sede the Holy See

santu'ario *sm* sanctuary

sanzio'nare [santsjo'nare] *vt* to sanction

sanzi'one [san'tsjone] *sf* sanction; (*penale, civile*) sanction, penalty

sa'pere *vt* to know; (*essere capace di*): so nuotare I know how to swim, I can swim ♦ *vi*: ~ di (*aver sapore*) to taste of; (*aver odore*) to smell of ♦ *sm* knowledge; far ~ qc a qn to inform sb about sth, let sb know sth; mi sa che non sia vero I don't think that's true

sapi'enza [sa'pjɛntsa] *sf* wisdom

sa'pone *sm* soap; ~ da bucato washing soap; sapo'netta *sf* cake o bar o tablet of soap

sa'pore *sm* taste, flavour; sapo'rito, a *ag* tasty

sappi'amo *vb vedi* sapere

saraci'nesca [saratʃi'neska] *sf* (*serranda*) rolling shutter

sar'casmo *sm* sarcasm *no pl*; sarcastic remark

Sar'degna [sar'deɲɲa] *sf*: la ~ Sardinia

sar'dina *sf* sardine

'sardo, a *ag, sm/f* Sardinian

'sarto, a *sm/f* tailor/dressmaker; sarto'ria *sf* tailor's (shop); dressmaker's (shop); (*casa di moda*) fashion house; (*arte*) couture

'sasso *sm* stone; (*ciottolo*) pebble; (*masso*) rock

sas'sofono *sm* saxophone

sas'soso, a *ag* stony; pebbly

'Satana *sm* Satan; sa'tanico, a, ci, che *ag* satanic, fiendish

sa'tellite *sm, ag* satellite

'satira *sf* satire

'saturo, a *ag* saturated; (*fig*): ~ di full of

'sauna *sf* sauna

Sa'voia *sf* Savoy

savoi'ardo, a *ag* of Savoy, Savoyard ♦ *sm* (*biscotto*) sponge finger

sazi'are [sat'tsjare] *vt* to satisfy, satiate; ~rsi *vr*: ~rsi (di) to eat one's fill (of); (*fig*): ~rsi di to grow tired o weary of

'sazio, a ['sattsjo] *ag*: ~ (di) sated (with), full (of); (*fig: stufo*) fed up (with), sick (of)

sba'dato, a *ag* careless, inattentive

sbadigli'are [zbadiʎ'ʎare] *vi* to yawn; **sba'diglio** *sm* yawn

sbagli'are [zbaʎ'ʎare] *vt* to make a mistake in, get wrong ♦ *vi* to make a mistake, be mistaken, be wrong; (*operare in modo non giusto*) to err; **~rsi** *vr* to make a mistake, be mistaken, be wrong; **~ la mira/strada** to miss one's aim/take the wrong road; **'sbaglio** *sm* mistake, error; (*morale*) error; **fare uno sbaglio** to make a mistake

sbal'lare *vt* (*merce*) to unpack ♦ *vi* (*nel fare un conto*) to overestimate; (*fam: gergo della droga*) to get high

sballot'tare *vt* to toss (about)

sbalor'dire *vt* to stun, amaze ♦ *vi* to be stunned, be amazed; **sbalordi'tivo, a** *ag* amazing; (*prezzo*) incredible, absurd

sbal'zare [zbal'tsare] *vt* to throw, hurl ♦ *vi* (*balzare*) to bounce; (*saltare*) to leap, bound; **'sbalzo** *sm* (*spostamento improvviso*) jolt, jerk; **a sbalzi** jerkily; (*fig*) in fits and starts; **uno sbalzo di temperatura** a sudden change in temperature

sban'dare *vi* (*NAUT*) to list; (*AER*) to bank; (*AUT*) to skid; **~rsi** *vr* (*folla*) to disperse

sbandie'rare *vt* (*bandiera*) to wave; (*fig*) to parade, show off

sbaragli'are [zbaraʎ'ʎare] *vt* (*MIL*) to rout; (*in gare sportive etc*) to beat, defeat

sba'raglio [zba'raʎʎo] *sm* rout; defeat; **gettarsi allo ~** to risk everything

sbaraz'zarsi [zbarat'tsarsi] *vr*: **~ di** to get rid of, rid o.s. of

sbar'care *vt* (*passeggeri*) to disembark; (*merci*) to unload ♦ *vi* to disembark; **'sbarco** *sm* disembarkation; (*MIL*) landing

'sbarra *sf* bar; (*di passaggio a livello*) barrier; (*DIR*): **presentarsi alla ~** to appear before the court

sbarra'mento *sm* (*stradale*) barrier; (*diga*) dam, barrage; (*MIL*) barrage

sbar'rare *vt* (*strada etc*) to block, bar; (*assegno*) to cross; **~ il passo** to bar the way; **~ gli occhi** to open one's eyes wide

'sbattere *vt* (*porta*) to slam, bang; (*tappeti, ali, CUC*) to beat; (*urtare*) to knock, hit ♦ *vi* (*porta, finestra*) to bang; (*agitarsi: ali, vele etc*) to flap; **me ne sbatto!** (*fam*) I don't give a damn!; **sbat'tuto, a** *ag* (*viso, aria*) dejected, worn out; (*uovo*) beaten

sba'vare *vi* to dribble; (*colore*) to smear, smudge

sbia'dire *vi, vt* to fade; **~rsi** *vr* to fade, **sbia'dito, a** *ag* faded; (*fig*) colourless, dull

sbian'care *vt* to whiten; (*tessuto*) to bleach ♦ *vi* (*impallidire*) to grow pale *o* white

sbi'eco, a, chi, che *ag* (*storto*) squint, askew; **di ~**: **guardare qn di ~** (*fig*) to look askance at sb; **tagliare una stoffa di ~** to cut

a material on the bias

sbigot'tire *vt* to dismay, stun ♦ *vi* (*anche*: **~rsi**) to be dismayed

sbilanci'are [zbilan'tʃare] *vt* to throw off balance; **~rsi** *vr* (*perdere l'equilibrio*) to overbalance, lose one's balance; (*fig*: *compromettersi*) to compromise o.s.

sbirci'are [zbir'tʃare] *vt* to cast sidelong glances at, eye

'sbirro (*peg*) *sm* cop

sbizzar'rirsi [zbiddzar'rirsi] *vr* to indulge one's whims

sbloc'care *vt* to unblock, free; (*freno*) to release; (*prezzi, affitti*) to decontrol

sboc'care *vi*: **~ in** (*fiume*) to flow into; (*strada*) to lead into; (*persona*) to come (out) into; (*fig*: *concludersi*) to end (up) in

sboc'cato, a *ag* (*persona*) foul-mouthed; (*linguaggio*) foul

sbocci'are [zbot'tʃare] *vi* (*fiore*) to bloom, open (out)

'sbocco, chi *sm* (*di fiume*) mouth; (*di strada*) end; (*di tubazione, COMM*) outlet; (*uscita: anche fig*) way out; **siamo in una situazione senza ~chi** there's no way out of this for us

sbol'lire *vi* (*fig*) to cool down, calm down

'sbornia (*fam*) *sf*: **prendersi una ~** to get plastered

sbor'sare *vt* (*denaro*) to pay out

sbot'tare *vi*: **~ in una risata/per la collera** to burst out laughing/explode with anger

sbotto'nare *vt* to unbutton, undo

sbrai'tare *vi* to yell, bawl

sbra'nare *vt* to tear to pieces

sbricio'lare [zbritʃo'lare] *vt* to crumble; **~rsi** *vr* to crumble

sbri'gare *vt* to deal with; **~rsi** *vr* to hurry (up); **sbriga'tivo, a** *ag* (*persona, modo*) quick, expeditious; (*giudizio*) hasty

sbrindel'lato, a *ag* tattered, in tatters

sbrodo'lare *vt* to stain, dirty

'sbronza ['zbrontsa] (*fam*) *sf* (*ubriaco*): **prendersi una ~** to get plastered

'sbronzo, a ['zbrontso] (*fam*) *ag* plastered

sbruf'fone, a *sm/f* boaster

sbu'care *vi* to come out, emerge; (*improvvisamente*) to pop out (*o* up)

sbucci'are [zbut'tʃare] *vt* (*arancia, patata*) to peel; (*piselli*) to shell; **~rsi un ginocchio** to graze one's knee

sbudel'larsi *vr*: **~ dalle risa** to split one's sides laughing

sbuf'fare *vi* (*persona, cavallo*) to snort; (: *ansimare*) to puff, pant; (*treno*) to puff; **'sbuffo** *sm* (*di aria, fumo, vapore*) puff; **maniche a sbuffo** puff(ed) sleeves

'scabbia *sf* (*MED*) scabies *sg*

sca'broso, a *ag* (*fig*: *difficile*) difficult,

thorny; (: *imbarazzante*) embarrassing; (: *sconcio*) indecent

scacchi'era [skak'kjɛra] *sf* chessboard

scacci'are [skat'tʃare] *vt* to chase away o out, drive away o out

'scacco, chi *sm* (*pezzo del gioco*) chessman; (*quadretto di scacchiera*) square; (*fig*) setback, reverse; **~chi** *smpl* (*gioco*) chess *sg*; **a ~chi** (*tessuto*) check(ed); **scacco'matto** *sm* checkmate

sca'dente *ag* shoddy, of poor quality

sca'denza [ska'dɛntsa] *sf* (*di cambiale, contratto*) maturity; (*di passaporto*) expiry date; **a breve/lunga ~** short-/long-term; **data di ~** expiry date

sca'dere *vi* (*contratto etc*) to expire; (*debito*) to fall due; (*valore, forze, peso*) to decline, go down

sca'fandro *sm* (*di palombaro*) diving suit; (*di astronauta*) space-suit

scaf'fale *sm* shelf; (*mobile*) set of shelves

'scafo *sm* (*NAUT, AER*) hull

scagio'nare [skadʒo'nare] *vt* to exonerate, free from blame

'scaglia ['skaʎʎa] *sf* (*ZOOL*) scale; (*scheggia*) chip, flake

scagli'are [skaʎ'ʎare] *vt* (*lanciare: anche fig*) to hurl, fling; **~rsi** *vr*: **~rsi su** o **contro** to hurl o fling o.s. at; (*fig*) to rail at

scaglio'nare [skaʎʎo'nare] *vt* (*pagamenti*) to space out, spread out; (*MIL*) to echelon; **scagli'one** *sm* echelon; (*GEO*) terrace; **a scaglioni** in groups

'scala *sf* (*a gradini etc*) staircase, stairs *pl*; (*a pioli, di corda*) ladder; (*MUS, GEO, di colori, valori, fig*) scale; **~e** *sfpl* (*scalinata*) stairs; **su vasta ~/~ ridotta** on a large/small scale; **~ a libretto** stepladder; **~ mobile** escalator; (*ECON*) sliding scale; **~ mobile (dei salari)** index-linked pay scale

sca'lare *vt* (*ALPINISMO, muro*) to climb, scale; (*debito*) to scale down, reduce; **sca'lata** *sf* scaling *no pl*, climbing *no pl*; (*arrampicata, fig*) climb; **scala'tore, 'trice** *sm/f* climber

scalda'bagno [skalda'baɲɲo] *sm* water-heater

scal'dare *vt* to heat; **~rsi** *vr* to warm up, heat up; (*al fuoco, al sole*) to warm o.s.; (*fig*) to get excited

scal'fire *vt* to scratch

scali'nata *sf* staircase

sca'lino *sm* (*anche fig*) step; (*di scala a pioli*) rung

'scalo *sm* (*NAUT*) slipway; (: *porto d'approdo*) port of call; (*AER*) stopover; **fare ~ (a)** (*NAUT*) to call (at), put in (at); (*AER*) to land (at), make a stop (at); **~ merci** (*FERR*) goods (*BRIT*) o freight yard

scalop'pina *sf* (*CUC*) escalope

scal'pello *sm* chisel

scal'pore *sm* noise, row; **far ~** (*notizia*) to cause a sensation o a stir

'scaltro, a *ag* cunning, shrewd

'scalzo, a ['skaltso] *ag* barefoot

scambi'are *vt* to exchange; (*confondere*): **~ qn/qc per** to mistake sb/sth for; **mi hanno scambiato il cappello** they've given me the wrong hat

scambi'evole *ag* mutual, reciprocal

'scambio *sm* exchange; (*FERR*) points *pl*; **fare (uno) ~** to make a swap

scampa'gnata [skampaɲ'ɲata] *sf* trip to the country

scam'pare *vt* (*salvare*) to rescue, save; (*evitare: morte, prigione*) to escape ♦ *vi*: **~ (a qc)** to survive (sth), escape (sth); **scamparla bella** to have a narrow escape

'scampo *sm* (*salvezza*) escape; (*ZOOL*) prawn; **cercare ~ nella fuga** to seek safety in flight

'scampolo *sm* remnant

scanala'tura *sf* (*incavo*) channel, groove

scandagli'are [skanda'ʎʎare] *vt* (*NAUT*) to sound; (*fig*) to sound out; to probe

scandaliz'zare [skandalid'dzare] *vt* to shock, scandalize; **~rsi** *vr* to be shocked

'scandalo *sm* scandal

Scandi'navia *sf*: **la ~** Scandinavia; **scandi'navo, a** *ag, sm/f* Scandinavian

scan'dire *vt* (*versi*) to scan; (*parole*) to articulate, pronounce distinctly; **~ il tempo** (*MUS*) to beat time

scan'nare *vt* (*animale*) to butcher, slaughter; (*persona*) to cut o slit the throat of

'scanno *sm* seat, bench

scansafa'tiche [skansafa'tike] *sm/f inv* idler, loafer

scan'sare *vt* (*rimuovere*) to move (aside), shift; (*schivare: schiaffo*) to dodge; (*fuggire*) to avoid; **~rsi** *vr* to move aside

scan'sia *sf* shelves *pl*; (*per libri*) bookcase

'scanso *sm*: **a ~ di** in order to avoid, as a precaution against

scanti'nato *sm* basement

scanto'nare *vi* to turn the corner; (*svignarsela*) to sneak off

scapacci'one [skapat'tʃone] *sm* clout

scapes'trato, a *ag* dissolute

'scapito *sm*: **a ~ di** to the detriment of

'scapola *sf* shoulder blade

'scapolo *sm* bachelor

scappa'mento *sm* (*AUT*) exhaust

scap'pare *vi* (*fuggire*) to escape; (*andare via in fretta*) to rush off; **lasciarsi ~ un'occasione** to let an opportunity go by; **~ di prigione** to escape from prison; **~ di mano** (*oggetto*) to slip out of one's hands; **~ di mente a qn** to slip sb's mind; **mi scappò detto** I let it slip;

scap'pata sf quick visit o call; **scappa'tella** sf escapade; **scappa'toia** sf way out

scara'beo sm beetle

scarabocchi'are [skarabok'kjare] vt to scribble, scrawl; **scara'bocchio** sm scribble, scrawl

scara'faggio [skara'faddʒo] sm cockroach

scaraven'tare vt to fling, hurl

scarce'rare [skartʃe'rare] vt to release (from prison)

scardi'nare vt: ~ **una porta** to take a door off its hinges

'scarica, che sf (di più armi) volley of shots; (di sassi, pugni) hail, shower; (ELETTR) discharge; ~ **di mitra** burst of machine-gun fire

scari'care vt (merci, camion etc) to unload; (passeggeri) to set down, put off; (arma) to unload; (: sparare, ELETTR) to discharge; (sog: corso d'acqua) to empty, pour; (fig: liberare da un peso) to unburden, relieve; **~rsi** vr (orologio) to run o wind down; (batteria, accumulatore) to go flat o dead; (fig: rilassarsi) to unwind; (: sfogarsi) to let off steam; **scarica'tore** sm (di porto) docker

'scarico, a, chi, che ag unloaded; (orologio) run down; (accumulatore) dead, flat ♦ sm (di merci, materiali) unloading; (di immondizie) dumping, tipping (BRIT); (TECN: deflusso) draining; (: dispositivo) drain; (AUT) exhaust

scarlat'tina sf scarlet fever

scar'latto, a ag scarlet

'scarno, a ag thin, bony

'scarpa sf shoe; **~e da ginnastica/tennis** gym/tennis shoes

scar'pata sf escarpment

scar'pone sm boot; **~i da sci** ski-boots

scarseggi'are [skarsed'dʒare] vi to be scarce; ~ **di** to be short of, lack

scar'sezza [skar'settsa] sf scarcity, lack

'scarso, a ag (insufficiente) insufficient, meagre; (povero: annata) poor, lean; (INS: voto) poor; ~ **di** lacking in; **3 chili ~i** just under 3 kilos, barely 3 kilos

scarta'mento sm (FERR) gauge; ~ **normale/ ridotto** standard/narrow gauge

scar'tare vt (pacco) to unwrap; (idea) to reject; (MIL) to declare unfit for military service; (carte da gioco) to discard; (CALCIO) to dodge (past) ♦ vi to swerve

'scarto sm (cosa scartata, anche COMM) reject; (di veicolo) swerve; (differenza) gap, difference

scassi'nare vt to break, force

'scasso sm vedi **furto**

scate'nare vt (fig) to incite, stir up; **~rsi** vr (temporale) to break; (rivolta) to break out; (persona: infuriarsi) to rage

'scatola sf box; (di latta) tin (BRIT); can; **cibi in ~** tinned (BRIT) o canned foods; ~ **cranica** cranium

scat'tare vt (fotografia) to take ♦ vi (congegno, molla etc) to be released; (balzare) to spring up; (SPORT) to put on a spurt; (fig: per l'ira) to fly into a rage; ~ **in piedi** to spring to one's feet

'scatto sm (dispositivo) release; (: di arma da fuoco) trigger mechanism; (rumore) click; (balzo) jump, start; (SPORT) spurt; (fig: di ira etc) fit; (: di stipendio) increment; **di ~** suddenly

scatu'rire vi to gush, spring

scaval'care vt (ostacolo) to pass (o climb) over; (fig) to get ahead of, overtake

sca'vare vt (terreno) to dig; (legno) to hollow out; (pozzo, galleria) to bore; (città sepolta etc) to excavate

'scavo sm excavating no pl; excavation

'scegliere ['ʃeʎʎere] vt to choose, select

sce'icco, chi [ʃe'ikko] sm sheik

scelle'rato, a [ʃelle'rato] ag wicked, evil

scel'lino [ʃel'lino] sm shilling

'scelta ['ʃelta] sf choice; selection; **di prima ~** top grade o quality; **frutta o formaggi a ~** choice of fruit or cheese

'scelto, a ['ʃelto] pp di **scegliere** ♦ ag (gruppo) carefully selected; (frutta, verdura) choice, top quality; (MIL: specializzato) crack cpd, highly skilled

sce'mare [ʃe'mare] vt, vi to diminish

'scemo, a ['ʃemo] ag stupid, silly

'scempio ['ʃempjo] sm slaughter, massacre; (fig) ruin; **far ~ di** (fig) to play havoc with, ruin

'scena ['ʃena] sf (gen) scene; (palcoscenico) stage; **le ~e** (fig: teatro) the stage; **fare una ~** to make a scene; **andare in ~** to be staged o put on o performed; **mettere in ~** to stage

sce'nario [ʃe'narjo] sm scenery; (di film) scenario

sce'nata [ʃe'nata] sf row, scene

'scendere ['ʃendere] vi to go (o come) down; (strada, sole) to go down; (notte) to fall; (passeggero: fermarsi) to get out, alight; (fig: temperatura, prezzi) to go o come down, fall, drop ♦ vt (scale, pendio) to go (o come) down; ~ **dalle scale** to go (o come) down the stairs; ~ **dal treno** to get off o out of the train; ~ **dalla macchina** to get out of the car; ~ **da cavallo** to dismount, get off one's horse

'scenico, a, ci, che ['ʃeniko] ag stage cpd, scenic

scervel'lato, a [ʃervel'lato] ag feather-brained, scatterbrained

'sceso, a ['ʃeso] pp di **scendere**

'scettico, a, ci, che ['ʃettiko] ag sceptical

'scettro ['ʃettro] sm sceptre

'**scheda** ['skeda] *sf* (index) card; **~ elettorale** ballot paper; **~ telefonica** phone card; **sche'dare** *vt* (*dati*) to file; (*libri*) to catalogue; (*registrare: anche* POLIZIA) to put on one's files; **sche'dario** *sm* file; (*mobile*) filing cabinet

'**scheggia, ge** ['skeddʒa] *sf* splinter, sliver

'**scheletro** ['skeletro] *sm* skeleton

'**schema, i** ['skema] *sm* (*diagramma*) diagram, sketch; (*progetto, abbozzo*) outline, plan

'**scherma** ['skerma] *sf* fencing

scher'maglia [sker'maʎʎa] *sf* (*fig*) skirmish

'**schermo** ['skermo] *sm* shield, screen; (CINEMA, TV) screen

scher'nire [sker'nire] *vt* to mock, sneer at; '**scherno** *sm* mockery, derision

scher'zare [sker'tsare] *vi* to joke

'**scherzo** ['skertso] *sm* joke; (*tiro*) trick; (MUS) scherzo; **è uno ~!** (*una cosa facile*) it's child's play!, it's easy!; **per ~** in jest; **for a joke o a laugh; fare un brutto ~ a qn** to play a nasty trick on sb; **scher'zoso, a** *ag* (*tono, gesto*) playful; (*osservazione*) facetious; **è un tipo scherzoso** he likes a joke

schiaccia'noci [skjattʃa'notʃi] *sm inv* nutcracker

schiacci'are [skjat'tʃare] *vt* (*dito*) to crush; (*noci*) to crack; **~ un pisolino** to have a nap

schiaffeggi'are [skjaffed'dʒare] *vt* to slap

schi'affo [skjaffo] *sm* slap

schiamaz'zare [skjamat'tsare] *vi* to squawk, cackle

schian'tare [skjan'tare] *vt* to break, tear apart; **~rsi** *vr* to break (up), shatter; **schi'anto** *sm* (*rumore*) crash; tearing sound; **è uno schianto!** (*fam*) it's (*o* he's *o* she's) terrific!; **di schianto** all of a sudden

schia'rire [skja'rire] *vt* to lighten, make lighter ♦ *vi* (*anche*: **~rsi**) to grow lighter; (*tornar sereno*) to clear, brighten up; **~rsi la voce** to clear one's throat

schiavitù [skjavi'tu] *sf* slavery

schi'avo, a ['skjavo] *sm/f* slave

schi'ena ['skjena] *sf* (ANAT) back; **schie'nale** *sm* (*di sedia*) back

schi'era ['skjera] *sf* (MIL) rank; (*gruppo*) group, band

schiera'mento [skjera'mento] *sm* (MIL, SPORT) formation; (*fig*) alliance

schie'rare [skje'rare] *vt* (*esercito*) to line up, draw up, marshal; **~rsi** *vr* to line up; (*fig*): **~rsi con** *o* **dalla parte di/contro qn** to side with/oppose sb

schi'etto, a ['skjetto] *ag* (*puro*) pure; (*fig*) frank, straightforward; sincere

'**schifo** ['skifo] *sm* disgust; **fare ~** (*essere fatto male, dare pessimi risultati*) to be awful; **mi fa ~** it makes me sick, it's disgusting; **quel libro è**

uno ~ that book's rotten; **schi'foso, a** *ag* disgusting, revolting; (*molto scadente*) rotten, lousy

schioc'care [skjok'kare] *vt* (*frusta*) to crack; (*dita*) to snap; (*lingua*) to click; **~ le labbra** to smack one's lips

schi'udere ['skjudere] *vt* to open; **~rsi** *vr* to open

schi'uma ['skjuma] *sf* foam; (*di sapone*) lather; (*di latte*) froth; (*fig: feccia*) scum; **schiu'mare** *vt* to skim ♦ *vi* to foam

schi'uso, a ['skjuso] *pp di* **schiudere**

schi'vare [ski'vare] *vt* to dodge, avoid

'**schivo, a** ['skivo] *ag* (*ritroso*) stand-offish, reserved; (*timido*) shy

schiz'zare [skit'tsare] *vt* (*spruzzare*) to spurt, squirt; (*sporcare*) to splash, spatter; (*fig: abbozzare*) to sketch ♦ *vi* to spurt, squirt; (*saltar fuori*) to dart up (*o* off *etc*)

schizzi'noso, a [skittsi'noso] *ag* fussy, finicky

'**schizzo** ['skittso] *sm* (*di liquido*) spurt; splash, spatter; (*abbozzo*) sketch

sci [ʃi] *sm* (*attrezzo*) ski; (*attività*) skiing; **~ nautico** water-skiing

'**scia** ['ʃia] (*pl* '**scie**) *sf* (*di imbarcazione*) wake; (*di profumo*) trail

scià [ʃa] *sm inv* shah

sci'abola ['ʃabola] *sf* sabre

scia'callo [ʃa'kallo] *sm* jackal

sciac'quare [ʃak'kware] *vt* to rinse

scia'gura [ʃa'gura] *sf* disaster, calamity; misfortune; **sciagu'rato, a** *ag* unfortunate; (*malvagio*) wicked

scialac'quare [ʃalak'kware] *vt* to squander

scia'lare [ʃa'lare] *vi* to lead a life of luxury

sci'albo, a ['ʃalbo] *ag* pale, dull; (*fig*) dull, colourless

sci'alle ['ʃalle] *sm* shawl

scia'luppa [ʃa'luppa] *sf* (*anche*: **~ di salvataggio**) lifeboat

sci'ame ['ʃame] *sm* swarm

scian'cato, a [ʃan'kato] *ag* lame

sci'are [ʃi'are] *vi* to ski

sci'arpa ['ʃarpa] *sf* scarf; (*fascia*) sash

scia'tore, 'trice [ʃia'tore] *sm/f* skier

sci'atto, a ['ʃatto] *ag* (*persona*) slovenly, unkempt

scien'tifico, a, ci, che [ʃen'tifiko] *ag* scientific

sci'enza ['ʃentsa] *sf* science; (*sapere*) knowledge; **~e** *sfpl* (INS) science *sg*; **~e naturali** natural sciences; **scienzi'ato, a** *sm/f* scientist

'**scimmia** ['ʃimmja] *sf* monkey; **scimmiot'tare** *vt* to ape, mimic

scimpanzé [ʃimpan'tse] *sm inv* chimpanzee

scimu'nito, a [ʃimu'nito] *ag* silly, idiotic

'**scindere** ['ʃindere] *vt* to split (up); **~rsi** *vr* to split (up)

scin'tilla [fin'tilla] *sf* spark; **scintil'lare** *vi* to spark; (*acqua, occhi*) to sparkle

scioc'chezza [fok'kettsa] *sf* stupidity *no pl*; stupid o foolish thing; **dire ~e** to talk nonsense

sci'occo, a, chi, che ['fɔkko] *ag* stupid, foolish

sci'ogliere ['fɔʎʎere] *vt* (*nodo*) to untie; (*capelli*) to loosen; (*persona, animale*) to untie, release; (*fig: persona*): **~ da** to release from; (*neve*) to melt; (*nell'acqua: zucchero etc*) to dissolve; (*fig: mistero*) to solve; (*porre fine a: contratto*) to cancel; (*: società, matrimonio*) to dissolve; (*: riunione*) to bring to an end; **~rsi** *vr* to loosen, come untied; to melt; to dissolve; (*assemblea etc*) to break up; **~ i muscoli** to limber up

sciol'tezza [fol'tettsa] *sf* agility; suppleness; ease

sci'olto, a ['fɔlto] *pp di* **sciogliere ♦** *ag* loose; (*agile*) agile, nimble; supple; (*disinvolto*) free and easy; **versi ~i** (*POESIA*) blank verse

sciope'rante [fope'rante] *sm/f* striker

sciope'rare [fope'rare] *vi* to strike, go on strike

sci'opero ['fopero] *sm* strike; **fare ~** to strike; **~ bianco** work-to-rule (*BRIT*), slowdown (*US*); **~ selvaggio** wildcat strike; **~ a singhiozzo** on-off strike

scip'pare [fip'pare] *vt*: **~ qn** to snatch sb's bag; **mi hanno scippato** they snatched my bag

sci'rocco [fi'rɔkko] *sm* sirocco

sci'roppo [fi'rɔppo] *sm* syrup

'scisma, i ['fizma] *sm* (*REL*) schism

scissi'one [fis'sjone] *sf* (*anche fig*) split, division; (*FISICA*) fission

'scisso, a ['fisso] *pp di* **scindere**

sciu'pare [fu'pare] *vt* (*abito, libro, appetito*) to spoil, ruin; (*tempo, denaro*) to waste; **~rsi** *vr* to get spoilt o ruined; (*rovinarsi la salute*) to ruin one's health

scivo'lare [fivo'lare] *vi* to slide o glide along; (*involontariamente*) to slip, slide; **'scivolo** *sm* slide; (*TECN*) chute; **scivo'loso, a** *ag* slippery

scle'rosi *sf* sclerosis

scoc'care *vt* (*freccia*) to shoot ♦ *vi* (*guizzare*) to shoot up; (*battere: ora*) to strike

scocci'are [skot'tfare] (*fam*) *vt* to bother, annoy; **~rsi** *vr* to be bothered o annoyed

sco'della *sf* bowl

scodinzo'lare [skodintso'lare] *vi* to wag its tail

scogli'era [skoʎ'ʎera] *sf* reef; cliff

'scoglio ['skɔʎʎo] *sm* (*al mare*) rock

scoi'attolo *sm* squirrel

scolapi'atti *sm inv* drainer (*for plates*)

sco'lare *ag*: **età ~** school age ♦ *vt* to drain

♦ *vi* to drip

scola'resca *sf* schoolchildren *pl*, pupils *pl*

sco'laro, a *sm/f* pupil, schoolboy/girl

sco'lastico, a, ci, che *ag* school *cpd*; scholastic

scol'lare *vt* (*staccare*) to unstick; **~rsi** *vr* to come unstuck

scolla'tura *sf* neckline

'scolo *sm* drainage

scolo'rire *vt* to fade; to discolour ♦ *vi* (*anche: ~rsi*) to fade; to become discoloured; (*impallidire*) to turn pale

scol'pire *vt* to carve, sculpt

scombi'nare *vt* to mess up, upset

scombusso'lare *vt* to upset

scom'messa *sf* bet, wager

scom'messo, a *pp di* **scommettere**

scom'mettere *vt, vi* to bet

scomo'dare *vt* to trouble, bother; to disturb; **~rsi** *vr* to put o.s. out; **~rsi a fare** to go to the bother o trouble of doing

'scomodo, a *ag* uncomfortable; (*sistemazione, posto*) awkward, inconvenient

scompa'rire *vi* (*sparire*) to disappear, vanish; (*fig*) to be insignificant; **scom'parsa** *sf* disappearance; **scom'parso, a** *pp di* **scomparire**

scomparti'mento *sm* compartment

scom'parto *sm* compartment, division

scompigli'are [skompiʎ'ʎare] *vt* (*cassetto, capelli*) to mess up, disarrange; (*fig: piani*) to upset; **scom'piglio** *sm* mess, confusion

scom'porre *vt* (*parola, numero*) to break up; (*CHIM*) to decompose; **scomporsi** *vr* (*fig*) to get upset, lose one's composure; **scom'posto, a** *pp di* **scomporre** ♦ *ag* (*gesto*) unseemly; (*capelli*) ruffled, dishevelled

sco'munica *sf* excommunication

scomuni'care *vt* to excommunicate

sconcer'tare [skontfer'tare] *vt* to disconcert, bewilder

'sconcio, a, ci, ce ['skontfo] *ag* (*osceno*) indecent, obscene ♦ *sm* disgrace

sconfes'sare *vt* to renounce, disavow; to repudiate

scon'figgere [skon'fiddʒere] *vt* to defeat, overcome

sconfi'nare *vi* to cross the border; (*in proprietà privata*) to trespass; (*fig*): **~ da** to stray o digress from; **sconfi'nato, a** *ag* boundless, unlimited

scon'fitta *sf* defeat

scon'fitto, a *pp di* **sconfiggere**

scon'forto *sm* despondency

scongiu'rare [skondʒu'rare] *vt* (*implorare*) to entreat, beseech, implore; (*eludere: pericolo*) to ward off, avert; **scongi'uro** *sm* entreaty; (*esorcismo*) exorcism; **fare gli scongiuri** to touch wood (*BRIT*), knock on wood (US)

scon'nesso, a ag incoherent

sconosci'uto, a [skonoʃʃuto] ag unknown; new, strange ♦ sm/f stranger; unknown person

sconquas'sare vt to shatter, smash

sconside'rato, a ag thoughtless, rash

sconsigli'are [skonsiʎʎare] vt: ~ qc a qn to advise sb against sth; ~ qn dal fare qc to advise sb not to do o against doing sth

sconso'lato, a ag inconsolable; desolate

scon'tare vt (COMM: detrarre) to deduct; (: debito) to pay off; (: cambiale) to discount; (pena) to serve; (colpa, errori) to pay for, suffer for

scon'tato, a ag (previsto) foreseen, taken for granted; **dare per ~ che** to take it for granted that

scon'tento, a ag: ~ (di) dissatisfied (with) ♦ sm dissatisfaction

'sconto sm discount; **fare uno ~** to give a discount

scon'trarsi vr (treni etc) to crash, collide; (venire ad uno scontro, fig) to clash; ~ con to crash into, collide with

scon'trino sm ticket

'scontro sm clash, encounter; crash, collision

scon'troso, a ag sullen, surly; (permaloso) touchy

sconveni'ente ag unseemly, improper

scon'volgere [skon'vɔldʒere] vt to throw into confusion, upset; (turbare) to shake, disturb, upset; **scon'volto, a** pp di sconvolgere

'scopa sf broom; (CARTE) Italian card game; **sco'pare** vt to sweep

sco'perta sf discovery

sco'perto, a pp di scoprire ♦ ag uncovered; (capo) uncovered, bare; (macchina) open; (MIL) exposed, without cover; (conto) overdrawn

'scopo sm aim, purpose; **a che ~?** what for?

scoppi'are vi (spaccarsi) to burst; (esplodere) to explode; (fig) to break out; ~ **in pianto** o **a piangere** to burst out crying; ~ **dalle risa** o **dal ridere** to split one's sides laughing

scoppiet'tare vi to crackle

'scoppio sm explosion; (di tuono, arma etc) crash, bang; (fig: di risa, ira) fit, outburst; (: di guerra) outbreak; **a ~ ritardato** delayed-action

sco'prire vt to discover; (liberare da ciò che copre) to uncover; (: monumento) to unveil; ~rsi vr to put on lighter clothes; (fig) to give o.s. away

scoraggi'are [skoradˈdʒare] vt to discourage; ~rsi vr to become discouraged, lose heart

scorcia'toia [skortʃaˈtoja] sf short cut

'scorcio ['skortʃo] sm (ARTE) foreshortening; (di secolo, periodo) end, close

scor'dare vt to forget; ~rsi vr: ~rsi di qc/di fare to forget sth/to do

'scorgere ['skɔrdʒere] vt to make out, distinguish, see

sco'ria sf (di metalli) slag; (vulcanica) scoria; ~e radioattive (FISICA) radioactive waste sg

'scorno sm ignominy, disgrace

scorpacci'ata [skorpatˈtʃata] sf: **fare una ~ (di)** to stuff o.s. (with), eat one's fill (of)

scorpi'one sm scorpion; (dello zodiaco): **S~** Scorpio

scorraz'zare [skorratˈtsare] vi to run about

'scorrere vt (giornale, lettera) to run o skim through ♦ vi (liquido, fiume) to run, flow; (fune) to run; (cassetto, porta) to slide easily; (tempo) to pass (by)

scor'retto, a ag incorrect; (sgarbato) impolite; (sconveniente) improper

scor'revole ag (porta) sliding; (fig: stile) fluent, flowing

scorri'banda sf (MIL) raid; (escursione) trip, excursion

'scorsa sf quick look, glance

'scorso, a pp di scorrere ♦ ag last

scor'soio, a ag: **nodo ~** noose

'scorta sf (di personalità, convoglio) escort; (provvista) supply, stock; **scor'tare** vt to escort

scor'tese ag discourteous, rude; **scorte'sia** sf discourtesy, rudeness; (azione) discourtesy

scorti'care vt to skin

'scorto, a pp di scorgere

'scorza ['skɔrdza] sf (di albero) bark; (di agrumi) peel, skin

sco'sceso, a [skoʃˈʃeso] ag steep

'scossa sf jerk, jolt, shake; (ELETTR, fig) shock

'scosso, a pp di scuotere ♦ ag (turbato) shaken, upset

scos'tante ag (fig) off-putting (BRIT), unpleasant

scos'tare vt to move (away), shift; ~rsi vr to move away

scostu'mato, a ag immoral, dissolute

scot'tare vt (ustionare) to burn; (: con liquido bollente) to scald ♦ vi to burn; (caffè) to be too hot; **scotta'tura** sf burn; scald

'scotto, a ag overcooked ♦ sm (fig): **pagare lo ~ (di)** to pay the penalty (for)

sco'vare vt to drive out, flush out; (fig) to discover

'Scozia ['skɔttsia] sf: **la ~** Scotland; **scoz'zese** ag Scottish ♦ sm/f Scot

scredi'tare vt to discredit

screpo'lare vt to crack; ~rsi vr to crack; **screpola'tura** sf cracking no pl; crack

screzi'ato, a [skretˈtsjato] ag streaked

'screzio ['skrɛttsjo] sm disagreement

scricchio'lare [skrikkjo'lare] *vi* to creak, squeak

'scricciolo ['skritt∫olo] *sm* wren

'scrigno ['skriɲɲo] *sm* casket

scrimina'tura *sf* parting

'scritta *sf* inscription

'scritto, a *pp di* **scrivere** ♦ *ag* written ♦ *sm* writing; (*lettera*) letter, note; **~i** *smpl* (*letterari etc*) writing *sg*

scrit'toio *sm* writing desk

scrit'tore, 'trice *sm/f* writer

scrit'tura *sf* writing; (*COMM*) entry; (*contratto*) contract; (*REL*): **la Sacra S~** the Scriptures *pl*; **~e** *sfpl* (*COMM*) accounts, books

scrittu'rare *vt* (*TEATRO, CINEMA*) to sign up, engage; (*COMM*) to enter

scriva'nia *sf* desk

'scrivere *vt* to write; **come si scrive?** how is it spelt?, how do you write it?

scroc'cone, a *sm/f* scrounger

'scrofa *sf* (*ZOOL*) sow

scrol'lare *vt* to shake; **~rsi** *vr* (*anche fig*) to give o.s. a shake; **~ le spalle/il capo** to shrug one's shoulders/shake one's head

scrosci'are [skro∫'∫are] *vi* (*pioggia*) to pour down, pelt down; (*torrente, fig: applausi*) to thunder, roar; **'scroscio** *sm* pelting; thunder, roar; (*di applausi*) burst

scros'tare *vt* (*intonaco*) to scrape off, strip; **~rsi** *vr* to peel off, flake off

'scrupolo *sm* scruple; (*meticolosità*) care, conscientiousness

scru'tare *vt* to scrutinize; (*intenzioni, causa*) to examine, scrutinize

scruti'nare *vt* (*voti*) to count; **scru'tinio** *sm* (*votazione*) ballot; (*insieme delle operazioni*) poll; (*INS*) (*meeting for*) assignment of marks at end of a term or year

scu'cire [sku't∫ire] *vt* (*orlo etc*) to unpick, undo

scude'ria *sf* stable

scu'detto *sm* (*SPORT*) (championship) shield; (*distintivo*) badge

'scudo *sm* shield

scul'tore, 'trice *sm/f* sculptor

scul'tura *sf* sculpture

scu'ola *sf* school; **~ elementare/materna/ media** primary (*BRIT*) o grade (*US*)/nursery/ secondary (*BRIT*) o high (*US*) school; **~ guida** driving school; **~ dell'obbligo** compulsory education; **~e serali** evening classes, night school *sg*; **~ tecnica** technical college

scu'otere *vt* to shake; **~rsi** *vr* to jump, be startled; (*fig: muoversi*) to rouse o.s., stir o.s.; (: *turbarsi*) to be shaken

'scure *sf* axe

'scuro, a *ag* dark; (*fig: espressione*) grim ♦ *sm* darkness; dark colour; (*imposta*) (window) shutter; **verde/rosso** *etc* **~** dark

green/red *etc*

scur'rile *ag* scurrilous

'scusa *sf* apology; (*pretesto*) excuse; **chie- dere ~ a qn (per)** to apologize to sb (for); **chiedo ~** I'm sorry; (*disturbando etc*) excuse me

scu'sare *vt* to excuse; **~rsi** *vr*: **~rsi (di)** to apologize (for); **(mi) scusi** I'm sorry; (*per richiamare l'attenzione*) excuse me

sde'gnato, a [zdeɲ'ɲato] *ag* indignant, angry

'sdegno ['zdeɲɲo] *sm* scorn, disdain; **sde'gnoso, a** *ag* scornful, disdainful

sdoga'nare *vt* (*merci*) to clear through customs

sdolci'nato, a [zdolt∫i'nato] *ag* mawkish, oversentimental

sdrai'arsi *vr* to stretch out, lie down

'sdraio *sm*: **sedia a ~** deck chair

sdruccio'levole [zdruttʃo'levole] *ag* slippery

PAROLA CHIAVE

se *pron vedi* **si**

♦ *cong* **1** (*condizionale, ipotetica*) if; **~ nevica non vengo** I won't come if it snows; **sarei rimasto ~ me l'avessero chiesto** I would have stayed if they'd asked me; **non puoi fare altro ~ non telefonare** all you can do is phone; **~ mai** if, if ever; **siamo noi ~ mai che le siamo grati** it is we who should be grateful to you; **~ no** (*altrimenti*) or (else), otherwise

2 (*in frasi dubitative, interrogative indirette*) if, whether; **non so ~ scrivere o telefonare** I don't know whether o if I should write or phone

---

sé *pron* (*gen*) oneself; (*esso, essa, lui, lei, loro*) itself; himself; herself; themselves; **~ stesso(a)** *pron* oneself; itself; himself; herself; **~ stessi(e)** *pron pl* themselves

seb'bene *cong* although, though

sec. *abbr* (= *secolo*) c

'secca *sf* (*del mare*) shallows *pl*; *vedi anche* **secco**

sec'care *vt* to dry; (*prosciugare*) to dry up; (*fig: importunare*) to annoy, bother ♦ *vi* to dry; to dry up; **~rsi** *vr* to dry; to dry up; (*fig*) to grow annoyed; **secca'tura** *sf* (*fig*) bother *no pl*, trouble *no pl*

secchi'ello *sm* bucket; **~ del ghiaccio** ice bucket

'secchio ['sekkjo] *sm* bucket, pail

'secco, a, chi, che *ag* dry; (*fichi, pesce*) dried; (*foglie, ramo*) withered; (*magro: persona*) thin, skinny; (*fig: risposta, modo di fare*) curt, abrupt; (: *colpo*) clean, sharp ♦ *sm* (*siccità*) drought; **restarci ~** (*fig: morire sul colpo*) to drop dead; **mettere in ~** (*barca*) to beach; **rimanere a ~** (*fig*) to be left in the lurch

seco'lare *ag* age-old, centuries-old; (*laico, mondano*) secular

'**secolo** *sm* century; (*epoca*) age

se'conda *sf* (AUT) second (gear); **viaggiare in ~ to** travel second-class; *vedi anche* **secondo**

secon'dario, a *ag* secondary

se'condo, a *ag* second ♦ *sm* second; (*di pranzo*) main course ♦ *prep* according to; (*nel modo prescritto*) in accordance with; **~ me** in my opinion, to my mind; **di ~a classe** second-class; **di ~a mano** second-hand; **a ~a di** according to; in accordance with

'**sedano** *sm* celery

seda'tivo, a *ag, sm* sedative

'**sede** *sf* seat; (*di ditta*) head office; (*di organizzazione*) headquarters *pl*; **~ sociale** registered office

seden'tario, a *ag* sedentary

se'dere *vi* to sit, be seated; **~rsi** *vr* to sit down ♦ *sm* (*deretano*) behind, bottom

'**sedia** *sf* chair

sedi'cente [sedi't͡ʃɛnte] *ag* self-styled

'**sedici** ['seditʃi] *num* sixteen

se'dile *sm* seat; (*panchina*) bench

se'dotto, a *pp di* **sedurre**

sedu'cente [sedu'tʃɛnte] *ag* seductive; (*proposta*) very attractive

se'durre *vt* to seduce

se'duta *sf* session, sitting; (*riunione*) meeting; **~ spiritica** séance; **~ stante** (*fig*) immediately

seduzi'one [sedut'tsjone] *sf* seduction; (*fascino*) charm, appeal

'**sega, ghe** *sf* saw

'**segale** *sf* rye

se'gare *vt* to saw; (*recidere*) to saw off; **sega'tura** *sf* (*residuo*) sawdust

'**seggio** ['sɛddʒo] *sm* seat; **~ elettorale** polling station

'**seggiola** ['sɛddʒola] *sf* chair; **seggio'lino** *sm* seat; (*per bambini*) child's chair; **seggio'lone** *sm* (*per bambini*) highchair

seggio'via [sɛddʒo'via] *sf* chairlift

seghe'ria [sege'ria] *sf* sawmill

segna'lare [seɲɲa'lare] *vt* (*manovra etc*) to signal; to indicate; (*annunciare*) to announce; to report; (*fig: far conoscere*) to point out; (*: persona*) to single out; **~rsi** *vr* (*distinguersi*) to distinguish o.s.

se'gnale [seɲ'ɲale] *sm* signal; (*cartello*): **~ stradale** road sign; **~ d'allarme** alarm; (FERR) communication cord; **~ orario** (RADIO) time signal; **segna'letica** *sf* signalling, sign-posting; **segnaletica stradale** road signs *pl*

segna'libro [seɲɲa'libro] *sm* bookmark

se'gnare [seɲ'ɲare] *vt* to mark; (*prendere nota*) to note; (*indicare*) to indicate, mark; (SPORT: *goal*) to score; **~rsi** *vr* (REL) to make the sign of the cross, cross o.s.

'**segno** ['seɲɲo] *sm* sign; (*impronta, contrassegno*) mark; (*limite*) limit, bounds *pl*; (*bersaglio*) target; **fare ~ di si/no** to nod (one's head)/shake one's head; **fare ~ a qn di fermarsi** to motion (to) sb to stop; **cogliere o colpire nel ~** (*fig*) to hit the mark

segre'gare *vt* to segregate, isolate; **segregazi'one** *sf* segregation

segre'tario, a *sm/f* secretary; **~ comunale** town clerk; **S~ di Stato** Secretary of State

segrete'ria *sf* (*di ditta, scuola*) (secretary's) office; (*d'organizzazione internazionale*) secretariat; (POL *etc*: *carica*) office of Secretary; **~ telefonica** answering service

segre'tezza [segre'tettsa] *sf* secrecy

se'greto, a *ag* secret ♦ *sm* secret; secrecy *no pl*; **in ~** in secret, secretly

segu'ace [se'gwat͡ʃe] *sm/f* follower, disciple

segu'ente *ag* following, next

segu'ire *vt* to follow; (*frequentare: corso*) to attend ♦ *vi* to follow; (*continuare: testo*) to continue

segui'tare *vt* to continue, carry on with ♦ *vi* to continue, carry on

'**seguito** *sm* (*scorta*) suite, retinue; (*discepoli*) followers *pl*; (*favore*) following; (*continuazione*) continuation; (*conseguenza*) result; **di ~** at a stretch, on end; **in ~** later on; **in ~ a, a ~ di** following; (*a causa di*) as a result of, owing to

'**sei** *vb vedi* **essere** ♦ *num* six

sei'cento [sei'tʃɛnto] *num* six hundred ♦ *sm*: **il S~** the seventeenth century

selci'ato [sel'tʃato] *sm* cobbled surface

selezio'nare [selettsjo'nare] *vt* to select

selezi'one [selet'tsjone] *sf* selection

'**sella** *sf* saddle; **sel'lare** *vt* to saddle

selvag'gina [selvad'dʒina] *sf* (*animali*) game

sel'vaggio, a, gi, ge [sel'vaddʒo] *ag* wild; (*tribù*) savage, uncivilized; (*fig*) savage, brutal ♦ *sm/f* savage

sel'vatico, a, ci, che *ag* wild

se'maforo *sm* (AUT) traffic lights *pl*

sem'brare *vi* to seem ♦ *vb impers*: **sembra che** it seems that; **mi sembra che** it seems to me that; I think (that); **~ di essere** to seem to be

'**seme** *sm* seed; (*sperma*) semen; (CARTE) suit

se'mestre *sm* half-year, six-month period

'**semi...** *prefisso* semi...; **semi'cerchio** *sm* semicircle; **semifi'nale** *sf* semifinal; **semi'freddo** *sm* ice-cream cake

'**semina** *sf* (AGR) sowing

semi'nare *vt* to sow

semi'nario *sm* seminar; (REL) seminary

seminter'rato *sm* basement; (*appartamento*) basement flat

sem'mai = **se mai**; *vedi* **se**

'**semola** *sf*: **~ di grano duro** durum wheat

semo'lino *sm* semolina

'semplice ['semplitʃe] *ag* simple; (*di un solo elemento*) single; **semplice'mente** *av* simply; **semplicità** *sf* simplicity

'sempre *av* always; (*ancora*) still; **posso ~ tentare** I can always o still try; **da ~** always; **per ~** forever; **una volta per ~** once and for all; **~ che** provided (that); **~ più** more and more; **~ meno** less and less

sempre'verde *ag, sm o f* (*BOT*) evergreen

'senape *sf* (*CUC*) mustard

se'nato *sm* senate; **sena'tore, 'trice** *sm/f* senator

'senno *sm* judgment, (*common*) sense; **col ~ di poi** with hindsight

sennò *av* = **se no**; *vedi* **se**

'seno *sm* (*ANAT: petto, mammella*) breast; (: *grembo, fig*) womb; (: *cavità*) sinus

sen'sato, a *ag* sensible

sensazio'nale [sensattsjo'nale] *ag* sensational

sensazi'one [sensat'tsjone] *sf* feeling, sensation; **avere la ~ che** to have a feeling that; **fare ~** to cause a sensation, create a stir

sen'sibile *ag* sensitive; (*ai sensi*) perceptible; (*rilevante, notevole*) appreciable, noticeable; **~ a** sensitive to; **sensibilità** *sf* sensitivity

'senso *sm* (*FISIOL, istinto*) sense; (*impressione, sensazione*) feeling, sensation; (*significato*) meaning, sense; (*direzione*) direction; **~i** *smpl* (*coscienza*) consciousness *sg*; (*sensualità*) senses; **ciò non ha ~** that doesn't make sense; **fare ~ a** (*ripugnare*) to disgust, repel; **~ comune** common sense; **in ~ orario/ antiorario** clockwise/anticlockwise; **a ~ unico** (*strada*) one-way

sensu'ale *ag* sensual; sensuous; **sensualità** *sf* sensuality; sensuousness

sen'tenza [sen'tentsa] *sf* (*DIR*) sentence; (*massima*) maxim; **sentenzi'are** *vi* (*DIR*) to pass judgment

senti'ero *sm* path

sentimen'tale *ag* sentimental; (*vita, avventura*) love *cpd*

senti'mento *sm* feeling

senti'nella *sf* sentry

sen'tire *vt* (*percepire al tatto, fig*) to feel; (*udire*) to hear; (*ascoltare*) to listen to; (*odore*) to smell; (*avvertire con il gusto, assaggiare*) to taste ♦ *vi*: **~ di** (*avere sapore*) to taste of; (*avere odore*) to smell of; **~rsi** *vr* (*uso reciproco*) to be in touch; **~rsi bene/male** to feel well/unwell o ill; **~rsi di fare qc** (*essere disposto*) to feel like doing sth

sen'tito, a *ag* (*sincero*) sincere, warm; **per ~ dire** by hearsay

'senza ['sentsa] *prep, cong* without; **~ dir nulla** without saying a word; **fare ~ qc** to do without sth; **~ di me** without me; **~ che io lo sapessi** without me o my knowing; **senz'altro** of course, certainly; **~ dubbio** no doubt; **~ scrupoli** unscrupulous; **~ amici** friendless

sepa'rare *vt* to separate; (*dividere*) to divide; (*tenere distinto*) to distinguish; **~rsi** *vr* (*coniugi*) to separate, part; (*amici*) to part, leave each other; **~rsi da** (*coniuge*) to separate o part from; (*amico, socio*) to part company with; (*oggetto*) to part with; **sepa'rato, a** *ag* (*letti, conto etc*) separate; (*coniugi*) separated; **separazi'one** *sf* separation

se'polcro *sm* sepulchre

se'polto, a *pp di* **seppellire**

seppel'lire *vt* to bury

'seppia *sf* cuttlefish ♦ *ag inv* sepia

se'quenza [se'kwentsa] *sf* sequence

seques'trare *vt* (*DIR*) to impound; (*rapire*) to kidnap; **se'questro** *sm* (*DIR*) impoundment; **sequestro di persona** kidnapping

'sera *sf* evening; **di ~** in the evening; **domani ~** tomorrow evening, tomorrow night; **se'rale** *ag* evening *cpd*; **se'rata** *sf* evening; (*ricevimento*) party

ser'bare *vt* to keep; (*mettere da parte*) to put aside; **~ rancore/odio verso qn** to bear sb a grudge/hate sb

serba'toio *sm* tank; (*cisterna*) cistern

'serbo *sm*: **mettere/tenere** o **avere in ~ qc** to put/keep sth aside

se'reno, a *ag* (*tempo, cielo*) clear; (*fig*) serene, calm

ser'gente [ser'dʒɛnte] *sm* (*MIL*) sergeant

'serie *sf inv* (*successione*) series *inv*; (*gruppo, collezione*) set; (*SPORT*) division; league; (*COMM*): **modello di ~/fuori ~** standard/ custom-built model; **in ~** in quick succession; (*COMM*) mass *cpd*

serietà *sf* seriousness; reliability

'serio, a *ag* serious; (*impiegato, ditta*) responsible, reliable; **sul ~** (*davvero*) really, truly; (*seriamente*) seriously

ser'mone *sm* sermon

serpeggi'are [serped'dʒare] *vi* to wind; (*fig*) to spread

ser'pente *sm* snake; **~ a sonagli** rattlesnake

'serra *sf* greenhouse; hothouse

ser'randa *sf* roller shutter

ser'rare *vt* to close, shut; (*a chiave*) to lock; (*stringere*) to tighten; **~ i pugni/i denti** to clench one's fists/teeth; **~ le file** to close ranks

serra'tura *sf* lock

'serva *sf vedi* **servo**

'server ['sɛrver] *sm inv* (*INFORM*) server

ser'vire *vt* to serve; (*clienti: al ristorante*) to wait on; (: *al negozio*) to serve, attend to; (*fig: giovare*) to aid, help; (*CARTE*) to deal ♦ *vi* (*TENNIS*) to serve; (*essere utile*): **~ a qn** to be of use to sb; ~ **a qc/a fare** (*utensile etc*) to be used for sth/for doing; ~ **(a qn) da** to serve as (for sb); **~rsi** *vr* (*usare*): **~rsi di** to use; (*prendere: cibo*): **~rsi (di)** to help o.s. (to); (*essere cliente abituale*): **~rsi da** to be a regular customer at, go to

servitù *sf* servitude; slavery; (*personale di servizio*) servants *pl*, domestic staff

servizi'evole [servit'tsjevole] *ag* obliging, willing to help

ser'vizio [ser'vittsjo] *sm* service; (*al ristorante: sul conto*) service (charge); (*STAMPA, TV, RADIO*) report; (*da tè, caffè etc*) set, service; ~ **smpl** (*di casa*) kitchen and bathroom; (*ECON*) services; **essere di** ~ to be on duty; **fuori** ~ (*telefono etc*) out of order; ~ **compreso** service included; ~ **militare** military service; **~i segreti** secret service *sg*

'servo, a *sm/f* servant

ses'santa *num* sixty; **sessan'tesimo, a** *num* sixtieth

sessan'tina *sf*: **una** ~ **(di)** about sixty

sessi'one *sf* session

'sesso *sm* sex; **sessu'ale** *ag* sexual, sex *cpd*

ses'tante *sm* sextant

'sesto, a *ag, sm* sixth

'seta *sf* silk

'sete *sf* thirst; **avere** ~ to be thirsty

'setola *sf* bristle

'setta *sf* sect

set'tanta *num* seventy; **settan'tesimo, a** *num* seventieth

settan'tina *sf*: **una** ~ **(di)** about seventy

'sette *num* seven

sette'cento [sette'tʃɛnto] *num* seven hundred ♦ *sm*: **il S~** the eighteenth century

set'tembre *sm* September

settentrio'nale *ag* northern

settentri'one *sm* north

setti'mana *sf* week; **settima'nale** *ag, sm* weekly

'settimo, a *ag, sm* seventh

set'tore *sm* sector

severità *sf* severity

se'vero, a *ag* severe

sevizi'are [sevit'tsjare] *vt* to torture

se'vizie [se'vittsje] *sfpl* torture *sg*

sezio'nare [settsjo'nare] *vt* to divide into sections; (*MED*) to dissect

sezi'one [set'tsjone] *sf* section

sfaccen'dato, a [sfattʃen'dato] *ag* idle

sfacci'ato, a [sfat'tʃato] *ag* (*maleducato*) cheeky, impudent; (*vistoso*) gaudy

sfa'celo [sfa'tʃɛlo] *sm* (*fig*) ruin, collapse

sfal'darsi *vr* to flake (off)

sfa'mare *vt* to feed; (*sog: cibo*) to fill

'sfarzo ['sfartso] *sm* pomp, splendour

sfasci'are [sfaʃ'ʃare] *vt* (*ferita*) to unbandage; (*distruggere*) to smash, shatter; **~rsi** *vr*

(*rompersi*) to smash, shatter

sfa'tare *vt* (*leggenda*) to explode

sfavil'lare *vi* to spark, send out sparks; (*risplendere*) to sparkle

sfavo'revole *ag* unfavourable

'sfera *sf* sphere; **'sferico, a, ci, che** *ag* spherical

sfer'rare *vt* (*fig: colpo*) to land, deal; (: *attacco*) to launch

sfer'zare [sfer'tsare] *vt* to whip; (*fig*) to lash out at

sfi'brare *vt* (*indebolire*) to exhaust, enervate

'sfida *sf* challenge

sfi'dare *vt* to challenge; (*fig*) to defy, brave

sfi'ducia [sfi'dutʃa] *sf* distrust, mistrust

sfigu'rare *vt* (*persona*) to disfigure; (*quadro, statua*) to deface ♦ *vi* (*far cattiva figura*) to make a bad impression

sfi'lare *vt* (*ago*) to unthread; (*abito, scarpe*) to slip off ♦ *vi* (*truppe*) to march past; (*atleti*) to parade; **~rsi** *vr* (*perle etc*) to come unstrung; (*orlo, tessuto*) to fray; (*calza*) to run, ladder; **sfi'lata** *sf* march past; parade; **sfilata di moda** fashion show

'sfinge ['sfindʒe] *sf* sphinx

sfi'nito, a *ag* exhausted

sfio'rare *vt* to brush (against); (*argomento*) to touch upon

sfio'rire *vi* to wither, fade

sfo'cato, a *ag* (*FOT*) out of focus

sfoci'are [sfo'tʃare] *vi*: ~ **in** to flow into; (*fig: malcontento*) to develop into

sfode'rato, a *ag* (*vestito*) unlined

sfo'gare *vt* to vent, pour out; **~rsi** *vr* (*sfogare la propria rabbia*) to give vent to one's anger; (*confidarsi*): **~rsi (con)** to pour out one's feelings (to); **non sfogarti su di me!** don't take your bad temper out on me!

sfoggi'are [sfod'dʒare] *vt, vi* to show off

'sfoglia ['sfoʎʎa] *sf* sheet of pasta dough; **pasta** ~ (*CUC*) puff pastry

sfogli'are [sfoʎ'ʎare] *vt* (*libro*) to leaf through

'sfogo, ghi *sm* (*eruzione cutanea*) rash; (*fig*) outburst; **dare** ~ **a** (*fig*) to give vent to

sfolgo'rante *ag* (*luce*) blazing; (*fig: vittoria*) brilliant

sfol'lare *vt* to empty, clear ♦ *vi* to disperse; ~ **da** (*città*) to evacuate

sfon'dare *vt* (*porta*) to break down; (*scarpe*) to wear a hole in; (*cesto, scatola*) to burst, knock the bottom out of; (*MIL*) to break through ♦ *vi* (*riuscire*) to make a name for o.s.

'sfondo *sm* background

sfor'mato *sm* (*CUC*) type of soufflé

sfor'nare *vt* (*pane etc*) to take out of the oven; (*fig*) to churn out

sfor'nito, a *ag*: ~ **di** lacking in, without;

(*negozio*) out of

sfor'tuna *sf* misfortune, ill luck *no pl*; **avere ~** to be unlucky; **sfortu'nato, a** *ag* unlucky; (*impresa, film*) unsuccessful

sfor'zare [sfor'tsare] *vt* to force; (*voce, occhi*) to strain; **~rsi** *vr*: **~rsi di** o **a** o **per fare** to try hard to do

'sforzo ['sfɔrtso] *sm* effort; (*tensione eccessiva, TECN*) strain; **fare uno ~** to make an effort

sfrat'tare *vt* to evict; **'sfratto** *sm* eviction

sfrecci'are [sfret'tʃare] *vi* to shoot o flash past

sfregi'are [sfre'dʒare] *vt* to slash, gash; (*persona*) to disfigure; (*quadro*) to deface; **'sfregio** *sm* gash; scar; (*fig*) insult

sfre'nato, a *ag* (*fig*) unrestrained, unbridled

sfron'tato, a *ag* shameless

sfrutta'mento *sm* exploitation

sfrut'tare *vt* (*terreno*) to overwork, exhaust; (*miniera*) to exploit, work; (*fig: operai, occasione, potere*) to exploit ·

sfug'gire [sfud'dʒire] *vi* to escape; **~ a** (*custode*) to escape (from); (*morte*) to escape; **~ a qn** (*dettaglio, nome*) to escape sb; **~ di mano a qn** to slip out of sb's hand (o hands); **sfug'gita: di sfuggita** *ad* (*rapidamente, in fretta*) in passing

sfu'mare *vt* (*colori, contorni*) to soften, shade off ♦ *vi* to shade (off), fade; (*fig: svanire*) to vanish, disappear; (: *speranze*) to come to nothing

sfuma'tura *sf* shading off *no pl*; (*tonalità*) shade, tone; (*fig*) touch, hint

sfuri'ata *sf* (*scatto di collera*) fit of anger; (*rimprovero*) sharp rebuke

sga'bello *sm* stool

sgabuz'zino [sgabud'dzino] *sm* lumber room

sgambet'tare *vi* to kick one's legs about

sgam'betto *sm*: **far lo ~ a qn** to trip sb up; (*fig*) to oust sb

sganasci'arsi [zganaʃ'ʃarsi] *vr*: **~ dalle risa** to roar with laughter

sganci'are [zgan'tʃare] *vt* to unhook; (*FERR*) to uncouple; (*bombe: da aereo*) to release, drop; (*fig: fam: soldi*) to fork out; **~rsi** *vr* (*fig*): **~rsi (da)** to get away (from)

sghe'rato, a [zgange'rato] *ag* (*porta*) off its hinges; (*auto*) ramshackle; (*risata*) wild, boisterous

sgar'bato, a *ag* rude, impolite

'sgarbo *sm*: **fare uno ~ a qn** to be rude to sb

sgattaio'lare *vi* to sneak away o off

sge'lare [zdʒe'lare] *vi, vt* to thaw

'sghembo, a ['zgembo] *ag* (*obliquo*) slanting; (*storto*) crooked

sghignaz'zare [zgiɲɲat'tsare] *vi* to laugh scornfully

sgob'bare (*fam*) *vi* (*scolaro*) to swot;

(*operaio*) to slog

sgoccio'lare [zgottʃo'lare] *vt* (*vuotare*) to drain (to the last drop) ♦ *vi* (*acqua*) to drip; (*recipiente*) to drain; **'sgoccioli** *smpl*: **essere agli sgoccioli** (*provviste*) to be nearly finished; (*periodo*) to be nearly over

sgo'larsi *vr* to talk (o shout o sing) o.s. hoarse

sgomb(e)'rare *vt* to clear; (*andarsene da: stanza*) to vacate; (*evacuare*) to evacuate

'sgombro, a *ag*: **~ (di)** clear (of), free (from) ♦ *sm* (*ZOOL*) mackerel; (*anche: sgombero*) clearing; vacating; evacuation; (: *trasloco*) removal

sgomen'tare *vt* to dismay; **sgo'mento, a** *ag* dismayed ♦ *sm* dismay, consternation

sgonfi'are *vt* to let down, deflate; **~rsi** *vr* to go down

'sgorbio *sm* blot; scribble

sgor'gare *vi* to gush (out)

sgoz'zare [zgot'tsare] *vt* to cut the throat of

sgra'devole *ag* unpleasant, disagreeable

sgra'dito, a *ag* unpleasant, unwelcome

sgra'nare *vt* (*piselli*) to shell; **~ gli occhi** to open one's eyes wide

sgran'chirsi [zgran'kirsi] *vr* to stretch; **~ le gambe** to stretch one's legs

sgranocchi'are [zgranok'kjare] *vt* to munch

'sgravio *sm*: **~ fiscale** tax relief

sgrazi'ato, a [zgrat'tsjato] *ag* clumsy, ungainly

sgreto'lare *vt* to cause to crumble; **~rsi** *vr* to crumble

sgri'dare *vt* to scold; **sgri'data** *sf* scolding

sguai'ato, a *ag* coarse, vulgar

sgual'cire [zgwal'tʃire] *vt* to crumple (up), crease

sgual'drina (*peg*) *sf* slut

sgu'ardo *sm* (*occhiata*) look, glance; (*espressione*) look (in one's eye)

'sguattero, a *sm/f* dishwasher (*person*)

sguaz'zare [zgwat'tsare] *vi* (*nell'acqua*) to splash about; (*nella melma*) to wallow; **~ nell'oro** to be rolling in money

sguinzagli'are [zgwintsaʎ'ʎare] *vt* to let off the leash; (*fig: persona*): **~ qn dietro a qn** to set sb on sb

sgusci'are [zguʃ'ʃare] *vt* to shell ♦ *vi* (*sfuggire di mano*) to slip; **~ via** to slip o slink away

'shampoo ['ʃampo] *sm inv* shampoo

shock [ʃɔk] *sm inv* shock

PAROLA CHIAVE

si¹ (*dav lo, la, li, le, ne diventa* **se**) *pron* **1** (*riflessivo: maschile*) himself; (: *femminile*) herself; (: *impersonale*) itself; (: *pl*) themselves; **lavarsi** to wash (oneself); **~ è tagliato** he has cut himself; **~ credono importanti** they think a lot of themselves

2 (*riflessivo: con complemento oggetto*): **lavarsi le mani** to wash one's hands; ~ **sta lavando i capelli** he (*o* she) is washing his (*o* her) hair

3 (*reciproco*) one another, each other; **si amano** they love one another *o* each other

4 (*passivo*): ~ **ripara facilmente** it is easily repaired

5 (*impersonale*): ~ **dice che ...** they *o* people say that ...; ~ **vede che è vecchio** one *o* you can see that it's old

6 (*noi*) we; **tra poco ~ parte** we're leaving soon

si² *sm* (*MUS*) B; (*solfeggiando la scala*) ti

sì *av* yes; **un giorno ~ e uno no** every other day

'sia *cong*: ~ ... ~ (*o* ... *o*): ~ **che lavori, ~ che non lavori** whether he works or not; (*tanto ... quanto*): **verranno ~ Luigi ~ suo fratello** both Luigi and his brother will be coming

si'amo *vb vedi* **essere**

sibi'lare *vi* to hiss; (*fischiare*) to whistle; **'sibilo** *sm* hiss; whistle

si'cario *sm* hired killer

sicché [sik'ke] *cong* (*perciò*) so (that), therefore; (*e quindi*) (and) so

siccità [sittʃi'ta] *sf* drought

sic'come *cong* since, as

Si'cilia [si'tʃilja] *sf*: **la ~** Sicily; **sicili'ano, a** *ag, sm/f* Sicilian

si'cura *sf* safety catch; (*AUT*) safety lock

sicu'rezza [siku'rettsa] *sf* safety; security; (*fiducia*) confidence; (*certezza*) certainty; **di ~** safety *cpd*; **la ~ stradale** road safety

si'curo, a *ag* safe; (*ben difeso*) secure; (*fiducioso*) confident; (*certo*) sure, certain; (*notizia, amico*) reliable; (*esperto*) skilled ♦ *av* (*anche: di ~*) certainly; **essere/mettere al ~ to** be safe/put in a safe place; ~ **di sé** self-confident, sure of o.s.; **sentirsi ~ to** feel safe *o* secure

siderur'gia [siderur'dʒia] *sf* iron and steel industry

'sidro *sm* cider

si'epe *sf* hedge

si'ero *sm* (*MED*) serum; **sieronega'tivo, a** *ag* HIV-negative; **sieroposi'tivo, a** *ag* HIV-positive

si'esta *sf* siesta, (afternoon) nap

si'ete *vb vedi* **essere**

si'filide *sf* syphilis

si'fone *sm* siphon

Sig. *abbr* (= *signore*) Mr

siga'retta *sf* cigarette

'sigaro *sm* cigar

Sigg. *abbr* (= *signori*) Messrs

sigil'lare [sidʒil'lare] *vt* to seal

si'gillo [si'dʒillo] *sm* seal

'sigla *sf* initials *pl*; acronym, abbreviation; ~ **automobilistica** abbreviation of province on vehicle number plate; ~ **musicale** signature tune

si'glare *vt* to initial

Sig.na *abbr* (= *signorina*) Miss

signifi'care [siɲɲifi'kare] *vt* to mean; **significa'tivo, a** *ag* significant; **signifi'cato** *sm* meaning

si'gnora [siɲ'ɲora] *sf* lady; **la ~ X** Mrs X; **buon giorno S~/Signore/Signorina** good morning; (*deferente*) good morning Madam/Sir/Madam; (*quando si conosce il nome*) good morning Mrs/Mr/Miss X; **Gentile S~/Signore/Signorina** (*in una lettera*) Dear Madam/Sir/Madam; **il signor Rossi e ~** Mr Rossi and his wife; **~e e signori** ladies and gentlemen

si'gnore [siɲ'ɲore] *sm* gentleman; (*padrone*) lord, master; (*REL*): **il S~** the Lord; **il signor X** Mr X; **i ~i Bianchi** (*coniugi*) Mr and Mrs Bianchi; *vedi anche* **signora**

signo'rile [siɲɲo'rile] *ag* refined

signo'rina [siɲɲo'rina] *sf* young lady; **la ~ X** Miss X; *vedi anche* **signora**

Sig.ra *abbr* (= *signora*) Mrs

silenzia'tore [silentsja'tore] *sm* silencer

si'lenzio [si'lentsjo] *sm* silence; **fare ~** to be quiet, stop talking; **silenzi'oso, a** *ag* silent, quiet

si'licio [si'litʃo] *sm* silicon

'sillaba *sf* syllable

silu'rare *vt* to torpedo; (*fig: privare del comando*) to oust

si'luro *sm* torpedo

simboleggi'are [simboled'dʒare] *vt* to symbolize

'simbolo *sm* symbol

'simile *ag* (*analogo*) similar; (*di questo tipo*): **un uomo ~** such a man, a man like this; **libri ~i** such books; ~ **a** similar to; **i suoi ~i** one's fellow men; one's peers

simme'tria *sf* symmetry

simpa'tia *sf* (*qualità*) pleasantness; (*inclinazione*) liking; **avere ~ per qn** to like sb, have a liking for sb; **sim'patico, a, ci, che** *ag* (*persona*) nice, pleasant, likeable; (*casa, albergo etc*) nice, pleasant

simpatiz'zare [simpatid'dzare] *vi*: ~ **con** to take a liking to

sim'posio *sm* symposium

simu'lare *vt* to sham, simulate; (*TECN*) to simulate; **simulazi'one** *sf* shamming; simulation

simul'taneo, a *ag* simultaneous

sina'goga, ghe *sf* synagogue

sincerità [sintʃeri'ta] *sf* sincerity

sin'cero, a [sin'tʃero] *ag* sincere; genuine; heartfelt

'sincope *sf* syncopation; (*MED*) blackout

sinda'cale *ag* (trade-)union *cpd*;
sindaca'lista, i, e *sm/f* trade unionist

sinda'cato *sm* (*di lavoratori*) (trade) union;
(*AMM, ECON, DIR*) syndicate, trust, pool

'sindaco, ci *sm* mayor

sinfo'nia *sf* (*MUS*) symphony

singhioz'zare [singjot'tsare] *vi* to sob; to
hiccup

singhi'ozzo [sin'gjottso] *sm* sob; (*MED*)
hiccup; **avere il ~** to have the hiccups; **a ~**
(*fig*) by fits and starts

singo'lare *ag* (*insolito*) remarkable, singular;
(*LING*) singular ♦ *sm* (*LING*) singular; (*TENNIS*):
~ maschile/femminile men's/women's singles

'singolo, a *ag* single, individual ♦ *sm*
(*persona*) individual; (*TENNIS*) = **singolare**

si'nistra *sf* (*POL*) left (wing); **a ~** on the left;
(*direzione*) to the left

si'nistro, a *ag* left, left-hand; (*fig*) sinister
♦ *sm* (*incidente*) accident

'sino *prep* = **fino**

si'nonimo *sm* synonym; **~ di** synonymous
with

sin'tassi *sf* syntax

'sintesi *sf* synthesis; (*riassunto*) summary,
résumé

sin'tetico, a, ci, che *ag* synthetic

sintetiz'zare [sintetid'dzare] *vt* to
synthesize; (*riassumere*) to summarize

sinto'matico, a, ci, che *ag* symptomatic

'sintomo *sm* symptom

sinu'oso, a *ag* (*strada*) winding

si'pario *sm* (*TEATRO*) curtain

si'rena *sf* (*apparecchio*) siren; (*nella mitologia,
fig*) siren, mermaid

'Siria *sf*: **la ~** Syria

si'ringa, ghe *sf* syringe

'sismico, a, ci, che *ag* seismic

sis'mografo *sm* seismograph

sis'tema, i *sm* system; method, way

siste'mare *vt* (*mettere a posto*) to tidy, put
in order; (*risolvere: questione*) to sort out, •
settle; (*procurare un lavoro a*) to find a job
for; (*dare un alloggio a*) to settle, find
accommodation for; **~rsi** *vr* (*problema*) to be
settled; (*persona: trovare alloggio*) to find
accommodation (*BRIT*) o accommodations
(*US*); (: *trovarsi un lavoro*) to get fixed up
with a job; **ti sistemo io!** I'll soon sort you
out!

siste'matico, a, ci, che *ag* systematic

sistemazi'one [sistemat'tsjone] *sf*
arrangement, order; settlement;
employment; accommodation (*BRIT*),
accommodations (*US*)

'sito *sm*: **~** (*Internet*) website

situ'are *vt* to site, situate; **situ'ato, a** *ag*:
situato a/su situated at/on

situazi'one [situat'tsjone] *sf* situation

ski-lift ['ski:lift] *sm inv* ski tow

slacci'are [zlat'tʃare] *vt* to undo, unfasten

slanci'ato, a [zlan'tʃato] *ag* slender

'slancio *sm* dash, leap; (*fig*) surge; **di ~**
impetuously

sla'vato, a *ag* faded, washed out; (*fig: viso,
occhi*) pale, colourless

'slavo, a *ag* Slav(onic), Slavic

sle'ale *ag* disloyal; (*concorrenza etc*) unfair

sle'gare *vt* to untie

slip [zlip] *sm inv* briefs *pl*

'slitta *sf* sledge; (*trainata*) sleigh

slit'tare *vi* to slip, slide; (*AUT*) to skid

slo'gare *vt* (*MED*) to dislocate

sloggi'are [zlod'dʒare] *vt* (*inquilino*) to turn
out ♦ *vi* to move out

slo'vacco, a, chi, che *ag, sm/f* Slovak

Slovenia [zlo'vɛnja] *sf* Slovenia

smacchi'are [zmak'kjare] *vt* to remove
stains from; **smacchia'tore** *sm* stain
remover

'smacco, chi *sm* humiliating defeat

smagli'ante [zmaʎ'ʎante] *ag* brilliant,
dazzling

smaglia'tura [zmaʎʎa'tura] *sf* (*su maglia,
calza*) ladder; (*della pelle*) stretch mark

smalizi'ato, a [zmalit'tsjato] *ag* shrewd,
cunning

smal'tare *vt* to enamel; (*ceramica*) to glaze;
(*unghie*) to varnish

smal'tire *vt* (*merce*) to sell off; (*rifiuti*) to
dispose of; (*cibo*) to digest; (*peso*) to lose;
(*rabbia*) to get over; **~ la sbornia** to sober up

'smalto *sm* (*anche: di denti*) enamel; (*per
ceramica*) glaze; **~ per unghie** nail varnish

'smania *sf* agitation, restlessness; (*fig*): **~ di**
thirst for, craving for; **avere la ~ addosso** to
have the fidgets; **avere la ~ di fare** to be
desperate to do

smantel'lare *vt* to dismantle

smarri'mento *sm* loss; (*fig*) bewilderment;
dismay

smar'rire *vt* to lose; (*non riuscire a trovare*)
to mislay; **~rsi** *vr* (*perdersi*) to lose one's way,
get lost; (: *oggetto*) to go astray; **smar'rito,
a** *ag* (*sbigottito*) bewildered

smasche'rare [zmaske'rare] *vt* to unmask

smemo'rato, a *ag* forgetful

smen'tire *vt* (*negare*) to deny;
(*testimonianza*) to refute; **smen'tita** *sf*
denial; retraction

sme'raldo *sm* emerald

smerci'are [zmer'tʃare] *vt* (*COMM*) to sell;
(: *svendere*) to sell off

'smesso, a *pp di* **smettere**

'smettere *vt* (*cessare*); (*vestiti*) to stop
wearing ♦ *vi* to stop, cease; **~ di fare** to stop
doing

'smilzo, a ['zmiltso] *ag* thin, lean

sminu'ire vt to diminish, lessen; (fig) to belittle

sminuz'zare [zminut'tsare] vt to break into small pieces; to crumble

smis'tare vt (pacchi etc) to sort; (FERR) to shunt

smisu'rato, a ag boundless, immeasurable; (grandissimo) immense, enormous

smobili'tare vt to demobilize

smo'dato, a ag immoderate

smoking ['smaukıŋ] sm inv dinner jacket

smon'tare vt (mobile, macchina etc) to take to pieces, dismantle; (fig: scoraggiare) to dishearten ♦ vi (scendere: da cavallo) to dismount; (: da treno) to get off; (terminare il lavoro) to stop (work); ~rsi vr to lose heart; to lose one's enthusiasm

'smorfia sf grimace; (atteggiamento lezioso) simpering; **fare ~e** to make faces; to simper; **smorfi'oso, a** ag simpering

'smorto, a ag (viso) pale, wan; (colore) dull

smor'zare [zmor'tsare] vt (suoni) to deaden; (colori) to tone down; (luce) to dim; (sete) to quench; (entusiasmo) to dampen; ~rsi vr (suono, luce) to fade; (entusiasmo) to dampen

'smosso, a pp di **smuovere**

smotta'mento sm landslide

'smunto, a ag haggard, pinched

smu'overe vt to move, shift; (fig: commuovere) to move; (: dall'inerzia) to rouse, stir; ~rsi vr to move, shift

smus'sare vt (angolo) to round off, smooth; (lama etc) to blunt; ~rsi vr to become blunt

snatu'rato, a ag inhuman, heartless

'snello, a ag (agile) agile; (svelto) slender, slim

sner'vare vt to enervate, wear out

sni'dare vt to drive out, flush out

snob'bare vt to snub

sno'bismo sm snobbery

snoccio'lare [znottfo'lare] vt (frutta) to stone; (fig: orazioni) to rattle off

sno'dare vt (rendere agile, mobile) to loosen; ~rsi vr to come loose; (articolarsi) to bend; (strada, fiume) to wind

so vb vedi **sapere**

so'ave ag sweet, gentle, soft

sobbal'zare [sobbal'tsare] vi to jolt, jerk; (trasalire) to jump, start; **sob'balzo** sm jerk, jolt; jump, start

sobbar'carsi vr: ~ **a** to take on, undertake

sob'borgo, ghi sm suburb

sobil'lare vt to stir up, incite

'sobrio, a ag sober

socchi'udere [sok'kjudere] vt (porta) to leave ajar; (occhi) to half-close; **socchi'uso, a** pp di **socchiudere**

soc'correre vt to help, assist; **soc'corso, a**

pp di **soccorrere** ♦ sm help, aid, assistance; **soccorsi** smpl relief sg, aid sg; **soccorso stradale** breakdown service

soci'ale [so'tʃale] ag social; (di associazione) club cpd, association cpd

socia'lismo [sotʃa'lizmo] sm socialism; **socia'lista, i, e** ag, sm/f socialist

società [sotʃe'ta] sf inv society; (sportiva) club; (COMM) company; ~ **per azioni** limited (BRIT) o incorporated (US) company; ~ **a responsabilità limitata** type of limited liability company

soci'evole [so'tʃevole] ag sociable

'socio ['sɔtʃo] sm (DIR, COMM) partner; (membro di associazione) member

'soda sf (CHIM) soda; (bibita) soda (water)

soda'lizio [soda'littsjo] sm association, society

soddisfa'cente [soddisfa'tʃɛnte] ag satisfactory

soddis'fare vt, vi: ~ **a** to satisfy; (impegno) to fulfil; (debito) to pay off; (richiesta) to meet, comply with; **soddis'fatto, a** pp di **soddisfare** ♦ ag satisfied; **soddisfatto di** happy o satisfied with; pleased with; **soddisfazi'one** sf satisfaction

'sodo, a ag firm, hard; (uovo) hard-boiled ♦ av (picchiare, lavorare) hard; (dormire) soundly

sofà sm inv sofa

soffe'renza [soffe'rɛntsa] sf suffering

sof'ferto, a pp di **soffrire**

soffi'are vt to blow; (notizia, segreto) to whisper ♦ vi to blow; (sbuffare) to puff (and blow); ~rsi **il naso** to blow one's nose; ~ **qc/ qn a qn** (fig) to pinch o steal sth/sb from sb; ~ **via qc** to blow sth away

'soffice ['sɔffitʃe] ag soft

'soffio sm (di vento) breath; ~ **al cuore** heart murmur

sof'fitta sf attic

sof'fitto sm ceiling

soffo'care vi (anche: ~rsi) to suffocate, choke ♦ vt to suffocate, choke; (fig) to stifle, suppress

sof'friggere [sof'friddʒere] vt to fry lightly

sof'frire vt to suffer, endure; (sopportare) to bear, stand ♦ vi to suffer; to be in pain; ~ **(di) qc** (MED) to suffer from sth

sof'fritto, a pp di **soffriggere** ♦ sm (CUC) fried mixture of herbs, bacon and onions

sofisti'cato, a ag sophisticated; (vino) adulterated

sogget'tivo, a [soddʒet'tivo] ag subjective

sog'getto, a [sod'dʒetto] ag: ~ **a** (sottomesso) subject to; (esposto: a variazioni, danni etc) subject o liable to ♦ sm subject

soggezi'one [soddʒet'tsjone] sf subjection; (timidezza) awe; **avere ~ di qn** to stand in awe of sb; to be ill at ease in sb's presence

sogghi'gnare [soggiɲ'ɲare] *vi* to sneer

soggior'nare [soddʒor'nare] *vi* to stay; **soggi'orno** *sm (invernale, marino)* stay; *(stanza)* living room

sog'giungere [sod'dʒundʒere] *vt* to add

'soglia ['sɔʎʎa] *sf* doorstep; *(anche fig)* threshold

'sogliola ['sɔʎʎola] *sf (ZOOL)* sole

so'gnare [soɲ'ɲare] *vt, vi* to dream; **~ a occhi aperti** to daydream; **sogna'tore, 'trice** *sm/f* dreamer

'sogno ['soɲɲo] *sm* dream

'soia *sf (BOT)* soya

sol *sm (MUS)* G; *(: solfeggiando)* so(h)

so'laio *sm (soffitta)* attic

sola'mente *av* only, just

so'lare *ag* solar, sun *cpd*

'solco, chi *sm (scavo, fig: ruga)* furrow; *(incavo)* rut, track; *(di disco)* groove

sol'dato *sm* soldier; **~ semplice** private

'soldo *sm (fig)*: **non avere un ~** to be penniless; **non vale un ~** it's not worth a penny; **~i** *smpl (denaro)* money *sg*

'sole *sm* sun; *(luce)* sun(light); *(tempo assolato)* sun(shine); **prendere il ~** to sunbathe

soleggi'ato, a [soled'dʒato] *ag* sunny

so'lenne *ag* solemn; **solennità** *sf* solemnity; *(festività)* holiday, feast day

sol'fato *sm (CHIM)* sulphate

soli'dale *ag*: **essere ~ (con)** to be in agreement (with)

solidarietà *sf* solidarity

'solido, a *ag* solid; *(forte, robusto)* sturdy, solid; *(fig: ditta)* sound, solid ♦ *sm (MAT)* solid

soli'loquio *sm* soliloquy

so'lista, i, e *ag* solo ♦ *sm/f* soloist

solita'mente *av* usually, as a rule

soli'tario, a *ag (senza compagnia)* solitary, lonely; *(solo, isolato)* solitary, lone; *(deserto)* lonely ♦ *sm (gioiello, gioco)* solitaire

'solito, a *ag* usual; **essere ~ fare** to be in the habit of doing; **di ~** usually; **più tardi del ~** later than usual; **come al ~** as usual

soli'tudine *sf* solitude

solleci'tare [solletʃi'tare] *vt (lavoro)* to speed up; *(persona)* to urge on; *(chiedere con insistenza)* to press for, request urgently; *(stimolare)*: **~ qn a fare** to urge sb to do; **sollecitazi'one** *sf* entreaty, request; *(fig)* incentive; *(TECN)* stress

sol'lecito, a [sol'letʃito] *ag* prompt, quick ♦ *sm (lettera)* reminder; **solleci'tudine** *sf* promptness, speed

solleti'care *vt* to tickle

sol'letico *sm* tickling; **soffrire il ~** to be ticklish

solleva'mento *sm* raising; lifting; revolt; **~ pesi** *(SPORT)* weight-lifting

solle'vare *vt* to lift, raise; *(fig: persona: alleggerire)*: **~ (da)** to relieve (of); *(: dar conforto)* to comfort, relieve; *(: questione)* to raise; *(: far insorgere)* to stir (to revolt); **~rsi** *vr* to rise; *(fig: riprendersi)* to recover; *(: ribellarsi)* to rise up

solli'evo *sm* relief; *(conforto)* comfort

'solo, a *ag* alone; *(in senso spirituale: isolato)* lonely; *(unico)*: **un ~ libro** only one book, a single book; *(con ag numerale)*: **veniamo noi tre ~i** just o only the three of us are coming ♦ *av (soltanto)* only, just; **non ~ ... ma anche** not only ... but also; **fare qc da ~** to do sth (all) by oneself

sol'tanto *av* only

so'lubile *ag (sostanza)* soluble

soluzi'one [solut'tsjone] *sf* solution

sol'vente *ag, sm* solvent

'soma *sf*: **bestia da ~** beast of burden

so'maro *sm* ass, donkey

somigli'anza [somiʎ'ʎantsa] *sf* resemblance

somigli'are [somiʎ'ʎare] *vi*: **~ a** to be like, resemble; *(nell'aspetto fisico)* to look like; **~rsi** *vr* to be (o look) alike

'somma *sf (MAT)* sum; *(di denaro)* sum (of money)

som'mare *vt* to add up; *(aggiungere)* to add; **tutto sommato** all things considered

som'mario, a *ag (racconto, indagine)* brief; *(giustizia)* summary ♦ *sm* summary

som'mergere [som'merdʒere] *vt* to submerge

sommer'gibile [sommer'dʒibile] *sm* submarine

som'merso, a *pp di* **sommergere**

som'messo, a *ag (voce)* soft, subdued

somminis'trare *vt* to give, administer

sommità *sf inv* summit, top; *(fig)* height

'sommo, a *ag* highest; *(rispetto etc)* highest, greatest; *(poeta, artista)* great, outstanding; **per ~i capi** briefly, covering the main points

som'mossa *sf* uprising

so'nare *etc* = **suonare** *etc*

son'daggio [son'daddʒo] *sm* sounding; probe; boring, drilling; *(indagine)* survey; **~ d'opinioni** opinion poll

son'dare *vt (NAUT)* to sound; *(atmosfera, piaga)* to probe; *(MINERALOGIA)* to bore, drill; *(fig: opinione etc)* to survey, poll

so'netto *sm* sonnet

son'nambulo, a *sm/f* sleepwalker

sonnecchi'are [sonnek'kjare] *vi* to doze, nod

son'nifero *sm* sleeping drug (*o* pill)

'sonno *sm* sleep; **prendere ~** to fall asleep; **aver ~** to be sleepy

'sono *vb vedi* **essere**

so'noro, a ag (ambiente) resonant; (voce) sonorous, ringing; (onde, film) sound cpd

sontu'oso, a ag sumptuous; lavish

sopo'rifero, a ag soporific

soppe'sare vt to weigh in one's hand(s), feel the weight of; (fig) to weigh up

soppi'atto: di ~ av secretly; furtively

soppor'tare vt (reggere) to support; (subire: perdita, spese) to bear, sustain; (soffrire: dolore) to bear, endure; (sog: cosa: freddo) to withstand; (sog: persona: freddo, vino) to take; (tollerare) to put up with, tolerate

sop'presso, a pp di **sopprimere**

sop'primere vt (carica, privilegi, testimone) to do away with; (pubblicazione) to suppress; (parola, frase) to delete

'sopra prep (gen) on; (al di sopra di, più in alto di) above; over; (riguardo a) on, about ♦ av on top; (attaccato, scritto) on it; (al di sopra) above; (al piano superiore) upstairs; **donne ~ i 30 anni** women over 30 (years of age); **abito di ~** I live upstairs; **dormirci ~** (fig) to sleep on it

so'prabito sm overcoat

soprac'ciglio [soprat'tʃiʎʎo] (pl(f) **soprac'ciglia**) sm eyebrow

sopracco'perta sf (di letto) bedspread; (di libro) jacket

sopraf'fare vt to overcome, overwhelm; **sopraf'fatto, a** pp di **sopraffare**

sopraf'fino, a ag (pranzo, vino) excellent

sopraggi'ungere [soprad'dʒundʒere] vi (giungere all'improvviso) to arrive (unexpectedly); (accadere) to occur (unexpectedly)

sopral'luogo, ghi sm (di esperti) inspection; (di polizia) on-the-spot investigation

sopram'mobile sm ornament

soprannatu'rale ag supernatural

sopran'nome sm nickname

so'prano, a sm/f (persona) soprano ♦ sm (voce) soprano

soprappensi'ero av lost in thought

sopras'salto sm: **di ~** with a start; suddenly

soprasse'dere vi: **~ a** to delay, put off

soprat'tutto av (anzitutto) above all; (specialmente) especially

sopravvalu'tare vt to overestimate

soprav'vento sm: **avere/prendere il ~ su** to have/get the upper hand over

sopravvis'suto, a pp di **sopravvivere**

soprav'vivere vi to survive; (continuare a vivere): **~ (in)** to live on (in); **~ a** (incidente etc) to survive; (persona) to outlive

soprele'vata sf (strada) flyover; (ferrovia) elevated railway

soprin'tendente sm/f supervisor; (statale: di belle arti etc) keeper; **soprinten'denza** sf supervision; (ente): **soprintendenza alle Belle**

Arti government department responsible for monuments and artistic treasures

so'pruso sm abuse of power; **subire un ~** to be abused

soq'quadro sm: **mettere a ~** to turn upside-down

sor'betto sm sorbet, water ice

sor'bire vt to sip; (fig) to put up with

'sorcio, ci ['sortʃo] sm mouse

'sordido, a ag sordid; (fig: gretto) stingy

sor'dina sf: **in ~** softly; (fig) on the sly

sordità sf deafness

'sordo, a ag deaf; (rumore) muffled; (dolore) dull; (odio, rancore) veiled ♦ sm/f deaf person; **sordo'muto, a** ag deaf-and-dumb ♦ sm/f deaf-mute

so'rella sf sister; **sorel'lastra** sf stepsister

sor'gente [sor'dʒɛnte] sf (d'acqua) spring; (di fiume, FISICA, fig) source

'sorgere ['sordʒere] vi to rise; (scaturire) to spring, rise; (fig: difficoltà) to arise

sormon'tare vt (fig) to overcome, surmount

sorni'one, a ag sly

sorpas'sare vt (AUT) to overtake; (fig) to surpass; (: eccedere) to exceed, go beyond; **~ in altezza** to be higher than; (persona) to be taller than; **sor'passo** sm (AUT) overtaking

sorpren'dente ag surprising

sor'prendere vt (cogliere: in flagrante etc) to catch; (stupire) to surprise; **~rsi** vr: **~rsi (di)** to be surprised (at); **sor'presa** sf surprise; **fare una sorpresa a qn** to give sb a surprise; **sor'preso, a** pp di **sorprendere**

sor'reggere [sor'reddʒere] vt to support, hold up; (fig) to sustain; **sor'retto, a** pp di **sorreggere**

sor'ridere vi to smile; **sor'riso, a** pp di **sorridere** ♦ sm smile

'sorso sm sip

'sorta sf sort, kind; **di ~** whatever, of any kind, at all

'sorte sf (fato) fate, destiny; (evento fortuito) chance; **tirare a ~** to draw lots

sor'teggio [sor'teddʒo] sm draw

sorti'legio [sorti'ledʒo] sm witchcraft no pl; (incantesimo) spell; **fare un ~ a qn** to cast a spell on sb

sor'tita sf (MIL) sortie

'sorto, a pp di **sorgere**

sorvegli'anza [sorveʎ'ʎantsa] sf watch; supervision; (POLIZIA, MIL) surveillance

sorvegli'are [sorveʎ'ʎare] vt (bambino, bagagli, prigioniero) to watch, keep an eye on; (malato) to watch over; (territorio, casa) to watch o keep watch over; (lavori) to supervise

sorvo'lare vt (territorio) to fly over ♦ vi: **~ su** (fig) to skim over

'sosia *sm inv* double

sos'pendere *vt* (*appendere*) to hang (up); (*interrompere, privare di una carica*) to suspend; (*rimandare*) to defer; (*appendere*) to hang; **sospensi'one** *sf* (*anche CHIM, AUT*) suspension; deferment; **sos'peso, a** *pp di* **sospendere ♦** *ag* (*appeso*): **sospeso a** hanging on (o from); (*treno, autobus*) cancelled; **in sospeso** in abeyance; (*conto*) outstanding; **tenere in sospeso** (*fig*) to keep in suspense

sospet'tare *vt* to suspect **♦** *vi*: **~ di** to suspect; (*diffidare*) to be suspicious of

sos'petto, a *ag* suspicious **♦** *sm* suspicion; **sospet'toso, a** *ag* suspicious

sos'pingere [sos'pindʒere] *vt* to drive, push; **sos'pinto, a** *pp di* **sospingere**

sospi'rare *vi* to sigh **♦** *vt* to long for, yearn for; **sos'piro** *sm* sigh

'sosta *sf* (*fermata*) stop, halt; (*pausa*) pause, break; **senza ~** non-stop, without a break

sostan'tivo *sm* noun, substantive

sos'tanza [sos'tantsa] *sf* substance; **~e** *sfpl* (*ricchezze*) wealth *sg*, possessions; **in ~** in short, to sum up; **sostanzi'oso, a** *ag* (*cibo*) nourishing, substantial

sos'tare *vi* (*fermarsi*) to stop (for a while), stay; (*fare una pausa*) to take a break

sos'tegno [sos'teɲɲo] *sm* support

soste'nere *vt* to support; (*prendere su di sé*) to take on, bear; (*resistere*) to withstand, stand up to; (*affermare*): **~ che** to maintain that; **~rsi** *vr* to hold o.s. up, support o.s.; (*fig*) to keep up one's strength; **~ gli esami** to sit exams; **sosteni'tore, 'trice** *sm/f* supporter

sostenta'mento *sm* maintenance, support

soste'nuto, a *ag* (*stile*) elevated; (*velocità, ritmo*) sustained; (*prezzo*) high **♦** *sm/f*: **fare il(la) ~(a)** to be standoffish, keep one's distance

sostitu'ire *vt* (*mettere al posto di*): **~ qn/qc a** to substitute sb/sth for; (*prendere il posto di: persona*) to substitute for; (: *cosa*) to take the place of

sosti'tuto, a *sm/f* substitute

sostituzi'one [sostitut'tsjone] *sf* substitution; **in ~ di** as a substitute for, in place of

sotta'ceti [sotta'tʃeti] *smpl* pickles

sot'tana *sf* (*sottoveste*) underskirt; (*gonna*) skirt; (*REL*) soutane, cassock

sotter'fugio [sotter'fudʒo] *sm* subterfuge

sotter'raneo, a *ag* underground **♦** *sm* cellar

sotter'rare *vt* to bury

sottigli'ezza [sotti λ 'λettsa] *sf* thinness; slimness; (*fig: acutezza*) subtlety; shrewdness; **~e** *sfpl* (*pedanteria*) quibbles

sot'tile *ag* thin; (*figura, caviglia*) thin, slim, slender; (*fine: polvere, capelli*) fine; (*fig:*

leggero) light; (: *vista*) sharp, keen; (: *olfatto*) fine, discriminating; (: *mente*) subtle; shrewd **♦** *sm*: **non andare per il ~** not to mince matters

sottin'tendere *vt* (*intendere qc non espresso*) to understand; (*implicare*) to imply; **sottin'teso, a** *pp di* **sottintendere ♦** *sm* allusion; **parlare senza sottintesi** to speak plainly

'sotto *prep* (*gen*) under; (*più in basso di*) below **♦** *av* underneath, beneath; below; (**al piano**) **di ~** downstairs; **~ forma di** in the form of; **~ il monte** at the foot of the mountain; **siamo ~ Natale** it's nearly Christmas; **~ la pioggia/il sole** in the rain/sun(shine); **~ terra** underground; **chiuso ~ vuoto** vacuum-packed

sottoline'are *vt* to underline; (*fig*) to emphasize, stress

sottoma'rino, a *ag* (*flora*) submarine; (*cavo, navigazione*) underwater **♦** *sm* (*NAUT*) submarine

sotto'messo, a *pp di* **sottomettere**

sotto'mettere *vt* to subdue, subjugate; **~rsi** *vr* to submit

sottopas'saggio [sottopas'saddʒo] *sm* (*AUT*) underpass; (*pedonale*) subway, underpass

sotto'porre *vt* (*costringere*) to subject; (*fig: presentare*) to submit; **sottoporsi** *vr* to submit; **sottoporsi a** (*subire*) to undergo; **sotto'posto, a** *pp di* **sottoporre**

sottos'critto, a *pp di* **sottoscrivere**

sottos'crivere *vt* to sign **♦** *vi*: **~ a** to subscribe to; **sottoscrizi'one** *sf* signing; subscription

sottosegre'tario *sm*: **~ di Stato** Under-Secretary of State (*BRIT*), Assistant Secretary of State (*US*)

sotto'sopra *av* upside-down

sotto'terra *av* underground

sotto'titolo *sm* subtitle

sottovalu'tare *vt* to underestimate

sotto'veste *sf* underskirt

sotto'voce [sotto'votʃe] *av* in a low voice .

sot'trarre *vt* to subtract, take away; **~ qn/qc a** (*togliere*) to remove sb/sth from; (*salvare*) to save o rescue sb/sth from; **~ qc a qn** (*rubare*) to steal sth from sb; **sottrarsi a** (*sfuggire*) to escape; (*evitare*) to avoid; **sot'tratto, a** *pp di* **sottrarre**; **sottrazi'one** *sf* subtraction; removal

sovi'etico, a, ci, che *ag* Soviet **♦** *sm/f* Soviet citizen

sovraccari'care *vt* to overload

sovrannatu'rale *ag* = **soprannaturale**

so'vrano, a *ag* sovereign; (*fig: sommo*) supreme **♦** *sm/f* sovereign, monarch

sovrap'porre *vt* to place on top of, put on top of

sovras'tare vi: ~ a (vallata, fiume) to overhang; (fig) to hang over, threaten ♦ vt to overhang; (fig) to hang over, threaten
sovrinten'dente etc = **soprintendente** etc
sovru'mano, a ag superhuman
sovvenzi'one |sovven'tsjone| sf subsidy, grant
sovver'sivo, a ag subversive
'sozzo, a |'sottso| ag filthy, dirty
S.p.A. abbr = **società per azioni**
spac'care vt to split, break; (legna) to chop; ~rsi vr to split, break; **spacca'tura** sf split
spacci'are |spat'tʃare| vt (vendere) to sell (off); (mettere in circolazione) to circulate; (droga) to peddle, push; ~rsi vr: ~rsi per (farsi credere) to pass o.s. off as, pretend to be; **spaccia'tore, 'trice** sm/f (di droga) pusher; (di denaro falso) dealer; **'spaccio** sm (di merce rubata, droga): **spaccio (di)** trafficking (in); (in denaro falso): **spaccio (di)** passing (of); (vendita) sale; (bottega) shop
'spacco, chi sm (fenditura) split, crack; (strappo) tear; (di gonna) slit
spac'cone sm/f boaster, braggart
'spada sf sword
spae'sato, a ag disorientated, lost
spa'ghetti |spa'getti| smpl (CUC) spaghetti sg
'Spagna |'spaɲɲa| sf: **la ~** Spain; **spa'gno-lo, a** ag Spanish ♦ sm/f Spaniard ♦ sm (LING) Spanish; **gli Spagnoli** the Spanish
'spago, ghi sm string, twine
spai'ato, a ag (calza, guanto) odd
spalan'care vt to open wide; ~rsi vr to open wide
spa'lare vt to shovel
'spalla sf shoulder; (fig: TEATRO) stooge; ~e sfpl (dorso) back; **spalleggi'are** vt to back up, support
spalli'era sf (di sedia etc) back; (di letto: da capo) head(board); (: da piedi) foot(board); (GINNASTICA) wall bars pl
spal'lina sf (bretella) strap; (imbottita) shoulder pad
spal'mare vt to spread
'spalti smpl (di stadio) terracing
'spandere vt to spread; (versare) to pour (out); ~rsi vr to spread; **'spanto, a** pp di **spandere**
spa'rare vt to fire ♦ vi (far fuoco) to fire; (tirare) to shoot; **spara'toria** sf exchange of shots
sparecchi'are |sparek'kjare| vt: ~ (la tavola) to clear the table
spa'reggio |spa'reddʒo| sm (SPORT) play-off
'spargere |'spardʒere| vt (sparpagliare) to scatter; (versare: vino) to spill; (: lacrime, sangue) to shed; (diffondere) to spread; (emanare) to give off (o out); ~rsi vr to

spread; **spargi'mento** sm scattering, strewing; spilling; shedding; **spargimento di sangue** bloodshed
spa'rire vi to disappear, vanish
spar'lare vi: ~ **di** to run down, speak ill of
'sparo sm shot
sparpagli'are |sparpaʎ'ʎare| vt to scatter; ~rsi vr to scatter
'sparso, a pp di **spargere** ♦ ag scattered; (sciolto) loose
spar'tire vt (eredità, bottino) to share out; (avversari) to separate
spar'tito sm (MUS) score
sparti'traffico sm inv (AUT) central reservation (BRIT), median (strip) (US)
spa'ruto, a ag (viso etc) haggard
sparvi'ero sm (ZOOL) sparrowhawk
spasi'mante sm suitor
'spasimo sm pang; **'spasmo** sm (MED) spasm; **spas'modico, a, ci, che** ag (angoscioso) agonizing; (MED) spasmodic
spassio'nato, a ag dispassionate, impartial
'spasso sm (divertimento) amusement, enjoyment; **andare a ~** to go out for a walk; **essere a ~** (fig) to be out of work; **mandare qn a ~** (fig) to give sb the sack
'spatola sf spatula; (di muratore) trowel
spau'racchio |spau'rakkjo| sm scarecrow
spau'rire vt to frighten, terrify
spa'valdo, a ag arrogant, bold
spaventa'passeri sm inv scarecrow
spaven'tare vt to frighten, scare; ~rsi vr to be frightened, be scared; to get a fright; **spa'vento** sm fear, fright; **far spavento a qn** to give sb a fright; **spaven'toso, a** ag frightening, terrible; (fig: fam) tremendous, fantastic
spazien'tire |spattsjen'tire| vi (anche: ~rsi) to lose one's patience
'spazio |'spattsjo| sm space; **~ aereo** airspace; **spazi'oso, a** ag spacious
spazzaca'mino |spattsaka'mino| sm chimney sweep
spazza'neve |spattsa'neve| sm inv snow-plough
spaz'zare |spat'tsare| vt to sweep; (foglie etc) to sweep up; (cacciare) to sweep away; **spazza'tura** sf sweepings pl; (immondizia) rubbish; **spaz'zino** sm street sweeper
'spazzola |'spattsola| sf brush; **~ per abiti** clothesbrush; **~ da capelli** hairbrush; **spazzo'lare** vt to brush; **spazzo'lino** sm (small) brush; **spazzolino da denti** toothbrush
specchi'arsi |spek'kjarsi| vr to look at o.s. in a mirror; (riflettersi) to be mirrored, be reflected
'specchio |'spekkjo| sm mirror
speci'ale |spe'tʃale| ag special; **specia'lista, i, e** sm/f specialist; **specialità** sf inv

speciality; (branca di studio) special field, speciality; **specializ'zarsi** vr: **specializzarsi (in)** to specialize (in); **special'mente** av especially, particularly

'specie ['spɛtʃe] sf inv (BIOL, BOT, ZOOL) species inv; (tipo) kind, sort ♦ av especially, particularly; **una ~ di** a kind of; **fare ~ a qn** to surprise sb; **la ~ umana** mankind

specifi'care [spetʃifi'kare] vt to specify, state

spe'cifico, a, ci, che [spe'tʃifiko] ag specific

specu'lare vi: **~ su** (COMM) to speculate in; (sfruttare) to exploit; (apparecchio elettrico) to turn o switch off; (gas) to turn off; (fig: (meditare) to speculate on; **speculazi'one** sf speculation

spe'dire vt to send; **spedizi'one** sf sending; (collo) consignment; (scientifica etc) expedition

'spegnere ['spɛɲɲere] vt (fuoco, sigaretta) to put out, extinguish; (apparecchio elettrico) to turn o switch off; (gas) to turn off; (fig: suoni, passioni) to stifle; (debito) to extinguish; **~rsi** vr to go out; to go off; (morire) to pass away

spel'lare vt (scuoiare) to skin; (scorticare) to graze; **~rsi** vr to peel

'spendere vt to spend

spen'nare vt to pluck

spensie'rato, a ag carefree

'spento, a pp di **spegnere** ♦ ag (suono) muffled; (colore) dull; (sigaretta) out; (civiltà, vulcano) extinct

spe'ranza [spe'rantsa] sf hope

spe'rare vt to hope for ♦ vi: **~ in** to trust in; **~ che/di fare** to hope that/to do; **lo spero, spero di sì** I hope so

sper'duto, a ag (isolato) out-of-the-way; (persona: smarrita, a disagio) lost

spergi'uro, a [sper'dʒuro] sm/f perjurer ♦ sm perjury

sperimen'tale ag experimental

sperimen'tare vt to experiment with, test; (fig) to test, put to the test

'sperma, i sm sperm

spe'rone sm spur

sperpe'rare vt to squander

'spesa sf (somma di denaro) expense; (costo) cost; (acquisto) purchase; (fam: acquisto del cibo quotidiano) shopping; **~e** sfpl (soldi spesi) expenses; (COMM) costs; charges; **fare la ~** to do the shopping; **a ~e di** (a carico di) at the expense of; **~e generali** overheads; **~e postali** postage sg; **~e di viaggio** travelling expenses

'speso, a pp di **spendere**

'spesso, a ag (fitto) thick; (frequente) frequent ♦ av often; **~e volte** frequently, often

spes'sore sm thickness

spet'tabile (abbr: **Spett.**: in lettere) ag: **~ ditta X** Messrs X and Co.

spet'tacolo sm (rappresentazione) performance, show; (vista, scena) sight; **dare ~ di sé** to make an exhibition o a spectacle of o.s.; **spettaco'loso, a** ag spectacular

spet'tare vi: **~ a** (decisione) to be up to; (stipendio) to be due to; **spetta a te decidere** it's up to you to decide

spetta'tore, 'trice sm/f (CINEMA, TEATRO) member of the audience; (di avvenimento) onlooker, witness

spetti'nare vt: **~ qn** to ruffle sb's hair; **~rsi** vr to get one's hair in a mess

'spettro sm (fantasma) spectre; (FISICA) spectrum

'spezie ['spɛttsje] sfpl (CUC) spices

spez'zare [spet'tsare] vt (rompere) to break; (fig: interrompere) to break up; **~rsi** vr to break

spezza'tino [spettsa'tino] sm (CUC) stew

spezzet'tare [spettset'tare] vt to break up (o chop) into small pieces

'spia sf spy; (confidente della polizia) informer; (ELETTR) indicating light; warning light; (fessura) peep-hole; (fig: sintomo) sign, indication

spia'cente [spja'tʃɛnte] ag sorry; **essere ~ di qc/di fare** qc to be sorry about sth/for doing sth

spia'cevole [spja'tʃevole] ag unpleasant

spi'aggia, ge ['spjaddʒa] sf beach; **~ libera** public beach

spia'nare vt (terreno) to level, make level; (edificio) to raze to the ground; (pasta) to roll out; (rendere liscio) to smooth (out)

spi'ano sm: **a tutto ~** (lavorare) non-stop, without a break; (spendere) lavishly

spian'tato, a ag penniless, ruined

spi'are vt to spy on

spi'azzo ['spjattso] sm open space; (radura) clearing

spic'care vt (assegno, mandato di cattura) to issue ♦ vi (risaltare) to stand out; **~ il volo** to fly off; (fig) to spread one's wings; **~ un balzo** to leap; **spic'cato, a** ag (marcato) marked, strong; (notevole) remarkable

'spicchio ['spikkjo] sm (di agrumi) segment; (di aglio) clove; (parte) piece, slice

spicci'are [spit'tʃare] vt to finish off quickly; **~rsi** vr to hurry up

'spicciolo, a ['spittʃolo] ag: **moneta ~a, ~i** smpl (small) change

'spicco, chi sm: **di ~** outstanding; (tema) main, principal; **fare ~** to stand out

spie'dino sm (utensile) skewer; (pietanza) kebab

spi'edo sm (CUC) spit

spie'gare vt (far capire) to explain; (tovaglia) to unfold; (vele) to unfurl; **~rsi** vr to explain o.s., make o.s. clear; **~ qc a qn** to explain sth to sb; **spiegazi'one** sf explanation

spiegaz'zare [spjegat'tsare] vt to crease, crumple

spie'tato, a ag ruthless, pitiless

spiffe'rare (fam) vt to blurt out, blab

'spiga, ghe sf (BOT) ear

spigli'ato, a [spiʎ'ʎato] ag self-possessed, self-confident

'spigolo sm corner; (MAT) edge

'spilla sf brooch; (da cravatta, cappello) pin; ~ **di sicurezza** o **da balia** safety pin

spil'lare vt (vino, fig) to tap; ~ **denaro/notizie a qn** to tap sb for money/information

'spillo sm pin

spi'lorcio, a, ci, ce [spi'lortʃo] ag mean, stingy

'spina sf (BOT) thorn; (ZOOL) spine, prickle; (di pesce) bone; (ELETTR) plug; (di botte) bunghole; **birra alla ~** draught beer; ~ **dorsale** (ANAT) backbone

spi'nacio [spi'natʃo] sm spinach; (CUC): ~**i** spinach sg

'spingere ['spindʒere] vt to push; (condurre: anche fig) to drive; (stimolare): ~ **qn a fare** to urge o press sb to do; ~**rsi** vr (inoltrarsi) to push on, carry on; ~**rsi troppo lontano** (anche fig) to go too far

spi'noso, a ag thorny, prickly

'spinta sf (urto) push; (FISICA) thrust; (fig: stimolo) incentive, spur; (: appoggio) string-pulling no pl; **dare una ~a a qn** (fig) to pull strings for sb

'spinto, a pp di **spingere**

spio'naggio [spio'naddʒo] sm espionage, spying

spi'overe vi to stop raining

'spira sf coil

spi'raglio [spi'raʎʎo] sm (fessura) chink, narrow opening; (raggio di luce, fig) glimmer, gleam

spi'rale sf spiral; (contraccettivo) coil; **a spirale** spiral(-shaped)

spi'rare vi (vento) to blow; (morire) to expire, pass away

spiri'tato, a ag possessed; (fig: persona, espressione) wild

spiri'tismo sm spiritualism

'spirito sm (REL, CHIM, disposizione d'animo, di legge etc, fantasma) spirit; (pensieri, intelletto) mind; (arguzia) wit; (umorismo) humour, wit; **lo S~ Santo** the Holy Spirit o Ghost

spirito'saggine [spirito'saddʒine] sf witticism; (peg) wisecrack

spiri'toso, a ag witty

spiritu'ale ag spiritual

'splendere vi to shine

'splendido, a ag splendid; (splendente) shining; (sfarzoso) magnificent, splendid

splen'dore sm splendour; (luce intensa)

brilliance, brightness

spodes'tare vt to deprive of power; (sovrano) to depose

spogli'are [spoʎ'ʎare] vt (svestire) to undress; (privare, fig: depredare): ~ **qn di qc** to deprive sb of sth; (togliere ornamenti: anche fig): ~ **qn/qc di** to strip sb/sth of; ~**rsi** vr to undress, strip; ~**rsi di** (ricchezze etc) to deprive o.s. of, give up; (pregiudizi) to rid o.s. of; **spoglia'toio** sm dressing room; (di scuola etc) cloakroom; (SPORT) changing room; **'spoglie** ['spoʎʎe] sfpl (salma) remains; (preda) spoils, booty sg; vedi anche spoglio; **'spoglio, a** ag (pianta, terreno) bare; (privo): **spoglio di** stripped of; lacking in, without ♦ sm (di voti) counting

'spola sf (bobina di filo) cop; **fare la ~** (fra) to go to and fro o shuttle (between)

spol'pare vt to strip the flesh off

spolve'rare vt (anche CUC) to dust; (con spazzola) to brush; (con battipanni) to beat; (fig) to polish off ♦ vi to dust

'sponda sf (di fiume) bank; (di mare, lago) shore; (bordo) edge

spon'taneo, a ag spontaneous; (persona) unaffected, natural

spopo'lare vt to depopulate ♦ vi (attirare folla) to draw the crowds; ~**rsi** vr to become depopulated

spor'care vt to dirty, make dirty; (fig) to sully, soil; ~**rsi** vr to get dirty

spor'cizia [spor'tʃittsja] sf (stato) dirtiness; (sudiciume) dirt, filth; (cosa sporca) dirt no pl, something dirty

'sporco, a, chi, che ag dirty, filthy

spor'genza [spor'dʒentsa] sf projection

'sporgere ['spordʒere] vt to put out, stretch out ♦ vi (venire in fuori) to stick out; ~**rsi** vr to lean out; ~ **querela contro qn** (DIR) to take legal action against sb

sport sm inv sport

'sporta sf shopping bag

spor'tello sm (di treno, auto etc) door; (di banca, ufficio) window, counter; ~ **automatico** (BANCA) cash dispenser, automated telling machine

spor'tivo, a ag (gara, giornale, centro) sports cpd; (persona) sporty; (abito) casual; (spirito, atteggiamento) sporting

'sporto, a pp di **sporgere**

'sposa sf bride; (moglie) wife

sposa'lizio [spoza'littsjo] sm wedding

spo'sare vt to marry; (fig: idea, fede) to espouse; ~**rsi** vr to get married, marry; ~**rsi con qn** to marry sb, get married to sb; **spo'sato, a** ag married

'sposo sm (bride)groom; (marito) husband; **gli ~i** smpl the newlyweds

spos'sato, a ag exhausted, weary

spos'tare *vt* to move, shift; (*cambiare: orario*) to change; **~rsi** *vr* to move

'spranga, ghe *sf* (*sbarra*) bar

'sprazzo ['sprattso] *sm* (*di sole etc*) flash; (*fig: di gioia etc*) burst

spre'care *vt* to waste; **~rsi** *vr* (*persona*) to waste one's energy; **'spreco** *sm* waste

spre'gevole [spre'dʒevole] *ag* contemptible, despicable

spregiudi'cato, a [spredʒudi'kato] *ag* unprejudiced, unbiased; (*peg*) unscrupulous

'spremere *vt* to squeeze

spre'muta *sf* fresh juice; **~ d'arancia** fresh orange juice

sprez'zante [spret'tsante] *ag* scornful, contemptuous

sprigio'nare [spridʒo'nare] *vt* to give off, emit; **~rsi** *vr* to emanate; (*uscire con impeto*) to burst out

spriz'zare [sprit'tsare] *vt, vi* to spurt; **~ gioia/salute** to be bursting with joy/health

sprofon'dare *vi* to sink; (*casa*) to collapse; (*suolo*) to give way, subside; **~rsi** *vr*: **~rsi in** (*poltrona*) to sink into; (*fig*) to become immersed *o* absorbed in

spro'nare *vt* to spur (on)

'sprone *sm* (*sperone, fig*) spur

sproporzio'nato, a [sproportsjo'nato] *ag* disproportionate, out of all proportion

sproporzi'one [spropor'tsjone] *sf* disproportion

sproposi'tato, a *ag* (*lettera, discorso*) full of mistakes; (*fig: costo*) excessive, enormous

spro'posito *sm* blunder; **a ~** at the wrong time; (*rispondere, parlare*) irrelevantly

sprovve'duto, a *ag* inexperienced, naïve

sprov'visto, a *ag* (*mancante*): **~ di** lacking in, without; **alla ~a** unawares

spruz'zare [sprut'tsare] *vt* (*a nebulizzazione*) to spray; (*aspergere*) to sprinkle; (*inzaccherare*) to splash; **'spruzzo** *sm* spray; splash

'spugna ['spuɲɲa] *sf* (*ZOOL*) sponge; (*tessuto*) towelling; **spu'gnoso, a** *ag* spongy

'spuma *sf* (*schiuma*) foam; (*bibita*) fizzy drink

spu'mante *sm* sparkling wine

spumeggi'ante [spumed'dʒante] *ag* (*birra*) foaming; (*vino, fig*) sparkling

spu'mone *sm* (*CUC*) mousse

spun'tare *vt* (*coltello*) to break the point of; (*capelli*) to trim ♦ *vi* (*uscire: germoglio*) to sprout; (*: capelli*) to begin to grow; (*: denti*) to come through; (*apparire*) to appear (suddenly); **~rsi** *vr* to become blunt, lose its point; **spuntarla** (*fig*) to make it, win through

spun'tino *sm* snack

'spunto *sm* (*TEATRO, MUS*) cue; (*fig*) starting point; **dare lo ~ a** (*fig*) to give rise to

spur'gare *vt* (*fogna*) to clean, clear

spu'tare *vt* to spit out; (*fig*) to belch (out)

♦ *vi* to spit; **'sputo** *sm* spittle *no pl*, spit *no pl*

'squadra *sf* (*strumento*) (set) square; (*gruppo*) team, squad; (*di operai*) gang, squad; (*MIL*) squad; (*: AER, NAUT*) squadron; (*SPORT*) team; **lavoro a ~e** teamwork

squa'drare *vt* to square, make square; (*osservare*) to look at closely

squa'driglia [skwa'driʎʎa] *sf* (*AER*) flight; (*NAUT*) squadron

squa'drone *sm* squadron

squagli'arsi [skwaʎ'ʎarsi] *vr* to melt; (*fig*) to sneak off

squa'lifica *sf* disqualification

squalifi'care *vt* to disqualify

'squallido, a *ag* wretched, bleak

squal'lore *sm* wretchedness, bleakness

'squalo *sm* shark

'squama *sf* scale; **squa'mare** *vt* to scale; **squamarsi** *vr* to flake *o* peel (off)

squarcia'gola [skwartʃa'gola]: **a ~** *av* at the top of one's voice

squarci'are [skwar'tʃare] *vt* to rip (open); (*fig*) to pierce

squar'tare *vt* to quarter, cut up

squattri'nato, a *ag* penniless

squili'brato, a *ag* (*PSIC*) unbalanced; **squi'librio** *sm* (*differenza, sbilancio*) imbalance; (*PSIC*) unbalance

squil'lante *ag* shrill, sharp

squil'lare *vi* (*campanello, telefono*) to ring (out); (*tromba*) to blare; **'squillo** *sm* ring, ringing *no pl*; blare; **ragazza f squillo** *inv* call girl

squi'sito, a *ag* exquisite; (*cibo*) delicious; (*persona*) delightful

squit'tire *vi* (*uccello*) to squawk; (*topo*) to squeak

sradi'care *vt* to uproot; (*fig*) to eradicate

sragio'nare [zradʒo'nare] *vi* to talk nonsense, rave

srego'lato, a *ag* (*senza ordine: vita*) disorderly; (*smodato*) immoderate; (*dissoluto*) dissolute

S.r.l. *abbr* = **società a responsabilità limitata**

'stabile *ag* stable, steady; (*tempo: non variabile*) settled; (*TEATRO: compagnia*) resident ♦ *sm* (*edificio*) building

stabili'mento *sm* (*edificio*) establishment; (*fabbrica*) plant, factory

stabi'lire *vt* to establish; (*fissare: prezzi, data*) to fix; (*decidere*) to decide; **~rsi** *vr* (*prendere dimora*) to settle

stac'care *vt* (*levare*) to detach, remove; (*separare: anche fig*) to separate, divide; (*strappare*) to tear off (*o* out); (*scandire: parole*) to pronounce clearly; (*SPORT*) to leave behind; **~rsi** *vr* (*bottone etc*) to come off; (*scostarsi*): **~rsi (da)** to move away (from); (*fig: separarsi*): **~rsi da** to leave; **non ~ gli**

occhi da qn not to take one's eyes off sb

'**stadio** *sm* (*SPORT*) stadium; (*periodo, fase*) phase, stage

'**staffa** *sf* (*di sella, TECN*) stirrup; **perdere le ~e** (*fig*) to fly off the handle

staf'fetta *sf* (*messo*) dispatch rider; (*SPORT*) relay race

stagio'nale [stadʒo'nale] *ag* seasonal

stagio'nare [stadʒo'nare] *vt* (*legno*) to season; (*formaggi, vino*) to mature

stagi'one [sta'dʒone] *sf* season; **alta/bassa ~** high/low season

stagli'arsi [staʎ'ʎarsi] *vr* to stand out, be silhouetted

'**stagno, a** ['staɲɲo] *ag* watertight; (*a tenuta d'aria*) airtight ♦ *sm* (*acquitrino*) pond; (*CHIM*) tin

sta'gnola [staɲ'ɲɔla] *sf* tinfoil

'**stalla** *sf* (*per bovini*) cowshed; (*per cavalli*) stable

stal'lone *sm* stallion

sta'mani *av* = **stamattina**

stamat'tina *av* this morning

stam'becco, chi *sm* ibex

'**stampa** *sf* (*TIP, FOT: tecnica*) printing; (*impressione, copia fotografica*) print; (*insieme di quotidiani, giornalisti etc*) press; "**~e**" *sfpl* "printed matter"

stam'pante *sf* (*INFORM*) printer

stam'pare *vt* to print; (*pubblicare*) to publish; (*coniare*) to strike, coin; (*imprimere: anche fig*) to impress

stampa'tello *sm* block letters *pl*

stam'pella *sf* crutch

'**stampo** *sm* mould; (*fig: indole*) type, kind, sort

sta'nare *vt* to drive out

stan'care *vt* to tire, make tired; (*annoiare*) to bore; (*infastidire*) to annoy; **~rsi** *vr* to get tired, tire o.s. out; **~rsi (di)** to grow weary (of), grow tired (of)

stan'chezza [stan'kettsa] *sf* tiredness, fatigue

'**stanco, a, chi, che** *ag* tired; **~ di** tired of, fed up with

'**stanga, ghe** *sf* bar; (*di carro*) shaft

stan'gata *sf* (*colpo: anche fig*) blow; (*cattivo risultato*) poor result; (*CALCIO*) shot

sta'notte *av* tonight; (*notte passata*) last night

'**stante** *prep*: **a sé ~** (*appartamento, casa*) independent, separate

stan'tio, a, 'tii, 'tie *ag* stale; (*burro*) rancid; (*fig*) old

stan'tuffo *sm* piston

'**stanza** ['stantsa] *sf* room; (*POESIA*) stanza; **~ da letto** bedroom

stanzi'are [stan'tsjare] *vt* to allocate

stap'pare *vt* to uncork; to uncap

'**stare** *vi* (*restare in un luogo*) to stay, remain; (*abitare*) to stay, live; (*essere situato*) to be, be situated; (*anche: ~ in piedi*) to be, stand; (*essere, trovarsi*) to be; (*dipendere*): **se stesse in me** if it were up to me, if it depended on me; (*seguito da gerundio*): **sta studiando** he's studying; **starci** (*esserci spazio*): **nel baule non ci sta più niente** there's no more room in the boot; (*accettare*) to accept; **ci stai?** is that okay with you?; **~ a** (*attenersi a*) to follow, stick to; (*seguito dall'infinito*): **stiamo a discutere** we're talking; (*toccare a*): **sta a te giocare** it's your turn to play; **~ per fare qc** to be about to do sth; **come sta?** how are you?; **io sto bene/male** I'm very well/not very well; **~ a qn** (*abiti etc*) to fit sb; **queste scarpe mi stanno strette** these shoes are tight for me; **il rosso ti sta bene** red suits you

starnu'tire *vi* to sneeze; **star'nuto** *sm* sneeze

sta'sera *av* this evening, tonight

sta'tale *ag* state *cpd*; government *cpd* ♦ *sm/f* state employee, local authority employee; (*nell'amministrazione*) ≈ civil servant

sta'tista, i *sm* statesman

sta'tistica *sf* statistics *sg*

'**stato, a** *pp di* **essere; stare** ♦ *sm* (*condizione*) state, condition; (*POL*) state; (*DIR*) status; **essere in ~ d'accusa** (*DIR*) to be committed for trial; **~ d'assedio/d'emergenza** state of siege/emergency; **~ civile** (*AMM*) marital status; **~ maggiore** (*MIL*) staff; **gli S~i Uniti (d'America)** the United States (of America)

'**statua** *sf* statue

statuni'tense *ag* United States *cpd*, of the United States

sta'tura *sf* (*ANAT*) height, stature; (*fig*) stature

sta'tuto *sm* (*DIR*) statute; constitution

sta'volta *av* this time

stazio'nario, a [stattsjo'narjo] *ag* stationary; (*fig*) unchanged

stazi'one [stat'tsjone] *sf* station; (*balneare, termale*) resort: **~ degli autobus** bus station; **~ balneare** seaside resort; **~ ferroviaria** railway (*BRIT*) o railroad (*US*) station; **~ invernale** winter sports resort; **~ di polizia** police station (*in small town*); **~ di servizio** service o petrol (*BRIT*) o filling station

'**stecca, che** *sf* stick; (*di ombrello*) rib; (*di sigarette*) carton; (*MED*) splint; (*stonatura*): **fare una ~** to sing (o play) a wrong note

stec'cato *sm* fence

stec'chito, a [stek'kito] *ag*: **lasciar ~ qn** (*fig*) to leave sb flabbergasted; **morto ~** stone dead

'**stella** *sf* star; **~ alpina** (*BOT*) edelweiss; **~ di mare** (*ZOOL*) starfish

'**stelo** *sm* stem; (*asta*) rod; **lampada a ~** standard lamp

'**stemma, i** *sm* coat of arms

stempe'rare *vt* to dilute; to dissolve; (*colori*)

to mix

sten'dardo sm standard

'stendere vt (braccia, gambe) to stretch (out); (tovaglia) to spread (out); (bucato) to hang out; (mettere a giacere) to lay (down); (spalmare: colore) to spread; (mettere per iscritto) to draw up; **~rsi** vr (coricarsi) to stretch out, lie down; (estendersi) to extend, stretch

stenodatti'lografo, a sm/f shorthand typist (BRIT), stenographer (US)

stenogra'fare vt to take down in shorthand; **stenogra'fia** sf shorthand

sten'tare vi: **~ a fare** to find it hard to do, have difficulty doing

'stento sm (fatica) difficulty; **~i** smpl (privazioni) hardship sg, privation sg; **a ~** with difficulty, barely

'sterco sm dung

stereo('fonico, a, ci, che) ag stereo(phonic)

'sterile ag sterile; (terra) barren; (fig) futile, fruitless; **sterilità** sf sterility

steriliz'zare [sterilid'dzare] vt to sterilize; **sterilizzazi'one** sf sterilization

ster'lina sf pound (sterling)

stermi'nare vt to exterminate, wipe out

stermi'nato, a ag immense; endless

ster'minio sm extermination, destruction

'sterno sm (ANAT) breastbone

'sterpo sm dry twig; **~i** smpl brushwood sg

ster'zare [ster'tsare] vt, vi (AUT) to steer; **'sterzo** sm steering; (volante) steering wheel

'steso, a pp di **stendere**

'stesso, a ag same; (rafforzativo: in persona, proprio): **il re ~** the king himself o in person ♦ pron: **lo(la) ~(a)** the same (one); **i suoi ~i avversari lo ammirano** even his enemies admire him; **fa lo ~** it doesn't matter; **per me è lo ~** it's all the same to me, it doesn't matter to me; vedi **io; tu** etc

ste'sura sf drafting no pl, drawing up no pl; draft

'stigmate sfpl (REL) stigmata

sti'lare vt to draw up, draft

'stile sm style; **sti'lista, i** sm designer

stil'lare vi (trasudare) to ooze; (gocciolare) to drip; **stilli'cidio** sm (fig) continual pestering (o moaning etc)

stilo'grafica, che sf (anche: penna ~) fountain pen

'stima sf esteem; valuation; assessment, estimate

sti'mare vt (persona) to esteem, hold in high regard; (terreno, casa etc) to value; (stabilire in misura approssimativa) to estimate, assess; (ritenere): **~ che** to consider that; **~rsi fortunato** to consider o.s. (to be) lucky

stimo'lare vt to stimulate; (incitare): **~ qn (a fare)** to spur sb on (to do)

'stimolo sm (anche fig) stimulus

'stinco, chi sm shin; shinbone

'stingere ['stindʒere] vt, vi (anche: **~rsi**) to fade; **'stinto, a** pp di **stingere**

sti'pare vt to cram, pack; **~rsi** vr (accalcarsi) to crowd, throng

sti'pendio sm salary

'stipite sm (di porta, finestra) jamb

stipu'lare vt (redigere) to draw up

sti'rare vt (abito) to iron; (distendere) to stretch; (strappare: muscolo) to strain; **~rsi** vr to stretch (o.s.); **stira'tura** sf ironing

'stirpe sf birth, stock; descendants pl

stiti'chezza [stiti'kettsa] sf constipation

'stitico, a, ci, che ag constipated

'stiva sf (di nave) hold

sti'vale sm boot

'stizza ['stittsa] sf anger, vexation; **stiz'zirsi** vr to lose one's temper; **stiz'zoso, a** ag (persona) quick-tempered, irascible; (risposta) angry

stocca'fisso sm stockfish, dried cod

stoc'cata sf (colpo) stab, thrust; (fig) gibe, cutting remark

'stoffa sf material, fabric; (fig): **aver la ~ di** to have the makings of

'stola sf stole

'stolto, a ag stupid, foolish

'stomaco, chi sm stomach; **dare di ~** to vomit, be sick

sto'nare vt to sing (o play) out of tune ♦ vi to be out of tune, sing (o play) out of tune; (fig) to be out of place, jar; (: colori) to clash; **stona'tura** sf (suono) false note

stop sm inv (TEL) stop; (AUT: cartello) stop sign; (: fanalino d'arresto) brake-light

'stoppa sf tow

stop'pino sm wick; (miccia) fuse

'storcere ['stortʃere] vt to twist; **~rsi** vr to writhe, twist; **~ il naso** (fig) to turn up one's nose; **~rsi la caviglia** to twist one's ankle

stor'dire vt (intontire) to stun, daze; **~rsi** vr: **~rsi col bere** to dull one's senses with drink; **stor'dito, a** ag stunned

'storia sf (scienza, avvenimenti) history; (racconto, bugia) story; (faccenda, questione) business no pl; (pretesto) excuse, pretext; **~e** sfpl (smancerie) fuss sg; **'storico, a, ci, che** ag historic(al) ♦ sm historian

stori'one sm (ZOOL) sturgeon

stor'mire vi to rustle

'stormo sm (di uccelli) flock

stor'nare vt (COMM) to transfer

'storno sm (ZOOL) starling

storpi'are vt to cripple, maim; (fig: parole) to mangle; (: significato) to twist

'storpio, a ag crippled, maimed

'storta sf (distorsione) sprain, twist

'storto, a *pp di* storcere ♦ *ag* (*chiodo*) twisted, bent; (*gamba, quadro*) crooked

sto'viglie [sto'viʎʎe] *sfpl* dishes *pl*, crockery

'strabico, a, ci, che *ag* squint-eyed; (*occhi*) squint

stra'bismo *sm* squinting

stra'carico, a, chi, che *ag* overloaded

strac'chino [strak'kino] *sm type of soft cheese*

stracci'are [strat'tʃare] *vt* to tear

'straccio, a, ci, ce ['strattʃo] *ag*: **carta ~a** waste paper ♦ *sm* rag; (*per pulire*) cloth, duster

stra'cotto, a *ag* overcooked ♦ *sm* (*CUC*) beef stew

'strada *sf* road; (*di città*) street; (*cammino, via, fig*) way; **farsi ~** (*fig*) to do well for o.s.; **essere fuori ~** (*fig*) to be on the wrong track; **~ facendo** on the way; **~ senza uscita** dead end; **stra'dale** *ag* road *cpd*

strafalci'one [strafal'tʃone] *sm* blunder, howler

stra'fare *vi* to overdo it; **stra'fatto, a** *pp di* strafare

strafot'tente *ag*: **è ~** he doesn't give a damn, he couldn't care less

'strage ['stradʒe] *sf* massacre, slaughter

stralu'nato, a *ag* (*occhi*) rolling; (*persona*) beside o.s., very upset

stramaz'zare [stramat'tsare] *vi* to fall heavily

'strambo, a *ag* strange, queer

strampa'lato, a *ag* odd, eccentric

stra'nezza [stra'nettsa] *sf* strangeness

strango'lare *vt* to strangle; **~rsi** *vr* to choke

strani'ero, a *ag* foreign ♦ *sm/f* foreigner

'strano, a *ag* strange, odd

straordi'nario, a *ag* extraordinary; (*treno etc*) special ♦ *sm* (*lavoro*) overtime

strapaz'zare [strapat'tsare] *vt* to ill-treat; **~rsi** *vr* to tire o.s. out, overdo things; **stra'pazzo** *sm* strain, fatigue; **da strapazzo** (*fig*) third-rate

strapi'ombo *sm* overhanging rock; **a ~** overhanging

strapo'tere *sm* excessive power

strap'pare *vt* (*gen*) to tear, rip; (*pagina etc*) to tear off, tear out; (*sradicare*) to pull up; (*togliere*): **~ qc a qn** to snatch sth from sb; (*fig*) to wrest sth from sb; **~rsi** *vr* (*lacerarsi*) to rip, tear; (*rompersi*) to break; **~rsi un muscolo** to tear a muscle; **'strappo** *sm* pull, tug; tear, rip; **fare uno strappo alla regola** to make an exception to the rule; **strappo muscolare** torn muscle

strari'pare *vi* to overflow

strasci'care [straʃʃi'kare] *vt* to trail; (*piedi*) to drag; **~ le parole** to drawl

'strascico, chi ['straʃʃiko] *sm* (*di abito*) train; (*conseguenza*) after-effect

strata'gemma, i [strata'dʒɛmma] *sm* stratagem

strate'gia, 'gie [strate'dʒia] *sf* strategy; **stra'tegico, a, ci, che** *ag* strategic

'strato *sm* layer; (*rivestimento*) coat, coating; (*GEO, fig*) stratum; (*METEOR*) stratus; **~ di ozono** ozòne layer

strava'gante *ag* odd, eccentric; **strava'ganza** *sf* eccentricity

stra'vecchio, a [stra'vɛkkjo] *ag* very old

stra'vizio [stra'vittsjo] *sm* excess

stra'volgere [stra'vɔldʒere] *vt* (*volto*) to contort; (*fig: animo*) to trouble deeply; (: *verità*) to twist, distort; **stra'volto, a** *pp di* stravolgere

strazi'are [strat'tsjare] *vt* to torture, torment; **'strazio** *sm* torture; (*fig: cosa fatta male*): **essere uno strazio** to be appalling

'strega, ghe *sf* witch

stre'gare *vt* to bewitch

stre'gone *sm* (*mago*) wizard; (*di tribù*) witch doctor

'stregua *sf*: **alla ~ di** by the same standard as

stre'mare *vt* to exhaust

'stremo *sm* very end; **essere allo ~** to be at the end of one's tether

'strenna *sf* Christmas present

strepi'toso, a *ag* clamorous, deafening; (*fig: successo*) resounding

stres'sante *ag* stressful

'stretta *sf* (*di mano*) grasp; (*finanziaria*) squeeze; (*fig: dolore, turbamento*) pang; **una ~ di mano** a handshake; **essere alle ~e** to have one's back to the wall; *vedi anche* **stretto**

stretta'mente *av* tightly; (*rigorosamente*) strictly

stret'tezza [stret'tettsa] *sf* narrowness

'stretto, a *pp di* stringere ♦ *ag* (*corridoio, limiti*) narrow; (*gonna, scarpe, nodo, curva*) tight; (*intimo: parente, amico*) close; (*rigoroso: osservanza*) strict; (*preciso: significato*) precise, exact ♦ *sm* (*braccio di mare*) strait; **a denti ~i** with clenched teeth; **lo ~ necessario** the bare minimum; **stret'toia** *sf* bottleneck; (*fig*) tricky situation

stri'ato, a *ag* streaked

'stridere *vi* (*porta*) to squeak; (*animale*) to screech, shriek; (*colori*) to clash; **'stridulo, a** *ag* shrill

stril'lare *vt, vi* to scream, shriek; **'strillo** *sm* scream, shriek

stril'lone *sm* newspaper seller

strimin'zito, a [strimin'tsito] *ag* (*misero*) shabby; (*molto magro*) skinny

strimpel'lare *vt* (*MUS*) to strum

'stringa, ghe *sf* lace

strin'gato, a *ag* (*fig*) concise

'stringere ['strindʒere] *vt* (*avvicinare due*

cose) to press (together), squeeze (together); (*tenere stretto*) to hold tight, clasp, clutch; (*pugno, mascella, denti*) to clench; (*labbra*) to compress; (*avvitare*) to tighten; (*abito*) to take in; (*sog: scarpe*) to pinch, be tight for; (*fig: concludere: patto*) to make; (: *accelerare: passo, tempo*) to quicken ♦ *vi* (*essere stretto*) to be tight; (*tempo: incalzare*) to be pressing; **~rsi** *vr* (*accostarsi*): **~rsi a** to press o.s. up against; **~ la mano a qn** to shake sb's hand; **~ gli occhi** to screw up one's eyes

'striscia, sce ['striʃʃa] *sf* (*di carta, tessuto etc*) strip; (*riga*) stripe; **~sce (pedonali)** zebra crossing *sg*

strisci'are [striʃ'ʃare] *vt* (*piedi*) to drag; (*muro, macchina*) to graze ♦ *vi* to crawl, creep

'striscio ['striʃʃo] *sm* graze; (*MED*) smear; **colpire di ~** to graze

strito'lare *vt* to grind

striz'zare [strit'tsare] *vt* (*panni*) to wring (out); **~ l'occhio** to wink

'strofa *sf* strophe

strofi'naccio [strofi'nattʃo] *sm* duster, cloth; (*per piatti*) dishcloth; (*per pavimenti*) floorcloth

strofi'nare *vt* to rub

stron'care *vt* to break off; (*fig: ribellione*) to suppress, put down; (: *film, libro*) to tear to pieces

stropicci'are [stropit'tʃare] *vt* to rub

stroz'zare [strot'tsare] *vt* (*soffocare*) to choke, strangle; **~rsi** *vr* to choke; **strozza'tura** *sf* (*restringimento*) narrowing; (*di strada etc*) bottleneck

'struggersi ['struddʒersi] *vr* (*fig*): **~ di** to be consumed with

strumen'tale *ag* (*MUS*) instrumental

strumentaliz'zare [strumentalid'dzare] *vt* to exploit, use to one's own ends

stru'mento *sm* (*arnese, fig*) instrument, tool; (*MUS*) instrument; **~ a corda** *o* **ad arco/a fiato** stringed/wind instrument

'strutto *sm* lard

strut'tura *sf* structure; **struttu'rare** *vt* to structure

'struzzo ['struttso] *sm* ostrich

stuc'care *vt* (*muro*) to plaster; (*vetro*) to putty; (*decorare con stucchi*) to stucco

stuc'chevole [stuk'kevole] *ag* nauseating; (*fig*) tedious, boring

'stucco, chi *sm* plaster; (*da vetri*) putty; (*ornamentale*) stucco; **rimanere di ~** (*fig*) to be dumbfounded

stu'dente, 'essa *sm/f* student; (*scolaro*) pupil, schoolboy/girl; **studen'tesco, a, schi, sche** *ag* student *cpd*; school *cpd*

studi'are *vt* to study

'studio *sm* studying; (*ricerca, saggio, stanza*) study; (*di professionista*) office; (*di artista, CINEMA, TV, RADIO*) studio; **~i** *smpl* (*INS*) studies; **~ medico** doctor's surgery (*BRIT*) *o* office (*US*)

studi'oso, a *ag* studious, hard-working ♦ *sm/f* scholar

'stufa *sf* stove; **~ elettrica** electric fire *o* heater

stu'fare *vt* (*CUC*) to stew; (*fig: fam*) to bore; **stu'fato** *sm* (*CUC*) stew; **'stufo, a** (*fam*) *ag*: **essere stufo di** to be fed up with, be sick and tired of

stu'oia *sf* mat

stupefa'cente [stupefa'tʃente] *ag* stunning, astounding ♦ *sm* drug, narcotic

stu'pendo, a *ag* marvellous, wonderful

stupi'daggine [stupi'daddʒine] *sf* stupid thing (to do *o* say)

stupidità *sf* stupidity

'stupido, a *ag* stupid

stu'pire *vt* to amaze, stun ♦ *vi* (*anche*: **~rsi**): **~ (di)** to be amazed (at), be stunned (by)

stu'pore *sm* amazement, astonishment

'stupro *sm* rape

stu'rare *vt* (*lavandino*) to clear

stuzzica'denti [stuttsika'denti] *sm* toothpick

stuzzi'care [stuttsi'kare] *vt* (*ferita etc*) to poke (at), prod (at); (*fig*) to tease; (: *appetito*) to whet; (: *curiosità*) to stimulate; **~ i denti** to pick one's teeth

---

PAROLA CHIAVE

su (*su +il* = **sul**, *su +lo* = **sullo**, *su +l'* = **sull'**, *su +la* = **sulla**, *su +i* = **sui**, *su +gli* = **sugli**, *su +le* = **sulle**) *prep* **1** (*gen*) on; (*moto*) on(to); (*in cima a*) on (top of); **mettilo sul tavolo** put it on the table; **un paesino sul mare** a village by the sea

2 (*argomento*) about, on; **un libro ~ Cesare** a book on *o* about Caesar

3 (*circa*) about; **costerà sui 3 milioni** it will cost about 3 million; **una ragazza sui 17 anni** a girl of about 17 (years of age)

4: **~ misura** made to measure; **~ richiesta** on request; **3 casi ~ dieci** 3 cases out of 10

♦ *av* **1** (*in alto, verso l'alto*) up; **vieni ~** come on up; **guarda ~** look up; **~ le mani!** hands up!; **in ~** (*verso l'alto*) up(wards); (*in poi*) onwards; **dai 20 anni in ~** from the age of 20 onwards

2 (*addosso*) on; **cos'hai ~?** what have you got on?

♦ *escl* come on!; **~ coraggio!** come on, cheer up!

'sua *vedi* **suo**

su'bacqueo, a *ag* underwater ♦ *sm* skindiver

sub'buglio [sub'buʎʎo] *sm* confusion,

turmoil

subcosci'ente [subkoʃ'ʃɛnte] *ag, sm* subconscious

'subdolo, a *ag* underhand, sneaky

suben'trare *vi:* ~ **a qn in qc** to take over sth from sb

su'bire *vt* to suffer, endure

subis'sare *vt (fig):* ~ **di** to overwhelm with, load with

subi'taneo, a *ag* sudden

'subito *av* immediately, at once, straight away

subodo'rare *vt (insidia etc)* to smell, suspect

subordi'nato, a *ag* subordinate; *(dipendente):* ~ **a** dependent on, subject to

subur'bano, a *ag* suburban

suc'cedere [sut'tʃedere] *vi (prendere il posto di qn):* ~ **a** to succeed; *(venire dopo):* ~ **a** to follow; *(accadere)* to happen; **~rsi** *vr* to follow each other; ~ **al trono** to succeed to the throne; **successi'one** *sf* succession; **succes'sivo, a** *ag* successive; **suc'cesso, a** *pp di* **succedere** ♦ *sm (esito)* outcome; *(buona riuscita)* success; **di successo** *(libro, personaggio)* successful

succhi'are [suk'kjare] *vt* to suck (up); **succhi'otto** *sm (per bambino)* dummy

suc'cinto, a [sut'tʃinto] *ag (discorso)* succinct; *(abito)* brief

'succo, chi *sm* juice; *(fig)* essence, gist; ~ **di frutta** fruit juice; **suc'coso, a** *ag* juicy; *(fig)* pithy

succur'sale *sf* branch (office)

sud *sm* south ♦ *ag inv* south; *(lato)* south, southern

Su'dafrica *sm:* **il** ~ South Africa; **sudafri'cano, a** *ag, sm/f* South African

Suda'merica *sm:* **il** ~ South America; **sudameri'cano, a** *ag, sm/f* South American

su'dare *vi* to perspire, sweat; ~ **freddo** to come out in a cold sweat; **su'data** *sf* sweat; **ho fatto una bella sudata per finirlo in tempo** it was a real sweat to get it finished in time

sud'detto, a *ag* above-mentioned

sud'dito, a *sm/f* subject

suddi'videre *vt* to subdivide

su'dest *sm* south-east

'sudicio, a, ci, ce ['suditʃo] *ag* dirty, filthy; **sudici'ume** *sm* dirt, filth

su'dore *sm* perspiration, sweat

su'dovest *sm* south-west

'sue *vedi* **suo**

suffici'ente [suffi'tʃɛnte] *ag* enough, sufficient; *(borioso)* self-important; *(INS)* satisfactory; **suffici'enza** *sf* self-importance; pass mark; **a sufficienza** enough; **ne ho avuto a sufficienza!** I've had enough of this!

suf'fisso *sm (LING)* suffix

suf'fragio [suf'fradʒo] *sm (voto)* vote;

~ **universale** universal suffrage

suggel'lare [suddʒel'lare] *vt (fig)* to seal

suggeri'mento [suddʒeri'mento] *sm* suggestion; *(consiglio)* piece of advice, advice *no pl*

sugge'rire [suddʒe'rire] *vt (risposta)* to tell; *(consigliare)* to advise; *(proporre)* to suggest; *(TEATRO)* to prompt; **suggeri'tore, 'trice** *sm/f (TEATRO)* prompter

suggestio'nare [suddʒestjo'nare] *vt* to influence

suggesti'one [suddʒes'tjone] *sf (PSIC)* suggestion

sugges'tivo, a [suddʒes'tivo] *ag (paesaggio)* evocative; *(teoria)* interesting, attractive

'sughero ['sugero] *sm* cork

'sugli ['suʎʎi] *prep* +*det vedi* **su**

'sugo, ghi *sm (succo)* juice; *(di carne)* gravy; *(condimento)* sauce; *(fig)* gist, essence

'sui *prep* +*det vedi* **su**

sui'cida, i, e [sui'tʃida] *ag* suicidal ♦ *sm/f* suicide

suici'darsi [suitʃi'darsi] *vr* to commit suicide

sui'cidio [sui'tʃidjo] *sm* suicide

su'ino, a *ag:* **carne ~a** pork ♦ *sm* pig; **~i** *smpl* swine *pl*

sul *prep* + *det vedi* **su**

sull' *prep* + *det vedi* **su**

'sulla *prep* + *det vedi* **su**

'sulle *prep* + *det vedi* **su**

'sullo *prep* + *det vedi* **su**

sulta'nina *ag f:* **(uva)** ~ sultana

sul'tano, a *sm/f* sultan/sultana

'sunto *sm* summary

'suo *(f* **'sua,** *pl* **'sue, su'oi)** *det:* **il** ~, **la sua** *etc (di lui)* his; *(di lei)* her; *(di esso)* its; *(con valore indefinito)* one's, his/her; *(forma di cortesia: anche:* S~) your ♦ *pron:* **il** ~, **la sua** *etc* his; hers; yours; **i suoi** his *(o* her *o* one's *o* your) family

su'ocero, a ['swɔtʃero] *sm/f* father/mother-in-law; **i ~i** *smpl* father- and mother-in-law

su'oi *vedi* **suo**

su'ola *sf (di scarpa)* sole

su'olo *sm (terreno)* ground; *(terra)* soil

suo'nare *vt (MUS)* to play; *(campana)* to ring; *(ore)* to strike; *(clacson, allarme)* to sound ♦ *vi* to play; *(telefono, campana)* to ring; *(ore)* to strike; *(clacson, fig: parole)* to sound

suone'ria *sf* alarm

su'ono *sm* sound

su'ora *sf (REL)* sister

'super *sf (anche: benzina ~)* ≈ four-star (petrol) *(BRIT)*, premium *(US)*

supe'rare *vt (oltrepassare: limite)* to exceed, surpass; *(percorrere)* to cover; *(attraversare: fiume)* to cross; *(sorpassare: veicolo)* to overtake; (*fig: essere più bravo di*) to surpass, outdo; (: *difficoltà*) to overcome; (: *esame*) to get through; ~ **qn in altezza/peso** to be taller/heavier than sb; **ha superato la cinquantina** he's over fifty (years of age)

su'**perbia** *sf* pride; **su'perbo, a** *ag* proud; (*fig*) magnificent, superb

supere'na'lotto *sm Italian national lottery*

superfici'ale [superfi'tʃale] *ag* superficial

super'ficie, ci [super'fitʃe] *sf* surface

su'perfluo, a *ag* superfluous

superi'ore *ag* (*piano, arto, classi*) upper; (*più elevato: temperatura, livello*): ~ (**a**) higher (than); (*migliore*): ~ (**a**) superior (to); ~, **a** *sm/f* (*anche REL*) superior; **superiorità** *sf* superiority

superla'tivo, a *ag, sm* superlative

supermer'cato *sm* supermarket

su'perstite *ag* surviving ♦ *sm/f* survivor

superstizi'one [superstit'tsjone] *sf* superstition; **superstizi'oso, a** *ag* superstitious

super'strada *sf* ≈ (toll-free) motorway

su'pino, a *ag* supine

suppel'lettile *sf* furnishings *pl*

suppergiù [supper'dʒu] *av* more or less, roughly

supplemen'tare *ag* extra; (*treno*) relief *cpd*; (*entrate*) additional

supple'mento *sm* supplement

sup'plente *sm/f* temporary member of staff; supply (o substitute) teacher

'supplica, che *sf* (*preghiera*) plea; (*domanda scritta*) petition, request

suppli'care *vt* to implore, beseech

sup'plire *vi*: ~ **a** to compensate for

sup'plizio [sup'plittsjo] *sm* torture

sup'porre *vt* to suppose

sup'porto *sm* (*sostegno*) support

sup'posta *sf* (*MED*) suppository

sup'posto, a *pp di* supporre

su'premo, a *ag* supreme

surge'lare [surdʒe'lare] *vt* to (deep-)freeze; **surge'lati** *smpl* frozen food *sg*

sur'plus *sm inv* (*ECON*) surplus

surriscal'dare *vt* to overheat

surro'gato *sm* substitute

suscet'tibile [suʃʃet'tibile] *ag* (*sensibile*) touchy, sensitive

susci'tare [suʃʃi'tare] *vt* to provoke, arouse

su'sina *sf* plum; **su'sino** *sm* plum (tree)

sussegu'ire *vt* to follow; **~rsi** *vr* to follow one another

sus'sidio *sm* subsidy

sus'sistere *vi* to exist; (*essere fondato*) to be valid o sound

sussul'tare *vi* to shudder

sussur'rare *vt, vi* to whisper, murmur; **sus'surro** *sm* whisper, murmur

sutu'rare *vt* (*MED*) to stitch up, suture

sva'gare *vt* (*distrarre*) to distract; (*divertire*) to amuse; **~rsi** *vr* to amuse o.s.; to enjoy o.s.

'svago, ghi *sm* (*riposo*) relaxation; (*ricreazione*) amusement; (*passatempo*) pastime

svaligi'are [zvali'dʒare] *vt* to rob, burgle (*BRIT*), burglarize (*US*)

svalu'tare *vt* (*ECON*) to devalue; (*fig*) to belittle; **~rsi** *vr* (*ECON*) to be devalued; **svalutazi'one** *sf* devaluation

sva'nire *vi* to disappear, vanish

svan'taggio [zvan'taddʒo] *sm* disadvantage; (*inconveniente*) drawback, disadvantage

svapo'rare *vi* to evaporate

svari'ato, a *ag* varied; various

'svastica *sf* swastika

sve'dese *ag* Swedish ♦ *sm/f* Swede ♦ *sm* (*LING*) Swedish

'sveglia ['zveʎʎa] *sf* waking up; (*orologio*) alarm (clock); ~ **telefonica** alarm call

svegli'are [zveʎ'ʎare] *vt* to wake up; (*fig*) to awaken, arouse; **~rsi** *vr* to wake up; (*fig*) to be revived, reawaken

'sveglio, a ['zveʎʎo] *ag* awake; (*fig*) quick-witted

sve'lare *vt* to reveal

'svelto, a *ag* (*passo*) quick; (*mente*) quick, alert; **alla ~a** quickly

'svendita *sf* (*COMM*) (clearance) sale

sveni'mento *sm* fainting fit, faint

sve'nire *vi* to faint

sven'tare *vt* to foil, thwart

sven'tato, a *ag* (*distratto*) scatterbrained; (*imprudente*) rash

svento'lare *vt, vi* to wave, flutter

sven'trare *vt* to disembowel

sven'tura *sf* misfortune; **sventu'rato, a** *ag* unlucky, unfortunate

sve'nuto, a *pp di* svenire

svergo'gnato, a [zvergoɲ'ɲato] *ag* shameless

sver'nare *vi* to spend the winter

sves'tire *vt* to undress; **~rsi** *vr* to get undressed

'Svezia ['zvettsja] *sf*: **la ~** Sweden

svez'zare [zvet'tsare] *vt* to wean

svi'are *vt* to divert; (*fig*) to lead astray; **~rsi** *vr* to go astray

svi'gnarsela [zviɲ'ɲarsela] *vr* to slip away, sneak off

svilup'pare *vt* to develop; **~rsi** *vr* to develop

svi'luppo *sm* development

'svincolo *sm* (*stradale*) motorway (*BRIT*) o expressway (*US*) intersection

svisce'rare [zviʃʃe'rare] *vt* (*fig: argomento*) to examine in depth; **svisce'rato, a** *ag* (*amore*) passionate; (*lodi*) obsequious

'svista *sf* oversight

svi'tare *vt* to unscrew

'Svizzera ['zvittsera] *sf*: la ~ Switzerland

'svizzero, a ['zvittsero] *ag, sm/f* Swiss

svogli'ato, a [zvoʎ'ʎato] *ag* listless; (*pigro*) lazy

svolaz'zare [zvolat'tsare] *vi* to flutter

'svolgere ['zvɔldʒere] *vt* to unwind; (*srotolare*) to unroll; (*fig: argomento*) to develop; (: *piano, programma*) to carry out; ~rsi *vr* to unwind; to unroll; (*fig: aver luogo*) to take place; (: *procedere*) to go on; svolgi'mento *sm* development; carrying out; (*andamento*) course

'svolta *sf* (*atto*) turning *no pl*; (*curva*) turn, bend; (*fig*) turning-point

svol'tare *vi* to turn

'svolto, a *pp di* svolgere

svuo'tare *vt* to empty (out)

T, t

tabac'caio, a *sm/f* tobacconist

tabacche'ria [tabakke'ria] *sf* tobacconist's (shop)

ta'bacco, chi *sm* tobacco

ta'bella *sf* (*tavola*) table; (*elenco*) list

tabel'lone *sm* (*pubblicitario*) billboard; (*con orario*) timetable board

taber'nacolo *sm* tabernacle

tabu'lato *sm* (INFORM) printout

'tacca, che *sf* notch, nick

tac'cagno, a [tak'kaɲɲo] *ag* mean, stingy

tac'chino [tak'kino] *sm* turkey

tacci'are [tat'tʃare] *vt*: ~ qn di to accuse sb of

'tacco, chi *sm* heel; ~chi a spillo stiletto heels

taccu'ino *sm* notebook

ta'cere [ta'tʃere] *vi* to be silent o quiet; (*smettere di parlare*) to fall silent ♦ *vt* to keep to oneself, say nothing about; far ~ qn to make sb be quiet; (*fig*) to silence sb

ta'chimetro [ta'kimetro] *sm* speedometer

'tacito, a ['tatʃito] *ag* silent; (*sottinteso*) tacit, unspoken

ta'fano *sm* horsefly

taffe'ruglio [taffe'ruʎʎo] *sm* brawl, scuffle

taffettà *sm* taffeta

'taglia ['taʎʎa] *sf* (*statura*) height; (*misura*) size; (*riscatto*) ransom; (*ricompensa*) reward; ~ forte (*di abito*) large size

taglia'carte [taʎʎa'karte] *sm inv* paperknife

tagli'ando [taʎʎ'ando] *sm* coupon

tagli'are [taʎ'ʎare] *vt* to cut; (*recidere, interrompere*) to cut off; (*intersecare*) to cut across, intersect; (*carne*) to carve; (*vini*) to blend ♦ *vi* to cut; (*prendere una scorciatoia*) to take a short-cut; ~ corto (*fig*) to cut short

taglia'telle [taʎʎa'telle] *sfpl* tagliatelle *pl*

taglia'unghie [taʎʎa'ungje] *sm inv* nail clippers *pl*

tagli'ente [taʎ'ʎɛnte] *ag* sharp

'taglio ['taʎʎo] *sm* cutting *no pl*; cut; (*parte tagliente*) cutting edge; (*di abito*) cut, style; (*di stoffa: lunghezza*) length; (*di vini*) blending; di ~ on edge, edgeways; banconote di piccolo/grosso ~ notes of small/large denomination

tagli'ola [taʎ'ʎola] *sf* trap, snare

tai'lleur [ta'jœr] *sm inv* suit (*for women*)

'talco *sm* talcum powder

'tale *det* 1 (*simile, così grande*) such; un(a) ~ ... such (a) ...; non accetto ~i discorsi I won't allow such talk; è di una ~ arroganza he is so arrogant; fa una ~ confusione! he makes such a mess!

2 (*persona o cosa indeterminata*) such-and-such; il giorno ~ all'ora ~ on such-and-such a day at such-and-such a time; la tal persona that person; ha telefonato una ~ Giovanna somebody called Giovanna phoned

3 (*nelle similitudini*): ~ ... ~ like ... like; ~ padre ~ figlio like father, like son; hai il vestito ~ quale il mio your dress is just o exactly like mine

♦ *pron* (*indefinito: persona*): un(a) ~ someone; quel (o quella) ~ that person, that man (o woman); il tal dei ~i what's-his-name

ta'lento *sm* talent

talis'mano *sm* talisman

tallon'cino [tallon'tʃino] *sm* counterfoil

tal'lone *sm* heel

tal'mente *av* so

ta'lora *av* = talvolta

'talpa *sf* (ZOOL) mole

tal'volta *av* sometimes, at times

tambu'rello *sm* tambourine

tam'buro *sm* drum

Ta'migi [ta'midʒi] *sm*: il ~ the Thames

tampona'mento *sm* (AUT) collision; ~ a catena pile-up

tampo'nare *vt* (*otturare*) to plug; (*urtare: macchina*) to crash o ram into

tam'pone *sm* (MED) wad, pad; (*per timbri*) ink-pad; (*respingente*) buffer; ~ assorbente tampon

'tana *sf* lair, den

'tanfo *sm* stench; musty smell

tan'gente [tan'dʒɛnte] *ag* (MAT): ~ a tangential to ♦ *sf* tangent; (*quota*) share

tangenzi'ale [tandʒen'tsjale] *sf* (AUT) bypass

'tanica *sf* (*contenitore*) jerry can

tan'tino: un ~ *av* a little, a bit

'tanto, a *det* 1 (*molto: quantità*) a lot of, much; (: *numero*) a lot of, many; (*così* ~:

quantità) so much, such a lot of; (: *numero*) so many, such a lot of; **~e volte** many times, so often; **~i auguri!** all the best!; **~e grazie** many thanks; **~ tempo** so long, such a long time; **ogni ~i chilometri** every so many kilometres

2: **~ ... quanto** (*quantità*) as much ... as; (*numero*) as many ... as; **ho ~a pazienza quanta ne hai tu** I have as much patience as you have *o* as you; **ha ~i amici quanti nemici** he has as many friends as he has enemies **3** (*rafforzativo*) such; **ho aspettato per ~ tempo** I waited so long *o* for such a long time

♦ *pron* **1** (*molto*) much, a lot; (*così ~*) so much, such a lot; **~i, e** many, a lot; so many, such a lot; **credevo ce ne fosse ~** I thought there was (such) a lot, I thought there was plenty

2: **~ quanto** (*denaro*) as much as; (*cioccolatini*) as many as; **ne ho ~ quanto basta** I have as much as I need; **due volte ~** twice as much

3 (*indeterminato*) so much; **~ per l'affitto, ~ per il gas** so much for the rent, so much for the gas; **costa un ~ al metro** it costs so much per metre; **di ~ in ~, ogni ~** every so often; **~ vale che ... I** (*o* we *etc*) may as well ...; **~ meglio!** so much the better!; **~ peggio per lui!** so much the worse for him!

♦ *av* **1** (*molto*) very; **vengo ~ volentieri** I'd be very glad to come; **non ci vuole ~ a capirlo** it doesn't take much to understand it

2 (*così ~*: con *ag, av*) so; (: con *vb*) so much, such a lot; **è ~ bella!** she's so beautiful!; **non urlare ~** don't shout so much; **sto ~ meglio adesso** I'm so much better now; **~ ... che** so ... (that); **~ ... da** so ... as

3: **~ ... quanto** as ... as; **conosco ~ Carlo quanto suo padre** I know both Carlo and his father; **non è poi ~ complicato quanto sembri** it's not as difficult as it seems; **~ più insisti, ~ più non mollerà** the more you insist, the more stubborn he'll be; **quanto più ... ~ meno** the more ... the less

4 (*solamente*) just; **~ per cambiare/scherzare** just for a change/a joke; **una volta ~** for once
5 (*a lungo*) (for) long
♦ *cong* after all

'tappa *sf* (*luogo di sosta, fermata*) stop, halt; (*parte di un percorso*) stage, leg; (*SPORT*) lap; **a ~e** in stages

tap'pare *vt* to plug, stop up; (*bottiglia*) to cork

tap'peto *sm* carpet; (*anche: tappetino*) rug; (*SPORT*): **andare al ~** to go down for the count; **mettere sul ~** (*fig*) to bring up for

discussion

tappez'zare [tappet'tsare] *vt* (*con carta*) to paper; (*rivestire*): **~ qc (di)** to cover sth (with); **tappezze'ria** *sf* (*tessuto*) tapestry; (*carta da parati*) wallpaper; (*arte*) upholstery; **far da tappezzeria** (*fig*) to be a wallflower; **tappezzi'ere** *sm* upholsterer

'tappo *sm* stopper; (*in sughero*) cork

tarchi'ato, a [tar'kjato] *ag* stocky, thickset

tar'dare *vi* to be late ♦ *vt* to delay; **~ a fare** to delay doing

'tardi *av* late; **più ~** later (on); **al più ~** at the latest; **sul ~** (*verso sera*) late in the day; **far ~** to be late; (*restare alzato*) to stay up late

tar'divo, a *ag* (*primavera*) late; (*rimedio*) belated, tardy; (*fig*) retarded

'tardo, a *ag* (*lento, fig: ottuso*) slow; (*tempo: avanzato*) late

'targa, ghe *sf* plate; (*AUT*) number (*BRIT*) *o* license (*US*) plate; **tar'ghetta** *sf* (*su bagaglio*) name tag; (*su porta*) nameplate

ta'riffa *sf* (*gen*) rate, tariff; (*di trasporti*) fare; (*elenco*) price list; tariff

'tarlo *sm* woodworm

'tarma *sf* moth

ta'rocco, chi *sm* tarot card; **~chi** *smpl* (*gioco*) tarot *sg*

tartagli'are [tartaʎ'ʎare] *vi* to stutter, stammer

'tartaro, a *ag, sm* (*in tutti i sensi*) tartar

tarta'ruga, ghe *sf* tortoise; (*di mare*) turtle; (*materiale*) tortoiseshell

tar'tina *sf* canapé

tar'tufo *sm* (*BOT*) truffle

'tasca, sche *sf* pocket; **tas'cabile** *ag* (*libro*) pocket *cpd*; **tasca'pane** *sm* haversack; **tas'chino** *sm* breast pocket

'tassa *sf* (*imposta*) tax; (*doganale*) duty; (*per iscrizione: a scuola etc*) fee; **~ di circolazione/ di soggiorno** road/tourist tax

tas'sametro *sm* taximeter

tas'sare *vt* to tax; to levy a duty on

tassa'tivo, a *ag* peremptory

tassazi'one [tassat'tsjone] *sf* taxation

tas'sello *sm* plug; wedge

tassi *sm inv* = **taxi**; **tas'sista, i, e** *sm/f* taxi driver

'tasso *sm* (*di natalità, d'interesse etc*) rate; (*BOT*) yew; (*ZOOL*) badger; **~ di cambio/ d'interesse** rate of exchange/interest

tas'tare *vt* to feel; **~ il terreno** (*fig*) to see how the land lies

tasti'era *sf* keyboard

'tasto *sm* key; (*tatto*) touch, feel

tas'toni *av*: **procedere (a) ~** to grope one's way forward

'tattica *sf* tactics *pl*

'tattico, a, ci, che *ag* tactical

'tatto *sm* (*senso*) touch; (*fig*) tact; **duro al ~**

hard to the touch; **aver ~** to be tactful, have tact

tatu'aggio [tatu'addʒo] *sm* tattooing; (*disegno*) tattoo

tatu'are *vt* to tattoo

'tavola *sf* table; (*asse*) plank, board; (*lastra*) tablet; (*quadro*) panel (painting); (*illustrazione*) plate; **~ calda** snack bar; **~ a vela** windsurfer

tavo'lato *sm* boarding; (*pavimento*) wooden floor

tavo'letta *sf* tablet, bar; **a ~** (AUT) flat out

tavo'lino *sm* small table; (*scrivania*) desk

'tavolo *sm* table

tavo'lozza [tavo'lɔttsa] *sf* (ARTE) palette

'taxi *sm inv* taxi

'tazza ['tattsa] *sf* cup; **~ da caffè/tè** coffee/tea cup; **una ~ di caffè/tè** a cup of coffee/tea

te *pron* (*soggetto: in forme comparative, oggetto*) you

tè *sm inv* tea; (*trattenimento*) tea party

tea'trale *ag* theatrical

te'atro *sm* theatre

'tecnica, che *sf* technique; (*tecnologia*) technology

'tecnico, a, ci, che *ag* technical ♦ *sm/f* technician

tecnolo'gia [teknolo'dʒia] *sf* technology

te'desco, a, schi, sche *ag, sm/f, sm* German

'tedio *sm* tedium, boredom

te'game *sm* (CUC) pan

'teglia ['teʎʎa] *sf* (*per dolci*) (baking) tin; (*per arrosti*) (roasting) tin

'tegola *sf* tile

tei'era *sf* teapot

'tela *sf* (*tessuto*) cloth; (*per vele, quadri*) canvas; (*dipinto*) canvas, painting; **di ~** (*calzoni*) (heavy) cotton *cpd*; (*scarpe, borsa*) canvas *cpd*; **~ cerata** oilcloth

te'laio *sm* (*apparecchio*) loom; (*struttura*) frame

tele'camera *sf* television camera

teleco'mando *sm* remote control

telecopia'trice *sf* fax (machine)

tele'cronaca, che *sf* television report

tele'ferica, che *sf* cableway

telefo'nare *vi* to telephone, ring; to make a phone call ♦ *vt* to telephone; **~ a** to phone up, ring up, call up

telefo'nata *sf* (telephone) call; **~ a carico del destinatario** reverse charge (BRIT) o collect (US) call

tele'fonico, a, ci, che *ag* (tele)phone *cpd*

telefon'ino *sm* mobile phone

telefo'nista, i, e *sm/f* telephonist; (*d'impresa*) switchboard operator

te'lefono *sm* telephone; **~ a gettoni** ≈ pay phone

telegior'nale [teledʒor'nale] *sm* television news (programme)

te'legrafo *sm* telegraph

tele'gramma, i *sm* telegram

telela'voro *sm* teleworking

tele'matica *sf* data transmission; telematics *sg*

teleobiet'tivo *sm* telephoto lens *sg*

telepa'tia *sf* telepathy

teles'copio *sm* telescope

teleselezi'one [teleselet'tsjone] *sf* direct dialling

telespetta'tore, 'trice *sm/f* (television) viewer

televisi'one *sf* television

televi'sore *sm* television set

'telex *sm inv* telex

'telo *sm* cloth; **~ da bagno** bath towel; **~ da spiaggia** beach towel

'tema, i *sm* theme; (INS) essay, composition

teme'rario, a *ag* rash, reckless

te'mere *vt* to fear, be afraid of; (*essere sensibile a: freddo, calore*) to be sensitive to ♦ *vi* to be afraid; (*essere preoccupato*): **~ per** to worry about, fear for; **~ di/che** to be afraid of/that

temperama'tite *sm inv* pencil sharpener

tempera'mento *sm* temperament

tempe'rato, a *ag* temperate

tempera'tura *sf* temperature

tempe'rino *sm* penknife

tem'pesta *sf* storm; **~ di sabbia/neve** sand/snowstorm

tempes'tare *vt*: **~ qn di domande** to bombard sb with questions; **~ qn di colpi** to rain blows on sb

tempes'tivo, a *ag* timely

tempes'toso, a *ag* stormy

'tempia *sf* (ANAT) temple

'tempio *sm* (*edificio*) temple

'tempo *sm* (METEOR) weather; (*cronologico*) time; (*epoca*) time, times *pl*; (*di film, gioco: parte*) part; (MUS) time; (: *battuta*) beat; (LING) tense; **un ~** once; **~ fa** some time ago; **al ~ stesso** o **a un ~** at the same time; **per ~** early; **ha fatto il suo ~** it has had its day; **~ libero** free time; **primo/secondo ~** (TEATRO) first/second part; (SPORT) first/second half; **in ~ utile** in due time o course; **a ~ pieno** full-time

tempo'rale *ag* temporal ♦ *sm* (METEOR) (thunder)storm

tempo'raneo, a *ag* temporary

temporeggi'are [tempored'dʒare] *vi* to play for time, temporize

tem'prare *vt* to temper

te'nace [te'natʃe] *ag* strong, tough; (*fig*) tenacious; **te'nacia** *sf* tenacity

te'naglie [te'naʎʎe] *sfpl* pincers *pl*

'tenda *sf* (*riparo*) awning; (*di finestra*) curtain; (*per campeggio etc*) tent

ten'denza [ten'dɛntsa] *sf* tendency; (*orientamento*) trend; **avere ~ a** o **per qc** to have a bent for sth

'tendere *vt* (*allungare al massimo*) to stretch, draw tight; (*porgere: mano*) to hold out; (*fig: trappola*) to lay, set ♦ *vi*: **~ qc/a fare** to tend towards sth/to do; **~ l'orecchio** to prick up one's ears; **il tempo tende al caldo** the weather is getting hot; **un blu che tende al verde** a greenish blue

ten'dina *sf* curtain

'tendine *sm* tendon, sinew

ten'done *sm* (*da circo*) tent

'tenebre *sfpl* darkness *sg*; **tene'broso, a** *ag* dark, gloomy

te'nente *sm* lieutenant

te'nere *vt* to hold; (*conservare, mantenere*) to keep; (*ritenere, considerare*) to consider; (*spazio: occupare*) to take up, occupy; (*seguire: strada*) to keep to ♦ *vi* to hold; (*colori*) to be fast; (*dare importanza*): **~ a** to care about; **~ a fare** to want to do, be keen to do; **~rsi** *vr* (*stare in una determinata posizione*) to stand; (*stimarsi*) to consider o.s.; (*aggrapparsi*): **~rsi a** to hold on to; (*attenersi*): **~rsi a** to stick to; **~ una conferenza** to give a lecture; **~ conto di qc** to take sth into consideration; **~ presente qc** to bear sth in mind

'tenero, a *ag* tender; (*pietra, cera, colore*) soft; (*fig*) tender, loving

'tenia *sf* tapeworm

'tennis *sm* tennis

te'nore *sm* (*tono*) tone; (*MUS*) tenor; **~ di vita** (*livello*) standard of living

tensi'one *sf* tension

ten'tare *vt* (*indurre*) to tempt; (*provare*): **~ qc/di fare** to attempt o try sth/to do; **tenta'tivo** *sm* attempt; **tentazi'one** *sf* temptation

tenten'nare *vi* to shake, be unsteady; (*fig*) to hesitate, waver

ten'toni *av*: **andare a ~** (*anche fig*) to grope one's way

'tenue *ag* (*sottile*) fine; (*colore*) soft; (*fig*) slender, slight

te'nuta *sf* (*capacità*) capacity; (*divisa*) uniform; (*abito*) dress; (*AGR*) estate; **a ~ d'aria** airtight; **~ di strada** roadholding power

teolo'gia [teolo'dʒia] *sf* theology; **te'ologo, gi** *sm* theologian

teo'rema, i *sm* theorem

teo'ria *sf* theory; **te'orico, a, ci, che** *ag* theoretic(al)

te'pore *sm* warmth

'teppa *sf* mob, hooligans *pl*; **tep'pismo** *sm* hooliganism; **tep'pista, i** *sm* hooligan

tera'pia *sf* therapy

tergicris'tallo [terdʒikris'tallo] *sm* windscreen (*BRIT*) o windshield (*US*) wiper

tergiver'sare [terdʒiver'sare] *vi* to shilly-shally

'tergo *sm*: **a ~** behind; **vedi a ~** please turn over

ter'male *ag* thermal; **stazione** *sf* **~ spa**

'terme *sfpl* thermal baths

'termico, a, ci, che *ag* thermic; (*unità*) thermal

termi'nale *ag, sm* terminal

termi'nare *vt* to end; (*lavoro*) to finish ♦ *vi* to end

'termine *sm* term; (*fine, estremità*) end; (*di territorio*) boundary, limit; **contratto a ~** (*COMM*) forward contract; **a breve/lungo ~** short-/long-term; **parlare senza mezzi ~i** to talk frankly, not to mince one's words

ter'mometro *sm* thermometer

termonucle'are *ag* thermonuclear

termosi'fone *sm* radiator

ter'mostato *sm* thermostat

'terra *sf* (*gen, ELETTR*) earth; (*sostanza*) soil, earth; (*opposto al mare*) land *no pl*; (*regione, paese*) land; (*argilla*) clay; **~e** *sfpl* (*possedimento*) lands, land *sg*; **a** o **per ~** (*stato*) on the ground (o floor); (*moto*) to the ground, down; **mettere a ~** (*ELETTR*) to earth

terra'cotta *sf* terracotta; **vasellame** *sm* **di ~** earthenware

terra'ferma *sf* dry land, terra firma; (*continente*) mainland

terrapi'eno *sm* embankment, bank

ter'razza [ter'rattsa] *sf* terrace

ter'razzo [ter'rattso] *sm* = **terrazza**

terre'moto *sm* earthquake

ter'reno, a *ag* (*vita, beni*) earthly ♦ *sm* (*suolo, fig*) ground; (*COMM*) land *no pl*, plot (of land); site; (*SPORT, MIL*) field

ter'restre *ag* (*superficie*) of the earth, earth's; (*di terra: battaglia, animale*) land *cpd*; (*REL*) earthly, worldly

ter'ribile *ag* terrible, dreadful

terrifi'cante *ag* terrifying

ter'rina *sf* tureen

territori'ale *ag* territorial

terri'torio *sm* territory

ter'rore *sm* terror; **terro'rismo** *sm* terrorism; **terro'rista, i, e** *sm/f* terrorist

'terso, a *ag* clear

'terzo, a ['tɛrtso] *ag* third ♦ *sm* (*frazione*) third; (*DIR*) third party; **la ~a pagina** (*STAMPA*) the Arts page

'tesa *sf* brim

'teschio ['teskjo] *sm* skull

'tesi *sf* thesis

'teso, a *pp di* **tendere** ♦ *ag* (*tirato*) taut,

tight; (fig) tense

tesore'ria sf treasury

tesori'ere sm treasurer

te'soro sm treasure; **il Ministero del T~** the Treasury

'tessera sf (documento) card

'tessere vt to weave; **'tessile** ag, sm textile; **tessi'tore**, **'trice** sm/f weaver; **tessi'tura** sf weaving

tes'suto sm fabric, material; (BIOL) tissue

'testa sf head; (di cose: estremità, parte anteriore) head, front; **di ~** (vettura etc) front; **tenere ~ a qn** (nemico etc) to stand up to sb; **fare di ~ propria** to go one's own way; **in ~** (SPORT) in the lead; **~ o croce?** heads or tails?; **avere la ~ dura** to be stubborn; **~ di serie** (TENNIS) seed, seeded player

testa'mento sm (atto) will; **l'Antico/il Nuovo T~** (REL) the Old/New Testament

tes'tardo, a ag stubborn, pig-headed

tes'tata sf (parte anteriore) head; (intestazione) heading

'teste sm/f witness

tes'ticolo sm testicle

testi'mone sm/f (DIR) witness

testimoni'anza [testimo'njantsa] sf testimony

testimoni'are vt to testify to; (fig) to bear witness to, testify to ♦ vi to give evidence, testify

tes'tina sf (TECN) head

'testo sm text; **fare ~** (opera, autore) to be authoritative; **questo libro non fa ~** this book is not essential reading; **testu'ale** ag textual; literal, word for word

tes'tuggine [tes'tuddʒine] sf tortoise; (di mare) turtle

'tetano sm (MED) tetanus

'tetro, a ag gloomy

'tetto sm roof; **tet'toia** sf roofing; canopy

'Tevere sm: **il ~** the Tiber

Tg abbr = **telegiornale**

'thermos ® ['tɛrmos] sm inv vacuum o Thermos ® flask

ti pron (dav lo, la, li, le, ne diventa **te**) pron (oggetto) you; (complemento di termine) (to) you; (riflessivo) yourself

'tibia sf tibia, shinbone

tic sm inv tic, (nervous) twitch; (fig) mannerism

ticchet'tio [tikket'tio] sm (di macchina da scrivere) clatter; (di orologio) ticking; (della pioggia) patter

'ticchio ['tikkjo] sm (ghiribizzo) whim; (tic) tic, (nervous) twitch

'ticket sm inv (su farmaci) prescription charge

ti'epido, a ag lukewarm, tepid

ti'fare vi: **~ per** to be a fan of; (parteggiare) to side with

'tifo sm (MED) typhus; (fig): **fare il ~ per** to be a fan of

tifoi'dea sf typhoid

ti'fone sm typhoon

ti'foso, a sm/f (SPORT etc) fan

'tiglio ['tiʎʎo] sm lime (tree), linden (tree)

'tigre sf tiger

tim'ballo sm (strumento) kettledrum; (CUC) timbale

'timbro sm stamp; (MUS) timbre, tone

'timido, a ag shy; timid

'timo sm thyme

ti'mone sm (NAUT) rudder; **timoni'ere** sm helmsman

ti'more sm (paura) fear; (rispetto) awe; **timo'roso, a** ag timid, timorous

'timpano sm (ANAT) eardrum; (MUS): **~i** smpl kettledrums, timpani

ti'nello sm small dining room

'tingere ['tindʒere] vt to dye

'tino sm vat

ti'nozza [ti'nɔttsa] sf tub

'tinta sf (materia colorante) dye; (colore) colour, shade; **tinta'rella** (fam) sf (sun)tan

tintin'nare vi to tinkle

'tinto, a pp di **tingere**

tinto'ria sf (lavasecco) dry cleaner's (shop)

tin'tura sf (operazione) dyeing; (colorante) dye; **~ di iodio** tincture of iodine

'tipico, a, ci, che ag typical

'tipo sm type; (genere) kind, type; (fam) chap, fellow

tipogra'fia sf typography; (procedimento) letterpress (printing); (officina) printing house; **tipo'grafico, a, ci, che** ag typographic(al); letterpress cpd; **ti'pografo** sm typographer

ti'ranno, a ag tyrannical ♦ sm tyrant

ti'rante sm (per tenda) guy

ti'rare vt (gen) to pull; (estrarre): **~ qc da** to take o pull sth out of; to get sth out of; to extract sth from; (chiudere: tenda etc) to draw, pull; (tracciare, disegnare) to draw, trace; (lanciare: sasso, palla) to throw; (stampare) to print; (pistola, freccia) to fire ♦ vi (pipa, camino) to draw; (vento) to blow; (abito) to be tight; (fare fuoco) to fire; (fare del tiro, CALCIO) to shoot; **~ avanti** vi to struggle on ♦ vt to keep going; **~ fuori** (estrarre) to take out, pull out; **~ giù** (abbassare) to bring down; **~ su** to pull up; (capelli) to put up; (fig: bambino) to bring up; **~rsi indietro** to move back

tira'tore sm gunman; **un buon ~** a good shot; **~ scelto** marksman

tira'tura sf (azione) printing; (di libro) (print) run; (di giornale) circulation

'tirchio, a ['tirkjo] ag mean, stingy

'tiro sm shooting no pl, firing no pl; (colpo,

sparo) shot; (*di palla: lancio*) throwing *no pl*;
throw; (*fig*) trick; **cavallo da ~** draught (*BRIT*)
o draft (*US*) horse; **~ a segno** target shooting;
(*luogo*) shooting range

tiro'cinio [tiro'tʃinjo] *sm* apprenticeship;
(*professionale*) training

ti'roide *sf* thyroid (gland)

Tir'reno *sm*: **il** (**mar**) **~** the Tyrrhenian Sea

ti'sana *sf* herb tea

tito'lare *sm/f* incumbent; (*proprietario*)
owner; (*CALCIO*) regular player

'titolo *sm* title; (*di giornale*) headline;
(*diploma*) qualification; (*COMM*) security;
(: *azione*) share; **a che ~?** for what reason?; **a
~ di amicizia** out of friendship; **a ~ di premio**
as a prize; **~ di credito** share

titu'bante *ag* hesitant, irresolute

'tizio, a ['tittsjo] *sm/f* fellow, chap

tiz'zone [tit'tsone] *sm* brand

toast [toust] *sm inv* toasted sandwich
(*generally with ham and cheese*)

toc'cante *ag* touching

toc'care *vt* to touch; (*tastare*) to feel; (*fig:
riguardare*) to concern; (: *commuovere*) to
touch, move; (: *pungere*) to hurt, wound;
(: *far cenno a: argomento*) to touch on, mention ♦ *vi*: **~ a** (*accadere*) to happen to; (*spettare*) to be up to; **~** (**il fondo**) (*in acqua*) to
touch the bottom; **tocca a te difenderci** it's
up to you to defend us; **a chi tocca?** whose
turn is it?; **mi toccò pagare** I had to pay

'tocco, chi *sm* touch; (*ARTE*) stroke, touch

'toga, ghe *sf* toga; (*di magistrato, professore*)
gown

'togliere ['tɔʎʎere] *vt* (*rimuovere*) to take
away (*o* off), remove; (*riprendere, non
concedere più*) to take away, remove; (*MAT*) to
take away, subtract; **~ qc a qn** to take sth
(*away*) from sb; **ciò non toglie che**
nevertheless, be that as it may; **~rsi il
cappello** to take off one's hat

toi'lette [twa'lɛt] *sf inv* toilet; (*mobile*)
dressing table

to'letta *sf* = **toilette**

tolle'ranza [tolle'rantsa] *sf* tolerance

tolle'rare *vt* to tolerate

'tolto, a *pp di* **togliere**

to'maia *sf* (*di scarpa*) upper

'tomba *sf* tomb

tom'bino *sm* manhole cover

'tombola *sf* (*gioco*) tombola; (*ruzzolone*)
tumble

'tomo *sm* volume

'tonaca, che *sf* (*REL*) habit

'tondo, a *ag* round

'tonfo *sm* splash; (*rumore sordo*) thud;
(*caduta*): **fare un ~** to take a tumble

'tonico, a, ci, che *ag, 'sm* tonic

tonifi'care *vt* (*muscoli, pelle*) to tone up;

(*irrobustire*) to invigorate, brace

tonnel'laggio [tonnel'laddʒo] *sm* (*NAUT*)
tonnage

tonnel'lata *sf* ton

'tonno *sm* tuna (fish)

'tono *sm* (*gen*) tone; (*MUS: di pezzo*) key; (*di
colore*) shade, tone

ton'silla *sf* tonsil; **tonsil'lite** *sf* tonsillitis

'tonto, a *ag* dull, stupid

to'pazio [to'pattsjo] *sm* topaz

'topo *sm* mouse

topogra'fia *sf* topography

'toppa *sf* (*serratura*) keyhole; (*pezza*) patch

to'race [to'ratʃe] *sm* chest

'torba *sf* peat

'torbido, a *ag* (*liquido*) cloudy; (: *fiume*)
muddy; (*fig*) dark; troubled ♦ *sm*: **pescare
nel ~** (*fig*) to fish in troubled water

'torcere ['tɔrtʃere] *vt* to twist; **~rsi** *vr* to twist,
writhe

torchi'are [tor'kjare] *vt* to press; **'torchio**
sm press

'torcia, ce ['tɔrtʃa] *sf* torch; **~ elettrica** torch
(*BRIT*), flashlight (*US*)

torci'collo [tortʃi'kɔllo] *sm* stiff neck

'tordo *sm* thrush

To'rino *sf* Turin

tor'menta *sf* snowstorm

tormen'tare *vt* to torment; **~rsi** *vr* to fret,
worry o.s.; **tor'mento** *sm* torment

torna'conto *sm* advantage, benefit

tor'nado *sm* tornado

tor'nante *sm* hairpin bend

tor'nare *vi* to return, go (*o* come) back;
(*ridiventare: anche fig*) to become (again);
(*riuscire giusto, esatto: conto*) to work out;
(*risultare*) to turn out (to be), prove (to be);
~ utile to prove *o* turn out (to be) useful; **~ a
casa** to go (*o* come) home

torna'sole *sm inv* litmus

tor'neo *sm* tournament

'tornio *sm* lathe

'toro *sm* bull; (*dello zodiaco*): **T~** Taurus

tor'pedine *sf* torpedo; **torpedini'era** *sf*
torpedo boat

'torre *sf* tower; (*SCACCHI*) rook, castle; **~ di
controllo** (*AER*) control tower

torrefazi'one [torrefat'tsjone] *sf* roasting

tor'rente *sm* torrent

tor'retta *sf* turret

torri'one *sm* keep

tor'rone *sm* nougat

torsi'one *sf* twisting; torsion

'torso *sm* torso, trunk; (*ARTE*) torso

'torsolo *sm* (*di cavolo etc*) stump; (*di frutta*)
core

'torta *sf* cake

'torto, a *pp di* **torcere** ♦ *ag* (*ritorto*) twisted;
(*storto*) twisted, crooked ♦ *sm* (*ingiustizia*)

wrong; (*colpa*) fault; **a ~** wrongly; **aver ~ to** be wrong

'tortora *sf* turtle dove

tortu'oso, a *ag* (*strada*) twisting; (*fig*) tortuous

tor'tura *sf* torture; **tortu'rare** *vt* to torture

'torvo, a *ag* menacing, grim

tosa'erba *sm o f inv* (lawn)mower

to'sare *vt* (*pecora*) to shear; (*siepe*) to clip

Tos'cana *sf*: **la ~** Tuscany; **tos'cano, a** *ag, sm/f* Tuscan ♦ *sm* (*sigaro*) strong Italian cigar

'tosse *sf* cough

'tossico, a, ci, che *ag* toxic

tossicodipen'dente *sm/f* drug addict

tossi'comane *sm/f* drug addict

tos'sire *vi* to cough

tosta'pane *sm inv* toaster

tos'tare *vt* to toast; (*caffè*) to roast

'tosto, a *ag*: **faccia ~a** cheek

to'tale *ag, sm* total; **totalità** *sf*: **la totalità di** all of, the total amount (*o* number) of; the whole **+sg**; **totaliz'zare** *vt* to total; (*SPORT: punti*) to score

toto'calcio [toto'kaltʃo] *sm* gambling pool betting on football results, ≈ (football) pools *pl* (*BRIT*)

to'vaglia [to'vaλλa] *sf* tablecloth; **tova-gli'olo** *sm* napkin

'tozzo, a ['tɔttso] *ag* squat ♦ *sm*: **~ di pane** crust of bread

tra *prep* (*di due persone, cose*) between; (*di più persone, cose*) among(st); (*tempo: entro*) within, in; **~ 5 giorni** in 5 days' time; **sia detto ~ noi ...** between you and me ...; **litigano ~ (di) loro** they're fighting amongst themselves; **~ breve** soon; **~ sé e sé** (*parlare etc*) to oneself

trabal'lare *vi* to stagger, totter

traboc'care *vi* to overflow

traboc'chetto [trabok'ketto] *sm* (*fig*) trap

tracan'nare *vt* to gulp down

'traccia, ce ['trattʃa] *sf* (*segno, striscia*) trail, track; (*orma*) tracks *pl*; (*residuo, testimonianza*) trace, sign; (*abbozzo*) outline

tracci'are [trat'tʃare] *vt* to trace, mark (out); (*disegnare*) to draw; (*fig: abbozzare*) to outline; **tracci'ato** *sm* (*grafico*) layout, plan

tra'chea [tra'kea] *sf* windpipe, trachea

tra'colla *sf* shoulder strap; **borsa a ~** shoulder bag

tra'collo *sm* (*fig*) collapse, crash

tradi'mento *sm* betrayal; (*DIR, MIL*) treason

tra'dire *vt* to betray; (*coniuge*) to be unfaithful to; (*doveri: mancare*) to fail in; (*rivelare*) to give away, reveal; **tradi'tore, 'trice** *sm/f* traitor

tradizio'nale [tradittsjo'nale] *ag* traditional

tradizi'one [tradit'tsjone] *sf* tradition

tra'dotto, a *pp di* **tradurre**

tra'durre *vt* to translate; (*spiegare*) to render, convey; **tradut'tore, 'trice** *sm/f* translator; **traduzi'one** *sf* translation

trafe'lato, a *ag* out of breath

traffi'cante *sm/f* dealer; (*peg*) trafficker

traffi'care *vi* (*commerciare*): **~ (in)** to trade (in), deal (in); (*affaccendarsi*) to busy o.s. ♦ *vt* (*peg*) to traffic in

'traffico, ci *sm* traffic; (*commercio*) trade, traffic

tra'figgere [tra'fiddʒere] *vt* to run through, stab; (*fig*) to pierce

tra'fitto, a *pp di* **trafiggere**

trafo'rare *vt* to bore, drill; **tra'foro** *sm* (*azione*) boring, drilling; (*galleria*) tunnel

tra'gedia [tra'dʒedja] *sf* tragedy

tra'ghetto [tra'getto] *sm* ferry(boat)

'tragico, a, ci, che ['tradʒiko] *ag* tragic

tra'gitto [tra'dʒitto] *sm* (*passaggio*) crossing; (*viaggio*) journey

tragu'ardo *sm* (*SPORT*) finishing line; (*fig*) goal, aim

traiet'toria *sf* trajectory

trai'nare *vt* to drag, haul; (*rimorchiare*) to tow; **'traino** *sm* (*carro*) wagon; (*slitta*) sledge; (*carico*) load

tralasci'are [tralaʃ'ʃare] *vt* (*studi*) to neglect; (*dettagli*) to leave out, omit

'tralcio ['traltʃo] *sm* (*BOT*) shoot

tra'liccio [tra'littʃo] *sm* (*ELETTR*) pylon

tram *sm inv* tram

'trama *sf* (*filo*) weft, woof; (*fig: argomento, maneggio*) plot

traman'dare *vt* to pass on, hand down

tra'mare *vt* (*fig*) to scheme, plot

tram'busto *sm* turmoil

trames'tio *sm* bustle

tramez'zino [tramed'dzino] *sm* sandwich

tra'mezzo [tra'mɛddzo] *sm* (*EDIL*) partition

tra'mite *prep* through

tramon'tare *vi* to set, go down; **tra'monto** *sm* setting; (*del sole*) sunset

tramor'tire *vi* to faint ♦ *vt* to stun

trampo'lino *sm* (*per tuffi*) springboard, diving board; (*per lo sci*) ski-jump

'trampolo *sm* stilt

tramu'tare *vt*: **~ in** to change into, turn into

tra'nello *sm* trap

trangugi'are [trangu'dʒare] *vt* to gulp down

'tranne *prep* except (for:), but (for); **~ che** unless

tranquil'lante *sm* (*MED*) tranquillizer

tranquillità *sf* calm, stillness; quietness; peace of mind

tranquilliz'zare [trankwillid'dzare] *vt* to reassure

tran'quillo, a *ag* calm, quiet; (*bambino, scolaro*) quiet; (*sereno*) with one's mind at rest; **sta' ~** don't worry

transat'lantico, ci sm transatlantic liner

transazi'one [transat'tsjone] sf compromise; (DIR) settlement; (COMM) transaction, deal

tran'senna sf barrier

tran'sigere [tran'sidʒere] vi (venire a patti) to compromise, come to an agreement

tran'sistor sm inv transistor

transi'tabile ag passable

transi'tare vi to pass

transi'tivo, a ag transitive

'transito sm transit; **di ~** (merci) in transit; (stazione) transit cpd; **"divieto di ~"** "no entry"

transi'torio, a ag transitory, transient; (provvisorio) provisional

'trapano sm (utensile) drill; (: MED) trepan

trapas'sare vt to pierce

tra'passo sm passage

trape'lare vi to leak, drip; (fig) to leak out

tra'pezio [tra'pettsjo] sm (MAT) trapezium; (attrezzo ginnico) trapeze

trapian'tare vt to transplant; **trapi'anto** sm transplanting; (MED) transplant

'trappola sf trap

tra'punta sf quilt

'trarre vt to draw, pull; (portare) to take; (prendere, tirare fuori) to take (out), draw; (derivare) to obtain; **~ origine da qc** to have its origins o originate in sth

trasa'lire vi to start, jump

trasan'dato, a ag shabby

tras'bordo sm transfer

trasci'nare [traʃʃi'nare] vt to drag; **~rsi** vr to drag o.s. along; (fig) to drag on

tras'correre vt (tempo) to spend, pass ♦ vi to pass; **tras'corso, a** pp di trascorrere

tras'critto, a pp di trascrivere

tras'crivere vt to transcribe

trascu'rare vt to neglect; (non considerare) to disregard; **trascura'tezza** sf carelessness, negligence; **trascu'rato, a** ag (casa) neglected; (persona) careless, negligent

trasfe'ribile ag transferable; **"non ~"** (su assegno) "account payee only"

trasferi'mento sm transfer; (trasloco) removal, move

trasfe'rire vt to transfer; **~rsi** vr to move; **tras'ferta** sf transfer; (indennità) travelling expenses pl; (SPORT) away game

trasfigu'rare vt to transfigure

trasfor'mare vt to transform, change; **trasforma'tore** sm (ELEC) transformer

trasfusi'one sf (MED) transfusion

trasgre'dire vt to disobey, contravene

tras'lato, a ag metaphorical, figurative

traslo'care vt to move, transfer; **~rsi** vr to move; **tras'loco, chi** sm removal

tras'messo, a pp di trasmettere

tras'mettere vt (passare): **~ qc a qn** to pass

sth on to sb; (mandare) to send; (TECN, TEL, MED) to transmit; (TV, RADIO) to broadcast; **trasmetti'tore** sm transmitter; **trasmissi'one** sf (gen, FISICA, TECN) transmission; (passaggio) transmission, passing on; (TV, RADIO) broadcast; **trasmit'tente** sf transmitting o broadcasting station

traso'gnato, a [trasoɲ'ɲato] ag dreamy

traspa'rente ag transparent

traspa'rire vi to show (through)

traspi'rare vi to perspire; (fig) to come to light, leak out; **traspirazi'one** sf perspiration

traspor'tare vt to carry, move; (merce) to transport, convey; **lasciarsi ~ (da qc)** (fig) to let o.s. be carried away (by sth); **tras'porto** sm transport

trastul'lare vt to amuse; **~rsi** vr to amuse o.s.

trasu'dare vi (filtrare) to ooze; (sudare) to sweat ♦ vt to ooze with

trasver'sale ag transverse, cross(-); running at right angles

trasvo'lare vt to fly over

'tratta sf (ECON) draft; (di persone): **la ~ delle bianche** the white slave trade

tratta'mento sm treatment; (servizio) service

trat'tare vt (gen) to treat; (commerciare) to deal in; (svolgere: argomento) to discuss, deal with; (negoziare) to negotiate ♦ vi: **~ di** to deal with; **~ con** (persona) to deal with; **si tratta di ...** it's about ...; **tratta'tive** sfpl negotiations; **trat'tato** sm (testo) treatise; (accordo) treaty; **trattazi'one** sf treatment

tratteggi'are [tratted'dʒare] vt (disegnare: a tratti) to sketch, outline; (: col tratteggio) to hatch

tratte'nere vt (far rimanere: persona) to detain; (intrattenere: ospiti) to entertain; (tenere, frenare, reprimere) to hold back, keep back; (astenersi dal consegnare) to hold, keep; (detrarre: somma) to deduct; **~rsi** vr (astenersi) to restrain o.s., stop o.s.; (soffermarsi) to stay, remain

tratteni'mento sm entertainment; (festa) party

tratte'nuta sf deduction

trat'tino sm dash; (in parole composte) hyphen

'tratto, a pp di trarre ♦ sm (di penna, matita) stroke; (parte) part, piece; (di strada) stretch; (di mare, cielo) expanse; (di tempo) period (of time); **~i** smpl (caratteristiche) features; (modo di fare) ways, manners; **a un ~, d'un ~** suddenly

trat'tore sm tractor

tratto'ria sf restaurant

'trauma, i sm trauma; **trau'matico, a, ci,**

che *ag* traumatic
tra'vaglio [tra'vaʎʎo] *sm* (*angoscia*) pain, suffering; (*MED*) pains *pl*
trava'sare *vt* to decant
'trave *sf* beam
tra'versa *sf* (*trave*) crosspiece; (*via*) sidestreet; (*FERR*) sleeper (*BRIT*), (railroad) tie (*US*); (*CALCIO*) crossbar
traver'sare *vt* to cross; **traver'sata** *sf* crossing; (*AER*) flight, trip
traver'sie *sfpl* mishaps, misfortunes
traver'sina *sf* (*FERR*) sleeper (*BRIT*), (railroad) tie (*US*)
tra'verso, a *ag* oblique; **di ~** *ag* askew ♦ *av* sideways; **andare di ~** (*cibo*) to go down the wrong way; **guardare di ~** to look askance at
travesti'mento *sm* disguise
traves'tire *vt* to disguise; **~rsi** *vr* to disguise o.s.
travi'are *vt* (*fig*) to lead astray
travi'sare *vt* (*fig*) to distort, misrepresent
tra'volgere [tra'vɔldʒere] *vt* to sweep away, carry away; (*fig*) to overwhelm; **tra'volto, a** *pp di* **travolgere**
tre *num* three
trebbi'are *vt* to thresh
'treccia, ce ['trettʃa] *sf* plait, braid
tre'cento [tre'tʃɛnto] *num* three hundred ♦ *sm*: **il T~** the fourteenth century
'tredici ['treditʃi] *num* thirteen
'tregua *sf* truce; (*fig*) respite
tre'mare *vi*: **~ di** (*freddo etc*) to shiver o tremble with; (*paura, rabbia*) to shake o tremble with
tre'mendo, a *ag* terrible, awful
tre'mila *num* three thousand
'tremito *sm* trembling *no pl*; shaking *no pl*; shivering *no pl*
tremo'lare *vi* to tremble; (*luce*) to flicker; (*foglie*) to quiver
tre'more *sm* tremor
'treno *sm* train; **~ di gomme** set of tyres (*BRIT*) o tires (*US*); **~ merci** goods (*BRIT*) o freight train; **~ viaggiatori** passenger train
'trenta *num* thirty; **tren'tesimo, a** *num* thirtieth; **tren'tina** *sf*: **una trentina (di)** thirty or so, about thirty
trepi'dante *ag* anxious
treppi'ede *sm* tripod; (*CUC*) trivet
'tresca, sche *sf* (*fig*) intrigue; (: *relazione amorosa*) affair
'trespolo *sm* trestle
tri'angolo *sm* triangle
tribù *sf inv* tribe
tri'buna *sf* (*podio*) platform; (*in aule etc*) gallery; (*di stadio*) stand
tribu'nale *sm* court
tribu'tare *vt* to bestow
tri'buto *sm* tax; (*fig*) tribute

tri'checo, chi [tri'kɛko] *sm* (*ZOOL*) walrus
tri'ciclo [tri'tʃiklo] *sm* tricycle
trico'lore *ag* three-coloured ♦ *sm* tricolour; (*bandiera italiana*) Italian flag
tri'dente *sm* trident
tri'foglio [tri'fɔʎʎo] *sm* clover
'triglia ['triʎʎa] *sf* red mullet
tril'lare *vi* (*MUS*) to trill
tri'mestre *sm* period of three months; (*INS*) term, quarter (*US*); (*COMM*) quarter
'trina *sf* lace
trin'cea [trin'tʃea] *sf* trench; **trince'rare** *vt* to entrench
trinci'are [trin'tʃare] *vt* to cut up
trion'fare *vi* to triumph, win; **~ su** to triumph over, overcome; **tri'onfo** *sm* triumph
tripli'care *vt* to triple
'triplice ['triplitʃe] *ag* triple; **in ~ copia** in triplicate
'triplo, a *ag* triple; treble ♦ *sm*: **il ~ (di)** three times as much (as); **la spesa è ~a** it costs three times as much
'trippa *sf* (*CUC*) tripe
'triste *ag* sad; (*luogo*) dreary, gloomy; **tris'tezza** *sf* sadness; gloominess
trita'carne *sm inv* mincer, grinder (*US*)
tri'tare *vt* to mince, grind (*US*)
'trito, a *ag* (*tritato*) minced, ground (*US*); **~ e ritrito** (*fig*) trite, hackneyed
'trittico, ci *sm* (*ARTE*) triptych
trivel'lare *vt* to drill
trivi'ale *ag* vulgar, low
tro'feo *sm* trophy
'tromba *sf* (*MUS*) trumpet; (*AUT*) horn; **~ d'aria** whirlwind; **~ delle scale** stairwell
trom'bone *sm* trombone
trom'bosi *sf* thrombosis
tron'care *vt* to cut off; (*spezzare*) to break off
'tronco, a, chi, che *ag* cut off; broken off; (*LING*) truncated; (*fig*) cut short ♦ *sm* (*BOT, ANAT*) trunk; (*fig*: *tratto*) section; **licenziare qn in ~** to fire sb on the spot
troneggi'are [troned'dʒare] *vi*: **~ (su)** to tower (over)
tron'fio, a *ag* conceited
'trono *sm* throne
tropi'cale *ag* tropical
'tropico, ci *sm* tropic; **~ci** *smpl* (*GEO*) tropics

PAROLA CHIAVE

'troppo, a *det* (*in eccesso*: *quantità*) too much; (: *numero*) too many; **c'era ~a gente** there were too many people; **fa ~ caldo** it's too hot
♦ *pron* (*in eccesso*: *quantità*) too much; (: *numero*) too many; **ne hai messo ~** you've put in too much; **meglio ~i che pochi** better too

many than too few

♦ av (eccessivamente: con ag, av) too; (: con vb) too much; ~ **amaro/tardi** too bitter/late; **lavora ~** he works too much; **di ~** too much; too many; **qualche tazza di ~** a few cups too many; **3000 lire di ~** 3000 lire too much; **essere di ~** to be in the way

'**trota** sf trout

trot'tare vi to trot; **trotterel'lare** vi to trot along; (bambino) to toddle; '**trotto** sm trot

'**trottola** sf spinning top

tro'vare vt to find; (giudicare): **trovo che I** find o think that; **~rsi** vr (reciproco: incontrarsi) to meet; (: essere, stare) to be; (arrivare, capitare) to find o.s.; **andare a ~ qn** to go and see sb; **~ qn colpevole** to find sb guilty; **~rsi bene** (in un luogo, con qn) to get on well; **tro'vata** sf good idea

truc'care vt (falsare) to fake; (attore etc) to make up; (travestire) to disguise; (SPORT) to fix; (AUT) to soup up; **~rsi** vr to make up (one's face); **trucca'tore, 'trice** sm/f (CINEMA, TEATRO) make-up artist

'**trucco, chi** sm trick; (cosmesi) make-up

'**truce** ['trutʃe] ag fierce

truci'dare [trutʃi'dare] vt to slaughter

truciolo ['trutʃolo] sm shaving

'**truffa** sf fraud, swindle; **truf'fare** vt to swindle, cheat

'**truppa** sf troop

tu pron you; **~ stesso(a)** you yourself; **dare del ~ a qn** to address sb as "tu"

'**tua** vedi **tuo**

'**tuba** sf (MUS) tuba; (cappello) top hat

tu'bare vi to coo

tuba'tura sf piping no pl, pipes pl

tu'betto sm tube

'**tubo** sm tube; pipe; **~ digerente** (ANAT) alimentary canal, digestive tract; **~ di scappamento** (AUT) exhaust pipe

'**tue** vedi **tuo**

tuf'fare vt to plunge, dip; **~rsi** vr to plunge, dive; '**tuffo** sm dive; (breve bagno) dip

tu'gurio sm hovel

tuli'pano sm tulip

tume'farsi vr (MED) to swell

'**tumido, a** ag swollen

tu'more sm (MED) tumour

tu'multo sm uproar, commotion; (sommossa) riot; (fig) turmoil; **tumultu'oso, a** ag rowdy, unruly; (fig) turbulent, stormy

'**tunica, che** sf tunic

Tuni'sia sf: **la ~** Tunisia

'**tuo** (f '**tua,** pl **'tuoi, 'tue**) det: **il ~, la tua** etc your ♦ pron: **il ~, la tua** etc yours

tuo'nare vi to thunder; **tuona** it is thundering, there's some thunder

tu'ono sm thunder

tu'orlo sm yolk

tu'racciolo [tu'rattʃolo] sm cap, top; (di sughero) cork

tu'rare vt to stop, plug; (con sughero) to cork; **~rsi il naso** to hold one's nose

turba'mento sm disturbance; (di animo) anxiety, agitation

tur'bante sm turban

tur'bare vt to disturb, trouble

'**turbine** sm whirlwind

turbo'lento, a ag turbulent; (ragazzo) boisterous, unruly

turbo'lenza [turbo'lɛntsa] sf turbulence

tur'chese [tur'kese] sf turquoise

Tur'chia [tur'kia] sf: **la ~** Turkey

tur'chino, a [tur'kino] ag deep blue

'**turco, a, chi, che** ag Turkish ♦ sm/f Turk/ Turkish woman ♦ sm (LING) Turkish; **parlare ~** (fig) to talk double-dutch

tu'rismo sm tourism; tourist industry; **tu'rista, i, e** sm/f tourist; **tu'ristico, a, ci, che** ag tourist cpd

'**turno** sm turn; (di lavoro) shift; **di ~** (soldato, medico, custode) on duty; **a ~** (rispondere) in turn; (lavorare) in shifts; **fare a ~ a fare qc** to take turns to do sth; **è il suo ~** it's your (o his etc) turn

'**turpe** ag filthy, vile; **turpi'loquio** sm obscene language

'**tuta** sf overalls pl; (SPORT) tracksuit

tu'tela sf (DIR: di minore) guardianship; (: protezione) protection; (difesa) defence; **tute'lare** vt to protect, defend

tu'tore, 'trice sm/f (DIR) guardian

tutta'via cong nevertheless, yet

PAROLA CHIAVE

'**tutto, a** det **1** (intero) all; **~ il latte** all the milk; **~a la notte** all night, the whole night; **~ il libro** the whole book; **~a una bottiglia** a whole bottle

2 (pl, collettivo) all; every; **~i i libri** all the books; **~e le notti** every night; **~i i venerdì** every Friday; **~i gli uomini** all the men; (collettivo) all men; **~ l'anno** all year long; **~i e due** both o each of us (o them o you); **~i e cinque** all five of us (o them o you)

3 (completamente): **era ~a sporca** she was all dirty; **tremava ~** he was trembling all over; **è ~a sua madre** she's just o exactly like her mother

4: a tutt'oggi so far, up till now; **a ~a velocità** at full o top speed

♦ pron **1** (ogni cosa) everything, all; (qualsiasi cosa) anything; **ha mangiato ~** he's eaten everything; **~ considerato** all things considered; **in ~: 10,000 lire in ~** 10.000 lire in all; **in ~ eravamo 50** there were 50 of us in all

2: ~i, e (ognuno) all, everybody; **vengono ~i**

they are all coming, everybody's coming; **~i quanti** all and sundry

♦ *av* (*completamente*) entirely, quite; **è ~ il contrario** it's quite o exactly the opposite; **tutt'al più: saranno stati tutt'al più una cinquantina** there were about fifty of them at (the very) most; **tutt'al più possiamo prendere un treno** if the worst comes to the worst we can take a train; **tutt'altro** on the contrary; **è tutt'altro che felice** he's anything but happy; **tutt'a un tratto** suddenly

♦ *sm*: **il ~ the** whole lot, all of it

tutto'fare *ag inv*: **domestica ~** general maid; **ragazzo ~** office boy ♦ *sm/f inv* handyman/ woman

tut'tora *av* still

U, u

ubbidi'ente *ag* obedient; **ubbidi'enza** *sf* obedience

ubbi'dire *vi* to obey; **~ a** to obey; (*sog: veicolo, macchina*) to respond to

ubria'care *vt*: **~ qn** to get sb drunk; (*sog: alcool*) to make sb drunk; (*fig*) to make sb's head spin o reel; **~rsi** *vr* to get drunk; **~rsi di** (*fig*) to become intoxicated with

ubri'aco, a, chi, che *ag, sm/f* drunk

uccelli'era [uttʃelˈljɛra] *sf* aviary

uccel'lino [uttʃelˈlino] *sm* baby bird, chick

uc'cello [utˈtʃɛllo] *sm* bird

uc'cidere [utˈtʃidere] *vt* to kill; **~rsi** *vr* (*suicidarsi*) to kill o.s.; (*perdere la vita*) to be killed; **uccisi'one** *sf* killing; **uc'ciso, a** *pp di* **uccidere**; **ucci'sore** *sm* killer

udi'enza [uˈdjɛntsa] *sf* audience, (*DIR*) hearing

u'dire *vt* to hear; **udi'tivo, a** *ag* auditory; **u'dito** *sm* (*sense of*) hearing; **udi'torio** *sm* (*persone*) audience

UE *sigla f* (= *Unione Europea*) EU

UEM *sigla f* (= *Unione economica e monetaria*) EMU

'uffa *escl* tut!

uffici'ale [uffiˈtʃale] *ag* official ♦ *sm* (*AMM*) official, officer; (*MIL*) officer; **~ di stato civile** registrar

uf'ficio [ufˈfitʃo] *sm* (*gen*) office; (*dovere*) duty; (*mansione*) task, function, job; (*agenzia*) agency, bureau; (*REL*) service; **d'~** *ag* office *cpd*; official ♦ *av* officially; **~ di collocamento** employment office; **~ informazioni** information bureau; **~ oggetti smarriti** lost property office (*BRIT*), lost and found (*US*); **~ postale** post office

uffici'oso, a [uffiˈtʃoso] *ag* unofficial

'UFO *sm inv* UFO

'ufo: **a ~** *av* free, for nothing

uguagli'anza [ugwaʎˈʎantsa] *sf* equality

uguagli'are [ugwaʎˈʎare] *vt* to make equal; (*essere uguale*) to equal, be equal to; (*livellare*) to level; **~rsi a o con qn** (*paragonarsi*) to compare o.s. with sb

ugu'ale *ag* equal; (*identico*) identical, the same; (*uniforme*) level, even ♦ *av*: **costano ~** they cost the same; **sono bravi ~** they're equally good; **ugual'mente** *av* equally; (*lo stesso*) all the same

'ulcera [ˈultʃera] *sf* ulcer

u'livo = **olivo**

ulteri'ore *ag* further

ulti'mare *vt* to finish, complete

'ultimo, a *ag* (*finale*) last; (*estremo*) farthest, utmost; (*recente: notizia, moda*) latest; (*fig: sommo, fondamentale*) ultimate ♦ *sm/f* last (one); **fino all'~** to the last, until the end; **da ~, in ~** in the end; **abitare all'~ piano** to live on the top floor; **per ~** (*entrare, arrivare*) last

ulu'lare *vi* to howl; **ulu'lato** *sm* howling *no pl*; howl

umanità *sf* humanity; **umani'tario, a** *ag* humanitarian

u'mano, a *ag* human; (*comprensivo*) humane

umet'tare *vt* to dampen, moisten

umidità *sf* dampness; humidity

'umido, a *ag* damp; (*mano, occhi*) moist; (*clima*) humid ♦ *sm* dampness, damp; **carne in ~** stew

'umile *ag* humble

umili'are *vt* to humiliate; **~rsi** *vr* to humble o.s.; **umiliazi'one** *sf* humiliation

umiltà *sf* humility, humbleness

u'more *sm* (*disposizione d'animo*) mood; (*carattere*) temper; **di buon/cattivo ~** in a good/bad mood

umo'rismo *sm* humour; **avere il senso dell'~** to have a sense of humour; **umo'ristico, a, ci, che** *ag* humorous, funny

un *vedi* **uno**

un' *vedi* **uno**

una *vedi* **uno**

u'nanime *ag* unanimous; **unanimità** *sf* unanimity; **all'unanimità** unanimously

unci'netto [untʃiˈnetto] *sm* crochet hook

un'cino [unˈtʃino] *sm* hook

'undici [ˈunditʃi] *num* eleven

'ungere [ˈundʒere] *vt* to grease, oil; (*REL*) to anoint; (*fig*) to flatter, butter up; **~rsi** *vr* (*sporcarsi*) to get covered in grease; **~rsi con la crema** to put on cream

unghe'rese [ungeˈrese] *ag, sm/f*, *sm* Hungarian

Unghe'ria [ungeˈria] *sf*: **l'~** Hungary

'unghia [ˈungja] *sf* (*ANAT*) nail; (*di animale*) claw; (*di rapace*) talon; (*di cavallo*) hoof;

unghi'ata *sf* (*graffio*) scratch

ungu'ento *sm* ointment

'unico, a, ci, che *ag* (*solo*) only; (*ineguagliabile*) unique; (*singolo*: *binario*) single; **figlio(a) ~(a)** only son/daughter, only child

unifamili'are *ag* one-family *cpd*

unificazi'one *sf* uniting; unification; standardization

uni'forme *ag* uniform; (*superficie*) even ♦ *sf* (*divisa*) uniform

unilate'rale *ag* one-sided; (*DIR*) unilateral

uni'one *sf* union; (*fig*: *concordia*) unity, harmony; **U~ Europea** European Union

u'nire *vt* to unite; (*congiungere*) to join, connect; (: *ingredienti*, *colori*) to combine; (*in matrimonio*) to unite, join together; **~rsi** *vr* to unite; (*in matrimonio*) to be joined together; **~ qc a** to unite sth with; to join *o* connect sth with; to combine sth with; **~rsi a** (*gruppo*, *società*) to join

unità *sf inv* (*unione*, *concordia*) unity; (*MAT*, *MIL*, *COMM*, *di misura*) unit; **uni'tario, a** *ag* unitary; **prezzo unitario** price per unit

u'nito, a *ag* (*paese*) united; (*amici*, *famiglia*) close; **in tinta ~a** plain, self-coloured

univer'sale *ag* universal; general

università *sf inv* university; **universi'tario, a** *ag* university *cpd* ♦ *sm/f* (*studente*) university student; (*insegnante*) academic, university lecturer

uni'verso *sm* universe

'uno, a (*dav sm* **un** +C, V, **uno** +s *impura*, *gn*, *pn*, *ps*, *x*, *z*; *dav sf* **un'** +V, **una** +C) *art indef*
1 a; (*dav vocale*) an; **un bambino** a child; **~a strada** a street; **~ zingaro** a gypsy
2 (*intensivo*): **ho avuto ~a paura!** I got such a fright!
♦ *pron* **1** one; **prendine ~** take one (of them); **l'~ o l'altro** either (of them); **l'~ e l'altro** both (of them); **aiutarsi l'un l'altro** to help one another *o* each other; **sono entrati l'~ dopo l'altro** they came in one after the other
2 (*un tale*) someone, somebody
3 (*con valore impersonale*) one, you; **se ~ vuole** if one wants, if you want
♦ *num one*; **~a mela e due pere** one apple and two pears; **~ più ~ fa due** one plus one equals two, one and one are two
♦ *sf*: **è l'~a** it's one (o'clock)

'unto, a *pp di* **ungere** ♦ *ag* greasy, oily ♦ *sm* grease; **untu'oso, a** *ag* greasy, oily

u'omo (*pl* **u'omini**) *sm* man; **da ~** (*abito*, *scarpe*) men's, for men; **~ d'affari** businessman; **~ di paglia** stooge; **~ rana** frogman

u'ovo (*pl*(*f*) **u'ova**) *sm* egg; **~ affogato** poached egg; **~ al tegame** fried egg; **~ alla coque** boiled egg; **~ bazzotto/sodo** soft-/hard-boiled egg; **~ di Pasqua** Easter egg; **~ in camicia** poached egg; **~a strapazzate** scrambled eggs

ura'gano *sm* hurricane

urba'nistica *sf* town planning

ur'bano, a *ag* urban, city *cpd*, town *cpd*; (*TEL*: *chiamata*) local; (*fig*) urbane

ur'gente [ur'dʒɛnte] *ag* urgent; **ur'genza** *sf* urgency; **in caso d'urgenza** (in case of) an emergency; **d'urgenza** *ag* emergency ♦ *av* urgently, as a matter of urgency

u'rina *sf* = **orina**

ur'lare *vi* (*persona*) to scream, yell; (*animale*, *vento*) to howl ♦ *vt* to scream, yell

'urlo (*pl*(*m*) **'urli**, *pl*(*f*) **'urla**) *sm* scream, yell; howl

'urna *sf* urn; (*elettorale*) ballot-box; **andare alle ~e** to go to the polls

urrà *escl* hurrah!

U.R.S.S. *abbr f*: **l'~** the USSR

ur'tare *vt* to bump into, knock against; (*fig*: *irritare*) to annoy ♦ *vi*: **~ contro** *o* **in** to bump into, knock against, crash into; (*fig*: *imbattersi*) to come up against; **~rsi** *vr* (*reciproco*: *scontrarsi*) to collide; (: *fig*) to clash; (*irritarsi*) to get annoyed; **'urto** *sm* (*colpo*) knock, bump; (*scontro*) crash, collision; (*fig*) clash

'U.S.A. ['uza] *smpl*: **gli ~** the USA

u'sanza [u'zantsa] *sf* custom; (*moda*) fashion

u'sare *vt* to use, employ ♦ *vi* (*servirsi*): **~ di** to use; (: *diritto*) to exercise; (*essere di moda*) to be fashionable; (*essere solito*): **~ fare** to be in the habit of doing, be accustomed to doing ♦ *vb impers*: **qui usa così** it's the custom round here; **u'sato, a** *ag* used; (*consumato*) worn; (*di seconda mano*) used, second-hand ♦ *sm* second-hand goods *pl*

usci'ere [uʃ'ʃɛre] *sm* usher

'uscio ['uʃʃo] *sm* door

u'scire [uʃ'ʃire] *vi* (*gen*) to come out; (*partire*, *andare a passeggio*, *a uno spettacolo etc*) to go out; (*essere sorteggiato*: *numero*) to come up; **~ da** (*gen*) to leave; (*posto*) to go (*o* come) out of, leave; (*solco*, *vasca etc*) to come out of; (*muro*) to stick out of; (*competenza etc*) to be outside; (*infanzia*, *adolescenza*) to leave behind; (*famiglia nobile etc*) to come from; **~ da** *o* **di casa** to go out; (*fig*) to leave home; **~ in automobile** to go out in the car, go for a drive; **~ di strada** (*AUT*) to go off *o* leave the road

u'scita [uʃ'ʃita] *sf* (*passaggio*, *varco*) exit, way out; (*per divertimento*) outing; (*ECON*: *somma*) expenditure; (*TEATRO*) entrance; (*fig*: *battuta*) witty remark; **~ di sicurezza**

emergency exit

usi'gnolo [uziɲ'ɲɔlo] *sm* nightingale

U.S.L. [uzl] *sigla f* (= *unità sanitaria locale*) local health centre

'uso *sm* (*utilizzazione*) use; (*esercizio*) practice; (*abitudine*) custom; **a ~ di** for (the use of); **d'~** (*corrente*) in use; **fuori ~** out of use

usti'one *sf* burn

usu'ale *ag* common, everyday

u'sura *sf* usury; (*logoramento*) wear (and tear)

uten'sile *sm* tool, implement; **~i da cucina** kitchen utensils

u'tente *sm/f* user

'utero *sm* uterus

'utile *ag* useful ♦ *sm* (*vantaggio*) advantage, benefit; (*ECON: profitto*) profit; **utilità** *sf* usefulness *no pl*; use; (*vantaggio*) benefit; **utili'taria** *sf* (*AUT*) economy car

utiliz'zare [utilid'dzare] *vt* to use, make use of, utilize

'uva *sf* grapes *pl*; **~ passa** raisins *pl*; **~ spina** gooseberry

V, v

v. *abbr* (= *vedi*) v

va *vb vedi* **andare**

va'cante *ag* vacant

va'canza [va'kantsa] *sf* (*l'essere vacante*) vacancy; (*riposo, ferie*) holiday(s *pl*) (*BRIT*), vacation (*US*); (*giorno di permesso*) day off, holiday; **~e** *sfpl* (*periodo di ferie*) holidays (*BRIT*), vacation *sg* (*US*); **essere/andare in ~** to be/go on holiday *o* vacation; **~e estive** summer holiday(s) *o* vacation

'vacca, che *sf* cow

vacci'nare [vattʃi'nare] *vt* to vaccinate

vac'cino [vat'tʃino] *sm* (*MED*) vaccine

vacil'lare [vatʃil'lare] *vi* to sway, wobble; (*luce*) to flicker; (*fig: memoria, coraggio*) to be failing, falter

'vacuo, a *ag* (*fig*) empty, vacuous

'vado *vb vedi* **andare**

vaga'bondo, a *sm/f* tramp, vagrant

va'gare *vi* to wander

va'gina [va'dʒina] *sf* vagina

va'gire [va'dʒire] *vi* to whimper

va'gito [va'dʒito] *sm* cry

'vaglia ['vaʎʎa] *sm inv* money order; **~ postale** postal order

vagli'are [vaʎ'ʎare] *vt* to sift; (*fig*) to weigh up; **'vaglio** *sm* sieve

'vago, a, ghi, ghe *ag* vague

va'gone *sm* (*FERR: per passeggeri*) coach; (: *per merci*) truck, wagon; **~ letto** sleeper, sleeping car; **~ ristorante** dining *o* restaurant car

'vai *vb vedi* **andare**

vai'olo *sm* smallpox

va'langa, ghe *sf* avalanche

va'lente *ag* able, talented

va'lere *vi* (*avere forza, potenza*) to have influence; (*essere valido*) to be valid; (*avere vigore, autorità*) to hold, apply; (*essere capace: poeta, studente*) to be good, be able ♦ *vt* (*prezzo, sforzo*) to be worth; (*corrispondere*) to correspond to; (*procurare*): **~ qc a qn** to earn sb sth; **~rsi di** to make use of, take advantage of; **far ~** (*autorità etc*) to assert; **vale a dire** that is to say; **~ la pena** to be worth the effort *o* worth it

va'levole *ag* valid

vali'care *vt* to cross

'valico, chi *sm* (*passo*) pass

'valido, a *ag* valid; (*rimedio*) effective; (*aiuto*) real; (*persona*) worthwhile

valige'ria [validʒe'ria] *sf* leather goods *pl*; leather goods factory; leather goods shop

vali'getta [vali'dʒetta] *sf* briefcase

va'ligia, gie *o* **ge** [va'lidʒa] *sf* (suit)case; **fare le ~gie** to pack (up)

val'lata *sf* valley

'valle *sf* valley; **a ~** (*di fiume*) downstream; **scendere a ~** to go downhill

va'lore *sm* (*gen*) value; (*merito*) merit, worth; (*coraggio*) valour, courage; (*COMM: titolo*) security; **~i** *smpl* (*oggetti preziosi*) valuables

valoriz'zare [valorid'dzare] *vt* (*terreno*) to develop; (*fig*) to make the most of

'valso, a *pp di* **valere**

va'luta *sf* currency, money; (*BANCA*): **~ 15 gennaio** interest to run from January 15th

valu'tare *vt* (*casa, gioiello, fig*) to value; (*stabilire: peso, entrate, fig*) to estimate; **valutazi'one** *sf* valuation; estimate

'valvola *sf* (*TECN, ANAT*) valve; (*ELETTR*) fuse

'valzer ['valtser] *sm inv* waltz

vam'pata *sf* (*di fiamma*) blaze; (*di calore*) blast; (: *al viso*) flush

vam'piro *sm* vampire

vanda'lismo *sm* vandalism

'vandalo *sm* vandal

vaneggi'are [vaned'dʒare] *vi* to rave

'vanga, ghe *sf* spade; **van'gare** *vt* to dig

van'gelo [van'dʒelo] *sm* gospel

va'niglia [va'niʎʎa] *sf* vanilla

vanità *sf* vanity; (*di promessa*) emptiness; (*di sforzo*) futility; **vani'toso, a** *ag* vain, conceited

'vanno *vb vedi* **andare**

'vano, a *ag* vain ♦ *sm* (*spazio*) space; (*apertura*) opening; (*stanza*) room

van'taggio [van'taddʒo] *sm* advantage; **essere/portarsi in ~** (*SPORT*) to be in/take the lead; **vantaggi'oso, a** *ag* advantageous;

favourable

van'tare vt to praise, speak highly of; **~rsi** vr: **~rsi (di/di aver fatto)** to boast o brag (about/ about having done); **vante'ria** sf boasting; **'vanto** sm boasting; (merito) virtue, merit; (gloria) pride

vanvera sf: **a ~** haphazardly; **parlare a ~** to talk nonsense

va'pore sm vapour; (anche: **~ acqueo**) steam; (nave) steamer; **a ~** (turbina etc) steam cpd; **al ~** (CUC) steamed; **vapo'retto** sm steamer; **vaporiz'zare** vt to vaporize; **vapo'roso, a** ag (tessuto) filmy; (capelli) soft and full

va'rare vt (NAUT, fig) to launch; (DIR) to pass

var'care vt to cross

'varco, chi sm passage; **aprirsi un ~ tra la folla** to push one's way through the crowd

vari'abile ag variable; (tempo, umore) changeable, variable ♦ sf (MAT) variable

vari'are vt, vi to vary; **~ di opinione** to change one's mind; **variazi'one** sf variation; change

va'rice [va'ritʃe] sf varicose vein

vari'cella [vari'tʃɛlla] sf chickenpox

vari'coso, a ag varicose

varie'gato, a ag variegated

varietà sf inv variety ♦ sm inv variety show

'vario, a ag varied; (parecchi: col sostantivo al pl) various; (mutevole: umore) changeable; **vario'pinto, a** ag multicoloured

'varo sm (NAUT, fig) launch; (di leggi) passing

va'saio sm potter

'vasca, sche sf basin; (anche: **~ da bagno**) bathtub, bath

va'scello [vaʃ'ʃɛllo] sm vessel, ship

vase'lina sf vaseline

vasel'lame sm (stoviglie) crockery; (: di porcellana) china; **~ d'oro/d'argento** gold/ silver plate

'vaso sm (recipiente) pot; (: barattolo) jar; (: decorativo) vase; (ANAT) vessel; **~ da fiori** vase; (per piante) flowerpot

vas'soio sm tray

'vasto, a ag vast, immense

Vati'cano sm: **il ~** the Vatican

ve pron, av vedi **vi**

vecchi'aia [vek'kjaja] sf old age

'vecchio, a ['vɛkkjo] ag old ♦ sm/f old man/woman; **i ~i** the old

'vece ['vetʃe] sf: **in ~ di** in the place of, for; **fare le ~i di qn** to take sb's place

ve'dere vt, vi to see; **~rsi** vr to meet, see one another; **avere a che ~ con** to have something to do with; **far ~ qc a qn** to show sb sth; **farsi ~** to show o.s.; (farsi vivo) to show one's face; **vedi di non farlo** make sure o see you don't do it; **non (ci) si vede** (è buio etc) you can't see a thing; **non lo posso ~** (fig) I can't stand him

ve'detta sf (sentinella, posto) look-out; (NAUT) patrol boat

'vedovo, a sm/f widower/widow

ve'duta sf view

vee'mente ag vehement; violent

vege'tale [vedʒe'tale] ag, sm vegetable

vegetari'ano, a [vedʒeta'rjano] ag, sm/f vegetarian

'vegeto, a ['vɛdʒeto] ag (pianta) thriving; (persona) strong, vigorous

'veglia ['veʎʎa] sf wakefulness; (sorveglianza) watch; (trattenimento) evening gathering; **fare la ~ a un malato** to watch over a sick person

vegli'are [veʎ'ʎare] vi to be awake; to stay o sit up; (stare vigile) to watch; to keep watch ♦ vt (malato, morto) to watch over, sit up with

ve'icolo sm vehicle

'vela sf (NAUT: tela) sail; (sport) sailing

ve'lare vt to veil; (occhi, luna) to mist over; (voce) to become husky; **~rsi il viso** to cover one's face (with a veil); **ve'lato, a** ag veiled

veleggi'are [veled'dʒare] vi to sail; (AER) to glide

ve'leno sm poison; **vele'noso, a** ag poisonous

veli'ero sm sailing ship

velleità sf inv vain ambition, vain desire

vel'luto sm velvet; **~ a coste** cord

'velo sm veil; (tessuto) voile

ve'loce [ve'lotʃe] ag fast, quick ♦ av fast, quickly; **velo'cista, i, e** sm/f (SPORT) sprinter; **velo'cità** sf speed; **a forte velocità** at high speed; **velocità di crociera** cruising speed

'vena sf (gen) vein; (filone) vein, seam; (fig: ispirazione) inspiration; (: umore) mood; **essere in ~ di qc** to be in the mood for sth

ve'nale ag (prezzo, valore) market cpd; (fig) venal; mercenary

ven'demmia sf (raccolta) grape harvest; (quantità d'uva) grape crop, grapes pl; (vino ottenuto) vintage; **vendemmi'are** vt to harvest ♦ vi to harvest the grapes

'vendere vt to sell; **"vendesi"** "for sale"

ven'detta sf revenge

vendi'care vt to avenge; **~rsi** vr: **~rsi (di)** to avenge o.s. (for); (per rancore) to take one's revenge (for); **~rsi su qn** to revenge o.s. on sb; **vendica'tivo, a** ag vindictive

'vendita sf sale; **la ~** (attività) selling; (smercio) sales pl; **in ~** on sale; **~ all'asta** sale by auction; **~ per telefono** telesales sg; **vendi'tore** sm seller, vendor; (gestore di negozio) trader, dealer

vene'rabile *ag* venerable

vene'rando, a *ag* = **venerabile**

vene'rare *vt* to venerate

venerdì *sm inv* Friday; **di ~ o il ~** on Fridays; **V~ Santo** Good Friday

ve'nereo, a *ag* venereal

'veneto, a *ag, sm/f* Venetian

Ve'nezia [ve'nɛttsja] *sf* Venice; **venezi'ana** *sf* Venetian blind; **venezi'ano, a** *ag, sm/f* Venetian

ve'nire *vi* to come; *(riuscire: dolce, fotografia)* to turn out; *(come ausiliare: essere)*: **viene ammirato da tutti** he is admired by everyone; **~ da** to come from; **quanto viene?** how much does it cost?; **far ~** *(mandare a chiamare)* to send for; **~ giù** to come down; **~ meno** *(svenire)* to faint; **~ meno a qc** not to fulfil sth; **~ su** to come up; **~ a trovare qn** to come and see sb; **~ via** to come away

ven'taglio [ven'taʎʎo] *sm* fan

ven'tata *sf* gust of wind

ven'tenne *ag*: **una ragazza ~** a twenty-year-old girl, a girl of twenty

ven'tesimo, a *num* twentieth

'venti *num* twenty

venti'lare *vt (stanza)* to air, ventilate; *(fig: idea, proposta)* to air; **ventila'tore** *sm* ventilator, fan

ven'tina *sf*: **una ~ (di)** around twenty, twenty or so

venti'sette *num* twenty-seven

'vento *sm* wind

'ventola *sf (AUT, TECN)* fan

ven'tosa *sf (ZOOL)* sucker; *(di gomma)* suction pad

ven'toso, a *ag* windy

'ventre *sm* stomach

ven'tura *sf*: **soldato di ~** mercenary

ven'turo, a *ag* next, coming

ve'nuta *sf* coming, arrival

ve'nuto, a *pp di* **venire**

vera'mente *av* really

ver'bale *ag* verbal ♦ *sm (di riunione)* minutes *pl*

'verbo *sm (LING)* verb; *(parola)* word; *(REL)*: **il V~** the Word

'verde *ag, sm* green; **essere al ~** to be broke; **~ bottiglia/oliva** bottle/olive green

verde'rame *sm* verdigris

ver'detto *sm* verdict

ver'dura *sf* vegetables *pl*

'verga, ghe *sf* rod

'vergine ['verdʒine] *sf* virgin; *(dello zodiaco)*: **V~** Virgo ♦ *ag* virgin; *(ragazza)*: **essere ~** to be a virgin

ver'gogna [ver'ɡoɲɲa] *sf* shame; *(timidezza)* shyness, embarrassment; **vergo'gnarsi** *vr*: **vergognarsi (di)** to be o feel ashamed (of); to be shy (about), be embarrassed (about);

vergo'gnoso, a *ag* ashamed; *(timido)* shy, embarrassed; *(causa di vergogna: azione)* shameful

ve'rifica, che *sf* checking *no pl*, check

verifi'care *vt (controllare)* to check; *(confermare)* to confirm, bear out

verità *sf inv* truth

veriti'ero, a *ag (che dice la verità)* truthful; *(conforme a verità)* true

'verme *sm* worm

vermi'celli [vermi'tʃelli] *smpl* vermicelli *sg*

ver'miglio [ver'miʎʎo] *sm* vermilion, scarlet

'vermut *sm inv* vermouth

ver'nice [ver'nitʃe] *sf (colorazione)* paint; *(trasparente)* varnish; *(pelle)* patent leather; **"~ fresca"** "wet paint"; **vernici'are** *vt* to paint; to varnish

'vero, a *ag (veridico: fatti, testimonianza)* true; *(autentico)* real ♦ *sm (verità)* truth; *(realtà) (real)* life; **un ~ e proprio delinquente** a real criminal, an out-and-out criminal

vero'simile *ag* likely, probable

ver'ruca, che *sf* wart

versa'mento *sm (pagamento)* payment; *(deposito di denaro)* deposit

ver'sante *sm* slopes *pl*, side

ver'sare *vt (fare uscire: vino, farina)* to pour (out); *(spargere: lacrime, sangue)* to shed; *(rovesciare)* to spill; *(ECON)* to pay; *(: depositare)* to deposit, pay in; **~rsi** *vr* *(rovesciarsi)* to spill; *(fiume, folla)*: **~rsi (in)** to pour (into)

versa'tile *ag* versatile

ver'setto *sm (REL)* verse

versi'one *sf* version; *(traduzione)* translation

'verso *sm (di poesia)* verse, line; *(di animale, uccello)* cry; *(direzione)* direction; *(modo)* way; *(di foglio di carta)* verso; *(di moneta)* reverse; **~i** *smpl (poesia)* verse *sg*; **non c'è ~ di persuaderlo** there's no way of persuading him, he can't be persuaded ♦ *prep (in direzione di)* toward(s); *(nei pressi di)* near, around (about); *(in senso temporale)* about, around; *(nei confronti di)* for; **~ di me** towards me; **~ sera** towards evening

'vertebra *sf* vertebra

verti'cale *ag, sf* vertical

'vertice ['vertitʃe] *sm* summit, top; *(MAT)* vertex; **conferenza al ~** *(POL)* summit conference

ver'tigine [ver'tidʒine] *sf* dizziness *no pl*; dizzy spell; *(MED)* vertigo; **avere le ~i** to feel dizzy; **vertigi'noso, a** *ag (altezza)* dizzy; *(fig)* breathtakingly high (o deep *etc*)

ve'scica, che [veʃ'ʃika] *sf (ANAT)* bladder; *(MED)* blister

'vescovo *sm* bishop

'vespa *sf* wasp

'vespro *sm (REL)* vespers *pl*

ves'sillo *sm* standard; (*bandiera*) flag

ves'taglia [ves'taʎʎa] *sf* dressing gown

'veste *sf* garment; (*rivestimento*) covering; (*qualità, facoltà*) capacity; in ~ ufficiale (*fig*) in an official capacity; in ~ di in the guise of, as; **vesti'ario** *sm* wardrobe, clothes *pl*

ves'tire *vt* (*bambino, malato*) to dress; (*avere indosso*) to have on, wear; ~rsi *vr* to dress, get dressed; **ves'tito, a** *ag* dressed ♦ *sm* garment; (*da donna*) dress; (*da uomo*) suit; **vestiti** *smpl* (*indumenti*) clothes; **vestito di bianco** dressed in white

Ve'suvio *sm*: il ~ Vesuvius

vete'rano, a *ag, sm/f* veteran

veteri'naria *sf* veterinary medicine

veteri'nario, a *ag* veterinary ♦ *sm* veterinary surgeon (*BRIT*), veterinarian (*US*), vet

'veto *sm inv* veto

ve'traio *sm* glassmaker; glazier

ve'trata *sf* glass door (o window); (*di chiesa*) stained glass window

vetre'ria *sf* (*stabilimento*) glassworks *sg*; (*oggetti di vetro*) glassware

ve'trina *sf* (*di negozio*) (shop) window; (*armadio*) display cabinet; **vetri'nista, i, e** *sm/f* window dresser

vetri'olo *sm* vitriol

'vetro *sm* glass; (*per finestra, porta*) pane (of glass)

'vetta *sf* peak, summit, top

vet'tore *sm* (*MAT, FISICA*) vector; (*chi trasporta*) carrier

vetto'vaglie [vetto'vaʎʎe] *sfpl* supplies

vet'tura *sf* (*carrozza*) carriage; (*FERR*) carriage (*BRIT*), car (*US*); (*auto*) car (*BRIT*), automobile (*US*)

vezzeggia'tivo [vettseddʒa'tivo] *sm* (*LING*) term of endearment

'vezzo ['vettso] *sm* habit; ~i *smpl* (*smancerie*) affected ways; (*leggiadria*) charms; **vez'zoso, a** *ag* (*grazioso*) charming, pretty; (*lezioso*) affected

vi (*dav lo, la, li, le, ne diventa ve*) *pron* (*oggetto*) you; (*complemento di termine*) (to) you; (*riflessivo*) yourselves; (*reciproco*) each other ♦ *av* (*lì*) there; (*qui*) here; (*per questo/ quel luogo*) through here/there; ~ è/sono there is/are

'via *sf* (*gen*) way; (*strada*) street; (*sentiero, pista*) path, track; (*AMM: procedimento*) channels *pl* ♦ *prep* (*passando per*) via, by way of ♦ *av* away ♦ *escl* go away!; (*suvvia*) come on!; (*SPORT*) go! ♦ *sm* (*SPORT*) starting signal; in ~ di guarigione on the road to recovery; per ~ di (*a causa di*) because of, on account of; in o per ~ on the way; per ~ aerea by air; (*lettere*) by airmail; andare/essere ~ to go/be away; ~ ~ che (*a mano a mano*) as; dare il ~

(*SPORT*) to give the starting signal; dare il ~ a (*fig*) to start; V~ lattea (*ASTR*) Milky Way; ~ di mezzo middle course; in ~ provvisoria provisionally

viabilità *sf* (*di strada*) practicability; (*rete stradale*) roads *pl*, road network

via'dotto *sm* viaduct

viaggi'are [viad'dʒare] *vi* to travel; **viaggia'tore, 'trice** *ag* travelling ♦ *sm* traveller; (*passeggero*) passenger

vi'aggio ['vjaddʒo] *sm* travel(ling); (*tragitto*) journey, trip; **buon ~!** have a good trip!; ~ **di nozze** honeymoon

vi'ale *sm* avenue

via'vai *sm* coming and going, bustle

vi'brare *vi* to vibrate

vi'cario *sm* (*apostolico etc*) vicar

vice ['vitʃe] *sm/f* deputy ♦ *prefisso:* ~'console *sm* vice-consul; ~diret'tore *sm* assistant manager

vi'cenda [vi'tʃɛnda] *sf* event; a ~ in turn; **vicen'devole** *ag* mutual, reciprocal

vice'versa [vitʃe'vɛrsa] *av* vice versa; da Roma a Pisa e ~ from Rome to Pisa and back

vici'nanza [vitʃi'nantsa] *sf* nearness, closeness; ~e *sfpl* (*paraggi*) neighbourhood, vicinity .

vici'nato [vitʃi'nato] *sm* neighbourhood; (*vicini*) neighbours *pl*

vi'cino, a [vi'tʃino] *ag* (*gen*) near; (*nello spazio*) near, nearby; (*accanto*) next; (*nel tempo*) near, close at hand ♦ *sm/f* neighbour ♦ *av* near, close; da ~ (*guardare*) close up; (*esaminare, seguire*) closely; (*conoscere*) well, intimately; ~ a near (to), close to; (*accanto a*) beside; ~ di casa neighbour

'vicolo *sm* alley; ~ cieco blind alley

'video *sm inv* (*TV: schermo*) screen; ~'camera *sf* camcorder; ~cas'setta *sf* videocassette; ~registra'tore *sm* video (recorder)

vie'tare *vt* to forbid; (*AMM*) to prohibit; ~ a qn di fare to forbid sb to do; to prohibit sb from doing; **"vietato fumare/l'ingresso"** "no smoking/admittance"

Viet'nam *sm*: il ~ Vietnam; **vietna'mita, i, e** *ag, sm/f, sm* Vietnamese *inv*

vi'gente [vi'dʒɛnte] *ag* in force

vigi'lare [vidʒi'lare] *vt* to watch over, keep an eye on; ~ che to make sure that, see to it that

'vigile ['vidʒile] *ag* watchful ♦ *sm* (*anche:* ~ urbano) policeman (*in towns*); ~ del fuoco fireman

vi'gilia [vi'dʒilja] *sf* (*giorno antecedente*) eve; la ~ di Natale Christmas Eve

vigli'acco, a, chi, che [viʎ'ʎakko] *ag* cowardly ♦ *sm/f* coward

'vigna ['viɲɲa] *sf* = vi'gneto

vi'gneto [viɲ'ɲeto] *sm* vineyard

vi'gnetta [viɲ'ɲetta] *sf* cartoon

vi'gore *sm* vigour; (*DIR*): **essere/entrare in ~** to be in/come into force; **vigo'roso, a** *ag* vigorous

'vile *ag* (*spregevole*) low, mean, base; (*codardo*) cowardly

vili'pendio *sm* contempt, scorn; public insult

'villa *sf* villa

vil'laggio [vil'laddʒo] *sm* village

villa'nia *sf* rudeness, lack of manners; **fare** (*o* **dire**) **una ~ a qn** to be rude to sb

vil'lano, a *ag* rude, ill-mannered

villeggia'tura [villeddʒa'tura] *sf* holiday(s *pl*) (*BRIT*), vacation (*US*)

vil'lino *sm* small house (with a garden), cottage

vil'loso, a *ag* hairy

viltà *sf* cowardice *no pl*; cowardly act

'vimine *sm* wicker; **mobili di ~i** wicker furniture *sg*

'vincere ['vintʃere] *vt* (*in guerra, al gioco, a una gara*) to defeat, beat; (*premio, guerra, partita*) to win; (*fig*) to overcome, conquer ♦ *vi* to win; **~ qn in bellezza** to be better-looking than sb; **'vincita** *sf* win; (*denaro vinto*) winnings *pl*; **vinci'tore** *sm* winner; (*MIL*) victor

vinco'lare *vt* to bind; (*COMM: denaro*) to tie up; **'vincolo** *sm* (*fig*) bond, tie; (*DIR: servitù*) obligation

vi'nicolo, a *ag* wine *cpd*

'vino *sm* wine; **~ bianco/rosso** white/red wine; **~ da pasto** table wine

'vinto, a *pp di* **vincere**

vi'ola *sf* (*BOT*) violet; (*MUS*) viola ♦ *ag, sm inv* (*colore*) purple

vio'lare *vt* (*chiesa*) to descrate, violate; (*giuramento, legge*) to violate

violen'tare *vt* to use violence on; (*donna*) to rape

vio'lento, a *ag* violent; **vio'lenza** *sf* violence; **violenza carnale** rape

vio'letta *sf* (*BOT*) violet

vio'letto, a *ag, sm* (*colore*) violet

violi'nista, i, e *sm/f* violinist

vio'lino *sm* violin

violon'cello [violon'tʃello] *sm* cello

vi'ottolo *sm* path, track

'vipera *sf* viper, adder

vi'rare *vt* (*NAUT, AER*) to turn; (*FOT*) to tone; **~ di bordo** (*NAUT*) to tack

'virgola *sf* (*LING*) comma; (*MAT*) point; **virgo'lette** *sfpl* inverted commas, quotation marks

vi'rile *ag* (*proprio dell'uomo*) masculine; (*non puerile, da uomo*) manly, virile

virtù *sf inv* virtue; **in** *o* **per ~ di** by virtue of, by

virtu'ale *ag* virtual

virtu'oso, a *ag* virtuous ♦ *sm/f* (*MUS etc*) virtuoso

'virus *sm inv* (*anche COMPUT*) virus

'viscere ['viʃʃere] *sfpl* (*di animale*) entrails *pl*; (*fig*) bowels *pl*

'vischio ['viskjo] *sm* (*BOT*) mistletoe; (*pania*) birdlime; **vischi'oso, a** *ag* sticky

'viscido, a ['viʃʃido] *ag* slimy

vi'sibile *ag* visible

visi'bilio *sm*: **andare in ~** to go into raptures

visibilità *sf* visibility

visi'era *sf* (*di elmo*) visor; (*di berretto*) peak

visi'one *sf* vision; **prendere ~ di qc** to examine sth, look sth over; **prima/seconda ~** (*CINEMA*) first/second showing

'visita *sf* visit; (*MED*) visit, call; (: *esame*) examination; **visi'tare** *vt* to visit; (*MED*) to visit, call on; (: *esaminare*) to examine; **visita'tore, 'trice** *sm/f* visitor

vi'sivo, a *ag* visual

'viso *sm* face

vi'sone *sm* mink

'vispo, a *ag* quick, lively

vis'suto, a *pp di* **vivere** ♦ *ag* (*aria, modo di fare*) experienced

'vista *sf* (*facoltà*) (eye)sight; (*fatto di vedere*): **la ~ di** the sight of; (*veduta*) view; **sparare a ~** to shoot on sight; **in ~** in sight; **perdere qn di ~** to lose sight of sb; (*fig*) to lose touch with sb; **a ~ d'occhio** as far as the eye can see; (*fig*) before one's very eyes; **far ~ di fare** to pretend to do

'visto, a *pp di* **vedere** ♦ *sm* visa; **~ che** seeing (that)

vis'toso, a *ag* gaudy, garish; (*ingente*) considerable

visu'ale *ag* visual; **visualizza'tore** *sm* (*INFORM*) visual display unit, VDU

'vita *sf* life; (*ANAT*) waist; **a ~** for life

vi'tale *ag* vital; **vita'lizio, a** *ag* life *cpd* ♦ *sm* life annuity

vita'mina *sf* vitamin

'vite *sf* (*BOT*) vine; (*TECN*) screw

vi'tello *sm* (*ZOOL*) calf; (*carne*) veal; (*pelle*) calfskin

vi'ticcio [vi'tittʃo] *sm* (*BOT*) tendril

viticol'tore *sm* wine grower; **viticol'tura** *sf* wine growing

'vitreo, a *ag* vitreous; (*occhio, sguardo*) glassy

'vittima *sf* victim

'vitto *sm* food; (*in un albergo etc*) board; **~ e alloggio** board and lodging

vit'toria *sf* victory

'viva *escl*: **~ il re!** long live the king!

vi'vace [vi'vatʃe] *ag* (*vivo, animato*) lively; (: *mente*) lively, sharp; (*colore*) bright; **viva-cità** *sf* vivacity; liveliness; brightness

vi'vaio *sm* (*di pesci*) hatchery; (*AGR*) nursery

vi'vanda sf food; (*piatto*) dish

vi'vente ag living, alive; **i ~i** the living

'vivere vi to live ♦ vt to live; (*passare: brutto momento*) to live through, go through; (*sentire: gioie, pene di qn*) to share ♦ sm life; (*anche: modo di ~*) way of life; **~i** smpl (*cibo*) food sg, provisions; **~ di** to live on

'vivido, a ag (*colore*) vivid, bright

'vivo, a ag (*vivente*) alive, living; (: *animale*) live; (*fig*) lively; (: *colore*) bright, brilliant; **i ~i** the living; **~ e vegeto** hale and hearty; **farsi ~** to show one's face; to be heard from; **ritrarre dal ~** to paint from life; **pungere qn nel ~** (*fig*) to cut sb to the quick

vizi'are [vit'tsjare] vt (*bambino*) to spoil; (*corrompere moralmente*) to corrupt; **vizi'ato, a** ag spoilt; (*aria, acqua*) polluted

'vizio ['vittsjo] sm (*morale*) vice; (*cattiva abitudine*) bad habit; (*imperfezione*) flaw, defect; (*errore*) fault, mistake; **vizi'oso, a** ag depraved; defective; (*inesatto*) incorrect, wrong

vocabo'lario sm (*dizionario*) dictionary; (*lessico*) vocabulary

vo'cabolo sm word

vo'cale ag vocal ♦ sf vowel

vocazi'one [vokat'tsjone] sf vocation; (*fig*) natural bent

'voce ['votʃe] sf voice; (*diceria*) rumour; (*di un elenco, in bilancio*) item; **aver ~ in capitolo** (*fig*) to have a say in the matter

voci'are [vo'tʃare] vi to shout, yell

'voga sf (*NAUT*) rowing; (*usanza*): **essere in ~** to be in fashion o in vogue

vo'gare vi to row

'voglia ['voʎʎa] sf desire, wish; (*macchia*) birthmark; **aver ~ di qc/di fare** to feel like sth/like doing; (*più forte*) to want sth/to do

'voi pron you; **voi'altri** pron you

vo'lano sm (*SPORT*) shuttlecock; (*TECN*) flywheel

vo'lante ag flying ♦ sm (steering) wheel

volan'tino sm leaflet

vo'lare vi (*uccello, aereo, fig*) to fly; (*cappello*) to blow away o off, fly away o off; **~ via** to fly away o off

vo'latile ag (*CHIM*) volatile ♦ sm (*ZOOL*) bird

volente'roso, a ag willing

volenti'eri av willingly; **"~"** "with pleasure", "I'd be glad to"

vo'lere sm will, wish(es); **contro il ~ di** against the wishes of; **per ~ di qn** in obedience to sb's will o wishes

♦ vt 1 (*esigere, desiderare*) to want; **voler fare/che qn faccia** to want to/sb to do; **volete del caffè?** would you like o do you want some coffee?; **vorrei questo/fare l**

would o I'd like this/to do; **come vuoi** as you like; **senza ~** (*inavvertitamente*) without meaning to, unintentionally

2 (*consentire*): **vogliate attendere, per piacere** please wait; **vogliamo andare?** shall we go?; **vuole essere così gentile da ...?** would you be so kind as to ...?; **non ha voluto ricevermi** he wouldn't see me

3: **volerci** (*essere necessario: materiale, attenzione*) to need; (: *tempo*) to take; **quanta farina ci vuole per questa torta?** how much flour do you need for this cake?; **ci vuole un'ora per arrivare a Venezia** it takes an hour to get to Venice

4: **voler bene a qn** (*amore*) to love sb; (*affetto*) to be fond of sb, like sb very much; **voler male a qn** to dislike sb; **volerne a qn** to bear sb a grudge; **voler dire** to mean

──────────────

vol'gare ag vulgar; **volgariz'zare** vt to popularize

'volgere ['vɔldʒere] vt to turn ♦ vi to turn; (*tendere*): **~ a: il tempo volge al brutto** the weather is breaking; **un rosso che volge al viola** a red verging on purple; **~rsi** vr to turn; **~ al peggio** to take a turn for the worse; **~ al termine** to draw to an end

'volgo sm common people

voli'era sf aviary

voli'tivo, a ag strong-willed

'volo sm flight; **al ~: colpire qc al ~** to hit sth as it flies past; **capire al ~** to understand straight away

volontà sf will; **a ~** (*mangiare, bere*) as much as one likes; **buona/cattiva ~** goodwill/lack of goodwill

volon'tario, a ag voluntary ♦ sm (*MIL*) volunteer

'volpe sf fox

'volta sf (*momento, circostanza*) time; (*turno, giro*) turn; (*curva*) turn, bend; (*ARCHIT*) vault; (*direzione*): **partire alla ~ di** to set off for; **a mia** (o **tua** etc) **~** in turn; **una ~** once; **una ~ sola** only once; **due ~e** twice; **una cosa per ~** one thing at a time; **una ~ per tutte** once and for all; **a ~e** at times, sometimes; **una ~ che** (*temporale*) once; (*causale*) since; **3 ~e 4** 3 times 4

volta'faccia [volta'fattʃa] sm inv (*fig*) volte-face

vol'taggio [vol'taddʒo] sm (*ELETTR*) voltage

vol'tare vt to turn; (*girare: moneta*) to turn over; (*rigirare*) to turn round ♦ vi to turn; **~rsi** vr to turn; to turn over; to turn round

volteggi'are [volted'dʒare] vi (*volare*) to circle; (*in equitazione*) to do trick riding; (*in ginnastica*) to vault; to perform acrobatics

'volto, a pp di **volgere** ♦ sm face

vo'lubile ag changeable, fickle

vo'lume sm volume; **volumi'noso, a** ag voluminous, bulky

voluttà sf sensual pleasure o delight; **voluttu'oso, a** ag voluptuous

vomi'tare vt, vi to vomit; **'vomito** sm vomiting no pl; vomit

'vongola sf clam

vo'race [vo'ratʃe] ag voracious, greedy

vo'ragine [vo'radʒine] sf abyss, chasm

'vortice ['vɔrtitʃe] sm whirlwind; whirlpool; (fig) whirl

'vostro, a det: **il(la) ~(a)** etc your ♦ pron: **il(la) ~(a)** etc yours

vo'tante sm/f voter

vo'tare vi to vote ♦ vt (sottoporre a votazione) to take a vote on; (approvare) to vote for; (REL): **~ qc a** to dedicate sth to; **votazi'one** sf vote, voting; **votazioni** sfpl (POL) votes; (INS) marks

'voto sm (POL) vote; (INS) mark; (REL) vow; (: offerta) votive offering; **aver ~i belli/brutti** (INS) to get good/bad marks

vs. abbr (COMM) = **vostro**

vul'cano sm volcano

vulne'rabile ag vulnerable

vuo'tare vt to empty; **~rsi** vr to empty

vu'oto, a ag empty; (fig: privo): **~ di** (senso etc) devoid of ♦ sm empty space, gap; (spazio in bianco) blank; (FISICA) vacuum; (fig: mancanza) gap, void; **a mani ~e** empty-handed; **~ d'aria** air pocket; **~ a rendere** returnable bottle

W, X, Y

'water ['wɔːtə*] sm inv toilet

watt [vat] sm inv watt

'weekend ['wiːkend] sm inv weekend

'whisky ['wiski] sm inv whisky

'windsurf ['windsəːf] sm inv (tavola) windsurfer; (sport) windsurfing

'würstel ['vyrstəl] sm inv frankfurter

xi'lofono [ksi'lɔfono] sm xylophone

yacht [jɔt] sm inv yacht

'yoghurt ['jɔgurt] sm inv yoghourt

Z, z

zabai'one [dzaba'jone] sm dessert made of egg yolks, sugar and marsala

zaf'fata [tsaf'fata] sf (tanfo) stench

zaffe'rano [dzaffe'rano] sm saffron

zaf'firo [dzaf'firo] sm sapphire

'zaino ['dzaino] sm rucksack

'zampa ['tsampa] sf (di animale: gamba) leg; (: piede) paw; **a quattro ~e** on all fours

zampil'lare [tsampil'lare] vi to gush, spurt;

zam'pillo sm gush, spurt

zam'pogna [tsam'pɔɲɲa] sf instrument similar to bagpipes

'zanna ['tsanna] sf (di elefante) tusk; (di carnivori) fang

zan'zara [dzan'dzara] sf mosquito; **zanzari'era** sf mosquito net

'zappa ['tsappa] sf hoe; **zap'pare** vt to hoe

'zapping ['tsapiŋ] sm (TV) channel-hopping

zar, za'rina [tsar, tsa'rina] sm/f tsar/tsarina

'zattera ['dzattera] sf raft

za'vorra [dza'vɔrra] sf ballast

'zazzera ['tsattsera] sf shock of hair

'zebra ['dzɛbra] sf zebra; **~e** sfpl (AUT) zebra crossing sg (BRIT), crosswalk sg (US)

'zecca, che ['tsekka] sf (ZOOL) tick; (officina di monete) mint

'zelo ['dzɛlo] sm zeal

'zenit ['dzenit] sm zenith

'zenzero ['dzendzero] sm ginger

'zeppa ['tseppa] sf wedge

'zeppo, a ['tseppo] ag: **~ di** crammed o packed with

zer'bino [dzer'bino] sm doormat

'zero ['dzɛro] sm zero, nought; **vincere per tre a ~** (SPORT) to win three-nil

'zeta ['dzeta] sm o f zed, (the letter) z

'zia ['tsia] sf aunt

zibel'lino [dzibel'lino] sm sable

'zigomo ['dzigomo] sm cheekbone

zig'zag [dzig'dzag] sm inv zigzag; **andare a ~** to zigzag

zim'bello [dzim'bɛllo] sm (oggetto di burle) laughing-stock

'zinco ['dzinko] sm zinc

'zingaro, a ['dzingaro] sm/f gipsy

'zio ['tsio] (pl **'zii**) sm uncle; **zii** smpl (zio e zia) uncle and aunt

zi'tella [dzi'tella] sf spinster; (peg) old maid

'zitto, a ['tsitto] ag quiet, silent; **sta' ~!** be quiet!

ziz'zania [dzid'dzanja] sf (fig): **gettare o seminare ~** to sow discord

'zoccolo ['tsɔkkolo] sm (calzatura) clog; (di cavallo etc) hoof; (basamento) base; plinth

zo'diaco [dzo'diako] sm zodiac

'zolfo ['tsolfo] sm sulphur

'zolla ['dzɔlla] sf clod (of earth)

zol'letta [dzol'letta] sf sugar lump

'zona ['dzɔna] sf zone, area; **~ di depressione** (METEOR) trough of low pressure; **~ disco** (AUT) ≈ meter zone; **~ pedonale** pedestrian precinct; **~ verde** (di abitato) green area

'zonzo ['dzondzo]: **a ~** av: **andare a ~** to wander about, stroll about

zoo ['dzɔo] sm inv zoo

zoolo'gia [dzoolo'dʒia] sf zoology

zoppi'care [tsoppi'kare] vi to limp; to be shaky, rickety '**zoppo, a** ['tsɔppo] *ag* lame; (*fig: mobile*) shaky, rickety

zoti'cone [dzoti'kone] *sm* lout

'**zucca, che** ['tsukka] *sf* (*BOT*) marrow; pumpkin

zucche'rare [tsukke'rare] *vt* to put sugar in; **zucche'rato, a** *ag* sweet, sweetened

zuccheri'era [tsukke'rjera] *sf* sugar bowl

zucche'rino, a [tsukke'rino] *ag* sugary, sweet

'**zucchero** ['tsukkero] *sm* sugar

zuc'china [tsuk'kina] *sf* courgette (*BRIT*), zucchini (*US*)

zuc'chino [tsuk'kino] *sm* = **zucchina**

'**zuffa** ['tsuffa] *sf* brawl

'**zuppa** ['tsuppa] *sf* soup; (*fig*) mixture, muddle; ~ **inglese** (*CUC*) dessert made with sponge cake, custard and chocolate, ≈ trifle (*BRIT*); **zuppi'era** *sf* soup tureen

'**zuppo, a** ['tsuppo] *ag*: ~ **(di)** drenched (with), soaked (with)

ENGLISH - ITALIAN

INGLESE - ITALIANO

A, a

A [eɪ] n (MUS) la m; (letter) A, a f or m inv; **~-road** n strada statale

a [ə] (before vowel or silent h: **an**) indef art **1** un (uno +s impure, gn, pn, ps, x, z), f una (un' +vowel); **~ book** un libro; **~ mirror** uno specchio; **an apple** una mela; **she's ~ doctor** è medico

2 (instead of the number "one") un(o), f una; **~ year ago** un anno fa; **~ hundred/thousand** etc **pounds** cento/mille etc sterline

3 (in expressing ratios, prices etc) a, per; **3 ~ day/week** 3 al giorno/alla settimana; **10 km an hour** 10 km all'ora; **£5 ~ person** 5 sterline a persona or per persona

A.A. n abbr (= Alcoholics Anonymous) AA; (BRIT: = Automobile Association) ≈ A.C.I. m

A.A.A. (US) n abbr (= American Automobile Association) ≈ A.C.I. m

aback [ə'bæk] adv: **to be taken ~** essere sbalordito(a)

abandon [ə'bændən] vt abbandonare ♦ n: **with ~** sfrenatamente, spensieratamente

abate [ə'beɪt] vi calmarsi

abattoir ['æbətwɑːʲ] (BRIT) n mattatoio

abbey ['æbɪ] n abbazia, badia

abbot ['æbət] n abate m

abbreviation [əbriːvɪ'eɪʃən] n abbreviazione f

abdicate ['æbdɪkeɪt] vt abdicare a ♦ vi abdicare

abdomen ['æbdəmən] n addome m

abduct [æb'dʌkt] vt rapire

abide [ə'baɪd] vt: **I can't ~ it/him** non lo posso soffrire or sopportare; **~ by** vt fus conformarsi a

ability [ə'bɪlɪtɪ] n abilità f inv

abject ['æbdʒɛkt] adj (poverty) abietto(a); (apology) umiliante

ablaze [ə'bleɪz] adj in fiamme

able ['eɪbl] adj capace; **to be ~ to do sth** essere capace di fare qc, poter fare qc; **~-bodied** adj robusto(a); **ably** adv abilmente

abnormal [æb'nɔːməl] adj anormale

aboard [ə'bɔːd] adv a bordo ♦ prep a bordo di

abode [ə'bəʊd] n: **of no fixed ~** senza fissa dimora

abolish [ə'bɒlɪʃ] vt abolire

abominable [ə'bɒmɪnəbl] adj abominevole

aborigine [æbə'rɪdʒɪnɪ] n aborigeno/a

abort [ə'bɔːt] vt abortire; **~ion** [ə'bɔːʃən] n aborto; **to have an ~ion** abortire; **~ive** adj abortivo(a)

abound [ə'baʊnd] vi abbondare; **to ~ in** or **with** abbondare di

about [ə'baʊt] adv **1** (approximately) circa, quasi; **~ a hundred/thousand** etc un centinaio/migliaio etc, circa cento/mille etc; **it takes ~ 10 hours** ci vogliono circa 10 ore; **at ~ 2 o'clock** verso le 2; **I've just ~ finished** ho quasi finito

2 (referring to place) qua e là, in giro; **to leave things lying ~** lasciare delle cose in giro; **to run ~** correre qua e là; **to walk ~** camminare

3: **to be ~ to do sth** stare per fare qc

♦ prep **1** (relating to) su, di; **a book ~ London** un libro su Londra; **what is it ~?** di che si tratta?; (book, film etc) di cosa tratta?; **we talked ~ it** ne abbiamo parlato; **what** or **how ~ doing this?** che ne dici di fare questo?

2 (referring to place): **to walk ~ the town** camminare per la città; **her clothes were scattered ~ the room** i suoi vestiti erano sparsi or in giro per tutta la stanza

about-face [ə'baʊt'feɪs] n dietro front m inv

about-turn [ə'baʊt'tɜːn] n dietro front m inv

above [ə'bʌv] adv, prep sopra; **mentioned ~** suddetto; **~ all** soprattutto; **~board** adj aperto(a); onesto(a)

abrasive [ə'breɪzɪv] adj abrasivo(a); (fig) caustico(a)

abreast [ə'brɛst] adv di fianco; **to keep ~ of** tenersi aggiornato su

abroad [ə'brɔːd] adv all'estero

abrupt [ə'brʌpt] adj (sudden) improvviso(a); (gruff, blunt) brusco(a)

abscess ['æbsɪs] n ascesso

absence ['æbsəns] n assenza

absent ['æbsənt] adj assente; **~ee** [-'tiː] n assente m/f; **~-minded** adj distratto(a)

absolute ['æbsəluːt] adj assoluto(a); **~ly** [-'luːtlɪ] adv assolutamente

absolve [əb'zɒlv] vt: **to ~ sb (from)** (sin)

assolvere qn (da); (*oath*) sciogliere qn (da)
absorb [əb'zɔ:b] *vt* assorbire; **to be ~ed in a book** essere immerso in un libro; **~ent cotton** (*US*) *n* cotone *m* idrofilo
absorption [əb'sɔ:pʃən] *n* assorbimento
abstain [əb'stein] *vi*: **to ~ (from)** astenersi (da)
abstract ['æbstrækt] *adj* astratto(a)
absurd [əb'sə:d] *adj* assurdo(a)
abuse [*n* ə'bju:s, *vb* ə'bju:z] *n* abuso; (*insults*) ingiurie *fpl* ♦ *vt* abusare di; **abusive** *adj* ingiurioso(a)
abysmal [ə'bizməl] *adj* spaventoso(a)
abyss [ə'bis] *n* abisso
AC *abbr* (= *alternating current*) c.a.
academic [ækə'demik] *adj* accademico(a); (*pej: issue*) puramente formale ♦ *n* universitario/a
academy [ə'kædəmi] *n* (*learned body*) accademia; (*school*) scuola privata; **~ of music** conservatorio
accelerate [æk'seləreit] *vt, vi* accelerare; **acceleration** *n* accelerazione *f*; **accelerator** *n* acceleratore *m*
accent ['æksənt] *n* accento
accept [ək'sept] *vt* accettare; **~able** *adj* accettabile; **~ance** *n* accettazione *f*
access ['æksɛs] *n* accesso; **~ible** [æk'sɛsəbl] *adj* accessibile
accessory [æk'sɛsəri] *n* accessorio; (*LAW*): **~ to** complice *m/f* di
accident ['æksidənt] *n* incidente *m*; (*chance*) caso; **by ~** per caso; **~al** [-'dentl] *adj* accidentale; **~ally** [-'dentəli] *adv* per caso; **~ insurance** *n* assicurazione *f* contro gli infortuni; **~-prone** *adj*: **he's very ~-prone** è un vero passaguai
acclaim [ə'kleim] *n* acclamazione *f*
accommodate [ə'kɔmədeit] *vt* alloggiare; (*oblige, help*) favorire
accommodating [ə'kɔmədeitiŋ] *adj* compiacente
accommodation [əkɔmə'deiʃən] *n* alloggio; **~s** (*US*) *npl* alloggio
accompany [ə'kʌmpəni] *vt* accompagnare
accomplice [ə'kʌmplis] *n* complice *m/f*
accomplish [ə'kʌmpliʃ] *vt* compiere; (*goal*) raggiungere; **~ed** *adj* esperto(a); **~ment** *n* compimento; realizzazione *f*
accord [ə'kɔ:d] *n* accordo ♦ *vt* accordare; **of his own ~** di propria iniziativa; **~ance** *n*: **in ~ance with** in conformità con; **~ing**: **~ing to** *prep* secondo; **~ingly** *adv* in conformità
accordion [ə'kɔ:diən] *n* fisarmonica
account [ə'kaunt] *n* (*COMM*) conto; (*report*) descrizione *f*; **~s** *npl* (*COMM*) conti *mpl*; **of no ~** di nessuna importanza; **on ~** in acconto; **on no ~** per nessun motivo; **on ~ of** a causa di; **to take into ~, take ~ of** tener conto di; **~ for**

vt fus spiegare; giustificare; **~able** *adj*: **~able (to)** responsabile (verso)
accountancy [ə'kauntənsi] *n* ragioneria
accountant [ə'kauntənt] *n* ragioniere/a
account number *n* numero di conto
accrued interest [ə'kru:d-] *n* interesse *m* maturato
accumulate [ə'kju:mjuleit] *vt* accumulare ♦ *vi* accumularsi
accuracy ['ækjurəsi] *n* precisione *f*
accurate ['ækjurit] *adj* preciso(a); **~ly** *adv* precisamente
accusation [ækju'zeiʃən] *n* accusa
accuse [ə'kju:z] *vt* accusare; **~d** *n* accusato/a
accustom [ə'kʌstəm] *vt* abituare; **~ed** *adj*: **~ed to** abituato(a) a
ace [eis] *n* asso
ache [eik] *n* male *m*, dolore *m* ♦ *vi* (*be sore*) far male, dolere; **my head ~s** mi fa male la testa
achieve [ə'tʃi:v] *vt* (*aim*) raggiungere; (*victory, success*) ottenere; **~ment** *n* compimento; successo
acid ['æsid] *adj* acido(a) ♦ *n* acido; **~ rain** *n* pioggia acida
acknowledge [ək'nɔlidʒ] *vt* (*letter: also*: **~ receipt of**) confermare la ricevuta di; (*fact*) riconoscere; **~ment** *n* conferma; riconoscimento
acne ['ækni] *n* acne *f*
acorn ['eikɔ:n] *n* ghianda
acoustic [ə'ku:stik] *adj* acustico(a); **~s** *n, npl* acustica
acquaint [ə'kweint] *vt*: **to ~ sb with sth** far sapere qc a qn; **to be ~ed with** (*person*) conoscere; **~ance** *n* conoscenza; (*person*) conoscente *m/f*
acquire [ə'kwaiə*] *vt* acquistare
acquit [ə'kwit] *vt* assolvere; **to ~ o.s. well** comportarsi bene; **~tal** *n* assoluzione *f*
acre ['eikə*] *n* acro (= *4047 m²*)
acrid ['ækrid] *adj* acre; pungente
acrobat ['ækrəbæt] *n* acrobata *m/f*
across [ə'krɔs] *prep* (*on the other side*) dall'altra parte di; (*crosswise*) attraverso ♦ *adv* dall'altra parte; in larghezza; **to run/swim ~** attraversare di corsa/a nuoto; **~ from** di fronte a
acrylic [ə'krilik] *adj* acrilico(a)
act [ækt] *n* atto; (*in music-hall etc*) numero; (*LAW*) decreto ♦ *vi* agire; (*THEATRE*) recitare; (*pretend*) fingere ♦ *vt* (*part*) recitare; **to ~ as** agire da; **~ing** *adj* che fa le funzioni di ♦ *n* (*of actor*) recitazione *f*; (*activity*): **to do some ~ing** fare del teatro (*or* del cinema)
action ['ækʃən] *n* azione *f*; (*MIL*) combattimento; (*LAW*) processo; **out of ~** fuori combattimento; fuori servizio; **to take ~** agire; **~ replay** *n* (*TV*) replay *m inv*

activate ['æktɪveɪt] vt (*mechanism*) attivare
active ['æktɪv] adj attivo(a); **~ly** adv (*participate*) attivamente; (*discourage, dislike*) vivamente
activity [æk'tɪvɪtɪ] n attività f inv; **~ holiday** n vacanza organizzata con attività ricreative per ragazzi
actor ['æktə*] n attore m
actress ['æktrɪs] n attrice f
actual ['æktjuəl] adj reale, vero(a); **~ly** adv veramente; (*even*) addirittura
acute [ə'kjuːt] adj acuto(a); (*mind, person*) perspicace
ad [æd] n abbr = **advertisement**
A.D. adv abbr (= *Anno Domini*) d.C.
adamant ['ædəmənt] adj irremovibile
adapt [ə'dæpt] vt adattare ♦ vi: **to ~ (to)** adattarsi (a); **~able** adj (*device*) adattabile; (*person*) che sa adattarsi; **~er** or **~or** n (ELEC) adattatore m
add [æd] vt aggiungere; (*figures: also: ~ up*) addizionare ♦ vi: **to ~ to** (*increase*) aumentare; **it doesn't ~ up** (*fig*) non quadra, non ha senso
adder ['ædə*] n vipera
addict ['ædɪkt] n tossicomane m/f; (*fig*) fanatico/a; **~ed** [ə'dɪktɪd] adj: **to be ~ed to** (*drink etc*) essere dedito(a) a; (*fig: football etc*) essere tifoso(a) di; **~ion** [ə'dɪkʃən] n (MED) tossicodipendenza; **~ive** [ə'dɪktɪv] adj che dà assuefazione
addition [ə'dɪʃən] n addizione f; (*thing added*) aggiunta; **in ~** inoltre; **in ~ to** oltre; **~al** adj supplementare
additive ['ædɪtɪv] n additivo
address [ə'drɛs] n indirizzo; (*talk*) discorso ♦ vt indirizzare; (*speak to*) fare un discorso a; (*issue*) affrontare
adept ['ædɛpt] adj: **~ at** esperto(a) in
adequate ['ædɪkwɪt] adj adeguato(a); sufficiente
adhere [əd'hɪə*] vi: **to ~ to** aderire a; (*fig: rule, decision*) seguire
adhesive [əd'hiːzɪv] n adesivo; **~ tape** n (BRIT: *for parcels etc*) nastro adesivo; (US: MED) cerotto adesivo
adjective ['ædʒɛktɪv] n aggettivo
adjoining [ə'dʒɔɪnɪŋ] adj accanto inv, adiacente
adjourn [ə'dʒɜːn] vt rimandare ♦ vi essere aggiornato(a)
adjust [ə'dʒʌst] vt aggiustare; (*change*) rettificare ♦ vi: **to ~ (to)** adattarsi (a); **~able** adj regolabile; **~ment** n (PSYCH) adattamento; (*of machine*) regolazione f; (*of prices, wages*) modifica
ad-lib [æd'lɪb] vi improvvisare ♦ adv: **ad lib** a piacere, a volontà
administer [əd'mɪnɪstə*] vt amministrare;

(*justice, drug*) somministrare
administration [ədmɪnɪs'treɪʃən] n amministrazione f
administrative [əd'mɪnɪstrətɪv] adj amministrativo(a)
admiral ['ædmərəl] n ammiraglio; **A~ty** (BRIT) n Ministero della Marina
admiration [ædmə'reɪʃən] n ammirazione f
admire [əd'maɪə*] vt ammirare
admission [əd'mɪʃən] n ammissione f; (*to exhibition, night club etc*) ingresso; (*confession*) confessione f
admit [əd'mɪt] vt ammettere; far entrare; (*agree*) riconoscere; **to ~ to** riconoscere; **~tance** n ingresso; **~tedly** adv bisogna pur riconoscere (che)
ad nauseam [æd'nɔːsɪæm] adv fino alla nausea, a non finire
ado [ə'duː] n: **without (any) more ~** senza più indugi
adolescence [ædəu'lɛsns] n adolescenza
adolescent [ædəu'lɛsnt] adj, n adolescente m/f
adopt [ə'dɔpt] vt adottare; **~ed** adj adottivo(a); **~ion** [ə'dɔpʃən] n adozione f
adore [ə'dɔː*] vt adorare
Adriatic [eɪdrɪ'ætɪk] n: **the ~ (Sea)** il mare Adriatico, l'Adriatico
adrift [ə'drɪft] adv alla deriva
adult ['ædʌlt] adj adulto(a); (*work, education*) per adulti ♦ n adulto/a
adultery [ə'dʌltərɪ] n adulterio
advance [əd'vɑːns] n avanzamento; (*money*) anticipo ♦ adj (*booking etc*) in anticipo ♦ vt (*money*) anticipare ♦ vi avanzare; **in ~** in anticipo; **~d** adj avanzato(a); (SCOL: *studies*) superiore
advantage [əd'vɑːntɪdʒ] n (*also*: TENNIS) vantaggio; **to take ~ of** approfittarsi di
advent ['ædvənt] n avvento; (REL) **A~** Avvento
adventure [əd'vɛntʃə*] n avventura
adverb ['ædvɜːb] n avverbio
adverse ['ædvɜːs] adj avverso(a)
advert ['ædvɜːt] (BRIT) n abbr = **advertisement**
advertise ['ædvətaɪz] vi (vt) fare pubblicità or réclame (a); fare un'inserzione (per vendere); **to ~ for** (*staff*) mettere un annuncio sul giornale per trovare
advertisement [əd'vɜːtɪsmənt] n (COMM) réclame f inv, pubblicità f inv; (*in classified ads*) inserzione f
advertising ['ædvətaɪzɪŋ] n pubblicità
advice [əd'vaɪs] n consigli mpl; (*notification*) avviso; **piece of ~** consiglio; **to take legal ~** consultare un avvocato
advisable [əd'vaɪzəbl] adj consigliabile
advise [əd'vaɪz] vt consigliare; **to ~ sb of sth**

informare qn di qc; **to ~ sb against sth/doing
sth** sconsigliare qc a qn/a qn di fare qc; **~r** or
advisor n consigliere/a; **advisory** [-ərɪ] adj
consultivo(a)

advocate [n 'ædvəkɪt, vb 'ædvəkeɪt] n
(upholder) sostenitore/trice; (LAW) avvocato
(difensore) ♦ vt propugnare

Aegean [iː'dʒiːən] n: **the ~ (Sea)** il mar Egeo,
l'Egeo

aerial ['ɛərɪəl] n antenna ♦ adj aereo(a)

aerobics [ɛə'rəubɪks] n aerobica

aeroplane ['ɛərəpleɪn] (BRIT) n aeroplano

aerosol ['ɛərəsɔl] (BRIT) n aerosol m inv

aesthetic [ɪs'θetɪk] adj estetico(a)

afar [ə'fɑː*] adv: **from ~** da lontano

affair [ə'fɛə*] n affare m; (also: love ~)
relazione f amorosa; **~s** (business) affari

affect [ə'fekt] vt toccare; (influence) influire
su, incidere su; (feign) fingere; **~ed** adj
affettato(a)

affection [ə'fekʃən] n affezione f; **~ate** adj
affettuoso(a)

afflict [ə'flɪkt] vt affliggere

affluence ['æfluəns] n abbondanza; opulenza

affluent ['æfluənt] adj ricco(a); **the ~ society**
la società del benessere

afford [ə'fɔːd] vt permettersi; (provide) fornire

afloat [ə'fləut] adv a galla

afoot [ə'fut] adv: **there is something ~** si sta
preparando qualcosa

afraid [ə'freɪd] adj impaurito(a); **to be ~ of** or
to/that aver paura di/che; **I am ~ so/not** ho
paura di sì/no

Africa ['æfrɪkə] n Africa; **~n** adj, n africano(a)

after ['ɑːftə*] prep, adv dopo ♦ conj dopo che;
what/who are you ~? che/chi cerca?; **~ he
left/having done** dopo che se ne fu andato/
dopo aver fatto; **to name sb ~ sb** dare a qn il
nome di qn; **it's twenty ~ eight** (US) sono le
otto e venti; **to ask ~ sb** chiedere di qn; **~ all**
dopo tutto; **~ you!** dopo di lei!; **~effects**
conseguenze fpl; (of illness) postumi mpl;
~math n conseguenze fpl; **in the ~math of**
nel periodo dopo; **~noon** n pomeriggio; **~s**
n (inf: dessert) dessert m inv; **~-sales
service** (BRIT) n servizio assistenza clienti; **~-
shave (lotion)** n dopobarba m inv; **~sun
(lotion/cream)** n doposole m inv;
~thought n: **as an ~thought** come aggiunta;
~wards (US **~ward**) adv dopo

again [ə'gen] adv di nuovo; **to begin/see ~**
ricominciare/rivedere; **not ... ~** non ... più; **~
and ~** ripetutamente

against [ə'genst] prep contro

age [eɪdʒ] n età f inv ♦ vt, vi invecchiare; **it's
been ~s since** sono secoli che; **he is 20 years
of ~** ha 20 anni; **to come of ~** diventare
maggiorenne; **~d 10** di 10 anni; **the ~d**
['eɪdʒɪd] gli anziani; **~ group** n generazione

f; **~ limit** n limite m d'età

agency ['eɪdʒənsɪ] n agenzia

agenda [ə'dʒendə] n ordine m del giorno

agent ['eɪdʒənt] n agente m

aggravate ['ægrəveɪt] vt aggravare; (person)
irritare

aggregate ['ægrɪgeɪt] n aggregato

aggressive [ə'gresɪv] adj aggressivo(a)

agitate ['ædʒɪteɪt] vt turbare; agitare ♦ vi: **to
~ for** agitarsi per

AGM n abbr = **annual general meeting**

ago [ə'gəu] adv: **2 days ~** 2 giorni fa; **not long
~** poco tempo fa; **how long ~?** quanto tempo
fa?

agonizing ['ægənaɪzɪŋ] adj straziante

agony ['ægənɪ] n dolore m atroce; **to be in ~**
avere dolori atroci

agree [ə'griː] vt (price) pattuire ♦ vi: **to ~
(with)** essere d'accordo (con); (LING)
concordare (con); **to ~ to sth/to do sth**
accettare qc/di fare qc; **to ~ that** (admit)
ammettere che; **to ~ on sth** accordarsi su qc;
garlic doesn't ~ with me l'aglio non mi va;
~able adj gradevole; (willing) disposto(a);
~d adj (time, place) stabilito(a); **~ment** n
accordo; **in ~ment** d'accordo

agricultural [ægrɪ'kʌltʃərəl] adj agricolo(a)

agriculture ['ægrɪkʌltʃə*] n agricoltura

aground [ə'graund] adv: **to run ~** arenarsi

ahead [ə'hed] adv avanti; davanti; **~ of**
davanti a; (fig: schedule etc) in anticipo su; **~
of time** in anticipo; **go right** or **straight ~** tiri
diritto

aid [eɪd] n aiuto ♦ vt aiutare; **in ~ of** a favore
di

aide [eɪd] n (person) aiutante m

AIDS [eɪdz] n abbr (= acquired immune
deficiency syndrome) AIDS f; **~-related** adj
(symptoms, illness) legato(a) all'AIDS;
(research) sull'AIDS

aim [eɪm] vt: **to ~ sth at** (such as gun) mirare
qc a, puntare qc a; (camera) rivolgere qc a;
(missile) lanciare qc contro ♦ vi (also: to take
~) prendere la mira ♦ n mira; **to ~ at** mirare;
to ~ to do aver l'intenzione di fare; **~less** adj
senza scopo

ain't [eɪnt] (inf) = **am not**; **aren't**; **isn't**

air [ɛə*] n aria ♦ vt (room) arieggiare; (clothes)
far prendere aria a; (grievances, ideas)
esprimere pubblicamente ♦ cpd (currents)
d'aria; (attack) aereo(a); **to throw sth into
the ~** lanciare qc in aria; **by ~** (travel) in
aereo; **on the ~** (RADIO, TV) in onda; **~bed**
(BRIT) n materassino; **~ conditioning** n
condizionamento d'aria; **~craft** n inv
apparecchio; **~craft carrier** n portaerei f inv;
~field n campo d'aviazione; **A~ Force** n
aviazione f militare; **~ freshener** n
deodorante m per ambienti; **~gun** n fucile m

ad aria compressa; **~ hostess** (*BRIT*) *n* hostess *f inv*; **~ letter** (*BRIT*) *n* aerogramma *m*; **~lift** *n* ponte *m* aereo; **~line** *n* linea aerea; **~liner** *n* aereo di linea; **~mail** *n*: **by ~mail** per via aerea; **~ mattress** *n* materassino gonfiabile; **~plane** (*US*) *n* aeroplano; **~port** *n* aeroporto; **~ raid** *n* incursione *f* aerea; **~sick** *adj*: **to be ~sick** soffrire di mal d'aria; **~tight** *adj* ermetico(a); **~ traffic controller** *n* controllore *m* del traffico aereo; **~y** *adj* arioso(a); (*manners*) noncurante

aisle [aɪl] *n* (*of church*) navata laterale; navata centrale; (*of plane*) corridoio; **~ seat** *n* (*on plane*) posto sul corridoio

ajar [ə'dʒɑ:*] *adj* socchiuso(a)

alarm [ə'lɑ:m] *n* allarme *m* ♦ *vt* allarmare; **~ call** *n* (*in hotel etc*) sveglia; **~ clock** *n* sveglia

alas [ə'læs] *excl* ohimè!, ahimè!

albeit [ɔːl'biːɪt] *conj* sebbene +*sub*, benché +*sub*

album ['ælbəm] *n* album *m inv*

alcohol ['ælkəhɔl] *n* alcool *m*; **~ic** [-'hɔlɪk] *adj* alcolico(a) ♦ *n* alcolizzato/a

ale [eɪl] *n* birra

alert [ə'lə:t] *adj* vigile ♦ *n* allarme *m* ♦ *vt* avvertire; mettere in guardia; **on the ~** all'erta

algebra ['ældʒɪbrə] *n* algebra

alias ['eɪlɪəs] *adv* alias ♦ *n* pseudonimo, falso nome *m*

alibi ['ælɪbaɪ] *n* alibi *m inv*

alien ['eɪlɪən] *n* straniero/a; (*extraterrestrial*) alieno/a ♦ *adj*: **~ (to)** estraneo(a) (a); **~ate** *vt* alienare

alight [ə'laɪt] *adj* acceso(a) ♦ *vi* scendere; (*bird*) posarsi

alike [ə'laɪk] *adj* simile ♦ *adv* sia ... sia; **to look ~** assomigliarsi

alimony ['ælɪmənɪ] *n* (*payment*) alimenti *mpl*

alive [ə'laɪv] *adj* vivo(a); (*lively*) vivace

KEYWORD

all [ɔ:l] *adj* tutto(a); **~ day** tutto il giorno; **~ night** tutta la notte; **~ men** tutti gli uomini; **~ five came** sono venuti tutti e cinque; **~ the books** tutti i libri; **~ the food** tutto il cibo; **~ the time** sempre; tutto il tempo; **~ his life** tutta la vita

♦ *pron* **1** tutto(a); **I ate it ~**, **I ate ~ of it** l'ho mangiato tutto; **~ of us went** tutti noi siamo andati; **~ of the boys went** tutti i ragazzi sono andati

2 (*in phrases*): **above ~** soprattutto; **after ~** dopotutto; **at ~: not at ~** (*in answer to question*) niente affatto; (*in answer to thanks*) prego!, di niente!, s'immagini!; **I'm not at ~ tired** non sono affatto stanco(a); **anything at ~ will do** andrà bene qualsiasi cosa; **~ in ~**

tutto sommato

♦ *adv*: **~ alone** tutto(a) solo(a); **it's not as hard as ~ that** non è poi così difficile; **~ the more/the better** tanto più/meglio; **~ but** quasi; **the score is two ~** il punteggio è di due a due

allay [ə'leɪ] *vt* (*fears*) dissipare

all clear *n* (*also fig*) segnale *m* di cessato allarme

allegation [ælɪ'geɪʃən] *n* asserzione *f*

allege [ə'ledʒ] *vt* asserire; **~dly** [ə'ledʒɪdlɪ] *adv* secondo quanto si asserisce

allegiance [ə'liːdʒəns] *n* fedeltà

allergic [ə'lə:dʒɪk] *adj*: **~ to** allergico(a) a

allergy ['ælədʒɪ] *n* allergia

alleviate [ə'liːvɪeɪt] *vt* sollevare

alley ['ælɪ] *n* vicolo

alliance [ə'laɪəns] *n* alleanza

allied ['ælaɪd] *adj* alleato(a)

all-in ['ɔːlɪn] *adj* (*BRIT: also adv: charge*) tutto compreso

all-night ['ɔːl'naɪt] *adj* aperto(a) (*or che dura*) tutta la notte

allocate ['æləkeɪt] *vt* assegnare

allot [ə'lɔt] *vt* assegnare; **~ment** *n* assegnazione *f*; (*garden*) lotto di terra

all-out ['ɔːl'aut] *adj* (*effort etc*) totale ♦ *adv*: **to go all out for** mettercela tutta per

allow [ə'lau] *vt* (*practice, behaviour*) permettere; (*sum to spend etc*) accordare; (*sum, time estimated*) dare; (*concede*): **to ~ that** ammettere che; **to ~ sb to do** permettere a qn di fare; **he is ~ed to do it** lo può fare; **~ for** *vt fus* tener conto di; **~ance** *n* (*money received*) assegno; indennità *f inv*; (*TAX*) detrazione *f* di imposta; **to make ~ances for** tener conto di

alloy ['ælɔɪ] *n* lega

all right *adv* (*feel, work*) bene; (*as answer*) va bene

all-round ['ɔːl'raund] *adj* completo(a)

all-time ['ɔːl'taɪm] *adj* (*record*) assoluto(a)

alluring [ə'ljuərɪŋ] *adj* seducente

ally ['ælaɪ] *n* alleato

almighty [ɔːl'maɪtɪ] *adj* onnipotente; (*row etc*) colossale

almond ['ɑːmənd] *n* mandorla

almost ['ɔːlməust] *adv* quasi

alone [ə'ləun] *adj*, *adv* solo(a); **to leave sb ~** lasciare qn in pace; **to leave sth ~** lasciare stare qc; **let ~ ...** figuriamoci poi ..., tanto meno ...

along [ə'lɔŋ] *prep* lungo ♦ *adv*: **is he coming ~?** viene con noi?; **he was limping ~** veniva zoppicando; **~ with** insieme con; **all ~** (*all the time*) sempre, fin dall'inizio; **~side** *prep* accanto a; lungo ♦ *adv* accanto

aloof [ə'luːf] *adj* distaccato(a) ♦ *adv*: **to stand**

~ tenersi a distanza *or* in disparte

aloud [ə'laud] *adv* ad alta voce

alphabet ['ælfəbɛt] *n* alfabeto

alpine ['ælpaɪn] *adj* alpino(a)

Alps [ælps] *npl*: **the ~** le Alpi

already [ɔːl'rɛdɪ] *adv* già

alright ['ɔːl'raɪt] (*BRIT*) *adv* = **all right**

Alsatian [æl'seɪʃən] (*BRIT*) *n* (*dog*) pastore *m* tedesco; (*cane m*) lupo

also ['ɔːlsəʊ] *adv* anche

altar ['ɔltə*] *n* altare *m*

alter ['ɔltə*] *vt*, *vi* alterare

alternate [*adj* ɔl'tɜːnɪt, *vb* 'ɔltəːneɪt] *adj* alterno(a); (*US*: *plan etc*) alternativo(a) ♦ *vi*: **to ~ (with)** alternarsi (a); **on ~ days** ogni due giorni; **alternating** *adj* (*current*) alternato(a)

alternative [ɔl'tɜːnətɪv] *adj* alternativo(a) ♦ *n* (*choice*) alternativa; **~ly** *adv*: **~ly one could ...** come alternativa si potrebbe ...; **~ medicine** *n* medicina alternativa

alternator ['ɔltəːneɪtə*] *n* (*AUT*) alternatore *m*

although [ɔːl'ðəʊ] *conj* benché +*sub*, sebbene +*sub*

altitude ['æltɪtjuːd] *n* altitudine *f*

alto ['æltəʊ] *n* contralto; (*male*) contraltino

altogether [ɔːltə'gɛðə*] *adv* del tutto, completamente; (*on the whole*) tutto considerato; (*in all*) in tutto

aluminium [ælju'mɪnɪəm] *n* alluminio

aluminum [ə'luːmɪnəm] (*US*) *n* = **aluminium**

always ['ɔːlweɪz] *adv* sempre

Alzheimer's (disease) ['æltshaɪməz-] *n* (malattia di) Alzheimer

AM *n abbr* (= (*Welsh*) *Assembly Member*) deputato/a del Parlamento gallese

am [æm] *vb see* **be**

a.m. *adv abbr* (= *ante meridiem*) della mattina

amalgamate [ə'mælgəmeɪt] *vt* amalgamare ♦ *vi* amalgamarsi

amateur ['æmətə*] *n* dilettante *m/f* ♦ *adj* (*SPORT*) dilettante; **~ish** (*pej*) *adj* da dilettante

amaze [ə'meɪz] *vt* stupire; **to be ~d (at)** essere sbalordito (da); **~ment** *n* stupore *m*; **amazing** *adj* sorprendente, sbalorditivo(a)

ambassador [æm'bæsədə*] *n* ambasciatore/trice

amber ['æmbə*] *n* ambra; **at ~** (*BRIT*: *AUT*) giallo

ambiguous [æm'bɪgjuəs] *adj* ambiguo(a)

ambition [æm'bɪʃən] *n* ambizione *f*

ambitious [æm'bɪʃəs] *adj* ambizioso(a)

ambulance ['æmbjuləns] *n* ambulanza

ambush ['æmbuʃ] *n* imboscata

amenable [ə'miːnəbl] *adj*: **~ to** (*advice etc*) ben disposto(a) a

amend [ə'mɛnd] *vt* (*law*) emendare; (*text*) correggere; **to make ~s** fare ammenda

amenities [ə'miːnɪtɪz] *npl* attrezzature *fpl* ricreative e culturali

America [ə'mɛrɪkə] *n* America; **~n** *adj*, *n* americano(a)

amiable ['eɪmɪəbl] *adj* amabile, gentile

amicable ['æmɪkəbl] *adj* amichevole

amid(st) [ə'mɪd(st)] *prep* in mezzo a

amiss [ə'mɪs] *adj*, *adv*: **there's something ~** c'è qualcosa che non va bene; **don't take it ~** non prendertela (a male)

ammonia [ə'məʊnɪə] *n* ammoniaca

ammunition [æmju'nɪʃən] *n* munizioni *fpl*

amok [ə'mɔk] *adv*: **to run ~** diventare pazzo(a) furioso(a)

among(st) [ə'mʌŋ(st)] *prep* fra, tra, in mezzo a

amorous ['æmərəs] *adj* amoroso(a)

amount [ə'maʊnt] *n* somma; ammontare *m*; quantità *f inv* ♦ *vi*: **to ~ to** (*total*) ammontare a; (*be same as*) essere come

amp(ère) ['æmp(ɛə*)] *n* ampère *m inv*

ample ['æmpl] *adj* ampio(a); spazioso(a); (*enough*): **this is ~** questo è più che sufficiente

amplifier ['æmplɪfaɪə*] *n* amplificatore *m*

amuse [ə'mjuːz] *vt* divertire; **~ment** *n* divertimento; **~ment arcade** *n* sala giochi; **~ment park** *n* luna park *m inv*

an [æn] *indef art see* **a**

anaemic [ə'niːmɪk] *adj* anemico(a)

anaesthetic [ænɪs'θɛtɪk] *adj* anestetico(a) ♦ *n* anestetico

analog(ue) ['ænəlɔg] *adj* (*watch, computer*) analogico(a)

analyse ['ænəlaɪz] (*BRIT*) *vt* analizzare

analysis [ə'næləsɪs] (*pl* **analyses**) *n* analisi *f inv*

analyst ['ænəlɪst] *n* (*POL etc*) analista *m/f*; (*US*) (*psic*)analista *m/f*

analyze ['ænəlaɪz] (*US*) *vt* = **analyse**

anarchy ['ænəkɪ] *n* anarchia

anatomy [ə'nætəmɪ] *n* anatomia

ancestor ['ænsɪstə*] *n* antenato/a

anchor ['æŋkə*] *n* ancora ♦ *vi* (*also*: **to drop ~**) gettare l'ancora ♦ *vt* ancorare; **to weigh ~** salpare *or* levare l'ancora

anchovy ['æntʃəvɪ] *n* acciuga

ancient ['eɪnʃənt] *adj* antico(a); (*person, car*) vecchissimo(a)

ancillary [æn'sɪlərɪ] *adj* ausiliario(a)

and [ænd] *conj* e (*often* ed *before vowel*); **~ so on** e così via; **try ~ come** cerca di venire; **he talked ~ talked** non la finiva di parlare; **better ~ better** sempre meglio

anemic [ə'niːmɪk] (*US*) *adj* = **anaemic**

anesthetic [ænɪs'θɛtɪk] (*US*) *adj*, *n* = **anaesthetic**

anew [ə'njuː] *adv* di nuovo

angel ['eɪndʒəl] *n* angelo

anger ['æŋgə*] *n* rabbia
angina [æn'dʒaɪnə] *n* angina pectoris
angle ['æŋgl] *n* angolo; **from their ~** dal loro punto di vista
Anglican ['æŋglɪkən] *adj, n* anglicano(a)
angling ['æŋglɪŋ] *n* pesca con la lenza
Anglo- ['æŋgləʊ] *prefix* anglo...
angrily ['æŋgrɪlɪ] *adv* con rabbia
angry ['æŋgrɪ] *adj* arrabbiato(a), furioso(a); (*wound*) infiammato(a); **to be ~ with sb/at sth** essere in collera con qn/per qc; **to get ~** arrabbiarsi; **to make sb ~** fare arrabbiare qn
anguish ['æŋgwɪʃ] *n* angoscia
animal ['ænɪməl] *adj* animale ♦ *n* animale *m*
animate ['ænɪmɪt] *adj* animato(a)
animated ['ænɪmeɪtɪd] *adj* animato(a)
aniseed ['ænɪsiːd] *n* semi *mpl* di anice
ankle ['æŋkl] *n* caviglia; **~ sock** *n* calzino
annex [*n* 'æneks, *vb* ə'neks] *n* (*also*: BRIT: **annexe**) (edificio) annesso ♦ *vt* annettere
anniversary [ænɪ'vɜːsərɪ] *n* anniversario
announce [ə'naʊns] *vt* annunciare; **~ment** *n* annuncio; (*letter, card*) partecipazione *f*; **~r** *n* (RADIO, TV: between programmes) annunciatore/trice; (: *in a programme*) presentatore/trice
annoy [ə'nɔɪ] *vt* dare fastidio a; **don't get ~ed!** non irritarti!; **~ance** *n* fastidio; (*cause of ~ance*) noia; **~ing** *adj* noioso(a)
annual ['ænjuəl] *adj* annuale ♦ *n* (BOT) pianta annua; (*book*) annuario
annul [ə'nʌl] *vt* annullare
annum ['ænəm] *n see* **per**
anonymous [ə'nɒnɪməs] *adj* anonimo(a)
anorak ['ænəræk] *n* giacca a vento
anorexia [ænə'reksɪə] *n* (MED: *also*: **~ nervosa**) anoressia
another [ə'nʌðə*] *adj*: **~ book** (*one more*) un altro libro, ancora un libro; (*a different one*) un altro libro ♦ *pron* un altro(un'altra), ancora uno(a); *see also* **one**
answer ['ɑːnsə*] *n* risposta; soluzione *f* ♦ *vi* rispondere ♦ *vt* (*reply to*) rispondere a; (*problem*) risolvere; (*prayer*) esaudire; **in ~ to your letter** in risposta alla sua lettera; **to ~ the phone** rispondere (al telefono); **to ~ the bell** rispondere al campanello; **to ~ the door** aprire la porta; **~ back** *vi* ribattere; **~ for** *vt fus* essere responsabile di; **~ to** *vt fus* (*description*) corrispondere a; **~able** *adj*: **~able (to sb/for sth)** responsabile (verso qn/di qc); **~ing machine** *n* segreteria (telefonica) automatica
ant [ænt] *n* formica
antagonism [æn'tægənɪzəm] *n* antagonismo
antagonize [æn'tægənaɪz] *vt* provocare l'ostilità di
Antarctic [ænt'ɑːktɪk] *n*: **the ~** l'Antartide *f*
antenatal ['æntɪ'neɪtl] *adj* prenatale;

~ clinic *n* assistenza medica preparto
anthem ['ænθəm] *n*: **national ~** inno nazionale
antibiotic ['æntɪbaɪ'ɔtɪk] *n* antibiotico
antibody ['æntɪbɔdɪ] *n* anticorpo
anticipate [æn'tɪsɪpeɪt] *vt* prevedere; pregustare; (*wishes, request*) prevenire
anticipation [æntɪsɪ'peɪʃən] *n* anticipazione *f*; (*expectation*) aspettative *fpl*
anticlimax ['æntɪ'klaɪmæks] *n*: **it was an ~** fu una completa delusione
anticlockwise ['æntɪ'klɔkwaɪz] *adj, adv* in senso antiorario
antics ['æntɪks] *npl* buffonerie *fpl*
antidepressant ['æntɪdɪ'presnt] *n* antidepressivo
antifreeze ['æntɪ'friːz] *n* anticongelante *m*
antihistamine [æntɪ'hɪstəmɪn] *n* antistaminico
antique [æn'tiːk] *n* antichità *f inv* ♦ *adj* antico(a); **~ dealer** *n* antiquario/a; **~ shop** *n* negozio d'antichità
anti-Semitism ['æntɪ'semɪtɪzəm] *n* antisemitismo
antiseptic [æntɪ'septɪk] *n* antisettico
antisocial ['æntɪ'səʊʃəl] *adj* asociale
antlers ['æntləz] *npl* palchi *mpl*
anvil ['ænvɪl] *n* incudine *f*
anxiety [æŋ'zaɪətɪ] *n* ansia; (*keenness*): **~ to do** smania di fare
anxious ['æŋkʃəs] *adj* ansioso(a), inquieto(a); (*worrying*) angosciante; (*keen*): **~ to do/that** impaziente di fare/che +*sub*

any ['enɪ] *adj* **1** (*in questions etc*): **have you ~ butter?** hai del burro?, hai un po' di burro?; **have you ~ children?** hai bambini?; **if there are ~ tickets left** se ci sono ancora (dei) biglietti, se c'è ancora qualche biglietto
2 (*with negative*): **I haven't ~ money/books** non ho soldi/libri
3 (*no matter which*) qualsiasi, qualunque; **choose ~ book you like** scegli un libro qualsiasi
4 (*in phrases*): **in ~ case** in ogni caso; **~ day now** da un giorno all'altro; **at ~ moment** in qualsiasi momento, da un momento all'altro; **at ~ rate** ad ogni modo
♦ *pron* **1** (*in questions, with negative*): **have you got ~?** ne hai?; **can ~ of you sing?** qualcuno di voi sa cantare?; **I haven't ~ (of them)** non ne ho
2 (*no matter which one(s)*): **take ~ of those books (you like)** prendi uno qualsiasi di quei libri
♦ *adv* **1** (*in questions etc*): **do you want ~ more soup/sandwiches?** vuoi ancora un po' di minestra/degli altri panini?; **are you feeling**

~ **better?** ti senti meglio?
2 (with negative): **I can't hear him ~ more**
non lo sento più; **don't wait ~ longer** non
aspettare più

anybody ['ɛnɪbɔdɪ] pron (in questions etc)
qualcuno, nessuno; (with negative) nessuno;
(no matter who) chiunque; **can you see ~?**
vedi qualcuno or nessuno?; **if ~ should phone**
... se telefona qualcuno ...; **I can't see ~** non
vedo nessuno; **~ could do it** chiunque
potrebbe farlo

anyhow ['ɛnɪhau] adv (at any rate) ad ogni
modo, comunque; (haphazard): **do it ~ you**
like fallo come ti pare; **I shall go ~** ci andrò lo
stesso or comunque; **she leaves things just ~**
lascia tutto come capita

anyone ['ɛnɪwʌn] pron = **anybody**

anything ['ɛnɪθɪŋ] pron (in question etc)
qualcosa, niente; (with negative) niente; (no
matter what): **you can say ~ you like** puoi dire
quello che ti pare; **can you see ~?** vedi niente
or qualcosa?; **if ~ happens to me ...** se mi
dovesse succedere qualcosa ...; **I can't see ~**
non vedo niente; **~ will do** va bene qualsiasi
cosa or tutto

anyway ['ɛnɪweɪ] adv (at any rate) ad ogni
modo, comunque; (besides) ad ogni modo

anywhere ['ɛnɪwɛə*] adv (in questions etc)
da qualche parte; (with negative) da nessuna
parte; (no matter where) da qualsiasi or
qualunque parte, dovunque; **can you see him**
~? lo vedi da qualche parte?; **I can't see him ~**
non lo vedo da nessuna parte; **~ in the world**
dovunque nel mondo

apart [ə'pɑːt] adv (to one side) a parte;
(separately) separatamente; **with one's legs ~**
con le gambe divaricate; **10 miles ~** a 10
miglia di distanza (l'uno dall'altro); **to take ~**
smontare; **~ from** a parte, eccetto

apartheid [ə'pɑːteɪt] n apartheid f

apartment [ə'pɑːtmənt] n (US)
appartamento; (room) locale m; **~ building**
(US) n stabile m, caseggiato

ape [eɪp] n scimmia ♦ vt scimmiottare

apéritif [ə'pɛrɪtɪv] n aperitivo

aperture ['æpətʃjuə*] n apertura

APEX ['eɪpɛks] n abbr (= advance purchase
excursion) APEX m inv

apologetic [əpɔlə'dʒɛtɪk] adj (tone, letter) di
scusa

apologize [ə'pɔlədʒaɪz] vi: **to ~ (for sth to**
sb) scusarsi (di qc a qn), chiedere scusa (a qn
per qc)

apology [ə'pɔlədʒɪ] n scuse fpl

apostle [ə'pɔsl] n apostolo

apostrophe [ə'pɔstrəfɪ] n (sign) apostrofo

appal [ə'pɔːl] vt scioccare; **~ling** adj
spaventoso(a)

apparatus [æpə'reɪtəs] n apparato; (in
gymnasium) attrezzatura

apparel [ə'pærl] (US) n abbigliamento,
confezioni fpl

apparent [ə'pærənt] adj evidente; **~ly** adv
evidentemente

appeal [ə'piːl] vi (LAW) appellarsi alla legge
♦ n (LAW) appello; (request) richiesta;
(charm) attrattiva; **to ~ for** chiedere (con
insistenza); **to ~ to** (subj: person) appellarsi a;
(subj: thing) piacere a; **it doesn't ~ to me** mi
dice poco; **~ing** adj (nice) attraente

appear [ə'pɪə*] vi apparire; (LAW) comparire;
(publication) essere pubblicato(a); (seem)
sembrare; **it would ~ that** sembra che; **~ance**
n apparizione f; apparenza; (look, aspect)
aspetto

appease [ə'piːz] vt calmare, appagare

appendicitis [əpɛndɪ'saɪtɪs] n appendicite f

appendix [ə'pɛndɪks] (pl **appendices**) n
appendice f

appetite ['æpɪtaɪt] n appetito

appetizer ['æpɪtaɪzə*] n stuzzichino

applaud [ə'plɔːd] vt, vi applaudire

applause [ə'plɔːz] n applauso

apple ['æpl] n mela; **~ tree** n melo

appliance [ə'plaɪəns] n apparecchio

applicant ['æplɪkənt] n candidato/a

application [æplɪ'keɪʃən] n applicazione f;
(for a job, a grant etc) domanda; **~ form** n
modulo per la domanda

applied [ə'plaɪd] adj applicato(a)

apply [ə'plaɪ] vt: **to ~ (to)** (paint, ointment)
dare (a); (theory, technique) applicare (a)
♦ vi: **to ~ to** (ask) rivolgersi a; (be suitable for,
relevant to) riguardare, riferirsi a; **to ~ (for)**
(permit, grant, job) fare domanda (per); **to**
~ o.s. to dedicarsi a

appoint [ə'pɔɪnt] vt nominare; **~ed** adj: **at**
the ~ed time all'ora stabilita; **~ment** n
nomina; (arrangement to meet)
appuntamento; **to make an ~ment (with)**
prendere un appuntamento (con)

appraisal [ə'preɪzl] n valutazione f

appreciate [ə'priːʃɪeɪt] vt (like) apprezzare;
(be grateful for) essere riconoscente di; (be
aware of) rendersi conto di ♦ vi (FINANCE)
aumentare; **I'd ~ your help** ti sono grato per
l'aiuto

appreciation [əpriːʃɪ'eɪʃən] n apprez-
zamento; (FINANCE) aumento del valore

appreciative [ə'priːʃɪətɪv] adj (person)
sensibile; (comment) elogiativo(a)

apprehend [æprɪ'hɛnd] vt (arrest) arrestare

apprehension [æprɪ'hɛnʃən] n (fear)
inquietudine f

apprehensive [æprɪ'hɛnsɪv] adj
apprensivo(a)

apprentice [ə'prɛntɪs] n apprendista m/f;

~ship n apprendistato
approach [ə'prəʊtʃ] vi avvicinarsi ♦ vt (come near) avvicinarsi a; (ask, apply to) rivolgersi a; (subject, passer-by) avvicinare ♦ n approccio; accesso; (to problem) modo di affrontare; **~able** adj accessibile
approach road n strada d'accesso
appropriate [adj ə'prəʊprɪɪt, vb ə'prəʊprɪeɪt] adj appropriato(a); adatto(a) ♦ vt (take) appropriarsi
approval [ə'pruːvəl] n approvazione f; **on ~** (COMM) in prova, in esame
approve [ə'pruːv] vt, vi approvare; **~ of** vt fus approvare
approximate [ə'prɒksɪmɪt] adj approssimativo(a); **~ly** adv circa
apricot ['eɪprɪkɒt] n albicocca
April ['eɪprəl] n aprile m; **~ fool!** pesce d'aprile!
apron ['eɪprən] n grembiule m
apt [æpt] adj (suitable) adatto(a); (able) capace; (likely): **to be ~ to do** avere tendenza a fare
aquarium [ə'kwɛərɪəm] n acquario
Aquarius [ə'kwɛərɪəs] n Acquario
Arab ['ærəb] adj, n arabo(a)
Arabian [ə'reɪbɪən] adj arabo(a)
Arabic ['ærəbɪk] adj arabico(a), arabo(a) ♦ n arabo; **~ numerals** numeri mpl arabi, numerazione f araba
arbitrary ['ɑːbɪtrərɪ] adj arbitrario(a)
arbitration [ɑːbɪ'treɪʃən] n (LAW) arbitrato; (INDUSTRY) arbitraggio
arcade [ɑː'keɪd] n portico; (passage with shops) galleria
arch [ɑːtʃ] n arco; (of foot) arco plantare ♦ vt inarcare
archaeologist [ɑːkɪ'ɒlədʒɪst] n archeologo/a
archaeology [ɑːkɪ'ɒlədʒɪ] n archeologia
archbishop [ɑːtʃ'bɪʃəp] n arcivescovo
archeology [ɑːkɪ'ɒlədʒɪ] etc (US) = **archaeology** etc
archery ['ɑːtʃərɪ] n tiro all'arco
architect ['ɑːkɪtɛkt] n architetto; **~ure** ['ɑːkɪtɛktʃə*] n architettura
archives ['ɑːkaɪvz] npl archivi mpl
Arctic ['ɑːktɪk] adj artico(a) ♦ n: **the ~** l'Artico
ardent ['ɑːdənt] adj ardente
are [ɑː*] vb see **be**
area ['ɛərɪə] n (GEOM) area; (zone) zona; (: smaller) settore m
aren't [ɑːnt] = **are not**
Argentina [ɑːdʒən'tiːnə] n Argentina; **Argentinian** [-'tɪnɪən] adj, n argentino(a)
arguably ['ɑːgjʊəblɪ] adv: **it is ~ ...** si può sostenere che sia ...
argue ['ɑːgjuː] vi (quarrel) litigare; (reason) ragionare; **to ~ that** sostenere che
argument ['ɑːgjʊmənt] n (reasons)

argomento; (quarrel) lite f; **~ative** [ɑːgjuː'mɛntətɪv] adj litigioso(a)
Aries ['ɛərɪz] n Ariete m
arise [ə'raɪz] (pt arose, pp arisen) vi (opportunity, problem) presentarsi
aristocrat ['ærɪstəkræt] n aristocratico/a
arithmetic [ə'rɪθmətɪk] n aritmetica
ark [ɑːk] n: **Noah's A~** l'arca di Noè
arm [ɑːm] n braccio ♦ vt armare; **~s** npl (weapons) armi fpl; **~ in ~** a braccetto
armaments ['ɑːməmənts] npl armamenti mpl
arm: ~chair n poltrona; **~ed** adj armato(a); **~ed robbery** n rapina a mano armata
armour ['ɑːmə*] (US armor) n armatura; (MIL: tanks) mezzi mpl blindati; **~ed car** n autoblinda f inv
armpit ['ɑːmpɪt] n ascella
armrest ['ɑːmrɛst] n bracciolo
army ['ɑːmɪ] n esercito
aroma [ə'rəʊmə] n aroma; **~therapy** n aromaterapia
arose [ə'rəʊz] pt of **arise**
around [ə'raʊnd] adv attorno, intorno ♦ prep intorno a; (fig: about): **~ £5/3 o'clock** circa 5 sterline/le 3; **is he ~?** è in giro?
arouse [ə'raʊz] vt (sleeper) svegliare; (curiosity, passions) suscitare
arrange [ə'reɪndʒ] vt sistemare; (programme) preparare; **to ~ to do sth** mettersi d'accordo per fare qc; **~ment** n sistemazione f; (agreement) accordo; **~ments** npl (plans) progetti mpl, piani mpl
array [ə'reɪ] n: **~ of** fila di
arrears [ə'rɪəz] npl arretrati mpl; **to be in ~ with one's rent** essere in arretrato con l'affitto
arrest [ə'rɛst] vt arrestare; (sb's attention) attirare ♦ n arresto; **under ~** in arresto
arrival [ə'raɪvəl] n arrivo; (person) arrivato/a; **a new ~** un nuovo venuto; (baby) un neonato
arrive [ə'raɪv] vi arrivare
arrogant ['ærəgənt] adj arrogante
arrow ['ærəʊ] n freccia
arse [ɑːs] (inf!) n culo (!)
arson ['ɑːsn] n incendio doloso
art [ɑːt] n arte f; (craft) mestiere m; **A~s** npl (SCOL) Lettere fpl
art gallery n galleria d'arte
arthritis [ɑː'θraɪtɪs] n artrite f
artichoke ['ɑːtɪtʃəʊk] n carciofo; **Jerusalem ~** topinambur m inv
article ['ɑːtɪkl] n articolo; **~s** npl (BRIT: LAW: training) contratto di tirocinio; **~ of clothing** capo di vestiario
articulate [adj ɑː'tɪkjulɪt, vb ɑː'tɪkjuleɪt] adj (person) che si esprime forbitamente; (speech) articolato(a) ♦ vi articolare; **~d**

lorry (*BRIT*) *n* autotreno
artificial [ɑːtɪˈfɪʃəl] *adj* artificiale;
 ~ respiration *n* respirazione *f* artificiale
artist [ˈɑːtɪst] *n* artista *m/f*; **~ic** [ɑːˈtɪstɪk] *adj*
 artistico(a); **~ry** *n* arte *f*
art school *n* scuola d'arte

KEYWORD
---

as [æz] *conj* 1 (*referring to time*) mentre; **~ the
 years went by** col passare degli anni; **he came
 in ~ I was leaving** arrivò mentre stavo
 uscendo; **~ from tomorrow** da domani
 2 (*in comparisons*): **~ big ~** grande come;
 twice ~ big ~ due volte più grande di; **~
 much/many ~** tanto quanto/tanti quanti; **~
 soon ~ possible** prima possibile
 3 (*since, because*) dal momento che, siccome
 4 (*referring to manner, way*) come; **do ~ you
 wish** fa' come vuoi; **~ she said** come ha detto
 lei
 5 (*concerning*): **~ for** or **to that** per quanto
 riguarda or quanto a quello
 6: **~ if** or **though** come se; **he looked ~ if he
 was ill** sembrava stare male; *see also* **long;
 such; well**
 ♦ *prep*: **he works ~ a driver** fa l'autista; **~
 chairman of the company, he ...** come
 presidente della compagnia, lui ...; **he gave
 me it ~ a present** me lo ha regalato

a.s.a.p. *abbr* = **as soon as possible**
ascend [əˈsɛnd] *vt* salire
ascertain [æsəˈteɪn] *vt* accertare
ash [æʃ] *n* (*dust*) cenere *f*; (*wood, tree*) frassino
ashamed [əˈʃeɪmd] *adj* vergognoso(a); **to be
 ~ of** vergognarsi di
ashore [əˈʃɔː*] *adv* a terra
ashtray [ˈæʃtreɪ] *n* portacenere *m*
Ash Wednesday *n* mercoledì *m inv* delle
 Ceneri
Asia [ˈeɪʃə] *n* Asia; **~n** *adj, n* asiatico(a)
aside [əˈsaɪd] *adv* da parte ♦ *n* a parte *m*
ask [ɑːsk] *vt* (*question*) domandare; (*invite*)
 invitare; **to ~ sb sth/sb to do sth** chiedere qc
 a qn/a qn di fare qc; **to ~ sb about sth**
 chiedere a qn di qc; **to ~ (sb) a question** fare
 una domanda (a qn); **to ~ sb out to dinner**
 invitare qn a mangiare fuori; **~ after** *vt fus*
 chiedere di; **~ for** *vt fus* chiedere; (*trouble
 etc*) cercare
asleep [əˈsliːp] *adj* addormentato(a); **to be ~**
 dormire; **to fall ~** addormentarsi
asparagus [əsˈpærəgəs] *n* asparagi *mpl*
aspect [ˈæspɛkt] *n* aspetto
aspersions [əsˈpɜːʃənz] *npl*: **to cast ~ on**
 diffamare
asphyxiation [æsfɪksɪˈeɪʃən] *n* asfissia
aspire [əsˈpaɪə*] *vi*: **to ~ to** aspirare a
aspirin [ˈæsprɪn] *n* aspirina

ass [æs] *n* asino; (*inf*) scemo/a; (*US: inf!*) culo
 (!)
assailant [əˈseɪlənt] *n* assalitore *m*
assassinate [əˈsæsɪneɪt] *vt* assassinare;
 assassination [əsæsɪˈneɪʃən] *n* assassinio
assault [əˈsɔːlt] *n* (*MIL*) assalto; (*gen: attack*)
 aggressione *f* ♦ *vt* assaltare; aggredire;
 (*sexually*) violentare
assemble [əˈsɛmbl] *vt* riunire; (*TECH*)
 montare ♦ *vi* riunirsi
assembly [əˈsɛmblɪ] *n* (*meeting*) assemblea;
 (*construction*) montaggio; **~ line** *n* catena di
 montaggio
assent [əˈsɛnt] *n* assenso, consenso
assert [əˈsɜːt] *vt* asserire; (*insist on*) far valere
assess [əˈsɛs] *vt* valutare; **~ment** *n*
 valutazione *f*
asset [ˈæsɛt] *n* vantaggio; **~s** *npl* (*FINANCE: of
 individual*) beni *mpl*; (: *of company*) attivo
assign [əˈsaɪn] *vt*: **to ~ (to)** (*task*) assegnare
 (a); (*resources*) riservare (a); (*cause,
 meaning*) attribuire (a); **to ~ a date to sth**
 fissare la data di qc; **~ment** *n* compito
assist [əˈsɪst] *vt* assistere, aiutare; **~ance** *n*
 assistenza, aiuto; **~ant** *n* assistente *m/f*; (*BRIT:
 also: shop ~ant*) commesso/a
associate [*adj, n* əˈsəʊʃɪɪt, *vb* əˈsəʊʃɪeɪt] *adj*
 associato(a); (*member*) aggiunto(a) ♦ *n*
 collega *m/f* ♦ *vt* associare ♦ *vi*: **to ~ with sb**
 frequentare qn
association [əsəʊsɪˈeɪʃən] *n* associazione *f*
assorted [əˈsɔːtɪd] *adj* assortito(a)
assortment [əˈsɔːtmənt] *n* assortimento
assume [əˈsjuːm] *vt* supporre; (*responsibilities
 etc*) assumere; (*attitude, name*) prendere
assumption [əˈsʌmpʃən] *n* supposizione *f*,
 ipotesi *f inv*; (*of power*) assunzione *f*
assurance [əˈʃʊərəns] *n* assicurazione *f*;
 (*self-confidence*) fiducia in se stesso
assure [əˈʃʊə*] *vt* assicurare
asthma [ˈæsmə] *n* asma
astonish [əˈstɒnɪʃ] *vt* stupire; **~ment** *n*
 stupore *m*
astound [əˈstaʊnd] *vt* sbalordire
astray [əˈstreɪ] *adv*: **to go ~** smarrirsi; **to lead
 ~** portare sulla cattiva strada
astride [əˈstraɪd] *prep* a cavalcioni di
astrology [əsˈtrɒlədʒɪ] *n* astrologia
astronaut [ˈæstrənɔːt] *n* astronauta *m/f*
astronomy [əsˈtrɒnəmɪ] *n* astronomia
asylum [əˈsaɪləm] *n* asilo; (*building*)
 manicomio

KEYWORD
---

at [æt] *prep* 1 (*referring to position, direction*) a;
 ~ the top in cima; **~ the desk** al banco, alla
 scrivania; **~ home/school** a casa/scuola; **~ the
 baker's** dal panettiere; **to look ~ sth** guardare
 qc; **to throw sth ~ sb** lanciare qc a qn

2 (*referring to time*) a; **~ 4 o'clock** alle 4; **~ night** di notte; **~ Christmas** a Natale; **~ times** a volte

3 (*referring to rates, speed etc*) a; **~ £1 a kilo** a 1 sterlina al chilo; **two ~ a time** due alla volta, due per volta; **~ 50 km/h** a 50 km/h

4 (*referring to manner*): **~ a stroke** d'un solo colpo; **~ peace** in pace

5 (*referring to activity*): **to be ~ work** essere al lavoro; **to play ~ cowboys** giocare ai cowboy; **to be good ~ sth/doing sth** essere bravo in qc/a fare qc

6 (*referring to cause*): **shocked/surprised/ annoyed ~ sth** colpito da/sorpreso da/ arrabbiato per qc; **I went ~ his suggestion** ci sono andato dietro suo consiglio

ate [eɪt] *pt of* **eat**
atheist ['eɪθɪɪst] *n* ateo/a
Athens ['æθɪnz] *n* Atene *f*
athlete ['æθliːt] *n* atleta *m/f*
athletic [æθ'lɛtɪk] *adj* atletico(a); **~s** *n* atletica
Atlantic [ət'læntɪk] *adj* atlantico(a) ♦ *n*: **the ~ (Ocean)** l'Atlantico, l'Oceano Atlantico
atlas ['ætləs] *n* atlante *m*
ATM *n abbr* (= *automated telling machine*) cassa automatica prelievi, sportello automatico
atmosphere ['ætməsfɪə*] *n* atmosfera
atom ['ætəm] *n* atomo; **~ic** [ə'tɒmɪk] *adj* atomico(a); **~(ic) bomb** *n* bomba atomica; **~izer** ['ætəmaɪzə*] *n* atomizzatore *m*
atone [ə'təʊn] *vi*: **to ~ for** espiare
atrocious [ə'trəʊʃəs] *adj* pessimo(a), atroce
attach [ə'tætʃ] *vt* attaccare; (*document, letter*) allegare; (*importance etc*) attribuire; **to be ~ed to sb/sth** (*to like*) essere affezionato(a) a qn/ qc
attaché case [ə'tæʃeɪ-] *n* valigetta per documenti
attachment [ə'tætʃmənt] *n* (*tool*) accessorio; (*love*): **~ (to)** affetto (per)
attack [ə'tæk] *vt* attaccare; (*person*) aggredire; (*task etc*) iniziare; (*problem*) affrontare ♦ *n* attacco; **heart ~** infarto; **~er** *n* aggressore *m*
attain [ə'teɪn] *vt* (*also*: **to ~ to**) arrivare a, raggiungere
attempt [ə'tɛmpt] *n* tentativo ♦ *vt* tentare; **to make an ~ on sb's life** attentare alla vita di qn
attend [ə'tɛnd] *vt* frequentare; (*meeting, talk*) andare a; (*patient*) assistere; **~ to** *vt fus* (*needs, affairs etc*) prendersi cura di; (*customer*) occuparsi di; **~ance** *n* (*being present*) presenza; (*people present*) gente *f* presente; **~ant** *n* custode *m/f*; persona di servizio ♦ *adj* concomitante
attention [ə'tɛnʃən] *n* attenzione *f* ♦ *excl*

(*MIL*) attenti!; **for the ~ of** (*ADMIN*) per l'attenzione di
attentive [ə'tɛntɪv] *adj* attento(a); (*kind*) premuroso(a)
attic ['ætɪk] *n* soffitta
attitude ['ætɪtjuːd] *n* atteggiamento; posa
attorney [ə'tɜːnɪ] *n* (*lawyer*) avvocato; (*having proxy*) mandatario; **A~ General** *n* (*BRIT*) Procuratore *m* Generale; (*US*) Ministro della Giustizia
attract [ə'trækt] *vt* attirare; **~ion** [ə'trækʃən] *n* (*gen pl*: *pleasant things*) attrattiva; (*PHYSICS, fig*: *towards sth*) attrazione *f*; **~ive** *adj* attraente
attribute [*n* 'ætrɪbjuːt, *vb* ə'trɪbjuːt] *n* attributo ♦ *vt*: **to ~ sth to** attribuire qc a
attrition [ə'trɪʃən] *n*: **war of ~** guerra di logoramento
aubergine ['əʊbəʒiːn] *n* melanzana
auburn ['ɔːbən] *adj* tizianesco(a)
auction ['ɔːkʃən] *n* (*also*: *sale by ~*) asta ♦ *vt* (*also*: *to sell by ~*) vendere all'asta; (*also*: *to put up for ~*) mettere all'asta; **~eer** [-'nɪə*] *n* banditore *m*
audible ['ɔːdɪbl] *adj* udibile
audience ['ɔːdɪəns] *n* (*people*) pubblico; spettatori *mpl*; ascoltatori *mpl*; (*interview*) udienza
audio-typist ['ɔːdɪəʊ'taɪpɪst] *n* dattilografo/a che trascrive da nastro
audio-visual [ɔːdɪəʊ'vɪzjuəl] *adj* audiovisivo(a); **~ aid** *n* sussidio audiovisivo
audit ['ɔːdɪt] *vt* rivedere, verificare
audition [ɔː'dɪʃən] *n* audizione *f*
auditor ['ɔːdɪtə*] *n* revisore *m*
augment [ɔːg'mɛnt] *vt*, *vi* aumentare
augur ['ɔːgə*] *vi*: **it ~s well** promette bene
August ['ɔːgəst] *n* agosto
aunt [ɑːnt] *n* zia; **~ie**, **~y** *n* zietta; **~y** *n* zietta
au pair ['əʊ'pɛə*] *n* (*also*: **~ girl**) (ragazza *f*) alla pari *inv*
auspicious [ɔːs'pɪʃəs] *adj* propizio(a)
Australia [ɒs'treɪlɪə] *n* Australia; **~n** *adj*, *n* australiano(a)
Austria ['ɒstrɪə] *n* Austria; **~n** *adj*, *n* austriaco(a)
authentic [ɔː'θɛntɪk] *adj* autentico(a)
author ['ɔːθə*] *n* autore/trice
authoritarian [ɔːθɔrɪ'tɛərɪən] *adj* autoritario(a)
authoritative [ɔː'θɔrɪtətɪv] *adj* (*account etc*) autorevole; (*manner*) autoritario(a)
authority [ɔː'θɔrɪtɪ] *n* autorità *f inv*; (*permission*) autorizzazione *f*; **the authorities** *npl* (*government etc*) le autorità
authorize ['ɔːθəraɪz] *vt* autorizzare
auto ['ɔːtəʊ] *n* (*US*) auto *f inv*
autobiography [ɔːtəbaɪ'ɒgrəfɪ] *n* autobiografia

autograph ['ɔ:təgrɑ:f] n autografo ♦ vt firmare

automatic [ɔ:tə'mætɪk] adj automatico(a) ♦ n (gun) arma automatica; (washing machine) lavatrice f automatica; (car) automobile f con cambio automatico; **~ally** adv automaticamente

automation [ɔ:tə'meɪʃən] n automazione f

automobile ['ɔ:təməbi:l] (US) n automobile f

autonomy [ɔ:'tɒnəmi] n autonomia

autumn ['ɔ:təm] n autunno

auxiliary [ɔ:g'zɪlɪərɪ] adj ausiliario(a) ♦ n ausiliare m/f

Av. abbr = **avenue**

avail [ə'veɪl] vt: **to ~ o.s. of** servirsi di; approfittarsi di ♦ n: **to no ~** inutilmente

available [ə'veɪləbl] adj disponibile

avalanche ['ævəlɑ:nʃ] n valanga

avant-garde ['ævɑ̃'gɑ:d] adj d'avanguardia

Ave. abbr = **avenue**

avenge [ə'vendʒ] vt vendicare

avenue ['ævənju:] n viale m; (fig) strada, via

average ['ævərɪdʒ] n media ♦ adj medio(a) ♦ vt (a certain figure) fare di or in media; **on ~ in** media; **~ out** vi: **to ~ out at** aggirarsi in media su, essere in media di

averse [ə'vɜ:s] adj: **to be ~ to sth/doing** essere contrario a qc/a fare

avert [ə'vɜ:t] vt evitare, prevenire; (one's eyes) distogliere

aviary ['eɪvɪərɪ] n voliera, uccelliera

avid ['ævɪd] adj (supporter etc) accanito(a)

avocado [ævə'kɑ:dəu] n (also: BRIT: ~ pear) avocado m inv

avoid [ə'vɔɪd] vt evitare

await [ə'weɪt] vt aspettare

awake [ə'weɪk] (pt **awoke**, pp **awoken**, **awaked**) adj sveglio(a) ♦ vt svegliare ♦ vi svegliarsi; **~ning** [ə'weɪknɪŋ] n risveglio

award [ə'wɔ:d] n premio; (LAW) risarcimento ♦ vt assegnare; (LAW: damages) accordare

aware [ə'wɛə*] adj: **~ of** (conscious) conscio(a) di; (informed) informato(a) di; **to become ~ of** accorgersi di; **~ness** n consapevolezza

away [ə'weɪ] adj, adv via; lontano(a); **two kilometres ~** a due chilometri di distanza; **two hours ~ by car** a due ore di distanza in macchina; **the holiday was two weeks ~** mancavano due settimane alle vacanze; **he's ~ for a week** è andato via per una settimana; **to take ~** togliere; **he was working/pedalling etc ~** la particella indica la continuità e l'energia dell'azione: lavorava/pedalava etc più che poteva; **to fade/wither etc ~** la particella rinforza l'idea della diminuzione; **~ game** n (SPORT) partita fuori casa

awe [ɔ:] n timore m; **~-inspiring** imponente; **~some** adj imponente

awful ['ɔ:fəl] adj terribile; **an ~ lot of** un mucchio di; **~ly** adv (very) terribilmente

awkward ['ɔ:kwəd] adj (clumsy) goffo(a); (inconvenient) scomodo(a); (embarrassing) imbarazzante

awning ['ɔ:nɪŋ] n (of shop, hotel etc) tenda

awoke [ə'wəuk] pt of **awake**

awoken [ə'wəukn] pp of **awake**

awry [ə'raɪ] adv di traverso

axe [æks] (US **ax**) n scure f ♦ vt (project etc) abolire; (jobs) sopprimere

axes ['æksi:z] npl of **axis**

axis ['æksɪs] (pl **axes**) n asse m

axle ['æksl] n (also: ~-tree) asse m

ay(e) [aɪ] excl (yes) sì

B, b

B [bi:] n (MUS) si m; (letter) B, b f or m inv; **~-road** n (BRIT: AUT) strada secondaria

B.A. n abbr = **Bachelor of Arts**

baby ['beɪbɪ] n bambino/a; **~ carriage** (US) n carrozzina; **~ food** n omogeneizzati mpl; **~-sit** vi fare il (or la) baby-sitter; **~-sitter** n baby-sitter m/f inv; **~-sitting** n: **to go ~-sitting** fare il (or la) baby-sitter; **~ wipe** n salvietta umidificata

bachelor ['bætʃələ*] n scapolo; **B~ of Arts/Science** ≈ laureato/a in lettere/scienze

back [bæk] n (of person, horse) dorso, schiena; (as opposed to front) dietro; (of hand) dorso; (of train) coda; (of chair) schienale m; (of page) rovescio; (of book) retro; (FOOTBALL) difensore m ♦ vt (candidate: also: ~ up) appoggiare; (horse: at races) puntare su; (car) guidare a marcia indietro ♦ vi indietreggiare; (car etc) fare marcia indietro ♦ cpd posteriore, di dietro; (AUT: seat, wheels) posteriore ♦ adv (not forward) indietro; (returned): **he's ~** è tornato; **he ran ~** tornò indietro di corsa; (restitution): **throw the ball ~** ritira la palla; **can I have it ~?** posso riaverlo?; (again): **he called ~** ha richiamato; **~ down** vi fare marcia indietro; **~ out** vi (of promise) tirarsi indietro; **~ up** vt (support) appoggiare, sostenere; (COMPUT) fare una copia di riserva di; **~bencher** (BRIT) n membro del Parlamento senza potere amministrativo; **~bone** n spina dorsale; **~date** vt (letter) retrodatare; **~dated pay rise** aumento retroattivo; **~fire** vi (AUT) dar ritorni di fiamma; (plans) fallire; **~ground** n sfondo; (of events) background m inv; (basic knowledge) base f; (experience) esperienza; **family ~ground** ambiente m familiare; **~hand** n (TENNIS: also: ~hand stroke) rovescio; **~handed** adj (fig) ambiguo(a); **~hander** (BRIT) n (bribe) bustarella; **~ing** n (fig) appoggio; **~lash** n contraccolpo, ripercussione f; **~log** n: **~log of work** lavoro arretrato; **~ number** n (of magazine etc) numero arretrato; **~pack** n zaino; **~packer** n chi viaggia con zaino e sacco a pelo; **~ pay** n arretrato di paga; **~ payments** npl arretrati mpl; **~side** (inf) n sedere m; **~stage** adv nel retroscena; **~stroke** n nuoto sul dorso; **~up** adj (train, plane) supplementare; (COMPUT) di riserva ♦ n (support) appoggio, sostegno; (also: ~up file) file m inv di riserva; **~ward** adj (movement) indietro inv; (person) tardivo(a); (country) arretrato(a); **~wards** adv indietro; (fall, walk) all'indietro; **~yard** n cortile m dietro la casa

bacon ['beɪkən] n pancetta

bad [bæd] adj cattivo(a); (accident, injury) brutto(a); (meat, food) andato(a) a male; **his ~ leg** la sua gamba malata; **to go ~** andare a male

badge [bædʒ] n insegna; (of policeman) stemma m

badger ['bædʒə*] n tasso

badly ['bædlɪ] adv (work, dress etc) male; **~ wounded** gravemente ferito; **he needs it ~** ne ha un gran bisogno; **~ off** adj povero(a)

badminton ['bædmɪntən] n badminton m

bad-tempered ['bæd'tempəd] adj irritabile; di malumore

baffle ['bæfl] vt (puzzle) confondere

bag [bæg] n sacco; (handbag etc) borsa; **~s of** (inf: lots of) un sacco di; **~gage** n bagagli mpl; **~gage allowance** n franchigia f bagaglio inv; **~gage reclaim** n ritiro m bagaglio inv; **~gy** adj largo(a), sformato(a); **~pipes** npl cornamusa

bail [beɪl] n cauzione f ♦ vt (prisoner: also: grant ~ to) concedere la libertà provvisoria su cauzione a; (boat: also: ~ out) aggottare; **on ~** in libertà provvisoria su cauzione; **~ out** vt (prisoner) ottenere la libertà provvisoria su cauzione di; see also **bale**

bailiff ['beɪlɪf] n (LAW: BRIT) ufficiale m giudiziario; (: US) usciere m

bait [beɪt] n esca ♦ vt (hook) innescare; (trap) munire di esca; (fig) tormentare

bake [beɪk] vt cuocere al forno ♦ vi cuocersi al forno; **~d beans** npl fagioli mpl in salsa di pomodoro; **~d potato** npl patata cotta al forno con la buccia; **~r** n fornaio/a, panettiere/a; **~ry** n panetteria; **baking** n cottura (al forno); **baking powder** n lievito in polvere

balance ['bæləns] n equilibrio; (COMM: sum) bilancio; (remainder) resto; (scales) bilancia ♦ vt tenere in equilibrio; (budget) far quadrare; (account) pareggiare; (compensate) contrappesare; **~ of trade/payments** bilancia commerciale/dei pagamenti; **~d** adj

(personality, diet) equilibrato(a); **~ sheet** n bilancio

balcony ['bælkənɪ] n balcone m; (in theatre) balconata

bald [bɔːld] adj calvo(a); (tyre) liscio(a)

bale [beɪl] n balla; **~ out** vi (of a plane) gettarsi col paracadute

ball [bɔːl] n palla; (football) pallone m; (for golf) pallina; (of wool, string) gomitolo; (dance) ballo; **to play ~** (fig) stare al gioco

ballast ['bæləst] n zavorra

ball bearings npl cuscinetti a sfere

ballerina [bælə'riːnə] n ballerina

ballet ['bæleɪ] n balletto; **~ dancer** n ballerino(a) classico(a)

balloon [bə'luːn] n pallone m

ballot paper ['bælət-] n scheda

ball-point pen ['bɔːlpɔɪnt-] n penna a sfera

ballroom ['bɔːlrum] n sala da ballo

balm [bɑːm] n balsamo

ban [bæn] n interdizione f ♦ vt interdire

banana [bə'nɑːnə] n banana

band [bænd] n insegna; (at a dance) orchestra; (MIL) fanfara; **~ together** vi collegarsi

bandage ['bændɪdʒ] n benda, fascia

Bandaid ® ['bændeɪd] (US) n cerotto

bandy-legged ['bændɪ'legɪd] adj dalle gambe storte

bang [bæŋ] n (of door) lo sbattere; (of gun, blow) colpo ♦ vt battere (violentemente); (door) sbattere ♦ vi scoppiare; sbattere

Bangladesh [bɑːŋglə'deʃ] n Bangladesh m

bangle ['bæŋgl] n braccialetto

bangs [bæŋz] (US) npl (fringe) frangia, frangetta

banish ['bænɪʃ] vt bandire

banister(s) ['bænɪstə(z)] n(pl) ringhiera

bank [bæŋk] n banca, banco; (of river, lake) riva, sponda; (of earth) banco ♦ vi (AVIAT) inclinarsi in virata; **~ on** vt fus contare su; **~ account** n conto in banca; **~ card** n carta f assegni inv; **~er** n banchiere m; **~er's card** (BRIT) n = **bank card**; **B~ holiday** (BRIT) n giorno di festa; **~ing** n attività bancaria; professione f di banchiere; **~note** n banconota; **~ rate** n tasso bancario

bankrupt ['bæŋkrʌpt] adj fallito(a); **to go ~** fallire; **~cy** n fallimento

bank statement n estratto conto

banner ['bænə*] n striscione m

baptism ['bæptɪzəm] n battesimo

bar [bɑː*] n (place) bar m inv; (counter) banco; (rod) barra; (of window etc) sbarra; (of chocolate) tavoletta; (fig) ostacolo; restrizione f; (MUS) battuta ♦ vt (road, window) sbarrare; (person) escludere; (activity) interdire; **~ of soap** saponetta; **the B~** (LAW) l'Ordine m degli avvocati; **behind ~s** (prisoner) dietro le sbarre; **~ none** senza eccezione

barbaric [bɑːˈbærɪk] *adj* barbarico(a)

barbecue [ˈbɑːbɪkjuː] *n* barbecue *m inv*

barbed wire [ˈbɑːbd-] *n* filo spinato

barber [ˈbɑːbəˈ] *n* barbiere *m*

bar code *n* (*on goods*) codice *m* a barre

bare [bɛəˈ] *adj* nudo(a) ♦ *vt* scoprire,
denudare; (*teeth*) mostrare; **the ~ necessities**
lo stretto necessario; **~back** *adv* senza sella;
~faced *adj* sfacciato(a); **~foot** *adj, adv*
scalzo(a); **~ly** *adv* appena

bargain [ˈbɑːgɪn] *n* (*transaction*) contratto;
(*good buy*) affare *m* ♦ *vi* trattare; **into the ~**
per giunta; **~ for** *vt fus*: **he got more than he
~ed for** gli è andata peggio di quel che si
aspettasse

barge [bɑːdʒ] *n* chiatta; **~ in** *vi* (*walk in*)
piombare dentro; (*interrupt talk*)
intromettersi a sproposito

bark [bɑːk] *n* (*of tree*) corteccia; (*of dog*)
abbaio ♦ *vi* abbaiare

barley [ˈbɑːlɪ] *n* orzo

barmaid [ˈbɑːmeɪd] *n* cameriera al banco

barman [ˈbɑːmən] *n* barista *m*

bar meal *n* spuntino servito al bar

barn [bɑːn] *n* granaio

barometer [bəˈrɒmɪtəˈ] *n* barometro

baron [ˈbærən] *n* barone *m*; **~ess** *n*
baronessa

barracks [ˈbærəks] *npl* caserma

barrage [ˈbærɑːʒ] *n* (*MIL, dam*) sbarramento;
(*fig*) fiume *m*

barrel [ˈbærəl] *n* barile *m*; (*of gun*) canna

barren [ˈbærən] *adj* sterile; (*soil*) arido(a)

barricade [bærɪˈkeɪd] *n* barricata

barrier [ˈbærɪəˈ] *n* barriera

barring [ˈbɑːrɪŋ] *prep* salvo

barrister [ˈbærɪstəˈ] (*BRIT*) *n* avvocato/essa
(*con diritto di parlare davanti a tutte le corti*)

barrow [ˈbærəu] *n* (*cart*) carriola

bartender [ˈbɑːtendəˈ] (*US*) *n* barista *m*

barter [ˈbɑːtəˈ] *vt*: **to ~ sth for** barattare qc
con

base [beɪs] *n* base *f* ♦ *vt*: **to ~ sth on** basare
qc su ♦ *adj* vile

baseball [ˈbeɪsbɔːl] *n* baseball *m*

basement [ˈbeɪsmənt] *n* seminterrato; (*of
shop*) interrato

bases¹ [ˈbeɪsiːz] *npl of* **basis**

bases² [ˈbeɪsɪz] *npl of* **base**

bash [bæʃ] (*inf*) *vt* picchiare

bashful [ˈbæʃful] *adj* timido(a)

basic [ˈbeɪsɪk] *adj* rudimentale; essenziale;
~ally [-lɪ] *adv* fondamentalmente;
sostanzialmente; **~s** *npl*: **the ~s** l'essenziale *m*

basil [ˈbæzl] *n* basilico

basin [ˈbeɪsn] *n* (*vessel, also GEO*) bacino;
(*also:* **wash~**) lavabo

basis [ˈbeɪsɪs] (*pl* **bases**) *n* base *f*; **on a part-**

time ~ part-time; **on a trial ~** in prova

bask [bɑːsk] *vi*: **to ~ in the sun** crogiolarsi al
sole

basket [ˈbɑːskɪt] *n* cesta; (*smaller*) cestino;
(*with handle*) paniere *m*; **~ball** *n* pallacanestro *f*

bass [beɪs] *n* (*MUS*) basso

bassoon [bəˈsuːn] *n* fagotto

bastard [ˈbɑːstəd] *n* bastardo/a; (*inf!*) stronzo
(!)

bat [bæt] *n* pipistrello; (*for baseball etc*)
mazza; (*BRIT: for table tennis*) racchetta ♦ *vt*:
he didn't ~ an eyelid non battè ciglio

batch [bætʃ] *n* (*of bread*) infornata; (*of
papers*) cumulo

bated [ˈbeɪtɪd] *adj*: **with ~ breath** col fiato
sospeso

bath [bɑːθ] *n* bagno; (*bathtub*) vasca da
bagno ♦ *vt* far fare il bagno a; **to have a ~**
fare un bagno; *see also* **baths**

bathe [beɪð] *vi* fare il bagno ♦ *vt* (*wound*)
lavare; **~r** *n* bagnante *m/f*

bathing [ˈbeɪðɪŋ] *n* bagni *mpl*; **~ costume**
(*US* **~ suit**) *n* costume *m* da bagno

bathrobe [ˈbɑːθrəub] *n* accappatoio

bathroom [ˈbɑːθrum] *n* stanza da bagno

baths [bɑːðz] *npl* bagni *mpl* pubblici

bath towel *n* asciugamano da bagno

baton [ˈbætən] *n* (*MUS*) bacchetta; (*ATHLETICS*)
testimone *m*; (*club*) manganello

batter [ˈbætəˈ] *vt* battere ♦ *n* pastetta; **~ed**
adj (*hat*) sformato(a); (*pan*) ammaccato(a)

battery [ˈbætərɪ] *n* batteria; (*of torch*) pila;
~ farming *n* allevamento in batteria

battle [ˈbætl] *n* battaglia ♦ *vi* battagliare,
lottare; **~field** *n* campo di battaglia; **~ship** *n*
nave *f* da guerra

bawl [bɔːl] *vi* urlare

bay [beɪ] *n* (*of sea*) baia; **to hold sb at ~** tenere
qn a bada; **~ leaf** *n* foglia d'alloro; **~
window** *n* bovindo

bazaar [bəˈzɑːˈ] *n* bazar *m inv*; vendita di
beneficenza

B. & B. *abbr* = **bed and breakfast**

BBC *n abbr* (= *British Broadcasting
Corporation*) rete nazionale di radiotelevisione
in Gran Bretagna

B.C. *adv abbr* (= *before Christ*) a.C.

KEYWORD

be [biː] (*pt* **was, were**, *pp* **been**) *aux vb* **1** (*with
present participle: forming continuous tenses*):
what are you doing? che fa?, che stai
facendo?; **they're coming tomorrow** vengono
domani; **I've been waiting for her for hours**
sono ore che l'aspetto

2 (*with pp: forming passives*) essere; **to
~ killed** essere *or* venire ucciso(a); **the box
had been opened** la scatola era stata aperta;

the thief was nowhere to ~ **seen** il ladro non si trovava da nessuna parte

3 (*in tag questions*): **it was fun, wasn't it?** è stato divertente, no?; **he's good-looking, isn't he?** è un bell'uomo, vero?; **she's back, is she?** così è tornata, eh?

4 (+ *to* + *infinitive*): **the house is to ~ sold** abbiamo (*or* hanno *etc*) intenzione di vendere casa; **you're to ~ congratulated for all your work** dovremo farvi i complimenti per tutto il vostro lavoro; **he's not to open it** non deve aprirlo

♦ *vb* + *complement* **1** (*gen*) essere; **I'm English** sono inglese; **I'm tired** sono stanco(a); **I'm hot/cold** ho caldo/freddo; **he's a doctor** è medico; **2 and 2 are 4** 2 più 2 fa 4; **~ careful!** sta attento(a)!; **~ good** sii buono(a) **2** (*of health*) stare; **how are you?** come sta?; **he's very ill** sta molto male

3 (*of age*): **how old are you?** quanti anni hai?; **I'm sixteen (years) old** ho sedici anni **4** (*cost*) costare; **how much was the meal?** quant'era *or* quanto costava il pranzo?; **that'll ~ £5, please** (fa) 5 sterline, per favore

♦ *vi* **1** (*exist, occur etc*) essere, esistere; **the best singer that ever was** il migliore cantante mai esistito *or* di tutti i tempi; **~ that as it may** comunque sia, sia come sia; **so ~ it** sia pure, e sia

2 (*referring to place*) essere, trovarsi; **I won't ~ here tomorrow** non ci sarò domani; **Edinburgh is in Scotland** Edimburgo si trova in Scozia

3 (*referring to movement*): **where have you been?** dov'è stato?; **I've been to China** sono stato in Cina

♦ *impers vb* **1** (*referring to time, distance*) essere; **it's 5 o'clock** sono le 5; **it's the 28th of April** è il 28 aprile; **it's 10 km to the village** di qui al paese sono 10 km

2 (*referring to the weather*) fare; **it's too hot/cold** fa troppo caldo/freddo; **it's windy** c'è vento

3 (*emphatic*): **it's me** sono io; **it was Maria who paid the bill** è stata Maria che ha pagato il conto

beach [biːtʃ] *n* spiaggia ♦ *vt* tirare in secco

beacon ['biːkən] *n* (*lighthouse*) faro; (*marker*) segnale *m*

bead [biːd] *n* perlina

beak [biːk] *n* becco

beaker ['biːkə*] *n* coppa

beam [biːm] *n* trave *f*; (*of light*) raggio ♦ *vi* brillare

bean [biːn] *n* fagiolo; (*of coffee*) chicco; **runner ~** fagiolino; **broad ~** fava; **~sprouts** *npl* germogli *mpl* di soia

bear [bɛə*] (*pt* **bore**, *pp* **borne**) *n* orso ♦ *vt*

portare; (*endure*) sopportare; (*produce*) generare ♦ *vi*: **to ~ right/left** piegare a destra/sinistra; **~ out** *vt* (*suspicions*) confermare, convalidare; (*person*) dare il proprio appoggio a; **~ up** *vi* (*person*) fare buon viso a cattiva sorte

beard [bɪəd] *n* barba

bearer ['bɛərə*] *n* portatore *m*

bearing ['bɛərɪŋ] *n* portamento; (*connection*) rapporto; **~s** *npl* (*also*: **ball ~s**) cuscinetti *mpl* a sfere; **to take a ~** fare un rilevamento; **to find one's ~s** orientarsi

beast [biːst] *n* bestia; **~ly** *adj* meschino(a); (*weather*) da cani

beat [biːt] (*pt* **beat**, *pp* **beaten**) *n* colpo; (*of heart*) battito; (*MUS*) tempo; battuta; (*of policeman*) giro ♦ *vt* battere; (*eggs, cream*) sbattere ♦ *vi* battere; **off the ~en track** fuori mano; **~ it!** (*inf*) fila!, fuori dai piedi!; **~ off** *vt* respingere; **~ up** *vt* (*person*) picchiare; (*eggs*) sbattere; **beaten** *pp* of **beat**; **~ing** *n* bastonata

beautiful ['bjuːtɪful] *adj* bello(a); **~ly** *adv* splendidamente

beauty ['bjuːtɪ] *n* bellezza; **~ salon** *n* istituto di bellezza; **~ spot** *n* (*BRIT*) *n* (*TOURISM*) luogo pittoresco

beaver ['biːvə*] *n* castoro

became [bɪ'keɪm] *pt* of **become**

because [bɪ'kɔz] *conj* perché; **~ of** a causa di

beckon ['bɛkən] *vt* (*also*: **~ to**) chiamare con un cenno

become [bɪ'kʌm] (*irreg*: *like* **come**) *vt* diventare; **to ~ fat/thin** ingrassarsi/dimagrire

becoming [bɪ'kʌmɪŋ] *adj* (*behaviour*) che si conviene; (*clothes*) grazioso(a)

bed [bɛd] *n* letto; (*of flowers*) aiuola; (*of coal, clay*) strato; **single/double ~** letto a una piazza/a due piazze *or* matrimoniale; **~ and breakfast** *n* (*place*) ≈ pensione *f* familiare; (*terms*) camera con colazione; **~clothes** ['bɛdkləuðz] *npl* biancheria e coperte *fpl* da letto; **~ding** *n* coperte e lenzuola *fpl*

bed linen *n* biancheria da letto

bedraggled [bɪ'dræɡld] *adj* fradicio(a)

bed: ~ridden *adj* costretto(a) a letto; **~room** *n* camera da letto; **~side** *n*: **at sb's ~side** al capezzale di qn; **~sit(ter)** (*BRIT*) *n* monolocale *m*; **~spread** *n* copriletto; **~time** *n*: **it's ~time** è ora di andare a letto

bee [biː] *n* ape *f*

beech [biːtʃ] *n* faggio

beef [biːf] *n* manzo; **roast ~** arrosto di manzo; **~burger** *n* hamburger *m inv*; **B~eater** *n* guardia della Torre di Londra

beehive ['biːhaɪv] *n* alveare *m*

beeline ['biːlaɪn] *n*: **to make a ~ for** buttarsi a capo fitto verso

been [biːn] *pp* of **be**

beer [bɪə*] n birra
beetle ['biːtl] n scarafaggio; coleottero
beetroot ['biːtruːt] (BRIT) n barbabietola
before [bɪ'fɔː*] prep (in time) prima di; (in space) davanti a ♦ conj prima che + sub; prima di ♦ adv prima; ~ going prima di andare; ~ she goes prima che vada; the week ~ la settimana prima; I've seen it ~ l'ho già visto; I've never seen it ~ è la prima volta che lo vedo; ~hand adv in anticipo
beg [bɛg] vi chiedere l'elemosina ♦ vt (also: ~ for) chiedere in elemosina; (: favour) chiedere; to ~ sb to do pregare qn di fare
began [bɪ'gæn] pt of begin
beggar ['bɛgə*] n mendicante m/f
begin [bɪ'gɪn] (pt began, pp begun) vt, vi cominciare; to ~ doing or to do sth incominciare or iniziare a fare qc; ~ner n principiante m/f; ~ning n inizio, principio
begun [bɪ'gʌn] pp of begin
behalf [bɪ'hɑːf] n: on ~ of per conto di; a nome di
behave [bɪ'heɪv] vi comportarsi; (well: also: ~ o.s.) comportarsi bene
behaviour [bɪ'heɪvjə*] (US behavior) n comportamento, condotta
behind [bɪ'haɪnd] prep dietro; (followed by pronoun) dietro a; (time) in ritardo con ♦ adv dietro; (leave, stay) indietro ♦ n didietro; to be ~ (schedule) essere in ritardo rispetto al programma; ~ the scenes (fig) dietro le quinte
behold [bɪ'həʊld] (irreg: like hold) vt vedere, scorgere
beige [beɪʒ] adj beige inv
Beijing ['beɪ'dʒɪŋ] n Pechino f
being ['biːɪŋ] n essere m
Beirut [beɪ'ruːt] n Beirut f
Belarus [bɛlə'ruːs] n Bielorussia
belated [bɪ'leɪtɪd] adj tardo(a)
belch [bɛltʃ] vi ruttare ♦ vt (gen: ~ out: smoke etc) eruttare
Belgian ['bɛldʒən] adj, n belga m/f
Belgium ['bɛldʒəm] n Belgio
belie [bɪ'laɪ] vt smentire
belief [bɪ'liːf] n (opinion) opinione f, convinzione f; (trust, faith) fede f
believe [bɪ'liːv] vt, vi credere; to ~ in (God) credere in; (ghosts) credere a; (method) avere fiducia in; ~r n (REL) credente m/f; (in idea, activity): to be a ~r in credere in
belittle [bɪ'lɪtl] vt sminuire
bell [bɛl] n campana; (small, on door, electric) campanello
belligerent [bɪ'lɪdʒərənt] adj bellicoso(a)
bellow ['bɛləʊ] vi muggire
bellows ['bɛləʊz] npl soffietto
belly ['bɛlɪ] n pancia
belong [bɪ'lɒŋ] vi: to ~ to appartenere a;

(club etc) essere socio di; this book ~s here questo libro va qui; ~ings npl cose fpl, roba
beloved [bɪ'lʌvɪd] adj adorato(a)
below [bɪ'ləʊ] prep sotto, al di sotto di ♦ adv sotto, di sotto; giù; see ~ vedi sotto or oltre
belt [bɛlt] n cintura; (TECH) cinghia ♦ vt (thrash) picchiare ♦ vi (inf) filarsela; ~way (US) n (AUT: ring road) circonvallazione f; (: motorway) autostrada
bemused [bɪ'mjuːzd] adj perplesso(a), stupito(a)
bench [bɛntʃ] n panca; (in workshop, POL) banco; the B~ (LAW) la Corte
bend [bɛnd] (pt, pp bent) vt curvare; (leg, arm) piegare ♦ vi curvarsi; piegarsi ♦ n (BRIT: in road) curva; (in pipe, river) gomito; ~ down vi chinarsi; ~ over vi piegarsi
beneath [bɪ'niːθ] prep sotto, al di sotto di; (unworthy of) indegno(a) di ♦ adv sotto, di sotto
benefactor ['bɛnɪfæktə*] n benefattore m
beneficial [bɛnɪ'fɪʃəl] adj che fa bene; vantaggioso(a)
benefit ['bɛnɪfɪt] n beneficio, vantaggio; (allowance of money) indennità f inv ♦ vt far bene a ♦ vi: he'll ~ from it ne trarrà beneficio or profitto
benevolent [bɪ'nɛvələnt] adj benevolo(a)
benign [bɪ'naɪn] adj (person, smile) benevolo(a); (MED) benigno(a)
bent [bɛnt] pt, pp of bend ♦ n inclinazione f ♦ adj (inf: dishonest) losco(a); to be ~ on essere deciso(a) a
bequest [bɪ'kwɛst] n lascito
bereaved [bɪ'riːvd] n: the ~ i familiari in lutto
beret ['bɛreɪ] n berretto
Berlin [bə:'lɪn] n Berlino f
berm [bə:m] (US) n (AUT) corsia d'emergenza
berry ['bɛrɪ] n bacca
berserk [bə'sə:k] adj: to go ~ montare su tutte le furie
berth [bə:θ] n (bed) cuccetta; (for ship) ormeggio ♦ vi (in harbour) entrare in porto; (at anchor) gettare l'ancora
beseech [bɪ'siːtʃ] (pt, pp besought) vt implorare
beset [bɪ'sɛt] (pt, pp beset) vt assalire
beside [bɪ'saɪd] prep accanto a; to be ~ o.s. (with anger) essere fuori di sé (dalla rabbia); that's ~ the point non c'entra
besides [bɪ'saɪdz] adv inoltre, per di più ♦ prep oltre a; a parte
besiege [bɪ'siːdʒ] vt (town) assediare; (fig) tempestare
best [bɛst] adj migliore ♦ adv meglio; the ~ part of (quantity) la maggior parte di; at ~ tutt'al più; to make the ~ of sth cavare il meglio possibile da qc; to do one's ~ fare del proprio meglio; to the ~ of my knowledge per

quel che ne so; **to the ~ of my ability** al massimo delle mie capacità; **~-before date** n scadenza; **~ man** n testimone m dello sposo

bestow [bɪ'stəu] vt accordare; (title) conferire

bet [bɛt] (pt, pp **bet** or **betted**) n scommessa ♦ vt, vi scommettere; **to ~ sb sth** scommettere qc con qn

betray [bɪ'treɪ] vt tradire; **~al** n tradimento

better ['bɛtə*] adj migliore ♦ adv meglio ♦ vt migliorare ♦ n: **to get the ~ of** avere la meglio su; **you had ~ do it** è meglio che lo faccia; **he thought ~ of it** cambiò idea; **to get ~** migliorare; **~ off** adj più ricco(a); (fig): **you'd be ~ off this way** starebbe meglio così

betting ['bɛtɪŋ] n scommesse fpl; **~ shop** (BRIT) n ufficio dell'allibratore

between [bɪ'twiːn] prep tra ♦ adv in mezzo, nel mezzo

beverage ['bɛvərɪdʒ] n bevanda

beware [bɪ'wɛə*] vt, vi: **to ~ (of)** stare attento(a) (a); **"~ of the dog"** "attenti al cane"

bewildered [bɪ'wɪldəd] adj sconcertato(a), confuso(a)

beyond [bɪ'jɔnd] prep (in space) oltre; (exceeding) al di sopra di ♦ adv di là; **~ doubt** senza dubbio; **~ repair** irreparabile

bias ['baɪəs] n (prejudice) pregiudizio; (preference) preferenza; **~(s)ed** adj parziale

bib [bɪb] n bavaglino

Bible ['baɪbl] n Bibbia

bicarbonate of soda [baɪ'kɑːbənɪt-] n bicarbonato (di sodio)

bicker ['bɪkə*] vi bisticciare

bicycle ['baɪsɪkl] n bicicletta

bid [bɪd] (pt **bade** or **bid**, pp **bidden** or **bid**) n offerta; (attempt) tentativo ♦ vi fare un'offerta ♦ vt fare un'offerta di; **to ~ sb good day** dire buon giorno a qn; **bidden** pp of bid; **~der** n: **the highest ~der** il maggior offerente; **~ding** n offerte fpl

bide [baɪd] vt: **to ~ one's time** aspettare il momento giusto

bifocals [baɪ'fəuklz] npl occhiali mpl bifocali

big [bɪg] adj grande; grosso(a)

big dipper [-'dɪpə*] n montagne fpl russe, otto m inv volante

bigheaded ['bɪg'hɛdɪd] adj presuntuoso(a)

bigot ['bɪgət] n persona gretta; **~ed** adj gretto(a); **~ry** n grettezza

big top n tendone m del circo

bike [baɪk] n bici f inv

bikini [bɪ'kiːnɪ] n bikini m inv

bilingual [baɪ'lɪŋgwəl] adj bilingue

bill [bɪl] n conto; (POL) atto; (US: banknote) banconota; (of bird) becco; (of show) locandina; **"post no ~s"** "divieto di affissione"; **to fit** or **fill the ~** (fig) fare al caso;

~board n tabellone m

billet ['bɪlɪt] n alloggio

billfold ['bɪlfəuld] (US) n portafoglio

billiards ['bɪljədz] n biliardo

billion ['bɪljən] n (BRIT) bilione m; (US) miliardo

bimbo ['bɪmbəu] n (pej, col) pollastrella, svampitella

bin [bɪn] n (for coal, rubbish) bidone m; (for bread) cassetta; (dust~) pattumiera; (litter ~) cestino

bind [baɪnd] (pt, pp **bound**) vt legare; (oblige) obbligare ♦ n (inf) scocciatura; **~ing** adj (contract) vincolante

binge [bɪndʒ] (inf) n: **to go on a ~** fare baldoria

bingo ['bɪŋgəu] n gioco simile alla tombola

binoculars [bɪ'nɔkjuləz] npl binocolo

bio... [baɪə'...] prefix: **~chemistry** n biochimica; **~degradable** adj biodegradabile; **~graphy** [baɪ'ɔgrəfɪ] n biografia; **~logical** adj biologico(a); **~logy** [baɪ'ɔlədʒɪ] n biologia

birch [bəːtʃ] n betulla

bird [bəːd] n uccello; (BRIT: inf: girl) bambola; **~'s eye view** n vista panoramica; **~ watcher** n ornitologo/a dilettante

Biro ® ['baɪrəu] n biro ® f inv

birth [bəːθ] n nascita; **to give ~ to** partorire; **~ certificate** n certificato di nascita; **~ control** n controllo delle nascite; contraccezione f; **~day** n compleanno ♦ cpd di compleanno; **~ rate** n indice m di natalità

biscuit ['bɪskɪt] (BRIT) n biscotto

bisect [baɪ'sɛkt] vt tagliare in due (parti)

bishop ['bɪʃəp] n vescovo

bit [bɪt] pt of bite ♦ n pezzo; (COMPUT) bit m inv; (of horse) morso; **a ~ of** un po' di; **a ~ mad** un po' matto; **~ by ~** a poco a poco

bitch [bɪtʃ] n (dog) cagna; (inf!) vacca

bite [baɪt] (pt **bit**, pp **bitten**) vt, vi mordere; (subj: insect) pungere ♦ n morso; (insect ~) puntura; (mouthful) boccone m; **let's have a ~ (to eat)** mangiamo un boccone; **to ~ one's nails** mangiarsi le unghie; **bitten** ['bɪtn] pp of bite

bitter ['bɪtə*] adj amaro(a); (wind, criticism) pungente ♦ n (BRIT: beer) birra amara; **~ness** n amarezza; gusto amaro

black [blæk] adj nero(a) ♦ n nero; (person): **B~** negro/a ♦ vt (BRIT: INDUSTRY) boicottare; **to give sb a ~ eye** fare un occhio nero a qn; **in the ~** (bank account) in attivo; **~ and blue** adj tutto(a) pesto(a); **~berry** n mora; **~bird** n merlo; **~board** n lavagna; **~ coffee** n caffè m inv nero; **~currant** n ribes m inv; **~en** vt annerire; **~ ice** n strato trasparente di ghiaccio; **~leg** (BRIT) n crumiro; **~list** n lista nera; **~mail** n ricatto ♦ vt ricattare;

~ **market** n mercato nero; **~out** n oscuramento; (TV, RADIO) interruzione f delle trasmissioni; (fainting) svenimento; **B~ Sea** n: **the B~ Sea** il Mar Nero; ~ **sheep** n pecora nera; **~smith** n fabbro ferraio; **~ spot** n (AUT) luogo famigerato per gli incidenti; (for unemployment etc) zona critica

bladder ['blædə*] n vescica

blade [bleɪd] n lama; (of oar) pala; ~ **of grass** filo d'erba

blame [bleɪm] n colpa ♦ vt: **to ~ sb/sth for sth** dare la colpa di qc a qn/qc; **who's to ~?** chi è colpevole?

bland [blænd] adj mite; (taste) blando(a)

blank [blæŋk] adj bianco(a); (look) distratto(a) ♦ n spazio vuoto; (cartridge) cartuccia a salve; ~ **cheque** n assegno in bianco

blanket ['blæŋkɪt] n coperta

blare [blɛa*] vi strombettare

blasphemy ['blæsfɪmɪ] n bestemmia

blast [blɑːst] n (of wind) raffica; (of bomb etc) esplosione f ♦ vt far saltare; **~-off** n (SPACE) lancio

blatant ['bleɪtənt] adj flagrante

blaze [bleɪz] n (fire) incendio; (fig) vampata; splendore m ♦ vi (fire) ardere, fiammeggiare; (guns) sparare senza sosta; (fig: eyes) ardere ♦ vt: **to ~ a trail** (fig) tracciare una via nuova; **in a ~ of publicity** circondato da grande pubblicità

blazer ['bleɪzə*] n blazer m inv

bleach [bliːtʃ] n (also: household ~) varechina ♦ vt (material) candeggiare; **~ed** adj (hair) decolorato(a); **~ers** (US) npl (SPORT) posti mpl di gradinata

bleak [bliːk] adj tetro(a)

bleat [bliːt] vi belare

bled [blɛd] pt, pp of **bleed**

bleed [bliːd] (pt, pp **bled**) vi sanguinare; **my nose is ~ing** mi viene fuori sangue dal naso

bleeper ['bliːpə*] n (device) cicalino

blemish ['blɛmɪʃ] n macchia

blend [blɛnd] n miscela ♦ vt mescolare ♦ vi (colours etc: also: ~ **in**) armonizzare

bless [blɛs] (pt, pp **blessed** or **blest**) vt benedire; ~ **you!** (after sneeze) salute!; **~ing** n benedizione f; fortuna; **blest** [blɛst] pt, pp of **bless**

blew [bluː] pt of **blow**

blight [blaɪt] vt (hopes etc) deludere; (life) rovinare

blimey ['blaɪmɪ] (BRIT: inf) excl accidenti!

blind [blaɪnd] adj cieco(a) ♦ n (for window) avvolgibile m; (Venetian ~) veneziana ♦ vt accecare; **the ~** npl i ciechi; ~ **alley** n vicolo cieco; ~ **corner** n (BRIT) svolta cieca; **~fold** n benda ♦ adj, adv bendato(a) ♦ vt bendare gli occhi a; **~ly** adv ciecamente; **~ness** n cecità;

~ **spot** n (AUT etc) punto cieco; (fig) punto debole

blink [blɪŋk] vi battere gli occhi; (light) lampeggiare; **~ers** npl paraocchi mpl

bliss [blɪs] n estasi f

blister ['blɪstə*] n (on skin) vescica; (on paintwork) bolla ♦ vi (paint) coprirsi di bolle

blizzard ['blɪzəd] n bufera di neve

bloated ['bləutɪd] adj gonfio(a)

blob [blɔb] n (drop) goccia; (stain, spot) macchia

bloc [blɔk] n (POL) blocco

block [blɔk] n blocco; (in pipes) ingombro; (toy) cubo; (of buildings) isolato ♦ vt bloccare; **~ade** [-'keɪd] n blocco; **~age** n ostacolo; **~buster** n (film, book) grande successo; ~ **letters** npl stampatello; ~ **of flats** (BRIT) n caseggiato.

bloke [bləuk] (BRIT: inf) n tizio

blond(e) [blɔnd] adj, n biondo(a)

blood [blʌd] n sangue m; ~ **donor** n donatore/trice di sangue; ~ **group** n gruppo sanguigno; **~hound** n segugio; ~ **poisoning** n setticemia; ~ **pressure** n pressione f sanguigna; **~shed** n spargimento di sangue; **~shot** adj: **~shot eyes** occhi iniettati di sangue; **~stream** n flusso del sangue; ~ **test** n analisi f inv del sangue; **~thirsty** adj assetato(a) di sangue; **~y** adj (fight) sanguinoso(a); (nose) sanguinante; (BRIT: inf!): **this ~y ...** questo maledetto ...; **~y awful/good** (inf!) veramente terribile/forte; **~y-minded** (BRIT: inf) adj indisponente

bloom [bluːm] n fiore m ♦ vi (tree) essere in fiore; (flower) aprirsi

blossom ['blɔsəm] n fiore m; (with pl sense) fiori mpl ♦ vi essere in fiore

blot [blɔt] n macchia ♦ vt macchiare; ~ **out** vt (memories) cancellare; (view) nascondere

blotchy ['blɔtʃɪ] adj (complexion) coperto(a) di macchie

blotting paper ['blɔtɪŋ-] n carta assorbente

blouse [blauz] n (feminine garment) camicetta

blow [bləu] (pt **blew**, pp **blown**) n colpo ♦ vi soffiare ♦ vt (fuse) far saltare; (subj: wind) spingere; (instrument) suonare; **to ~ one's nose** soffiarsi il naso; **to ~ a whistle** fischiare; ~ **away** vt portare via; ~ **down** vt abbattere; ~ **off** vt far volare via; ~ **out** vi scoppiare; ~ **over** vi calmarsi; ~ **up** vi saltare in aria ♦ vt far saltare in aria; (tyre) gonfiare; (PHOT) ingrandire; **~-dry** n messa in piega a föhn; **~lamp** (BRIT) n lampada a benzina per saldare; **blown** pp of **blow**; **~-out** n (of tyre) scoppio; **~torch** n = **~lamp**

blue [bluː] adj azzurro(a); (depressed) giù inv; ~ **film/joke** film/ barzelletta pornografico(a); **out of the ~** (fig) all'improvviso; **~bell** n giacinto dei boschi; **~bottle** n moscone m;

~print n (fig): **~print (for)** formula (di)

bluff [blʌf] vi bluffare ♦ n bluff m inv ♦ adj (person) brusco(a); **to call sb's ~** mettere alla prova il bluff di qn

blunder ['blʌndə*] n abbaglio ♦ vi prendere un abbaglio

blunt [blʌnt] adj smussato(a); spuntato(a); (person) brusco(a)

blur [blə:*] n forma indistinta ♦ vt offuscare

blush [blʌʃ] vi arrossire ♦ n rossore m

blustering ['blʌstərɪŋ] adj infuriato(a)

blustery ['blʌstərɪ] adj (weather) burrascoso(a)

boar [bɔ:*] n cinghiale m

board [bɔ:d] n tavola; (on wall) tabellone m; (committee) consiglio, comitato; (in firm) consiglio d'amministrazione; (NAUT, AVIAT): **on ~ a bordo** ♦ vt (ship) salire a bordo di; (train) salire su; **full ~** (BRIT) pensione completa; **half ~** (BRIT) mezza pensione; **~ and lodging** vitto e alloggio; **which goes by the ~** (fig) che viene abbandonato; **~ up** vt (door) chiudere con assi; **~er** n (SCOL) convittore/trice; **~ing card** n = **~ing pass**; **~ing house** n pensione f; **~ing pass** n (AVIAT, NAUT) carta d'imbarco; **~ing school** n collegio; **~ room** n sala del consiglio

boast [bəust] vi: **to ~ (about** or **of)** vantarsi (di)

boat [bəut] n nave f; (small) barca; **~swain** ['bəusn] n nostromo

bob [bɔb] vi (boat, cork on water: also: **~ up and down)** andare su e giù; **~ up** vi saltare fuori

bobby ['bɔbɪ] (BRIT: inf) n poliziotto

bobsleigh ['bɔbsleɪ] n bob m inv

bode [bəud] vi: **to ~ well/ill (for)** essere di buon/cattivo auspicio (per)

bodily ['bɔdɪlɪ] adj fisico(a), corporale ♦ adv corporalmente; interamente; in persona

body ['bɔdɪ] n corpo; (of car) carrozzeria; (of plane) fusoliera; (fig: group) gruppo; (: organization) organizzazione f; (: quantity) quantità f inv; **~-building** n culturismo; **~guard** n guardia del corpo; **~work** n carrozzeria

bog [bɔg] n palude f ♦ vt: **to get ~ged down** (fig) impantanarsi

bogus ['bəugəs] adj falso(a); finto(a)

boil [bɔɪl] vt, vi bollire ♦ n (MED) foruncolo; **to come to the (BRIT)** or **a (US) ~** raggiungere l'ebollizione; **~ down to** vt fus (fig) ridursi a; **~ over** vi trabboccare (bollendo); **~ed egg** n uovo alla coque; **~ed potatoes** npl patate fpl bollite or lesse; **~er** n caldaia; **~er suit** (BRIT) n tuta; **~ing point** n punto di ebollizione

boisterous ['bɔɪstərəs] adj chiassoso(a)

bold [bəuld] adj audace; (child) impudente;

(colour) deciso(a)

bollard ['bɔləd] (BRIT) n (AUT) colonnina luminosa

bolt [bəult] n chiavistello; (with nut) bullone m ♦ adv: **~ upright** diritto(a) come un fuso ♦ vt serrare; (also: **~ together)** imbullonare; (food) mangiare in fretta ♦ vi scappare via

bomb [bɔm] n bomba ♦ vt bombardare

bombastic [bɔm'bæstɪk] adj magniloquente

bomb: **~ disposal unit** n corpo degli artificieri; **~er** n (AVIAT) bombardiere m; **~shell** n (fig) notizia bomba

bond [bɔnd] n legame m; (binding promise, FINANCE) obbligazione f; (COMM): **in ~** in attesa di sdoganamento

bondage ['bɔndɪdʒ] n schiavitù f

bone [bəun] n osso; (of fish) spina, lisca ♦ vt disossare; togliere le spine a; **~ idle** adj pigrissimo(a); **~ marrow** n midollo osseo

bonfire ['bɔnfaɪə*] n falò m inv

bonnet ['bɔnɪt] n cuffia; (BRIT: of car) cofano

bonus ['bəunəs] n premio; (fig) sovrappiù m inv

bony ['bəunɪ] adj (MED: tissue) osseo(a); (arm, face) ossuto(a); (meat) pieno(a) di ossi; (fish) pieno(a) di spine

boo [bu:] excl ba! ♦ vt fischiare

booby trap ['bu:bɪ-] n trappola

book [buk] n libro; (of stamps etc) blocchetto ♦ vt (ticket, seat, room) prenotare; (driver) multare; (football player) ammonire; **~s** npl (COMM) conti mpl; **~case** n scaffale m; **~ing office** (BRIT) n (RAIL) biglietteria; (THEATRE) botteghino; **~-keeping** n contabilità; **~let** n libricino; **~maker** n allibratore m; **~seller** n libraio; **~shop**, **~store** n libreria

boom [bu:m] n (noise) rimbombo; (in prices etc) boom m inv ♦ vi rimbombare; andare a gonfie vele

boon [bu:n] n vantaggio

boost [bu:st] n spinta ♦ vt spingere; **~er** n (MED) richiamo

boot [bu:t] n stivale m; (for hiking) scarpone m da montagna; (for football etc) scarpa; (BRIT: of car) portabagagli m inv ♦ vt (COMPUT) inizializzare; **to ~** (in addition) per giunta, in più

booth [bu:ð] n cabina; (at fair) baraccone m

booty ['bu:tɪ] n bottino

booze [bu:z] (inf) n alcool m

border ['bɔ:də*] n orlo; margine m; (of a country) frontiera; (for flowers) aiuola (laterale) ♦ vt (road) costeggiare; (another country: also: **~ on)** confinare con; **the B~s** la zona di confine tra l'Inghilterra e la Scozia; **~ on** vt fus (fig: insanity etc) sfiorare; **~line** n (fig): **on the ~line** incerto(a); **~line case** n caso incerto

bore [bɔ:*] pt of **bear** ♦ vt (hole etc) scavare;

(person) annoiare ♦ n (person) seccatore/trice; (of gun) calibro; **to be ~d** annoiarsi; **~dom** n noia; **boring** adj noioso(a)

born [bɔːn] adj: **to be ~** nascere; **I was ~ in 1960** sono nato nel 1960

borne [bɔːn] pp of **bear**

borough ['bʌrə] n comune m

borrow ['bɔrəu] vt: **to ~ sth (from sb)** prendere in prestito qc (da qn)

Bosnia(-Herzegovina) ['bɔznɪə(hɜːzəˈgəuviːnə)] n Bosnia-Erzegovina

Bosnian ['bɔznɪən] n, adj bosniaco(a) m/f

boss [bɔs] n capo ♦ vt comandare; **~y** adj prepotente

bosun ['bəusn] n nostromo

botany ['bɔtənɪ] n botanica

botch [bɔtʃ] vt (also: **~ up**) fare un pasticcio di

both [bəuθ] adj entrambi(e), tutt'e due ♦ pron: **~ (of them)** entrambi(e); **~ of us went, we ~ went** ci siamo andati tutt'e due ♦ adv: **they sell ~ meat and poultry** vendono insieme la carne ed il pollame

bother ['bɔðə*] vt (worry) preoccupare; (annoy) infastidire ♦ vi (also: **~ o.s.**) preoccuparsi ♦ n: **it is a ~ to have to do** è una seccatura dover fare; **it was no ~** non c'era problema; **to ~ doing sth** darsi la pena di fare qc

bottle ['bɔtl] n bottiglia; (baby's) biberon m inv ♦ vt imbottigliare; **~ up** vt contenere; **~ bank** n contenitore m per la raccolta del vetro; **~neck** n imbottigliamento; **~-opener** n apribottiglie m inv

bottom ['bɔtəm] n fondo; (buttocks) sedere m ♦ adj più basso(a); ultimo(a); **at the ~ of** in fondo a

bough [bau] n ramo

bought [bɔːt] pt, pp of **buy**

boulder ['bəuldə*] n masso (tondeggiante)

bounce [bauns] vi (ball) rimbalzare; (cheque) essere restituito(a) ♦ vt far rimbalzare ♦ n (rebound) rimbalzo; **~r** (inf) n buttafuori m inv

bound [baund] pt, pp of **bind** ♦ n (gen pl) limite m; (leap) salto ♦ vi saltare ♦ vt (limit) delimitare ♦ adj: **~ by law** obbligato(a) per legge; **to be ~ to do sth** (obliged) essere costretto(a) a fare qc; **he's ~ to fail** (likely) fallirà di certo; **~ for** diretto(a) a; **out of ~s** il cui accesso è vietato

boundary ['baundrɪ] n confine m

boundless ['baundlɪs] adj senza limiti

bourgeois ['buəʒwaː] adj borghese

bout [baut] n periodo; (of malaria etc) attacco; (BOXING etc) incontro

bow[1] [bəu] n (knot) nodo; (weapon) arco; (MUS) archetto

bow[2] [bau] n (with body) inchino; (NAUT: also:

~s) prua ♦ vi inchinarsi; (yield): **to ~ to** or **before** sottomettersi a

bowels ['bauəlz] npl intestini mpl; (fig) viscere fpl

bowl [bəul] n (for eating) scodella; (for washing) bacino; (ball) boccia ♦ vi (CRICKET) servire (la palla)

bow-legged ['bəuˈlɛgɪd] adj dalle gambe storte

bowler ['bəulə*] n (CRICKET, BASEBALL) lanciatore m; (BRIT: also: **~ hat**) bombetta

bowling ['bəulɪŋ]-n (game) gioco delle bocce; **~ alley** n pista da bowling; **~ green** n campo di bocce

bowls [bəulz] n gioco delle bocce

bow tie n cravatta a farfalla

box [bɔks] n scatola; (also: cardboard **~**) cartone m; (THEATRE) palco ♦ vt inscatolare ♦ vi fare del pugilato; **~er** n (person) pugile m; **~ing** n (SPORT) pugilato; **B~ing Day** (BRIT) n ≈ Santo Stefano; **~ing gloves** npl guantoni mpl da pugile; **~ing ring** n ring m inv; **~ office** n biglietteria; **~ room** n ripostiglio

boy [bɔɪ] n ragazzo

boycott ['bɔɪkɔt] n boicottaggio ♦ vt boicottare

boyfriend ['bɔɪfrɛnd] n ragazzo

boyish ['bɔɪʃ] adj da ragazzo

B.R. abbr (formerly) = **British Rail**

bra [braː] n reggipetto, reggiseno

brace [breɪs] n (on teeth) apparecchio correttore; (tool) trapano ♦ vt rinforzare, sostenere; **~s** (BRIT) npl (DRESS) bretelle fpl; **to ~ o.s.** (also fig) tenersi forte

bracelet ['breɪslɪt] n braccialetto

bracing ['breɪsɪŋ] adj invigorante

bracken ['brækən] n felce f

bracket ['brækɪt] n (TECH) mensola; (group) gruppo; (TYP) parentesi f inv ♦ vt mettere fra parentesi

brag [bræg] vi vantarsi

braid [breɪd] n (trimming) passamano; (of hair) treccia

brain [breɪn] n cervello; **~s** npl (intelligence) cervella fpl; **he's got ~s** è intelligente; **~wash** vt fare un lavaggio di cervello a; **~wave** n lampo di genio; **~y** adj intelligente

braise [breɪz] vt brasare

brake [breɪk] n (on vehicle) freno ♦ vi frenare; **~ fluid** n liquido dei freni; **~ light** n (fanalino dello) stop m inv

bramble ['bræmbl] n rovo

bran [bræn] n crusca

branch [braːntʃ] n ramo; (COMM) succursale f; **~ out** vi (fig) intraprendere una nuova attività

brand [brænd] n (also: **~ name**) marca; (fig) tipo ♦ vt (cattle) marcare (a ferro rovente)

brand-new ['brænd'njuː] *adj* nuovo(a) di zecca

brandy ['brændɪ] *n* brandy *m inv*

brash [bræʃ] *adj* sfacciato(a)

brass [brɑːs] *n* ottone *m*; **the ~** (*MUS*) gli ottoni; **~ band** *n* fanfara

brat [bræt] (*pej*) *n* marmocchio, monello/a

bravado [brə'vɑːdəu] *n* spavalderia

brave [breɪv] *adj* coraggioso(a) ♦ *vt* affrontare; **~ry** *n* coraggio

brawl [brɔːl] *n* rissa

brawny ['brɔːnɪ] *adj* muscoloso(a)

bray [breɪ] *vi* ragliare

brazen ['breɪzn] *adj* sfacciato(a) ♦ *vt*: **to ~ it out** fare lo sfacciato

brazier ['breɪzɪə*] *n* braciere *m*

Brazil [brə'zɪl] *n* Brasile *m*

breach [briːtʃ] *vt* aprire una breccia in ♦ *n* (*gap*) breccia, varco; (*breaking*): **~ of contract** rottura di contratto; **~ of the peace** violazione *f* dell'ordine pubblico

bread [brɛd] *n* pane *m*; **~ and butter** *n* pane e burro; (*fig*) mezzi *mpl* di sussistenza; **~bin** *n* cassetta *f* portapane *inv*; **~crumbs** *npl* briciole *fpl*; (*CULIN*) pangrattato; **~line** *n*: **to be on the ~line** avere appena il denaro per vivere

breadth [brɛtθ] *n* larghezza; (*fig: of knowledge etc*) ampiezza

breadwinner ['brɛdwɪnə*] *n* chi guadagna il pane per tutta la famiglia

break [breɪk] (*pt* **broke**, *pp* **broken**) *vt* rompere; (*law*) violare; (*record*) battere ♦ *vi* rompersi; (*storm*) scoppiare; (*weather*) cambiare; (*dawn*) spuntare; (*news*) saltare fuori ♦ *n* (*gap*) breccia; (*fracture*) rottura; (*rest, also SCOL*) intervallo; (*: short*) pausa; (*chance*) possibilità *f inv*; **to ~ one's leg etc** rompersi la gamba *etc*; **to ~ the news to sb** comunicare per primo la notizia a qn; **to ~ even** coprire le spese; **to ~ free *or* loose** spezzare i legami; **to ~ open** (*door etc*) sfondare; **~ down** *vt* (*figures, data*) analizzare ♦ *vi* (*person*) avere un esaurimento (nervoso); (*AUT*) guastarsi; **~ in** *vt* (*horse etc*) domare ♦ *vi* (*burglar*) fare irruzione; (*interrupt*) interrompere; **~ into** *vt fus* (*house*) fare irruzione in; **~ off** *vi* (*speaker*) interrompersi; (*branch*) troncarsi; **~ out** *vi* evadere; (*war, fight*) scoppiare; **to ~ out in spots** coprirsi di macchie; **~ up** *vi* (*ship*) sfondarsi; (*meeting*) sciogliersi; (*crowd*) disperdersi; (*marriage*) andare a pezzi; (*SCOL*) chiudere ♦ *vt* fare a pezzi, spaccare; (*fight etc*) interrompere, far cessare; **~age** *n* rottura; (*object broken*) cosa rotta; **~down** *n* (*AUT*) guasto; (*in communications*) interruzione *f*; (*of marriage*) rottura; (*MED: also: nervous ~down*) esaurimento nervoso; (*of*

statistics*) resoconto; **~down van** (*BRIT*) *n* carro *m* attrezzi *inv*; **~er** *n* frangente *m*

breakfast ['brɛkfəst] *n* colazione *f*

break: **~-in** *n* irruzione *f*; **~ing and entering** *n* (*LAW*) violazione *f* di domicilio con scasso; **~through** *n* (*fig*) passo avanti; **~water** *n* frangiflutti *m inv*

breast [brɛst] *n* (*of woman*) seno; (*chest, CULIN*) petto; **~-feed** (*irreg: like* feed) *vt, vi* allattare (al seno); **~-stroke** *n* nuoto a rana

breath [brɛθ] *n* respiro; **out of ~** senza fiato

Breathalyser ® ['brɛθəlaɪzə*] (*BRIT*) *n* alcoltest *m inv*

breathe [briːð] *vt, vi* respirare; **~ in** *vt* respirare ♦ *vi* inspirare; **~ out** *vt, vi* espirare; **~r** *n* attimo di respiro; **breathing** *n* respiro, respirazione *f*

breathless ['brɛθlɪs] *adj* senza fiato

breathtaking ['brɛθteɪkɪŋ] *adj* mozzafiato *inv*

bred [brɛd] *pt, pp of* **breed**

breed [briːd] (*pt, pp* **bred**) *vt* allevare ♦ *vi* riprodursi ♦ *n* razza; (*type, class*) varietà *f inv*; **~ing** *n* riproduzione *f*; allevamento; (*upbringing*) educazione *f*

breeze [briːz] *n* brezza

breezy ['briːzɪ] *adj* allegro(a); ventilato(a)

brew [bruː] *vt* (*tea*) fare un infuso di; (*beer*) fare ♦ *vi* (*storm, fig: trouble etc*) prepararsi; **~ery** *n* fabbrica di birra

bribe [braɪb] *n* bustarella ♦ *vt* comprare; **~ry** *n* corruzione *f*

brick [brɪk] *n* mattone *m*; **~layer** *n* muratore *m*

bridal ['braɪdl] *adj* nuziale

bride [braɪd] *n* sposa; **~groom** *n* sposo; **~smaid** *n* damigella d'onore

bridge [brɪdʒ] *n* ponte *m*; (*NAUT*) ponte di comando; (*of nose*) dorso; (*CARDS*) bridge *m inv* ♦ *vt* (*fig: gap*) colmare

bridle ['braɪdl] *n* briglia; **~ path** *n* sentiero (per cavalli)

brief [briːf] *adj* breve ♦ *n* (*LAW*) comparsa; (*gen*) istruzioni *fpl* ♦ *vt* mettere al corrente; **~s** *npl* (*underwear*) mutande *fpl*; **~case** *n* cartella; **~ing** *n* briefing *m inv*; **~ly** *adv* (*glance*) di sfuggita; (*explain, say*) brevemente

bright [braɪt] *adj* luminoso(a); (*clever*) sveglio(a); (*lively*) vivace; **~en** (*also: ~en up*) *vt* (*room*) rendere luminoso(a) ♦ *vi* schiarirsi; (*person*) rallegrarsi

brilliance ['brɪljəns] *n* splendore *m*

brilliant ['brɪljənt] *adj* brillante; (*light, smile*) radioso(a); (*inf*) splendido(a)

brim [brɪm] *n* orlo

brine [braɪn] *n* (*CULIN*) salamoia

bring [brɪŋ] (*pt, pp* **brought**) *vt* portare; **~ about** *vt* causare; **~ back** *vt* riportare;

~ **down** vt portare giù; abbattere;
~ **forward** vt (proposal) avanzare; (meeting) anticipare; ~ **off** vt (task, plan) portare a compimento; ~ **out** vt tirar fuori; (meaning) mettere in evidenza; (book, album) far uscire; ~ **round** vt (unconscious person) far rinvenire; ~ **up** vt (carry up) portare su; (child) allevare; (question) introdurre; (food: vomit) rimettere, rigurgitare

brink [brɪŋk] n orlo

brisk [brɪsk] adj (manner) spiccio(a); (trade) vivace; (pace) svelto(a)

bristle ['brɪsl] n setola ♦ vi rizzarsi; **bristling with** irto(a) di

Britain ['brɪtən] n (also: Great ~) Gran Bretagna

British ['brɪtɪʃ] adj britannico(a); **the ~** npl i Britannici; **the ~ Isles** npl le Isole Britanniche; ~ **Rail** n compagnia ferroviaria britannica, ≈ Ferrovie fpl dello Stato

Briton ['brɪtən] n britannico/a

brittle ['brɪtl] adj fragile

broach [brəʊtʃ] vt (subject) affrontare

broad [brɔːd] adj largo(a); (distinction) generale; (accent) spiccato(a); **in ~ daylight** in pieno giorno; ~**cast** (pt, pp ~**cast**) n trasmissione f ♦ vt trasmettere per radio (or per televisione) ♦ vi fare una trasmissione; ~**en** vt allargare ♦ vi allargarsi; ~**ly** adv (fig) in generale; ~**minded** adj di mente aperta

broccoli ['brɒkəlɪ] n broccoli mpl

brochure ['brəʊʃjʊə*] n dépliant m inv

broil [brɔɪl] vt cuocere a fuoco vivo

broke [brəʊk] pt of **break** ♦ adj (inf) squattrinato(a)

broken ['brəʊkn] pp of **break** ♦ adj rotto(a); **a ~ leg** una gamba rotta; **in ~ English** in un inglese stentato; ~-**hearted** adj: **to be ~-hearted** avere il cuore spezzato

broker ['brəʊkə*] n agente m

brolly ['brɒlɪ] (BRIT: inf) n ombrello

bronchitis [brɒŋ'kaɪtɪs] n bronchite f

bronze [brɒnz] n bronzo

brooch [brəʊtʃ] n spilla

brood [bruːd] n covata ♦ vi (person) rimuginare

brook [brʊk] n ruscello

broom [brum] n scopa; (BOT) ginestra

Bros. abbr (= Brothers) F.lli

broth [brɒθ] n brodo

brothel ['brɒθl] n bordello

brother ['brʌðə*] n fratello; ~-**in-law** n cognato

brought [brɔːt] pt, pp of **bring**

brow [braʊ] n fronte f; (rare, gen: eye~) sopracciglio; (of hill) cima

brown [braʊn] adj bruno(a), marrone; (tanned) abbronzato(a) ♦ n (colour) color m bruno or marrone ♦ vt (CULIN) rosolare;

~ **bread** n pane m integrale, pane nero

Brownie ['braʊnɪ] n giovane esploratrice f; **b~** (US: cake) dolce al cioccolato e nocciole

brown paper n carta da pacchi or da imballaggio

brown sugar n zucchero greggio

browse [braʊz] vi (among books) curiosare fra i libri; **to ~ through a book** sfogliare un libro; ~**r** n (COMPUT) browser m inv

bruise [bruːz] n (on person) livido ♦ vt farsi un livido a

brunette [bruː'nɛt] n bruna

brunt [brʌnt] n: **the ~ of** (attack, criticism etc) il peso maggiore di

brush [brʌʃ] n spazzola; (for painting, shaving) pennello; (quarrel) schermaglia ♦ vt spazzolare; (also: ~ against) sfiorare; ~ **aside** vt scostare; ~ **up** vt (knowledge) rinfrescare; ~**wood** n macchia

Brussels ['brʌslz] n Bruxelles f; ~ **sprout** n cavolo di Bruxelles

brutal ['bruːtl] adj brutale

brute [bruːt] n bestia ♦ adj: **by ~ force** con la forza, a viva forza

B.Sc. n abbr (UNIV) = **Bachelor of Science**

BSE n abbr (= bovine spongiform encephalopathy) encefalite f bovina spongiforme

bubble ['bʌbl] n bolla ♦ vi ribollire; (sparkle, fig) essere effervescente; ~ **bath** n bagnoschiuma m inv; ~ **gum** n gomma americana

buck [bʌk] n maschio (di camoscio, caprone, coniglio etc); (US: inf) dollaro ♦ vi sgroppare; **to pass the ~ (to sb)** scaricare (su di qn) la propria responsabilità; ~ **up** vi (cheer up) rianimarsi

bucket ['bʌkɪt] n secchio

buckle ['bʌkl] n fibbia ♦ vt allacciare ♦ vi (wheel etc) piegarsi

bud [bʌd] n gemma; (of flower) bocciolo ♦ vi germogliare; (flower) sbocciare

Buddhism ['bʊdɪzəm] n buddismo

budding ['bʌdɪŋ] adj (poet etc) in erba

buddy ['bʌdɪ] (US) n compagno

budge [bʌdʒ] vt scostare; (fig) smuovere ♦ vi spostarsi; smuoversi

budgerigar ['bʌdʒərɪgɑː*] n pappagallino

budget ['bʌdʒɪt] n bilancio preventivo ♦ vi: **to ~ for sth** fare il bilancio per qc

budgie ['bʌdʒɪ] n = **budgerigar**

buff [bʌf] adj color camoscio ♦ n (inf: enthusiast) appassionato/a

buffalo ['bʌfələʊ] (pl ~ or ~es) n bufalo; (US) bisonte m

buffer ['bʌfə*] n respingente m; (COMPUT) memoria tampone, buffer m inv

buffet¹ ['bʊfeɪ] n (food, BRIT: bar) buffet m inv; ~ **car** (BRIT) n (RAIL) ≈ servizio ristoro

buffet² ['bʌfɪt] vt sferzare

bug [bʌg] n (esp US: insect) insetto; (COMPUT, fig: germ) virus m inv; (spy device) microfono spia ♦ vt mettere sotto controllo; (inf: annoy) scocciare

buggy ['bʌgɪ] n (baby ~) passeggino

bugle ['bju:gl] n tromba

build [bɪld] (pt, pp built) n (of person) corporatura ♦ vt costruire; ~ **up** vt accumulare; aumentare; **~er** n costruttore m; **~ing** n costruzione f; edificio; (industry) edilizia; **~ing society** (BRIT) n società f inv immobiliare

built [bɪlt] pt, pp of build ♦ adj: **~-in** (cupboard) a muro; (device) incorporato(a); **~-up area** n abitato

bulb [bʌlb] n (BOT) bulbo; (ELEC) lampadina

bulge [bʌldʒ] n rigonfiamento ♦ vi essere protuberante or rigonfio(a); **to be bulging with** essere pieno(a) or zeppo(a) di

bulk [bʌlk] n massa, volume m; **in ~** a pacchi (or cassette etc); (COMM) all'ingrosso; **the ~ of** il grosso di; **~y** adj grosso(a); voluminoso(a)

bull [bul] n toro; (male elephant, whale) maschio; **~dog** n bulldog m inv

bulldozer ['buldəuzə*] n bulldozer m inv

bullet ['bulɪt] n pallottola

bulletin ['bulɪtɪn] n bollettino

bulletproof ['bulɪtpru:f] adj (car) blindato(a); (vest etc) antiproiettile inv

bullfight ['bulfaɪt] n corrida; **~er** n torero; **~ing** n tauromachia

bullion ['buljən] n oro or argento in lingotti

bullock ['bulək] n manzo

bullring ['bulrɪŋ] n arena (per corride)

bull's-eye ['bulzaɪ] n centro del bersaglio

bully ['bulɪ] n prepotente m ♦ vt angariare; (frighten) intimidire

bum [bʌm] (inf) n (backside) culo; (tramp) vagabondo/a

bumblebee ['bʌmblbi:] n bombo

bump [bʌmp] n (in car) piccolo tamponamento; (jolt) scossa; (on road etc) protuberanza; (on head) bernoccolo ♦ vt battere; **~ into** vt fus scontrarsi con; (person) imbattersi in; **~er** n paraurti m inv ♦ adj: **~er harvest** raccolto eccezionale; **~er cars** npl autoscontri mpl

bumpy ['bʌmpɪ] adj (road) dissestato(a)

bun [bʌn] n focaccia; (of hair) crocchia

bunch [bʌntʃ] n (of flowers, keys) mazzo; (of bananas) casco; (of people) gruppo; **~ of grapes** grappolo d'uva; **~es** npl (in hair) codine fpl

bundle ['bʌndl] n fascio ♦ vt (also: ~ up) legare in un fascio; (put): **to ~ sth/sb into** spingere qc/qn in

bungalow ['bʌŋgələu] n bungalow m inv

bungle ['bʌŋgl] vt fare un pasticcio di

bunion ['bʌnjən] n callo (al piede)

bunk [bʌŋk] n cuccetta; **~ beds** npl letti mpl a castello

bunker ['bʌŋkə*] n (coal store) ripostiglio per il carbone; (MIL, GOLF) bunker m inv

bunny ['bʌnɪ] n (also: ~ rabbit) coniglietto

bunting ['bʌntɪŋ] n pavesi mpl, bandierine fpl

buoy [bɔɪ] n boa; **~ant** adj galleggiante; (fig) vivace

burden ['bə:dn] n carico, fardello ♦ vt: **to ~ sb with** caricare qn di

bureau [bjuə'rəu] (pl bureaux) n (BRIT: writing desk) scrivania; (US: chest of drawers) cassettone m; (office) ufficio, agenzia

bureaucracy [bjuə'rɔkrəsɪ] n burocrazia

bureaux [bjuə'rəuz] npl of bureau

burglar ['bə:glə*] n scassinatore m; **~ alarm** n campanello antifurto; **~y** n furto con scasso

burial ['berɪəl] n sepoltura

burly ['bə:lɪ] adj robusto(a)

Burma ['bə:mə] n Birmania

burn [bə:n] (pt, pp burned or burnt) vt, vi bruciare ♦ n bruciatura, scottatura; **~ down** vt distruggere col fuoco; **~er** n (on cooker) fornello; (TECH) bruciatore m, becco (a gas); **~ing** adj in fiamme; (sand) che scotta; (ambition) bruciante; **burnt** pt, pp of burn

burrow ['bʌrəu] n tana ♦ vt scavare

bursary ['bə:sərɪ] (BRIT) n (SCOL) borsa di studio

burst [bə:st] (pt, pp burst) vt far scoppiare ♦ vi esplodere; (tyre) scoppiare ♦ n scoppio; (also: ~ pipe) rottura nel tubo, perdita; **a ~ of speed** uno scatto di velocità; **to ~ into flames/tears** scoppiare in fiamme/lacrime; **to ~ out laughing** scoppiare a ridere; **to be ~ing with** scoppiare di; **~ into** vt fus (room etc) irrompere in

bury ['berɪ] vt seppellire

bus [bʌs] (pl ~es) n autobus m inv

bush [buʃ] n cespuglio; (scrub land) macchia; **to beat about the ~** menare il cane per l'aia

bushy ['buʃɪ] adj cespuglioso(a)

busily ['bɪzɪlɪ] adv con impegno, alacremente

business ['bɪznɪs] n (matter) affare m; (trading) affari mpl; (firm) azienda; (job, duty) lavoro; **to be away on ~** essere andato via per affari; **it's none of my ~** questo non mi riguarda; **he means ~** non scherza; **~like** adj serio(a); efficiente; **~man/woman** (irreg) n uomo/donna d'affari; **~ trip** n viaggio d'affari

busker ['bʌskə*] (BRIT) n suonatore/trice ambulante

bus: **~ shelter** n pensilina (alla fermata dell'autobus); **~ station** n stazione f delle corriere, autostazione f; **~-stop** n fermata d'autobus

bust [bʌst] n busto; (ANAT) seno ♦ adj (inf:

broken) rotto(a); **to go ~** fallire
bustle ['bʌsl] n movimento, attività ♦ vi darsi
da fare; **bustling** adj movimentato(a).
busy ['bɪzɪ] adj occupato(a); (*shop, street*)
molto frequentato(a) ♦ vt: **to ~ o.s.** darsi da
fare; **~body** n ficcanaso m/f inv; **~ signal**
(*US*) n (*TEL*) segnale m di occupato

KEYWORD

but [bʌt] conj ma; **I'd love to come, ~ I'm busy**
vorrei tanto venire, ma ho da fare
♦ prep (*apart from, except*) eccetto, tranne,
meno; **he was nothing ~ trouble** non dava
altro che guai; **no-one ~ him can do it**
nessuno può farlo tranne lui; **~ for you/your
help** se non fosse per te/per il tuo aiuto;
anything ~ that tutto ma non questo
♦ adv (*just, only*) solo, soltanto; **she's ~ a
child** è solo una bambina; **had I ~ known** se
solo avessi saputo; **I can ~ try** tentar non
nuoce; **all ~ finished** quasi finito

butcher ['butʃə*] n macellaio ♦ vt macellare;
~'s (shop) n macelleria
butler ['bʌtlə*] n maggiordomo
butt [bʌt] n (*cask*) grossa botte f; (*of gun*)
calcio; (*of cigarette*) mozzicone m; (*BRIT: fig:
target*) oggetto ♦ vt cozzare; **~ in** vi
(*interrupt*) interrompere
butter ['bʌtə*] n burro ♦ vt imburrare; **~cup**
n ranuncolo
butterfly ['bʌtəflaɪ] n farfalla; (*SWIMMING:
also: ~ stroke*) (nuoto a) farfalla
buttocks ['bʌtəks] npl natiche fpl
button ['bʌtn] n bottone m; (*US: badge*)
distintivo ♦ vt (*also: ~ up*) abbottonare ♦ vi
abbottonarsi
buttress ['bʌtrɪs] n contrafforte f
buy [baɪ] (*pt, pp bought*) vt comprare ♦ n
acquisto; **to ~ sb sth/sth from sb** comprare
qc per qn/qc da qn; **to ~ sb a drink** offrire da
bere a qn; **~er** n compratore/trice
buzz [bʌz] n ronzio; (*inf: phone call*) colpo di
telefono ♦ vi ronzare
buzzer ['bʌzə*] n cicalino
buzz word (*inf*) n termine m di gran moda

KEYWORD

by [baɪ] prep **1** (*referring to cause, agent*) da;
killed ~ lightning ucciso da un fulmine;
surrounded ~ a fence circondato da uno
steccato; **a painting ~ Picasso** un quadro di
Picasso
2 (*referring to method, manner, means*):
~ bus/car/train in autobus/macchina/treno,
con l'autobus/la macchina/il treno; **to pay
~ cheque** pagare con (un) assegno;
~ moonlight al chiaro di luna; **~ saving hard,
he ...** risparmiando molto, lui ...

3 (*via, through*) per; **we came ~ Dover** siamo
venuti via Dover
4 (*close to, past*) accanto a; **the house ~ the
river** la casa sul fiume; **a holiday ~ the sea**
una vacanza al mare; **she sat ~ his bed** si
sedette accanto al suo letto; **she rushed ~ me**
mi è passata accanto correndo; **I go ~ the
post office every day** passo davanti all'ufficio
postale ogni giorno
5 (*not later than*) per, entro; **~ 4 o'clock** per
or entro le 4; **~ this time tomorrow** domani a
quest'ora; **~ the time I got here it was too
late** quando sono arrivato era ormai troppo
tardi
6 (*during*): **~ day/night** di giorno/notte
7 (*amount*) a; **~ the kilo/metre** a chili/metri;
paid ~ the hour pagato all'ora; **one ~ one** uno
per uno; **little ~ little** a poco a poco
8 (*MATH, measure*): **to divide/multiply ~ 3**
dividere/moltiplicare per 3; **it's broader ~ a
metre** è un metro più largo, è più largo di un
metro
9 (*according to*) per; **to play ~ the rules**
attenersi alle regole; **it's all right ~ me** per me
va bene
10: (**all**) **~ oneself** etc (tutto(a)) solo(a); **he
did it (all) ~ himself** lo ha fatto (tutto) da
solo
11: **~ the way** a proposito; **this wasn't my
idea ~ the way** tra l'altro l'idea non è stata
mia
♦ adv **1** see **go; pass** etc
2: **~ and ~** (*in past*) poco dopo; (*in future*)
fra breve; **~ and large** nel complesso

bye(-bye) ['baɪ('baɪ)] excl ciao!, arrivederci!
by(e)-law ['baɪlɔ:] n legge f locale
by-election ['baɪɪlekʃən] (*BRIT*) n elezione f
straordinaria
bygone ['baɪgɔn] adj passato(a) ♦ n: **let ~s
be ~s** mettiamoci una pietra sopra
bypass ['baɪpɑ:s] n circonvallazione f; (*MED*)
by-pass m inv ♦ vt fare una deviazione
intorno a
by-product ['baɪprɔdʌkt] n sottoprodotto;
(*fig*) conseguenza secondaria
bystander ['baɪstændə*] n spettatore/trice
byte [baɪt] n (*COMPUT*) byte m inv, bicarattere
m
byword ['baɪwə:d] n: **to be a ~ for** essere
sinonimo di

C, c

C [si:] n (*MUS*) do
C. abbr (= *centigrade*) C.
C.A. n abbr = **chartered accountant**
cab [kæb] n taxi m inv; (*of train, truck*) cabina

cabaret ['kæbəreɪ] n cabaret m inv
cabbage ['kæbɪdʒ] n cavolo
çabin ['kæbɪn] n capanna; (on ship) cabina; ~ **crew** n equipaggio; ~ **cruiser** n cabinato
cabinet ['kæbɪnɪt] n (POL) consiglio dei ministri; (furniture) armadietto; (also: display ~) vetrinetta
cable ['keɪbl] n cavo; fune f; (TEL) cablogramma m ♦ vt telegrafare; **~-car** n funivia; ~ **television** n televisione f via cavo
cache [kæʃ] n deposito segreto
cackle ['kækl] vi schiamazzare
cactus ['kæktəs] (pl **cacti**) n cactus m inv
cadet [kə'dɛt] n (MIL) cadetto
cadge [kædʒ] (inf) vt scroccare
café ['kæfeɪ] n caffè m inv
cafeteria [kæfɪ'tɪərɪə] n self-service m inv
cage [keɪdʒ] n gabbia
cagey ['keɪdʒɪ] (inf) adj chiuso(a); guardingo(a)
cagoule [kə'guːl] n K-way ® m inv
cajole [kə'dʒəul] vt allettare
cake [keɪk] n (large) torta; (small) pasticcino; ~ **of soap** saponetta; **~d** adj: **~d with** incrostato(a) di
calculate ['kælkjuleɪt] vt calcolare; **calculation** [-'leɪʃən] n calcolo; **calculator** n calcolatrice f
calendar ['kæləndə*] n calendario; ~ **year** n anno civile
calf [kɑːf] (pl **calves**) n (of cow) vitello; (of other animals) piccolo; (also: ~**skin**) (pelle f di) vitello; (ANAT) polpaccio
calibre ['kælɪbə*] (US **caliber**) n calibro
call [kɔːl] vt (gen, also TEL) chiamare; (meeting) indire ♦ vi chiamare; (visit: also: ~ **in**, ~ **round**) passare ♦ n (shout) grido, urlo; (TEL) telefonata; **to be ~ed** (person, object) chiamarsi; **to be on** ~ essere a disposizione; ~ **back** vi (return) ritornare; (TEL) ritelefonare, richiamare; ~ **for** vt fus richiedere; (fetch) passare a prendere; ~ **off** vt disdire; ~ **on** vt fus (visit) passare da; (appeal to) chiedere a; ~ **out** vi (in pain) urlare; (to person) chiamare; ~ **up** vt (MIL) richiamare; (TEL) telefonare a; **~box** (BRIT) n cabina telefonica; ~ **centre** n centro informazioni telefoniche; **~er** n persona che chiama; visitatore/trice; ~ **girl** n ragazza f squillo inv; **~-in** (US) n (phone-in) trasmissione f a filo diretto con gli ascoltatori; **~ing** n vocazione f; **~ing card** (US) n biglietto da visita
callous ['kæləs] adj indurito(a), insensibile
calm [kɑːm] adj calmo(a) ♦ n calma ♦ vt calmare; ~ **down** vi calmarsi ♦ vt calmare
Calor gas ® ['kælə*-] n butano
calorie ['kælərɪ] n caloria
calves [kɑːvz] npl of **calf**

Cambodia [kæm'bəudjə] n Cambogia
camcorder ['kæmkɔːdə*] n camcorder f inv
came [keɪm] pt of **come**
camel ['kæməl] n cammello
camera ['kæmərə] n macchina fotografica; (CINEMA, TV) cinepresa; **in** ~ a porte chiuse; **~man** (irreg) n cameraman m inv
camouflage ['kæməflɑːʒ] n (MIL, ZOOL) mimetizzazione f ♦ vt mimetizzare
camp [kæmp] n campeggio; (MIL) campo ♦ vi accamparsi ♦ adj effeminato(a)
campaign [kæm'peɪn] n (MIL, POL etc) campagna ♦ vi (also fig) fare una campagna
camp bed (BRIT) n brandina
camper ['kæmpə*] n campeggiatore/trice; (vehicle) camper m inv
camping ['kæmpɪŋ] n campeggio; **to go** ~ andare in campeggio
campsite ['kæmpsaɪt] n campeggio
campus ['kæmpəs] n campus m inv
can¹ [kæn] n (of milk) scatola; (of oil) bidone m; (of water) tanica; (tin) scatola ♦ vt mettere in scatola

can² [kæn] (negative **cannot**, **can't**; conditional and pt **could**) aux vb **1** (be able to) potere; **I ~'t go any further** non posso andare oltre; **you ~ do it if you try** sei in grado di farlo — basta provarci; **I'll help you all I ~** ti aiuterò come potrò; **I ~'t see you** non ti vedo
2 (know how to) sapere, essere capace di; **I ~ swim** so nuotare; ~ **you speak French?** parla francese?
3 (may) potere; **could I have a word with you?** posso parlarle un momento?
4 (expressing disbelief, puzzlement etc): **it ~'t be true!** non può essere vero!; **what** CAN **he want?** cosa può mai volere?
5 (expressing possibility, suggestion etc): **he could be in the library** può darsi che sia in biblioteca; **she could have been delayed** può aver avuto un contrattempo

Canada ['kænədə] n Canada m
Canadian [kə'neɪdɪən] adj, n canadese m/f
canal [kə'næl] n canale m
canary [kə'nɛərɪ] n canarino
cancel ['kænsəl] vt annullare; (train) sopprimere; (cross out) cancellare; **~lation** [-'leɪʃən] n annullamento; soppressione f; cancellazione f; (TOURISM) prenotazione f annullata
cancer ['kænsə*] n cancro; **C~** (sign) Cancro
candid ['kændɪd] adj onesto(a)
candidate ['kændɪdeɪt] n candidato/a
candle ['kændl] n candela; (in church) cero; **~light** n: **by ~light** a lume di candela; **~stick** n bugia; (bigger, ornate) candeliere m

candour ['kændə*] (US **candor**) n sincerità

candy ['kændɪ] n zucchero candito; (US) caramella; caramelle fpl; **~-floss** (BRIT) n zucchero filato

cane [keɪn] n canna; (for furniture) bambù m; (stick) verga ♦ vt (BRIT: SCOL) punire a colpi di verga

canister ['kænɪstə*] n scatola metallica

cannabis ['kænəbɪs] n canapa indiana

canned ['kænd] adj (food) in scatola

cannon ['kænən] (pl ~ or ~s) n (gun) cannone m

cannot ['kænɔt] = **can not**

canny ['kænɪ] adj furbo(a)

canoe [kə'nu:] n canoa; **~ing** n canottaggio

canon ['kænən] n (clergyman) canonico; (standard) canone m

can opener [-'əupnə*] n apriscatole m inv

canopy ['kænəpɪ] n baldacchino

cant [kænt] n gergo ♦ vt inclinare ♦ vi inclinarsi

can't [kænt] = **can not**

canteen [kæn'ti:n] n mensa; (BRIT: of cutlery) portaposate m inv

canter ['kæntə*] vi andare al piccolo galoppo

canvas ['kænvəs] n tela

canvass ['kænvəs] vi (POL): **to ~ for** raccogliere voti per ♦ vt fare un sondaggio di

cap [kæp] n (hat) berretto; (of pen) coperchio; (of bottle, toy gun) tappo; (contraceptive) diaframma m ♦ vt (outdo) superare; (limit) fissare un tetto a

capability [keɪpə'bɪlɪtɪ] n capacità f inv, abilità f inv

capable ['keɪpəbl] adj capace

capacity [kə'pæsɪtɪ] n capacità f inv; (of lift etc) capienza

cape [keɪp] n (garment) cappa; (GEO) capo

caper ['keɪpə*] n (CULIN) cappero; (prank) scherzetto

capital ['kæpɪtl] n (also: ~ city) capitale f; (money) capitale m; (also: ~ letter) maiuscola; **~ gains tax** n imposta sulla plusvalenza; **~ism** n capitalismo; **~ist** adj, n capitalista (m/f); **~ize: to ~ize on** vt fus trarre vantaggio da; **~ punishment** n pena capitale

Capitol ['kæpɪtl] n: **the ~** il Campidoglio

Capricorn ['kæprɪkɔ:n] n Capricorno

capsize [kæp'saɪz] vt capovolgere ♦ vi capovolgersi

capsule ['kæpsju:l] n capsula

captain ['kæptɪn] n capitano

caption ['kæpʃən] n leggenda

captivate ['kæptɪveɪt] vt avvincere

captive ['kæptɪv] adj, n prigioniero(a)

captivity [kæp'tɪvɪtɪ] n cattività

capture ['kæptʃə*] vt catturare; (COMPUT) registrare ♦ n cattura; (data ~) registrazione

f or rilevazione f di dati

car [kɑ:*] n (AUT) macchina, automobile f; (RAIL) vagone m

carafe [kə'ræf] n caraffa

caramel ['kærəməl] n caramello

caravan ['kærəvæn] n (BRIT) roulotte f inv; (of camels) carovana; **~ning** n vacanze fpl in roulotte; **~ site** (BRIT) n campeggio per roulotte

carbohydrates [kɑ:bəu'haɪdreɪts] npl (foods) carboidrati mpl

carbon ['kɑ:bən] n carbonio; **~ paper** n carta carbone

car boot sale n mercatino dell'usato dove la merce viene esposta nei bagagliai delle macchine

carburettor [kɑ:bju'retə*] (US **carburetor**) n carburatore m

card [kɑ:d] n carta; (visiting ~ etc) biglietto; (Christmas ~ etc) cartolina; **~board** n cartone m; **~ game** n gioco di carte

cardiac ['kɑ:dɪæk] adj cardiaco(a)

cardigan ['kɑ:dɪgən] n cardigan m inv

cardinal ['kɑ:dɪnl] adj cardinale ♦ n cardinale m

card index n schedario

cardphone ['kɑ:dfəun] n telefono a scheda

care [kɛə*] n cura, attenzione f; (worry) preoccupazione f ♦ vi: **to ~ about** curarsi di; (thing, idea) interessarsi di; **~ of** presso; **in sb's ~** alle cure di qn; **to take ~ (to do)** fare attenzione (a fare); **to take ~ of** curarsi di; (bill, problem) occuparsi di; **I don't ~** non me ne importa; **I couldn't ~ less** non m'interessa affatto; **~ for** vt fus aver cura di; (like) volere bene a

career [kə'rɪə*] n carriera ♦ vi (also: ~ along) andare di (gran) carriera

carefree ['kɛəfri:] adj sgombro(a) di preoccupazioni

careful ['kɛəful] adj attento(a); (cautious) cauto(a); **(be) ~!** attenzione!; **~ly** adv con cura; cautamente

careless ['kɛəlɪs] adj negligente; (heedless) spensierato(a)

carer ['kɛərə*] n assistente m/f (di persone malata o handicappata)

caress [kə'rɛs] n carezza ♦ vt accarezzare

caretaker ['kɛəteɪkə*] n custode m

car-ferry ['kɑ:fɛrɪ] n traghetto

cargo ['kɑ:gəu] (pl ~es) n carico

car hire n autonoleggio

Caribbean [kærɪ'bi:ən] adj: **the ~ (Sea)** il Mar dei Caraibi

caring ['kɛərɪŋ] adj (person) premuroso(a); (society, organization) umanitario(a)

carnage ['kɑ:nɪdʒ] n carneficina

carnation [kɑ:'neɪʃən] n garofano

carnival ['kɑ:nɪvəl] n (public celebration)

carnevale m; (US: funfair) luna park m inv

carol ['kærəl] n: (Christmas) ~ canto di Natale

carp [kɑːp] n (fish) carpa

car park (BRIT) n parcheggio

carpenter ['kɑːpɪntə*] n carpentiere m

carpentry ['kɑːpɪntrɪ] n carpenteria

carpet ['kɑːpɪt] n tappeto ♦ vt coprire con tappeto

car phone n telefonino per auto, cellulare m per auto

car rental (US) n autonoleggio

carriage ['kærɪdʒ] n vettura; (of goods) trasporto; **~way** (BRIT) n (part of road) carreggiata

carrier ['kærɪə*] n (of disease) portatore/trice; (COMM) impresa di trasporti; **~ bag** (BRIT) n sacchetto

carrot ['kærət] n carota

carry ['kærɪ] vt (subj: person) portare; (: vehicle) trasportare; (involve: responsibilities etc) comportare; (MED) essere portatore/trice di ♦ vi (sound) farsi sentire; **to be** or **get carried away** (fig) entusiasmarsi; **~ on** vi: **to ~ on with sth/doing** continuare qc/a fare ♦ vt mandare avanti; **~ out** vt (orders) eseguire; (investigation) svolgere; **~cot** (BRIT) n culla portabile; **~-on** (inf) n (fuss) casino, confusione f

cart [kɑːt] n carro ♦ vt (inf) trascinare

carton ['kɑːtən] n (box) scatola di cartone; (of yogurt) cartone m; (of cigarettes) stecca

cartoon [kɑːˈtuːn] n (PRESS) disegno umoristico; (comic strip) fumetto; (CINEMA) disegno animato

cartridge ['kɑːtrɪdʒ] n (for gun, pen) cartuccia; (music tape) cassetta

carve [kɑːv] vt (meat) trinciare; (wood, stone) intagliare; **~ up** vt (fig: country) suddividere; **carving** n (in wood etc) scultura; **carving knife** n trinciante m

car wash n lavaggio auto

cascade [kæsˈkeɪd] n cascata

case [keɪs] n caso; (LAW) causa, processo; (box) scatola; (BRIT: also: suit~) valigia; **in ~ of** in caso di; **in ~** he caso mai lui; **in any ~** in ogni caso; **just in ~** in caso di bisogno

cash [kæʃ] n denaro; (coins, notes) denaro liquido ♦ vt incassare; **to pay (in) ~** pagare in contanti; **~ on delivery** pagamento alla consegna; **~-book** n giornale m di cassa; **~ card** (BRIT) n tesserino di prelievo; **~ desk** (BRIT) n cassa; **~ dispenser** (BRIT) n sportello automatico

cashew [kæˈʃuː] n (also: ~ nut) anacardio

cashier [kæˈʃɪə*] n cassiere/a

cashmere ['kæʃmɪə*] n cachemire m

cash register n registratore m di cassa

casing ['keɪsɪŋ] n rivestimento

casino [kəˈsiːnəʊ] n casinò m inv

cask [kɑːsk] n botte f

casket ['kɑːskɪt] n cofanetto; (US: coffin) bara

casserole ['kæsərəʊl] n casseruola; (food): **chicken ~** pollo in casseruola

cassette [kæˈset] n cassetta; **~ player** n riproduttore m a cassette; **~ recorder** n registratore m a cassette

cast [kɑːst] (pt, pp cast) vt (throw) gettare; (metal) gettare, fondere; (THEATRE): **to ~ sb as Hamlet** scegliere qn per la parte di Amleto ♦ n (THEATRE) cast m inv; (also: plaster ~) ingessatura; **to ~ one's vote** votare, dare il voto; **~ off** vi (NAUT) salpare; (KNITTING) calare; **~ on** vi (KNITTING) avviare le maglie

castaway ['kɑːstəwəɪ] n naufrago/a

caster sugar ['kɑːstə*-] (BRIT) n zucchero semolato

casting vote ['kɑːstɪŋ-] (BRIT) n voto decisivo

cast iron n ghisa

castle ['kɑːsl] n castello

castor oil ['kɑːstə*-] n olio di ricino

casual ['kæʒjul] adj (by chance) casuale, fortuito(a); (irregular: work etc) avventizio(a); (unconcerned) noncurante, indifferente; **~ wear** casual m; **~ly** adv (in a relaxed way) con noncuranza; (dress) casual

casualty ['kæʒjultɪ] n ferito/a; (dead) morto/a, vittima; (MED: department) pronto soccorso

cat [kæt] n gatto

catalogue ['kætəlɒg] (US **catalog**) n catalogo ♦ vt catalogare

catalyst ['kætəlɪst] n catalizzatore m

catalytic convertor [kætəˈlɪtɪkkənˈvɜːtə*] n marmitta catalitica, catalizzatore m

catapult ['kætəpʌlt] n catapulta; fionda

cataract ['kætərækt] n (also MED) cateratta

catarrh [kəˈtɑː*] n catarro

catastrophe [kəˈtæstrəfɪ] n catastrofe f

catch [kætʃ] (pt, pp caught) vt prendere; (ball) afferrare; (surprise: person) sorprendere; (attention) attirare; (comment, whisper) cogliere; (person: also: ~ up) raggiungere ♦ vi (fire) prendere ♦ n (fish etc caught) retata; (of ball) presa; (trick) inganno; (TECH) gancio; (game) catch m inv: **to ~ fire** prendere fuoco; **to ~ sight of** scorgere; **~ on** vi capire; (become popular) affermarsi, far presa; **~ up** vi mettersi in pari ♦ vt (also: ~ up with) raggiungere

catching ['kætʃɪŋ] adj (MED) contagioso(a)

catchment area ['kætʃmənt-] (BRIT) n (SCOL) circoscrizione f scolare

catch phrase n slogan m inv; frase f fatta

catchy ['kætʃɪ] adj orecchiabile

category ['kætɪgərɪ] n categoria

cater ['keɪtə*] vi: **~ for** (BRIT: needs) provvedere a; (: readers, consumers)

incontrare i gusti di; (COMM: provide food)
provvedere alla ristorazione di; **~er** n
fornitore m; **~ing** n approvvigionamento
caterpillar ['kætəpɪlə*] n bruco
cathedral [kə'θi:drəl] n cattedrale f, duomo
catholic ['kæθəlɪk] adj universale; aperto(a);
eclettico(a); **C~** adj, n (REL) cattolico(a)
CAT scan [kæt-] n (= computerized axial
tomography) TAC f inv
Catseye ® [kæts'aɪ] (BRIT) n (AUT)
catarifrangente m
cattle ['kætl] npl bestiame m, bestie fpl
catty ['kætɪ] adj maligno(a), dispettoso(a)
caucus ['kɔ:kəs] n (POL: group) comitato di
dirigenti; (: US) (riunione f del) comitato
elettorale
caught [kɔ:t] pt, pp of catch
cauliflower ['kɒlɪflauə*] n cavolfiore m
cause [kɔ:z] n causa ♦ vt causare
caution ['kɔ:ʃən] n prudenza; (warning)
avvertimento ♦ vt avvertire; ammonire
cautious ['kɔ:ʃəs] adj cauto(a), prudente
cavalry ['kævəlrɪ] n cavalleria
cave [keɪv] n caverna, grotta; **~ in** vi (roof
etc) crollare; **~man** (irreg) n uomo delle
caverne
caviar(e) ['kævɪa:*] n caviale m
CB n abbr (= Citizens' Band (Radio)): **~ radio**
(set) baracchino
CBI n abbr (= Confederation of British
Industries) ≈ Confindustria
cc abbr = cubic centimetres; carbon copy
CD abbr (disc) CD m inv; (player) lettore m CD
inv
CDI n abbr (= compact disk interactive) CD-I m
inv, compact disc m inv interattivo
CD player n lettore m CD
CD-ROM [si:di:'rɔm] n abbr CD-ROM m inv
cease [si:s] vt, vi cessare; **~fire** n cessate il
fuoco m inv; **~less** adj incessante,
continuo(a)
cedar ['si:də*] n cedro
ceiling ['si:lɪŋ] n soffitto; (on wages etc) tetto
celebrate ['sɛlɪbreɪt] vt, vi celebrare; **~d** adj
celebre; **celebration** [-'breɪʃən] n
celebrazione f
celery ['sɛlərɪ] n sedano
cell [sɛl] n cella; (of revolutionaries, BIOL)
cellula; (ELEC) elemento (di batteria)
cellar ['sɛlə*] n sottosuolo; cantina
'cello ['tʃɛləu] n violoncello
cellphone [sɛl,faun] n cellulare m
Celt [kɛlt, sɛlt] n celta m/f
Celtic ['kɛltɪk, 'sɛltɪk] adj celtico(a)
cement [sə'mɛnt] n cemento; **~ mixer** n
betoniera
cemetery ['sɛmɪtrɪ] n cimitero
censor ['sɛnsə*] n censore m ♦ vt censurare;
~ship n censura

censure ['sɛnʃə*] vt riprovare, censurare
census ['sɛnsəs] n censimento
cent [sɛnt] n (US: coin) centesimo (= 1:100 di
un dollaro); see also **per**
centenary [sɛn'ti:nərɪ] n centenario
center ['sɛntə*] (US) n, vt = **centre**
centigrade ['sɛntɪɡreɪd] adj centigrado(a)
centimetre ['sɛntɪmi:tə*] (US **centimeter**) n
centimetro
centipede ['sɛntɪpi:d] n centopiedi m inv
central ['sɛntrəl] adj centrale; **C~ America** n
America centrale; **~ heating** n riscaldamento
centrale; **~ize** vt accentrare
centre ['sɛntə*] (US **center**) n centro ♦ vt
centrare; **~-forward** n (SPORT) centroavanti
m inv; **~-half** n (SPORT) centromediano
century ['sɛntjurɪ] n secolo; **20th ~** ventesimo
secolo
ceramic [sɪ'ræmɪk] adj ceramico(a); **~s** npl
ceramica
cereal ['si:rɪəl] n cereale m
ceremony ['sɛrɪmənɪ] n cerimonia; **to stand
on ~** fare complimenti
certain ['sə:tən] adj certo(a); **to make ~ of**
assicurarsi di; **for ~** per certo, di sicuro; **~ly**
adv certamente, certo; **~ty** n certezza
certificate [sə'tɪfɪkɪt] n certificato; diploma m
certified ['sə:tɪfaɪd]: **~ mail** (US) n posta
raccomandata con ricevuta di ritorno;
~ public accountant (US) n ≈ com-
mercialista m/f
certify ['sə:tɪfaɪ] vt certificare; (award diploma
to) conferire un diploma a; (declare insane)
dichiarare pazzo(a)
cervical ['sə:vɪkl] adj: **~ cancer** cancro della
cervice; **~ smear** Pap-test m inv
cervix ['sə:vɪks] n cervice f
cf. abbr (= compare) cfr
CFC n (= chlorofluorocarbon) CFC m inv
ch. abbr (= chapter) cap
chafe [tʃeɪf] vt fregare, irritare
chain [tʃeɪn] n catena ♦ vt (also: ~ up)
incatenare; **~ reaction** n reazione f a catena;
~-smoke vi fumare una sigaretta dopo
l'altra; **~ store** n negozio a catena
chair [tʃɛə*] n sedia; (armchair) poltrona; (of
university) cattedra; (of meeting) presidenza
♦ vt (meeting) presiedere; **~lift** n seggiovia;
~man (irreg) n presidente m
chalet ['ʃæleɪ] n chalet m inv
chalk [tʃɔ:k] n gesso
challenge ['tʃælɪndʒ] n sfida ♦ vt sfidare;
(statement, right) mettere in dubbio; **to ~ sb
to do** sfidare qn a fare; **challenging** adj
(task) impegnativo(a); (look) di sfida
chamber ['tʃeɪmbə*] n camera; **~ of
commerce** n camera di commercio; **~maid**
n cameriera; **~ music** n musica da camera
chamois ['ʃæmwa:] n camoscio; (also:

~ *leather*) panno in pelle di camoscio

champagne [ʃæm'peɪn] *n* champagne *m inv*

champion ['tʃæmpɪən] *n* campione/essa; **~ship** *n* campionato

chance [tʃɑːns] *n* caso; (*opportunity*) occasione *f*; (*likelihood*) possibilità *f inv* ♦ *vt*: **to ~ it** rischiare, provarci ♦ *adj* fortuito(a); **to take a ~** rischiare; **by ~** per caso

chancellor ['tʃɑːnsələ*] *n* cancelliere *m*; **C~ of the Exchequer** (*BRIT*) *n* Cancelliere dello Scacchiere

chandelier [ʃændə'lɪə*] *n* lampadario

change [tʃeɪndʒ] *vt* cambiare; (*transform*): **to ~ sb into** trasformare qn in ♦ *vi* cambiare; (*~ one's clothes*) cambiarsi; (*be transformed*): **to ~ into** trasformarsi in ♦ *n* cambiamento; (*of clothes*) cambio; (*money*) resto; **to ~ one's mind** cambiare idea; **for a ~** tanto per cambiare; **~able** *adj* (*weather*) variabile; **~ machine** *n* distributore automatico di monete; **~over** *n* cambiamento, passaggio

changing ['tʃeɪndʒɪŋ] *adj* che cambia; (*colours*) cangiante; **~ room** *n* (*BRIT: in shop*) camerino; (: *SPORT*) spogliatoio

channel ['tʃænl] *n* canale *m*; (*of river, sea*) alveo ♦ *vt* canalizzare; **the (English) C~** *n* la Manica; **~-hopping** *n* (*TV*) zapping *m inv*; **the C~ Islands** *npl* le Isole Normanne; **the C~ Tunnel** *n* il tunnel sotto la Manica

chant [tʃɑːnt] *n* canto; salmodia ♦ *vt* cantare; salmodiare

chaos ['keɪɒs] *n* caos *m*

chap [tʃæp] (*BRIT: inf*) *n* (*man*) tipo

chapel ['tʃæpəl] *n* cappella

chaperone ['ʃæpərəun] *n* accompagnatrice *f* ♦ *vt* accompagnare

chaplain ['tʃæplɪn] *n* cappellano

chapped [tʃæpt] *adj* (*skin, lips*) screpolato(a)

chapter ['tʃæptə*] *n* capitolo

char [tʃɑː*] *vt* (*burn*) carbonizzare

character ['kærɪktə*] *n* carattere *m*; (*in novel, film*) personaggio; **~istic** [-'rɪstɪk] *adj* caratteristico(a) ♦ *n* caratteristica

charcoal ['tʃɑːkəul] *n* carbone *m* di legna

charge [tʃɑːdʒ] *n* accusa; (*cost*) prezzo; (*responsibility*) responsabilità ♦ *vt* (*gun, battery, MIL: enemy*) caricare; (*customer*) fare pagare a; (*sum*) fare pagare; (*LAW*) accusare; **to ~ sb (with)** accusare qn (di) ♦ *vi* (*gen with: up, along etc*) lanciarsi; **~s** *npl* (*bank ~s etc*) tariffe *fpl*; **to reverse the ~s** (*TEL*) fare una telefonata a carico del destinatario; **to take ~ of** incaricarsi di; **to be in ~ of** essere responsabile per; **how much do you ~?** quanto chiedete?; **to ~ an expense (up) to sb** addebitare una spesa a qn; **~ card** *n* carta *f* clienti *inv*

charitable ['tʃærɪtəbl] *adj* caritatevole

charity ['tʃærɪtɪ] *n* carità; (*organization*) opera pia

charm [tʃɑːm] *n* fascino; (*on bracelet*) ciondolo ♦ *vt* affascinare, incantare; **~ing** *adj* affascinante

chart [tʃɑːt] *n* tabella; grafico; (*map*) carta nautica ♦ *vt* fare una carta nautica di; **~s** *npl* (*MUS*) hit parade *f*

charter ['tʃɑːtə*] *vt* (*plane*) noleggiare ♦ *n* (*document*) carta; **~ed accountant** (*BRIT*) *n* ragioniere/a professionista; **~ flight** *n* volo *m* charter *inv*

charwoman ['tʃɑːwumən] *n* domestica a ore

chase [tʃeɪs] *vt* inseguire; (*also: ~ away*) cacciare ♦ *n* caccia

chasm ['kæzəm] *n* abisso

chassis ['ʃæsɪ] *n* telaio

chat [tʃæt] *vi* (*also: have a ~*) chiacchierare ♦ *n* chiacchierata; **~ show** (*BRIT*) *n* talk show *m inv*

chatter ['tʃætə*] *vi* (*person*) ciarlare; (*bird*) cinguettare; (*teeth*) battere ♦ *n* ciarle *fpl*; cinguettio; **~box** (*inf*) *n* chiacchierone/a

chatty ['tʃætɪ] *adj* (*style*) familiare; (*person*) chiacchierino/a

chauffeur ['ʃəufə*] *n* autista *m*

chauvinist ['ʃəuvɪnɪst] *n* (*male ~*) maschilista *m*; (*nationalist*) sciovinista *m/f*

cheap [tʃiːp] *adj* a buon mercato; (*joke*) grossolano(a); (*poor quality*) di cattiva qualità ♦ *adv* a buon mercato; **~ day return** *n* biglietto ridotto di andata e ritorno valido in giornata; **~er** *adj* meno caro(a); **~ly** *adv* a buon prezzo, a buon mercato

cheat [tʃiːt] *vi* imbrogliare; (*at school*) copiare ♦ *vt* ingannare ♦ *n* imbroglione *m*; **to ~ sb out of sth** defraudare qn di qc

check [tʃɛk] *vt* verificare; (*passport, ticket*) controllare; (*halt*) fermare; (*restrain*) contenere ♦ *n* verifica; controllo; (*curb*) freno; (*US: bill*) conto; (*pattern: gen pl*) quadretti *mpl*; (*US*) = **cheque** ♦ *adj* (*pattern, cloth*) a quadretti; **~ in** *vi* (*in hotel*) registrare; (*at airport*) presentarsi all'accettazione ♦ *vt* (*luggage*) depositare; **~ out** *vi* (*in hotel*) saldare il conto; **~ up** *vi*: **to ~ up (on sth)** investigare (qc); **to ~ up on sb** informarsi sul conto di qn; **~ered** (*US*) *adj* = **chequered**; **~ers** (*US*) *n* dama; **~-in (desk)** *n* check-in *m inv*, accettazione *f* (*bagagli inv*); **~ing account** (*US*) *n* conto corrente; **~mate** *n* scaccomatto; **~out** *n* (*in supermarket*) cassa; **~point** *n* posto di blocco; **~room** (*US*) *n* deposito *m* bagagli *inv*; **~up** *n* (*MED*) controllo medico

cheek [tʃiːk] *n* guancia; (*impudence*) faccia tosta; **~bone** *n* zigomo; **~y** *adj* sfacciato(a)

cheep [tʃiːp] *vi* pigolare

cheer [tʃɪə*] *vt* applaudire; (*gladden*) rallegrare ♦ *vi* applaudire ♦ *n* grido (di incoraggiamento); **~s** *npl* (*of approval*, *encouragement*) applausi *mpl*; evviva *mpl*; **~s!** salute!; **~ up** *vi* rallegrarsi, farsi animo ♦ *vt* rallegrare; **~ful** *adj* allegro(a)

cheerio ['tʃɪərɪ'əʊ] (*BRIT*) *excl* ciao!

cheese [tʃiːz] *n* formaggio; **~board** *n* piatto del (*or* per il) formaggio

cheetah ['tʃiːtə] *n* ghepardo

chef [ʃef] *n* capocuoco

chemical ['kemɪkəl] *adj* chimico(a) ♦ *n* prodotto chimico

chemist ['kemɪst] *n* (*BRIT: pharmacist*) farmacista *m/f*; (*scientist*) chimico/a; **~ry** *n* chimica; **~'s (shop)** (*BRIT*) *n* farmacia

cheque [tʃek] (*BRIT*) *n* assegno; **~book** *n* libretto degli assegni; **~ card** *n* carta *f* assegni *inv*

chequered ['tʃekəd] (*US* **checkered**) *adj* (*fig*) movimentato(a)

cherish ['tʃerɪʃ] *vt* aver caro

cherry ['tʃerɪ] *n* ciliegia; (*also: ~ tree*) ciliegio

chess [tʃes] *n* scacchi *mpl*; **~board** *n* scacchiera

chest [tʃest] *n* petto; (*box*) cassa; **~ of drawers** *n* cassettone *m*

chestnut ['tʃesnʌt] *n* castagna; (*also: ~ tree*) castagno

chew [tʃuː] *vt* masticare; **~ing gum** *n* chewing gum *m*

chic [ʃiːk] *adj* elegante

chick [tʃɪk] *n* pulcino; (*inf*) pollastrella

chicken ['tʃɪkɪn] *n* pollo; (*inf: coward*) coniglio; **~ out** (*inf*) *vi* avere fifa; **~pox** *n* varicella

chicory ['tʃɪkərɪ] *n* cicoria

chief [tʃiːf] *n* capo ♦ *adj* principale; **~ executive** *n* direttore *m* generale; **~ly** *adv* per lo più, soprattutto

chilblain ['tʃɪlblɪn] *n* gelone *m*

child [tʃaɪld] (*pl* **~ren**) *n* bambino/a; **~birth** *n* parto; **~hood** *n* infanzia; **~ish** *adj* puerile; **~like** *adj* fanciullesco(a); **~ minder** (*BRIT*) *n* bambinaia

children ['tʃɪldrən] *npl of* **child**

child seat *n* seggiolino per bambini (*in auto*)

Chile ['tʃɪlɪ] *n* Cile *m*

chill [tʃɪl] *n* freddo; (*MED*) infreddatura ♦ *vt* raffreddare

chilli ['tʃɪlɪ] *n* peperoncino

chilly ['tʃɪlɪ] *adj* freddo(a), fresco(a); **to feel ~** sentirsi infreddolito(a)

chime [tʃaɪm] *n* carillon *m inv* ♦ *vi* suonare, scampanare

chimney ['tʃɪmnɪ] *n* camino; **~ sweep** *n* spazzacamino

chimpanzee [tʃɪmpæn'ziː] *n* scimpanzé *m inv*

chin [tʃɪn] *n* mento

China ['tʃaɪnə] *n* Cina

china ['tʃaɪnə] *n* porcellana

Chinese [tʃaɪ'niːz] *adj* cinese ♦ *n inv* cinese *m/f*; (*LING*) cinese *m*

chink [tʃɪŋk] *n* (*opening*) fessura; (*noise*) tintinnio

chip [tʃɪp] *n* (*gen pl*: *CULIN*) patatina fritta; (: *US: also: potato ~*) patatina; (*of wood, glass, stone*) scheggia; (*also: micro~*) chip *m inv* ♦ *vt* (*cup, plate*) scheggiare

chiropodist [kɪ'rɒpədɪst] (*BRIT*) *n* pedicure *m/f inv*

chirp [tʃəːp] *vi* cinguettare; fare cri cri

chisel ['tʃɪzl] *n* cesello

chit [tʃɪt] *n* biglietto

chitchat ['tʃɪttʃæt] *n* chiacchiere *fpl*

chivalry ['ʃɪvəlrɪ] *n* cavalleria; cortesia

chives [tʃaɪvz] *npl* erba cipollina

chock-a-block ['tʃɒkə'blɒk] *adj* pieno(a) zeppo(a)

chock-full ['tʃɒk'ful] *adj* = **chock-a-block**

chocolate ['tʃɒklɪt] *n* (*substance*) cioccolato, cioccolata; (*drink*) cioccolata; (*a sweet*) cioccolatino

choice [tʃɔɪs] *n* scelta ♦ *adj* scelto(a)

choir ['kwaɪə*] *n* coro; **~boy** *n* corista *m* fanciullo

choke [tʃəʊk] *vi* soffocare ♦ *vt* soffocare; (*block*): **to be ~d with** essere intasato(a) di ♦ *n* (*AUT*) valvola dell'aria

cholera ['kɒlərə] *n* colera *m*

cholesterol [kə'lestərɒl] *n* colesterolo

choose [tʃuːz] (*pt* **chose**, *pp* **chosen**) *vt* scegliere; **to ~ to do** decidere di fare; preferire fare

choosy ['tʃuːzɪ] *adj* schizzinoso(a)

chop [tʃɒp] *vt* (*wood*) spaccare; (*CULIN: also: ~ up*) tritare ♦ *n* (*CULIN*) costoletta; **~s** *npl* (*jaws*) mascelle *fpl*

chopper ['tʃɒpə*] *n* (*helicopter*) elicottero

choppy ['tʃɒpɪ] *adj* (*sea*) mosso(a)

chopsticks ['tʃɒpstɪks] *npl* bastoncini *mpl* cinesi

choral ['kɔːrəl] *adj* corale

chord [kɔːd] *n* (*MUS*) accordo

chore [tʃɔː*] *n* faccenda; **household ~s** faccende *fpl* domestiche

chortle ['tʃɔːtl] *vi* ridacchiare

chorus ['kɔːrəs] *n* coro; (*repeated part of song, also fig*) ritornello

chose [tʃəʊz] *pt of* **choose**

chosen ['tʃəʊzn] *pp of* **choose**

chowder ['tʃaʊdə*] *n* (*esp US*) zuppa di pesce

Christ [kraɪst] *n* Cristo

christen ['krɪsn] *vt* battezzare

Christian ['krɪstɪən] *adj, n* cristiano(a); **~ity** [-'ænɪtɪ] *n* cristianesimo; **~ name** *n* nome *m* (di battesimo)

Christmas ['krɪsməs] *n* Natale *m*; **Merry ~!** Buon Natale!; **~ card** *n* cartolina di Natale; **~ Day** *n* il giorno di Natale; **~ Eve** *n* la vigilia di Natale; **~ tree** *n* albero di Natale

chrome [krəum] *n* cromo

chromium ['krəumɪəm] *n* cromo

chronic ['krɒnɪk] *adj* cronico(a)

chronological [krɒnə'lɒdʒɪkəl] *adj* cronologico(a)

chrysanthemum [krɪ'sænθəməm] *n* crisantemo

chubby ['tʃʌbɪ] *adj* paffuto(a)

chuck [tʃʌk] (*inf*) *vt* buttare, gettare; (*BRIT: also*: ~ *up*) piantare; **~ out** *vt* buttar fuori

chuckle ['tʃʌkl] *vi* ridere sommessamente

chug [tʃʌg] *vi* fare ciuf ciuf

chum [tʃʌm] *n* compagno/a

chunk [tʃʌŋk] *n* pezzo

church [tʃɜːtʃ] *n* chiesa; **~yard** *n* sagrato

churn [tʃɜːn] *n* (*for butter*) zangola; (*for milk*) bidone *m*; **~ out** *vt* sfornare

chute [ʃuːt] *n* (*also: rubbish* ~) canale *m* di scarico; (*BRIT: children's slide*) scivolo

chutney ['tʃʌtnɪ] *n* salsa piccante (*di frutta, zucchero e spezie*)

CIA (*US*) *n abbr* (= *Central Intelligence Agency*) CIA *f*

CID (*BRIT*) *n abbr* (= *Criminal Investigation Department*) ≈ polizia giudiziaria

cider ['saɪdə*] *n* sidro

cigar [sɪ'gɑː*] *n* sigaro

cigarette [sɪgə'ret] *n* sigaretta; **~ case** *n* portasigarette *m inv*; **~ end** *n* mozzicone *m*

Cinderella [sɪndə'relə] *n* Cenerentola

cinders ['sɪndəz] *npl* ceneri *fpl*

cine camera ['sɪnɪ-] (*BRIT*) *n* cinepresa

cine film ['sɪnɪ-] (*BRIT*) *n* pellicola

cinema ['sɪnəmə] *n* cinema *m inv*

cinnamon ['sɪnəmən] *n* cannella

cipher ['saɪfə*] *n* cifra

circle ['sɜːkl] *n* cerchio; (*of friends etc*) circolo; (*in cinema*) galleria ♦ *vi* girare in circolo ♦ *vt* (*surround*) circondare; (*move round*) girare intorno a

circuit ['sɜːkɪt] *n* circuito; **~ous** [sɜː'kjuːtəs] *adj* indiretto(a)

circular ['sɜːkjulə*] *adj* circolare ♦ *n* circolare *f*

circulate ['sɜːkjuleɪt] *vi* circolare ♦ *vt* far circolare; **circulation** [-'leɪʃən] *n* circolazione *f*; (*of newspaper*) tiratura

circumstances ['sɜːkəmstənsɪz] *npl* circostanze *fpl*; (*financial condition*) condizioni *fpl* finanziarie

circus ['sɜːkəs] *n* circo

CIS *n abbr* (= *Commonwealth of Independent States*) CSI *f*

cistern ['sɪstən] *n* cisterna; (*in toilet*) serbatoio d'acqua

citizen ['sɪtɪzn] *n* (*of country*) cittadino/a; (*of town*) abitante *m/f*; **~ship** *n* cittadinanza

citrus fruit ['sɪtrəs-] *n* agrume *m*

city ['sɪtɪ] *n* città *f inv*; **the C~** la Città di Londra (*centro commerciale*)

civic ['sɪvɪk] *adj* civico(a); **~ centre** (*BRIT*) *n* centro civico

civil ['sɪvɪl] *adj* civile; **~ engineer** *n* ingegnere *m* civile; **~ian** [sɪ'vɪlɪən] *adj*, *n* borghese *m/f*

civilization [sɪvɪlaɪ'zeɪʃən] *n* civiltà *f inv*

civilized ['sɪvɪlaɪzd] *adj* civilizzato(a); (*fig*) cortese

civil: **~ law** *n* codice *m* civile; (*study*) diritto civile; **~ servant** *n* impiegato/a statale; **C~ Service** *n* amministrazione *f* statale; **~ war** *n* guerra civile

clad [klæd] *adj*: **~ (in)** vestito(a) (di)

claim [kleɪm] *vt* (*assert*): **to ~ (that)/to be** sostenere (che)/di essere; (*credit, rights etc*) rivendicare; (*damages*) richiedere ♦ *vi* (*for insurance*) fare una domanda d'indennizzo ♦ *n* pretesa; rivendicazione *f*; richiesta; **~ant** *n* (*ADMIN, LAW*) richiedente *m/f*

clairvoyant [kleə'vɔɪənt] *n* chiaroveggente *m/f*

clam [klæm] *n* vongola

clamber ['klæmbə*] *vi* arrampicarsi

clammy ['klæmɪ] *adj* (*weather*) caldo(a) umido(a); (*hands*) viscido(a)

clamour ['klæmə*] (*US* **clamor**) *vi*: **to ~ for** chiedere a gran voce

clamp [klæmp] *n* pinza; morsa ♦ *vt* stringere con una morsa; (*AUT: wheel*) applicare i ceppi bloccaruote a; **~ down on** *vt fus* dare un giro di vite a

clan [klæn] *n* clan *m inv*

clang [klæŋ] *vi* emettere un suono metallico

clap [klæp] *vi* applaudire; **~ping** *n* applausi *mpl*

claret ['klærət] *n* vino di Bordeaux

clarify ['klærɪfaɪ] *vt* chiarificare, chiarire

clarinet [klærɪ'net] *n* clarinetto

clarity ['klærɪtɪ] *n* chiarità

clash [klæʃ] *n* frastuono; (*fig*) scontro ♦ *vi* scontrarsi; cozzare

clasp [klɑːsp] *n* (*hold*) stretta; (*of necklace, bag*) fermaglio, fibbia ♦ *vt* stringere

class [klɑːs] *n* classe *f* ♦ *vt* classificare

classic ['klæsɪk] *adj* classico(a) ♦ *n* classico; **~al** *adj* classico(a)

classified ['klæsɪfaɪd] *adj* (*information*) segreto(a), riservato(a); **~ advertisement** *n* annuncio economico

classmate ['klɑːsmeɪt] *n* compagno/a di classe

classroom ['klɑːsrum] *n* aula

clatter ['klætə*] *n* tintinnio; scalpitio ♦ *vi* tintinnare; scalpitare

clause [klɔːz] *n* clausola; (*LING*) proposizione *f*

claw [klɔː] *n* (*of bird of prey*) artiglio; (*of lobster*) pinza

clay [kleɪ] *n* argilla

clean [kli:n] adj pulito(a); (clear, smooth) liscio(a) ♦ vt pulire; ~ **out** vt ripulire; ~ **up** vt (also fig) ripulire; **~-cut** adj (man) curato(a); **~er** n (person) donna delle pulizie; **~er's** n (also: dry ~er's) tintoria; **~ing** n pulizia; **~liness** ['klɛnlɪnɪs] n pulizia

cleanse [klɛnz] vt pulire; purificare; **~r** n detergente m

clean-shaven [-'ʃeɪvn] adj sbarbato(a)

cleansing department ['klɛnzɪŋ-] (BRIT) n nettezza urbana

clear [klɪə*] adj chiaro(a); (glass etc) trasparente; (road, way) libero(a); (conscience) pulito(a) ♦ vt sgombrare; liberare; (table) sparecchiare; (cheque) fare la compensazione di; (LAW: suspect) discolpare; (obstacle) superare ♦ vi (weather) rasserenarsi; (fog) andarsene ♦ adv: ~ **of** distante da; ~ **up** vt mettere in ordine; (mystery) risolvere; **~ance** n (removal) sgombro; (permission) autorizzazione f, permesso; **~-cut** adj ben delineato(a), distinto(a); **~ing** n radura; **~ing bank** (BRIT) n banca (che fa uso della camera di compensazione); **~ly** adv chiaramente; **~way** (BRIT) n strada con divieto di sosta

cleaver ['kli:və*] n mannaia

clef [klɛf] n (MUS) chiave f

cleft [klɛft] n (in rock) crepa, fenditura

clench [klɛntʃ] vt stringere

clergy ['klɜ:dʒɪ] n clero; **~man** (irreg) n ecclesiastico

clerical ['klɛrɪkəl] adj d'impiegato; (REL) clericale

clerk [klɑ:k, (US) klɜ:rk] n (BRIT) impiegato/a; (US) commesso/a

clever ['klɛvə*] adj (mentally) intelligente; (deft, skilful) abile; (device, arrangement) ingegnoso(a)

click [klɪk] vi scattare ♦ vt (heels etc) battere; (tongue) far schioccare

client ['klaɪənt] n cliente m/f

cliff [klɪf] n scogliera scoscesa, rupe f

climate ['klaɪmɪt] n clima m

climax ['klaɪmæks] n culmine m; (sexual) orgasmo

climb [klaɪm] vi salire; (clamber) arrampicarsi ♦ vt salire; (CLIMBING) scalare ♦ n salita; arrampicata; scalata; **~-down** n marcia indietro; **~er** n rocciatore/trice; alpinista m/f; **~ing** n alpinismo

clinch [klɪntʃ] vt (deal) concludere

cling [klɪŋ] (pt, pp clung) vi: **to ~ (to)** aggrapparsi (a); (of clothes) aderire strettamente (a)

clinic ['klɪnɪk] n clinica; **~al** adj clinico(a); (fig) distaccato(a); (: room) freddo(a)

clink [klɪŋk] vi tintinnare

clip [klɪp] n (for hair) forcina; (also: paper ~)

graffetta; (TV, CINEMA) sequenza ♦ vt attaccare insieme; (hair, nails) tagliare; (hedge) tosare; **~pers** npl (for gardening) cesoie fpl; (also: nail ~pers) forbicine fpl per le unghie; **~ping** n (from newspaper) ritaglio

clique [kli:k] n cricca

cloak [kləuk] n mantello ♦ vt avvolgere; **~room** n (for coats etc) guardaroba m inv; (BRIT: W.C.) gabinetti mpl

clock [klɔk] n orologio; ~ **in** or **on** vi timbrare il cartellino (all'entrata); ~ **off** or **out** vi timbrare il cartellino (all'uscita); **~wise** adv in senso orario; **~work** n movimento or meccanismo a orologeria ♦ adj a molla

clog [klɔg] n zoccolo ♦ vt intasare ♦ vi (also: ~ up) intasarsi, bloccarsi

cloister ['klɔɪstə*] n chiostro

clone [kləun] n clone m

close¹ [kləus] adj: ~ **(to)** vicino(a) (a); (watch, link, relative) stretto(a); (examination) attento(a); (contest) combattuto(a); (weather) afoso(a) ♦ adv vicino, dappresso; ~ **to** vicino a; ~ **by**, ~ **at hand** a portata di mano; **a ~ friend** un amico intimo; **to have a ~ shave** (fig) scamparla bella

close² [kləuz] vt chiudere ♦ vi (shop etc) chiudere; (lid, door etc) chiudersi; (end) finire ♦ n (end) fine f; ~ **down** vi cessare (definitivamente); **~d** adj chiuso(a); **~d shop** n azienda o fabbrica che impiega solo aderenti ai sindacati

close-knit [kləus'nɪt] adj (family, community) molto unito(a)

closely ['kləuslɪ] adv (examine, watch) da vicino; (related) strettamente

closet ['klɔzɪt] n (cupboard) armadio

close-up ['kləusʌp] n primo piano

closure ['kləuʒə*] n chiusura

clot [klɔt] n (also: blood ~) coagulo; (inf: idiot) scemo ♦ vi coagularsi

cloth [klɔθ] n (material) tessuto, stoffa; (rag) strofinaccio

clothe [kləuð] vt vestire; **~s** npl abiti mpl, vestiti mpl; **~s brush** n spazzola per abiti; **~s line** n corda (per stendere il bucato); **~s peg** (US **~s pin**) n molletta

clothing ['kləuðɪŋ] n = **clothes**

cloud [klaud] n nuvola; **~burst** n acquazzone m; **~y** adj nuvoloso(a); (liquid) torbido(a)

clout [klaut] vt dare un colpo a

clove [kləuv] n chiodo di garofano; ~ **of garlic** spicchio d'aglio

clover ['kləuvə*] n trifoglio

clown [klaun] n pagliaccio ♦ vi (also: ~ about, ~ around) fare il pagliaccio

cloying ['klɔɪɪŋ] adj (taste, smell) nauseabondo(a)

club [klʌb] n (society) club m inv, circolo; (weapon, GOLF) mazza ♦ vt bastonare ♦ vi: **to**

~ **together** associarsi; ~**s** npl (CARDS) fiori mpl;
~ **class** n (AVIAT) classe f club inv; ~**house** n
sede f del circolo

cluck [klʌk] vi chiocciare

clue [klu:] n indizio; (in crosswords)
definizione f; **I haven't a** ~ non ho la minima
idea

clump [klʌmp] n (of flowers, trees) gruppo;
(of grass) ciuffo

clumsy [ˈklʌmzɪ] adj goffo(a)

clung [klʌŋ] pt, pp of **cling**

cluster [ˈklʌstə*] n gruppo ♦ vi raggrupparsi

clutch [klʌtʃ] n (grip, grasp) presa, stretta;
(AUT) frizione f ♦ vt afferrare, stringere forte

clutter [ˈklʌtə*] vt ingombrare

CND n abbr = **Campaign for Nuclear
Disarmament**

Co. abbr = **county; company**

c/o abbr (= care of) presso

coach [kəʊtʃ] n (bus) pullman m inv; (horse-
drawn, of train) carrozza; (SPORT) allenatore/
trice; (tutor) chi dà ripetizioni ♦ vt allenare;
dare ripetizioni a; ~ **trip** n viaggio in pullman

coal [kəʊl] n carbone m; ~ **face** n fronte f;
~**field** n bacino carbonifero

coalition [kəʊəˈlɪʃən] n coalizione f

coalman [ˈkəʊlmən] (irreg) n negoziante m
di carbone

coalmine [ˈkəʊlmaɪn] n miniera di carbone

coarse [kɔ:s] adj (salt, sand etc) grosso(a);
(cloth, person) rozzo(a)

coast [kəʊst] n costa ♦ vi (with cycle etc)
scendere a ruota libera; ~**al** adj costiero(a);
~**guard** n guardia costiera; ~**line** n linea
costiera

coat [kəʊt] n cappotto; (of animal) pelo; (of
paint) mano f ♦ vt coprire; ~ **of arms** n
stemma m; ~ **hanger** n attaccapanni m inv;
~**ing** n rivestimento

coax [kəʊks] vt indurre (con moine)

cobbler [ˈkɔblə*] n calzolaio

cobbles [ˈkɔblz] npl ciottoli mpl

cobblestones [ˈkɔblstəʊnz] npl ciottoli mpl

cobweb [ˈkɔbwɛb] n ragnatela

cocaine [kəˈkeɪn] n cocaina

cock [kɔk] n (rooster) gallo; (male bird)
maschio ♦ vt (gun) armare; ~**erel** n galletto

cockle [ˈkɔkl] n cardio

cockney [ˈkɔknɪ] n cockney m/f inv (abitante
dei quartieri popolari dell'East End di Londra)

cockpit [ˈkɔkpɪt] n abitacolo

cockroach [ˈkɔkrəʊtʃ] n blatta

cocktail [ˈkɔkteɪl] n cocktail m inv; ~ **cabinet**
n mobile m bar inv; ~ **party** n cocktail m inv

cocoa [ˈkəʊkəʊ] n cacao

coconut [ˈkəʊkənʌt] n noce f di cocco

cocoon [kəˈku:n] n bozzolo

cod [kɔd] n merluzzo

C.O.D. abbr = **cash on delivery**

code [kəʊd] n codice m

cod-liver oil [ˈkɔdlɪvə*-] n olio di fegato di
merluzzo

coercion [kəʊˈə:ʃən] n coercizione f

coffee [ˈkɔfɪ] n caffè m inv; ~ **bar** (BRIT) n
caffè m inv; ~ **break** n pausa per il caffè;
~**pot** n caffettiera; ~ **table** n tavolino

coffin [ˈkɔfɪn] n bara

cog [kɔg] n dente m

cogent [ˈkəʊdʒənt] adj convincente

coherent [kəʊˈhɪərənt] adj coerente

coil [kɔɪl] n rotolo; (ELEC) bobina;
(contraceptive) spirale f ♦ vt avvolgere

coin [kɔɪn] n moneta ♦ vt (word) coniare;
~**age** n sistema m monetario; ~-**box** (BRIT) n
telefono a gettoni

coincide [kəʊɪnˈsaɪd] vi coincidere; **coincidence** [kəʊˈɪnsɪdəns] n combinazione f

Coke ® [kəʊk] n coca

coke [kəʊk] n coke m

colander [ˈkɔləndə*] n colino

cold [kəʊld] adj freddo(a) ♦ n freddo; (MED)
raffreddore m; **it's** ~ fa freddo; **to be** ~
(person) aver freddo; (object) essere
freddo(a); **to catch** ~ prendere freddo; **to
catch a** ~ prendere un raffreddore; **in** ~ **blood**
a sangue freddo; ~-**shoulder** vt trattare con
freddezza; ~ **sore** n erpete m

coleslaw [ˈkəʊlslɔ:] n insalata di cavolo bianco

colic [ˈkɔlɪk] n colica

collapse [kəˈlæps] vi crollare ♦ n crollo;
(MED) collasso

collapsible [kəˈlæpsəbl] adj pieghevole

collar [ˈkɔlə*] n (of coat, shirt) colletto; (of
dog, cat) collare m; ~**bone** n clavicola

collateral [kəˈlætərl] n garanzia

colleague [ˈkɔli:g] n collega m/f

collect [kəˈlekt] vt (gen) raccogliere; (as a
hobby) fare collezione di; (BRIT: call and pick
up) prendere; (money owed, pension)
riscuotere; (donations, subscriptions) fare una
colletta di ♦ vi adunarsi, riunirsi; ammucchiarsi; **to call** ~ (US: TEL) fare una
chiamata a carico del destinatario; ~**ion**
[kəˈlekʃən] n raccolta; collezione f; (for
money) colletta

collector [kəˈlektə*] n collezionista m/f

college [ˈkɔlidʒ] n college m inv; (of
technology etc) istituto superiore

collide [kəˈlaɪd] vi: **to** ~ (**with**) scontrarsi
(con)

colliery [ˈkɔlɪərɪ] (BRIT) n miniera di carbone

collision [kəˈlɪʒən] n collisione f, scontro

colloquial [kəˈləʊkwɪəl] adj familiare

colon [ˈkəʊlən] n (sign) due punti mpl; (MED)
colon m inv

colonel [ˈkə:nl] n colonnello

colonial [kəˈləʊnɪəl] adj coloniale

colony [ˈkɔlənɪ] n colonia

colour ['kʌlə*] (US **color**) n colore m ♦ vt colorare; (tint, dye) tingere; (fig: affect) influenzare ♦ vi (blush) arrossire; **~s** npl (of party, club) colori mpl; **in ~** a colori; **~ in** vt colorare; **~ bar** n discriminazione f razziale (in locali etc); **~-blind** adj daltonico(a); **~ed** adj (photo) a colori; (person) di colore; **~ film** n (for camera) pellicola a colori; **~ful** adj pieno(a) di colore, a vivaci colori; (personality) colorato(a); **~ing** n (substance) colorante m; (complexion) colorito; **~ scheme** n combinazione f di colori; **~ television** n televisione f a colori

colt [kəult] n puledro

column ['kɔləm] n colonna; **~ist** ['kɔləmnɪst] n articolista m/f

coma ['kəumə] n coma m inv

comb [kəum] n pettine m ♦ vt (hair) pettinare; (area) battere a tappeto

combat ['kɔmbæt] n combattimento ♦ vt combattere, lottare contro

combination [kɔmbɪ'neɪʃən] n combinazione f

combine [vb kəm'baɪn, n 'kɔmbaɪn] vt: **to ~ (with)** combinare (con); (one quality with another) unire (a) ♦ vi unirsi; (CHEM) combinarsi ♦ n (ECON) associazione f; **~ (harvester)** n mietitrebbia

come [kʌm] (pt **came**, pp **come**) vi venire; arrivare; **to ~ to** (decision etc) raggiungere; **I've ~ to like him** ha cominciato a piacermi; **to ~ undone** slacciarsi; **to ~ loose** allentarsi; **~ about** vi succedere; **~ across** vt fus trovare per caso; **~ away** vi venire via; staccarsi; **~ back** vi ritornare; **~ by** vt fus (acquire) ottenere; procurarsi; **~ down** vi scendere; (prices) calare; (buildings) essere demolito(a); **~ forward** vi farsi avanti, presentarsi; **~ from** vt fus venire da; provenire da; **~ in** vi entrare; **~ in for** vt fus (criticism etc) ricevere; **~ into** vt fus (money) ereditare; **~ off** vi (button) staccarsi; (stain) andar via; (attempt) riuscire; **~ on** vi (pupil, work, project) fare progressi; (lights) accendersi; (electricity) entrare in funzione; **~ on!** avanti!, andiamo!, forza!; **~ out** vi uscire; (stain) andare via; **~ round** vi (after faint, operation) riprendere conoscenza, rinvenire; **~ to** vi rinvenire; **~ up** vi (sun) salire; (problem) sorgere; (event) essere in arrivo; (in conversation) saltar fuori; **~ up against** vt fus (resistance, difficulties) urtare contro; **~ up with** vt fus: **he came up with an idea** venne fuori con un'idea; **~ upon** vt fus trovare per caso; **~back** n (THEATRE etc) ritorno

comedian [kə'miːdɪən] n comico

comedienne [kəmiːdɪ'ɛn] n attrice f comica

comedy ['kɔmɪdɪ] n commedia

comeuppance [kʌm'ʌpəns] n: **to get one's ~** ricevere ciò che si merita

comfort ['kʌmfət] n comodità f inv, benessere m; (relief) consolazione f, conforto ♦ vt consolare, confortare; **~s** npl comodità fpl; **~able** adj comodo(a); (financially) agiato(a); **~ably** adv (sit etc) comodamente; (live) bene; **~ station** n (US) gabinetti mpl

comic ['kɔmɪk] adj (also: **~al**) comico(a) ♦ n comico; (BRIT: magazine) giornaletto; **~ strip** n fumetto

coming ['kʌmɪŋ] n arrivo ♦ adj (next) prossimo(a); (future) futuro(a); **~(s) and going(s)** n(pl) andirivieni m inv

comma ['kɔmə] n virgola

command [kə'mɑːnd] n ordine m, comando; (MIL: authority) comando; (mastery) padronanza ♦ vt comandare; **to ~ sb to do** ordinare a qn di fare; **~eer** [kɔmən'dɪə*] vt requisire; **~er** n capo; (MIL) comandante m

commando [kə'mɑːndəu] n commando m inv; membro di un commando

commence [kə'mɛns] vt, vi cominciare

commend [kə'mɛnd] vt lodare; raccomandare

commensurate [kə'mɛnʃərɪt] adj: **~ with** proporzionato(a) a

comment ['kɔmɛnt] n commento ♦ vi: **to ~ (on)** fare commenti (su); **~ary** ['kɔməntərɪ] n commentario; (SPORT) radiocronaca, telecronaca; **~ator** ['kɔməntertə*] n commentatore/trice; radiocronista m/f; telecronista m/f

commerce ['kɔmə:s] n commercio

commercial [kə'mə:ʃəl] adj commerciale ♦ n (TV, RADIO: advertisement) pubblicità f inv; **~ radio/television** n radio f inv/televisione f privata

commiserate [kə'mɪzəreɪt] vi: **to ~ with** partecipare al dolore di

commission [kə'mɪʃən] n commissione f ♦ vt (work of art) commissionare; **out of ~** (NAUT) in disarmo; **~aire** [kəmɪʃə'neə*] (BRIT) n (at shop, cinema etc) portiere m in livrea; **~er** n (POLICE) questore m

commit [kə'mɪt] vt (act) commettere; (to sb's care) affidare; **to ~ o.s. (to do)** impegnarsi (a fare); **to ~ suicide** suicidarsi; **~ment** n impegno; promessa

committee [kə'mɪtɪ] n comitato

commodity [kə'mɔdɪtɪ] n prodotto, articolo

common ['kɔmən] adj comune; (pej) volgare; (usual) normale ♦ n terreno comune; **the C~s** (BRIT) npl la Camera dei Comuni; **in ~** in comune; **~er** n cittadino/a (non nobile); **~ law** n diritto consuetudinario; **~ly** adv comunemente, usualmente; **C~ Market** n Mercato Comune;

~place adj banale, ordinario(a); **~room** n sala di riunione; (SCOL) sala dei professori; **~ sense** n buon senso; **the C~wealth** n il Commonwealth

commotion [kə'məuʃən] n confusione f, tumulto

communal ['kɔmjuːnl] adj (for common use) pubblico(a)

commune [n 'kɔmjuːn, vb kə'mjuːn] n (group) comune f ♦ vi: **to ~ with** mettersi in comunione con

communicate [kə'mjuːnɪkeɪt] vt comunicare, trasmettere ♦ vi: **to ~ (with)** comunicare (con)

communication [kəmjuːnɪ'keɪʃən] n comunicazione f; **~ cord** n (BRIT) segnale m d'allarme

communion [kə'mjuːnɪən] n (also: Holy C~) comunione f

communiqué [kə'mjuːnɪkeɪ] n comunicato

communism ['kɔmjunɪzəm] n comunismo; **communist** adj, n comunista m/f

community [kə'mjuːnɪtɪ] n comunità f inv; **~ centre** n circolo ricreativo; **~ chest** (US) n fondo di beneficenza

commutation ticket [kɔmjuːˈteɪʃən-] (US) n biglietto di abbonamento

commute [kə'mjuːt] vi fare il pendolare ♦ vt (LAW) commutare; **~r** n pendolare m/f

compact [adj kəmˈpækt, n 'kɔmpækt] adj compatto(a) ♦ n (also: powder ~) portacipria m inv; **~ disc** n compact disc m inv; **~ disc player** n lettore m CD inv

companion [kəmˈpænɪən] n compagno/a; **~ship** n compagnia

company ['kʌmpənɪ] n (also COMM, MIL, THEATRE) compagnia; **to keep sb ~** tenere compagnia a qn; **~ secretary** (BRIT) n segretario/a generale

comparable ['kɔmpərəbl] adj simile

comparative [kəmˈpærətɪv] adj relativo(a); (adjective etc) comparativo(a); **~ly** adv relativamente

compare [kəmˈpeə*] vt: **to ~ sth/sb with/to** confrontare qc/qn con/a ♦ vi: **to ~ (with)** reggere il confronto (con); **comparison** [-ˈpærɪsn] n confronto; **in comparison (with)** in confronto (a)

compartment [kəmˈpɑːtmənt] n compartimento; (RAIL) scompartimento

compass ['kʌmpəs] n bussola; **~es** npl (MATH) compasso

compassion [kəmˈpæʃən] n compassione f

compatible [kəmˈpætɪbl] adj compatibile

compel [kəmˈpel] vt costringere, obbligare

compensate ['kɔmpənseɪt] vt risarcire ♦ vi: **to ~ for** compensare; **compensation** [-ˈseɪʃən] n compensazione f; (money) risarcimento

compère ['kɔmpeə*] n presentatore/trice

compete [kəmˈpiːt] vi (take part) concorrere; (vie): **to ~ (with)** fare concorrenza (a)

competent ['kɔmpɪtənt] adj competente

competition [kɔmpɪ'tɪʃən] n gara; concorso; (ECON) concorrenza

competitive [kəmˈpetɪtɪv] adj (ECON) concorrenziale; (sport) agonistico(a); (person) che ha spirito di competizione; che ha spirito agonistico

competitor [kəmˈpetɪtə*] n concorrente m/f

complacency [kəmˈpleɪsnsɪ] n compiacenza di sé

complain [kəmˈpleɪn] vi lagnarsi, lamentarsi; **~t** n lamento; (in shop etc) reclamo; (MED) malattia

complement [n 'kɔmplɪmənt, vb 'kɔmplɪment] n complemento; (especially of ship's crew etc) effettivo ♦ vt (enhance) accompagnarsi bene a; **~ary** [kɔmplɪ'mentərɪ] adj complementare

complete [kəmˈpliːt] adj completo(a) ♦ vt completare; (a form) riempire; **~ly** adv completamente; **completion** n completamento

complex ['kɔmpleks] adj complesso(a) ♦ n (PSYCH, buildings etc) complesso

complexion [kəmˈplekʃən] n (of face) carnagione f

compliance [kəmˈplaɪəns] n acquiescenza, in ~ with (orders, wishes etc) in conformità con

complicate ['kɔmplɪkeɪt] vt complicare; **~d** adj complicato(a); **complication** [-ˈkeɪʃən] n complicazione f

compliment [n 'kɔmplɪmənt, vb 'kɔmplɪment] n complimento ♦ vt fare un complimento a; **~s** npl (greetings) complimenti mpl; rispetti mpl; **to pay sb a ~** fare un complimento a qn; **~ary** [-ˈmentərɪ] adj complimentoso(a), elogiativo(a); (free) in omaggio; **~ary ticket** n biglietto omaggio

comply [kəmˈplaɪ] vi: **to ~ with** assentire a; conformarsi a

component [kəmˈpəunənt] a componente ♦ n componente m

compose [kəmˈpəuz] vt (form): **to be ~d of** essere composto di; (music, poem etc) comporre; **to ~ o.s.** ricomporsi; **~d** adj calmo(a); **~r** n (MUS) compositore/trice

composition [kɔmpə'zɪʃən] n composizione f

composure [kəmˈpəuʒə*] n calma

compound ['kɔmpaund] n (CHEM, LING) composto; (enclosure) recinto ♦ adj composto(a); **~ fracture** n frattura esposta

comprehend [kɔmprɪ'hend] vt comprendere, capire; **comprehension** [-ˈhenʃən] n comprensione f

comprehensive [kɔmprɪ'hensɪv] *adj*
comprensivo(a); **~ policy** *n* (*INSURANCE*)
polizza che copre tutti i rischi; **~ (school)**
(*BRIT*) *n* scuola secondaria aperta a tutti

compress [*vb* kəm'pres, *n* 'kɔmpres] *vt*
comprimere ♦ *n* (*MED*) compressa

comprise [kəm'praɪz] *vt* (*also:* **be ~d of**)
comprendere

compromise ['kɔmprəmaɪz] *n* compromesso
♦ *vt* compromettere ♦ *vi* venire a un
compromesso

compulsion [kəm'pʌlʃən] *n* costrizione *f*

compulsive [kəm'pʌlsɪv] *adj* (*liar, gambler*)
che non riesce a controllarsi; (*viewing,
reading*) cui non si può fare a meno

compulsory [kəm'pʌlsərɪ] *adj*
obbligatorio(a)

computer [kəm'pjuːtə*] *n* computer *m inv*,
elaboratore *m* elettronico; **~ game** *n* gioco
per computer; **~-generated** *adj* realizzato(a)
al computer; **~ize** *vt* computerizzare;
~ programmer *n* programmatore/trice;
~ programming *n* programmazione *f* di
computer; **~ science** *n* informatica; **computing** *n* informatica

comrade ['kɔmrɪd] *n* compagno/a; **~ship** *n*
cameratismo

con [kɔn] (*inf*) *vt* truffare ♦ *n* truffa

conceal [kən'siːl] *vt* nascondere

concede [kən'siːd] *vt* ammettere

conceit [kən'siːt] *n* presunzione *f*, vanità;
~ed *adj* presuntuoso(a), vanitoso(a)

conceive [kən'siːv] *vt* concepire ♦ *vi*
concepire un bambino

concentrate ['kɔnsəntreɪt] *vi* concentrarsi
♦ *vt* concentrare

concentration [kɔnsən'treɪʃən] *n*
concentrazione *f*; **~ camp** *n* campo di
concentramento

concept ['kɔnsept] *n* concetto

concern [kən'səːn] *n* affare *m*; (*COMM*)
azienda, ditta; (*anxiety*) preoccupazione *f*
♦ *vt* riguardare; **to be ~ed** (*about*)
preoccuparsi (di); **~ing** *prep* riguardo a, circa

concert ['kɔnsət] *n* concerto; **~ed**
[kən'səːtɪd] *adj* concertato(a); **~ hall** *n* sala
da concerti

concertina [kɔnsə'tiːnə] *n* piccola
fisarmonica

conclude [kən'kluːd] *vt* concludere;
conclusion [-'kluːʒən] *n* conclusione *f*;
conclusive [-'kluːsɪv] *adj* conclusivo(a)

concoct [kən'kɔkt] *vt* inventare; **~ion**
[-'kɔkʃən] *n* miscuglio

concourse ['kɔŋkɔːs] *n* (*hall*) atrio

concrete ['kɔŋkriːt] *n* calcestruzzo ♦ *adj*
concreto(a); di calcestruzzo

concur [kən'kəː*] *vi* concordare

concurrently [kən'kʌrntlɪ] *adv*
simultaneamente

concussion [kən'kʌʃən] *n* commozione *f*
cerebrale

condemn [kən'dem] *vt* condannare;
(*building*) dichiarare pericoloso(a)

condensation [kɔnden'seɪʃən] *n*
condensazione *f*

condense [kən'dens] *vi* condensarsi ♦ *vt*
condensare; **~d milk** *n* latte *m* condensato

condescending [kɔndɪ'sendɪŋ] *adj* (*person*)
che ha un'aria di superiorità

condition [kən'dɪʃən] *n* condizione *f*; (*MED*)
malattia ♦ *vt* condizionare; **on ~ that** a
condizione che + *sub*, a condizione di; **~er** *n*
(*for hair*) balsamo; (*for fabrics*) ammorbidente
m

condolences [kən'dəʊlənsɪz] *npl*
condoglianze *fpl*

condom ['kɔndəm] *n* preservativo

condominium [kɔndə'mɪnɪəm] (*US*) *n*
condominio

conducive [kən'djuːsɪv] *adj*: **~ to** favorevole
a

conduct [*n* 'kɔndʌkt, *vb* kən'dʌkt] *n*
condotta ♦ *vt* condurre; (*manage*) dirigere,
amministrare; (*MUS*) dirigere; **to ~ o.s.**
comportarsi; **~ed tour** *n* gita accompagnata;
~or *n* (*of orchestra*) direttore *m* d'orchestra;
(*on bus*) bigliettaio; (*US: on train*) controllore
m; (*ELEC*) conduttore *m*; **~ress** *n* (*on bus*)
bigliettaia

cone [kəʊn] *n* cono; (*BOT*) pigna; (*traffic ~*)
birillo

confectioner [kən'fekʃənə*] *n* pasticciere *m*;
~'s (shop) *n* ≈ pasticceria; **~y** *n* dolciumi
mpl

confer [kən'fəː*] *vt*: **to ~ sth on** conferire qc a
♦ *vi* conferire

conference ['kɔnfərns] *n* congresso

confess [kən'fes] *vt* confessare, ammettere
♦ *vi* confessare; **~ion** [-'feʃən] *n* confessione *f*

confetti [kən'fetɪ] *n* coriandoli *mpl*

confide [kən'faɪd] *vi*: **to ~ in** confidarsi con

confidence ['kɔnfɪdns] *n* confidenza; (*trust*)
fiducia; (*self-assurance*) sicurezza di sé; **in ~**
(*speak, write*) in confidenza, con-
fidenzialmente; **~ trick** *n* truffa; **confident**
adj sicuro(a); sicuro(a) di sé; **confidential**
[kɔnfɪ'denʃəl] *adj* riservato(a), confidenziale

confine [kən'faɪn] *vt* limitare; (*shut up*)
rinchiudere; **~d** *adj* (*space*) ristretto(a);
~ment *n* prigionia; **~s** ['kɔnfaɪnz] *npl* confini
mpl

confirm [kən'fəːm] *vt* confermare; **~ation**
[kɔnfə'meɪʃən] *n* conferma; (*REL*) cresima;
~ed *adj* inveterato(a)

confiscate ['kɔnfɪskeɪt] *vt* confiscare

conflict [*n* 'kɔnflɪkt, *vb* kən'flɪkt] *n* conflitto
♦ *vi* essere in conflitto; **~ing** *adj* contrastante

conform [kən'fɔːm] vi: **to ~ (to)** conformarsi (a)

confound [kən'faund] vt confondere

confront [kən'frʌnt] vt (enemy, danger) affrontare; [kɒnfrʌn'teɪʃən] n scontro

confuse [kən'fjuːz] vt (one thing with another) confondere; **~d** adj confuso(a); **confusing** adj che fa confondere; **confusion** [-'fjuːʒən] n confusione f

congeal [kən'dʒiːl] vi (blood) congelarsi

congenial [kən'dʒiːnɪəl] adj (person) simpatico(a); (thing) congeniale

congested [kən'dʒestɪd] adj congestionato(a)

congestion [kən'dʒestʃən] n congestione f

congratulate [kən'grætjuleɪt] vt: **to ~ sb (on)** congratularsi con qn (per or di); **congratulations** [-'leɪʃənz] npl auguri mpl; (on success) complimenti mpl, congratulazioni fpl

congregate ['kɒŋgrɪgeɪt] vi congregarsi, riunirsi

congress ['kɒŋgres] n congresso; **C~man** (US) n membro del Congresso

conjunction [kən'dʒʌŋkʃən] n congiunzione f

conjunctivitis [kəndʒʌŋktɪ'vaɪtɪs] n congiuntivite f

conjure ['kʌndʒə*] vi fare giochi di prestigio; **~ up** vt (ghost, spirit) evocare; (memories) rievocare; **~r** n prestidigitatore/trice, prestigiatore/trice

conk out [kɒŋk-] (inf) vi andare in panne

con man n truffatore m

connect [kə'nekt] vt connettere, collegare; (ELEC, TEL) collegare; (fig) associare ♦ vi (train): **to ~ with** essere in coincidenza con; **to be ~ed with** (associated) aver rapporti con; **~ion** [-ʃən] n relazione f, rapporto; (ELEC) connessione f; (train, plane) coincidenza; (TEL) collegamento

connive [kə'naɪv] vi: **to ~ at** essere connivente in

connoisseur [kɒnɪ'sə*] n conoscitore/trice

conquer ['kɒŋkə*] vt conquistare; (feelings) vincere

conquest ['kɒŋkwest] n conquista

cons [kɒnz] npl see **convenience; pro**

conscience ['kɒnʃəns] n coscienza

conscientious [kɒnʃɪ'enʃəs] adj coscienzioso(a)

conscious ['kɒnʃəs] adj consapevole; (MED) cosciente; **~ness** n consapevolezza; coscienza

conscript ['kɒnskrɪpt] n coscritto; **~ion** [-'skrɪpʃən] n arruolamento (obbligatorio)

consent [kən'sent] n consenso ♦ vi: **to ~ (to)** acconsentire (a)

consequence ['kɒnsɪkwəns] n conseguenza,

risultato; importanza

consequently ['kɒnsɪkwəntlɪ] adv di conseguenza, dunque

conservation [kɒnsə'veɪʃən] n conservazione f

conservative [kən'sə:vətɪv] adj conservatore(trice); (cautious) cauto(a); **C~** (BRIT) adj, n (POL) conservatore(trice)

conservatory [kən'sə:vətrɪ] n (greenhouse) serra; (MUS) conservatorio

conserve [kən'sə:v] vt conservare ♦ n conserva

consider [kən'sɪdə*] vt considerare; (take into account) tener conto di; **to ~ doing sth** considerare la possibilità di fare qc

considerable [kən'sɪdərəbl] adj considerevole, notevole; **considerably** adv notevolmente, decisamente

considerate [kən'sɪdərɪt] adj premuroso(a)

consideration [kənsɪdə'reɪʃən] n considerazione f

considering [kən'sɪdərɪŋ] prep in considerazione di

consign [kən'saɪn] vt: **to ~ to** (sth unwanted) relegare in; (person: to sb's care) consegnare a; (: to poverty) condannare a; **~ment** n (of goods) consegna; spedizione f

consist [kən'sɪst] vi: **to ~ of** constare di, essere composto(a) di

consistency [kən'sɪstənsɪ] n consistenza; (fig) coerenza

consistent [kən'sɪstənt] adj coerente

consolation [kɒnsə'leɪʃən] n consolazione f

console[1] [kən'səul] vt consolare

console[2] ['kɒnsəul] n quadro di comando

consonant ['kɒnsənənt] n consonante f

consortium [kən'sɔːtɪəm] n consorzio

conspicuous [kən'spɪkjuəs] adj cospicuo(a)

conspiracy [kən'spɪrəsɪ] n congiura, cospirazione f

constable ['kʌnstəbl] (BRIT) n ≈ poliziotto, agente m di polizia; **chief ~** ≈ questore m

constabulary [kən'stæbjulərɪ] n forze fpl dell'ordine

constant ['kɒnstənt] adj costante; continuo(a); **~ly** adv costantemente; continuamente

constipated ['kɒnstɪpeɪtɪd] adj stitico(a)

constipation [kɒnstɪ'peɪʃən] n stitichezza

constituency [kən'stɪtjuənsɪ] n collegio elettorale

constituent [kən'stɪtjuənt] n elettore/trice; (part) elemento componente

constitution [kɒnstɪ'tjuːʃən] n costituzione f; **~al** adj costituzionale

constraint [kən'streɪnt] n costrizione f

construct [kən'strʌkt] vt costruire; **~ion** [-ʃən] n costruzione f; **~ive** adj costruttivo(a)

consul ['kɒnsl] n console m; **~ate** ['kɒnsjulɪt]

n consolato

consult [kənˈsʌlt] *vt* consultare; **~ant** *n* (*MED*) consulente *m* medico; (*other specialist*) consulente; **~ation** [-ˈteɪʃən] *n* (*MED*) consulto; (*discussion*) consultazione *f*; **~ing room** (*BRIT*) *n* ambulatorio

consume [kənˈsjuːm] *vt* consumare; **~r** *n* consumatore/trice; **~r goods** *npl* beni *mpl* di consumo; **~r society** *n* società dei consumi

consumption [kənˈsʌmpʃən] *n* consumo

cont. *abbr* = **continued**

contact [ˈkɔntækt] *n* contatto; (*person*) conoscenza ♦ *vt* mettersi in contatto con; **~ lenses** *npl* lenti *fpl* a contatto

contagious [kənˈteɪdʒəs] *adj* (*also fig*) contagioso(a)

contain [kənˈteɪn] *vt* contenere; **to ~ o.s.** contenersi; **~er** *n* recipiente *m*; (*for shipping etc*) container *m inv*

contaminate [kənˈtæmɪneɪt] *vt* contaminare

cont'd *abbr* = **continued**

contemplate [ˈkɔntəmpleɪt] *vt* contemplare; (*consider*) pensare a (*or* di)

contemporary [kənˈtempərəri] *adj, n* contemporaneo(a)

contempt [kənˈtempt] *n* disprezzo; **~ of court** (*LAW*) oltraggio alla Corte; **~ible** *adj* deprecabile

contend [kənˈtend] *vt*: **to ~ that** sostenere che ♦ *vi*: **to ~ with** lottare contro; **~er** *n* contendente *m/f*; concorrente *m/f*

content¹ [ˈkɔntent] *n* contenuto; **~s** *npl* (*of box, case etc*) contenuto; (**table of**) **~s** indice *m*

content² [kənˈtent] *adj* contento(a), soddisfatto(a) ♦ *vt* contentare, soddisfare; **~ed** *adj* contento(a), soddisfatto(a)

contention [kənˈtenʃən] *n* contesa; (*assertion*) tesi *f inv*

contentment [kənˈtentmənt] *n* contentezza

contest [*n* ˈkɔntest, *vb* kənˈtest] *n* lotta; (*competition*) gara, concorso ♦ *vt* contestare; impugnare; (*compete for*) essere in lizza per; **~ant** [kənˈtestənt] *n* concorrente *m/f*; (*in fight*) avversario/a

context [ˈkɔntekst] *n* contesto

continent [ˈkɔntɪnənt] *n* continente *m*; **the C~** (*BRIT*) l'Europa continentale; **~al** [-ˈnentl] *adj* continentale; **~al breakfast** *n* colazione *f* all'europea (*senza piatti caldi*); **~al quilt** (*BRIT*) *n* piumino

contingency [kənˈtɪndʒənsɪ] *n* eventualità *f inv*

continual [kənˈtɪnjuəl] *adj* continuo(a)

continuation [kəntɪnjuˈeɪʃən] *n* continuazione *f*; (*after interruption*) ripresa; (*of story*) seguito

continue [kənˈtɪnjuː] *vi* continuare ♦ *vt* continuare; (*start again*) riprendere

continuity [kɔntɪˈnjuːɪtɪ] *n* continuità; (*TV, CINEMA*) (ordine *m* della) sceneggiatura

continuous [kənˈtɪnjuəs] *adj* continuo(a); ininterrotto(a)

contort [kənˈtɔːt] *vt* contorcere

contour [ˈkɔntuə*] *n* contorno, profilo; (*also:* ~ **line**) curva di livello

contraband [ˈkɔntrəbænd] *n* contrabbando

contraceptive [kɔntrəˈseptɪv] *adj* contraccettivo(a) ♦ *n* contraccettivo

contract [*n* ˈkɔntrækt, *vb* kənˈtrækt] *n* contratto ♦ *vi* (*become smaller*) contrarsi; (*COMM*): **to ~ to do sth** fare un contratto per fare qc ♦ *vt* (*illness*) contrarre; **~ion** [-ʃən] *n* contrazione *f*; **~or** *n* imprenditore *m*

contradict [kɔntrəˈdɪkt] *vt* contraddire

contraflow [ˈkɔntrəfləu] *n* (*AUT*) senso unico alternato

contraption [kənˈtræpʃən] (*pej*) *n* aggeggio

contrary¹ [ˈkɔntrərɪ] *adj* contrario(a); (*unfavourable*) avverso(a), contrario(a) ♦ *n* contrario; **on the ~** al contrario; **unless you hear to the ~** salvo contrordine

contrary² [kənˈtreərɪ] *adj* (*perverse*) bisbetico(a)

contrast [*n* ˈkɔntrɑːst, *vb* kənˈtrɑːst] *n* contrasto ♦ *vt* mettere in contrasto; **in ~ to** contrariamente a

contribute [kənˈtrɪbjuːt] *vi* contribuire ♦ *vt*: **to ~ £10/an article to** dare 10 sterline/un articolo a; **to ~ to** contribuire a; (*newspaper*) scrivere per; **contribution** [kɔntrɪˈbjuːʃən] *n* contributo; **contributor** *n* (*to newspaper*) collaboratore/trice

contrivance [kənˈtraɪvəns] *n* congegno; espediente *m*

contrive [kənˈtraɪv] *vi*: **to ~ to do** fare in modo di fare

control [kənˈtrəul] *vt* controllare; (*firm, operation etc*) dirigere ♦ *n* controllo; **~s** *npl* (*of vehicle etc*) comandi *mpl*; (*governmental*) controlli *mpl*; **under ~** sotto controllo; **to be in ~ of** avere il controllo di; **to go out of ~** (*car*) non rispondere ai comandi; (*situation*) sfuggire di mano; **~led substance** *n* sostanza stupefacente; **~ panel** *n* quadro dei comandi; **~ room** *n* (*NAUT, MIL*) sala di comando; (*RADIO, TV*) sala di regia; **~ tower** *n* (*AVIAT*) torre *f* di controllo

controversial [kɔntrəˈvəːʃl] *adj* controverso(a), polemico(a)

controversy [ˈkɔntrəvəːsɪ] *n* controversia, polemica

convalesce [kɔnvəˈles] *vi* rimettersi in salute

convene [kənˈviːn] *vt* convocare ♦ *vi* convenire, adunarsi

convenience [kənˈviːnɪəns] *n* comodità *f inv*; **at your ~** a suo comodo; **all modern ~s**, (*BRIT*) **all mod cons** tutte le comodità moderne

convenient [kən'viːnɪənt] *adj* conveniente, comodo(a)

convent ['kɔnvənt] *n* convento

convention [kən'venʃən] *n* convenzione *f*; (*meeting*) convegno; **~al** *adj* convenzionale

conversant [kən'vɑːsnt] *adj*: **to be ~ with** essere al corrente di; essere pratico(a) di

conversation [kɔnvə'seɪʃən] *n* conversazione *f*; **~al** *adj* non formale

converse[1] [kən'vɑːs] *vi* conversare

converse[2] ['kɔnvɑːs] *n* contrario, opposto; **~ly** [-'vɑːslɪ] *adv* al contrario, per contro

convert [*vb* kən'vɑːt, *n* 'kɔnvɑːt] *vt* (*COMM, REL*) convertire; (*alter*) trasformare ♦ *n* convertito/a; **~ible** *n* macchina decappottabile

convex ['kɔnveks] *adj* convesso(a)

convey [kən'veɪ] *vt* trasportare; (*thanks*) comunicare; (*idea*) dare; **~or belt** *n* nastro trasportatore

convict [*vb* kən'vɪkt, *n* 'kɔnvɪkt] *vt* dichiarare colpevole ♦ *n* carcerato/a; **~ion** [-ʃən] *n* condanna; (*belief*) convinzione *f*

convince [kən'vɪns] *vt* convincere, persuadere; **convincing** *adj* convincente

convoluted [kɔnvə'luːtɪd] *adj* (*argument etc*) involuto(a)

convoy ['kɔnvɔɪ] *n* convoglio

convulse [kən'vʌls] *vt*: **to be ~d with laughter** contorcersi dalle risa

cook [kuk] *vt* cucinare, cuocere ♦ *vi* cuocere; (*person*) cucinare ♦ *n* cuoco/a; **~book** *n* libro di cucina; **~er** *n* fornello, cucina; **~ery** *n* cucina; **~ery book** (*BRIT*) *n* = **~book**; **~ie** (*US*) *n* biscotto; **~ing** *n* cucina

cool [kuːl] *adj* fresco(a); (*not afraid, calm*) calmo(a); (*unfriendly*) freddo(a) ♦ *vt* raffreddare; (*room*) rinfrescare ♦ *vi* (*water*) raffreddarsi; (*air*) rinfrescarsi

coop [kuːp] *n* stia ♦ *vt*: **to ~ up** (*fig*) rinchiudere

cooperate [kəu'ɔpəreɪt] *vi* cooperare, collaborare; **cooperation** [-'reɪʃən] *n* cooperazione *f*, collaborazione *f*

cooperative [kəu'ɔpərətɪv] *adj* cooperativo(a) ♦ *n* cooperativa

coordinate [*vb* kəu'ɔːdɪneɪt, *n* kəu'ɔːdɪnət] *vt* coordinare ♦ *n* (*MATH*) coordinata; **~s** *npl* (*clothes*) coordinati *mpl*

co-ownership [kəu'əunəʃɪp] *n* comproprietà

cop [kɔp] (*inf*) *n* sbirro

cope [kəup] *vi*: **to ~ with** (*problems*) far fronte a

copper ['kɔpə*] *n* rame *m*; (*inf: policeman*) sbirro; **~s** *npl* (*coins*) spiccioli *mpl*

copse [kɔps] *n* bosco ceduo

copy ['kɔpɪ] *n* copia ♦ *vt* copiare; **~right** *n* diritto d'autore

coral ['kɔrəl] *n* corallo

cord [kɔːd] *n* corda; (*ELEC*) filo

cordial ['kɔːdɪəl] *adj* cordiale ♦ *n* (*BRIT*) cordiale *m*

cordon ['kɔːdn] *n* cordone *m*; **~ off** *vt* fare cordone a

corduroy ['kɔːdərɔɪ] *n* fustagno

core [kɔː*] *n* (*of fruit*) torsolo; (*of organization etc*) cuore *m* ♦ *vt* estrarre il torsolo da

cork [kɔːk] *n* sughero; (*of bottle*) tappo; **~screw** *n* cavatappi *m inv*

corn [kɔːn] *n* (*BRIT: wheat*) grano; (*US: maize*) granturco; (*on foot*) callo; **~ on the cob** (*CULIN*) pannocchia cotta

corned beef ['kɔːnd-] *n* carne *f* di manzo in scatola

corner ['kɔːnə*] *n* angolo; (*AUT*) curva ♦ *vt* intrappolare; mettere con le spalle al muro; (*COMM: market*) accaparrare ♦ *vi* prendere una curva; **~stone** *n* pietra angolare

cornet ['kɔːnɪt] *n* (*MUS*) cornetta; (*BRIT: of ice-cream*) cono

cornflakes ['kɔːnfleɪks] *npl* fiocchi *mpl* di granturco

cornflour ['kɔːnflauə*] (*BRIT*) *n* farina finissima di granturco

cornstarch ['kɔːnstɑːtʃ] (*US*) *n* = **cornflour**

Cornwall ['kɔːnwəl] *n* Cornovaglia

corny ['kɔːnɪ] (*inf*) *adj* trito(a)

coronary ['kɔrənərɪ] *n*: **~ (thrombosis)** trombosi *f* coronaria

coronation [kɔrə'neɪʃən] *n* incoronazione *f*

coroner ['kɔrənə*] *n* magistrato incaricato di indagare la causa di morte in circostanze sospette

coronet ['kɔrənɪt] *n* diadema *f*

corporal ['kɔːpərl] *n* caporalmaggiore *m* ♦ *adj*: **~ punishment** pena corporale

corporate ['kɔːpərɪt] *adj* costituito(a) (in corporazione); comune

corporation [kɔːpə'reɪʃən] *n* (*of town*) consiglio comunale; (*COMM*) ente *m*

corps [kɔː*, *pl* kɔːz] *n inv* corpo

corpse [kɔːps] *n* cadavere *m*

correct [kə'rekt] *adj* (*accurate*) corretto(a), esatto(a); (*proper*) corretto(a) ♦ *vt* correggere; **~ion** [-ʃən] *n* correzione *f*

correspond [kɔrɪs'pɔnd] *vi* corrispondere; **~ence** *n* corrispondenza; **~ence course** *n* corso per corrispondenza; **~ent** *n* corrispondente *m/f*

corridor ['kɔrɪdɔː*] *n* corridoio

corrode [kə'rəud] *vt* corrodere ♦ *vi* corrodersi

corrugated ['kɔrəgeɪtɪd] *adj* increspato(a); ondulato(a); **~ iron** *n* lamiera di ferro ondulata

corrupt [kə'rʌpt] *adj* corrotto(a); (*COMPUT*) alterato(a) ♦ *vt* corrompere

corset ['kɔːsɪt] *n* busto

Corsica ['kɔːsɪkə] n Corsica

cosh [kɔʃ] (BRIT) n randello (corto)

cosmetic [kɔz'metɪk] n cosmetico ♦ adj (fig: measure etc) superficiale

cost [kɔst] (pt, pp cost) n costo ♦ vt costare; (find out the ~ of) stabilire il prezzo di; ~s npl (COMM, LAW) spese fpl; **how much does it ~?** quanto costa?; **at all ~s** a ogni costo

co-star ['kəustɑː*] n attore/trice della stessa importanza del protagonista

cost-effective [kɔstɪ'fektɪv] adj conveniente

costly ['kɔstlɪ] adj costoso(a), caro(a)

cost-of-living [kɔstəv'lɪvɪŋ] adj: ~ **allowance** indennità f inv di contingenza

cost price (BRIT) n prezzo all'ingrosso

costume ['kɔstjuːm] n costume m; (lady's suit) tailleur m inv; (BRIT: also: swimming ~) costume da bagno; ~ **jewellery** n bigiotteria

cosy ['kəuzɪ] (US **cozy**) adj intimo(a); **I'm very ~ here** sto proprio bene qui

cot [kɔt] n (BRIT: child's) lettino; (US: campbed) brandina

cottage ['kɔtɪdʒ] n cottage m inv; ~ **cheese** n fiocchi mpl di latte magro

cotton ['kɔtn] n cotone m; ~ **on to** (inf) vt fus afferrare; ~ **candy** (US) n zucchero filato; ~ **wool** (BRIT) n cotone idrofilo

couch [kautʃ] n sofà m inv

couchette [kuː'ʃet] n (on train, boat) cuccetta

cough [kɔf] vi tossire ♦ n tosse f; ~ **drop** n pasticca per la tosse

could [kud] pt of **can²**; ~**n't** = **could not**

council ['kaunsl] n consiglio; **city** or **town ~** consiglio comunale; ~ **estate** (BRIT) n quartiere m di case popolari; ~ **house** (BRIT) n casa popolare; ~**lor** n consigliere/a

counsel ['kaunsl] n avvocato; consultazione f ♦ vt consigliare; ~**lor** n (US: ~**or**) consigliere/a; (US) avvocato

count [kaunt] vt, vi contare ♦ n (of votes etc) conteggio; (of pollen etc) livello; (nobleman) conte m; ~ **on** vt fus contare su; ~**down** n conto alla rovescia

countenance ['kauntɪnəns] n volto, aspetto ♦ vt approvare

counter ['kauntə*] n banco ♦ vt opporsi a ♦ adv: ~ **to** contro; in opposizione a; ~**act** vt agire in opposizione a; (poison etc) annullare gli effetti di; ~**-espionage** n contro-spionaggio

counterfeit ['kauntəfɪt] n contraffazione f, falso ♦ vt contraffare, falsificare ♦ adj falso(a)

counterfoil ['kauntəfɔɪl] n matrice f

counterpart ['kauntəpaːt] n (of document etc) copia; (of person) corrispondente m/f

counter-productive [kauntəprə'dʌktɪv] adj controproducente

countersign ['kauntəsaɪn] vt controfirmare

countess ['kauntɪs] n contessa

countless ['kauntlɪs] adj innumerevole

country ['kʌntrɪ] n paese m; (native land) patria; (as opposed to town) campagna; (region) regione f; ~ **dancing** (BRIT) n danza popolare; ~ **house** n villa in campagna; ~**man** (irreg) n (national) compatriota m; (rural) contadino; ~**side** n campagna

county ['kauntɪ] n contea

coup [kuː] (pl **coups**) n colpo; (also: ~ **d'état**) colpo di Stato

couple ['kʌpl] n coppia; **a ~ of** un paio di

coupon ['kuːpɔn] n buono; (detachable form) coupon m inv

courage ['kʌrɪdʒ] n coraggio

courgette [kuə'ʒet] (BRIT) n zucchina

courier ['kurɪə*] n corriere m; (for tourists) guida

course [kɔːs] n corso; (of ship) rotta; (for golf) campo; (part of meal) piatto; **of ~** senz'altro, naturalmente; ~ **of action** modo d'agire; **a ~ of treatment** (MED) una cura

court [kɔːt] n corte f; (TENNIS) campo ♦ vt (woman) fare la corte a; **to take to ~** citare in tribunale

courteous ['kəːtɪəs] adj cortese

courtesy ['kəːtəsɪ] n cortesia; (by) ~ **of** per gentile concessione di; ~ **bus**, ~ **coach** n autobus m inv gratuito (di hotel, aeroporto)

court-house ['kɔːthaus] (US) n palazzo di giustizia

courtier ['kɔːtɪə*] n cortigiano/a

court-martial ['kɔːt'maːʃəl] (pl **courts-martial**) n corte f marziale

courtroom ['kɔːtrum] n tribunale m

courtyard ['kɔːtjaːd] n cortile m

cousin ['kʌzn] n cugino/a; **first ~** cugino di primo grado

cove [kəuv] n piccola baia

covenant ['kʌvənənt] n accordo

cover ['kʌvə*] vt coprire; (book, table) rivestire; (include) comprendere; (PRESS) fare un servizio su ♦ n (of pan) coperchio; (over furniture) fodera; (of bed) copriletto; (over book) copertina; (shelter) riparo; (COMM, INSURANCE, of spy) copertura; **to take ~** (shelter) ripararsi; **under ~** al riparo; **under ~ of darkness** protetto dall'oscurità; **under separate ~** (COMM) a parte, in plico separato; ~ **up** vi: **to ~ up for sb** coprire qn; ~**age** n (PRESS, RADIO, TV): **to give full ~age to sth** fare un ampio servizio su qc; ~ **charge** n coperto; ~**ing** n copertura; ~**ing letter** (US ~ **letter**) n lettera d'accompagnamento; ~ **note** n (INSURANCE) polizza (di assi-curazione) provvisoria

covert ['kʌvət] adj (hidden) nascosto(a); (glance) furtivo(a)

cover-up ['kʌvərʌp] n occultamento (di

informazioni)

cow [kau] n vacca ♦ vt (person) intimidire

coward ['kauəd] n vigliacco/a; **~ice** [-ɪs] n vigliaccheria; **~ly** adj vigliacco(a)

cowboy ['kaubɔɪ] n cow-boy m inv

cower ['kauə*] vi acquattarsi

coxswain ['kɔksn] (abbr: **cox**) n timoniere m

coy [kɔɪ] adj falsamente timido(a)

cozy ['kəuzɪ] (US) adj = **cosy**

CPA (US) n abbr = **certified public accountant**

crab [kræb] n granchio; **~ apple** n mela selvatica

crack [kræk] n fessura, crepa; incrinatura; (noise) schiocco; (: of gun) scoppio; (drug) crack m inv ♦ vt spaccare; incrinare; (whip) schioccare; (nut) schiacciare; (problem) risolvere; (code) decifrare ♦ adj (troops) fuori classe; **to ~ a joke** fare una battuta; **~ down on** vt fus porre freno a; **~ up** vi crollare; **~er** n cracker m inv; petardo

crackle ['krækl] vi crepitare

cradle ['kreɪdl] n culla

craft [krɑːft] n mestiere m; (cunning) astuzia; (boat) naviglio; **~sman** (irreg) n artigiano; **~smanship** n abilità; **~y** adj furbo(a), astuto(a)

crag [kræg] n roccia

cram [kræm] vt (fill): **to ~ sth with** riempire qc di; (put): **to ~ sth into** stipare qc in ♦ vi (for exams) prepararsi (in gran fretta)

cramp [kræmp] n crampo; **~ed** adj ristretto(a)

crampon ['kræmpən] n (CLIMBING) rampone m

cranberry ['krænbərɪ] n mirtillo

crane [kreɪn] n gru f inv

crank [kræŋk] n manovella; (person) persona stramba

cranny ['krænɪ] n see **nook**

crash [kræʃ] n fragore m; (of car) incidente m; (of plane) caduta; (of business etc) crollo ♦ vt fracassare ♦ vi (plane) fracassarsi; (car) avere un incidente; (two cars) scontrarsi; (business etc) fallire, andare in rovina; **~ course** n corso intensivo; **~ helmet** n casco; **~ landing** n atterraggio di fortuna

crate [kreɪt] n cassa

cravat(e) [krə'væt] n fazzoletto da collo

crave [kreɪv] vt, vi: **to ~ (for)** desiderare ardentemente

crawl [krɔːl] vi strisciare carponi; (vehicle) avanzare lentamente ♦ n (SWIMMING) crawl m

crayfish ['kreɪfɪʃ] n inv (freshwater) gambero (d'acqua dolce); (saltwater) gambero

crayon ['kreɪən] n matita colorata

craze [kreɪz] n mania

crazy ['kreɪzɪ] adj matto(a); (inf: keen): **~ about sb** pazzo(a) di qn; **~ about sth** matto(a) per qc

creak [kriːk] vi cigolare, scricchiolare

cream [kriːm] n crema; (fresh) panna ♦ adj (colour) color crema inv; **~ cake** n torta alla panna; **~ cheese** n formaggio fresco; **~y** adj cremoso(a)

crease [kriːs] n grinza; (deliberate) piega ♦ vt sgualcire ♦ vi sgualcirsi

create [kriː'eɪt] vt creare; **creation** [-ʃən] n creazione f; **creative** adj creativo(a)

creature ['kriːtʃə*] n creatura

crèche [kreʃ] n asilo infantile

credence ['kriːdns] n: **to lend** or **give ~ to** prestar fede a

credentials [krɪ'denʃlz] npl credenziali fpl

credit ['krɛdɪt] n credito; onore m ♦ vt (COMM) accreditare; (believe: also: **give ~ to**) credere, prestar fede a; **~s** npl (CINEMA) titoli mpl; **to ~ sb with** (fig) attribuire a qn; **to be in ~** (person) essere creditore (trice); (bank account) essere coperto(a); **~ card** n carta di credito; **~or** n creditore/trice

creed [kriːd] n credo; dottrina

creek [kriːk] n insenatura; (US) piccolo fiume m

creep [kriːp] (pt, pp **crept**) vi avanzare furtivamente (or pian piano); **~er** n pianta rampicante; **~y** adj (frightening) che fa accaponare la pelle

crematorium [krɛmə'tɔːrɪəm] (pl **crematoria**) n forno crematorio

crêpe [kreɪp] n crespo; **~ bandage** (BRIT) n fascia elastica

crept [krɛpt] pt, pp of **creep**

crescent ['krɛsnt] n (shape) mezzaluna; (street) strada semicircolare

cress [krɛs] n crescione m

crest [krɛst] n cresta; (of coat of arms) cimiero; **~fallen** adj mortificato(a)

Crete [kriːt] n Creta

crevasse [krɪ'væs] n crepaccio

crevice ['krɛvɪs] n fessura, crepa

crew [kruː] n equipaggio; **~-cut** n: **to have a ~-cut** avere i capelli a spazzola; **~-neck** n girocollo

crib [krɪb] n culla ♦ vt (inf) copiare

crick [krɪk] n crampo

cricket ['krɪkɪt] n (insect) grillo; (game) cricket m

crime [kraɪm] n crimine m; **criminal** ['krɪmɪnl] adj, n criminale m/f

crimson ['krɪmzn] adj color cremisi inv

cringe [krɪndʒ] vi acquattarsi; (in embarrassment) sentirsi sprofondare

crinkle ['krɪŋkl] vt arricciare, increspare

cripple ['krɪpl] n zoppo/a ♦ vt azzoppare

crises ['kraɪsiːz] npl of **crisis**

crisis ['kraɪsɪs] (pl **crises**) n crisi f inv

crisp [krɪsp] adj croccante; (fig) frizzante; vivace; deciso(a); **~s** (BRIT) npl patatine fpl

criss-cross ['krɪskrɔs] adj incrociato(a)
criteria [kraɪ'tɪərɪə] npl of criterion
criterion [kraɪ'tɪərɪən] (pl criteria) n criterio
critic ['krɪtɪk] n critico; **~al** adj critico(a);
~ally adv (speak etc) criticamente; **~ally ill**
gravemente malato; **~ism** ['krɪtɪsɪzm] n
critica; **~ize** ['krɪtɪsaɪz] vt criticare
croak [krəuk] vi gracchiare; (frog) gracidare
Croatia [krəu'eɪʃə] n Croazia
crochet ['krəuʃeɪ] n lavoro all'uncinetto
crockery ['krɔkərɪ] n vasellame m
crocodile ['krɔkədaɪl] n coccodrillo
crocus ['krəukəs] n croco
croft [krɔft] (BRIT) n piccolo podere m
crony ['krəunɪ] (inf: pej) n compare m
crook [kruk] n truffatore m; (of shepherd)
bastone m; **~ed** ['krukɪd] adj curvo(a),
storto(a); (action) disonesto(a)
crop [krɔp] n (produce) coltivazione f;
(amount produced) raccolto; (riding ~)
frustino ♦ vt (hair) rapare; **~ up** vi presentarsi
croquette [krə'ket] n crocchetta
cross [krɔs] n croce f; (BIOL) incrocio ♦ vt
(street etc) attraversare; (arms, legs, BIOL)
incrociare; (cheque) sbarrare ♦ adj di cattivo
umore; **~ out** vt cancellare; **~ over** vi
attraversare; **~bar** n traversa; **~country
(race)** n cross-country m inv; **~-examine** vt
(LAW) interrogare in contraddittorio; **~-eyed**
adj strabico(a); **~fire** n fuoco incrociato;
~ing n incrocio; (sea passage) traversata;
(also: pedestrian ~ing) passaggio pedonale;
~ing guard (US) n dipendente comunale che
aiuta i bambini ad attraversare la strada;
~ purposes npl: **to be at ~ purposes** non
parlare della stessa cosa; **~reference** n
rinvio, rimando; **~roads** n incrocio;
~ section n sezione f trasversale; (in
population) settore m rappresentativo;
~walk (US) n strisce fpl pedonali, passaggio
pedonale; **~wind** n vento di traverso;
~word n cruciverba m inv
crotch [krɔtʃ] n (ANAT) inforcatura; (of
garment) pattina
crotchet ['krɔtʃɪt] n (MUS) semiminima
crouch [krautʃ] vi accuattarsi; rannicchiarsi
crow [krəu] n (bird) cornacchia; (of cock)
canto del gallo ♦ vi (cock) cantare
crowbar ['krəubɑ:*] n piede m di porco
crowd [kraud] n folla ♦ vt affollare, stipare
♦ vi: **to ~ round/in** affollarsi intorno a/in;
~ed adj affollato(a); **~ed with** stipato(a) di
crown [kraun] n corona; (of head) calotta
cranica; (of hat) cocuzzolo; (of hill) cima ♦ vt
incoronare; (fig: career) coronare; **~ jewels**
npl gioielli mpl della Corona; **~ prince** n
principe m ereditario
crow's feet npl zampe fpl di gallina
crucial ['kru:ʃl] adj cruciale, decisivo(a)

crucifix ['kru:sɪfɪks] n crocifisso; **~ion**
[-'fɪkʃən] n crocifissione f
crude [kru:d] adj (materials) greggio(a); non
raffinato(a); (fig: basic) crudo(a),
primitivo(a); (: vulgar) rozzo(a),
grossolano(a); **~ (oil)** n (petrolio) greggio
cruel ['kruəl] adj crudele; **~ty** n crudeltà f inv
cruise [kru:z] n crociera ♦ vi andare a velocità
di crociera; (taxi) circolare; **~r** n incrociatore
m
crumb [krʌm] n briciola
crumble ['krʌmbl] vt sbriciolare ♦ vi
sbriciolarsi; (plaster etc) sgretolarsi; (land,
earth) franare; (building, fig) crollare;
crumbly adj friabile
crumpet ['krʌmpɪt] n specie di frittella
crumple ['krʌmpl] vt raggrinzare, spiegazzare
crunch [krʌntʃ] vt sgranocchiare; (underfoot)
scricchiolare ♦ n (fig) punto or momento
cruciale; **~y** adj croccante
crusade [kru:'seɪd] n crociata
crush [krʌʃ] n folla; (love): **to have a ~ on sb**
avere una cotta per qn; (drink): **lemon ~**
spremuta di limone ♦ vt schiacciare;
(crumple) sgualcire
crust [krʌst] n crosta
crutch [krʌtʃ] n gruccia
crux [krʌks] n nodo
cry [kraɪ] vi piangere; (shout: also: ~ out)
urlare ♦ n urlo, grido; **~ off** vi ritirarsi
cryptic ['krɪptɪk] adj ermetico(a)
crystal ['krɪstl] n cristallo; **~-clear** adj
cristallino(a)
cub [kʌb] n cucciolo; (also: ~ scout) lupetto
Cuba ['kju:bə] n Cuba
cube [kju:b] n cubo ♦ vt (MATH) elevare al
cubo; **cubic** adj cubico(a); (metre, foot)
cubo(a); **cubic capacity** n cilindrata
cubicle ['kju:bɪkl] n scompartimento
separato; cabina
cuckoo ['kuku:] n cucù m inv; **~ clock** n
orologio a cucù
cucumber ['kju:kʌmbə*] n cetriolo
cuddle ['kʌdl] vt abbracciare, coccolare ♦ vi
abbracciarsi
cue [kju:] n (snooker ~) stecca; (THEATRE etc)
segnale m
cuff [kʌf] n (BRIT: of shirt, coat etc) polsino;
(US: of trousers) risvolto; **off the ~**
improvvisando; **~link** n gemello
cuisine [kwɪ'zi:n] n cucina
cul-de-sac ['kʌldəsæk] n vicolo cieco
cull [kʌl] vt (ideas etc) scegliere ♦ n (of
animals) abbattimento selettivo
culminate ['kʌlmɪneɪt] vi: **to ~ in** culminare
con; **culmination** [-'neɪʃən] n culmine m
culottes [kju:'lɔts] npl gonna f pantalone inv
culpable ['kʌlpəbl] adj colpevole
culprit ['kʌlprɪt] n colpevole m/f

cult [kʌlt] n culto
cultivate ['kʌltɪveɪt] vt (also fig) coltivare;
   cultivation [-'veɪʃən] n coltivazione f
cultural ['kʌltʃərəl] adj culturale
culture ['kʌltʃə*] n (also fig) cultura; **~d** adj
   colto(a)
cumbersome ['kʌmbəsəm] adj ingombrante
cunning ['kʌnɪŋ] n astuzia, furberia ♦ adj
   astuto(a), furbo(a)
cup [kʌp] n tazza; (prize, of bra) coppa
cupboard ['kʌbəd] n armadio
cup-tie ['kʌptaɪ] (BRIT) n partita di coppa
curate ['kjuərɪt] n cappellano
curator [kjuə'reɪtə*] n direttore m (di museo
   etc)
curb [kə:b] vt tenere a freno ♦ n freno; (US)
   bordo del marciapiede
curdle ['kə:dl] vi cagliare
cure [kjuə*] vt guarire; (CULIN) trattare;
   affumicare; essiccare ♦ n rimedio
curfew ['kə:fju:] n coprifuoco
curiosity [kjuərɪ'ɒsɪtɪ] n curiosità
curious ['kjuərɪəs] adj curioso(a)
curl [kə:l] n riccio ♦ vt ondulare; (tightly)
   arricciare ♦ vi arricciarsi; **~ up** vi
   rannicchiarsi; **~er** n bigodino
curly ['kə:lɪ] adj ricciuto(a)
currant ['kʌrnt] n (dried) sultanina; (bush,
   fruit) ribes m inv
currency ['kʌrnsɪ] n moneta; **to gain ~** (fig)
   acquistare larga diffusione
current ['kʌrnt] adj corrente ♦ n corrente f;
   ~ account (BRIT) n conto corrente; **~
   affairs** npl attualità fpl; **~ly** adv attualmente
curricula [kə'rɪkjulə] npl of **curriculum**
curriculum [kə'rɪkjuləm] (pl **~s** or **curricula**)
   n curriculum m inv; **~ vitae** n curriculum
   vitae m inv
curry ['kʌrɪ] n curry m inv ♦ vt: **to ~ favour
   with** cercare di attirarsi i favori di; **~
   powder** n curry m
curse [kə:s] vt maledire ♦ vi bestemmiare ♦ n
   maledizione f; bestemmia
cursor ['kə:sə*] n (COMPUT) cursore m
cursory ['kə:sərɪ] adj superficiale
curt [kə:t] adj secco(a)
curtail [kə:'teɪl] vt (visit etc) accorciare;
   (expenses etc) ridurre
curtain ['kə:tn] n tenda; (THEATRE) sipario
curts(e)y ['kə:tsɪ] vi fare un inchino or una
   riverenza
curve [kə:v] n curva ♦ vi curvarsi
cushion ['kuʃən] n cuscino ♦ vt (shock) fare
   da cuscinetto a
custard ['kʌstəd] n (for pouring) crema
custodian [kʌs'təudɪən] n custode m/f
custody ['kʌstədɪ] n (of child) tutela; **to take
   into ~** (suspect) mettere in detenzione
   preventiva

custom ['kʌstəm] n costume m,
   consuetudine f; (COMM) clientela; **~ary** adj
   consueto(a)
customer ['kʌstəmə*] n cliente m/f
customized ['kʌstəmaɪzd] adj (car etc)
   fuoriserie inv
custom-made ['kʌstəm'meɪd] adj (clothes)
   fatto(a) su misura; (other goods) fatto(a) su
   ordinazione
customs ['kʌstəmz] npl dogana; **~ duty** n
   tassa doganale; **~ officer** n doganiere m
cut [kʌt] (pt, pp **cut**) vt tagliare; (shape, make)
   intagliare; (reduce) ridurre ♦ vi tagliare ♦ n
   taglio; (in salary etc) riduzione f; **to ~ a tooth**
   mettere un dente; **~ down** vt (tree etc)
   abbattere ♦ vt fus (also: **~ down on**) ridurre;
   ~ off vt tagliare; (fig) isolare; **~ out** vt tagliare fuori; eliminare; ritagliare; **~ up** vt tagliare
   a pezzi; **~back** n riduzione f
cute [kju:t] adj (sweet) carino(a)
cuticle ['kju:tɪkl] n (on nail) pellicina, cuticola
cutlery ['kʌtlərɪ] n posate fpl
cutlet ['kʌtlɪt] n costoletta; (nut etc ~)
   cotoletta vegetariana
cut: **~out** n interruttore m; (cardboard ~out)
   ritaglio; **~-price** (US **~-rate**) adj a prezzo
   ridotto(a); **~throat** n assassino ♦ adj
   (competition) spietato(a)
cutting ['kʌtɪŋ] adj tagliente ♦ n (from
   newspaper) ritaglio (di giornale); (from plant)
   talea
CV n abbr = **curriculum vitae**
cwt abbr = **hundredweight(s)**
cyanide ['saɪənaɪd] n cianuro
cybercafé ['saɪbækæfeɪ] n cybercaffè m inv
cycle ['saɪkl] n ciclo; (bicycle) bicicletta ♦ vi
   andare in bicicletta; **~ hire** n noleggio m
   biciclette inv; **~ lane**, **~ path** n pista ciclabile
cycling ['saɪklɪŋ] n ciclismo
cyclist ['saɪklɪst] n ciclista m/f
cygnet ['sɪgnɪt] n cigno giovane
cylinder ['sɪlɪndə*] n cilindro; **~-head
   gasket** n guarnizione f della testata del
   cilindro
cymbals ['sɪmblz] npl cembali mpl
cynic ['sɪnɪk] n cinico/a; **~al** adj cinico(a);
   ~ism ['sɪnɪsɪzəm] n cinismo
Cyprus ['saɪprəs] n Cipro
cyst [sɪst] n cisti f inv
cystitis [sɪs'taɪtɪs] n cistite f
czar [zɑ:*] n zar m inv
Czech [tʃɛk] adj ceco(a) ♦ n ceco/a; (LING)
   ceco
Czech Republic n: **the ~** la Repubblica
   Ceca

D, d

D [di:] n (MUS) re m

dab [dæb] vt (eyes, wound) tamponare; (paint, cream) applicare (con leggeri colpetti)

dabble ['dæbl] vi: **to ~ in** occuparsi (da dilettante) di

dad(dy) [dæd(ɪ)] (inf) n babbo, papà m inv

daffodil ['dæfədɪl] n trombone m, giunchiglia

daft [dɑ:ft] adj sciocco(a)

dagger ['dægə*] n pugnale m

daily ['deɪlɪ] adj quotidiano(a), giornaliero(a) ♦ n quotidiano ♦ adv tutti i giorni

dainty ['deɪntɪ] adj delicato(a), grazioso(a)

dairy ['dɛərɪ] n (BRIT: shop) latteria; (on farm) caseificio ♦ adj caseario(a); **~ farm** n caseificio; **~ products** npl latticini mpl; **~ store** (US) n latteria

daisy ['deɪzɪ] n margherita

dale [deɪl] (BRIT) n valle f

dam [dæm] n diga ♦ vt sbarrare; costruire dighe su

damage ['dæmɪdʒ] n danno, danni mpl; (fig) danno ♦ vt danneggiare; **~s** npl (LAW) danni

damn [dæm] vt condannare; (curse) maledire ♦ n (inf): **I don't give a ~** non me ne frega niente ♦ adj (inf: also: ~ed): **this ~ ...** questo maledetto ...; **~ (it)!** accidenti!; **~ing** adj (evidence) schiacciante

damp [dæmp] adj umido(a) ♦ n umidità, umido ♦ vt (also: ~en: cloth, rag) inumidire, bagnare; (: enthusiasm etc) spegnere

damson ['dæmzən] n susina damaschina

dance [dɑ:ns] n danza, ballo; (ball) ballo ♦ vi ballare; **~ hall** n dancing m inv, sala da ballo; **~r** n danzatore/trice; (professional) ballerino/a

dancing ['dɑ:nsɪŋ] n danza, ballo

dandelion ['dændɪlaɪən] n dente m di leone

dandruff ['dændrəf] n forfora

Dane [deɪn] n danese m/f

danger ['deɪndʒə*] n pericolo; **there is a ~ of fire** c'è pericolo di incendio; **in ~** in pericolo; **he was in ~ of falling** rischiava di cadere; **~ous** adj pericoloso(a)

dangle ['dæŋgl] vt dondolare; (fig) far balenare ♦ vi pendolare

Danish ['deɪnɪʃ] adj danese ♦ n (LING) danese m

dare [dɛə*] vt: **to ~ sb to do** sfidare qn a fare ♦ vi: **to ~ (to) do sth** osare fare qc; **I ~ say** (I suppose) immagino (che); **daring** adj audace, ardito(a) ♦ n audacia

dark [dɑ:k] adj (night, room) buio(a), scuro(a); (colour, complexion) scuro(a); (fig) cupo(a), tetro(a), nero(a) ♦ n: **in the ~** al buio; **in the ~ about** (fig) all'oscuro di; **after ~** a notte fatta; **~en** vt (colour) scurire ♦ vi (sky, room) oscurarsi; **~ glasses** npl occhiali mpl scuri; **~ness** n oscurità, buio; **~room** n camera oscura

darling ['dɑ:lɪŋ] adj caro(a) ♦ n tesoro

darn [dɑ:n] vt rammendare

dart [dɑ:t] n freccetta; (SEWING) pince f inv ♦ vi: **to ~ towards** precipitarsi verso; **to ~ away/along** sfrecciare via/lungo; **~board** n bersaglio (per freccette); **~s** n tiro al bersaglio (con freccette)

dash [dæʃ] n (sign) lineetta; (small quantity) punta ♦ vt (missile) gettare; (hopes) infrangere ♦ vi: **to ~ towards** precipitarsi verso; **~ away** or **off** vi scappare via

dashboard ['dæʃbɔ:d] n (AUT) cruscotto

dashing ['dæʃɪŋ] adj ardito(a)

data ['deɪtə] npl dati mpl; **~base** n base f di dati, data base m inv; **~ processing** n elaborazione f (elettronica) dei dati

date [deɪt] n data; appuntamento; (fruit) dattero ♦ vt datare; (person) uscire con; **~ of birth** data di nascita; **to ~** (until now) fino a oggi; **~d** [deɪtɪd] passato(a) di moda; **~ rape** n stupro perpetrato da persona conosciuta

daub [dɔ:b] vt imbrattare

daughter ['dɔ:tə*] n figlia; **~-in-law** n nuora

daunting ['dɔ:ntɪŋ] adj non invidiabile

dawdle ['dɔ:dl] vi bighellonare

dawn [dɔ:n] n alba ♦ vi (day) spuntare; (fig): **it ~ed on him that ...** gli è venuto in mente che ....

day [deɪ] n giorno; (as duration) giornata; (period of time, age) tempo, epoca; **the ~ before** il giorno avanti o prima; **the ~ after, the following ~** il giorno dopo or seguente; **the ~ after tomorrow** dopodomani; **the ~ before yesterday** l'altroieri; **by ~** di giorno; **~break** n spuntar m del giorno; **~dream** vi sognare a occhi aperti; **~light** n luce f del giorno; **~ return** (BRIT) n biglietto giornaliero di andata e ritorno; **~time** n giorno; **~-to-~** adj (life, organization) quotidiano(a)

daze [deɪz] vt (subject: drug) inebetire; (: blow) stordire ♦ n: **in a ~** inebetito(a); stordito(a)

dazzle ['dæzl] vt abbagliare

DC abbr (= direct current) c.c.

D-day n giorno dello sbarco alleato in Normandia

dead [dɛd] adj morto(a); (numb) intirizzito(a); (telephone) muto(a); (battery) scarico(a) ♦ adv assolutamente, perfettamente ♦ npl: **the ~** i morti; **he was shot ~** fu colpito a morte; **~ tired** stanco(a) morto(a); **to stop ~** fermarsi di colpo; **~en** vt (blow, sound) ammortire; **~ end** n vicolo cieco; **~ heat** n (SPORT): **to finish in a ~ heat** finire alla pari; **~line** n scadenza; **~lock** n punto morto; **~ loss** n: **to be a ~ loss** (inf:

person, thing) non valere niente; **~ly** *adj*
mortale; (*weapon, poison*) micidiale; **~pan**
adj a faccia impassibile

deaf [dɛf] *adj* sordo(a); **~en** *vt* assordare;
~ness *n* sordità

deal [diːl] (*pt, pp* dealt) *n* accordo; (*business*
~) affare *m* ♦ *vt* (*blow, cards*) dare; **a great**
~ (of) molto(a); **~ in** *vt fus* occuparsi di;
~ with *vt fus* (*COMM*) fare affari con, trattare
con; (*handle*) occuparsi di; (*be about: book*
etc) trattare di; **~er** *n* commerciante *m/f*;
~ings *npl* (*COMM*) relazioni *fpl*; (*relations*)
rapporti *mpl*; **dealt** [dɛlt] *pt, pp* of **deal**

dean [diːn] *n* (*REL*) decano; (*SCOL*) preside *m*
di facoltà (*or* di collegio)

dear [dɪə*] *adj* caro(a) ♦ *n*: **my ~** caro mio/
cara mia ♦ *excl*: **~ me!** Dio mio!; **D~ Sir/**
Madam (*in letter*) Egregio Signore/Egregia
Signora; **D~ Mr/Mrs X** Gentile Signor/Signora
X; **~ly** *adv* (*love*) moltissimo; (*pay*) a caro
prezzo

death [dɛθ] *n* morte *f*; (*ADMIN*) decesso;
~ certificate *n* atto di decesso; **~ly** *adj* di
morte; **~ penalty** *n* pena di morte; **~ rate** *n*
indice *m* di mortalità; **~ toll** *n* vittime *fpl*

debacle [dɪ'bækl] *n* fiasco

debase [dɪ'beɪs] *vt* (*currency*) adulterare;
(*person*) degradare

debatable [dɪ'beɪtəbl] *adj* discutibile

debate [dɪ'beɪt] *n* dibattito ♦ *vt* dibattere;
discutere

debit ['dɛbɪt] *n* debito ♦ *vt*: **to ~ a sum to sb**
or **to sb's account** addebitare una somma a
qn

debris ['dɛbriː] *n* detriti *mpl*

debt [dɛt] *n* debito; **to be in ~** essere
indebitato(a); **~or** *n* debitore/trice

début ['deɪbjuː] *n* debutto

decade ['dɛkeɪd] *n* decennio

decadence ['dɛkədəns] *n* decadenza

decaff ['diːkæf] (*inf*) *n* decaffeinato

decaffeinated [dɪ'kæfɪneɪtɪd] *adj*
decaffeinato(a)

decanter [dɪ'kæntə*] *n* caraffa

decay [dɪ'keɪ] *n* decadimento; (*also: tooth* ~)
carie *f* ♦ *vi* (*rot*) imputridire

deceased [dɪ'siːst] *n* defunto/a

deceit [dɪ'siːt] *n* inganno; **~ful** *adj*
ingannevole, perfido(a)

deceive [dɪ'siːv] *vt* ingannare

December [dɪ'sɛmbə*] *n* dicembre *m*

decent ['diːsənt] *adj* decente; (*respectable*)
per bene; (*kind*) gentile

deception [dɪ'sɛpʃən] *n* inganno

deceptive [dɪ'sɛptɪv] *adj* ingannevole

decide [dɪ'saɪd] *vt* (*person*) far prendere una
decisione a; (*question, argument*) risolvere,
decidere ♦ *vi* decidere, decidersi; **to ~ to do/**
that decidere di fare/che; **to ~ on** decidere

per; **~d** *adj* (*resolute*) deciso(a); (*clear,*
definite) netto(a), chiaro(a); **~dly** [-dɪdlɪ] *adv*
indubbiamente; decisamente

decimal ['dɛsɪməl] *adj* decimale ♦ *n* decimale
m; **~ point** *n* ≈ virgola

decipher [dɪ'saɪfə*] *vt* decifrare

decision [dɪ'sɪʒən] *n* decisione *f*

decisive [dɪ'saɪsɪv] *adj* decisivo(a); (*person*)
deciso(a)

deck [dɛk] *n* (*NAUT*) ponte *m*; (*of bus*): **top ~**
imperiale *m*; (*record* ~) piatto; (*of cards*)
mazzo; **~chair** *n* sedia a sdraio

declaration [dɛklə'reɪʃən] *n* dichiarazione *f*

declare [dɪ'klɛə*] *vt* dichiarare

decline [dɪ'klaɪn] *n* (*decay*) declino;
(*lessening*) ribasso ♦ *vt* declinare; rifiutare ♦ *vi*
declinare; diminuire

decode [diː'kəud] *vt* decifrare

decoder [diː'kəudə*] *n* (*TV*) decodificatore *m*

decompose [diːkəm'pəuz] *vi* decomporre

décor ['deɪkɔː*] *n* decorazione *f*

decorate ['dɛkəreɪt] *vt* (*adorn, give a medal*
to) decorare; (*paint and paper*) tinteggiare e
tappezzare; **decoration** [-'reɪʃən] *n* (*medal*
etc, adornment) decorazione *f*; **decorator** *n*
decoratore *m*

decorum [dɪ'kɔːrəm] *n* decoro

decoy ['diːkɔɪ] *n* zimbello

decrease [*n* 'diːkriːs, *vb* diː'kriːs] *n*
diminuzione *f* ♦ *vt, vi* diminuire

decree [dɪ'kriː] *n* decreto; **~ nisi** [-'naɪsaɪ] *n*
sentenza provvisoria di divorzio

dedicate ['dɛdɪkeɪt] *vt* consacrare; (*book etc*)
dedicare

dedication [dɛdɪ'keɪʃən] *n* (*devotion*)
dedizione *f*; (*in book etc*) dedica

deduce [dɪ'djuːs] *vt* dedurre

deduct [dɪ'dʌkt] *vt*: **to ~ sth (from)** dedurre
qc (da); **~ion** [dɪ'dʌkʃən] *n* deduzione *f*

deed [diːd] *n* azione *f*, atto; (*LAW*) atto

deep [diːp] *adj* profondo(a); **4 metres ~**
profondo(a) 4 metri ♦ *adv*: **spectators stood**
20 ~ c'erano 20 file di spettatori; **~en** *vt*
(*hole*) approfondire ♦ *vi* approfondirsi;
(*darkness*) farsi più buio; **~ end** *n*: **the ~ end**
(*of swimming pool*) la parte più profonda; **~-**
freeze *n* congelatore *m*; **~-fry** *vt* friggere in
olio abbondante; **~ly** *adv* profondamente;
~-sea diving *n* immersione *f* in alto mare;
~-seated *adj* radicato(a)

deer [dɪə*] *n inv*: **the ~** i cervidi; (*red*) ~ cervo;
(*fallow*) ~ daino; (*roe*) ~ capriolo; **~skin** *n*
pelle *f* di daino

deface [dɪ'feɪs] *vt* imbrattare

default [dɪ'fɔːlt] *n* (*COMPUT: also*: ~ *value*)
default *m inv*; **by ~** (*SPORT*) per abbandono

defeat [dɪ'fiːt] *n* sconfitta ♦ *vt* (*team,*
opponents) sconfiggere; **~ist** *adj*, *n* disfattista
m/f

defect [n 'di:fɛkt, vb dɪ'fɛkt] n difetto ♦ vi:
to ~ to the enemy passare al nemico; **~ive**
[dɪ'fɛktɪv] adj difettoso(a)

defence [dɪ'fɛns] (US **defense**) n difesa; **~less**
adj senza difesa

defend [dɪ'fɛnd] vt difendere; **~ant** n
imputato/a; **~er** n difensore/a

defense [dɪ'fɛns] (US) n = **defence**

defensive [dɪ'fɛnsɪv] adj difensivo(a) ♦ n:
on the ~ sulla difensiva

defer [dɪ'fə:*] vt (postpone) differire, rinviare

defiance [dɪ'faɪəns] n sfida; in ~ of a dispetto
di

defiant [dɪ'faɪənt] adj (attitude) di sfida;
(person) ribelle

deficiency [dɪ'fɪʃənsɪ] n deficienza; carenza

deficit ['dɛfɪsɪt] n deficit m inv

define [dɪ'faɪn] vt definire

definite ['dɛfɪnɪt] adj (fixed) definito(a),
preciso(a); (clear, obvious) ben definito(a),
esatto(a); (LING) determinativo(a); he was
~ about it ne era sicuro; **~ly** adv
indubbiamente

definition [dɛfɪ'nɪʃən] n definizione f

deflate [di:'fleɪt] vt sgonfiare

deflect [dɪ'flɛkt] vt deflettere, deviare

deformed [dɪ'fɔ:md] adj deforme

defraud [dɪ'frɔ:d] vt defraudare

defrost [di:'frɔst] vt (fridge) disgelare; **~er**
(US) n (demister) sbrinatore m

deft [dɛft] adj svelto(a), destro(a)

defunct [dɪ'fʌŋkt] adj che non esiste più

defuse [di:'fju:z] vt disinnescare; (fig)
distendere

defy [dɪ'faɪ] vt sfidare; (efforts etc) resistere a;
it defies description supera ogni descrizione

degenerate [vb dɪ'dʒɛnəreɪt, adj dɪ'dʒɛnərɪt]
vi degenerare ♦ adj degenere

degree [dɪ'gri:] n grado; (SCOL) laurea
(universitaria); a (first) ~ in maths una laurea
in matematica; by **~s** (gradually) gradualmente, a poco a poco; to some ~ fino a
un certo punto, in certa misura

dehydrated [di:haɪ'dreɪtɪd] adj
disidratato(a); (milk, eggs) in polvere

de-ice [di:'aɪs] vt (windscreen) disgelare

deign [deɪn] vi: to ~ to do degnarsi di fare

deity ['di:ɪtɪ] n divinità f inv

dejected [dɪ'dʒɛktɪd] adj abbattuto(a),
avvilito(a)

delay [dɪ'leɪ] vt ritardare ♦ vi: to ~ (in doing
sth) ritardare (a fare qc) ♦ n ritardo; to be
~ed subire un ritardo; (person) essere
trattenuto(a)

delectable [dɪ'lɛktəbl] adj (person, food)
delizioso(a)

delegate [n 'dɛlɪgɪt, vb 'dɛlɪgeɪt] n delegato/a
♦ vt delegare; **delegation** [-'geɪʃən] n
(group) delegazione f; (by manager) delega

delete [dɪ'li:t] vt cancellare

deliberate [adj dɪ'lɪbərɪt, vb dɪ'lɪbəreɪt] adj
(intentional) intenzionale; (slow) misurato(a)
♦ vi deliberare, riflettere; **~ly** adv (on
purpose) deliberatamente

delicacy ['dɛlɪkəsɪ] n delicatezza

delicate ['dɛlɪkɪt] adj delicato(a)

delicatessen [dɛlɪkə'tɛsn] n ≈ salumeria

delicious [dɪ'lɪʃəs] adj delizioso(a),
squisito(a)

delight [dɪ'laɪt] n delizia, gran piacere m ♦ vt
dilettare; to take (a) ~ in dilettarsi in; **~ed**
adj: **~ed (at** or **with)** contentissimo(a) (di),
felice (di); **~ed to do** felice di fare; **~ful** adj
delizioso(a); incantevole

delinquent [dɪ'lɪŋkwənt] adj, n delinquente
m/f

delirious [dɪ'lɪrɪəs] adj: to be ~ delirare

deliver [dɪ'lɪvə*] vt (mail) distribuire; (goods)
consegnare; (speech) pronunciare; (MED) far
partorire; **~y** n distribuzione f; consegna; (of
speaker) dizione f; (MED) parto

delude [dɪ'lu:d] vt illudere

deluge ['dɛlju:dʒ] n diluvio

delusion [dɪ'lu:ʒən] n illusione f

demand [dɪ'mɑ:nd] vt richiedere; (rights)
rivendicare ♦ n domanda; (claim) rivendicazione f; in ~ ricercato(a), richiesto(a);
on ~ a richiesta; **~ing** adj (boss) esigente;
(work) impegnativo(a)

demean [dɪ'mi:n] vt: to ~ o.s. umiliarsi

demeanour [dɪ'mi:nə*] (US **demeanor**) n
comportamento; contegno

demented [dɪ'mɛntɪd] adj demente,
impazzito(a)

demise [dɪ'maɪz] n decesso

demister [di:'mɪstə*] (BRIT) n (AUT)
sbrinatore m

demo ['dɛməu] (inf) n abbr (= demonstration) manifestazione f

democracy [dɪ'mɔkrəsɪ] n democrazia

democrat ['dɛməkræt] n democratico/a; **~ic**
[dɛmə'krætɪk] adj democratico(a)

demolish [dɪ'mɔlɪʃ] vt demolire

demonstrate ['dɛmənstreɪt] vt dimostrare,
provare ♦ vi dimostrare, manifestare;
demonstration [-'streɪʃən] n dimostrazione
f; (POL) dimostrazione, manifestazione f;
demonstrator n (POL) dimostrante m/f;
(COMM) dimostratore/trice

demote [dɪ'məut] vt far retrocedere

demure [dɪ'mjuə*] adj contegnoso(a)

den [dɛn] n tana, covo; (room) buco

denial [dɪ'naɪəl] n diniego; rifiuto

denim ['dɛnɪm] n tessuto di cotone ritorto; **~s**
npl (jeans) blue jeans mpl

Denmark ['dɛnmɑ:k] n Danimarca

denomination [dɪnɔmɪ'neɪʃən] n (money)
valore m; (REL) confessione f

denounce [dɪ'naʊns] vt denunciare

dense [dɛns] adj fitto(a); (smoke) denso(a); (inf: person) ottuso(a), duro(a)

density ['dɛnsɪtɪ] n densità f inv

dent [dɛnt] n ammaccatura ♦ vt (also: make a ~ in) ammaccare

dental ['dɛntl] adj dentale; ~ **surgeon** n medico/a dentista

dentist ['dɛntɪst] n dentista m/f

dentures ['dɛntʃəz] npl dentiera

deny [dɪ'naɪ] vt negare; (refuse) rifiutare

deodorant [diː'əʊdərənt] n deodorante m

depart [dɪ'pɑːt] vi partire; **to ~ from** (fig) deviare da

department [dɪ'pɑːtmənt] n (COMM) reparto; (SCOL) sezione f, dipartimento; (POL) ministero; ~ **store** n grande magazzino

departure [dɪ'pɑːtʃə*] n partenza; (fig): ~ **from** deviazione f da; **a new ~** una svolta (decisiva); ~ **lounge** n (at airport) sala d'attesa

depend [dɪ'pɛnd] vi: **to ~ on** dipendere da; (rely on) contare su; **it ~s** dipende; **~ing on the result ...** a seconda del risultato ...; **~able** adj fidato(a); (car etc) affidabile; **~ant** n persona a carico; **~ent** adj: **to be ~ent on** dipendere da; (child, relative) essere a carico di ♦ n = **~ant**

depict [dɪ'pɪkt] vt (in picture) dipingere; (in words) descrivere

depleted [dɪ'pliːtɪd] adj diminuito(a)

deploy [dɪ'plɔɪ] vt dispiegare

depopulation ['diːpɔpju'leɪʃən] n spopolamento

deport [dɪ'pɔːt] vt deportare; espellere

deportment [dɪ'pɔːtmənt] n portamento

deposit [dɪ'pɔzɪt] n (COMM, GEO) deposito; (of ore, oil) giacimento; (CHEM) sedimento; (part payment) acconto; (for hired goods etc) cauzione f ♦ vt depositare; dare in acconto; mettere or lasciare in deposito; ~ **account** n conto vincolato

depot ['dɛpəʊ] n deposito; (US) stazione f ferroviaria

depreciate [dɪ'priːʃɪeɪt] vi svalutarsi

depress [dɪ'prɛs] vt deprimere; (price, wages) abbassare; (press down) premere; **~ed** adj (person) depresso(a), abbattuto(a); (price) in ribasso; (industry) in crisi; **~ing** adj deprimente; **~ion** [dɪ'prɛʃən] n depressione f

deprivation [dɛprɪ'veɪʃən] n privazione f

deprive [dɪ'praɪv] vt: **to ~ sb of** privare qn di; **~d** adj disgraziato(a)

depth [dɛpθ] n profondità f inv; **in the ~s of** nel profondo di; **out of one's ~** (in water) dove non si tocca; (fig) a disagio

deputize ['dɛpjutaɪz] vi: **to ~ for** svolgere le funzioni di

deputy ['dɛpjutɪ] adj: ~ **head** (BRIT: SCOL)

vicepreside m/f ♦ n (assistant) vice m/f inv; (US: also: ~ sheriff) vice-sceriffo

derail [dɪ'reɪl] vt: **to be ~ed** deragliare

deranged [dɪ'reɪndʒd] adj: **to be (mentally) ~** essere pazzo(a)

derby ['dɜːbɪ] (US) n (bowler hat) bombetta

derelict ['dɛrɪlɪkt] adj abbandonato(a)

derisory [dɪ'raɪsərɪ] adj (sum) irrisorio(a); (laughter, person) beffardo(a)

derive [dɪ'raɪv] vt: **to ~ sth from** derivare qc da; trarre qc da ♦ vi: **to ~ from** derivare da

derogatory [dɪ'rɔgətərɪ] adj denigratorio(a)

derv [dɜːv] (BRIT) n gasolio

descend [dɪ'sɛnd] vt, vi discendere, scendere; **to ~ from** discendere da; **to ~ to** (lying, begging) abbassarsi a; **~ant** n discendente m/f

descent [dɪ'sɛnt] n discesa; (origin) discendenza, famiglia

describe [dɪs'kraɪb] vt descrivere; **description** [-'krɪpʃən] n descrizione f; (sort) genere m, specie f

desecrate ['dɛsɪkreɪt] vt profanare

desert [n 'dɛzət, vb dɪ'zɜːt] n deserto ♦ vt lasciare, abbandonare ♦ vi (MIL) disertare; **~er** n disertore m; **~ion** [dɪ'zɜːʃən] n (MIL) diserzione f; (LAW) abbandono del tetto coniugale; ~ **island** n isola deserta; **~s** [dɪ'zɜːts] npl: **to get one's just ~s** avere ciò che si merita

deserve [dɪ'zɜːv] vt meritare; **deserving** adj (person) meritevole, degno(a); (cause) meritorio(a)

design [dɪ'zaɪn] n (art, sketch) disegno; (layout, shape) linea; (pattern) fantasia; (intention) intenzione f ♦ vt disegnare; progettare

designer [dɪ'zaɪnə*] n (ART, TECH) disegnatore/trice; (of fashion) modellista m/f

desire [dɪ'zaɪə*] n desiderio, voglia ♦ vt desiderare, volere

desk [dɛsk] n (in office) scrivania; (for pupil) banco; (BRIT: in shop, restaurant) cassa; (in hotel) ricevimento; (at airport) accettazione f

desolate ['dɛsəlɪt] adj desolato(a)

despair [dɪs'pɛə*] n disperazione f ♦ vi: **to ~ of** disperare di

despatch [dɪs'pætʃ] n, vt = **dispatch**

desperate ['dɛspərɪt] adj disperato(a); (fugitive) capace di tutto; **to be ~ for sth/to do** volere disperatamente qc/fare; **~ly** adv disperatamente; (very) terribilmente, estremamente

desperation [dɛspə'reɪʃən] n disperazione f

despicable [dɪs'pɪkəbl] adj disprezzabile

despise [dɪs'paɪz] vt disprezzare, sdegnare

despite [dɪs'paɪt] prep malgrado, a dispetto di, nonostante

despondent [dɪs'pɔndənt] adj abbattuto(a),

scoraggiato(a)

dessert [dɪ'zɜ:t] n dolce m; frutta; **~spoon** n cucchiaio da dolci

destination [dɛstɪ'neɪʃən] n destinazione f

destined ['dɛstɪnd] adj: **to be ~ to** do/for essere destinato(a) a fare/per

destiny ['dɛstɪnɪ] n destino

destitute ['dɛstɪtjuːt] adj indigente, bisognoso(a)

destroy [dɪs'trɔɪ] vt distruggere; **~er** n (NAUT) cacciatorpediniere m

destruction [dɪs'trʌkʃən] n distruzione f

detach [dɪ'tætʃ] vt staccare, distaccare; **~ed** adj (attitude) distante; **~ed house** n villa; **~ment** n (MIL) distaccamento; (fig) distacco

detail ['diːteɪl] n particolare m, dettaglio ♦ vt dettagliare, particolareggiare; **in ~** nei particolari; **~ed** adj particolareggiato(a)

detain [dɪ'teɪn] vt trattenere; (in captivity) detenere

detect [dɪ'tɛkt] vt scoprire, scorgere; (MED, POLICE, RADAR etc) individuare; **~ion** [dɪ'tɛkʃən] n scoperta; individuazione f; **~ive** n investigatore/trice; **~ive story** n giallo

détente [deɪ'tɑːnt] n (POL) distensione f

detention [dɪ'tɛnʃən] n detenzione f; (SCOL) permanenza forzata per punizione

deter [dɪ'tɜːʳ] vt dissuadere

detergent [dɪ'tɜːdʒənt] n detersivo

deteriorate [dɪ'tɪərɪəreɪt] vi deteriorarsi

determine [dɪ'tɜːmɪn] vt determinare; **~d** adj (person) risoluto(a), deciso(a); **~d to do** deciso(a) a fare

detour ['diːtuəʳ] n deviazione f

detract [dɪ'trækt] vi: **to ~ from** detrarre da

detriment ['dɛtrɪmənt] n: **to the ~ of** a detrimento di; **~al** [dɛtrɪ'mɛntl] adj: **~al to** dannoso(a) a, nocivo(a) a

devaluation [diːvæljuˈeɪʃən] n svalutazione f

devastate ['dɛvəsteɪt] vt devastare; (fig): **~d by** sconvolto(a) da; **devastating** adj devastatore(trice); sconvolgente

develop [dɪ'vɛləp] vt sviluppare; (habit) prendere (gradualmente) ♦ vi svilupparsi; (facts, symptoms: appear) manifestarsi, rivelarsi; **~er** n (also: property ~er) costruttore m edile; **~ing country** n paese m in via di sviluppo; **~ment** n sviluppo

device [dɪ'vaɪs] n (apparatus) congegno

devil ['dɛvl] n diavolo; demonio

devious ['diːvɪəs] adj (person) subdolo(a)

devise [dɪ'vaɪz] vt escogitare, concepire

devoid [dɪ'vɔɪd] adj: **~ of** privo(a) di

devolution [diːvə'luːʃən] n (POL) decentramento

devote [dɪ'vəut] vt: **to ~ sth to** dedicare qc a; **~d** adj devoto(a); **to be ~d to sb** essere molto affezionato(a) a qn; **~e** [dɛvəu'tiː] n (MUS, SPORT) appassionato/a

devotion [dɪ'vəuʃən] n devozione f, attaccamento f; (REL) atto di devozione, preghiera

devour [dɪ'vauəʳ] vt divorare

devout [dɪ'vaut] adj pio(a), devoto(a)

dew [djuː] n rugiada

dexterity [dɛks'tɛrɪtɪ] n destrezza

diabetes [daɪə'biːtiːz] n diabete m; **diabetic** [-'bɛtɪk] adj, n diabetico(a)

diabolical [daɪə'bɔlɪkl] (inf) adj (weather, behaviour) orribile

diagnosis [daɪəg'nəusɪs] (pl **diagnoses**) n diagnosi f inv

diagonal [daɪ'ægənl] adj diagonale ♦ n diagonale f

diagram ['daɪəgræm] n diagramma m

dial ['daɪəl] n quadrante m; (on radio) lancetta; (on telephone) disco combinatore ♦ vt (number) fare

dialect ['daɪəlɛkt] n dialetto

dialling code ['daɪəlɪŋ-] (US **area code**) n prefisso

dialling tone ['daɪəlɪŋ-] (US **dial tone**) n segnale m di linea libera

dialogue ['daɪəlɔg] (US **dialog**) n dialogo

diameter [daɪ'æmɪtəʳ] n diametro

diamond ['daɪəmənd] n diamante m; (shape) rombo; **~s** npl (CARDS) quadri mpl

diaper ['daɪəpəʳ] (US) n pannolino

diaphragm ['daɪəfræm] n diaframma m

diarrhoea [daɪə'riːə] (US **diarrhea**) n diarrea

diary ['daɪərɪ] n (daily account) diario; (book) agenda

dice [daɪs] n inv dado ♦ vt (CULIN) tagliare a dadini

Dictaphone ® ['dɪktəfəun] n dittafono ®

dictate [dɪk'teɪt] vt dettare

dictation [dɪk'teɪʃən] n dettatura; (SCOL) dettato

dictator [dɪk'teɪtəʳ] n dittatore m; **~ship** n dittatura

dictionary ['dɪkʃənrɪ] n dizionario

did [dɪd] pt of **do**

didn't [dɪdnt] = **did not**

die [daɪ] vi morire; **to be dying for sth/to do sth** morire dalla voglia di qc/di fare qc; **~ away** vi spegnersi a poco a poco; **~ down** vi abbassarsi; **~ out** vi estinguersi

diesel ['diːzəl] n (vehicle) diesel m inv; **~ engine** n motore m diesel inv; **~ (oil)** n gasolio (per motori diesel), diesel m inv

diet ['daɪət] n alimentazione f; (restricted food) dieta ♦ vi (also: **be on a ~**) stare a dieta

differ ['dɪfəʳ] vi: **to ~ from sth** differire da qc; essere diverso(a) da qc; **to ~ from sb over sth** essere in disaccordo con qn su qc; **~ence** n differenza; (disagreement) screzio; **~ent** adj diverso(a); **~entiate** [-'rɛnʃɪeɪt] vi: **to ~entiate between** discriminare or fare differenza fra

difficult ['dɪfɪkəlt] *adj* difficile; **~y** *n* difficoltà *f inv*

diffident ['dɪfɪdənt] *adj* sfiduciato(a)

diffuse [*adj* dɪ'fju:s, *vb* dɪ'fju:z] *adj* diffuso(a) ♦ *vt* diffondere

dig [dɪg] (*pt, pp* **dug**) *vt* (*hole*) scavare; (*garden*) vangare ♦ *n* (*prod*) gomitata; (*archaeological*) scavo; (*fig*) frecciata; **~ into** *vt fus* (*savings*) scavare in; **to ~ one's nails into** conficcare le unghie in; **~ up** *vt* (*tree etc*) sradicare; (*information*) scavare fuori

digest [*vb* daɪ'dʒɛst, *n* 'daɪdʒɛst] *vt* digerire ♦ *n* compendio; **~ion** [dɪ'dʒɛstʃən] *n* digestione *f*; **~ive** *adj* (*juices, system*) digerente

digit ['dɪdʒɪt] *n* cifra; (*finger*) dito; **~al** *adj* digitale; **~al TV** *n* televisione *f* digitale

dignified ['dɪgnɪfaɪd] *adj* dignitoso(a)

dignity ['dɪgnɪtɪ] *n* dignità

digress [daɪ'grɛs] *vi*: **to ~ from** divagare da

digs [dɪgz] (*BRIT: inf*) *npl* camera ammobiliata

dike [daɪk] *n* = **dyke**

dilapidated [dɪ'læpɪdeɪtɪd] *adj* cadente

dilemma [daɪ'lɛmə] *n* dilemma *m*

diligent ['dɪlɪdʒənt] *adj* diligente

dilute [daɪ'lu:t] *vt* diluire; (*with water*) annacquare

dim [dɪm] *adj* (*light*) debole; (*outline, figure*) vago(a); (*room*) in penombra; (*inf: person*) tonto(a) ♦ *vt* (*light*) abbassare

dime [daɪm] (*US*) *n* = 10 cents

dimension [daɪ'mɛnʃən] *n* dimensione *f*

diminish [dɪ'mɪnɪʃ] *vt, vi* diminuire

diminutive [dɪ'mɪnjutɪv] *adj* minuscolo(a) ♦ *n* (*LING*) diminutivo

dimmers ['dɪməz] (*US*) *npl* (*AUT*) anabbaglianti *mpl*; luci *fpl* di posizione

dimple ['dɪmpl] *n* fossetta

din [dɪn] *n* chiasso, fracasso

dine [daɪn] *vi* pranzare; **~r** *n* (*person*) cliente *m/f*; (*US: place*) tavola calda

dinghy ['dɪŋgɪ] *n* battello pneumatico; (*also: rubber ~*) gommone *m*

dingy ['dɪndʒɪ] *adj* grigio(a)

dining car ['daɪnɪŋ-] (*BRIT*) *n* vagone *m* ristorante

dining room ['daɪnɪŋ-] *n* sala da pranzo

dinner ['dɪnə*] *n* (*lunch*) pranzo; (*evening meal*) cena; (*public*) banchetto; **~ jacket** *n* smoking *m inv*; **~ party** *n* cena; **~ time** *n* ora di pranzo (*or* cena)

dip [dɪp] *n* discesa; (*in sea*) bagno; (*CULIN*) salsetta ♦ *vt* immergere; bagnare; (*BRIT: AUT: lights*) abbassare ♦ *vi* abbassarsi

diploma [dɪ'pləumə] *n* diploma *m*

diplomacy [dɪ'pləuməsɪ] *n* diplomazia

diplomat ['dɪpləmæt] *n* diplomatico; **~ic** [dɪplə'mætɪk] *adj* diplomatico(a)

diprod ['dɪprɔd] (*US*) *n* = **dipstick**

dipstick ['dɪpstɪk] *n* (*AUT*) indicatore *m* di livello dell'olio

dipswitch ['dɪpswɪtʃ] (*BRIT*) *n* (*AUT*) levetta dei fari

dire [daɪə*] *adj* terribile; estremo(a)

direct [daɪ'rɛkt] *adj* diretto(a) ♦ *vt* dirigere; (*order*): **to ~ sb to do sth** dare direttive a qn di fare qc ♦ *adv* direttamente; **can you ~ me to ...?** mi può indicare la strada per ...?

direction [dɪ'rɛkʃən] *n* direzione *f*; **~s** *npl* (*advice*) chiarimenti *mpl*; **sense of ~** senso dell'orientamento; **~s for use** istruzioni *fpl*

directly [dɪ'rɛktlɪ] *adv* (*in straight line*) direttamente; (*at once*) subito

director [dɪ'rɛktə*] *n* direttore/trice; amministratore/trice; (*THEATRE, CINEMA*) regista *m/f*

directory [dɪ'rɛktərɪ] *n* elenco; **~ enquiries, ~ assistance** (*US*) *n* informazioni *fpl* elenco abbonati *inv*

dirt [də:t] *n* sporcizia; immondizia; (*earth*) terra; **~-cheap** *adj* da due soldi; **~y** *adj* sporco(a) ♦ *vt* sporcare; **~y trick** *n* brutto scherzo

disability [dɪsə'bɪlɪtɪ] *n* invalidità *f inv*; (*LAW*) incapacità *f inv*

disabled [dɪs'eɪbld] *adj* invalido(a); (*mentally*) ritardato(a) ♦ *npl*: **the ~** gli invalidi

disadvantage [dɪsəd'vɑ:ntɪdʒ] *n* svantaggio

disagree [dɪsə'gri:] *vi* (*differ*) discordare; (*be against, think otherwise*): **to ~ (with)** essere in disaccordo (con), dissentire (da); **~able** *adj* sgradevole; (*person*) antipatico(a); **~ment** *n* disaccordo; (*argument*) dissapore *m*

disallow [dɪsə'lau] *vt* (*appeal*) respingere

disappear [dɪsə'pɪə*] *vi* scomparire; **~ance** *n* scomparsa

disappoint [dɪsə'pɔɪnt] *vt* deludere; **~ed** *adj* deluso(a); **~ing** *adj* deludente; **~ment** *n* delusione *f*

disapproval [dɪsə'pru:vəl] *n* disapprovazione *f*

disapprove [dɪsə'pru:v] *vi*: **to ~ of** disapprovare

disarm [dɪs'ɑ:m] *vt* disarmare; **~ament** *n* disarmo

disarray [dɪsə'reɪ] *n*: **in ~** (*army*) in rotta; (*organization*) in uno stato di confusione; (*clothes, hair*) in disordine

disaster [dɪ'zɑ:stə*] *n* disastro

disband [dɪs'bænd] *vt* sbandare; (*MIL*) congedare ♦ *vi* sciogliersi

disbelief ['dɪsbə'li:f] *n* incredulità

disc [dɪsk] *n* disco; (*COMPUT*) = **disk**

discard [dɪs'kɑ:d] *vt* (*old things*) scartare; (*fig*) abbandonare

discern [dɪ'sə:n] *vt* discernere, distinguere; **~ing** *adj* perspicace

discharge [vb dɪs'tʃɑːdʒ, n 'dɪstʃɑːdʒ] vt (duties) compiere; (ELEC, waste etc) scaricare; (MED) emettere; (patient) dimettere; (employee) licenziare; (soldier) congedare; (defendant) liberare ♦ n (ELEC) scarica; (MED) emissione f; (dismissal) licenziamento; congedo; liberazione f

disciple [dɪ'saɪpl] n discepolo

discipline ['dɪsɪplɪn] n disciplina ♦ vt disciplinare; (punish) punire

disc jockey n disc jockey m inv

disclaim [dɪs'kleɪm] vt negare, smentire

disclose [dɪs'kləʊz] vt rivelare, svelare; **disclosure** [-'kləʊʒə*] n rivelazione f

disco ['dɪskəʊ] n abbr = **discotheque**

discoloured [dɪs'kʌləd] (US **discolored**) adj scolorito(a); ingiallito(a)

discomfort [dɪs'kʌmfət] n disagio; (lack of comfort) scomodità f inv

disconcert [dɪskən'sɜːt] vt sconcertare

disconnect [dɪskə'nekt] vt sconnettere, staccare; (ELEC, RADIO) staccare; (gas, water) chiudere

discontent [dɪskən'tent] n scontentezza; **~ed** adj scontento(a)

discontinue [dɪskən'tɪnjuː] vt smettere, cessare; **"~d"** (COMM) "fuori produzione"

discord ['dɪskɔːd] n disaccordo; (MUS) dissonanza

discotheque ['dɪskəʊtek] n discoteca

discount [n 'dɪskaʊnt, vb dɪs'kaʊnt] n sconto ♦ vt scontare; (idea) non badare a

discourage [dɪs'kʌrɪdʒ] vt scoraggiare

discourteous [dɪs'kɜːtɪəs] adj scortese

discover [dɪs'kʌvə*] vt scoprire; **~y** n scoperta

discredit [dɪs'kredɪt] vt screditare; mettere in dubbio

discreet [dɪ'skriːt] adj discreto(a)

discrepancy [dɪ'skrepənsɪ] n discrepanza

discriminate [dɪ'skrɪmɪneɪt] vi: to **~ between** distinguere tra; **to ~ against** discriminare contro; **discriminating** adj fine, giudizioso(a); **discrimination** [-'neɪʃən] n discriminazione f; (judgment) discernimento

discuss [dɪ'skʌs] vt discutere; (debate) dibattere; **~ion** [dɪ'skʌʃən] n discussione f

disdain [dɪs'deɪn] n disdegno

disease [dɪ'ziːz] n malattia

disembark [dɪsɪm'bɑːk] vt, vi sbarcare

disentangle [dɪsɪn'tæŋgl] vt liberare; (wool etc) sbrogliare

disfigure [dɪs'fɪgə*] vt sfigurare

disgrace [dɪs'greɪs] n vergogna; (disfavour) disgrazia ♦ vt disonorare, far cadere in disgrazia; **~ful** adj scandaloso(a), vergognoso(a)

disgruntled [dɪs'grʌntld] adj scontento(a), di cattivo umore

disguise [dɪs'gaɪz] n travestimento ♦ vt: to **~ (as)** travestire (da); **in ~** travestito(a)

disgust [dɪs'gʌst] n disgusto, nausea ♦ vt disgustare, far schifo a; **~ing** adj disgustoso(a); ripugnante

dish [dɪʃ] n piatto; **to do** or **wash the ~es** fare i piatti; **~ out** vt distribuire; **~ up** vt servire; **~cloth** n strofinaccio

dishearten [dɪs'hɑːtn] vt scoraggiare

dishevelled [dɪ'ʃevəld] (US **disheveled**) adj arruffato(a); scapigliato(a)

dishonest [dɪs'ɒnɪst] adj disonesto(a)

dishonour [dɪs'ɒnə*] (US **dishonor**) n disonore m; **~able** adj disonorevole

dishtowel ['dɪʃtaʊəl] (US) n strofinaccio dei piatti

dishwasher ['dɪʃwɒʃə*] n lavastoviglie f inv

disillusion [dɪsɪ'luːʒən] vt disilludere, disingannare

disinfect [dɪsɪn'fekt] vt disinfettare; **~ant** n disinfettante m

disintegrate [dɪs'ɪntɪgreɪt] vi disintegrarsi

disinterested [dɪs'ɪntrəstɪd] adj disinteressato(a)

disjointed [dɪs'dʒɔɪntɪd] adj sconnesso(a)

disk [dɪsk] n (COMPUT) disco; **single-/double-sided ~** disco a facciata singola/doppia; **~ drive** n lettore m; **~ette** (US) n = **disk**

dislike [dɪs'laɪk] n antipatia, avversione f; (gen pl) cosa che non piace ♦ vt: **he ~s it** non gli piace

dislocate ['dɪsləkeɪt] vt slogare

dislodge [dɪs'lɒdʒ] vt rimuovere

disloyal [dɪs'lɔɪəl] adj sleale

dismal ['dɪzml] adj triste, cupo(a)

dismantle [dɪs'mæntl] vt (machine) smontare

dismay [dɪs'meɪ] n costernazione f ♦ vt sgomentare

dismiss [dɪs'mɪs] vt congedare; (employee) licenziare; (idea) scacciare; (LAW) respingere; **~al** n congedo; licenziamento

dismount [dɪs'maʊnt] vi scendere

disobedience [dɪsə'biːdɪəns] n disubbidienza

disobedient [dɪsə'biːdɪənt] adj disubbidiente

disobey [dɪsə'beɪ] vt disubbidire a

disorder [dɪs'ɔːdə*] n disordine m; (rioting) tumulto; (MED) disturbo; **~ly** adj disordinato(a); tumultuoso(a)

disorientated [dɪs'ɔːrɪenteɪtɪd] adj disorientato(a)

disown [dɪs'əʊn] vt rinnegare

disparaging [dɪs'pærɪdʒɪŋ] adj spregiativo(a), sprezzante

dispassionate [dɪs'pæʃənət] adj calmo(a), freddo(a); imparziale

dispatch [dɪs'pætʃ] vt spedire, inviare ♦ n spedizione f, invio; (MIL, PRESS) dispaccio

dispel [dɪs'pɛl] vt dissipare, scacciare

dispense [dɪs'pɛns] vt distribuire, amministrare; **~ with** vt fus fare a meno di; **~r** n (container) distributore m; **dispensing chemist** (BRIT) n farmacista m/f

disperse [dɪs'pɔːs] vt disperdere; (knowledge) disseminare ♦ vi disperdersi

dispirited [dɪs'pɪrɪtɪd] adj scoraggiato(a), abbattuto(a)

displace [dɪs'pleɪs] vt spostare; **~d person** n (POL) profugo/a

display [dɪs'pleɪ] n esposizione f; (of feeling etc) manifestazione f; (screen) schermo ♦ vt mostrare; (goods) esporre; (pej) ostentare

displease [dɪs'pliːz] vt dispiacere a, scontentare; **~d with** scontento di; **displeasure** [-'plɛʒə*] n dispiacere m

disposable [dɪs'pəuzəbl] adj (pack etc) a perdere; (income) disponibile; **~ nappy** n pannolino di carta

disposal [dɪs'pəuzl] n eliminazione f; (of property) cessione f; **at one's ~** alla sua disposizione

dispose [dɪs'pəuz] vi: **~ of** sbarazzarsi di; **~d** adj: **~d to do** disposto(a) a fare; **disposition** [-'zɪʃən] n disposizione f; (temperament) carattere m

disproportionate [dɪsprə'pɔːʃənət] adj sproporzionato(a)

disprove [dɪs'pruːv] vt confutare

dispute [dɪs'pjuːt] n disputa; (also: industrial ~) controversia (sindacale) ♦ vt contestare; (matter) discutere; (victory) disputare

disqualify [dɪs'kwɔlɪfaɪ] vt (SPORT) squalificare; **to ~ sb from sth/from doing** rendere qn incapace a qc/a fare; squalificare qn da qc/da fare; **to ~ sb from driving** ritirare la patente a qn

disquiet [dɪs'kwaɪət] n inquietudine f

disregard [dɪsrɪ'gɑːd] vt non far caso a, non badare a

disrepair [dɪsrɪ'pɛə*] n: **to fall into ~** (building) andare in rovina; (machine) deteriorarsi

disreputable [dɪs'rɛpjutəbl] adj poco raccomandabile; indecente

disrupt [dɪs'rʌpt] vt disturbare; creare scompiglio in

dissatisfaction [dɪssætɪs'fækʃən] n scontentezza, insoddisfazione f

dissect [dɪ'sɛkt] vt sezionare

dissent [dɪ'sɛnt] n dissenso

dissertation [dɪsə'teɪʃən] n tesi f inv, dissertazione f

disservice [dɪs'sɔːvɪs] n: **to do sb a ~** fare un cattivo servizio a qn

dissimilar [dɪ'sɪmɪlə*] adj: **~ (to)** dissimile or diverso(a) (da)

dissipate ['dɪsɪpeɪt] vt dissipare

dissolve [dɪ'zɔlv] vt dissolvere, sciogliere; (POL, marriage etc) sciogliere ♦ vi dissolversi, sciogliersi

distance ['dɪstns] n distanza; **in the ~** in lontananza

distant ['dɪstnt] adj lontano(a), distante; (manner) riservato(a), freddo(a)

distaste [dɪs'teɪst] n ripugnanza; **~ful** adj ripugnante, sgradevole

distended [dɪs'tɛndɪd] adj (stomach) dilatato(a)

distil [dɪs'tɪl] (US **distill**) vt distillare; **~lery** n distilleria

distinct [dɪs'tɪŋkt] adj distinto(a); **as ~ from** a differenza di; **~ion** [dɪs'tɪŋkʃən] n distinzione f; (in exam) lode f; **~ive** adj distintivo(a)

distinguish [dɪs'tɪŋgwɪʃ] vt distinguere; **~ed** adj (eminent) eminente; **~ing** adj (feature) distinto(a), caratteristico(a)

distort [dɪs'tɔːt] vt distorcere; (TECH) deformare

distract [dɪs'trækt] vt distrarre; **~ed** adj distratto(a); **~ion** [dɪs'trækʃən] n distrazione f

distraught [dɪs'trɔːt] adj stravolto(a)

distress [dɪs'trɛs] n angoscia ♦ vt affliggere; **~ing** adj doloroso(a); **~ signal** n segnale m di soccorso

distribute [dɪs'trɪbjuːt] vt distribuire; **distribution** [-'bjuːʃən] n distribuzione f; **distributor** n distributore m

district ['dɪstrɪkt] n (of country) regione f; (of town) quartiere m; (ADMIN) distretto; **~ attorney** (US) n ≈ sostituto procuratore m della Repubblica; **~ nurse** (BRIT) n infermiera di quartiere

distrust [dɪs'trʌst] n diffidenza, sfiducia ♦ vt non aver fiducia in

disturb [dɪs'tɔːb] vt disturbare; **~ance** n disturbo; (political etc) disordini mpl; **~ed** adj (worried, upset) turbato(a); **emotionally ~ed** con turbe emotive; **~ing** adj sconvolgente

disuse [dɪs'juːs] n: **to fall into ~** cadere in disuso

disused [dɪs'juːzd] adj abbandonato(a)

ditch [dɪtʃ] n fossa ♦ vt (inf) piantare in asso

dither ['dɪðə*] (pej) vi vacillare

ditto ['dɪtəu] adv idem

dive [daɪv] n tuffo; (of submarine) immersione f ♦ vi tuffarsi; immergersi; **~r** n tuffatore /trice; palombaro

diverse [daɪ'vɔːs] adj vario(a)

diversion [daɪ'vɔːʃən] n (BRIT: AUT) deviazione f; (distraction) divertimento

divert [daɪ'vɔːt] vt deviare

divide [dɪ'vaɪd] vt dividere; (separate) separare ♦ vi dividersi; **~d highway** (US) n strada a doppia carreggiata

dividend ['dɪvɪdɛnd] n dividendo; (fig): **to**

pay **~s** dare dei frutti

divine [dɪ'vaɪn] adj divino(a)

diving ['daɪvɪŋ] n tuffo; **~ board** n trampolino

divinity [dɪ'vɪnɪtɪ] n divinità f inv; teologia

division [dɪ'vɪʒən] n divisione f; separazione f; (esp FOOTBALL) serie f

divorce [dɪ'vɔːs] n divorzio ♦ vt divorziare da; (dissociate) separare; **~d** adj divorziato(a); **~e** [-'siː] n divorziato/a

D.I.Y. (BRIT) n abbr = **do-it-yourself**

dizzy ['dɪzɪ] adj: **to feel ~** avere il capogiro

DJ n abbr = **disc jockey**

KEYWORD

do [duː] (pt **did**, pp **done**) n (inf: party etc) festa; **it was rather a grand ~** è stato un ricevimento piuttosto importante
♦ vb **1** (in negative constructions) non tradotto; **I don't understand** non capisco
2 (to form questions) non tradotto; **didn't you know?** non lo sapevi?; **why didn't you come?** perché non sei venuto?
3 (for emphasis, in polite expressions): **she does seem rather late** sembra essere piuttosto in ritardo; **~ sit down** si accomodi la prego, prego si sieda; **~ take care!** mi raccomando, sta attento!
4 (used to avoid repeating vb): **she swims better than I ~** lei nuota meglio di me; **~ you agree? — yes, I ~/no, I don't** sei d'accordo? — si/no; **she lives in Glasgow — so ~ I** lei vive a Glasgow — anch'io; **he asked me to help him and I did** mi ha chiesto di aiutarlo ed io l'ho fatto
5 (in question tags): **you like him, don't you?** ti piace, vero?; **I don't know him, ~ I?** non lo conosco, vero?
♦ vt (gen, carry out, perform etc) fare; **what are you ~ing tonight?** che fa stasera?; **to ~ the cooking** cucinare; **to ~ the washing-up** fare i piatti; **to ~ one's teeth** lavarsi i denti; **to ~ one's hair/nails** farsi i capelli/le unghie; **the car was ~ing 100** la macchina faceva i 100 all'ora
♦ vi **1** (act, behave) fare; **~ as I ~** faccia come me, faccia come faccio io
2 (get on, fare) andare; **he's ~ing well/badly at school** va bene/male a scuola; **how ~ you ~?** piacere!
3 (suit) andare bene; **this room will ~** questa stanza va bene
4 (be sufficient) bastare; **will £10 ~?** basteranno 10 sterline?; **that'll ~** basta così; **that'll ~!** (in annoyance) ora basta!; **to make ~ (with)** arrangiarsi (con)
do away with vt fus (kill) far fuori; (abolish) abolire
do up vt (laces) allacciare; (dress, buttons)

abbottonare; (renovate: room, house) rimettere a nuovo, rifare
do with vt fus (need) aver bisogno di; (be connected): **what has it got to ~ with you?** e tu che c'entri?; **I won't have anything to ~ with it** non voglio avere niente a che farci; **it has to ~ with money** si tratta di soldi
do without vi fare senza ♦ vt fus fare a meno di

dock [dɒk] n (NAUT) bacino; (LAW) banco degli imputati ♦ vi entrare in bacino; (SPACE) agganciarsi; **~s** npl (NAUT) dock m inv; **~er** n scaricatore m; **~yard** n cantiere m (navale)

doctor ['dɒktə*] n medico/a; (Ph.D. etc) dottore/essa ♦ vt (drink etc) adulterare; **D~ of Philosophy** n dottorato di ricerca; (person) titolare m/f di un dottorato di ricerca

doctrine ['dɒktrɪn] n dottrina

document ['dɒkjumənt] n documento; **~ary** [-'mɛntərɪ] adj (evidence) documentato(a) ♦ n documentario

dodge [dɒdʒ] n trucco; schivata ♦ vt schivare, eludere

dodgems ['dɒdʒəmz] (BRIT) npl autoscontri mpl

doe [dəʊ] n (deer) femmina di daino; (rabbit) coniglia

does [dʌz] vb see **do**; **doesn't** = **does not**

dog [dɒg] n cane m ♦ vt (follow closely) pedinare; (fig: memory etc) perseguitare; **~ collar** n collare m di cane; (fig) collarino; **~-eared** adj (book) con orecchie

dogged ['dɒgɪd] adj ostinato(a), tenace

dogsbody ['dɒgzbɒdɪ] (BRIT: inf) n factotum m inv

doing ['duːɪŋ] n: **this is your ~** è opera tua, sei stato tu

do-it-yourself [duːɪtjɔː'self] n il far da sé

doldrums ['dɒldrəmz] npl (fig): **to be in the ~** avere un brutto periodo

dole [dəʊl] (BRIT) n sussidio di disoccupazione; **to be on the ~** vivere del sussidio; **~ out** vt distribuire

doll [dɒl] n bambola; **~ed up** (inf) adj in ghingheri

dollar ['dɒlə*] n dollaro

dolly ['dɒlɪ] n bambola

dolphin ['dɒlfɪn] n delfino

domain [də'meɪn] n dominio

dome [dəʊm] n cupola

domestic [də'mɛstɪk] adj (duty, happiness, animal) domestico(a); (policy, affairs, flights) nazionale; **~ated** adj addomesticato(a)

dominant ['dɒmɪnənt] adj dominante

dominate ['dɒmɪneɪt] vt dominare

domineering [dɒmɪ'nɪərɪŋ] adj dispotico(a), autoritario(a)

dominion [də'mɪnɪən] n dominio; sovranità;

dominion *m inv*
domino ['dɔminəu] (*pl* ~es) *n* domino; ~es *n* (*game*) gioco del domino
don [dɔn] (*BRIT*) *n* docente *m/f* universitario(a)
donate [də'neit] *vt* donare
done [dʌn] *pp of* do
donkey ['dɔŋki] *n* asino
donor ['dəunə*] *n* donatore/trice; ~ **card** *n* tessera di donatore di organi
don't [dəunt] = do not
doodle ['du:dl] *vi* scarabocchiare
doom [du:m] *n* destino; rovina ♦ *vt*: to be ~ed (to failure) essere predestinato(a) (a fallire)
door [dɔ:*] *n* porta; ~bell *n* campanello; ~ handle *n* maniglia; ~man (*irreg*) *n* (*in hotel*) portiere *m* in livrea; ~mat *n* stuoia della porta; ~step *n* gradino della porta; ~way *n* porta
dope [dəup] *n* (*inf*: *drugs*) roba ♦ *vt* (*horse etc*) drogare
dormant ['dɔ:mənt] *adj* inattivo(a)
dormitory ['dɔ:mitri] *n* dormitorio; (*US*) casa dello studente
dormouse ['dɔ:maus] (*pl* dormice) *n* ghiro
dosage ['dəusidʒ] *n* posologia
dose [dəus] *n* dose *f*; (*bout*) attacco
doss house ['dɔs-] (*BRIT*) *n* asilo notturno
dot [dɔt] *n* punto; macchiolina ♦ *vt*: ~ted with punteggiato(a) di; on the ~ in punto
dotted line ['dɔtid-] *n* linea punteggiata
double ['dʌbl] *adj* doppio(a) ♦ *adv* (*twice*): to cost ~ (sth) costare il doppio (di qc) ♦ *n* sosia *m inv* ♦ *vt* raddoppiare; (*fold*) piegare doppio *or* in due ♦ *vi* raddoppiarsi; at the ~ (*BRIT*), on the ~ a passo di corsa; ~ bass *n* contrabbasso; ~ bed *n* letto matrimoniale; ~-breasted *adj* a doppio petto; ~cross *vt* fare il doppio gioco con; ~decker *n* autobus *m inv* a due piani; ~ glazing (*BRIT*) *n* doppi vetri *mpl*; ~ room *n* camera per due; ~s *n* (*TENNIS*) doppio; **doubly** *adv* doppiamente
doubt [daut] *n* dubbio ♦ *vt* dubitare di; to ~ that dubitare che + *sub*; ~ful *adj* dubbioso(a), incerto(a); (*person*) equivoco(a); ~less *adv* indubbiamente
dough [dəu] *n* pasta, impasto; ~nut *n* bombolone *m*
dove [dʌv] *n* colombo/a
Dover ['dəuvə*] *n* Dover *f*
dovetail ['dʌvteil] *vi* (*fig*) combaciare
dowdy ['daudi] *adj* trasandato(a); malvestito(a)
down [daun] *n* piume *fpl* ♦ *adv* giù, di sotto ♦ *prep* giù per ♦ *vt* (*inf*: *drink*) scolarsi; ~ with X! abbasso X!; ~-and-out *n* barbone *m*; ~-at-heel *adj* scalcagnato(a); ~cast *adj* abbattuto(a); ~fall *n* caduta; rovina; ~hearted *adj* scoraggiato(a); ~hill *adv*: to

go ~hill andare in discesa; (*fig*) lasciarsi andare; andare a rotoli; ~ payment *n* acconto; ~pour *n* scroscio di pioggia; ~right *adj* franco(a); (*refusal*) assoluto(a); ~size *vi* (*ECON*: *company*) ridurre il personale; ~stairs *adv* di sotto; al piano inferiore; ~stream *adv* a valle; ~-to-earth *adj* pratico(a); ~town *adv* in città; ~ under *adv* (*Australia etc*) agli antipodi; ~ward ['daunwəd] *adj*, *adv* in giù, in discesa; ~wards ['daunwədz] *adv* = downward
dowry ['dauri] *n* dote *f*
doz. *abbr* = dozen
doze [dəuz] *vi* sonnecchiare; ~ off *vi* appisolarsi
dozen ['dʌzn] *n* dozzina; a ~ books una dozzina di libri; ~s of decine *fpl* di
Dr. *abbr* (= *doctor*) dott.; (*in street names*) = drive *n*
drab [dræb] *adj* tetro(a), grigio(a)
draft [drɑːft] *n* abbozzo; (*POL*) bozza; (*COMM*) tratta; (*US*: *call-up*) leva ♦ *vt* abbozzare; *see also* draught
draftsman ['drɑːftsmən] (*US*) *n* = draughtsman
drag [dræg] *vt* trascinare; (*river*) dragare ♦ *vi* trascinarsi ♦ *n* (*inf*) noioso/a; noia, fatica; (*women's clothing*): in ~ travestito (da donna); ~ on *vi* tirar avanti lentamente
dragon ['drægən] *n* drago
dragonfly ['drægənflai] *n* libellula
drain [drein] *n* (*for sewage*) fogna; (*on resources*) salasso ♦ *vt* (*land*, *marshes*) prosciugare; (*vegetables*) scolare ♦ *vi* (*water*) defluire (via); ~age *n* prosciugamento; fognatura; ~ing board (*US* ~board) *n* piano del lavello; ~pipe *n* tubo di scarico
drama ['drɑːmə] *n* (*art*) dramma *m*, teatro; (*play*) commedia; (*event*) dramma; ~tic [drə'mætik] *adj* drammatico(a); ~tist ['dræmətist] *n* drammaturgo/a; ~tize *vt* (*events*) drammatizzare
drank [dræŋk] *pt of* drink
drape [dreip] *vt* drappeggiare; ~r (*BRIT*) *n* negoziante *m/f* di stoffe; ~s (*US*) *npl* (*curtains*) tende *fpl*
drastic ['dræstik] *adj* drastico(a)
draught [drɑːft] (*US* draft) *n* corrente *f* d'aria; (*NAUT*) pescaggio; (*on* ~) (*beer*) alla spina; ~ beer *n* birra alla spina; ~board (*BRIT*) *n* scacchiera; ~s (*BRIT*) *n* (gioco della) dama
draughtsman ['drɑːftsmən] (*US* draftsman) (*irreg*) *n* disegnatore *m*
draw [drɔː] (*pt* drew, *pp* drawn) *vt* tirare; (*take out*) estrarre; (*attract*) attirare; (*picture*) disegnare; (*line*, *circle*) tracciare; (*money*) ritirare ♦ *vi* (*SPORT*) pareggiare ♦ *n* pareggio; (*in lottery*) estrazione *f*; to ~ near avvicinarsi; ~ out *vi* (*lengthen*) allungarsi ♦ *vt* (*money*)

ritirare; **~ up** vi (stop) arrestarsi, fermarsi ♦ vt
(chair) avvicinare; (document) compilare;
~back n svantaggio, inconveniente m;
~bridge n ponte m levatoio
drawer [drɔ:*] n cassetto
drawing ['drɔ:ɪŋ] n disegno; **~ board** n
tavola da disegno; **~ pin** (BRIT) n puntina da
disegno; **~ room** n salotto
drawl [drɔ:l] n pronuncia strascicata
drawn [drɔ:n] pp of draw
dread [drɛd] n terrore m ♦ vt tremare all'idea
di; **~ful** adj terribile
dream [dri:m] (pt, pp dreamed or dreamt) n
sogno ♦ vt, vi sognare; **~y** adj sognante
dreary ['drɪərɪ] adj tetro(a); monotono(a)
dredge [drɛdʒ] vt dragare
dregs [drɛgz] npl feccia
drench [drɛntʃ] vt inzuppare
dress [drɛs] n vestito; (no pl: clothing)
abbigliamento ♦ vt vestire; (wound) fasciare
♦ vi vestirsi; **to get ~ed** vestirsi; **~ up** vi
vestirsi a festa; (in fancy dress) vestirsi in
costume; **~ circle** (BRIT) n prima galleria; **~er**
n (BRIT: cupboard) credenza; (US) cassettone
m; **~ing** n (MED) benda; (CULIN) condimento;
~ing gown (BRIT) n vestaglia; **~ing room** n
(THEATRE) camerino; (SPORT) spogliatoio; **~ing
table** n toilette f inv; **~maker** n sarta;
~ rehearsal n prova generale; **~y** (inf) adj
elegante
drew [dru:] pt of draw
dribble ['drɪbl] vi (baby) sbavare ♦ vt (ball)
dribblare
dried [draɪd] adj (fruit, beans) secco(a); (eggs,
milk) in polvere
drier ['draɪə*] n = dryer
drift [drɪft] n (of current etc) direzione f; forza;
(of snow) cumulo; turbine m, (general
meaning) senso ♦ vi (boat) essere
trasportato(a) dalla corrente; (sand, snow)
ammucchiarsi; **~wood** n resti mpl della
mareggiata
drill [drɪl] n trapano; (MIL) esercitazione f ♦ vt
trapanare; (troops) addestrare ♦ vi (for oil)
fare trivellazioni
drink [drɪŋk] (pt drank, pp drunk) n bevanda,
bibita; (alcoholic ~) bicchierino; (sip) sorso
♦ vt, vi bere; **to have a ~** bere qualcosa; **a
~ of water** un bicchier d'acqua; **~er** n bevitore/
trice; **~ing water** n acqua potabile
drip [drɪp] n goccia; gocciolamento; (MED)
fleboclisi f inv ♦ vi gocciolare; (tap)
sgocciolare; **~-dry** adj (shirt) che non si stira;
~ping n grasso d'arrosto
drive [draɪv] (pt drove, pp driven) n
passeggiata o giro in macchina; (also: ~way)
viale m d'accesso; (energy) energia;
(campaign) campagna; (also: disk ~) lettore
m ♦ vt guidare; (nail) piantare; (push)

cacciare, spingere; (TECH: motor) azionare;
far funzionare ♦ vi (AUT: at controls) guidare;
(: travel) andare in macchina; **left-/right-hand
~** guida a sinistra/destra; **to ~ sb mad** far
impazzire qn
drivel ['drɪvl] (inf) n idiozie fpl
driven ['drɪvn] pp of drive
driver ['draɪvə*] n conducente m/f; (of taxi)
tassista m; (chauffeur, of bus) autista m/f; **~'s
license** (US) n patente f di guida
driveway ['draɪvweɪ] n viale m d'accesso
driving ['draɪvɪŋ] n guida; **~ instructor** n
istruttore/trice di scuola guida; **~ lesson** n
lezione f di guida; **~ licence** (BRIT) n patente
f di guida; **~ mirror** n specchietto
retrovisore; **~ school** n scuola f guida inv;
~ test n esame m di guida
drizzle ['drɪzl] n pioggerella
drool [dru:l] vi sbavare
droop [dru:p] vi (flower) appassire; (head,
shoulders) chinarsi
drop [drɔp] n (of water) goccia; (lessening)
diminuzione f; (fall) caduta ♦ vt lasciare
cadere; (voice, eyes, price) abbassare; (set
down from car) far scendere; (name from list)
lasciare fuori ♦ vi cascare; (wind) abbassarsi;
~s npl (MED) gocce fpl; **~ off** vi (sleep)
addormentarsi ♦ vt (passenger) far scendere;
~ out vi (withdraw) ritirarsi; (student etc)
smettere di studiare; **~out** n (from society/
from university) chi ha abbandonato (la
società/gli studi); **~per** n contagocce m inv;
~pings npl sterco
drought [draut] n siccità f inv
drove [drəuv] pt of drive
drown [draun] vt affogare; (fig: noise)
soffocare ♦ vi affogare
drowsy ['drauzi] adj sonnolento(a),
assonnato(a)
drug [drʌg] n farmaco; (narcotic) droga ♦ vt
drogare; **to be on ~s** drogarsi; (MED) prendere
medicinali; **hard/soft ~s** droghe pesanti/
leggere; **~ addict** n tossicomane m/f; **~gist**
(US) n persona che gestisce un drugstore;
~store (US) n drugstore m inv
drum [drʌm] n tamburo; (for oil, petrol) fusto
♦ vi tamburellare; **~s** npl (set of ~s) batteria;
~mer n batterista m/f
drunk [drʌŋk] pp of drink ♦ adj ubriaco(a);
ebbro(a) ♦ n (also: ~ard) ubriacone/a; **~en**
adj ubriaco(a); da ubriaco
dry [draɪ] adj secco(a); (day, clothes)
asciutto(a) ♦ vt seccare; (clothes, hair, hands)
asciugare ♦ vi asciugarsi; **~ up** vi seccarsi; **~-
cleaner's** n lavasecco m inv; **~-cleaning** n
pulitura a secco; **~er** n (for hair) föhn m inv,
asciugacapelli m inv; (for clothes) asciu-
gabiancheria; (US: spin-dryer) centrifuga;
~ goods store (US) n negozio di stoffe;

~ rot n fungo del legno
DSS n abbr (= Department of Social Security)
ministero della Previdenza sociale
DTP n abbr (= desk-top publishing) desktop
publishing m inv
dual ['djuəl] adj doppio(a); ~ **carriageway**
(BRIT) n strada a doppia carreggiata; ~-
purpose adj a doppio uso
dubbed [dʌbd] adj (CINEMA) doppiato(a)
dubious ['dju:bɪəs] adj dubbio(a)
Dublin ['dʌblɪn] n Dublino f
duchess ['dʌtʃɪs] n duchessa
duck [dʌk] n anatra ♦ vi abbassare la testa;
~**ling** n anatroccolo
duct [dʌkt] n condotto; (ANAT) canale m
dud [dʌd] n (object, tool): **it's a ~** è inutile,
non funziona ♦ adj: ~ **cheque** (BRIT) assegno
a vuoto
due [dju:] adj dovuto(a); (expected) atteso(a);
(fitting) giusto(a) ♦ n dovuto ♦ adv: ~ **north**
diritto verso nord; ~**s** npl (for club, union)
quota; (in harbour) diritti mpl di porto; **in
~ course** a tempo debito; finalmente; ~ **to**
dovuto a; a causa di; **to be ~ to do** dover fare
duet [dju:'et] n duetto
duffel bag ['dʌfl-] n sacca da viaggio di tela
duffel coat ['dʌfl-] n montgomery m inv
dug [dʌg] pt, pp of **dig**
duke [dju:k] n duca m
dull [dʌl] adj (light) debole; (boring)
noioso(a); (slow-witted) ottuso(a); (sound,
pain) sordo(a); (weather, day) fosco(a),
scuro(a) ♦ vt (pain, grief) attutire; (mind,
senses) intorpidire
duly ['dju:lɪ] adv (on time) a tempo debito;
(as expected) debitamente
dumb [dʌm] adj muto(a); (pej) stupido(a);
~**founded** [dʌm'faundɪd] adj stupito(a),
stordito(a)
dummy ['dʌmɪ] n (tailor's model) manichino;
(TECH, COMM) riproduzione f; (BRIT: for baby)
tettarella ♦ adj falso(a), finto(a)
dump [dʌmp] n (also: rubbish ~) discarica di
rifiuti; (inf: place) buco ♦ vt (put down)
scaricare; mettere giù; (get rid of) buttar via
dumpling ['dʌmplɪŋ] n specie di gnocco
dumpy ['dʌmpɪ] adj tracagnotto(a)
dunce [dʌns] n (SCOL) somaro/a
dung [dʌŋ] n concime m
dungarees [dʌŋɡə'ri:z] npl tuta
dungeon ['dʌndʒən] n prigione f sotterranea
dupe [dju:p] n zimbello ♦ vt gabbare,
ingannare
duplex ['dju:pleks] (US) n (house) casa con
muro divisorio in comune con un'altra;
(apartment) appartamento su due piani
duplicate [n 'dju:plɪkət, vb 'dju:plɪkeɪt] n
doppio ♦ vt duplicare; **in ~** in doppia copia
durable ['djuərəbl] adj durevole; (clothes,

metal) resistente
duration [djuə'reɪʃən] n durata
during ['djuərɪŋ] prep durante, nel corso di
dusk [dʌsk] n crepuscolo
dust [dʌst] n polvere f ♦ vt (furniture)
spolverare; (cake etc): **to ~ with** cospargere
con; ~**bin** (BRIT) n pattumiera; ~**er** n straccio
per la polvere; ~**man** (BRIT irreg) n
netturbino; ~**y** adj polveroso(a)
Dutch [dʌtʃ] adj olandese ♦ n (LING) olandese
m; **the ~** npl gli Olandesi; **to go ~** (inf) fare
alla romana; ~**man/woman** (irreg) n
olandese m/f
duty ['dju:tɪ] n dovere m; (tax) dazio, tassa;
on ~ di servizio; **off ~** libero(a), fuori servizio;
~ **chemist's** n farmacia di turno; ~-**free** adj
esente da dazio
duvet ['du:veɪ] (BRIT) n piumino, piumone m
DVD n abbr (= digital versatile disk) DVD m
inv
dwarf [dwɔ:f] n nano/a ♦ vt far apparire
piccolo
dwell [dwel] (pt, pp **dwelt**) vi dimorare; ~ **on**
vt fus indugiare su
dwindle ['dwɪndl] vi diminuire
dye [daɪ] n tinta ♦ vt tingere
dying ['daɪɪŋ] adj morente, moribondo(a)
dyke [daɪk] (BRIT) n diga
dynamic [daɪ'næmɪk] adj dinamico(a)
dynamite ['daɪnəmaɪt] n dinamite f
dynamo ['daɪnəməu] n dinamo f inv
dyslexia [dɪs'leksɪə] n dislessia

E, e

E [i:] n (MUS) mi m
each [i:tʃ] adj ogni, ciascuno(a) ♦ pron
ciascuno(a), ognuno(a); ~ **one** ognuno(a);
~ **other** si (or ci etc); **they hate ~ other** si
odiano (l'un l'altro); **you are jealous of**
~ **other** siete gelosi l'uno dell'altro; **they have
2 books ~** hanno 2 libri ciascuno
eager ['i:ɡə*] adj impaziente; desideroso(a);
ardente; **to be ~ for** essere desideroso di, aver
gran voglia di
eagle ['i:ɡl] n aquila
ear [ɪə*] n orecchio; (of corn) pannocchia;
~**ache** n mal d'orecchi; ~**drum** n timpano
earl [ə:l] (BRIT) n conte m
earlier ['ə:lɪə*] adj precedente ♦ adv prima
early ['ə:lɪ] adv presto, di buon'ora; (ahead of
time) in anticipo ♦ adj (near the beginning)
primo(a); (sooner than expected) pre-
maturo(a); (quick: reply) veloce; **at an ~ hour**
di buon'ora; **to have an ~ night** andare a letto
presto; **in the ~ or ~ in the spring/19th
century** all'inizio della primavera/dell'Otto-
cento; ~ **retirement** n ritiro anti-

cipato

earmark ['ɪəmɑ:k] vt: **to ~ sth for** destinare qc a

earn [ə:n] vt guadagnare; (rest, reward) meritare

earnest ['ə:nɪst] adj serio(a); **in ~** sul serio

earnings ['ə:nɪŋz] npl guadagni mpl; (salary) stipendio

earphones ['ɪəfəunz] npl cuffia

earring ['ɪərɪŋ] n orecchino

earshot ['ɪəʃɔt] n: **within ~** a portata d'orecchio

earth [ə:θ] n terra ♦ vt (BRIT: ELEC) mettere a terra; **~enware** n terracotta; stoviglie fpl di terracotta; **~quake** n terremoto; **~y** adj (fig) grossolano(a)

ease [i:z] n agio, comodo ♦ vt (soothe) calmare; (loosen) allentare; **to ~ sth out/in** tirare fuori/infilare qc con delicatezza; facilitare l'uscita/l'entrata di qc; **at ~** a proprio agio; (MIL) a riposo; **~ off** or **up** vi diminuire; (slow down) rallentare

easel ['i:zl] n cavalletto

easily ['i:zɪlɪ] adv facilmente

east [i:st] n est m ♦ adj dell'est ♦ adv a oriente; **the E~** l'Oriente m; (POL) l'Est

Easter ['i:stə*] n Pasqua; **~ egg** n uovo di Pasqua

easterly ['i:stəlɪ] adj dall'est, d'oriente

eastern ['i:stən] adj orientale, d'oriente; dell'est

East Germany n Germania dell'Est

eastward(s) ['i:stwəd(z)] adv verso est, verso levante

easy ['i:zɪ] adj facile; (manner) disinvolto(a) ♦ adv: **to take it** or **things ~** prendersela con calma; **~ chair** n poltrona; **~-going** adj accomodante

eat [i:t] (pt **ate**, pp **eaten**) vt, vi mangiare; **~ away at** vt fus rodere; **~ into** vt fus rodere

eaves [i:vz] npl gronda

eavesdrop ['i:vzdrɔp] vi: **to ~ (on a conversation)** origliare (una conversazione)

ebb [ɛb] n riflusso ♦ vi rifluire; (fig: also: **~ away**) declinare

ebony ['ɛbənɪ] n ebano

EC n abbr (= European Community) CEE f

ECB n abbr (= European Central Bank) BCE f

eccentric [ɪk'sɛntrɪk] adj, n eccentrico(a)

echo ['ɛkəu] (pl **~es**) n eco m or f ♦ vt ripetere; fare eco a ♦ vi echeggiare; dare un eco

éclair [eɪ'klɛə*] n ≈ bignè m inv

eclipse [ɪ'klɪps] n eclissi f inv

ecology [ɪ'kɔlədʒɪ] n ecologia

e-commerce ['i:'kɔmə:s] n commercio elettronico

economic [i:kə'nɔmɪk] adj economico(a);

~al adj economico(a); (person) economo(a); **~s** n economia ♦ npl lato finanziario

economize [ɪ'kɔnəmaɪz] vi risparmiare, fare economia

economy [ɪ'kɔnəmɪ] n economia; **~ class** n (AVIAT) classe f turistica; **~ size** n (COMM) confezione f economica

ecstasy ['ɛkstəsɪ] n estasi f inv

ECU ['eɪkju:] n abbr (= European Currency Unit) ECU m inv

eczema ['ɛksɪmə] n eczema m

edge [ɛdʒ] n margine m; (of table, plate, cup) orlo; (of knife etc) taglio ♦ vt bordare; **on ~** (fig) = **edgy**; **to ~ away from** sgattaiolare da; **~ways** adv: **he couldn't get a word in ~ways** non riuscì a dire una parola; **edgy** adj nervoso(a)

edible ['ɛdɪbl] adj commestibile; (meal) mangiabile

edict ['i:dɪkt] n editto

Edinburgh ['ɛdɪnbərə] n Edimburgo f

edit ['ɛdɪt] vt curare; **~ion** [ɪ'dɪʃən] n edizione f; **~or** n (in newspaper) redattore/trice; redattore/trice capo; (of sb's work) curatore/trice; **~orial** [-'tɔ:rɪəl] adj redazionale, editoriale ♦ n editoriale m

educate ['ɛdjukeɪt] vt istruire; educare

education [ɛdju'keɪʃən] n educazione f; (schooling) istruzione f; **~al** adj pedagogico(a); scolastico(a); istruttivo(a)

EEC n abbr = **EC**

eel [i:l] n anguilla

eerie ['ɪərɪ] adj che fa accapponare la pelle

effect [ɪ'fɛkt] n effetto ♦ vt effettuare; **to take ~** (law) entrare in vigore; (drug) fare effetto; **in ~** effettivamente; **~ive** adj efficace; (actual) effettivo(a); **~ively** adv efficacemente; effettivamente; **~iveness** n efficacia

effeminate [ɪ'fɛmɪnɪt] adj effeminato(a)

efficiency [ɪ'fɪʃənsɪ] n efficienza; rendimento effettivo

efficient [ɪ'fɪʃənt] adj efficiente

effort ['ɛfət] n sforzo

effusive [ɪ'fju:sɪv] adj (handshake, welcome) caloroso(a)

e.g. adv abbr (= exempli gratia) per esempio, p.es.

egg [ɛg] n uovo; **hard-boiled/soft-boiled ~** uovo sodo/alla coque; **~ on** vt incitare; **~cup** n portauovo m inv; **~plant** n (especially US) melanzana; **~shell** n guscio d'uovo

ego ['i:gəu] n ego m inv

egotism ['ɛgəutɪzəm] n egotismo

Egypt ['i:dʒɪpt] n Egitto; **~ian** [ɪ'dʒɪpʃən] adj, n egiziano(a)

eiderdown ['aɪdədaun] n piumino

eight [eɪt] num otto; **~een** num diciotto; **eighth** [eɪtθ] num ottavo(a); **~y** num ottanta

Eire ['ɛərə] n Repubblica d'Irlanda
either ['aɪðə*] adj l'uno(a) o l'altro(a); (both,
    each) ciascuno(a) ♦ pron: ~ (of them) (o)
    l'uno(a) o l'altro(a) ♦ adv neanche ♦ conj:
    ~ good or bad o buono o cattivo; on ~ side
    su ciascun lato; I don't like ~ non mi piace né
    l'uno né l'altro; no, I don't ~ no, neanch'io
eject [ɪ'dʒɛkt] vt espellere; lanciare
elaborate [adj ɪ'læbərɪt, vb ɪ'læbəreɪt] adj
    elaborato(a), minuzioso(a) ♦ vt elaborare
    ♦ vi fornire i particolari
elastic [ɪ'læstɪk] adj elastico(a) ♦ n elastico;
    ~ **band** (BRIT) n elastico
elated [ɪ'leɪtɪd] adj pieno(a) di gioia
elbow ['ɛlbəu] n gomito
elder ['ɛldə*] adj maggiore, più vecchio(a)
    ♦ n (tree) sambuco; **one's** ~s i più anziani;
    ~ly adj anziano(a) ♦ npl: the ~ly gli anziani
eldest ['ɛldɪst] adj, n: the ~ (child) il(la)
    maggiore (dei bambini)
elect [ɪ'lɛkt] vt eleggere ♦ adj: the president ~
    il presidente designato; to ~ to do decidere di
    fare; ~ion [ɪ'lɛkʃən] n elezione f; ~ioneering
    [ɪlɛkʃə'nɪərɪŋ] n propaganda elettorale; ~or n
    elettore/trice; ~orate n elettorato
electric [ɪ'lɛktrɪk] adj elettrico(a); ~al adj
    elettrico(a); ~ **blanket** n coperta elettrica;
    ~ **fire** n stufa elettrica
electrician [ɪlɛk'trɪʃən] n elettricista m
electricity [ɪlɛk'trɪsɪtɪ] n elettricità
electrify [ɪ'lɛktrɪfaɪ] vt (RAIL) elettrificare;
    (audience) elettrizzare
electrocute [ɪ'lɛktraukju:t] vt fulminare
electronic [ɪlɛk'trɒnɪk] adj elettronico(a);
    ~ **mail** n posta elettronica; ~s n elettronica
elegant ['ɛlɪgənt] adj elegante
element ['ɛlɪmənt] n elemento; (of heater,
    kettle etc) resistenza; ~ary [-'mɛntərɪ] adj
    elementare
elephant ['ɛlɪfənt] n elefante/essa
elevation [ɛlɪ'veɪʃən] n elevazione f
elevator ['ɛlɪveɪtə*] n elevatore m; (US: lift)
    ascensore m
eleven [ɪ'lɛvn] num undici; ~ses (BRIT) n
    caffè m a metà mattina; ~th adj
    undicesimo(a)
elicit [ɪ'lɪsɪt] vt: to ~ (from) trarre (da), cavare
    fuori (da)
eligible ['ɛlɪdʒəbl] adj eleggibile; (for
    membership) che ha i requisiti
elm [ɛlm] n olmo
elocution [ɛlə'kju:ʃən] n dizione f
elongated ['i:lɒŋgeɪtɪd] adj allungato(a)
elope [ɪ'ləup] vi (lovers) scappare; ~ment n
    fuga
eloquent ['ɛləkwənt] adj eloquente
else [ɛls] adv altro; **something** ~ qualcos'altro;
    somewhere ~ altrove; **everywhere** ~ in
    qualsiasi altro luogo; **nobody** ~ nessun altro;

where ~? in quale altro luogo?; **little** ~ poco
    altro; ~**where** adv altrove
elude [ɪ'lu:d] vt eludere
elusive [ɪ'lu:sɪv] adj elusivo(a)
emaciated [ɪ'meɪsɪeɪtɪd] adj emaciato(a)
E-mail, e-mail ['i:meɪl] n abbr (= electronic
    mail) posta elettronica
emanate ['ɛmaneɪt] vi: to ~ from provenire
    da
emancipate [ɪ'mænsɪpeɪt] vt emancipare
embankment [ɪm'bæŋkmənt] n (of road,
    railway) terrapieno
embark [ɪm'bɑːk] vi: to ~ (on) imbarcarsi
    (su) ♦ vt imbarcare; to ~ on (fig) imbarcarsi
    in; ~**ation** [ɛmbɑːˈkeɪʃən] n imbarco
embarrass [ɪm'bærəs] vt imbarazzare; ~**ed**
    adj imbarazzato(a); ~**ing** adj imbarazzante;
    ~**ment** n imbarazzo
embassy ['ɛmbəsɪ] n ambasciata
embedded [ɪm'bɛdɪd] adj incastrato(a)
embellish [ɪm'bɛlɪʃ] vt abbellire
embers ['ɛmbəz] npl braci fpl
embezzle [ɪm'bɛzl] vt appropriarsi
    indebitamente di
embitter [ɪm'bɪtə*] vt amareggiare; inasprire
embody [ɪm'bɒdɪ] vt (features) racchiudere,
    comprendere; (ideas) dar forma concreta a,
    esprimere
embossed [ɪm'bɒst] adj in rilievo;
    goffrato(a)
embrace [ɪm'breɪs] vt abbracciare ♦ vi
    abbracciarsi ♦ n abbraccio
embroider [ɪm'brɔɪdə*] vt ricamare; ~**y** n
    ricamo
embryo ['ɛmbrɪəu] n embrione m
emerald ['ɛmərəld] n smeraldo
emerge [ɪ'mɜːdʒ] vi emergere
emergency [ɪ'mɜːdʒənsɪ] n emergenza; **in
    an** ~ in caso di emergenza; ~ **cord** (US) n
    segnale m d'allarme; ~ **exit** n uscita di
    sicurezza; ~ **landing** n atterraggio forzato;
    ~ **services** npl (fire, police, ambulance) servizi
    mpl di pronto intervento
emery board ['ɛmərɪ-] n limetta di carta
    smerigliata
emigrate ['ɛmɪgreɪt] vi emigrare
eminent ['ɛmɪnənt] adj eminente
emissions [ɪ'mɪʃənz] npl emissioni fpl
emit [ɪ'mɪt] vt emettere
emotion [ɪ'məuʃən] n emozione f; ~**al** adj
    (person) emotivo(a); (scene) commovente;
    (tone, speech) carico(a) d'emozione
emperor ['ɛmpərə*] n imperatore m
emphasis ['ɛmfəsɪs] n (pl -ases) enfasi f inv;
    importanza
emphasize ['ɛmfəsaɪz] vt (word, point)
    sottolineare; (feature) mettere in evidenza
emphatic [ɛm'fætɪk] adj (strong)
    vigoroso(a); (unambiguous, clear) netto(a)

empire |'ɛmpaɪə*| n impero

employ |ɪm'plɔɪ| vt impiegare; **~ee** [-'i:] n impiegato/a; **~er** n principale m/f, datore m di lavoro; **~ment** n impiego; **~ment agency** n agenzia di collocamento

empower |ɪm'pauə*| vt: **to ~ sb to do** concedere autorità a qn dal fare

empress |'ɛmprɪs| n imperatrice f

emptiness |'ɛmptɪnɪs| n vuoto

empty |'ɛmptɪ| adj vuoto(a); (threat, promise) vano(a) ♦ vt vuotare ♦ vi vuotarsi; (liquid) scaricarsi; **~-handed** adj a mani vuote

EMU n abbr (= economic and monetary union) unione f economica e monetaria

emulate |'ɛmjuleɪt| vt emulare

emulsion |ɪ'mʌlʃən| n emulsione f; **~ (paint)** n colore m a tempera

enable |ɪ'neɪbl| vt: **to ~ sb to do** permettere a qn di fare

enamel |ɪ'næməl| n smalto; (also: ~ paint) vernice f a smalto

enchant |ɪn'tʃɑːnt| vt incantare; (subj: magic spell) catturare; **~ing** adj incantevole, affascinante

encircle |ɪn'səːkl| vt accerchiare

encl. abbr (= enclosed) all

enclave |'ɛnkleɪv| n enclave f

enclose |ɪn'kləuz| vt (land) circondare, recingere; (letter etc): **to ~ (with)** allegare (con); **please find ~d** trovi qui accluso

enclosure |ɪn'kləuʒə*| n recinto

encompass |ɪn'kʌmpəs| vt comprendere

encore |ɔŋ'kɔː*| excl bis ♦ n bis m inv

encounter |ɪn'kauntə*| n incontro ♦ vt incontrare

encourage |ɪn'kʌrɪdʒ| vt incoraggiare; **~ment** n incoraggiamento

encroach |ɪn'krəutʃ| vi: **to ~ (up)on** (rights) usurpare; (time) abusare di; (land) oltrepassare i limiti di

encyclop(a)edia |ɛnsaɪkləu'piːdɪə| n enciclopedia

end |ɛnd| n fine f; (aim) fine m; (of table) bordo estremo; (of pointed object) punta ♦ vt finire; (also: bring to an ~, put an ~ to) mettere fine a ♦ vi finire; **in the ~** alla fine; **on ~** (object) ritto(a); **to stand on ~** (hair) rizzarsi; **for hours on ~** per ore ed ore; **~ up** vi: **to ~ up in** finire in

endanger |ɪn'deɪndʒə*| vt mettere in pericolo

endearing |ɪn'dɪərɪŋ| adj accattivante

endeavour |ɪn'dɛvə*| (US **endeavor**) n sforzo, tentativo ♦ vi: **to ~ to do** cercare or sforzarsi di fare

ending |'ɛndɪŋ| n fine f, conclusione f; (LING) desinenza

endive |'ɛndaɪv| n (curly) indivia (riccia); (smooth, flat) indivia belga

endless |'ɛndlɪs| adj senza fine

endorse |ɪn'dɔːs| vt (cheque) girare; (approve) approvare, appoggiare; **~ment** n approvazione f; (on driving licence) contravvenzione registrata sulla patente

endurance |ɪn'djuərəns| n resistenza; pazienza

endure |ɪn'djuə*| vt sopportare, resistere a ♦ vi durare

enemy |'ɛnəmɪ| adj, n nemico(a)

energetic |ɛnə'dʒɛtɪk| adj energico(a); attivo(a)

energy |'ɛnədʒɪ| n energia

enforce |ɪn'fɔːs| vt (LAW) applicare, far osservare

engage |ɪn'geɪdʒ| vt (hire) assumere; (lawyer) incaricare; (attention, interest) assorbire; (TECH): **to ~ gear/the clutch** innestare la marcia/la frizione ♦ vi (TECH) ingranare; **to ~ in** impegnarsi in; **~d** adj (BRIT: busy, in use) occupato(a); (betrothed) fidanzato(a); **to get ~d** fidanzarsi; **~d tone** (BRIT) n (TEL) segnale m di occupato; **~ment** n impegno, obbligo; appuntamento; (to marry) fidanzamento; **~ment ring** n anello di fidanzamento

engaging |ɪn'geɪdʒɪŋ| adj attraente

engine |'ɛndʒɪn| n (AUT) motore m; (RAIL) locomotiva; **~ driver** n (of train) macchinista m

engineer |ɛndʒɪ'nɪə*| n ingegnere m; (BRIT: for repairs) tecnico; (on ship, US: RAIL) macchinista m; **~ing** n ingegneria

England |'ɪŋglənd| n Inghilterra

English |'ɪŋglɪʃ| adj inglese ♦ n (LING) inglese m; **the ~** npl gli Inglesi; **the ~ Channel** n la Manica; **~man/woman** (irreg) n inglese m/f

engraving |ɪn'greɪvɪŋ| n incisione f

engrossed |ɪn'grəust| adj: **~ in** assorbito(a) da, preso(a) da

engulf |ɪn'gʌlf| vt inghiottire

enhance |ɪn'hɑːns| vt accrescere

enjoy |ɪn'dʒɔɪ| vt godere; (have: success, fortune) avere; **to ~ o.s.** godersela, divertirsi; **~able** adj piacevole; **~ment** n piacere m, godimento

enlarge |ɪn'lɑːdʒ| vt ingrandire ♦ vi: **to ~ on** (subject) dilungarsi su

enlighten |ɪn'laɪtn| vt illuminare; dare schiarimenti a; **~ed** adj illuminato(a); **~ment** n: **the E~ment** (HISTORY) l'Illuminismo

enlist |ɪn'lɪst| vt arruolare; (support) procurare ♦ vi arruolarsi

enmity |'ɛnmɪtɪ| n inimicizia

enormous |ɪ'nɔːməs| adj enorme

enough |ɪ'nʌf| adj, n: **~ time/books** assai tempo/libri; **have you got ~?** ne ha abbastanza or a sufficienza? ♦ adv: **big ~** abbastanza grande; **he has not worked ~** non ha lavorato abbastanza; **~! basta!**; **that's ~, thanks** basta così, grazie; **I've had ~ of him** ne ho abbastanza di lui; **... which, funnily** or **oddly ~ ...** che, strano a dirsi

enquire [ɪnˈkwaɪə*] vt, vi = **inquire**

enrage [ɪnˈreɪdʒ] vt fare arrabbiare

enrich [ɪnˈrɪtʃ] vt arricchire

enrol [ɪnˈrəul] (US enroll) vt iscrivere ♦ vi iscriversi; **~ment** (US enrollment) n iscrizione f

en suite [ɔnˈswiːt] adj: **room with ~ bathroom** camera con bagno

ensure [ɪnˈʃuə*] vt assicurare; garantire

entail [ɪnˈteɪl] vt comportare

entangled [ɪnˈtæŋgld] adj: **to become ~ (in)** impigliarsi (in)

enter [ˈentə*] vt entrare in; (army) arruolarsi in; (competition) partecipare a; (sb for a competition) iscrivere; (write down) registrare; (COMPUT) inserire ♦ vi entrare; **~ for** vt fus iscriversi a; **~ into** vt fus (explanation) cominciare a dare; (debate) partecipare a; (agreement) concludere

enterprise [ˈentəpraɪz] n (undertaking, company) impresa; (spirit) iniziativa; **free ~** liberalismo economico; **private ~** iniziativa privata

enterprising [ˈentəpraɪzɪŋ] adj intraprendente

entertain [entəˈteɪn] vt divertire; (invite) ricevere; (idea, plan) nutrire; **~er** n comico/a; **~ing** adj divertente; **~ment** n (amusement) divertimento; (show) spettacolo

enthralled [ɪnˈθrɔːld] adj affascinato(a)

enthusiasm [ɪnˈθuːzɪæzəm] n entusiasmo

enthusiast [ɪnˈθuːzɪæst] n entusiasta m/f; **~ic** [-ˈæstɪk] adj entusiasta, entusiastico(a); **to be ~ic about sth/sb** essere appassionato(a) di qc/entusiasta di qn

entire [ɪnˈtaɪə*] adj intero(a); **~ly** adv completamente, interamente; **~ty** [ɪnˈtaɪərətɪ] n: **in its ~ty** nel suo complesso

entitle [ɪnˈtaɪtl] vt (give right): **to ~ sb to sth/ to do** dare diritto a qn a qc/a fare; **~d** adj (book) che si intitola; **to be ~d to do** avere il diritto di fare

entrails [ˈentreɪlz] npl interiora fpl

entrance [n ˈentrns, vb ɪnˈtrɑːns] n entrata, ingresso; (of person) entrata ♦ vt incantare, rapire; **to gain ~ to** (university etc) essere ammesso a; **~ examination** n esame m di ammissione; **~ fee** n tassa d'iscrizione; (to museum etc) prezzo d'ingresso; **~ ramp** (US) n (AUT) rampa di accesso

entrant [ˈentrnt] n partecipante m/f; concorrente m/f

entreat [enˈtriːt] vt supplicare

entrenched [enˈtrentʃt] adj radicato(a)

entrepreneur [ɔntrəprəˈnəː*] n

imprenditore m

entrust [ɪnˈtrʌst] vt: **to ~ sth to** affidare qc a

entry [ˈentrɪ] n entrata; (way in) entrata, ingresso; (item: on list) iscrizione f; (in dictionary) voce f; **no ~** vietato l'ingresso; (AUT) divieto di accesso; **~ form** n modulo d'iscrizione; **~ phone** n citofono

envelop [ɪnˈveləp] vt avvolgere, avviluppare

envelope [ˈenvələup] n busta

envious [ˈenvɪəs] adj invidioso(a)

environment [ɪnˈvaɪərnmənt] n ambiente m; **~al** [-ˈmentl] adj ecologico(a); ambientale; **~-friendly** adj che rispetta l'ambiente

envisage [ɪnˈvɪzɪdʒ] vt immaginare; prevedere

envoy [ˈenvɔɪ] n inviato/a

envy [ˈenvɪ] n invidia ♦ vt invidiare; **to ~ sb sth** invidiare qn per qc

epic [ˈepɪk] n poema m epico ♦ adj epico(a)

epidemic [epɪˈdemɪk] n epidemia

epilepsy [ˈepɪlepsɪ] n epilessia

episode [ˈepɪsəud] n episodio

epistle [ɪˈpɪsl] n epistola

epitome [ɪˈpɪtəmɪ] n epitome f; quintessenza; **epitomize** vt (fig) incarnare

equal [ˈiːkwl] adj uguale ♦ n pari m/f inv ♦ vt uguagliare; **~ to** (task) all'altezza di; **~ity** [iːˈkwɔlɪtɪ] n uguaglianza; **~ize** vi pareggiare; **~ly** adv ugualmente

equanimity [ekwəˈnɪmɪtɪ] n serenità

equate [ɪˈkweɪt] vt: **to ~ sth with** considerare qc uguale a; (compare) paragonare qc con; **equation** [ɪˈkweɪʃən] n (MATH) equazione f

equator [ɪˈkweɪtə*] n equatore m

equilibrium [iːkwɪˈlɪbrɪəm] n equilibrio

equip [ɪˈkwɪp] vt equipaggiare, attrezzare; **to ~ sb/sth with** fornire qn/qc di; **to be well ~ped** (office etc) essere ben attrezzato(a); **he is well ~ped for the job** ha i requisiti necessari per quel lavoro; **~ment** n attrezzatura; (electrical etc) apparecchiatura

equitable [ˈekwɪtəbl] adj equo(a), giusto(a)

equities [ˈekwɪtɪz] (BRIT) npl (COMM) azioni fpl ordinarie

equivalent [ɪˈkwɪvəlnt] adj equivalente ♦ n equivalente m; **to be ~ to** equivalere a

era [ˈɪərə] n era, età f inv

eradicate [ɪˈrædɪkeɪt] vt sradicare

erase [ɪˈreɪz] vt cancellare; **~r** n gomma

erect [ɪˈrekt] adj eretto(a) ♦ vt costruire; (assemble) montare; **~ion** [ɪˈrekʃən] n costruzione f; montaggio; (PHYSIOL) erezione f

ERM n (= Exchange Rate Mechanism) ERM m

ermine [ˈəːmɪn] n ermellino

erode [ɪˈrəud] vt erodere; (metal) corrodere

erotic [ɪˈrɔtɪk] adj erotico(a)

errand [ˈernd] n commissione f

erratic [ɪˈrætɪk] adj imprevedibile; (person,

mood) incostante
error ['ɛrə*] *n* errore *m*
erupt [ɪ'rʌpt] *vi* (*volcano*) mettersi (*or* essere) in eruzione; (*war, crisis*) scoppiare; **~ion** [ɪ'rʌpʃən] *n* eruzione *f*; scoppio
escalate ['ɛskəleɪt] *vi* intensificarsi
escalator ['ɛskəleɪtə*] *n* scala mobile
escapade [ɛskə'peɪd] *n* scappatella; avventura
escape [ɪ'skeɪp] *n* evasione *f*; fuga; (*of gas etc*) fuga, fuoriuscita ♦ *vi* fuggire; (*from jail*) evadere, scappare; (*leak*) uscire ♦ *vt* sfuggire a; **to ~ from** (*place*) fuggire da; (*person*) sfuggire a; **escapism** *n* evasione *f* (dalla realtà)
escort [*n* 'ɛskɔ:t, *vb* ɪ'skɔ:t] *n* scorta; (*male companion*) cavaliere *m* ♦ *vt* scortare; accompagnare
Eskimo ['ɛskɪməu] *n* eschimese *m/f*
especially [ɪ'spɛʃlɪ] *adv* specialmente; soprattutto; espressamente
espionage ['ɛspɪənɑ:ʒ] *n* spionaggio
esplanade [ɛsplə'neɪd] *n* lungomare *m inv*
Esq. *abbr* = **Esquire**
Esquire [ɪ'skwaɪə*] *n*: **J. Brown, ~ Signor J. Brown**
essay ['ɛseɪ] *n* (*SCOL*) composizione *f*; (*LITERATURE*) saggio
essence ['ɛsns] *n* essenza
essential [ɪ'sɛnʃl] *adj* essenziale ♦ *n* elemento essenziale; **~ly** *adv* essenzialmente
establish [ɪ'stæblɪʃ] *vt* stabilire; (*business*) mettere su; (*one's power etc*) affermare; **~ed** *adj* (*business etc*) affermato(a); **~ment** *n* stabilimento; **the E~ment** la classe dirigente, l'establishment *m*
estate [ɪ'steɪt] *n* proprietà *f inv*; beni *mpl*, patrimonio; (*BRIT: also: housing ~*) complesso edilizio; **~ agent** (*BRIT*) *n* agente *m* immobiliare; **~ car** (*BRIT*) *n* giardiniera
esteem [ɪ'sti:m] *n* stima ♦ *vt* (*think highly of*) stimare; (*consider*) considerare
esthetic [ɪs'θɛtɪk] (*US*) *adj* = **aesthetic**
estimate [*n* 'ɛstɪmət, *vb* 'ɛstɪmeɪt] *n* stima; (*COMM*) preventivo ♦ *vt* stimare, valutare; **estimation** [-'meɪʃən] *n* stima; opinione *f*
estranged [ɪ'streɪndʒd] *adj* separato(a)
etc *abbr* (= *et cetera*) etc, ecc
eternal [ɪ'tə:nl] *adj* eterno(a)
eternity [ɪ'tə:nɪtɪ] *n* eternità
ether ['i:θə*] *n* etere *m*
ethical ['ɛθɪkl] *adj* etico(a), morale
ethics ['ɛθɪks] *n* etica ♦ *npl* morale *f*
Ethiopia [i:θɪ'əupɪə] *n* Etiopia
ethnic ['ɛθnɪk] *adj* etnico(a); **~ minority** *n* minoranza etnica
ethos ['i:θɔs] *n* norma di vita
etiquette ['ɛtɪkɛt] *n* etichetta
EU *n abbr* (= *European Union*) UE

euro ['juərəu] *n* (*currency*) euro *m inv*
Eurocheque ['juərəutʃɛk] *n* eurochèque *m inv*
Euroland ['juərəulænd] *n* Eurolandia
Europe ['juərəp] *n* Europa; **European** [-'pi:ən] *adj, n* europeo(a); **European Community** *n* Comunità Europea
evacuate [ɪ'vækjueɪt] *vt* evacuare
evade [ɪ'veɪd] *vt* (*tax*) evadere; (*duties etc*) sottrarsi a; (*person*) schivare
evaluate [ɪ'væljueɪt] *vt* valutare
evaporate [ɪ'væpəreɪt] *vi* evaporare; **~d milk** *n* latte *m* concentrato
evasion [ɪ'veɪʒən] *n* evasione *f*
evasive [ɪ'veɪsɪv] *adj* evasivo(a)
eve [i:v] *n*: **on the ~ of** alla vigilia di
even ['i:vn] *adj* regolare; (*number*) pari *inv* ♦ *adv* anche, perfino; **~ if, ~ though** anche se; **~ more** ancora di più; **~ so** ciò nonostante; **not ~** nemmeno; **to get ~ with sb** dare la pari a qn
evening ['i:vnɪŋ] *n* sera; (*as duration, event*) serata; **in the ~** la sera; **~ class** *n* corso serale; **~ dress** *n* (*woman's*) abito da sera; **in ~ dress** (*man*) in abito scuro; (*woman*) in abito lungo
event [ɪ'vɛnt] *n* avvenimento; (*SPORT*) gara; **in the ~ of** in caso di; **~ful** *adj* denso(a) di eventi
eventual [ɪ'vɛntʃuəl] *adj* finale; **~ity** [-'ælɪtɪ] *n* possibilità *f inv*, eventualità *f inv*; **~ly** *adv* alla fine
ever ['ɛvə*] *adv* mai; (*at all times*) sempre; **the best ~** il migliore che ci sia mai stato; **have you ~ seen it?** l'ha mai visto?; **~ since** *adv* da allora ♦ *conj* sin da quando; **~ so pretty** così bello(a); **~green** *n* sempreverde *m*; **~lasting** *adj* eterno(a)
every ['ɛvrɪ] *adj* ogni; **~ day** tutti i giorni, ogni giorno; **~ other/third day** ogni due/tre giorni; **~ other car** una macchina su due; **~ now and then** ogni tanto, di quando in quando; **~body** *pron* = **~one**; **~day** *adj* quotidiano(a); di ogni giorno; **~one** *pron* ognuno, tutti *pl*; **~thing** *pron* tutto, ogni cosa; **~where** *adv* (*gen*) dappertutto; (*wherever*) ovunque
evict [ɪ'vɪkt] *vt* sfrattare
evidence ['ɛvɪdns] *n* (*proof*) prova; (*of witness*) testimonianza; (*sign*): **to show ~ of** dare segni di; **to give ~** deporre
evident ['ɛvɪdnt] *adj* evidente; **~ly** *adv* evidentemente
evil ['i:vl] *adj* cattivo(a), maligno(a) ♦ *n* male *m*
evoke [ɪ'vəuk] *vt* evocare
evolution [i:və'lu:ʃən] *n* evoluzione *f*
evolve [ɪ'vɔlv] *vt* elaborare ♦ *vi* svilupparsi, evolversi

ewe [juː] n pecora

ex- [ɛks] prefix ex

exacerbate [ɛksˈæsəbeɪt] vt aggravare

exact [ɪgˈzækt] adj esatto(a) ♦ vt: **to ~ sth (from)** estorcere qc (da); esigere qc (da); **~ing** adj esigente; (work) faticoso(a); **~ly** adv esattamente

exaggerate [ɪgˈzædʒəreɪt] vt, vi esagerare; **exaggeration** [-ˈreɪʃən] n esagerazione f

exalted [ɪgˈzɔːltɪd] adj esaltato(a); elevato(a)

exam [ɪgˈzæm] n abbr (SCOL) = examination

examination [ɪgzæmɪˈneɪʃən] n (SCOL) esame m; (MED) controllo

examine [ɪgˈzæmɪn] vt esaminare; **~r** n esaminatore/trice

example [ɪgˈzɑːmpl] n esempio; **for ~** ad or per esempio

exasperate [ɪgˈzɑːspəreɪt] vt esasperare; **exasperating** adj esasperante; **exasperation** [-ˈreɪʃən] n esasperazione f

excavate [ˈɛkskəveɪt] vt scavare

exceed [ɪkˈsiːd] vt superare; (one's powers, time limit) oltrepassare; **~ingly** adv eccessivamente

excellent [ˈɛksələnt] adj eccellente

except [ɪkˈsɛpt] prep (also: ~ for, ~ing) salvo, all'infuori di, eccetto ♦ vt escludere; **~ if/when** salvo se/quando; **~ that** salvo che; **~ion** [ɪkˈsɛpʃən] n eccezione f; **to take ~ion to** trovare a ridire su; **~ional** [ɪkˈsɛpʃənl] adj eccezionale

excerpt [ˈɛksəːpt] n estratto

excess [ɪkˈsɛs] n eccesso; **~ baggage** n bagaglio in eccedenza; **~ fare** n supplemento; **~ive** adj eccessivo(a)

exchange [ɪksˈtʃeɪndʒ] n scambio; (also: telephone ~) centralino ♦ vt: **to ~ (for)** scambiare (con); **~ rate** n tasso di cambio

Exchequer [ɪksˈtʃɛkə*] n: **the ~** (BRIT) lo Scacchiere, ≈ il ministero delle Finanze

excise [ˈɛksaɪz] n imposta, dazio

excite [ɪkˈsaɪt] vt eccitare; **to get ~d** eccitarsi; **~ment** n eccitazione f; agitazione f; **exciting** adj avventuroso(a); (film, book) appassionante

exclaim [ɪkˈskleɪm] vi esclamare; **exclamation** [ɛkskləˈmeɪʃən] n esclamazione f; **exclamation mark** n punto esclamativo

exclude [ɪkˈskluːd] vt escludere

exclusive [ɪkˈskluːsɪv] adj esclusivo(a); **~ of VAT** I.V.A. esclusa

excommunicate [ɛkskəˈmjuːnɪkeɪt] vt scomunicare

excruciating [ɪkˈskruːʃieɪtɪŋ] adj straziante, atroce

excursion [ɪkˈskəːʃən] n escursione f, gita

excuse [n ɪkˈskjuːs, vb ɪkˈskjuːz] n scusa ♦ vt scusare; **to ~ sb from** (activity) dispensare qn da; **~ me!** mi scusi!; **now, if you will ~ me ...** ora, mi scusi ma ....

ex-directory [ˈɛksdɪˈrɛktərɪ] (BRIT) adj (TEL): **to be ~** non essere sull'elenco

execute [ˈɛksɪkjuːt] vt (prisoner) giustiziare; (plan etc) eseguire

execution [ɛksɪˈkjuːʃən] n esecuzione f; **~er** n boia m inv

executive [ɪgˈzɛkjutɪv] n (COMM) dirigente m; (POL) esecutivo ♦ adj esecutivo(a)

exemplify [ɪgˈzɛmplɪfaɪ] vt esemplificare

exempt [ɪgˈzɛmpt] adj esentato(a) ♦ vt: **to ~ sb from** esentare qn da; **~ion** [ɪgˈzɛmpʃən] n esenzione f

exercise [ˈɛksəsaɪz] n (keep fit) moto; (SCOL, MIL etc) esercizio ♦ vt esercitare; (patience) usare; (dog) portar fuori ♦ vi fare del moto; **~bike** n cyclette f inv; **~ book** n quaderno

exert [ɪgˈzəːt] vt esercitare; **to ~ o.s.** sforzarsi; **~ion** [-ʃən] n sforzo

exhale [ɛksˈheɪl] vt, vi espirare

exhaust [ɪgˈzɔːst] n (also: ~ fumes) scappamento; (also: ~ pipe) tubo di scappamento ♦ vt esaurire; **~ed** adj esaurito(a); **~ion** [ɪgˈzɔːstʃən] n esaurimento; **nervous ~ion** sovraffaticamento mentale; **~ive** adj esauriente

exhibit [ɪgˈzɪbɪt] n (ART) oggetto esposto; (LAW) documento or oggetto esibito ♦ vt esporre; (courage, skill) dimostrare; **~ion** [ɛksɪˈbɪʃən] n mostra, esposizione f

exhilarating [ɪgˈzɪləreɪtɪŋ] adj esilarante; stimolante

exhort [ɪgˈzɔːt] vt esortare

exile [ˈɛksaɪl] n esilio; (person) esiliato/a ♦ vt esiliare

exist [ɪgˈzɪst] vi esistere; **~ence** n esistenza; **~ing** adj esistente

exit [ˈɛksɪt] n uscita ♦ vi (THEATRE, COMPUT) uscire; **~ poll** n exit poll m inv; **~ ramp** (US) n (AUT) rampa di uscita

exodus [ˈɛksədəs] n esodo

exonerate [ɪgˈzɔnəreɪt] vt: **to ~ from** discolpare da

exotic [ɪgˈzɔtɪk] adj esotico(a)

expand [ɪkˈspænd] vt espandere; estendere; allargare ♦ vi (business, gas) espandersi; (metal) dilatarsi

expanse [ɪkˈspæns] n distesa, estensione f

expansion [ɪkˈspænʃən] n (gen) espansione f; (of town, economy) sviluppo; (of metal) dilatazione f

expect [ɪkˈspɛkt] vt (anticipate) prevedere, aspettarsi, prevedere or aspettarsi che + sub; (require) richiedere, esigere; (suppose) supporre; (await, also baby) aspettare ♦ vi: **to be ~ing** essere in stato interessante; **to ~ sb to do** aspettarsi che qn faccia; **~ancy** n (anticipation) attesa; **life ~ancy** probabilità fpl

di vita; **~ant mother** n gestante f; **~ation**
[ekspek'teɪʃən] n aspettativa; speranza

expediency [ɪk'spiːdɪənsɪ] n convenienza

expedient [ɪk'spiːdɪənt] adj conveniente;
vantaggioso(a) ♦ n espediente m

expedition [ekspə'dɪʃən] n spedizione f

expel [ɪk'spɛl] vt espellere

expend [ɪk'spɛnd] vt spendere; (use up)
consumare; **~iture** [ɪk'spɛndɪtʃə*] n spesa

expense [ɪk'spɛns] n spesa; (high cost) costo;
~s npl (COMM) spese fpl, indennità fpl; **at the
~ of** a spese di; **~ account** n conto m spese
inv

expensive [ɪk'spɛnsɪv] adj caro(a),
costoso(a)

experience [ɪk'spɪərɪəns] n esperienza ♦ vt
(pleasure) provare; (hardship) soffrire; **~d** adj
esperto(a)

experiment [n ɪk'spɛrɪmənt, vb
ɪk'spɛrɪmənt] n esperimento, esperienza ♦ vi:
to ~ (with/on) fare esperimenti (con/su)

expert ['ɛkspəːt] adj, n esperto(a); **~ise**
[-'tiːz] n competenza

expire [ɪk'spaɪə*] vi (period of time, licence)
scadere; **expiry** n scadenza

explain [ɪk'splɛɪn] vt spiegare; **explanation**
[eksplə'neɪʃən] n spiegazione f; **explanatory**
[ɪk'splænətrɪ] adj esplicativo(a)

explicit [ɪk'splɪsɪt] adj esplicito(a)

explode [ɪk'spləʊd] vi esplodere

exploit [n 'ɛksplɔɪt, vb ɪk'splɔɪt] n impresa
♦ vt sfruttare; **~ation** [-'teɪʃən] n
sfruttamento

exploratory [ɪk'splɔrətrɪ] adj esplorativo(a)

explore [ɪk'splɔː*] vt esplorare; (possibilities)
esaminare; **~r** n esploratore/trice

explosion [ɪk'spləʊʒən] n esplosione f

explosive [ɪk'spləʊsɪv] adj esplosivo(a) ♦ n
esplosivo

exponent [ɪk'spəʊnənt] n esponente m/f

export [vb ɛk'spɔːt, n 'ɛkspɔːt] vt esportare
♦ n esportazione f; articolo di esportazione
♦ cpd d'esportazione; **~er** n esportatore m

expose [ɪk'spəʊz] vt esporre; (unmask)
smascherare; **~d** adj (position) esposto(a)

exposure [ɪk'spəʊʒə*] n esposizione f; (PHOT)
posa; (MED) assideramento; **~ meter** n
esposimetro

express [ɪk'sprɛs] adj (definite) chiaro(a),
espresso(a); (BRIT: letter etc) espresso inv ♦ n
(train) espresso ♦ vt esprimere; **~ion**
[ɪk'sprɛʃən] n espressione f; **~ive** adj
espressivo(a); **~ly** adv espressamente;
~way (US) n (urban motorway) autostrada
che attraversa la città

exquisite [ɛk'skwɪzɪt] adj squisito(a)

extend [ɪk'stɛnd] vt (visit) protrarre; (road,
deadline) prolungare; (building) ampliare;
(offer) offrire, porgere ♦ vi (land, period)

estendersi

extension [ɪk'stɛnʃən] n (of road, term)
prolungamento; (of contract, deadline)
proroga; (building) annesso; (to wire, table)
prolunga; (telephone) interno; (: in private
house) apparecchio supplementare

extensive [ɪk'stɛnsɪv] adj esteso(a),
ampio(a); (damage) su larga scala; (coverage,
discussion) esauriente; (use) grande; **~ly** adv:
he's travelled ~ly ha viaggiato molto

extent [ɪk'stɛnt] n estensione f; **to some
~** fino a un certo punto; **to such an ~ that** ... a
un tal punto che ...; **to what ~?** fino a che
punto?; **to the ~ of** ... fino al punto di ...

extenuating [ɪks'tɛnjʊeɪtɪŋ] adj:
~ circumstances attenuanti fpl

exterior [ek'stɪərɪə*] adj esteriore, esterno(a)
♦ n esteriore m, esterno; aspetto (esteriore)

exterminate [ɪk'stəːmɪneɪt] vt sterminare

external [ek'stəːnl] adj esterno(a), esteriore

extinct [ɪk'stɪŋkt] adj estinto(a)

extinguish [ɪk'stɪŋgwɪʃ] vt estinguere; **~er** n
estintore m

extort [ɪk'stɔːt] vt: **to ~ sth (from)** estorcere
qc (da); **~ionate** [ɪk'stɔːʃnət] adj esorbitante

extra ['ɛkstrə] adj extra inv, supplementare
♦ adv (in addition) di più ♦ n extra m inv;
(surcharge) supplemento; (CINEMA, THEATRE)
comparsa

extra... ['ɛkstrə] prefix extra...

extract [vb ɪk'strækt, n 'ɛkstrækt] vt estrarre;
(money, promise) strappare ♦ n estratto;
(passage) brano

extracurricular ['ɛkstrəkə'rɪkjʊlə*] adj
extrascolastico(a)

extradite ['ɛkstrədaɪt] vt estradare

extramarital [ekstrə'mærɪtl] adj
extraconiugale

extramural [ekstrə'mjʊərl] adj fuori
dell'università

extraordinary [ɪk'strɔːdnrɪ] adj
straordinario(a)

extravagance [ɪk'strævəgəns] n sperpero;
stravaganza

extravagant [ɪk'strævəgənt] adj (lavish)
prodigo(a); (wasteful) dispendioso(a)

extreme [ɪk'striːm] adj estremo(a) ♦ n
estremo; **~ly** adv estremamente

extricate ['ɛkstrɪkeɪt] vt: **to ~ sth (from)**
districare qc (da)

extrovert ['ɛkstrəvəːt] n estroverso/a

exude [ɪg'zjuːd] vt trasudare; (fig) emanare

eye [aɪ] n occhio; (of needle) cruna ♦ vt
osservare; **to keep an ~ on** tenere d'occhio;
~brow n sopracciglio; **~drops** npl gocce fpl
oculari, collirio; **~lash** n ciglio; **~lid** n
palpebra, **~liner** n eye-liner m inv; **~opener**
n rivelazione f; **~shadow** n ombretto;
~sight n vista; **~sore** n pugno nell'occhio;

~ **witness** n testimone m/f oculare

F, f

F [ɛf] n (MUS) fa m
fable ['feɪbl] n favola
fabric ['fæbrɪk] n stoffa, tessuto
fabulous ['fæbjuləs] adj favoloso(a); (super) favoloso(a), fantastico(a)
façade [fə'sɑːd] n (also fig) facciata
face [feɪs] n faccia, viso, volto; (expression) faccia; (of clock) quadrante m; (of building) facciata ♦ vt essere di fronte a; (facts, situation) affrontare; ~ **down** a faccia in giù; **to make** or **pull a** ~ fare una smorfia; **in the** ~ **of** (difficulties etc) di fronte a; **on the** ~ **of it** a prima vista; ~ **to** ~ faccia a faccia; ~ **up to** vt fus affrontare, far fronte a; ~ **cloth** (BRIT) n guanto di spugna; ~ **cream** n crema per il viso; ~ **lift** n lifting m inv; (of façade etc) ripulita; ~ **powder** n cipria; ~**-saving** adj per salvare la faccia
facet ['fæsɪt] n sfaccettatura
facetious [fə'siːʃəs] adj faceto(a)
face value n (of coin) valore m facciale or nominale; **to take sth at** ~ (fig) giudicare qc dalle apparenze
facial ['feɪʃəl] adj del viso
facile ['fæsaɪl] adj superficiale
facilities [fə'sɪlɪtɪz] npl attrezzature fpl; **credit** ~ facilitazioni fpl di credito
facing ['feɪsɪŋ] prep di fronte a
facsimile [fæk'sɪmɪlɪ] n facsimile m inv; ~ **machine** n telecopiatrice f
fact [fækt] n fatto; **in** ~ infatti
factor ['fæktə*] n fattore m
factory ['fæktərɪ] n fabbrica, stabilimento
factual ['fæktjuəl] adj che si attiene ai fatti
faculty ['fækəltɪ] n facoltà f inv; (US) corpo insegnante
fad [fæd] n mania; capriccio
fade [feɪd] vi sbiadire, sbiadirsi; (light, sound, hope) attenuarsi, affievolirsi; (flower) appassire
fag [fæg] (BRIT: inf) n (cigarette) cicca
fail [feɪl] vt (exam) non superare; (candidate) bocciare; (subj: courage, memory) mancare a ♦ vi fallire; (student) essere respinto(a); (eyesight, health, light) venire a mancare; **to** ~ **to do sth** (neglect) mancare di fare qc; (be unable) non riuscire a fare qc; **without** ~ senza fallo; certamente; ~**ing** n difetto ♦ prep in mancanza di; ~**ure** ['feɪljə*] n fallimento; (person) fallito/a; (mechanical etc) guasto
faint [feɪnt] adj debole; (recollection) vago(a); (mark) indistinto(a) ♦ n (MED) svenimento ♦ vi svenire; **to feel** ~ sentirsi svenire
fair [feə*] adj (person, decision) giusto(a), equo(a); (quite large, quite good) discreto(a);

(hair etc) biondo(a); (skin, complexion) chiaro(a); (weather) bello(a), clemente ♦ adv (play) lealmente ♦ n fiera; (BRIT: funfair) luna park m inv; ~**ly** adv equamente; (quite) abbastanza; ~**ness** n equità, giustizia; ~ **play** n correttezza
fairy ['feərɪ] n fata; ~ **tale** n fiaba
faith [feɪθ] n fede f; (trust) fiducia; (sect) religione f, fede f; ~**ful** adj fedele; ~**fully** adv fedelmente; **yours** ~**fully** (BRIT: in letters) distinti saluti
fake [feɪk] n imitazione f; (picture) falso; (person) impostore/a ♦ adj falso(a) ♦ vt (accounts) falsificare; (illness) fingere; (painting) contraffare
fall [fɔːl] (pt fell, pp fallen) n caduta; (in temperature) abbassamento; (in price) ribasso; (US: autumn) autunno ♦ vi cadere; (temperature, price, night) scendere; ~**s** npl (waterfall) cascate fpl; **to** ~ **flat** (on one's face) cadere bocconi; (joke) fare cilecca; (plan) fallire; ~ **back** vi (retreat) indietreggiare; (MIL) ritirarsi; ~ **back on** vt fus (remedy etc) ripiegare su; ~ **behind** vi rimanere indietro; ~ **down** vi (person) cadere; (building) crollare; ~ **for** vt fus (person) prendere una cotta per; **to** ~ **for a trick** (or story etc) cascarci; ~ **in** vi crollare; (MIL) mettersi in riga; ~ **off** vi cadere; (diminish) diminuire, abbassarsi; ~ **out** vi (hair, teeth) cadere; (friends etc) litigare; ~ **through** vi (plan, project) fallire
fallacy ['fæləsɪ] n errore m
fallen ['fɔːlən] pp of **fall**
fallout ['fɔːlaut] n fall-out m
fallow ['fæləu] adj incolto(a), a maggese
false [fɔːls] adj falso(a); **under** ~ **pretences** con l'inganno; ~ **teeth** (BRIT) npl denti mpl finti
falter ['fɔːltə*] vi esitare, vacillare
fame [feɪm] n fama, celebrità
familiar [fə'mɪlɪə*] adj familiare; (close) intimo(a); **to be** ~ **with** (subject) conoscere; ~**ize** [fə'mɪlɪəraɪz] vt: **to** ~**ize o.s. with** familiarizzare con
family ['fæmɪlɪ] n famiglia; ~ **business** n ditta a conduzione familiare
famine ['fæmɪn] n carestia
famished ['fæmɪʃt] adj affamato(a)
famous ['feɪməs] adj famoso(a); ~**ly** adv (get on) a meraviglia
fan [fæn] n (folding) ventaglio; (ELEC) ventilatore m; (person) ammiratore/trice, tifoso/a ♦ vt far vento a; (fire, quarrel) alimentare
fanatic [fə'nætɪk] n fanatico/a
fan belt n cinghia del ventilatore
fanciful ['fænsɪful] adj fantasioso(a)
fancy ['fænsɪ] n immaginazione f, fantasia; (whim) capriccio ♦ adj (hat) stravagante;

(*hotel, food*) speciale ♦ *vt* (*feel like, want*) aver voglia di; (*imagine, think*) immaginare; **to take a ~ to** incapricciarsi di; **he fancies her** (*inf*) gli piace; **~ dress** *n* costume *m* (per maschera); **~-dress ball** *n* ballo in maschera

fang [fæŋ] *n* zanna; (*of snake*) dente *m*

fantastic [fæn'tæstɪk] *adj* fantastico(a)

fantasy ['fæntəsɪ] *n* fantasia, immaginazione *f*; fantasticheria; chimera

far [fɑː*] *adj* lontano(a) ♦ *adv* lontano; (*much, greatly*) molto; **~ away, ~ off** lontano, distante; **~ better** assai migliore; **~ from** lontano da; **by ~** di gran lunga; **go as ~ as the farm** vada fino alla fattoria; **as ~ as I know** per quel che so; **how ~?** quanto lontano?; (*referring to activity etc*) fino a dove?; **~away** *adj* lontano(a)

farce [fɑːs] *n* farsa

fare [fɛə*] *n* (*on trains, buses*) tariffa; (*in taxi*) prezzo della corsa; (*food*) vitto, cibo; **half ~** metà tariffa; **full ~** tariffa intera

Far East *n*: **the ~** l'Estremo Oriente *m*

farewell [fɛə'wɛl] *excl, n* addio

farm [fɑːm] *n* fattoria, podere *m* ♦ *vt* coltivare; **~er** *n* coltivatore/trice; agricoltore/trice; **~hand** *n* bracciante *m* agricolo; **~house** *n* fattoria; **~ing** *n* (*gen*) agricoltura; (*of crops*) coltivazione *f*; (*of animals*) allevamento; **~land** *n* terreno coltivabile; **~ worker** *n* = **~hand**; **~yard** *n* aia

far-reaching [-'riːtʃɪŋ] *adj* di vasta portata

fart [fɑːt] (*inf!*) *vi* scoreggiare (!)

farther ['fɑːðə*] *adv* più lontano ♦ *adj* più lontano(a)

farthest ['fɑːðɪst] *superl* of **far**

fascinate ['fæsɪneɪt] *vt* affascinare; **fascinating** *adj* affascinante; **fascination** [-'neɪʃən] *n* fascino

fascism ['fæʃɪzəm] *n* fascismo

fashion ['fæʃən] *n* (*in*) moda; (*manner*) maniera, modo ♦ *vt* foggiare, formare; **in ~** alla moda; **out of ~** passato(a) di moda; **~able** *adj* alla moda, di moda; **~ show** *n* sfilata di moda

fast [fɑːst] *adj* rapido(a), svelto(a), veloce; (*clock*): **to be ~** andare avanti; (*dye, colour*) solido(a) ♦ *adv* rapidamente, in fretta; (*stuck, held*) saldamente ♦ *n* digiuno ♦ *vi* digiunare; **~ asleep** profondamente addormentato

fasten ['fɑːsn] *vt* chiudere, fissare; (*coat*) abbottonare, allacciare ♦ *vi* chiudersi, fissarsi; abbottonarsi, allacciarsi; **~er** *n* fermaglio, chiusura; **~ing** *n* = **~er**

fast food *n* fast food *m*

fastidious [fæs'tɪdɪəs] *adj* esigente, difficile

fat [fæt] *adj* grasso(a); (*book, profit etc*) grosso(a) ♦ *n* grasso

fatal ['feɪtl] *adj* fatale; mortale; disastroso(a); **~ity** [fə'tælɪtɪ] *n* (*road death etc*) morto/a, vittima; **~ly** *adv* a morte

fate [feɪt] *n* destino; (*of person*) sorte *f*; **~ful** *adj* fatidico(a)

father ['fɑːðə*] *n* padre *m*; **~-in-law** *n* suocero; **~ly** *adj* paterno(a)

fathom ['fæðəm] *n* braccio (= *1828 mm*) ♦ *vt* (*mystery*) penetrare, sondare

fatigue [fə'tiːg] *n* stanchezza

fatten ['fætn] *vt, vi* ingrassare

fatty ['fætɪ] *adj* (*food*) grasso(a) ♦ *n* (*inf*) ciccione/a

fatuous ['fætjuəs] *adj* fatuo(a)

faucet ['fɔːsɪt] (*US*) *n* rubinetto

fault [fɔːlt] *n* colpa; (*TENNIS*) fallo; (*defect*) difetto; (*GEO*) faglia ♦ *vt* criticare; **it's my ~** è colpa mia; **to find ~ with** trovare da ridire su; **at ~** in fallo; **~y** *adj* difettoso(a)

fauna ['fɔːnə] *n* fauna

favour ['feɪvə*] (*US* favor) *n* favore *m* ♦ *vt* (*proposition*) favorire, essere favorevole a; (*pupil etc*) favorire; (*team, horse*) dare per vincente; **to do sb a ~** fare un favore or una cortesia a qn; **to find ~ with** (*subj: person*) entrare nelle buone grazie di; (: *suggestion*) avere l'approvazione di; **in ~ of** in favore di; **~able** *adj* favorevole; **~ite** [-rɪt] *adj, n* favorito(a)

fawn [fɔːn] *n* daino ♦ *adj* (*also*: **~-coloured**) marrone chiaro *inv* ♦ *vi*: **to ~ (up)on** adulare servilmente

fax [fæks] *n* (*document*) facsimile *m inv*, telecopia; (*machine*) telecopiatrice *f* ♦ *vt* telecopiare, trasmettere in facsimile

FBI (*US*) *n abbr* (= *Federal Bureau of Investigation*) F.B.I. *f*

fear [fɪə*] *n* paura, timore *m* ♦ *vt* aver paura di, temere; **for ~ of** per paura di; **~ful** *adj* pauroso(a); (*sight, noise*) terribile, spaventoso(a)

feasible ['fiːzəbl] *adj* possibile, realizzabile

feast [fiːst] *n* festa, banchetto; (*REL: also*: **~ day**) festa ♦ *vi* banchettare

feat [fiːt] *n* impresa, fatto insigne

feather ['fɛðə*] *n* penna

feature ['fiːtʃə*] *n* caratteristica; (*PRESS, TV*) articolo ♦ *vt* (*subj: film*) avere come protagonista ♦ *vi* figurare; **~s** *npl* (*of face*) fisionomia; **~ film** *n* film *m inv* principale

February ['fɛbruərɪ] *n* febbraio

fed [fɛd] *pt, pp of* **feed**

federal ['fɛdərəl] *adj* federale

fed-up [fɛd'ʌp] *adj*: **to be ~** essere stufo(a)

fee [fiː] *n* pagamento; (*of doctor, lawyer*) onorario; (*for examination*) tassa d'esame; **school ~s** tasse *fpl* scolastiche

feeble ['fiːbl] *adj* debole

feed [fiːd] *n* (*of baby*) pappa; (*of animal*) mangime *m*; (*on printer*) meccanismo di alimentazione ♦ *vt* nutrire; (*baby*) allattare; (*horse etc*) dare da mangiare a; (*fire,* *machine*) alimentare; (*data, information*): to ~ **into** inserire in; ~ **on** vt fus nutrirsi di; ~**back** n feed-back m

feel [fi:l] (*pt, pp* **felt**) n consistenza; (*sense of touch*) tatto ♦ vt toccare; palpare; tastare; (*cold, pain, anger*) sentire; (*think, believe*): to ~ (*that*) pensare che; to ~ **hungry/cold** aver fame/freddo; to ~ **lonely/better** sentirsi solo/meglio; I **don't** ~ **well** non mi sento bene; it ~**s soft** è morbido al tatto; to ~ **like** (*want*) aver voglia di; to ~ **about** or **around for** cercare a tastoni; ~**er** n (*of insect*) antenna; ~**ing** n sensazione f; (*emotion*) sentimento

feet [fi:t] npl of **foot**

feign [fein] vt fingere, simulare

fell [fel] pt of **fall** ♦ vt (*tree*) abbattere

fellow ['feləʊ] n individuo, tipo; compagno; (*of learned society*) membro ♦ cpd: ~ **citizen** n concittadino/a; ~ **countryman** (*irreg*) n compatriota m; ~ **men** npl simili mpl; ~**ship** n associazione f; compagnia; *specie di borsa di studio universitaria*

felony ['felənı] n reato, crimine m

felt [felt] pt, pp of **feel** ♦ n feltro; ~-**tip pen** n pennarello

female ['fi:meil] n (*ZOOL*) femmina, (*pej: woman*) donna, femmina ♦ adj (*BIOL, ELEC*) femmina inv; (*sex, character*) femminile; (*vote etc*) di donne

feminine ['feminin] adj femminile

feminist ['feminist] n femminista m/f

fence [fens] n recinto ♦ vt (*also:* ~ **in**) recingere ♦ vi (*SPORT*) tirare di scherma; **fencing** n (*SPORT*) scherma

fend [fend] vi: to ~ **for o.s.** arrangiarsi; ~ **off** vt (*attack, questions*) respingere, difendersi da

fender ['fendə*] n parafuoco; (*on boat*) parabordo; (*US*) parafango; paraurti m inv

ferment [vb fə'mɛnt, n 'fə:mɛnt] vi fermentare ♦ n (*fig*) agitazione f, eccitazione f

fern [fə:n] n felce f

ferocious [fə'rəʊʃəs] adj feroce

ferret ['ferit] n furetto; ~ **out** vt (*information*) scovare

ferry ['feri] n (*small*) traghetto; (*large: also:* ~**boat**) nave f traghetto inv ♦ vt traghettare

fertile ['fə:tail] adj fertile; (*BIOL*) fecondo(a); **fertilizer** ['fə:tilaizə*] n fertilizzante m

fester ['festə*] vi suppurare

festival ['festivəl] n (*REL*) festa; (*ART, MUS*) festival m inv

festive ['festiv] adj di festa; **the ~ season** (*BRIT: Christmas*) il periodo delle feste

festivities [fes'tivitiz] npl festeggiamenti mpl

festoon [fes'tu:n] vt: to ~ **with** ornare di

fetch [fetʃ] vt andare a prendere; (*sell for*) essere venduto(a) per

fête [feit] n festa

fetus ['fi:təs] (*US*) n = **foetus**

feud [fju:d] n contesa, lotta

feudal ['fju:dl] adj feudale

fever ['fi:və*] n febbre f; ~**ish** adj febbrile

few [fju:] adj pochi(e); **a** ~ adj qualche inv ♦ pron alcuni(e); ~**er** adj meno inv; meno numerosi(e); ~**est** adj il minor numero di

fiancé [fɪ'ɑ̃:ŋseɪ] n fidanzato; ~**e** n fidanzata

fib [fɪb] n piccola bugia

fibre ['faɪbə*] (*US* **fiber**) n fibra; **F~glass** ® n fibra di vetro

fickle ['fɪkl] adj incostante, capriccioso(a)

fiction ['fɪkʃən] n narrativa, romanzi mpl; (*sth made up*) finzione f; ~**al** adj immaginario(a)

fictitious [fɪk'tɪʃəs] adj fittizio(a)

fiddle ['fɪdl] n (*MUS*) violino; (*cheating*) imbroglio; truffa ♦ vt (*BRIT: accounts*) falsificare, falsare; ~ **with** vt fus gingillarsi con

fidelity [fɪ'dɛlɪtɪ] n fedeltà; (*accuracy*) esattezza

fidget ['fɪdʒɪt] vi agitarsi

field [fi:ld] n campo; ~ **marshal** n feldmaresciallo; ~**work** n ricerche fpl esterne

fiend [fi:nd] n demonio

fierce [fiəs] adj (*animal, person, fighting*) feroce; (*loyalty*) assoluto(a); (*wind*) furioso(a); (*heat*) intenso(a)

fiery ['faiəri] adj ardente; infocato(a)

fifteen [fɪf'ti:n] num quindici

fifth [fɪfθ] num quinto(a)

fifty ['fɪftɪ] num cinquanta; ~-~ adj: **a ~-~ chance** una possibilità su due ♦ adv fifty-fifty, metà per ciascuno

fig [fɪg] n fico

fight [fait] (*pt, pp* **fought**) n zuffa, rissa; (*MIL*) battaglia, combattimento; (*against cancer etc*) lotta ♦ vt (*person*) azzuffarsi con; (*enemy: also: MIL*) combattere; (*cancer, alcoholism, emotion*) lottare contro, combattere; (*election*) partecipare a ♦ vi combattere; ~**er** n combattente m; (*plane*) aeroplano da caccia; ~**ing** n combattimento

figment ['fɪgmənt] n: **a ~ of the imagination** un parto della fantasia

figurative ['fɪgjʊrətɪv] adj figurato(a)

figure ['fɪgə*] n figura; (*number, cipher*) cifra ♦ vt (*think: esp US*) pensare ♦ vi (*appear*) figurare; ~ **out** vt riuscire a capire; calcolare; ~**head** n (*NAUT*) polena; (*pej*) prestanome m/f inv; ~ **of speech** n figura retorica

file [fail] n (*tool*) lima; (*dossier*) incartamento; (*folder*) cartellina; (*COMPUT*) archivio; (*row*) fila ♦ vt (*nails, wood*) limare; (*papers*) archiviare; (*LAW: claim*) presentare; passare agli atti; ~ **in/out** vi entrare/uscire in fila

filing cabinet ['failɪŋ-] n casellario

fill [fɪl] vt riempire; (*job*) coprire ♦ n: **to eat one's ~** mangiare a sazietà; ~ **in** vt (*hole*) riempire; (*form*) compilare; ~ **up** vt riempire ♦ vi (*AUT*) fare il pieno

fillet ['fılıt] n filetto; ~ **steak** n bistecca di filetto

filling ['fılıŋ] n (CULIN) impasto, ripieno; (for tooth) otturazione f; ~ **station** n stazione f di rifornimento

film [fılm] n (CINEMA) film m inv; (PHOT) pellicola; (of powder, liquid) sottile strato ♦ vt, vi girare; ~ **star** n divo/a dello schermo

filter ['fıltə*] n filtro ♦ vt filtrare; ~ **lane** (BRIT) n (AUT) corsia di svincolo; ~**-tipped** adj con filtro

filth [fılθ] n sporcizia; ~**y** adj lordo(a), sozzo(a); (language) osceno(a)

fin [fın] n (of fish) pinna

final ['faınl] adj finale, ultimo(a); definitivo(a) ♦ n (SPORT) finale f; ~**s** npl (SCOL) esami mpl finali

finale [fı'nɑːlı] n finale m

finalize ['faınəlaız] vt mettere a punto

finally ['faınəlı] adv (lastly) alla fine; (eventually) finalmente

finance [faı'næns] n finanza; (capital) capitale m ♦ vt finanziare; ~**s** npl (funds) finanze fpl

financial [faı'nænʃəl] adj finanziario(a)

financier [faı'nænsıə*] n finanziatore m

find [faınd] (pt, pp **found**) vt trovare; (lost object) ritrovare ♦ n trovata, scoperta; **to ~ sb guilty** (LAW) giudicare qn colpevole; ~ **out** vt (truth, secret) scoprire; (person) cogliere in fallo; **to ~ out about** informarsi su; (by chance) scoprire; ~**ings** npl (LAW) sentenza, conclusioni fpl; (of report) conclusioni

fine [faın] adj bello(a); ottimo(a); (thin, subtle) fine ♦ adv (well) molto bene ♦ n (LAW) multa ♦ vt (LAW) multare; **to be ~** (person) stare bene; (weather) far bello; ~ **arts** npl belle arti fpl

finery ['faınərı] n abiti mpl eleganti

finger ['fıŋgə*] n dito ♦ vt toccare, tastare; **little/index ~** mignolo/(dito) indice m; ~**nail** n unghia; ~**print** n impronta digitale; ~**tip** n punta del dito

finish ['fınıʃ] n fine f; (polish etc) finitura ♦ vt, vi finire; **to ~ doing sth** finire di fare qc; **to ~ third** arrivare terzo(a); ~ **off** vt compiere; (kill) uccidere; ~ **up** vi, vt finire; ~**ing line** n linea d'arrivo

finite ['faınaıt] adj limitato(a); (verb) finito(a)

Finland ['fınlənd] n Finlandia

Finn [fın] n finlandese m/f; ~**ish** adj finlandese ♦ n (LING) finlandese m

fir [fəː*] n abete m

fire [faıə*] n fuoco; (destructive) incendio; (gas ~, electric ~) stufa ♦ vt (gun) far fuoco con; (arrow) sparare; (fig) infiammare; (inf: dismiss) licenziare ♦ vi sparare, far fuoco; **on ~** in fiamme; ~ **alarm** n allarme m d'incendio; ~**arm** n arma da fuoco; ~ **brigade** (US

~ **department**) n (corpo dei) pompieri mpl; ~ **engine** n autopompa; ~ **escape** n scala di sicurezza; ~ **extinguisher** n estintore m; ~**guard** n parafuoco; ~**man** (irreg) n pompiere m; ~**place** n focolare m; ~**side** n angolo del focolare; ~ **station** n caserma dei pompieri; ~**wood** n legna; ~**works** npl fuochi mpl d'artificio

firing squad ['faıərıŋ-] n plotone m d'esecuzione

firm [fəːm] adj fermo(a) ♦ n ditta, azienda; ~**ly** adv fermamente

first [fəːst] adj primo(a) ♦ adv (before others) il primo, la prima; (before other things) per primo; (when listing reasons etc) per prima cosa ♦ n (person: in race) primo/a; (BRIT: SCOL) laurea con lode; (AUT) prima; **at ~** dapprima, all'inizio; ~ **of all** prima di tutto; ~ **aid** n pronto soccorso; ~**-aid kit** n cassetta pronto soccorso; ~**-class** adj di prima classe; ~ **floor** n il primo piano (BRIT); il pianterreno (US); ~**-hand** adj di prima mano; ~ **lady** (US) n moglie f del presidente; ~**ly** adv in primo luogo; ~ **name** n prenome m; ~**-rate** adj di prima qualità, ottimo(a)

fish [fıʃ] n inv pesce m ♦ vt (river, area) pescare in ♦ vi pescare; **to go ~ing** andare a pesca; ~**erman** n pescatore m; ~ **farm** n vivaio; ~ **fingers** (BRIT) npl bastoncini mpl di pesce (surgelati); ~**ing boat** n barca da pesca; ~**ing line** n lenza; ~**ing rod** n canna da pesca; ~**monger** n pescivendolo; ~**monger's (shop)** n pescheria; ~ **sticks** (US) npl = ~ **fingers**; ~**y** (inf) adj (tale, story) sospetto(a)

fist [fıst] n pugno

fit [fıt] adj (MED, SPORT) in forma; (proper) adatto(a), appropriato(a); conveniente ♦ vt (subj: clothes) stare bene a; (put in, attach) mettere, installare; (equip) fornire, equipaggiare ♦ vi (clothes) stare bene; (parts) andare bene, adattarsi; (in space, gap) entrare ♦ n (MED) accesso, attacco; ~ **to** in grado di; ~ **for** adatto(a) a; degno(a) di; **a ~ of anger** un accesso d'ira; **this dress is a good ~** questo vestito sta bene; **by ~s and starts** a sbalzi; ~ **in** vi accordarsi; adattarsi; ~**ful** adj saltuario(a); ~**ness** n (MED) forma fisica; ~**ted carpet** n moquette f; ~**ted kitchen** n cucina componibile; ~**ter** n aggiustatore m or montatore m meccanico; ~**ting** adj appropriato(a) ♦ n (of dress) prova; (of piece of equipment) montaggio, aggiustaggio; ~**tings** npl (in building) impianti mpl; ~**ting room** n camerino

five [faıv] num cinque; ~**r** (inf) n (BRIT) biglietto da cinque sterline; (US) biglietto da cinque dollari

fix [fıks] vt fissare; (mend) riparare; (meal,

drink) preparare ♦ n: **to be in a ~** essere nei guai; **~ up** vt (meeting) fissare; **to ~ sb up with sth** procurare qc a qn; **~ation** n fissazione f; **~ed** [fɪkst] adj (prices etc) fisso(a); **~ture** [ˈfɪkstʃə*] n impianto (fisso); (SPORT) incontro (del calendario sportivo)

fizzy [ˈfɪzɪ] adj frizzante; gassato(a)

flabbergasted [ˈflæbəgɑːstɪd] adj sbalordito(a)

flabby [ˈflæbɪ] adj flaccido(a)

flag [flæg] n bandiera; (also: ~stone) pietra da lastricare ♦ vi stancarsi; affievolirsi; **~ down** vt fare segno (di fermarsi) a

flagpole [ˈflægpəul] n albero

flagship [ˈflægʃɪp] n nave f ammiraglia

flair [fleə*] n (for business etc) fiuto; (for languages etc) facilità; (style) stile m

flak [flæk] n (MIL) fuoco d'artiglieria; (inf: criticism) critiche fpl

flake [fleɪk] n (of rust, paint) scaglia; (of snow, soap powder) fiocco ♦ vi (also: ~ off) sfaldarsi

flamboyant [flæmˈbɔɪənt] adj sgargiante

flame [fleɪm] n fiamma

flamingo [fləˈmɪŋgəu] n fenicottero, fiammingo

flammable [ˈflæməbl] adj infiammabile

flan [flæn] (BRIT) n flan m inv

flank [flæŋk] n fianco ♦ vt fiancheggiare

flannel [ˈflænl] n (BRIT: also: face ~) guanto di spugna; (fabric) flanella

flap [flæp] n (of pocket) patta; (of envelope) lembo ♦ vt (wings) battere ♦ vi (sail, flag) sbattere; (inf: also: be in a ~) essere in agitazione

flare [fleə*] n razzo; (in skirt etc) svasatura; **~ up** vi andare in fiamme; (fig: person) infiammarsi di rabbia; (: revolt) scoppiare

flash [flæʃ] n vampata; (also: news ~) notizia f lampo inv; (PHOT) flash m inv ♦ vt accendere e spegnere; (send: message) trasmettere; (: look, smile) lanciare ♦ vi brillare; (light on ambulance, eyes etc) lampeggiare; **in a ~** in un lampo; **to ~ one's headlights** lampeggiare; **he ~ed by** or **past** ci passò davanti come un lampo; **~bulb** n cubo m flash inv; **~cube** n flash m inv; **~light** n lampadina tascabile

flashy [ˈflæʃɪ] (pej) adj vistoso(a)

flask [flɑːsk] n fiasco; (also: vacuum ~) thermos ® m inv

flat [flæt] adj piatto(a); (tyre) sgonfio(a), a terra; (battery) scarico(a); (beer) svampito(a); (denial) netto(a); (MUS) bemolle inv; (: voice) stonato(a); (rate, fee) unico(a) ♦ n (BRIT: rooms) appartamento; (AUT) pneumatico sgonfio; (MUS) bemolle m; **to work ~ out** lavorare a più non posso; **~ly** adv categoricamente; **~ten** vt (also: ~ten out) appiattire; (building, city) spianare

flatter [ˈflætə*] vt lusingare; **~ing** adj

lusinghiero(a); (dress) che dona; **~y** n adulazione f

flaunt [flɔːnt] vt fare mostra di

flavour [ˈfleɪvə*] (US **flavor**) n gusto ♦ vt insaporire, aggiungere sapore a; **strawberry-~ed** al gusto di fragola; **~ing** n essenza (artificiale)

flaw [flɔː] n difetto

flax [flæks] n lino

flea [fliː] n pulce f

fleck [flek] n (mark) macchiolina; (pattern) screziatura

fled [fled] pt, pp of **flee**

flee [fliː] (pt, pp **fled**) vt fuggire da ♦ vi fuggire, scappare

fleece [fliːs] n vello ♦ vt (inf) pelare

fleet [fliːt] n flotta; (of lorries etc) convoglio; parco

fleeting [ˈfliːtɪŋ] adj fugace, fuggitivo(a); (visit) volante

Flemish [ˈflemɪʃ] adj fiammingo(a)

flesh [fleʃ] n carne f; (of fruit) polpa; **~ wound** n ferita superficiale

flew [fluː] pt of **fly**

flex [fleks] n filo (flessibile) ♦ vt flettere; (muscles) contrarre; **~ible** adj flessibile

flick [flɪk] n colpetto; scarto ♦ vt dare un colpetto a; **~ through** vt fus sfogliare

flicker [ˈflɪkə*] vi tremolare

flier [ˈflaɪə*] n aviatore m

flight [flaɪt] n volo; (escape) fuga; (also: ~ of steps) scalinata; **~ attendant** (US) n steward m inv, hostess f inv; **~ deck** n (AVIAT) cabina di controllo; (NAUT) ponte m di comando

flimsy [ˈflɪmzɪ] adj (shoes, clothes) leggero(a); (building) poco solido(a); (excuse) che non regge

flinch [flɪntʃ] vi ritirarsi; **to ~ from** tirarsi indietro di fronte a

fling [flɪŋ] (pt, pp **flung**) vt lanciare, gettare

flint [flɪnt] n selce f; (in lighter) pietrina

flip [flɪp] vt (switch) far scattare; (coin) lanciare in aria

flippant [ˈflɪpənt] adj senza rispetto, irriverente

flipper [ˈflɪpə*] n pinna

flirt [flɜːt] vi flirtare ♦ n civetta

float [fləut] n galleggiante m; (in procession) carro; (money) somma ♦ vi galleggiare

flock [flɔk] n (of sheep, REL) gregge m; (of birds) stormo ♦ vi: **to ~ to** accorrere in massa a

flog [flɔg] vt flagellare

flood [flʌd] n alluvione m; (of letters etc) marea f allagare; (subj: people) invadere ♦ vi (place) allagarsi; (people): **to ~ into** riversarsi in; **~ing** n inondazione f; **~light** n riflettore m ♦ vt illuminare a giorno

floor [flɔː*] n pavimento; (storey) piano; (of

sea, valley) fondo ♦ *vt* (*subj: blow*) atterrare; (: *question*) ridurre al silenzio; **ground ~**, (*US*) **first ~** pianterreno; **first ~**, (*US*) **second ~** primo piano; **~ show** *n* spettacolo di varietà

flop [flɔp] *n* fiasco ♦ *vi* far fiasco; (*fall*) lasciarsi cadere

floppy ['flɔpɪ] *adj* floscio(a), molle; **~ (disk)** *n* (*COMPUT*) floppy disk *m inv*

Florence ['flɔrəns] *n* Firenze *f*; **Florentine** ['flɔrəntaɪn] *adj* fiorentino(a)

florid ['flɔrɪd] *adj* (*complexion*) florido(a); (*style*) fiorito(a)

florist ['flɔrɪst] *n* fioraio/a

flounder ['flaundə*] *vi* annaspare ♦ *n* (*ZOOL*) passera di mare

flour ['flauə*] *n* farina

flourish ['flʌrɪʃ] *vi* fiorire ♦ *n* (*bold gesture*): **with a ~** con ostentazione; **~ing** *adj* florido(a)

flout [flaut] *vt* (*order*) contravvenire a

flow [fləu] *n* flusso; circolazione *f* ♦ *vi* fluire; (*traffic, blood in veins*) circolare; (*hair*) scendere; **~ chart** *n* schema *m* di flusso

flower ['flauə*] *n* fiore *m* ♦ *vi* fiorire; **~ bed** *n* aiuola; **~pot** *n* vaso da fiori; **~y** *adj* (*perfume*) di fiori; (*pattern*) a fiori; (*speech*) fiorito(a)

flown [fləun] *pp of* **fly**

flu [flu:] *n* influenza

fluctuate ['flʌktjueɪt] *vi* fluttuare, oscillare

fluent ['flu:ənt] *adj* (*speech*) facile, sciolto(a); corrente; **he speaks ~ Italian, he's ~ in Italian** parla l'italiano correntemente

fluff [flʌf] *n* lanugine *f*; **~y** *adj* lanuginoso(a); (*toy*) di peluche

fluid ['flu:ɪd] *adj* fluido(a) ♦ *n* fluido

fluke [flu:k] (*inf*) *n* colpo di fortuna

flung [flʌŋ] *pt, pp of* **fling**

fluoride ['fluəraɪd] *n* fluoruro; **~ toothpaste** dentifricio al fluoro

flurry ['flʌrɪ] *n* (*of snow*) tempesta; **a ~ of activity** una scoppio di attività

flush [flʌʃ] *n* rossore *m*; (*fig: of youth, beauty etc*) rigoglio, pieno vigore ♦ *vt* ripulire con un getto d'acqua ♦ *vi* arrossire ♦ *adj:* **~ with** a livello di, pari a; **to ~ the toilet** tirare l'acqua; **~ed** *adj* tutto(a) rosso(a)

flustered ['flʌstəd] *adj* sconvolto(a)

flute [flu:t] *n* flauto

flutter ['flʌtə*] *n* agitazione *f*; (*of wings*) battito ♦ *vi* (*bird*) battere le ali

flux [flʌks] *n*: **in a state of ~** in continuo mutamento

fly [flaɪ] (*pt* **flew**, *pp* **flown**) *n* (*insect*) mosca; (*on trousers: also:* **flies**) chiusura ♦ *vt* pilotare; (*passengers, cargo*) trasportare (in aereo); (*distances*) percorrere ♦ *vi* volare; (*passengers*) andare in aereo; (*escape*) fuggire; (*flag*) sventolare; **~ away** *or* **off** *vi*

volare via; **~ing** *n* (*activity*) aviazione *f*; (*action*) volo ♦ *adj:* **~ing visit** visita volante; **with ~ing colours** con risultati brillanti; **~ing saucer** *n* disco volante; **~ing start** *n*: **to get off to a ~ing start** partire come un razzo; **~over** (*BRIT*) *n* (*bridge*) cavalcavia *m inv*; **~sheet** *n* (*for tent*) sopratetto

foal [fəul] *n* puledro

foam [fəum] *n* schiuma; (*also:* **~ rubber**) gommapiuma ® ♦ *vi* schiumare; (*soapy water*) fare la schiuma

fob [fɔb] *vt:* **to ~ sb off with** rifilare a qn

focus ['fəukəs] (*pl* **~es**) *n* fuoco; (*of interest*) centro ♦ *vt* (*field glasses etc*) mettere a fuoco ♦ *vi:* **to ~ on** (*with camera*) mettere a fuoco; (*person*) fissare lo sguardo su; **in ~** a fuoco; **out of ~** sfocato(a)

fodder ['fɔdə*] *n* foraggio

foe [fəu] *n* nemico

foetus ['fi:təs] (*US* **fetus**) *n* feto

fog [fɔg] *n* nebbia; **~gy** *adj:* **it's ~gy** c'è nebbia; **~ lamp** (*US* **~ light**) *n* (*AUT*) faro *m* antinebbia *inv*

foil [fɔɪl] *vt* confondere, frustrare ♦ *n* lamina di metallo; (*kitchen ~*) foglio di alluminio; (*FENCING*) fioretto; **to act as a ~ to** (*fig*) far risaltare

fold [fəuld] *n* (*bend, crease*) piega; (*AGR*) ovile *m*; (*fig*) gregge *m* ♦ *vt* piegare; (*arms*) incrociare; **~ up** *vi* (*map, bed, table*) piegarsi; (*business*) crollare ♦ *vt* (*map etc*) piegare, ripiegare; **~er** *n* (*for papers*) cartella; cartellina; **~ing** *adj* (*chair, bed*) pieghevole

foliage ['fəulɪdʒ] *n* fogliame *m*

folk [fəuk] *npl* gente *f* ♦ *adj* popolare; **~s** *npl* (*family*) famiglia; **~lore** ['fəuklɔ:*] *n* folclore *m*; **~ song** *n* canto popolare

follow ['fɔləu] *vt* seguire ♦ *vi* seguire; (*result*) conseguire, risultare; **to ~ suit** fare lo stesso; **~ up** *vt* (*letter, offer*) fare seguito a; (*case*) seguire; **~er** *n* seguace *m/f*, discepolo/a; **~ing** *adj* seguente ♦ *n* seguito, discepoli *mpl*; **~-on call** *n* chiamata successiva

folly ['fɔlɪ] *n* pazzia, follia

fond [fɔnd] *adj* (*memory, look*) tenero(a), affettuoso(a); **to be ~ of sb** volere bene a qn; **he's ~ of walking** gli piace fare camminate

fondle ['fɔndl] *vt* accarezzare

font [fɔnt] *n* (*in church*) fonte *m* battesimale; (*TYP*) caratteri *mpl*

food [fu:d] *n* cibo; **~ mixer** *n* frullatore *m*; **~ poisoning** *n* intossicazione *f*; **~ processor** *n* tritatutto *m inv* elettrico; **~stuffs** *npl* generi *fpl* alimentari

fool [fu:l] *n* sciocco/a; (*CULIN*) frullato ♦ *vt* ingannare ♦ *vi* (*gen: ~ around*) fare lo sciocco; **~hardy** *adj* avventato(a); **~ish** *adj* scemo(a), stupido(a); imprudente; **~proof** *adj* (*plan etc*) sicurissimo(a)

foot [fut] (*pl* **feet**) *n* piede *m*; (*measure*) piede (= 304 *mm*; 12 *inches*); (*of animal*) zampa ♦ *vt* (*bill*) pagare; **on ~** a piedi; **~age** *n* (*CINEMA*: *length*) ≈ metraggio; (: *material*) sequenza; **~ball** *n* pallone *m*; (*sport*: *BRIT*) calcio; (: *US*) football *m* americano; **~ball player** *n* (*BRIT*: *also*: **~baller**) calciatore *m*; (*US*) giocatore *m* di football americano; **~brake** *n* freno a pedale; **~bridge** *n* passerella; **~hills** *npl* contrafforti *fpl*; **~hold** *n* punto d'appoggio; **~ing** *n* (*fig*) posizione *f*; **to lose one's ~ing** mettere un piede in fallo; **~lights** *npl* luci *fpl* della ribalta; **~note** *n* nota (a piè di pagina); **~path** *n* sentiero; (*in street*) marciapiede *m*; **~print** *n* orma, impronta; **~step** *n* passo; (*~print*) orma, impronta; **~wear** *n* calzatura

KEYWORD

for [fɔː*] *prep* **1** (*indicating destination, intention, purpose*) per; **the train ~ London** il treno per Londra; **he went ~ the paper** è andato a prendere il giornale; **it's time ~ lunch** è ora di pranzo; **what's it ~?** a che serve?; **what ~?** (*why*) perché?
2 (*on behalf of, representing*) per; **to work ~ sb/sth** lavorare per qn/qc; **I'll ask him ~ you** glielo chiederò a nome tuo; **G ~ George** G come George
3 (*because of*) per, a causa di; **~ this reason** per questo motivo
4 (*with regard to*) per; **it's cold ~ July** è freddo per luglio; **~ everyone who voted yes, 50 voted no** per ogni voto a favore ce n'erano 50 contro
5 (*in exchange for*) per; **I sold it ~ £5** l'ho venduto per 5 sterline
6 (*in favour of*) per, a favore di; **are you ~ or against us?** è con noi o contro di noi?; **I'm all ~ it** sono completamente a favore
7 (*referring to distance, time*) per; **there are roadworks ~ 5 km** ci sono lavori in corso per 5 km; **he was away ~ 2 years** è stato via per 2 anni; **she will be away ~ a month** starà via un mese; **it hasn't rained ~ 3 weeks** non piove da 3 settimane; **can you do it ~ tomorrow?** può farlo per domani?
8 (*with infinitive clauses*): **it is not ~ me to decide** non sta a me decidere; **it would be best ~ you to leave** sarebbe meglio che lei se ne andasse; **there is still time ~ you to do it** ha ancora tempo per farlo; **~ this to be possible ...** perché ciò sia possibile ...
9 (*in spite of*) nonostante; **~ all his complaints, he's very fond of her** nonostante tutte le sue lamentele, le vuole molto bene ♦ *conj* (*since, as*: *rather formal*) dal momento che, poiché

forage ['fɔrɪdʒ] *vi*: **to ~ (for)** andare in cerca (di)
foray ['fɔreɪ] *n* incursione *f*
forbid [fə'bɪd] (*pt* **forbad(e)**, *pp* **forbidden**) *vt* vietare, interdire; **to ~ sb to do sth** proibire a qn di fare qc; **~ding** *adj* minaccioso(a)
force [fɔːs] *n* forza ♦ *vt* forzare; **the F~s** (*BRIT*) *npl* le forze armate; **to ~ o.s. to do** costringersi a fare; **in ~** (*in large numbers*) in gran numero; (*law*) in vigore; **~d** *adj* forzato(a); **~-feed** *vt* (*animal, prisoner*) sottoporre ad alimentazione forzata; **~ful** *adj* forte, vigoroso(a)
forceps ['fɔːsɛps] *npl* forcipe *m*
forcibly ['fɔːsəblɪ] *adv* con la forza; (*vigorously*) vigorosamente
ford [fɔːd] *n* guado
fore [fɔː*] *n*: **to come to the ~** mettersi in evidenza
forearm ['fɔːrɑːm] *n* avambraccio
foreboding [fɔː'bəudɪŋ] *n* cattivo presagio
forecast ['fɔːkɑːst] (*irreg*: *like* **cast**) *n* previsione *f* ♦ *vt* prevedere
forecourt ['fɔːkɔːt] *n* (*of garage*) corte *f* esterna
forefinger ['fɔːfɪŋgə*] *n* (dito) indice *m*
forefront ['fɔːfrʌnt] *n*: **in the ~ of** all'avanguardia in
forego [fɔː'gəu] (*irreg*: *like* **go**) *vt* rinunciare a
foregone [fɔː'gɒn] *pp of* **forego** ♦ *adj*: **it's a ~ conclusion** è una conclusione scontata
foreground ['fɔːgraund] *n* primo piano
forehead ['fɔrɪd] *n* fronte *f*
foreign ['fɔrɪn] *adj* straniero(a); (*trade*) estero(a); (*object, matter*) estraneo(a); **~er** *n* straniero/a; **~ exchange** *n* cambio con l'estero; (*currency*) valuta estera; **F~ Office** (*BRIT*) *n* Ministero degli Esteri; **F~ Secretary** (*BRIT*) *n* ministro degli Affari esteri
foreleg ['fɔːlɛg] *n* zampa anteriore
foreman ['fɔːmən] (*irreg*) *n* caposquadra *m*
foremost ['fɔːməust] *adj* principale; più in vista ♦ *adv*: **first and ~** innanzitutto
forensic [fə'rɛnsɪk] *adj*: **~ medicine** medicina legale
forerunner ['fɔːrʌnə*] *n* precursore *m*
foresaw [fɔː'sɔː] *pt of* **foresee**
foresee [fɔː'siː] (*irreg*: *like* **see**) *vt* prevedere; **~able** *adj* prevedibile; **foreseen** *pp of* **foresee**
foreshadow [fɔː'ʃædəu] *vt* presagire, far prevedere
foresight ['fɔːsaɪt] *n* previdenza
forest ['fɔrɪst] *n* foresta
forestry ['fɔrɪstrɪ] *n* silvicoltura
foretaste ['fɔːteɪst] *n* pregustazione *f*
foretell [fɔː'tɛl] (*irreg*: *like* **tell**) *vt* predire; **foretold** [fɔː'təuld] *pt, pp of* **foretell**
forever [fə'rɛvə*] *adv* per sempre; (*endlessly*)

sempre, di continuo

foreword ['fɔːwəːd] n prefazione f

forfeit ['fɔːfɪt] vt perdere; (one's happiness, health) giocarsi

forgave [fəˈgeɪv] pt of **forgive**

forge [fɔːdʒ] n fucina ♦ vt (signature, money) contraffare, falsificare; (wrought iron) fucinare, foggiare; **~ ahead** vi tirare avanti; **~ry** n falso; (activity) contraffazione f

forget [fəˈɡet] (pt **forgot**, pp **forgotten**) vt, vi dimenticare; **~ful** adj di corta memoria; **~ful of** dimentico(a) di; **~-me-not** n nontiscordardimé m inv

forgive [fəˈɡɪv] (pt **forgave**, pp **forgiven**) vt perdonare; **to ~ sb for sth** perdonare qc a qn; **~ness** n perdono

forgo [fɔːˈɡəu] = **forego**

forgot [fəˈɡɔt] pt of **forget**

forgotten [fəˈɡɔtn] pp of **forget**

fork [fɔːk] n (for eating) forchetta; (for gardening) forca; (of roads, rivers, railways) biforcazione f ♦ vi (road etc) biforcarsi; **~ out** (inf) vt (pay) sborsare; **~-lift truck** n carrello elevatore

forlorn [fəˈlɔːn] adj (person) sconsolato(a); (place) abbandonato(a); (attempt) disperato(a); (hope) vano(a)

form [fɔːm] n forma; (SCOL) classe f; (questionnaire) scheda ♦ vt formare; **in top ~** in gran forma

formal ['fɔːməl] adj formale; (gardens) simmetrico(a), regolare; **~ly** adv formalmente

format ['fɔːmæt] n formato ♦ vt (COMPUT) formattare

formation [fɔːˈmeɪʃən] n formazione f

formative ['fɔːmətɪv] adj: **~ years** anni mpl formativi

former ['fɔːmə*] adj vecchio(a) (before n), ex inv (before n); **the ~ ... the latter** quello ... questo; **~ly** adv in passato

formula ['fɔːmjulə] n formula

forsake [fəˈseɪk] (pt **forsook**, pp **forsaken**) vt abbandonare

fort [fɔːt] n forte m

forth [fɔːθ] adv in avanti; **back and ~** avanti e indietro; **and so ~** e così via; **~coming** adj (event) prossimo(a); (help) disponibile; (character) aperto(a), comunicativo(a); **~right** adj franco(a), schietto(a); **~with** adv immediatamente, subito

fortify ['fɔːtɪfaɪ] vt (city) fortificare; (person) armare

fortitude ['fɔːtɪtjuːd] n forza d'animo

fortnight ['fɔːtnaɪt] (BRIT) n quindici giorni mpl, due settimane fpl; **~ly** adj bimensile ♦ adv ogni quindici giorni

fortress ['fɔːtrɪs] n fortezza, rocca

fortunate ['fɔːtʃənɪt] adj fortunato(a); **it is ~ that** è una fortuna che; **~ly** adv fortunatamente

fortune ['fɔːtʃən] n fortuna; **~-teller** n indovino/a

forty ['fɔːtɪ] num quaranta

forum ['fɔːrəm] n foro

forward ['fɔːwəd] adj (ahead of schedule) in anticipo; (movement, position) in avanti; (not shy) aperto(a); diretto(a) ♦ n (SPORT) avanti m inv ♦ vt (letter) inoltrare; (parcel, goods) spedire; (career, plans) promuovere, appoggiare; **to move ~** avanzare; **~(s)** adv avanti

fossil ['fɔsl] adj fossile ♦ n fossile m

foster ['fɔstə*] vt incoraggiare, nutrire; (child) avere in affidamento; **~ child** n bambino(a) preso(a) in affidamento

fought [fɔːt] pt, pp of **fight**

foul [faul] adj (smell, food, temper etc) cattivo(a); (weather) brutto(a); (language) osceno(a) ♦ n (SPORT) fallo ♦ vt sporcare; **~ play** n (LAW): **the police suspect ~ play** la polizia sospetta un atto criminale

found [faund] pt, pp of **find** ♦ vt (establish) fondare; **~ation** [-ˈdeɪʃən] n (act) fondazione f; (base) base f; (also: **~ation cream**) fondo tinta; **~ations** npl (of building) fondamenta fpl

founder ['faundə*] n fondatore/trice ♦ vi affondare

foundry ['faundrɪ] n fonderia

fountain ['fauntɪn] n fontana; **~ pen** n penna stilografica

four [fɔː*] num quattro; **on all ~s** a carponi; **~-poster** n (also: **~-poster bed**) letto a quattro colonne; **~teen** num quattordici; **~th** num quarto(a)

fowl [faul] n pollame m; volatile m

fox [fɔks] n volpe f ♦ vt confondere

foyer ['fɔɪeɪ] n atrio; (THEATRE) ridotto

fraction ['frækʃən] n frazione f

fracture ['fræktʃə*] n frattura

fragile ['frædʒaɪl] adj fragile

fragment ['frægmənt] n frammento

fragrant ['freɪɡrənt] adj fragrante, profumato(a)

frail [freɪl] adj debole, delicato(a)

frame [freɪm] n (of building) armatura; (of human, animal) ossatura, corpo; (of picture) cornice f; (of door, window) telaio; (of spectacles: also: **~s**) montatura ♦ vt (picture) incorniciare; **~ of mind** n stato d'animo; **~work** n struttura

France [frɑːns] n Francia

franchise ['fræntʃaɪz] n (POL) diritto di voto; (COMM) concessione f

frank [fræŋk] adj franco(a), aperto(a) ♦ vt (letter) affrancare; **~ly** adv francamente, sinceramente

frantic ['fræntɪk] adj frenetico(a)

fraternity [frəˈtəːnɪtɪ] n (club) associazione f;

(*spirit*) fratellanza

fraud [frɔːd] *n* truffa; (*LAW*) frode *f*; (*person*) impostore/a

fraught [frɔːt] *adj*: ~ **with** pieno(a) di, intriso(a) da

fray [freɪ] *vt* logorare ♦ *vi* logorarsi

freak [friːk] *n* fenomeno, mostro

freckle ['frɛkl] *n* lentiggine *f*

free [friː] *adj* libero(a); (*gratis*) gratuito(a) ♦ *vt* (*prisoner, jammed person*) liberare; (*jammed object*) districare; ~ (**of charge**), **for** ~ gratuitamente; **~dom** ['friːdəm] *n* libertà; **F~fone** ® *n* numero verde; **~-for-all** *n* parapiglia *m* generale; ~ **gift** *n* regalo, -omaggio; **~hold** *n* proprietà assoluta; ~ **kick** *n* calcio libero; **~lance** *adj* indipendente; **~ly** *adv* liberamente; (*liberally*) liberalmente; **F~mason** *n* massone *m*; **F~post** ® *n* affrancatura a carico del destinatario; **~-range** *adj* (*hen*) ruspante; (*eggs*) di gallina ruspante; **~style** *n* (*SPORT*) stile *m* libero; ~ **trade** *n* libero scambio; **~way** *n* (*US*) *n* superstrada; ~ **will** *n* libero arbitrio; **of one's own** ~ **will** di spontanea volontà

freeze [friːz] (*pt* **froze**, *pp* **frozen**) *vi* gelare ♦ *vt* gelare; (*food*) congelare; (*prices, salaries*) bloccare ♦ *n* gelo; blocco; **~-dried** *adj* liofilizzato(a); **~r** *n* congelatore *m*

freezing ['friːzɪŋ] *adj* (*wind, weather*) gelido(a); ~ **point** *n* punto di congelamento; **3 degrees below** ~ **point** 3 gradi sotto zero

freight [freɪt] *n* (*goods*) merce *f*, merci *fpl*; (*money charged*) spese *fpl* di trasporto; ~ **train** *n* (*US*) *n* treno *m* merci *inv*

French [frɛntʃ] *adj* francese ♦ *n* (*LING*) francese *m*; **the** ~ *npl* i Francesi; ~ **bean** *n* fagiolino; ~ **fried potatoes** (*US* = **fries**) *npl* patate *fpl* fritte; **~man** (*irreg*) *n* francese *m*; ~ **window** *n* portafinestra; **~woman** (*irreg*) *n* francese *f*

frenzy ['frɛnzɪ] *n* frenesia

frequency ['friːkwənsɪ] *n* frequenza

frequent [*adj* 'friːkwənt, *vb* frɪ'kwɛnt] *adj* frequente ♦ *vt* frequentare; **~ly** *adv* frequentemente, spesso

fresco ['frɛskəʊ] *n* affresco

fresh [frɛʃ] *adj* fresco(a); (*new*) nuovo(a); (*cheeky*) sfacciato(a); **~en** *vi* (*wind, air*) rinfrescare; **~en up** *vi* rinfrescarsi; **~er** (*BRIT*: *inf*) *n* (*SCOL*) matricola; **~ly** *adv* di recente, di fresco; **~man** (*irreg*) (*US*) *n* = **~er**; **~ness** *n* freschezza; **~water** *adj* (*fish*) d'acqua dolce

fret [frɛt] *vi* agitarsi, affliggersi

friar ['fraɪə*] *n* frate *m*

friction ['frɪkʃən] *n* frizione *f*, attrito

Friday ['fraɪdɪ] *n* venerdì *m inv*

fridge [frɪdʒ] (*BRIT*) *n* frigo, frigorifero

fried [fraɪd] *pt*, *pp* of **fry** ♦ *adj* fritto(a)

friend [frɛnd] *n* amico/a; **~ly** *adj* amichevole; **~ly fire** *n* (*MIL*) fuoco amico; **~ship** *n* amicizia

frieze [friːz] *n* fregio

fright [fraɪt] *n* paura, spavento; **to take** ~ spaventarsi; **~en** *vt* spaventare, far paura a; **~ened** *adj* spaventato(a); **~ening** *adj* spaventoso(a), pauroso(a); **~ful** *adj* orribile

frill [frɪl] *n* balza

fringe [frɪndʒ] *n* (*decoration, BRIT*: *of hair*) frangia; (*edge*: *of forest etc*) margine *m*; ~ **benefits** *npl* vantaggi *mpl*

frisk [frɪsk] *vt* perquisire

frisky ['frɪskɪ] *adj* vivace, vispo(a)

fritter ['frɪtə*] *n* frittella; ~ **away** *vt* sprecare

frivolous ['frɪvələs] *adj* frivolo(a)

frizzy ['frɪzɪ] *adj* crespo(a)

fro [frəʊ] *see* **to**

frock [frɒk] *n* vestito

frog [frɒg] *n* rana; **~man** (*irreg*) *n* uomo *m* rana *inv*

frolic ['frɒlɪk] *vi* sgambettare

KEYWORD

---

from [frɒm] *prep* **1** (*indicating starting place, origin etc*) da; **where do you come** ~?, **where are you** ~? da dove viene?, di dov'è?; ~ **London to Glasgow** da Londra a Glasgow; **a letter** ~ **my sister** una lettera da mia sorella; **tell him** ~ **me that** ... gli dica da parte mia che ...

2 (*indicating time*) da; ~ **one o'clock to** or **until** or **till two** dall'una alle due; ~ **January (on)** da gennaio, a partire da gennaio

3 (*indicating distance*) da; **the hotel is 1 km** ~ **the beach** l'albergo è a 1 km dalla spiaggia

4 (*indicating price, number etc*) da; **prices range** ~ **£10 to £50** i prezzi vanno dalle 10 alle 50 sterline

5 (*indicating difference*) da; **he can't tell red** ~ **green** non sa distinguere il rosso dal verde

6 (*because of, on the basis of*): ~ **what he says** da quanto dice lui; **weak** ~ **hunger** debole per la fame

---

front [frʌnt] *n* (*of house, dress*) davanti *m inv*; (*of train*) testa; (*of book*) copertina; (*promenade*: *also*: **sea** ~) lungomare *m*; (*MIL, POL, METEOR*) fronte *m*; (*fig*: *appearances*) fronte *f* ♦ *adj* primo(a); anteriore, davanti *inv*; **in** ~ **of** davanti a; ~ **door** *n* porta d'entrata; (*of car*) sportello anteriore; **~ier** ['frʌntɪə*] *n* frontiera; ~ **page** *n* prima pagina; ~ **room** (*BRIT*) *n* salotto; **~-wheel drive** *n* trasmissione *f* anteriore

frost [frɒst] *n* gelo; (*also*: **hoar~**) brina; **~bite** *n* congelamento; **~ed** *adj* (*glass*) smerigliato(a); **~y** *adj* (*weather, look*) gelido(a)

froth [frɔθ] n spuma; schiuma

frown [fraun] vi accigliarsi

froze [frəuz] pt of **freeze**; **frozen** pp of **freeze**

fruit [fru:t] n inv (also fig) frutto; (collectively) frutta; **~erer** n fruttivendolo; **~erer's (shop)** n: **at the ~erer's (shop)** dal fruttivendolo; **~ful** adj fruttuoso(a); **~ion** [fru:'ɪʃən] n: **to come to ~ion** realizzarsi; **~ juice** n succo di frutta; **~ machine** (BRIT) n macchina f mangiasoldi inv; **~ salad** n macedonia

frustrate [frʌs'treɪt] vt frustrare

fry [fraɪ] (pt, pp **fried**) vt friggere; see also **small**; **~ing pan** n padella

ft. abbr = **foot**; **feet**

fudge [fʌdʒ] n (CULIN) specie di caramella a base di latte, burro e zucchero

fuel [fjuəl] n (for heating) combustibile m; (for propelling) carburante m; **~ tank** n deposito m nafta inv; (on vehicle) serbatoio (della benzina)

fugitive [fju:dʒɪtɪv] n fuggitivo/a, profugo/a

fulfil [ful'fil] vt (function) compiere; (order) eseguire; (wish, desire) soddisfare, appagare; **~ment** (US **fulfillment**) n (of wishes) soddisfazione f, appagamento; **sense of ~ment** soddisfazione

full [ful] adj pieno(a); (details, skirt) ampio(a) ♦ adv: **to know ~ well that** sapere benissimo che; **I'm ~ (up)** sono pieno; **a ~ two hours** due ore intere; **at ~ speed** a tutta velocità; **in ~** per intero; **~ board** (BRIT) n pensione f completa; **~ employment** n piena occupazione; **~-length** adj (film) a lungometraggio; (coat, novel) lungo(a); (portrait) in piedi; **~ moon** n luna piena; **~-scale** adj (attack, war) su larga scala; (model) in grandezza naturale; **~ stop** n punto; **~-time** adj, adv (work) a tempo pieno; **~y** adv interamente, pienamente, completamente; (at least) almeno; **~y-fledged** adj (teacher, member etc) a tutti gli effetti; **~y licensed** adj (hotel, restaurant) autorizzato(a) alla vendita di alcolici

fumble [fʌmbl] vi: **to ~ with sth** armeggiare con qc

fume [fju:m] vi essere furioso(a); **~s** npl esalazioni fpl, vapori mpl

fun [fʌn] n divertimento, spasso; **to have ~** divertirsi; **for ~** per scherzo; **to make ~ of** prendersi gioco di

function ['fʌŋkʃən] n funzione f; cerimonia, ricevimento ♦ vi funzionare; **~al** adj funzionale

fund [fʌnd] n fondo, cassa; (source) fondo; (store) riserva; **~s** npl (money) fondi mpl

fundamental [fʌndə'mentl] adj fondamentale

funeral ['fju:nərəl] n funerale m; **~ parlour** n

impresa di pompe funebri; **~ service** n ufficio funebre

fun fair (BRIT) n luna park m inv

fungus ['fʌŋgəs] (pl **fungi**) n fungo; (mould) muffa

funnel ['fʌnl] n imbuto; (of ship) ciminiera

funny ['fʌnɪ] adj divertente, buffo(a); (strange) strano(a), bizzarro(a)

fur [fə:*] n pelo; pelliccia; (BRIT: in kettle etc) deposito calcare; **~ coat** n pelliccia

furious ['fjuərɪəs] adj furioso(a); (effort) accanito(a)

furlong ['fə:lɔŋ] n = 201.17 m (termine ippico)

furnace ['fə:nɪs] n fornace f

furnish ['fə:nɪʃ] vt ammobiliare; (supply) fornire; **~ings** npl mobili mpl, mobilia

furniture ['fə:nɪtʃə*] n mobili mpl; **piece of ~** mobile m

furrow ['fʌrəu] n solco

furry ['fə:rɪ] adj (animal) peloso(a)

further ['fə:ðə*] adj supplementare, altro(a); nuovo(a); più lontano(a) ♦ adv più lontano; (more) di più; (moreover) inoltre ♦ vt favorire, promuovere; **college of ~ education** n istituto statale con corsi specializzati (di formazione professionale, aggiornamento professionale etc); **~more** [fə:ðə'mɔ:*] adv inoltre, per di più

furthest ['fə:ðɪst] superl of **far**

fury ['fjuərɪ] n furore m

fuse [fju:z] n fusibile m; (for bomb etc) miccia, spoletta ♦ vt fondere ♦ vi fondersi; **to ~ the lights** (BRIT: ELEC) far saltare i fusibili; **~ box** n cassetta dei fusibili

fuselage ['fju:zəlɑ:ʒ] n fusoliera

fuss [fʌs] n agitazione f; (complaining) storie fpl; **to make a ~** fare delle storie; **~y** adj (person) puntiglioso(a), esigente; che fa le storie; (dress) carico(a) di fronzoli; (style) elaborato(a)

future ['fju:tʃə*] adj futuro(a) ♦ n futuro, avvenire m; (LING) futuro; **in ~** in futuro

fuze [fju:z] (US) = **fuse**

fuzzy ['fʌzɪ] adj (PHOT) indistinto(a), sfocato(a); (hair) crespo(a)

G, g

G [dʒi:] n (MUS) sol m

G8 abbr (= Group of Eight) G8

gabble ['gæbl] vi borbottare; farfugliare

gable ['geɪbl] n frontone m

gadget ['gædʒɪt] n aggeggio

Gaelic ['geɪlɪk] adj gaelico(a) ♦ n (LING) gaelico

gag [gæg] n bavaglio; (joke) facezia, scherzo ♦ vt imbavagliare

gaiety ['geɪtɪ] n gaiezza
gaily ['geɪlɪ] adv allegramente
gain [geɪn] n guadagno, profitto ♦ vt guadagnare ♦ vi (clock, watch) andare avanti; (benefit): **to ~ (from)** trarre beneficio (da); **to ~ 3lbs (in weight)** aumentare di 3 libbre; **to ~ on sb** (in race etc) guadagnare su qn
gal. abbr = **gallon**
galaxy ['gæləksɪ] n galassia
gale [geɪl] n vento forte; burrasca
gallant ['gælənt] adj valoroso(a); (towards ladies) galante, cortese
gall bladder ['gɔːl-] n cistifellea
gallery ['gælərɪ] n galleria
gallon ['gælən] n gallone m (= 8 pints; BRIT = 4.543l; US = 3.785l)
gallop ['gæləp] n galoppo ♦ vi galoppare
gallows ['gæləʊz] n forca
gallstone ['gɔːlstəʊn] n calcolo biliare
galore [gə'lɔː*] adv a iosa, a profusione
galvanize ['gælvənaɪz] vt galvanizzare
gambit ['gæmbɪt] n (fig): **(opening) ~** prima mossa
gamble ['gæmbl] n azzardo, rischio calcolato ♦ vt, vi giocare; **to ~ on** (fig) giocare su; **~r** n giocatore/trice d'azzardo; **gambling** n gioco d'azzardo
game [geɪm] n gioco; (event) partita; (TENNIS) game m inv; (CULIN, HUNTING) selvaggina ♦ adj (ready): **to be ~ (for sth/to do)** essere pronto(a) (a qc/a fare); **big ~** selvaggina grossa; **~keeper** n guardacaccia m inv
gammon ['gæmən] n (bacon) quarto di maiale; (ham) prosciutto affumicato
gamut ['gæmət] n gamma
gang [gæŋ] n banda, squadra ♦ vi: **to ~ up on sb** far combutta contro qn
gangrene ['gæŋgriːn] n cancrena
gangster ['gæŋstə*] n gangster m inv
gangway ['gæŋweɪ] n passerella; (BRIT: of bus) corridoio
gaol [dʒeɪl] (BRIT) n, vt = **jail**
gap [gæp] n (space) buco; (in time) intervallo; (difference): **~ (between)** divario (tra)
gape [geɪp] vi (person) restare a bocca aperta; (shirt, hole) essere spalancato(a); **gaping** adj spalancato(a)
garage ['gærɑːʒ] n garage m inv
garbage ['gɑːbɪdʒ] n (US) immondizie fpl, rifiuti mpl; (inf) sciocchezze fpl; **~ can** (US) n bidone m della spazzatura
garbled ['gɑːbld] adj deformato(a); ingarbugliato(a)
garden ['gɑːdn] n giardino; **~s** npl (public park) giardini pubblici; **~er** n giardiniere/a; **~ing** n giardinaggio
gargle ['gɑːgl] vi fare gargarismi
garish ['gɛərɪʃ] adj vistoso(a)
garland ['gɑːlənd] n ghirlanda; corona

garlic ['gɑːlɪk] n aglio
garment ['gɑːmənt] n indumento
garnish ['gɑːnɪʃ] vt (food) guarnire
garrison ['gærɪsn] n guarnigione f
garter ['gɑːtə*] n giarrettiera
gas [gæs] n gas m inv; (US: gasoline) benzina ♦ vt asfissiare con il gas; **~ cooker** (BRIT) n cucina a gas; **~ cylinder** n bombola del gas; **~ fire** (BRIT) n radiatore m a gas
gash [gæʃ] n sfregio ♦ vt sfregiare
gasket ['gæskɪt] n (AUT) guarnizione f
gas mask n maschera f antigas inv
gas meter n contatore m del gas
gasoline ['gæsəliːn] (US) n benzina
gasp [gɑːsp] n respiro affannoso, ansito ♦ vi ansare, ansimare; (in surprise) restare senza fiato
gas station (US) n distributore m di benzina
gassy ['gæsɪ] adj gassoso(a)
gate [geɪt] n cancello; (at airport) uscita; **~crash** (BRIT) vt partecipare senza invito a; **~way** n porta
gather ['gæðə*] vt (flowers, fruit) cogliere; (pick up) raccogliere; (assemble) radunare; raccogliere; (understand) capire; (SEWING) increspare ♦ vt (assemble) radunarsi; **to ~ speed** acquistare velocità; **~ing** n adunanza
gauche [gəʊʃ] adj goffo(a), maldestro(a)
gaudy ['gɔːdɪ] adj vistoso(a)
gauge [geɪdʒ] n (instrument) indicatore m ♦ vt misurare; (fig) valutare
gaunt [gɔːnt] adj scarno(a); (grim, desolate) desolato(a)
gauntlet ['gɔːntlɪt] n guanto; (fig): **to run the ~ through an angry crowd** passare sotto il fuoco di una folla ostile; **to throw down the ~** gettare il guanto
gauze [gɔːz] n garza
gave [geɪv] pt of **give**
gay [geɪ] adj (homosexual) omosessuale; (cheerful) gaio(a), allegro(a); (colour) vivace, vivo(a)
gaze [geɪz] n sguardo fisso ♦ vi: **to ~ at** guardare fisso
GB abbr = **Great Britain**
GCE (BRIT) n abbr (= General Certificate of Education) ≈ maturità
GCSE (BRIT) n abbr (= General Certificate of Secondary Education)
gear [gɪə*] n attrezzi mpl, equipaggiamento; (TECH) ingranaggio; (AUT) marcia ♦ vt (fig: adapt): **to ~ sth to** adattare qc a; **in top** or (US) **high/low ~** in quarta (or quinta)/ seconda; **in ~** in marcia; **~ box** n scatola del cambio; **~ lever** (US = **shift**) n leva del cambio
geese [giːs] npl of **goose**
gel [dʒel] n gel m inv
gem [dʒɛm] n gemma

Gemini ['dʒɛmɪnaɪ] n Gemelli mpl

gender ['dʒɛndə*] n genere m

general ['dʒɛnərl] n generale m ♦ adj
generale; **in ~** in genere; **~ delivery** (US) n
fermo posta m; **~ election** n elezioni fpl
generali; **~ly** adv generalmente

general practitioner n medico generico

generate ['dʒɛnəreɪt] vt generare

generation [dʒɛnə'reɪʃən] n generazione f

generator ['dʒɛnəreɪtə*] n generatore m

generosity [dʒɛnə'rɔsɪtɪ] n generosità

generous ['dʒɛnərəs] adj generoso(a);
(copious) abbondante

genetic engineering [dʒɪ'nɛtɪk-
ɛndʒɪ'nɪərɪŋ] n ingegneria genetica

genetic fingerprinting [-'fɪŋgəprɪntɪŋ] n
rilevamento delle impronte genetiche

Geneva [dʒɪ'niːvə] n Ginevra

genial ['dʒiːnɪəl] adj geniale, cordiale

genitals ['dʒɛnɪtlz] npl genitali mpl

genius ['dʒiːnɪəs] n genio

Genoa ['dʒɛnəuə] n Genova

gent [dʒɛnt] n abbr = **gentleman**

genteel [dʒɛn'tiːl] adj raffinato(a), distinto(a)

gentle ['dʒɛntl] adj delicato(a); (person)
dolce

gentleman ['dʒɛntlmən] n signore m; (well-
bred man) gentiluomo

gently ['dʒɛntlɪ] adv delicatamente

gentry ['dʒɛntrɪ] n nobiltà minore

gents [dʒɛnts] n W.C. m (per signori)

genuine ['dʒɛnjuɪn] adj autentico(a);
sincero(a)

geography [dʒɪ'ɔgrəfɪ] n geografia

geology [dʒɪ'ɔlədʒɪ] n geologia

geometric(al) [dʒɪə'mɛtrɪk(l)] adj
geometrico(a)

geometry [dʒɪ'ɔmətrɪ] n geometria

geranium [dʒɪ'reɪnjəm] n geranio

geriatric [dʒɛrɪ'ætrɪk] adj geriatrico(a)

germ [dʒəːm] n (MED) microbo; (BIOL, fig)
germe m

German ['dʒəːmən] adj tedesco(a) ♦ n
tedesco/a; (LING) tedesco; **~ measles** (BRIT)
n rosolia

Germany ['dʒəːmənɪ] n Germania

gesture ['dʒɛstjə*] n gesto

KEYWORD

get [gɛt] (pt, pp **got**, (US) pp **gotten**) vi **1**
(become, be) diventare, farsi; **to ~ old**
invecchiare; **to ~ tired** stancarsi; **to ~ drunk**
ubriacarsi; **to ~ killed** venire or rimanere
ucciso(a); **when do I ~ paid?** quando mi
pagate?; **it's ~ting late** si sta facendo tardi

2 (go): **to ~ to/from** andare a/da; **to ~ home**
arrivare or tornare a casa; **how did you
~ here?** come sei venuto?

3 (begin) mettersi a, cominciare a; **to ~ to**

---

know sb incominciare a conoscere qn; **let's
~ going** or **started** muoviamoci

4 (modal aux vb): **you've got to do it** devi
farlo

♦ vt **1**: **to ~ sth done** (do) fare qc; (have
done) far fare qc; **to ~ one's hair cut** farsi
tagliare i capelli; **to ~ sb to do sth** far fare qc
a qn

2 (obtain: money, permission, results)
ottenere; (find: job, flat) trovare; (fetch:
person, doctor) chiamare; (: object) prendere;
to ~ sth for sb prendere or procurare qc a qn;
~ me Mr Jones, please (TEL) mi passi il signor
Jones, per favore; **can I ~ you a drink?** le
posso offrire da bere?

3 (receive: present, letter, prize) ricevere;
(acquire: reputation) farsi; **how much did you
~ for the painting?** quanto le hanno dato per
il quadro?

4 (catch) prendere; (hit: target etc) colpire;
to ~ sb by the arm/throat afferrare qn per un
braccio/alla gola; **~ him!** prendetelo!

5 (take, move) portare; **to ~ sth to sb** far
avere qc a qn; **do you think we'll ~ it through
the door?** pensi che riusciremo a farlo passare
per la porta?

6 (catch, take: plane, bus etc) prendere

7 (understand) afferrare; (hear) sentire; **I've
got it!** ci sono arrivato!, ci sono!; **I'm sorry, I
didn't ~ your name** scusi, non ho capito (or
sentito) il suo nome

8 (have, possess): **to have got** avere; **how
many have you got?** quanti ne ha?

get about vi muoversi; (news) diffondersi

get along vi (agree) andare d'accordo;
(depart) andarsene; (manage) = **get by**

get at vt fus (attack) prendersela con;
(reach) raggiungere, arrivare a

get away vi partire, andarsene; (escape)
scappare

get away with vt fus cavarsela; farla franca

get back vi (return) ritornare, tornare ♦ vt
riottenere, riavere

get by vi (pass) passare; (manage) farcela

get down vi, vt fus scendere ♦ vt far
scendere; (depress) buttare giù

get down to vt fus (work) mettersi a (fare)

get in vi entrare; (train) arrivare; (arrive
home) ritornare, tornare

get into vt fus entrare in; **to ~ into a rage**
incavolarsi

get off vi (from train etc) scendere; (depart:
person, car) andare via; (escape) cavarsela
♦ vt (remove: clothes, stain) levare ♦ vt fus
(train, bus) scendere da

get on vi (at exam etc) andare; (agree): **to
~ on (with)** andare d'accordo (con) ♦ vt fus
montare in; (horse) montare su

get out vi uscire; (of vehicle) scendere ♦ vt

tirar fuori, far uscire
get out of *vt fus* uscire da; (*duty etc*) evitare
get over *vt fus* (*illness*) riaversi da
get round *vt fus* aggirare; (*fig: person*) rigirare
get through *vi* (*TEL*) avere la linea
get through to *vt fus* (*TEL*) parlare a
get together *vi* riunirsi ♦ *vt* raccogliere; (*people*) adunare
get up *vi* (*rise*) alzarsi ♦ *vt fus* salire su per
get up to *vt fus* (*reach*) raggiungere; (*prank etc*) fare

getaway ['gɛtəweɪ] *n* fuga
geyser ['giːzə*] *n* (*BRIT*) scaldabagno; (*GEO*) geyser *m inv*
Ghana ['gɑːnə] *n* Ghana *m*
ghastly ['gɑːstlɪ] *adj* orribile, orrendo(a); (*pale*) spettrale
gherkin ['gəːkɪn] *n* cetriolino
ghetto blaster ['gɛtəublɑːstə*] *n* maxistereo *m inv* portatile
ghost [gəust] *n* fantasma *m*, spettro
giant ['dʒaɪənt] *n* gigante *m* ♦ *adj* gigantesco(a), enorme
gibberish ['dʒɪbərɪʃ] *n* parole *fpl* senza senso
gibe [dʒaɪb] *n* = **jibe**
giblets ['dʒɪblɪts] *npl* frattaglie *fpl*
Gibraltar [dʒɪ'brɔːltə*] *n* Gibilterra
giddy ['gɪdɪ] *adj* (*dizzy*): **to be ~** aver le vertigini
gift [gɪft] *n* regalo; (*donation, ability*) dono; **~ed** *adj* dotato(a); **~ token** *n* buono *m* omaggio *inv*; **~ voucher** *n* = **~ token**
gigantic [dʒaɪ'gæntɪk] *adj* gigantesco(a)
giggle ['gɪgl] *vi* ridere scioccamente
gill [dʒɪl] *n* (*measure*) = 0.25 pints (*BRIT* = 0.148l, *US* = 0.118l)
gills [gɪlz] *npl* (*of fish*) branchie *fpl*
gilt [gɪlt] *n* doratura ♦ *adj* dorato(a); **~-edged** *adj* (*COMM*) della massima sicurezza
gimmick ['gɪmɪk] *n* trucco
gin [dʒɪn] *n* (*liquor*) gin *m inv*
ginger ['dʒɪndʒə*] *n* zenzero; **~ ale, ~ beer** *n* bibita gassosa allo zenzero; **~bread** *n* pan *m* di zenzero
gingerly ['dʒɪndʒəlɪ] *adv* cautamente
gipsy ['dʒɪpsɪ] *n* zingaro/a
giraffe [dʒɪ'rɑːf] *n* giraffa
girder ['gəːdə*] *n* trave *f*
girl [gəːl] *n* ragazza; (*young unmarried woman*) signorina; (*daughter*) figlia, figliola; **~friend** *n* (*of girl*) amica; (*of boy*) ragazza; **~ish** *adj* da ragazza
giro ['dʒaɪrəu] *n* (*bank ~*) versamento bancario; (*post office ~*) postagiro; (*BRIT: welfare cheque*) assegno del sussidio di assistenza sociale
gist [dʒɪst] *n* succo

give [gɪv] (*pt* **gave**, *pp* **given**) *vt* dare ♦ *vi* cedere; **to ~ sb sth, ~ sth to sb** dare qc a qn; **I'll ~ you £5 for it** te lo pago 5 sterline; **to ~ a cry/sigh** emettere un grido/sospiro; **to ~ a speech** fare un discorso; **~ away** *vt* dare via; (*disclose*) rivelare; (*bride*) condurre all'altare; **~ back** *vt* rendere; **~ in** *vi* cedere ♦ *vt* consegnare; **~ off** *vt* emettere; **~ out** *vt* distribuire; annunciare; **~ up** *vi* rinunciare ♦ *vt* rinunciare a; **to ~ up smoking** smettere di fumare; **to ~ o.s. up** arrendersi; **~ way** *vi* cedere; (*BRIT: AUT*) dare la precedenza
glacier ['glæsɪə*] *n* ghiacciaio
glad [glæd] *adj* lieto(a), contento(a)
gladly ['glædlɪ] *adv* volentieri
glamorous ['glæmərəs] *adj* affascinante, seducente
glamour ['glæmə*] *n* fascino
glance [glɑːns] *n* occhiata, sguardo ♦ *vi*: **to ~ at** dare un'occhiata a; **to ~ off** (*bullet*) rimbalzare su; **glancing** *adj* (*blow*) che colpisce di striscio
gland [glænd] *n* ghiandola
glare [glɛə*] *n* (*of anger*) sguardo furioso; (*of light*) riverbero, luce *f* abbagliante; (*of publicity*) chiasso ♦ *vi* abbagliare; **to ~ at** guardare male; **glaring** *adj* (*mistake*) madornale
glass [glɑːs] *n* (*substance*) vetro; (*tumbler*) bicchiere *m*; **~es** *npl* (*spectacles*) occhiali *mpl*; **~ware** *n* vetrame *m*; **~y** *adj* (*eyes*) vitreo(a)
glaze [gleɪz] *vt* (*door*) fornire di vetri; (*pottery*) smaltare ♦ *n* smalto; **~d** *adj* (*eyes*) vitreo(a); (*pottery*) smaltato(a)
glazier ['gleɪzɪə*] *n* vetraio
gleam [gliːm] *vi* luccicare
glean [gliːn] *vt* (*information*) racimolare
glee [gliː] *n* allegrezza, gioia
glen [glɛn] *n* valletta
glib [glɪb] *adj* dalla parola facile; facile
glide [glaɪd] *vi* scivolare; (*AVIAT, birds*) planare; **~r** *n* (*AVIAT*) aliante *m*; **gliding** *n* (*AVIAT*) volo a vela
glimmer ['glɪmə*] *n* barlume *m*
glimpse [glɪmps] *n* impressione *f* fugace ♦ *vt* vedere al volo
glint [glɪnt] *vi* luccicare
glisten ['glɪsn] *vi* luccicare
glitter ['glɪtə*] *vi* scintillare
gloat [gləut] *vi*: gongolare
global ['gləubl] *adj* globale; **~ warming** *n* effetto *m* serra *inv*
globe [gləub] *n* globo, sfera
gloom [gluːm] *n* oscurità, buio; (*sadness*) tristezza, malinconia; **~y** *adj* scuro(a); fosco(a), triste
glorious ['glɔːrɪəs] *adj* glorioso(a); magnifico(a)
glory ['glɔːrɪ] *n* gloria; splendore *m*

gloss [glɔs] n (shine) lucentezza; (also:
~ paint) vernice f a olio; ~ over vt fus
scivolare su

glossary ['glɔsərɪ] n glossario

glossy ['glɔsɪ] adj lucente

glove [glʌv] n guanto; ~ compartment n
(AUT) vano portaoggetti

glow [gləu] vi ardere; (face) essere
luminoso(a)

glower ['glauə*] vi: to ~ (at sb) guardare
(qn) in cagnesco

glucose ['glu:kəus] n glucosio

glue [glu:] n colla ♦ vt incollare

glum [glʌm] adj abbattuto(a)

glut [glʌt] n eccesso

glutton ['glʌtn] n ghiottone/a; a ~ for work
un(a) patito(a) del lavoro

GM adj abbr (= genetically modified)
geneticamente modificato(a)

gnat [næt] n moscerino

gnaw [nɔ:] vt rodere

go [gəu] (pt went, pp gone; pl ~es) vi andare;
(depart) partire, andarsene; (work)
funzionare; (time) passare; (break etc)
rompersi; (be sold): to ~ for £10 essere
venduto per 10 sterline; (fit, suit): to ~ with
andare bene con; (become): to ~ pale
diventare pallido(a); to ~ mouldy ammuffire
♦ n: to have a ~ (at) provare; to be on the ~
essere in moto; whose ~ is it? a chi tocca?;
he's going to do sta per fare; to ~ for a walk
andare a fare una passeggiata; to ~ dancing/
shopping andare a ballare/fare la spesa; just
then the bell went proprio allora suonò il
campanello; how did it ~? com'è andato?; to
~ round the back/by the shop passare da
dietro/davanti al negozio; ~ about vi (also:
~ round: rumour) correre, circolare ♦ vt fus:
how do I ~ about this? qual'è la prassi per
questo?; ~ ahead vi andare avanti; ~ along
vi andare, avanzare ♦ vt fus percorrere; to
~ along with (plan, idea) appoggiare;
~ away vi partire, andarsene; ~ back vi
tornare, ritornare; ~ back on vt fus (promise)
non mantenere; ~ by vi (years, time) scorrere
♦ vt fus attenersi a, seguire (alla lettera);
prestar fede a; ~ down vi scendere; (ship)
affondare; (sun) tramontare ♦ vt fus
scendere; ~ for vt fus (fetch) andare a
prendere; (like) andar matto(a) per; (attack)
attaccare; saltare addosso a; ~ in vi entrare;
~ in for vt fus (competition) iscriversi a; (be
interested in) interessarsi di; ~ into vt fus
entrare in; (investigate) indagare, esaminare;
(embark on) lanciarsi in; ~ off vi partire,
andar via; (food) guastarsi; (explode)
esplodere, scoppiare; (event) passare ♦ vt fus:
I've gone off chocolate la cioccolata non mi
piace più; the gun went off il fucile si scaricò;

~ on vi continuare; (happen) succedere; to
~ on doing continuare a fare; ~ out vi uscire;
(couple): they went out for 3 years sono stati
insieme per 3 anni; (fire, light) spegnersi;
~ over vi (ship) ribaltarsi ♦ vt fus (check)
esaminare; ~ through vt fus (town etc)
attraversare; (files, papers) passare in
rassegna; (examine: list etc) leggere da cima a
fondo; ~ up vi salire; ~ without vt fus fare a
meno di

goad [gəud] vt spronare

go-ahead ['gəuəhɛd] adj intraprendente ♦ n
via m

goal [gəul] n (SPORT) gol m, rete f; (: place)
porta; (fig: aim) fine m, scopo; ~keeper n
portiere m; ~-post n palo (della porta)

goat [gəut] n capra

gobble ['gɔbl] vt (also: ~ down, ~ up)
ingoiare

go-between ['gəubɪtwi:n] n intermediario/a

god [gɔd] n dio; G~ n Dio; ~child n
figlioccio/a; ~daughter n figlioccia; ~dess n
dea; ~father n padrino; ~-forsaken adj
desolato(a), sperduto(a); ~mother n
madrina; ~send n dono del cielo; ~son n
figlioccio

goggles ['gɔglz] npl occhiali mpl (di
protezione)

going ['gəuɪŋ] n (conditions) andare m, stato
del terreno ♦ adj: the ~ rate la tariffa in
vigore

gold [gəuld] n oro ♦ adj d'oro; ~en adj
(made of ~) d'oro; (~ in colour) dorato(a);
~fish n pesce m dorato o rosso; ~mine n
(also fig) miniera d'oro; ~-plated adj
placcato(a) oro inv; ~smith n orefice m,
orafo

golf [gɔlf] n golf m; ~ ball n (for game)
pallina da golf; (on typewriter) pallina; ~ club
n circolo di golf; (stick) bastone m or mazza
da golf; ~ course n campo di golf; ~er n
giocatore/trice di golf

gondola ['gɔndələ] n gondola

gone [gɔn] pp of go ♦ adj partito(a)

gong [gɔŋ] n gong m inv

good [gud] adj buono(a); (kind) buono(a),
gentile; (child) bravo(a) ♦ n bene m; ~s npl
(COMM etc) beni mpl; merci fpl; ~! bene!,
ottimo!; to be ~ at essere bravo(a) in; to be
~ for andare bene per; it's ~ for you fa bene;
would you be ~ enough to ...? avrebbe la
gentilezza di ...?; a ~ deal (of) molto(a), una
buona quantità (di); a ~ many molti(e); to
make ~ (loss, damage) compensare; it's no
~ complaining brontolare non serve a niente;
for ~ per sempre, definitivamente; ~ morning!
buon giorno!; ~ afternoon/evening! buona
sera!; ~ night! buona notte!; ~bye excl
arrivederci!; G~ Friday n Venerdì Santo; ~-

looking adj bello(a); **~-natured** adj affabile; **~ness** n (of person) bontà; **for ~ness sake!** per amor di Dio!; **~ness gracious!** santo cielo!, mamma mia!; **~s train** (BRIT) n treno m merci inv; **~will** n amicizia, benevolenza

goose [guːs] (pl **geese**) n oca

gooseberry ['guzbəri] n uva spina; **to play ~** (BRIT) tenere la candela

gooseflesh ['guːsfleʃ] n pelle f d'oca

goose pimples npl pelle f d'oca

gore [gɔː*] vt incornare ♦ n sangue m (coagulato)

gorge [gɔːdʒ] n gola ♦ vt: **to ~ o.s. (on)** ingozzarsi (di)

gorgeous ['gɔːdʒəs] adj magnifico(a)

gorilla [gə'rɪlə] n gorilla m inv

gorse [gɔːs] n ginestrone m

gory ['gɔːrɪ] adj sanguinoso(a)

go-slow ['gəu'sləu] (BRIT) n rallentamento dei lavori (per agitazione sindacale)

gospel ['gɔspl] n vangelo

gossip ['gɔsɪp] n chiacchiere fpl; pettegolezzi mpl; (person) pettegolo/a ♦ vi chiacchierare

got [gɔt] pt, pp of **get**; **~ten** (US) pp of **get**

gout [gaut] n gotta

govern ['gʌvn] vt governare

governess ['gʌvənɪs] n governante f

government ['gʌvnmənt] n governo

governor ['gʌvənə*] n (of state, bank) governatore m; (of school, hospital) amministratore m; (BRIT: of prison) direttore/trice

gown [gaun] n vestito lungo; (of teacher, BRIT: of judge) toga

G.P. n abbr = **general practitioner**

grab [græb] vt afferrare, arraffare; (property, power) impadronirsi di ♦ vi: **to ~ at** cercare di afferrare

grace [greɪs] n grazia ♦ vt onorare; **5 days' ~** dilazione f di 5 giorni; **~ful** adj elegante, aggraziato(a); **gracious** ['greɪʃəs] adj grazioso(a); misericordioso(a)

grade [greɪd] n (COMM) qualità f inv; classe f; categoria; (in hierarchy) grado; (SCOL: mark) voto; (US: school class) classe ♦ vt classificare; ordinare; graduare; **~ crossing** (US) n passaggio a livello; **~ school** (US) n scuola elementare

gradient ['greɪdɪənt] n pendenza, inclinazione f

gradual ['grædjuəl] adj graduale; **~ly** adv man mano, a poco a poco

graduate [n 'grædjuɪt, vb 'grædjueɪt] n (of university) laureato/a; (US: of high school) diplomato/a ♦ vi laurearsi; diplomarsi; **graduation** [-'eɪʃən] n (ceremony) consegna delle lauree (or dei diplomi)

graffiti [grə'fiːtɪ] npl graffiti mpl

graft [grɑːft] n (AGR, MED) innesto; (bribery)

corruzione f; (BRIT: hard work): **it's hard ~** è un lavoraccio ♦ vt innestare

grain [greɪn] n grano; (of sand) granello; (of wood) venatura

gram [græm] n grammo

grammar ['græmə*] n grammatica; **~ school** (BRIT) n ≈ liceo

grammatical [grə'mætɪkl] adj grammaticale

gramme [græm] n = **gram**

grand [grænd] adj grande, magnifico(a); grandioso(a); **~children** npl nipoti mpl; **~dad** (inf) n nonno; **~daughter** n nipote f; **~eur** ['grændjə*] n grandiosità; **~father** n nonno; **~ma** (inf) n nonna; **~mother** n nonna; **~pa** (inf) n = **~dad**; **~parents** npl nonni mpl; **~ piano** n pianoforte m a coda; **~son** n nipote m; **~stand** n (SPORT) tribuna

granite ['grænɪt] n granito

granny ['grænɪ] (inf) n nonna

grant [grɑːnt] vt accordare; (admit) ammettere, concedere ♦ n (SCOL) borsa; (ADMIN) sussidio, sovvenzione f; **to take sth for ~ed** dare qc per scontato; **to take sb for ~ed** dare per scontata la presenza di qn

granulated ['grænjuleɪtɪd] adj: **~ sugar** zucchero cristallizzato

granule ['grænjuːl] n granello

grape [greɪp] n chicco d'uva, acino

grapefruit ['greɪpfruːt] n pompelmo

graph [grɑːf] n grafico; **~ic** adj grafico(a); (vivid) vivido(a); **~ics** n grafica ♦ npl illustrazioni fpl

grapple ['græpl] vi: **to ~ with** essere alle prese con

grasp [grɑːsp] vt afferrare ♦ n (grip) presa; (fig) potere m; comprensione f; **~ing** adj avido(a)

grass [grɑːs] n erba; **~hopper** n cavalletta; **~-roots** adj di base

grate [greɪt] n graticola (del focolare) ♦ vi cigolare, stridere ♦ vt (CULIN) grattugiare

grateful ['greɪtful] adj grato(a), riconoscente

grater ['greɪtə*] n grattugia

grating ['greɪtɪŋ] n (iron bars) grata ♦ adj (noise) stridente, stridulo(a)

gratitude ['grætɪtjuːd] n gratitudine f

gratuity [grə'tjuːɪtɪ] n mancia

grave [greɪv] n tomba ♦ adj grave, serio(a)

gravel ['grævl] n ghiaia

gravestone ['greɪvstəun] n pietra tombale

graveyard ['greɪvjɑːd] n cimitero

gravity ['grævɪtɪ] n (PHYSICS) gravità; pesantezza; (seriousness) gravità, serietà

gravy ['greɪvɪ] n intingolo della carne; salsa

gray [greɪ] adj = **grey**

graze [greɪz] vi pascolare, pascere ♦ vt (touch lightly) sfiorare; (scrape) escoriare ♦ n (MED) escoriazione f

grease [gri:s] n (fat) grasso; (lubricant) lubrificante m ♦ vt ingrassare; lubrificare; **~proof paper** (BRIT) n carta oleata; **greasy** adj grasso(a), untuoso(a)

great [greɪt] adj grande; (inf) magnifico(a), meraviglioso(a); **G~ Britain** n Gran Bretagna; **~-grandfather** n bisnonno; **~-grandmother** n bisnonna; **~ly** adv molto; **~ness** n grandezza

Greece [gri:s] n Grecia

greed [gri:d] n (also: **~iness**) avarizia; (for food) golosità, ghiottoneria; **~y** adj avido(a); goloso(a), ghiotto(a)

Greek [gri:k] adj greco(a) ♦ n greco/a; (LING) greco

green [gri:n] adj verde; (inexperienced) inesperto(a), ingenuo(a) ♦ n verde m; (stretch of grass) prato; (on golf course) green m inv; **~s** npl (vegetables) verdura; **~ belt** n (round town) cintura di verde; **~ card** n (BRIT: AUT) carta verde; (US: ADMIN) permesso di soggiorno e di lavoro; **~ery** n verde m; **~grocer** (BRIT) n fruttivendolo/a, erbivendolo/a; **~house** n serra; **~house effect** n effetto serra; **~house gas** n gas responsabile dell'effetto serra; **~ish** adj verdastro(a)

Greenland ['gri:nlənd] n Groenlandia

greet [gri:t] vt salutare; **~ing** n saluto; **~ing(s) card** n cartolina d'auguri

gregarious [grə'gɛərɪəs] adj (person) socievole

grenade [grə'neɪd] n (also: hand ~) granata

grew [gru:] pt of **grow**

grey [greɪ] adj grigio(a); **~-haired** adj dai capelli grigi; **~hound** n levriere m

grid [grɪd] n grata; (ELEC) rete f

gridlock ['grɪdlɒk] n (traffic jam) paralisi f inv del traffico; **~ed** adj paralizzato(a) dal traffico; (talks etc) in fase di stallo

grief [gri:f] n dolore m

grievance ['gri:vəns] n lagnanza

grieve [gri:v] vi addolorarsi; rattristarsi ♦ vt addolorare; **to ~ for sb** (dead person) piangere qn

grievous ['gri:vəs] adj: **~ bodily harm** (LAW) aggressione f

grill [grɪl] n (on cooker) griglia; (also: mixed ~) grigliata mista ♦ vt (BRIT) cuocere ai ferri; (inf: question) interrogare senza sosta

grille [grɪl] n grata; (AUT) griglia

grim [grɪm] adj sinistro(a), brutto(a)

grimace [grɪ'meɪs] n smorfia ♦ vi fare smorfie; fare boccacce

grime [graɪm] n sudiciume m

grin [grɪn] n sorriso smagliante ♦ vi fare un gran sorriso

grind [graɪnd] (pt, pp **ground**) vt macinare; (make sharp) arrotare ♦ n (work) sgobbata

grip [grɪp] n impugnatura; presa; (holdall) borsa da viaggio ♦ vt (object) afferrare; (attention) catturare; **to come to ~s with** affrontare; cercare di risolvere

gripping ['grɪpɪŋ] adj avvincente

grisly ['grɪzlɪ] adj macabro(a), orrido(a)

gristle ['grɪsl] n cartilagine f

grit [grɪt] n ghiaia; (courage) fegato ♦ vt (road) coprire di sabbia; **to ~ one's teeth** stringere i denti

groan [grəun] n gemito ♦ vi gemere

grocer ['grəusə*] n negoziante m di generi alimentari; **~ies** npl provviste fpl; **~'s (shop)** n negozio di (generi) alimentari

groggy ['grɒgɪ] adj barcollante

groin [grɔɪn] n inguine m

groom [gru:m] n palafreniere m; (also: bride~) sposo ♦ vt (horse) strigliare; (fig): **to ~ sb for** avviare qn a; **well-~ed** (person) curato(a)

groove [gru:v] n scanalatura, solco

grope [grəup] vi: **to ~ for** cercare a tastoni

gross [grəus] adj grossolano(a); (COMM) lordo(a); **~ly** adv (greatly) molto

grotesque [grəu'tɛsk] adj grottesco(a)

grotto ['grɒtəu] n grotta

grotty ['grɒtɪ] (inf) adj terribile

ground [graund] pt, pp of **grind** ♦ n suolo, terra; (land) terreno; (SPORT) campo; (reason: gen pl) ragione f; (US: also: ~ wire) terra ♦ vt (plane) tenere a terra; (US: ELEC) mettere la presa a terra a; **~s** npl (of coffee etc) fondi mpl; (gardens etc) terreno, giardini mpl; **on/to the ~** per/a terra; **to gain/lose ~** guadagnare/perdere terreno; **~ cloth** (US) n = **~sheet**; **~ing** n (in education) basi fpl; **~less** adj infondato(a); **~sheet** (BRIT) n telone m impermeabile; **~ staff** n personale m di terra; **~work** n preparazione f

group [gru:p] n gruppo ♦ vt (also: ~ together) raggruppare ♦ vi (also: ~ together) raggrupparsi

grouse [graus] n inv (bird) tetraone m ♦ vi (complain) brontolare

grove [grəuv] n boschetto

grovel ['grɒvl] vi (fig): **to ~ (before)** strisciare (di fronte a)

grow [grəu] (pt **grew**, pp **grown**) vi crescere; (increase) aumentare; (develop): **to ~ rich/weak** arricchirsi/indebolirsi ♦ vt coltivare, far crescere; **~ up** vi farsi grande, crescere; **~er** n coltivatore/trice; **~ing** adj (fear, amount) crescente

growl [graul] vi ringhiare

grown [grəun] pp of **grow**; **~-up** n adulto/a, grande m/f

growth [grəuθ] n crescita, sviluppo; (what has grown) crescita; (MED) escrescenza, tumore m

grub [grʌb] *n* larva; (*inf: food*) roba (da mangiare)

grubby ['grʌbɪ] *adj* sporco(a)

grudge [grʌdʒ] *n* rancore *m* ♦ *vt*: **to ~ sb sth** dare qc a qn di malavoglia; invidiare qc a qn; **to bear sb a ~ (for)** serbar rancore a qn (per)

gruelling ['gruəlɪŋ] (*US* **grueling**) *adj* estenuante

gruesome ['gru:səm] *adj* orribile

gruff [grʌf] *adj* rozzo(a)

grumble ['grʌmbl] *vi* brontolare, lagnarsi

grumpy ['grʌmpɪ] *adj* scorbutico(a)

grunt [grʌnt] *vi* grugnire

G-string ['dʒi:strɪŋ] *n* tanga *m inv*

guarantee [gærən'ti:] *n* garanzia ♦ *vt* garantire

guard [gɑ:d] *n* guardia; (*one man*) guardia, sentinella; (*BRIT: RAIL*) capotreno; (*on machine*) schermo protettivo; (*also: fire~*) parafuoco ♦ *vt* fare la guardia a; (*protect*): **to ~ (against)** proteggere (da); **to be on one's ~** stare in guardia; **~ against** *vt fus* guardarsi da; **~ed** *adj* (*fig*) cauto(a), guardingo(a); **~ian** *n* custode *m*; (*of minor*) tutore/trice; **~'s van** (*BRIT*) *n* (*RAIL*) vagone *m* di servizio

guerrilla [gə'rɪlə] *n* guerrigliero

guess [ges] *vi* indovinare ♦ *vt* indovinare; (*US*) credere, pensare ♦ *n*: **to take** *or* **have a ~** provare a indovinare; **~work** *n*: **I got the answer by ~work** ho azzeccato la risposta

guest [gest] *n* ospite *m/f*; (*in hotel*) cliente *m/f*; **~-house** *n* pensione *f*; **~ room** *n* camera degli ospiti

guffaw [gʌ'fɔ:] *vi* scoppiare in una risata sonora

guidance ['gaɪdəns] *n* guida, direzione *f*

guide [gaɪd] *n* (*person, book etc*) guida; (*BRIT: also: girl ~*) giovane esploratrice *f* ♦ *vt* guidare; **~book** *n* guida; **~ dog** *n* cane *m* guida *inv*; **~lines** *npl* (*fig*) indicazioni *fpl*, linee *fpl* direttive

guild [gɪld] *n* arte *f*, corporazione *f*; associazione *f*

guillotine ['gɪləti:n] *n* ghigliottina; (*for paper*) taglierina

guilt [gɪlt] *n* colpevolezza; **~y** *adj* colpevole

guinea pig ['gɪnɪ-] *n* cavia

guise [gaɪz] *n* maschera

guitar [gɪ'tɑ:*] *n* chitarra

gulf [gʌlf] *n* golfo; (*abyss*) abisso

gull [gʌl] *n* gabbiano

gullible ['gʌlɪbl] *adj* credulo(a)

gully ['gʌlɪ] *n* burrone *m*; gola; canale *m*

gulp [gʌlp] *vi* deglutire; (*from emotion*) avere il nodo in gola ♦ *vt* (*also: ~ down*) tracannare, inghiottire

gum [gʌm] *n* (*ANAT*) gengiva; (*glue*) colla; (*also: ~drop*) caramella gommosa; (*also: chewing ~*) chewing-gum ♦ *vt*: **to**

~ (together) incollare; **~boots** (*BRIT*) *npl* stivali *mpl* di gomma

gumption ['gʌmpʃən] *n* spirito d'iniziativa, buonsenso

gun [gʌn] *n* fucile *m*; (*small*) pistola, rivoltella; (*rifle*) carabina; (*shotgun*) fucile da caccia; (*cannon*) cannone *m*; **~boat** *n* cannoniera; **~fire** *n* spari *mpl*; **~man** *n* bandito armato; **~point** *n*: **at ~point** sotto minaccia di fucile; **~powder** *n* polvere *f* da sparo; **~shot** *n* sparo

gurgle ['gə:gl] *vi* gorgogliare

gush [gʌʃ] *vi* sgorgare; (*fig*) abbandonarsi ad effusioni

gusset ['gʌsɪt] *n* gherone *m*

gust [gʌst] *n* (*of wind*) raffica; (*of smoke*) buffata

gusto ['gʌstəu] *n* entusiasmo

gut [gʌt] *n* intestino, budello; **~s** *npl* (*ANAT*) interiora *fpl*; (*courage*) fegato

gutter ['gʌtə*] *n* (*of roof*) grondaia; (*in street*) cunetta

guy [gaɪ] *n* (*inf: man*) tipo, elemento; (*also: ~rope*) cavo *or* corda di fissaggio; (*figure*) effigie di Guy Fawkes

guzzle ['gʌzl] *vt* tranguggiare

gym [dʒɪm] *n* (*also: gymnasium*) palestra; (*also: gymnastics*) ginnastica

gymnast ['dʒɪmnæst] *n* ginnasta *m/f*; **~ics** [-'næstɪks] *n*, *npl* ginnastica

gym shoes *npl* scarpe *fpl* da ginnastica

gym slip (*BRIT*) *n* grembiule *m* da scuola (*per ragazze*)

gynaecologist [gaɪnɪ'kɔlədʒɪst] (*US* **gynecologist**) *n* ginecologo/a

gypsy ['dʒɪpsɪ] *n* = **gipsy**

gyrate [dʒaɪ'reɪt] *vi* girare

H, h

haberdashery ['hæbə'dæʃərɪ] (*BRIT*) *n* merceria

habit ['hæbɪt] *n* abitudine *f*; (*costume*) abito; (*REL*) tonaca

habitual [hə'bɪtjuəl] *adj* abituale; (*drinker, liar*) inveterato(a)

hack [hæk] *vt* tagliare, fare a pezzi ♦ *n* (*pej: writer*) scribacchino/a

hacker ['hækə*] *n* (*COMPUT*) pirata *m* informatico

hackney cab ['hæknɪ-] *n* carrozza a nolo

hackneyed ['hæknɪd] *adj* comune, trito(a)

had [hæd] *pt, pp of* **have**

haddock ['hædək] (*pl* **~** *or* **~s**) *n* eglefino

hadn't ['hædnt] = **had not**

haemorrhage ['hemərɪdʒ] (*US* **hemorrhage**) *n* emorragia

haemorrhoids ['hemərɔɪdz] (*US*

hemorrhoids) npl emorroidi fpl

haggard ['hægəd] adj smunto(a)

haggle ['hægl] vi mercanteggiare

Hague [heɪg] n: The ~ L'Aia

hail [heɪl] n grandine f; (of criticism etc) pioggia ♦ vt (call) chiamare; (flag down: taxi) fermare; (greet) salutare ♦ vi grandinare; **~stone** n chicco di grandine

hair [heə*] n capelli mpl; (single hair: on head) capello; (: on body) pelo; **to do one's ~** pettinarsi; **~brush** n spazzola per capelli; **~cut** n taglio di capelli; **~do** ['heədu:] n acconciatura, pettinatura; **~dresser** n parrucchiere/a; **~dryer** n asciugacapelli m inv; **~ grip** n forcina; **~net** n retina per capelli; **~pin** n forcina; **~pin bend** (US **~pin curve**) n tornante m; **~raising** adj orripilante; **~ removing cream** n crema depilatoria; **~ spray** n lacca per capelli; **~style** n pettinatura, acconciatura; **~y** adj irsuto(a); peloso(a); (inf: frightening) spaventoso(a)

hake [heɪk] (pl ~ or ~s) n nasello

half [hɑːf] (pl **halves**) n mezzo, metà f inv ♦ adj mezzo(a) ♦ adv a mezzo, a metà; **~ an hour** mezz'ora; **~ a dozen** mezza dozzina; **~ a pound** mezza libbra; **two and a ~** due e mezzo; **a week and a ~** una settimana e mezza; **~ (of it)** la metà; **~ (of)** la metà di; **to cut sth in ~** tagliare qc in due; **~ asleep** mezzo(a) addormentato(a); **~-baked** adj (scheme) che non sta in piedi; **~ board** (BRIT) n mezza pensione; **~-caste** ['hɑːfkɑːst] n meticcio/a; **~ fare** n tariffa a metà prezzo; **~-hearted** adj tiepido(a); **~-hour** n mezz'ora; **~-mast: at ~-mast** adv (flag) a mezz'asta; **~penny** ['heɪpnɪ] (BRIT) n mezzo penny m inv; **~-price** adj, adv a metà prezzo; **~ term** (BRIT) n (SCOL) vacanza a or di metà trimestre; **~-time** n (SPORT) intervallo; **~way** adv a metà strada

halibut ['hælɪbət] n inv ippoglosso

hall [hɔːl] n sala, salone m; (entrance way) entrata; **~ of residence** (BRIT) n casa dello studente

hallmark ['hɔːlmɑːk] n marchio di garanzia; (fig) caratteristica

hallo [hə'ləu] excl = hello

Hallowe'en [hæləu'iːn] n vigilia d'Ognissanti

hallucination [həluːsɪ'neɪʃən] n allucinazione f

hallway ['hɔːlweɪ] n corridoio; (entrance) ingresso

halo ['heɪləu] n (of saint etc) aureola

halt [hɔːlt] n fermata ♦ vt fermare ♦ vi fermarsi

halve [hɑːv] vt (apple etc) dividere a metà; (expense) ridurre di metà

halves [hɑːvz] npl of **half**

ham [hæm] n prosciutto

Hamburg ['hæmbəːg] n Amburgo f

hamburger ['hæmbəːgə*] n hamburger m inv

hamlet ['hæmlɪt] n paesetto

hammer ['hæmə*] n martello ♦ vt martellare ♦ vi: **to ~ on** or **at the door** picchiare alla porta

hammock ['hæmək] n amaca

hamper ['hæmpə*] vt impedire ♦ n cesta

hamster ['hæmstə*] n criceto

hand [hænd] n mano f; (of clock) lancetta; (handwriting) scrittura; (at cards) mano; (: game) partita; (worker) operaio/a ♦ vt dare, passare; **to give sb a ~** dare una mano a qn; **at ~** a portata di mano; **in ~** a disposizione; (work) in corso; **on ~** (person) disponibile; (services) pronto(a) a intervenire; **to ~** (information etc) a portata di mano; **on the one ~ ...**, **on the other ~** da un lato ..., dall'altro; **~ in** vt consegnare; **~ out** vt distribuire; **~ over** vt passare; cedere; **~bag** n borsetta; **~book** n manuale m; **~brake** n freno a mano; **~cuffs** npl manette fpl; **~ful** n manciata, pugno

handicap ['hændɪkæp] n handicap m inv ♦ vt handicappare; **to be physically ~ped** essere handicappato(a); **to be mentally ~ped** essere un(a) handicappato(a) mentale

handicraft ['hændɪkrɑːft] n lavoro d'artigiano

handiwork ['hændɪwəːk] n opera

handkerchief ['hæŋkətʃɪf] n fazzoletto

handle ['hændl] n (of door etc) maniglia; (of cup etc) ansa; (of knife etc) impugnatura; (of saucepan) manico; (for winding) manovella ♦ vt toccare, maneggiare; (deal with) occuparsi di; (treat: people) trattare; "**~ with care**" "fragile"; **to fly off the ~** (fig) perdere le staffe, uscire dai gangheri; **~bar(s)** n(pl) manubrio

hand: ~ luggage n bagagli mpl a mano; **~made** adj fatto(a) a mano; **~out** n (money, food) elemosina; (leaflet) volantino; (at lecture) prospetto; **~rail** n corrimano; **~set** n (TEL) ricevitore m; **please replace the ~set** riagganciare il ricevitore; **~shake** n stretta di mano

handsome ['hænsəm] adj bello(a); (profit, fortune) considerevole

handwriting ['hændraɪtɪŋ] n scrittura

handy ['hændɪ] adj (person) bravo(a); (close at hand) a portata di mano; (convenient) comodo(a)

hang [hæŋ] (pt, pp hung) vt appendere; (criminal: pt, pp hanged) impiccare ♦ vi (painting) essere appeso(a); (hair) scendere; (drapery) cadere; **to get the ~ of sth** (inf) capire come qc funziona; **~ about** or

around *vi* bighellonare, ciondolare; **~ on** *vi* (*wait*) aspettare; **~ up** *vi* (*TEL*) riattaccare ♦ *vt* appendere

hangar ['hæŋə*] *n* hangar *m inv*

hanger ['hæŋə*] *n* gruccia

hanger-on [hæŋər'ɔn] *n* parassita *m*

hang-gliding ['hæŋglaɪdɪŋ] *n* volo col deltaplano

hangover ['hæŋəuvə*] *n* (*after drinking*) postumi *mpl* di sbornia

hang-up ['hæŋʌp] *n* complesso

hanker ['hæŋkə*] *vi*: **to ~ after** bramare

hankie ['hæŋkɪ] *n abbr* = **handkerchief**

hanky ['hæŋkɪ] *n abbr* = **handkerchief**

haphazard [hæp'hæzəd] *adj* a casaccio, alla carlona

happen ['hæpən] *vi* accadere, succedere; (*chance*): **to ~ to do sth** fare qc per caso; **as it ~s** guarda caso; **~ing** *n* avvenimento

happily ['hæpɪlɪ] *adv* felicemente; fortunatamente

happiness ['hæpɪnɪs] *n* felicità, contentezza

happy ['hæpɪ] *adj* felice, contento(a); **~ with** (*arrangements etc*) soddisfatto(a) di; **to be ~ to do** (*willing*) fare volentieri; **~ birthday!** buon compleanno!; **~-go-lucky** *adj* spensierato(a); **~ hour** *n* orario in cui i bar hanno prezzi ridotti

harangue [hə'ræŋ] *vt* arringare

harass ['hærəs] *vt* molestare; **~ment** *n* molestia

harbour ['hɑːbə*] (*US* **harbor**) *n* porto ♦ *vt* (*hope, fear*) nutrire; (*criminal*) dare rifugio a

hard [hɑːd] *adj* duro(a) ♦ *adv* (*work*) sodo; (*think, try*) bene; **to look ~ at** guardare fissamente; esaminare attentamente; **no ~ feelings!** senza rancore!; **to be ~ of hearing** essere duro(a) d'orecchio; **to be ~ done by** essere trattato(a) ingiustamente; **~back** *n* libro rilegato; **~ cash** *n* denaro in contanti; **~ disk** *n* (*COMPUT*) disco rigido; **~en** *vt, vi* indurire; **~-headed** *adj* pratico(a); **~ labour** *n* lavori forzati *mpl*

hardly ['hɑːdlɪ] *adv* (*scarcely*) appena; **it's ~ the case** non è proprio il caso; **~ anyone/ anywhere** quasi nessuno/da nessuna parte; **~ ever** quasi mai

hardship ['hɑːdʃɪp] *n* avversità *f inv*; privazioni *fpl*

hard shoulder (*BRIT*) *n* (*AUT*) corsia d'emergenza

hard-up [hɑːd'ʌp] (*inf*) *adj* al verde

hardware ['hɑːdwεə*] *n* ferramenta *fpl*; (*COMPUT*) hardware *m*; (*MIL*) armamenti *mpl*; **~ shop** *n* (negozio di) ferramenta *fpl*

hard-wearing [hɑːd'wεərɪŋ] *adj* resistente; (*shoes*) robusto(a)

hard-working [hɑːd'wəːkɪŋ] *adj* lavoratore(trice)

hardy ['hɑːdɪ] *adj* robusto(a); (*plant*) resistente al gelo

hare [hεə*] *n* lepre *f*; **~-brained** *adj* folle; scervellato(a)

harm [hɑːm] *n* male *m*; (*wrong*) danno ♦ *vt* (*person*) fare male a; (*thing*) danneggiare; **out of ~'s way** al sicuro; **~ful** *adj* dannoso(a); **~less** *adj* innocuo(a); inoffensivo(a)

harmonica [hɑː'mɔnɪkə] *n* armonica

harmonious [hɑː'məunɪəs] *adj* armonioso(a)

harmony ['hɑːmənɪ] *n* armonia

harness ['hɑːnɪs] *n* (*for horse*) bardatura, finimenti *mpl*; (*for child*) briglie *fpl*; (*safety ~*) imbracatura ♦ *vt* (*horse*) bardare; (*resources*) sfruttare

harp [hɑːp] *n* arpa ♦ *vi*: **to ~ on about** insistere tediosamente su

harpoon [hɑː'puːn] *n* arpione *m*

harrowing ['hærəuɪŋ] *adj* straziante

harsh [hɑːʃ] *adj* (*life, winter*) duro(a); (*judge, criticism*) severo(a); (*sound*) rauco(a); (*light*) violento(a)

harvest ['hɑːvɪst] *n* raccolto; (*of grapes*) vendemmia ♦ *vt* fare il raccolto di, raccogliere; vendemmiare

has [hæz] *vb see* **have**

hash [hæʃ] *n* (*CULIN*) specie di spezzatino fatto con carne già cotta; (*fig*: *mess*) pasticcio

hasn't ['hæznt] = **has not**

hassle ['hæsl] (*inf*) *n* sacco di problemi

haste [heɪst] *n* fretta; precipitazione *f*; **~n** ['heɪsn] *vt* affrettare ♦ *vi*: **to ~n (to)** affrettarsi (a); **hastily** *adv* in fretta; precipitosamente; **hasty** *adj* affrettato(a); precipitoso(a)

hat [hæt] *n* cappello

hatch [hætʃ] *n* (*NAUT*: *also*: **~way**) boccaporto; (*also*: **service ~**) portello di servizio ♦ *vi* (*bird*) uscire dal guscio; (*egg*) schiudersi

hatchback ['hætʃbæk] *n* (*AUT*) tre (*or* cinque) porte *f inv*

hatchet ['hætʃɪt] *n* accetta

hate [heɪt] *vt* odiare, detestare ♦ *n* odio; **~ful** *adj* odioso(a), detestabile

hatred ['heɪtrɪd] *n* odio

haughty ['hɔːtɪ] *adj* altero(a), arrogante

haul [hɔːl] *vt* trascinare, tirare ♦ *n* (*of fish*) pescata; (*of stolen goods etc*) bottino; **~age** *n* trasporto; autotrasporto; **~ier** (*US* **~er**) *n* trasportatore *m*

haunch [hɔːntʃ] *n* anca; (*of meat*) coscia

haunt [hɔːnt] *vt* (*subj*: *fear*) pervadere; (: *person*) frequentare ♦ *n* rifugio; **this house is ~ed** questa casa è abitata da un fantasma

KEYWORD

have [hæv] (*pt, pp* **had**) *aux vb* **1** (*gen*) avere; essere; **to ~ arrived/gone** essere arrivato(a)/

andato(a); **to ~ eaten/slept** avere mangiato/
dormito; **he has been kind/promoted** è stato
gentile/promosso; **having finished** or **when he
had finished, he left** dopo aver finito, se n'è
andato

2 (*in tag questions*): **you've done it, ~n't you?**
l'hai fatto, (non è) vero?; **he hasn't done it,
has he?** non l'ha fatto, vero?

3 (*in short answers and questions*): **you've
made a mistake — no I ~n't/so I ~** ha fatto un
errore — ma no, niente affatto/sì, è vero; **we
~n't paid — yes we ~!** I non abbiamo pagato
— ma sì che abbiamo pagato!; **I've been
there before, ~ you?** ci sono già stato, e lei?

♦ *modal aux vb* (*be obliged*): **to ~ (got) to do
sth** dover fare qc; **I ~n't got** or **I don't ~ to
wear glasses** non ho bisogno di portare gli
occhiali

♦ *vt* **1** (*possess, obtain*) avere; **he has (got)
blue eyes/dark hair** ha gli occhi azzurri/i
capelli scuri; **do you ~** or **~ you got a car/
phone?** ha la macchina/il telefono?; **may I
~ your address?** potrebbe darmi il suo
indirizzo?; **you can ~ it for £5** te lo lascio per
5 sterline

2 (+ *noun: take, hold etc*): **to ~ breakfast/a
swim/a bath** fare colazione/una nuotata/un
bagno; **to ~ lunch** pranzare; **to ~ dinner**
cenare; **to ~ a drink** bere qualcosa; **to ~ a
cigarette** fumare una sigaretta

3: **to ~ sth done** far fare qc; **to ~ one's hair
cut** farsi tagliare i capelli; **to ~ sb do sth** far
fare qc a qn

4 (*experience, suffer*) avere; **to ~ a cold/flu**
avere il raffreddore/l'influenza; **she had her
bag stolen** le hanno rubato la borsa

5 (*inf: dupe*): **you've been had!** ci sei cascato!

have out *vt*: **to ~ it out with sb** (*settle a
problem etc*) mettere le cose in chiaro con qn

haven ['heɪvn] *n* porto; (*fig*) rifugio
haven't ['hævnt] = **have not**
havoc ['hævək] *n* caos *m*
hawk [hɔːk] *n* falco
hay [heɪ] *n* fieno; **~ fever** *n* febbre *f* da fieno;
~stack *n* pagliaio
haywire ['heɪwaɪə*] (*inf*) *adj*: **to go ~**
impazzire
hazard ['hæzəd] *n* azzardo, ventura; pericolo,
rischio ♦ *vt* (*guess etc*) azzardare; **~ous** *adj*
pericoloso(a); **~ (warning) lights** *npl* (*AUT*)
luci *fpl* di emergenza
haze [heɪz] *n* foschia
hazelnut ['heɪzlnʌt] *n* nocciola
hazy ['heɪzɪ] *adj* fosco(a); (*idea*) vago(a)
he [hiː] *pronoun* lui, egli; **it is ~ who ...** è lui
che ....
head [hɛd] *n* testa; (*leader*) capo; (*of school*)
preside *m/f* ♦ *vt* (*list*) essere in testa a;

(*group*) essere a capo di; **~s (or tails)** testa (o
croce), pari (o dispari); **~ first** a capofitto, di
testa; **~ over heels in love** pazzamente
innamorato(a); **to ~ the ball** colpire una palla
di testa; **~ for** *vt fus* dirigersi verso; **~ache** *n*
mal *m* di testa; **~dress** (*BRIT*) *n* (*of bride*)
acconciatura; **~ing** *n* titolo; intestazione *f*;
~lamp (*BRIT*) *n* = **~light**; **~land** *n*
promontorio; **~light** *n* fanale *m*; **~line** *n*
titolo; **~long** *adv* (*fall*) a capofitto; (*rush*)
precipitosamente; **~master/~mistress** *n*
preside *m/f*; **~ office** *n* sede *f* (centrale); **~
on** *adj* (*collision*) frontale; **~phones** *npl*
cuffia; **~quarters** *npl* ufficio centrale; (*MIL*)
quartiere *m* generale; **~-rest** *n* poggiacapo;
~room *n* (*in car*) altezza dell'abitacolo;
(*under bridge*) altezza limite; **~scarf** *n* foulard
m inv; **~strong** *adj* testardo(a); **~ waiter** *n*
capocameriere *m*; **~way** *n*: **to make ~way**
fare progressi; **~wind** *n* controvento; **~y** *adj*
(*experience, period*) inebriante

heal [hiːl] *vt, vi* guarire
health [hɛlθ] *n* salute *f*; **~ centre** (*BRIT*) *n*
poliambulatorio; **~ food(s)** *n(pl)* cibo
macrobiotico; **~ food store** *n* negozio di
alimenti dietetici e macrobiotici; **the
H~ Service** (*BRIT*) *n* ≈ il Servizio Sanitario
Statale; **~y** *adj* (*person*) sano(a), in buona
salute; (*climate*) salubre; (*appetite, economy
etc*) sano(a)
heap [hiːp] *n* mucchio ♦ *vt* (*stones, sand*): **to
~ (up)** ammucchiare; (*plate, sink*): **to ~ sth
with** riempire qc di; **~s of** (*inf*) un mucchio di
hear [hɪə*] (*pt, pp* **heard**) *vt* sentire; (*news*)
ascoltare ♦ *vi* sentire; **to ~ about** avere notizie
di; sentire parlare di; **to ~ from sb** ricevere
notizie da qn; **~ing** *n* (*sense*) udito; (*of
witnesses*) audizione *f*; (*of a case*) udienza;
~ing aid *n* apparecchio acustico; **~say** *n*
dicerie *fpl*, chiacchiere *fpl*
hearse [hɜːs] *n* carro funebre
heart [hɑːt] *n* cuore *m*; **~s** *npl* (*CARDS*) cuori
mpl; **to lose ~** scoraggiarsi; **to take ~** farsi
coraggio; **at ~** in fondo; **by ~** (*learn, know*) a
memoria; **~ attack** *n* attacco di cuore;
~beat *n* battito del cuore; **~breaking** *adj*
straziante; **~broken** *adj*: **to be ~broken** avere
il cuore spezzato; **~burn** *n* bruciore *m* di
stomaco; **~ failure** *n* arresto cardiaco; **~felt**
adj sincero(a)
hearth [hɑːθ] *n* focolare *m*
heartland ['hɑːtlænd] *n* regione *f* centrale
heartless ['hɑːtlɪs] *adj* senza cuore
hearty ['hɑːtɪ] *adj* caloroso(a); robusto(a),
sano(a); vigoroso(a)
heat [hiːt] *n* calore *m*; (*fig*) ardore *m*; fuoco;
(*SPORT: also: qualifying ~*) prova eliminatoria
♦ *vt* scaldare; **~ up** *vi* (*liquids*) scaldarsi;
(*room*) riscaldarsi ♦ *vt* riscaldare; **~ed** *adj*

riscaldato(a); (*argument*) acceso(a); **~er** *n* radiatore *m*; (*stove*) stufa

heath [hiːθ] (*BRIT*) *n* landa

heathen ['hiːðn] *n* pagano/a

heather ['hɛðə*] *n* erica

heating ['hiːtɪŋ] *n* riscaldamento

heatstroke ['hiːtstrəuk] *n* colpo di sole

heatwave ['hiːtweɪv] *n* ondata di caldo

heave [hiːv] *vt* (*pull*) tirare (con forza); (*push*) spingere (con forza); (*lift*) sollevare (con forza) ♦ *vi* sollevarsi; (*retch*) aver conati di vomito ♦ *n* (*push*) grande spinta; **to ~ a sigh** emettere un sospiro

heaven ['hɛvn] *n* paradiso, cielo; **~ly** *adj* divino(a), celeste

heavily ['hɛvɪlɪ] *adv* pesantemente; (*drink, smoke*) molto

heavy ['hɛvɪ] *adj* pesante; (*sea*) grosso(a); (*rain, blow*) forte; (*weather*) afoso(a); (*drinker, smoker*) gran (*before noun*); **~ goods vehicle** *n* veicolo per trasporti pesanti; **~weight** *n* (*SPORT*) peso massimo

Hebrew ['hiːbruː] *adj* ebreo(a) ♦ *n* (*LING*) ebraico

Hebrides ['hɛbrɪdiːz] *npl*: **the ~** le Ebridi

heckle ['hɛkl] *vt* interpellare e dare noia a (*un oratore*)

hectic ['hɛktɪk] *adj* movimentato(a)

he'd [hiːd] = **he would; he had**

hedge [hɛdʒ] *vt* siepe f ♦ *vi* essere elusivo(a); **to ~ one's bets** (*fig*) coprirsi dai rischi

hedgehog ['hɛdʒhɔg] *n* riccio

heed [hiːd] *vt* (*also*: *take ~ of*) badare a, far conto di; **~less** *adj*: **~less (of)** sordo(a) (a)

heel [hiːl] *n* (*ANAT*) calcagno; (*of shoe*) tacco ♦ *vt* (*shoe*) rifare i tacchi a

hefty ['hɛftɪ] *adj* (*person*) robusto(a); (*parcel*) pesante; (*profit*) grosso(a)

heifer ['hɛfə*] *n* giovenca

height [haɪt] *n* altezza; (*high ground*) altura; (*fig*: *of glory*) apice *m*; (: *of stupidity*) colmo; **~en** *vt* (*fig*) accrescere

heir [ɛə*] *n* erede *m*; **~ess** *n* erede f; **~loom** *n* mobile *m* (or gioiello or quadro) di famiglia

held [hɛld] *pt, pp* of **hold**

helicopter ['hɛlɪkɔptə*] *n* elicottero

heliport ['hɛlɪpɔːt] *n* eliporto

helium ['hiːlɪəm] *n* elio

hell [hɛl] *n* inferno; **~!** (*inf*) porca miseria!, accidenti!

he'll [hiːl] = **he will; he shall**

hellish ['hɛlɪʃ] (*inf*) *adj* infernale

hello [hə'ləu] *excl* buon giorno!; ciao! (*to sb one addresses as "tu"*); (*surprise*) ma guarda!

helm [hɛlm] *n* (*NAUT*) timone *m*

helmet ['hɛlmɪt] *n* casco

help [hɛlp] *n* aiuto; (*charwoman*) donna di servizio ♦ *vt* aiutare; **~!** aiuto!; **~ yourself (to bread)** si serva (del pane); **he can't ~ it** non

ci può far niente; **~er** *n* aiutante *m/f*, assistente *m/f*; **~ful** *adj* di grande aiuto; (*useful*) utile; **~ing** *n* porzione f; **~less** *adj* impotente; debole

hem [hɛm] *n* orlo ♦ *vt* fare l'orlo a; **~ in** *vt* cingere

hemisphere ['hɛmɪsfɪə*] *n* emisfero

hemorrhage ['hɛmərɪdʒ] (*US*) *n* = **haemorrhage**

hemorrhoids ['hɛmərɔɪdz] (*US*) *npl* = **haemorroids**

hen [hɛn] *n* gallina; (*female bird*) femmina

hence [hɛns] *adv* (*therefore*) dunque; **2 years ~** di qui a 2 anni; **~forth** *adv* d'ora in poi

henpecked ['hɛnpɛkt] *adj* dominato dalla moglie

hepatitis [hɛpə'taɪtɪs] *n* epatite f

her [həː*] *pron* (*direct*) la, l' + *vowel*; (*indirect*) le; (*stressed, after prep*) lei ♦ *adj* il(la) suo(a), i(le) suoi(sue); *see also* **my**

herald ['hɛrəld] *n* araldo ♦ *vt* annunciare

heraldry ['hɛrəldrɪ] *n* araldica

herb [həːb] *n* erba

herd [həːd] *n* mandria

here [hɪə*] *adv* qui, qua ♦ *excl* ehi!; **~!** (*at roll call*) presente!; **~ is/are** ecco; **~ he/she is** eccolo/eccola; **~after** *adv* in futuro; dopo questo; **~by** *adv* (*in letter*) con la presente

hereditary [hɪ'rɛdɪtrɪ] *adj* ereditario(a)

heresy ['hɛrəsɪ] *n* eresia

heretic ['hɛrətɪk] *n* eretico/a

heritage ['hɛrɪtɪdʒ] *n* eredità; (*fig*) retaggio

hermetically [həː'mɛtɪklɪ] *adv*: **~ sealed** ermeticamente chiuso(a)

hermit ['həːmɪt] *n* eremita *m*

hernia ['həːnɪə] *n* ernia

hero ['hɪərəu] (*pl* **~es**) *n* eroe *m*

heroin ['hɛrəuɪn] *n* eroina

heroine ['hɛrəuɪn] *n* eroina

heron ['hɛrən] *n* airone *m*

herring ['hɛrɪŋ] *n* aringa

hers [həːz] *pron* il(la) suo(a), i(le) suoi(sue); *see also* **mine[1]**

herself [həː'sɛlf] *pron* (*reflexive*) si; (*emphatic*) lei stessa; (*after prep*) se stessa, sé; *see also* **oneself**

he's [hiːz] = **he is; he has**

hesitant ['hɛzɪtənt] *adj* esitante, indeciso(a)

hesitate ['hɛzɪteɪt] *vi*: **to ~ (about/to do)** esitare (su/a fare); **hesitation** [-'teɪʃən] *n* esitazione f

heterosexual ['hɛtərəu'sɛksjuəl] *adj, n* eterosessuale *m/f*

hexagonal [hɛk'sægənəl] *adj* esagonale

heyday ['heɪdeɪ] *n*: **the ~ of** i bei giorni di, l'età d'oro di

HGV *n abbr* = **heavy goods vehicle**

hi [haɪ] *excl* ciao!

hiatus [haɪ'eɪtəs] *n* vuoto; (*LING*) iato

hibernate ['haɪbəneɪt] vi ibernare

hiccough ['hɪkʌp] vi singhiozzare; **~s** npl: **to have ~s** avere il singhiozzo

hiccup ['hɪkʌp] = **hiccough**

hid [hɪd] pt of **hide**; **~den** ['hɪdn] pp of **hide**

hide [haɪd] (pt **hid**, pp **hidden**) n (skin) pelle f ♦ vt: **to ~ sth (from sb)** nascondere qc (a qn) ♦ vi: **to ~ (from sb)** nascondersi (da qn); **~-and-seek** n rimpiattino

hideous ['hɪdɪəs] adj laido(a); orribile

hiding ['haɪdɪŋ] n (beating) bastonata; **to be in ~** (concealed) tenersi nascosto(a)

hierarchy ['haɪərɑːkɪ] n gerarchia

hi-fi ['haɪfaɪ] n stereo ♦ adj ad alta fedeltà, hi-fi inv

high [haɪ] adj alto(a); (speed, respect, number) grande; (wind) forte; (voice) acuto(a) ♦ adv alto, in alto; **20m ~** alto(a) 20m; **~brow** adj, n intellettuale m/f; **~chair** n seggiolone m; **~er education** n studi mpl superiori; **~-handed** adj prepotente; **~-heeled** adj con i tacchi alti; **~ jump** n (SPORT) salto in alto; **the H~lands** npl le Highlands scozzesi; **~light** n (fig: of event) momento culminante; (in hair) colpo di sole ♦ vt mettere in evidenza; **~ly** adv molto; **to speak ~ly of** parlare molto bene di; **~ly strung** adj teso(a) di nervi, eccitabile; **~ness** n: **Her H~ness** Sua Altezza; **~-pitched** adj acuto(a); **~-rise block** n palazzone m; **~ school** n scuola secondaria; (US) istituto superiore d'istruzione; **~ season** (BRIT) n alta stagione; **~ street** (BRIT) n strada principale

highway ['haɪweɪ] n strada maestra; **H~ Code** (BRIT) n codice m della strada

hijack ['haɪdʒæk] vt dirottare; **~er** n dirottatore/trice

hike [haɪk] vi fare un'escursione a piedi ♦ n escursione f a piedi; **~r** n escursionista m/f; **hiking** n escursioni fpl a piedi

hilarious [hɪ'lɛərɪəs] adj (behaviour, event) spassosissimo(a)

hill [hɪl] n collina, colle m; (fairly high) montagna; (on road) salita; **~side** n fianco della collina; **~ walking** n escursioni fpl in collina; **~y** adj collinoso(a); montagnoso(a)

hilt [hɪlt] n (of sword) elsa; **to the ~** (fig: support) fino in fondo

him [hɪm] pron (direct) lo, l' + vowel; (indirect) gli; (stressed, after prep) lui; see also **me**; **~self** pron (reflexive) si; (emphatic) lui stesso; (after prep) se stesso, sé; see also **oneself**

hinder ['hɪndə*] vt ostacolare; **hindrance** ['hɪndrəns] n ostacolo, impedimento

hindsight ['haɪndsaɪt] n: **with ~** con il senno di poi

Hindu ['hɪnduː] n indù m/f inv

hinge [hɪndʒ] n cardine m ♦ vi (fig): **to ~ on** dipendere da

hint [hɪnt] n (suggestion) allusione f; (advice) consiglio; (sign) accenno ♦ vt: **to ~ that** lasciar capire che ♦ vi: **to ~ at** alludere a

hip [hɪp] n anca, fianco

hippopotamus [hɪpə'pɔtəməs] (pl **~es** or **hippopotami**) n ippopotamo

hire ['haɪə*] vt (BRIT: car, equipment) noleggiare; (worker) assumere, dare lavoro a ♦ n nolo, noleggio; **for ~** a nolo; (taxi) libero(a); **~(d) car** (BRIT) n macchina a nolo; **~ purchase** (BRIT) n acquisto (or vendita) rateale

his [hɪz] adj, pron il(la) suo(sua), i(le) suoi(sue); see also **my**; **mine**[1]

hiss [hɪs] vi fischiare; (cat, snake) sibilare

historic(al) [hɪ'stɔrɪk(l)] adj storico(a)

history ['hɪstərɪ] n storia

hit [hɪt] (pt, pp **hit**) vt colpire, picchiare; (knock against) battere; (reach: target) raggiungere; (collide with: car) urtare contro; (fig: affect) colpire; (find: problem etc) incontrare ♦ n colpo; (success, song) successo; **to ~ it off with sb** andare molto d'accordo con qn; **~-and-run driver** n pirata m della strada

hitch [hɪtʃ] vt (fasten) attaccare; (also: ~ up) tirare su ♦ n (difficulty) intoppo, difficoltà f inv; **to ~ a lift** fare l'autostop

hitch-hike ['hɪtʃhaɪk] vi fare l'autostop; **~r** n autostoppista m/f; **hitch-hiking** n autostop m

hi-tech ['haɪtɛk] adj di alta tecnologia ♦ n alta tecnologia

hitherto [hɪðə'tuː] adv in precedenza

HIV abbr: **HIV-negative/-positive** adj sieronegativo(a)/sieropositivo(a)

hive [haɪv] n alveare m

H.M.S. abbr = **His(Her) Majesty's Ship**

hoard [hɔːd] n (of food) provviste fpl; (of money) gruzzolo ♦ vt ammassare

hoarding ['hɔːdɪŋ] (BRIT) n (for posters) tabellone m per affissioni

hoarse [hɔːs] adj rauco(a)

hoax [həuks] n scherzo; falso allarme

hob [hɔb] n piastra (con fornelli)

hobble ['hɔbl] vi zoppicare

hobby ['hɔbɪ] n hobby m inv, passatempo

hobo ['həubəu] (US) n vagabondo

hockey ['hɔkɪ] n hockey m

hoe [həu] n zappa

hog [hɔg] n maiale m ♦ vt (fig) arraffare; **to go the whole ~** farlo fino in fondo

hoist [hɔɪst] n paranco ♦ vt issare

hold [həuld] (pt, pp **held**) vt tenere; (contain) contenere; (keep back) trattenere; (believe) mantenere, considerare; (possess) avere, possedere; detenere ♦ vi (withstand pressure) tenere; (be valid) essere valido(a) ♦ n presa;

(*control*): **to have a ~ over** avere controllo su; (*NAUT*) stiva; **~ the line!** (*TEL*) resti in linea!; **to ~ one's own** (*fig*) difendersi bene; **to catch** *or* **get (a) ~ of** afferrare; **~ back** *vt* trattenere; (*secret*) tenere celato(a); **~ down** *vt* (*person*) tenere a terra; (*job*) tenere; **~ off** *vt* tener lontano; **~ on** *vi* tener fermo; (*wait*) aspettare; **~ on!** (*TEL*) resti in linea!; **~ on to** *vt fus* tenersi stretto(a) a; (*keep*) conservare; **~ out** *vt* offrire ♦ *vi* (*resist*) resistere; **~ up** *vt* (*raise*) alzare; (*support*) sostenere; (*delay*) ritardare; (*rob*) assaltare; **~all** (*BRIT*) *n* borsone *m*; **~er** *n* (*container*) contenitore *m*; (*of ticket, title*) possessore/posseditrice; (*of office etc*) incaricato/a; (*of record*) detentore/trice; **~ing** *n* (*share*) azioni *fpl*, titoli *mpl*; (*farm*) podere *m*, tenuta; **~up** *n* (*robbery*) rapina a mano armata; (*delay*) ritardo; (*BRIT: in traffic*) blocco

hole [həʊl] *n* buco, buca

holiday ['hɔlədɪ] *n* vacanza; (*day off*) giorno di vacanza; (*public*) giorno festivo; **on ~** in vacanza; **~ camp** (*BRIT*) *n* (*also: ~ centre*) ≈ villaggio (di vacanze); **~-maker** (*BRIT*) *n* villeggiante *m/f*; **~ resort** *n* luogo di villeggiatura

holiness ['həʊlɪnɪs] *n* santità

Holland ['hɔlənd] *n* Olanda

hollow ['hɔləʊ] *adj* cavo(a); (*container, claim*) vuoto(a); (*laugh, sound*) cupo(a) ♦ *n* cavità *f inv*; (*in land*) valletta, depressione *f* ♦ *vt*: **to ~ out** scavare

holly ['hɔlɪ] *n* agrifoglio

holocaust ['hɔləkɔːst] *n* olocausto

holster ['həʊlstə*] *n* fondina (di pistola)

holy ['həʊlɪ] *adj* santo(a); (*bread, ground*) benedetto(a), consacrato(a)

homage ['hɔmɪdʒ] *n* omaggio; **to pay ~ to** rendere omaggio a

home [həʊm] *n* casa; (*country*) patria; (*institution*) casa, ricovero ♦ *cpd* familiare; (*cooking etc*) casalingo(a); (*ECON, POL*) nazionale, interno(a); (*SPORT*) di casa ♦ *adv* a casa; in patria; (*right in: nail etc*) fino in fondo; **at ~** a casa; (*in situation*) a proprio agio; **to go** (*or* **come**) **~** tornare a casa (or in patria); **make yourself at ~** si metta a suo agio; **~ address** *n* indirizzo di casa; **~land** *n* patria; **~less** *adj* senza tetto; spatriato(a); **~ly** *adj* semplice, alla buona; accogliente; **~-made** *adj* casalingo(a); **H~ Office** (*BRIT*) *n* ministero degli Interni; **~ page** *n* (*COMPUT*) home page *f inv*; **~ rule** *n* autogoverno; **H~ Secretary** (*BRIT*) *n* ministro degli Interni; **~sick** *adj*: **to be ~sick** avere la nostalgia; **~ town** *n* città *f inv* natale; **~ward** ['həʊmwəd] *adj* (*journey*) di ritorno; **~work** *n* compiti *mpl* (per casa)

homicide ['hɔmɪsaɪd] (*US*) *n* omicidio

homoeopathic [həʊmɪə'pæθɪk] (*US* **homeopathic**) *adj* omeopatico(a)

homosexual [hɔməʊ'sɛksjuəl] *adj, n* omosessuale *m/f*

honest ['ɔnɪst] *adj* onesto(a); sincero(a); **~ly** *adv* onestamente; sinceramente; **~y** *n* onestà

honey ['hʌnɪ] *n* miele *m*; **~comb** *n* favo; **~moon** *n* luna di miele, viaggio di nozze; **~suckle** *n* (*BOT*) caprifoglio

honk [hɔŋk] *vi* suonare il clacson

honorary ['ɔnərərɪ] *adj* onorario(a); (*duty, title*) onorifico(a)

honour ['ɔnə*] (*US* **honor**) *vt* onorare ♦ *n* onore *m*; **~able** *adj* onorevole; **~s degree** *n* (*SCOL*) laurea specializzata

hood [hud] *n* cappuccio; (*on cooker*) cappa; (*BRIT: AUT*) capote *f*; (*US: AUT*) cofano

hoodlum ['huːdləm] *n* teppista *m/f*

hoof [huːf] (*pl* **hooves**) *n* zoccolo

hook [huk] *n* gancio; (*for fishing*) amo ♦ *vt* uncinare; (*dress*) agganciare

hooligan ['huːlɪgən] *n* giovinastro, teppista *m*

hoop [huːp] *n* cerchio

hooray [huː'reɪ] *excl* = **hurray**

hoot [huːt] *vi* (*AUT*) suonare il clacson; (*siren*) ululare; (*owl*) gufare; **~er** *n* (*BRIT: AUT*) clacson *m inv*; (*NAUT*) sirena

Hoover ® ['huːvə*] (*BRIT*) *n* aspirapolvere *m inv* ♦ *vt*: **h~** pulire con l'aspirapolvere

hooves [huːvz] *npl of* **hoof**

hop [hɔp] *vi* saltellare, saltare; (*on one foot*) saltare su una gamba

hope [həʊp] *vt*: **to ~ that/to do** sperare che/di fare ♦ *vi* sperare ♦ *n* speranza; **I ~ so/not** spero di sì/no; **~ful** *adj* (*person*) pieno(a) di speranza; (*situation*) promettente; **~fully** *adv* con speranza; **~fully he will recover** speriamo che si riprenda; **~less** *adj* senza speranza, disperato(a); (*useless*) inutile

hops [hɔps] *npl* luppoli *mpl*

horde [hɔːd] *n* orda

horizon [hə'raɪzn] *n* orizzonte *m*; **~tal** [hɔrɪ'zɔntl] *adj* orizzontale

hormone ['hɔːməʊn] *n* ormone *m*

horn [hɔːn] *n* (*ZOOL, MUS*) corno; (*AUT*) clacson *m inv*

hornet ['hɔːnɪt] *n* calabrone *m*

horoscope ['hɔrəskəʊp] *n* oroscopo

horrendous [hə'rɛndəs] *adj* orrendo(a)

horrible ['hɔrɪbl] *adj* orribile, tremendo(a)

horrid ['hɔrɪd] *adj* orrido(a); (*person*) odioso(a)

horrify ['hɔrɪfaɪ] *vt* scandalizzare

horror ['hɔrə*] *n* orrore *m*; **~ film** *n* film *m inv* dell'orrore

hors d'œuvre [ɔː'dəːvrə] *n* antipasto

horse [hɔːs] *n* cavallo; **~back: on ~back** *adj, adv* a cavallo; **~ chestnut** *n* ippocastano;

~man (*irreg*) *n* cavaliere *m*; **~power** *n* cavallo (vapore); **~-racing** *n* ippica; **~radish** *n* rafano; **~shoe** *n* ferro di cavallo; **~woman** (*irreg*) *n* amazzone *f*

horticulture ['hɔːtɪkʌltʃə*] *n* orticoltura

hose [həuz] *n* (*also:* ~*pipe*) tubo; (*also: garden* ~) tubo per annaffiare

hosiery ['həuʒərɪ] *n* maglieria

hospice ['hɔspɪs] *n* ricovero, ospizio

hospitable [hɔs'pɪtəbl] *adj* ospitale

hospital ['hɔspɪtl] *n* ospedale *m*

hospitality [hɔspɪ'tælɪtɪ] *n* ospitalità

host [həust] *n* ospite *m*; (*REL*) ostia; (*large number*): **a ~ of** una schiera di

hostage ['hɔstɪdʒ] *n* ostaggio/a

hostel ['hɔstl] *n* ostello; (*also: youth* ~) ostello della gioventù

hostess ['həustɪs] *n* ospite *f*; (*BRIT: air* ~) hostess *f inv*

hostile ['hɔstaɪl] *adj* ostile

hostility [hɔ'stɪlɪtɪ] *n* ostilità *f inv*

hot [hɔt] *adj* caldo(a); (*as opposed to only warm*) molto caldo(a); (*spicy*) piccante; (*fig*) accanito(a); ardente; violento(a), focoso(a); **to be ~** (*person*) aver caldo; (*object*) essere caldo(a); (*weather*) far caldo; **~bed** *n* (*fig*) focolaio; **~ dog** *n* hot dog *m inv*

hotel [həu'tɛl] *n* albergo; **~ier** *n* albergatore/trice

hot: **~house** *n* serra; **~ line** *n* (*POL*) telefono rosso; **~ly** *adv* violentemente; **~plate** *n* (*on cooker*) piastra riscaldante; **~pot** (*BRIT*) *n* stufato coperto da uno strato di patate; **~water bottle** *n* borsa dell'acqua calda

hound [haund] *vt* perseguitare ♦ *n* segugio

hour ['auə*] *n* ora; **~ly** *adj* all'ora

house [*n* haus, *pl* 'hauzɪz, *vb* hauz] *n* (*also: firm*) casa; (*POL*) camera; (*THEATRE*) sala; pubblico; spettacolo; (*dynasty*) casata ♦ *vt* (*person*) ospitare, alloggiare; **on the ~** (*fig*) offerto(a) dalla casa; **~ arrest** *n* arresti *mpl* domiciliari; **~boat** *n* house boat *f inv*; **~bound** *adj* confinato(a) in casa; **~breaking** *n* furto con scasso; **~hold** *n* famiglia; casa; **~keeper** *n* governante *f*; **~keeping** *n* (*work*) governo della casa; (*money*) soldi *mpl* per le spese di casa; **~warming party** *n* festa per inaugurare la casa nuova; **~wife** (*irreg*) *n* massaia, casalinga; **~work** *n* faccende *fpl* domestiche

housing ['hauzɪŋ] *n* alloggio; **~ development** (*BRIT* ~ *estate*) *n* zona residenziale con case popolari e/o private

hovel ['hɔvl] *n* casupola

hover ['hɔvə*] *vi* (*bird*) librarsi; **~craft** *n* hovercraft *m inv*

how [hau] *adv* come; **~ are you?** come sta?; **~ do you do?** piacere!; **~ far is it to the river?** quanto è lontano il fiume?; **~ long have you been here?** da quando è qui?; **~ lovely!/awful!** che bello!/orrore!; **~ many?** quanti(e)?; **~ much?** quanto(a)?; **~ much milk?** quanto latte?; **~ many people?** quante persone?; **~ old are you?** quanti anni ha?; **~ever** *adv* in qualsiasi modo *or* maniera che; (*+ adjective*) per quanto + *sub*; (*in questions*) come ♦ *conj* comunque, però

howl [haul] *vi* ululare; (*baby, person*) urlare

H.P. *abbr* = hire purchase; horsepower

h.p. *n abbr* = H.P

HQ *n abbr* = headquarters

hub [hʌb] *n* (*of wheel*) mozzo; (*fig*) fulcro

hubcap ['hʌbkæp] *n* coprimozzo

huddle ['hʌdl] *vi*: **to ~ together** rannicchiarsi l'uno contro l'altro

hue [hjuː] *n* tinta

huff [hʌf] *n*: **in a ~** stizzito(a)

hug [hʌg] *vt* abbracciare; (*shore, kerb*) stringere

huge [hjuːdʒ] *adj* enorme, immenso(a)

hulk [hʌlk] *n* (*ship*) nave *f* in disarmo; (*building, car*) carcassa; (*person*) mastodonte *m*

hull [hʌl] *n* (*of ship*) scafo

hullo [hə'ləu] *excl* = hello

hum [hʌm] *vt* (*tune*) canticchiare ♦ *vi* canticchiare; (*insect, plane, tool*) ronzare

human ['hjuːmən] *adj* umano(a) ♦ *n* essere *m* umano

humane [hjuː'meɪn] *adj* umanitario(a)

humanitarian [hjuːmænɪ'tɛərɪən] *adj* umanitario(a)

humanity [hjuː'mænɪtɪ] *n* umanità

humble ['hʌmbl] *adj* umile, modesto(a) ♦ *vt* umiliare

humdrum ['hʌmdrʌm] *adj* monotono(a), tedioso(a)

humid ['hjuːmɪd] *adj* umido(a)

humiliate [hjuː'mɪlɪeɪt] *vt* umiliare; **humiliation** [-'eɪʃən] *n* umiliazione *f*

humility [hjuː'mɪlɪtɪ] *n* umiltà

humorous ['hjuːmərəs] *adj* umoristico(a); (*person*) buffo(a)

humour ['hjuːmə*] (*US* humor) *n* umore *m* ♦ *vt* accontentare

hump [hʌmp] *n* gobba

hunch [hʌntʃ] *n* (*premonition*) intuizione *f*; **~ed** *adj* incurvato(a)

hundred ['hʌndrəd] *num* cento; **~s of** centinaia *fpl* di; **~weight** *n* (*BRIT*) = 50.8 kg; 112 lb; (*US*) = 45.3 kg; 100 lb

hung [hʌŋ] *pt, pp* of hang

Hungary ['hʌŋgərɪ] *n* Ungheria

hunger ['hʌŋgə*] *n* fame *f* ♦ *vi*: **to ~ for** desiderare ardentemente; **~ strike** *n* sciopero della fame

hungry ['hʌŋgrɪ] *adj* affamato(a); **to be ~** aver fame

hunk [hʌŋk] n (of bread etc) bel pezzo

hunt [hʌnt] vt (seek) cercare; (SPORT) cacciare
♦ vi: **to ~ (for)** andare a caccia (di) ♦ n
caccia; **~er** n cacciatore m; **~ing** n caccia

hurdle ['hə:dl] n (SPORT, fig) ostacolo

hurl [hə:l] vt lanciare con violenza

hurrah [hu'rɑ:] excl = **hurray**

hurray [hu'reɪ] excl urra!, evviva!

hurricane ['hʌrɪkən] n uragano

hurried ['hʌrɪd] adj affrettato(a); (work)
fatto(a) in fretta; **~ly** adv in fretta

hurry ['hʌrɪ] n fretta ♦ vi (also: ~ up)
affrettarsi ♦ vt (also: ~ up: person) affrettare;
(: work) far in fretta; **to be in a ~** aver fretta

hurt [hə:t] (pt, pp hurt) vt (cause pain to) far
male a; (injure, fig) ferire ♦ vi far male; **~ful**
adj (remark) che ferisce

hurtle ['hə:tl] vi: **to ~ past/down** passare/
scendere a razzo

husband ['hʌzbənd] n marito

hush [hʌʃ] n silenzio, calma ♦ vt zittire; **~ up**
vt (scandal) mettere a tacere

husk [hʌsk] n (of wheat) cartoccio; (of rice,
maize) buccia

husky ['hʌskɪ] adj roco(a) ♦ n cane m
eschimese

hustle ['hʌsl] vt spingere, incalzare ♦ n:
~ and bustle trambusto

hut [hʌt] n rifugio; (shed) ripostiglio

hutch [hʌtʃ] n gabbia

hyacinth ['haɪəsɪnθ] n giacinto

hybrid ['haɪbrɪd] n ibrido

hydrant ['haɪdrənt] n (also: fire ~) idrante m

hydraulic [haɪ'drɔ:lɪk] adj idraulico(a)

hydroelectric [haɪdrəʊ'lektrɪk] adj
idroelettrico(a)

hydrofoil ['haɪdrəfɔɪl] n aliscafo

hydrogen ['haɪdrədʒən] n idrogeno

hyena [haɪ'i:nə] n iena

hygiene ['haɪdʒi:n] n igiene f

hymn [hɪm] n inno; cantica

hype [haɪp] (inf) n campagna pubblicitaria

hypermarket ['haɪpəmɑ:kɪt] (BRIT) n
ipermercato

hypertext ['haɪpətekst] n (COMPUT) ipertesto

hyphen ['haɪfn] n trattino

hypnotize ['hɪpnətaɪz] vt ipnotizzare

hypocrisy [hɪ'pɔkrɪsɪ] n ipocrisia

hypocrite ['hɪpəkrɪt] n ipocrita m/f;
hypocritical [-'krɪtɪkl] adj ipocrita

hypothermia [haɪpəʊ'θə:mɪə] n ipotermia

hypothesis [haɪ'pɔθɪsɪs] (pl **hypotheses**) n
ipotesi f inv

hypothetical [haɪpəʊ'θetɪkl] adj ipotetico(a)

hysterical [hɪ'sterɪkl] adj isterico(a)

hysterics [hɪ'sterɪks] npl accesso di isteria;
(laughter) attacco di riso

I, i

I [aɪ] pron io

ice [aɪs] n ghiaccio; (on road) gelo; (~ cream)
gelato ♦ vt (cake) glassare ♦ vi (also: ~ over)
ghiacciare; (also: ~ up) gelare; **~berg** n
iceberg m inv; **~box** n (US) frigorifero; (BRIT)
reparto ghiaccio; (insulated box) frigo
portatile; **~ cream** n gelato; **~ hockey** n
hockey m su ghiaccio

Iceland ['aɪslənd] n Islanda

ice: **~ lolly** (BRIT) n ghiacciolo; **~ rink** n pista
di pattinaggio; **~ skating** n pattinaggio sul
ghiaccio

icicle ['aɪsɪkl] n ghiacciolo

icing ['aɪsɪŋ] n (CULIN) glassa; **~ sugar** (BRIT)
n zucchero a velo

icy ['aɪsɪ] adj ghiacciato(a); (weather,
temperature) gelido(a)

I'd [aɪd] = **I would; I had**

idea [aɪ'dɪə] n idea

ideal [aɪ'dɪəl] adj ideale ♦ n ideale m

identical [aɪ'dentɪkl] adj identico(a)

identification [aɪdentɪfɪ'keɪʃən] n
identificazione f; **(means of)** ~ carta d'identità

identify [aɪ'dentɪfaɪ] vt identificare

Identikit picture ® [aɪ'dentɪkɪt-] n identikit
m inv

identity [aɪ'dentɪtɪ] n identità f inv; **~ card** n
carta d'identità

ideology [aɪdɪ'ɔlədʒɪ] n ideologia

idiom ['ɪdɪəm] n idioma m; (phrase)
espressione f idiomatica

idiot ['ɪdɪət] n idiota m/f; **~ic** [-'ɔtɪk] adj idiota

idle ['aɪdl] adj inattivo(a); (lazy) pigro(a),
ozioso(a); (unemployed) disoccupato(a);
(question, pleasures) ozioso(a) ♦ vi (engine)
girare al minimo

idol ['aɪdl] n idolo; **~ize** vt idoleggiare

i.e. adv abbr (= that is) cioè

if [ɪf] conj se; **~ I were you** ... se fossi in te ..., io
al tuo posto ...; **~ so** se è così; **~ not** se no;
~ only se solo or soltanto

ignite [ɪg'naɪt] vt accendere ♦ vi accendersi

ignition [ɪg'nɪʃən] n (AUT) accensione f; **to
switch on/off the ~** accendere/spegnere il
motore; **~ key** n (AUT) chiave f
dell'accensione

ignorant ['ɪgnərənt] adj ignorante; **to be ~ of**
(subject) essere ignorante in; (events) essere
ignaro(a) di

ignore [ɪg'nɔ:*] vt non tener conto di;
(person, fact) ignorare

I'll [aɪl] = **I will; I shall**

ill [ɪl] adj (sick) malato(a); (bad) cattivo(a) ♦ n
male m ♦ adv: **to speak** etc ~ **of sb** parlare etc
male di qn; **to take** or **be taken** ~ ammalarsi;

~-advised adj (decision) poco giudizioso(a); (person) mal consigliato(a); **~-at-ease** adj a disagio

illegal [ɪ'li:gl] adj illegale

illegible [ɪ'lɛdʒɪbl] adj illeggibile

illegitimate [ɪlɪ'dʒɪtɪmət] adj illegittimo(a)

ill-fated [ɪl'feɪtɪd] adj nefasto(a)

ill feeling n rancore m

illiterate [ɪ'lɪtərət] adj analfabeta, illetterato(a); (letter) scorretto(a)

ill-mannered [ɪl'mænəd] adj maleducato(a)

illness ['ɪlnɪs] n malattia

ill-treat [ɪl'tri:t] vt maltrattare

illuminate [ɪ'lu:mɪneɪt] vt illuminare; **illumination** [-'neɪʃən] n illuminazione f; **illuminations** npl (decorative) luminarie fpl

illusion [ɪ'lu:ʒən] n illusione f

illustrate ['ɪləstreɪt] vt illustrare

illustration [ɪlə'streɪʃən] n illustrazione f

I'm [aɪm] = **I am**

image ['ɪmɪdʒ] n immagine f; (public face) immagine (pubblica); **~ry** n immagini fpl

imaginary [ɪ'mædʒɪnərɪ] adj immaginario(a)

imagination [ɪmædʒɪ'neɪʃən] n immaginazione f, fantasia

imaginative [ɪ'mædʒɪnətɪv] adj immaginoso(a)

imagine [ɪ'mædʒɪn] vt immaginare

imbalance [ɪm'bæləns] n squilibrio

imbue [ɪm'bju:] vt: **to ~ sb/sth with** permeare qn/qc di

imitate ['ɪmɪteɪt] vt imitare; **imitation** [-'teɪʃən] n imitazione f

immaculate [ɪ'mækjulət] adj immacolato(a); (dress, appearance) impeccabile

immaterial [ɪmə'tɪərɪəl] adj immateriale, indifferente

immature [ɪmə'tjuə*] adj immaturo(a)

immediate [ɪ'mi:dɪət] adj immediato(a); **~ly** adv (at once) subito, immediatamente; **~ly next to** proprio accanto a

immense [ɪ'mɛns] adj immenso(a); enorme

immerse [ɪ'mɜːs] vt immergere

immersion heater [ɪ'mɜːʃən-] (BRIT) n scaldaacqua m inv a immersione

immigrant ['ɪmɪgrənt] n immigrante m/f; immigrato/a

immigration [ɪmɪ'greɪʃən] n immigrazione f

imminent ['ɪmɪnənt] adj imminente

immoral [ɪ'mɔrl] adj immorale

immortal [ɪ'mɔːtl] adj, n immortale m/f

immune [ɪ'mju:n] adj: **~ (to)** immune (da); **immunity** n immunità

impact ['ɪmpækt] n impatto

impair [ɪm'pɛə*] vt danneggiare

impart [ɪm'pɑːt] vt (make known) comunicare; (bestow) impartire

impartial [ɪm'pɑːʃl] adj imparziale

impassable [ɪm'pɑːsəbl] adj insuperabile; (road) impraticabile

impassive [ɪm'pæsɪv] adj impassibile

impatience [ɪm'peɪʃəns] n impazienza

impatient [ɪm'peɪʃənt] adj impaziente; **to get or grow ~** perdere la pazienza

impeccable [ɪm'pɛkəbl] adj impeccabile

impede [ɪm'pi:d] vt impedire

impediment [ɪm'pɛdɪmənt] n impedimento; (also: speech ~) difetto di pronuncia

impending [ɪm'pɛndɪŋ] adj imminente

imperative [ɪm'pɛrətɪv] adj imperativo(a); necessario(a), urgente; (voice) imperioso(a)

imperfect [ɪm'pə:fɪkt] adj imperfetto(a); (goods etc) difettoso(a) ♦ n (LING: also: ~ tense) imperfetto

imperial [ɪm'pɪərɪəl] adj imperiale; (measure) legale

impersonal [ɪm'pə:sənl] adj impersonale

impersonate [ɪm'pə:səneɪt] vt impersonare; (THEATRE) fare la mimica di

impertinent [ɪm'pə:tɪnənt] adj insolente, impertinente

impervious [ɪm'pə:vɪəs] adj (fig): **~ to** insensibile a; impassibile di fronte a

impetuous [ɪm'pɛtjuəs] adj impetuoso(a), precipitoso(a)

impetus ['ɪmpətəs] n impeto

impinge on [ɪm'pɪndʒ-] vt fus (person) colpire; (rights) ledere

implement [n 'ɪmplɪmənt, vb 'ɪmplɪment] n attrezzo; (for cooking) utensile m ♦ vt effettuare

implicit [ɪm'plɪsɪt] adj implicito(a); (complete) completo(a)

imply [ɪm'plaɪ] vt insinuare; suggerire

impolite [ɪmpə'laɪt] adj scortese

import [vb ɪm'pɔːt, n 'ɪmpɔːt] vt importare ♦ n (COMM) importazione f

importance [ɪm'pɔːtns] n importanza

important [ɪm'pɔːtnt] adj importante; **it's not ~** non ha importanza

importer [ɪm'pɔːtə*] n importatore/trice

impose [ɪm'pəuz] vt imporre ♦ vi: **to ~ on sb** sfruttare la bontà di qn

imposing [ɪm'pəuzɪŋ] adj imponente

imposition [ɪmpə'zɪʃən] n (of tax etc) imposizione f; **to be an ~ on** (person) abusare della gentilezza di

impossibility [ɪmpɔsə'bɪlɪtɪ] n impossibilità

impossible [ɪm'pɔsɪbl] adj impossibile

impotent ['ɪmpətnt] adj impotente

impound [ɪm'paund] vt confiscare

impoverished [ɪm'pɔvərɪʃt] adj impoverito(a)

impracticable [ɪm'præktɪkəbl] adj inattuabile

impractical [ɪm'præktɪkl] adj non pratico(a)

impress [ɪm'prɛs] vt impressionare; (mark)

imprimere, stampare; **to ~ sth on sb** far capire qc a qn

impression [ɪmˈprɛʃən] n impressione f; **to be under the ~ that** avere l'impressione che

impressive [ɪmˈprɛsɪv] adj notevole

imprint [ˈɪmprɪnt] n (of hand etc) impronta; (PUBLISHING) sigla editoriale

imprison [ɪmˈprɪzn] vt imprigionare; **~ment** n imprigionamento

improbable [ɪmˈprɔbəbl] adj improbabile; (excuse) inverosimile

impromptu [ɪmˈprɔmptjuː] adj improvvisato(a)

improper [ɪmˈprɔpə*] adj scorretto(a); (unsuitable) inadatto(a), improprio(a); sconveniente, indecente

improve [ɪmˈpruːv] vt migliorare ♦ vi migliorare; (pupil etc) fare progressi; **~ment** n miglioramento; progresso

improvise [ˈɪmprəvaɪz] vt, vi improvvisare

impudent [ˈɪmpjudnt] adj impudente, sfacciato(a)

impulse [ˈɪmpʌls] n impulso; **on ~** d'impulso, impulsivamente

impulsive [ɪmˈpʌlsɪv] adj impulsivo(a)

KEYWORD

in [ɪn] prep **1** (indicating place, position) in; **~ the house/garden** in casa/giardino; **~ the box** nella scatola; **~ the fridge** nel frigorifero; **I have it ~ my hand** ce l'ho in mano; **~ town/ the country** in città/campagna; **~ school** a scuola; **~ here/there** qui/lì dentro
2 (with place names: of town, region, country): **~ London** a Londra; **~ England** in Inghilterra; **~ the United States** negli Stati Uniti; **~ Yorkshire** nello Yorkshire
3 (indicating time: during, in the space of) in; **~ spring/summer** in primavera/estate; **~ 1988** nel 1988; **~ May** in o a maggio; **I'll see you ~ July** ci vediamo a luglio; **~ the afternoon** nel pomeriggio; **at 4 o'clock ~ the afternoon** alle 4 del pomeriggio; **I did it ~ 3 hours/days** l'ho fatto in 3 ore/giorni; **I'll see you ~ 2 weeks** or **~ 2 weeks' time** ci vediamo tra 2 settimane
4 (indicating manner etc) a; **~ a loud/soft voice** a voce alta/bassa; **~ pencil** a matita; **~ English/French** in inglese/francese; **the boy ~ the blue shirt** il ragazzo con la camicia blu
5 (indicating circumstances): **~ the sun** al sole; **~ the shade** all'ombra; **~ the rain** sotto la pioggia; **a rise ~ prices** un aumento dei prezzi
6 (indicating mood, state): **~ tears** in lacrime; **~ anger** per la rabbia; **~ despair** disperato(a); **~ good condition** in buono stato, in buone condizioni; **to live ~ luxury** vivere nel lusso
7 (with ratios, numbers): **1 ~ 10** 1 su 10; **20 pence ~ the pound** 20 pence per sterlina;

they lined up **~ twos** si misero in fila a due a due
8 (referring to people, works) in; **the disease is common ~ children** la malattia è comune nei bambini; **~ (the works of) Dickens** in Dickens
9 (indicating profession etc) in; **to be ~ teaching** fare l'insegnante, insegnare; **to be ~ publishing** essere nell'editoria
10 (after superlative) di; **the best ~ the class** il migliore della classe
11 (with present participle): **~ saying this** dicendo questo, nel dire questo
♦ adv: **to be ~** (person: at home, work) esserci; (train, ship, plane) essere arrivato(a); (in fashion) essere di moda; **to ask sb ~** invitare qn ad entrare; **to run/limp** etc **~** entrare di corsa/zoppicando etc
♦ n: **the ~s and outs of the problem** tutti i particolari del problema

---

in. abbr = inch

inability [ɪnəˈbɪlɪtɪ] n: **~ (to do)** incapacità (di fare)

inaccurate [ɪnˈækjurət] adj inesatto(a), impreciso(a)

inadequate [ɪnˈædɪkwət] adj insufficiente

inadvertently [ɪnədˈvəːtntlɪ] adv senza volerlo

inadvisable [ɪnədˈvaɪzəbl] adj consigliabile

inane [ɪˈneɪn] adj vacuo(a), stupido(a)

inanimate [ɪnˈænɪmət] adj inanimato(a)

inappropriate [ɪnəˈprəuprɪət] adj non adatto(a); (word, expression) improprio(a)

inarticulate [ɪnɑːˈtɪkjulət] adj (person) che si esprime male; (speech) inarticolato(a)

inasmuch as [ɪnəzˈmʌtʃæz] adv in quanto che; (insofar as) poiché

inaudible [ɪnˈɔːdɪbl] adj che non si riesce a sentire

inauguration [ɪnɔːgjuˈreɪʃən] n inaugurazione f; insediamento in carica

in-between [ɪnbɪˈtwiːn] adj fra i (or le) due

inborn [ɪnˈbɔːn] adj innato(a)

inbred [ɪnˈbred] adj innato(a); (family) connaturato(a)

Inc. (US) abbr (= incorporated) S.A

incapable [ɪnˈkeɪpəbl] adj incapace

incapacitate [ɪnkəˈpæsɪteɪt] vt: **to ~ sb from doing** rendere qn incapace di fare

incense [n ˈɪnsɛns, vb ɪnˈsɛns] n incenso ♦ vt (anger) infuriare

incentive [ɪnˈsɛntɪv] n incentivo

incessant [ɪnˈsɛsnt] adj incessante; **~ly** adv di continuo, senza sosta

inch [ɪntʃ] n pollice m (= 25 mm; 12 in a foot); **within an ~ of** a un pelo da; **he didn't give an ~** non ha ceduto di un millimetro

incidence [ˈɪnsɪdns] n (of crime, disease) incidenza

incident ['ɪnsɪdnt] n incidente m; (in book) episodio

incidental [ɪnsɪ'dɛntl] adj accessorio(a), d'accompagnamento; (unplanned) incidentale; ~ **to** marginale a; **~ly** [-'dɛntəlɪ] adv (by the way) a proposito

inclination [ɪnklɪ'neɪʃən] n inclinazione f

incline [n 'ɪnklaɪn, vb ɪn'klaɪn] n pendenza, pendio ♦ vt inclinare ♦ vi (surface) essere inclinato(a); **to be ~d to do** tendere a fare; essere propenso(a) a fare

include [ɪn'kluːd] vt includere, comprendere; **including** prep compreso(a), incluso(a)

inclusive [ɪn'kluːsɪv] adj incluso(a), compreso(a); ~ **of tax** etc tasse etc comprese

incoherent [ɪnkəʊ'hɪərənt] adj incoerente

income ['ɪnkʌm] n reddito; ~ **tax** n imposta sul reddito

incoming ['ɪnkʌmɪŋ] adj (flight, mail) in arrivo; (government) subentrante; (tide) montante

incompetent [ɪn'kɔmpɪtnt] adj incompetente, incapace

incomplete [ɪnkəm'pliːt] adj incompleto(a)

incongruous [ɪn'kɔŋgruəs] adj poco appropriato(a); (remark, act) incongruo(a)

inconsiderate [ɪnkən'sɪdərət] adj sconsiderato(a)

inconsistency [ɪnkən'sɪstənsɪ] n incoerenza

inconsistent [ɪnkən'sɪstənt] adj incoerente; ~ **with** non coerente con

inconspicuous [ɪnkən'spɪkjuəs] adj incospicuo(a); (colour) poco appariscente; (dress) dimesso(a)

inconvenience [ɪnkən'viːnjəns] n inconveniente m; (trouble) disturbo ♦ vt disturbare

inconvenient [ɪnkən'viːnjənt] adj scomodo(a)

incorporate [ɪn'kɔːpəreɪt] vt incorporare; (contain) contenere; **~d** adj: **~d company** (US) società f inv anonima

incorrect [ɪnkə'rɛkt] adj scorretto(a); (statement) inesatto(a)

increase [n 'ɪnkriːs, vb ɪn'kriːs] n aumento ♦ vi, vt aumentare

increasing [ɪn'kriːsɪŋ] adj (number) crescente; **~ly** adv sempre più

incredible [ɪn'krɛdɪbl] adj incredibile

increment ['ɪnkrɪmənt] n aumento, incremento

incriminate [ɪn'krɪmɪneɪt] vt compromettere

incubator ['ɪnkjubeɪtə*] n incubatrice f

incumbent [ɪn'kʌmbənt] adj: **to be ~ on sb** spettare a qn

incur [ɪn'kə:*] vt (expenses) incorrere; (anger, risk) esporsi a; (debt) contrarre; (loss) subire

indebted [ɪn'dɛtɪd] adj: **to be ~ to sb** (for) essere obbligato(a) verso qn (per)

indecent [ɪn'diːsnt] adj indecente; ~ **assault** (BRIT) n aggressione f a scopo di violenza sessuale; ~ **exposure** n atti mpl osceni in luogo pubblico

indecisive [ɪndɪ'saɪsɪv] adj indeciso(a)

indeed [ɪn'diːd] adv infatti; veramente; **yes ~!** certamente!

indefinite [ɪn'dɛfɪnɪt] adj indefinito(a); (answer) vago(a); (period, number) indeterminato(a); **~ly** adv (wait) indefinitamente

indemnity [ɪn'dɛmnɪtɪ] n (insurance) assicurazione f; (compensation) indennità, indennizzo

independence [ɪndɪ'pɛndns] n indipendenza

independent [ɪndɪ'pɛndnt] adj indipendente

index ['ɪndɛks] (pl ~es) n (in book) indice m; (: in library etc) catalogo; (pl indices: ratio, sign) indice m; ~ **card** n scheda; ~ **finger** n (dito) indice m; **~-linked** (US **~ed**) adj legato(a) al costo della vita

India ['ɪndɪə] n India; **~n** adj, n indiano(a)

indicate ['ɪndɪkeɪt] vt indicare; **indication** [-'keɪʃən] n indicazione f, segno

indicative [ɪn'dɪkətɪv] adj: ~ **of** indicativo(a) di

indicator ['ɪndɪkeɪtə*] n indicatore m; (AUT) freccia

indices ['ɪndɪsiːz] npl of **index**

indictment [ɪn'daɪtmənt] n accusa

indifference [ɪn'dɪfrəns] n indifferenza

indifferent [ɪn'dɪfrənt] adj indifferente; (poor) mediocre

indigenous [ɪn'dɪdʒɪnəs] adj indigeno(a)

indigestion [ɪndɪ'dʒɛstʃən] n indigestione f

indignant [ɪn'dɪgnənt] adj: ~ (**at sth/with sb**) indignato(a) (per qc/contro qn)

indignity [ɪn'dɪgnɪtɪ] n umiliazione f

indigo ['ɪndɪgəu] n indaco

indirect [ɪndɪ'rɛkt] adj indiretto(a)

indiscreet [ɪndɪ'skriːt] adj indiscreto(a); (rash) imprudente

indiscriminate [ɪndɪ'skrɪmɪnət] adj indiscriminato(a)

indisputable [ɪndɪ'spjuːtəbl] adj incontestabile, indiscutibile

individual [ɪndɪ'vɪdjuəl] n individuo ♦ adj individuale; (characteristic) particolare, originale

indoctrination [ɪndɔktrɪ'neɪʃən] n indottrinamento

Indonesia [ɪndə'niːzɪə] n Indonesia

indoor ['ɪndɔ:*] adj da interno; (plant) d'appartamento; (swimming pool) coperto(a); (sport, games) fatto(a) al coperto; **~s** [ɪn'dɔ:z] adv all'interno

induce [ɪn'djuːs] vt persuadere; (bring about,

MED) provocare

indulge [ɪnˈdʌldʒ] *vt* (*whim*) compiacere, soddisfare; (*child*) viziare ♦ *vi*: **to ~ in sth** concedersi qc; abbandonarsi a qc; **~nce** *n* lusso (che uno si permette); (*leniency*) indulgenza; **~nt** *adj* indulgente

industrial [ɪnˈdʌstrɪəl] *adj* industriale; (*injury*) sul lavoro; **~ action** *n* azione *f* rivendicativa; **~ estate** (*BRIT*) *n* zona industriale; **~ park** (*US*) *n* = **~ estate**

industrious [ɪnˈdʌstrɪəs] *adj* industrioso(a), assiduo(a)

industry [ˈɪndəstrɪ] *n* industria; (*diligence*) operosità

inedible [ɪnˈɛdɪbl] *adj* immangiabile; (*poisonous*) non commestibile

ineffective [ɪnɪˈfɛktɪv] *adj* inefficace; incompetente

ineffectual [ɪnɪˈfɛktjuəl] *adj* inefficace; incompetente

inefficient [ɪnɪˈfɪʃənt] *adj* inefficiente

inept [ɪˈnɛpt] *adj* inetto(a)

inequality [ɪnɪˈkwɔlɪtɪ] *n* ineguaglianza

inescapable [ɪnɪˈskeɪpəbl] *adj* inevitabile

inevitable [ɪnˈɛvɪtəbl] *adj* inevitabile; **inevitably** *adv* inevitabilmente

inexact [ɪnɪgˈzækt] *adj* inesatto(a)

inexcusable [ɪnɪksˈkjuːzəbl] *adj* ingiustificabile

inexpensive [ɪnɪkˈspɛnsɪv] *adj* poco costoso(a)

inexperienced [ɪnɪksˈpɪərɪənst] *adj* inesperto(a), senza esperienza

infallible [ɪnˈfælɪbl] *adj* infallibile

infamous [ˈɪnfəməs] *adj* infame

infancy [ˈɪnfənsɪ] *n* infanzia

infant [ˈɪnfənt] *n* bambino/a; **~ school** (*BRIT*) scuola elementare (*per bambini dall'età di 5 a 7 anni*)

infantry [ˈɪnfəntrɪ] *n* fanteria

infatuated [ɪnˈfætjueɪtɪd] *adj*: **~ with** infatuato(a) di

infatuation [ɪnfætjuˈeɪʃən] *n* infatuazione *f*

infect [ɪnˈfɛkt] *vt* infettare; **~ion** [ɪnˈfɛkʃən] *n* infezione *f*; **~ious** [ɪnˈfɛkʃəs] *adj* (*disease*) infettivo(a), contagioso(a); (*person, fig*: *enthusiasm*) contagioso(a)

infer [ɪnˈfəː*] *vt* inferire, dedurre

inferior [ɪnˈfɪərɪə*] *adj* inferiore; (*goods*) di qualità scadente ♦ *n* inferiore *m/f*; (*in rank*) subalterno/a; **~ity** [ɪnfɪərɪˈɔrɪtɪ] *n* inferiorità; **~ity complex** *n* complesso di inferiorità

infertile [ɪnˈfəːtaɪl] *adj* sterile

in-fighting [ˈɪnfaɪtɪŋ] *n* lotte *fpl* intestine

infiltrate [ˈɪnfɪltreɪt] *vt* infiltrarsi in

infinite [ˈɪnfɪnɪt] *adj* infinito(a)

infinitive [ɪnˈfɪnɪtɪv] *n* infinito

infinity [ɪnˈfɪnɪtɪ] *n* infinità; (*also MATH*) infinito

infirmary [ɪnˈfəːmərɪ] *n* ospedale *m*; (*in school, factory*) infermeria

inflamed [ɪnˈfleɪmd] *adj* infiammato(a)

inflammable [ɪnˈflæməbl] *adj* infiammabile

inflammation [ɪnfləˈmeɪʃən] *n* infiammazione *f*

inflatable [ɪnˈfleɪtəbl] *adj* gonfiabile

inflate [ɪnˈfleɪt] *vt* (*tyre, balloon*) gonfiare; (*fig*) esagerare; gonfiare; **inflation** [ɪnˈfleɪʃən] *n* (*ECON*) inflazione *f*; **inflationary** [ɪnˈfleɪʃnərɪ] *adj* inflazionistico(a)

inflict [ɪnˈflɪkt] *vt*: **to ~ on** infliggere a

influence [ˈɪnfluəns] *n* influenza ♦ *vt* influenzare; **under the ~ of alcohol** sotto l'effetto dell'alcool

influential [ɪnfluˈɛnʃl] *adj* influente

influenza [ɪnfluˈɛnzə] *n* (*MED*) influenza

influx [ˈɪnflʌks] *n* afflusso

inform [ɪnˈfɔːm] *vt*: **to ~ sb** (**of**) informare qn (di) ♦ *vi*: **to ~ on sb** denunciare qn

informal [ɪnˈfɔːml] *adj* informale; (*announcement, invitation*) non ufficiale; **~ity** [-ˈmælɪtɪ] *n* informalità; carattere *m* non ufficiale

informant [ɪnˈfɔːmənt] *n* informatore/trice

information [ɪnfəˈmeɪʃən] *n* informazioni *fpl*; particolari *mpl*; **a piece of ~** un'informazione; **~ desk** *n* banco *m* informazioni; **~ office** *n* ufficio *m* informazioni *inv*

informative [ɪnˈfɔːmətɪv] *adj* istruttivo(a)

informer [ɪnˈfɔːmə*] *n* (*also: police ~*) informatore/trice

infringe [ɪnˈfrɪndʒ] *vt* infrangere ♦ *vi*: **to ~ on** calpestare; **~ment** *n* infrazione *f*

infuriating [ɪnˈfjuərɪeɪtɪŋ] *adj* molto irritante

ingenious [ɪnˈdʒiːnjəs] *adj* ingegnoso(a)

ingenuity [ɪndʒɪˈnjuːɪtɪ] *n* ingegnosità

ingenuous [ɪnˈdʒɛnjuəs] *adj* ingenuo(a)

ingot [ˈɪŋgət] *n* lingotto

ingrained [ɪnˈgreɪnd] *adj* radicato(a)

ingratiate [ɪnˈgreɪʃɪeɪt] *vt*: **to ~ o.s. with sb** ingraziarsi qn

ingredient [ɪnˈgriːdɪənt] *n* ingrediente *m*; elemento

inhabit [ɪnˈhæbɪt] *vt* abitare

inhabitant [ɪnˈhæbɪtnt] *n* abitante *m/f*

inhale [ɪnˈheɪl] *vt* inalare ♦ *vi* (*in smoking*) aspirare

inherent [ɪnˈhɪərənt] *adj*: **~ (in** *or* **to)** inerente (a)

inherit [ɪnˈhɛrɪt] *vt* ereditare; **~ance** *n* eredità

inhibit [ɪnˈhɪbɪt] *vt* (*PSYCH*) inibire; **~ion** [-ˈbɪʃən] *n* inibizione *f*

inhospitable [ɪnhɔsˈpɪtəbl] *adj* inospitale

inhuman [ɪnˈhjuːmən] *adj* inumano(a)

initial [ɪˈnɪʃl] *adj* iniziale ♦ *n* iniziale *f* ♦ *vt* siglare; **~s** *npl* (*of name*) iniziali *fpl*; (*as signature*) sigla; **~ly** *adv* inizialmente, all'inizio

initiate [ɪ'nɪʃɪeɪt] vt (start) avviare; intraprendere; iniziare; (person) iniziare; **to ~ sb into a secret** mettere qn a parte di un segreto; **to ~ proceedings against sb** (LAW) intentare causa contro qn

initiative [ɪ'nɪʃətɪv] n iniziativa

inject [ɪn'dʒekt] vt (liquid) iniettare; (patient): **to ~ sb with sth** fare a qn un'iniezione di qc; (funds) immettere; **~ion** [ɪn'dʒekʃən] n iniezione f, puntura

injure ['ɪndʒə*] vt ferire; (damage: reputation etc) nuocere a; **~d** adj ferito(a)

injury ['ɪndʒərɪ] n ferita; **~ time** n (SPORT) tempo di recupero

injustice [ɪn'dʒʌstɪs] n ingiustizia

ink [ɪŋk] n inchiostro

inkling ['ɪŋklɪŋ] n sentore m, vaga idea

inlaid ['ɪnleɪd] adj incrostato(a); (table etc) intarsiato(a)

inland [adj 'ɪnlənd, adv ɪn'lænd] adj interno(a) ♦ adv all'interno; **I~ Revenue** (BRIT) n Fisco

in-laws ['ɪnlɔːz] npl suoceri mpl; famiglia del marito (or della moglie)

inlet ['ɪnlet] n (GEO) insenatura, baia

inmate ['ɪnmeɪt] n (in prison) carcerato/a; (in asylum) ricoverato/a

inn [ɪn] n locanda

innate [ɪ'neɪt] adj innato(a)

inner ['ɪnə*] adj interno(a), interiore; **~ city** n centro di una zona urbana; **~ tube** n camera d'aria

innings ['ɪnɪŋz] n (CRICKET) turno di battuta

innocence ['ɪnəsns] n innocenza

innocent ['ɪnəsnt] adj innocente

innocuous [ɪ'nɒkjuəs] adj innocuo(a)

innuendo [ɪnju'endəu] (pl **~es**) n insinuazione f

innumerable [ɪ'njuːmrəbl] adj innumerevole

in-patient ['ɪnpeɪʃənt] n ricoverato/a

input ['ɪnput] n input m

inquest ['ɪnkwest] n inchiesta

inquire [ɪn'kwaɪə*] vi informarsi ♦ vt domandare, informarsi su; **~ about** vt fus informarsi di or su; **~ into** vt fus fare indagini su; **inquiry** n domanda; (LAW) indagine f, investigazione f; **"inquiries"** "informazioni"; **inquiry office** (BRIT) n ufficio m informazioni inv

inquisitive [ɪn'kwɪzɪtɪv] adj curioso(a)

ins. abbr = **inches**

insane [ɪn'seɪn] adj matto(a), pazzo(a); (MED) alienato(a)

insanity [ɪn'sænɪtɪ] n follia; (MED) alienazione f mentale

inscription [ɪn'skrɪpʃən] n iscrizione f; dedica

insect ['ɪnsekt] n insetto; **~icide** [ɪn'sektɪsaɪd] n insetticida m; **~ repellent** n insettifugo

insecure [ɪnsɪ'kjuə*] adj malsicuro(a); (person) insicuro(a)

insemination [ɪnsemɪ'neɪʃən] n: **artificial ~** fecondazione f artificiale

insensible [ɪn'sensɪbl] adj (unconscious) privo(a) di sensi

insensitive [ɪn'sensɪtɪv] adj insensibile

insert [ɪn'sɜːt] vt inserire, introdurre; **~ion** [ɪn'sɜːʃən] n inserzione f

in-service [ɪn'sɜːvɪs] adj (training, course) durante l'orario di lavoro

inshore [ɪn'ʃɔː*] adj costiero(a) ♦ adv presso la riva; verso la riva

inside ['ɪn'saɪd] n interno, parte f interiore ♦ adj interno(a), interiore ♦ adv dentro, all'interno ♦ prep dentro, all'interno di; (of time): **~ 10 minutes** entro 10 minuti; **~s** npl (inf: stomach) ventre m; **~ forward** n (SPORT) mezzala, interno; **~ lane** n (AUT) corsia di marcia; **~ out** adv (turn) a rovescio; (know) in fondo

insider dealing [ɪn'saɪdə'diːlɪŋ] n insider dealing m inv

insider trading [ɪn'saɪdə'treɪdɪŋ] n insider trading m inv

insight ['ɪnsaɪt] n acume m, perspicacia; (glimpse, idea) percezione f

insignia [ɪn'sɪgnɪə] npl insegne fpl

insignificant [ɪnsɪg'nɪfɪknt] adj insignificante

insincere [ɪnsɪn'sɪə*] adj insincero(a)

insinuate [ɪn'sɪnjueɪt] vt insinuare

insist [ɪn'sɪst] vi insistere; **to ~ on doing** insistere per fare; **to ~ that** insistere perché + sub; (claim) sostenere che; **~ent** adj insistente

insole ['ɪnsəul] n soletta

insolent ['ɪnsələnt] adj insolente

insomnia [ɪn'sɒmnɪə] n insonnia

inspect [ɪn'spekt] vt ispezionare; (BRIT: ticket) controllare; **~ion** [ɪn'spekʃən] n ispezione f; controllo; **~or** n ispettore/trice; (BRIT: on buses, trains) controllore m

inspire [ɪn'spaɪə*] vt ispirare

install [ɪn'stɔːl] vt installare; **~ation** [ɪnstə'leɪʃən] n installazione f

instalment [ɪn'stɔːlmənt] (US **installment**) n rata; (of TV serial etc) puntata; **in ~s** (pay) a rate; (receive) una parte per volta; (: publication) a fascicoli

instance ['ɪnstəns] n esempio, caso; **for ~** per or ad esempio; **in the first ~** in primo luogo

instant ['ɪnstənt] n istante m, attimo ♦ adj immediato(a); urgente; (coffee, food) in polvere; **~ly** adv immediatamente, subito

instead [ɪn'sted] adv invece; **~ of** invece di

instep ['ɪnstep] n collo del piede; (of shoe) collo della scarpa

instil [ɪn'stɪl] vt: **to ~ (into)** inculcare (in)

instinct ['ɪnstɪŋkt] n istinto

institute ['ɪnstɪtjuːt] n istituto ♦ vt istituire, stabilire; (inquiry) avviare; (proceedings) iniziare

institution [ɪnstɪ'tjuːʃən] n istituzione f; (educational ~, mental ~) istituto

instruct [ɪn'strʌkt] vt: **to ~ sb in sth** insegnare qc a qn; **to ~ sb to do** dare ordini a qn di fare; **~ion** [ɪn'strʌkʃən] n istruzione f; **~ions (for use)** istruzioni per l'uso; **~or** n istruttore/trice; (for skiing) maestro/a

instrument ['ɪnstrəmənt] n strumento; **~al** [-'mentl] adj (MUS) strumentale; **to be ~al in** essere d'aiuto in; **~ panel** n quadro m portastrumenti inv

insufferable [ɪn'sʌfərəbl] adj insopportabile

insufficient [ɪnsə'fɪʃənt] adj insufficiente

insular ['ɪnsjulə*] adj insulare; (person) di mente ristretta

insulate ['ɪnsjuleɪt] vt isolare; **insulation** [-'leɪʃən] n isolamento

insulin ['ɪnsjulɪn] n insulina

insult [n 'ɪnsʌlt, vb ɪn'sʌlt] n insulto, affronto ♦ vt insultare; **~ing** adj offensivo(a), ingiurioso(a)

insuperable [ɪn'sjuːprəbl] adj insormontabile, insuperabile

insurance [ɪn'ʃuərəns] n assicurazione f; **fire/life ~** assicurazione contro gli incendi/sulla vita; **~ policy** n polizza d'assicurazione

insure [ɪn'ʃuə*] vt assicurare

intact [ɪn'tækt] adj intatto(a)

intake ['ɪnteɪk] n (TECH) immissione f; (of food) consumo; (BRIT: of pupils etc) afflusso

integral ['ɪntɪgrəl] adj integrale; (part) integrante

integrate ['ɪntɪgreɪt] vt integrare ♦ vi integrarsi

integrity [ɪn'tegrɪtɪ] n integrità

intellect ['ɪntəlekt] n intelletto; **~ual** [-'lektjuəl] adj, n intellettuale m/f

intelligence [ɪn'telɪdʒəns] n intelligenza; (MIL etc) informazioni fpl; **~ service** n servizio segreto

intelligent [ɪn'telɪdʒənt] adj intelligente

intend [ɪn'tend] vt (gift etc): **to ~ sth for** destinare qc a; **to ~ to do** aver l'intenzione di fare; **~ed** adj (effect) voluto(a)

intense [ɪn'tens] adj intenso(a); (person) di forti sentimenti; **~ly** adv intensamente; profondamente

intensive [ɪn'tensɪv] adj intensivo(a); **~ care unit** n reparto terapia intensiva

intent [ɪn'tent] n intenzione f ♦ adj: **~ (on)** intento(a) (a), immerso(a) (in); **to all ~s and purposes** a tutti gli effetti; **to be ~ on doing sth** essere deciso a fare qc

intention [ɪn'tenʃən] n intenzione f; **~al** adj intenzionale, deliberato(a); **~ally** adv apposta

intently [ɪn'tentlɪ] adv attentamente

interact [ɪntər'ækt] vi interagire

interactive [ɪntər'æktɪv] adj (COMPUT) interattivo(a)

interchange ['ɪntətʃeɪndʒ] n (exchange) scambio; (on motorway) incrocio pluridirezionale; **~able** [-'tʃeɪndʒəbl] adj intercambiabile

intercom ['ɪntəkɔm] n interfono

intercourse ['ɪntəkɔːs] n rapporti mpl

interest ['ɪntrɪst] n interesse m; (COMM: share) interessi mpl ♦ vt interessare; **~ed** adj interessato(a); **to be ~ed in** interessarsi di; **~ing** adj interessante; **~ rate** n tasso di interesse

interface ['ɪntəfeɪs] n (COMPUT) interfaccia

interfere [ɪntə'fɪə*] vi: **to ~ in** (quarrel, other people's business) immischiarsi in; **to ~ with** (object) toccare; (plans, duty) interferire con

interference [ɪntə'fɪərəns] n interferenza

interim ['ɪntərɪm] adj provvisorio(a) ♦ n: **in the ~** nel frattempo

interior [ɪn'tɪərɪə*] n interno; (of country) entroterra ♦ adj interno(a); (minister) degli Interni; **~ designer** n arredatore/trice

interlock [ɪntə'lɔk] vi ingranarsi

interlude ['ɪntəluːd] n intervallo; (THEATRE) intermezzo

intermediate [ɪntə'miːdɪət] adj intermedio(a)

intermission [ɪntə'mɪʃən] n pausa; (THEATRE, CINEMA) intermissione f, intervallo

intern [vb ɪn'təːn, n 'ɪntəːn] vt internare ♦ n (US) medico interno

internal [ɪn'təːnl] adj interno(a); **~ly** adv: **"not to be taken ~ly"** "per uso esterno"; **I~ Revenue Service** (US) n Fisco

international [ɪntə'næʃənl] adj internazionale ♦ n (BRIT: SPORT) incontro internazionale

Internet ['ɪntənet] n: **the ~** Internet f

interplay ['ɪntəpleɪ] n azione e reazione f

interpret [ɪn'təːprɪt] vt interpretare ♦ vi fare da interprete; **~er** n interprete m/f

interrogate [ɪn'terəugeɪt] vt interrogare; **interrogation** [-'geɪʃən] n interrogazione f; (of suspect etc) interrogatorio

interrupt [ɪntə'rʌpt] vt, vi interrompere; **~ion** [-'rʌpʃən] n interruzione f

intersect [ɪntə'sekt] vi (roads) incrociarsi; **~ion** [-'sekʃən] n intersezione f; (of roads) incrocio

intersperse [ɪntə'spəːs] vt: **to ~ with** costellare di

intertwine [ɪntə'twaɪn] vi intrecciarsi

interval ['ɪntəvl] n intervallo; **at ~s** a intervalli

intervene [ɪntə'viːn] vi (time) intercorrere; (event, person) intervenire; **intervention** [-'venʃən] n intervento

interview ['ɪntəvjuː] n (RADIO, TV etc) intervista; (for job) colloquio ♦ vt intervistare;

avere un colloquio con; **~er** n intervistatore/
trice

intestine [ɪn'testɪn] n intestino

intimacy ['ɪntɪməsɪ] n intimità

intimate [adj 'ɪntɪmət, vb 'ɪntɪmeɪt] adj
intimo(a); (knowledge) profondo(a) ♦ vt
lasciar capire

into ['ɪntu:] prep dentro, in; **come ~ the house**
entra in casa; **he worked late ~ the night**
lavorò fino a tarda notte; **~ Italian** in italiano

intolerable [ɪn'tɔlərəbl] adj intollerabile

intolerance [ɪn'tɔlərns] n intolleranza

intolerant [ɪn'tɔlərnt] adj: **~ of** intollerante di

intoxicated [ɪn'tɔksɪkeɪtɪd] adj inebriato(a)

intractable [ɪn'træktəbl] adj intrattabile

intranet ['ɪntrənet] n intranet f

intransitive [ɪn'trænsɪtɪv] adj intransitivo(a)

intravenous [ɪntrə'viːnəs] adj
endovenoso(a)

in-tray ['ɪntreɪ] n contenitore m per la
corrispondenza in arrivo

intricate ['ɪntrɪkət] adj intricato(a),
complicato(a)

intrigue [ɪn'triːg] n intrigo ♦ vt affascinare;
intriguing adj affascinante

intrinsic [ɪn'trɪnsɪk] adj intrinseco(a)

introduce [ɪntrə'djuːs] vt introdurre; **to ~ sb**
(to sb) presentare qn (a qn); **to ~ sb to**
(pastime, technique) iniziare qn a;
introduction [-'dʌkʃən] n introduzione f; (of
person) presentazione f; (to new experience)
iniziazione f; **introductory** adj
introduttivo(a)

intrude [ɪn'truːd] vi (person): **to ~ (on)**
intromettersi (in); **~r** n intruso/a

intuition [ɪntjuː'ɪʃən] n intuizione f

inundate ['ɪnʌndeɪt] vt: **to ~ with** inondare
di

invade [ɪn'veɪd] vt invadere

invalid [n 'ɪnvəlɪd, adj ɪn'vælɪd] n malato/a;
(with disability) invalido/a ♦ adj (not valid)
invalido(a), non valido(a)

invaluable [ɪn'væljuəbl] adj prezioso(a);
inestimabile

invariably [ɪn'veərɪəblɪ] adv invariabilmente;
sempre

invasion [ɪn'veɪʒən] n invasione f

invent [ɪn'vent] vt inventare; **~ion**
[ɪn'venʃən] n invenzione f; **~ive** adj
inventivo(a); **~or** n inventore m

inventory ['ɪnvəntrɪ] n inventario

invert [ɪn'vɜːt] vt invertire; (cup, object)
rovesciare; **~ed commas** (BRIT) npl virgolette
fpl

invest [ɪn'vest] vt investire ♦ vi: **to ~ (in)**
investire (in)

investigate [ɪn'vestɪgeɪt] vt investigare,
indagare; (crime) fare indagini su;
investigation [-'geɪʃən] n investigazione f;

(of crime) indagine f

investment [ɪn'vestmənt] n investimento

investor [ɪn'vestə*] n investitore/trice;
azionista m/f

invidious [ɪn'vɪdɪəs] adj odioso(a); (task)
spiacevole

invigilator [ɪn'vɪdʒɪleɪtə*] n (in exam)
sorvegliante m/f

invigorating [ɪn'vɪgəreɪtɪŋ] adj stimolante;
vivificante

invisible [ɪn'vɪzɪbl] adj invisibile

invitation [ɪnvɪ'teɪʃən] n invito

invite [ɪn'vaɪt] vt invitare; (opinions etc)
sollecitare; **inviting** adj invitante, attraente

invoice ['ɪnvɔɪs] n fattura ♦ vt fatturare

involuntary [ɪn'vɔləntrɪ] adj involontario(a)

involve [ɪn'vɔlv] vt (entail) richiedere,
comportare; (associate): **to ~ sb (in)** implicare
qn (in); coinvolgere qn (in); **~d** adj
involuto(a), complesso(a); **to be ~d in** essere
coinvolto(a) in; **~ment** n implicazione f;
coinvolgimento

inward ['ɪnwəd] adj (movement) verso
l'interno; (thought, feeling) interiore,
intimo(a); **~(s)** adv verso l'interno

I/O abbr (COMPUT: = input/output) I/O

iodine ['aɪəudiːn] n iodio

ioniser ['aɪənaɪzə*] n ionizzatore m

iota [aɪ'əutə] n (fig) briciolo

IOU n abbr (= I owe you) pagherò m inv

IQ n abbr (= intelligence quotient) quoziente m
d'intelligenza

IRA n abbr (= Irish Republican Army) IRA f

Iran [ɪ'rɑːn] n Iran m; **~ian** adj, n iraniano(a)

Iraq [ɪ'rɑːk] n Iraq m; **~i** adj, n iracheno(a)

irate [aɪ'reɪt] adj adirato(a)

Ireland ['aɪələnd] n Irlanda

iris ['aɪrɪs] (pl **~es**) n iride f; (BOT) giaggiolo,
iride

Irish ['aɪrɪʃ] adj irlandese ♦ npl: **the ~** gli
Irlandesi; **~man** (irreg) n irlandese m; **~ Sea**
n Mar m d'Irlanda; **~woman** (irreg) n
irlandese f

irksome ['ɜːksəm] adj seccante

iron ['aɪən] n ferro; (for clothes) ferro da stiro
♦ adj di or in ferro ♦ vt (clothes) stirare;
~ out vt (crease) appianare; (fig) spianare;
far sparire

ironic(al) [aɪ'rɔnɪk(l)] adj ironico(a)

ironing ['aɪənɪŋ] n (act) stirare m; (clothes)
roba da stirare; **~ board** n asse f da stiro

ironmonger's (shop) ['aɪənmʌŋgəz-]
(BRIT) n negozio di ferramenta

irony ['aɪrənɪ] n ironia

irrational [ɪ'ræʃənl] adj irrazionale

irregular [ɪ'regjulə*] adj irregolare

irrelevant [ɪ'reləvənt] adj non pertinente

irreplaceable [ɪrɪ'pleɪsəbl] adj insostituibile

irrepressible [ɪrɪ'presəbl] adj irrefrenabile

irresistible [ɪrɪˈzɪstɪbl] adj irresistibile
irrespective [ɪrɪˈspektɪv]: ~ **of** prep senza
  riguardo a
irresponsible [ɪrɪˈspɔnsɪbl] adj irresponsabile
irrigate [ˈɪrɪɡeɪt] vt irrigare; **irrigation**
  [-ˈɡeɪʃən] n irrigazione f
irritable [ˈɪrɪtəbl] adj irritabile
irritate [ˈɪrɪteɪt] vt irritare; **irritating** adj
  (person, sound etc) irritante; **irritation**
  [-ˈteɪʃən] n irritazione f
IRS (US) n abbr = **Internal Revenue Service**
is [ɪz] vb see **be**
Islam [ˈɪzlɑːm] n Islam m
island [ˈaɪlənd] n isola; **~er** n isolano/a
isle [aɪl] n isola
isn't [ˈɪznt] = **is not**
isolate [ˈaɪsəleɪt] vt isolare; **~d** adj isolato(a);
  isolation [-ˈleɪʃən] n isolamento
Israel [ˈɪzreɪl] n Israele m; **~i** [ɪzˈreɪlɪ] adj, n
  israeliano(a)
issue [ˈɪʃuː] n questione f, problema m; (of
  banknotes etc) emissione f; (of newspaper etc)
  numero ♦ vt (statement) rilasciare; (rations,
  equipment) distribuire; (book) pubblicare;
  (banknotes, cheques, stamps) emettere; **at ~**
  in gioco, in discussione; **to take ~ with sb**
  (**over sth**) prendere posizione contro qn
  (riguardo a qc); **to make an ~ of sth** fare un
  problema di qc
isthmus [ˈɪsməs] n istmo

> **KEYWORD**

it [ɪt] pron 1 (specific: subject) esso(a); (: direct
  object) lo(la), l'; (: indirect object) gli(le);
  where's my book? — ~'s on the table dov'è il
  mio libro? — è sulla tavola; **I can't find ~** non
  lo (or la) trovo; **give ~ to me** dammelo (or
  dammela); **about/from/of ~** ne; **I spoke to
  him about ~** gliene ho parlato; **what did you
  learn from ~?** quale insegnamento ne hai
  tratto?; **I'm proud of ~** ne sono fiero; **did you
  go to ~?** ci sei andato?; **put the book in ~**
  mettici il libro
2 (impers): **~'s raining** piove; **~'s Friday
  tomorrow** domani è venerdì; **~'s 6 o'clock**
  sono le 6; **who is ~? — ~'s me** chi è? — sono
  io

Italian [ɪˈtæljən] adj italiano(a) ♦ n italiano/a;
  (LING) italiano; **the ~s** gli Italiani
italics [ɪˈtælɪks] npl corsivo
Italy [ˈɪtəlɪ] n Italia
itch [ɪtʃ] n prurito ♦ vi (person) avere il
  prurito; (part of body) prudere; **to ~ to do sth**
  aver una gran voglia di fare qc; **~y** adj che
  prude; **to be ~y** = **to ~**
it'd [ˈɪtd] = **it would**; **it had**
item [ˈaɪtəm] n articolo; (on agenda) punto;
  (also: news ~) notizia; **~ize** vt specificare,

---

dettagliare
itinerant [ɪˈtɪnərənt] adj ambulante
itinerary [aɪˈtɪnərərɪ] n itinerario
it'll [ˈɪtl] = **it will**; **it shall**
its [ɪts] adj il(la) suo(a), i(le) suoi(sue)
it's [ɪts] = **it is**; **it has**
itself [ɪtˈself] pron (emphatic) esso(a)
  stesso(a); (reflexive) si
ITV (BRIT) n abbr (= Independent Television)
  rete televisiva in concorrenza con la BBC
I.U.D. n abbr (= intra-uterine device) spirale f
I've [aɪv] = **I have**
ivory [ˈaɪvərɪ] n avorio
ivy [ˈaɪvɪ] n edera

J, j

jab [dʒæb] vt dare colpetti a ♦ n (MED: inf)
  puntura; **to ~ sth into** affondare or piantare
  qc dentro
jack [dʒæk] n (AUT) cricco; (CARDS) fante m;
  ~ up vt sollevare col cricco
jackal [ˈdʒækl] n sciacallo
jackdaw [ˈdʒækdɔː] n taccola
jacket [ˈdʒækɪt] n giacca; (of book) copertura
jack-knife [ˈdʒæknaɪf] vi: **the lorry ~d**
  l'autotreno si è piegato su se stesso
jack plug n (ELEC) jack m inv
jackpot [ˈdʒækpɔt] n primo premio (in
  denaro)
jade [dʒeɪd] n (stone) giada
jaded [ˈdʒeɪdɪd] adj sfinito(a), spossato(a)
jagged [ˈdʒæɡɪd] adj seghettato(a); (cliffs etc)
  frastagliato(a)
jail [dʒeɪl] n prigione f ♦ vt mandare in
  prigione
jam [dʒæm] n marmellata; (also: traffic ~)
  ingorgo; (inf) pasticcio ♦ vt (passage etc)
  ingombrare, ostacolare; (mechanism, drawer
  etc) bloccare; (RADIO) disturbare con
  interferenze ♦ vi incepparsi; **to ~ sth into**
  forzare qc dentro; infilare qc a forza dentro
Jamaica [dʒəˈmeɪkə] n Giamaica
jangle [ˈdʒæŋɡl] vi risuonare; (bracelet)
  tintinnare
janitor [ˈdʒænɪtə*] n (caretaker) portiere m;
  (: SCOL) bidello
January [ˈdʒænjuərɪ] n gennaio
Japan [dʒəˈpæn] n Giappone m; **~ese**
  [dʒæpəˈniːz] adj giapponese ♦ n inv
  giapponese m/f; (LING) giapponese m
jar [dʒɑː*] n (glass) barattolo, vasetto ♦ vi
  (sound) stridere; (colours etc) stonare
jargon [ˈdʒɑːɡən] n gergo
jasmin(e) [ˈdʒæzmɪn] n gelsomino
jaundice [ˈdʒɔːndɪs] n itterizia
jaunt [dʒɔːnt] n gita
javelin [ˈdʒævlɪn] n giavellotto

jaw [dʒɔː] n mascella

jay [dʒeɪ] n ghiandaia

jaywalker ['dʒeɪwɔːkə*] n pedone(a) indisciplinato(a)

jazz [dʒæz] n jazz m; ~ **up** vt rendere vivace

jealous ['dʒeləs] adj geloso(a); ~**y** n gelosia

jeans [dʒiːnz] npl (blue-)jeans mpl

jeer [dʒɪə*] vi: **to ~ (at)** fischiare; beffeggiare

jelly ['dʒelɪ] n gelatina; ~**fish** n medusa

jeopardy ['dʒepədɪ] n: **in ~** in pericolo

jerk [dʒəːk] n sobbalzo, scossa; sussulto; (inf: idiot) tonto/a ♦ vt dare una scossa a ♦ vi (vehicles) sobbalzare

jersey ['dʒəːzɪ] n maglia; (fabric) jersey m

jest [dʒest] n scherzo

Jesus ['dʒiːzəs] n Gesù m

jet [dʒet] n (of gas, liquid) getto; (AVIAT) aviogetto; ~**-black** adj nero(a) come l'ebano, corvino(a); ~ **engine** n motore m a reazione; ~ **lag** n (problemi mpl dovuti allo) sbalzo dei fusi orari

jettison ['dʒetɪsn] vt gettare in mare

jetty ['dʒetɪ] n molo

Jew [dʒuː] n ebreo

jewel ['dʒuːəl] n gioiello; ~**ler** (US ~**er**) n orefice m, gioielliere/a; ~**(l)er's (shop)** n oreficeria, gioielleria; ~**lery** (US ~**ery**) n gioielli mpl

Jewess ['dʒuːɪs] n ebrea

Jewish ['dʒuːɪʃ] adj ebreo(a), ebraico(a)

jibe [dʒaɪb] n beffa

jiffy ['dʒɪfɪ] (inf) n: **in a ~** in un batter d'occhio

jig [dʒɪg] n giga

jigsaw ['dʒɪgsɔː] n (also: ~ **puzzle**) puzzle m inv

jilt [dʒɪlt] vt piantare in asso

jingle ['dʒɪŋgl] n (for advert) sigla pubblicitaria ♦ vi tintinnare, scampanellare

jinx [dʒɪŋks] n iettatura; (person) iettatore/trice

jitters ['dʒɪtəz] (inf) npl: **to get the ~** aver fifa

job [dʒɔb] n lavoro; (employment) impiego, posto; **it's not my ~** (duty) non è compito mio; **it's a good ~ that ...** meno male che ...; **just the ~!** proprio quello che ci vuole; ~ **centre** (BRIT) n ufficio di collocamento; ~**less** adj senza lavoro, disoccupato(a)

jockey ['dʒɔkɪ] n fantino, jockey m inv ♦ vi: **to ~ for position** manovrare per una posizione di vantaggio

jog [dʒɔg] vt urtare ♦ vi (SPORT) fare footing, fare jogging; **to ~ sb's memory** rinfrescare la memoria a qn; **to ~ along** trottare; (fig) andare avanti piano piano; ~**ging** n footing m, jogging m

join [dʒɔɪn] vt unire, congiungere; (become member of) iscriversi a; (meet) raggiungere; riunirsi a ♦ vi (roads, rivers) confluire ♦ n

giuntura; ~ **in** vi partecipare ♦ vt fus unirsi a; ~ **up** vi incontrarsi; (MIL) arruolarsi

joiner ['dʒɔɪnə*] (BRIT) n falegname m

joint [dʒɔɪnt] n (TECH) giuntura; giunto; (ANAT) articolazione f, giuntura; (BRIT: CULIN) arrosto; (inf: place) locale m; (: of cannabis) spinello ♦ adj comune; ~ **account** n (at bank etc) conto in partecipazione, conto comune

joist [dʒɔɪst] n trave f

joke [dʒəuk] n scherzo; (funny story) barzelletta; (also: practical ~) beffa ♦ vi scherzare; **to play a ~ on sb** fare uno scherzo a qn; ~**r** n (CARDS) matta, jolly m inv

jolly ['dʒɔlɪ] adj allegro(a), gioioso(a) ♦ adv (BRIT: inf) veramente, proprio

jolt [dʒəult] n scossa, sobbalzo ♦ vt urtare

Jordan ['dʒɔːdən] n (country) Giordania; (river) Giordano

jostle ['dʒɔsl] vt spingere coi gomiti

jot [dʒɔt] n: **not one ~** nemmeno un po'; ~ **down** vt annotare in fretta, buttare giù; ~**ter** (BRIT) n blocco

journal ['dʒəːnl] n giornale m; rivista; diario; ~**ism** n giornalismo; ~**ist** n giornalista m/f

journey ['dʒəːnɪ] n viaggio; (distance covered) tragitto

joy [dʒɔɪ] n gioia; ~**ful** adj gioioso(a), allegro(a); ~**rider** n chi ruba un'auto per farvi un giro; ~**stick** n (AVIAT) barra di comando; (COMPUT) joystick m inv

JP n abbr = **Justice of the Peace**

Jr abbr = **junior**

jubilant ['dʒuːbɪlnt] adj giubilante; trionfante

jubilee ['dʒuːbɪliː] n giubileo; **silver ~** venticinquesimo anniversario

judge [dʒʌdʒ] n giudice m/f ♦ vt giudicare; **judg(e)ment** n giudizio

judiciary [dʒuː'dɪʃərɪ] n magistratura

judo ['dʒuːdəu] n judo

jug [dʒʌg] n brocca, bricco

juggernaut ['dʒʌgənɔːt] (BRIT) n (huge truck) bestione m

juggle ['dʒʌgl] vi fare giochi di destrezza; ~**r** n giocoliere/a

juice [dʒuːs] n succo

juicy ['dʒuːsɪ] adj succoso(a)

jukebox ['dʒuːkbɔks] n juke-box m inv

July [dʒuː'laɪ] n luglio

jumble ['dʒʌmbl] n miscuglio ♦ vt (also: ~ up) mischiare; ~ **sale** (BRIT) n vendita di beneficenza

jumbo (jet) ['dʒʌmbəu-] n jumbo-jet m inv

jump [dʒʌmp] vi saltare, balzare; (start) sobbalzare; (increase) rincarare ♦ vt saltare ♦ n salto, balzo; sobbalzo

jumper ['dʒʌmpə*] n (BRIT: pullover) maglione m, pullover m inv; (US: dress) scamiciato; ~ **cables** (US) npl = **jump leads**

jump leads [-liːdz] (*BRIT*) *npl* cavi *mpl* per batteria

jumpy ['dʒʌmpɪ] *adj* nervoso(a), agitato(a)

Jun. *abbr* = **junior**

junction ['dʒʌŋkʃən] *n* (*BRIT*: of roads) incrocio; (*of rails*) nodo ferroviario

juncture ['dʒʌŋktʃə*] *n*: **at this ~** in questa congiuntura

June [dʒuːn] *n* giugno

jungle ['dʒʌŋgl] *n* giungla

junior ['dʒuːnɪə*] *adj, n*: **he's ~ to me (by 2 years)**, **he's my ~ (by 2 years)** è più giovane di me (di 2 anni); **he's ~ to me** (*seniority*) è al di sotto di me, ho più anzianità di lui; **~ school** (*BRIT*) *n* scuola elementare (*da 8 a 11 anni*)

junk [dʒʌŋk] *n* cianfrusaglie *fpl*; (*cheap goods*) robaccia; **~ food** *n* porcherie *fpl*

junkie ['dʒʌŋkɪ] (*inf*) *n* drogato/a

junk mail *n* stampe *fpl* pubblicitarie

junk shop *n* chincaglieria

Junr *abbr* = **junior**

juror ['dʒuərə*] *n* giurato/a

jury ['dʒuərɪ] *n* giuria

just [dʒʌst] *adj* giusto(a) ♦ *adv*: **he's ~ done it/left** lo ha appena fatto/è appena partito; **~ right** proprio giusto; **~ 2 o'clock** le 2 precise; **she's ~ as clever as you** è in gamba proprio quanto te; **it's ~ as well that ...** meno male che ...; **~ as I arrived** proprio mentre arrivavo; **it was ~ before/enough/here** era poco prima/appena assai/proprio qui; **it's ~ me** sono solo io; **~ missed/caught** appena perso/preso; **~ listen to this!** senta un po' questo!

justice ['dʒʌstɪs] *n* giustizia; **J~ of the Peace** *n* giudice *m* conciliatore

justify ['dʒʌstɪfaɪ] *vt* giustificare

jut [dʒʌt] *vi* (*also*: **~ out**) sporgersi

juvenile ['dʒuːvənaɪl] *adj* giovane, giovanile; (*court*) dei minorenni; (*books*) per ragazzi ♦ *n* giovane *m/f*, minorenne *m/f*

juxtapose ['dʒʌkstəpəuz] *vt* giustapporre

K, k

K *abbr* (= *one thousand*) mille; (= *kilobyte*) K

Kampuchea [kæmpuˈtʃɪə] *n* Cambogia

kangaroo [kæŋgəˈruː] *n* canguro

karate [kəˈrɑːtɪ] *n* karatè *m*

kebab [kəˈbæb] *n* spiedino

keel [kiːl] *n* chiglia; **on an even ~** (*fig*) in uno stato normale

keen [kiːn] *adj* (*interest, desire*) vivo(a); (*eye, intelligence*) acuto(a); (*competition*) serrato(a); (*edge*) affilato(a); (*eager*) entusiasta; **to be ~ to do** *or* **on doing sth** avere una gran voglia di fare qc; **to be ~ on**

sth essere appassionato(a) di qc; **to be ~ on sb** avere un debole per qn

keep [kiːp] (*pt, pp* **kept**) *vt* tenere; (*hold back*) trattenere; (*feed: one's family etc*) mantenere, sostentare; (*a promise*) mantenere; (*chickens, bees, pigs etc*) allevare ♦ *vi* (*food*) mantenersi; (*remain: in a certain state or place*) restare ♦ *n* (*of castle*) maschio; (*food etc*): **enough for his ~** abbastanza per vitto e alloggio; (*inf*): **for ~s** per sempre; **to ~ doing sth** continuare a fare qc; fare qc di continuo; **to ~ sb from doing sth** impedire a qn di fare; **to ~ sb busy/a place tidy** tenere qn occupato(a)/un luogo in ordine; **to ~ sth to o.s.** tenere qc per sé; **to ~ sth (back) from sb** celare qc a qn; **to ~ time** (*clock*) andar bene; **~ on** *vi*: **to ~ on doing** continuare a fare; **to ~ on (about sth)** continuare a insistere (su qc); **~ out** *vt* tener fuori; **"~ out"** "vietato l'accesso"; **~ up** *vt* continuare, mantenere ♦ *vi*: **to ~ up with** tener dietro a, andare di pari passo con; (*work etc*) farcela a seguire; **~er** *n* custode *m/f*, guardiano/a; **~-fit** *n* ginnastica; **~ing** *n* (*care*) custodia; **in ~ing with** in armonia con; in accordo con; **~sake** *n* ricordo

kennel ['kɛnl] *n* canile *m*; **to put a dog in ~s** mettere un cane al canile

kept [kɛpt] *pt, pp of* **keep**

kerb [kəːb] (*BRIT*) *n* orlo del marciapiede

kernel ['kəːnl] *n* nocciolo

kettle ['kɛtl] *n* bollitore *m*

kettle drum *n* timpano

key [kiː] *n* (*gen, MUS*) chiave *f*; (*of piano, typewriter*) tasto ♦ *adj* chiave *inv* ♦ *vt* (*also*: **~ in**) digitare; **~board** *n* tastiera; **~ed up** *adj* (*person*) agitato(a); **~hole** *n* buco della serratura; **~hole surgery** *n* chirurgia non invasiva; **~note** *n* (*MUS*) tonica; (*fig*) nota dominante; **~ring** *n* portachiavi *m inv*

khaki ['kɑːkɪ] *adj* cachi ♦ *n* cachi *m*

kick [kɪk] *vt* calciare, dare calci a; (*inf: habit etc*) liberarsi di ♦ *vi* (*horse*) tirar calci ♦ *n* calcio; (*thrill*): **he does it for ~s** lo fa giusto per il piacere di farlo; **~ off** *vi* (*SPORT*) dare il primo calcio

kid [kɪd] *n* (*inf: child*) ragazzino/a; (*animal, leather*) capretto ♦ *vi* (*inf*) scherzare

kidnap ['kɪdnæp] *vt* rapire, sequestrare; **~per** *n* rapitore/trice; **~ping** *n* sequestro (di persona)

kidney ['kɪdnɪ] *n* (*ANAT*) rene *m*; (*CULIN*) rognone *m*

kill [kɪl] *vt* uccidere, ammazzare ♦ *n* uccisione *f*; **~er** *n* uccisore *m*, killer *m inv*; assassino/a; **~ing** *n* assassinio; **to make a ~ing** (*inf*) fare un bel colpo; **~joy** *n* guastafeste *m/f inv*

kiln [kɪln] *n* forno

kilo ['kiːləu] *n* chilo; **~byte** *n* (*COMPUT*) kilobyte *m inv*; **~gram(me)** ['kɪləugræm] *n*

chilogrammo; **~metre** ['kɪləmiːtə*] (US
~**meter**) n chilometro; **~watt** ['kɪləuwɒt] n
chilowatt m inv

kilt [kɪlt] n gonnellino scozzese

kin [kɪn] n see **next**; **kith**

kind [kaɪnd] adj gentile, buono(a) ♦ n sorta,
specie f; (species) genere m; **to be two of a ~**
essere molto simili; **in ~** (COMM) in natura

kindergarten ['kɪndəgɑːtn] n giardino
d'infanzia

kind-hearted [kaɪnd'hɑːtɪd] adj di buon
cuore

kindle ['kɪndl] vt accendere, infiammare

kindly ['kaɪndlɪ] adj pieno(a) di bontà,
benevolo(a) ♦ adv con bontà, gentilmente;
will you ~ ... vuole ... per favore

kindness ['kaɪndnɪs] n bontà, gentilezza

king [kɪŋ] n re m inv; **~dom** n regno, reame
m; **~fisher** n martin m inv pescatore; **~-size**
adj super inv; gigante

kiosk ['kiːɒsk] n edicola, chiosco; (BRIT: TEL)
cabina (telefonica)

kipper ['kɪpə*] n aringa affumicata

kiss [kɪs] n bacio ♦ vt baciare; **to ~ (each
other)** baciarsi; **~ of life** n respirazione f
bocca a bocca

kit [kɪt] n equipaggiamento, corredo; (set of
tools etc) attrezzi mpl; (for assembly) scatola
di montaggio

kitchen ['kɪtʃɪn] n cucina; **~ sink** n acquaio

kite [kaɪt] n (toy) aquilone m

kitten ['kɪtn] n gattino/a, micino/a

kitty ['kɪtɪ] n (money) fondo comune

knack [næk] n: **to have the ~ of** avere l'abilità
di

knapsack ['næpsæk] n zaino, sacco da
montagna

knead [niːd] vt impastare

knee [niː] n ginocchio; **~cap** n rotula

kneel [niːl] (pt, pp **knelt**) vi (also: ~ **down**)
inginocchiarsi

knew [njuː] pt of **know**

knickers ['nɪkəz] (BRIT) npl mutandine fpl

knife [naɪf] (pl **knives**) n coltello ♦ vt
accoltellare, dare una coltellata a

knight [naɪt] n cavaliere m; (CHESS) cavallo;
~hood (BRIT) n (title): **to get a ~hood** essere
fatto cavaliere

knit [nɪt] vt fare a maglia ♦ vi lavorare a
maglia; (broken bones) saldarsi; **to ~ one's
brows** aggrottare le sopracciglia; **~ting** n
lavoro a maglia; **~ting machine** n macchina
per maglieria; **~ting needle** n ferro (da
calza); **~wear** n maglieria

knives [naɪvz] npl of **knife**

knob [nɒb] n bottone m; manopola

knock [nɒk] vt colpire; urtare; (fig: inf)
criticare ♦ vi (at door etc): **to ~ at/on** bussare
a ♦ n bussata; colpo, botta; **~ down** vt

abbattere; **~ off** vi (inf: finish) smettere (di
lavorare), ♦ vt (from price) far abbassare; (inf:
steal) sgraffignare; **~ out** vt stendere;
(BOXING) mettere K.O.; (defeat) battere;
~ over vt (person) investire; (object) far
cadere; **~er** n (on door) battente m; **~out** n
(BOXING) knock out m inv ♦ cpd a
eliminazione

knot [nɒt] n nodo ♦ vt annodare

know [nəu] (pt **knew**, pp **known**) vt sapere;
(person, author, place) conoscere; **to ~ how to
do** sapere fare; **to ~ about** or **of sth/sb**
conoscere qc/qn; **~-all** n sapientone/a; **~-
how** n tecnica; pratica; **~ing** adj (look etc)
d'intesa; **~ingly** adv (purposely)
consapevolmente; (smile, look) con aria
d'intesa

knowledge ['nɒlɪdʒ] n consapevolezza;
(learning) conoscenza, sapere m; **~able** adj
ben informato(a)

known [nəun] pp of **know**

knuckle ['nʌkl] n nocca

Koran [kɔ'rɑːn] n Corano

Korea [kə'rɪə] n Corea

kosher ['kəuʃə*] adj kasher inv

L, l

L (BRIT) abbr = **learner driver**

lab [læb] n abbr (= laboratory) laboratorio

label ['leɪbl] n etichetta, cartellino; (brand: of
record) casa ♦ vt etichettare

labor etc ['leɪbə*] (US) = **labour** etc

laboratory [lə'bɒrətərɪ] n laboratorio

labour ['leɪbə*] (US **labor**) n (task) lavoro;
(workmen) manodopera; (MED): **to be in ~**
avere le doglie ♦ vi: **to ~ (at)** lavorare duro
(a); **L~, the L~ party** (BRIT) il partito laburista,
i laburisti; **hard ~** lavori mpl forzati; **~ed** adj
(breathing) affannoso(a); **~er** n manovale m;
farm ~er lavoratore m agricolo

lace [leɪs] n merletto, pizzo; (of shoe etc)
laccio ♦ vt (shoe: also: ~ **up**) allacciare

lack [læk] n mancanza ♦ vt mancare di;
through or **for ~ of** per mancanza di; **to be
~ing** mancare; **to be ~ing in** mancare di

lackadaisical [lækə'deɪzɪkl] adj
disinteressato(a), noncurante

lacquer ['lækə*] n lacca

lad [læd] n ragazzo, giovanotto

ladder ['lædə*] n scala; (BRIT: in tights)
smagliatura

laden ['leɪdn] adj: **~ (with)** carico(a) or
caricato(a) (di)

ladle ['leɪdl] n mestolo

lady ['leɪdɪ] n signora; dama; **L~ Smith** lady
Smith; **the ladies' (room)** i gabinetti per
signore; **~bird** (US **~bug**) n coccinella; **~like**

adj da signora, distinto(a); **~ship** *n*: your **~ship** signora contessa (*or* baronessa *etc*)

lag [læg] *n* (*of time*) lasso, intervallo ♦ *vi* (*also*: ~ *behind*) trascinarsi ♦ *vt* (*pipes*) rivestire di materiale isolante

lager ['lɑːɡə*] *n* lager *m inv*

lagoon [lə'ɡuːn] *n* laguna

laid [leɪd] *pt*, *pp* of **lay**; **~ back** (*inf*) *adj* rilassato(a), tranquillo(a); **~ up** *adj*: **~ up** (**with**) costretto(a) a letto (da)

lain [leɪn] *pp* of **lie**

lair [lɛə*] *n* covo, tana

lake [leɪk] *n* lago

lamb [læm] *n* agnello

lame [leɪm] *adj* zoppo(a); (*excuse etc*) zoppicante

lament [lə'mɛnt] *n* lamento ♦ *vt* lamentare, piangere

laminated ['læmɪneɪtɪd] *adj* laminato(a)

lamp [læmp] *n* lampada

lamppost ['læmppəʊst] (*BRIT*) *n* lampione *m*

lampshade ['læmpʃeɪd] *n* paralume *m*

lance [lɑːns] *vt* (*MED*) incidere

land [lænd] *n* (*as opposed to sea*) terra (ferma); (*country*) paese *m*; (*soil*) terreno; suolo; (*estate*) terreni *mpl*, terre *fpl* ♦ *vi* (*from ship*) sbarcare; (*AVIAT*) atterrare; (*fig*: *fall*) cadere ♦ *vt* (*passengers*) sbarcare; (*goods*) scaricare; **to ~ sb with sth** affibbiare qc a qn; **~ up** *vi* andare a finire; **~fill site** *n* discarica; **~ing** *n* atterraggio; (*of staircase*) pianerottolo; **~ing gear** *n* carrello di atterraggio; **~lady** *n* padrona *or* proprietaria di casa; **~locked** *adj* senza sbocco sul mare; **~lord** *n* padrone *m or* proprietario di casa; (*of pub etc*) padrone *m*; **~mark** *n* punto di riferimento; (*fig*) pietra miliare; **~owner** *n* proprietario(a) terriero(a); **~scape** *n* paesaggio; **~slide** *n* (*GEO*) frana; (*fig*: *POL*) valanga

lane [leɪn] *n* stradina; (*AUT*, *in race*) corsia; "get in lane" "immettersi in corsia"

language ['læŋɡwɪdʒ] *n* lingua; (*way one speaks*) linguaggio; **bad ~** linguaggio volgare; **~ laboratory** *n* laboratorio linguistico

languid ['læŋɡwɪd] *adj* languido(a)

lank [læŋk] *adj* (*hair*) liscio(a) e opaco(a)

lanky ['læŋkɪ] *adj* allampanato(a)

lantern ['læntən] *n* lanterna

lap [læp] *n* (*of track*) giro; (*of body*): **in** *or* **on one's ~** in grembo ♦ *vt* (*also*: ~ *up*) papparsi, leccare ♦ *vi* (*waves*) sciabordare; **~ up** *vt* (*fig*) bearsi di

lapel [lə'pɛl] *n* risvolto

Lapland ['læplænd] *n* Lapponia

lapse [læps] *n* lapsus *m inv*; (*longer*) caduta ♦ *vi* (*law*) cadere; (*membership*, *contract*) scadere; **to ~ into bad habits** pigliare cattive abitudini; **~ of time** spazio di tempo

laptop (computer) ['læp,tɒp-] *n* laptop *m inv*

larch [lɑːtʃ] *n* larice *m*

lard [lɑːd] *n* lardo

larder ['lɑːdə*] *n* dispensa

large [lɑːdʒ] *adj* grande; (*person*, *animal*) grosso(a); **at ~** (*free*) in libertà; (*generally*) in generale; nell'insieme; **~ly** *adv* in gran parte

largesse [lɑː'ʒɛs] *n* generosità

lark [lɑːk] *n* (*bird*) allodola; (*joke*) scherzo, gioco

laryngitis [lærɪn'dʒaɪtɪs] *n* laringite *f*

laser ['leɪzə*] *n* laser *m*; **~ printer** *n* stampante *f* laser *inv*

lash [læʃ] *n* frustata; (*also*: *eye~*) ciglio ♦ *vt* frustare; (*tie*): **to ~ to/together** legare a insieme; **~ out** *vi*: **to ~ out** (**at** *or* **against sb**) attaccare violentemente (qn)

lass [læs] *n* ragazza

lasso [læ'suː] *n* laccio

last [lɑːst] *adj* ultimo(a); (*week*, *month*, *year*) scorso(a), passato(a) ♦ *adv* per ultimo ♦ *vi* durare; **~ week** la settimana scorsa; **~ night** ieri sera, la notte scorsa; **at ~** finalmente, alla fine; **~ but one** penultimo(a); **~-ditch** *adj* (*attempt*) estremo(a); **~ing** *adj* durevole; **~ly** *adv* infine, per finire; **~-minute** *adj* fatto(a) (*or* preso(a) *etc*) all'ultimo momento

latch [lætʃ] *n* chiavistello

late [leɪt] *adj* (*not on time*) in ritardo; (*far on in day etc*) tardi *inv*; tardo(a); (*former*) ex; (*dead*) defunto(a) ♦ *adv* tardi; (*behind time*, *schedule*) in ritardo; **of ~** di recente; **in the ~ afternoon** nel tardo pomeriggio; **in ~ May** verso la fine di maggio; **~comer** *n* ritardatario(a); **~ly** *adv* recentemente

later ['leɪtə*] *adj* (*date etc*) posteriore; (*version etc*) successivo(a) ♦ *adv* più tardi; **~ on** più avanti

lateral ['lætərl] *adj* laterale

latest ['leɪtɪst] *adj* ultimo(a), più recente; **at the ~** al più tardi

lathe [leɪð] *n* tornio

lather ['lɑːðə*] *n* schiuma di sapone ♦ *vt* insaponare

Latin ['lætɪn] *n* latino ♦ *adj* latino(a); **~ America** *n* America Latina; **~-American** *adj*, *n* sudamericano(a)

latitude ['lætɪtjuːd] *n* latitudine *f*; (*fig*) libertà d'azione

latter ['lætə*] *adj* secondo(a); più recente ♦ *n*: **the ~** quest'ultimo, il secondo; **~ly** *adv* recentemente, negli ultimi tempi

lattice ['lætɪs] *n* traliccio; graticolato

laudable ['lɔːdəbl] *adj* lodevole

laugh [lɑːf] *n* risata ♦ *vi* ridere; **~ at** *vt fus* (*misfortune etc*) ridere di; **~ off** *vt* prendere alla leggera; **~able** *adj* ridicolo(a); **~ing stock** *n*: **the ~ing stock of** lo zimbello di;

~ter n riso; risate fpl

launch [lɔːntʃ] n (of rocket, COMM) lancio; (of new ship) varo; (also: motor ~) lancia ♦ vt (rocket, COMM) lanciare; (ship, plan) varare; **~ into** vt fus lanciarsi in; **~(ing) pad** n rampa di lancio

launder [ˈlɔːndə*] vt lavare e stirare

launderette [lɔːnˈdrɛt] (BRIT) n lavanderia (automatica)

Laundromat ® [ˈlɔːndrəmæt] (US) n lavanderia automatica

laundry [ˈlɔːndrɪ] n lavanderia; (clothes) biancheria; (: dirty) panni mpl da lavare

laurel [ˈlɔrl] n lauro

lava [ˈlɑːvə] n lava

lavatory [ˈlævətərɪ] n gabinetto

lavender [ˈlævəndə*] n lavanda

lavish [ˈlævɪʃ] adj copioso(a); abbondante; (giving freely): **~ with** prodigo(a) di, largo(a) in ♦ vt: **to ~ sth on sb** colmare qn di qc

law [lɔː] n legge f; civil/criminal ~ diritto civile/penale; **~-abiding** adj ubbidiente alla legge; **~ and order** n l'ordine m pubblico; **~ court** n tribunale m, corte f di giustizia; **~ful** adj legale; lecito(a); **~less** adj che non conosce nessuna legge

lawn [lɔːn] n tappeto erboso; **~ mower** n tosaerba m or f inv; **~ tennis** n tennis m su prato

law school n facoltà f inv di legge

lawsuit [ˈlɔːsuːt] n processo, causa

lawyer [ˈlɔːjə*] n (for sales, wills etc) ≈ notaio; (partner, in court) ≈ avvocato/essa

lax [læks] adj rilassato(a); negligente

laxative [ˈlæksətɪv] n lassativo

lay [leɪ] (pt, pp laid) pt of **lie** ♦ adj laico(a); (not expert) profano(a) ♦ vt posare, mettere; (eggs) fare; (trap) tendere; (plans) fare, elaborare; **to ~ the table** apparecchiare la tavola; **~ aside** or **by** vt mettere da parte; **~ down** vt mettere giù; (rules etc) formulare, fissare; **to ~ down the law** dettar legge; **to ~ down one's life** dare la propria vita; **~ off** vt (workers) licenziare; **~ on** vt (provide) fornire; **~ out** vt (display) presentare, disporre; **~about** n sfaccendato/a, fannullone/a; **~-by** (BRIT) n piazzola (di sosta)

layer [ˈleɪə*] n strato

layman [ˈleɪmən] n laico; profano

layout [ˈleɪaut] n lay-out m inv, disposizione f; (PRESS) impaginazione f

laze [leɪz] vi oziare

lazy [ˈleɪzɪ] adj pigro(a)

lb. abbr = **pound** (weight)

lead¹ [liːd] n (front position) posizione f di testa; (distance, time ahead) vantaggio; (clue) indizio; (ELEC) filo (elettrico); (for dog) guinzaglio; (THEATRE) parte f principale ♦ vt guidare, condurre;

(induce) indurre; (be leader of) essere a capo di ♦ vi condurre; (SPORT) essere in testa; **in the ~** in testa; **to ~ the way** fare strada; **~ away** vt condurre via; **~ back** vt: **to ~ back to** ricondurre a; **~ on** vt (tease) tenere sulla corda; **~ to** vt fus condurre a; portare a; **~ up to** vt fus portare a

lead² [lɛd] n (metal) piombo; (in pencil) mina; **~ed petrol** n benzina con piombo

leaden [ˈlɛdn] adj (sky, sea) plumbeo(a)

leader [ˈliːdə*] n capo; leader m inv; (in newspaper) articolo di fondo; (SPORT) chi è in testa; **~ship** n direzione f; capacità f di comando

leading [ˈliːdɪŋ] adj primo(a); principale; **~ light** n (person) personaggio di primo piano; **~ man/lady** n (THEATRE) primo attore/prima attrice

lead singer n cantante alla testa di un gruppo

leaf [liːf] (pl **leaves**) n foglia ♦ vi: **to ~ through** sth sfogliare qc; **to turn over a new ~** cambiar vita

leaflet [ˈliːflɪt] n dépliant m inv; (POL, REL) volantino

league [liːg] n lega; (FOOTBALL) campionato; **to be in ~ with** essere in lega con

leak [liːk] n (out) fuga; (in) infiltrazione f; (security ~) fuga d'informazioni ♦ vi (roof, bucket) perdere; (liquid) uscire; (shoes) lasciar passare l'acqua ♦ vt (information) divulgare; **~ out** vi uscire; (information) trapelare

lean [liːn] (pt, pp leaned or leant) adj magro(a) ♦ vt: **to ~ sth on** appoggiare qc su qc ♦ vi (slope) pendere; (rest): **to ~ against** appoggiarsi contro; essere appoggiato(a); **to ~ on** appoggiarsi a; **~ back/forward** vi sporgersi indietro/in avanti; **~ out** vi sporgersi; **~ over** vi inclinarsi; **~ing** n: **~ing (towards)** propensione f (per)

leap [liːp] (pt, pp leaped or leapt) n salto, balzo ♦ vi saltare, balzare; **~frog** n gioco della cavallina; **~ year** n anno bisestile

learn [lɜːn] (pt, pp learned or learnt) vt, vi imparare; **to ~ about sth** (hear, read) apprendere qc; **to ~ to do sth** imparare a fare qc; **~ed** [ˈlɜːnɪd] adj erudito(a), dotto(a); **~er** n principiante m/f; apprendista m/f; (BRIT: also: **~er driver**) guidatore/trice principiante; **~ing** n erudizione f, sapienza

lease [liːs] n contratto d'affitto ♦ vt affittare

leash [liːʃ] n guinzaglio

least [liːst] adj: **the ~** (+ noun) il(la) più piccolo(a), il(la) minimo(a); (smallest amount of) il(la) meno (+ verb) meno; **the ~** (+ adjective): **the ~ beautiful girl** la ragazza meno bella; **the ~ possible effort** il minimo sforzo possibile; **I have the ~ money** ho meno

denaro di tutti; **at ~** almeno; **not in the ~**
affatto, per nulla
leather ['leðə*] n cuoio
leave [li:v] (pt, pp **left**) vt lasciare; (go away
from) partire da ♦ vi partire, andarsene; (bus,
train) partire ♦ n (time off) congedo; (MIL,
also: consent) licenza; **to be left** rimanere;
there's some milk left over c'è rimasto del
latte; **on ~** in congedo; **~ behind** vt (person,
object) lasciare; (: forget) dimenticare; **~ out**
vt omettere, tralasciare; **~ of absence** n
congedo
leaves [li:vz] npl of **leaf**
Lebanon ['lebənən] n Libano
lecherous ['letʃərəs] adj lascivo(a), lubrico(a)
lecture ['lektʃə*] n conferenza; (SCOL) lezione
f ♦ vi fare conferenze; fare lezioni ♦ vt
(scold): **to ~ sb on** or **about sth** rimproverare
qn or fare una ramanzina a qn per qc; **to give
a ~ on** tenere una conferenza su
lecturer ['lektʃərə*] (BRIT) n (at university)
professore/essa, docente m/f
led [led] pt, pp of **lead**
ledge [ledʒ] n (of window) davanzale m; (on
wall etc) sporgenza; (of mountain) cornice f,
cengia
ledger ['ledʒə*] n libro maestro, registro
lee [li:] n lato sottovento
leech [li:tʃ] n sanguisuga
leek [li:k] n porro
leer [liə*] vi: **to ~ at sb** gettare uno sguardo
voglioso (or maligno) su qn
leeway ['li:wei] n (fig): **to have some ~** avere
una certa libertà di azione
left [left] pt, pp of **leave** ♦ adj sinistro(a) ♦ adv
a sinistra ♦ n sinistra; **on the ~, to the ~** a
sinistra; **the L~** (POL) la sinistra; **~-hand** adj:
~-hand drive guida a sinistra; **~-handed**
adj mancino(a); **~-hand side** n lato or
fianco sinistro; **~-luggage locker** n
armadietto per deposito bagagli; **~ luggage
(office)** (BRIT) n deposito m bagagli inv;
~overs npl avanzi mpl, resti mpl; **~-wing** adj
(POL) di sinistra
leg [leg] n gamba; (of animal) zampa; (of
furniture) piede m; (CULIN: of chicken) coscia;
(of journey) tappa; **lst/2nd ~** (SPORT) partita di
andata/ritorno
legacy ['legəsi] n eredità f inv
legal ['li:gl] adj legale; **~ holiday** (US) n
giorno festivo, festa nazionale; **~ tender** n
moneta legale
legend ['ledʒənd] n leggenda
legislation [ledʒis'leiʃən] n legislazione f;
legislature ['ledʒislətʃə*] n corpo legislativo
legitimate [li'dʒitimət] adj legittimo(a)
leg-room ['legru:m] n spazio per le gambe
leisure ['leʒə*] n agio, tempo libero;
ricreazioni fpl; **at ~** con comodo; **~ centre** n

centro di ricreazione; **~ly** adj tranquillo(a);
fatto(a) con comodo or senza fretta
lemon ['lemən] n limone m; **~ade** [-'neid] n
limonata; **~ tea** n tè m inv al limone
lend [lend] (pt, pp lent) vt: **to ~ sth (to sb)**
prestare qc (a qn); **~ing library** n biblioteca
che consente prestiti di libri
length [leŋθ] n lunghezza; (distance)
distanza; (section: of road, pipe etc) pezzo,
tratto; (of time) periodo; **at ~** (at last)
finalmente, alla fine; (lengthily) a lungo; **~en**
vt allungare, prolungare ♦ vi allungarsi;
~ways adv per il lungo; **~y** adj molto
lungo(a)
lenient ['li:niənt] adj indulgente, clemente
lens [lenz] n lente f; (of camera) obiettivo
Lent [lent] n Quaresima
lent [lent] pt, pp of **lend**
lentil ['lentl] n lenticchia
Leo ['li:əu] n Leone m
leotard ['li:əta:d] n calzamaglia
leprosy ['leprəsi] n lebbra
lesbian ['lezbiən] n lesbica
less [les] adj, pron, adv meno ♦ prep: **~ tax/
10% discount** meno tasse/il 10% di sconto;
~ than ever meno che mai; **~ than half** meno
della metà; **~ and ~** sempre meno; **the ~ he
works ...** meno lavora ....
lessen ['lesn] vi diminuire, attenuarsi ♦ vt
diminuire, ridurre
lesser ['lesə*] adj minore, più piccolo(a); **to a
~ extent** in grado or misura minore
lesson ['lesn] n lezione f; **to teach sb a ~** dare
una lezione a qn
let [let] (pt, pp let) vt lasciare; (BRIT: lease)
dare in affitto; **to ~ sb do sth** lasciar fare qc a
qn, lasciare che qn faccia qc; **to ~ sb know
sth** far sapere qc a qn; **~'s go** andiamo; **~ him
come** lo lasci venire; "**to ~**" "affittasi";
~ down vt (lower) abbassare; (dress)
allungare; (hair) sciogliere; (tyre) sgonfiare;
(disappoint) deludere; **~ go** vt, vi mollare;
~ in vt lasciare entrare; (visitor etc) far
entrare; **~ off** vt (allow to go) lasciare andare;
(firework etc) far partire; **~ on** (inf) vi dire;
~ out vt lasciare uscire; (scream) emettere;
~ up vi diminuire
lethal ['li:θl] adj letale, mortale
lethargic [le'θɑ:dʒik] adj letargico(a)
letter ['letə*] n lettera; **~ bomb** n lettera
esplosiva; **~box** (BRIT) n buca delle lettere;
~ing n iscrizione f; caratteri mpl
lettuce ['letis] n lattuga, insalata
let-up ['letʌp] n pausa
leukaemia [lu:'ki:miə] (US **leukemia**) n
leucemia
level ['levl] adj piatto(a), piano(a); orizzontale
♦ adv: **to draw ~ with** mettersi alla pari di
♦ n livello ♦ vt livellare, spianare; **to be**

~ **with** essere alla pari di; **A ~s** (BRIT) npl ≈ esami mpl di maturità; **O ~s** (BRIT) npl esami fatti in Inghilterra all'età di 16 anni; **on the ~** piatto(a); (fig) onesto(a); ~ **off** or **out** vi (prices etc) stabilizzarsi; ~ **crossing** (BRIT) n passaggio a livello; ~**-headed** adj equilibrato(a)

lever ['li:vər] n leva; ~**age** n: ~**age** (on or with) forza (su); (fig) ascendente m (su)

levy ['levi] n tassa, imposta ♦ vt imporre

lewd [lu:d] adj osceno(a), lascivo(a)

liability [laɪə'bɪlətɪ] n responsabilità f inv; (handicap) peso; **liabilities** npl debiti mpl; (on balance sheet) passivo

liable ['laɪəbl] adj (subject): ~ **to** soggetto(a) a; passibile di; (responsible): ~ **(for)** responsabile (di); (likely): ~ **to do** propenso(a) a fare

liaise [li:'eɪz] vi: **to ~ (with)** mantenere i contatti (con)

liaison [li:'eɪzɒn] n relazione f; (MIL) collegamento

liar ['laɪə*] n bugiardo/a

libel ['laɪbl] n libello, diffamazione f ♦ vt diffamare

liberal ['lɪbərl] adj liberale; (generous): **to be ~ with** distribuire liberalmente

liberation [lɪbə'reɪʃən] n liberazione f

liberty ['lɪbətɪ] n libertà f inv; **at ~** (criminal) in libertà; **at ~ to do** libero(a) di fare

Libra ['li:brə] n Bilancia

librarian [laɪ'breərɪən] n bibliotecario/a

library ['laɪbrərɪ] n biblioteca

Libya ['lɪbɪə] n Libia; ~**n** adj, n libico(a)

lice [laɪs] npl of **louse**

licence ['laɪsns] (US **license**) n autorizzazione f, permesso; (COMM) licenza; (RADIO, TV) canone m, abbonamento; (also: driving ~, (US) driver's ~) patente f di guida; (excessive freedom) licenza; ~ **number** n numero di targa; ~ **plate** n targa

license ['laɪsns] n (US) = **licence** ♦ vt dare una licenza a; ~**d** adj (for alcohol) che ha la licenza di vendere bibite alcoliche

lick [lɪk] vt leccare; (inf: defeat) stracciare; **to ~ one's lips** (fig) leccarsi i baffi

licorice ['lɪkərɪs] (US) n = **liquorice**

lid [lɪd] n coperchio; (eye~) palpebra

lie [laɪ] (pt **lay**, pp **lain**) vi (rest) giacere; (of object: be situated) trovarsi, essere; (tell lies: pt, pp **lied**) mentire, dire bugie ♦ n bugia, menzogna; **to ~ low** (fig) latitare; ~ **about** or **around** vi (things) essere in giro; (person) bighellonare; ~**-down** (BRIT) n: **to have a ~-down** sdraiarsi, riposarsi; ~**-in** (BRIT) n: **to have a ~-in** rimanere a letto

lieu [lu:]: **in ~ of** prep invece di, al posto di

lieutenant [lɛf'tɛnənt, (US) lu:'tɛnənt] n

tenente m

life [laɪf] (pl **lives**) n vita ♦ cpd di vita; della vita; **a ~** a vita; **to come to ~** rianimarsi; ~ **assurance** (BRIT) n = **~ insurance**; ~**belt** (BRIT) n salvagente m; ~**boat** n scialuppa di salvataggio; ~**guard** n bagnino; ~ **imprisonment** n carcere m a vita; ~ **insurance** n assicurazione f sulla vita; ~ **jacket** n giubbotto di salvataggio; ~**less** adj senza vita; ~**like** adj verosimile; rassomigliante; ~**long** adj per tutta la vita; ~ **preserver** (US) n salvagente m; giubbotto di salvataggio; ~ **sentence** n ergastolo; ~**size(d)** adj a grandezza naturale; ~ **span** n (durata della) vita; ~**style** n stile m di vita; ~ **support system** n respiratore m automatico; ~**time** n: **in his ~time** durante la sua vita; **once in a ~time** una volta nella vita

lift [lɪft] vt sollevare; (ban, rule) levare ♦ vi (fog) alzarsi ♦ n (BRIT: elevator) ascensore m; **to give sb a ~** (BRIT) dare un passaggio a qn; ~**-off** n decollo

light [laɪt] (pt, pp **lighted** or **lit**) n luce f, lume m; (daylight) luce f, giorno; (lamp) lampada; (AUT: rear ~) luce f di posizione; (: headlamp) fanale m; (for cigarette etc): **have you got a ~?** ha da accendere?; ~**s** npl (AUT: traffic ~s) semaforo ♦ vt (candle, cigarette, fire) accendere; (room): **to be lit by** essere illuminato(a) da ♦ adj (room, colour) chiaro(a); (not heavy, also fig) leggero(a); **to come to ~** venire alla luce, emergere; ~ **up** vi illuminarsi ♦ vt illuminare; ~ **bulb** n lampadina; ~**en** vt (make less heavy) alleggerire; ~**er** n (also: cigarette ~er) accendino; ~**-headed** adj stordito(a); ~**-hearted** adj gioioso(a), gaio(a); ~**house** n faro; ~**ing** n illuminazione f; ~**ly** adv leggermente; **to get off ~ly** cavarsela a buon mercato, ~ **meter** n (PHOT) esposimetro; ~**ness** n chiarezza; (in weight) leggerezza

lightning ['laɪtnɪŋ] n lampo, fulmine m; ~ **conductor** (US ~ **rod**) n parafulmine m

light pen n penna ottica

lightweight ['laɪtweɪt] adj (suit) leggero(a) ♦ n (BOXING) peso leggero

light year n anno m luce inv

like [laɪk] vt (person) volere bene a; (activity, object, food): **I ~ swimming/that book/chocolate** mi piace nuotare/quel libro/il cioccolato ♦ prep come ♦ adj simile, uguale ♦ n: the ~ uno(a) uguale; **his ~s and dislikes** i suoi gusti; **I would ~**, **I'd ~** mi piacerebbe, vorrei; **would you ~ a coffee?** gradirebbe un caffè?; **to be/look ~ sb/sth** somigliare a qn/ qc; **what does it look/taste ~?** che aspetto/ gusto ha?; **what does it sound ~?** come fa?; **that's just ~ him** è proprio di lui; **do it ~ this** fallo così; **it is nothing ~ ...** non è affatto come

...; **~able** adj simpatico(a)

likelihood ['laɪklɪhud] n probabilità

likely ['laɪklɪ] adj probabile; plausibile; he's
~ to leave probabilmente partirà, è probabile
che parta; **not ~!** neanche per sogno!

likeness ['laɪknɪs] n somiglianza

likewise ['laɪkwaɪz] adv similmente, nello
stesso modo

liking ['laɪkɪŋ] n: ~ **(for)** debole m (per); **to
be to sb's ~** piacere a qn

lilac ['laɪlək] n lilla m inv

lily ['lɪlɪ] n giglio; ~ **of the valley** n
mughetto

limb [lɪm] n arto

limber up ['lɪmbə*-] vi riscaldarsi i muscoli

limbo ['lɪmbəu] n: **to be in ~** (fig) essere
lasciato(a) nel dimenticatoio

lime [laɪm] n (tree) tiglio; (fruit) limetta; (GEO)
calce f

limelight ['laɪmlaɪt] n: **in the ~** (fig) alla
ribalta, in vista

limerick ['lɪmərɪk] n poesiola umoristica di 5
versi

limestone ['laɪmstəun] n pietra calcarea;
(GEO) calcare m

limit ['lɪmɪt] n limite m ♦ vt limitare; **~ed** adj
limitato(a), ristretto(a); **to be ~ed to** limitarsi
a; **~ed (liability) company** (BRIT) n ≈
società f inv a responsabilità limitata

limp [lɪmp] n: **to have a ~** zoppicare ♦ vi
zoppicare ♦ adj floscio(a), flaccido(a)

limpet ['lɪmpɪt] n patella

line [laɪn] n linea; (rope) corda; (for fishing)
lenza; (wire) filo; (of poem) verso; (row,
series) fila, riga; (on face) ruga ♦ vt
(clothes): **to ~ (with)** foderare (di); (box): **to
~ (with)** rivestire or foderare (di); (subj: trees,
crowd) fiancheggiare; ~ **of business** settore m
or ramo d'attività; **in ~ with** in linea con;
~ **up** vi allinearsi, mettersi in fila ♦ vt mettere
in fila; (event, celebration) preparare

lined [laɪnd] adj (face) rugoso(a); (paper) a
righe, rigato(a)

linen ['lɪnɪn] n biancheria, panni mpl; (cloth)
tela di lino

liner ['laɪnə*] n nave f di linea; (for bin)
sacchetto

linesman ['laɪnzmən] n guardalinee m inv

line-up ['laɪnʌp] n allineamento, fila; (SPORT)
formazione f di gioco

linger ['lɪŋgə*] vi attardarsi; indugiare; (smell,
tradition) persistere

lingerie ['lænʒəriː] n biancheria intima
femminile

linguistics [lɪŋ'gwɪstɪks] n linguistica

lining ['laɪnɪŋ] n fodera

link [lɪŋk] n (of a chain) anello; (relationship)
legame m; (connection) collegamento ♦ vt
collegare, unire, congiungere; (associate): **to**

~ **with** or **to** collegare a; **~s** npl (GOLF) pista or
terreno da golf; ~ **up** vt collegare, unire ♦ vi
riunirsi; associarsi

lino ['laɪnəu] n = **linoleum**

linoleum [lɪ'nəulɪəm] n linoleum m inv

lion ['laɪən] n leone m; **~ess** n leonessa

lip [lɪp] n labbro; (of cup etc) orlo

liposuction ['lɪpəusʌkʃən] n liposuzione f

lip: **~read** vi leggere sulle labbra; ~ **salve** n
burro di cacao; ~ **service** n: **to pay ~ service
to sth** essere favorevole a qc solo a parole;
~stick n rossetto

liqueur [lɪ'kjuə*] n liquore m

liquid ['lɪkwɪd] n liquido ♦ adj liquido(a)

liquidize ['lɪkwɪdaɪz] vt (CULIN) passare al
frullatore; **~r** n frullatore m (a brocca)

liquor ['lɪkə*] n alcool m

liquorice ['lɪkərɪs] (BRIT) n liquirizia

liquor store (US) n negozio di liquori

lisp [lɪsp] n pronuncia blesa della "s"

list [lɪst] n lista, elenco ♦ vt (write down)
mettere in lista; fare una lista di; (enumerate)
elencare; **~ed building** (BRIT) n edificio sotto
la protezione delle Belle Arti

listen ['lɪsn] vi ascoltare; **to ~ to** ascoltare;
~er n ascoltatore/trice

listless ['lɪstlɪs] adj apatico(a)

lit [lɪt] pt, pp of **light**

liter ['liːtə*] (US) n = **litre**

literacy ['lɪtərəsɪ] n il sapere leggere e scrivere

literal ['lɪtərl] adj letterale; **~ly** adv alla
lettera, letteralmente

literary ['lɪtərərɪ] adj letterario(a)

literate ['lɪtərət] adj che sa leggere e scrivere

literature ['lɪtərɪtʃə*] n letteratura; (brochures
etc) materiale m

lithe [laɪð] adj agile, snello(a)

litigation [lɪtɪ'geɪʃən] n causa

litre ['liːtə*] (US **liter**) n litro

litter ['lɪtə*] n (rubbish) rifiuti mpl; (young
animals) figliata; ~ **bin** (BRIT) n cestino per
rifiuti; **~ed** adj: **~ed with** coperto(a) di

little ['lɪtl] adj (small) piccolo(a); (not much)
poco(a) ♦ adv poco; **a ~** un po' (di); **a ~ bit**
un pochino; ~ **by** ~ a poco a poco; ~ **finger**
n mignolo

live¹ [lɪv] vi vivere; (reside) vivere, abitare;
~ **down** vt far dimenticare (alla gente);
~ **on** vt fus (food) vivere di; ~ **together** vi
vivere insieme, convivere; ~ **up to** vt fus
tener fede a, non venir meno a

live² [laɪv] adj (animal) vivo(a); (wire) sotto
tensione; (bullet, missile) inesploso(a);
(broadcast) diretto(a); (performance) dal vivo

livelihood ['laɪvlɪhud] n mezzi mpl di
sostentamento

lively ['laɪvlɪ] adj vivace, vivo(a)

liven up ['laɪvn'ʌp] vt (discussion, evening)
animare ♦ vi ravvivarsi

liver ['lɪvə*] n fegato
lives [laɪvz] npl of **life**
livestock ['laɪvstɔk] n bestiame m
livid ['lɪvɪd] adj livido(a); (furious) livido(a) di rabbia, furibondo(a)
living ['lɪvɪŋ] adj vivo(a), vivente ♦ n: **to earn** or **make a ~** guadagnarsi la vita; **~ conditions** npl condizioni fpl di vita; **~ room** n soggiorno; **~ standards** npl tenore m di vita; **~ wage** n salario sufficiente per vivere
lizard ['lɪzəd] n lucertola
load [ləud] n (weight) peso; (thing carried) carico ♦ vt (also: **~ up**): **to ~ (with)** (lorry, ship) caricare (di); (gun, camera, COMPUT) caricare (con); **a ~ of**, **~s of** (fig) un sacco di; **~ed** adj (vehicle): **~ed (with)** carico(a) (di); (question) capzioso(a); (inf: rich) carico(a) di soldi
loaf [ləuf] (pl **loaves**) n pane m, pagnotta
loan [ləun] n prestito ♦ vt dare in prestito; **on ~** in prestito
loath [ləuθ] adj: **to be ~ to do** essere restio(a) a fare
loathe [ləuð] vt detestare, aborrire
loaves [ləuvz] npl of **loaf**
lobby ['lɔbɪ] n atrio, vestibolo; (POL: pressure group) gruppo di pressione ♦ vt fare pressione su
lobster ['lɔbstə*] n aragosta
local ['ləukl] adj locale ♦ n (BRIT: pub) ≈ bar m inv all'angolo; **the ~s** npl (local inhabitants) la gente della zona; **~ anaesthetic** n anestesia locale; **~ authority** n ente m locale; **~ call** n (TEL) telefonata urbana; **~ government** n amministrazione f locale
locality [ləu'kælɪtɪ] n località f inv; (position) posto, luogo
locally ['ləukəlɪ] adv da queste parti; nel vicinato
locate [ləu'keɪt] vt (find) trovare; (situate) collocare; situare
location [ləu'keɪʃən] n posizione f; **on ~** (CINEMA) all'esterno
loch [lɔx] n lago
lock [lɔk] n (of door, box) serratura; (of canal) chiusa; (of hair) ciocca, riccio ♦ vt (with key) chiudere a chiave ♦ vi (door etc) chiudersi; (wheels) bloccarsi, incepparsi; **~ in** vt chiudere dentro (a chiave); **~ out** vt chiudere fuori; **~ up** vt (criminal, mental patient) rinchiudere; (house) chiudere (a chiave) ♦ vi chiudere tutto (a chiave)
locker ['lɔkə*] n armadietto
locket ['lɔkɪt] n medaglione m
locksmith ['lɔksmɪθ] n magnano
lockup ['lɔkʌp] n (US) prigione f; guardina
locum ['ləukəm] n (MED) medico sostituto
locust ['ləukəst] n locusta

lodge [lɔdʒ] n casetta, portineria; (hunting ~) casino di caccia ♦ vi (person): **to ~ (with)** essere a pensione (presso or da); (bullet etc) conficcarsi ♦ vt (appeal etc) presentare, fare; **to ~ a complaint** presentare un reclamo; **~r** n affittuario/a; (with room and meals) pensionante m/f
lodgings ['lɔdʒɪŋz] npl camera d'affitto; camera ammobiliata
loft [lɔft] n solaio, soffitta
lofty ['lɔftɪ] adj alto(a); (haughty) altezzoso(a)
log [lɔg] n (of wood) ceppo; (book) = **logbook** ♦ vt registrare
logbook ['lɔgbuk] n (NAUT, AVIAT) diario di bordo; (AUT) libretto di circolazione
loggerheads ['lɔgəhedz] npl: **at ~ (with)** ai ferri corti (con)
logic ['lɔdʒɪk] n logica; **~al** adj logico(a)
loin [lɔɪn] n (CULIN) lombata
loiter ['lɔɪtə*] vi attardarsi
loll [lɔl] vi (also: **~ about**) essere stravaccato(a)
lollipop ['lɔlɪpɔp] n lecca lecca m inv; **~ man/lady** (BRIT irreg) n impiegato/a che aiuta i bambini ad attraversare la strada
London ['lʌndən] n Londra; **~er** n londinese m/f
lone [ləun] adj solitario(a)
loneliness ['ləunlɪnɪs] n solitudine f, isolamento
lonely ['ləunlɪ] adj solo(a); solitario(a), isolato(a)
long [lɔŋ] adj lungo(a) ♦ adv a lungo, per molto tempo ♦ vi: **to ~ for sth/to do** desiderare qc/di fare; non veder l'ora di aver qc/di fare; **so** or **as ~ as** (while) finché; (provided that) sempre che + sub; **don't be ~!** fai presto!; **how ~ is this river/course?** quanto è lungo questo fiume/corso?; **6 metres ~** lungo 6 metri; **6 months ~** che dura 6 mesi, di 6 mesi; **all night ~** tutta la notte; **he no ~er comes** non viene più; **~ before** molto tempo prima; **before ~** (+ future) presto, fra poco; (+ past) poco tempo dopo; **at ~ last** finalmente; **~-distance** adj (race) di fondo; (call) interurbano(a); **~-haired** adj dai capelli lunghi; **~hand** n scrittura normale; **~ing** n desiderio, voglia, brama
longitude ['lɔŋgɪtjuːd] n longitudine f
long: **~ jump** n salto in lungo; **~-life** adj (milk) a lunga conservazione; (batteries) di lunga durata; **~-lost** adj perduto(a) da tempo; **~-range** adj a lunga portata; **~-sighted** adj presbite; **~-standing** adj di vecchia data; **~-suffering** adj estremamente paziente; infinitamente tollerante; **~-term** adj a lungo termine; **~ wave** n onde fpl lunghe; **~-winded** adj prolisso(a), interminabile
loo [luː] (BRIT: inf) n W.C. m inv, cesso
look [luk] vi guardare; (seem) sembrare,

parere; (*building etc*): **to ~ south/on to the sea** dare a sud/sul mare ♦ *n* sguardo; (*appearance*) aspetto, aria; **~s** *npl* (*good ~s*) bellezza; **~ after** *vt fus* occuparsi di, prendere cura di; (*keep an eye on*) guardare, badare a; **~ at** *vt fus* guardare; **~ back** *vi*: **to ~ back on** (*event etc*) ripensare a; **~ down on** *vt fus* (*fig*) guardare dall'alto, disprezzare; **~ for** *vt fus* cercare; **~ forward to** *vt fus* non veder l'ora di; (*in letters*): **we ~ forward to hearing from you** in attesa di una vostra gentile risposta; **~ into** *vt fus* esaminare; **~ on** *vi* fare da spettatore; **~ out** *vi* (*beware*): **to ~ out** (**for**) stare in guardia (per); **~ out for** *vt fus* cercare; **~ round** *vi* (*turn*) girarsi, voltarsi; (*in shop*) dare un'occhiata; **~ to** *vt fus* (*rely on*) contare su; **~ up** *vi* alzare gli occhi; (*improve*) migliorare ♦ *vt* (*word*) cercare; (*friend*) andare a trovare; **~ up to** *vt fus* avere rispetto per; **~-out** *n* posto d'osservazione; guardia; **to be on the ~-out (for)** stare in guardia (per)

loom [luːm] *n* telaio ♦ *vi* (*also*: **~ up**) apparire minaccioso(a); (*event*) essere imminente

loony ['luːnɪ] (*inf*) *n* pazzo/a

loop [luːp] *n* cappio ♦ *vt*: **to ~ sth round sth** passare qc intorno a qc; **~hole** *n* via d'uscita; scappatoia

loose [luːs] *adj* (*knot*) sciolto(a); (*screw*) allentato(a); (*stone*) cadente; (*clothes*) ampio(a), largo(a); (*animal*) in libertà, scappato(a); (*life, morals*) dissoluto(a) ♦ *n*: **to be on the ~** essere in libertà; **~ change** *n* spiccioli *mpl*, moneta; **~ chippings** *npl* (*on road*) ghiaino; **~ end** *n*: **to be at a ~ end** (*BRIT*) or **at ~ ends** (*US*) non saper che fare; **~ly** *adv* senza stringere; approssimativamente; **~n** *vt* sciogliere; (*belt etc*) allentare

loot [luːt] *n* bottino ♦ *vt* saccheggiare

lop [lɔp] *vt* (*also*: **~ off**) tagliare via, recidere

lop-sided ['lɔp'saɪdɪd] *adj* non equilibrato(a), asimmetrico(a)

lord [lɔːd] *n* signore *m*; **L~ Smith** lord Smith; **the L~** il Signore; **good L~!** buon Dio!; **the (House of) L~s** (*BRIT*) la Camera dei Lord; **~ship** *n*: **your L~ship** Sua Eccellenza

lore [lɔː*] *n* tradizioni *fpl*

lorry ['lɔrɪ] (*BRIT*) *n* camion *m inv*; **~ driver** (*BRIT*) *n* camionista *m*

lose [luːz] (*pt, pp* **lost**) *vt* perdere ♦ *vi* perdere; **to ~ (time)** (*clock*) ritardare; **~r** *n* perdente *m/f*

loss [lɔs] *n* perdita; **to be at a ~** essere perplesso(a)

lost [lɔst] *pt, pp of* **lose** ♦ *adj* perduto(a); **~ property** (*US* **~ and found**) *n* oggetti *mpl* smarriti

lot [lɔt] *n* (*at auctions*) lotto; (*destiny*) destino,

sorte *f*; **the ~** tutto(a) quanto(a); tutti(e) quanti(e); **a ~** molto; **a ~ of** una gran quantità di, un sacco di; **~s of** molto(a); **to draw ~s** (**for sth**) tirare a sorte (per qc)

lotion ['ləʊʃən] *n* lozione *f*

lottery ['lɔtərɪ] *n* lotteria

loud [laʊd] *adj* forte, alto(a); (*gaudy*) vistoso(a), sgargiante ♦ *adv* (*speak etc*) forte; **out ~** (*read etc*) ad alta voce; **~hailer** (*BRIT*) *n* portavoce *m inv*; **~ly** *adv* fortemente, ad alta voce; **~speaker** *n* altoparlante *m*

lounge [laʊndʒ] *n* salotto, soggiorno; (*at airport, station*) sala d'attesa; (*BRIT*: *also*: **~ bar**) bar *m inv* con servizio a tavolino ♦ *vi* oziare; **~ about** or **around** *vi* starsene colle mani in mano

louse [laʊs] (*pl* **lice**) *n* pidocchio

lousy ['laʊzɪ] (*inf*) *adj* orrendo(a), schifoso(a); **to feel ~** stare da cani

lout [laʊt] *n* zoticone *m*

lovable ['lʌvəbl] *adj* simpatico(a), carino(a); amabile

love [lʌv] *n* amore *m* ♦ *vt* amare; voler bene a; **to ~ to do**: **I ~ to do** mi piace fare; **to be/fall in ~ with** essere innamorato(a)/ innamorarsi di; **to make ~** fare l'amore; **"15 ~"** (*TENNIS*) "15 a zero"; **~ affair** *n* relazione *f*; **~ life** *n* vita sentimentale

lovely ['lʌvlɪ] *adj* bello(a); (*delicious*: *smell, meal*) buono(a)

lover ['lʌvə*] *n* amante *m/f*; (*person in love*) innamorato/a; (*amateur*): **a ~ of** un(un')amante di; un(un')appassionato(a) di

loving ['lʌvɪŋ] *adj* affettuoso(a)

low [ləʊ] *adj* basso(a) ♦ *adv* in basso ♦ *n* (*METEOR*) depressione *f*; **to be ~ on** (*supplies etc*) avere scarsità di; **to feel ~** sentirsi giù; **~-alcohol** *adj* a basso contenuto alcolico; **~-calorie** *adj* a basso contenuto calorico; **~-cut** *adj* (*dress*) scollato(a); **~er** *adj* (*bottom: of 2 things*) più basso; (*less important*) meno importante ♦ *vt* calare; (*prices, voice*) abbassare; **~-fat** *adj* magro(a); **~lands** *npl* (*GEO*) pianura; **~ly** *adj* umile, modesto(a)

loyal ['lɔɪəl] *adj* fedele, leale; **~ty** *n* fedeltà, lealtà; **~ty card** *n* carta che offre sconti a clienti abituali

lozenge ['lɔzɪndʒ] *n* (*MED*) pastiglia

L.P. *n abbr* = **long-playing record**

L-plates ['ɛlpleɪts] (*BRIT*) *npl* contrassegno P principiante

Ltd *abbr* (= *limited*) ≈ S.r.l.

lubricate ['luːbrɪkeɪt] *vt* lubrificare

luck [lʌk] *n* fortuna, sorte *f*; **bad ~** sfortuna, mala sorte; **good ~!** buona fortuna!; **~ily** *adv* fortunatamente, per fortuna; **~y** *adj* fortunato(a); (*number etc*) che porta fortuna

ludicrous ['luːdɪkrəs] *adj* ridicolo(a)

lug [lʌg] (*inf*) *vt* trascinare

luggage ['lʌgɪdʒ] n bagagli mpl; ~ **rack** n portabagagli m inv

lukewarm ['luːkwɔːm] adj tiepido(a)

lull [lʌl] n intervallo di calma ♦ vt: **to ~ sb to sleep** cullare qn finché si addormenta

lullaby ['lʌləbaɪ] n ninnananna

lumbago [lʌm'beɪgəu] n lombaggine f

lumber ['lʌmbə*] n (wood) legname m; (junk) roba vecchia; ~ **with** vt: **to be ~ed with sth** doversi sorbire qc; **~jack** n boscaiolo

luminous ['luːmɪnəs] adj luminoso(a)

lump [lʌmp] n pezzo; (in sauce) grumo; (swelling) gonfiore m; (also: sugar ~) zolletta ♦ vt (also: ~ together) riunire, mettere insieme; **a ~ sum** una somma globale; **~y** adj (sauce) pieno(a) di grumi; (bed) bitorzoluto(a)

lunatic ['luːnətɪk] adj pazzo(a), matto(a)

lunch [lʌntʃ] n pranzo, colazione f

luncheon ['lʌntʃən] n pranzo; ~ **voucher** (BRIT) n buono m pasto inv

lunch time n ora di pranzo

lung [lʌŋ] n polmone m

lunge [lʌndʒ] vi (also: ~ forward) fare un balzo in avanti; **to ~ at** balzare su

lurch [ləːtʃ] vi vacillare, barcollare ♦ n scatto improvviso; **to leave sb in the ~** piantare in asso qn

lure [luə*] n richiamo; lusinga ♦ vt attirare (con l'inganno)

lurid ['luərɪd] adj sgargiante; (details etc) impressionante

lurk [ləːk] vi stare in agguato

luscious ['lʌʃəs] adj succulento(a); delizioso(a)

lush [lʌʃ] adj lussureggiante

lust [lʌst] n lussuria; cupidigia; desiderio; (fig): ~ **for** sete f di

lusty ['lʌstɪ] adj vigoroso(a), robusto(a)

Luxembourg ['lʌksəmbəːg] n (state) Lussemburgo m; (city) Lussemburgo f

luxuriant [lʌg'zjuərɪənt] adj lussureggiante; (hair) folto(a)

luxurious [lʌg'zjuərɪəs] adj sontuoso(a), di lusso

luxury ['lʌkʃərɪ] n lusso ♦ cpd di lusso

lying ['laɪɪŋ] n bugie fpl, menzogne fpl ♦ adj bugiardo(a)

lynch [lɪntʃ] vt linciare

lyrical ['lɪrɪkl] adj lirico(a); (fig) entusiasta

lyrics ['lɪrɪks] npl (of song) parole fpl

M, m

m. abbr = metre; mile; million

M.A. abbr = Master of Arts

mac [mæk] (BRIT) n impermeabile m

macaroni [mækə'rəunɪ] n maccheroni mpl

machine [mə'ʃiːn] n macchina ♦ vt (TECH) lavorare a macchina; (dress etc) cucire a macchina; ~ **gun** n mitragliatrice f; **~ry** n macchinario, macchine fpl; (fig) macchina

mackerel ['mækrl] n inv sgombro

mackintosh ['mækɪntɒʃ] (BRIT) n impermeabile m

mad [mæd] adj matto(a), pazzo(a); (foolish) sciocco(a); (angry) furioso(a); **to be ~ about** (keen) andare pazzo(a) per

madam ['mædəm] n signora

madden ['mædn] vt fare infuriare

made [meɪd] pt, pp of **make**

Madeira [mə'dɪərə] n (GEO) Madera; (wine) madera

made-to-measure ['meɪdtəmeʒə*] (BRIT) adj fatto(a) su misura

madly ['mædlɪ] adv follemente

madman ['mædmən] (irreg) n pazzo, alienato

madness ['mædnɪs] n pazzia

magazine [mægə'ziːn] n (PRESS) rivista; (RADIO, TV) rubrica

maggot ['mægət] n baco, verme m

magic ['mædʒɪk] n magia ♦ adj magico(a); **~al** adj magico(a); **~ian** [mə'dʒɪʃən] n mago/a

magistrate ['mædʒɪstreɪt] n magistrato; giudice m/f

magnet ['mægnɪt] n magnete m, calamita; **~ic** [-'netɪk] adj magnetico(a)

magnificent [mæg'nɪfɪsnt] adj magnifico(a)

magnify ['mægnɪfaɪ] vt ingrandire; **~ing glass** n lente f d'ingrandimento

magnitude ['mægnɪtjuːd] n grandezza; importanza

magpie ['mægpaɪ] n gazza

mahogany [mə'hɒgənɪ] n mogano

maid [meɪd] n domestica; (in hotel) cameriera

maiden ['meɪdn] n fanciulla ♦ adj (aunt etc) nubile; (speech, voyage) inaugurale; ~ **name** n nome m da nubile or da ragazza

mail [meɪl] n posta ♦ vt spedire (per posta); **~box** (US) n cassetta delle lettere; **~ing list** n elenco d'indirizzi; **~-order** n vendita (or acquisto) per corrispondenza

maim [meɪm] vt mutilare

main [meɪn] adj principale ♦ n (pipe) conduttura principale; **the ~s** npl (ELEC) la linea principale; **in the ~** nel complesso, nell'insieme; **~frame** n (COMPUT) mainframe m inv; **~land** n continente m; **~ly** adv principalmente, soprattutto; ~ **road** n strada principale; **~stay** n (fig) sostegno principale; **~stream** n (fig) corrente f principale

maintain [meɪn'teɪn] vt mantenere; (affirm) sostenere; **maintenance** ['meɪntənəns] n manutenzione f; (alimony) alimenti mpl

maize [meɪz] n granturco, mais m

majestic [mə'dʒestɪk] adj maestoso(a)

majesty ['mædʒɪstɪ] n maestà f inv

major ['meɪdʒə*] n (MIL) maggiore m ♦ adj (greater, MUS) maggiore; (in importance) principale, importante

Majorca [mə'jɔːkə] n Maiorca

majority [mə'dʒɒrɪtɪ] n maggioranza

make [meɪk] (pt, pp made) vt fare; (manufacture) fare, fabbricare; (cause to be): **to ~ sb sad** etc rendere qn triste etc; (force): **to ~ sb do sth** costringere qn a fare qc, far fare qc a qn; (equal): **2 and 2 ~ 4** 2 più 2 fa 4 ♦ n fabbricazione f; (brand) marca; **to ~ a fool of sb** far fare a qn la figura dello scemo; **to ~ a profit** realizzare un profitto; **to ~ a loss** subire una perdita; **to ~ it** (arrive) arrivare; (achieve sth) farcela; **what time do you ~ it?** che ora fai?; **to ~ do with** arrangiarsi con; **~ for** vt fus (place) avviarsi verso; **~ out** vt (write out) scrivere; (: cheque) emettere; (understand) capire; (see) distinguere; (: numbers) decifrare; **~ up** vt (constitute) formare; (invent) inventare; (parcel) fare ♦ vi conciliarsi; (with cosmetics) truccarsi; **~ up for** vt fus compensare; ricuperare; **~-believe** n: **a world of ~-believe** un mondo di favole; **it's just ~-believe** è tutta un'invenzione; **~r** n (of programme etc) creatore/trice; (manufacturer) fabbricante m; **~shift** adj improvvisato(a); **~-up** n trucco; **~-up remover** n struccatore m

making ['meɪkɪŋ] n (fig): **in the ~** in formazione; **to have the ~s of** (actor, athlete etc) avere la stoffa di

maladjusted [mælə'dʒʌstɪd] adj disadattato(a)

malaria [mə'leərɪə] n malaria

Malaysia [mə'leɪzɪə] n Malaysia

male [meɪl] n (BIOL) maschio ♦ adj maschile; maschio(a)

malfunction [mæl'fʌŋkʃən] n funzione f difettosa

malice ['mælɪs] n malevolenza; **malicious** [mə'lɪʃəs] adj malevolo(a); (LAW) doloso(a)

malignant [mə'lɪgnənt] adj (MED) maligno(a)

mall [mɔːl] n (also: shopping ~) centro commerciale

mallet ['mælɪt] n maglio

malnutrition [mælnjuː'trɪʃən] n denutrizione f

malpractice [mæl'præktɪs] n prevaricazione f; negligenza

malt [mɔːlt] n malto

Malta ['mɔːltə] n Malta

mammal ['mæml] n mammifero

mammoth ['mæməθ] adj enorme, gigantesco(a)

man [mæn] (pl **men**) n uomo ♦ vt fornire d'uomini; stare a; **an old ~** un vecchio; **~ and wife** marito e moglie

manage ['mænɪdʒ] vi farcela ♦ vt (be in charge of) occuparsi di; gestire; **to ~ to do sth** riuscire a far qc; **~able** adj maneggevole; fattibile; **~ment** n amministrazione f, direzione f; **~r** n direttore m; (of shop, restaurant) gerente m; (of artist, SPORT) manager m inv; **~ress** [-ə'res] n direttrice f; gerente f; **~rial** [-ə'dʒɪərɪəl] adj dirigenziale; **managing director** n amministratore m delegato

mandarin ['mændərɪn] n (person, fruit) mandarino

mandatory ['mændətərɪ] adj obbligatorio(a); ingiuntivo(a)

mane [meɪn] n criniera

maneuver etc [mə'nuːvə*] (US) = **manoeuvre** etc

manfully ['mænfəlɪ] adv valorosamente

mangle ['mæŋgl] vt straziare; mutilare

mango ['mæŋgəʊ] (pl **~es**) n mango

mangy ['meɪndʒɪ] adj rognoso(a)

manhandle ['mænhændl] vt malmenare

manhole ['mænhəʊl] n botola stradale

manhood ['mænhʊd] n età virile; virilità

man-hour ['mæn'aʊə*] n ora di lavoro

manhunt ['mænhʌnt] n caccia all'uomo

mania ['meɪnɪə] n mania; **~c** ['meɪnɪæk] n maniaco/a

manic ['mænɪk] adj (behaviour, activity) maniacale

manicure ['mænɪkjʊə*] n manicure f inv; **~ set** n trousse f inv della manicure

manifest ['mænɪfest] vt manifestare ♦ adj manifesto(a), palese

manifesto [mænɪ'festəʊ] n manifesto

manipulate [mə'nɪpjʊleɪt] vt manipolare

mankind [mæn'kaɪnd] n umanità, genere m umano

manly ['mænlɪ] adj virile; coraggioso(a)

man-made ['mæn'meɪd] adj sintetico(a); artificiale

manner ['mænə*] n maniera, modo; (behaviour) modo di fare; (type, sort): **all ~ of things** ogni genere di cosa; **~s** npl (conduct) maniere fpl; **bad ~s** maleducazione f; **~ism** n vezzo, tic m inv

manoeuvre [mə'nuːvə*] (US **maneuver**) vt manovrare ♦ vi far manovre ♦ n manovra

manor ['mænə*] n (also: ~ house) maniero

manpower ['mænpaʊə*] n manodopera

mansion ['mænʃən] n casa signorile

manslaughter ['mænslɔːtə*] n omicidio preterintenzionale

mantelpiece ['mæntlpiːs] n mensola del caminetto

manual ['mænjʊəl] adj manuale ♦ n

manuale m

manufacture [mænju'fæktʃə*] vt fabbricare ♦ n fabbricazione f, manifattura; **~r** n fabbricante m

manure [mə'njuə*] n concime m

manuscript ['mænjuskrɪpt] n manoscritto

many ['menɪ] adj molti(e) ♦ pron molti(e); **a great ~** moltissimi(e), un gran numero (di); **~ a time** molte volte

map [mæp] n carta (geografica); **~ out** vt tracciare un piano di

maple ['meɪpl] n acero

mar [mɑ:*] vt sciupare

marathon ['mærəθən] n maratona

marauder [mə'rɔ:də*] n saccheggiatore m

marble ['mɑ:bl] n marmo; (toy) pallina, bilia

March [mɑ:tʃ] n marzo

march [mɑ:tʃ] vi marciare; sfilare ♦ n marcia

mare [meə*] n giumenta

margarine [mɑ:dʒə'ri:n] n margarina

margin ['mɑ:dʒɪn] n margine m; **~al (seat)** n (POL) seggio elettorale ottenuto con una stretta maggioranza

marigold ['mærɪgəuld] n calendola

marina [mə'ri:nə] n marina

marine [mə'ri:n] adj (animal, plant) marino(a); (forces, engineering) marittimo(a) ♦ n (BRIT) fante m di marina; (US) marine m inv

marital ['mærɪtl] adj maritale, coniugale; **~ status** stato coniugale

mark [mɑ:k] n segno; (stain) macchia; (of skid etc) traccia; (BRIT: SCOL) voto; (SPORT) bersaglio; (currency) marco ♦ vt segnare; (stain) macchiare; (indicate) indicare; (BRIT: SCOL) dare un voto a; correggere; **to ~ time** segnare il passo; **~ed** adj spiccato(a), chiaro(a); **~er** n (sign) segno; (bookmark) segnalibro

market ['mɑ:kɪt] n mercato ♦ vt (COMM) mettere in vendita; **~ garden** (BRIT) n orto industriale; **~ing** n marketing m; **~ place** n piazza del mercato; (COMM) piazza, mercato; **~ research** n indagine f or ricerca di mercato

marksman ['mɑ:ksmən] n tiratore m scelto

marmalade ['mɑ:məleɪd] n marmellata d'arance

maroon [mə'ru:n] vt (also fig): **to be ~ed (in or at)** essere abbandonato(a) (in) ♦ adj bordeaux inv

marquee [mɑ:'ki:] n padiglione m

marquess ['mɑ:kwɪs] n = **marquis**

marquis ['mɑ:kwɪs] n marchese m

marriage ['mærɪdʒ] n matrimonio; **~ certificate** n certificato di matrimonio

married ['mærɪd] adj sposato(a); (life, love) coniugale, matrimoniale

marrow ['mærəu] n midollo; (vegetable) zucca

marry ['mærɪ] vt sposare, sposarsi con; (subj: vicar, priest etc) dare in matrimonio ♦ vi (also: **get married**) sposarsi

Mars [mɑ:z] n (planet) Marte m

marsh [mɑ:ʃ] n palude f

marshal ['mɑ:ʃl] n maresciallo; (US: fire) capo; (: police) capitano ♦ vt (thoughts, support) ordinare; (soldiers) adunare

martyr ['mɑ:tə*] n martire m/f; **~dom** n martirio

marvel ['mɑ:vl] n meraviglia ♦ vi: **to ~ (at)** meravigliarsi (di); **~lous** (US **~ous**) adj meraviglioso(a)

Marxist ['mɑ:ksɪst] adj, n marxista m/f

marzipan ['mɑ:zɪpæn] n marzapane m

mascara [mæs'kɑ:rə] n mascara m

masculine ['mæskjulɪn] adj maschile; (woman) mascolino(a)

mash [mæʃ] vt passare, schiacciare; **~ed potatoes** npl purè m di patate

mask [mɑ:sk] n maschera ♦ vt mascherare

mason ['meɪsn] n (also: stone~) scalpellino; (also: free~) massone m; **~ry** n muratura

masquerade [mæskə'reɪd] vi: **to ~ as** farsi passare per

mass [mæs] n moltitudine f, massa; (PHYSICS) massa; (REL) messa ♦ vi ammassarsi; **the ~es** npl (ordinary people) le masse; **~es of** (inf) una montagna di

massacre ['mæsəkə*] n massacro

massage ['mæsɑ:ʒ] n massaggio

masseur [mæ'sə:*] n massaggiatore m; **masseuse** [-'sə:z] n massaggiatrice f

massive ['mæsɪv] adj enorme, massiccio(a)

mass media npl mass media mpl

mass-production ['mæsprə'dʌkʃən] n produzione f in serie

mast [mɑ:st] n albero

master ['mɑ:stə*] n padrone m; (ART etc, teacher: in primary school) maestro; (: in secondary school) professore m; (title for boys): **M~ X** Signorino X ♦ vt domare; (learn) imparare a fondo; (understand) conoscere a fondo; **~ key** n chiave f maestra; **~ly** adj magistrale; **~mind** n mente f superiore ♦ vt essere il cervello di; **M~ of Arts/Science** n Master m inv in lettere/scienze; **~piece** n capolavoro; **~y** n dominio; padronanza

mat [mæt] n stuoia; (also: door~) stoino, zerbino; (also: table ~) sottopiatto ♦ adj = **matt**

match [mætʃ] n fiammifero; (game) partita, incontro; (fig) uguale m/f; matrimonio; partito ♦ vt intonare; (go well with) andare benissimo con; (equal) uguagliare; (correspond to) corrispondere a; (pair: also: ~ up) accoppiare ♦ vi combaciare; **to be a good ~** andare bene; **~box** n scatola per fiammiferi; **~ing** adj ben assortito(a)

mate [meɪt] *n* compagno/a di lavoro; (*inf*: *friend*) amico/a; (*animal*) compagno/a; (*in merchant navy*) secondo ♦ *vi* accoppiarsi

material [mə'tɪərɪəl] *n* (*substance*) materiale *m*, materia; (*cloth*) stoffa ♦ *adj* materiale; **~s** *npl* (*equipment*) materiali *mpl*

maternal [mə'təːnl] *adj* materno(a)

maternity [mə'təːnɪtɪ] *n* maternità; **~ dress** *n* vestito *m* pre-maman *inv*; **~ hospital** *n* ≈ clinica ostetrica

math [mæθ] (*US*) *n* = **maths**

mathematical [mæθə'mætɪkl] *adj* matematico(a)

mathematics [mæθə'mætɪks] *n* matematica

maths [mæθs] (*US* **math**) *n* matematica

matinée ['mætɪneɪ] *n* matinée *f inv*

mating call ['meɪtɪŋ-] *n* richiamo sessuale

matriculation [mətrɪkju'leɪʃən] *n* immatricolazione *f*

matrimonial [mætrɪ'məʊnɪəl] *adj* matrimoniale, coniugale

matrimony ['mætrɪmənɪ] *n* matrimonio

matron ['meɪtrən] *n* (*in hospital*) capoinfermiera; (*in school*) infermiera

mat(t) [mæt] *adj* opaco(a)

matted ['mætɪd] *adj* ingarbugliato(a)

matter ['mætə*] *n* questione *f*; (*PHYSICS*) materia, sostanza; (*content*) contenuto; (*MED*: *pus*) pus *m* ♦ *vi* importare; **it doesn't ~** non importa; (*I don't mind*) non fa niente; **what's the ~?** che cosa c'è?; **no ~ what** qualsiasi cosa accada; **as a ~ of course** come cosa naturale; **as a ~ of fact** in verità; **~-of-fact** *adj* prosaico(a)

mattress ['mætrɪs] *n* materasso

mature [mə'tjuə*] *adj* maturo(a); (*cheese*) stagionato(a) ♦ *vi* maturare; stagionare

maul [mɔːl] *vt* lacerare

mauve [məʊv] *adj* malva *inv*

maxim ['mæksɪm] *n* massima

maximum ['mæksɪməm] (*pl* **maxima**) *adj* massimo(a) ♦ *n* massimo

May [meɪ] *n* maggio

may [meɪ] (*conditional*: **might**) *vi* (*indicating possibility*): **he ~ come** può darsi che venga; (*be allowed to*): **~ I smoke?** posso fumare?; (*wishes*): **~ God bless you!** Dio la benedica!; **you ~ as well go** tanto vale che tu te ne vada

maybe ['meɪbiː] *adv* forse, può darsi; **~ he'll ... può darsi che lui ... + *sub*, forse lui ....

May Day *n* il primo maggio

mayhem ['meɪhɛm] *n* cagnara

mayonnaise [meɪə'neɪz] *n* maionese *f*

mayor [mɛə*] *n* sindaco; **~ess** *n* sindaco (*donna*); moglie *f* del sindaco

maze [meɪz] *n* labirinto, dedalo

M.D. *abbr* = **Doctor of Medicine**

me [miː] *pron* mi, m' + *vowel or silent "h"*; (*stressed, after prep*) me; **he heard ~** mi ha or

m'ha sentito; **give ~ a book** dammi (*or* mi dia) un libro; **it's ~** sono io; **with ~** con me; **without ~** senza di me

meadow ['mɛdəʊ] *n* prato

meagre ['miːgə*] (*US* **meager**) *adj* magro(a)

meal [miːl] *n* pasto; (*flour*) farina; **~time** *n* l'ora di mangiare

mean [miːn] (*pt*, *pp* **meant**) *adj* (*with money*) avaro(a), gretto(a); (*unkind*) meschino(a), maligno(a); (*shabby*) misero(a); (*average*) medio(a) ♦ *vt* (*signify*) significare, voler dire; (*intend*): **to ~ to do** aver l'intenzione di fare ♦ *n* mezzo; (*MATH*) media; **~s** *npl* (*way*, *money*) mezzi *mpl*; **by ~s of** per mezzo di; **by all ~s** ma certo, prego; **to be meant for** essere destinato(a) a; **do you ~ it?** dice sul serio?; **what do you ~?** che cosa vuol dire?

meander [mɪ'ændə*] *vi* far meandri

meaning ['miːnɪŋ] *n* significato, senso; **~ful** *adj* significativo(a); **~less** *adj* senza senso

means [miːnz] *npl* mezzi *mpl*; **by ~ of** per mezzo di; (*person*) a mezzo di; **by all ~** ma certo, prego

meant [mɛnt] *pt*, *pp of* **mean**

meantime ['miːntaɪm] *adv* (*also: in the ~*) nel frattempo

meanwhile ['miːnwaɪl] *adv* nel frattempo

measles ['miːzlz] *n* morbillo

measure ['mɛʒə*] *vt*, *vi* misurare ♦ *n* misura; (*also: tape ~*) metro; **~ments** *npl* (*size*) misure *fpl*

meat [miːt] *n* carne *f*; **cold ~** affettato; **~ball** *n* polpetta di carne; **~ pie** *n* pasticcio di carne in crosta

Mecca ['mɛkə] *n* (*also fig*) la Mecca

mechanic [mɪ'kænɪk] *n* meccanico; **~al** *adj* meccanico(a); **~s** *n* meccanica ♦ *npl* meccanismo

mechanism ['mɛkənɪzəm] *n* meccanismo

medal ['mɛdl] *n* medaglia; **~lion** [mɪ'dælɪən] *n* medaglione *m*; **~list** (*US* **~ist**) *n* (*SPORT*): **to be a gold ~list** essere medaglia d'oro

meddle ['mɛdl] *vi*: **to ~ in** immischiarsi in, mettere le mani in; **to ~ with** toccare

media ['miːdɪə] *npl* media *mpl*

mediaeval [mɛdɪ'iːvl] *adj* = **medieval**

median ['miːdɪən] *n* (*also: ~ strip*) banchina *f* spartitraffico

mediate ['miːdɪeɪt] *vi* fare da mediatore/trice

Medicaid ® ['mɛdɪkeɪd] (*US*) *n* assistenza medica ai poveri

medical ['mɛdɪkl] *adj* medico(a) ♦ *n* visita medica

Medicare ® ['mɛdɪkeə*] (*US*) *n* assistenza medica agli anziani

medication [mɛdɪ'keɪʃən] *n* medicinali *mpl*, farmaci *mpl*

medicine ['mɛdsɪn] *n* medicina

medieval [mɛdɪ'iːvl] *adj* medievale

mediocre [miːdɪˈəʊkə*] adj mediocre

meditate [ˈmedɪteɪt] vi: **to ~ (on)** meditare (su)

Mediterranean [medɪtəˈreɪnɪən] adj mediterraneo(a); **the ~ (Sea)** il (mare) Mediterraneo

medium [ˈmiːdɪəm] (pl **media**) adj medio(a) ♦ n (means) mezzo; (pl **mediums**: person) medium m inv; **~ wave** n onde fpl medie

meek [miːk] adj dolce, umile

meet [miːt] (pt, pp **met**) vt incontrare; (for the first time) fare la conoscenza di; (go and fetch) andare a prendere; (fig) affrontare; soddisfare; raggiungere ♦ vi incontrarsi; (in session) riunirsi; (join: objects) unirsi; **~ with** vt fus incontrare; **~ing** n incontro; (session: of club etc) riunione f; (interview) intervista; **she's at a ~ing** (COMM) è in riunione

megabyte [ˈmegəbaɪt] n (COMPUT) megabyte m inv

megaphone [ˈmegəfəun] n megafono

melancholy [ˈmelənkəlɪ] n malinconia ♦ adj malinconico(a)

mellow [ˈmeləʊ] adj (wine, sound) ricco(a); (light) dolce; (colour) caldo(a) ♦ vi (person) addolcirsi

melody [ˈmelədɪ] n melodia

melon [ˈmelən] n melone m

melt [melt] vi (gen) sciogliersi, struggersi; (metals) fondersi ♦ vt sciogliere, struggere; fondere; **~ down** vt fondere; **~down** n (in nuclear reactor) fusione f (dovuta a surriscaldamento); **~ing pot** n (fig) crogiolo

member [ˈmembə*] n membro; **M~ of the European Parliament** (BRIT) n eurodeputato/a; **M~ of Parliament** (BRIT) n deputato/a; **M~ of the Scottish Parliament** (BRIT) n deputato/a del Parlamento scozzese; **~ship** n iscrizione f; (numero d')iscritti mpl, membri mpl; **~ship card** n tessera (di iscrizione)

memento [məˈmentəu] n ricordo, souvenir m inv

memo [ˈmeməu] n appunto; (COMM etc) comunicazione f di servizio

memoirs [ˈmemwɑːz] npl memorie fpl, ricordi mpl

memoranda [meməˈrændə] npl of **memorandum**

memorandum [meməˈrændəm] (pl **memoranda**) n appunto; (COMM etc) comunicazione f di servizio

memorial [mɪˈmɔːrɪəl] n monumento commemorativo ♦ adj commemorativo(a)

memorize [ˈmeməraɪz] vt memorizzare

memory [ˈmemərɪ] n (also COMPUT) memoria; (recollection) ricordo

men [men] npl of **man**

menace [ˈmenəs] n minaccia ♦ vt minacciare

mend [mend] vt aggiustare, riparare; (darn) rammendare ♦ n: **on the ~** in via di guarigione

menial [ˈmiːnɪəl] adj da servo, domestico(a); umile

meningitis [menɪnˈdʒaɪtɪs] n meningite f

menopause [ˈmenəupɔːz] n menopausa

menstruation [menstruˈeɪʃən] n mestruazione f

mental [ˈmentl] adj mentale

mentality [menˈtælɪtɪ] n mentalità f inv

menthol [ˈmenθɒl] n mentolo

mention [ˈmenʃən] n menzione f ♦ vt menzionare, far menzione di; **don't ~ it!** non c'è di che!, prego!

menu [ˈmenjuː] n (set ~, COMPUT) menù m inv; (printed) carta

MEP n abbr = **Member of the European Parliament**

merchandise [ˈmɜːtʃəndaɪz] n merci fpl

merchant [ˈmɜːtʃənt] n mercante m, commerciante m; **~ bank** (BRIT) n banca d'affari; **~ navy** (US **~ marine**) n marina mercantile

merciful [ˈmɜːsɪful] adj pietoso(a), clemente

merciless [ˈmɜːsɪlɪs] adj spietato(a)

mercury [ˈmɜːkjurɪ] n mercurio

mercy [ˈmɜːsɪ] n pietà; (REL) misericordia; **at the ~ of** alla mercè di

mere [mɪə*] adj semplice; **by a ~ chance** per mero caso; **~ly** adv semplicemente, non ... che

merge [mɜːdʒ] vt unire ♦ vi fondersi, unirsi; (COMM) fondersi; **~r** n (COMM) fusione f

meringue [məˈræŋ] n meringa

merit [ˈmerɪt] n merito, valore m ♦ vt meritare

mermaid [ˈmɜːmeɪd] n sirena

merry [ˈmerɪ] adj gaio(a), allegro(a); **M~ Christmas!** Buon Natale!; **~-go-round** n carosello

mesh [meʃ] n maglia; rete f

mesmerize [ˈmezməraɪz] vt ipnotizzare; affascinare

mess [mes] n confusione f, disordine m; (fig) pasticcio; (dirt) sporcizia; (MIL) mensa; **~ about** (inf) vi (also: ~ around) trastullarsi; **~ about with** (inf) vt fus (also: ~ around with) gingillarsi con; (plans) fare un pasticcio di; **~ up** vt sporcare; fare un pasticcio di; rovinare

message [ˈmesɪdʒ] n messaggio

messenger [ˈmesɪndʒə*] n messaggero/a

Messrs [ˈmesəz] abbr (on letters) Spett

messy [ˈmesɪ] adj sporco(a); disordinato(a)

met [met] pt, pp of **meet**

metal [ˈmetl] n metallo; **~lic** [-ˈtælɪk] adj metallico(a)

metaphor [ˈmetəfə*] n metafora

meteorology [miːtɪəˈrɒlədʒɪ] n

meteorologia

meter ['miːtə*] n (instrument) contatore m; (parking ~) parchimetro; (US: unit) = **metre**

method ['mɛθəd] n metodo; **~ical** [mɪ'θɔdɪkl] adj metodico(a)

Methodist ['mɛθədɪst] n metodista m/f

meths [mɛθs] (BRIT) n = **methylated spirit**

methylated spirit ['mɛθɪleɪtɪd-] (BRIT) n alcool m denaturato

metre ['miːtə*] (US meter) n metro

metric ['mɛtrɪk] adj metrico(a)

metropolitan [mɛtrə'pɔlɪtən] adj metropolitano(a); **the M~ Police** (BRIT) n la polizia di Londra

mettle ['mɛtl] n: **to be on one's ~** essere pronto(a) a dare il meglio di se stesso(a)

mew [mjuː] vi (cat) miagolare

mews [mjuːz] (BRIT) n: **~ flat** appartamento ricavato da un'antica scuderia

Mexico ['mɛksɪkəʊ] n Messico

miaow [miːˈaʊ] vi miagolare

mice [maɪs] npl of **mouse**

micro... ['maɪkrəʊ] prefix micro...; **~chip** n microcircuito integrato; **~(computer)** n microcomputer m inv; **~phone** n microfono; **~scope** n microscopio; **~wave** n (also: ~wave oven) n forno a microonde

mid [mɪd] adj: **~ May** metà maggio; **~ afternoon** metà pomeriggio; **in ~ air** a mezz'aria; **~day** n mezzogiorno

middle ['mɪdl] n mezzo; centro; (waist) vita ♦ adj di mezzo; **in the ~ of the night** nel bel mezzo della notte; **~-aged** adj di mezza età; **the M~ Ages** npl il Medioevo; **~-class** adj ≈ borghese; **the ~ class(es)** n(pl) ≈ la borghesia; **M~ East** n Medio Oriente m; **~man** (irreg) n intermediario; agente m rivenditore; **~ name** n secondo nome m; **~of-the-road** adj moderato(a); **~weight** n (BOXING) peso medio

middling ['mɪdlɪŋ] adj medio(a)

midge [mɪdʒ] n moscerino

midget ['mɪdʒɪt] n nano/a

Midlands ['mɪdləndz] npl contee del centro dell'Inghilterra

midnight ['mɪdnaɪt] n mezzanotte f

midriff ['mɪdrɪf] n diaframma m

midst [mɪdst] n: **in the ~ of** in mezzo a

midsummer [mɪd'sʌmə*] n mezza or piena estate f

midway [mɪd'weɪ] adj, adv: **~ (between)** a mezza strada (fra); **~ (through)** a metà (di)

midweek [mɪd'wiːk] adv a metà settimana

midwife ['mɪdwaɪf] (pl midwives) n levatrice f

might [maɪt] vb see **may** ♦ n potere m, forza; **~y** adj forte, potente

migraine ['miːgreɪn] n emicrania

migrant ['maɪgrənt] adj (bird)

migratore(trice); (worker) emigrato(a)

migrate [maɪ'greɪt] vi (bird) migrare; (person) emigrare

mike [maɪk] n abbr (= microphone) microfono

Milan [mɪ'læn] n Milano f

mild [maɪld] adj mite; (person, voice) dolce; (flavour) delicato(a); (illness) leggero(a); (interest) blando(a) ♦ n (beer) birra leggera

mildew ['mɪldjuː] n muffa

mildly ['maɪldlɪ] adv mitemente; dolcemente; delicatamente; leggermente; blandamente; **to put it ~** a dire poco

mile [maɪl] n miglio; **~age** n distanza in miglia, ≈ chilometraggio

mileometer [maɪ'lɔmɪtə*] n ≈ contachilometri m inv

milestone ['maɪlstəʊn] n pietra miliare

milieu ['miːljə:] n ambiente m

militant ['mɪlɪtnt] adj militante

military ['mɪlɪtərɪ] adj militare

milk [mɪlk] n latte m ♦ vt (cow) mungere; (fig) sfruttare; **~ chocolate** n cioccolato al latte; **~man** (irreg) n lattaio; **~ shake** n frappé m inv; **~y** adj lattiginoso(a); (colour) latteo(a); **M~y Way** n Via Lattea

mill [mɪl] n mulino; (small: for coffee, pepper etc) macinino; (factory) fabbrica; (spinning ~) filatura ♦ vt macinare ♦ vi (also: ~ about) brulicare

millennia [mɪ'lɛnɪə] npl of **millennium**

millennium [mɪ'lɛnɪəm] (pl ~s or millennia) n millennio; **~ bug** n baco di fine millennio

miller ['mɪlə*] n mugnaio

milli... ['mɪlɪ] prefix: **~gram(me)** n milligrammo; **~metre** (US ~meter) n millimetro

million ['mɪljən] n milione m; **~aire** n milionario, ≈ miliardario

milometer [maɪ'lɔmɪtə*] n = **mileometer**

mime [maɪm] n mimo ♦ vt, vi mimare

mimic ['mɪmɪk] n imitatore/trice ♦ vt fare la mimica di

min. abbr = minute(s); minimum

mince [mɪns] vt tritare, macinare ♦ n (BRIT: CULIN) carne f tritata or macinata; **~meat** n frutta secca tritata per uso in pasticceria; (US) carne f tritata or macinata; **~ pie** n specie di torta con frutta secca; **~r** n tritacarne m inv

mind [maɪnd] n mente f ♦ vt (attend to, look after) badare a, occuparsi di; (be careful) fare attenzione a, stare attento(a) a; (object to): **I don't ~ the noise** il rumore non mi dà alcun fastidio; **I don't ~** non m'importa; **it is on my ~** mi preoccupa; **to my ~** secondo me, a mio parere; **to be out of one's ~** essere uscito(a) di mente; **to keep** or **bear sth in ~** non dimenticare qc; **to make up one's ~** decidersi; **~ you, ... sì**, però va detto che ...; **never ~** non importa, non fa niente; (don't worry) non preoccuparti; "~ **the step**" "attenzione allo scalino"; ~**er** n (child ~er) bambinaia; (bodyguard) guardia del corpo

mine¹ [main] pron il(la) mio(a), pl i(le) miei(mie); **that book is** ~ quel libro è mio; **yours is red,** ~ **is green** il tuo è rosso, il mio è verde; **a friend of** ~ un mio amico

mine² [main] n miniera; (explosive) mina ♦ vt (coal) estrarre; (ship, beach) minare; ~**field** n (also fig) campo minato

miner ['mainə*] n minatore m

mineral ['minərəl] adj minerale ♦ n minerale m; ~**s** npl (BRIT: soft drinks) bevande fpl gasate; ~ **water** n acqua minerale

mingle ['miŋgl] vi: **to** ~ **with** mescolarsi a, mischiarsi con

miniature ['minətʃə*] adj in miniatura ♦ n miniatura

minibus ['minibʌs] n minibus m inv

minim ['minim] n (MUS) minima

minimum ['miniməm] (pl minima) n minimo ♦ adj minimo(a)

mining ['mainiŋ] n industria mineraria

miniskirt ['miniskə:t] n minigonna

minister ['ministə*] n (BRIT: POL) ministro; (REL) pastore m

ministry ['ministri] n ministero

mink [miŋk] n visone m

minnow ['minəu] n pesciolino d'acqua dolce

minor ['mainə*] adj minore, di poca importanza; (MUS) minore ♦ n (LAW) minorenne m/f

minority [mai'nɔriti] n minoranza

mint [mint] n (plant) menta; (sweet) pasticca di menta ♦ vt (coins) battere; **the (Royal) M~** (BRIT), **the (US) M~** (US) la Zecca; **in ~ condition** come nuovo(a) di zecca

minus ['mainəs] n (also: ~ sign) segno meno ♦ prep meno

minute [adj mai'nju:t, n 'minit] adj minuscolo(a); (detail) minuzioso(a) ♦ n minuto; ~**s** npl (of meeting) verbale m

miracle ['mirəkl] n miracolo

mirage ['mira:ʒ] n miraggio

mirror ['mirə*] n specchio; (in car) specchietto

mirth [mə:θ] n ilarità

misadventure [misəd'ventʃə*] n disavventura; **death by** ~ morte f accidentale

misapprehension ['misæpri'henʃən] n malinteso

misappropriate [misə'prəuprieit] vt appropriarsi indebitamente di

misbehave [misbi'heiv] vi comportarsi male

miscarriage ['miskærɪdʒ] n (MED) aborto spontaneo; ~ **of justice** errore m giudiziario

miscellaneous [misi'leiniəs] adj (items) vario(a); (selection) misto(a)

mischance [mis'tʃɑ:ns] n sfortuna

mischief ['mistʃif] n (naughtiness) birichineria; (maliciousness) malizia; **mischievous** adj birichino(a)

misconception ['miskən'sepʃən] n idea sbagliata

misconduct [mis'kɔndʌkt] n cattiva condotta; **professional** ~ reato professionale

misdemeanour [misdi'mi:nə*] (US **misdemeanor**) n misfatto; infrazione f

miser ['maizə*] n avaro

miserable ['mizərəbl] adj infelice; (wretched) miserabile; (weather) deprimente; (offer, failure) misero(a)

miserly ['maizəli] adj avaro(a)

misery ['mizəri] n (unhappiness) tristezza; (wretchedness) miseria

misfire [mis'faiə*] vi far cilecca; (car engine) perdere colpi

misfit ['misfit] n (person) spostato/a

misfortune [mis'fɔ:tʃən] n sfortuna

misgiving [mis'giviŋ] n apprensione f; **to have ~s about** avere dei dubbi per quanto riguarda

misguided [mis'gaidid] adj sbagliato(a); poco giudizioso(a)

mishandle [mis'hændl] vt (mismanage) trattare male

mishap ['mishæp] n disgrazia

misinterpret [misin'tə:prit] vt interpretare male

misjudge [mis'dʒʌdʒ] vt giudicare male

mislay [mis'lei] (irreg) vt smarrire

mislead [mis'li:d] (irreg) vt sviare; ~**ing** adj ingannevole

mismanage [mis'mænidʒ] vt gestire male

misplace [mis'pleis] vt smarrire

misprint ['misprint] n errore m di stampa

Miss [mis] n Signorina

miss [mis] vt (fail to get) perdere; (fail to hit) mancare; (fail to see): **you can't** ~ **it** non puoi non vederlo; (regret the absence of): **I** ~ **him** sento la sua mancanza ♦ vi mancare ♦ n (shot) colpo mancato; ~ **out** (BRIT) vt omettere

misshapen [mis'ʃeipən] adj deforme

missile ['misail] n (MIL) missile m; (object thrown) proiettile m

missing ['misiŋ] adj perso(a), smarrito(a); (person) scomparso(a); (: after disaster, MIL) disperso(a); (removed) mancante; **to be** ~ mancare

mission ['miʃən] n missione f; ~**ary** n missionario/a

mist [mist] n nebbia, foschia ♦ vi (also: ~ over, ~ up) annebbiarsi; (: BRIT: windows) appannarsi

mistake [mis'teik] (irreg: like **take**) n sbaglio, errore m ♦ vt sbagliarsi di; fraintendere; **to make a** ~ fare uno sbaglio, sbagliare; **by** ~ per

sbaglio; **to ~ for** prendere per; **mistaken** pp
of **mistake ♦** adj (idea etc) sbagliato(a); **to
be mistaken** sbagliarsi

mister ['mɪstə*] (inf) n signore m; see **Mr**

mistletoe ['mɪsltəu] n vischio

mistook [mɪs'tuk] pt of **mistake**

mistress ['mɪstrɪs] n padrona; (lover) amante
f; (BRIT: SCOL) insegnante f

mistrust [mɪs'trʌst] vt diffidare di

misty ['mɪstɪ] adj nebbioso(a), brumoso(a)

misunderstand [mɪsʌndə'stænd] (irreg) vt,
vi capire male, fraintendere; **~ing** n
malinteso, equivoco

misuse [n mɪs'juːs, vb mɪs'juːz] n cattivo uso;
(of power) abuso ♦ vt far cattivo uso di;
abusare di

mitigate ['mɪtɪgeɪt] vt mitigare

mitt(en) ['mɪt(n)] n mezzo guanto;
manopola

mix [mɪks] vt mescolare ♦ vi (people): **to
~ with** avere a che fare con ♦ n mescolanza;
preparato; **~ up** vt mescolare; (confuse)
confondere; **~ed** adj misto(a); **~ed-up** adj
(confused) confuso(a); **~er** n (for food:
electric) frullatore m; (: hand) frullino;
(person): **he is a good ~er** è molto socievole;
~ture n mescolanza; (blend: of tobacco etc)
miscela; (MED) sciroppo; **~-up** n confusione f

moan [məun] n gemito ♦ vi (inf: complain):
to ~ (about) lamentarsi (di)

moat [məut] n fossato

mob [mɔb] n calca ♦ vt accalcarsi intorno a

mobile ['məubaɪl] adj mobile ♦ n (decoration)
mobile m; **~ home** n grande roulotte f inv
(utilizzata come domicilio); **~ phone**
telefono portatile, telefonino

mock [mɔk] vt deridere, burlarsi di ♦ adj
falso(a); **~ery** n derisione f; **to make a ~ery
of** burlarsi di; (exam) rendere una farsa; **~-up**
n modello

mod [mɔd] adj see **convenience**

mode [məud] n modo

model ['mɔdl] n modello; (person: for
fashion) indossatore/trice; (: for artist)
modello/a ♦ adj (small-scale: railway etc) in
miniatura; (child, factory) modello inv ♦ vt
modellare ♦ vi fare l'indossatore (or
l'indossatrice); **to ~ clothes** presentare degli
abiti

modem ['məudɛm] n modem m inv

moderate [adj 'mɔdərət, vb 'mɔdəreɪt] adj
moderato(a) ♦ vi moderarsi, placarsi ♦ vt
moderare

modern ['mɔdən] adj moderno(a); **~ize** vt
modernizzare

modest ['mɔdɪst] adj modesto(a); **~y** n
modestia

modify ['mɔdɪfaɪ] vt modificare

mogul ['məugl] n (fig) magnate m, pezzo

grosso

mohair ['məuhɛə*] n mohair m

moist [mɔɪst] adj umido(a); **~en** ['mɔɪsn] vt
inumidire; **~ure** ['mɔɪstʃə*] n umidità; (on
glass) goccioline fpl di vapore; **~urizer**
['mɔɪstʃəraɪzə*] n idratante f

molar ['məulə*] n molare m

mold [məuld] (US) n, vt = **mould**

mole [məul] n (animal, fig) talpa; (spot) neo

molest [məu'lɛst] vt molestare

mollycoddle ['mɔlɪkɔdl] vt coccolare,
vezzeggiare

molt [məult] (US) vi = **moult**

molten ['məultən] adj fuso(a)

mom [mɔm] (US) n = **mum**

moment ['məumənt] n momento, istante m;
at that ~ in quel momento; **at the ~** al
momento, in questo momento; **~ary** adj
momentaneo(a), passeggero(a); **~ous**
[-'mɛntəs] adj di grande importanza

momentum [məu'mɛntəm] n (PHYSICS)
momento; (fig) impeto; **to gather ~**
aumentare di velocità

mommy ['mɔmɪ] (US) n = **mummy**

Monaco ['mɔnəkəu] n Principato di Monaco

monarch ['mɔnək] n monarca m; **~y** n
monarchia

monastery ['mɔnəstərɪ] n monastero

Monday ['mʌndɪ] n lunedì m inv

monetary ['mʌnɪtərɪ] adj monetario(a)

money ['mʌnɪ] n denaro, soldi mpl; **~ belt** n
marsupio (per soldi); **~ order** n vaglia m inv;
~-spinner (inf) n miniera d'oro (fig)

mongol ['mɔngəl] adj, n (MED) mongoloide
m/f

mongrel ['mʌngrəl] n (dog) cane m bastardo

monitor ['mɔnɪtə*] n (TV, COMPUT) monitor m
inv ♦ vt controllare

monk [mʌŋk] n monaco

monkey ['mʌŋkɪ] n scimmia; **~ nut** (BRIT) n
nocciolina americana; **~ wrench** n chiave f a
rullino

mono ['mɔnəu] adj (recording) (in) mono inv

monopoly [mə'nɔpəlɪ] n monopolio

monotone ['mɔnətəun] n pronunzia (or
voce f) monotona

monotonous [mə'nɔtənəs] adj
monotono(a)

monsoon [mɔn'suːn] n monsone m

monster ['mɔnstə*] n mostro

monstrous ['mɔnstrəs] adj mostruoso(a);
(huge) gigantesco(a)

month [mʌnθ] n mese m; **~ly** adj mensile
♦ adv al mese; ogni mese

monument ['mɔnjumənt] n monumento

moo [muː] vi muggire, mugghiare

mood [muːd] n umore m; **to be in a good/
bad ~** essere di buon/cattivo umore; **~y** adj
(variable) capriccioso(a), lunatico(a); (sullen)

imbronciato(a)

moon [mu:n] n luna; **~light** n chiaro di luna; **~lighting** n lavoro nero; **~lit** adj: a **~lit night** una notte rischiarata dalla luna

Moor [muə*] n moro/a

moor [muə*] n brughiera ♦ vt (ship) ormeggiare ♦ vi ormeggiarsi

moorland ['muələnd] n brughiera

moose [mu:s] n inv alce m

mop [mɔp] n lavapavimenti m inv; (also: ~ of hair) zazzera ♦ vt lavare con lo straccio; (face) asciugare; ~ **up** vt asciugare con uno straccio

mope [məup] vi fare il broncio

moped ['məupɛd] n (BRIT) ciclomotore m

moral ['mɔrl] adj morale ♦ n morale f; ~s npl (principles) moralità

morality [mə'rælɪt] n moralità

morass [mə'ræs] n palude f, pantano

morbid ['mɔ:bɪd] adj morboso(a)

---

more [mɔ:*] adj **1** (greater in number etc) più; **~ people/letters than we expected** più persone/lettere di quante ne aspettavamo; I have ~ **wine/money than you** ho più vino/ soldi di te; I have ~ **wine than beer** ho più vino che birra

2 (additional) altro(a), ancora; **do you want (some) ~ tea?** vuole dell'altro tè?, vuole ancora del tè?; **I have no** or **I don't have any ~ money** non ho più soldi

♦ pron **1** (greater amount) più; ~ **than 10** più di 10; **it cost ~ than we expected** ha costato più di quanto ci aspettavamo

2 (further or additional amount) ancora; **is there any ~?** ce n'è ancora?; **there's no ~** non ce n'è più; **a little ~** ancora un po'; **many/ much ~** molti(e)/molto(a) di più

♦ adv: ~ **dangerous/easily (than)** più pericoloso/facilmente (di); ~ **and ~** sempre di più; ~ **and ~ difficult** sempre più difficile; ~ **or less** più o meno; ~ **than ever** più che mai

---

moreover [mɔ:'rəuvə*] adv inoltre, di più

morgue [mɔ:g] n obitorio

morning ['mɔ:nɪŋ] n mattina, mattino; (duration) mattinata ♦ cpd del mattino; **in the ~** la mattina; **7 o'clock in the ~** le 7 di o della mattina; ~ **sickness** n nausee fpl mattutine

Morocco [mə'rɔkəu] n Marocco

moron ['mɔ:rɔn] (inf) n deficiente m/f

morose [mə'rəus] adj cupo(a), tetro(a)

Morse [mɔ:s] n (also: ~ code) alfabeto Morse

morsel ['mɔ:sl] n boccone m

mortal ['mɔ:tl] adj mortale ♦ n mortale m

mortgage ['mɔ:gɪdʒ] n ipoteca; (loan) prestito ipotecario ♦ vt ipotecare; ~ **company** n (US) società f inv di credito

immobiliare

mortuary ['mɔ:tjuərɪ] n camera mortuaria; obitorio

mosaic [məu'zeɪk] n mosaico

Moscow ['mɔskəu] n Mosca

Moslem ['mɔzləm] adj, n = **Muslim**

mosque [mɔsk] n moschea

mosquito [mɔs'ki:təu] (pl ~es) n zanzara

moss [mɔs] n muschio

most [məust] adj (almost all) la maggior parte di; (largest, greatest): **who has (the) ~ money?** chi ha più soldi di tutti? ♦ pron la maggior parte ♦ adv più; (work, sleep etc) di più; (very) molto, estremamente; **the ~** (also: + adjective) il(la) più; ~ **of** la maggior parte di; ~ **of them** quasi tutti; **I saw (the) ~** ho visto più io; **at (the ~ very) ~** al massimo; **to make the ~ of** trarre il massimo vantaggio da; **a ~ interesting book** un libro estremamente interessante; **~ly** adv per lo più

MOT (BRIT) n abbr (= Ministry of Transport): **the ~ (test)** revisione annuale obbligatoria degli autoveicoli

motel [məu'tɛl] n motel m inv

moth [mɔθ] n farfalla notturna; tarma

mother ['mʌðə*] n madre f ♦ vt (care for) fare da madre a; **~hood** n maternità; **~-in-law** n suocera; **~ly** adj materno(a); **~-of-pearl** [mʌðərəv'pə:l] n madreperla; **~-to-be** [mʌðətə'bi:] n futura mamma; ~ **tongue** n madrelingua

motion ['məuʃən] n movimento, moto; (gesture) gesto; (at meeting) mozione f ♦ vt, vi: **to ~ (to) sb to do** fare cenno a qn di fare; **~less** adj immobile; ~ **picture** n film m inv

motivated ['məutɪveɪtɪd] adj motivato(a)

motive ['məutɪv] n motivo

motley ['mɔtlɪ] adj eterogeneo(a), molto vario(a)

motor ['məutə*] n motore m; (BRIT: inf: vehicle) macchina ♦ cpd automobilistico(a); **~bike** n moto f inv; **~boat** n motoscafo; **~car** (BRIT) n automobile f; **~cycle** n motocicletta; **~cyclist** n motociclista m/f; **~ing** (BRIT) n turismo automobilistico; **~ist** n automobilista m/f; ~ **racing** (BRIT) n corse fpl automobilistiche; **~way** (BRIT) n autostrada

mottled ['mɔtld] adj chiazzato(a), marezzato(a)

motto ['mɔtəu] (pl ~es) n motto

mould [məuld] (US mold) n forma, stampo; (mildew) muffa ♦ vt formare; (fig) foggiare; **~y** adj ammuffito(a); (smell) di muffa

moult [məult] (US molt) vi far la muta

mound [maund] n rialzo, collinetta; (heap) mucchio

mount [maunt] n (GEO) monte m ♦ vt montare; (horse) montare a ♦ vi (increase) aumentare; ~ **up** vi (build up) accumularsi

mountain ['mauntɪn] n montagna ♦ cpd di montagna; **~ bike** n mountain bike f inv; **~eer** [-'nɪə*] n alpinista m/f; **~eering** [-'nɪərɪŋ] n alpinismo; **~ous** adj montagnoso(a); **~ rescue team** n squadra di soccorso alpino; **~side** n fianco della montagna

mourn [mɔːn] vt piangere, lamentare ♦ vi: **to ~ (for sb)** piangere (la morte di qn); **~er** n parente m/f or amico/a del defunto; **~ing** n lutto; **in ~ing** in lutto

mouse [maus] (pl **mice**) n topo; (COMPUT) mouse m inv; **~trap** n trappola per i topi

mousse [muːs] n mousse f inv

moustache [məs'tɑːʃ] (US **mustache**) n baffi mpl

mousy ['mausɪ] adj (hair) né chiaro(a) né scuro(a)

mouth [mauθ, pl mauðz] n bocca; (of river) bocca, foce f; (opening) orifizio; **~ful** n boccata; **~ organ** n armonica; **~piece** n (MUS) imboccatura, bocchino; (spokesman) portavoce m/f inv; **~wash** n collutorio; **~-watering** adj che fa venire l'acquolina in bocca

movable ['muːvəbl] adj mobile

move [muːv] n (movement) movimento; (in game) mossa; (: turn to play) turno; (change: of house) trasloco; (: of job) cambiamento ♦ vt muovere, spostare; (emotionally) commuovere; (POL: resolution etc) proporre ♦ vi (gen) muoversi, spostarsi; (also: ~ house) cambiar casa, traslocare; **to get a ~ on** affrettarsi, sbrigarsi; **to ~ sb to do sth** indurre or spingere qn a fare qc; **to ~ towards** andare verso; **~ about or around** vi spostarsi; **~ along** vi muoversi avanti; **~ away** vi allontanarsi, andarsene; **~ back** vi (return) ritornare; **~ forward** vi avanzare; **~ in** vi (to a house) entrare (in una nuova casa); (police etc) intervenire; **~ on** vi riprendere la strada; **~ out** vi (of house) sgombrare; **~ over** vi spostarsi; **~ up** vi avanzare

moveable ['muːvəbl] adj = **movable**

movement ['muːvmənt] n (gen) movimento; (gesture) gesto; (of stars, water, physical) moto

movie ['muːvɪ] n film m inv; **the ~s** il cinema

movie camera n cinepresa

moving ['muːvɪŋ] adj mobile; (causing emotion) commovente

mow [məu] (pt **mowed**, pp **mowed** or **mown**) vt (grass) tagliare; (corn) mietere; **~ down** vt falciare; **~er** n (also: lawnmower) tagliaerba m inv

MP n abbr = Member of Parliament

m.p.h. n abbr = miles per hour (60 m.p.h. = 96 km/h)

Mr ['mɪstə*] (US **Mr.**) n: **~ X** Signor X, Sig. X

Mrs ['mɪsɪz] (US **Mrs.**) n: **~ X** Signora X, Sig.ra X

Ms [mɪz] (US **Ms.**) n (= Miss or Mrs): **~ X** ≈ Signora X, Sig.ra X

M.Sc. abbr = Master of Science

MSP n abbr = Member of the Scottish Parliament

KEYWORD

much [mʌtʃ] adj, pron molto(a); **he's done so ~ work** ha lavorato così tanto; **I have as ~ money as you** ho tanti soldi quanti ne hai tu; **how ~ is it?** quant'è?; **it costs too ~** costa troppo; **as ~ as you want** quanto vuoi
♦ adv **1** (greatly) molto, tanto; **thank you very ~** molte grazie; **he's very ~ the gentleman** è il vero gentiluomo; **I read as ~ as I can** leggo quanto posso; **as ~ as you** tanto quanto te
2 (by far) molto; **it's ~ the biggest company in Europe** è di gran lunga la più grossa società in Europa
3 (almost) grossomodo, praticamente; **they're ~ the same** sono praticamente uguali

muck [mʌk] n (dirt) sporcizia; **~ about or around** (inf) vi fare lo stupido; (waste time) gingillarsi; **~ up** (inf) vt (ruin) rovinare

mud [mʌd] n fango

muddle ['mʌdl] n confusione f, disordine m; pasticcio ♦ vt (also: ~ up) confondere; **~ through** vi cavarsela alla meno peggio

muddy ['mʌdɪ] adj fangoso(a)

mudguard ['mʌdgɑːd] n parafango

muesli ['mjuːzlɪ] n muesli m

muffin ['mʌfɪn] n specie di pasticcino soffice da tè

muffle ['mʌfl] vt (sound) smorzare, attutire; (against cold) imbacuccare

muffler ['mʌflə*] (US) n (AUT) marmitta; (: on motorbike) silenziatore m

mug [mʌg] n (cup) tazzone m; (for beer) boccale m; (inf: face) muso; (: fool) scemo/a ♦ vt (assault) assalire; **~ging** n assalto

muggy ['mʌgɪ] adj afoso(a)

mule [mjuːl] n mulo

multi-level ['mʌltɪ-] (US) adj = **multistorey**

multiple ['mʌltɪpl] adj multiplo(a); molteplice ♦ n multiplo; **~ sclerosis** n sclerosi f a placche

multiplex cinema ['mʌltɪpleks-] n cinema m inv multisala inv

multiplication [mʌltɪplɪ'keɪʃən] n moltiplicazione f

multiply ['mʌltɪplaɪ] vt moltiplicare ♦ vi moltiplicarsi

multistorey ['mʌltɪ'stɔːrɪ] (BRIT) adj (building, car park) a più piani

mum [mʌm] (BRIT: inf) n mamma ♦ adj: **to**

keep ~ non aprire bocca

mumble ['mʌmbl] vt, vi borbottare

mummy ['mʌmɪ] n (BRIT: mother) mamma; (embalmed) mummia

mumps [mʌmps] n orecchioni mpl

munch [mʌntʃ] vt, vi sgranocchiare

mundane [mʌn'deɪn] adj terra a terra inv

municipal [mju:'nɪsɪpl] adj municipale

mural ['mjuərl] n dipinto murale

murder ['mɜːdə*] n assassinio, omicidio ♦ vt assassinare; **~er** n omicida m, assassino; **~ous** adj omicida

murky ['mɜːkɪ] adj tenebroso(a)

murmur ['mɜːmə*] n mormorio ♦ vt, vi mormorare

muscle ['mʌsl] n muscolo; (fig) forza; ~ **in** vi immischiarsi

muscular ['mʌskjʊlə*] adj muscolare; (person, arm) muscoloso(a)

muse [mju:z] vi meditare, sognare ♦ n musa

museum [mju:'zɪəm] n museo

mushroom ['mʌʃrum] n fungo ♦ vi crescere in fretta

music ['mju:zɪk] n musica; **~al** adj musicale; (person) portato(a) per la musica ♦ n (show) commedia musicale; **~ instrument** n strumento musicale; **~ hall** n teatro di varietà; **~ian** [-'zɪʃən] n musicista m/f

Muslim ['mʌzlɪm] adj, n musulmano(a)

muslin ['mʌzlɪn] n mussola

mussel ['mʌsl] n cozza

must [mʌst] aux vb (obligation): **I ~ do it** devo farlo; (probability): **he ~ be there by now** dovrebbe essere arrivato ormai; **I ~ have made a mistake** devo essermi sbagliato ♦ n: **it's a ~** è d'obbligo

mustache ['mʌstæʃ] (US) n = moustache

mustard ['mʌstəd] n senape f, mostarda

muster ['mʌstə*] vt radunare

mustn't ['mʌsnt] = must not

musty ['mʌstɪ] adj che sa di muffa or di rinchiuso

mute [mju:t] adj, n muto(a)

muted ['mju:tɪd] adj smorzato(a)

mutiny ['mju:tɪnɪ] n ammutinamento

mutter ['mʌtə*] vt, vi borbottare, brontolare

mutton ['mʌtn] n carne f di montone

mutual ['mju:tʃuəl] adj mutuo(a), reciproco(a); **~ly** adv reciprocamente

muzzle ['mʌzl] n muso; (protective device) museruola; (of gun) bocca ♦ vt mettere la museruola a

my [maɪ] adj il(la) mio(a), pl i(le) miei(mie); ~ **house** la mia casa; ~ **books** i miei libri; ~ **brother** mio fratello; **I've washed** ~ **hair/cut** ~ **finger** mi sono lavato i capelli/tagliato il dito

myself [maɪ'self] pron (reflexive) mi; (emphatic) io stesso(a); (after prep) me; see also oneself

mysterious [mɪs'tɪərɪəs] adj misterioso(a)

mystery ['mɪstərɪ] n mistero

mystify ['mɪstɪfaɪ] vt mistificare; (puzzle) confondere

mystique [mɪs'ti:k] n fascino

myth [mɪθ] n mito

mythology [mɪ'θɒlədʒɪ] n mitologia

N, n

n/a abbr = not applicable

nag [næg] vt tormentare ♦ vi brontolare in continuazione; **~ging** adj (doubt, pain) persistente

nail [neɪl] n (human) unghia; (metal) chiodo ♦ vt inchiodare; **to ~ sb down to (doing) sth** costringere qn a (fare) qc; **~brush** n spazzolino da or per unghie; **~file** n lima da or per unghie; **~ polish** n smalto da or per unghie; **~ polish remover** n acetone m, solvente m; **~ scissors** npl forbici fpl da or per unghie; **~ varnish** (BRIT) n = ~ polish

naïve [naɪ'i:v] adj ingenuo(a)

naked ['neɪkɪd] adj nudo(a)

name [neɪm] n nome m; (reputation) nome, reputazione f ♦ vt (baby etc) chiamare; (plant, illness) nominare; (person, object) identificare; (price, date) fissare; **what's your ~?** come si chiama?; **by ~** di nome; **she knows them all by ~** li conosce tutti per nome; **~ly** adv cioè; **~sake** n omonimo

nanny ['nænɪ] n bambinaia

nap [næp] n (sleep) pisolino; (of cloth) peluria; **to be caught ~ping** essere preso alla sprovvista

nape [neɪp] n: ~ **of the neck** nuca

napkin ['næpkɪn] n (also: table ~) tovagliolo

nappy ['næpɪ] (BRIT) n pannolino; ~ **rash** n arrossamento (causato dal pannolino)

narcissus [nɑː'sɪsəs] (pl **narcissi**) n narciso

narcotic [nɑː'kɒtɪk] n narcotico ♦ adj narcotico(a)

narrative ['nærətɪv] n narrativa

narrow ['nærəu] adj stretto(a); (fig) limitato(a), ristretto(a) ♦ vi restringersi; **to have a ~ escape** farcela per un pelo; **to ~ sth down to** ridurre qc a; **~ly** adv per un pelo; (time) per poco; **~-minded** adj meschino(a)

nasty ['nɑːstɪ] adj (person, remark: unpleasant) cattivo(a); (: rude) villano(a); (smell, wound, situation) brutto(a)

nation ['neɪʃən] n nazione f

national ['næʃənl] adj nazionale ♦ n cittadino/a; ~ **dress** n costume m nazionale; **N~ Health Service** (BRIT) n servizio nazionale di assistenza sanitaria, ≈ S.S.N. m; **N~ Insurance** (BRIT) n ≈ Previdenza Sociale; **~ism** n nazionalismo; **~ity** [-'nælɪtɪ] n nazionalità f inv; **~ize** vt nazionalizzare; **~ly**

adv a livello nazionale; **~ park** *n* parco nazionale

nationwide ['neɪʃənwaɪd] *adj* diffuso(a) in tutto il paese ♦ *adv* in tutto il paese

native ['neɪtɪv] *n* abitante *m/f* del paese ♦ *adj* indigeno(a); (*country*) natio(a); (*ability*) innato(a); **a ~ of Russia** un nativo della Russia; **a ~ speaker of French** una persona di madrelingua francese; **N~ American** *n* discendente di tribù dell'America settentrionale; **~ language** *n* madrelingua

Nativity [nə'tɪvɪtɪ] *n*: **the ~** la Natività

NATO ['neɪtəʊ] *n abbr* (= *North Atlantic Treaty Organization*) N.A.T.O. *f*

natural ['nætʃrəl] *adj* naturale; (*ability*) innato(a); (*manner*) semplice; **~ gas** *n* gas *m* metano; **~ly** *adv* naturalmente; (*by nature: gifted*) di natura

nature ['neɪtʃə*] *n* natura; (*character*) natura, indole *f*; **by ~** di natura

naught [nɔːt] *n* = **nought**

naughty ['nɔːtɪ] *adj* (*child*) birichino(a), cattivello(a); (*story, film*) spinto(a)

nausea ['nɔːsɪə] *n* (*MED*) nausea; (*fig: disgust*) schifo

nautical ['nɔːtɪkl] *adj* nautico(a)

naval ['neɪvl] *adj* navale; **~ officer** *n* ufficiale *m* di marina

nave [neɪv] *n* navata centrale

navel ['neɪvl] *n* ombelico

navigate ['nævɪgeɪt] *vt* percorrere navigando ♦ *vi* navigare; (*AUT*) fare da navigatore; **navigation** [-'geɪʃən] *n* navigazione *f*; **navigator** *n* (*NAUT, AVIAT*) ufficiale *m* di rotta; (*explorer*) navigatore *m*; (*AUT*) copilota *m/f*

navvy ['nævɪ] (*BRIT*) *n* manovale *m*

navy ['neɪvɪ] *n* marina; **~(-blue)** *adj* blu scuro *inv*

Nazi ['nɑːtsɪ] *n* nazista *m/f*

NB *abbr* (= *nota bene*) N.B.

near [nɪə*] *adj* vicino(a); (*relation*) prossimo(a) ♦ *adv* vicino ♦ *prep* (*also: ~ to*) vicino a, presso; (: *time*) verso ♦ *vt* avvicinarsi a; **~by** [nɪə'baɪ] *adj* vicino(a) ♦ *adv* vicino; **~ly** *adv* quasi; **I ~ly fell** per poco non sono caduto; **~ miss** *n*: **that was a ~ miss** c'è mancato poco; **~side** *n* (*AUT: in Britain*) lato sinistro; (: *in US, Europe etc*) lato destro; **~-sighted** [nɪə'saɪtɪd] *adj* miope

neat [niːt] *adj* (*person, room*) ordinato(a); (*work*) pulito(a); (*solution, plan*) ben indovinato(a), azzeccato(a); (*spirits*) liscio(a); **~ly** *adv* con ordine; (*skilfully*) abilmente

necessarily ['nesɪsrɪlɪ] *adv* necessariamente

necessary ['nesɪsrɪ] *adj* necessario(a)

necessity [nɪ'sesɪtɪ] *n* necessità *f inv*

neck [nek] *n* collo; (*of garment*) colletto ♦ *vi* (*inf*) pomiciare, sbaciucchiarsi; **~ and ~** testa

a testa

necklace ['neklɪs] *n* collana

neckline ['neklaɪn] *n* scollatura

necktie ['nektaɪ] *n* cravatta

née [neɪ] *adj*: **~ Scott** nata Scott

need [niːd] *n* bisogno ♦ *vt* aver bisogno di; **to ~ to do** dover fare; aver bisogno di fare; **you don't ~ to go** non devi andare, non c'è bisogno che tu vada

needle ['niːdl] *n* ago; (*on record player*) puntina ♦ *vt* punzecchiare

needless ['niːdlɪs] *adj* inutile

needlework ['niːdlwɜːk] *n* cucito

needn't ['niːdnt] = **need not**

needy ['niːdɪ] *adj* bisognoso(a)

negative ['negətɪv] *n* (*LING*) negazione *f*; (*PHOT*) negativo ♦ *adj* negativo(a); **~ equity** *n* situazione in cui l'ammontare del mutuo su un immobile supera il suo valore sul mercato

neglect [nɪ'glekt] *vt* trascurare ♦ *n* (*of person, duty*) negligenza; (*of child, house etc*) scarsa cura; **state of ~** stato di abbandono

negligence ['neglɪdʒəns] *n* negligenza

negligible ['neglɪdʒɪbl] *adj* insignificante, trascurabile

negotiable [nɪ'gəʊʃɪəbl] *adj* (*cheque*) trasferibile

negotiate [nɪ'gəʊʃɪeɪt] *vi*: **to ~ (with)** negoziare (con) ♦ *vt* (*COMM*) negoziare; (*obstacle*) superare; **negotiation** [-'eɪʃən] *n* negoziato, trattativa

Negro ['niːgrəʊ] (*pl* **~es**) *n* negro(a)

neigh [neɪ] *vi* nitrire

neighbour ['neɪbə*] (*US* **neighbor**) *n* vicino/a; **~hood** *n* vicinato; **~ing** *adj* vicino(a); **~ly** *adj*: **he is a ~ly person** è un buon vicino

neither ['naɪðə*] *adj, pron* né l'uno(a) né l'altro(a), nessuno(a) dei(delle) due ♦ *conj* neanche, nemmeno, neppure ♦ *adv*: **~ good nor bad** né buono né cattivo; **I didn't move and ~ did Claude** io non mi mossi e nemmeno Claude; ..., **~ did I refuse** ..., ma non ho nemmeno rifiutato

neon light ['niːɔn-] *n* luce *f* al neon

nephew ['nevjuː] *n* nipote *m*

nerve [nɜːv] *n* nervo; (*fig*) coraggio; (*impudence*) faccia tosta; **a fit of ~s** una crisi di nervi; **~-racking** *adj* che spezza i nervi

nervous ['nɜːvəs] *adj* nervoso(a); (*anxious*) agitato(a), in apprensione; **~ breakdown** *n* esaurimento nervoso

nest [nest] *n* nido ♦ *vi* fare il nido, nidificare; **~ egg** *n* (*fig*) gruzzolo

nestle ['nesl] *vi* accoccolarsi

net [net] *n* rete *f* ♦ *adj* netto(a) ♦ *vt* (*fish etc*) prendere con la rete; (*profit*) ricavare un netto di; **the N~** (*Internet*) Internet *f*; **~ball** *n* specie di pallacanestro

Netherlands ['neðələndz] *npl*: **the ~** i Paesi

Bassi

nett [nɛt] adj = net

netting ['nɛtɪŋ] n (for fence etc) reticolato

nettle ['nɛtl] n ortica

network ['nɛtwəːk] n rete f

neurotic [njuə'rɔtɪk] adj, n nevrotico(a)

neuter ['njuːtə*] adj neutro(a) ♦ vt (cat etc) castrare

neutral ['njuːtrəl] adj neutro(a); (person, nation) neutrale ♦ n (AUT): **in ~** in folle; **~ize** vt neutralizzare

never ['nɛvə*] adv (non...) mai; **~ again** mai più; **I'll ~ go there again** non ci vado più; **~ in my life** mai in vita mia; see also **mind**; **~-ending** adj interminabile; **~theless** [nɛvəðə'lɛs] adv tuttavia, ciò nonostante, ciò nondimeno

new [njuː] adj nuovo(a); (brand new) nuovo(a) di zecca; **N~ Age** n New Age f inv; **~born** adj neonato(a); **~comer** ['njuːkʌmə*] n nuovo(a) venuto(a); **~-fangled** ['njuːfæŋgld] (pej) adj stramoderno(a); **~-found** adj nuovo(a); **~ly** adv di recente; **~ly-weds** npl sposini mpl, sposi mpl novelli

news [njuːz] n notizie fpl; (RADIO) giornale m radio; (TV) telegiornale m; **a piece of ~** una notizia; **~ agency** n agenzia di stampa; **~agent** (BRIT) n giornalaio; **~caster** n (RADIO, TV) annunciatore/trice; **~ flash** n notizia f lampo inv; **~letter** n bollettino; **~paper** n giornale m; **~print** n carta da giornale; **~reader** n = **~caster**; **~reel** n cinegiornale m; **~ stand** n edicola

newt [njuːt] n tritone m

New Year n Anno Nuovo; **~'s Day** n il Capodanno; **~'s Eve** n la vigilia di Capodanno

New York [-'jɔːk] n New York f

New Zealand [-'ziːlənd] n Nuova Zelanda; **~er** n neozelandese m/f

next [nɛkst] adj prossimo(a) ♦ adv accanto; (in time) dopo; **the ~ day** il giorno dopo, l'indomani; **~ time** la prossima volta; **~ year** l'anno prossimo; **when do we meet ~?** quando ci rincontriamo?; **~ to** accanto a; **~ to nothing** quasi niente; **~ please!** (avanti) il prossimo!; **~ door** adv, adj accanto inv; **~-of-kin** n parente m/f prossimo(a)

NHS n abbr = **National Health Service**

nib [nɪb] n (of pen) pennino

nibble ['nɪbl] vt mordicchiare

Nicaragua [nɪkə'ræɡjuə] n Nicaragua m

nice [naɪs] adj (holiday, trip) piacevole; (flat, picture) bello(a); (person) simpatico(a), gentile; **~ly** adv bene

niceties ['naɪsɪtɪz] npl finezze fpl

nick [nɪk] n taglietto; tacca ♦ vt (inf) rubare; **in the ~ of time** appena in tempo

nickel ['nɪkl] n nichel m; (US) moneta da cinque centesimi di dollaro

nickname ['nɪkneɪm] n soprannome m

niece [niːs] n nipote f

Nigeria [naɪ'dʒɪərɪə] n Nigeria

niggling ['nɪɡlɪŋ] adj insignificante; (annoying) irritante

night [naɪt] n notte f; (evening) sera; **at ~** la sera; **by ~** di notte; **the ~ before last** l'altro ieri notte (or sera); **~cap** n bicchierino prima di andare a letto; **~ club** n locale m notturno; **~dress** n camicia da notte; **~fall** n crepuscolo; **~gown** n = **~dress**; **~ie** ['naɪtɪ] n = **~dress**

nightingale ['naɪtɪŋɡeɪl] n usignolo

nightlife ['naɪtlaɪf] n vita notturna

nightly ['naɪtlɪ] adj di ogni notte or sera; (by night) notturno(a) ♦ adv ogni notte or sera

nightmare ['naɪtmɛə*] n incubo

night: ~ porter n portiere m di notte; **~ school** n scuola serale; **~ shift** n turno di notte; **~-time** n notte f

nil [nɪl] n nulla m; (BRIT: SPORT) zero

Nile [naɪl] n: **the ~** il Nilo

nimble ['nɪmbl] adj agile

nine [naɪn] num nove; **~teen** num diciannove; **~ty** num novanta

ninth [naɪnθ] adj nono(a)

nip [nɪp] vt pizzicare; (bite) mordere

nipple ['nɪpl] n (ANAT) capezzolo

nitrogen ['naɪtrədʒən] n azoto

--- KEYWORD ---

no [nəu] (pl **~es**) adv (opposite of "yes") no; **are you coming? — ~ (I'm not)** viene? — no (non vengo); **would you like some more? — ~ thank you** ne vuole ancora un po'? — no, grazie

♦ adj (not any) nessuno(a); **I have ~ money/time/books** non ho soldi/tempo/libri; **~ student would have done it** nessuno studente lo avrebbe fatto; **"~ parking"** "divieto di sosta"; **"~ smoking"** "vietato fumare"

♦ n no m inv

---

nobility [nəu'bɪlɪtɪ] n nobiltà

noble ['nəubl] adj nobile

nobody ['nəubədɪ] pron nessuno

nod [nɔd] vi accennare col capo, fare un cenno; (in agreement) annuire con un cenno del capo; (sleep) sonnecchiare ♦ vt: **to ~ one's head** fare di sì col capo ♦ n cenno; **~ off** vi assopirsi

noise [nɔɪz] n rumore m; (din, racket) chiasso; **noisy** adj (street, car) rumoroso(a); (person) chiassoso(a)

nominal ['nɔmɪnl] adj nominale; (rent) simbolico(a)

nominate ['nɔmɪneɪt] vt (propose) proporre

come candidato; (*elect*) nominare
nominee [nɔmɪ'niː] *n* persona nominata; candidato/a
non... [nɔn] *prefix* non...; **~-alcoholic** *adj* analcolico(a)
nonchalant ['nɔnʃələnt] *adj* disinvolto(a), noncurante
non-committal ['nɔnkə'mɪtl] *adj* evasivo(a)
nondescript ['nɔndɪskrɪpt] *adj* qualunque *inv*
none [nʌn] *pron* (*not one thing*) niente; (*not one person*) nessuno(a); **~ of you** nessuno(a) di voi; **I've ~ left** non ne ho più; **he's ~ the worse for it** non ne ha risentito
nonentity [nɔ'nentɪtɪ] *n* persona insignificante
nonetheless [nʌnðə'les] *adv* nondimeno
non-existent [-ɪg'zɪstənt] *adj* inesistente
non-fiction [nɔn'fɪkʃən] *n* saggistica
nonplussed [nɔn'plʌst] *adj* sconcertato(a)
nonsense ['nɔnsəns] *n* sciocchezze *fpl*
non: **~-smoker** *n* non fumatore/trice; **~-smoking** *adj* (*person*) che non fuma; (*area, section*) per non fumatori; **~-stick** *adj* antiaderente, antiadesivo(a); **~-stop** *adj* continuo(a); (*train, bus*) direttissimo(a) ♦ *adv* senza sosta
noodles ['nuːdlz] *npl* taglierini *mpl*
nook [nuk] *n*: **~s and crannies** angoli *mpl*
noon [nuːn] *n* mezzogiorno
no one ['nəuwʌn] *pron* = **nobody**
noose [nuːs] *n* nodo scorsoio; (*hangman's*) cappio
nor [nɔː*] *conj* = **neither** ♦ *adv see* **neither**
norm [nɔːm] *n* norma
normal ['nɔːml] *adj* normale; **~ly** *adv* normalmente
north [nɔːθ] *n* nord *m*, settentrione *m* ♦ *adj* nord *inv*, del nord, settentrionale ♦ *adv* verso nord; **N~ America** *n* America del Nord; **~-east** *n* nord-est *m*; **~erly** ['nɔːðəlɪ] *adj* (*point, direction*) verso nord; **~ern** ['nɔːðən] *adj* del nord, settentrionale; **N~ern Ireland** *n* Irlanda del Nord; **N~ Pole** *n* Polo Nord; **N~ Sea** *n* Mare *m* del Nord; **~ward(s)** ['nɔːθwəd(z)] *adv* verso nord; **~-west** *n* nord-ovest *m*
Norway ['nɔːweɪ] *n* Norvegia
Norwegian [nɔː'wiːdʒən] *adj* norvegese ♦ *n* norvegese *m/f*; (*LING*) norvegese *m*
nose [nəuz] *n* naso; (*of animal*) muso ♦ *vi*: **to ~ about** aggirarsi; **~bleed** *n* emorragia nasale; **~-dive** *n* picchiata; **~y** (*inf*) *adj* = **nosy**
nostalgia [nɔs'tældʒɪə] *n* nostalgia
nostril ['nɔstrɪl] *n* narice *f*; (*of horse*) frogia
nosy ['nəuzɪ] (*inf*) *adj* curioso(a)
not [nɔt] *adv* non; **he is ~ or isn't here** non è qui, non c'è; **you must ~ or you mustn't do**

that non devi fare quello; **it's too late, isn't it** *or* **is it ~?** è troppo tardi, vero?; **~ that I don't like him** non che (lui) non mi piaccia; **~ yet/now** non ancora/ora; *see also* **all; only**
notably ['nəutəblɪ] *adv* (*markedly*) notevolmente; (*particularly*) in particolare
notary ['nəutərɪ] *n* notaio
notch [nɔtʃ] *n* tacca; (*in saw*) dente *m*
note [nəut] *n* nota; (*letter, banknote*) biglietto ♦ *vt* (*also*: **~ down**) prendere nota di; **to take ~s** prendere appunti; **~book** *n* taccuino; **~d** ['nəutɪd] *adj* celebre; **~pad** *n* bloc-notes *m inv*; **~paper** *n* carta da lettere
nothing ['nʌθɪŋ] *n* nulla *m*, niente *m*; (*zero*) zero; **he does ~** non fa niente; **~ new/much** *etc* niente di nuovo/speciale *etc*; **for ~** per niente
notice ['nəutɪs] *n* avviso; (*of leaving*) preavviso ♦ *vt* notare, accorgersi di; **to take ~ of** fare attenzione a; **to bring sth to sb's ~** far notare qc a qn; **at short ~** con un breve preavviso; **until further ~** fino a nuovo avviso; **to hand in one's ~** licenziarsi; **~able** *adj* evidente; **~ board** (*BRIT*) *n* tabellone *m* per affissi
notify ['nəutɪfaɪ] *vt*: **to ~ sth to sb** far sapere qc a qn; **to ~ sb of sth** avvisare qn di qc
notion ['nəuʃən] *n* idea; (*concept*) nozione *f*
notorious [nəu'tɔːrɪəs] *adj* famigerato(a)
nougat ['nuːgaː] *n* torrone *m*
nought [nɔːt] *n* zero
noun [naun] *n* nome *m*, sostantivo
nourish ['nʌrɪʃ] *vt* nutrire
novel ['nɔvl] *n* romanzo ♦ *adj* nuovo(a); **~ist** *n* romanziere/a; **~ty** *n* novità *f inv*
November [nəu'vembə*] *n* novembre *m*
novice ['nɔvɪs] *n* principiante *m/f*; (*REL*) novizio/a
now [nau] *adv* ora, adesso ♦ *conj*: **~ (that)** adesso che, ora che; **by ~** ormai; **just ~** proprio ora; **right ~** subito, immediatamente; **~ and then, ~ and again** ogni tanto; **from ~ on** da ora in poi; **~adays** ['nauədeɪz] *adv* oggidì
nowhere ['nəuweə*] *adv* in nessun luogo, da nessuna parte
nozzle ['nɔzl] *n* (*of hose etc*) boccaglio; (*of fire extinguisher*) lancia
nuance ['njuːɑːns] *n* sfumatura
nuclear ['njuːklɪə*] *adj* nucleare
nucleus ['njuːklɪəs] (*pl* **nuclei**) *n* nucleo
nude [njuːd] *adj* nudo(a) ♦ *n* (*ART*) nudo; **in the ~** tutto(a) nudo(a)
nudge [nʌdʒ] *vt* dare una gomitata a
nudist ['njuːdɪst] *n* nudista *m/f*
nuisance ['njuːsns] *n*: **it's a ~** è una seccatura; **he's a ~** è uno scocciatore
null [nʌl] *adj*: **~ and void** nullo(a)
numb [nʌm] *adj*: **~ (with)** intorpidito(a) (da);

(*with fear*) impietrito(a) (da); **~ with cold** intirizzito(a) (dal freddo)

number ['nʌmbə*] *n* numero ♦ *vt* numerare; (*include*) contare; **a ~ of** un certo numero di; **to be ~ed among** venire annoverato(a) tra; **they were 10 in ~** erano in tutto 10; **~ plate** (*BRIT*) *n* (*AUT*) targa

numeral ['nju:mərəl] *n* numero, cifra

numerate ['nju:mərɪt] *adj*: **to be ~** avere nozioni di aritmetica

numerical [nju:'mɛrɪkl] *adj* numerico(a)

numerous ['nju:mərəs] *adj* numeroso(a)

nun [nʌn] *n* suora, monaca

nurse [nəːs] *n* infermiere/a; (*also*: ~*maid*) bambinaia ♦ *vt* (*patient, cold*) curare; (*baby*: *BRIT*) cullare; (: *US*) allattare, dare il latte a

nursery ['nəːsəri] *n* (*room*) camera dei bambini; (*institution*) asilo; (*for plants*) vivaio; **~ rhyme** *n* filastrocca; **~ school** *n* scuola materna; **~ slope** (*BRIT*) *n* (*SKI*) pista per principianti

nursing ['nəːsɪŋ] *n* (*profession*) professione *f* di infermiere (*or* di infermiera); (*care*) cura; **~ home** *n* casa di cura

nurture ['nəːtʃə*] *vt* allevare; nutrire

nut [nʌt] *n* (*of metal*) dado; (*fruit*) noce *f*; **~crackers** *npl* schiaccianoci *m inv*

nutmeg ['nʌtmɛg] *n* noce *f* moscata

nutritious [nju:'trɪʃəs] *adj* nutriente

nuts [nʌts] (*inf*) *adj* matto(a)

nutshell ['nʌtʃɛl] *n*: **in a ~** in poche parole

nylon ['naɪlɔn] *n* nailon *m* ♦ *adj* di nailon

O, o

oak [əuk] *n* quercia ♦ *adj* di quercia

O.A.P. (*BRIT*) *n abbr* = **old age pensioner**

oar [ɔː*] *n* remo

oasis [əu'eɪsɪs] (*pl* **oases**) *n* oasi *f inv*

oath [əuθ] *n* giuramento; (*swear word*) bestemmia

oatmeal ['əutmiːl] *n* farina d'avena

oats [əuts] *npl* avena

obedience [ə'biːdɪəns] *n* ubbidienza

obedient [ə'biːdɪənt] *adj* ubbidiente

obey [ə'beɪ] *vt* ubbidire a; (*instructions, regulations*) osservare

obituary [ə'bɪtjuərɪ] *n* necrologia

object [*n* 'ɔbdʒɪkt, *vb* əb'dʒɛkt] *n* oggetto; (*purpose*) scopo, intento; (*LING*) complemento oggetto ♦ *vi*: **to ~ to** (*attitude*) disapprovare; (*proposal*) protestare contro, sollevare delle obiezioni contro; **expense is no ~** non si bada a spese; **to ~ that** obiettare che; **I ~!** mi oppongo!; **~ion** [əb'dʒɛkʃən] *n* obiezione *f*; **~ionable** [əb'dʒɛkʃənəbl] *adj* antipatico(a); (*language*) scostumato(a); **~ive** *n* obiettivo

obligation [ɔblɪ'geɪʃən] *n* obbligo, dovere *m*; **without ~** senza impegno

oblige [ə'blaɪdʒ] *vt* (*force*): **to ~ sb to do** costringere qn a fare; (*do a favour*) fare una cortesia a; **to be ~d to sb for sth** essere grato a qn per qc; **obliging** *adj* servizievole, compiacente

oblique [ə'bliːk] *adj* obliquo(a); (*allusion*) indiretto(a)

obliterate [ə'blɪtəreɪt] *vt* cancellare

oblivion [ə'blɪvɪən] *n* oblio

oblivious [ə'blɪvɪəs] *adj*: **~ of** incurante di; inconscio(a) di

oblong ['ɔblɔŋ] *adj* oblungo(a) ♦ *n* rettangolo

obnoxious [əb'nɔkʃəs] *adj* odioso(a); (*smell*) disgustoso(a), ripugnante

oboe ['əubəu] *n* oboe *m*

obscene [əb'siːn] *adj* osceno(a)

obscure [əb'skjuə*] *adj* oscuro(a) ♦ *vt* oscurare; (*hide*: *sun*) nascondere

observant [əb'zəːvnt] *adj* attento(a)

observation [ɔbzə'veɪʃən] *n* osservazione *f*; (*by police etc*) sorveglianza

observatory [əb'zəːvətrɪ] *n* osservatorio

observe [əb'zəːv] *vt* osservare; (*remark*) fare osservare; **~r** *n* osservatore/trice

obsess [əb'sɛs] *vt* ossessionare; **~ive** *adj* ossessivo(a)

obsolescence [ɔbsə'lɛsns] *n* obsolescenza

obsolete ['ɔbsəliːt] *adj* obsoleto(a)

obstacle ['ɔbstəkl] *n* ostacolo

obstinate ['ɔbstɪnɪt] *adj* ostinato(a)

obstruct [əb'strʌkt] *vt* (*block*) ostruire, ostacolare; (*halt*) fermare; (*hinder*) impedire

obtain [əb'teɪn] *vt* ottenere; **~able** *adj* ottenibile

obvious ['ɔbvɪəs] *adj* ovvio(a), evidente; **~ly** *adv* ovviamente; certo

occasion [ə'keɪʒən] *n* occasione *f*; (*event*) avvenimento; **~al** *adj* occasionale; **~ally** *adv* ogni tanto

occupation [ɔkju'peɪʃən] *n* occupazione *f*; (*job*) mestiere *m*, professione *f*; **~al hazard** *n* rischio del mestiere

occupier ['ɔkjupaɪə*] *n* occupante *m/f*

occupy ['ɔkjupaɪ] *vt* occupare; **to ~ o.s. in doing** occuparsi a fare

occur [ə'kəː*] *vi* accadere, capitare; **to ~ to sb** venire in mente a qn; **~rence** *n* caso, fatto; presenza

ocean ['əuʃən] *n* oceano

o'clock [ə'klɔk] *adv*: **it is 5 ~** sono le 5

OCR *n abbr* (= *optical character recognition*) lettura ottica; (= *optical character reader*) lettore *m* ottico

octave ['ɔktɪv] *n* ottavo

October [ɔk'təubə*] *n* ottobre *m*

octopus ['ɔktəpəs] *n* polpo, piovra

odd [ɔd] adj (strange) strano(a), bizzarro(a);
(number) dispari inv; (not of a set) spaiato(a);
60-~ 60 e oltre; **at ~ times** di tanto in tanto;
the ~ one out l'eccezione f; **~ity** n bizzarria;
(person) originale m; **~-job man** n tuttofare
m inv; **~ jobs** npl lavori mpl occasionali; **~ly**
adv stranamente; **~ments** npl (COMM)
rimanenze fpl; **at ~s** in contesa
odometer [ɔ'dɔmitə*] n odometro
odour ['əudə*] (US **odor**) n odore m;
(unpleasant) cattivo odore

KEYWORD
---

of [ɔv, əv] prep **1** (gen) di; **a boy ~ 10** un
ragazzo di 10 anni; **a friend ~ ours** un nostro
amico; **that was kind ~ you** è stato molto
gentile da parte sua
2 (expressing quantity, amount, dates etc) di;
a kilo ~ flour un chilo di farina; **how much
~ this do you need?** quanto gliene serve?;
there were 3 ~ them (people) erano in 3;
(objects) ce n'erano 3; **3 ~ us went** 3 di noi
sono andati; **the 5th ~ July** il 5 luglio
3 (from, out of) di, in; **made ~ wood** (fatto)
di or in legno

KEYWORD
---

off [ɔf] adv **1** (distance, time): **it's a long way ~**
è lontano; **the game is 3 days ~** la partita è
tra 3 giorni
2 (departure, removal) via; **to go ~ to Paris**
andarsene a Parigi; **I must be ~** devo andare
via; **to take ~ one's coat** togliersi il cappotto;
the button came ~ il bottone è venuto via or
si è staccato; **10% ~** con lo sconto del 10%
3 (not at work): **to have a day ~** avere un
giorno libero; **to be ~ sick** essere assente per
malattia
♦ adj (engine) spento(a); (tap) chiuso(a);
(cancelled) sospeso(a); (BRIT: food) andato(a)
a male; **on the ~ chance** nel caso; **to have an
~ day** non essere in forma
♦ prep **1** (motion, removal etc) da; (distant
from) a poca distanza da; **a street ~ the
square** una strada che parte dalla piazza
2: to be ~ meat non mangiare più la carne

offal ['ɔfl] n (CULIN) frattaglie fpl
off-colour ['ɔf'kʌlə*] (BRIT) adj (ill)
malato(a), indisposto(a)
offence [ə'fɛns] (US **offense**) n (LAW)
contravvenzione f; (: more serious) reato f; **to
take ~ at** offendersi per
offend [ə'fɛnd] vt (person) offendere; **~er** n
delinquente m/f; (against regulations)
contravventore/trice

offense [ə'fɛns] (US) n = **offence**
offensive [ə'fɛnsɪv] adj offensivo(a); (smell
etc) sgradevole, ripugnante ♦ n (MIL)
offensiva
offer ['ɔfə*] n offerta, proposta ♦ vt offrire;
"on ~" (COMM) "in offerta speciale"; **~ing** n
offerta
offhand [ɔf'hænd] adj disinvolto(a),
noncurante ♦ adv su due piedi
office ['ɔfɪs] n (place) ufficio; (position) carica;
doctor's ~ (US) studio; **to take ~** entrare in
carica; **~ automation** n automazione f
d'ufficio; burotica; **~ block** (US **~ building**) n
complesso di uffici; **~ hours** npl orario
d'ufficio; (US: MED) orario di visite
officer ['ɔfɪsə*] n (MIL etc) ufficiale m; (also:
police ~) agente m di polizia; (of
organization) funzionario
office worker n impiegato/a d'ufficio
official [ə'fɪʃl] adj (authorized) ufficiale n
ufficiale m; (civil servant) impiegato/a statale;
funzionario
officiate [ə'fɪʃɪeɪt] vi presenziare
officious [ə'fɪʃəs] adj invadente
offing ['ɔfɪŋ] n: **in the ~** (fig) in vista
off: **~-licence** (BRIT) n (shop) spaccio di
bevande alcoliche; **~-line** adj, adv (COMPUT)
off-line inv, fuori linea; (: switched off)
spento(a); **~-peak** adj (ticket, heating etc) a
tariffa ridotta; (time) non di punta; **~-
putting** (BRIT) adj sgradevole, antipatico(a);
~-road vehicle n fuoristrada m inv; **~-
season** adj, adv fuori stagione
offset ['ɔfset] (irreg) vt (counteract)
controbilanciare, compensare
offshoot ['ɔfʃuːt] n (fig) diramazione f
offshore [ɔf'ʃɔː*] adj (breeze) di terra;
(island) vicino alla costa; (fishing) costiero(a)
offside ['ɔf'saɪd] adj (SPORT) fuori gioco; (AUT:
in Britain) destro(a); (: in Italy etc) sinistro(a)
offspring ['ɔfsprɪŋ] n inv prole f, discendenza
off: **~-stage** adv dietro le quinte; **~-the-peg**
(US **~-the-rack**) adv prêt-à-porter; **~-white**
adj bianco sporco inv
often ['ɔfn] adv spesso; **how ~ do you go?**
quanto spesso ci vai?
oh [əu] excl oh!
oil [ɔɪl] n olio; (petroleum) petrolio; (for central
heating) nafta ♦ vt (machine) lubrificare;
~can n oliatore m a mano; (for storing) latta
da olio; **~field** n giacimento petrolifero;
~ filter n (AUT) filtro dell'olio; **~ painting** n
quadro a olio; **~ refinery** [-rɪ'faɪnərɪ] n
raffineria di petrolio; **~ rig** n derrick m inv;
(at sea) piattaforma per trivellazioni
subacquee; **~ tanker** n (ship) petroliera;
(truck) autocisterna per petrolio; **~ well** n
pozzo petrolifero; **~y** adj unto(a), oleoso(a);
(food) grasso(a)

ointment [ˈɔɪntmənt] n unguento

O.K., okay [ˈəuˈkeɪ] excl d'accordo! ♦ adj non male inv ♦ vt approvare; **is it ~?, are you ~?** tutto bene?

old [əuld] adj vecchio(a); (ancient) antico(a), vecchio(a); (person) vecchio(a), anziano(a); **how ~ are you?** quanti anni ha?; **he's 10 years ~** ha 10 anni; **~er brother** fratello maggiore; **~ age** n vecchiaia; **~ age pensioner** (BRIT) n pensionato/a; **~-fashioned** adj antiquato(a), fuori moda; (person) all'antica

olive [ˈɔlɪv] n (fruit) oliva; (tree) olivo ♦ adj (also: **~-green**) verde oliva inv; **~ oil** n olio d'oliva

Olympic [əuˈlɪmpɪk] adj olimpico(a); **the ~ Games, the ~s** i giochi olimpici, le Olimpiadi

omelet(te) [ˈɔmlɪt] n omelette f inv

omen [ˈəumən] n presagio, augurio

ominous [ˈɔmɪnəs] adj minaccioso(a); (event) di malaugurio

omit [əuˈmɪt] vt omettere

on [ɔn] prep 1 (indicating position) su; **~ the wall** sulla parete; **~ the left** a or sulla sinistra

2 (indicating means, method, condition etc): **~ foot** a piedi; **~ the train/plane** in treno/aereo; **~ the telephone** al telefono; **~ the radio/television** alla radio/televisione; **to be ~ drugs** drogarsi; **~ holiday** in vacanza

3 (of time): **~ Friday** venerdì; **~ Fridays** il or di venerdì; **~ June 20th** il 20 giugno; **~ Friday, June 20th** venerdì, 20 giugno; **a week ~ Friday** venerdì a otto; **~ his arrival** al suo arrivo; **~ seeing this** vedendo ciò

4 (about, concerning) su, di; **information ~ train services** informazioni sui collegamenti ferroviari; **a book ~ Goldoni/physics** un libro su Goldoni/di or sulla fisica

♦ adv 1 (referring to dress, covering): **to have one's coat ~** avere indosso il cappotto; **to put one's coat ~** mettersi il cappotto; **what's she got ~?** cosa indossa?; **she put her boots/gloves/hat ~** si mise gli stivali/i guanti/il cappello

2 (further, continuously): **to walk ~, go ~** etc continuare, proseguire etc; **to read ~** continuare a leggere; **~ and off** ogni tanto

♦ adj 1 (in operation: machine, TV, light) acceso(a); (: tap) aperto(a); (: brake) inserito(a); **is the meeting still ~?** (in progress) la riunione è ancora in corso?; (not cancelled) è confermato l'incontro?; **there's a good film ~ at the cinema** danno un buon film al cinema

2 (inf): **that's not ~!** (not acceptable) non si fa così!; (not possible) non se ne parla neanche!

once [wʌns] adv una volta ♦ conj non appena, quando; **~ he had left/it was done** dopo che se n'era andato/fu fatto; **at ~** subito; (simultaneously) a un tempo; **~ a week** una volta per settimana; **~ more** ancora una volta; **~ and for all** una volta per sempre; **~ upon a time** c'era una volta

oncoming [ˈɔnkʌmɪŋ] adj (traffic) che viene in senso opposto

one [wʌn] num uno(a); **~ hundred and fifty** centocinquanta; **~ day** un giorno

♦ adj 1 (sole) unico(a); **the ~ book which** l'unico libro che; **the ~ man who** l'unico che

2 (same) stesso(a); **they came in the ~ car** sono venuti nella stessa macchina

♦ pron 1: **this ~** questo/a; **that ~** quello/a; **I've already got ~/a red ~** ne ho già uno/uno rosso; **~ by ~** uno per uno

2: **~ another** l'un l'altro; **to look at ~ another** guardarsi; **to help ~ another** aiutarsi l'un l'altro or a vicenda

3 (impersonal) si; **~ never knows** non si sa mai; **to cut ~'s finger** tagliarsi un dito; **~ needs to eat** bisogna mangiare

one: **~-day excursion** (US) n biglietto giornaliero di andata e ritorno; **~-man** adj (business) diretto(a) etc da un solo uomo; **~-man band** n suonatore ambulante con vari strumenti; **~-off** (BRIT: inf) n fatto eccezionale

oneself [wʌnˈsɛlf] pron (reflexive) si; (after prep) se stesso(a), sé; **to do sth (by) ~** fare qc da sé; **to hurt ~** farsi male; **to keep sth for ~** tenere qc per sé; **to talk to ~** parlare da solo

one: **~-sided** adj (argument) unilaterale; **~-to-~** adj (relationship) univoco(a); **~-way** adj (street, traffic) a senso unico

ongoing [ˈɔngəuɪŋ] adj in corso; in attuazione

onion [ˈʌnjən] n cipolla

online [ˈɔnlaɪn] adj, adv (COMPUT) on-line inv

onlooker [ˈɔnlukə*] n spettatore/trice

only [ˈəunlɪ] adv solo, soltanto ♦ adj solo(a), unico(a) ♦ conj solo che, ma; **an ~ child** un figlio unico; **not ~ ... but also** non solo ... ma anche

onset [ˈɔnsɛt] n inizio

onshore [ˈɔnʃɔː*] adj (wind) di mare

onslaught [ˈɔnslɔːt] n attacco, assalto

onto [ˈɔntu] prep = **on to**

onus [ˈəunəs] n onere m, peso

onward(s) [ˈɔnwəd(z)] adv (move) in avanti; **from that time ~** da quella volta in poi

onyx [ˈɔnɪks] n onice f

ooze [uːz] vi stillare

OPEC ['əupɛk] n abbr (= Organization of Petroleum-Exporting Countries) O.P.E.C. f

open ['əupn] adj aperto(a); (road) libero(a); (meeting) pubblico(a) ♦ vt aprire ♦ vi (eyes, door, debate) aprirsi; (flower) sbocciare; (shop, bank, museum) aprire; (book etc: commence) cominciare; **in the ~ (air)** all'aperto; **~ on to** vt fus (subj: room, door) dare su; **~ up** vt aprire; (blocked road) sgombrare ♦ vi (shop, business) aprire; **~ing** adj (speech) di apertura ♦ n apertura, (opportunity) occasione f, opportunità f inv; sbocco; **~ing hours** npl orario d'apertura; **~ learning centre** n sistema educativo nel quale lo studente ha maggiore controllo e gestione delle modalità di apprendimento; **~ly** adv apertamente; **~-minded** adj che ha la mente aperta; **~-necked** adj col collo slacciato; **~-plan** adj senza pareti divisorie

opera ['ɔpərə] n opera

operate ['ɔpəreɪt] vt (machine) azionare, far funzionare; (system) usare ♦ vi funzionare; (drug) essere efficace; **to ~ on sb (for)** (MED) operare qn (di)

operatic [ɔpə'rætɪk] adj dell'opera, lirico(a)

operating ['ɔpəreɪtɪŋ] adj: **~ table** tavolo operatorio; **~ theatre** sala operatoria

operation [ɔpə'reɪʃən] n operazione f; **to be in ~** (machine) essere in azione or funzionamento; (system) essere in vigore; **to have an ~** (MED) subire un'operazione; **~al** adj in funzione; d'esercizio

operative ['ɔpərətɪv] adj (measure) operativo(a)

operator ['ɔpəreɪtə*] n (of machine) operatore/trice; (TEL) centralinista m/f

opinion [ə'pɪnɪən] n opinione f, parere m; **in my ~** secondo me, a mio avviso; **~ated** adj dogmatico(a); **~ poll** n sondaggio di opinioni

opium ['əupɪəm] n oppio

opponent [ə'pəunənt] n avversario/a

opportunist [ɔpə'tju:nɪst] n opportunista m/f

opportunity [ɔpə'tju:nɪtɪ] n opportunità f inv, occasione f; **to take the ~ of doing** cogliere l'occasione per fare

oppose [ə'pəuz] vt opporsi a; **~d to** contrario(a) a; **as ~d to** in contrasto con; **opposing** adj opposto(a); (team) avversario(a)

opposite ['ɔpəzɪt] adj opposto(a); (house etc) di fronte ♦ adv di fronte, dirimpetto ♦ prep di fronte a ♦ n: **the ~** il contrario, l'opposto; **the ~ sex** l'altro sesso

opposition [ɔpə'zɪʃən] n opposizione f

opt [ɔpt] vi: **to ~ for** optare per; **to ~ to do** scegliere di fare; **~ out** vi: **to ~ out of** ritirarsi da

optical ['ɔptɪkl] adj ottico(a)

optician [ɔp'tɪʃən] n ottico

optimist ['ɔptɪmɪst] n ottimista m/f; **~ic** [-'mɪstɪk] adj ottimistico(a)

optimum ['ɔptɪməm] adj ottimale

option ['ɔpʃən] n scelta; (SCOL) materia facoltativa; (COMM) opzione f; **~al** adj facoltativo(a); (COMM) a scelta

or [ɔː*] conj o, oppure; (with negative): **he hasn't seen ~ heard anything** non ha visto né sentito niente; **~ else** se no, altrimenti; oppure

oral ['ɔːrəl] adj orale ♦ n esame m orale

orange ['ɔrɪndʒ] n (fruit) arancia ♦ adj arancione

orbit ['ɔːbɪt] n orbita ♦ vt orbitare intorno a

orbital (motorway) ['ɔːbɪtl-] n raccordo anulare

orchard ['ɔːtʃəd] n frutteto

orchestra ['ɔːkɪstrə] n orchestra; (US: seating) platea

orchid ['ɔːkɪd] n orchidea

ordain [ɔː'deɪn] vt (REL) ordinare; (decide) decretare

ordeal [ɔː'diːl] n prova, travaglio

order ['ɔːdə*] n ordine m; (COMM) ordinazione f ♦ vt ordinare; **in ~** in ordine; (of document) in regola; **in (working) ~** funzionante; **in ~ to do** per fare; **in ~ that** affinché + sub; **on ~** (COMM) in ordinazione; **out of ~** non in ordine; (not working) guasto; **to ~ sb to do** ordinare a qn di fare; **~ form** n modulo d'ordinazione; **~ly** n (MIL) attendente m; (MED) inserviente m ♦ adj (room) in ordine; (mind) metodico(a); (person) ordinato(a), metodico(a)

ordinary ['ɔːdnrɪ] adj normale, comune; (pej) mediocre; **out of the ~** diverso dal solito, fuori dell'ordinario

Ordnance Survey ['ɔːdnəns-] (BRIT) n istituto cartografico britannico

ore [ɔː*] n minerale m grezzo

organ ['ɔːgən] n organo; **~ic** [ɔː'gænɪk] adj organico(a); (of food) biologico(a)

organization [ɔːgənaɪ'zeɪʃən] n organizzazione f

organize ['ɔːgənaɪz] vt organizzare; **to get ~d** organizzarsi; **~r** n organizzatore/trice

orgasm ['ɔːgæzəm] n orgasmo

orgy ['ɔːdʒɪ] n orgia

Orient ['ɔːrɪənt] n: **the ~** l'Oriente m; **oriental** [-'ɛntl] adj, n orientale m/f

origin ['ɔrɪdʒɪn] n origine f

original [ə'rɪdʒɪnl] adj originale; (earliest) originario(a) ♦ n originale m; **~ly** adv (at first) all'inizio

originate [ə'rɪdʒɪneɪt] vi: **to ~ from** essere originario(a) di; (suggestion) provenire da; **to ~ in** avere origine in

Orkneys ['ɔːknɪz] npl: **the ~** (also: the Orkney Islands) le Orcadi

ornament ['ɔːnəmənt] n ornamento; (trinket) ninnolo; **~al** [-'mɛntl] adj ornamentale

ornate [ɔː'neɪt] adj molto ornato(a)

orphan ['ɔːfn] n orfano/a

orthodox ['ɔːθədɔks] adj ortodosso(a)

orthopaedic [ɔːθə'piːdɪk] (US **orthopedic**) adj ortopedico(a)

ostensibly [ɔs'tɛnsɪblɪ] adv all'apparenza

ostentatious [ɔstɛn'teɪʃəs] adj pretenzioso(a); ostentato(a)

ostrich ['ɔstrɪtʃ] n struzzo

other ['ʌðə*] adj altro(a) ♦ pron: **the ~** (one) l'altro(a); **~s** (~ people) altri mpl; **~ than** altro che; a parte; **~wise** adv, conj altrimenti

otter ['ɔtə*] n lontra

ouch [autʃ] excl ohi!, ahi!

ought [ɔːt] (pt ought) aux vb: **I ~ to do it** dovrei farlo; **this ~ to have been corrected** questo avrebbe dovuto essere corretto; **he ~ to win** dovrebbe vincere

ounce [auns] n oncia (= 28.35 g; 16 in a pound)

our ['auə*] adj il(la) nostro(a), pl i(le) nostri(e); see also **my**; **~s** pron il(la) nostro(a), pl i(le) nostri(e); see also **mine**; **~selves** pron pl (reflexive) ci; (after preposition) noi; (emphatic) noi stessi(e); see also **oneself**

oust [aust] vt cacciare, espellere

KEYWORD

out [aut] adv (gen) fuori; **~ here/there** qui/là fuori; **to speak ~ loud** parlare forte; **to have a night ~** uscire una sera; **the boat was 10 km ~** la barca era a 10 km dalla costa; **3 days ~ from Plymouth** a 3 giorni da Plymouth
♦ adj: **to be ~** (gen) essere fuori; (unconscious) aver perso i sensi; (style, singer) essere fuori moda; **before the week was ~** prima che la settimana fosse finita; **to be ~ to do sth** avere intenzione di fare qc; **to be ~ in one's calculations** aver sbagliato i calcoli
♦ **out of** prep 1 (outside, beyond) fuori di; **to go ~ of the house** uscire di casa; **to look ~ of the window** guardare fuori dalla finestra
2 (because of) per
3 (origin) da; **to drink ~ of a cup** bere da una tazza
4 (from among): **~ of 10** su 10
5 (without) senza; **~ of petrol** senza benzina

out-and-out ['autənaut] adj (liar, thief etc) vero(a) e proprio(a)

outback ['autbæk] n (in Australia) interno, entroterra

outboard ['autbɔːd] n: **~ (motor)** (motore

m) fuoribordo

outbreak ['autbreɪk] n scoppio; epidemia

outburst ['autbɜːst] n scoppio

outcast ['autkɑːst] n esule m/f; (socially) paria m inv

outcome ['autkʌm] n esito, risultato

outcrop ['autkrɔp] n (of rock) affioramento

outcry ['autkraɪ] n protesta, clamore m

outdated [aut'deɪtɪd] adj (custom, clothes) fuori moda; (idea) sorpassato(a)

outdo [aut'duː] (irreg) vt sorpassare

outdoor [aut'dɔː*] adj all'aperto; **~s** adv fuori; all'aria aperta

outer ['autə*] adj esteriore; **~ space** n spazio cosmico

outfit ['autfɪt] n (clothes) completo; (: for sport) tenuta

outgoing ['autgəuɪŋ] adj (character) socievole; **~s** (BRIT) npl (expenses) spese fpl, uscite fpl

outgrow [aut'grəu] (irreg) vt: **he has ~n his clothes** tutti i vestiti gli sono diventati piccoli

outhouse ['authaus] n costruzione f annessa

outing ['autɪŋ] n gita; escursione f

outlaw ['autlɔː] n fuorilegge m/f ♦ vt bandire

outlay ['autleɪ] n spese fpl; (investment) sborsa, spesa

outlet ['autlɛt] n (for liquid etc) sbocco, scarico; (US: ELEC) presa di corrente; (also: retail ~) punto di vendita

outline ['autlaɪn] n contorno, profilo; (summary) abbozzo, grandi linee fpl ♦ vt (fig) descrivere a grandi linee

outlive [aut'lɪv] vt sopravvivere a

outlook ['autluk] n prospettiva, vista

outlying ['autlaɪɪŋ] adj periferico(a)

outmoded [aut'məudɪd] adj passato(a) di moda; antiquato(a)

outnumber [aut'nʌmbə*] vt superare in numero

out-of-date [autəv'deɪt] adj (passport) scaduto(a); (clothes) fuori moda inv

out-of-the-way [autəvðə'weɪ] adj (place) fuori mano inv

outpatient ['autpeɪʃənt] n paziente m/f esterno/a

outpost ['autpəust] n avamposto

output ['autput] n produzione f; (COMPUT) output m inv

outrage ['autreɪdʒ] n oltraggio; scandalo ♦ vt oltraggiare; **~ous** [-'reɪdʒəs] adj oltraggioso(a); scandaloso(a)

outreach worker ['autriːtʃ-] n assistente sociale che opera direttamente nei luoghi di aggregazione di emarginati, tossicodipendenti ecc

outright [adv aut'raɪt, adj 'autraɪt] adv completamente; schiettamente; apertamente; sul colpo ♦ adj completo(a); schietto(a) e netto(a)

outset ['autsɛt] n inizio

outside [aut'saɪd] n esterno, esteriore m ♦ adj esterno(a), esteriore ♦ adv fuori, all'esterno ♦ prep fuori di, all'esterno di; **at the ~** (fig) al massimo; **~ lane** n (AUT) corsia di sorpasso; **~ line** n (TEL) linea esterna; **~r** n (in race etc) outsider m inv; (stranger) estraneo/a

outsize ['autsaɪz] adj (clothes) per taglie forti

outskirts ['autskə:ts] npl sobborghi mpl

outspoken [aut'spəukən] adj molto franco(a)

outstanding [aut'stændɪŋ] adj eccezionale, di rilievo; (unfinished) non completo(a); non evaso(a); non regolato(a)

outstay [aut'steɪ] vt: **to ~ one's welcome** diventare un ospite sgradito

outstretched [aut'strɛtʃt] adj (hand) teso(a); (body) disteso(a)

outstrip [aut'strɪp] vt (competitors, demand) superare

out-tray ['auttreɪ] n contenitore m per la corrispondenza in partenza

outward ['autwəd] adj (sign, appearances) esteriore; (journey) d'andata

outweigh [aut'weɪ] vt avere maggior peso di

outwit [aut'wɪt] vt superare in astuzia

oval ['əuvl] adj ovale ♦ n ovale m

ovary ['əuvəri] n ovaia

oven ['ʌvn] n forno; **~proof** adj da forno

over ['əuvə*] adv al di sopra ♦ adj (or adv) (finished) finito(a), terminato(a); (too) troppo; (remaining) che avanza ♦ prep su; sopra; (above) al di sopra di; (on the other side of) di là di; (more than) più di; (during) durante; **~ here** qui; **~ there** là; **all ~** (everywhere) dappertutto; (finished) finito(a) finito(a); **~ and ~ (again)** più e più volte; **~ and above** oltre (a); **to ask sb ~** invitare qn (a passare)

overall [adj, n 'əuvərɔ:l, adv əuvər'ɔ:l] adj totale ♦ n (BRIT) grembiule m ♦ adv nell'insieme, complessivamente; **~s** npl (worker's ~s) tuta (da lavoro)

overawe [əuvər'ɔ:] vt intimidire

overbalance [əuvə'bæləns] vi perdere l'equilibrio

overboard ['əuvəbɔ:d] adv (NAUT) fuori bordo, in mare

overbook [əuvə'buk] vt: **the hotel was ~ed** le prenotazioni all'albergo superavano i posti disponibili

overcast ['əuvəka:st] adj (sky) coperto(a)

overcharge [əuvə'tʃa:dʒ] vt: **to ~ sb for sth** far pagare troppo caro a qn per qc

overcoat ['əuvəkəut] n soprabito, cappotto

overcome [əuvə'kʌm] (irreg) vt superare; sopraffare

overcrowded [əuvə'kraudɪd] adj sovraffollato(a)

overdo [əuvə'du:] (irreg) vt esagerare; (overcook) cuocere troppo

overdose ['əuvədəus] n dose f eccessiva

overdraft ['əuvədra:ft] n scoperto (di conto)

overdrawn [əuvə'drɔ:n] adj (account) scoperto(a)

overdue [əuvə'dju:] adj in ritardo

overestimate [əuvər'estɪmeɪt] vt sopravvalutare

overflow [vb əuvə'fləu, n 'əuvəfləu] vi traboccare ♦ n (also: **~ pipe**) troppopieno

overgrown [əuvə'grəun] adj (garden) ricoperto(a) di vegetazione

overhaul [vb əuvə'hɔ:l, n 'əuvəhɔ:l] vt revisionare ♦ n revisione f

overhead [adv əuvə'hɛd, adj, n 'əuvəhɛd] adv di sopra ♦ adj aereo(a); (lighting) verticale ♦ n (US) = **~s**; **~s** npl spese fpl generali

overhear [əuvə'hɪə*] (irreg) vt sentire (per caso)

overheat [əuvə'hi:t] vi (engine) surriscaldare

overjoyed [əuvə'dʒɔɪd] adj pazzo(a) di gioia

overlap [əuvə'læp] vi sovrapporsi

overleaf [əuvə'li:f] adv a tergo

overload [əuvə'ləud] vt sovraccaricare

overlook [əuvə'luk] vt (have view of) dare su; (miss) trascurare; (forgive) passare sopra a

overnight [əuvə'naɪt] adv (happen) durante la notte; (fig) tutto ad un tratto ♦ adj di notte; **he stayed there ~** ci ha passato la notte

overpass ['əuvəpa:s] n cavalcavia m inv

overpower [əuvə'pauə*] vt sopraffare; **~ing** adj irresistibile; (heat, stench) soffocante

overrate [əuvə'reɪt] vt sopravvalutare

override [əuvə'raɪd] (irreg: like **ride**) vt (order, objection) passar sopra a; (decision) annullare; **overriding** adj preponderante

overrule [əuvə'ru:l] vt (decision) annullare; (claim) respingere

overrun [əuvə'rʌn] (irreg: like **run**) vt (country) invadere; (time limit) superare

overseas [əuvə'si:z] adv oltremare; (abroad) all'estero ♦ adj (trade) estero(a); (visitor) straniero(a)

overshadow [əuvə'ʃædəu] vt far ombra su; (fig) eclissare

overshoot [əuvə'ʃu:t] (irreg) vt superare

oversight ['əuvəsaɪt] n omissione f, svista

oversleep [əuvə'sli:p] (irreg) vt dormire troppo a lungo

overstep [əuvə'stɛp] vt: **to ~ the mark** superare ogni limite

overt [əu'və:t] adj palese

overtake [əuvə'teɪk] (irreg) vt sorpassare

overthrow [əuvə'θrəu] (irreg) vt (government) rovesciare

overtime ['əuvətaɪm] n (lavoro) straordinario

overtone ['əuvətəun] n sfumatura

overture ['əuvətʃuə*] n (MUS) ouverture f inv; (fig) approccio

overturn [əuvə'tə:n] vt rovesciare ♦ vi rovesciarsi

overweight [əuvə'weit] adj (person) troppo grasso(a)

overwhelm [əuvə'wɛlm] vt sopraffare; sommergere; schiacciare; ~ing adj (victory, defeat) schiacciante; (heat, desire) intenso(a)

overwrought [əuvə'rɔ:t] adj molto agitato(a)

owe [əu] vt: to ~ sb sth, to ~ sth to sb dovere qc a qn; **owing to** prep a causa di

owl [aul] n gufo

own [əun] vt possedere ♦ adj proprio(a); **a room of my ~** la mia propria camera; **to get one's ~ back** vendicarsi; **on one's ~** tutto(a) solo(a); **~ up** vi confessare; **~er** n proprietario/a; **~ership** n possesso

ox [ɔks] pl **oxen** n bue m

oxen ['ɔksn] npl of **ox**

oxtail ['ɔksteil] n: **~ soup** minestra di coda di bue

oxygen ['ɔksidʒən] n ossigeno; **~ mask/tent** n maschera/tenda ad ossigeno

oyster ['ɔistə*] n ostrica

oz. abbr = **ounce(s)**

ozone ['əuzəun] n ozono; **~-friendly** adj che non danneggia l'ozono; **~ hole** n buco nell'ozono

P, p

p [pi:] abbr = **penny; pence**

P.A. n abbr = **personal assistant; public address system**

p.a. abbr = **per annum**

pa [pɑ:] (inf) n papà m inv, babbo

pace [peis] n passo; (speed) velocità ♦ vi: **to ~ up and down** camminare su e giù; **to keep ~ with** camminare di pari passo a; (events) tenersi al corrente di; **~maker** n (MED) segnapasso; (SPORT: also: ~ setter) battistrada m inv

pacific [pə'sifik] n: **the P~ (Ocean)** il Pacifico, l'Oceano Pacifico

pacify ['pæsifai] vt calmare, placare

pack [pæk] n pacco; (US: of cigarettes) pacchetto; (back~) zaino; (of hounds) muta; (of thieves) banda; (of cards) mazzo ♦ vt (in suitcase etc) mettere; (box) riempire; (cram) stipare, pigiare; **to ~ (one's bags)** fare la valigia; **to ~ sb off** spedire via qn; **~ it in!** (inf) dacci un taglio!

package ['pækidʒ] n pacco; balla; (also: ~ deal) pacchetto; forfait m inv; **~ holiday** n vacanza organizzata; **~ tour** n viaggio organizzato

packed lunch ['pækt-] n pranzo al sacco

packet ['pækit] n pacchetto

packing ['pækiŋ] n imballaggio; **~ case** n cassa da imballaggio

pact [pækt] n patto, accordo; trattato

pad [pæd] n blocco; (to prevent friction) cuscinetto; (inf: flat) appartamentino ♦ vt imbottire; **~ding** n imbottitura

paddle ['pædl] n (oar) pagaia; (US: for table tennis) racchetta da ping-pong ♦ vi sguazzare ♦ vt: **to ~ a canoe** etc vogare con la pagaia; **paddling pool** (BRIT) n piscina per bambini

paddock ['pædək] n prato recintato; (at racecourse) paddock m inv

padlock ['pædlɔk] n lucchetto

paediatrics [pi:di'ætriks] (US **pediatrics**) n pediatria

pagan ['peigən] adj, n pagano(a)

page [peidʒ] n pagina; (also: ~ boy) paggio ♦ vt (in hotel etc) (far) chiamare

pageant ['pædʒənt] n spettacolo storico; grande cerimonia; **~ry** n pompa

pager ['peidʒə*] n (TEL) cercapersone m inv

paging device ['peidʒiŋ-] n (TEL) cercapersone m inv

paid [peid] pt, pp of **pay** ♦ adj (work, official) rimunerato(a); **to put ~ to** (BRIT) mettere fine a

pail [peil] n secchio

pain [pein] n dolore m; **to be in ~** soffrire, aver male; **to take ~s to do** mettercela tutta per fare; **~ed** adj addolorato(a), afflitto(a); **~ful** adj doloroso(a), che fa male; difficile, penoso(a); **~fully** adv (fig: very) fin troppo; **~killer** n antalgico, antidolorifico; **~less** adj indolore

painstaking ['peinzteikiŋ] adj (person) sollecito(a); (work) accurato(a)

paint [peint] n vernice f, colore m ♦ vt dipingere; (walls, door etc) verniciare; **to ~ the door blue** verniciare la porta di azzurro; **~brush** n pennello; **~er** n (artist) pittore m; (decorator) imbianchino; **~ing** n pittura; verniciatura; (picture) dipinto, quadro; **~work** n tinta; (of car) vernice f

pair [pɛə*] n (of shoes, gloves etc) paio; (of people) coppia; duo m inv; **a ~ of scissors/trousers** un paio di forbici/pantaloni

pajamas [pi'dʒɑ:məz] (US) npl pigiama m

Pakistan [pɑ:ki'stɑ:n] n Pakistan m; **~i** adj, n pakistano(a)

pal [pæl] (inf) n amico/a, compagno/a

palace ['pæləs] n palazzo

palatable ['pælitəbl] adj gustoso(a)

palate ['pælit] n palato

palatial [pə'leiʃəl] adj sontuoso(a), sfarzoso(a)

pale [peil] adj pallido(a) ♦ n: **to be beyond**

the ~ aver oltrepassato ogni limite
Palestine ['pælɪstaɪn] n Palestina;
Palestinian [-'tɪnɪən] adj, n palestinese m/f
palette ['pælɪt] n tavolozza
palings ['peɪlɪŋz] npl (fence) palizzata
pallet ['pælɪt] n (for goods) paletta
pallid ['pælɪd] adj pallido(a), smorto(a)
pallor ['pælə*] n pallore m
palm [pɑ:m] n (ANAT) palma, palmo; (also:
~ tree) palma ♦ vt: to ~ sth off on sb (inf)
rifilare qc a qn; **P~ Sunday** n Domenica
delle Palme
paltry ['pɔːltrɪ] adj irrisorio(a); insignificante
pamper ['pæmpə*] vt viziare, coccolare
pamphlet ['pæmflət] n dépliant m inv
pan [pæn] n (also: sauce~) casseruola; (also:
frying ~) padella
panache [pə'næʃ] n stile m
pancake ['pænkeɪk] n frittella
pancreas ['pænkrɪəs] n pancreas m inv
panda ['pændə] n panda m inv; ~ **car** (BRIT) n
auto f della polizia
pandemonium [pændɪ'məʊnɪəm] n
pandemonio
pander ['pændə*] vi: to ~ to lusingare;
concedere tutto a
pane [peɪn] n vetro
panel ['pænl] n (of wood, cloth etc) pannello;
(RADIO, TV) giuria; **~ling** (US **~ing**) n
rivestimento a pannelli
pang [pæŋ] n: a ~ of regret un senso di
rammarico; **hunger ~s** morsi mpl della fame
panic ['pænɪk] n panico ♦ vi perdere il sangue
freddo; **~ky** adj (person) pauroso(a); **~-
stricken** adj (person) preso(a) dal panico, in
preda al panico; (look) terrorizzato(a)
pansy ['pænzɪ] n (BOT) viola del pensiero,
pensée f inv; (inf: pej) femminuccia
pant [pænt] vi ansare
panther ['pænθə*] n pantera
panties ['pæntɪz] npl slip m, mutandine fpl
pantihose ['pæntɪhəʊz] (US) n collant m inv
pantomime ['pæntəmaɪm] (BRIT) n
pantomima
pantry ['pæntrɪ] n dispensa
pants [pænts] npl mutande fpl, slip m; (US:
trousers) pantaloni mpl
papal ['peɪpəl] adj papale, pontificio(a)
paper ['peɪpə*] n carta; (also: wall~) carta da
parati, tappezzeria; (also: news~) giornale m;
(study, article) saggio; (exam) prova scritta
♦ adj di carta ♦ vt tappezzare; **~s** npl (also:
identity ~s) carte fpl, documenti mpl; **~back**
n tascabile m; edizione f economica; **~ bag**
n sacchetto di carta; ~ **clip** n graffetta, clip f
inv; ~ **hankie** n fazzolettino di carta;
~weight n fermacarte m inv; **~work** n
lavoro amministrativo
papier-mâché ['pæpɪeɪ'mæʃeɪ] n cartapesta

par [pɑ:*] n parità, pari f; (GOLF) norma; **on a
~ with** alla pari con
parachute ['pærəʃuːt] n paracadute m inv
parade [pə'reɪd] n parata ♦ vt (fig) fare
sfoggio di ♦ vi sfilare in parata
paradise ['pærədaɪs] n paradiso
paradox ['pærədɒks] n paradosso; **~ically**
[-'dɒksɪklɪ] adv paradossalmente
paraffin ['pærəfɪn] (BRIT) n: ~ **(oil)** paraffina
paragon ['pærəgən] n modello di perfezione
or di virtù
paragraph ['pærəgrɑːf] n paragrafo
parallel ['pærəlel] adj parallelo(a); (fig)
analogo(a) ♦ n (line) parallela; (fig, GEO)
parallelo
paralyse ['pærəlaɪz] (US **paralyze**) vt
paralizzare
paralysis [pə'rælɪsɪs] n paralisi f inv
paralyze ['pærəlaɪz] (US) vt = **paralyse**
paramount ['pærəmaʊnt] adj: **of
~ importance** di capitale importanza
paranoid ['pærənɔɪd] adj paranoico(a)
paraphernalia [pærəfə'neɪlɪə] n attrezzi mpl,
roba
parasol ['pærəsɒl] n parasole m
paratrooper ['pærətruːpə*] n paracadutista
m (soldato)
parcel ['pɑːsl] n pacco, pacchetto ♦ vt (also:
~ up) impaccare
parched [pɑːtʃt] adj (person) assetato(a)
parchment ['pɑːtʃmənt] n pergamena
pardon ['pɑːdn] n perdono; grazia ♦ vt
perdonare; (LAW) graziare; ~ **me!** mi scusi; **I
beg your ~!** scusi; **I beg your ~?** (BRIT), ~ **me?**
(US) prego?
parent ['pɛərənt] n genitore m; **~s** npl
(mother and father) genitori mpl; **~al**
[pə'rentl] adj dei genitori
parentheses [pə'renθɪsiːz] npl of **parenthesis**
parenthesis [pə'renθɪsɪs] (pl **parentheses**) n
parentesi f inv
Paris ['pærɪs] n Parigi f
parish ['pærɪʃ] n parrocchia; (BRIT: civil) ≈
municipio
park [pɑːk] n parco ♦ vt, vi parcheggiare
parka ['pɑːkə] n eskimo
parking ['pɑːkɪŋ] n parcheggio; "**no ~**"
"sosta vietata"; ~ **lot** (US) n posteggio,
parcheggio; ~ **meter** n parchimetro;
~ **ticket** n multa per sosta vietata
parliament ['pɑːləmənt] n parlamento
parliamentary [pɑːlə'mentərɪ] adj
parlamentare
parlour ['pɑːlə*] (US **parlor**) n salotto
parochial [pə'rəʊkɪəl] (pej) adj provinciale
parole [pə'rəʊl] n: **on ~** in libertà per buona
condotta
parrot ['pærət] n pappagallo
parry ['pærɪ] vt parare

parsley ['pɑːslɪ] n prezzemolo
parsnip ['pɑːsnɪp] n pastinaca
parson ['pɑːsn] n prete m; (Church of England) parroco
part [pɑːt] n parte f; (of machine) pezzo; (US: in hair) scriminatura ♦ adj in parte ♦ adv = **partly** ♦ vt separare ♦ vi (people) separarsi; **to take ~ in** prendere parte a; **for my ~** per parte mia; **to take sth in good ~** prendere bene qc; **to take sb's ~** parteggiare per or prendere le parti di qn; **for the most ~** in generale; nella maggior parte dei casi; **~ with** vt fus separarsi da; rinunciare a; **~ exchange** (BRIT) n: **in ~ exchange** in pagamento parziale
partial ['pɑːʃl] adj parziale; **to be ~ to** avere un debole per
participate [pɑː'tɪsɪpeɪt] vi: **to ~ (in)** prendere parte (a), partecipare (a); **participation** [-'peɪʃən] n partecipazione f
participle ['pɑːtɪsɪpl] n participio
particle ['pɑːtɪkl] n particella
particular [pə'tɪkjulə*] adj particolare; speciale; (fussy) difficile; meticoloso(a); **in ~** in particolare, particolarmente; **~ly** adv particolarmente; in particolare; **~s** npl particolari mpl, dettagli mpl; (information) informazioni fpl
parting ['pɑːtɪŋ] n separazione f; (BRIT: in hair) scriminatura ♦ adj d'addio
partisan [pɑːtɪ'zæn] n partigiano/a ♦ adj partigiano(a); di parte
partition [pɑː'tɪʃən] n (POL) partizione f; (wall) tramezzo
partly ['pɑːtlɪ] adv parzialmente; in parte
partner ['pɑːtnə*] n (COMM) socio/a; (wife, husband etc, SPORT) compagno/a; (at dance) cavaliere/dama; **~ship** n associazione f; (COMM) società f inv
partridge ['pɑːtrɪdʒ] n pernice f
part-time ['pɑːt'taɪm] adj, adv a orario ridotto
party ['pɑːtɪ] n (POL) partito; (group) gruppo; (LAW) parte f; (celebration) ricevimento; serata; festa ♦ cpd (POL) del partito, di partito; **~ dress** n vestito della festa
pass [pɑːs] vt (gen) passare; (place) passare davanti a; (exam) passare, superare; (candidate) promuovere; (overtake, surpass) sorpassare, superare; (approve) approvare ♦ vi passare ♦ n (permit) lasciapassare m inv; permesso; (in mountains) passo, gola; (SPORT) passaggio; (SCOL): **to get a ~** prendere la sufficienza; **to ~ sth through a hole** etc far passare qc attraverso un buco etc; **to make a ~ at sb** (inf) fare delle proposte or delle avances a qn; **~ away** vi morire; **~ by** vi passare ♦ vt trascurare; **~ on** vt passare; **~ out** vi svenire; **~ up** vt (opportunity) lasciarsi sfuggire, perdere; **~able** adj (road)

praticabile; (work) accettabile
passage ['pæsɪdʒ] n (gen) passaggio; (also: ~way) corridoio; (in book) brano, passo; (by boat) traversata
passbook ['pɑːsbuk] n libretto di risparmio
passenger ['pæsɪndʒə*] n passeggero/a
passer-by [pɑːsə'baɪ] n passante m/f
passing ['pɑːsɪŋ] adj (fig) fuggevole; **to mention sth in ~** accennare a qc di sfuggita; **~ place** n (AUT) piazzola di sosta
passion ['pæʃən] n passione f; amore m; **~ate** adj appassionato(a)
passive ['pæsɪv] adj (also LING) passivo(a); **~ smoking** n fumo passivo
Passover ['pɑːsəuvə*] n Pasqua ebraica
passport ['pɑːspɔːt] n passaporto; **~ control** n controllo m passaporti inv; **~ office** n ufficio m passaporti inv
password ['pɑːswɜːd] n parola d'ordine
past [pɑːst] prep (further than) oltre, di là di; dopo; (later than) dopo ♦ adj passato(a); (president etc) ex inv ♦ n passato; **he's ~ forty** ha più di quarant'anni; **ten ~ eight** le otto e dieci; **for the ~ few days** da qualche giorno; in questi ultimi giorni; **to run ~** passare di corsa
pasta ['pæstə] n pasta
paste [peɪst] n (glue) colla; (CULIN) pâté m inv; pasta ♦ vt collare
pastel ['pæstl] adj pastello inv
pasteurized ['pæstəraɪzd] adj pastorizzato(a)
pastille ['pæstl] n pastiglia
pastime ['pɑːstaɪm] n passatempo
pastry ['peɪstrɪ] n pasta
pasture ['pɑːstʃə*] n pascolo
pasty¹ ['pæstɪ] n pasticcio di carne
pasty² ['peɪstɪ] adj (face etc) smorto(a)
pat [pæt] vt accarezzare, dare un colpetto (affettuoso) a
patch [pætʃ] n (of material, on tyre) toppa; (eye ~) benda; (spot) macchia ♦ vt (clothes) rattoppare; (to go through) a bad ~ (attraversare) un brutto periodo; **~ up** vt rappezzare; (quarrel) appianare; **~y** adj irregolare
pâté ['pæteɪ] n pâté m inv
patent ['peɪtnt] n brevetto ♦ vt brevettare ♦ adj patente, manifesto(a); **~ leather** n cuoio verniciato
paternal [pə'tɜːnl] adj paterno(a)
path [pɑːθ] n sentiero, viottolo; viale m; (fig) via, strada; (of planet, missile) traiettoria
pathetic [pə'θetɪk] adj (pitiful) patetico(a); (very bad) penoso(a)
pathological [pæθə'lɔdʒɪkl] adj patologico(a)
pathway ['pɑːθweɪ] n sentiero
patience ['peɪʃns] n pazienza; (BRIT: CARDS) solitario

patient ['peɪʃnt] n paziente m/f; malato/a
♦ adj paziente

patio ['pætɪəʊ] n terrazza

patriot ['peɪtrɪət] n patriota m/f; **~ic**
[pætrɪ'ɔtɪk] adj patriottico(a); **~ism** n
patriottismo

patrol [pə'trəʊl] n pattuglia ♦ vt pattugliare;
~ car n autoradio f inv (della polizia); **~man**
(US irreg) n poliziotto

patron ['peɪtrən] n (in shop) cliente m/f; (of
charity) benefattore/trice; **~ of the arts**
mecenate m/f; **~ize** ['pætrənaɪz] vt essere
cliente abituale di; (fig) trattare dall'alto in
basso

patter ['pætə*] n picchiettio; (sales talk)
propaganda di vendita ♦ vi picchiettare; a
~ of footsteps un rumore di passi

pattern ['pætən] n modello; (design) disegno,
motivo

pauper ['pɔ:pə*] n indigente m/f

pause [pɔ:z] n pausa ♦ vi fare una pausa,
arrestarsi

pave [peɪv] vt pavimentare; **to ~ the way for**
aprire la via a

pavement ['peɪvmənt] (BRIT) n marciapiede
m

pavilion [pə'vɪlɪən] n (SPORT) edificio annesso
a campo sportivo

paving ['peɪvɪŋ] n pavimentazione f; **~ stone**
n lastra di pietra

paw [pɔ:] n zampa

pawn [pɔ:n] n (CHESS) pedone m; (fig) pedina
♦ vt dare in pegno; **~broker** n prestatore m
su pegno; **~shop** n monte m di pietà

pay [peɪ] (pt, pp paid) n stipendio, paga ♦ vt
pagare ♦ vi (be profitable) rendere; **to
~ attention (to)** fare attenzione (a); **to ~ sb
a visit** far visita a qn; **to ~ one's respects to sb**
porgere i propri rispetti a qn; **~ back** vt
rimborsare; **~ for** vt fus pagare; **~ in** vt
versare; **~ off** vt (debt) saldare; (person)
pagare; (employee) pagare e licenziare ♦ vi
(scheme, decision) dare dei frutti; **~ up** vt
saldare; **~able** adj pagabile; **~ee** n
beneficiario/a; **~ envelope** (US) n =
~ packet; **~ing** adj: **~ing guest** ospite m/f
pagante, pensionante m/f; **~ment** n
pagamento; versamento; saldo; **~ packet**
(BRIT) n busta f paga inv; **~ phone** n cabina
telefonica; **~roll** n ruolo (organico); **~ slip** n
foglio m paga inv; **~ television** n televisione
f a pagamento, pay-tv f inv

PC n abbr = **personal computer**; adv abbr =
politically correct

p.c. abbr = **per cent**

pea [pi:] n pisello

peace [pi:s] n pace f; **~ful** adj pacifico(a),
calmo(a)

peach [pi:tʃ] n pesca

peacock ['pi:kɔk] n pavone m

peak [pi:k] n (of mountain) cima, vetta;
(mountain itself) picco; (of cap) visiera; (fig)
apice m, culmine m; **~ hours** npl ore fpl di
punta; **~ period** n = **~ hours**

peal [pi:l] n (of bells) scampanio, carillon m
inv; **~s of laughter** scoppi mpl di risa

peanut ['pi:nʌt] n arachide f, nocciolina
americana; **~ butter** n burro di arachidi

pear [pɛə*] n pera

pearl [pɜ:l] n perla

peasant ['pɛznt] n contadino/a

peat [pi:t] n torba

pebble ['pɛbl] n ciottolo

peck [pɛk] vt (also: **~ at**) beccare ♦ n colpo di
becco; (kiss) bacetto; **~ing order** n ordine
m gerarchico; **~ish** (BRIT: inf) adj: **I feel ~ish**
ho un languorino

peculiar [pɪ'kju:lɪə*] adj strano(a),
bizzarro(a); peculiare; **~ to** peculiare di

pedal ['pɛdl] n pedale m ♦ vi pedalare

pedantic [pɪ'dæntɪk] adj pedantesco(a)

peddler ['pɛdlə*] n (also: drug **~**)
spacciatore/trice

pedestal ['pɛdəstl] n piedestallo

pedestrian [pɪ'dɛstrɪən] n pedone/a ♦ adj
pedonale; (fig) prosaico(a), pedestre;
~ crossing (BRIT) n passaggio pedonale;
~ precinct (BRIT), **~ zone** (US) n zona
pedonale

pediatrics [pi:dɪ'ætrɪks] (US) n = **paediatrics**

pedigree ['pɛdɪgri:] n (of animal) pedigree m
inv; (fig) background m inv ♦ cpd (animal) di
razza

pee [pi:] (inf) vi pisciare

peek [pi:k] vi guardare furtivamente

peel [pi:l] n buccia; (of orange, lemon) scorza
♦ vt sbucciare ♦ vi (paint etc) staccarsi

peep [pi:p] n (BRIT: look) sguardo furtivo,
sbirciata; (sound) pigolio ♦ vi (BRIT) guardare
furtivamente; **~ out** vi mostrarsi
furtivamente; **~hole** n spioncino

peer [pɪə*] vi: **to ~ at** scrutare ♦ n (noble) pari
m inv; (equal) pari m/f inv, uguale m/f;
(contemporary) contemporaneo/a; **~age** n
dignità di pari; pari mpl

peeved [pi:vd] adj stizzito(a)

peevish ['pi:vɪʃ] adj stizzoso(a)

peg [pɛg] n caviglia; (for coat etc)
attaccapanni m inv; (BRIT: also: clothes **~**)
molletta

Peking [pi:'kɪŋ] n Pechino f

pelican ['pɛlɪkən] n pellicano; **~ crossing**
(BRIT) n (AUT) attraversamento pedonale con
semaforo a controllo manuale

pellet ['pɛlɪt] n pallottola, pallina

pelt [pɛlt] vt: **to ~ sb (with)** bombardare qn
(con) ♦ vi (rain) piovere a dirotto; (inf: run)
filare ♦ n pelle f

pelvis ['pelvɪs] n pelvi f inv, bacino

pen [pɛn] n penna; (for sheep) recinto

penal ['piːnl] adj penale; **~ize** vt punire; (SPORT, fig) penalizzare

penalty ['pɛnltɪ] n penalità f inv; sanzione f penale; (fine) ammenda; (SPORT) penalizzazione f; **~ (kick)** n (SPORT) calcio di rigore

penance ['pɛnəns] n penitenza

pence [pɛns] (BRIT) npl of **penny**

pencil ['pɛnsl] n matita; **~ case** n astuccio per matite; **~ sharpener** n temperamatite m inv

pendant ['pɛndnt] n pendaglio

pending ['pɛndɪŋ] prep in attesa di ♦ adj in sospeso

pendulum ['pɛndjuləm] n pendolo

penetrate ['pɛnɪtreɪt] vt penetrare

penfriend ['pɛnfrɛnd] (BRIT) n corrispondente m/f

penguin ['pɛŋgwɪn] n pinguino

penicillin [pɛnɪ'sɪlɪn] n penicillina

peninsula [pə'nɪnsjulə] n penisola

penis ['piːnɪs] n pene m

penitentiary [pɛnɪ'tɛnʃərɪ] (US) n carcere m

penknife ['pɛnnaɪf] n temperino

pen name n pseudonimo

penniless ['pɛnɪlɪs] adj senza un soldo

penny ['pɛnɪ] (pl **pennies** or **pence** (BRIT)) n penny m; (US) centesimo

penpal ['pɛnpæl] n corrispondente m/f

pension ['pɛnʃən] n pensione f; **~er** (BRIT) n pensionato/a

pensive ['pɛnsɪv] adj pensoso(a)

penthouse ['pɛnthaus] n appartamento (di lusso) nell'attico

pent-up ['pɛntʌp] adj (feelings) represso(a)

people ['piːpl] npl gente f; persone fpl; (citizens) popolo ♦ n (nation, race) popolo; 4/several ~ came 4/parecchie persone sono venute; **~ say that …** si dice che ….

pep [pɛp] (inf): **~ up** vt vivacizzare; (food) rendere più gustoso(a)

pepper ['pɛpə*] n pepe m; (vegetable) peperone m ♦ vt (fig): **to ~ with** spruzzare di; **~mint** n (sweet) pasticca di menta

peptalk ['pɛptɔːk] (inf) n discorso di incoraggiamento

per [pɜː*] prep per; a; **~ hour** all'ora; **~ kilo** etc il chilo etc; **~ day** al giorno; **~ annum** adv all'anno; **~ capita** adj, adv pro capite inv

perceive [pə'siːv] vt percepire; (notice) accorgersi di

per cent [pə'sɛnt] adv per cento

percentage [pə'sɛntɪdʒ] n percentuale f

perception [pə'sɛpʃən] n percezione f; sensibilità; perspicacia

perceptive [pə'sɛptɪv] adj percettivo(a); perspicace

perch [pɜːtʃ] n (fish) pesce m persico; (for bird) sostegno, ramo ♦ vi appollaiarsi

percolator ['pɜːkəleɪtə*] n (also: coffee ~) caffettiera a pressione; caffettiera elettrica

percussion [pə'kʌʃən] n percussione f; (MUS) strumenti mpl a percussione

perennial [pə'rɛnɪəl] adj perenne

perfect [adj, n 'pɜːfɪkt, vb pə'fɛkt] adj perfetto(a) ♦ n (also: ~ tense) perfetto, passato prossimo ♦ vt perfezionare; mettere a punto; **~ly** adv perfettamente, alla perfezione

perforate ['pɜːfəreɪt] vt perforare; **perforation** [-'reɪʃən] n perforazione f

perform [pə'fɔːm] vt (carry out) eseguire, fare; (symphony etc) suonare; (play, ballet) dare; (opera) fare ♦ vi suonare; recitare; **~ance** n esecuzione f; (at theatre etc) rappresentazione f, spettacolo, f; (of an artist) interpretazione f; (of player etc) performance f; (of car, engine) prestazione f; **~er** n artista m/f

perfume ['pɜːfjuːm] n profumo

perhaps [pə'hæps] adv forse

peril ['pɛrɪl] n pericolo

perimeter [pə'rɪmɪtə*] n perimetro

period ['pɪərɪəd] n periodo; (HISTORY) epoca; (SCOL) lezione f; (full stop) punto; (MED) mestruazioni fpl ♦ adj (costume, furniture) d'epoca; **~ic(al)** [-'ɔdɪk(l)] adj periodico(a); **~ical** [-'ɔdɪkl] n periodico

peripheral [pə'rɪfərəl] adj periferico(a) ♦ n (COMPUT) unità f inv periferica

perish ['pɛrɪʃ] vi perire, morire; (decay) deteriorarsi; **~able** adj deperibile

perjury ['pɜːdʒərɪ] n spergiuro

perk [pɜːk] (inf) n vantaggio; **~ up** vi (cheer up) rianimarsi

perm [pɜːm] n (for hair) permanente f

permanent ['pɜːmənənt] adj permanente

permeate ['pɜːmɪeɪt] vi penetrare ♦ vt permeare

permissible [pə'mɪsɪbl] adj permissibile, ammissibile

permission [pə'mɪʃən] n permesso

permissive [pə'mɪsɪv] adj permissivo(a)

permit [n 'pɜːmɪt, vb pə'mɪt] n permesso ♦ vt permettere; **to ~ sb to do** permettere a qn di fare

perpendicular [pɜːpən'dɪkjulə*] adj perpendicolare ♦ n perpendicolare f

perplex [pə'plɛks] vt lasciare perplesso(a)

persecute ['pɜːsɪkjuːt] vt perseguitare

persevere [pɜːsɪ'vɪə*] vi perseverare

Persian ['pɜːʃən] adj persiano(a) ♦ n (LING) persiano; **the (~) Gulf** n il Golfo Persico

persist [pə'sɪst] vi: **to ~ (in doing)** persistere (nel fare); ostinarsi (a fare); **~ent** adj persistente; ostinato(a)

person ['pɜːsn] n persona; **in ~** di or in

persona, personalmente; **~al** adj personale; individuale; **~al assistant** n segretaria personale; **~al column** n ≈ messaggi mpl personali; **~al computer** n personal computer m inv; **~ality** [-'næliti] n personalità f inv; **~ally** adv personalmente; **to take sth ~ally** prendere qc come una critica personale; **~al organizer** n (Filofax ®) Fulltime ®; (electronic) agenda elettronica; **~al stereo** n Walkman ® m inv

personnel [pəːsə'nɛl] n personale m

perspective [pə'spɛktɪv] n prospettiva

Perspex ® ['pəːspɛks] (BRIT) n tipo di resina termoplastica

perspiration [pəːspɪ'reɪʃən] n traspirazione f, sudore m

persuade [pə'sweɪd] vt: **to ~ sb to do sth** persuadere qn a fare qc

perturb [pə'təːb] vt turbare

pervert [n 'pəːvəːt, vb pə'vəːt] n pervertito/a ♦ vt pervertire

pessimism ['pɛsɪmɪzəm] n pessimismo

pessimist ['pɛsɪmɪst] n pessimista m/f; **~ic** [-'mɪstɪk] adj pessimistico(a)

pest [pɛst] n animale m (or insetto) pestifero; (fig) peste f

pester ['pɛstə*] vt tormentare, molestare

pet [pɛt] n animale m domestico ♦ cpd favorito(a) ♦ vt accarezzare; **teacher's ~** favorito/a del maestro

petal ['pɛtl] n petalo

peter ['piːtə*]: **to ~ out** vi esaurirsi; estinguersi

petite [pə'tiːt] adj piccolo(a) e aggraziato(a)

petition [pə'tɪʃən] n petizione f

petrified ['pɛtrɪfaɪd] adj (fig) morto(a) di paura

petrol ['pɛtrəl] (BRIT) n benzina; **two/four-star ~** ≈ benzina normale/super; **~ can** n tanica per benzina

petroleum [pə'trəuliəm] n petrolio

petrol: **~ pump** (BRIT) n (in car, at garage) pompa di benzina; **~ station** (BRIT) n stazione f di rifornimento; **~ tank** (BRIT) n serbatoio della benzina

petticoat ['pɛtɪkəut] n sottana

petty ['pɛtɪ] adj (mean) meschino(a); (unimportant) insignificante; **~ cash** n piccola cassa; **~ officer** n sottufficiale m di marina

petulant ['pɛtjulənt] adj irritabile

pew [pjuː] n panca (di chiesa)

pewter ['pjuːtə*] n peltro

phallic ['fælɪk] adj fallico(a)

phantom ['fæntəm] n fantasma m

pharmaceutical [faːmə'sjuːtɪkl] adj farmaceutico(a)

pharmacy ['faːməsɪ] n farmacia

phase [feɪz] n fase f, periodo ♦ vt: **to ~ sth in/out** introdurre/eliminare qc

progressivamente

Ph.D. n abbr = Doctor of Philosophy

pheasant ['fɛznt] n fagiano

phenomena [fə'nɔmɪnə] npl of **phenomenon**

phenomenon [fə'nɔmɪnən] (pl **phenomena**) n fenomeno

Philippines ['fɪlɪpiːnz] npl: **the ~** le Filippine

philosophical [fɪlə'sɔfɪkl] adj filosofico(a)

philosophy [fɪ'lɔsəfɪ] n filosofia

phobia ['fəubjə] n fobia

phone [fəun] n telefono ♦ vt telefonare; **to be on the ~** avere il telefono; (be calling) essere al telefono; **~ back** vt, vi richiamare; **~ up** vt telefonare a ♦ vi telefonare; **~ book** n guida del telefono, elenco telefonico; **~ booth** n = **~ box;** **~ box** n cabina telefonica; **~ call** n telefonata; **~card** n scheda telefonica; **~-in** n (BRIT: RADIO, TV) trasmissione f a filo diretto con gli ascoltatori

phonetics [fə'nɛtɪks] n fonetica

phoney ['fəunɪ] adj falso(a), fasullo(a)

phosphorus ['fɔsfərəs] n fosforo

photo ['fəutəu] n foto f inv

photo... ['fəutəu] prefix: **~copier** n fotocopiatrice f; **~copy** n fotocopia ♦ vt fotocopiare; **~graph** n fotografia ♦ vt fotografare; **~grapher** [fə'tɔgrəfə*] n fotografo; **~graphy** [fə'tɔgrəfɪ] n fotografia

phrase [freɪz] n espressione f; (LING) locuzione f; (MUS) frase f ♦ vt esprimere; **~ book** n vocabolarietto

physical ['fɪzɪkl] adj fisico(a); **~ education** n educazione f fisica; **~ly** adv fisicamente

physician [fɪ'zɪʃən] n medico

physicist ['fɪzɪsɪst] n fisico

physics ['fɪzɪks] n fisica

physiology [fɪzɪ'ɔlədʒɪ] n fisiologia

physique [fɪ'ziːk] n fisico; costituzione f

pianist ['piːənɪst] n pianista m/f

piano [pɪ'ænəu] n pianoforte m

piccolo ['pɪkələu] n ottavino

pick [pɪk] n (tool: also: ~-axe) piccone m ♦ vt scegliere; (gather) cogliere; (remove) togliere; (lock) far scattare; **take your ~** scegliere; **the ~ of** il fior fiore di; **to ~ one's nose** mettersi le dita nel naso; **to ~ one's teeth** pulirsi i denti con lo stuzzicadenti; **to ~ a quarrel** attaccar briga; **~ at** vt fus: **to ~ at one's food** piluccare; **~ on** vt fus (person) avercela con; **~ out** vt scegliere; (distinguish) distinguere; **~ up** vi (improve) migliorarsi ♦ vt raccogliere; (POLICE, RADIO) prendere; (collect) passare a prendere; (AUT: give lift to) far salire; (person: for sexual encounter) rimorchiare; (learn) imparare; **to ~ up speed** acquistare velocità; **to ~ o.s. up** rialzarsi

picket ['pɪkɪt] n (in strike) scioperante m/f che fa parte di un picchetto; picchetto ♦ vt picchettare

pickle ['pɪkl] n (also: ~s: as condiment) sottaceti mpl; (fig: mess) pasticcio ♦ vt mettere sottaceto; mettere in salamoia

pickpocket ['pɪkpɔkɪt] n borsaiolo

pickup ['pɪkʌp] n (small truck) camioncino

picnic ['pɪknɪk] n picnic m inv

picture ['pɪktʃə*] n quadro; (painting) pittura; (photograph) foto(grafia); (drawing) disegno; (film) film m inv ♦ vt raffigurarsi; ~s (BRIT) npl (cinema): **the ~s** il cinema; ~ **book** n libro illustrato

picturesque [pɪktʃə'rɛsk] adj pittoresco(a)

pie [paɪ] n torta; (of meat) pasticcio

piece [pi:s] n pezzo; (of land) appezzamento; (item): **a ~ of furniture/advice** un mobile/ consiglio ♦ vt: **to ~ together** mettere insieme; **to take to ~s** smontare; **~meal** adv pezzo a pezzo, a spizzico; **~work** n (lavoro a) cottimo

pie chart n grafico a torta

pier [pɪə*] n molo; (of bridge etc) pila

pierce [pɪəs] vt forare; (with arrow etc) trafiggere

piercing ['pɪəsɪŋ] adj (cry) acuto(a); (eyes) penetrante; (wind) pungente

pig [pɪg] n maiale m, porco

pigeon ['pɪdʒən] n piccione m; **~hole** n casella

piggy bank ['pɪgɪ-] n salvadanaio

pigheaded ['pɪg'hɛdɪd] adj caparbio(a), cocciuto(a)

piglet ['pɪglɪt] n porcellino

pigskin ['pɪgskɪn] n cinghiale m

pigsty ['pɪgstaɪ] n porcile m

pigtail ['pɪgteɪl] n treccina

pike [paɪk] n (fish) luccio

pilchard ['pɪltʃəd] n specie di sardina

pile [paɪl] n (pillar, of books) pila; (heap) mucchio; (of carpet) pelo ♦ vt (also: ~ up) ammucchiare ♦ vi (also: ~ up) ammucchiarsi; **to ~ into** (car) stiparsi or ammucchiarsi in

piles [paɪlz] npl emorroidi fpl

pile-up ['paɪlʌp] n (AUT) tamponamento a catena

pilfering ['pɪlfərɪŋ] n rubacchiare m

pilgrim ['pɪlgrɪm] n pellegrino/a; **~age** n pellegrinaggio

pill [pɪl] n pillola; **the ~** la pillola

pillage ['pɪlɪdʒ] vt saccheggiare

pillar ['pɪlə*] n colonna; ~ **box** (BRIT) n cassetta postale

pillion ['pɪljən] n: **to ride ~** (on motor cycle) viaggiare dietro

pillow ['pɪləu] n guanciale m; **~case** n federa

pilot ['paɪlət] n pilota m/f ♦ cpd (scheme etc) pilota inv ♦ vt pilotare; ~ **light** n fiamma pilota

pimp [pɪmp] n mezzano

pimple ['pɪmpl] n foruncolo

pin [pɪn] n spillo; (TECH) perno ♦ vt attaccare con uno spillo; **~s and needles** formicolio; **to ~ sb down** (fig) obbligare qn a pronunziarsi; **to ~ sth on sb** (fig) addossare la colpa di qc a qn

pinafore ['pɪnəfɔ:*] n (also: ~ dress) grembiule m (senza maniche)

pinball ['pɪnbɔ:l] n flipper m inv

pincers ['pɪnsəz] npl pinzette fpl

pinch [pɪntʃ] n pizzicotto, pizzico ♦ vt pizzicare; (inf: steal) grattare; **at a ~** in caso di bisogno

pincushion ['pɪnkuʃən] n puntaspilli m inv

pine [paɪn] n (also: ~ tree) pino ♦ vi: **to ~ for** struggersi dal desiderio di; ~ **away** vi languire

pineapple ['paɪnæpl] n ananas m inv

ping [pɪŋ] n (noise) tintinnio; **~-pong** ® n ping-pong ® m

pink [pɪŋk] adj rosa inv ♦ n (colour) rosa m inv; (BOT) garofano

PIN (number) [pɪn-] n abbr codice m segreto

pinpoint ['pɪnpɔɪnt] vt indicare con precisione

pint [paɪnt] n pinta (BRIT = 0.57l; US = 0.47l); (BRIT: inf) ≈ birra da mezzo

pioneer [paɪə'nɪə*] n pioniere/a

pious ['paɪəs] adj pio(a)

pip [pɪp] n (seed) seme m; (BRIT: time signal on radio) segnale m orario

pipe [paɪp] n tubo; (for smoking) pipa ♦ vt portare per mezzo di tubazione; **~s** npl (also: bag~s) cornamusa (scozzese); ~ **cleaner** n scovolino; ~ **dream** n vana speranza; **~line** n conduttura; (for oil) oleodotto; **~r** n piffero; suonatore/trice di cornamusa

piping ['paɪpɪŋ] adv: ~ **hot** caldo bollente

pique [pi:k] n picca

pirate ['paɪərət] n pirata m ♦ vt riprodurre abusivamente

Pisces ['paɪsi:z] n Pesci mpl

piss [pɪs] (inf) vi pisciare; **~ed** (inf) adj (drunk) ubriaco(a) fradicio(a)

pistol ['pɪstl] n pistola

piston ['pɪstən] n pistone m

pit [pɪt] n buca, fossa; (also: coal ~) miniera; (quarry) cava ♦ vt: **to ~ sb against sb** opporre qn a qn; **~s** npl (AUT) box m

pitch [pɪtʃ] n (BRIT: SPORT) campo; (MUS) tono; (tar) pece f; (fig) grado, punto ♦ vt (throw) lanciare ♦ vi (fall) cascare; **to ~ a tent** piantare una tenda; **~ed battle** n battaglia campale

pitfall ['pɪtfɔ:l] n trappola

pith [pɪθ] n (of plant) midollo; (of orange) parte f interna della scorza; (fig) essenza, succo; vigore m

pithy ['pɪθɪ] adj conciso(a); vigoroso(a)

pitiful ['pɪtɪful] adj (touching) pietoso(a)
pitiless ['pɪtɪlɪs] adj spietato(a)
pittance ['pɪtns] n miseria, magro salario
pity ['pɪtɪ] n pietà ♦ vt aver pietà di; **what a ~**! che peccato!
pivot ['pɪvət] n perno
pizza ['pi:tsə] n pizza
placard ['plækɑ:d] n affisso
placate [plə'keɪt] vt placare, calmare
place [pleɪs] n posto, luogo; (proper position, rank, seat) posto; (house) casa, alloggio; (home): **at/to his ~** a casa sua ♦ vt (object) posare, mettere; (identify) riconoscere; individuare; **to take ~** aver luogo; succedere; **to change ~s with sb** scambiare il posto con qn; **out of ~** (not suitable) inopportuno(a); **in the first ~** in primo luogo; **to ~ an order** dare un'ordinazione; **to be ~d** (in race, exam) classificarsi
placid ['plæsɪd] adj placido(a), calmo(a)
plagiarism ['pleɪdʒjarɪzəm] n plagio
plague [pleɪg] n peste f ♦ vt tormentare
plaice [pleɪs] n inv pianuzza
plaid [plæd] n plaid m inv
plain [pleɪn] adj (clear) chiaro(a), palese; (simple) semplice; (frank) franco(a), aperto(a); (not handsome) bruttino(a); (without seasoning etc) scondito(a); naturale; (in one colour) tinta unita inv ♦ adv francamente, chiaramente ♦ n pianura; **~ chocolate** n cioccolato fondente; **~ clothes** npl: **in ~ clothes** (police) in borghese; **~ly** adv chiaramente; (frankly) francamente
plaintiff ['pleɪntɪf] n attore/trice
plaintive ['pleɪntɪv] adj (cry, voice) dolente, lamentoso(a)
plait [plæt] n treccia
plan [plæn] n pianta; (scheme) progetto, piano ♦ vt (think in advance) progettare; (prepare) organizzare ♦ vi far piani or progetti; **to ~ to do** progettare di fare
plane [pleɪn] n (AVIAT) aereo; (tree) platano; (tool) pialla; (ART, MATH etc) piano ♦ adj piano(a), piatto(a) ♦ vt (with tool) piallare
planet ['plænɪt] n pianeta m
plank [plæŋk] n tavola, asse f
planner ['plænə*] n pianificatore/trice
planning ['plænɪŋ] n progettazione f; **family ~** pianificazione f delle nascite; **~ permission** n permesso di costruzione
plant [plɑ:nt] n pianta; (machinery) impianto; (factory) fabbrica ♦ vt piantare; (bomb) mettere
plantation [plæn'teɪʃən] n piantagione f
plaque [plæk] n placca
plaster ['plɑ:stə*] n intonaco; (also: ~ of Paris) gesso; (BRIT: also: sticking ~) cerotto ♦ vt intonacare; ingessare; (cover): **to ~ with**

coprire di; **~ed** (inf) adj ubriaco(a) fradicio(a)
plastic ['plæstɪk] n plastica ♦ adj (made of ~) di or in plastica; **~ bag** n sacchetto di plastica
Plasticine ® ['plæstɪsi:n] n plastilina ®
plastic surgery n chirurgia plastica
plate [pleɪt] n (dish) piatto; (in book) tavola; (dental ~) dentiera; **gold/silver ~** vasellame m d'oro/d'argento
plateau ['plætəu] (pl ~s or ~x) n altipiano
plateaux ['plætəuz] npl of **plateau**
plate glass n vetro piano
platform ['plætfɔ:m] n (stage, at meeting) palco; (RAIL) marciapiede m; (BRIT: of bus) piattaforma
platinum ['plætɪnəm] n platino
platitude ['plætɪtju:d] n luogo comune
platoon [plə'tu:n] n plotone m
platter ['plætə*] n piatto
plausible ['plɔ:zɪbl] adj plausibile, credibile; (person) convincente
play [pleɪ] n gioco; (THEATRE) commedia ♦ vt (game) giocare a; (team, opponent) giocare contro; (instrument, piece of music) suonare; (record, tape) ascoltare; (role, part) interpretare ♦ vi giocare; suonare; recitare; **to ~ safe** giocare sul sicuro; **~ down** vt minimizzare; **~ up** vi (cause trouble) fare i capricci; **~boy** n playboy m inv; **~er** n giocatore/trice; (THEATRE) attore/trice; (MUS) musicista m/f; **~ful** adj giocoso(a); **~ground** n (in school) cortile m per la ricreazione; (in park) parco m giochi inv; **~group** n giardino d'infanzia; **~ing card** n carta da gioco; **~ing field** n campo sportivo; **~mate** n compagno/a di gioco; **~-off** n (SPORT) bella; **~pen** n box m inv; **~thing** n giocattolo; **~time** n (SCOL) ricreazione f; **~wright** n drammaturgo/a
plc abbr (= public limited company) società per azioni a responsabilità limitata quotata in borsa
plea [pli:] n (request) preghiera, domanda; (LAW) (argomento di) difesa; **~ bargaining** n (LAW) patteggiamento (della pena)
plead [pli:d] vt patrocinare; (give as excuse) addurre a pretesto ♦ vi (LAW) perorare la causa; (beg): **to ~ with sb** implorare qn
pleasant ['plɛznt] adj piacevole, gradevole; **~ries** npl (polite remarks): **to exchange ~ries** scambiarsi i convenevoli
please [pli:z] excl per piacere!, per favore!; (acceptance): **yes, ~** sì, grazie ♦ vt piacere a ♦ vi piacere; (think fit): **do as you ~** faccia come le pare; **~ yourself!** come ti (or le) pare!; **~d** adj: **~d (with)** contento(a) (di); **~d to meet you!** piacere!; **pleasing** adj piacevole, che fa piacere
pleasure ['plɛʒə*] n piacere m; **"it's a ~"** "prego"

pleat [pli:t] n piega

pledge [plɛdʒ] n pegno; (promise) promessa ♦ vt impegnare; promettere

plentiful ['plɛntɪful] adj abbondante, copioso(a)

plenty ['plɛntɪ] n: ~ **of** tanto(a), molto(a); un'abbondanza di

pleurisy ['pluǝrɪsɪ] n pleurite f

pliable ['plaɪǝbl] adj flessibile; (fig: person) malleabile

pliant [plaɪǝnt] adj = **pliable**

pliers ['plaɪǝz] npl pinza

plight [plaɪt] n situazione f critica

plimsolls ['plɪmsǝlz] (BRIT) npl scarpe fpl da tennis

plinth [plɪnθ] n plinto; piedistallo

plod [plɔd] vi camminare a stento; (fig) sgobbare

plonk [plɔŋk] (inf) n (BRIT: wine) vino da poco ♦ vt: **to ~ sth down** buttare giù qc bruscamente

plot [plɔt] n congiura, cospirazione f; (of story, play) trama; (of land) lotto ♦ vt (mark out) fare la pianta di; rilevare; (: diagram etc) tracciare; (conspire) congiurare, cospirare ♦ vi congiurare

plough [plau] (US **plow**) n aratro ♦ vt (earth) arare; **to ~ money into** (company etc) investire denaro in; ~ **through** vt fus (snow etc) procedere a fatica in; ~**man's lunch** (BRIT) n pasto a base di pane, formaggio e birra

ploy [plɔɪ] n stratagemma m

pluck [plʌk] vt (fruit) cogliere; (musical instrument) pizzicare; (bird) spennare; (hairs) togliere ♦ n coraggio, fegato; **to ~ up courage** farsi coraggio

plug [plʌg] n tappo; (ELEC) spina; (AUT: also: **spark(ing) ~**) candela ♦ vt (hole) tappare; (inf: advertise) spingere; ~ **in** vt (ELEC) attaccare a una presa

plum [plʌm] n (fruit) susina

plumb [plʌm] vt: **to ~ the depths** (fig) toccare il fondo

plumber ['plʌmǝ*] n idraulico

plumbing ['plʌmɪŋ] n (trade) lavoro di idraulico; (piping) tubature fpl

plummet ['plʌmɪt] vi: **to ~ (down)** cadere a piombo

plump [plʌmp] adj grassoccio(a) ♦ vi: **to ~ for** (inf: choose) decidersi per; ~ **up** vt (cushion etc) sprimacciare

plunder ['plʌndǝ*] n saccheggio ♦ vt saccheggiare

plunge [plʌndʒ] n tuffo; (fig) caduta ♦ vt immergere ♦ vi (fall) cadere, precipitare; (dive) tuffarsi; **to take the ~** saltare il fosso; **plunging** adj (neckline) profondo(a)

pluperfect [plu:'pǝ:fɪkt] n piucchepperfetto

plural ['pluǝrl] adj plurale ♦ n plurale m

plus [plʌs] n (also: ~ **sign**) segno più ♦ prep più; **ten/twenty ~** più di dieci/venti

plush [plʌʃ] adj lussuoso(a)

ply [plaɪ] vt (a trade) esercitare ♦ vi (ship) fare il servizio ♦ n (of wool, rope) capo; **to ~ sb with drink** dare di bere continuamente a qn; ~**wood** n legno compensato

P.M. n abbr = **prime minister**

p.m. adv abbr (= post meridiem) del pomeriggio

pneumatic drill [nju:'mætɪk-] n martello pneumatico

pneumonia [nju:'mǝunɪǝ] n polmonite f

poach [pǝutʃ] vt (cook: egg) affogare; (: fish) cuocere in bianco; (steal) cacciare (or pescare) di frodo ♦ vi fare il bracconiere; ~**er** n bracconiere m

P.O. Box n abbr = **Post Office Box**

pocket ['pɔkɪt] n tasca ♦ vt intascare; **to be out of ~** (BRIT) rimetterci; ~**book** (US) n (wallet) portafoglio; ~ **knife** n temperino; ~ **money** n paghetta, settimana

pod [pɔd] n guscio

podgy ['pɔdʒɪ] adj grassoccio(a)

podiatrist [pɔ'di:ǝtrɪst] (US) n callista m/f, pedicure m/f

poem ['pǝuɪm] n poesia

poet ['pǝuɪt] n poeta/essa; ~**ic** [-'ɛtɪk] adj poetico(a); ~**ry** n poesia

poignant ['pɔɪnjǝnt] adj struggente

point [pɔɪnt] n (gen) punto; (tip: of needle etc) punta; (in time) punto, momento; (SCOL) voto; (main idea, important part) nocciolo; (ELEC) presa (di corrente); (also: decimal ~): **2 ~ 3 (2.3)** 2 virgola 3 (2,3) ♦ vt (show) indicare; (gun etc) **to ~ sth at** puntare qc contro ♦ vi: **to ~ at** mostrare a dito; ~**s** npl (AUT) puntine fpl; (RAIL) scambio; **to be on the ~ of doing sth** essere sul punto di or stare per fare qc; **to make a ~** fare un'osservazione; **to get/miss the ~** capire/non capire; **to come to the ~** venire al fatto; **there's no ~ (in doing)** è inutile (fare); ~ **out** vt far notare; ~ **to** vt fus indicare; (fig) dimostrare; ~**blank** adv (also: **at ~-blank range**) a bruciapelo; (fig) categoricamente; ~**ed** adj (shape) aguzzo(a), appuntito(a); (remark) specifico(a); ~**edly** adv in maniera inequivocabile; ~**er** n (needle) lancetta; (fig) indicazione f, consiglio; ~**less** adj inutile, vano(a); ~ **of view** n punto di vista

poise [pɔɪz] n (composure) portamento; ~**d** adj: **to be ~d to do** tenersi pronto(a) a fare

poison ['pɔɪzn] n veleno ♦ vt avvelenare; ~**ing** n avvelenamento; ~**ous** adj velenoso(a)

poke [pǝuk] vt (fire) attizzare; (jab with finger, stick etc) punzecchiare; (put) **to ~ sth in(to)** spingere qc dentro; ~ **about** vi frugare

poker ['pǝukǝ*] n attizzatoio; (CARDS) poker m

poky ['pəʊkɪ] adj piccolo(a) e stretto(a)
Poland ['pəʊlənd] n Polonia
polar ['pəʊlə*] adj polare; **~ bear** n orso bianco
Pole [pəʊl] n polacco/a
pole [pəʊl] n (of wood) palo; (ELEC, GEO) polo; **~ bean** (US) n (runner bean) fagiolino; **~ vault** n salto con l'asta
police [pə'liːs] n polizia ♦ vt mantenere l'ordine in; **~ car** n macchina della polizia; **~man** (irreg) n poliziotto, agente m di polizia; **~ station** n posto di polizia; **~woman** (irreg) n donna f poliziotto inv
policy ['pɒlɪsɪ] n politica; (also: insurance ~) polizza (d'assicurazione)
polio ['pəʊlɪəʊ] n polio f
Polish ['pəʊlɪʃ] adj polacco(a) ♦ n (LING) polacco
polish ['pɒlɪʃ] n (for shoes) lucido; (for floor) cera; (for nails) smalto; (shine) lucentezza, lustro; (fig: refinement) raffinatezza ♦ vt lucidare; (fig: improve) raffinare; **~ off** vt (food) mangiarsi; **~ed** adj (fig) raffinato(a)
polite [pə'laɪt] adj cortese; **~ness** n cortesia
political [pə'lɪtɪkl] adj politico(a); **~ly** adv politicamente; **~ly correct** politicamente corretto(a)
politician [pɒlɪ'tɪʃən] n politico
politics ['pɒlɪtɪks] n politica ♦ npl (views, policies) idee fpl politiche
poll [pəʊl] n scrutinio; (votes cast) voti mpl; (also: opinion ~) sondaggio (d'opinioni) ♦ vt ottenere
pollen ['pɒlən] n polline m
polling day ['pəʊlɪŋ-] (BRIT) n giorno delle elezioni
polling station ['pəʊlɪŋ-] (BRIT) n sezione f elettorale
pollute [pə'luːt] vt inquinare
pollution [pə'luːʃən] n inquinamento
polo ['pəʊləʊ] n polo; **~-necked** adj a collo alto risvoltato; **~ shirt** n polo f inv
polyester [pɒlɪ'estə*] n poliestere m
polystyrene [pɒlɪ'staɪriːn] n polistirolo
polytechnic [pɒlɪ'teknɪk] n (college) istituto superiore ad indirizzo tecnologico
polythene ['pɒlɪθiːn] n politene m; **~ bag** n sacco di plastica
pomegranate ['pɒmɪɡrænɪt] n melagrana
pomp [pɒmp] n pompa, fasto
pompom ['pɒmpɒm] n pompon m inv
pompon ['pɒmpɒn] n = pompom
pompous ['pɒmpəs] adj pomposo(a)
pond [pɒnd] n pozza; stagno
ponder ['pɒndə*] vt ponderare, riflettere su; **~ous** adj ponderoso(a), pesante
pong [pɒŋ] (BRIT: inf) n puzzo
pony ['pəʊnɪ] n pony m inv; **~tail** n coda di cavallo; **~ trekking** (BRIT) n escursione f a

cavallo
poodle ['puːdl] n barboncino, barbone m
pool [puːl] n (puddle) pozza; (pond) stagno; (also: swimming ~) piscina; (fig: of light) cerchio; (billiards) specie di biliardo a buca ♦ vt mettere in comune; **~s** npl (football ~s) ≈ totocalcio; **typing ~** servizio comune di dattilografia
poor [pʊə*] adj povero(a); (mediocre) mediocre, cattivo(a) ♦ npl: **the ~** i poveri; **~ in** povero(a) di; **~ly** adv poveramente; male ♦ adj indisposto(a), malato(a)
pop [pɒp] n (noise) schiocco; (MUS) musica pop; (drink) bibita gasata; (US: inf: father) babbo ♦ vt (put) mettere (in fretta) ♦ vi scoppiare; (cork) schioccare; **~ in** vi passare; **~ out** vi fare un salto fuori; **~ up** vi apparire, sorgere; **~corn** n pop-corn m
pope [pəʊp] n papa m
poplar ['pɒplə*] n pioppo
popper ['pɒpə*] n bottone m a pressione
poppy ['pɒpɪ] n papavero
Popsicle ® ['pɒpsɪkl] (US) n (ice lolly) ghiacciolo
populace ['pɒpjʊlɪs] n popolino
popular ['pɒpjʊlə*] adj popolare; (fashionable) in voga; **~ity** [-'lærɪtɪ] n popolarità
population [pɒpjʊ'leɪʃən] n popolazione f
porcelain ['pɔːslɪn] n porcellana
porch [pɔːtʃ] n veranda
porcupine ['pɔːkjupaɪn] n porcospino
pore [pɔː*] n poro ♦ vi: to **~ over** essere immerso(a) in
pork [pɔːk] n carne f di maiale
pornographic [pɔːnə'ɡræfɪk] adj pornografico(a)
pornography [pɔː'nɒɡrəfɪ] n pornografia
porpoise ['pɔːpəs] n focena
porridge ['pɒrɪdʒ] n porridge m
port [pɔːt] n (gen, wine) porto; (NAUT: left side) babordo; **~ of call** (porto di) scalo
portable ['pɔːtəbl] adj portatile
porter ['pɔːtə*] n (for luggage) facchino, portabagagli m inv; (doorkeeper) portiere m, portinaio
portfolio [pɔːt'fəʊlɪəʊ] n (case) cartella; (POL, FINANCE) portafoglio; (of artist) raccolta dei propri lavori
porthole ['pɔːthəʊl] n oblò m inv
portion ['pɔːʃən] n porzione f
portrait ['pɔːtreɪt] n ritratto
portray [pɔː'treɪ] vt fare il ritratto di; (character on stage) rappresentare; (in writing) ritrarre
Portugal ['pɔːtjʊɡl] n Portogallo
Portuguese [pɔːtjʊ'ɡiːz] adj portoghese ♦ n inv portoghese m/f; (LING) portoghese m
pose [pəʊz] n posa ♦ vi posare; (pretend): **to**

~ **as** atteggiarsi a, posare a ♦ vt porre
posh [pɔʃ] (inf) adj elegante; (family) per
bene
position [pə'zɪʃən] n posizione f; (job) posto
♦ vt sistemare
positive ['pɔzɪtɪv] adj positivo(a); (certain)
sicuro(a), certo(a); (definite) preciso(a),
definitivo(a)
posse ['pɔsɪ] (US) n drappello
possess [pə'zɛs] vt possedere; **~ion**
[pə'zɛʃən] n possesso; **~ions** npl (belongings)
beni mpl; **~ive** adj possessivo(a)
possibility [pɔsɪ'bɪlɪtɪ] n possibilità f inv
possible ['pɔsɪbl] adj possibile; **as big as ~** il
più grande possibile
possibly ['pɔsɪblɪ] adv (perhaps) forse; **if you**
~ can se le è possibile; **I cannot ~ come**
proprio non posso venire
post [pəust] n (BRIT) posta; (: collection)
levata; (job, situation) posto; (MIL) postazione
f; (pole) palo ♦ vt (BRIT: send by post)
impostare; (: appoint): **to ~ to** assegnare a;
~age n affrancatura; **~age stamp** n
francobollo; **~al order** n vaglia m inv
postale; **~box** (BRIT) n cassetta postale;
~card n cartolina; **~ code** (BRIT) n codice m
(di avviamento) postale
poster ['pəustə*] n manifesto, affisso
poste restante [pəust'rɛstɑ:nt] (BRIT) n
fermo posta m
postgraduate ['pəust'grædjuət] n laureato/a
che continua gli studi
posthumous ['pɔstjuməs] adj postumo(a)
postman ['pəustmən] (irreg) n postino
postmark ['pəustmɑ:k] n bollo or timbro
postale
post-mortem [pəust'mɔːtəm] n autopsia
post office n (building) ufficio postale;
(organization): **the Post Office** ≈ le Poste e
Telecomunicazioni; **Post Office Box** n
casella postale
postpone [pəs'pəun] vt rinviare
postscript ['pəustskrɪpt] n poscritto
posture ['pɔstʃə*] n portamento; (pose) posa,
atteggiamento
postwar ['pəust'wɔː*] adj del dopoguerra
posy ['pəuzɪ] n mazzetto di fiori
pot [pɔt] n (for cooking) pentola, casseruola;
(tea~) teiera; (coffee~) caffettiera; (for plants,
jam) vaso; (inf: marijuana) erba ♦ vt (plant)
piantare in vaso; **a ~ of tea for two** tè per
due; **to go to ~** (inf: work, performance)
andare in malora
potato [pə'teɪtəu] (pl **~es**) n patata; **~ peeler**
n sbucciapatate m inv
potent ['pəutnt] adj potente, forte
potential [pə'tɛnʃl] adj potenziale ♦ n
possibilità fpl
pothole ['pɔthəul] n (in road) buca; (BRIT:

underground) caverna; **potholing** (BRIT) n:
to go potholing fare speleologia
potluck [pɔt'lʌk] n: **to take ~** tentare la sorte
potted ['pɔtɪd] adj (food) in conserva; (plant)
in vaso; (account etc) condensato(a)
potter ['pɔtə*] n vasaio ♦ vi: **to ~ around,**
~ about (BRIT) lavoracchiare; **~y** n ceramiche
fpl; (factory) fabbrica di ceramiche
potty ['pɔtɪ] adj (inf: mad) tocco(a) ♦ n
(child's) vasino
pouch [pautʃ] n borsa; (ZOOL) marsupio
poultry ['pəultrɪ] n pollame m
pounce [pauns] vi: **to ~ (on)** piombare (su)
pound [paund] n (weight) libbra; (money)
(lira) sterlina ♦ vt (beat) battere; (crush)
pestare, polverizzare ♦ vi (beat) battere,
martellare; **~ sterling** n sterlina (inglese)
pour [pɔː*] vt versare ♦ vi riversarsi; (rain)
piovere a dirotto; **~ away** vt vuotare; **~ in** vi
affluire in gran quantità; **~ off** vt vuotare;
~ out vi (people) uscire a fiumi ♦ vt vuotare;
versare; (fig) sfogare; **~ing** adj: **~ing rain**
pioggia torrenziale
pout [paut] vi sporgere le labbra; fare il
broncio
poverty ['pɔvətɪ] n povertà, miseria; **~-
stricken** adj molto povero(a), misero(a)
powder ['paudə*] n polvere f ♦ vt: **to ~ one's**
face incipriarsi il viso; **~ compact** n
portacipria m inv; **~ed milk** n latte m in
polvere; **~ room** n toilette f inv (per signore)
power ['pauə*] n (strength) potenza, forza;
(ability, POL) potere m; (of party, leader) potere m; (ELEC)
corrente f; **to be in ~** (POL etc) essere al
potere; **~ cut** (BRIT) n interruzione f or
mancanza di corrente; **~ed** adj: **~ed by**
azionato(a) da; **~ failure** n interruzione f
della corrente elettrica; **~ful** adj potente,
forte; **~less** adj impotente; **~less to do**
impossibilitato(a) a fare; **~ point** (BRIT) n
presa di corrente; **~ station** n centrale f
elettrica
p.p. abbr (= per procurationem): **~ J. Smith**
per J. Smith; (= pages) p.p.
PR abbr = public relations
practicable ['præktɪkəbl] adj (scheme)
praticabile
practical ['præktɪkl] adj pratico(a); **~ity**
[-'kælɪtɪ] (no pl) n (of situation etc) lato
pratico; **~ joke** n beffa; **~ly** adv
praticamente
practice ['præktɪs] n pratica; (of profession)
esercizio; (at football etc) allenamento;
(business) gabinetto; cliientela ♦ vt, vi (US) =
practise; in ~ (in reality) in pratica; **out of ~**
fuori esercizio
practise ['præktɪs] (US **practice**) vt (work at:
piano, one's backhand etc) esercitarsi a; (train
for: skiing, running etc) allenarsi a; (a sport,

religion) praticare; (*method*) usare;
(*profession*) esercitare ♦ *vi* esercitarsi; (*train*)
allenarsi; (*lawyer, doctor*) esercitare;
practising *adj* (*Christian etc*) praticante;
(*lawyer*) che esercita la professione
practitioner [præk'tɪʃənə*] *n* professionista
m/f
pragmatic [præg'mætɪk] *adj* pragmatico(a)
prairie ['prɛərɪ] *n* prateria
praise [preɪz] *n* elogio, lode *f* ♦ *vt* elogiare,
lodare; **~worthy** *adj* lodevole
pram [præm] (*BRIT*) *n* carrozzina
prank [præŋk] *n* burla
prawn [prɔ:n] *n* gamberetto
pray [preɪ] *vi* pregare
prayer [prɛə*] *n* preghiera
preach [pri:tʃ] *vt*, *vi* predicare
precarious [prɪ'kɛərɪəs] *adj* precario(a)
precaution [prɪ'kɔ:ʃən] *n* precauzione *f*
precede [prɪ'si:d] *vt* precedere
precedent ['presɪdənt] *n* precedente *m*
precept ['pri:sept] *n* precetto
precinct [prɪ'sɪŋkt] *n* (*US*) circoscrizione *f*;
~s *npl* (*of building*) zona recintata; **pedestrian**
~ (*BRIT*) zona pedonale; **shopping ~** (*BRIT*)
centro commerciale (chiuso al traffico)
precious ['prɛʃəs] *adj* prezioso(a)
precipitate [prɪ'sɪpɪteɪt] *vt* precipitare
precise [prɪ'saɪs] *adj* preciso(a); **~ly** *adv*
precisamente
precocious [prɪ'kəʊʃəs] *adj* precoce
precondition [pri:kən'dɪʃən] *n* condizione *f*
necessaria
predecessor ['pri:dɪsesə*] *n* predecessore/a
predicament [prɪ'dɪkəmənt] *n* situazione *f*
difficile
predict [prɪ'dɪkt] *vt* predire; **~able** *adj*
prevedibile
predominantly [prɪ'dɔmɪnəntlɪ] *adv* in
maggior parte; soprattutto
predominate [prɪ'dɔmɪneɪt] *vi* predominare
pre-empt [pri:'empt] *vt* pregiudicare
preen [pri:n] *vt*: **to ~ itself** (*bird*) lisciarsi le
penne; **to ~ o.s.** agghindarsi
prefab ['pri:fæb] *n* casa prefabbricata
preface ['prɛfəs] *n* prefazione *f*
prefect ['pri:fɛkt] *n* (*BRIT*: *in school*)
studente/essa con funzioni disciplinari;
(*French etc, Admin*) prefetto
prefer [prɪ'fə:*] *vt* preferire; **to ~ doing** or **to**
do preferire fare; **~ably** ['prɛfrəblɪ] *adv*
preferibilmente; **~ence** ['prɛfrəns] *n*
preferenza; **~ential** [prɛfə'rɛnʃəl] *adj*
preferenziale
prefix ['pri:fɪks] *n* prefisso
pregnancy ['prɛgnənsɪ] *n* gravidanza
pregnant ['prɛgnənt] *adj* incinta *f*
prehistoric ['pri:hɪs'tɔrɪk] *adj* preistorico(a)
prejudice ['prɛdʒudɪs] *n* pregiudizio; (*harm*)

torto, danno; **~d** *adj*: **~d (against)** pre-
venuto(a) (contro); **~d (in favour of)** ben
disposto(a) (verso)
preliminary [prɪ'lɪmɪnərɪ] *adj* preliminare
premarital ['pri:'mærɪtl] *adj* prematrimoniale
premature ['prɛmətʃuə*] *adj* prematuro(a)
premenstrual syndrome [pri:-
'menstruəl-] *n* (*MED*) sindrome *f* premestruale
premier ['prɛmɪə*] *adj* primo(a) ♦ *n* (*POL*)
primo ministro
première ['prɛmɪɛə*] *n* prima
premise ['prɛmɪs] *n* premessa; **~s** *npl* (*of*
business, institution) locale *m*; **on the ~s** sul
posto
premium ['pri:mɪəm] *n* premio; **to be at a ~**
essere ricercatissimo; **~ bond** (*BRIT*) *n*
obbligazione *f* a premio
premonition [prɛmə'nɪʃən] *n* premonizione
f
preoccupied [pri:'ɔkjupaɪd] *adj*
preoccupato(a)
prep [prɛp] *n* (*SCOL*: *study*) studio
prepaid [pri:'peɪd] *adj* pagato(a) in anticipo
preparation [prɛpə'reɪʃən] *n* preparazione *f*;
~s *npl* (*for trip, war*) preparativi *mpl*
preparatory [prɪ'pærətərɪ] *adj*
preparatorio(a); **~ school** *n* scuola
elementare privata
prepare [prɪ'pɛə*] *vt* preparare ♦ *vi*: **to ~ for**
prepararsi a; **~d to** pronto(a) a
preposition [prɛpə'zɪʃən] *n* preposizione *f*
preposterous [prɪ'pɔstərəs] *adj* assurdo(a)
prep school *n* = **preparatory school**
prerequisite [pri:'rɛkwɪzɪt] *n* requisito
indispensabile
prescribe [prɪ'skraɪb] *vt* (*MED*) prescrivere
prescription [prɪ'skrɪpʃən] *n* prescrizione *f*;
(*MED*) ricetta
presence ['prɛzns] *n* presenza; **~ of mind**
presenza di spirito
present [*adj, n* 'prɛznt, *vb* prɪ'zɛnt] *adj*
presente; (*wife, residence, job*) attuale ♦ *n*
(*actuality*): **the ~** il presente; (*gift*) regalo ♦ *vt*
presentare; (*give*): **to ~ sb with sth** offrire qc
a qn; **to give sb a ~** fare un regalo a qn; **at ~**
al momento; **~ation** [-'teɪʃən] *n* presentazione *f*; (*ceremony*) consegna ufficiale;
~-day *adj* attuale, d'oggigiorno; **~er** *n*
(*RADIO, TV*) presentatore/trice; **~ly** *adv* (*soon*)
fra poco, presto; (*at present*) al momento
preservative [prɪ'zə:vətɪv] *n* conservante *m*
preserve [prɪ'zə:v] *vt* (*keep safe*) preservare,
proteggere; (*maintain*) conservare; (*food*)
mettere in conserva ♦ *n* (*often pl*: *jam*)
marmellata; (: *fruit*) frutta sciroppata
preside [prɪ'zaɪd] *vi*: **to ~ (over)** presiedere
(a)
president ['prɛzɪdənt] *n* presidente *m*; **~ial**
[-'dɛnʃl] *adj* presidenziale

press [prɛs] n (newspapers etc): **the P~** la stampa; (tool, machine) pressa; (for wine) torchio ♦ vt (push) premere, pigiare; (squeeze) spremere; (: hand) stringere; (clothes: iron) stirare; (pursue) incalzare; (insist): **to ~ sth on sb** far accettare qc da qn ♦ vi premere; accalcare; **we are ~ed for time** ci manca il tempo; **to ~ for sth** insistere per avere qc; **~ on** vi continuare; **~ conference** n conferenza f stampa inv; **~ing** adj urgente; **~ stud** (BRIT) n bottone m a pressione; **~-up** (BRIT) n flessione f sulle braccia

pressure ['prɛʃə*] n pressione f; **to put ~ on sb (to do)** mettere qn sotto pressione (affinché faccia); **~ cooker** n pentola a pressione; **~ gauge** n manometro; **~ group** n gruppo di pressione

prestige [prɛs'tiːʒ] n prestigio

presumably [prɪ'zjuːməblɪ] adv presumibilmente

presume [prɪ'zjuːm] vt supporre

presumption [prɪ'zʌmpʃən] n presunzione f

presumptuous [prɪ'zʌmpʃəs] adj presuntuoso(a)

pretence [prɪ'tɛns] (US **pretense**) n (claim) pretesa; **to make a ~ of doing** far finta di fare; **under false ~s** con l'inganno

pretend [prɪ'tɛnd] vt (feign) fingere ♦ vi far finta; **to ~ to do** far finta di fare

pretense [prɪ'tɛns] (US) n = **pretence**

pretentious [prɪ'tɛnʃəs] adj pretenzioso(a)

pretext ['priːtɛkst] n pretesto

pretty ['prɪtɪ] adj grazioso(a), carino(a) ♦ adv abbastanza, assai

prevail [prɪ'veɪl] vi (win, be usual) prevalere; (persuade): **to ~ (up)on sb to do** persuadere qn a fare; **~ing** adj dominante

prevalent ['prɛvələnt] adj (belief) predominante; (customs) diffuso(a); (fashion) corrente; (disease) comune

prevent [prɪ'vɛnt] vt: **to ~ sb from doing** impedire a qn di fare; **to ~ sth from happening** impedire che qc succeda; **~ative** adj = **~ive**; **~ion** [-'vɛnʃən] n prevenzione f; **~ive** adj preventivo(a)

preview ['priːvjuː] n (of film) anteprima

previous ['priːvɪəs] adj precedente, anteriore; **~ly** adv prima

prewar ['priː'wɔː*] adj anteguerra inv

prey [preɪ] n preda ♦ vi: **to ~ on** far preda di; **it was ~ing on his mind** lo stava ossessionando

price [praɪs] n prezzo ♦ vt (goods) fissare il prezzo di; valutare; **~less** adj inapprezzabile; **~ list** n listino (dei) prezzi

prick [prɪk] n puntura ♦ vt pungere; **to ~ up one's ears** drizzare gli orecchi

prickle ['prɪkl] n (of plant) spina; (sensation) pizzicore m

prickly ['prɪklɪ] adj spinoso(a); **~ heat** n sudamina

pride [praɪd] n orgoglio; superbia ♦ vt: **to ~ o.s. on** essere orgoglioso(a) di; vantarsi di

priest [priːst] n prete m, sacerdote m; **~hood** n sacerdozio

prim [prɪm] adj pudico(a); contegnoso(a)

primarily ['praɪmərɪlɪ] adv principalmente, essenzialmente

primary ['praɪmərɪ] adj primario(a); (first in importance) primo(a) ♦ n (US: election) primarie fpl; **~ school** (BRIT) n scuola elementare

prime [praɪm] adj primario(a), fondamentale; (excellent) di prima qualità ♦ vt (wood) preparare; (fig) mettere al corrente ♦ n: **in the ~ of life** nel fiore della vita; **P~ Minister** n primo ministro

primeval [praɪ'miːvl] adj primitivo(a)

primitive ['prɪmɪtɪv] adj primitivo(a)

primrose ['prɪmrəuz] n primavera

primus (stove) ® ['praɪməs(-)] (BRIT) n fornello a petrolio

prince [prɪns] n principe m

princess [prɪn'sɛs] n principessa

principal ['prɪnsɪpl] adj principale ♦ n (headmaster) preside m

principle ['prɪnsɪpl] n principio; **in ~** in linea di principio; **on ~** per principio

print [prɪnt] n (mark) impronta; (letters) caratteri mpl; (fabric) tessuto stampato; (ART, PHOT) stampa ♦ vt imprimere; (publish) stampare, pubblicare; (write in capitals) scrivere in stampatello; **out of ~** esaurito(a); **~ed matter** n stampe fpl; **~er** n tipografo; (machine) stampante f; **~ing** n stampa; **~-out** n (COMPUT) tabulato

prior ['praɪə*] adj precedente; (claim etc) più importante; **~ to doing** prima di fare

priority [praɪ'ɔrɪtɪ] n priorità f inv; precedenza

prise [praɪz] vt: **to ~ open** forzare

prison ['prɪzn] n prigione f ♦ cpd (system) carcerario(a); (conditions, food) nelle or delle prigioni; **~er** n prigioniero/a

pristine ['prɪstiːn] adj immacolato(a)

privacy ['prɪvəsɪ] n solitudine f, intimità

private ['praɪvɪt] adj privato(a); personale ♦ n soldato semplice; **"~"** (on envelope) "riservata"; (on door) "privato"; **in ~** in privato; **~ enterprise** n iniziativa privata; **~ eye** n investigatore m privato; **~ly** adv in privato; (within oneself) dentro di sé; **~ property** n proprietà privata; **privatize** vt privatizzare

privet ['prɪvɪt] n ligustro

privilege ['prɪvɪlɪdʒ] n privilegio

privy ['prɪvɪ] adj: **to be ~ to** essere al corrente di

prize [praɪz] n premio ♦ adj (example, idiot)

perfetto(a); (*bull, novel*) premiato(a) ♦ *vt*
apprezzare, pregiare; **~-giving** *n* premiazione
f; **~winner** *n* premiato/a

pro [prəʊ] *n* (*SPORT*) professionista *m/f* ♦ *prep*
pro; **the ~s and cons** il pro e il contro

probability [prɔbə'bɪlɪtɪ] *n* probabilità *f inv*;
in all ~ con tutta probabilità

probable ['prɔbəbl] *adj* probabile; **probably**
adv probabilmente

probation [prə'beɪʃən] *n*: **on ~** (*employee*) in
prova; (*LAW*) in libertà vigilata

probe [prəʊb] *n* (*MED, SPACE*) sonda; (*enquiry*)
indagine *f*, investigazione *f* ♦ *vt* sondare,
esplorare; indagare

problem ['prɔbləm] *n* problema *m*

procedure [prə'siːdʒə*] *n* (*ADMIN, LAW*)
procedura; (*method*) metodo, procedimento

proceed [prə'siːd] *vi* (*go forward*) avanzare,
andare avanti; (*go about it*) procedere;
(*continue*): **to ~ (with)** continuare; **to ~ to**
andare a; passare a; **to ~ to do** mettersi a
fare; **~ings** *npl* misure *fpl*; (*LAW*)
procedimento; (*meeting*) riunione *f*; (*records*)
rendiconti *mpl*; atti *mpl*; **~s** ['prəʊsiːdz] *npl*
profitto, incasso

process ['prəʊses] *n* processo; (*method*)
metodo, sistema *m* ♦ *vt* trattare;
(*information*) elaborare; **~ing** *n* trattamento;
elaborazione *f*

procession [prə'seʃən] *n* processione *f*,
corteo; **funeral ~** corteo funebre

pro-choice [prəʊ'tʃɔɪs] *adj* per la libertà di
scelta di gravidanza

proclaim [prə'kleɪm] *vt* proclamare,
dichiarare

procrastinate [prəʊ'kræstɪneɪt] *vi*
procrastinare

prod [prɔd] *vt* dare un colpetto a; pungolare
♦ *n* colpetto

prodigal ['prɔdɪgl] *adj* prodigo(a)

prodigy ['prɔdɪdʒɪ] *n* prodigio

produce [*n* 'prɔdjuːs, *vb* prə'djuːs] *n* (*AGR*)
prodotto, prodotti *mpl* ♦ *vt* produrre; (*to
show*) esibire, mostrare; (*cause*) cagionare,
causare; **~r** *n* (*THEATRE*) regista *m/f*; (*AGR,
CINEMA*) produttore *m*

product ['prɔdʌkt] *n* prodotto

production [prə'dʌkʃən] *n* produzione *f*;
~ line *n* catena di lavorazione

productivity [prɔdʌk'tɪvɪtɪ] *n* produttività

profane [prə'feɪn] *adj* profano(a); (*language*)
empio(a)

profess [prə'fes] *vt* (*claim*) dichiarare;
(*opinion etc*) professare

profession [prə'feʃən] *n* professione *f*; **~al**
n professionista *m/f* ♦ *adj* professionale; (*work*)
da professionista

professor [prə'fesə*] *n* professore *m* (*titolare
di una cattedra*); (*US*) professore/essa

proficiency [prə'fɪʃənsɪ] *n* competenza,
abilità

profile ['prəʊfaɪl] *n* profilo

profit ['prɔfɪt] *n* profitto; beneficio ♦ *vi*: **to ~
(by** *or* **from)** approfittare (di); **~ability** [-'bɪ-
lɪtɪ] *n* redditività; **~able** *adj* redditizio(a)

profound [prə'faʊnd] *adj* profondo(a)

profusely [prə'fjuːslɪ] *adv* con grande
effusione

programme ['prəʊgræm] (*US* **program**) *n*
programma *m* ♦ *vt* programmare; **~r** (*US*
programer) *n* programmatore/trice

progress [*n* 'prəʊgres, *vb* prə'gres] *n*
progresso ♦ *vi* avanzare, procedere; **in ~** in
corso; **to make ~** far progressi; **~ive** [-'gresɪv]
adj progressivo(a); (*person*) progressista

prohibit [prə'hɪbɪt] *vt* proibire, vietare; **~ion**
[prəʊɪ'bɪʃən] *n* proibizione *f*, divieto; (*US*):
P~ion proibizionismo; **~ive** *adj* (*price etc*)
proibitivo(a)

project [*n* 'prɔdʒekt, *vb* prə'dʒekt] *n* (*plan*)
piano; (*venture*) progetto; (*SCOL*) studio ♦ *vt*
proiettare ♦ *vi* (*stick out*) sporgere

projectile [prə'dʒektaɪl] *n* proiettile *m*

projector [prə'dʒektə*] *n* proiettore *m*

pro-life [prəʊ'laɪf] *adj* per il diritto alla vita

prolific [prə'lɪfɪk] *adj* (*artist etc*) fecondo(a)

prolong [prə'lɔŋ] *vt* prolungare

prom [prɔm] *n abbr* = **promenade**; (*US*: *ball*)
ballo studentesco

promenade [prɔmə'nɑːd] *n* (*by sea*)
lungomare *m*; **~ concert** *n* concerto (*con
posti in piedi*)

prominent ['prɔmɪnənt] *adj* (*standing out*)
prominente; (*important*) importante

promiscuous [prə'mɪskjuəs] *adj* (*sexually*)
di facili costumi

promise ['prɔmɪs] *n* promessa ♦ *vt, vi*
promettere; **to ~ sb sth, ~ sth to sb**
promettere qc a qn; **to ~ (sb) that/to do sth**
promettere a qn che/di fare qc; **promising**
adj promettente

promote [prə'məʊt] *vt* promuovere; (*venture,
event*) organizzare; **~r** *n* promotore/trice; (*of
sporting event*) organizzatore/trice;
promotion [-'məʊʃən] *n* promozione *f*

prompt [prɔmpt] *adj* rapido(a), svelto(a);
puntuale; (*reply*) sollecito(a) ♦ *adv*
(*punctually*) in punto ♦ *n* (*COMPUT*) prompt *m*
♦ *vt* incitare; provocare; (*THEATRE*) suggerire
a; **to ~ sb to do** incitare qn a fare; **~ly** *adv*
prontamente; puntualmente

prone [prəʊn] *adj* (*lying*) prono(a); **~ to**
propenso(a) a, incline a

prong [prɔŋ] *n* rebbio, punta

pronoun ['prəʊnaʊn] *n* pronome *m*

pronounce [prə'naʊns] *vt* pronunciare

pronunciation [prənʌnsɪ'eɪʃən] *n* pronuncia

proof [pruːf] *n* prova; (*of book*) bozza; (*PHOT*)

provino ♦ adj: ~ **against** a prova di

prop [prɔp] n sostegno, appoggio ♦ vt (also: ~ **up**) sostenere, appoggiare; (lean): **to ~ sth against** appoggiare qc contro or a

propaganda [prɔpə'gændə] n propaganda

propel [prə'pɛl] vt spingere (in avanti), muovere; **~ler** n elica

propensity [prə'pɛnsɪtɪ] n tendenza

proper ['prɔpə*] adj (suited, right) adatto(a), appropriato(a); (seemly) decente; (authentic) vero(a); (inf: real) noun + vero(a) e proprio(a); **~ly** ['prɔpəlɪ] adv (eat, study) bene; (behave) come si deve; **~ noun** n nome m proprio

property ['prɔpətɪ] n (things owned) beni mpl; (land, building) proprietà f inv; (CHEM etc: quality) proprietà; **~ owner** n proprietario/a

prophecy ['prɔfɪsɪ] n profezia

prophesy ['prɔfɪsaɪ] vt predire

prophet ['prɔfɪt] n profeta m

proportion [prə'pɔːʃən] n proporzione f; (share) parte f; **~al** adj proporzionale; **~ate** adj proporzionato(a)

proposal [prə'pəuzl] n proposta; (plan) progetto; (of marriage) proposta di matrimonio

propose [prə'pəuz] vt proporre, suggerire ♦ vi fare una proposta di matrimonio; **to ~ to do** proporsi di fare, aver l'intenzione di fare

proposition [prɔpə'zɪʃən] n proposizione f; (offer) proposta

proprietor [prə'praɪətə*] n proprietario/a

propriety [prə'praɪətɪ] n (seemliness) decoro, rispetto delle convenienze sociali

pro rata ['prəu'rɑːtə] adv in proporzione

prose [prəuz] n prosa

prosecute ['prɔsɪkjuːt] vt processare; **prosecution** [-'kjuːʃən] n processo; (accusing side) accusa; **prosecutor** n (also: public prosecutor) ≈ procuratore m della Repubblica

prospect [n 'prɔspɛkt, vb prə'spɛkt] n prospettiva; (hope) speranza ♦ vi: **to ~ for** cercare; **~s** npl (for work etc) prospettive fpl; **~ive** [-'spɛktɪv] adj possibile; futuro(a)

prospectus [prə'spɛktəs] n prospetto, programma m

prosperity [prɔ'spɛrɪtɪ] n prosperità

prostitute ['prɔstɪtjuːt] n prostituta; **male ~** uomo che si prostituisce

protect [prə'tɛkt] vt proteggere, salvaguardare; **~ed species** n specie f protetta; **~ion** n protezione f; **~ive** adj protettivo(a)

protégé ['prəutəʒeɪ] n protetto

protein ['prəutiːn] n proteina

protest [n 'prəutɛst, vb prə'tɛst] n protesta ♦ vt, vi protestare

Protestant ['prɔtɪstənt] adj, n protestante m/f

protester [prə'tɛstə*] n dimostrante m/f

prototype ['prəutətaɪp] n prototipo

protracted [prə'træktɪd] adj tirato(a) per le lunghe

protrude [prə'truːd] vi sporgere

proud [praud] adj fiero(a), orgoglioso(a); (pej) superbo(a)

prove [pruːv] vt provare, dimostrare ♦ vi: **to ~ (to be) correct** etc risultare vero(a) etc; **to ~ o.s.** mostrare le proprie capacità

proverb ['prɔvəːb] n proverbio

provide [prə'vaɪd] vt fornire, provvedere; **to ~ sb with sth** fornire or provvedere qn di qc; **~ for** vt fus provvedere a; (future event) prevedere; **~d (that)** conj purché + sub, a condizione che + sub

providing [prə'vaɪdɪŋ] conj purché + sub, a condizione che + sub

province ['prɔvɪns] n provincia; **provincial** [prə'vɪnʃəl] adj provinciale

provision [prə'vɪʒən] n (supply) riserva; (supplying) provvista; rifornimento; (stipulation) condizione f; **~s** npl (food) provviste fpl; **~al** adj provvisorio(a)

proviso [prə'vaɪzəu] n condizione f

provocative [prə'vɔkətɪv] adj (aggressive) provocatorio(a); (thought-provoking) stimolante; (seductive) provocante

provoke [prə'vəuk] vt provocare; incitare

prowess ['prauɪs] n prodezza

prowl [praul] vi (also: ~ **about**, ~ **around**) aggirarsi ♦ n: **to be on the ~** aggirarsi; **~er** n tipo sospetto (che s'aggira con l'intenzione di rubare, aggredire etc)

proximity [prɔk'sɪmɪtɪ] n prossimità

proxy ['prɔksɪ] n: **by ~** per procura

prude [pruːd] n puritano/a

prudent ['pruːdnt] adj prudente

prudish ['pruːdɪʃ] adj puritano(a)

prune [pruːn] n prugna secca ♦ vt potare

pry [praɪ] vi: **to ~ into** ficcare il naso in

PS abbr (= postscript) P.S.

psalm [sɑːm] n salmo

pseudonym ['sjuːdənɪm] n pseudonimo

psyche ['saɪkɪ] n psiche f

psychiatric [saɪkɪ'ætrɪk] adj psichiatrico(a)

psychiatrist [saɪ'kaɪətrɪst] n psichiatra m/f

psychic ['saɪkɪk] adj (also: ~al) psichico(a); (person) dotato(a) di qualità telepatiche

psychoanalyst [saɪkəu'ænəlɪst] n psicanalista m/f

psychological [saɪkə'lɔdʒɪkl] adj psicologico(a)

psychologist [saɪ'kɔlədʒɪst] n psicologo/a

psychology [saɪ'kɔlədʒɪ] n psicologia

psychopath ['saɪkəupæθ] n psicopatico/a

P.T.O. abbr (= please turn over) v.r.

pub [pʌb] n abbr (= public house) pub m inv
pubic ['pju:bɪk] adj pubico(a), del pube
public ['pʌblɪk] adj pubblico(a) ♦ n pubblico;
in ~ in pubblico; **~ address system** n
impianto di amplificazione
publican ['pʌblɪkən] n proprietario di un pub
publication [pʌblɪ'keɪʃən] n pubblicazione f
public: ~ company n società f inv per azioni
(costituita tramite pubblica sottoscrizione);
~ convenience (BRIT) n gabinetti mpl;
~ holiday n giorno festivo, festa nazionale;
~ house (BRIT) n pub m inv
publicity [pʌb'lɪsɪtɪ] n pubblicità
publicize ['pʌblɪsaɪz] vt rendere pubblico(a)
publicly ['pʌblɪklɪ] adv pubblicamente
public: ~ opinion n opinione f pubblica;
~ relations n pubbliche relazioni fpl;
~ school n (BRIT) scuola privata; (US) scuola
statale; **~-spirited** adj che ha senso civico;
~ transport n mezzi mpl pubblici
publish ['pʌblɪʃ] vt pubblicare; **~er** n editore
m; **~ing** n (industry) editoria; (of a book)
pubblicazione f
pub lunch n pranzo semplice ed economico
servito nei pub
puce [pju:s] adj marroncino rosato inv
pucker ['pʌkə*] vt corrugare
pudding ['pudɪŋ] n budino; (BRIT: dessert)
dolce m; **black ~**, (US) **blood ~** sanguinaccio
puddle ['pʌdl] n pozza, pozzanghera
puff [pʌf] n sbuffo ♦ vt: **to ~ one's pipe** tirare
sboccate di fumo ♦ vi (pant) ansare; **~ out**
vt (cheeks etc) gonfiare; **~ pastry** n pasta
sfoglia; **~y** adj gonfio(a)
pull [pul] n (tug): **to give sth a ~** tirare su qc
♦ vt tirare; (muscle) strappare; (trigger)
premere ♦ vi tirare; **to ~ to pieces** fare a
pezzi; **to ~ one's punches** (BOXING)
risparmiare l'avversario; **to ~ one's weight**
dare il proprio contributo; **to ~ o.s. together**
ricomporsi, riprendersi; **to ~ sb's leg** prendere
in giro qn; **~ apart** vt (break) fare a pezzi;
~ down vt (house) demolire; (tree)
abbattere; **~ in** vi (AUT: at the kerb)
accostarsi, (RAIL) entrare in stazione; **~ off** vt
(clothes) togliere; (deal etc) portare a
compimento; **~ out** vi partire; (AUT: come out
of line) spostarsi sulla mezzeria ♦ vt staccare;
far uscire; (withdraw) ritirare; **~ over** vi (AUT)
accostare; **~ through** vi farcela; **~ up** vi
(stop) fermarsi ♦ vt (raise) sollevare; (uproot)
sradicare
pulley ['pulɪ] n puleggia, carrucola
pullover ['puləuvə*] n pullover m inv
pulp [pʌlp] n (of fruit) polpa
pulpit ['pulpɪt] n pulpito
pulsate [pʌl'seɪt] vi battere, palpitare
pulse [pʌls] n polso; (BOT) legume m
pummel ['pʌml] vt dare pugni a

pump [pʌmp] n pompa; (shoe) scarpetta ♦ vt
pompare; **~ up** vt gonfiare
pumpkin ['pʌmpkɪn] n zucca
pun [pʌn] n gioco di parole
punch [pʌntʃ] n (blow) pugno; (tool)
punzone m; (drink) ponce m ♦ vt (hit): **to
~ sb/sth** dare un pugno a qn/qc; **~ line** n (of
joke) battuta finale; **~-up** (BRIT: inf) n rissa
punctual ['pʌŋktjuəl] adj puntuale
punctuation [pʌŋktju'eɪʃən] n interpunzione
f, punteggiatura
puncture ['pʌŋktʃə*] n foratura ♦ vt forare
pundit ['pʌndɪt] n sapientone/a
pungent ['pʌndʒənt] adj pungente
punish ['pʌnɪʃ] vt punire; **~ment** n punizione
f
punk [pʌŋk] n (also: ~ rocker) punk m/f inv;
(also: ~ rock) musica punk, punk rock m; (US:
inf: hoodlum) teppista m
punt [pʌnt] n (boat) barchino
punter ['pʌntə*] (BRIT) n (gambler)
scommettitore/trice; (: inf) cliente m/f
puny ['pju:nɪ] adj gracile
pup [pʌp] n cucciolo/a
pupil ['pju:pl] n (of school) allievo/a; (ANAT) pupilla
puppet ['pʌpɪt] n burattino
puppy ['pʌpɪ] n cucciolo/a, cagnolino/a
purchase ['pɜ:tʃɪs] n acquisto, compera ♦ vt
comprare; **~r** n compratore/trice
pure [pjuə*] adj puro(a)
purée ['pjuəreɪ] n (of potatoes) purè m; (of
tomatoes) passato; (of apples) crema
purely ['pjuəlɪ] adv puramente
purge [pɜ:dʒ] n (MED) purga; (POL)
epurazione f ♦ vt purgare
puritan ['pjuərɪtən] adj, n puritano(a)
purity ['pjuərɪtɪ] n purezza
purple ['pɜ:pl] adj di porpora; viola inv
purpose ['pɜ:pəs] n intenzione f, scopo; **on ~**
apposta; **~ful** adj deciso(a), risoluto(a)
purr [pɜ:*] vi fare le fusa
purse [pɜ:s] n (BRIT) borsellino; (US) borsetta
♦ vt contrarre
purser ['pɜ:sə*] n (NAUT) commissario di
bordo
pursue [pə'sju:] vt inseguire; (fig: activity etc)
continuare con; (: aim etc) perseguire
pursuit [pə'sju:t] n inseguimento; (fig)
ricerca; (pastime) passatempo
push [puʃ] n spinta; (effort) grande sforzo;
(drive) energia f ♦ vt (button)
premere; (thrust): **to ~ sth (into)** ficcare qc
(in); (fig) fare pubblicità a ♦ vi spingere;
premere; **to ~ for** (fig) insistere per; **~ aside**
vt scostare; **~ off** (inf) vi filare; **~ on** vi
(continue) continuare; **~ through** vi farsi
largo spingendo ♦ vt (measure) far appro-
vare; **~ up** vt (total, prices) far salire; **~chair**
(BRIT) n passeggino; **~er** n (drug ~er)

spacciatore/trice; **~over** (*inf*) *n*: it's a **~over** è un lavoro da bambini; **~-up** (*US*) *n* (*press-up*) flessione *f* sulle braccia; **~y** (*pej*) *adj* opportunista

puss [pus] (*inf*) *n* = **pussy(-cat)**

pussy(-cat) [ˈpusɪ(-)] (*inf*) *n* micio

put [put] (*pt, pp* put) *vt* mettere, porre; (*say*) dire, esprimere; (*a question*) fare; (*estimate*) stimare; **~ about** or **around** *vt* (*rumour*) diffondere; **~ across** *vt* (*ideas etc*) comunicare; far capire; **~ away** *vt* (*return*) mettere a posto; **~ back** *vt* (*replace*) rimettere (a posto); (*postpone*) rinviare; (*delay*) ritardare; **~ by** *vt* (*money*) mettere da parte; **~ down** *vt* (*parcel etc*) posare, mettere giù; (*pay*) versare; (*in writing*) mettere per iscritto; (*revolt, animal*) sopprimere; (*attribute*) attribuire; **~ forward** *vt* (*ideas*) avanzare, proporre; **~ in** *vt* (*application, complaint*) presentare; (*time, effort*) mettere; **~ off** *vt* (*postpone*) rimandare, rinviare; (*discourage*) dissuadere; **~ on** *vt* (*clothes, lipstick etc*) mettere; (*light etc*) accendere; (*play etc*) mettere in scena; (*food, meal*) mettere su; (*brake*) mettere; **to ~ on weight** ingrassare; **to ~ on airs** darsi delle arie; **~ out** *vt* mettere fuori; (*one's hand*) porgere; (*light etc*) spegnere; (*person: inconvenience*) scomodare; **~ through** *vt* (*TEL: call*) passare; (*: person*) mettere in comunicazione; (*plan*) far approvare; **~ up** *vt* (*raise*) sollevare, alzare; (*: umbrella*) aprire; (*: tent*) montare; (*pin up*) affiggere; (*hang*) appendere; (*build*) costruire, erigere; (*increase*) aumentare; (*accommodate*) alloggiare; **~ up with** *vt fus* sopportare

putt [pʌt] *n* colpo leggero; **~ing green** *n* green *m inv*; campo da putting

putty [ˈpʌtɪ] *n* stucco

puzzle [ˈpʌzl] *n* enigma *m*, mistero; (*jigsaw*) puzzle *m*; (*also: crossword ~*) parole *fpl* incrociate, cruciverba *m inv* ♦ *vt* confondere, rendere perplesso(a) ♦ *vi* scervellarsi

pyjamas [pɪˈdʒɑːməz] (*BRIT*) *npl* pigiama *m*

pylon [ˈpaɪlən] *n* pilone *m*

pyramid [ˈpɪrəmɪd] *n* piramide *f*

Pyrenees [pɪrɪˈniːz] *npl*: **the ~** i Pirenei

Q, q

quack [kwæk] *n* (*of duck*) qua qua *m inv*; (*pej: doctor*) dottoruccio/a

quad [kwɒd] *n abbr* = **quadrangle; quadruplet**

quadrangle [ˈkwɒdræŋgl] *n* (*courtyard*) cortile *m*

quadruple [kwɔˈdrupl] *vt* quadruplicare ♦ *vi* quadruplicarsi

quadruplets [kwɔˈdruːplɪts] *npl* quattro gemelli *mpl*

quail [kweɪl] *n* (*ZOOL*) quaglia ♦ *vi* (*person*): **to ~ at** or **before** perdersi d'animo davanti a

quaint [kweɪnt] *adj* bizzarro(a); (*old-fashioned*) antiquato(a); grazioso(a), pittoresco(a)

quake [kweɪk] *vi* tremare ♦ *n abbr* = **earthquake**

Quaker [ˈkweɪkə*] *n* quacchero/a

qualification [kwɔlɪfɪˈkeɪʃən] *n* (*degree etc*) qualifica, titolo; (*ability*) competenza, qualificazione *f*; (*limitation*) riserva, restrizione *f*

qualified [ˈkwɔlɪfaɪd] *adj* qualificato(a); (*able*): **~ to** competente in, qualificato(a) a; (*limited*) condizionato(a)

qualify [ˈkwɔlɪfaɪ] *vt* abilitare; (*limit: statement*) modificare, precisare ♦ *vi*: **to ~ (as)** qualificarsi (come); **to ~ (for)** acquistare i requisiti necessari (per); (*SPORT*) qualificarsi (per or a)

quality [ˈkwɔlɪtɪ] *n* qualità *f inv*

qualm [kwɑːm] *n* dubbio; scrupolo

quandary [ˈkwɔndrɪ] *n*: **in a ~** in un dilemma

quantity [ˈkwɔntɪtɪ] *n* quantità *f inv*

quantity surveyor [-səˈveɪə*] *n* geometra *m* (*specializzato nel calcolare la quantità e il costo del materiale da costruzione*)

quarantine [ˈkwɔrəntiːn] *n* quarantena

quarrel [ˈkwɔrl] *n* lite *f*, disputa ♦ *vi* litigare

quarry [ˈkwɔrɪ] *n* (*for stone*) cava; (*animal*) preda

quart [kwɔːt] *n* ≈ litro

quarter [ˈkwɔːtə*] *n* quarto; (*US: coin*) quarto di dollaro; (*of year*) trimestre *m*; (*district*) quartiere *m* ♦ *vt* dividere in quattro; (*MIL*) alloggiare; **~s** *npl* (*living ~s*) alloggio; (*MIL*) alloggi *mpl*, quadrato; **a ~ of an hour** un quarto d'ora; **~ final** *n* quarto di finale; **~ly** *adj* trimestrale ♦ *adv* trimestralmente

quartet(te) [kwɔːˈtɛt] *n* quartetto

quartz [kwɔːts] *n* quarzo

quash [kwɔʃ] *vt* (*verdict*) annullare

quaver [ˈkweɪvə*] *n* (*BRIT: MUS*) croma ♦ *vi* tremolare

quay [kiː] *n* (*also: ~side*) banchina

queasy [ˈkwiːzɪ] *adj* (*stomach*) delicato(a); **to feel ~** aver la nausea

queen [kwiːn] *n* (*gen*) regina; (*CARDS etc*) regina, donna; **~ mother** *n* regina madre

queer [kwɪə*] *adj* strano(a), curioso(a) ♦ *n* (*inf*) finocchio

quell [kwɛl] *vt* domare

quench [kwɛntʃ] *vt*: **to ~ one's thirst** dissetarsi

query [ˈkwɪərɪ] *n* domanda, questione *f* ♦ *vt* mettere in questione

quest [kwɛst] *n* cerca, ricerca

question [ˈkwɛstʃən] *n* domanda, questione *f* ♦ *vt* (*person*) interrogare; (*plan, idea*) mettere in questione or in dubbio; **it's a ~ of doing** si tratta di fare; **beyond ~** fuori di dubbio; **out of the ~** fuori discussione, impossibile; **~able** adj discutibile; **~ mark** n punto interrogativo

questionnaire [kwestʃə'neə*] n questionario

queue [kjuː] (BRIT) n coda, fila ♦ vi fare la coda

quibble ['kwɪbl] vi cavillare

quiche [kiːʃ] n torta salata a base di uova, formaggio, prosciutto o altro

quick [kwɪk] adj rapido(a), veloce; (reply) pronto(a); (mind) pronto(a), acuto(a) ♦ n: **cut to the ~** (fig) toccato(a) sul vivo; **be ~!** fa presto!; **~en** vt accelerare, affrettare ♦ vi accelerare, affrettarsi; **~ly** adv rapidamente, velocemente; **~sand** n sabbie fpl mobili; **~-witted** adj pronto(a) d'ingegno

quid [kwɪd] (BRIT: inf) n inv sterlina

quiet ['kwaɪət] adj tranquillo(a), quieto(a); (ceremony) semplice ♦ n tranquillità, calma ♦ vt, vi (US) = **~en**; **keep ~!** sta zitto!; **~en** (also: **~en down**) vi calmarsi, chetarsi ♦ vt calmare, chetare; **~ly** adv tranquillamente, calmamente; sommessamente

quilt [kwɪlt] n trapunta; (continental ~) piumino

quin [kwɪn] n abbr = **quintuplet**

quintuplets [kwɪn'tjuːplɪts] npl cinque gemelli mpl

quip [kwɪp] n frizzo

quirk [kwəːk] n ghiribizzo

quit [kwɪt] (pt, pp quit or quitted) vt mollare; (premises) lasciare, partire da ♦ vi (give up) mollare; (resign) dimettersi

quite [kwaɪt] adv (rather) assai; (entirely) completamente, del tutto; **I ~ understand** capisco perfettamente; **that's not ~ big enough** non è proprio sufficiente; **~ a few of them** non pochi di loro; **~ (so)!** esatto!

quits [kwɪts] adj: **~ (with)** pari (con); **let's call it ~** adesso siamo pari

quiver ['kwɪvə*] vi tremare, fremere

quiz [kwɪz] n (game) quiz m inv; indovinello ♦ vt interrogare; **~zical** adj enigmatico(a)

quota ['kwəʊtə] n quota

quotation [kwəʊ'teɪʃən] n citazione f; (of shares etc) quotazione f; (estimate) preventivo; **~ marks** npl virgolette fpl

quote [kwəʊt] n citazione f ♦ vt (sentence) citare; (price) dare, fissare; (shares) quotare ♦ vi: **to ~ from** citare; **~s** npl = **quotation marks**

R, r

rabbi ['ræbaɪ] n rabbino

rabbit ['ræbɪt] n coniglio; **~ hutch** n conigliera

rabble ['ræbl] (pej) n canaglia, plebaglia

rabies ['reɪbiːz] n rabbia

RAC (BRIT) n abbr = **Royal Automobile Club**

rac(c)oon [rə'kuːn] n procione m

race [reɪs] n razza; (competition, rush) corsa ♦ vt (horse) far correre ♦ vi correre; (engine) imballarsi; **~ car** (US) n = **racing car**; **~ car driver** (US) n = **racing driver**; **~course** n campo di corse, ippodromo; **~horse** n cavallo da corsa; **~track** n pista

racial ['reɪʃl] adj razziale

racing ['reɪsɪŋ] n corsa; **~ car** (BRIT) n macchina da corsa; **~ driver** (BRIT) n corridore m automobilista

racism ['reɪsɪzəm] n razzismo; **racist** adj, n razzista m/f

rack [ræk] n rastrelliera; (also: luggage ~) rete f, portabagagli m inv; (also: roof ~) portabagagli; (dish ~) scolapiatti m inv ♦ vt: **~ed by** torturato(a) da; **to ~ one's brains** scervellarsi

racket ['rækɪt] n (for tennis) racchetta; (noise) fracasso; baccano; (swindle) imbroglio, truffa; (organized crime) racket m inv

racoon [rə'kuːn] n = **raccoon**

racquet ['rækɪt] n racchetta

racy ['reɪsɪ] adj brioso(a); piccante

radar ['reɪdɑː*] n radar m

radial ['reɪdɪəl] adj (also: ~-ply) radiale

radiant ['reɪdɪənt] adj raggiante; (PHYSICS) radiante

radiate ['reɪdɪeɪt] vt (heat) irraggiare, irradiare ♦ vi (lines) irradiarsi

radiation [reɪdɪ'eɪʃən] n irradiamento; (radioactive) radiazione f

radiator ['reɪdɪeɪtə*] n radiatore m

radical ['rædɪkl] adj radicale

radii ['reɪdɪaɪ] npl of **radius**

radio ['reɪdɪəʊ] n radio f inv; **on the ~** alla radio

radioactive [reɪdɪəʊ'æktɪv] adj radioattivo(a)

radio station n stazione f radio inv

radish ['rædɪʃ] n ravanello

radius ['reɪdɪəs] (pl **radii**) n raggio

RAF n abbr = **Royal Air Force**

raffle ['ræfl] n lotteria

raft [rɑːft] n zattera; (also: life ~) zattera di salvataggio

rafter ['rɑːftə*] n trave f

rag [ræg] n straccio, cencio; (pej: newspaper) giornalaccio, bandiera; (for charity) iniziativa studentesca a scopo benefico; **~s** npl (torn clothes) stracci mpl, brandelli mpl; **~ doll** n bambola di pezza

rage [reɪdʒ] n (fury) collera, furia ♦ vi (person) andare su tutte le furie; (storm) infuriare; **it's all the ~** fa furore

ragged ['rægɪd] adj (edge) irregolare; (clothes) logoro(a); (appearance) pezzente

raid [reɪd] n (MIL) incursione f; (criminal) rapina; (by police) irruzione f ♦ vt fare un'incursione in; rapinare; fare irruzione in

rail [reɪl] n (on stair) ringhiera; (on bridge, balcony) parapetto; (of ship) battagliola; **~s** npl (for train) binario, rotaie fpl; **by ~** per ferrovia; **~ing(s)** n(pl) ringhiere fpl; **~road** (US) n = **~way**; **~way** (BRIT) n ferrovia; **~way line** (BRIT) n linea ferroviaria; **~wayman** (BRIT irreg) n ferroviere m; **~way station** (BRIT) n stazione f ferroviaria

rain [reɪn] n pioggia ♦ vi piovere; **in the ~** sotto la pioggia; **it's ~ing** piove; **~bow** n arcobaleno; **~coat** n impermeabile m; **~drop** n goccia di pioggia; **~fall** n pioggia; (measurement) piovosità; **~forest** n foresta pluviale; **~y** adj piovoso(a)

raise [reɪz] n aumento ♦ vt (lift) alzare; sollevare; (increase) aumentare; (a protest, doubt, question) sollevare; (cattle, family) allevare; (crop) coltivare; (army, funds) raccogliere; (loan) ottenere; **to ~ one's voice** alzare la voce

raisin ['reɪzn] n uva secca

rake [reɪk] n (tool) rastrello ♦ vt (garden) rastrellare

rally ['rælɪ] n (POL etc) riunione f; (AUT) rally m inv; (TENNIS) scambio ♦ vt riunire, radunare ♦ vi (sick person, Stock Exchange) riprendersi; **~ round** vt fus raggrupparsi intorno a; venire in aiuto di

RAM [ræm] n abbr (= random access memory) memoria ad accesso casuale

ram [ræm] n montone m, ariete m ♦ vt conficcare; (crash into) cozzare, sbattere contro; percuotere; speronare

ramble ['ræmbl] n escursione f ♦ vi (pej: also: ~ on) divagare; **~r** n escursionista m/f; (BOT) rosa rampicante; **rambling** adj (speech) sconnesso(a); (house) tutto(a) a nicchie e corridoi; (BOT) rampicante

ramp [ræmp] n rampa; **on/off ~** (US: AUT) raccordo di entrata/uscita

rampage [ræm'peɪdʒ] n: **to go on the ~** scatenarsi in modo violento

rampant ['ræmpənt] adj (disease etc) che infierisce

rampart ['ræmpɑːt] n bastione m

ram raiding [-reɪdɪŋ] n il rapinare un negozio o una banca sfondandone la vetrina con un'auto-ariete

ramshackle ['ræmʃækl] adj (house) cadente; (car etc) sgangherato(a)

ran [ræn] pt of **run**

ranch [rɑːntʃ] n ranch m inv; **~er** n proprietario di un ranch; cowboy m inv

rancid ['rænsɪd] adj rancido(a)

rancour ['ræŋkə*] (US **rancor**) n rancore m

random ['rændəm] adj fatto(a) or detto(a) per caso; (COMPUT, MATH) casuale ♦ n: **at ~** a casaccio; **~ access** n (COMPUT) accesso casuale

randy ['rændɪ] (BRIT: inf) adj arrapato(a); lascivo(a)

rang [ræŋ] pt of **ring**

range [reɪndʒ] n (of mountains) catena; (of missile, voice) portata; (of proposals, products) gamma; (MIL: also: shooting ~) campo di tiro; (also: kitchen ~) fornello, cucina economica ♦ vt disporre ♦ vi: **to ~ over** coprire; **to ~ from ... to** andare da ... a

ranger ['reɪndʒə*] n guardia forestale

rank [ræŋk] n fila; (status, MIL) grado; (BRIT: also: taxi ~) posteggio di taxi ♦ vi: **to ~ among** essere tra ♦ adj puzzolente; vero(a) e proprio(a); **the ~ and file** (fig) la gran massa

ransack ['rænsæk] vt rovistare; (plunder) saccheggiare

ransom ['rænsəm] n riscatto; **to hold sb to ~** (fig) esercitare pressione su qn

rant [rænt] vi vociare

rap [ræp] vt bussare a; picchiare su ♦ n (music) rap m inv

rape [reɪp] n violenza carnale, stupro; (BOT) ravizzone m ♦ vt violentare; **~(seed) oil** n olio di ravizzone

rapid ['ræpɪd] adj rapido(a); **~s** npl (GEO) rapida; **~ly** adv rapidamente

rapist ['reɪpɪst] n violentatore m

rapport [ræ'pɔː*] n rapporto

rare [rɛə*] adj raro(a); (CULIN: steak) al sangue

rarely ['rɛəlɪ] adv raramente

raring ['rɛərɪŋ] adj: **to be ~ to go** (inf) non veder l'ora di cominciare

rascal ['rɑːskl] n mascalzone m

rash [ræʃ] adj imprudente, sconsiderato(a) ♦ n (MED) eruzione f; (of events etc) scoppio

rasher ['ræʃə*] n fetta sottile (di lardo or prosciutto)

raspberry ['rɑːzbərɪ] n lampone m

rasping ['rɑːspɪŋ] adj stridulo(a)

rat [ræt] n ratto

rate [reɪt] n (proportion) tasso, percentuale f; (speed) velocità f inv; (price) tariffa ♦ vt giudicare; stimare; **~s** npl (BRIT: property tax) imposte fpl comunali; (fees) tariffe fpl; **to ~ sb/sth as** valutare qn/qc come; **~able value** (BRIT) n valore m imponibile or locativo (di una proprietà); **~payer** (BRIT) n contribuente m/f (che paga le imposte comunali)

rather ['rɑːðə*] adv piuttosto; **it's ~ expensive** è piuttosto caro; (too) è un po' caro; **there's ~ a lot** ce n'è parecchio; **I would** or **I'd ~ go** preferirei andare

rating ['reɪtɪŋ] n (assessment) valutazione f; (score) punteggio di merito

ratio ['reɪʃɪəu] n proporzione f, rapporto

ration ['ræʃən] n (gen pl) razioni fpl ♦ vt razionare

rational ['ræʃənl] adj razionale, ragionevole; (solution, reasoning) logico(a); **~e** [-'nɑːl] n fondamento logico; giustificazione f; **~ize** vt razionalizzare

rat race n carrierismo, corsa al successo

rattle ['rætl] n tintinnio; (louder) strepito; (for baby) sonaglino ♦ vi risuonare, tintinnare; fare un rumore di ferraglia ♦ vt scuotere (con strepito); **~snake** n serpente m a sonagli

raucous ['rɔːkəs] adj rumoroso(a), fragoroso(a)

ravage ['rævɪdʒ] vt devastare; **~s** npl danni mpl

rave [reɪv] vi (in anger) infuriarsi; (with enthusiasm) andare in estasi; (MED) delirare ♦ (BRIT: inf) n (party) rave m inv

raven ['reɪvən] n corvo

ravenous ['rævənəs] adj affamato(a)

ravine [rə'viːn] n burrone m

raving ['reɪvɪŋ] adj: **~ lunatic** pazzo(a) furioso(a)

ravishing ['rævɪʃɪŋ] adj incantevole

raw [rɔː] adj (uncooked) crudo(a); (not processed) greggio(a); (sore) vivo(a); (inexperienced) inesperto(a); (weather, day) gelido(a); **~ deal** (inf) n bidonata; **~ material** n materia prima

ray [reɪ] n raggio; **a ~ of hope** un barlume di speranza

rayon ['reɪɔn] n raion m

raze [reɪz] vt radere, distruggere

razor ['reɪzə*] n rasoio; **~ blade** n lama di rasoio

Rd abbr = **road**

re [riː] prep con riferimento a

reach [riːtʃ] n portata; (of river etc) tratto ♦ vt raggiungere; arrivare a ♦ vi stendersi; **out of/within ~** fuori/a portata di mano; **within ~ of the shops/station** vicino ai negozi/alla stazione; **~ out** vt (hand) allungare ♦ vi: **to ~ out for** stendere la mano per prendere

react [riː'ækt] vi reagire; **~ion** [-'ækʃən] n reazione f

reactor [riː'æktə*] n reattore m

read [riːd, pt, pp red] (pt, pp **read**) vi leggere ♦ vt leggere; (understand) intendere, interpretare; (study) studiare; **~ out** vt leggere ad alta voce; **~able** adj (writing) leggibile; (book etc) che si legge volentieri; **~er** n lettore/trice; (BRIT: at university) professore con funzioni preminenti di ricerca; **~ership** n (of paper etc) numero di lettori

readily ['rɛdɪlɪ] adv volentieri; (easily) facilmente; (quickly) prontamente

readiness ['rɛdɪnɪs] n prontezza; **in ~** (prepared) pronto(a)

reading ['riːdɪŋ] n lettura; (understanding) interpretazione f; (on instrument) indicazione f

readjust [riːə'dʒʌst] vt riaggiustare ♦ vi (person): **to ~ (to)** riadattarsi (a)

ready ['rɛdɪ] adj pronto(a); (willing) pronto(a), disposto(a); (available) disponibile ♦ n: **at the ~** (MIL) pronto a sparare; **to get ~** vi prepararsi ♦ vt preparare; **~-made** adj prefabbricato(a); (clothes) confezionato(a); **~ reckoner** n prontuario di calcolo; **~-to-wear** adj prêt-à-porter inv

reaffirm [riːə'fəːm] vt riaffermare

real [rɪəl] adj reale; vero(a); **in ~ terms** in realtà; **~ estate** n beni mpl immobili; **~ism** n (also ART) realismo; **~ist** n realista m/f; **~istic** [-'lɪstɪk] adj realistico(a)

reality [riː'ælɪtɪ] n realtà f inv

realization [rɪəlaɪ'zeɪʃən] n presa di coscienza; realizzazione f

realize ['rɪəlaɪz] vt (understand) rendersi conto di

really ['rɪəlɪ] adv veramente, davvero; **~!** (indicating annoyance) oh, insomma!

realm [rɛlm] n reame m, regno

Realtor ® ['rɪəltɔː*] (US) n agente m immobiliare

reap [riːp] vt mietere; (fig) raccogliere

reappear [riːə'pɪə*] vi ricomparire, riapparire

rear [rɪə*] adj di dietro; (AUT: wheel etc) posteriore ♦ n didietro, parte f posteriore ♦ vt (cattle, family) allevare ♦ vi (also: ~ up: animal) impennarsi

rearmament [riː'ɑːməmənt] n riarmo

rearrange [riːə'reɪndʒ] vt riordinare

rear-view ['rɪəvjuː]: **~ mirror** n (AUT) specchio retrovisore

reason ['riːzn] n ragione f; (cause, motive) ragione, motivo ♦ vi: **to ~ with sb** far ragionare qn; **it stands to ~ that** è ovvio che; **~able** adj ragionevole; (not bad) accettabile; **~ably** adv ragionevolmente; **~ed** adj: **a well-~ed argument** una forte argomentazione; **~ing** n ragionamento

reassurance [riːə'ʃuərəns] n rassicurazione f

reassure [riːə'ʃuə*] vt rassicurare; **to ~ sb of** rassicurare qn di or su

rebate ['riːbeɪt] n (on tax etc) sgravio

rebel [n 'rɛbl, vb rɪ'bel] n ribelle m/f ♦ vi ribellarsi; **~lion** n ribellione f; **~lious** adj ribelle

rebound [vb rɪ'baund, n 'riːbaund] vi (ball) rimbalzare ♦ n: **on the ~** di rimbalzo

rebuff [rɪ'bʌf] n secco rifiuto

rebuke [rɪ'bjuːk] vt rimproverare

rebut [rɪ'bʌt] vt rifiutare

recall [rɪ'kɔːl] vt richiamare; (remember) ricordare, richiamare alla mente ♦ n richiamo

recap ['riːkæp], **recapitulate** [riːkə'pɪtjuleɪt]

vt ricapitolare ♦ *vi* riassumere

rec'd *abbr* = **received**

recede [rɪ'siːd] *vi* allontanarsi; ritirarsi; calare; **receding** *adj* (*forehead, chin*) sfuggente; **he's got a receding hairline** sta stempiando

receipt [rɪ'siːt] *n* (*document*) ricevuta; (*act of receiving*) ricevimento; **~s** *npl* (COMM) introiti *mpl*

receive [rɪ'siːv] *vt* ricevere; (*guest*) ricevere, accogliere

receiver [rɪ'siːvə*] *n* (TEL) ricevitore *m*; (RADIO, TV) apparecchio ricevente; (*of stolen goods*) ricettatore/trice; (COMM) curatore *m* fallimentare

recent ['riːsnt] *adj* recente; **~ly** *adv* recentemente

receptacle [rɪ'sɛptɪkl] *n* recipiente *m*

reception [rɪ'sɛpʃən] *n* ricevimento; (*welcome*) accoglienza; (TV etc) ricezione *f*; **~ desk** *n* (*in hotel*) reception *f inv*; (*in hospital, at doctor's*) accettazione *f*; (*in offices etc*) portineria; **~ist** *n* receptionist *m/f inv*

receptive [rɪ'sɛptɪv] *adj* ricettivo(a)

recess [rɪ'sɛs] *n* (*in room, secret place*) alcova; (POL etc: *holiday*) vacanze *fpl*; **~ion** [-'sɛʃən] *n* recessione *f*

recharge [riː'tʃɑːdʒ] *vt* (*battery*) ricaricare

recipe ['rɛsɪpɪ] *n* ricetta

recipient [rɪ'sɪpɪənt] *n* beneficiario/a; (*of letter*) destinatario/a

recital [rɪ'saɪtl] *n* recital *m inv*

recite [rɪ'saɪt] *vt* (*poem*) recitare

reckless ['rɛkləs] *adj* (*driver etc*) spericolato(a); (*spending*) folle

reckon ['rɛkən] *vt* (*count*) calcolare; (*think*): **I ~ that ...** penso che ....; **~ on** *vt fus* contare su; **~ing** *n* conto; stima

reclaim [rɪ'kleɪm] *vt* (*demand back*) richiedere, reclamare; (*land*) bonificare; (*materials*) recuperare; **reclamation** [rɛklə'meɪʃən] *n* bonifica

recline [rɪ'klaɪn] *vi* stare sdraiato(a); **reclining** *adj* (*seat*) ribaltabile

recognition [rɛkəg'nɪʃən] *n* riconoscimento; **transformed beyond ~** irriconoscibile

recognize ['rɛkəgnaɪz] *vt*: **to ~ (by/as)** riconoscere (a *or* da/come)

recoil [rɪ'kɔɪl] *vi* (*person*): **to ~ from doing sth** rifuggire dal fare qc ♦ *n* (*of gun*) rinculo

recollect [rɛkə'lɛkt] *vt* ricordare; **~ion** [-'lɛkʃən] *n* ricordo

recommend [rɛkə'mɛnd] *vt* raccomandare; (*advise*) consigliare

reconcile ['rɛkənsaɪl] *vt* (*two people*) riconciliare; (*two facts*) conciliare, quadrare; **to ~ o.s. to** rassegnarsi a

recondition [riːkən'dɪʃən] *vt* rimettere a nuovo

reconnoitre [rɛkə'nɔɪtə*] (US **reconnoiter**) *vt* (MIL) fare una ricognizione di

reconstruct [riːkən'strʌkt] *vt* ricostruire

record [*n* 'rɛkɔːd, *vb* rɪ'kɔːd] *n* ricordo, documento; (*of meeting etc*) nota, verbale *m*; (*register*) registro; (*file*) pratica, dossier *m inv*; (COMPUT) record *m inv*; (*also: criminal ~*) fedina penale sporca; (MUS: *disc*) disco; (SPORT) record *m inv*, primato ♦ *vt* (*set down*) prendere nota di, registrare; (MUS: *song etc*) registrare; **in ~ time** a tempo di record; **off the ~** *adj* ufficioso(a) ♦ *adv* ufficiosamente; **~ card** *n* (*in file*) scheda; **~ed delivery** (BRIT) *n* (POST): **~ed delivery letter** *etc* lettera *etc* raccomandata; **~er** *n* (MUS) flauto diritto; **~ holder** *n* (SPORT) primatista *m/f*; **~ing** *n* (MUS) registrazione *f*; **~ player** *n* giradischi *m inv*

recount [rɪ'kaunt] *vt* raccontare, narrare

re-count ['riːkaunt] *n* (POL: *of votes*) nuovo computo

recoup [rɪ'kuːp] *vt* ricuperare

recourse [rɪ'kɔːs] *n*: **to have ~ to** ricorrere a, far ricorso a

recover [rɪ'kʌvə*] *vt* ricuperare ♦ *vi*: **to ~ (from)** riprendersi (da)

recovery [rɪ'kʌvərɪ] *n* ricupero; ristabilimento; ripresa

recreation [rɛkrɪ'eɪʃən] *n* ricreazione *f*; svago; **~al** *adj* ricreativo(a); **~al drug** *n* sostanza stupefacente usata a scopo ricreativo

recrimination [rɪkrɪmɪ'neɪʃən] *n* recriminazione *f*

recruit [rɪ'kruːt] *n* recluta; (*in company*) nuovo(a) assunto(a) ♦ *vt* reclutare

rectangle ['rɛktæŋgl] *n* rettangolo; **rectangular** [-'tæŋgjulə*] *adj* rettangolare

rectify ['rɛktɪfaɪ] *vt* (*error*) rettificare; (*omission*) riparare

rector ['rɛktə*] *n* (REL) parroco (*anglicano*); **~y** *n* presbiterio

recuperate [rɪ'kjuːpəreɪt] *vi* ristabilirsi

recur [rɪ'kə:*] *vi* riaccadere; (*symptoms*) ripresentarsi; **~rent** *adj* ricorrente; periodico(a)

recycle [riː'saɪkl] *vt* riciclare

red [rɛd] *n* rosso; (POL: *pej*) rosso/a ♦ *adj* rosso(a); **in the ~** (*account*) scoperto; (*business*) in deficit; **~ carpet treatment** *n* cerimonia col gran pavese; **R~ Cross** *n* Croce *f* Rossa; **~currant** *n* ribes *m inv*; **~den** *vt* arrossare ♦ *vi* arrossire

redeem [rɪ'diːm] *vt* (*debt*) riscattare; (*sth in pawn*) ritirare; (*fig, also* REL) redimere; **~ing** *adj*: **~ing feature** unico aspetto positivo

redeploy [riːdɪ'plɔɪ] *vt* (*resources*) riorganizzare

red-haired [rɛd'hɛəd] *adj* dai capelli rossi

red-handed [rɛd'hændɪd] *adj*: **to be caught ~** essere preso(a) in flagrante *or* con le mani nel sacco

redhead ['rɛdhɛd] n rosso/a

red herring n (fig) falsa pista

red-hot [rɛd'hɔt] adj arroventato(a)

redirect [ri:daɪ'rɛkt] vt (mail) far seguire

red light n: **to go through a ~** (AUT) passare col rosso; **red-light district** n quartiere m a luci rosse

redo [ri:'du:] (irreg) vt rifare

redouble [ri:'dʌbl] vt: **to ~ one's efforts** raddoppiare gli sforzi

redress [rɪ'drɛs] vt riparare

Red Sea n: **the ~** il Mar Rosso

redskin ['rɛdskɪn] n pellerossa m/f

red tape n (fig) burocrazia

reduce [rɪ'dju:s] vt ridurre; (lower) ridurre, abbassare; **"~ speed now"** (AUT) "rallentare"; **at a ~d price** scontato(a); **reduction** [rɪ'dʌkʃən] n riduzione f; (of price) ribasso; (discount) sconto

redundancy [rɪ'dʌndənsɪ] n licenziamento

redundant [rɪ'dʌndnt] adj (worker) licenziato(a); (detail, object) superfluo(a); **to be made ~** essere licenziato (per eccesso di personale)

reed [ri:d] n (BOT) canna; (MUS: of clarinet etc) ancia

reef [ri:f] n (at sea) scogliera

reek [ri:k] vi: **to ~ (of)** puzzare (di)

reel [ri:l] n bobina, rocchetto; (FISHING) mulinello; (CINEMA) rotolo; (dance) danza veloce scozzese ♦ vi (sway) barcollare; **~ in** vt tirare su

ref [rɛf] (inf) n abbr (= referee) arbitro

refectory [rɪ'fɛktərɪ] n refettorio

refer [rɪ'fɔ:*] vt: **to ~ sth to** (dispute, decision) deferire qc a; **to ~ sb to** (inquirer, MED: patient) indirizzare qn a; (reader: to text) rimandare qn a ♦ vi: **to ~ to** (allude to) accennare a; (consult) rivolgersi a

referee [rɛfə'ri:] n arbitro; (BRIT: for job application) referenza ♦ vt arbitrare

reference ['rɛfrəns] n riferimento; (mention) menzione f, allusione f; (for job application) referenza; **with ~ to** (COMM: in letter) in or con riferimento a; **~ book** n libro di consultazione; **~ number** n numero di riferimento

referenda [rɛfə'rɛndə] npl of **referendum**

referendum [rɛfə'rɛndəm] (pl **referenda**) n referendum m inv

refill [vb ri:'fɪl, n 'ri:fɪl] vt riempire di nuovo; (pen, lighter etc) ricaricare ♦ n (for pen etc) ricambio

refine [rɪ'faɪn] vt raffinare; **~d** adj (person, taste) raffinato(a)

reflect [rɪ'flɛkt] vt (light, image) riflettere; (fig) rispecchiare ♦ vi (think) riflettere, considerare; **it ~s badly/well on him** si

ripercuote su di lui in senso negativo/positivo; **~ion** [-'flɛkʃən] n riflessione f; (image) riflesso; (criticism): **~ion on** giudizio su; attacco a; **on ~ion** pensandoci sopra

reflex ['ri:flɛks] adj riflesso(a) ♦ n riflesso; **~ive** [rɪ'flɛksɪv] adj (LING) riflessivo(a)

reform [rɪ'fɔ:m] n (of sinner etc) correzione f; (of law etc) riforma ♦ vt correggere; riformare; **~atory** (US) n riformatorio

refrain [rɪ'freɪn] vi: **to ~ from doing** trattenersi dal fare ♦ n ritornello

refresh [rɪ'frɛʃ] vt rinfrescare; (subj: food, sleep) ristorare; **~er course** (BRIT) n corso di aggiornamento; **~ing** adj (drink) rinfrescante; (sleep) riposante, ristoratore(trice); **~ments** npl rinfreschi mpl

refrigerator [rɪ'frɪdʒəreɪtə*] n frigorifero

refuel [ri:'fjuəl] vi far rifornimento (di carburante)

refuge ['rɛfju:dʒ] n rifugio; **to take ~ in** rifugiarsi in

refugee [rɛfju'dʒi:] n rifugiato/a, profugo/a

refund [n 'ri:fʌnd, vb rɪ'fʌnd] n rimborso ♦ vt rimborsare

refurbish [ri:'fə:bɪʃ] vt rimettere a nuovo

refusal [rɪ'fju:zəl] n rifiuto; **to have first ~ on** avere il diritto d'opzione su

refuse [n 'rɛfju:s, vb rɪ'fju:z] n rifiuti mpl ♦ vt, vi rifiutare; **to ~ to do** rifiutare di fare; **~ collection** n raccolta di rifiuti

refute [rɪ'fju:t] vt confutare

regain [rɪ'geɪn] vt riguadagnare; riacquistare, ricuperare

regal ['ri:gl] adj regale; **~ia** [rɪ'geɪlɪə] n insegne fpl regie

regard [rɪ'gɑ:d] n riguardo, stima ♦ vt considerare, stimare; **to give one's ~s to** porgere i suoi saluti a; **"with kindest ~s"** "cordiali saluti"; **~ing, as ~s, with ~ to** riguardo a; **~less** adv lo stesso; **~less of a** dispetto di, nonostante

regenerate [rɪ'dʒɛnəreɪt] vt rigenerare

régime [reɪ'ʒi:m] n regime m

regiment ['rɛdʒɪmənt] n reggimento; **~al** [-'mɛntl] adj reggimentale

region ['ri:dʒən] n regione f; **in the ~ of** (fig) all'incirca di; **~al** adj regionale

register ['rɛdʒɪstə*] n registro; (also: electoral ~) lista elettorale ♦ vt registrare; (vehicle) immatricolare; (letter) assicurare; (subj: instrument) segnare ♦ vi iscriversi; (at hotel) firmare il registro; (make impression) entrare in testa; **~ed** (BRIT) adj (letter) assicurato(a); **~ed trademark** n marchio depositato

registrar ['rɛdʒɪstrɑ:*] n ufficiale m di stato civile; segretario

registration [rɛdʒɪs'treɪʃən] n (act) registrazione f; iscrizione f; (AUT: also: ~ number) numero di targa

registry ['rɛdʒɪstrɪ] n ufficio del registro; **~ office** (BRIT) n anagrafe f; **to get married in a ~ office** ≈ sposarsi in municipio

regret [rɪ'grɛt] n rimpianto, rincrescimento ♦ vt rimpiangere; **~fully** adv con rincrescimento; **~table** adj deplorevole

regular ['rɛgjulə*] adj regolare; (usual) abituale, normale; (soldier) dell'esercito regolare ♦ n (client etc) cliente m/f abituale; **~ly** adv regolarmente

regulate ['rɛgjuleɪt] vt regolare; **regulation** [-'leɪʃən] n regolazione f; (rule) regola, regolamento

rehabilitation ['riːhəbɪlɪ'teɪʃən] n (of offender) riabilitazione f; (of disabled) riadattamento

rehearsal [rɪ'həːsəl] n prova

rehearse [rɪ'həːs] vt provare

reign [reɪn] n regno ♦ vi regnare

reimburse [riːɪm'bəːs] vt rimborsare

rein [reɪn] n (for horse) briglia

reindeer ['reɪndɪə*] n inv renna

reinforce [riːɪn'fɔːs] vt rinforzare; **~d concrete** n cemento armato; **~ment** n rinforzo; **~ments** npl (MIL) rinforzi mpl

reinstate [riːɪn'steɪt] vt reintegrare

reiterate [riː'ɪtəreɪt] vt reiterare, ripetere

reject [n 'riːdʒɛkt, vb rɪ'dʒɛkt] n (COMM) scarto ♦ vt rifiutare, respingere; (COMM: goods) scartare; **~ion** [rɪ'dʒɛkʃən] n rifiuto

rejoice [rɪ'dʒɔɪs] vi: **to ~ (at or over)** provare diletto in

rejuvenate [rɪ'dʒuːvəneɪt] vt ringiovanire

relapse [rɪ'læps] n (MED) ricaduta

relate [rɪ'leɪt] vt (tell) raccontare; (connect) collegare ♦ vi: **to ~ to** (connect) riferirsi a; (get on with) stabilire un rapporto con; **relating to** che riguarda, rispetto a; **~d** adj: **~d (to)** imparentato(a) (con); collegato(a) or connesso(a) (a)

relation [rɪ'leɪʃən] n (person) parente m/f; (link) rapporto, relazione f; **~ship** n rapporto; (personal ties) rapporti mpl, relazioni fpl; (also: family ~ship) legami mpl di parentela

relative ['rɛlatɪv] n parente m/f ♦ adj relativo(a); (respective) rispettivo(a); **~ly** adv relativamente; (fairly, rather) abbastanza

relax [rɪ'læks] vi rilassarsi; (person: unwind) rilassarsi ♦ vt rilasciare; (mind, person) rilassare; **~ation** [riːlæk'seɪʃən] n rilassamento; rilassamento; (entertainment) ricreazione f, svago; **~ed** adj rilassato(a); **~ing** adj rilassante

relay ['riːleɪ] n (SPORT) corsa a staffetta ♦ vt (message) trasmettere

release [rɪ'liːs] n (from prison) rilascio; (from obligation) liberazione f; (of gas etc) emissione f; (of film etc) distribuzione f;

(record) disco; (device) disinnesto ♦ vt (prisoner) rilasciare; (from obligation, wreckage etc) liberare; (book, film) fare uscire; (news) rendere pubblico(a); (gas etc) emettere; (TECH: catch, spring etc) disinnestare

relegate ['rɛləgeɪt] vt relegare; (BRIT: SPORT): **to be ~d** essere retrocesso(a)

relent [rɪ'lɛnt] vi cedere; **~less** adj implacabile

relevant ['rɛləvənt] adj pertinente; (chapter) in questione; **~ to** pertinente a

reliability [rɪlaɪə'bɪlɪtɪ] n (of person) serietà; (of machine) affidabilità

reliable [rɪ'laɪəbl] adj (person, firm) fidato(a), che dà affidamento; (method) sicuro(a); (machine) affidabile; **reliably** adv: **to be reliably informed** sapere da fonti sicure

reliance [rɪ'laɪəns] n: **~ (on)** fiducia (in); bisogno (di)

relic ['rɛlɪk] n (REL) reliquia; (of the past) resto

relief [rɪ'liːf] n (from pain, anxiety) sollievo; (help, supplies) soccorsi mpl; (ART, GEO) rilievo

relieve [rɪ'liːv] vt (pain, patient) sollevare; (bring help) soccorrere; (take over from: gen) sostituire; (: guard) rilevare; **to ~ sb of sth** (load) alleggerire qn di qc; **to ~ o.s.** fare i propri bisogni

religion [rɪ'lɪdʒən] n religione f; **religious** adj religioso(a)

relinquish [rɪ'lɪŋkwɪʃ] vt abbandonare; (plan, habit) rinunziare a

relish ['rɛlɪʃ] n (CULIN) condimento; (enjoyment) gran piacere m ♦ vt (food etc) godere; **to ~ doing** adorare fare

relocate ['riːləʊ'keɪt] vt trasferire ♦ vi trasferirsi

reluctance [rɪ'lʌktəns] n riluttanza

reluctant [rɪ'lʌktənt] adj riluttante, mal disposto(a); **~ly** adv di mala voglia, a malincuore

rely [rɪ'laɪ]: **to ~ on** vt fus contare su; (be dependent) dipendere da

remain [rɪ'meɪn] vi restare, rimanere; **~der** n resto; (COMM) rimanenza; **~ing** adj che rimane; **~s** npl resti mpl

remand [rɪ'mɑːnd] n: **on ~** in detenzione preventiva ♦ vt: **to ~ in custody** rinviare in carcere; trattenere a disposizione della legge; **~ home** (BRIT) n riformatorio, casa di correzione

remark [rɪ'mɑːk] n osservazione f ♦ vt osservare, dire; **~able** adj notevole; eccezionale

remedial [rɪ'miːdɪəl] adj (tuition, classes) di riparazione; (exercise) correttivo(a)

remedy ['rɛmədɪ] n: **~ (for)** rimedio (per) ♦ vt rimediare a

remember [rɪ'mɛmbə*] vt ricordare, ricordarsi di; **~ me to him** salutalo da parte

mia; **remembrance** n memoria; ricordo;
Remembrance Day n 11 novembre, giorno
della commemorazione dei caduti in guerra
remind [rɪ'maɪnd] vt: **to ~ sb of sth** ricordare
qc a qn; **to ~ sb to do** ricordare a qn di fare;
~er n richiamo; (note etc) promemoria m inv
reminisce [rɛmɪ'nɪs] vi: **to ~ (about)**
abbandonarsi ai ricordi (di)
reminiscent [rɛmɪ'nɪsnt] adj: **~ of** che fa
pensare a, che richiama
remiss [rɪ'mɪs] adj negligente
remission [rɪ'mɪʃən] n remissione f
remit [rɪ'mɪt] vt (send: money) rimettere;
~tance n rimessa
remnant ['rɛmnənt] n resto, avanzo; **~s** npl
(COMM) scampoli mpl; fine f serie
remorse [rɪ'mɔːs] n rimorso; **~ful** adj
pieno(a) di rimorsi; **~less** adj (fig)
spietato(a)
remote [rɪ'məut] adj remoto(a), lontano(a);
(person) distaccato(a); **~ control** n
telecomando; **~ly** adv remotamente;
(slightly) vagamente
remould ['riːməuld] (BRIT) n (tyre) gomma
rivestita
removable [rɪ'muːvəbl] adj (detachable)
staccabile
removal [rɪ'muːvəl] n (taking away)
rimozione f; soppressione f; (BRIT: from house)
trasloco; (from office: dismissal) destituzione f;
(MED) ablazione f; **~ van** (BRIT) n furgone m
per traslochi
remove [rɪ'muːv] vt togliere, rimuovere;
(employee) destituire; (stain) far sparire;
(doubt, abuse) sopprimere, eliminare; **~rs**
(BRIT) npl (company) ditta or impresa di
traslochi
Renaissance [rɪ'neɪsɑ̃ːns] n: **the ~** il
Rinascimento
render ['rɛndə*] vt rendere; **~ing** n (MUS etc)
interpretazione f
rendez-vous ['rɒndɪvuː] n appuntamento;
(place) luogo d'incontro; (meeting) incontro
renegade ['rɛnɪɡeɪd] n rinnegato/a
renew [rɪ'njuː] vt rinnovare; (negotiations)
riprendere; **~able** adj rinnovabile; **~al** n
rinnovo; ripresa
renounce [rɪ'nauns] vt rinunziare a
renovate ['rɛnəveɪt] vt rinnovare; (art work)
restaurare; **renovation** [-'veɪʃən] n
rinnovamento; restauro
renown [rɪ'naun] n rinomanza; **~ed** adj
rinomato(a)
rent [rɛnt] n affitto ♦ vt (take for ~) prendere
in affitto; (also: ~ out) dare in affitto; **~al** n
(for television, car) fitto
renunciation [rɪnʌnsɪ'eɪʃən] n rinunzia
rep [rɛp] n abbr (COMM: = representative)
rappresentante m/f; (THEATRE: = repertory)

teatro di repertorio
repair [rɪ'pɛə*] n riparazione f ♦ vt riparare; **in
good/bad ~** in buone/cattive condizioni; **~ kit**
n corredo per riparazioni
repatriate [riː'pætrɪeɪt] vt rimpatriare
repay [riː'peɪ] (irreg) vt (money, creditor)
rimborsare, ripagare; (sb's efforts)
ricompensare; (favour) ricambiare; **~ment** n
pagamento; rimborso
repeal [rɪ'piːl] n (of law) abrogazione f ♦ vt
abrogare
repeat [rɪ'piːt] n (RADIO, TV) replica ♦ vt
ripetere; (pattern) riprodurre; (promise,
attack, also COMM: order) rinnovare ♦ vi
ripetere; **~edly** adv ripetutamente, spesso
repel [rɪ'pɛl] vt respingere; (disgust) ripugnare
a; **~lent** adj repellente ♦ n: **insect ~lent**
prodotto m anti-insetti inv
repent [rɪ'pɛnt] vi: **to ~ (of)** pentirsi (di);
~ance n pentimento
repertoire ['rɛpətwɑː*] n repertorio
repertory ['rɛpətəri] n (also: ~ **theatre**) teatro
di repertorio
repetition [rɛpɪ'tɪʃən] n ripetizione f
repetitive [rɪ'pɛtɪtɪv] adj (movement) che si
ripete; (work) monotono(a); (speech)
pieno(a) di ripetizioni
replace [rɪ'pleɪs] vt (put back) rimettere a
posto; (take the place of) sostituire; **~ment** n
rimessa; sostituzione f; (person) sostituto/a
replay ['riːpleɪ] n (of match) partita ripetuta;
(of tape, film) replay m inv
replenish [rɪ'plɛnɪʃ] vt (glass) riempire;
(stock etc) rifornire
replete [rɪ'pliːt] adj (well-fed) sazio(a)
replica ['rɛplɪkə] n replica, copia
reply [rɪ'plaɪ] n risposta ♦ vi rispondere;
~ coupon n buono di risposta
report [rɪ'pɔːt] n rapporto; (PRESS etc)
cronaca; (BRIT: also: school ~) pagella; (of
gun) sparo ♦ vt riportare; (PRESS etc) fare una
cronaca su; (bring to notice: occurrence)
segnalare; (: person) denunciare ♦ vi (make a
report) fare un rapporto (or una cronaca);
(present o.s.): **to ~ (to sb)** presentarsi (a qn);
~ card (US, SCOTTISH) n pagella; **~edly** adv
stando a quanto si dice; **he ~edly told them
to ...** avrebbe detto loro di ...; **~er** n reporter
m inv
repose [rɪ'pəuz] n: **in ~** (face, mouth) in
riposo
reprehensible [rɛprɪ'hɛnsɪbl] adj riprovevole
represent [rɛprɪ'zɛnt] vt rappresentare;
~ation [-'teɪʃən] n rappresentazione f;
(petition) rappresentanza; **~ations** npl
(protest) protesta; **~ative** n rappresentante
m/f; (US: POL) deputato/a ♦ adj
rappresentativo(a)
repress [rɪ'prɛs] vt reprimere; **~ion** [-'prɛʃən]

n repressione f

reprieve [rɪ'priːv] n (LAW) sospensione f dell'esecuzione della condanna; (fig) dilazione f

reprimand ['reprɪmɑːnd] n rimprovero ♦ vt rimproverare

reprint ['riːprɪnt] n ristampa

reprisal [rɪ'praɪzl] n rappresaglia

reproach [rɪ'prəutʃ] n rimprovero ♦ vt: to ~ sb for sth rimproverare qn di qc; ~ful adj di rimprovero

reproduce [riːprə'djuːs] vt riprodurre ♦ vi riprodursi; **reproduction** [-'dʌkʃən] n riproduzione f

reproof [rɪ'pruːf] n riprovazione f

reprove [rɪ'pruːv] vt: to ~ (for) biasimare (per)

reptile ['reptaɪl] n rettile m

republic [rɪ'pʌblɪk] n repubblica; ~an adj, n repubblicano(a)

repudiate [rɪ'pjuːdɪeɪt] vt (accusation) respingere

repulse [rɪ'pʌls] vt respingere

repulsive [rɪ'pʌlsɪv] adj ripugnante, ripulsivo(a)

reputable ['repjutəbl] adj di buona reputazione; (occupation) rispettabile

reputation [repju'teɪʃən] n reputazione f

reputed [rɪ'pjuːtɪd] adj reputato(a); ~ly adv secondo quanto si dice

request [rɪ'kwest] n domanda; (formal) richiesta ♦ vt: to ~ (of or from sb) chiedere (a qn); ~ stop (BRIT) n (for bus) fermata facoltativa or a richiesta

require [rɪ'kwaɪə*] vt (need: subj: person) aver bisogno di; (: thing, situation) richiedere; (want) volere; esigere; (order): to ~ sb to do sth ordinare a qn di fare qc; ~ment n esigenza; bisogno; requisito

requisition [rekwɪ'zɪʃən] n: ~ (for) richiesta (di) ♦ vt (MIL) requisire

rescue ['reskjuː] n salvataggio; (help) soccorso ♦ vt salvare; ~ party n squadra di salvataggio; ~r n salvatore/trice

research [rɪ'səːtʃ] n ricerca, ricerche fpl ♦ vt fare ricerche su; ~er n ricercatore/trice

resemblance [rɪ'zembləns] n somiglianza

resemble [rɪ'zembl] vt assomigliare a

resent [rɪ'zent] vt risentirsi di; ~ful adj pieno(a) di risentimento; ~ment n risentimento

reservation [rezə'veɪʃən] n (booking) prenotazione f; (doubt) dubbio; (protected area); (BRIT: on road: also: central ~) spartitraffico m inv

reserve [rɪ'zəːv] n riserva ♦ vt (seats etc) prenotare; ~s npl (MIL) riserve fpl; in ~ in serbo; ~d adj (shy) riservato(a)

reservoir ['rezəvwɑː*] n serbatoio

reshuffle [riː'ʃʌfl] n: Cabinet ~ (POL) rimpasto governativo

reside [rɪ'zaɪd] vi risiedere

residence ['rezɪdəns] n residenza; ~ permit (BRIT) n permesso di soggiorno

resident ['rezɪdənt] n residente m/f; (in hotel) cliente m/f fisso(a) ♦ adj residente; (doctor) fisso(a); (course, college) a tempo pieno con pernottamento; ~ial [-'denʃəl] adj di residenza; (area) residenziale

residue ['rezɪdjuː] n resto; (CHEM, PHYSICS) residuo

resign [rɪ'zaɪn] vt (one's post) dimettersi da ♦ vi dimettersi; to ~ o.s. to rassegnarsi a; ~ation [rezɪg'neɪʃən] n dimissioni fpl; rassegnazione f; ~ed adj rassegnato(a)

resilience [rɪ'zɪlɪəns] n (of material) elasticità, resilienza; (of person) capacità di recupero

resilient [rɪ'zɪlɪənt] adj elastico(a); (person) che si riprende facilmente

resin ['rezɪn] n resina

resist [rɪ'zɪst] vt resistere a; ~ance n resistenza

resolution [rezə'luːʃən] n risoluzione f

resolve [rɪ'zɔlv] n risoluzione f ♦ vi (decide): to ~ to do decidere di fare ♦ vt (problem) risolvere

resort [rɪ'zɔːt] n (town) stazione f; (recourse) ricorso ♦ vi: to ~ to aver ricorso a; in the last ~ come ultima risorsa

resounding [rɪ'zaundɪŋ] adj risonante; (fig) clamoroso(a)

resource [rɪ'sɔːs] n risorsa; ~s npl (coal, iron etc) risorse fpl; ~ful adj pieno(a) di risorse, intraprendente

respect [rɪs'pekt] n rispetto ♦ vt rispettare; ~s npl (greetings) ossequi mpl; with ~ to rispetto a, riguardo a; in this ~ per questo riguardo; ~able adj rispettabile; ~ful adj rispettoso(a)

respective [rɪs'pektɪv] adj rispettivo(a)

respite ['respaɪt] n respiro, tregua

respond [rɪs'pɔnd] vi rispondere

response [rɪs'pɔns] n risposta

responsibility [rɪspɔnsɪ'bɪlɪtɪ] n responsabilità f inv

responsible [rɪs'pɔnsɪbl] adj (trustworthy) fidato(a); (job) di (grande) responsabilità; ~ (for) responsabile (di)

responsive [rɪs'pɔnsɪv] adj che reagisce

rest [rest] n riposo; (stop) sosta, pausa; (MUS) pausa; (object: to support sth) appoggio, sostegno; (remainder) resto, avanzi mpl ♦ vi riposarsi; (remain) rimanere, restare; (be supported): to ~ on appoggiarsi su ♦ vt (far) riposare; (lean): to ~ sth on/against appoggiare qc su/contro; the ~ of them gli altri; it ~s with him to decide sta a lui decidere

restaurant ['restərɔŋ] n ristorante m; ~ car

(BRIT) n vagone m ristorante

restful ['restful] adj riposante

rest home n casa di riposo

restitution [rɛstɪ'tjuːʃən] n: **to make ~ to sb for sth** compensare qn di qc

restive ['rɛstɪv] adj agitato(a), impaziente

restless ['rɛstlɪs] adj agitato(a), irrequieto(a)

restoration [rɛstə'reɪʃən] n restauro; restituzione f

restore [rɪ'stɔː*] vt (building, to power) restaurare; (sth stolen) restituire; (peace, health) ristorare

restrain [rɪs'treɪn] vt (feeling, growth) contenere, frenare; (person): **to ~ (from doing)** trattenere (dal fare); **~ed** adj (style) contenuto(a), sobrio(a); (person) riservato(a); **~t** n (restriction) limitazione f; (moderation) ritegno; (of style) contenutezza

restrict [rɪs'trɪkt] vt restringere, limitare; **~ion** [-kʃən] n: **~ion (on)** restrizione f (di), limitazione f

rest room (US) n toletta

restructure [riː'strʌktʃə*] vt ristrutturare

result [rɪ'zʌlt] n risultato ♦ vi: **to ~ in** avere per risultato; **as a ~ of** in or di conseguenza a, in seguito a

resume [rɪ'zjuːm] vt, vi (work, journey) riprendere

résumé ['reɪzjumeɪ] n riassunto; (US) curriculum m inv vitae

resumption [rɪ'zʌmpʃən] n ripresa

resurgence [rɪ'səːdʒəns] n rinascita

resurrection [rɛzə'rekʃən] n risurrezione f

resuscitate [rɪ'sʌsɪteɪt] vt (MED) risuscitare; **resuscitation** [-'teɪʃən] n rianimazione f

retail ['riːteɪl] adj, adv al minuto ♦ vt vendere al minuto; **~er** n commerciante m/f al minuto, dettagliante m/f; **~ price** n prezzo al minuto

retain [rɪ'teɪn] vt (keep) tenere, serbare; **~er** n (fee) onorario

retaliate [rɪ'tælɪeɪt] vi: **to ~ (against)** vendicarsi (di); **retaliation** [-'eɪʃən] n rappresaglie fpl

retarded [rɪ'tɑːdɪd] adj ritardato(a)

retch [rɛtʃ] vi aver conati di vomito

retire [rɪ'taɪə*] vi (give up work) andare in pensione; (withdraw) ritirarsi, andarsene; (go to bed) andare a letto, ritirarsi; **~d** adj (person) pensionato(a); **~ment** n pensione f; (act) pensionamento; **retiring** adj (leaving) uscente; (shy) riservato(a)

retort [rɪ'tɔːt] vi rimbeccare

retrace [riː'treɪs] vt: **to ~ one's steps** tornare sui passi

retract [rɪ'trækt] vt (statement) ritrattare; (claws, undercarriage, aerial) ritrarre, ritirare

retrain [riː'treɪn] vt (worker) riaddestrare

retread ['riːtrɛd] n (tyre) gomma rigenerata

retreat [rɪ'triːt] n ritirata; (ᵖ battere in ritirata

retribution [rɛtrɪ'bjuːʃən] n castigo

retrieval [rɪ'triːvəl] n (see vb) ricupero; riparazione f

retrieve [rɪ'triːv] vt (sth lost) ricuperare; ritrovare; (situation, honour) salvare; (error, loss) rimediare a; **~r** n cane m da riporto

retrospect ['rɛtrəspekt] n: **in ~** guardando indietro; **~ive** [-'spektɪv] adj retrospettivo(a); (law) retroattivo(a)

return [rɪ'təːn] n (going or coming back) ritorno; (of sth stolen etc) restituzione f; (FINANCE: from land, shares) profitto, reddito ♦ cpd (journey, match) di ritorno; (BRIT: ticket) di andata e ritorno ♦ vi tornare, ritornare ♦ vt rendere, restituire; (bring back) riportare; (send back) mandare indietro; (put back) rimettere; (POL: candidate) eleggere; **~s** npl (COMM) incassi mpl; profitti mpl; **in ~ (for)** in cambio (di); **by ~ of post** a stretto giro di posta; **many happy ~s (of the day)!** cento di questi giorni!

reunion [riː'juːnɪən] n riunione f

reunite [riːju:'naɪt] vt riunire

rev [rev] n abbr (AUT: = revolution) giro ♦ vt (also: ~ up) imballare

revamp ['riː'væmp] vt (firm) riorganizzare

reveal [rɪ'viːl] vt (make known) rivelare, svelare; (display) rivelare, mostrare; **~ing** adj rivelatore(trice); (dress) scollato(a)

revel ['rɛvl] vi: **to ~ in sth/in doing** dilettarsi di qc/a fare

revelation [rɛvə'leɪʃən] n rivelazione f

revenge [rɪ'vɛndʒ] n vendetta ♦ vt vendicare; **to take ~ on** vendicarsi di

revenue ['rɛvənjuː] n reddito

reverberate [rɪ'vəːbəreɪt] vi (sound) rimbombare; (light) riverberarsi; (fig) ripercuotersi

revere [rɪ'vɪə*] vt venerare

reverence ['rɛvərəns] n venerazione f, riverenza

Reverend ['rɛvərənd] adj (in titles) reverendo(a)

reverie ['rɛvərɪ] n fantasticheria

reversal [rɪ'vəːsl] n capovolgimento

reverse [rɪ'vəːs] n contrario, opposto; (back, defeat) rovescio; (AUT: also: ~ gear) marcia indietro ♦ adj (order, direction) contrario(a), opposto(a) ♦ vt (turn) invertire, rivoltare; (change) capovolgere, rovesciare; (LAW: judgment) cassare; (car) fare marcia indietro con ♦ vi (BRIT: AUT, person etc) fare marcia indietro; **~-charge call** (BRIT) n (TEL) telefonata con addebito al ricevente; **reversing lights** (BRIT) npl (AUT) luci fpl per la retromarcia

revert [rɪ'vəːt] vi: **to ~ to** tornare a

review [rɪ'vjuː] n rivista; (of book, film) recensione f; (of situation) esame m ♦ vt passare in rivista; fare la recensione di; fare il punto di; **~er** n recensore/a

revise [rɪ'vaɪz] vt (manuscript) rivedere, correggere; (opinion) emendare, modificare; (study: subject, notes) ripassare; **revision** [rɪ'vɪʒən] n revisione f; ripasso

revitalize [riː'vaɪtəlaɪz] vt ravvivare

revival [rɪ'vaɪvəl] n ripresa; ristabilimento; (of faith) risveglio

revive [rɪ'vaɪv] vt (person) rianimare; (custom) far rivivere; (hope, courage, economy) ravvivare; (play, fashion) riesumare ♦ vi (person) rianimarsi; (hope) ravvivarsi; (activity) riprendersi

revolt [rɪ'vəult] n rivolta, ribellione f ♦ vi rivoltarsi, ribellarsi ♦ vt (far) rivoltare; **~ing** adj ripugnante

revolution [revə'luːʃən] n rivoluzione f; (of wheel etc) rivoluzione, giro; **~ary** adj, n rivoluzionario/a

revolve [rɪ'vɔlv] vi girare

revolver [rɪ'vɔlvə*] n rivoltella

revolving [rɪ'vɔlvɪŋ] adj girevole

revue [rɪ'vjuː] n (THEATRE) rivista

revulsion [rɪ'vʌlʃən] n ripugnanza

reward [rɪ'wɔːd] n ricompensa, premio ♦ vt: **to ~ (for)** ricompensare (per); **~ing** adj (fig) gratificante

rewind [riː'waɪnd] (irreg) vt (watch) ricaricare; (ribbon etc) riavvolgere

rewire [riː'waɪə*] vt (house) rifare l'impianto elettrico di

reword [riː'wɔːd] vt formulare or esprimere con altre parole

rheumatism ['ruːmətɪzəm] n reumatismo

Rhine [raɪn] n: **the ~** il Reno

rhinoceros [raɪ'nɔsərəs] n rinoceronte m

rhododendron [rəudə'dendrən] n rododendro

Rhone [rəun] n: **the ~** il Rodano

rhubarb ['ruːbɑːb] n rabarbaro

rhyme [raɪm] n rima; (verse) poesia

rhythm ['rɪðm] n ritmo

rib [rɪb] n (ANAT) costola ♦ vt (tease) punzecchiare

ribbon ['rɪbən] n nastro; **in ~s** (torn) a brandelli

rice [raɪs] n riso; **~ pudding** n budino di riso

rich [rɪtʃ] adj ricco(a); (clothes) sontuoso(a); (abundant): **~ in** ricco(a) di; **the ~** npl (wealthy people) i ricchi; **~es** npl ricchezze fpl; **~ly** adv riccamente; (dressed) sontuosamente; (deserved) pienamente

rickets ['rɪkɪts] n rachitismo

ricochet ['rɪkəʃeɪ] vi rimbalzare

rid [rɪd] (pt, pp rid) vt: **to ~ sb of** sbarazzare or liberare qn di; **to get ~ of** sbarazzarsi di

ridden ['rɪdn] pp of ride

riddle ['rɪdl] n (puzzle) indovinello ♦ vt: **to be ~d with** (holes) essere crivellato(a) di; (doubts) essere pieno(a) di

ride [raɪd] (pt rode, pp ridden) n (on horse) cavalcata; (outing) passeggiata; (distance covered) cavalcata; corsa ♦ vi (as sport) cavalcare; (go somewhere: on horse, bicycle) andare (a cavallo or in bicicletta etc); (journey: on bicycle, motorcycle, bus) andare, viaggiare ♦ vt (a horse) montare, cavalcare; **to take sb for a ~** (fig) prendere in giro qn; fregare qn; **to ~ a horse/bicycle/camel** montare a cavallo/in bicicletta/in groppa a un cammello; **~r** n cavalcatore/trice; (in race) fantino; (on bicycle) ciclista m/f; (on motorcycle) motociclista m/f

ridge [rɪdʒ] n (of hill) cresta; (of roof) colmo; (on object) riga (in rilievo)

ridicule ['rɪdɪkjuːl] n ridicolo; scherno ♦ vt mettere in ridicolo

ridiculous [rɪ'dɪkjuləs] adj ridicolo(a)

riding ['raɪdɪŋ] n equitazione f; **~ school** n scuola d'equitazione

rife [raɪf] adj diffuso(a); **to be ~ with** abbondare di

riffraff ['rɪfræf] n canaglia

rifle ['raɪfl] n carabina ♦ vt vuotare; **~ through** vt fus frugare tra; **~ range** n campo di tiro; (at fair) tiro a segno

rift [rɪft] n fessura, crepatura; (fig: disagreement) incrinatura, disaccordo

rig [rɪg] n (also: oil ~: on land) derrick m inv; (: at sea) piattaforma di trivellazione ♦ vt (election etc) truccare; **to ~ out** (BRIT) vt: **to ~ out as/in** vestire da/in; **~ up** vt allestire; **~ging** n (NAUT) attrezzatura

right [raɪt] adj giusto(a); (suitable) appropriato(a); (not left) destro(a) ♦ n giusto; (title, claim) diritto; (not left) destra ♦ adv (answer) correttamente; (not on the left) a destra ♦ vt raddrizzare; (fig) riparare ♦ excl bene!; **to be ~** (person) aver ragione; (answer) essere giusto(a) or corretto(a); **by ~s** di diritto; **on the ~** a destra; **to be in the ~** aver ragione, essere nel giusto; **~ now** proprio adesso; subito; **~ away** subito; **~ angle** n angolo retto; **~eous** ['raɪtʃəs] adj retto(a), virtuoso(a); (anger) giusto(a), giustificato(a); **~ful** adj (heir) legittimo(a); **~-handed** adj (person) che adopera la mano destra; **~-hand man** n braccio destro; **~-hand side** n il lato destro; **~ly** adv bene, correttamente; (with reason) a ragione; **~ of way** n diritto di passaggio; (AUT) precedenza; **~-wing** adj (POL) di destra

rigid ['rɪdʒɪd] adj rigido(a); (principle) rigoroso(a)

rigmarole ['rɪgmərəul] n tiritera; commedia

rile [raɪl] vt irritare, seccare

rim [rɪm] n orlo; (of spectacles) montatura; (of wheel) cerchione m

rind [raɪnd] n (of bacon) cotenna; (of lemon etc) scorza

ring [rɪŋ] (pt **rang**, pp **rung**) n anello; (of people, objects) cerchio; (of spies) giro; (of smoke etc) spirale m; (arena) pista, arena; (for boxing) ring m inv; (sound of bell) scampanio ♦ vi (person, bell, telephone) suonare; (also: ~ out: voice, words) risuonare; (TEL) telefonare; (ears) fischiare ♦ vt (BRIT: TEL) telefonare a; (bell, doorbell) suonare; **to give sb a ~** (BRIT: TEL) dare un colpo di telefono a qn; ~ **back** vt, vi (TEL) richiamare; ~ **off** (BRIT) vi (TEL) mettere giù, riattaccare; ~ **up** (BRIT) vt (TEL) telefonare a; **~ing** n (of bell) scampanio; (of telephone) squillo; (in ears) ronzio; **~ing tone** (BRIT) n (TEL) segnale m di libero; **~leader** n (of gang) capobanda m

ringlets ['rɪŋlɪts] npl boccoli mpl

ring road (BRIT) n raccordo anulare

rink [rɪŋk] n (also: ice ~) pista di pattinaggio

rinse [rɪns] n risciacquatura; (hair tint) cachet m inv ♦ vt sciacquare

riot ['raɪət] n sommossa, tumulto; (of colours) orgia ♦ vi tumultuare; **to run ~** creare disordine; **~ous** adj tumultuoso(a); (living) sfrenato(a); (party) scatenato(a)

rip [rɪp] n strappo ♦ vt strappare ♦ vi strapparsi; **~cord** n cavo di sfilamento

ripe [raɪp] adj (fruit, grain) maturo(a); (cheese) stagionato(a); **~n** vt maturare ♦ vi maturarsi

ripple ['rɪpl] n increspamento, ondulazione f; mormorio ♦ vi incresparsi

rise [raɪz] (pt **rose**, pp **risen**) n (slope) salita, pendio; (hill) altura; (increase: in wages: BRIT) aumento; (: in prices, temperature) rialzo, aumento; (fig: to power etc) ascesa ♦ vi alzarsi, levarsi; (prices) aumentare; (waters, river) crescere; (sun, wind, person: from chair, bed) levarsi; (also: ~ up: building) ergersi; (: rebel) insorgere; ribellarsi; (in rank) salire; **to give ~ to** provocare, dare origine a; **to ~ to the occasion** essere all'altezza; **risen** ['rɪzn] pp of **rise**; **rising** adj (increasing: number) sempre crescente; (: prices) in aumento; (tide) montante; (sun, moon) nascente, che sorge

risk [rɪsk] n rischio; pericolo ♦ vt rischiare; **to take or run the ~ of doing** correre il rischio di fare; **at ~** in pericolo; **at one's own ~** a proprio rischio e pericolo; **~y** adj rischioso(a)

risqué ['riːskeɪ] adj (joke) spinto(a)

rissole ['rɪsəʊl] n crocchetta

rite [raɪt] n rito; **last ~s** l'estrema unzione

ritual ['rɪtjuəl] adj rituale ♦ n rituale m

rival ['raɪvl] n rivale m/f; (in business) concorrente m/f ♦ adj rivale; che fa concorrenza ♦ vt essere in concorrenza con; **to ~ sb/sth in** competere con qn/qc in; **~ry** n rivalità; concorrenza

river ['rɪvə*] n fiume m ♦ cpd (port, traffic) fluviale; **up/down ~** a monte/valle; **~bank** n argine m; **~bed** n letto di fiume

rivet ['rɪvɪt] n ribattino, rivetto ♦ vt (fig) concentrare, fissare

Riviera [rɪvɪ'ɛərə] n: **the (French) ~** la Costa Azzurra; **the Italian ~** la Riviera

road [rəʊd] n strada; (small) cammino; (in town) via ♦ cpd stradale; **major/minor ~** strada con/senza diritto di precedenza; **~ accident** n incidente m stradale; **~block** n blocco stradale; **~hog** n guidatore m egoista e spericolato; **~ map** n carta stradale; **~ rage** n comportamento aggressivo al volante; **~ safety** n sicurezza sulle strade; **~side** n margine m della strada; **~sign** n cartello stradale; **~ user** n chi usa la strada; **~way** n carreggiata; **~works** npl lavori mpl stradali; **~worthy** adj in buono stato di marcia

roam [rəʊm] vi errare, vagabondare

roar [rɔː*] n ruggito; (of crowd) tumulto; (of thunder, storm) muggito; (of laughter) scoppio ♦ vi ruggire; tumultuare; muggire; **to ~ with laughter** scoppiare dalle risa; **to do a ~ing trade** fare affari d'oro

roast [rəʊst] n arrosto ♦ vt arrostire; (coffee) tostare, torrefare; ~ **beef** n arrosto di manzo

rob [rɒb] vt (person) rubare; (bank) svaligiare; **to ~ sb of sth** derubare qn di qc; (fig: deprive) privare qn di qc; **~ber** n ladro; (armed) rapinatore m; **~bery** n furto; rapina

robe [rəʊb] n (for ceremony etc) abito; (also: bath ~) accappatoio; (US: also: lap ~) coperta

robin ['rɒbɪn] n pettirosso

robot ['rəʊbɒt] n robot m inv

robust [rəʊ'bʌst] adj robusto(a); (economy) solido(a)

rock [rɒk] n (substance) roccia; (boulder) masso, roccia; (in sea) scoglio; (US: pebble) ciottolo; (BRIT: sweet) zucchero candito ♦ vt (swing gently: cradle) dondolare; (: child) cullare; (shake) scrollare, far tremare ♦ vi dondolarsi; scrollarsi, tremare; **on the ~s** (drink) col ghiaccio; (marriage etc) in crisi; ~ **and roll** n rock and roll m; **~-bottom** adj bassissimo(a); **~ery** n giardino roccioso

rocket ['rɒkɪt] n razzo

rock fall n parete f della roccia

rocking ['rɒkɪŋ]: ~ **chair** n sedia a dondolo; ~ **horse** n cavallo a dondolo

rocky ['rɒkɪ] adj (hill) roccioso(a); (path) sassoso(a); (marriage etc) instabile

rod [rɒd] n (metallic, TECH) asta; (wooden) bacchetta; (also: fishing ~) canna da pesca

rode [rəud] *pt of* **ride**

rodent ['rəudnt] *n* roditore *m*

rodeo ['rəudɪəu] *n* rodeo

roe [rəu] *n* (*species: also:* ~ **deer**) capriolo; (*of fish, also:* hard ~) uova *fpl* di pesce; **soft ~** latte *m* di pesce

rogue [rəug] *n* mascalzone *m*

role [rəul] *n* ruolo

roll [rəul] *n* rotolo; (*of banknotes*) mazzo; (*also:* bread ~) panino; (*register*) lista; (*sound: of drums etc*) rullo ♦ *vt* rotolare; (*also:* ~ up: string) aggomitolare; (*also:* ~ up: sleeves) rimboccare; (*cigarettes*) arrotolare; (*eyes*) roteare; (*also:* ~ out: pastry*) stendere; (*lawn, road etc*) spianare ♦ *vi* rotolare; (*wheel*) girare; (*drum*) rullare; (*vehicle: also:* ~ along*) avanzare; (*ship*) rollare; ~ **about** *or* **around** *vi* rotolare qua e là; (*person*) rotolarsi; ~ **by** *vi* (*time*) passare; ~ **over** *vi* rivoltarsi; ~ **up** (*inf*) *vi* (*arrive*) arrivare ♦ *vt* (*carpet*) arrotolare; ~ **call** *n* appello; **~er** *n* rullo; (*wheel*) rotella; (*for hair*) bigodino; **R~erblades** ® *npl* pattini *mpl* in linea; **~er coaster** *n* montagne *fpl* russe; **~er skates** *npl* pattini *mpl* a rotelle

rolling ['rəulɪŋ] *adj* (*landscape*) ondulato(a); ~ **pin** *n* matterello; ~ **stock** *n* (*RAIL*) materiale *m* rotabile

ROM [rɔm] *n abbr* (= read only memory) memoria *f* di sola lettura

Roman ['rəumən] *adj, n* romano(a); ~ **Catholic** *adj, n* cattolico(a)

romance [rə'mæns] *n* storia (*or* avventura *or* film *m inv*) romantico(a); (*charm*) poesia; (*love affair*) idillio

Romania [rəu'meɪnɪə] *n* = **Rumania**

Roman numeral *n* numero romano

romantic [rə'mæntɪk] *adj* romantico(a); sentimentale

Rome [rəum] *n* Roma

romp [rɔmp] *n* gioco rumoroso ♦ *vi* (*also:* ~ about*) far chiasso, giocare in un modo rumoroso

rompers ['rɔmpəz] *npl* pagliaccetto

roof [ru:f] *n* tetto; (*of tunnel, cave*) volta ♦ *vt* coprire (con un tetto); ~ **of the mouth** palato; **~ing** *n* materiale *m* per copertura; ~ **rack** *n* (*AUT*) portabagagli *m inv*

rook [ruk] *n* (*bird*) corvo nero; (*CHESS*) torre *f*

room [ru:m] *n* (*in house*) stanza; (*bed~, in hotel*) camera; (*in school etc*) sala; (*space*) posto, spazio; **~s** *npl* (*lodging*) alloggio; "**~s to let**" (*BRIT*), "**~s for rent**" (*US*) "si affittano camere"; **there is ~ for improvement** si potrebbe migliorare; **~ing house** (*US*) *n* casa in cui si affittano camere *o* appartamentini ammobiliati; **~mate** *n* compagno/a di stanza; ~ **service** *n* servizio da camera; **~y** *adj* spazioso(a); (*garment*) ampio(a)

roost [ru:st] *vi* appollaiarsi

rooster ['ru:stə*] *n* gallo

root [ru:t] *n* radice *f* ♦ *vi* (*plant, belief*) attecchire; ~ **about** *vi* (*fig*) frugare; ~ **for** *vt fus* fare il tifo per; ~ **out** *vt* estirpare

rope [rəup] *n* corda, fune *f*; (*NAUT*) cavo ♦ *vt* (*box*) legare; (*climbers*) legare in cordata; (*area: also:* ~ off*) isolare cingendo con cordoni; **to know the ~s** (*fig*) conoscere i trucchi del mestiere; ~ **in** *vt* (*fig*) coinvolgere; ~ **ladder** *n* scala a corda

rosary ['rəuzərɪ] *n* rosario; roseto

rose [rəuz] *pt of* **rise** ♦ *n* rosa; (*also:* ~ **bush**) rosaio; (*on watering can*) rosetta

rosé ['rəuzeɪ] *n* vino rosato

rosebud ['rəuzbʌd] *n* bocciolo di rosa

rosebush ['rəuzbuʃ] *n* rosaio

rosemary ['rəuzmərɪ] *n* rosmarino

rosette [rəu'zet] *n* coccarda

roster ['rɔstə*] *n*: **duty ~** ruolino di servizio

rostrum ['rɔstrəm] *n* tribuna

rosy ['rəuzɪ] *adj* roseo(a)

rot [rɔt] *n* (*decay*) putrefazione *f*; (*inf: nonsense*) stupidaggini *fpl* ♦ *vt, vi* imputridire, marcire

rota ['rəutə] *n* tabella dei turni

rotary ['rəutərɪ] *adj* rotante

rotate [rəu'teɪt] *vt* (*revolve*) far girare; (*change round: jobs*) fare a turno ♦ *vi* (*revolve*) girare; **rotating** *adj* (*movement*) rotante

rotten ['rɔtn] *adj* (*decayed*) putrido(a), marcio(a); (*dishonest*) corrotto(a); (*inf: bad*) brutto(a); (: *action*) vigliacco(a); **to feel ~** (*ill*) sentirsi da cani

rouble ['ru:bl] (*US* **ruble**) *n* rublo

rouge [ru:ʒ] *n* belletto

rough [rʌf] *adj* (*skin, surface*) ruvido(a); (*terrain, road*) accidentato(a); (*voice*) rauco(a); (*person, manner: coarse*) rozzo(a), aspro(a); (: *violent*) brutale; (*district*) malfamato(a); (*weather*) cattivo(a); (*sea*) mosso(a); (*plan*) abbozzato(a); (*guess*) approssimativo(a) ♦ *n* (*GOLF*) macchia; **to ~ it** far vita dura; **to sleep ~** (*BRIT*) dormire all'addiaccio; **~age** *n* alimenti *mpl* ricchi di cellulosa; **~-and-ready** *adj* rudimentale; **~cast** *n* intonaco grezzo; ~ **copy** *n* brutta copia; **~ly** *adv* (*handle*) rudemente, brutalmente; (*make*) grossolanamente; (*speak*) bruscamente; (*approximately*) approssimativamente; **~ness** *n* ruvidità; (*of manner*) rozzezza

roulette [ru:'let] *n* roulette *f*

Roumania [ru:'meɪnɪə] *n* = **Rumania**

round [raund] *adj* rotondo(a); (*figures*) tondo(a) ♦ *n* (*BRIT:* of toast*) fetta; (*duty: of policeman, milkman etc*) giro; (: *of doctor*) visite *fpl*; (*game: of cards, golf, in competition*) partita; (*of ammunition*) cartuccia; (*BOXING*) round *m inv*; (*of talks*) serie *f inv* ♦ *vt* (*corner*) girare; (*bend*) prendere ♦ *prep* intorno a ♦ *adv*: **all ~** tutt'attorno; **to go the long way ~** fare il giro più lungo; **all the year ~** tutto l'anno; **it's just ~ the corner** (*also fig*) è dietro l'angolo; **~ the clock** ininterrottamente; **to go ~ to sb's house** andare da qn; **go ~ the back** passi dietro; **enough to go ~** abbastanza per tutti; **~ of applause** applausi *mpl*; **~ of drinks** giro di bibite; **~ of sandwiches** sandwich *m inv*; **~ off** *vt* (*speech etc*) finire; **~ up** *vt* radunare; (*criminals*) fare una retata di; (*prices*) arrotondare; **~about** *n* (*BRIT: AUT*) rotatoria; (: *at fair*) giostra ♦ *adj* (*route, means*) indiretto(a); **~ers** *npl* (*game*) gioco simile al baseball; **~ly** *adv* (*fig*) chiaro e tondo; **~ trip** *n* (*viaggio di*) andata e ritorno; **~up** *n* raduno; (*of criminals*) retata

rouse [rauz] *vt* (*wake up*) svegliare; (*stir up*) destare; provocare; risvegliare; **rousing** *adj* (*speech, applause*) entusiastico(a)

route [ruːt] *n* itinerario; (*of bus*) percorso.

routine [ruːˈtiːn] *adj* (*work*) corrente, abituale; (*procedure*) solito(a) ♦ *n* (*pej*) routine *f*, tran tran *m*; (*THEATRE*) numero

rove [rəuv] *vt* vagabondare per

row[1] [rəu] *n* (*line*) riga, fila; (*KNITTING*) ferro; (*behind one another: of cars, people*) fila; (*in boat*) remata ♦ *vi* (*in boat*) remare; (*as sport*) vogare ♦ *vt* (*boat*) manovrare a remi; **in a ~** (*fig*) di fila

row[2] [rau] *n* (*racket*) baccano, chiasso; (*dispute*) lite *f*; (*scolding*) sgridata ♦ *vi* (*argue*) litigare

rowboat [ˈrəubəut] (*US*) *n* barca a remi

rowdy [ˈraudɪ] *adj* chiassoso(a); turbolento(a) ♦ *n* teppista *m/f*

rowing [ˈrəuɪŋ] *n* canottaggio; **~ boat** (*BRIT*) *n* barca a remi

royal [ˈrɔɪəl] *adj* reale; **R~ Air Force** *n* aeronautica militare britannica

royalty [ˈrɔɪəltɪ] *n* (*royal persons*) (membri *mpl* della) famiglia reale; (*payment: to author*) diritti *mpl* d'autore

r.p.m. *abbr* (= *revolutions per minute*) giri/min

R.S.V.P. *abbr* (= *répondez s'il vous plaît*) R.S.V.P.

Rt Hon. (*BRIT*) *abbr* (= *Right Honourable*) ≈ Onorevole

rub [rʌb] *n*: **to give sth a ~** strofinare qc; (*sore place*) massaggiare qc ♦ *vt* strofinare; massaggiare; (*hands: also*: ~ **together**) sfregarsi; **to ~ sb up** (*BRIT*) *or* ~ **sb the wrong way** (*US*) lisciare qn contro pelo; **~ off** *vi* andare via; **~ off on** *vt fus* lasciare una traccia su; **~ out** *vt* cancellare

rubber [ˈrʌbə*] *n* gomma; **~ band** *n* elastico; **~ plant** *n* ficus *m inv*

rubbish [ˈrʌbɪʃ] *n* (*from household*)

immondizie *fpl*, rifiuti *mpl*; (*fig: pej*) cose *fpl* senza valore; robaccia; sciocchezze *fpl*; **~ bin** (*BRIT*) *n* pattumiera; **~ dump** *n* (*in town*) immondezzaio

rubble [ˈrʌbl] *n* macerie *fpl*; (*smaller*) pietrisco

ruble [ˈruːbl] (*US*) *n* = **rouble**

ruby [ˈruːbɪ] *n* rubino

rucksack [ˈrʌksæk] *n* zaino

rudder [ˈrʌdə*] *n* timone *m*

ruddy [ˈrʌdɪ] *adj* (*face*) rubicondo(a); (*inf: damned*) maledetto(a)

rude [ruːd] *adj* (*impolite: person*) scortese, rozzo(a); (: *word, manners*) grossolano(a), rozzo(a); (*shocking*) indecente; **~ness** *n* scortesia; grossolanità

ruffle [ˈrʌfl] *vt* (*hair*) scompigliare; (*clothes, water*) increspare; (*fig: person*) turbare

rug [rʌg] *n* tappeto; (*BRIT: for knees*) coperta

rugby [ˈrʌgbɪ] *n* (*also*: ~ *football*) rugby *m*

rugged [ˈrʌgɪd] *adj* (*landscape*) aspro(a); (*features, determination*) duro(a); (*character*) brusco(a)

ruin [ˈruːɪn] *n* rovina ♦ *vt* rovinare; **~s** *npl* (*of building, castle etc*) rovine *fpl*, ruderi *mpl*; **~ous** *adj* rovinoso(a); (*expenditure*) inverosimile

rule [ruːl] *n* regola; (*regulation*) regolamento, regola; (*government*) governo; (~*r*) riga ♦ *vt* (*country*) governare; (*person*) dominare ♦ *vi* regnare; decidere; (*LAW*) dichiarare; **as a ~** normalmente; **~ out** *vt* escludere; **~d** *adj* (*paper*) vergato(a); **~r** *n* (*sovereign*) sovrano a; (*for measuring*) regolo, riga; **ruling** *adj* (*party*) al potere; (*class*) dirigente ♦ *n* (*LAW*) decisione *f*

rum [rʌm] *n* rum *m*

Rumania [ruːˈmeɪnɪə] *n* Romania

rumble [ˈrʌmbl] *n* rimbombo; brontolio ♦ *vi* rimbombare; (*stomach, pipe*) brontolare

rummage [ˈrʌmɪdʒ] *vi* frugare

rumour [ˈruːmə*] (*US* **rumor**) *n* voce *f* ♦ *vt*: **it is ~ed that** corre voce che

rump [rʌmp] *n* groppa; **~ steak** *n* bistecca di girello

rumpus [ˈrʌmpəs] (*inf*) *n* baccano; (*quarrel*) rissa

run [rʌn] (*pt* **ran**, *pp* **run**) *n* corsa; (*outing*) gita (*in macchina*); (*distance travelled*) percorso, tragitto; (*SKI*) pista; (*CRICKET, BASEBALL*) meta; (*series*) serie *f*; (*THEATRE*) periodo di rappresentazione; (*in tights, stockings*) smagliatura ♦ *vt* (*distance*) correre; (*operate: business*) gestire, dirigere; (: *competition, course*) organizzare; (: *hotel*) gestire; (: *house*) governare; (*COMPUT*) eseguire; (*water, bath*) far scorrere; (*force through: rope, pipe*) far passare qc attraverso; (*pass: hand, finger*): **to ~ sth over** passare qc su; (*PRESS: feature*) presentare ♦ *vi*

correre; (*flee*) scappare; (*pass: road etc*)
passare; (*work: machine, factory*) funzionare,
andare; (*bus, train: operate*) far servizio;
(: *travel*) circolare; (*continue: play, contract*)
durare; (*slide: drawer; flow: river, bath*)
scorrere; (*colours, washing*) stemperarsi; (*in
election*) presentarsi candidato; (*nose*) colare;
there was a ~ on ... c'era una corsa a ...; **in
the long ~** a lungo andare; **on the ~** in fuga;
to ~ a race partecipare ad una gara; **I'll ~ you
to the station** la porto alla stazione; **to ~ a
risk** correre un rischio; **~ about** *or* **around**
vi (*children*) correre qua e là; **~ across** *vt fus*
(*find*) trovare per caso; **~ away** *vi* fuggire;
~ down *vt* (*production*) ridurre gradualmente; (*factory*) rallentare l'attività di;
(*AUT*) investire; (*criticize*) criticare; **to be
~ down** (*person: tired*) essere esausto(a); **~
in** (*BRIT*) *vt* (*car*) rodare, fare il rodaggio di;
~ into *vt fus* (*meet: person*) incontrare per
caso; (: *trouble*) incontrare, trovare; (*collide
with*) andare a sbattere contro; **~ off** *vi*
fuggire ♦ *vt* (*water*) far scolare; (*copies*) fare;
~ out *vi* (*person*) uscire di corsa; (*liquid*)
colare; (*lease*) scadere; (*money*) esaurirsi;
~ out of *vt fus* rimanere a corto di; **~
over** *vt* (*AUT*) investire, mettere sotto ♦ *vt fus*
(*revise*) rivedere; **~ through** *vt fus*
(*instructions*) dare una scorsa a; (*rehearse:
play*) riprovare, ripetere; **~ up** *vt* (*debt*)
lasciar accumulare; **to ~ up against**
(*difficulties*) incontrare; **~away** *adj* (*person*)
fuggiasco(a); (*horse*) in libertà; (*truck*) fuori
controllo

rung [rʌŋ] *pp of* **ring** ♦ *n* (*of ladder*) piolo
runner ['rʌnə*] *n* (*in race*) corridore *m*;
(: *horse*) partente *m/f*; (*on sledge*) pattino;
(*for drawer etc*) guida; **~ bean** (*BRIT*) *n*
fagiolo rampicante; **~-up** *n* secondo(a)
arrivato(a)
running ['rʌnɪŋ] *n* corsa; direzione *f*;
organizzazione *f*; funzionamento ♦ *adj*
(*water*) corrente; (*commentary*) si-
multaneo(a); **to be in/out of the ~ for sth**
essere/non essere più in lizza per qc; **6 days
~** 6 giorni di seguito; **~ costs** *npl* costi *mpl*
d'esercizio; (*of car*) spese *fpl* di man-
tenimento
runny ['rʌnɪ] *adj* che cola
run-of-the-mill ['rʌnəvðə'mɪl] *adj* solito(a),
banale
runt [rʌnt] *n* (*also pej*) omuncolo; (*ZOOL*)
animale *m* più piccolo del normale
run-through ['rʌnθru:] *n* prova
run-up ['rʌnʌp] *n*: **~ to** (*election etc*) periodo
che precede
runway ['rʌnweɪ] *n* (*AVIAT*) pista (di decollo)
rupture ['rʌptʃə*] *n* (*MED*) ernia
rural ['rʊərl] *adj* rurale

ruse [ru:z] *n* trucco
rush [rʌʃ] *n* corsa precipitosa; (*hurry*) furia,
fretta; (*sudden demand*): **~ for** corsa a;
(*current*) flusso; (*of emotion*) impeto; (*BOT*)
giunco ♦ *vt* mandare o spedire velocemente;
(*attack: town etc*) prendere d'assalto ♦ *vi*
precipitarsi; **~ hour** *n* ora di punta
rusk [rʌsk] *n* biscotto
Russia ['rʌʃə] *n* Russia; **~n** *adj* russo(a) ♦ *n*
russo/a; (*LING*) russo
rust [rʌst] *n* ruggine *f* ♦ *vi* arrugginirsi
rustic ['rʌstɪk] *adj* rustico(a)
rustle ['rʌsl] *vi* frusciare ♦ *vt* (*paper*) far
frusciare
rustproof ['rʌstpruːf] *adj* inossidabile
rusty ['rʌstɪ] *adj* arrugginito(a)
rut [rʌt] *n* solco; (*ZOOL*) fregola; **to get into a ~**
(*fig*) adagiarsi troppo
ruthless ['ru:θlɪs] *adj* spietato(a)
rye [raɪ] *n* segale *f*; **~ bread** *n* pane *m* di
segale

S, s

Sabbath ['sæbəθ] *n* (*Jewish*) sabato;
(*Christian*) domenica
sabotage ['sæbətɑːʒ] *n* sabotaggio ♦ *vt*
sabotare
saccharin(e) ['sækərɪn] *n* saccarina
sachet ['sæʃeɪ] *n* bustina
sack [sæk] *n* (*bag*) sacco ♦ *vt* (*dismiss*)
licenziare, mandare a spasso; (*plunder*)
saccheggiare; **to get the ~** essere mandato a
spasso; **~ing** *n* tela di sacco; (*dismissal*)
licenziamento
sacrament ['sækrəmənt] *n* sacramento
sacred ['seɪkrɪd] *adj* sacro(a)
sacrifice ['sækrɪfaɪs] *n* sacrificio ♦ *vt*
sacrificare
sad [sæd] *adj* triste
saddle ['sædl] *n* sella ♦ *vt* (*horse*) sellare; **to
be ~d with sth** (*inf*) avere qc sulle spalle;
~bag *n* (*on bicycle*) borsa
sadistic [sə'dɪstɪk] *adj* sadico(a)
sadness ['sædnɪs] *n* tristezza
s.a.e. *n abbr* = **stamped addressed envelope**
safe [seɪf] *adj* sicuro(a); (*out of danger*)
salvo(a), al sicuro; (*cautious*) prudente ♦ *n*
cassaforte *f*; **~ from** al sicuro da; **~ and sound**
sano(a) e salvo(a); (**just**) **to be on the ~ side**
per non correre rischi; **~-conduct** *n*
salvacondotto; **~-deposit** *n* (*vault*) caveau *m
inv*; (*box*) cassetta di sicurezza; **~guard** *n*
salvaguardia ♦ *vt* salvaguardare; **~keeping** *n*
custodia; **~ly** *adv* sicuramente; sano(a) e
salvo(a); prudentemente; **~ sex** *n* sesso
sicuro
safety ['seɪftɪ] *n* sicurezza; **~ belt** *n* cintura di

sicurezza; **~ pin** n spilla di sicurezza; **~ valve** n valvola di sicurezza

saffron ['sæfrən] n zafferano

sag [sæg] vi incurvarsi; afflosciarsi

sage [seidʒ] n (herb) salvia; (man) saggio

Sagittarius [sædʒɪ'tɛərɪəs] n Sagittario

Sahara [sə'hɑːrə] n: **the ~ (Desert)** il (deserto del) Sahara

said [sed] pt, pp of **say**

sail [seɪl] n (on boat) vela; (trip): **to go for a ~** fare un giro in barca a vela ♦ vt (boat) condurre, governare ♦ vi (travel: ship) navigare; (: passenger) viaggiare per mare; (set off) salpare; (sport) fare della vela; **they ~ed into Genoa** entrarono nel porto di Genova; **~ through** vt fus (fig) superare senza difficoltà; **~boat** (US) n barca a vela; **~ing** n (sport) vela; **to go ~ing** fare della vela; **~ing boat** n barca a vela; **~ing ship** n veliero; **~or** n marinaio

saint [seɪnt] n santo/a; **~ly** adj santo(a)

sake [seɪk] n: **for the ~ of** per, per amore di

salad ['sæləd] n insalata; **~ bowl** n insalatiera; **~ cream** (BRIT) n (tipo di) maionese f; **~ dressing** n condimento per insalata

salami [sə'lɑːmɪ] n salame m

salary ['sælərɪ] n stipendio

sale [seɪl] n vendita; (at reduced prices) svendita, liquidazione f; (auction) vendita all'asta; **"for ~"** "in vendita"; **on ~** in vendita; **on ~ or return** da vendere o rimandare; **~room** n sala delle aste; **~s assistant** (US **~s clerk**) n commesso/a; **~sman/swoman** (irreg) n commesso/a; (representative) rappresentante m/f

salmon ['sæmən] n inv salmone m

saloon [sə'luːn] n (US) saloon m inv, bar m inv; (BRIT: AUT) berlina; (ship's lounge) salone m

salt [sɔlt] n sale m ♦ vt salare; **~ cellar** n saliera; **~water** adj di mare; **~y** adj salato(a)

salute [sə'luːt] n saluto ♦ vt salutare

salvage ['sælvɪdʒ] n (saving) salvataggio; (things saved) beni mpl salvati o recuperati ♦ vt salvare, mettere in salvo

salvation [sæl'veɪʃən] n salvezza; **S~ Army** n Esercito della Salvezza

same [seɪm] adj stesso(a), medesimo(a) ♦ pron: **the ~** lo(la) stesso(a), gli(le) stessi(e); **the ~ book as** lo stesso libro di (o che); **at the ~ time** allo stesso tempo; **all** or **just the ~** tuttavia; **to do the ~ as sb** fare come qn; **the ~ to you!** altrettanto a te!

sample ['sɑːmpl] n campione m ♦ vt (food) assaggiare; (wine) degustare

sanction ['sæŋkʃən] n sanzione f ♦ vt sancire, sanzionare

sanctity ['sæŋktɪtɪ] n santità

sanctuary ['sæŋktjuərɪ] n (holy place) santuario; (refuge) rifugio; (for wildlife) riserva

sand [sænd] n sabbia ♦ vt (also: ~ **down**) cartavetrare

sandal ['sændl] n sandalo

sandbox ['sændbɔks] (US) n = **sandpit**

sandcastle ['sændkɑːsl] n castello di sabbia

sandpaper ['sændpeɪpə*] n carta vetrata

sandpit ['sændpɪt] n (for children) buca di sabbia

sandstone ['sændstəun] n arenaria

sandwich ['sændwɪtʃ] n tramezzino, panino, sandwich m inv ♦ vt: **~ed between** incastrato(a) fra; **cheese/ham ~** sandwich al formaggio/prosciutto; **~ course** (BRIT) n corso di formazione professionale

sandy ['sændɪ] adj sabbioso(a); (colour) color sabbia inv, biondo(a) rossiccio(a)

sane [seɪn] adj (person) sano(a) di mente; (outlook) sensato(a)

sang [sæŋ] pt of **sing**

sanitary ['sænɪtərɪ] adj (system, arrangements) sanitario(a); (clean) igienico(a); **~ towel** (US **~ napkin**) n assorbente m (igienico)

sanitation [sænɪ'teɪʃən] n (in house) impianti mpl sanitari; (in town) fognature fpl; **~ department** (US) n nettezza urbana

sanity ['sænɪtɪ] n sanità mentale; (common sense) buon senso

sank [sæŋk] pt of **sink**

Santa Claus [sæntə'klɔːz] n Babbo Natale

sap [sæp] n (of plants) linfa ♦ vt (strength) fiaccare

sapling ['sæplɪŋ] n alberello

sapphire ['sæfaɪə*] n zaffiro

sarcasm ['sɑːkæzm] n sarcasmo

sardine [sɑː'diːn] n sardina

Sardinia [sɑː'dɪnɪə] n Sardegna

sash [sæʃ] n fascia

sat [sæt] pt, pp of **sit**

Satan ['seɪtən] n Satana m

satchel ['sætʃl] n cartella

satellite ['sætəlaɪt] adj satellite ♦ n satellite m; **~ dish** n antenna parabolica; **~ television** n televisione f via satellite

satin ['sætɪn] n raso ♦ adj di raso

satire ['sætaɪə*] n satira

satisfaction [sætɪs'fækʃən] n soddisfazione f

satisfactory [sætɪs'fæktərɪ] adj soddisfacente

satisfy ['sætɪsfaɪ] vt soddisfare; (convince) convincere; **~ing** adj soddisfacente

Saturday ['sætədɪ] n sabato

sauce [sɔːs] n salsa; (containing meat, fish) sugo; **~pan** n casseruola

saucer ['sɔːsə*] n sottocoppa m, piattino

Saudi ['saudɪ]: **~ Arabia** n Arabia Saudita; **~ (Arabian)** adj, n arabo(a) saudita

sauna ['sɔːnə] n sauna

saunter ['sɔːntə*] vi andare a zonzo, bighellonare

sausage ['sɔsɪdʒ] n salsiccia; ~ **roll** n rotolo di pasta sfoglia ripieno di salsiccia

sauté ['səʊteɪ] adj: ~ **potatoes** patate fpl saltate in padella

savage ['sævɪdʒ] adj (cruel, fierce) selvaggio(a), feroce; (primitive) primitivo(a) ♦ n selvaggio/a ♦ vt attaccare selvaggiamente

save [seɪv] vt (person, belongings, COMPUT) salvare; (money) risparmiare, mettere da parte; (time) risparmiare; (food) conservare; (avoid: trouble) evitare; (SPORT) parare ♦ vi (also: ~ up) economizzare ♦ n (SPORT) parata ♦ prep salvo, a eccezione di

saving ['seɪvɪŋ] n risparmio ♦ adj: **the ~ grace** of l'unica cosa buona di; ~**s** npl (money) risparmi mpl; ~**s account** n libretto di risparmio; ~**s bank** n cassa di risparmio

saviour ['seɪvjə*] (US **savior**) n salvatore m

savour ['seɪvə*] (US **savor**) vt gustare; ~**y** adj (dish: not sweet) salato(a)

saw [sɔː] (pt **sawed**, pp **sawed** or **sawn**) pt of **see** ♦ n (tool) sega ♦ vt segare; ~**dust** n segatura; ~**mill** n segheria; **sawn** pp of **saw**; ~**n-off shotgun** n fucile m a canne mozze

saxophone ['sæksəfəun] n sassofono

say [seɪ] (pt, pp **said**) n: **to have one's ~** fare sentire il proprio parere; **to have a** or **some ~** avere voce in capitolo ♦ vt dire; **could you ~ that again?** potrebbe ripeterlo?; **that goes without ~ing** va da sé; ~**ing** n proverbio, detto

scab [skæb] n crosta; (pej) crumiro/a

scaffold ['skæfəuld] n (gallows) patibolo; ~**ing** n impalcatura

scald [skɔːld] n scottatura ♦ vt scottare

scale [skeɪl] n scala; (of fish) squama ♦ vt (mountain) scalare; ~**s** npl (for weighing) bilancia; **on a large** ~ su vasta scala; ~ **of charges** tariffa; ~ **down** vt ridurre (proporzionalmente)

scallop ['skɔləp] n (ZOOL) pettine m; (SEWING) smerlo

scalp [skælp] n cuoio capelluto ♦ vt scotennare

scalpel ['skælpl] n bisturi m inv

scampi ['skæmpɪ] npl scampi mpl

scan [skæn] vt scrutare; (glance at quickly) scorrere, dare un'occhiata a; (TV) analizzare; (RADAR) esplorare ♦ n (MED) ecografia

scandal ['skændl] n scandalo; (gossip) pettegolezzi mpl

Scandinavia [skændɪ'neɪvɪə] n Scandinavia; ~**n** adj, n scandinavo(a)

scant [skænt] adj scarso(a); ~**y** adj insufficiente; (swimsuit) ridotto(a)

scapegoat ['skeɪpgəut] n capro espiatorio

scar [skɑː] n cicatrice f ♦ vt sfregiare

scarce [skɛəs] adj scarso(a); (copy, edition) raro(a); **to make o.s. ~** (inf) squagliarsela; ~**ly** adv appena; **scarcity** n scarsità, mancanza

scare [skɛə*] n spavento; panico ♦ vt spaventare, atterrire; **there was a bomb ~ at the bank** hanno evacuato la banca per paura di un attentato dinamitardo; **to ~ sb stiff** spaventare a morte qn; ~ **off** or **away** vt mettere in fuga; ~**crow** n spaventapasseri m inv; ~**d** adj: **to be ~d** aver paura

scarf [skɑːf] (pl **scarves** or ~**s**) n (long) sciarpa; (square) fazzoletto da testa, foulard m inv

scarlet ['skɑːlɪt] adj scarlatto(a); ~ **fever** n scarlattina

scarves [skɑːvz] npl of **scarf**

scary ['skɛərɪ] adj che spaventa

scathing ['skeɪðɪŋ] adj aspro(a)

scatter ['skætə*] vt spargere; (crowd) disperdere ♦ vi disperdersi; ~**brained** adj sbadato(a)

scavenger ['skævəndʒə*] n (person) accattone/a

scenario [sɪ'nɑːrɪəu] n (THEATRE, CINEMA) copione m; (fig) situazione f

scene [siːn] n (THEATRE, fig etc) scena; (of crime, accident) scena, luogo; (sight, view) vista, veduta; ~**ry** n (THEATRE) scenario; (landscape) panorama m; **scenic** adj scenico(a); panoramico(a)

scent [sɛnt] n profumo; (sense of smell) olfatto, odorato; (fig: track) pista

sceptical ['skɛptɪkəl] (US **skeptical**) adj scettico(a)

sceptre ['sɛptə*] (US **scepter**) n scettro

schedule ['ʃɛdjuːl, (US) 'skɛdjuːl] n programma m, piano; (of trains) orario; (of prices etc) lista, tabella ♦ vt fissare; **on ~** in orario; **to be ahead of/behind ~** essere in anticipo/ritardo sul previsto; ~**d flight** n volo di linea

scheme [skiːm] n piano, progetto; (method) sistema m; (dishonest plan, plot) intrigo, trama; (arrangement) disposizione f, sistemazione f; (pension ~ etc) programma m ♦ vi fare progetti; (intrigue) complottare; **scheming** adj intrigante ♦ n intrighi mpl, macchinazioni fpl

schism ['skɪzəm] n scisma m

scholar ['skɔlə*] n erudito/a; (pupil) scolaro/a; ~**ship** n erudizione f; (grant) borsa di studio

school [skuːl] n (primary, secondary) scuola; (university: US) università f inv ♦ cpd scolare, scolastico(a) ♦ vt (animal) addestrare; ~ **age** n età scolare; ~**bag** n cartella; ~**book** n libro scolastico; ~**boy** n scolaro; ~**children** npl scolari mpl; ~**girl** n scolara; ~**ing** n istruzione f; ~**master** n (primary) maestro; (secondary) insegnante *m*; **~mistress** *n* maestra; insegnante *f*; **~teacher** *n* insegnante *m/f*, docente *m/f*; (*primary*) maestro/a

sciatica [saɪˈætɪkə] *n* sciatica

science [ˈsaɪəns] *n* scienza; **~ fiction** *n* fantascienza; **scientific** [-ˈtɪfɪk] *adj* scientifico(a); **scientist** *n* scienziato/a

scissors [ˈsɪzəz] *npl* forbici *fpl*

scoff [skɔf] *vt* (*BRIT: inf: eat*) trangugiare, ingozzare ♦ *vi*: **to ~ (at)** (*mock*) farsi beffe (di)

scold [skəuld] *vt* rimproverare

scone [skɔn] *n* focaccina da tè

scoop [sku:p] *n* mestolo; (*for ice cream*) cucchiaio dosatore; (*PRESS*) colpo giornalistico, notizia (in) esclusiva; **~ out** *vt* scavare; **~ up** *vt* tirare su, sollevare

scooter [ˈsku:tə*] *n* (*motor cycle*) motoretta, scooter *m inv*; (*toy*) monopattino

scope [skəup] *n* (*capacity: of plan, undertaking*) portata; (: *of person*) capacità *fpl*; (*opportunity*) possibilità *fpl*

scorch [skɔ:tʃ] *vt* (*clothes*) strinare, bruciacchiare; (*earth, grass*) bruciare

score [skɔ:*] *n* punti *mpl*, punteggio; (*MUS*) partitura, spartito; (*twenty*) venti ♦ *vt* (*goal, point*) segnare, fare; (*success*) ottenere ♦ *vi* segnare; (*FOOTBALL*) fare un goal; (*keep score*) segnare i punti; **~s of** (*very many*) un sacco di; **on that ~** a questo riguardo; **to ~ 6 out of 10** prendere 6 su 10; **~ out** *vt* cancellare con un segno; **~board** *n* tabellone *m* segnapunti

scorn [skɔ:n] *n* disprezzo ♦ *vt* disprezzare

scornful [ˈskɔ:nful] *adj* sprezzante

Scorpio [ˈskɔ:piəu] *n* Scorpione *m*

scorpion [ˈskɔ:piən] *n* scorpione *m*

Scot [skɔt] *n* scozzese *m/f*

Scotch [skɔtʃ] *n* whisky *m* scozzese, scotch *m*

scot-free [ˈskɔtˈfri:] *adv*: **to get off ~** farla franca

Scotland [ˈskɔtlənd] *n* Scozia

Scots [skɔts] *adj* scozzese; **~man/woman** (*irreg*) *n* scozzese *m/f*

Scottish [ˈskɔtɪʃ] *adj* scozzese; **~ Parliament** *n* Parlamento scozzese

scoundrel [ˈskaundrl] *n* farabutto/a; (*child*) furfantello/a

scour [ˈskauə*] *vt* (*search*) battere, perlustrare

scout [skaut] *n* (*MIL*) esploratore *m*; (*also: boy ~*) giovane esploratore, scout *m inv*; **~ around** *vi* cercare in giro; **girl ~** (*US*) *n* giovane esploratrice *f*

scowl [skaul] *vi* accigliarsi, aggrottare le sopracciglia; **to ~ at** guardare torvo

scrabble [ˈskræbl] *vi* (*claw*): **to ~ (at)** graffiare, grattare; (*also: ~ around: search*) cercare a tentoni ♦ *n*: **S~** ® Scarabeo ®

scraggy [ˈskrægɪ] *adj* scarno(a), molto magro(a)

scram [skræm] (*inf*) *vi* filare via

scramble [ˈskræmbl] *n* arrampicata ♦ *vi* inerpicarsi; **to ~ out** *etc* uscire *etc* in fretta; **to ~ for** azzuffarsi per; **~d eggs** *npl* uova *fpl* strapazzate

scrap [skræp] *n* pezzo, pezzetto; (*fight*) zuffa; (*also:* ~ iron) rottami *mpl* di ferro, ferraglia ♦ *vt* demolire; (*fig*) scartare ♦ *vi*: **to ~ (with sb)** fare a botte (con qn); **~s** *npl* (*waste*) scarti *mpl*; **~book** *n* album *m inv* di ritagli; **~ dealer** *n* commerciante *m* di ferraglia

scrape [skreɪp] *vt, vi* raschiare, grattare ♦ *n*: **to get into a ~** cacciarsi in un guaio; **~ through** *vi* farcela per un pelo; **~ together** *vt* (*money*) raggranellare; **~r** *n* raschietto

scrap: ~ heap *n*: **on the ~ heap** (*fig*) nel dimenticatoio; **~ merchant** (*BRIT*) *n* commerciante *m* di ferraglia; **~ paper** *n* cartaccia

scratch [skrætʃ] *n* graffio ♦ *cpd*: **~ team** squadra raccogliticcia ♦ *vt* graffiare, rigare ♦ *vi* grattare; (*paint, car*) graffiare; **to start from ~** cominciare *or* partire da zero; **to be up to ~** essere all'altezza

scrawl [skrɔ:l] *n* scarabocchio ♦ *vi* scarabocchiare

scrawny [ˈskrɔ:nɪ] *adj* scarno(a), pelle e ossa *inv*

scream [skri:m] *n* grido, urlo ♦ *vi* urlare, gridare

scree [skri:] *n* ghiaione *m*

screech [skri:tʃ] *vi* stridere

screen [skri:n] *n* schermo; (*fig*) muro, cortina, velo ♦ *vt* schermare, fare schermo a; (*from the wind etc*) riparare; (*film*) proiettare; (*book*) adattare per lo schermo; (*candidates etc*) selezionare; **~ing** *n* (*MED*) dépistage *m inv*; **~play** *n* sceneggiatura; **~ saver** *n* (*COMPUT*) screen saver *m inv*

screw [skru:] *n* vite *f* ♦ *vt* avvitare; **~ up** *vt* (*paper etc*) spiegazzare; (*inf: ruin*) rovinare; **to ~ up one's eyes** strizzare gli occhi; **~driver** *n* cacciavite *m*

scribble [ˈskrɪbl] *n* scarabocchio ♦ *vt* scribacchiare in fretta ♦ *vi* scarabocchiare

script [skrɪpt] *n* (*CINEMA etc*) copione *m*; (*in exam*) elaborato *or* compito d'esame

scripture(s) [ˈskrɪptʃə(z)] *n(pl)* sacre Scritture *fpl*

scroll [skrəul] *n* rotolo di carta

scrounge [skraundʒ] (*inf*) *vt*: **to ~ sth (off** *or* **from sb)** scroccare qc (a qn) ♦ *n*: **on the ~** a sbafo

scrub [skrʌb] *n* (*land*) boscaglia ♦ *vt* pulire strofinando; (*reject*) annullare

scruff [skrʌf] *n*: **by the ~ of the neck** per la collottola

scruffy [ˈskrʌfɪ] *adj* sciatto(a)

scrum(mage) ['skrʌm(ɪdʒ)] n mischia
scruple ['skru:pl] n scrúpolo
scrutiny ['skru:tɪnɪ] n esame m accurato
scuff [skʌf] vt (shoes) consumare strasciando
scuffle ['skʌfl] n baruffa, tafferuglio
sculptor ['skʌlptə*] n scultore m
sculpture ['skʌlptʃə*] n scultura
scum [skʌm] n schiuma; (pej: people) feccia
scupper ['skʌpə*] (BRIT: inf) vt far naufragare
scurry ['skʌrɪ] vi sgambare, affrettarsi; ~ **off** vi andarsene a tutta velocità
scuttle ['skʌtl] n (also: coal ~) secchio del carbone ♦ vt (ship) autoaffondare ♦ vi (scamper): **to ~ away, ~ off** darsela a gambe, scappare
scythe [saɪð] n falce f
SDP (BRIT) n abbr = **Social Democratic Party**
sea [si:] n mare m ♦ cpd marino(a), del mare; (bird, fish) di mare; (route, transport) marittimo(a); **by ~** (travel) per mare; **on the ~** (boat) in mare; (town) di mare; **to be all at ~** (fig) non sapere che pesci pigliare; **out to ~** al largo; **(out) at ~** in mare; **~board** n costa; **~food** n frutti mpl di mare; **~ front** n lungomare m; **~gull** n gabbiano
seal [si:l] n (animal) foca; (stamp) sigillo; (impression) impronta del sigillo ♦ vt sigillare; **~ off** vt (close) sigillare; (forbid entry to) bloccare l'accesso a
sea level n livello del mare
seam [si:m] n cucitura; (of coal) filone m
seaman ['si:mən] (irreg) n marinaio
seance ['seɪɒns] n seduta spiritica
seaplane ['si:pleɪn] n idrovolante m
seaport ['si:pɔ:t] n porto di mare
search [sə:tʃ] n ricerca; (LAW: at sb's home) perquisizione f ♦ vt frugare ♦ vi: **to ~ for** ricercare; **in ~ of** alla ricerca di; **~ through** vt fus frugare; **~ing** adj minuzioso(a); penetrante; **~light** n proiettore m; **~ party** n squadra di soccorso; **~ warrant** n mandato di perquisizione
seashore ['si:ʃɔ:*] n spiaggia
seasick ['si:sɪk] adj che soffre il mal di mare
seaside ['si:saɪd] n spiaggia; **~ resort** n stazione f balneare
season ['si:zn] n stagione f ♦ vt condire, insaporire; **~al** adj stagionale; **~ed** adj (fig) con esperienza; **~ing** n condimento; **~ ticket** n abbonamento
seat [si:t] n sedile m; (in bus, train: place) posto; (PARLIAMENT) seggio; (buttocks) didietro; (of trousers) fondo ♦ vt far sedere; (have room for) avere o essere fornito(a) di posti a sedere per; **to be ~ed** essere seduto(a); **~ belt** n cintura di sicurezza
sea water n acqua di mare
seaweed ['si:wi:d] n alghe fpl
seaworthy ['si:wə:ðɪ] adj atto(a) alla

navigazione
sec. abbr = **second(s)**
secluded [sɪ'klu:dɪd] adj isolato(a), appartato(a)
seclusion [sɪ'klu:ʒən] n isolamento
second¹ [sɪ'kɒnd] (BRIT) vt (worker) distaccare
second² ['sɛkənd] num secondo(a) ♦ adv (in race etc) al secondo posto ♦ n (unit of time) secondo; (AUT: also: ~ gear) seconda; (COMM: imperfect) scarto; (BRIT: SCOL: degree) laurea con punteggio discreto ♦ vt (motion) appoggiare; **~ary** adj secondario(a); **~ary school** n scuola secondaria; **~-class** adj di seconda classe ♦ adv in seconda classe; **~er** n sostenitore/trice; **~hand** adj di seconda mano, usato(a); **~ hand** n (on clock) lancetta dei secondi; **~ly** adv in secondo luogo; **~ rate** adj scadente; **~ thoughts** npl ripensamenti mpl; **on ~ thoughts** (BRIT) or **thought** (US) ripensandoci bene
secrecy ['si:krəsɪ] n segretezza
secret ['si:krɪt] adj segreto(a) ♦ n segreto; **in ~** in segreto
secretarial [sɛkrɪ'tɛərɪəl] adj di segretario(a)
secretariat [sɛkrɪ'tɛərɪət] n segretariato
secretary ['sɛkrətrɪ] n segretario/a; **S~ of State (for)** (BRIT: POL) ministro (di)
secretive ['si:krətɪv] adj riservato(a)
sect [sɛkt] n setta; **~arian** [-'tɛərɪən] adj settario(a)
section ['sɛkʃən] n sezione f
sector ['sɛktə*] n settore m
secure [sɪ'kjuə*] adj sicuro(a); (firmly fixed) assicurato(a), ben fermato(a); (in safe place) al sicuro ♦ vt (fix) fissare, assicurare; (get) ottenere, assicurarsi
security [sɪ'kjuərɪtɪ] n sicurezza; (for loan) garanzia
sedate [sɪ'deɪt] adj posato(a); calmo(a) ♦ vt calmare
sedation [sɪ'deɪʃən] n (MED) effetto dei sedativi
sedative ['sɛdɪtɪv] n sedativo, calmante m
seduce [sɪ'dju:s] vt sedurre; **seduction** [-'dʌkʃən] n seduzione f; **seductive** [-'dʌktɪv] adj seducente
see [si:] (pt saw, pp seen) vt vedere; (accompany): **to ~ sb to the door** accompagnare qn alla porta ♦ vi vedere; (understand) capire ♦ n sede f vescovile; **to ~ that** (ensure) badare che + sub, fare in modo che + sub; **~ you soon!** a presto!; **~ about** vt fus occuparsi di; **~ off** vt salutare alla partenza; **~ through** vt portare a termine ♦ vt fus non lasciarsi ingannare da; **~ to** vt fus occuparsi di
seed [si:d] n seme m; (fig) germe m; (TENNIS etc) testa di serie; **to go to ~** fare seme; (fig) scadere; **~ling** n piantina di semenzaio; **~y**

adj (*shabby: person*) sciatto(a); (: *place*) cadente

seeing ['si:ɪŋ] *conj*: ~ (**that**) visto che

seek [si:k] (*pt, pp* **sought**) *vt* cercare

seem [si:m] *vi* sembrare, parere; **there ~s to be** ... sembra che ci sia ...; **~ingly** *adv* apparentemente

seen [si:n] *pp of* **see**

seep [si:p] *vi* filtrare, trapelare

seesaw ['si:sɔ:] *n* altalena a bilico

seethe [si:ð] *vi* ribollire; **to ~ with anger** fremere di rabbia

see-through ['si:θru:] *adj* trasparente

segregate ['sɛgrɪgeɪt] *vt* segregare, isolare

seize [si:z] *vt* (*grasp*) afferrare; (*take possession of*) impadronirsi di; (*LAW*) sequestrare; ~ (**up)on** *vt fus* ricorrere a; ~ **up** *vi* (*TECH*) grippare

seizure ['si:ʒə*] *n* (*MED*) attacco; (*LAW*) confisca, sequestro

seldom ['sɛldəm] *adv* raramente

select [sɪ'lɛkt] *adj* scelto(a) ♦ *vt* scegliere, selezionare; **~ion** [-'lɛkʃən] *n* selezione *f*, scelta

self [sɛlf] *n*: **the** ~ l'io *m* ♦ *prefix* auto...; **~-assured** *adj* sicuro(a) di sé; **~-catering** (*BRIT*) *adj* in cui ci si cucina da sé; **~-centred** (*US* **~-centered**) *adj* egocentrico(a); **~-confidence** *n* sicurezza di sé; **~-conscious** *adj* timido(a); **~-contained** (*BRIT*) *adj* (*flat*) indipendente; **~-control** *n* autocontrollo; **~-defence** (*US* **~-defense**) *n* autodifesa; (*LAW*) legittima difesa; **~-discipline** *n* auto-disciplina; **~-employed** *adj* che lavora in proprio; **~-evident** *adj* evidente; **~-governing** *adj* autonomo(a); **~-indulgent** *adj* indulgente verso se stesso(a); **~-interest** *n* interesse m personale; **~-ish** *adj* egoista; **~ishness** *n* egoismo; **~-less** *adj* dimentico(a) di sé, altruista; **~-pity** *n* autocommiserazione *f*; **~-portrait** *n* autoritratto; **~-possessed** *adj* controllato(a); **~-preservation** *n* istinto di conservazione; **~-respect** *n* rispetto di sé, amor proprio; **~-righteous** *adj* sod-disfatto(a) di sé; **~-sacrifice** *n* abnegazione *f*; **~-satisfied** *adj* compiaciuto(a) di sé; **~-service** *n* autoservizio, self-service *m*; **~-sufficient** *adj* autosufficiente; **~-taught** *adj* autodidatta

sell [sɛl] (*pt, pp* **sold**) *vt* vendere ♦ *vi* vendersi; **to ~ at** *or* **for 1000 lire** essere in vendita a 1000 lire; ~ **off** *vt* svendere, liquidare; ~ **out** *vi*: **to ~ out (of sth)** esaurire (qc); **the tickets are all sold out** i biglietti sono esauriti; **~-by date** *n* data di scadenza; **~er** *n* venditore/trice; **~ing price** *n* prezzo di vendita

Sellotape ® ['sɛləʊteɪp] (*BRIT*) *n* nastro adesivo, scotch ® *m*

selves [sɛlvz] *npl of* **self**

semaphore ['sɛməfɔ:*] *n* segnalazioni *fpl* con bandierine; (*RAIL*) semaforo (ferroviario)

semblance ['sɛmbləns] *n* parvenza, apparenza

semen ['si:mən] *n* sperma *m*

semester [sɪ'mɛstə*] (*US*) *n* semestre *m*

semi... ['sɛmɪ] *prefix* semi...; **~circle** *n* semicerchio; **~colon** *n* punto e virgola; **~detached (house)** (*BRIT*) *n* casa gemella; **~final** *n* semifinale *f*

seminar ['sɛmɪnɑ:*] *n* seminario

seminary ['sɛmɪnərɪ] *n* (*REL*) seminario

semiskilled ['sɛmɪ'skɪld] *adj* (*worker*) parzialmente qualificato(a); (*work*) che richiede una qualificazione parziale

semi-skimmed ['sɛmɪ'skɪmd] *adj* (*milk*) parzialmente scremato(a)

senate ['sɛnɪt] *n* senato; **senator** *n* senatore/trice

send [sɛnd] (*pt, pp* **sent**) *vt* mandare; ~ **away** *vt* (*letter, goods*) spedire; (*person*) mandare via; ~ **away for** *vt fus* richiedere per posta, farsi spedire; ~ **back** *vt* rimandare; ~ **for** *vt fus* mandare a chiamare, far venire; ~ **off** *vt* (*goods*) spedire; (*BRIT: SPORT: player*) espellere; ~ **out** *vt* (*invitation*) diramare; ~ **up** *vt* (*person, price*) far salire; (*BRIT: parody*) mettere in ridicolo; **~er** *n* mittente *m/f*; **~off** *n*: **to give sb a good ~off** festeggiare la partenza di qn

senior ['si:nɪə*] *adj* (*older*) più vecchio(a); (*of higher rank*) di grado più elevato; ~ **citizen** *n* persona anziana; **~ity** [-'ɔrɪtɪ] *n* anzianità

sensation [sɛn'seɪʃən] *n* sensazione *f*; **~al** *adj* sensazionale; (*marvellous*) eccezionale

sense [sɛns] *n* senso; (*feeling*) sensazione *f*, senso; (*meaning*) senso, significato; (*wisdom*) buonsenso ♦ *vt* sentire, percepire; **it makes ~** ha senso; **~less** *adj* sciocco(a); (*unconscious*) privo(a) di sensi

sensible ['sɛnsɪbl] *adj* sensato(a), ragionevole

sensitive ['sɛnsɪtɪv] *adj* sensibile; (*skin, question*) delicato(a)

sensual ['sɛnsjuəl] *adj* sensuale

sensuous ['sɛnsjuəs] *adj* sensuale

sent [sɛnt] *pt, pp of* **send**

sentence ['sɛntns] *n* (*LING*) frase *f*; (*LAW: judgment*) sentenza; (: *punishment*) condanna ♦ *vt*: **to ~ sb to death/to 5 years** condannare qn a morte/a 5 anni

sentiment ['sɛntɪmənt] *n* sentimento; (*opinion*) opinione *f*; **~al** [-'mɛntl] *adj* sentimentale

sentry ['sɛntrɪ] *n* sentinella

separate [*adj* 'sɛprɪt, *vb* 'sɛpəreɪt] *adj* separato(a) ♦ *vt* separare ♦ *vi* separarsi; **~ly** *adv* separatamente; **~s** *npl* (*clothes*) coordinati *mpl*; **separation** [-'reɪʃən] *n* separazione *f*

September [sɛp'tɛmbə*] *n* settembre *m*

septic ['sɛptɪk] *adj* settico(a); (*wound*) infettato(a); **~ tank** *n* fossa settica

sequel ['si:kwl] *n* conseguenza; (*of story*) seguito; (*of film*) sequenza

sequence ['si:kwəns] *n* (*series*) serie *f*; (*order*) ordine *m*

sequin ['si:kwɪn] *n* lustrino, paillette *f inv*

serene [sə'ri:n] *adj* sereno(a), calmo(a)

sergeant ['sɑ:dʒənt] *n* sergente *m*; (*POLICE*) brigadiere *m*

serial ['sɪərɪəl] *n* (*PRESS*) romanzo a puntate; (*RADIO, TV*) trasmissione *f* a puntate, serial *m inv*; **~ize** *vt* pubblicare (*or* trasmettere) a puntate; **~ killer** *n* serial-killer *m/f inv*; **~ number** *n* numero di serie

series ['sɪəri:z] *n inv* serie *f inv*; (*PUBLISHING*) collana

serious ['sɪərɪəs] *adj* serio(a), grave; **~ly** *adv* seriamente

sermon ['sə:mən] *n* sermone *m*

serrated [sɪ'reɪtɪd] *adj* seghettato(a)

serum ['sɪərəm] *n* siero

servant ['sə:vənt] *n* domestico/a

serve [sə:v] *vt* (*employer etc*) servire, essere a servizio di; (*purpose*) servire a; (*customer, food, meal*) servire; (*apprenticeship*) fare; (*prison term*) scontare ♦ *vi* (*also TENNIS*) servire; (*be useful*): **to ~ as/for/to do** servire da/per/per fare ♦ *n* (*TENNIS*) servizio; **it ~s him right** ben gli sta, se l'è meritata; **~ out, ~ up** *vt* (*food*) servire

service ['sə:vɪs] *n* servizio; (*AUT: maintenance*) assistenza, revisione *f* ♦ *vt* (*car, washing machine*) revisionare; **the S~s** le forze armate; **to be of ~ to sb** essere d'aiuto a qn; **~ included/not included** servizio compreso/escluso; **~able** *adj* pratico(a), utile; **~ area** *n* (*on motorway*) area di servizio; **~ charge** (*BRIT*) *n* servizio; **~man** (*irreg*) *n* militare *m*; **~ station** *n* stazione *f* di servizio

serviette [sə:vɪ'ɛt] (*BRIT*) *n* tovagliolo

session ['sɛʃən] *n* (*sitting*) seduta, sessione *f*; (*SCOL*) anno scolastico (*or* accademico)

set [sɛt] (*pt, pp* **set**) *n* serie *f inv*; (*of cutlery etc*) servizio; (*RADIO, TV*) apparecchio; (*TENNIS*) set *m inv*; (*group of people*) mondo, ambiente *m*; (*CINEMA*) scenario; (*THEATRE: stage*) scene *fpl*; (*: scenery*) scenario; (*MATH*) insieme *m*; (*HAIRDRESSING*) messa in piega ♦ *adj* (*fixed*) stabilito(a), determinato(a); (*ready*) pronto(a) ♦ *vt* (*place*) posare, mettere; (*arrange*) sistemare; (*fix*) fissare; (*adjust*) regolare; (*decide: rules etc*) stabilire, fissare ♦ *vi* (*sun*) tramontare; (*jam, jelly*) rapprendersi; (*concrete*) fare presa; **to be ~ on doing** essere deciso a fare; **to ~ to music** mettere in musica; **to ~ on fire** dare fuoco a; **to ~ free** liberare; **to ~ sth going** mettere in

moto qc; **to ~ sail** prendere il mare; **~ about** *vt fus* (*task*) intraprendere, mettersi a; **~ aside** *vt* mettere da parte; **~ back** *vt* (*in time*): **to ~ back (by)** mettere indietro (di); (*inf: cost*): **it ~ me back £5** mi è costato la bellezza di 5 sterline; **~ off** *vi* partire ♦ *vt* (*bomb*) far scoppiare; (*cause to start*) mettere in moto; (*show up well*) dare risalto a; **~ out** *vi* partire ♦ *vt* (*arrange*) disporre; (*state*) esporre, presentare; **to ~ out to do** proporsi di fare; **~ up** *vt* (*organization*) fondare, costituire; **~back** *n* (*hitch*) contrattempo, inconveniente *m*; **~ menu** *n* menù *m inv* fisso

settee [sɛ'ti:] *n* divano, sofà *m inv*

setting ['sɛtɪŋ] *n* (*background*) ambiente *m*; (*of controls*) posizione *f*; (*of sun*) tramonto; (*of jewel*) montatura

settle ['sɛtl] *vt* (*argument, matter*) appianare; (*accounts*) regolare; (*MED: calm*) calmare ♦ *vi* (*bird, dust etc*) posarsi; (*sediment*) depositarsi; (*also: ~ down*) sistemarsi, stabilirsi; calmarsi; **to ~ for sth** accontentarsi di qc; **to ~ on sth** decidersi per qc; **~ in** *vi* sistemarsi; **~ up** *vi*: **to ~ up with sb** regolare i conti con qn; **~ment** *n* (*payment*) pagamento, saldo; (*agreement*) accordo; (*colony*) colonia; (*village etc*) villaggio, comunità *f inv*; **~r** *n* colonizzatore/trice

setup ['sɛtʌp] *n* (*arrangement*) sistemazione *f*; (*situation*) situazione *f*

seven ['sɛvn] *num* sette; **~teen** *num* diciassette; **~th** *num* settimo(a); **~ty** *num* settanta

sever ['sɛvə*] *vt* recidere, tagliare; (*relations*) troncare

several ['sɛvərl] *adj, pron* alcuni(e), diversi(e); **~ of us** alcuni di noi

severance ['sɛvərəns] *n* (*of relations*) rottura; **~ pay** *n* indennità di licenziamento

severe [sɪ'vɪə*] *adj* severo(a); (*serious*) serio(a), grave; (*hard*) duro(a); (*plain*) semplice, sobrio(a); **severity** [sɪ'vɛrɪtɪ] *n* severità; gravità; (*of weather*) rigore *m*

sew [səu] (*pt* sewed, *pp* sewn) *vt, vi* cucire; **~ up** *vt* ricucire

sewage ['su:ɪdʒ] *n* acque *fpl* di scolo

sewer ['su:ə*] *n* fogna

sewing ['səuɪŋ] *n* cucitura; cucito; **~ machine** *n* macchina da cucire

sewn [səun] *pp* of **sew**

sex [sɛks] *n* sesso; **to have ~ with** avere rapporti sessuali con; **~ist** *adj, n* sessista *m/f*

sexual ['sɛksjuəl] *adj* sessuale

sexy ['sɛksɪ] *adj* provocante, sexy *inv*

shabby ['ʃæbɪ] *adj* malandato(a); (*behaviour*) vergognoso(a)

shack [ʃæk] *n* baracca, capanna

shackles ['ʃæklz] *npl* ferri *mpl*, catene *fpl*

shade [ʃeɪd] n ombra; (for lamp) paralume m; (of colour) tonalità f inv; (small quantity): **a ~ (more/too large)** un po' (di più/troppo grande) ♦ vt ombreggiare, fare ombra a; **in the ~** all'ombra

shadow ['ʃædəu] n ombra ♦ vt (follow) pedinare; **~ cabinet** (BRIT) n (POL) governo m ombra inv; **~y** adj ombreggiato(a), ombroso(a); (dim) vago(a), indistinto(a)

shady ['ʃeɪdɪ] adj ombroso(a); (fig: dishonest) losco(a), equivoco(a)

shaft [ʃɑːft] n (of arrow, spear) asta; (AUT, TECH) albero; (of mine) pozzo; (of lift) tromba; (of light) raggio

shaggy ['ʃægɪ] adj ispido(a)

shake [ʃeɪk] (pt shook, pp shaken) vt scuotere; (bottle, cocktail) agitare ♦ vi tremare; **to ~ one's head** (in refusal, dismay) scuotere la testa; **to ~ hands with sb** stringere or dare la mano a qn; **~ off** vt scrollare (via); (fig) sbarazzarsi di; **~ up** vt scuotere; **~n** pp of shake; **shaky** adj (hand, voice) tremante; (building) traballante

shall [ʃæl] aux vb: **I ~ go** andrò; **~ I open the door?** apro la porta?; **I'll get some, ~ I?** ne prendo un po', va bene?

shallow ['ʃæləu] adj poco profondo(a); (fig) superficiale

sham [ʃæm] n finzione f, messinscena; (jewellery, furniture) imitazione f

shambles ['ʃæmblz] n confusione f, baraonda, scompiglio

shame [ʃeɪm] n vergogna ♦ vt far vergognare; **it is a ~ (that/to do)** è un peccato (che + sub/fare); **what a ~!** che peccato!; **~ful** adj vergognoso(a); **~less** adj sfrontato(a); (immodest) spudorato(a)

shampoo [ʃæm'puː] n shampoo m inv ♦ vt fare lo shampoo a; **~ and set** n shampoo e messa in piega

shamrock ['ʃæmrɔk] n trifoglio (simbolo nazionale dell'Irlanda)

shandy ['ʃændɪ] n birra con gassosa

shan't [ʃɑːnt] = shall not

shanty town ['ʃæntɪ-] n bidonville f inv

shape [ʃeɪp] n forma ♦ vt formare; (statement) formulare; (sb's ideas) condizionare; **to take ~** prendere forma; **~ up** vi (events) andare, mettersi; (person) cavarsela; **-shaped** suffix: heart-shaped a forma di cuore; **~less** adj senza forma, informe; **~ly** adj ben proporzionato(a)

share [ʃɛə*] n (thing received, contribution) parte f; (COMM) azione f ♦ vt dividere; (have in common) condividere, avere in comune; **~ out** vt dividere; **~holder** n azionista m/f

shark [ʃɑːk] n squalo, pescecane m

sharp [ʃɑːp] adj (razor, knife) affilato(a); (point) acuto(a), acuminato(a); (nose, chin) aguzzo(a); (outline, contrast) netto(a); (cold, pain) pungente; (voice) stridulo(a); (person: quick-witted) sveglio(a); (: unscrupulous) disonesto(a); (MUS): **C ~** do diesis ♦ n (MUS) diesis m inv ♦ adv: **at 2 o'clock** alle due in punto; **~en** vt affilare; (pencil) fare la punta a; (fig) acuire; **~ener** n (also: pencil ~ener) temperamatite m inv; **~-eyed** adj dalla vista acuta; **~ly** adv (turn, stop) bruscamente; (stand out, contrast) nettamente; (criticize, retort) duramente, aspramente

shatter ['ʃætə*] vt mandare in frantumi, frantumare; (fig: upset) distruggere; (: ruin) rovinare ♦ vi frantumarsi, andare in pezzi

shave [ʃeɪv] vt radere, rasare ♦ vi radersi, farsi la barba ♦ n: **to have a ~** farsi la barba; **~r** n (also: electric ~r) rasoio elettrico

shaving ['ʃeɪvɪŋ] n (action) rasatura; **~s** npl (of wood etc) trucioli mpl; **~ brush** n pennello da barba; **~ cream** n crema da barba; **~ foam** n = ~ cream

shawl [ʃɔːl] n scialle m

she [ʃiː] pron ella, lei; **~-cat** gatta; **~-elephant** elefantessa

sheaf [ʃiːf] (pl sheaves) n covone m; (of papers) fascio

shear [ʃɪə*] (pt ~ed, pp ~ed or shorn) vt (sheep) tosare; **~s** npl (for hedge) cesoie fpl

sheath [ʃiːθ] n fodero, guaina; (contraceptive) preservativo

sheaves [ʃiːvz] npl of sheaf

shed [ʃed] (pt, pp shed) n capannone m ♦ vt (leaves, fur etc) perdere; (tears, blood) versare; (workers) liberarsi di

she'd [ʃiːd] = she had; she would

sheen [ʃiːn] n lucentezza

sheep [ʃiːp] n inv pecora; **~dog** n cane m da pastore; **~skin** n pelle f di pecora

sheer [ʃɪə*] adj (utter) vero(a) (e proprio(a)); (steep) a picco, perpendicolare; (almost transparent) sottile ♦ adv a picco

sheet [ʃiːt] n (on bed) lenzuolo; (of paper) foglio; (of glass, ice) lastra; (of metal) foglio, lamina; **~ lightning** n lampo diffuso

sheik(h) [ʃeɪk] n sceicco

shelf [ʃelf] (pl shelves) n scaffale m, mensola

shell [ʃel] n (on beach) conchiglia; (of egg, nut etc) guscio; (explosive) granata; (of building) scheletro ♦ vt (peas) sgranare; (MIL) bombardare; **~ suit** n (lightweight) tuta di acetato; (heavier) tuta di trilobato

she'll [ʃiːl] = she will; she shall

shellfish ['ʃelfɪʃ] n inv (crab etc) crostaceo; (scallop etc) mollusco; (pl: as food) crostacei; molluschi

shelter ['ʃeltə*] n riparo, rifugio ♦ vt riparare, proteggere; (give lodging to) dare rifugio or asilo a ♦ vi ripararsi, mettersi al riparo; **~ed** adj riparato(a); **~ed housing** (BRIT) n alloggi dotati di strutture per anziani o handicappati

shelve [ʃɛlv] vt (fig) accantonare, rimandare; **~s** npl of **shelf**

shepherd [ˈʃɛpəd] n pastore m ♦ vt (guide) guidare; **~'s pie** (BRIT) n timballo di carne macinata e purè di patate

sheriff [ˈʃɛrɪf] (US) n sceriffo

sherry [ˈʃɛrɪ] n sherry m inv

she's [ʃiːz] = **she is; she has**

Shetland [ˈʃɛtlənd] n (also: the **~s**, the ~ Isles) le isole Shetland, le Shetland

shield [ʃiːld] n scudo; (trophy) scudetto; (protection) schermo ♦ vt: **to ~ (from)** riparare (da), proteggere (da or contro)

shift [ʃɪft] n (change) cambiamento; (of workers) turno ♦ vt spostare, muovere; (remove) rimuovere ♦ vi spostarsi, muoversi; **~ work** n lavoro a squadre; **~y** adj ambiguo(a); (eyes) sfuggente

shilling [ˈʃɪlɪŋ] (BRIT) n scellino (= 12 old pence; 20 in a pound)

shimmer [ˈʃɪmə*] vi brillare, luccicare

shin [ʃɪn] n tibia

shine [ʃaɪn] (pt, pp **shone**) n splendore m, lucentezza ♦ vi (ri)splendere, brillare ♦ vt far brillare, far risplendere; (torch): **to ~ sth on** puntare qc verso

shingle [ˈʃɪŋgl] n (on beach) ciottoli mpl; **~s** n (MED) herpes zoster m

shiny [ˈʃaɪnɪ] adj lucente, lucido(a)

ship [ʃɪp] n nave f ♦ vt trasportare (via mare); (send) spedire (via mare); **~building** n costruzione f navale; **~ment** n carico; **~ping** n (ships) naviglio; (traffic) navigazione f; **~shape** adj in perfetto ordine; **~wreck** n relitto; (event) naufragio ♦ vt: **to be ~wrecked** naufragare, fare naufragio; **~yard** n cantiere m navale

shire [ʃaɪə*] (BRIT) n contea

shirt [ʃəːt] n camicia; **in ~ sleeves** in maniche di camicia

shit [ʃɪt] (inf!) excl merda (!)

shiver [ˈʃɪvə*] n brivido ♦ vi rabbrividire, tremare

shoal [ʃəul] n (of fish) banco; (fig) massa

shock [ʃɔk] n (impact) urto, colpo; (ELEC) scossa; (emotional) colpo, shock m inv; (MED) shock ♦ vt colpire, scioccare; scandalizzare; **~ absorber** n ammortizzatore m; **~ing** adj scioccante, traumatizzante; scandaloso(a)

shoddy [ˈʃɔdɪ] adj scadente

shoe [ʃuː] (pt, pp **shod**) n scarpa; (also: horse~) ferro di cavallo ♦ vt (horse) ferrare; **~brush** n spazzola per scarpe; **~lace** n stringa; **~ polish** n lucido per scarpe; **~shop** n calzoleria; **~string** n (fig): **on a ~string** con quattro soldi

shone [ʃɔn] pt, pp of **shine**

shook [ʃuk] pt of **shake**

shoot [ʃuːt] (pt, pp **shot**) n (on branch, seedling) germoglio ♦ vt (game) cacciare, andare a caccia di; (person) sparare a; (execute) fucilare; (film) girare ♦ vi (with gun): **to ~ (at)** sparare (a), fare fuoco (su); (with bow): **to ~ (at)** tirare (su); (FOOTBALL) sparare, tirare (forte); **~ down** vt (plane) abbattere; **~ in/out** vi entrare/uscire come una freccia; **~ up** vi (fig) salire alle stelle; **~ing** n (shots) sparatoria; (HUNTING) caccia; **~ing star** n stella cadente

shop [ʃɔp] n negozio; (workshop) officina ♦ vi (also: go ~ping) fare spese; **~ assistant** (BRIT) n commesso/a; **~ floor** n officina; (BRIT: fig) operai mpl, maestranze fpl; **~keeper** n negoziante m/f, bottegaio/a; **~lifting** n taccheggio; **~per** n compratore/trice; **~ping** n (goods) spesa, acquisti mpl; **~ping bag** n borsa per la spesa; **~ping centre** (US **~ping center**) n centro commerciale; **~-soiled** adj sciupato(a) a forza di stare in vetrina; **~ steward** (BRIT) n (INDUSTRY) rappresentante m sindacale; **~ window** n vetrina

shore [ʃɔ:*] n (of sea) riva, spiaggia; (of lake) riva ♦ vt: **to ~ (up)** puntellare; **on ~** a riva

shorn [ʃɔːn] pp of **shear**

short [ʃɔːt] adj (not long) corto(a); (soon finished) breve; (person) basso(a); (curt) brusco(a), secco(a); (insufficient) insufficiente ♦ n (also: ~ film) cortometraggio; (a pair of) **~s** (i) calzoncini; **to be ~ of sth** essere a corto di or mancare di qc; **in ~** in breve; **~ of doing** a meno che non si faccia; **everything ~ of** tutto fuorché; **it is ~ for** è l'abbreviazione or il diminutivo di; **to cut ~** (speech, visit) accorciare, abbreviare; **to fall ~ of** venir meno a; non soddisfare; **to run ~ of** rimanere senza; **to stop ~** fermarsi di colpo; **to stop ~ of** non arrivare fino a; **~age** n scarsezza, carenza; **~bread** n biscotto di pasta frolla; **~-change** vt: **to ~-change sb** imbrogliare qn sul resto; **~-circuit** n cortocircuito; **~coming** n difetto; **~(crust) pastry** (BRIT) n pasta frolla; **~cut** n scorciatoia; **~en** vt accorciare, ridurre; **~fall** n deficit m; **~hand** (BRIT) n stenografia; **~hand typist** (BRIT) n stenodattilografo/a; **~ list** (BRIT) n (for job) rosa dei candidati; **~-lived** adj di breve durata; **~ly** adv fra poco; **~-sighted** (BRIT) adj miope; **~-staffed** adj a corto di personale; **~-stay** adj (car park) a tempo limitato; **~ story** n racconto, novella; **~-tempered** adj irascibile; **~-term** adj (effect) di or a breve durata; (borrowing) a breve scadenza; **~ wave** n (RADIO) onde fpl corte

shot [ʃɔt] pt, pp of **shoot** ♦ n sparo, colpo; (try) prova; (FOOTBALL) tiro; (injection) iniezione f; (PHOT) foto f inv; **like a ~** come un

razzo; (*very readily*) immediatamente; **~gun**
n fucile *m* da caccia

should [fud] *aux vb*: **I ~ go now** dovrei
andare ora; **he ~ be there now** dovrebbe
essere arrivato ora; **I ~ go if I were you** se fossi
in te andrei; **I ~ like to** mi piacerebbe

shoulder ['ʃəuldə*] *n* spalla; (*BRIT: of road*):
hard ~ banchina ♦ *vt* (*fig*) addossarsi,
prendere sulle proprie spalle; **~ bag** *n* borsa
a tracolla; **~ blade** *n* scapola

shouldn't ['ʃudnt] = **should not**

shout [faut] *n* urlo, grido ♦ *vt* gridare ♦ *vi*
(*also*: **~ out**) urlare, gridare; **~ down** *vt*
zittire gridando; **~ing** *n* urli *mpl*

shove [fʌv] *vt* spingere; (*inf: put*): **to ~ sth in**
ficcare qc in; **~ off** (*inf*) *vi* sloggiare,
smammare

shovel ['ʃʌvl] *n* pala ♦ *vt* spalare

show [ʃəu] (*pt ~ed, pp shown*) *n* (*of emotion*)
dimostrazione *f*, manifestazione *f*; (*semblance*)
apparenza; (*exhibition*) mostra, esposizione *f*;
(*THEATRE, CINEMA*) spettacolo ♦ *vt* far vedere,
mostrare; (*courage etc*) dimostrare, dar prova
di; (*exhibit*) esporre ♦ *vi* vedersi, essere
visibile; **for ~** per fare scena; **on ~** (*exhibits
etc*) esposto(a); **~ in** *vt* (*person*) far entrare;
~ off *vi* (*pej*) esibirsi, mettersi in mostra ♦ *vt*
(*display*) mettere in risalto; (*pej*) mettere in
mostra; **~ out** *vt* (*person*) accompagnare alla
porta; **~ up** *vi* (*stand out*) essere ben visibile;
(*inf: turn up*) farsi vedere ♦ *vt* mettere in
risalto; **~ business** *n* industria dello
spettacolo; **~down** *n* prova di forza

shower ['ʃauə*] *n* (*rain*) acquazzone *m*; (*of
stones etc*) pioggia; (*also: ~bath*) doccia ♦ *vi*
fare la doccia ♦ *vt*: **to ~ sb with** (*gifts, abuse
etc*) coprire qn di; (*missiles*) lanciare contro
qn una pioggia di; **to have a ~** fare la doccia;
~proof *adj* impermeabile

showing ['ʃəuɪŋ] *n* (*of film*) proiezione *f*

show jumping [-dʒʌmpɪŋ] *n* concorso
ippico (di salto ad ostacoli)

shown [ʃəun] *pp of* **show**

show-off ['ʃəuɔf] (*inf*) *n* (*person*) esibizionista
m/f

showpiece ['ʃəupiːs] *n* pezzo forte

showroom ['ʃəurum] *n* sala d'esposizione

shrank [fræŋk] *pt of* **shrink**

shrapnel ['ʃræpnl] *n* shrapnel *m*

shred [ʃred] *n* (*gen pl*) brandello ♦ *vt* fare a
brandelli; (*CULIN*) sminuzzare, tagliuzzare;
~der *n* (*vegetable ~der*) grattugia; (*document
~der*) distruttore *m* di documenti

shrewd [ʃruːd] *adj* astuto(a), scaltro(a)

shriek [ʃriːk] *n* strillo ♦ *vi* strillare

shrill [ʃrɪl] *adj* acuto(a), stridulo(a), stridente

shrimp [ʃrɪmp] *n* gamberetto

shrine [ʃraɪn] *n* reliquiario; (*place*) santuario

shrink [ʃrɪŋk] (*pt shrank, pp shrunk*) *vi*

restringersi; (*fig*) ridursi; (*also: ~ away*)
ritrarsi ♦ *vt* (*wool*) far restringere ♦ *n* (*inf:
pej*) psicanalista *m/f*; **to ~ from doing sth**
rifuggire dal fare qc; **~wrap** *vt* confezionare
con pellicola di plastica

shrivel ['ʃrɪvl] (*also: ~ up*) *vt* raggrinzare,
avvizzire ♦ *vi* raggrinzirsi, avvizzire

shroud [ʃraud] *n* lenzuolo funebre ♦ *vt*: **~ed
in mystery** avvolto(a) nel mistero

Shrove Tuesday ['ʃrəuv-] *n* martedì *m*
grasso

shrub [ʃrʌb] *n* arbusto; **~bery** *n* arbusti *mpl*

shrug [ʃrʌg] *n* scrollata di spalle ♦ *vt*, *vi*: **to
~ (one's shoulders)** alzare le spalle, fare
spallucce; **~ off** *vt* passare sopra a

shrunk [ʃrʌŋk] *pp of* **shrink**

shudder ['ʃʌdə*] *n* brivido ♦ *vi* rabbrividire

shuffle ['ʃʌfl] *vt* (*cards*) mescolare; **to
~ (one's feet)** strascicare i piedi

shun [ʃʌn] *vt* sfuggire, evitare

shunt [ʃʌnt] *vt* (*RAIL: direct*) smistare; (*: divert*)
deviare; (*object*) spostare

shut [ʃʌt] (*pt, pp shut*) *vt* chiudere ♦ *vi*
chiudersi, chiudere; **~ down** *vt*, *vi* chiudere
definitivamente; **~ off** *vt* fermare, bloccare;
~ up (*inf: keep quiet*) stare zitto(a), fare
silenzio ♦ *vt* (*close*) chiudere; (*silence*) far
tacere; **~ter** *n* imposta; (*PHOT*) otturatore *m*

shuttle ['ʃʌtl] *n* spola, navetta; (*space ~*)
navetta (spaziale); (*also: ~ service*) servizio *m*
navetta *inv*

shuttlecock ['ʃʌtlkɔk] *n* volano

shuttle diplomacy *n* la gestione dei
rapporti diplomatici caratterizzata da frequenti
viaggi e incontri dei rappresentanti del governo

shy [ʃaɪ] *adj* timido(a)

Sicily ['sɪsɪlɪ] *n* Sicilia

sick [sɪk] *adj* (*ill*) malato(a); (*vomiting*): **to be
~** vomitare; (*humour*) macabro(a); **to feel ~**
avere la nausea; **to be ~ of** (*fig*) averne
abbastanza di; **~ bay** *n* infermeria; **~en** *vt*
nauseare ♦ *vi*: **to be ~ening for sth** (*cold etc*)
covare qc

sickle ['sɪkl] *n* falcetto

sick: ~ leave *n* congedo per malattia; **~ly** *adj*
malaticcio(a); (*causing nausea*) nauseante;
~ness *n* malattia; (*vomiting*) vomito; **~ pay**
n sussidio per malattia

side [saɪd] *n* lato; (*of lake*) riva; (*team*)
squadra ♦ *cpd* (*door, entrance*) laterale ♦ *vi*:
to ~ with sb parteggiare per qn, prendere le
parti di qn; **by the ~ of** a fianco di; (*road*) sul
ciglio di; **~ by ~** fianco a fianco; **from ~ to ~**
da una parte all'altra; **to take ~s (with)**
schierarsi (con); **~board** *n* credenza;
~burns (*BRIT* **~boards**) *npl* (*whiskers*) basette
fpl; **~ effect** *n* (*MED*) effetto collaterale;
~light *n* (*AUT*) luce *f* di posizione; **~line** *n*
(*SPORT*) linea laterale; (*fig*) attività secondaria;

~long adj obliquo(a); **~ order** n contorno (pietanza); **~ show** n attrazione f; **~step** vt (question) eludere; (problem) scavalcare; **~ street** n traversa; **~track** vt (fig) distrarre; **~walk** (US) n marciapiede m; **~ways** adv (move) di lato, di fianco

siding ['saɪdɪŋ] n (RAIL) binario di raccordo

siege [siːdʒ] n assedio

sieve [sɪv] n setaccio ♦ vt setacciare

sift [sɪft] vt passare al crivello; (fig) vagliare

sigh [saɪ] n sospiro ♦ vi sospirare

sight [saɪt] n (faculty) vista; (spectacle) spettacolo; (on gun) mira ♦ vt avvistare; **in ~** in vista; **on ~** a vista; **out of ~** non visibile; **~seeing** n giro turistico; **to go ~seeing** visitare una località

sign [saɪn] n segno; (with hand etc) segno, gesto; (notice) insegna, cartello ♦ vt firmare; (player) ingaggiare; **~ on** vi (MIL) arruolarsi; (as unemployed) iscriversi sulla lista (dell'ufficio di collocamento) ♦ vt (MIL) arruolare; (employee) assumere; **~ over** vt: **to ~ sth over to sb** cedere qc con scrittura legale a qn; **~ up** vi (MIL) arruolarsi; (for course) iscriversi ♦ vt (player) ingaggiare; (recruits) reclutare

signal ['sɪgnl] n segnale m ♦ vi (AUT) segnalare, mettere la freccia ♦ vt (person) fare segno a; (message) comunicare per mezzo di segnali; **~man** (irreg) n (RAIL) deviatore m

signature ['sɪgnətʃə*] n firma; **~ tune** n sigla musicale

signet ring ['sɪgnət-] n anello con sigillo

significance [sɪg'nɪfɪkəns] n significato; importanza

significant [sɪg'nɪfɪkənt] adj significativo(a)

sign language n linguaggio dei muti

signpost ['saɪnpəust] n cartello indicatore

silence ['saɪlns] n silenzio ♦ vt far tacere, ridurre al silenzio; **~r** n (on gun, BRIT: AUT) silenziatore m

silent ['saɪlnt] adj silenzioso(a); (film) muto(a); **to remain ~** tacere, stare zitto; **~ partner** n (COMM) socio inattivo

silhouette [sɪlu'et] n silhouette f inv

silicon chip ['sɪlɪkən-] n piastrina di silicio

silk [sɪlk] n seta ♦ adj di seta; **~y** adj di seta

silly ['sɪlɪ] adj stupido(a), sciocco(a)

silt [sɪlt] n limo

silver ['sɪlvə*] n argento; (money) monete da 5, 10 or 50 pence; (also: ~ware) argenteria ♦ adj d'argento; **~ paper** (BRIT) n carta argentata, (carta) stagnola; **~-plated** adj argentato(a); **~smith** n argentiere m; **~y** adj (colour) argenteo(a); (sound) argentino(a)

similar ['sɪmɪlə*] adj: **~ (to)** simile (a); **~ly** adv allo stesso modo; così pure

simmer ['sɪmə*] vi cuocere a fuoco lento

simple ['sɪmpl] adj semplice; **simplicity**

[-'plɪsɪtɪ] n semplicità; **simply** adv semplicemente

simultaneous [sɪməl'teɪnɪəs] adj simultaneo(a)

sin [sɪn] n peccato ♦ vi peccare

since [sɪns] adv da allora ♦ prep da ♦ conj (time) da quando; (because) poiché, dato che; **~ then, ever ~** da allora

sincere [sɪn'sɪə*] adj sincero(a); **~ly** adv: **yours ~ly** (in letters) distinti saluti; **sincerity** [-'serɪtɪ] n sincerità

sinew ['sɪnju:] n tendine m

sing [sɪŋ] (pt sang, pp sung) vt, vi cantare

singe [sɪndʒ] vt bruciacchiare

singer ['sɪŋə*] n cantante m/f

singing ['sɪŋɪŋ] n canto

single ['sɪŋgl] adj solo(a), unico(a); (unmarried: man) celibe; (: woman) nubile; (not double) semplice ♦ n (BRIT: also: ~ ticket) biglietto di (sola) andata; (record) 45 giri m; **~s** n (TENNIS) singolo; **~ out** vt scegliere; (distinguish) distinguere; **~ bed** n letto singolo; **~-breasted** adj a un petto; **~ file** n: **in ~ file** in fila indiana; **~-handed** adv senza aiuto, da solo(a); **~-minded** adj tenace, risoluto(a); **~ parent** n (mother) ragazza f madre inv; (father) ragazzo m padre inv; **~ room** n camera singola; **~-track road** n strada a una carreggiata

singly ['sɪŋglɪ] adv separatamente

singular ['sɪŋgjulə*] adj (exceptional, LING) singolare ♦ n (LING) singolare m

sinister ['sɪnɪstə*] adj sinistro(a)

sink [sɪŋk] (pt sank, pp sunk) n lavandino, acquaio ♦ vt (ship) (fare) affondare, colare a picco; (foundations) scavare; (piles etc): **to ~ sth into** conficcare qc in ♦ vi affondare, andare a fondo; (ground etc) cedere, avvallarsi; **my heart sank** mi sentii venir meno; **~ in** vi penetrare

sinner ['sɪnə*] n peccatore/trice

sinus ['saɪnəs] n (ANAT) seno

sip [sɪp] n sorso ♦ vt sorseggiare

siphon ['saɪfən] n sifone m; **~ off** vt travasare (con un sifone)

sir [sə*] n signore m; **S~ John Smith** Sir John Smith; **yes ~** sì, signore

sirloin ['sə:lɔɪn] n controfiletto

sissy ['sɪsɪ] (inf) n femminuccia

sister ['sɪstə*] n sorella; (nun) suora; (BRIT: nurse) infermiera f caposala inv; **~-in-law** n cognata

sit [sɪt] (pt, pp sat) vi sedere, sedersi; (assembly) essere in seduta; (for painter) posare ♦ vt (exam) sostenere, dare; **~ down** vi sedersi; **~ in on** vt fus assistere a; **~ up** vi tirarsi su a sedere; (not go to bed) stare alzato(a) fino a tardi

sitcom ['sɪtkɔm] n abbr (= situation comedy)

commedia di situazione; (*TV*) telefilm *m inv* comico d'interni

site [saɪt] *n* posto; (*also:* building ~) cantiere *m* ♦ *vt* situare

sit-in ['sɪtɪn] *n* (demonstration) sit-in *m inv*

sitting ['sɪtɪŋ] *n* (of assembly etc) seduta; (in canteen) turno; ~ **room** *n* soggiorno

situated ['sɪtjʊeɪtɪd] *adj* situato(a)

situation [sɪtjuˈeɪʃən] *n* situazione *f*; (job) lavoro; (location) posizione *f*; "~s vacant" (*BRIT*) "offerte fpl di impiego"

six [sɪks] *num* sei; **~teen** *num* sedici; **~th** *num* sesto(a); **~ty** *num* sessanta

size [saɪz] *n* dimensioni fpl; (of clothing) taglia, misura; (of shoes) numero; (glue) colla; ~ **up** *vt* giudicare, farsi un'idea di; **~able** *adj* considerevole

sizzle ['sɪzl] *vi* sfrigolare

skate [skeɪt] *n* pattino; (fish: pl inv) razza ♦ *vi* pattinare; **~board** *n* skateboard *m inv*; **~r** *n* pattinatore/trice; **skating** *n* pattinaggio; **skating rink** *n* pista di pattinaggio

skeleton ['skɛlɪtn] *n* scheletro; ~ **staff** *n* personale *m* ridotto

skeptical ['skɛptɪkl] (*US*) *adj* = **sceptical**

sketch [skɛtʃ] *n* (drawing) schizzo, abbozzo; (*THEATRE*) scenetta comica, sketch *m inv* ♦ *vt* abbozzare, schizzare; ~ **book** *n* album *m inv* per schizzi; **~y** *adj* incompleto(a), lacunoso(a)

skewer ['skjuːə*] *n* spiedo

ski [skiː] *n* sci *m* ♦ *vi* sciare; ~ **boot** *n* scarpone *m* da sci

skid [skɪd] *n* slittamento ♦ *vi* slittare

skier ['skiːə*] *n* sciatore/trice

skiing ['skiːɪŋ] *n* sci *m*

ski jump *n* (ramp) trampolino; (event) salto con gli sci

skilful ['skɪlful] (*US* **skillful**) *adj* abile

ski lift *n* sciovia

skill [skɪl] *n* abilità *f inv*, capacità *f inv*; **~ed** *adj* esperto(a); (worker) qualificato(a), specializzato(a); **~ful** (*US*) *adj* = **skilful**

skim [skɪm] *vt* (milk) scremare; (glide over) sfiorare ♦ *vi*: **to ~ through** (fig) scorrere, dare una scorsa a; **~med milk** *n* latte *m* scremato

skimp [skɪmp] *vt* (work: also: ~ on) fare alla carlona; (cloth etc) lesinare; **~y** *adj* misero(a), striminzito(a); frugale

skin [skɪn] *n* pelle *f* ♦ *vt* (fruit etc) sbucciare; (animal) scuoiare, spellare; ~ **cancer** *n* cancro alla pelle; **~-deep** *adj* superficiale; ~ **diving** *n* nuoto subacqueo; **~ny** *adj* molto magro(a), pelle e ossa *inv*; **~tight** *adj* (dress etc) aderente

skip [skɪp] *n* saltello, balzo; (*BRIT:* container) benna ♦ *vi* saltare; (with rope) saltare la corda ♦ *vt* saltare

ski pass *n* ski pass *m inv*

ski pole *n* racchetta (da sci)

skipper ['skɪpə*] *n* (*NAUT*, *SPORT*) capitano

skipping rope ['skɪpɪŋ-] (*BRIT*) *n* corda per saltare

skirmish ['skəːmɪʃ] *n* scaramuccia

skirt [skəːt] *n* gonna, sottana ♦ *vt* fiancheggiare, costeggiare; **~ing board** (*BRIT*) *n* zoccolo

ski slope *n* pista da sci

ski suit *n* tuta da sci

skit [skɪt] *n* parodia; scenetta satirica

ski tow *n* sciovia, ski-lift *m inv*

skittle ['skɪtl] *n* birillo; **~s** *n* (game) (gioco dei) birilli *mpl*

skive [skaɪv] (*BRIT:* inf) *vi* fare il lavativo

skull [skʌl] *n* cranio, teschio

skunk [skʌŋk] *n* moffetta

sky [skaɪ] *n* cielo; **~light** *n* lucernario; **~scraper** *n* grattacielo

slab [slæb] *n* lastra; (of cake, cheese) fetta

slack [slæk] *adj* (loose) allentato(a); (slow) lento(a); (careless) negligente; **~en** (*also:* ~en off) *vi* rallentare, diminuire ♦ *vt* allentare; (speed) diminuire; **~s** *npl* (trousers) pantaloni *mpl*

slag heap [slæg-] *n* ammasso di scorie

slag off [slæg-] (*BRIT:* inf) *vt* sparlare di

slam [slæm] *vt* (door) sbattere; (throw) scaraventare; (criticize) stroncare ♦ *vi* sbattere

slander ['slɑːndə*] *n* calunnia; diffamazione *f*

slang [slæŋ] *n* gergo, slang *m*

slant [slɑːnt] *n* pendenza, inclinazione *f*; (fig) angolazione *f*, punto di vista; **~ed** *adj* in pendenza, inclinato(a); (eyes) obliquo(a); **~ing** *adj* = **~ed**

slap [slæp] *n* manata, pacca; (on face) schiaffo ♦ *vt* dare una manata a; schiaffeggiare ♦ *adv* (directly) in pieno; ~ **a coat of paint on it** dagli una mano di vernice; **~dash** *adj* negligente; (work) raffazzonato(a); **~stick** *n* (comedy) farsa grossolana; **~-up** (*BRIT*) *adj*: **a ~-up meal** un pranzo (*o* una cena) coi fiocchi

slash [slæʃ] *vt* tagliare; (face) sfregiare; (fig: prices) ridurre drasticamente, tagliare

slat [slæt] *n* (of wood) stecca; (of plastic) lamina

slate [sleɪt] *n* ardesia; (piece) lastra di ardesia ♦ *vt* (fig: criticize) stroncare, distruggere

slaughter ['slɔːtə*] *n* strage *f*, massacro ♦ *vt* (animal) macellare; (people) trucidare, massacrare

slave [sleɪv] *n* schiavo/a ♦ *vi* (also: ~ away) lavorare come uno schiavo; **~ry** *n* schiavitù *f*;

slavish *adj* servile; (copy) pedissequo(a)

slay [sleɪ] (pt **slew**, pp **slain**) *vt* (formal) uccidere

sleazy ['sliːzɪ] *adj* trasandato(a)

sledge [slɛdʒ] *n* slitta; **~hammer** *n* mazza, martello da fabbro

sleek [sli:k] *adj* (*hair, fur*) lucido(a), lucente; (*car, boat*) slanciato(a), affusolato(a)

sleep [sli:p] (*pt, pp* **slept**) *n* sonno ♦ *vi* dormire; **to go to ~** addormentarsi; **~ around** *vi* andare a letto con tutti; **~ in** *vi* (*oversleep*) dormire fino a tardi; **~er** (*BRIT*) *n* (*RAIL: on track*) traversina; (: *train*) treno di vagoni letto; **~ing bag** *n* sacco a pelo; **~ing car** *n* vagone *m* letto *inv*, carrozza *f* letto *inv*; **~ing partner** (*BRIT*) *n* (*COMM*) socio inattivo; **~ing pill** *n* sonnifero; **~less** *adj*: a **~less night** una notte in bianco; **~walker** *n* sonnambulo/a; **~y** *adj* assonnato(a), sonnolento(a); (*fig*) addormentato(a)

sleet [sli:t] *n* nevischio

sleeve [sli:v] *n* manica; (*of record*) copertina

sleigh [sleɪ] *n* slitta

sleight [slaɪt] *n*: **~ of hand** gioco di destrezza

slender ['slɛndə*] *adj* snello(a), sottile; (*not enough*) scarso(a), esiguo(a)

slept [slɛpt] *pt, pp of* **sleep**

slew [slu:] *pt of* **slay** ♦ *vi* (*BRIT*) girare

slice [slaɪs] *n* fetta ♦ *vt* affettare, tagliare a fette

slick [slɪk] *adj* (*skilful*) brillante; (*clever*) furbo(a) ♦ *n* (*also*: oil ~) chiazza di petrolio

slide [slaɪd] (*pt, pp* **slid**) *n* scivolone *m*; (*in playground*) scivolo; (*PHOT*) diapositiva; (*BRIT: also*: hair ~) fermaglio (per capelli) ♦ *vt* far scivolare ♦ *vi* scivolare; **~ rule** *n* regolo calcolatore; **sliding** *adj* (*door*) scorrevole; **sliding scale** *n* scala mobile

slight [slaɪt] *adj* (*slim*) snello(a), sottile; (*frail*) delicato(a), fragile; (*trivial*) insignificante; (*small*) piccolo(a) ♦ *n* offesa, affronto; **not in the ~est** affatto, neppure per sogno; **~ly** *adv* lievemente, un po'

slim [slɪm] *adj* magro(a), snello(a) ♦ *vi* dimagrire; fare (*or* seguire) una dieta dimagrante

slime [slaɪm] *n* limo, melma; viscidume *m*

slimming ['slɪmɪŋ] *adj* (*diet*) dimagrante; (*food*) ipocalorico(a)

sling [slɪŋ] (*pt, pp* **slung**) *n* (*MED*) fascia al collo; (*for baby*) marsupio ♦ *vt* lanciare, tirare

slip [slɪp] *n* scivolata, scivolone *m*; (*mistake*) errore *m*, sbaglio; (*underskirt*) sottoveste *f*; (*of paper*) striscia di carta; tagliando, scontrino ♦ *vt* (*slide*) far scivolare ♦ *vi* (*slide*) scivolare; (*move smoothly*): **to ~ into/out of** scivolare in/fuori da; (*decline*) declinare; **to ~ sth on/off** infilarsi/togliersi qc; **to give sb the ~** sfuggire qn; **a ~ of the tongue** un lapsus linguae; **~ away** *vi* svignarsela; **~ in** *vt* infilare ♦ *vi* (*error*) scivolare; **~ out** *vi* scivolare fuori; **~ up** *vi* sbagliarsi; **~ped disc** *n* spostamento delle vertebre

slipper ['slɪpə*] *n* pantofola

slippery ['slɪpərɪ] *adj* scivoloso(a)

slip road (*BRIT*) *n* (*to motorway*) rampa di accesso

slip-up ['slɪpʌp] *n* granchio (*fig*)

slipway ['slɪpweɪ] *n* scalo di costruzione

slit [slɪt] (*pt, pp* **slit**) *n* fessura, fenditura; (*cut*) taglio ♦ *vt* fendere; tagliare

slither ['slɪðə*] *vi* scivolare, sdrucciolare

sliver ['slɪvə*] *n* (*of glass, wood*) scheggia; (*of cheese etc*) fettina

slob [slɔb] (*inf*) *n* sciattone/a

slog [slɔg] (*BRIT*) *n* faticata ♦ *vi* lavorare con accanimento, sgobbare

slogan ['sləugən] *n* motto, slogan *m inv*

slope [sləup] *n* pendio; (*side of mountain*) versante *m*; (*ski ~*) pista; (*of roof*) pendenza; (*of floor*) inclinazione *f* ♦ *vi*: **to ~ down** declinare; **to ~ up** essere in salita; **sloping** *adj* inclinato(a)

sloppy ['slɔpɪ] *adj* (*work*) tirato(a) via; (*appearance*) sciatto(a)

slot [slɔt] *n* fessura ♦ *vt*: **to ~ sth into** infilare qc in

sloth [sləuθ] *n* (*laziness*) pigrizia, accidia

slot machine *n* (*BRIT: vending machine*) distributore *m* automatico; (*for gambling*) slot-machine *f inv*

slouch [slautʃ] *vi* (*when walking*) camminare dinoccolato(a); **she was ~ing in a chair** era sprofondata in una poltrona

Slovenia [sləu'vi:nɪə] *n* Slovenia

slovenly ['slʌvənlɪ] *adj* sciatto(a), trasandato(a)

slow [sləu] *adj* lento(a); (*watch*): **to be ~** essere indietro ♦ *adv* lentamente ♦ *vt, vi* (*also*: ~ down, ~ up) rallentare; "~" (*road sign*) "rallentare"; **~ly** *adv* lentamente; **~ motion** *n*: **in ~ motion** al rallentatore

sludge [slʌdʒ] *n* fanghiglia

slug [slʌg] *n* lumaca; (*bullet*) pallottola; **~gish** *adj* lento(a); (*trading*) stagnante

sluice [slu:s] *n* chiusa

slum [slʌm] *n* catapecchia

slumber ['slʌmbə*] *n* sonno

slump [slʌmp] *n* crollo, caduta; (*economic*) depressione *f*, crisi *f inv* ♦ *vi* crollare

slung [slʌŋ] *pt, pp of* **sling**

slur [slə:*] *n* (*fig*): ~ (**on**) calunnia (su) ♦ *vt* pronunciare in modo indistinto

slush [slʌʃ] *n* neve *f* mista a fango; **~ fund** *n* fondi *mpl* neri

slut [slʌt] *n* donna trasandata, sciattona

sly [slaɪ] *adj* (*smile, remark*) sornione(a); (*person*) furbo(a)

smack [smæk] *n* (*slap*) pacca; (*on face*) schiaffo ♦ *vt* schiaffeggiare; (*child*) picchiare ♦ *vi*: **to ~ of** puzzare di

small [smɔ:l] *adj* piccolo(a); **~ ads** (*BRIT*) *npl* piccola pubblicità; **~ change** *n* moneta, spiccioli *mpl*; **~-holder** *n* piccolo proprietario; **~ hours** npl: **in the ~ hours** alle ore piccole; **~pox** n vaiolo; **~ talk** n chiacchiere fpl

smart [smɑːt] adj elegante; (fashionable) alla moda; (clever) intelligente; (quick) sveglio(a) ♦ vi bruciare; **~ card** n carta intelligente; **~en up** vi farsi bello(a) ♦ vt (people) fare bello(a); (things) abbellire

smash [smæʃ] n (also: ~-up) scontro, collisione f; (~ hit) successone m ♦ vt frantumare, fracassare; (SPORT: record) battere ♦ vi frantumarsi, andare in pezzi; **~ing** (inf) adj favoloso(a), formidabile

smattering ['smætərɪŋ] n: **a ~ of** un'infarinatura di

smear [smɪə*] n macchia; (MED) striscio ♦ vt spalmare; (make dirty) sporcare; **~ campaign** n campagna diffamatoria

smell [smɛl] (pt, pp smelt or smelled) n odore m; (sense) olfatto, odorato ♦ vt sentire (l')odore di ♦ vi (food etc): **to ~ (of)** avere odore (di); (pej) puzzare, avere un cattivo odore; **~y** adj puzzolente

smile [smaɪl] n sorriso ♦ vi sorridere

smirk [smɜːk] n sorriso furbo; sorriso compiaciuto

smog [smɒg] n smog m

smoke [sməuk] n fumo ♦ vt, vi fumare; **~d** adj (bacon, glass) affumicato(a); **~r** n (person) fumatore/trice; (RAIL) carrozza per fumatori; **~ screen** n (MIL) cortina fumogena or di fumo; (fig) copertura; **smoking** n fumo; **"no smoking"** (sign) "vietato fumare"; **smoking compartment** (BRIT), **smoking car** (US) n scompartimento (per) fumatori; **smoky** adj fumoso(a); (taste) affumicato(a)

smolder ['sməuldə*] (US) vi = smoulder

smooth [smuːð] adj liscio(a); (sauce) omogeneo(a); (flavour, whisky) amabile; (movement) regolare; (person) mellifluo(a) ♦ vt (also: ~ out) lisciare, spianare; (: difficulties) appianare

smother ['smʌðə*] vt soffocare

smoulder ['sməuldə*] (US smolder) vi covare sotto la cenere

smudge [smʌdʒ] n macchia; sbavatura ♦ vt imbrattare, sporcare

smug [smʌg] adj soddisfatto(a), compiaciuto(a)

smuggle ['smʌgl] vt contrabbandare; **~r** n contrabbandiere/a; **smuggling** n contrabbando

smutty ['smʌtɪ] adj (fig) osceno(a), indecente

snack [snæk] n spuntino; **~ bar** n tavola calda, snack bar m inv

snag [snæg] n intoppo, ostacolo imprevisto

snail [sneɪl] n chiocciola

snake [sneɪk] n serpente m

snap [snæp] n (sound) schianto, colpo secco; (photograph) istantanea ♦ adj improvviso(a) ♦ vt (far) schioccare; (break) spezzare di netto ♦ vi spezzarsi con un rumore secco; (fig: person) parlare con tono secco; **to ~ shut** chiudersi di scatto; **~ at** vt fus (subj: dog) cercare di mordere; **~ off** vt (break) schiantare; **~ up** vt afferrare; **~py** (inf) adj (answer, slogan) d'effetto; **make it ~py!** (hurry up) sbrigati!, svelto!; **~shot** n istantanea

snare [snɛə*] n trappola

snarl [snɑːl] vi ringhiare

snatch [snætʃ] n (small amount) frammento ♦ vt strappare (con violenza); (fig) rubare

sneak [sniːk] (pt (US) snuck) vi: **to ~ in/out** entrare/uscire di nascosto ♦ n spione/a; **to ~ up on sb** avvicinarsi quatto quatto a qn; **~ers** npl scarpe fpl da ginnastica

sneer [snɪə*] vi sogghignare; **to ~ at** farsi beffe di

sneeze [sniːz] n starnuto ♦ vi starnutire

sniff [snɪf] n fiutata, annusata ♦ vi tirare su col naso ♦ vt fiutare, annusare

snigger ['snɪgə*] vi ridacchiare, ridere sotto i baffi

snip [snɪp] n pezzetto; (bargain) (buon) affare m, occasione f ♦ vt tagliare

sniper ['snaɪpə*] n (marksman) franco tiratore m, cecchino

snippet ['snɪpɪt] n frammento

snob [snɒb] n snob m/f inv; **~bery** n snobismo; **~bish** adj snob inv

snooker ['snuːkə*] n tipo di gioco del biliardo

snoop ['snuːp] vi: **to ~ about** curiosare

snooze [snuːz] n sonnellino, pisolino ♦ vi fare un sonnellino

snore [snɔː*] vi russare

snorkel ['snɔːkl] n (of swimmer) respiratore m a tubo

snort [snɔːt] n sbuffo ♦ vi sbuffare

snout [snaut] n muso

snow [snəu] n neve f ♦ vi nevicare; **~ball** n palla di neve ♦ vi (fig) crescere a vista d'occhio; **~bound** adj bloccato(a) dalla neve; **~drift** n cumulo di neve (ammucchiato dal vento); **~drop** n bucaneve m inv; **~fall** n nevicata; **~flake** n fiocco di neve; **~man** (irreg) n pupazzo di neve; **~plough** (US ~plow) n spazzaneve m inv; **~shoe** n racchetta da neve; **~storm** n tormenta

snub [snʌb] vt snobbare ♦ n offesa, affronto; **~-nosed** adj dal naso camuso

snuff [snʌf] n tabacco da fiuto

snug [snʌg] adj comodo(a); (room, house) accogliente, comodo(a)

snuggle ['snʌgl] vi: **to ~ up to sb** stringersi a qn

so [səʊ] adv **1** (thus, likewise) così; **if ~** se è così, quand'è così; **I didn't do it — you did ~!** non l'ho fatto io — sì che l'hai fatto!; **~ do I,** **~ am I** etc anch'io; **it's 5 o'clock — ~ it is!** sono le 5 — davvero!; **I hope ~** lo spero; **I think ~** penso di sì; **~ far** finora, fin qui; (in past) fino ad allora

2 (in comparisons etc: to such a degree) così; **~ big (that)** così grande (che); **she's not ~ clever as her brother** lei non è (così) intelligente come suo fratello

3: **~ much** adj tanto(a) ♦ adv tanto; **I've got ~ much work/money** ho tanto lavoro/tanti soldi; **I love you ~ much** ti amo tanto; **~ many** tanti(e)

4 (phrases): **10 or ~** circa 10; **~ long!** (inf: goodbye) ciao!, ci vediamo!

♦ conj **1** (expressing purpose): **~ as to do** in modo or così da fare; **we hurried ~ as not to be late** ci affrettammo per non fare tardi; **~ (that)** affinché + sub, perché + sub

2 (expressing result): **he didn't arrive ~ I left** non è venuto così me ne sono andata; **~ you see, I could have gone** vedi, sarei potuto andare

soak [səʊk] vt inzuppare; (clothes) mettere a mollo ♦ vi (clothes etc) essere a mollo; **~ in** vi penetrare; **~ up** vt assorbire

soap [səʊp] n sapone m; **~flakes** npl sapone m in scaglie; **~ opera** n soap opera f inv; **~ powder** n detersivo; **~y** adj insaponato(a)

soar [sɔː*] vi volare in alto; (price etc) salire alle stelle; (building) ergersi

sob [sɔb] n singhiozzo ♦ vi singhiozzare

sober ['səʊbə*] adj sobrio(a); (not drunk) non ubriaco(a); (moderate) moderato(a); **~ up** vt far passare la sbornia a ♦ vi farsi passare la sbornia

so-called ['səʊ'kɔːld] adj cosiddetto(a)

soccer ['sɔkə*] n calcio

sociable ['səʊʃəbl] adj socievole

social ['səʊʃl] adj sociale ♦ n festa, serata; **~ club** n club m inv sociale; **~ism** n socialismo; **~ist** adj, n socialista m/f; **~ize** vi: **to ~ize (with)** socializzare (con); **~ security** (BRIT) n previdenza sociale; **~ work** n servizio sociale; **~ worker** n assistente m/f sociale

society [sə'saɪətɪ] n società f inv; (club) società, associazione f; (also: high ~) alta società

sociology [səʊsɪ'ɔlədʒɪ] n sociologia

sock [sɔk] n calzino

socket ['sɔkɪt] n cavità f inv; (of eye) orbita; (BRIT: ELEC: also: wall ~) presa di corrente

sod [sɔd] n (of earth) zolla erbosa; (BRIT: inf!) bastardo/a (!)

soda ['səʊdə] n (CHEM) soda; (also: ~ water) acqua di seltz; (US: also: ~ pop) gassosa

sodium ['səʊdɪəm] n sodio

sofa ['səʊfə] n sofà m inv

soft [sɔft] adj (not rough) morbido(a); (not hard) soffice; (not loud) sommesso(a); (not bright) tenue; (kind) gentile; **~ drink** n analcolico; **~en** ['sɔfn] vt ammorbidire; addolcire; attenuare ♦ vi ammorbidirsi; addolcirsi; attenuarsi; **~ly** adv dolcemente, morbidamente; **~ness** n dolcezza; morbidezza

software* ['sɔftwεə*] n (COMPUT) software m

soggy ['sɔgɪ] adj inzuppato(a)

soil [sɔɪl] n terreno ♦ vt sporcare

solar ['səʊlə*] adj solare; **~ panel** n pannello solare; **~ power** n energie solare

sold [səʊld] pt, pp of **sell**; **~ out** adj (COMM) esaurito(a)

solder ['səʊldə*] vt saldare ♦ n saldatura

soldier ['səʊldʒə*] n soldato, militare m

sole [səʊl] n (of foot) pianta (del piede); (of shoe) suola; (fish: pl inv) sogliola ♦ adj solo(a), unico(a)

solemn ['sɔləm] adj solenne

sole trader n (COMM) commerciante m in proprio

solicit [sə'lɪsɪt] vt (request) richiedere, sollecitare ♦ vi (prostitute) adescare i passanti

solicitor [sə'lɪsɪtə*] (BRIT) n (for wills etc) ≈ notaio; (in court) ≈ avvocato

solid ['sɔlɪd] adj solido(a); (not hollow) pieno(a); (meal) sostanzioso(a) ♦ n solido

solidarity [sɔlɪ'dærɪtɪ] n solidarietà

solitaire [sɔlɪ'tεə*] n (games, gem) solitario

solitary ['sɔlɪtərɪ] adj solitario(a); **~ confinement** n (LAW) isolamento

solo ['səʊləʊ] n assolo; **~ist** n solista m/f

soluble ['sɔljʊbl] adj solubile

solution [sə'luːʃən] n soluzione f

solve [sɔlv] vt risolvere

solvent ['sɔlvənt] adj (COMM) solvibile ♦ n (CHEM) solvente m

sombre ['sɔmbə*] (US **somber**) adj scuro(a); (mood, person) triste

some [sʌm] adj **1** (a certain amount or number of): **~ tea/water/cream** del tè/ dell'acqua/della panna; **~ children/apples** dei bambini/delle mele

2 (certain: in contrasts) certo(a); **~ people say that ...** alcuni dicono che ..., certa gente dice che ...

3 (unspecified) un(a) certo(a), qualche; **~ woman was asking for you** una tale chiedeva di lei; **~ day** un giorno; **~ day next week** un giorno della prossima settimana

♦ pron **1** (a certain number) alcuni(e),

certi(e); **I've got ~** (*books etc*) ne ho alcuni;
~ (of them) have been sold alcuni sono stati
venduti

2 (*a certain amount*) un po'; **I've got ~**
(*money, milk*) ne ho un po'; **I've read ~ of
the book** ho letto parte del libro
♦ *adv*: **~ 10 people** circa 10 persone

somebody ['sʌmbədɪ] *pron* = **someone**

somehow ['sʌmhau] *adv* in un modo o
nell'altro, in qualche modo; (*for some reason*)
per qualche ragione

someone ['sʌmwʌn] *pron* qualcuno

someplace ['sʌmpleɪs] (*US*) *adv* =
somewhere

somersault ['sʌməsɔːlt] *n* capriola; salto
mortale ♦ *vi* fare una capriola (*or* un salto
mortale); (*car*) cappottare

something ['sʌmθɪŋ] *pron* qualcosa, qualche
cosa; **~ nice** qualcosa di bello; **~ to do**
qualcosa da fare

sometime ['sʌmtaɪm] *adv* (*in future*) una
volta o l'altra; (*in past*): **~ last month** durante
il mese scorso

sometimes ['sʌmtaɪmz] *adv* qualche volta

somewhat ['sʌmwɔt] *adv* piuttosto

somewhere ['sʌmwɛə*] *adv* in *or* da
qualche parte

son [sʌn] *n* figlio

song [sɒŋ] *n* canzone *f*

sonic ['sɒnɪk] *adj* (*boom*) sonico(a)

son-in-law ['sʌnɪnlɔː] *n* genero

sonnet ['sɒnɪt] *n* sonetto

sonny ['sʌnɪ] (*inf*) *n* ragazzo mio

soon [suːn] *adv* presto, fra poco; (*early, a
short time after*) presto; **~ afterwards** poco
dopo; *see also* **as**; **~er** *adv* (*time*) prima;
(*preference*): **I would ~er do** preferirei fare; **~er
or later** prima o poi

soot [sut] *n* fuliggine *f*

soothe [suːð] *vt* calmare

sophisticated [sə'fɪstɪkeɪtɪd] *adj*
sofisticato(a); raffinato(a); complesso(a)

sophomore ['sɒfəmɔː*] (*US*) *n* studente/essa
del secondo anno

sopping ['sɒpɪŋ] *adj* (*also:* **~ wet**) bagnato(a)
fradicio(a)

soppy ['sɒpɪ] (*pej*) *adj* sentimentale

soprano [sə'prɑːnəu] *n* (*voice*) soprano *m*;
(*singer*) soprano *m/f*

sorcerer ['sɔːsərə*] *n* stregone *m*, mago

sore [sɔː*] *adj* (*painful*) dolorante ♦ *n* piaga;
~ly *adv* (*tempted*) fortemente

sorrow ['sɒrəu] *n* dolore *m*; **~ful** *adj*
doloroso(a)

sorry ['sɒrɪ] *adj* spiacente; (*condition, excuse*)
misero(a); **~!** scusa! (*or* scusi! *or* scusate!); **to
feel ~ for sb** rincrescersi per qn

sort [sɔːt] *n* specie *f*, genere *m* ♦ *vt* (*also:*

~ out: *papers*) classificare; ordinare; (*: letters
etc*) smistare; (*: problems*) risolvere; **~ing
office** *n* ufficio *m* smistamento *inv*

SOS *n abbr* (= *save our souls*) S.O.S. *m inv*

so-so ['səusəu] *adv* così così

sought [sɔːt] *pt, pp of* **seek**

soul [səul] *n* anima; **~ful** *adj* pieno(a) di
sentimento

sound [saund] *adj* (*healthy*) sano(a); (*safe,
not damaged*) solido(a), in buono stato;
(*reliable, not superficial*) solido(a); (*sensible*)
giudizioso(a), di buon senso ♦ *adv*: **~ asleep**
profondamente addormentato ♦ *n* suono;
(*noise*) rumore *m*; (*GEO*) stretto ♦ *vt* (*alarm*)
suonare ♦ *vi* suonare; (*fig: seem*) sembrare;
to ~ like rassomigliare a; **~ out** *vt* sondare;
~ barrier *n* muro del suono; **~bite** *n*
dichiarazione breve ed incisiva (*trasmessa per
radio o per TV*); **~ effects** *npl* effetti sonori;
~ly *adv* (*sleep*) profondamente; (*beat*)
duramente; **~proof** *adj* insonorizzato(a),
isolato(a) acusticamente; **~track** *n* (*of film*)
colonna sonora

soup [suːp] *n* minestra; brodo; zuppa;
~ plate *n* piatto fondo; **~spoon** *n* cucchiaio
da minestra

sour ['sauə*] *adj* aspro(a); (*fruit*) acerbo(a);
(*milk*) acido(a); (*fig*) arcigno(a); acido(a);
it's ~ grapes è soltanto invidia

source [sɔːs] *n* fonte *f*, sorgente *f*; (*fig*) fonte
f

south [sauθ] *n* sud *m*, meridione *m*,
mezzogiorno ♦ *adj* del sud, sud, del sud,
meridionale ♦ *adv* verso sud; **S~ Africa** *n*
Sudafrica *m*; **S~ African** *adj, n*
sudafricano(a); **S~ America** *n* Sudamerica
m, America del sud; **S~ American** *adj, n*
sudamericano(a); **~-east** *n* sud-est *m*; **~erly**
['sʌðəlɪ] *adj* del sud; **~ern** ['sʌðən] *adj* del
sud, meridionale; esposto(a) a sud; **S~ Pole**
n Polo Sud; **~ward(s)** *adv* verso sud; **~-
west** *n* sud-ovest *m*

souvenir [suːvə'nɪə*] *n* ricordo, souvenir *m*
inv

sovereign ['sɒvrɪn] *adj, n* sovrano(a)

soviet ['səuvɪət] *adj* sovietico(a); **the
S~ Union** l'Unione *f* Sovietica

sow¹ [səu] (*pt* **~ed**, *pp* **sown**) *vt* seminare

sow² [sau] *n* scrofa

sown [səun] *pp of* **sow**

soy [sɔɪ] (*US*) *n* = **soya**

soya ['sɔɪə] (*US* **soy**) *n*: **~ bean** *n* seme *m* di
soia; **~ sauce** *n* salsa di soia

spa [spɑː] *n* (*resort*) stazione *f* termale; (*US:
also: health ~*) centro di cure estetiche

space [speɪs] *n* spazio; (*room*) posto; spazio;
(*length of time*) intervallo ♦ *cpd* spaziale ♦ *vt*
(*also: ~ out*) distanziare; **~craft** *n inv* veicolo
spaziale; **~man/woman** (*irreg*) *n* astronauta
m/f, cosmonauta *m/f*; **~ship** *n* = **~craft**;

spacing n spaziatura
spacious ['speɪʃəs] adj spazioso(a), ampio(a)
spade [speɪd] n (tool) vanga; pala; (child's) paletta; **~s** npl (CARDS) picche fpl
Spain [speɪn] n Spagna
span [spæn] n (of bird, plane) apertura alare; (of arch) campata; (in time) periodo; durata ♦ vt attraversare; (fig) abbracciare
Spaniard ['spænjəd] n spagnolo/a
spaniel ['spænjəl] n spaniel m inv
Spanish ['spænɪʃ] adj spagnolo(a) ♦ n (LING) spagnolo; **the ~** npl gli Spagnoli
spank [spæŋk] vt sculacciare
spanner ['spænə*] (BRIT) n chiave f inglese
spare [spɛə*] adj di riserva, di scorta; (surplus) in più, d'avanzo ♦ n (part) pezzo di ricambio ♦ vt (do without) fare a meno di; (afford to give) concedere; (refrain from hurting, using) risparmiare; **to ~** (surplus) d'avanzo; **~ part** n pezzo di ricambio; **~ time** n tempo libero; **~ wheel** n (AUT) ruota di scorta
sparingly ['spɛərɪŋlɪ] adv moderatamente
spark [spɑːk] n scintilla; **~(ing) plug** n candela
sparkle ['spɑːkl] n scintillio, sfavillio ♦ vi scintillare, sfavillare; **sparkling** adj scintillante, sfavillante; (conversation, wine, water) frizzante
sparrow ['spærəu] n passero
sparse [spɑːs] adj sparso(a), rado(a)
spartan ['spɑːtən] adj (fig) spartano(a)
spasm ['spæzəm] n (MED) spasmo; (fig) accesso, attacco; **~odic** [spæz'mɔdɪk] adj spasmodico(a); (fig) intermittente
spastic ['spæstɪk] n spastico/a
spat [spæt] pt, pp of **spit**
spate [speɪt] n (fig): **~ of** diluvio or fiume m di
spawn [spɔːn] vi deporre le uova ♦ n uova fpl
speak [spiːk] (pt **spoke**, pp **spoken**) vt (language) parlare; (truth) dire ♦ vi parlare; **to ~ to sb/of** or **about sth** parlare a qn/di qc; **~ up!** parla più forte!; **~er** n (in public) oratore/trice; (also: loud~er) altoparlante m; (POL): **the S~er** il presidente della Camera dei Comuni (BRIT) or dei Rappresentanti (US)
spear [spɪə*] n lancia ♦ vt infilzare; **~head** vt (attack etc) condurre
spec [spɛk] (inf) n: **on ~** sperando bene
special ['spɛʃl] adj speciale; **~ist** n specialista m/f; **~ity** [spɛʃɪ'ælɪtɪ] n specialità f inv; **~ize** vi: **to ~ize (in)** specializzarsi (in); **~ly** adv specialmente, particolarmente; **~ needs** adj: **~ needs children** bambini mpl con difficoltà di apprendimento; **~ty** n = **speciality**
species ['spiːʃiːz] n inv specie f inv
specific [spə'sɪfɪk] adj specifico(a); preciso(a); **~ally** adv esplicitamente; (especially) appositamente
specimen ['spɛsɪmən] n esemplare m,

modello; (MED) campione m
speck [spɛk] n puntino, macchiolina; (particle) granello
speckled ['spɛkld] adj macchiettato(a)
specs [spɛks] (inf) npl occhiali mpl
spectacle ['spɛktəkl] n spettacolo; **~s** npl (glasses) occhiali mpl; **spectacular** [-'tækjulə*] adj spettacolare
spectator [spɛk'teɪtə*] n spettatore m
spectra ['spɛktrə] npl of **spectrum**
spectre ['spɛktə*] (US **specter**) n spettro
spectrum ['spɛktrəm] (pl **spectra**) n spettro
speculation [spɛkju'leɪʃən] n speculazione f; congetture fpl
speech [spiːtʃ] n (faculty) parola; (talk, THEATRE) discorso; (manner of speaking) parlata; **~less** adj ammutolito(a), muto(a)
speed [spiːd] n velocità f inv; (promptness) prontezza; **at full** or **top ~** a tutta velocità; **~ up** vi, vt accelerare; **~boat** n motoscafo; **~ily** adv velocemente; prontamente; **~ing** n (AUT) eccesso di velocità; **~ limit** n limite m di velocità; **~ometer** [spɪ'dɔmɪtə*] n tachimetro; **~way** n (SPORT) corsa motociclistica (su pista); **~y** adj veloce, rapido(a); pronto(a)
spell [spɛl] (pt, pp **spelt** (BRIT) or **~ed**) n (also: magic ~) incantesimo; (period of time) (breve) periodo ♦ vt (in writing) scrivere (lettera per lettera); (aloud) dire lettera per lettera; (fig) significare; **to cast a ~ on sb** fare un incantesimo a qn; **he can't ~** fa errori di ortografia; **~bound** adj incantato(a); affascinato(a); **~ing** n ortografia; **spelt** (BRIT) pt, pp of **spell**
spend [spɛnd] (pt, pp **spent**) vt (money) spendere; (time, life) passare; **~thrift** n spendaccione/a; **spent** pt, pp of **spend**
sperm [spɜːm] n sperma m
sphere [sfɪə*] n sfera
spice [spaɪs] n spezia ♦ vt aromatizzare
spicy ['spaɪsɪ] adj piccante
spider ['spaɪdə*] n ragno
spike [spaɪk] n punta
spill [spɪl] (pt, pp **spilt** or **~ed**) vt versare, rovesciare ♦ vi versarsi, rovesciarsi; **~ over** vi (liquid) versarsi; (crowd) riversarsi; **spilt** pt, pp of **spill**
spin [spɪn] (pt, pp **spun**) n (revolution of wheel) rotazione f; (AVIAT) avvitamento; (trip in car) giretto ♦ vt (wool etc) filare; (wheel) far girare ♦ vi girare
spinach ['spɪnɪtʃ] n spinacio; (as food) spinaci mpl
spinal ['spaɪnl] adj spinale; **~ cord** n midollo spinale
spin doctor n esperto di comunicazioni responsabile dell'immagine di un partito politico
spin-dryer [spɪn'draɪə*] (BRIT) n centrifuga

spine [spaɪn] n spina dorsale; (thorn) spina
spinning ['spɪnɪŋ] n filatura; ~ **top** n trottola
spin-off ['spɪnɔf] n (product) prodotto secondario
spinster ['spɪnstə*] n nubile f; zitella
spiral ['spaɪərl] n spirale f ♦ vi (fig) salire a spirale; ~ **staircase** n scala a chiocciola
spire ['spaɪə*] n guglia
spirit ['spɪrɪt] n spirito; (ghost) spirito, fantasma m; (mood) stato d'animo, umore m; (courage) coraggio; ~**s** npl (drink) alcolici mpl; **in good ~s** di buon umore; ~**ed** adj vivace, vigoroso(a); (horse) focoso(a); ~ **level** n livella a bolla (d'aria)
spiritual ['spɪrɪtjuəl] adj spirituale
spit [spɪt] (pt, pp **spat**) n (for roasting) spiedo; (saliva) sputo; saliva ♦ vi sputare; (fire, fat) scoppiettare
spite [spaɪt] n dispetto ♦ vt contrariare, far dispetto a; **in ~ of** nonostante, malgrado; ~**ful** adj dispettoso(a)
spittle ['spɪtl] n saliva; sputo
splash [splæʃ] n spruzzo; (sound) splash m inv; (of colour) schizzo ♦ vt spruzzare ♦ vi (also: ~ **about**) sguazzare
spleen [spli:n] n (ANAT) milza
splendid ['splendɪd] adj splendido(a), magnifico(a)
splint [splɪnt] n (MED) stecca
splinter ['splɪntə*] n scheggia ♦ vi scheggiarsi
split [splɪt] (pt, pp **split**) n spaccatura; (fig: division, quarrel) scissione f ♦ vt spaccare; (party) dividere; (work, profits) spartire, ripartire ♦ vi (divide) dividersi; ~ **up** vi (couple) separarsi, rompere; (meeting) sciogliersi
spoil [spɔɪl] (pt, pp **spoilt** or ~**ed**) vt (damage) rovinare, guastare; (mar) sciupare; (child) viziare; ~**s** npl bottino; ~**sport** n guastafeste m/f inv; **spoilt** pt, pp of **spoil**
spoke [spəuk] pt of **speak** ♦ n raggio
spoken ['spəukn] pp of **speak**
spokesman ['spəuksmən] (irreg) n portavoce m inv
spokeswoman ['spəukswumən] (irreg) n portavoce f inv
sponge [spʌndʒ] n spugna; (also: ~ **cake**) pan m di spagna ♦ vt spugnare, pulire con una spugna ♦ vi: **to ~ off** or **on** scroccare a; ~ **bag** (BRIT) n nécessaire m inv
sponsor ['spɔnsə*] n (RADIO, TV, SPORT etc) sponsor m inv; (POL: of bill) promotore/trice ♦ vt sponsorizzare; (bill) presentare; ~**ship** n sponsorizzazione f
spontaneous [spɔn'teɪnɪəs] adj spontaneo(a)
spooky ['spu:kɪ] (inf) adj che fa accapponare la pelle
spool [spu:l] n bobina

spoon [spu:n] n cucchiaio; ~-**feed** vt nutrire con il cucchiaio; (fig) imboccare; ~**ful** n cucchiaiata
sport [spɔ:t] n sport m inv; (person) persona di spirito ♦ vt sfoggiare; ~**ing** adj sportivo(a); **to give sb a ~ing chance** dare a qn una possibilità (di vincere); ~ **jacket** (US) n = ~**s jacket**; ~**s car** n automobile f sportiva; ~**s jacket** (BRIT) n giacca sportiva; ~**sman** (irreg) n sportivo; ~**smanship** n spirito sportivo; ~**swear** n abiti mpl sportivi; ~**swoman** (irreg) n sportiva; ~**y** adj sportivo(a)
spot [spɔt] n punto; (mark) macchia; (dot: on pattern) pallino; (pimple) foruncolo; (place) posto; (RADIO, TV) spot m inv; (small amount): **a ~ of** un po' di ♦ vt (notice) individuare, distinguere; **on the ~** sul posto; (immediately) su due piedi; (in difficulty) nei guai; ~ **check** n controllo senza preavviso; ~**less** adj immacolato(a); ~**light** n proiettore m; (AUT) faro ausiliario; ~**ted** adj macchiato(a); a puntini, a pallini; ~**ty** adj (face) foruncoloso(a)
spouse [spauz] n sposo/a
spout [spaut] n (of jug) beccuccio; (of pipe) scarico ♦ vi zampillare
sprain [spreɪn] n storta, distorsione f ♦ vt: **to ~ one's ankle** storcersi una caviglia
sprang [spræŋ] pt of **spring**
sprawl [sprɔ:l] vi sdraiarsi (in modo scomposto); (place) estendersi (disordinatamente)
spray [spreɪ] n spruzzo; (container) nebulizzatore m, spray m inv; (of flowers) mazzetto ♦ vt spruzzare; (crops) irrorare
spread [spred] (pt, pp **spread**) n diffusione f; (distribution) distribuzione f; (CULIN) pasta (da spalmare); (inf: food) banchetto ♦ vt (cloth) stendere, distendere; (butter etc) spalmare; (disease, knowledge) propagare, diffondere ♦ vi stendersi, distendersi; spalmarsi; propagarsi, diffondersi; ~ **out** vi (move apart) separarsi; ~-**eagled** ['spredɪ:gld] adj a gambe e braccia aperte; ~**sheet** n foglio elettronico ad espansione
spree [spri:] n: **to go on a ~** fare baldoria
sprightly ['spraɪtlɪ] adj vivace
spring [sprɪŋ] (pt **sprang**, pp **sprung**) n (leap) salto, balzo; (coiled metal) molla; (season) primavera; (of water) sorgente f ♦ vi saltare, balzare; ~ **up** vi (problem) presentarsi; ~**board** n trampolino; ~-**clean(ing)** n grandi pulizie fpl di primavera; ~**time** n primavera
sprinkle ['sprɪŋkl] vt spruzzare; spargere; **to ~ water etc on, ~ with water etc** spruzzare dell'acqua etc su; ~**r** n (for lawn) irrigatore m; (to put out fire) sprinkler m inv

sprint [sprɪnt] *n* scatto ♦ *vi* scattare; **~er** *n* (*SPORT*) velocista *m/f*

sprout [spraʊt] *vi* germogliare; **~s** *npl* (*also: Brussels ~s*) cavolini *mpl* di Bruxelles

spruce [spruːs] *n inv* abete *m* rosso ♦ *adj* lindo(a); azzimato(a)

sprung [sprʌŋ] *pp of* **spring**

spun [spʌn] *pt, pp of* **spin**

spur [spəː*] *n* sperone *m*; (*fig*) sprone *m*, incentivo ♦ *vt* (*also: ~ on*) spronare; **on the ~ of the moment** lì per lì

spurious ['spjʊərɪəs] *adj* falso(a)

spurn [spəːn] *vt* rifiutare con disprezzo, sdegnare

spurt [spəːt] *n* (*of water*) getto; (*of energy*) scatto ♦ *vi* sgorgare

spy [spaɪ] *n* spia ♦ *vi*: **to ~ on** spiare ♦ *vt* (*see*) scorgere; **~ing** *n* spionaggio

sq. *abbr* = **square**

squabble ['skwɔbl] *vi* bisticciarsi

squad [skwɔd] *n* (*MIL*) plotone *m*; (*POLICE*) squadra

squadron ['skwɔdrn] *n* (*MIL*) squadrone *m*; (*AVIAT, NAUT*) squadriglia

squalid ['skwɔlɪd] *adj* squallido(a)

squall [skwɔːl] *n* raffica; burrasca

squalor ['skwɔlə*] *n* squallore *m*

squander ['skwɔndə*] *vt* dissipare

square [skwɛə*] *n* quadrato; (*in town*) piazza ♦ *adj* quadrato(a); (*inf: ideas, person*) di vecchio stampo ♦ *vt* (*arrange*) regolare; (*MATH*) elevare al quadrato; (*reconcile*) conciliare; **all ~** pari; **a ~ meal** un pasto abbondante; **2 metres ~** di 2 metri per 2; **1 ~ metre** 1 metro quadrato; **~ly** *adv* diritto; fermamente

squash [skwɔʃ] *n* (*SPORT*) squash *m*; (*BRIT: drink*): **lemon/orange ~** sciroppo di limone/arancia; (*US*) zucca; (*SPORT*) squash *m* ♦ *vt* schiacciare

squat [skwɔt] *adj* tarchiato(a), tozzo(a) ♦ *vi* (*also: ~ down*) accovacciarsi; **~ter** *n* occupante *m/f* abusivo(a)

squeak [skwiːk] *vi* squittire

squeal [skwiːl] *vi* strillare

squeamish ['skwiːmɪʃ] *adj* schizzinoso(a); disgustato(a)

squeeze [skwiːz] *n* pressione *f*; (*also ECON*) stretta ♦ *vt* premere; (*hand, arm*) stringere; **~ out** *vt* spremere

squelch [skwɛltʃ] *vi* fare ciac; sguazzare

squid [skwɪd] *n* calamaro

squiggle ['skwɪgl] *n* ghirigoro

squint [skwɪnt] *vi* essere strabico(a) ♦ *n*: **he has a ~** è strabico

squirm [skwəːm] *vi* contorcersi

squirrel ['skwɪrəl] *n* scoiattolo

squirt [skwəːt] *vi* schizzare; zampillare ♦ *vt* spruzzare

Sr *abbr* = **senior**

St *abbr* = **saint**; **street**

stab [stæb] *n* (*with knife etc*) pugnalata; (*of pain*) fitta; (*inf: try*): **to have a ~ at (doing) sth** provare (a fare) qc ♦ *vt* pugnalare

stable ['steɪbl] *n* (*for horses*) scuderia; (*for cattle*) stalla ♦ *adj* stabile

stack [stæk] *n* catasta, pila ♦ *vt* accatastare, ammucchiare

stadium ['steɪdɪəm] *n* stadio

staff [stɑːf] *n* (*work force: gen*) personale *m*; (*: BRIT: SCOL*) personale insegnante ♦ *vt* fornire di personale

stag [stæg] *n* cervo

stage [steɪdʒ] *n* palcoscenico; (*profession*): **the ~** il teatro, la scena; (*point*) punto; (*platform*) palco ♦ *vt* (*play*) allestire, mettere in scena; (*demonstration*) organizzare; **in ~s** per gradi; **a tappe;** **~coach** *n* diligenza; **~ manager** *n* direttore *m* di scena

stagger ['stægə*] *vi* barcollare ♦ *vt* (*person*) sbalordire; (*hours, holidays*) scaglionare; **~ing** *adj* (*amazing*) sbalorditivo(a)

stagnate [stæg'neɪt] *vi* stagnare

stag party *n* festa di addio al celibato

staid [steɪd] *adj* posato(a), serio(a)

stain [steɪn] *n* macchia; (*colouring*) colorante *m* ♦ *vt* macchiare; (*wood*) tingere; **~ed glass window** *n* vetrata; **~less** *adj* (*steel*) inossidabile; **~ remover** *n* smacchiatore *m*

stair [stɛə*] *n* (*step*) gradino; **~s** *npl* (*flight of ~s*) scale *fpl*, scala; **~case** *n* scale *fpl*, scala; **~way** *n* = **~case**

stake [steɪk] *n* palo, piolo; (*COMM*) interesse *m*; (*BETTING*) puntata, scommessa ♦ *vt* (*bet*) scommettere; (*risk*) rischiare; **to be at ~** essere in gioco

stale [steɪl] *adj* (*bread*) raffermo(a); (*food*) stantio(a); (*air*) viziato(a); (*beer*) svaporato(a); (*smell*) di chiuso

stalemate ['steɪlmeɪt] *n* stallo; (*fig*) punto morto

stalk [stɔːk] *n* gambo, stelo ♦ *vt* inseguire; **~ off** *vi* andarsene impettito(a)

stall [stɔːl] *n* bancarella; (*in stable*) box *m inv* di stalla ♦ *vt* (*AUT*) far spegnere; (*fig*) bloccare ♦ *vi* (*AUT*) spegnersi, fermarsi; (*fig*) temporeggiare; **~s** *npl* (*BRIT: in cinema, theatre*) platea

stallion ['stælɪən] *n* stallone *m*

stalwart ['stɔːlwət] *adj* fidato(a); risoluto(a)

stamina ['stæmɪnə] *n* vigore *m*, resistenza

stammer ['stæmə*] *n* balbuzie *f* ♦ *vi* balbettare

stamp [stæmp] *n* (*postage ~*) francobollo; (*implement*) timbro; (*mark, also fig*) marchio, impronta; (*on document*) bollo; timbro ♦ *vi* (*also: ~ one's foot*) battere il piede ♦ *vt* battere; (*letter*) affrancare; (*mark with a ~*)

timbrare; **~ album** n album m inv per
francobolli; **~ collecting** n filatelia

stampede [stæm'piːd] n fuggi fuggi m inv

stance [stæns] n posizione f

stand [stænd] n (pt, pp **stood**) n (position)
posizione f; (for taxis) posteggio; (structure)
supporto, sostegno; (at exhibition) stand m
inv; (in shop) banco; (at market) bancarella;
(booth) chiosco; (SPORT) tribuna ♦ vi stare in
piedi; (rise) alzarsi in piedi; (be placed)
trovarsi ♦ vt (place) mettere, porre; (tolerate,
withstand) resistere, sopportare; (treat)
offrire; **to make a ~** prendere posizione; **to
~ for parliament** (BRIT) presentarsi come
candidato (per il parlamento); **~ by** vi (be
ready) tenersi pronto(a) ♦ vt fus (opinion)
sostenere; **~ down** vi (withdraw) ritirarsi;
~ for vt fus (signify) rappresentare,
significare; (tolerate) sopportare, tollerare;
~ in for vt fus sostituire; **~ out** vi (be
prominent) spiccare; **~ up** vi (rise) alzarsi in
piedi; **~ up for** vt fus difendere; **~ up to** vt
fus tener testa a, resistere a

standard ['stændəd] n modello, standard m
inv; (level) livello; (flag) stendardo ♦ adj (size
etc) normale, standard inv; **~s** npl (morals)
principi mpl, valori mpl; **~ lamp** (BRIT) n
lampada a stelo; **~ of living** n livello di vita

stand-by ['stændbaɪ] n riserva, sostituto; **to
be on ~** (gen) tenersi pronto(a); (doctor)
essere di guardia; **~ ticket** n (AVIAT) biglietto
senza garanzia

stand-in ['stændɪn] n sostituto/a

standing ['stændɪŋ] adj diritto(a), in piedi;
(permanent) permanente ♦ n rango,
condizione f, posizione f; **of many years' ~**
che esiste da molti anni; **~ joke** n barzelletta;
~ order (BRIT) n (at bank) ordine m di
pagamento (permanente); **~ room** n posto
all'impiedi

standpoint ['stændpɔɪnt] n punto di vista

standstill ['stændstɪl] n: **at a ~** fermo(a);
(fig) a un punto morto; **to come to a ~**
fermarsi; giungere a un punto morto

stank [stæŋk] pt of **stink**

staple ['steɪpl] n (for papers) graffetta ♦ adj
(food etc) di base ♦ vt cucire; **~r** n cucitrice f

star [stɑː*] n stella; (celebrity) divo/a ♦ vi: **to
~ (in)** essere il (or la) protagonista (di) ♦ vt
(CINEMA) essere interpretato(a) da

starboard ['stɑːbəd] n dritta

starch [stɑːtʃ] n amido

stardom ['stɑːdəm] n celebrità

stare [stɛə*] n sguardo fisso ♦ vi: **to ~** at
fissare

starfish ['stɑːfɪʃ] n stella di mare

stark [stɑːk] adj (bleak) desolato(a) ♦ adv:
~ naked completamente nudo(a)

starling ['stɑːlɪŋ] n storno

starry ['stɑːrɪ] adj stellato(a); **~-eyed** adj
(innocent) ingenuo(a)

start [stɑːt] n inizio; (of race) partenza;
(sudden movement) sobbalzo; (advantage)
vantaggio ♦ vt cominciare, iniziare; (car)
mettere in moto ♦ vi cominciare; (on journey)
partire, mettersi in viaggio; (jump)
sobbalzare; **to ~ doing** or **to do sth**
(in)cominciare a fare qc; **~ off** vi cominciare;
(leave) partire; **~ up** vi cominciare; (car)
avviarsi ♦ vt iniziare; (car) avviare; **~er** n
(AUT) motorino d'avviamento; (SPORT: official)
starter m inv; (BRIT: CULIN) primo piatto; **~ing
point** n punto di partenza

startle ['stɑːtl] vt far trasalire; **startling** adj
sorprendente

starvation [stɑː'veɪʃən] n fame f, inedia

starve [stɑːv] vi morire di fame; soffrire la
fame ♦ vt far morire di fame, affamare

state [steɪt] n stato ♦ vt dichiarare, affermare;
annunciare; **the S~s** (USA) gli Stati Uniti; **to
be in a ~** essere agitato(a); **~ly** adj
maestoso(a), imponente; **~ly home** n
residenza nobiliare (d'interesse storico e
artistico); **~ment** n dichiarazione f; **~sman**
(irreg) n statista m

static ['stætɪk] n (RADIO) scariche fpl ♦ adj
statico(a)

station ['steɪʃən] n stazione f ♦ vt collocare,
disporre

stationary ['steɪʃənərɪ] adj fermo(a),
immobile

stationer ['steɪʃənə*] n cartolaio/a; **~'s
(shop)** n cartoleria; **~y** n articoli mpl di
cancelleria

station master n (RAIL) capostazione m

station wagon n (US) n giardinetta

statistic [stə'tɪstɪk] n statistica; **~s** n (science)
statistica

statue ['stætjuː] n statua

status ['steɪtəs] n posizione f, condizione f
sociale; prestigio; stato; **~ symbol** n simbolo
di prestigio

statute ['stætjuːt] n legge f; **statutory** adj
stabilito(a) dalla legge, statutario(a)

staunch [stɔːntʃ] adj fidato(a), leale

stay [steɪ] n (period of time) soggiorno,
permanenza ♦ vi rimanere; (reside)
alloggiare, stare; (spend some time)
trattenersi, soggiornare; **to ~ put** non
muoversi; **to ~ the night** fermarsi per la notte;
~ behind vi restare indietro; **~ in** vi (at
home) stare in casa; **~ on** vi restare,
rimanere; **~ out** vi (of house) rimanere fuori
(di casa); **~ up** vi (at night) rimanere
alzato(a); **~ing power** n capacità di
resistenza

stead [stɛd] n: **in sb's ~** al posto di qn; **to
stand sb in good ~** essere utile a qn

steadfast ['stedfɑːst] adj fermo(a), risoluto(a)

steadily ['stedɪlɪ] adv (firmly) saldamente; (constantly) continuamente; (fixedly) fisso; (walk) con passo sicuro

steady ['stedɪ] adj (not wobbling) fermo(a); (regular) costante; (person, character) serio(a); (: calm) calmo(a), tranquillo(a) ♦ vt stabilizzare; calmare

steak [steɪk] n (meat) bistecca; (fish) trancia

steal [stiːl] (pt stole, pp stolen) vt rubare ♦ vi rubare; (move) muoversi furtivamente

stealth [stelθ] n: by ~ furtivamente; ~y adj furtivo(a)

steam [stiːm] n vapore m ♦ vt (CULIN) cuocere a vapore ♦ vi fumare; ~ engine n macchina a vapore; (RAIL) locomotiva a vapore; ~er n piroscafo, vapore m; ~roller n rullo compressore; ~ship n = ~er; ~y adj (room) pieno(a) di vapore; (window) appannato(a)

steel [stiːl] n acciaio ♦ adj di acciaio; ~works n acciaieria

steep [stiːp] adj ripido(a), scosceso(a); (price) eccessivo(a) ♦ vt inzuppare; (washing) mettere a mollo

steeple ['stiːpl] n campanile m

steer [stɪə*] vt guidare ♦ vi (NAUT: person) governare; (car) guidarsi; ~ing n (AUT) sterzo; ~ing wheel n volante m

stem [stem] n (of flower, plant) stelo; (of tree) fusto; (of glass) gambo; (of fruit, leaf) picciolo ♦ vt contenere, arginare; ~ from vt fus provenire da, derivare da

stench [stentʃ] n puzzo, fetore m

stencil ['stensl] n (of metal, cardboard) stampino, mascherina; (in typing) matrice f ♦ vt disegnare con stampino

stenographer [ste'nɔgrəfə*] (US) n stenografo/a

step [step] n passo; (stair) gradino, scalino; (action) mossa, azione f ♦ vi: to ~ forward/back fare un passo avanti/indietro; ~s npl (BRIT) = **stepladder**; to be in/out of ~ (with) stare/non stare al passo (con); ~ down vi (fig) ritirarsi; ~ on vt fus calpestare; ~ up vt aumentare; intensificare; ~brother n fratellastro; ~daughter n figliastra; ~father n patrigno; ~ladder n scala a libretto; ~mother n matrigna; ~ping stone n pietra di un guado; ~sister n sorellastra; ~son n figliastro

stereo ['steriəu] n (system) sistema m stereofonico; (record player) stereo m inv ♦ adj (also: ~phonic) stereofonico(a)

sterile ['steraɪl] adj sterile; **sterilize** ['sterɪlaɪz] vt sterilizzare

sterling ['stɜːlɪŋ] adj (gold, silver) di buona lega ♦ n (ECON) (lira) sterlina; **a pound ~** una lira sterlina

stern [stɜːn] adj severo(a) ♦ n (NAUT) poppa

stew [stjuː] n stufato ♦ vt cuocere in umido

steward ['stjuːəd] n (AVIAT, NAUT, RAIL) steward m inv; (in club etc) dispensiere m; ~ess n assistente f di volo, hostess f inv

stick [stɪk] (pt, pp stuck) n bastone m; (of rhubarb, celery) gambo; (of dynamite) candelotto ♦ vt (glue) attaccare; (thrust): to ~ sth into conficcare or piantare or infiggere qc in; (inf: put) ficcare; (inf: tolerate) sopportare ♦ vi attaccarsi; (remain) restare, rimanere; ~ out vi sporgere, spuntare; ~ up vi sporgere, spuntare; ~ up for vt fus difendere; ~er n cartellino adesivo; ~ing plaster n cerotto adesivo

stick-up ['stɪkʌp] (inf) n rapina a mano armata

sticky ['stɪkɪ] adj attaccaticcio(a), vischioso(a); (label) adesivo(a); (fig: situation) difficile

stiff [stɪf] adj rigido(a), duro(a); (muscle) legato(a), indolenzito(a); (difficult) difficile, arduo(a); (cold) freddo(a), formale; (strong) forte; (high: price) molto alto(a) ♦ adv: **bored** ~ annoiato(a) a morte; ~en vt irrigidire; rinforzare ♦ vi irrigidirsi; indurirsi; ~ neck n torcicollo

stifle ['staɪfl] vt soffocare

stigma ['stɪgmə] n (fig) stigma m

stile [staɪl] n cavalcasiepe m; cavalcastecato

stiletto [stɪ'letəu] (BRIT) n (also: ~ heel) tacco a spillo

still [stɪl] adj fermo(a); silenzioso(a) ♦ adv (up to this time, even) ancora; (nonetheless) tuttavia, ciò nonostante; ~born adj nato(a) morto(a); ~ life n natura morta

stilt [stɪlt] n trampolo; (pile) palo

stilted ['stɪltɪd] adj freddo(a), formale; artificiale

stimulate ['stɪmjuleɪt] vt stimolare

stimuli ['stɪmjulaɪ] npl of **stimulus**

stimulus ['stɪmjuləs] (pl **stimuli**) n stimolo

sting [stɪŋ] (pt, pp stung) n puntura; (organ) pungiglione m ♦ vt pungere

stingy ['stɪndʒɪ] adj spilorcio(a), tirchio(a)

stink [stɪŋk] (pt stank, pp stunk) n fetore m, puzzo ♦ vi puzzare; ~ing (inf) adj (fig): **a ~ing ...** uno schifo di ..., un(a) maledetto(a) ....

stint [stɪnt] n lavoro, compito ♦ vi: to ~ on lesinare su

stir [stɜː*] n agitazione f, clamore m ♦ vt mescolare; (fig) risvegliare ♦ vi muoversi; ~ up vt provocare, suscitare

stirrup ['stɪrəp] n staffa

stitch [stɪtʃ] n (SEWING) punto; (KNITTING) maglia; (MED) punto (di sutura); (pain) fitta ♦ vt cucire, attaccare; suturare

stoat [stəut] n ermellino
stock [stɔk] n riserva, provvista; (COMM) giacenza, stock m inv; (AGR) bestiame m; (CULIN) brodo; (descent) stirpe f; (FINANCE) titoli mpl, azioni fpl ♦ adj (fig: reply etc) consueto(a); classico(a) ♦ vt (have in stock) avere, vendere; **~s and shares** valori mpl di borsa; **in ~** in magazzino; **out of ~** esaurito(a); **~ up** vi: **to ~ up (with)** fare provvista (di)
stockbroker ['stɔkbrəukə*] n agente m di cambio
stock cube (BRIT) n dado
stock exchange n Borsa (valori)
stocking ['stɔkɪŋ] n calza
stock: **~ market** n Borsa, mercato finanziario; **~pile** n riserva ♦ vt accumulare riserve di; **~taking** (BRIT) n (COMM) inventario
stocky ['stɔkɪ] adj tarchiato(a), tozzo(a)
stodgy ['stɔdʒɪ] adj pesante, indigesto(a)
stoke [stəuk] vt alimentare
stole [stəul] pt of **steal** ♦ n stola
stolen ['stəuln] pp of **steal**
stomach ['stʌmək] n stomaco; (belly) pancia ♦ vt sopportare, digerire; **~ ache** n mal m di stomaco
stone [stəun] n pietra; (pebble) sasso, ciottolo; (in fruit) nocciolo; (MED) calcolo; (BRIT: weight) = 6.348 kg.; 14 libbre ♦ adj di pietra ♦ vt lapidare; (fruit) togliere il nocciolo a; **~-cold** adj gelido(a); **~-deaf** adj sordo(a) come una campana; **~work** n muratura; **stony** adj sassoso(a); (fig) di pietra
stood [stud] pt, pp of **stand**
stool [stu:l] n sgabello
stoop [stu:p] vi (also: **have a ~**) avere una curvatura; (also: **~ down**) chinarsi, curvarsi
stop [stɔp] n arresto, fermata; (stopping place) fermata; (in punctuation) punto ♦ vt arrestare, fermare; (break off) interrompere; (also: **put a ~ to**) porre fine a ♦ vi fermarsi; (rain, noise etc) cessare, finire; **to ~ doing sth** cessare or finire di fare qc; **to ~ dead** fermarsi di colpo; **~ off** vi sostare brevemente; **~ up** vt (hole) chiudere, turare; **~gap** n tappabuchi m inv; **~lights** npl (AUT) stop mpl; **~over** n breve sosta; (AVIAT) scalo
stoppage ['stɔpɪdʒ] n arresto, fermata; (of pay) trattenuta; (strike) interruzione f del lavoro
stopper ['stɔpə*] n tappo
stop press n ultimissime fpl
stopwatch ['stɔpwɔtʃ] n cronometro
storage ['stɔːrɪdʒ] n immagazzinamento; **~ heater** n radiatore m elettrico che accumula calore
store [stɔː*] n provvista, riserva; (depot) deposito; (BRIT: department ~) grande magazzino; (US: shop) negozio ♦ vt immagazzinare; **~s** npl (provisions) rifornimenti mpl, scorte fpl; **in ~** di riserva; in serbo; **~ up** vt conservare; mettere in serbo; **~room** n dispensa
storey ['stɔːrɪ] (US **story**) n piano
stork [stɔːk] n cicogna
storm [stɔːm] n tempesta, temporale m, burrasca; uragano ♦ vi (fig) infuriarsi ♦ vt prendere d'assalto; **~y** adj tempestoso(a), burrascoso(a)
story ['stɔːrɪ] n storia; favola; racconto; (US) = **storey**; **~book** n libro di racconti
stout [staut] adj solido(a), robusto(a); (friend, supporter) tenace; (fat) corpulento(a), grasso(a) ♦ n birra scura
stove [stəuv] n (for cooking) fornello; (: small) fornelletto; (for heating) stufa
stow [stəu] vt (also: **~ away**) mettere via; **~away** n passeggero/a clandestino(a)
straddle ['strædl] vt stare a cavalcioni di; (fig) essere a cavallo di
straggle ['strægl] vi crescere (or estendersi) disordinatamente; trascinarsi; rimanere indietro; **straggly** adj (hair) in disordine
straight [streɪt] adj dritto(a); (frank) onesto(a), franco(a); (simple) semplice ♦ adv diritto; (drink) liscio; **to put** or **get ~** mettere in ordine, mettere ordine in; **~ away**, **~ off** (at once) immediatamente; **~en** vt (also: **~en out**) raddrizzare; **~-faced** adj impassibile, imperturbabile; **~forward** adj semplice; onesto(a), franco(a)
strain [streɪn] n (TECH) sollecitazione f; (physical) sforzo; (mental) tensione f; (MED) strappo; distorsione f; (streak, trace) tendenza; elemento ♦ vt tendere; (muscle) sforzare; (ankle) storcere; (resources) pesare su; (food) colare; passare; **~s** npl (MUS) note fpl; **~ed** adj (muscle) stirato(a); (laugh etc) forzato(a); (relations) teso(a); **~er** n passino, colino
strait [streɪt] n (GEO) stretto; **~s** npl: **to be in dire ~s** (fig) essere nei guai; **~jacket** n camicia di forza; **~-laced** adj bacchettone(a)
strand [strænd] n (of thread) filo; **~ed** adj nei guai; senza mezzi di trasporto
strange [streɪndʒ] adj (not known) sconosciuto(a); (odd) strano(a), bizzarro(a); **~ly** adv stranamente; **~r** n sconosciuto/a; estraneo/a
strangle ['stræŋgl] vt strangolare; **~hold** n (fig) stretta (mortale)
strap [stræp] n cinghia; (of slip, dress) spallina, bretella
strategic [strə'tiːdʒɪk] adj strategico(a)
strategy ['strætɪdʒɪ] n strategia
straw [strɔː] n paglia; (drinking ~) cannuccia; **that's the last ~!** è la goccia che fa traboccare

il vaso!

strawberry ['strɔːbərɪ] n fragola

stray [streɪ] adj (animal) randagio(a); (bullet) vagante; (scattered) sparso(a) ♦ vi perdersi

streak [striːk] n striscia; (of hair) mèche f inv ♦ vt striare, screziare ♦ vi: **to ~ past** passare come un fulmine

stream [striːm] n ruscello; corrente f; (of people, smoke etc) fiume m ♦ vt (SCOL) dividere in livelli di rendimento ♦ vi scorrere; **to ~ in/out** entrare/uscire a fiotti

streamer ['striːmə*] n (of paper) stella filante

streamlined ['striːmlaɪnd] adj aerodinamico(a), affusolato(a)

street [striːt] n strada, via; **~car** (US) n tram m inv; **~ lamp** n lampione m; **~ plan** n pianta (di una città); **~wise** (inf) adj esperto(a) dei bassifondi

strength [strɛŋθ] n forza; **~en** vt rinforzare; fortificare; consolidare

strenuous ['strɛnjuəs] adj vigoroso(a), energico(a); (tiring) duro(a), pesante

stress [strɛs] n (force, pressure) pressione f; (mental strain) tensione f; (accent) accento ♦ vt insistere su, sottolineare; accentare

stretch [strɛtʃ] n (of sand etc) distesa ♦ vi stirarsi; (extend): **to ~ to** or **as far as** estendersi fino a ♦ vt tendere, allungare; (spread) distendere; (fig) spingere (al massimo); **~ out** vi allungarsi, estendersi ♦ vt (arm etc) allungare, tendere; (to spread) distendere

stretcher ['strɛtʃə*] n barella, lettiga

strewn [struːn] adj: **~ with** cosparso(a) di

stricken ['strɪkən] adj (person) provato(a); (city, industry etc) colpito(a); **~ with** (disease etc) colpito(a) da

strict [strɪkt] adj (severe) rigido(a), severo(a); (precise) preciso(a), stretto(a); **~ly** adv severamente; rigorosamente; strettamente

stridden ['strɪdn] pp of stride

stride [straɪd] (pt **strode**, pp **stridden**) n passo lungo ♦ vi camminare a grandi passi

strife [straɪf] n conflitto; litigi mpl

strike [straɪk] (pt, pp **struck**) n sciopero; (of oil etc) scoperta; (attack) attacco ♦ vt colpire; (oil etc) scoprire, trovare (bargain) fare; (fig): **the thought** or **it ~s me that** ... mi viene in mente che ... ♦ vi scioperare; (attack) attaccare; (clock) suonare; **on ~** (workers) in sciopero; **to ~ a match** accendere un fiammifero; **~ down** vt (fig) atterrare; **~ up** vt (MUS, conversation) attaccare; **to ~ up a friendship with** fare amicizia con; **~r** n scioperante m/f; (SPORT) attaccante m; **striking** adj che colpisce

string [strɪŋ] (pt, pp **strung**) n spago; (row) fila; sequenza; catena; (MUS) corda ♦ vt: **to ~ out** disporre di fianco a; **to ~ together** (words,

ideas) mettere insieme; **the ~s** npl (MUS) gli archi; **to pull ~s for sb** (fig) raccomandare qn; **~ bean** n fagiolino; **~(ed) instrument** n (MUS) strumento a corda

stringent ['strɪndʒənt] adj rigoroso(a)

strip [strɪp] n striscia ♦ vt spogliare; (paint) togliere; (also: ~ down: machine) smontare ♦ vi spogliarsi; **~ cartoon** n fumetto

stripe [straɪp] n striscia, riga; (MIL, POLICE) gallone m; **~d** adj a strisce or righe

strip lighting n illuminazione f al neon

stripper ['strɪpə*] n spogliarellista m/f

strip-search ['strɪpsɜːtʃ] vt: **to ~ sb** perquisire qn facendolo(a) spogliare ♦ n perquisizione (facendo spogliare il perquisito)

striptease ['strɪptiːz] n spogliarello

strive [straɪv] (pt **strove**, pp **striven**) vi: **to ~ to do** sforzarsi di fare; **striven** ['strɪvn] pp of strive

strode [strəud] pt of stride

stroke [strəuk] n colpo; (SWIMMING) bracciata; (: style) stile m; (MED) colpo apoplettico ♦ vt accarezzare; **at a ~** in un attimo

stroll [strəul] n giretto, passeggiatina ♦ vi andare a spasso; **~er** n (US) passeggino

strong [strɔŋ] adj (gen) forte; (sturdy: table, fabric etc) robusto(a); **they are 50 ~** sono in 50; **~box** n cassaforte f; **~hold** n (also fig) roccaforte f; **~ly** adv fortemente, con forza; energicamente; vivamente; **~room** n camera di sicurezza

strove [strəuv] pt of strive

struck [strʌk] pt, pp of strike

structural ['strʌktʃərəl] adj strutturale

structure ['strʌktʃə*] n struttura; (building) costruzione f, fabbricato

struggle ['strʌgl] n lotta ♦ vi lottare

strum [strʌm] vt (guitar) strimpellare

strung [strʌŋ] pt, pp of string

strut [strʌt] n sostegno, supporto ♦ vi pavoneggiarsi

stub [stʌb] n mozzicone m; (of ticket etc) matrice f, talloncino ♦ vt: **to ~ one's toe** urtare or sbattere il dito del piede; **~ out** vt schiacciare

stubble ['stʌbl] n stoppia; (on chin) barba ispida

stubborn ['stʌbən] adj testardo(a), ostinato(a)

stuck [stʌk] pt, pp of stick ♦ adj (jammed) bloccato(a); **~-up** adj presuntuoso(a)

stud [stʌd] n bottoncino, borchia; (also: ~ earring) orecchino a pressione; (also: ~ farm) scuderia, allevamento di cavalli; (also: ~ horse) stallone m ♦ vt (fig): **~ded with** tempestato(a) di

student ['stjuːdənt] n studente/essa ♦ cpd studentesco(a); universitario(a); degli studenti; **~ driver** (US) n conducente m/f principiante

studio ['stju:dɪəʊ] n studio; **~ flat** (US **~ apartment**) n monolocale m

studious ['stju:dɪəs] adj studioso(a); (studied) studiato(a), voluto(a); **~ly** adv (carefully) deliberatamente, di proposito

study ['stʌdɪ] n studio ♦ vt studiare; esaminare ♦ vi studiare

stuff [stʌf] n roba; (substance) sostanza, materiale m ♦ vt imbottire; (CULIN) farcire; (dead animal) impagliare; (inf: push) ficcare; **~ing** n imbottitura; (CULIN) ripieno; **~y** adj (room) mal ventilato(a), senz'aria; (ideas) antiquato(a)

stumble ['stʌmbl] vi inciampare; **to ~ across** (fig) imbattersi in; **stumbling block** n ostacolo, scoglio

stump [stʌmp] n ceppo; (of limb) moncone m ♦ vt: **to be ~ed** essere sconcertato(a)

stun [stʌn] vt stordire; (amaze) sbalordire

stung [stʌŋ] pt, pp of **sting**

stunk [stʌŋk] pp of **stink**

stunning ['stʌnɪŋ] adj sbalorditivo(a); (girl etc) fantastico(a)

stunt [stʌnt] n bravata; trucco pubblicitario; **~man** (irreg) n cascatore m

stupefy ['stju:pɪfaɪ] vt stordire; intontire; (fig) stupire

stupendous [stju:'pɛndəs] adj stupendo(a), meraviglioso(a)

stupid ['stju:pɪd] adj stupido(a); **~ity** [-'pɪdɪtɪ] n stupidità f inv, stupidaggine f

stupor ['stju:pə*] n torpore m

sturdy ['stɜ:dɪ] adj robusto(a), vigoroso(a); solido(a)

stutter ['stʌtə*] n balbuzie f ♦ vi balbettare

sty [staɪ] n (of pigs) porcile m

stye [staɪ] n (MED) orzaiolo

style [staɪl] n stile m; (distinction) eleganza, classe f; **stylish** adj elegante

stylus ['staɪləs] n (of record player) puntina

suave [swɑ:v] adj untuoso(a)

sub... [sʌb] prefix sub..., sotto...; **~conscious** adj subcosciente ♦ n subcosciente m; **~contract** vt subappaltare

subdue [səb'dju:] vt sottomettere, soggiogare; **~d** adj pacato(a); (light) attenuato(a)

subject [n 'sʌbdʒɪkt, vb səb'dʒɛkt] n soggetto; (citizen etc) cittadino/a; (SCOL) materia ♦ vt: **to ~ to** sottomettere a; esporre a; **to be ~ to** (law) essere sottomesso(a) a; (disease) essere soggetto(a) a; **~ive** [-'dʒɛktɪv] adj soggettivo(a); **~ matter** n argomento; contenuto

sublet [sʌb'lɛt] vt subaffittare

submachine gun ['sʌbməʃi:n-] n mitra m inv

submarine [sʌbmə'ri:n] n sommergibile m

submerge [səb'mɜ:dʒ] vt sommergere; immergere ♦ vi immergersi

submission [səb'mɪʃən] n sottomissione f; (claim) richiesta

submissive [səb'mɪsɪv] adj remissivo(a)

submit [səb'mɪt] vt sottomettere ♦ vi sottomettersi

subnormal [sʌb'nɔ:məl] adj subnormale

subordinate [sə'bɔ:dɪnət] adj, n subordinato(a)

subpoena [səb'pi:nə] n (LAW) citazione f, mandato di comparizione

subscribe [səb'skraɪb] vi contribuire; **to ~ to** (opinion) approvare, condividere; (fund) sottoscrivere a; (newspaper) abbonarsi a; essere abbonato(a) a; **~r** n (to periodical, telephone) abbonato/a

subscription [səb'skrɪpʃən] n sottoscrizione f; abbonamento

subsequent ['sʌbsɪkwənt] adj successivo(a), seguente; conseguente; **~ly** adv in seguito, successivamente

subside [səb'saɪd] vi cedere, abbassarsi; (flood) decrescere; (wind) calmarsi; **~nce** [-'saɪdns] n cedimento, abbassamento

subsidiary [səb'sɪdɪərɪ] adj sussidiario(a); accessorio(a) ♦ n filiale f

subsidize ['sʌbsɪdaɪz] vt sovvenzionare

subsidy ['sʌbsɪdɪ] n sovvenzione f

subsistence [səb'sɪstəns] n esistenza; mezzi mpl di sostentamento; **~ allowance** n indennità f inv di trasferta

substance ['sʌbstəns] n sostanza

substantial [səb'stænʃl] adj solido(a); (amount, progress etc) notevole; (meal) sostanzioso(a)

substantiate [səb'stænʃɪeɪt] vt comprovare

substitute ['sʌbstɪtju:t] n (person) sostituto/a; (thing) succedaneo, surrogato ♦ vt: **to ~ sth/sb for** sostituire qc/qn a

subterfuge ['sʌbtəfju:dʒ] n sotterfugio

subterranean [sʌbtə'reɪnɪən] adj sotterraneo(a)

subtitle ['sʌbtaɪtl] n (CINEMA) sottotitolo; **~d** adj sottotitolato(a)

subtle ['sʌtl] adj sottile; **~ty** n sottigliezza

subtotal [sʌb'təʊtl] n somma parziale

subtract [səb'trækt] vt sottrarre; **~ion** [-'trækʃən] n sottrazione f

suburb ['sʌbɜ:b] n sobborgo; **the ~s** la periferia; **~an** [sə'bɜ:bən] adj suburbano(a); **~ia** n periferia, sobborghi mpl

subversive [səb'vɜ:sɪv] adj sovversivo(a)

subway ['sʌbweɪ] n (US: underground) metropolitana; (BRIT: underpass) sottopassaggio

succeed [sək'si:d] vi riuscire; avere successo ♦ vt succedere a; **to ~ in doing** riuscire a fare;

~ing adj (following) successivo(a)

success [sək'sɛs] n successo; **~ful** adj (venture) coronato(a) da successo, riuscito(a); **to be ~ful (in doing)** riuscire (a fare); **~fully** adv con successo

succession [sək'sɛʃən] n successione f

successive [sək'sɛsɪv] adj successivo(a); consecutivo(a)

succumb [sə'kʌm] vi soccombere

such [sʌtʃ] adj tale; (of that kind): ~ **a book** un tale libro, un libro del genere; ~ **books** tali libri, libri del genere; (so much): ~ **courage** tanto coraggio ♦ adv talmente, così; ~ **a long trip** un viaggio così lungo; ~ **a lot of** talmente or così tanto(a); ~ **as** (like) come; **as** ~ come or in quanto tale; **~-and-~** adj tale (after noun)

suck [sʌk] vt succhiare; (breast, bottle) poppare; **~er** n (ZOOL, TECH) ventosa; (inf) gonzo/a, babbeo/a

suction ['sʌkʃən] n succhiamento; (TECH) aspirazione f

sudden ['sʌdn] adj improvviso(a); **all of a** ~ improvvisamente, all'improvviso; **~ly** adv bruscamente, improvvisamente, di colpo

suds [sʌdz] npl schiuma (di sapone)

sue [su:] vt citare in giudizio

suede [sweɪd] n pelle f scamosciata

suet ['suɪt] n grasso di rognone

suffer ['sʌfə*] vt soffrire, patire; (bear) sopportare, tollerare ♦ vi soffrire; **to ~ from** soffrire di; **~er** n malato/a; **~ing** n sofferenza

suffice [sə'faɪs] vi essere sufficiente, bastare

sufficient [sə'fɪʃənt] adj sufficiente; ~ **money** abbastanza soldi; **~ly** adv sufficientemente, abbastanza

suffocate ['sʌfəkeɪt] vi (have difficulty breathing) soffocare; (die through lack of air) asfissiare

sugar ['ʃugə*] n zucchero ♦ vt zuccherare; ~ **beet** n barbabietola da zucchero; ~ **cane** n canna da zucchero

suggest [sə'dʒɛst] vt proporre, suggerire; indicare; **~ion** [-'dʒɛstʃən] n suggerimento, proposta; indicazione f; **~ive** (pej) adj indecente

suicide ['suɪsaɪd] n (person) suicida m/f; (act) suicidio; see also **commit**

suit [su:t] n (man's) vestito; (woman's) completo, tailleur m inv; (LAW) causa; (CARDS) seme m, colore m ♦ vt andar bene a or per; essere adatto(a) a or per; (adapt): **to** ~ **sth to** adattare qc a; **well ~ed** ben assortito(a); **~able** adj adatto(a); appropriato(a); **~ably** adv (dress) in modo adatto; (impressed) favorevolmente

suitcase ['su:tkeɪs] n valigia

suite [swi:t] n (of rooms) appartamento; (MUS) suite f inv; (furniture): **bedroom/dining room** ~ arredo or mobilia per la camera da letto/sala da pranzo

suitor ['su:tə*] n corteggiatore m, spasimante m

sulfur ['sʌlfə*] (US) n = **sulphur**

sulk [sʌlk] vi fare il broncio; **~y** adj imbronciato(a)

sullen ['sʌlən] adj scontroso(a); cupo(a)

sulphur ['sʌlfə*] (US **sulfur**) n zolfo

sultana [sʌl'tɑːnə] n (fruit) uva (secca) sultanina

sultry ['sʌltrɪ] adj afoso(a)

sum [sʌm] n somma; (SCOL etc) addizione f; ~ **up** vt, vi riassumere

summarize ['sʌmaraɪz] vt riassumere, riepilogare

summary ['sʌmərɪ] n riassunto

summer ['sʌmə*] n estate f ♦ cpd d'estate, estivo(a); ~ **holidays** npl vacanze fpl estive; **~house** n (in garden) padiglione m; **~time** n (season) estate f; ~ **time** n (by clock) ora legale (estiva)

summit ['sʌmɪt] n cima, sommità; (POL) vertice m

summon ['sʌmən] vt chiamare, convocare; ~ **up** vt raccogliere, fare appello a; **~s** n ordine m di comparizione ♦ vt citare

sump [sʌmp] (BRIT) n (AUT) coppa dell'olio

sumptuous ['sʌmptjuəs] adj sontuoso(a)

sun [sʌn] n sole m; **~bathe** vi prendere un bagno di sole; **~block** n protezione f solare totale; **~burn** n (painful) scottatura; **~burnt** adj abbronzato(a); (painfully) scottato(a)

Sunday ['sʌndɪ] n domenica; ~ **school** n ≈ scuola di catechismo

sundial ['sʌndaɪəl] n meridiana

sundown ['sʌndaun] n tramonto

sundry ['sʌndrɪ] adj vari(e), diversi(e); **all and** ~ tutti quanti; **sundries** npl articoli diversi, cose diverse

sunflower ['sʌnflauə*] n girasole m

sung [sʌŋ] pp of **sing**

sunglasses ['sʌnglɑːsɪz] npl occhiali mpl da sole

sunk [sʌŋk] pp of **sink**

sun: **~light** n (luce f del) sole m; **~lit** adj soleggiato(a); **~ny** adj assolato(a), soleggiato(a); (fig) allegro(a), felice; **~rise** n levata del sole, alba; ~ **roof** n (AUT) tetto apribile; **~screen** n (protective ingredient) filtro solare; (cream) crema solare protettiva; **~set** n tramonto; **~shade** n parasole m; **~shine** n (luce f del) sole m; **~stroke** n insolazione f, colpo di sole; **~tan** n abbronzatura; **~tan lotion** n lozione f solare; **~tan oil** n olio solare

super ['su:pə*] (inf) adj fantastico(a)

superannuation [su:pərænju'eɪʃən] n contributi mpl pensionistici; pensione f

superb [su:'pə:b] *adj* magnifico(a)

supercilious [su:pə'sɪlɪəs] *adj* sprezzante, sdegnoso(a)

superficial [su:pə'fɪʃəl] *adj* superficiale

superhuman [su:pə'hju:mən] *adj* sovrumano(a)

superimpose ['su:pərɪm'pəuz] *vt* sovrapporre

superintendent [su:pərɪn'tɛndənt] *n* direttore/trice; (*POLICE*) ≈ commissario (capo)

superior [su'pɪərɪə*] *adj, n* superiore *m/f*; **~ity** [-'ɔrɪtɪ] *n* superiorità

superlative [su'pə:lətɪv] *adj* superlativo(a), supremo(a) ♦ *n* (*LING*) superlativo

superman ['su:pəmæn] (*irreg*) *n* superuomo

supermarket ['su:pəmɑ:kɪt] *n* supermercato

supernatural [su:pə'nætʃərəl] *adj* soprannaturale ♦ *n* soprannaturale *m*

superpower ['su:pəpauə*] *n* (*POL*) superpotenza

supersede [su:pə'si:d] *vt* sostituire, soppiantare

superstitious [su:pə'stɪʃəs] *adj* superstizioso(a)

supertanker ['su:pətæŋkə*] *n* superpetroliera

supervise ['su:pəvaɪz] *vt* (*person etc*) sorvegliare; (*organization*) soprintendere a; **supervision** [-'vɪʒən] *n* sorveglianza; supervisione *f*; **supervisor** *n* sorvegliante *m/f*; soprintendente *m/f*; (*in shop*) capocommesso/a

supine ['su:paɪn] *adj* supino(a)

supper ['sʌpə*] *n* cena

supplant [sə'plɑ:nt] *vt* (*person, thing*) soppiantare

supple ['sʌpl] *adj* flessibile; agile

supplement [*n* 'sʌplɪmənt, *vb* sʌplɪ'mɛnt] *n* supplemento ♦ *vt* completare, integrare; **~ary** [-'mɛntərɪ] *adj* supplementare

supplier [sə'plaɪə*] *n* fornitore *m*

supply [sə'plaɪ] *vt* (*provide*) fornire; (*equip*): **to ~ (with)** approvvigionare (di); attrezzare (con) ♦ *n* riserva, provvista; (*supplying*) approvvigionamento; (*TECH*) alimentazione *f*; **supplies** *npl* (*food*) viveri *mpl*; (*MIL*) sussistenza; **~ teacher** (*BRIT*) *n* supplente *m/f*

support [sə'pɔ:t] *n* (*moral, financial etc*) sostegno, appoggio; (*TECH*) supporto ♦ *vt* sostenere; (*financially*) mantenere; (*uphold*) sostenere, difendere; **~er** *n* (*POL etc*) sostenitore/trice, fautore/trice; (*SPORT*) tifoso/a

suppose [sə'pəuz] *vt* supporre; immaginare; **to be ~d to do** essere tenuto(a) a fare; **~dly** [sə'pəuzɪdlɪ] *adv* presumibilmente; **supposing** *conj* se, ammesso che + *sub*

suppository [sə'pɔzɪtərɪ] *n* suppositorio

suppress [sə'prɛs] *vt* reprimere; sopprimere;

occultare

supreme [su'pri:m] *adj* supremo(a)

surcharge ['sə:tʃɑ:dʒ] *n* supplemento

sure [ʃuə*] *adj* sicuro(a); (*definite, convinced*) sicuro(a), certo(a); **~! (***of course***)** senz'altro!, certo!; **~ enough** infatti; **to make ~ of sth/that** assicurarsi di qc/che; **~-footed** *adj* dal passo sicuro; **~ly** *adv* sicuramente; certamente

surf [sə:f] *n* (*waves*) cavalloni *mpl*; (*foam*) spuma

surface ['sə:fɪs] *n* superficie *f* ♦ *vt* (*road*) asfaltare ♦ *vi* risalire alla superficie; (*fig: news, feeling*) venire a galla; **~ mail** *n* posta ordinaria

surfboard ['sə:fbɔ:d] *n* tavola per surfing

surfeit ['sə:fɪt] *n*: **a ~ of** un eccesso di; un'indigestione di

surfing ['sə:fɪŋ] *n* surfing *m*

surge [sə:dʒ] *n* (*strong movement*) ondata; (*of feeling*) impeto ♦ *vi* gonfiarsi; (*people*) riversarsi

surgeon ['sə:dʒən] *n* chirurgo

surgery ['sə:dʒərɪ] *n* chirurgia; (*BRIT: room*) studio *or* gabinetto medico, ambulatorio; (: *also*: **~ hours**) orario delle visite *or* di consultazione; **to undergo ~** subire un intervento chirurgico

surgical ['sə:dʒɪkl] *adj* chirurgico(a); **~ spirit** (*BRIT*) *n* alcool *m* denaturato

surname ['sə:neɪm] *n* cognome *m*

surpass [sə:'pɑ:s] *vt* superare

surplus ['sə:pləs] *n* eccedenza; (*ECON*) surplus *m inv* ♦ *adj* eccedente, d'avanzo

surprise [sə'praɪz] *n* sorpresa; (*astonishment*) stupore *m* ♦ *vt* sorprendere; stupire; **surprising** *adj* sorprendente, stupefacente; **surprisingly** *adv* (*easy, helpful*) sorprendentemente

surrender [sə'rɛndə*] *n* resa, capitolazione *f* ♦ *vi* arrendersi

surreptitious [sʌrəp'tɪʃəs] *adj* furtivo(a)

surrogate ['sʌrəgɪt] *n* surrogato; **~ mother** *n* madre *f* provetta

surround [sə'raund] *vt* circondare; (*MIL etc*) accerchiare; **~ing** *adj* circostante; **~ings** *npl* dintorni *mpl*; (*fig*) ambiente *m*

surveillance [sə:'veɪləns] *n* sorveglianza, controllo

survey [*n* 'sə:veɪ, *vb* sə:'veɪ] *n* quadro generale; (*study*) esame *m*; (*in housebuying etc*) perizia; (*of land*) rilevamento, rilievo topografico ♦ *vt* osservare; esaminare; valutare; rilevare; **~or** *n* perito; geometra *m*; (*of land*) agrimensore *m*

survival [sə'vaɪvl] *n* sopravvivenza; (*relic*) reliquia, vestigio

survive [sə'vaɪv] *vi* sopravvivere ♦ *vt* sopravvivere a; **survivor** *n* superstite *m/f*, sopravvissuto/a

susceptible [sə'sɛptəbl] *adj*: ~ **(to)** sensibile (a); (*disease*) predisposto(a) (a)

suspect [*adj*, *n* 'sʌspɛkt, *vb* səs'pɛkt] *adj* sospetto(a) ♦ *n* persona sospetta ♦ *vt* sospettare; (*think likely*) supporre; (*doubt*) dubitare

suspend [səs'pɛnd] *vt* sospendere; **~ed sentence** *n* condanna con la condizionale; **~er belt** *n* reggicalze *m inv*; **~ers** *npl* (*BRIT*) giarrettiere *fpl*; (*US*) bretelle *fpl*

suspense [səs'pɛns] *n* apprensione *f*; (*in film etc*) suspense *m*; **to keep sb in ~** tenere qn in sospeso

suspension [səs'pɛnʃən] *n* (*gen AUT*) sospensione *f*; (*of driving licence*) ritiro temporaneo; **~ bridge** *n* ponte *m* sospeso

suspicion [səs'pɪʃən] *n* sospetto

suspicious [səs'pɪʃəs] *adj* (*suspecting*) sospettoso(a); (*causing suspicion*) sospetto(a)

sustain [səs'teɪn] *vt* sostenere; sopportare; (*LAW: charge*) confermare; (*suffer*) subire; **~able** *adj* sostenibile; **~ed** *adj* (*effort*) prolungato(a)

sustenance ['sʌstɪnəns] *n* nutrimento; mezzi *mpl* di sostentamento

swab [swɔb] *n* (*MED*) tampone *m*

swagger ['swægə*] *vi* pavoneggiarsi

swallow ['swɔləu] *n* (*bird*) rondine *f* ♦ *vt* inghiottire; (*fig: story*) bere; **~ up** *vt* inghiottire

swam [swæm] *pt of* swim

swamp [swɔmp] *n* palude *f* ♦ *vt* sommergere

swan [swɔn] *n* cigno

swap [swɔp] *vt*: **to ~ (for)** scambiare (con)

swarm [swɔːm] *n* sciame *m* ♦ *vi* (*bees*) sciamare; (*people*) brulicare; (*place*): **to be ~ing with** brulicare di

swastika ['swɔstɪkə] *n* croce *f* uncinata, svastica

swat [swɔt] *vt* schiacciare

sway [sweɪ] *vi* (*tree*) ondeggiare; (*person*) barcollare ♦ *vt* (*influence*) influenzare, dominare

swear [swɛə*] (*pt* swore, *pp* sworn) *vi* (*curse*) bestemmiare, imprecare ♦ *vt* (*promise*) giurare; **~word** *n* parolaccia

sweat [swɛt] *n* sudore *m*, traspirazione *f* ♦ *vi* sudare

sweater ['swɛtə*] *n* maglione *m*

sweatshirt ['swɛtʃəːt] *n* felpa

sweaty ['swɛtɪ] *adj* sudato(a); bagnato(a) di sudore

Swede [swiːd] *n* svedese *m/f*

swede [swiːd] (*BRIT*) *n* rapa svedese

Sweden ['swiːdn] *n* Svezia

Swedish ['swiːdɪʃ] *adj* svedese ♦ *n* (*LING*) svedese *m*

sweep [swiːp] (*pt*, *pp* swept) *n* spazzata; (*also: chimney ~*) spazzacamino ♦ *vt*

spazzare, scopare; (*current*) spazzare ♦ *vi* (*hand*) muoversi con gesto ampio; (*wind*) infuriare; **~ away** *vt* spazzare via; trascinare via; **~ past** *vi* sfrecciare accanto; passare accanto maestosamente; **~ up** *vt*, *vi* spazzare; **~ing** *adj* (*gesture*) ampio(a); circolare; **a ~ing statement** un'affermazione generica

sweet [swiːt] *n* (*BRIT: pudding*) dolce *m*; (*candy*) caramella ♦ *adj* dolce; (*fresh*) fresco(a); (*fig*) piacevole; delicato(a), grazioso(a); gentile; **~corn** *n* granturco dolce; **~en** *vt* addolcire; zuccherare; **~heart** *n* innamorato/a; **~ness** *n* sapore *m* dolce; dolcezza; **~ pea** *n* pisello odoroso

swell [swɛl] (*pt* ~ed, *pp* swollen, ~ed) *n* (*of sea*) mare *m* lungo ♦ *adj* (*US: inf: excellent*) favoloso(a) ♦ *vt* gonfiare, ingrossare; aumentare ♦ *vi* gonfiarsi, ingrossarsi; (*sound*) crescere; (*also: ~ up*) gonfiarsi; **~ing** *n* (*MED*) tumefazione *f*, gonfiore *m*

sweltering ['swɛltərɪŋ] *adj* soffocante

swept [swɛpt] *pt*, *pp of* sweep

swerve [swəːv] *vi* deviare; (*driver*) sterzare; (*boxer*) scartare

swift [swɪft] *n* (*bird*) rondone *m* ♦ *adj* rapido(a), veloce

swig [swɪg] (*inf*) *n* (*drink*) sorsata

swill [swɪl] *vt* (*also: ~ out, ~ down*) risciacquare

swim [swɪm] (*pt* swam, *pp* swum) *n*: **to go for a ~** andare a fare una nuotata ♦ *vi* nuotare; (*SPORT*) fare del nuoto; (*head, room*) girare ♦ *vt* (*river, channel*) attraversare or percorrere a nuoto; (*length*) nuotare; **~mer** *n* nuotatore/trice; **~ming** *n* nuoto; **~ming cap** *n* cuffia; **~ming costume** (*BRIT*) *n* costume *m* da bagno; **~ming pool** *n* piscina; **~ming trunks** *npl* costume *m* da bagno (da uomo); **~suit** *n* costume *m* da bagno

swindle ['swɪndl] *n* truffa ♦ *vt* truffare

swine [swaɪn] (*inf!*) *n inv* porco (!)

swing [swɪŋ] (*pt*, *pp* swung) *n* altalena; (*movement*) oscillazione *f*; (*MUS*) ritmo; swing *m* ♦ *vt* dondolare, far oscillare; (*also: ~ round*) far girare ♦ *vi* oscillare, dondolare; (*also: ~ round: object*) roteare; (*: person*) girarsi, voltarsi; **to be in full ~** (*activity*) essere in piena attività; (*party etc*) essere nel pieno; **~ door** (*US* **~ing door**) *n* porta battente

swingeing ['swɪndʒɪŋ] *adj* (*BRIT: defeat*) violento(a); (*: cuts*) enorme

swipe [swaɪp] *vt* (*hit*) colpire con forza; dare uno schiaffo a; (*inf: steal*) sgraffignare

swirl [swəːl] *vi* turbinare, far mulinello

Swiss [swɪs] *adj*, *n inv* svizzero(a)

switch [swɪtʃ] *n* (*for light, radio etc*) interruttore *m*; (*change*) cambiamento ♦ *vt* (*change*) cambiare; scambiare; **~ off** *vt* spegnere; **~ on** *vt* accendere; (*engine,*

machine) mettere in moto, avviare; **~board** n
(TEL) centralino

Switzerland ['switsələnd] n Svizzera

swivel ['swivl] vi (also: ~ round) girare

swollen ['swəulən] pp of **swell**

swoon [swuːn] vi svenire

swoop [swuːp] n incursione f ♦ vi (also:
~ down) scendere in picchiata, piombare

swop [swɔp] n, vt = **swap**

sword [sɔːd] n spada; **~fish** n pesce m spada
inv

swore [swɔː*] pt of **swear**

sworn [swɔːn] pp of **swear** ♦ adj giurato(a)

swot [swɔt] vi sgobbare

swum [swʌm] pp of **swim**

swung [swʌŋ] pt, pp of **swing**

syllable ['siləbl] n sillaba

syllabus ['siləbəs] n programma m

symbol ['simbl] n simbolo

symmetry ['simitri] n simmetria

sympathetic [simpə'θetik] adj (showing
pity) compassionevole; (kind) com-
prensivo(a); **~ towards** ben disposto(a) verso

sympathize ['simpəθaiz] vi: **to ~ with**
(person) compatire; partecipare al dolore di;
(cause) simpatizzare per; **~r** n (POL)
simpatizzante m/f

sympathy ['simpəθi] n compassione f;
sympathies npl (support, tendencies) simpatie
fpl; **in ~ with** (strike) per solidarietà con; **with
our deepest ~** con le nostre più sincere
condoglianze

symphony ['simfəni] n sinfonia

symptom ['simptəm] n sintomo; indizio

synagogue ['sinəgɔg] n sinagoga

syndicate ['sindikit] n sindacato

synopses [si'nɔpsiːz] npl of **synopsis**

synopsis [si'nɔpsis] (pl **synopses**) n
sommario, sinossi f inv

syntheses ['sinθəsiːz] npl of **synthesis**

synthesis ['sinθəsis] (pl **syntheses**) n sintesi
f inv

synthetic [sin'θetik] adj sintetico(a)

syphon ['saifən] n, vb = **siphon**

Syria ['siriə] n Siria

syringe [si'rindʒ] n siringa

syrup ['sirəp] n sciroppo; (also: golden ~)
melassa raffinata

system ['sistəm] n sistema m; (order)
metodo; (ANAT) organismo; **~atic** [-'mætik]
adj sistematico(a); metodico(a); **~ disk** n
(COMPUT) disco del sistema; **~s analyst** n
analista m di sistemi

T, t

ta [tɑː] (BRIT: inf) excl grazie!

tab [tæb] n (loop on coat etc) laccetto; (label)

etichetta; **to keep ~s on** (fig) tenere d'occhio

tabby ['tæbi] n (also: ~ cat) (gatto) soriano,
gatto tigrato

table ['teibl] n tavolo, tavola; (MATH, CHEM etc)
tavola ♦ vt (BRIT: motion etc) presentare; **to
lay** or **set the ~** apparecchiare or preparare la
tavola; **~cloth** n tovaglia; **~ of contents** n
indice m; **~ d'hôte** [tɑːbl'dəut] adj (meal) a
prezzo fisso; **~ lamp** n lampada da tavolo;
~mat n sottopiatto; **~spoon** n cucchiaio da
tavola; (also: ~spoonful: as measurement)
cucchiaiata

tablet ['tæblit] n (MED) compressa; (of stone)
targa

table: ~ tennis n tennis m da tavolo, ping-
pong ® m; **~ wine** n vino da tavola

tacit ['tæsit] adj tacito(a)

tack [tæk] n (nail) bulletta; (fig) approccio
♦ vt imbullettare; imbastire ♦ vi bordeggiare

tackle ['tækl] n attrezzatura, equipaggiamento; (for lifting) paranco; (FOOTBALL)
contrasto; (RUGBY) placcaggio ♦ vt (difficulty)
affrontare; (FOOTBALL) contrastare; (RUGBY)
placcare

tacky ['tæki] adj appiccicaticcio(a); (pej)
scadente

tact [tækt] n tatto; **~ful** adj delicato(a),
discreto(a)

tactical ['tæktikl] adj tattico(a)

tactics ['tæktiks] n, npl tattica

tactless ['tæktlis] adj che manca di tatto

tadpole ['tædpəul] n girino

tag [tæg] n etichetta; **~ along** vi seguire

tail [teil] n coda; (of shirt) falda ♦ vt (follow)
seguire, pedinare; **~ away** vi = **~ off**; **~ off**
vi (in size, quality etc) diminuire
gradatamente; **~back** (BRIT) n (AUT) ingorgo;
~ end n (of train, procession etc) coda; (of
meeting etc) fine f; **~gate** n (AUT) portellone
m posteriore

tailor ['teilə*] n sarto; **~ing** n (cut) stile m;
(craft) sartoria; **~-made** adj (also fig) fatto(a)
su misura

tailwind ['teilwind] n vento di coda

tainted ['teintid] adj (food) guasto(a);
(water, air) infetto(a); (fig) corrotto(a)

take [teik] (pt **took**, pp **taken**) vt prendere;
(gain: prize) ottenere, vincere; (require: effort,
courage) occorrere, volerci; (tolerate)
accettare, sopportare; (hold: passengers etc)
contenere; (accompany) accompagnare;
(bring, carry) portare; (exam) sostenere,
presentarsi a; **to ~ a photo/a shower** fare una
fotografia/una doccia; **I ~ it that** suppongo
che; **~ after** vt fus assomigliare a; **~ apart** vt
smontare; **~ away** vt portare via; togliere;
~ back vt (return) restituire; riportare; (one's
words) ritirare; **~ down** vt (building)
demolire; (letter etc) scrivere; **~ in** vt

(*deceive*) imbrogliare, abbindolare; (*understand*) capire; (*include*) comprendere, includere; (*lodger*) prendere, ospitare; **~ off** *vi* (*AVIAT*) decollare; (*go away*) andarsene ♦ *vt* (*remove*) togliere; **~ on** *vt* (*work*) accettare, intraprendere; (*employee*) assumere; (*opponent*) sfidare, affrontare; **~ out** *vt* portare fuori; (*remove*) togliere; (*licence*) prendere, ottenere; **to ~ sth out of sth** (*drawer, pocket etc*) tirare qc fuori da qc; estrarre qc da qc; **~ over** *vt* (*business*) rilevare ♦ *vi*: **to ~ over from sb** prendere le consegne *or* il controllo da qn; **~ to** *vt fus* (*person*) prendere in simpatia; (*activity*) prendere gusto a; **~ up** *vt* (*dress*) accorciare; (*occupy: time, space*) occupare; (*engage in: hobby etc*) mettersi a; **to ~ sb up on sth** accettare qc da qn; **~away** (*BRIT*) *n* (*shop etc*) ≈ rosticceria; (*food*) pasto per asporto; **~off** *n* (*AVIAT*) decollo; **~out** (*US*) *n* = **~away**; **~over** *n* (*COMM*) assorbimento

takings ['teɪkɪŋz] *npl* (*COMM*) incasso

talc [tælk] *n* (*also*: ~**um powder**) talco

tale [teɪl] *n* racconto, storia; **to tell ~s** (*fig*: *to teacher, parent etc*) fare la spia

talent ['tælnt] *n* talento; **~ed** *adj* di talento

talk [tɔːk] *n* discorso; (*gossip*) chiacchiere *fpl*; (*conversation*) conversazione *f*; (*interview*) discussione *f* ♦ *vi* parlare; **~s** *npl* (*POL etc*) colloqui *mpl*; **to ~ about** parlare di; **to ~ sb out of/into doing** dissuadere qn da/convincere qn a fare; **to ~ shop** parlare di lavoro *or* di affari; **~ over** *vt* discutere; **~ative** *adj* loquace, ciarliero(a); **~ show** *n* conversazione *f* televisiva, talk show *m inv*

tall [tɔːl] *adj* alto(a); **to be 6 feet ~** ≈ essere alto 1 metro e 80; **~ story** *n* panzana, frottola

tally ['tælɪ] *n* conto, conteggio ♦ *vi*: **to ~ (with)** corrispondere (a)

talon ['tælən] *n* artiglio

tambourine [tæmbə'riːn] *n* tamburello

tame [teɪm] *adj* addomesticato(a); (*fig*: *story, style*) insipido(a), scialbo(a)

tamper ['tæmpə*] *vi*: **to ~ with** manomettere

tampon ['tæmpɔn] *n* tampone *m*

tan [tæn] *n* (*also*: sun~) abbronzatura ♦ *vi* abbronzarsi ♦ *adj* (*colour*) marrone rossiccio *inv*

tang [tæŋ] *n* odore *m* penetrante; sapore *m* piccante

tangent ['tændʒənt] *n*: **to go off at a ~** (*fig*) partire per la tangente

tangerine [tændʒə'riːn] *n* mandarino

tangle ['tæŋgl] *n* groviglio; **to get into a ~** aggrovigliarsi; (*fig*) combinare un pasticcio

tank [tæŋk] *n* serbatoio; (*for fish*) acquario; (*MIL*) carro armato

tanker ['tæŋkə*] *n* (*ship*) nave *f* cisterna *inv*;

(*truck*) autobotte *f*, autocisterna

tanned [tænd] *adj* abbronzato(a)

tantalizing ['tæntəlaɪzɪŋ] *adj* allettante

tantamount ['tæntəmaunt] *adj*: **~ to** equivalente a

tantrum ['tæntrəm] *n* accesso di collera

tap [tæp] *n* (*on sink etc*) rubinetto; (*gentle blow*) colpetto ♦ *vt* dare un colpetto a; (*resources*) sfruttare, utilizzare; (*telephone*) mettere sotto controllo; **on ~** (*fig*: *resources*) a disposizione; **~ dancing** *n* tip tap *m*

tape [teɪp] *n* nastro; (*also*: magnetic ~) nastro (magnetico); (*sticky ~*) nastro adesivo ♦ *vt* (*record*) registrare (su nastro); (*stick*) attaccare con nastro adesivo; **~ deck** *n* piastra; **~ measure** *n* metro a nastro

taper ['teɪpə*] *n* candelina ♦ *vi* assottigliarsi

tape recorder *n* registratore *m* (a nastro)

tapestry ['tæpɪstrɪ] *n* arazzo; tappezzeria

tar [tɑː*] *n* catrame *m*

target ['tɑːgɪt] *n* bersaglio; (*fig*: *objective*) obiettivo

tariff ['tærɪf] *n* tariffa

tarmac ['tɑːmæk] *n* (*BRIT*: on road) macadam *m al* catrame; (*AVIAT*) pista di decollo

tarnish ['tɑːnɪʃ] *vt* offuscare, annerire; (*fig*) macchiare

tarpaulin [tɑː'pɔːlɪn] *n* tela incatramata

tarragon ['tærəgən] *n* dragoncello

tart [tɑːt] *n* (*CULIN*) crostata; (*BRIT*: *inf*: *pej*: *woman*) sgualdrina ♦ *adj* (*flavour*) aspro(a), agro(a); **~ up** (*inf*) *vt* agghindare

tartan ['tɑːtn] *n* tartan *m inv*

tartar ['tɑːtə*] *n* (*on teeth*) tartaro; **~(e) sauce** *n* salsa tartara

task [tɑːsk] *n* compito; **to take to ~** rimproverare; **~ force** *n* (*MIL, POLICE*) unità operativa

taste [teɪst] *n* gusto; (*flavour*) sapore *m*, gusto; (*sample*) assaggio; (*fig*: *glimpse, idea*) idea ♦ *vt* gustare; (*sample*) assaggiare ♦ *vi*: **to ~ of** *or* **like** (*fish etc*) sapere *or* avere sapore di; **you can ~ the garlic (in it)** (ci) si sente il sapore dell'aglio; **in good/bad ~** di buon/cattivo gusto; **~ful** *adj* di buon gusto; **~less** *adj* (*food*) insipido(a); (*remark*) di cattivo gusto; **tasty** *adj* saporito(a), gustoso(a)

tatters ['tætəz] *npl*: **in ~** a brandelli

tattoo [tə'tuː] *n* tatuaggio; (*spectacle*) parata militare ♦ *vt* tatuare

tatty ['tætɪ] *adj* malridotto(a)

taught [tɔːt] *pt*, *pp of* **teach**

taunt [tɔːnt] *n* scherno ♦ *vt* schernire

Taurus ['tɔːrəs] *n* Toro

taut [tɔːt] *adj* teso(a)

tax [tæks] *n* (*on goods*) imposta; (*on services*) tassa; (*on income*) imposte *fpl*, tasse *fpl* ♦ *vt* tassare; (*fig*: *strain: patience etc*) mettere alla prova; **~able** *adj* (*income*) imponibile;

~ation [-'seɪʃən] n tassazione f; tasse fpl; imposte fpl; **~ avoidance** n elusione f fiscale; **~ disc** (BRIT) n (AUT) ≈ bollo; **~ evasion** n evasione f fiscale; **~-free** adj esente da imposte

taxi ['tæksɪ] n taxi m inv ♦ vi (AVIAT) rullare; **~ driver** n tassista m/f; **~ rank** (BRIT) n = **~ stand**; **~ stand** n posteggio dei taxi

tax: **~ payer** n contribuente m/f; **~ relief** n agevolazioni fpl fiscali; **~ return** n dichiarazione f dei redditi

TB n abbr = **tuberculosis**

tea [ti:] n tè m inv; (BRIT: snack: for children) merenda; **high ~** (BRIT) cena leggera (presa nel tardo pomeriggio); **~ bag** n bustina di tè; **~ break** (BRIT) n intervallo per il tè

teach [ti:tʃ] (pt, pp **taught**) vt: **to ~ sb sth, ~ sth to sb** insegnare qc a qn ♦ vi insegnare; **~er** n insegnante m/f; (in secondary school) professore/essa, (in primary school) maestro/a; **~ing** n insegnamento

tea cosy n copriteiera m inv

teacup ['ti:kʌp] n tazza da tè

teak [ti:k] n teak m

tea leaves npl foglie fpl di tè

team [ti:m] n squadra; (of animals) tiro; **~work** n lavoro di squadra

teapot ['ti:pɒt] n teiera

tear[1] [tɛə*] (pt **tore**, pp **torn**) n strappo ♦ vt strappare ♦ vi strapparsi; **~ along** vi (rush) correre all'impazzata; **~ up** vt (sheet of paper etc) strappare

tear[2] [tɪə*] n lacrima; **in ~s** in lacrime; **~ful** adj piangente, lacrimoso(a); **~ gas** n gas m lacrimogeno

tearoom ['ti:ru:m] n sala da tè

tease [ti:z] vt canzonare; (unkindly) tormentare

tea set n servizio da tè

teaspoon ['ti:spu:n] n cucchiaino da tè; (also: **~ful**: as measurement) cucchiaino

teat [ti:t] n capezzolo

teatime ['ti:taɪm] n ora del tè

tea towel (BRIT) n strofinaccio (per i piatti)

technical ['tɛknɪkl] adj tecnico(a); **~ college** (BRIT) n ≈ istituto tecnico; **~ity** [-'kælɪtɪ] n tecnicità; (detail) dettaglio tecnico; (legal) cavillo

technician [tɛk'nɪʃən] n tecnico/a

technique [tɛk'ni:k] n tecnica

technological [tɛknə'lɒdʒɪkl] adj tecnologico(a)

technology [tɛk'nɒlədʒɪ] n tecnologia

teddy (bear) ['tɛdɪ-] n orsacchiotto

tedious ['ti:dɪəs] adj noioso(a), tedioso(a)

tee [ti:] n (GOLF) tee m inv

teem [ti:m] vi: **to ~ with** brulicare di; **it is ~ing (with rain)** piove a dirotto

teenage ['ti:neɪdʒ] adj (fashions etc) per giovani, per adolescenti; **~r** n adolescente m/f

teens [ti:nz] npl: **to be in one's ~** essere adolescente

tee-shirt ['ti:ʃə:t] n = **T-shirt**

teeter ['ti:tə*] vi barcollare, vacillare

teeth [ti:θ] npl of **tooth**

teethe [ti:ð] vi mettere i denti

teething ring ['ti:ðɪŋ-] n dentaruolo

teething troubles ['ti:ðɪŋ-] npl (fig) difficoltà fpl iniziali

teetotal ['ti:'təutl] adj astemio(a)

tele: **~conferencing** n teleconferenza; **~gram** n telegramma m; **~graph** n telegrafo; **~pathy** [tə'lɛpəθɪ] n telepatia

telephone ['tɛlɪfəun] n telefono ♦ vt (person) telefonare a; (message) comunicare per telefono; **~ booth** (BRIT **~ box**) n cabina telefonica; **~ call** n telefonata; **~ directory** n elenco telefonico; **~ number** n numero di telefono; **telephonist** [tə'lɛfənɪst] (BRIT) n telefonista m/f

telesales ['tɛlɪseɪlz] n vendita per telefono

telescope ['tɛlɪskəup] n telescopio

television ['tɛlɪvɪʒən] n televisione f; **on ~** alla televisione; **~ set** n televisore m

teleworking ['tɛlɪwə:kɪŋ] n telelavoro

telex ['tɛlɛks] n telex m inv ♦ vt trasmettere per telex

tell [tɛl] (pt, pp **told**) vt dire; (relate: story) raccontare; (distinguish): **to ~ sth from** distinguere qc da ♦ vi (talk): **to ~ (of)** parlare (di); (have effect) farsi sentire, avere effetto; **to ~ sb to do** dire a qn di fare; **~ off** vt rimproverare, sgridare; **~er** n (in bank) cassiere/a; **~ing** adj (remark, detail) rivelatore(trice); **~tale** adj (sign) rivelatore(trice)

telly ['tɛlɪ] (BRIT: inf) n abbr (= television) tivù f inv

temerity [tə'mɛrɪtɪ] n temerarietà

temp [tɛmp] n abbr (= temporary) segretaria temporanea

temper ['tɛmpə*] n (nature) carattere m; (mood) umore m; (fit of anger) collera ♦ vt (moderate) moderare; **to be in a ~** essere in collera; **to lose one's ~** andare in collera

temperament ['tɛmprəmənt] n (nature) temperamento; **~al** [-'mɛntl] adj capriccioso(a)

temperate ['tɛmprət] adj temperato(a)

temperature ['tɛmprətʃə*] n temperatura; **to have or run a ~** avere la febbre

tempest ['tɛmpɪst] n tempesta

template ['tɛmplɪt] n sagoma

temple ['tɛmpl] n (building) tempio; (ANAT) tempia

temporary ['tɛmpərərɪ] adj temporaneo(a); (job, worker) avventizio(a), temporaneo(a)

tempt [tɛmpt] vt tentare; **to ~ sb into doing**

indurre qn a fare; **~ation** [-'teɪʃən] *n*
tentazione *f*; **~ing** *adj* allettante

ten [tɛn] *num* dieci

tenacity [tə'næsɪtɪ] *n* tenacia

tenancy ['tɛnənsɪ] *n* affitto; condizione *f* di
inquilino

tenant ['tɛnənt] *n* inquilino/a

tend [tɛnd] *vt* badare a, occuparsi di ♦ *vi*: to
~ to do tendere a fare

tendency ['tɛndənsɪ] *n* tendenza

tender ['tɛndə*] *adj* tenero(a); (*sore*)
dolorante ♦ *n* (*COMM: offer*) offerta; (*money*):
legal ~ moneta in corso legale ♦ *vt* offrire

tendon ['tɛndən] *n* tendine *m*

tenement ['tɛnəmənt] *n* casamento

tennis ['tɛnɪs] *n* tennis *m*; **~ ball** *n* palla da
tennis; **~ court** *n* campo da tennis; **~ player**
n tennista *m/f*; **~ racket** *n* racchetta da
tennis; **~ shoes** *npl* scarpe *fpl* da tennis

tenor ['tɛnə*] *n* (*MUS*) tenore *m*

tenpin bowling ♦ ['tɛnpɪn-] *n* bowling *m*

tense [tɛns] *adj* teso(a) ♦ *n* (*LING*) tempo

tension ['tɛnʃən] *n* tensione *f*

tent [tɛnt] *n* tenda

tentative ['tɛntətɪv] *adj* esitante, incerto(a);
(*conclusion*) provvisorio(a)

tenterhooks ['tɛntəhuks] *npl*: **on ~** sulle
spine

tenth [tɛnθ] *num* decimo(a)

tent: **~ peg** *n* picchetto da tenda; **~ pole** *n*
palo da tenda, montante *m*

tenuous ['tɛnjuəs] *adj* tenue

tenure ['tɛnjuə*] *n* (*of property*) possesso; (*of
job*) permanenza; titolarità

tepid ['tɛpɪd] *adj* tiepido(a)

term [tə:m] *n* termine *m*; (*SCOL*) trimestre *m*;
(*LAW*) sessione *f* ♦ *vt* chiamare, definire; **~s**
npl (*conditions*) condizioni *fpl*; (*COMM*) prezzi
mpl, tariffe *fpl*; **in the short/long ~** a breve/
lunga scadenza; **to be on good ~s with sb**
essere in buoni rapporti con qn; **to come to
~s with** (*problem*) affrontare

terminal ['tə:mɪnl] *adj* finale, terminale;
(*disease*) terminale ♦ *n* (*ELEC*) morsetto;
(*COMPUT*) terminale *m*; (*AVIAT, for oil, ore etc*)
terminal *m inv*; (*BRIT: also: coach ~*) capolinea
m

terminate ['tə:mɪneɪt] *vt* mettere fine a

termini ['tə:mɪnaɪ] *npl of* **terminus**

terminus ['tə:mɪnəs] (*pl* **termini**) *n* (*for
buses*) capolinea *m*; (*for trains*) stazione *f*
terminale

terrace ['tɛrəs] *n* terrazza; (*BRIT: row of
houses*) fila di case a schiera; **the ~s** *npl* (*BRIT:
SPORT*) le gradinate; **~d** *adj* (*garden*) a
terrazze

terracotta ['tɛrə'kɔtə] *n* terracotta

terrain [tɛ'reɪn] *n* terreno

terrible ['tɛrɪbl] *adj* terribile; **terribly** *adv*

terribilmente; (*very badly*) malissimo

terrier ['tɛrɪə*] *n* terrier *m inv*

terrific [tə'rɪfɪk] *adj* incredibile, fantastico(a);
(*wonderful*) formidabile, eccezionale

terrify ['tɛrɪfaɪ] *vt* terrorizzare

territory ['tɛrɪtərɪ] *n* territorio

terror ['tɛrə*] *n* terrore *m*; **~ism** *n* terrorismo;
~ist *n* terrorista *m/f*

Terylene ® ['tɛrɪliːn] *n* terital ® *m*, terilene
® *m*

test [tɛst] *n* (*trial, check, of courage etc*) prova;
(*MED*) esame *m*; (*CHEM*) analisi *f inv*; (*exam:
of intelligence etc*) test *m inv*; (: *in school*)
compito in classe; (*also: driving ~*) esame *m*
di guida ♦ *vt* provare; esaminare; analizzare;
sottoporre ad esame; **to ~ sb in history**
esaminare qn in storia

testament ['tɛstəmənt] *n* testamento; **the
Old/New T~** il Vecchio/Nuovo testamento

testicle ['tɛstɪkl] *n* testicolo

testify ['tɛstɪfaɪ] *vi* (*LAW*) testimoniare,
deporre; **to ~ to sth** (*LAW*) testimoniare qc;
(*gen*) comprovare *or* dimostrare qc

testimony ['tɛstɪmənɪ] *n* (*LAW*)
testimonianza, deposizione *f*

test match *n* (*CRICKET, RUGBY*) partita
internazionale

test tube *n* provetta

tetanus ['tɛtənəs] *n* tetano

tether ['tɛðə*] *vt* legare ♦ *n*: **at the end of
one's ~** al limite (della pazienza)

text [tɛkst] *n* testo; **~book** *n* libro di testo

textiles ['tɛkstaɪlz] *npl* tessuti *mpl*; (*industry*)
industria tessile

texture ['tɛkstʃə*] *n* tessitura; (*of skin, paper
etc*) struttura

Thames [tɛmz] *n*: **the ~** il Tamigi

than [ðæn, ðən] *conj* (*in comparisons*) che;
(*with numerals, pronouns, proper names*) di;
more ~ 10/once più di 10/una volta; **I have
more/less ~ you** ne ho più/meno di te; **I have
more pens ~ pencils** ho più penne che
matite; **she is older ~ you think** è più vecchia
di quanto tu (non) pensi

thank [θæŋk] *vt* ringraziare; **~ you (very
much)** grazie (tante); **~s** *npl* ringraziamenti
mpl, grazie *fpl* ♦ *excl* grazie!; **~s to** grazie a;
~ful *adj*: **~ful (for)** riconoscente (per); **~less**
adj ingrato(a); **T~sgiving (Day)** *n* giorno
del ringraziamento

KEYWORD

---

that [ðæt] (*pl* **those**) *adj* (*demonstrative*)
quel(quell', quello) *m*; quella(quell') *f*;
~ man/woman/book quell'uomo/quella
donna/quel libro; (*not "this"*) quell'uomo/
quella donna/quel libro là; **~ one** quello(a) là
♦ *pron* **1** (*demonstrative*) ciò; (*not "this one"*)
quello(a); **who's ~?** chi è?; **what's ~?** cos'è

quello?; **is ~ you?** sei tu?; **I prefer this to ~** preferisco questo a quello; **~'s what he said** questo è ciò che ha detto; **what happened after ~?** che è successo dopo?; **~ is (to say)** cioè

2 (*relative: direct*) che; (*: indirect*) cui; **the book (~) I read** il libro che ho letto; **the box (~) I put it in** la scatola in cui l'ho messo; **the people (~) I spoke to** le persone con cui or con le quali ho parlato

3 (*relative: of time*) in cui; **the day (~) he came** il giorno in cui è venuto
♦ *conj* che; **he thought ~ I was ill** pensava che io fossi malato
♦ *adv* (*demonstrative*) così; **I can't work ~ much** non posso lavorare (così) tanto; **~ high** così alto; **the wall's about ~ high and ~ thick** il muro è alto circa così e spesso circa così

thatched [θætʃt] *adj* (*roof*) di paglia; **~ cottage** *n* cottage *m inv* col tetto di paglia
thaw [θɔː] *n* disgelo ♦ *vi* (*ice*) sciogliersi; (*food*) scongelarsi ♦ *vt* (*food: also:* **~ out**) (fare) scongelare

KEYWORD

the [ðiː, ðə] *def art* **1** (*gen*) il(lo, l') *m*; la(l') *f*; i(gli) *mpl*; le *fpl*; **~ boy/girl/ink** il ragazzo/la ragazza/l'inchiostro; **~ books/pencils** i libri/le matite; **~ history of ~ world** la storia del mondo; **give it to ~ postman** dallo al postino; **I haven't ~ time/money** non ho tempo/soldi; **~ rich and ~ poor** i ricchi e i poveri
2 (*in titles*): **Elizabeth ~ First** Elisabetta prima; **Peter ~ Great** Pietro il grande
3 (*in comparisons*): **~ more he works, ~ more he earns** più lavora più guadagna

theatre ['θɪətə*] (*US* **theater**) *n* teatro; (*also: lecture ~*) aula magna; (*also: operating ~*) sala operatoria; **~-goer** *n* frequentatore/trice di teatri
theatrical [θɪ'ætrɪkl] *adj* teatrale
theft [θeft] *n* furto
their [ðɛə*] *adj* il(la) loro, *pl* i(le) loro; **~s** *pron* il(la) loro, *pl* i(le) loro; *see also* **my**; **mine**
them [ðɛm, ðəm] *pron* (*direct*) li(le); (*indirect*) gli, loro (*after vb*); (*stressed, after prep: people*) loro; (*: people, things*) essi(e); *see also* **me**
theme [θiːm] *n* tema *m*; **~ park** *n* parco di divertimenti (*intorno a un tema centrale*); **~ song** *n* tema musicale
themselves [ðəm'sɛlvz] *pl pron* (*reflexive*) si; (*emphatic*) loro stessi(e); (*after prep*) se stessi(e)
then [ðɛn] *adv* (*at that time*) allora; (*next*) poi, dopo; (*and also*) e poi ♦ *conj* (*therefore*)

perciò, dunque, quindi ♦ *adj*: **the ~ president** il presidente di allora; **by ~** allora; **from ~ on** da allora in poi
theology [θɪ'ɔlədʒiː] *n* teologia
theorem ['θɪərəm] *n* teorema *m*
theoretical [θɪə'rɛtɪkl] *adj* teorico(a)
theory ['θɪərɪ] *n* teoria
therapy ['θɛrəpɪ] *n* terapia

KEYWORD

there [ðɛə*] *adv* **1**: **~ is, ~ are** c'è, ci sono; **~ are 3 of them** (*people*) sono in 3; (*things*) ce ne sono 3; **~ is no-one here** non c'è nessuno qui; **~ has been an accident** c'è stato un incidente
2 (*referring to place*) là, lì; **up/in/down ~** lassù/là dentro/laggiù; **he went ~ on Friday** ci è andato venerdì; **I want that book ~** voglio quel libro là or lì; **~ he is!** eccolo!
3: **~, ~** (*esp to child*) su, su

thereabouts [ðɛərə'bauts] *adv* (*place*) nei pressi, da quelle parti; (*amount*) giù di lì, all'incirca
thereafter [ðɛər'ɑːftə*] *adv* da allora in poi
thereby [ðɛə'baɪ] *adv* con ciò
therefore ['ðɛəfɔː*] *adv* perciò, quindi
there's [ðɛəz] = **there is**; **there has**
thermal ['θəːml] *adj* termico(a)
thermometer [θə'mɔmɪtə*] *n* termometro
Thermos ® ['θəːməs] *n* (*also: ~ flask*) thermos ® *m inv*
thesaurus [θɪ'sɔːrəs] *n* dizionario dei sinonimi
these [ðiːz] *pl pron, adj* questi(e)
theses ['θiːsiːz] *npl of* **thesis**
thesis ['θiːsɪs] (*pl* **theses**) *n* tesi *f inv*
they [ðeɪ] *pl pron* essi(esse); (*people only*) loro; **~ say that ...** (*it is said that*) si dice che ...; **~'d** = **they had**; **they would**; **~'ll** = **they shall**; **they will**; **~'re** = **they are**; **~'ve** = **they have**
thick [θɪk] *adj* spesso(a); (*crowd*) compatto(a); (*stupid*) ottuso(a), lento(a) ♦ *n*: **in the ~ of** nel folto di; **it's 20 cm ~** ha uno spessore di 20 cm; **~en** *vi* ispessirsi ♦ *vt* (*sauce etc*) ispessire, rendere più denso(a); **~ly** *adv* (*spread*) a strati spessi; (*cut*) a fette grosse; (*populated*) densamente; **~ness** *n* spessore *m*; **~set** *adj* tarchiato(a), tozzo(a)
thief [θiːf] (*pl* **thieves**) *n* ladro/a
thieves [θiːvz] *npl of* **thief**
thigh [θaɪ] *n* coscia
thimble ['θɪmbl] *n* ditale *m*
thin [θɪn] *adj* sottile; (*person*) magro(a); (*soup*) poco denso(a) ♦ *vt*: **to ~ (down)** (*sauce, paint*) diluire
thing [θɪŋ] *n* cosa; (*object*) oggetto; (*mania*): **to have a ~ about** essere fissato(a) con; **~s** *npl*

(*belongings*) cose *fpl*; **poor ~** poverino(a); **the best ~ would be to** la cosa migliore sarebbe di; **how are ~s?** come va?

think [θɪŋk] (*pt, pp* **thought**) *vi* pensare, riflettere ♦ *vt* pensare, credere; (*imagine*) immaginare; **to ~ of** pensare a; **what did you ~ of them?** cosa ne ha pensato?; **to ~ about sth/sb** pensare a qc/qn; **I'll ~ about it** ci penserò; **to ~ of doing** pensare di fare; **I ~ so/not** penso di sì/no; **to ~ well of** avere una buona opinione di; **~ out** *vt* (*plan*) elaborare; (*solution*) trovare; **~ over** *vt* riflettere su; **~ through** *vt* riflettere a fondo su; **~ up** *vt* ideare; **~ tank** *n* commissione *f* di esperti

third [θəːd] *num* terzo(a) ♦ *n* terzo/a; (*fraction*) terzo, terza parte *f*; (AUT) terza; (BRIT: SCOL: *degree*) laurea col minimo dei voti; **~ly** *adv* in terzo luogo; **~ party insurance** (BRIT) *n* assicurazione *f* contro terzi; **~-rate** *adj* di qualità scadente; **the T~ World** *n* il Terzo Mondo

thirst [θəːst] *n* sete *f*; **~y** *adj* (*person*) assetato(a), che ha sete

thirteen [θəːˈtiːn] *num* tredici

thirty [ˈθəːtɪ] *num* trenta

KEYWORD

---

this [ðɪs] (*pl* **these**) *adj* (*demonstrative*) questo(a); **~ man/woman/book** quest'uomo/ questa donna/questo libro; (*not "that"*) quest'uomo/questa donna/questo libro qui; **~ one** questo(a) qui

♦ *pron* (*demonstrative*) questo(a); (*not "that one"*) questo(a) qui; **who/what is ~?** chi è/ che cos'è questo?; **I prefer ~ to that** preferisco questo a quello; **~ is where I live** io abito qui; **~ is what he said** questo è ciò che ha detto; **~ is Mr Brown** (*in introductions, photo*) questo è il signor Brown; (*on telephone*) sono il signor Brown

♦ *adv* (*demonstrative*): **~ high/long** *etc* alto/ lungo *etc* così; **I didn't know things were ~ bad** non sapevo andasse così male

---

thistle [ˈθɪsl] *n* cardo

thong [θɔŋ] *n* cinghia

thorn [θɔːn] *n* spina; **~y** *adj* spinoso(a)

thorough [ˈθʌrə] *adj* (*search*) minuzioso(a); (*knowledge, research*) approfondito(a), profondo(a); (*person*) coscienzioso(a); (*cleaning*) a fondo; **~bred** *n* (*horse*) purosangue *m/f inv*; **~fare** *n* strada transitabile; **"no ~fare"** "divieto di transito"; **~ly** *adv* (*search*) minuziosamente; (*wash, study*) a fondo; (*very*) assolutamente

those [ðəuz] *pl pron* quelli(e) ♦ *pl adj* quei(quegli) *mpl*; quelle *fpl*

though [ðəu] *conj* benché, sebbene ♦ *adv*

comunque

thought [θɔːt] *pt, pp of* **think** ♦ *n* pensiero; (*opinion*) opinione *f*; **~ful** *adj* pensieroso(a), pensoso(a); (*considerate*) premuroso(a); **~less** *adj* sconsiderato(a); (*behaviour*) scortese

thousand [ˈθauzənd] *num* mille; **one ~** mille; **~s of** migliaia di; **~th** *num* millesimo(a)

thrash [θræʃ] *vt* picchiare; bastonare; (*defeat*) battere; **~ about** *vi* dibattersi; **~ out** *vt* dibattere

thread [θrɛd] *n* filo; (*of screw*) filetto ♦ *vt* (*needle*) infilare; **~bare** *adj* consumato(a), logoro(a)

threat [θrɛt] *n* minaccia; **~en** *vi* (*storm*) minacciare ♦ *vt*: **to ~en sb with/to do** minacciare qn con/di fare

three [θriː] *num* tre; **~-dimensional** *adj* tridimensionale; (*film*) stereoscopico(a); **~-piece suit** *n* completo (con gilè); **~-piece suite** *n* salotto comprendente un divano e due poltrone; **~-ply** *adj* (*wool*) a tre fili

threshold [ˈθrɛʃhəuld] *n* soglia

threw [θruː] *pt of* **throw**

thrifty [ˈθrɪftɪ] *adj* economico(a)

thrill [θrɪl] *n* brivido ♦ *vt* (*audience*) elettrizzare; **to be ~ed** (*with gift etc*) essere elettrizzato(a); **~er** *n* thriller *m inv*; **~ing** *adj* (*book*) pieno(a) di suspense; (*news, discovery*) elettrizzante

thrive [θraɪv] (*pt, pp* **thrived**) *vi* crescere *or* svilupparsi bene; (*business*) prosperare; **he ~s on it** gli fa bene, ne gode; **thriving** *adj* fiorente

throat [θrəut] *n* gola; **to have a sore ~** avere (un *or* il) mal di gola

throb [θrɔb] *vi* palpitare; pulsare; vibrare

throes [θrəuz] *npl*: **in the ~ of** alle prese con; in preda a

thrombosis [θrɔmˈbəusɪs] *n* trombosi *f*

throne [θrəun] *n* trono

throng [θrɔŋ] *n* moltitudine *f* ♦ *vt* affollare

throttle [ˈθrɔtl] *n* (AUT) valvola a farfalla ♦ *vt* strangolare

through [θruː] *prep* attraverso; (*time*) per, durante; (*by means of*) per mezzo di; (*owing to*) a causa di ♦ *adj* (*ticket, train, passage*) diretto(a) ♦ *adv* attraverso; **to put sb ~ to sb** (TEL) passare qn a qn; **to be ~** (TEL) ottenere la comunicazione; (*have finished*) aver finito(a); **"no ~ road"** (BRIT) "strada senza sbocco"; **~out** *prep* (*place*) dappertutto in; (*time*) per *or* durante tutto(a) ♦ *adv* dappertutto; sempre

throw [θrəu] (*pt* **threw**, *pp* **thrown**) *n* (SPORT) lancio, tiro ♦ *vt* tirare, gettare; (SPORT) lanciare, tirare; (*rider*) disarcionare; (*fig*) confondere; **to ~ a party** dare una festa; **~ away** *vt* gettare *or* buttare via; **~ off** *vt* sbarazzarsi di; **~ out** *vt* buttare fuori; (*reject*) respingere; **~ up** *vi* vomitare; **~away** *adj* da buttare; **~-in** *n* (*SPORT*) rimessa in gioco; **thrown** *pp of* throw

thru [θru:] (*US*) *prep, adj, adv* = **through**

thrush [θrʌʃ] *n* tordo

thrust [θrʌst] (*pt, pp* thrust) *vt* spingere con forza; (*push in*) conficcare

thud [θʌd] *n* tonfo

thug [θʌg] *n* delinquente *m*

thumb [θʌm] *n* (*ANAT*) pollice *m*; **to ~ a lift** fare l'autostop; **~ through** *vt fus* (*book*) sfogliare; **~tack** (*US*) *n* puntina da disegno

thump [θʌmp] *n* colpo forte; (*sound*) tonfo ♦ *vt* (*person*) picchiare; (*object*) battere su ♦ *vi* picchiare, battere

thunder ['θʌndə*] *n* tuono ♦ *vi* tuonare; (*train etc*): **to ~ past** passare con un rombo; **~bolt** *n* fulmine *m*; **~clap** *n* rombo di tuono; **~storm** *n* temporale *m*; **~y** *adj* temporalesco(a)

Thursday ['θə:zdɪ] *n* giovedì *m inv*

thus [ðʌs] *adv* così

thwart [θwɔ:t] *vt* contrastare

thyme [taɪm] *n* timo

thyroid ['θaɪrɔɪd] *n* (*also*: ~ gland) tiroide *f*

tiara [tɪ'ɑ:rə] *n* (*woman's*) diadema *m*

Tiber ['taɪbə*] *n*: **the ~** il Tevere

tick [tɪk] *n* (*sound: of clock*) tic tac *m inv*; (*mark*) segno; spunta; (*ZOOL*) zecca; (*BRIT: inf*): **in a ~** in un attimo ♦ *vi* fare tic tac ♦ *vt* spuntare; **~ off** *vt* spuntare; (*person*) sgridare; **~ over** *vi* (*engine*) andare al minimo; (*fig*) andare avanti come al solito

ticket ['tɪkɪt] *n* biglietto; (*in shop: on goods*) etichetta; (*parking ~*) multa; (*for library*) scheda; **~ collector** *n* bigliettaio; **~ office** *n* biglietteria

tickle ['tɪkl] *vt* fare il solletico a; (*fig*) solleticare ♦ *vi*: **it ~s mi** (*or gli etc*) fa il solletico; **ticklish** [-lɪʃ] *adj* che soffre di solletico; (*problem*) delicato(a)

tidal ['taɪdl] *adj* di marea; (*estuary*) soggetto(a) alla marea; **~ wave** *n* onda anomala

tidbit ['tɪdbɪt] (*US*) *n* (*food*) leccornia; (*news*) notizia ghiotta

tiddlywinks ['tɪdlɪwɪŋks] *n* gioco della pulce

tide [taɪd] *n* marea; (*fig: of events*) corso; **high/low ~** alta/bassa marea; **~ over** *vt* dare una mano a

tidy ['taɪdɪ] *adj* (*room*) ordinato(a), lindo(a); (*dress, work*) curato(a), in ordine; (*person*) ordinato(a) ♦ *vt* (*also*: ~ up) riordinare, mettere in ordine

tie [taɪ] *n* (*string etc*) legaccio; (*BRIT: also*: neck~) cravatta; (*fig: link*) legame *m*; (*SPORT: draw*) pareggio ♦ *vt* (*parcel*) legare; (*ribbon*) annodare ♦ *vi* (*SPORT*) pareggiare; **to ~ sth in**

a bow annodare qc; **to ~ a knot in sth** fare un nodo a qc; **~ down** *vt* legare; (*to price etc*) costringere ad accettare; **~ up** *vt* (*parcel, dog*) legare; (*boat*) ormeggiare; (*arrangements*) concludere; **to be ~d up** (*busy*) essere occupato(a) *or* preso(a)

tier [tɪə*] *n* fila; (*of cake*) piano, strato

tiger ['taɪgə*] *n* tigre *f*

tight [taɪt] *adj* (*rope*) teso(a), tirato(a); (*money*) poco(a); (*clothes, budget, bend etc*) stretto(a); (*control*) severo(a), fermo(a); (*inf: drunk*) sbronzo(a) ♦ *adv* (*squeeze*) fortemente; (*shut*) ermeticamente; **~s** (*BRIT*) *npl* collant *m inv*; **~en** *vt* (*rope*) tendere; (*screw*) stringere; (*control*) rinforzare ♦ *vi* tendersi; stringersi; **~-fisted** *adj* avaro(a); **~ly** *adv* (*grasp*) bene, saldamente; **~rope** *n* corda (da acrobata)

tile [taɪl] *n* (*on roof*) tegola; (*on wall or floor*) piastrella, mattonella; **~d** *adj* di tegole; a piastrelle, a mattonelle

till [tɪl] *n* registratore *m* di cassa ♦ *vt* (*land*) coltivare ♦ *prep, conj* = **until**

tiller ['tɪlə*] *n* (*NAUT*) barra del timone

tilt [tɪlt] *vt* inclinare, far pendere ♦ *vi* inclinarsi, pendere

timber ['tɪmbə*] *n* (*material*) legname *m*

time [taɪm] *n* tempo; (*epoch: often pl*) epoca, tempo; (*by clock*) ora; (*moment*) momento; (*occasion*) volta; (*MUS*) tempo ♦ *vt* (*race*) cronometrare; (*programme*) calcolare la durata di; (*fix moment for*) programmare; (*remark etc*) dire (*or* fare) al momento giusto; **a long ~** molto tempo; **for the ~ being** per il momento; **4 at a ~** 4 per *or* alla volta; **from ~ to ~** ogni tanto; **at ~s** a volte; **in ~** (*soon enough*) in tempo; (*after some ~*) col tempo; (*MUS*) a tempo; **in a week's ~** fra una settimana; **in no ~** in un attimo; **any ~** in qualsiasi momento; **on ~** puntualmente; **5 ~s 5** 5 volte 5, 5 per 5; **what ~ is it?** che ora è?, che ore sono?; **to have a good ~** divertirsi; **~ bomb** *n* bomba a orologeria; **~less** *adj* eterno(a); **~ly** *adj* opportuno(a); **~ off** *n* tempo libero; **~r** *n* (~ switch) temporizzatore *m*; (*in kitchen*) contaminuti *m inv*; **~ scale** *n* periodo; **~-share** *adj*: **~-share apartment/villa** appartamento/villa in multiproprietà; **~ switch** (*BRIT*) *n* temporizzatore *m*; **~table** *n* orario; **~ zone** *n* fuso orario

timid ['tɪmɪd] *adj* timido(a); (*easily scared*) pauroso(a)

timing ['taɪmɪŋ] *n* (*SPORT*) cronometraggio; (*fig*) scelta del momento opportuno

timpani ['tɪmpənɪ] *npl* timpani *mpl*

tin [tɪn] *n* stagno; (*also*: ~ plate) latta; (*container*) scatola; (*BRIT: can*) barattolo (di latta), lattina; **~foil** *n* stagnola

tinge [tɪndʒ] *n* sfumatura ♦ *vt*: **~d with**

tinto(a) di

tingle ['tɪŋgl] vi pizzicare

tinker ['tɪŋkə*]: ~ **with** vt fus armeggiare intorno a; cercare di riparare

tinned [tɪnd] (BRIT) adj (food) in scatola

tin opener ['-əupnə*] (BRIT) n apriscatole m inv

tinsel ['tɪnsl] n decorazioni fpl natalizie (argentate)

tint [tɪnt] n tinta; **~ed** adj (hair) tinto(a); (spectacles, glass) colorato(a)

tiny ['taɪnɪ] adj minuscolo(a)

tip [tɪp] n (end) punta; (gratuity) mancia; (BRIT: for rubbish) immondezzaio; (advice) suggerimento ♦ vt (waiter) dare la mancia a; (tilt) inclinare; (overturn: also: ~ over) capovolgere; (empty: also: ~ out) scaricare; **~-off** n (hint) soffiata; **~ped** (BRIT) adj (cigarette) col filtro

Tipp-Ex ® ['tɪpɛks] n correttore m

tipsy ['tɪpsɪ] adj brillo(a)

tiptoe ['tɪptəu] n: **on ~** in punta di piedi

tiptop ['tɪp'tɔp] adj: **in ~ condition** in ottime condizioni

tire ['taɪə*] n (US) = **tyre** ♦ vt stancare ♦ vi stancarsi; **~d** adj stanco(a); **to be ~d of** essere stanco or stufo di; **~less** adj instancabile; **~some** adj noioso(a); **tiring** adj faticoso(a)

tissue ['tɪʃu:] n tessuto; (paper handkerchief) fazzoletto di carta; **~ paper** n carta velina

tit [tɪt] n (bird) cinciallegra; **to give ~ for tat** rendere pan per focaccia

titbit ['tɪtbɪt] (BRIT) n (food) leccornia; (news) notizia ghiotta

title ['taɪtl] n titolo; **~ deed** n (LAW) titolo di proprietà; **~ role** n ruolo or parte f principale

TM abbr = **trademark**

to [tu:, tə] prep **1** (direction) a; **to go ~ France/ London/school** andare in Francia/a Londra/a scuola; **to go ~ Paul's/the doctor's** andare da Paul/dal dottore; **the road ~ Edinburgh** la strada per Edimburgo; **~ the left/right** a sinistra/destra

2 (as far as) (fino) a; **from here ~ London** da qui a Londra; **to count ~ 10** contare fino a 10; **from 40 ~ 50 people** da 40 a 50 persone

3 (with expressions of time): **a quarter ~ 5** le 5 meno un quarto; **it's twenty ~ 3** sono le 3 meno venti

4 (for, of): **the key ~ the front door** la chiave della porta d'ingresso; **a letter ~ his wife** una lettera per la moglie

5 (expressing indirect object) a; **to give sth ~ sb** dare qc a qn; **to talk ~ sb** parlare a qn; **to be a danger ~ sb/sth** rappresentare un pericolo per qn/qc

6 (in relation to) a; **3 goals ~ 2** 3 goal a 2; **30**

miles ~ the gallon ≈ 11 chilometri con un litro

7 (purpose, result): **to come ~ sb's aid** venire in aiuto a qn; **to sentence sb ~ death** condannare a morte qn; **~ my surprise** con mia sorpresa

♦ with vb **1** (simple infinitive): **~ go/eat** etc andare/mangiare etc

2 (following another vb): **to want/try/start ~ do** volere/cercare di/cominciare a fare

3 (with vb omitted): **I don't want ~** non voglio (farlo); **you ought ~** devi (farlo)

4 (purpose, result) per; **I did it ~ help you** l'ho fatto per aiutarti

5 (equivalent to relative clause): **I have things ~ do** ho da fare; **the main thing is ~ try** la cosa più importante è provare

6 (after adjective etc): **ready ~ go** pronto a partire; **too old/young ~ ...** troppo vecchio/giovane per ...

♦ adv: **to push the door ~** accostare la porta

toad [təud] n rospo; **~stool** n fungo (velenoso)

toast [təust] n (CULIN) pane m tostato; (drink, speech) brindisi m inv ♦ vt (CULIN) tostare; (drink to) brindare a; **a piece** or **slice of ~** una fetta di pane tostato; **~er** n tostapane m inv

tobacco [tə'bækəu] n tabacco; **~nist** n tabaccaio/a; **~nist's (shop)** n tabaccheria

toboggan [tə'bɔgən] n toboga m inv

today [tə'deɪ] adv oggi ♦ n (also fig) oggi m

toddler ['tɔdlə*] n bambino/a che impara a camminare

toe [təu] n dito del piede; (of shoe) punta; **to ~ the line** (fig) stare in riga, conformarsi; **~nail** n unghia del piede

toffee ['tɔfɪ] n caramella; **~ apple** n mela caramellata

toga ['təugə] n toga

together [tə'geðə*] adv insieme; (at same time) allo stesso tempo; **~ with** insieme a

toil [tɔɪl] n travaglio, fatica ♦ vi affannarsi; sgobbare

toilet ['tɔɪlət] n (BRIT: lavatory) gabinetto ♦ cpd (bag, soap etc) da toletta; **~ paper** n carta igienica; **~ries** npl articoli mpl da toletta; **~ roll** n rotolo di carta igienica; **~ water** n acqua di colonia

token ['təukən] n (sign) segno; (substitute coin) gettone m; **book/record/gift ~** (BRIT) buono-libro/disco/regalo

told [təuld] pt, pp of **tell**

tolerable ['tɔlərəbl] adj (bearable) tollerabile; (fairly good) passabile

tolerant ['tɔlərnt] adj: **~ (of)** tollerante (nei confronti di)

tolerate ['tɔləreɪt] vt sopportare; (MED, TECH) tollerare

toll [təul] n (tax, charge) pedaggio ♦ vi (bell) suonare; **the accident ~ on the roads** il numero delle vittime della strada

tomato [tə'mɑːtəu] (pl **~es**) n pomodoro

tomb [tuːm] n tomba

tomboy ['tɔmbɔɪ] n maschiaccio

tombstone ['tuːmstəun] n pietra tombale

tomcat ['tɔmkæt] n gatto

tomorrow [tə'mɔrəu] adv domani ♦ n (also fig) domani m inv; **the day after ~** dopodomani; **~ morning** domani mattina

ton [tʌn] n tonnellata (BRIT = 1016 kg; US = 907 kg; metric = 1000 kg); **~s of** (inf) un mucchio or sacco di

tone [təun] n tono ♦ vi (also: ~ in) intonarsi; **~ down** vt (colour, criticism, sound) attenuare; **~ up** vt (muscles) tonificare; **~-deaf** adj che non ha orecchio (musicale)

tongs [tɔŋz] npl tenaglie fpl; (for coal) molle fpl; (for hair) arricciacapelli m inv

tongue [tʌŋ] n lingua; **~ in cheek** (say, speak) ironicamente; **~-tied** adj (fig) muto(a); **~-twister** n scioglilingua m inv

tonic ['tɔnɪk] n (MED) tonico; (also: ~ water) acqua tonica

tonight [tə'naɪt] adv stanotte; (this evening) stasera ♦ n questa notte; questa sera

tonnage ['tʌnɪdʒ] n (NAUT) tonnellaggio, stazza

tonsil ['tɔnsl] n tonsilla; **~litis** [-'laɪtɪs] n tonsillite f

too [tuː] adv (excessively) troppo; (also) anche; **~ much** adv troppo ♦ adj troppo(a); **~ many** troppi(e)

took [tuk] pt of **take**

tool [tuːl] n utensile m, attrezzo; **~ box** n cassetta f portautensili

toot [tuːt] n (of horn) colpo di clacson; (of whistle) fischio ♦ vi suonare; (with car horn) suonare il clacson

tooth [tuːθ] (pl **teeth**) n (ANAT, TECH) dente m; **~ache** n mal m di denti; **~brush** n spazzolino da denti; **~paste** n dentifricio; **~pick** n stuzzicadenti m inv

top [tɔp] n (of mountain, page, ladder) cima; (of box, cupboard, table) sopra m inv, parte f superiore; (lid: of box, jar) coperchio; (: of bottle) tappo; (blouse etc) sopra m inv; (toy) trottola ♦ adj più alto(a); (in rank) primo(a); (best) migliore ♦ vt (exceed) superare; (be first in) essere in testa a; **on ~ of** sopra, in cima a; (in addition to) oltre a; **from ~ to bottom** da cima a fondo; **~ up** (US **~ off**) vt riempire; (salary) integrare; **~ floor** n ultimo piano; **~ hat** n cilindro; **~-heavy** adj (object) con la parte superiore troppo pesante

topic ['tɔpɪk] n argomento; **~al** adj d'attualità

top: **~less** adj (bather etc) col seno scoperto; **~-level** adj (talks) ad alto livello; **~most** adj

il(la) più alto(a)

topple ['tɔpl] vt rovesciare, far cadere ♦ vi cadere; traballare

top-secret ['tɔp'siːkrɪt] adj segretissimo(a)

topsy-turvy ['tɔpsɪ'təːvɪ] adj, adv sottosopra inv

torch [tɔːtʃ] n torcia; (BRIT: electric) lampadina tascabile

tore [tɔː*] pt of **tear¹**

torment [n 'tɔːment, vb tɔː'ment] n tormento ♦ vt tormentare

torn [tɔːn] pp of **tear¹**

torpedo [tɔː'piːdəu] (pl **~es**) n siluro

torrent ['tɔrnt] n torrente m

torrid ['tɔrɪd] adj torrido(a); (love affair) infuocato(a)

tortoise ['tɔːtəs] n tartaruga; **~shell** ['tɔːtəʃel] adj di tartaruga

torture ['tɔːtʃə*] n tortura ♦ vt torturare

Tory ['tɔːrɪ] (BRIT: POL) adj dei tories, conservatore(trice) ♦ n tory m/f inv, conservatore/trice

toss [tɔs] vt gettare, lanciare; (one's head) scuotere; **to ~ a coin** fare a testa o croce; **to ~ up for sth** fare a testa o croce per qc; **to ~ and turn** (in bed) girarsi e rigirarsi

tot [tɔt] n (BRIT: drink) bicchierino; (child) bimbo/a

total ['təutl] adj totale ♦ n totale m ♦ vt (add up) sommare; (amount to) ammontare a

totally ['təutəlɪ] adv completamente

touch [tʌtʃ] n tocco; (sense) tatto; (contact) contatto ♦ vt toccare; **a ~ of** (fig) un tocco di; un pizzico di; **to get in ~ with** mettersi in contatto con; **to lose ~** (friends) perdersi di vista; **~ on** vt fus (topic) sfiorare, accennare a; **~ up** vt (paint) ritoccare; **~-and-go** adj incerto(a); **~down** n atterraggio; (on sea) ammaraggio; (US: FOOTBALL) meta; **~ed** adj commosso(a); **~ing** adj commovente; **~line** n (SPORT) linea laterale; **~y** adj (person) suscettibile

tough [tʌf] adj duro(a); (resistant) resistente; **~en** vt rinforzare

toupee ['tuːpeɪ] n parrucchino

tour ['tuə*] n viaggio; (also: package ~) viaggio organizzato or tutto compreso; (of town, museum) visita; (by artist) tournée f inv ♦ vt visitare; **~ guide** n guida turistica; **~ing** n turismo

tourism ['tuərɪzəm] n turismo

tourist ['tuərɪst] n turista m/f ♦ adv (travel) in classe turistica ♦ cpd turistico(a); **~ office** n pro loco f inv

tournament ['tuənəmənt] n torneo

tousled ['tauzld] adj (hair) arruffato(a)

tout [taut] vi: **to ~ for** procacciare, raccogliere; cercare clienti per ♦ n (also: ticket ~) bagarino

tow [təu] vt rimorchiare; "**on ~**" (BRIT), "**in ~**" (US) "veicolo rimorchiato"

toward(s) [tə'wɔːd(z)] prep verso; (of attitude) nei confronti di; (of purpose) per

towel ['tauəl] n asciugamano; (also: tea ~) strofinaccio; **~ling** n (fabric) spugna; **~ rail** (US ~ **rack**) n portasciugamano

tower ['tauə*] n torre f; **~ block** (BRIT) n palazzone m; **~ing** adj altissimo(a), imponente

town [taun] n città f inv; **to go to ~** andare in città; (fig) mettercela tutta; **~ centre** n centro (città); **~ council** n consiglio comunale; **~ hall** n ≈ municipio; **~ plan** n pianta della città; **~ planning** n urbanistica

towrope ['təurəup] n (cavo da) rimorchio

tow truck (US) n carro m attrezzi inv

toxic ['tɔksɪk] adj tossico(a)

toy [tɔɪ] n giocattolo; **~ with** vt fus giocare con; (idea) accarezzare, trastullarsi con; **~ shop** n negozio di giocattoli

trace [treɪs] n traccia ♦ vt (draw) tracciare; (follow) seguire; (locate) rintracciare; **tracing paper** n carta da ricalco

track [træk] n (of person, animal) traccia; (on tape, SPORT, path: gen) pista; (: of bullet etc) traiettoria; (: of suspect, animal) pista, tracce fpl; (RAIL) binario, rotaie fpl ♦ vt seguire le tracce di; **to keep ~** of seguire; **~ down** vt (prey) scovare; snidare; (sth lost) rintracciare; **~suit** n tuta sportiva

tract [trækt] n (GEO) tratto, estensione f

tractor ['træktə*] n trattore m

trade [treɪd] n commercio; (skill, job) mestiere m ♦ vi commerciare ♦ vt: **to ~ sth (for sth)** barattare qc (con qc); **to ~ with/in** commerciare con/in; **~ in** vt (old car etc) dare come pagamento parziale; **~ fair** n fiera commerciale; **~mark** n marchio di fabbrica; **~ name** n marca, nome m depositato; **~r** n commerciante m/f; **~sman** (irreg) n fornitore m; (shopkeeper) negoziante m; **~ union** n sindacato; **~ unionist** sindacalista m/f

tradition [trə'dɪʃən] n tradizione f; **~al** adj tradizionale

traffic ['træfɪk] n traffico ♦ vi: **to ~ in** (pej: liquor, drugs) trafficare in; **~ circle** (US) n isola rotatoria; **~ jam** n ingorgo (del traffico); **~ lights** npl semaforo; **~ warden** n addetto/a al controllo del traffico e del parcheggio

tragedy ['trædʒədɪ] n tragedia

tragic ['trædʒɪk] adj tragico(a)

trail [treɪl] n (tracks) tracce fpl, pista; (path) sentiero; (of smoke etc) scia ♦ vt trascinare, strascicare; (follow) seguire ♦ vi essere al traino; (dress etc) strusciare; (plant) arrampicarsi; strisciare; (in game) essere in svantaggio; **~ behind** vi essere al traino; **~er**

n (AUT) rimorchio; (US) roulotte f inv; (CINEMA) prossimamente m inv; **~er truck** (US) n (articulated lorry) autoarticolato

train [treɪn] n treno; (of dress) coda, strascico ♦ vt (apprentice, doctor etc) formare; (sportsman) allenare; (dog) addestrare; (memory) esercitare; (point: gun etc): **to ~ sth on** puntare qc contro ♦ vi formarsi; allenarsi; **one's ~ of thought** il filo dei propri pensieri; **~ed** adj qualificato(a); allenato(a); addestrato(a); **~ee** [treɪ'niː] n (in trade) apprendista m/f; **~er** n (SPORT) allenatore/ trice; (: shoe) scarpa da ginnastica; (of dogs etc) addestratore/trice; **~ing** n formazione f; allenamento; addestramento; **in ~ing** (SPORT) in allenamento; **~ing college** n istituto professionale; (for teachers) ≈ istituto magistrale; **~ing shoes** npl scarpe fpl da ginnastica

trait [treɪt] n tratto

traitor ['treɪtə*] n traditore m

tram [træm] (BRIT) n (also: ~car) tram m inv

tramp [træmp] n (person) vagabondo/a; (inf: pej: woman) sgualdrina

trample ['træmpl] vt: **to ~ (underfoot)** calpestare

trampoline ['træmpəliːn] n trampolino

tranquil ['træŋkwɪl] adj tranquillo(a); **~lizer** n (MED) tranquillante m

transact [træn'zækt] vt (business) trattare; **~ion** [-'zækʃən] n transazione f

transatlantic ['trænzət'læntɪk] adj transatlantico(a)

transfer [n 'trænsfə*, vb træns'fə*] n (gen, also SPORT) trasferimento; (POL: of power) passaggio; (picture, design) decalcomania; (: stick-on) autoadesivo ♦ vt trasferire; passare; **to ~ the charges** (BRIT: TEL) fare una chiamata a carico del destinatario; **~ desk** n (AVIAT) banco m transiti inv

transform [træns'fɔːm] vt trasformare

transfusion [træns'fjuːʒən] n trasfusione f

transient ['trænzɪənt] adj transitorio(a), fugace

transistor [træn'zɪstə*] n (ELEC) transistor m inv; (also: ~ radio) radio f inv a transistor

transit ['trænzɪt] n: **in ~** in transito

transitive ['trænzɪtɪv] adj (LING) transitivo(a)

translate [trænz'leɪt] vt tradurre; **translation** [-'leɪʃən] n traduzione f; **translator** n traduttore/trice

transmission [trænz'mɪʃən] n trasmissione f

transmit [trænz'mɪt] vt trasmettere; **~ter** n trasmettitore m

transparency [træns'pɛrənsɪ] n trasparenza; (BRIT: PHOT) diapositiva

transparent [træns'pærnt] adj trasparente

transpire [træn'spaɪə*] vi (happen) succedere; (turn out): **it ~d that** si venne a sapere che

transplant [*vb* træns'plɑːnt, *n* 'trænsplɑːnt] *vt* trapiantare ♦ *n* (MED) trapianto

transport [*n* 'trænspɔːt, *vb* træns'pɔːt] *n* trasporto ♦ *vt* trasportare; **~ation** [-'teɪʃən] *n* (mezzo di) trasporto; **~ café** (BRIT) *n* trattoria per camionisti

trap [træp] *n* (snare, trick) trappola; (carriage) calesse *m* ♦ *vt* prendere in trappola, intrappolare; **~ door** *n* botola

trapeze [trə'piːz] *n* trapezio

trappings ['træpɪŋz] *npl* ornamenti *mpl*; indoratura, sfarzo

trash [træʃ] (*pej*) *n* (goods) ciarpame *m*; (nonsense) sciocchezze *fpl*; **~ can** (US) *n* secchio della spazzatura

trauma ['trɔːmə] *n* trauma *m*; **~tic** [-'mætɪk] *adj* traumatico(a)

travel ['trævl] *n* viaggio; viaggi *mpl* ♦ *vi* viaggiare ♦ *vt* (distance) percorrere; **~ agency** *n* agenzia (di) viaggi; **~ agent** *n* agente *m* di viaggio; **~ler** (US **~er**) *n* viaggiatore/trice; **~ler's cheque** (US **~er's check**) *n* assegno turistico; **~ling** (US **~ing**) *n* viaggi *mpl*; **~ sickness** *n* mal *m* d'auto (or di mare or d'aria)

travesty ['trævəstɪ] *n* parodia

trawler ['trɔːlə*] *n* peschereccio (a strascico)

tray [treɪ] *n* (for carrying) vassoio; (on desk) vaschetta

treacherous ['tretʃərəs] *adj* infido(a)

treachery ['tretʃərɪ] *n* tradimento

treacle ['triːkl] *n* melassa

tread [tred] (*pt* **trod**, *pp* **trodden**) *n* passo; (sound) rumore *m* di passi; (of stairs) pedata; (of tyre) battistrada *m inv* ♦ *vi* camminare; **~ on** *vt fus* calpestare

treason ['triːzn] *n* tradimento

treasure ['treʒə*] *n* tesoro ♦ *vt* (value) tenere in gran conto, apprezzare molto; (store) custodire gelosamente

treasurer ['treʒərə*] *n* tesoriere/a

treasury ['treʒərɪ] *n*: **the T~** (BRIT), **the T~ Department** (US) il ministero del Tesoro

treat [triːt] *n* regalo ♦ *vt* trattare; (MED) curare; **to ~ sb to sth** offrire qc a qn

treatment ['triːtmənt] *n* trattamento

treaty ['triːtɪ] *n* patto, trattato

treble ['trebl] *adj* triplo(a), triplice ♦ *vt* triplicare ♦ *vi* triplicarsi; **~ clef** *n* chiave *f* di violino

tree [triː] *n* albero; **~ trunk** *n* tronco d'albero

trek [trek] *n* escursione *f* a piedi; escursione *f* in macchina; (tiring walk) camminata sfiancante ♦ *vi* (as holiday) fare dell'escursionismo

trellis ['trelɪs] *n* graticcio

tremble ['trembl] *vi* tremare

tremendous [trɪ'mendəs] *adj* (enormous)

enorme; (excellent) meraviglioso(a), formidabile

tremor ['tremə*] *n* tremore *m*, tremito; (also: earth ~) scossa sismica

trench [trentʃ] *n* trincea

trend [trend] *n* (tendency) tendenza; (of events) corso; (fashion) moda; **~y** *adj* (idea) di moda; (clothes) all'ultima moda

trespass ['trespəs] *vi*: **to ~ on** entrare abusivamente in; **"no ~ing"** "proprietà privata", "vietato l'accesso"

trestle ['tresl] *n* cavalletto

trial ['traɪəl] *n* (LAW) processo; (test: of machine etc) collaudo; **~s** *npl* (unpleasant experiences) dure prove *fpl*; **on ~** (LAW) sotto processo; **by ~ and error** a tentoni; **~ period** *n* periodo di prova

triangle ['traɪæŋgl] *n* (MATH, MUS) triangolo

tribe [traɪb] *n* tribù *f inv*; **~sman** (irreg) *n* membro di tribù

tribunal [traɪ'bjuːnl] *n* tribunale *m*

tributary ['trɪbjutərɪ] *n* (river) tributario, affluente *m*

tribute ['trɪbjuːt] *n* tributo, omaggio; **to pay ~ to** rendere omaggio a

trick [trɪk] *n* trucco; (joke) tiro; (CARDS) presa ♦ *vt* imbrogliare, ingannare; **to play a ~ on sb** giocare un tiro a qn; **that should do the ~** vedrai che funziona; **~ery** *n* inganno

trickle ['trɪkl] *n* (of water etc) rivolo; gocciolio ♦ *vi* gocciolare

tricky ['trɪkɪ] *adj* difficile, delicato(a)

tricycle ['traɪsɪkl] *n* triciclo

trifle ['traɪfl] *n* sciocchezza; (BRIT: CULIN) ≈ zuppa inglese ♦ *adv*: **a ~ long** un po' lungo; **trifling** *adj* insignificante

trigger ['trɪgə*] *n* (of gun) grilletto; **~ off** *vt* dare l'avvio a

trim [trɪm] *adj* (house, garden) ben tenuto(a); (figure) snello(a) ♦ *n* (haircut etc) spuntata, regolata; (embellishment) finiture *fpl*; (on car) guarnizioni *fpl* ♦ *vt* spuntare; (decorate): **to ~ (with)** decorare (con); (NAUT: a sail) orientare; **~mings** *npl* decorazioni *fpl*; (extras: gen CULIN) guarnizione *f*

trinket ['trɪŋkɪt] *n* gingillo; (piece of jewellery) ciondolo

trip [trɪp] *n* viaggio; (excursion) gita, escursione *f*; (stumble) passo falso ♦ *vi* inciampare; (go lightly) camminare con passo leggero; **on a ~** in viaggio; **~ up** *vi* inciampare ♦ *vt* fare lo sgambetto a

tripe [traɪp] *n* (CULIN) trippa; (pej: rubbish) sciocchezze *fpl*, fesserie *fpl*

triple ['trɪpl] *adj* triplo(a)

triplets ['trɪplɪts] *npl* bambini(e) trigemini(e)

triplicate ['trɪplɪkət] *n*: **in ~** in triplice copia

tripod ['traɪpɔd] *n* treppiede *m*

trite [traɪt] *adj* banale, trito(a)

triumph ['traɪʌmf] n trionfo ♦ vi: **to ~ (over)** trionfare (su)

trivia ['trɪvɪə] npl banalità fpl

trivial ['trɪvɪəl] adj insignificante; (commonplace) banale

trod [trɒd] pt of **tread**; **~den** pp of **tread**

trolley ['trɒlɪ] n carrello; **~ bus** n filobus m inv

trombone [trɒm'bəʊn] n trombone m

troop [truːp] n gruppo; (MIL) squadrone m; **~s** npl (MIL) truppe fpl; **~ in/out** vi entrare/ uscire a frotte; **~ing the colour** n (ceremony) sfilata della bandiera

trophy ['trəʊfɪ] n trofeo

tropic ['trɒpɪk] n tropico; **~al** adj tropicale

trot [trɒt] n trotto ♦ vi trottare; **on the ~** (BRIT: fig) di fila, uno(a) dopo l'altro(a)

trouble ['trʌbl] n difficoltà f inv, problema m; difficoltà fpl, problemi; (worry) preoc- cupazione f; (bother, effort) sforzo; (POL) conflitti mpl, disordine m; (MED): **stomach etc ~** disturbi mpl gastrici etc ♦ vt disturbare; (worry) preoccupare ♦ vi: **to ~ to do** disturbarsi a fare; **~s** npl (POL etc) disordini mpl; **to be in ~** avere dei problemi; **it's no ~!** di niente!; **what's the ~?** cosa c'è che non va?; **~d** adj (person) preoccupato(a), inquieto(a); (epoch, life) agitato(a), difficile; **~maker** n elemento disturbatore, agitatore/ trice; (child) disloco/a; **~shooter** n (in conflict) conciliatore m; **~some** adj fastidioso(a), seccante

trough [trɒf] n (also: drinking ~) abbeveratoio; (also: feeding ~) trogolo, mangiatoia; (channel) canale m

trousers ['traʊzəz] npl pantaloni mpl, calzoni mpl; **short ~** calzoncini mpl

trousseau ['truːsəʊ] n (pl **~x** or **~s**) corredo da sposa

trousseaux ['truːsəʊz] npl of **trousseau**

trout [traʊt] n inv trota

trowel ['traʊəl] n cazzuola

truant ['truːənt] (BRIT) n: **to play ~** marinare la scuola

truce [truːs] n tregua

truck [trʌk] n autocarro, camion m inv; (RAIL) carro merci aperto; (for luggage) carrello m portabagagli inv; **~ driver** n camionista m/f; **~ farm** (US) n orto industriale

true [truː] adj vero(a); (accurate) accurato(a), esatto(a); (genuine) reale; (faithful) fedele; **to come ~** avverarsi

truffle ['trʌfl] n tartufo

truly ['truːlɪ] adv veramente; (truthfully) sinceramente; (faithfully): **yours ~** (in letter) distinti saluti

trump [trʌmp] n (also: ~ card) atout m inv

trumpet ['trʌmpɪt] n tromba

truncheon ['trʌntʃən] n sfollagente m inv

trundle ['trʌndl] vt far rotolare rumorosamente ♦ vi: **to ~ along** rotolare rumorosamente

trunk [trʌŋk] n (of tree, person) tronco; (of elephant) proboscide f; (case) baule m; (US: AUT) bagagliaio; **~s** npl (also: swimming ~s) calzoncini mpl da bagno

truss [trʌs] vt: **~ (up)** (CULIN) legare

trust [trʌst] n fiducia; (LAW) amministrazione f fiduciaria; (COMM) trust m inv ♦ vt (rely on) contare su; (hope) sperare; (entrust): **to ~ sth to sb** affidare qc a qn; **~ed** adj fidato(a); **~ee** [trʌs'tiː] n (LAW) amministratore(trice) fiduciario(a); (of school etc) amministratore/ trice; **~ful** adj fiducioso(a); **~ing** adj = **~ful**; **~worthy** adj fidato(a), degno(a) di fiducia

truth [truːθ, pl truːðz] n verità f inv; **~ful** adj (person) sincero(a); (description) veritiero(a), esatto(a)

try [traɪ] n prova, tentativo; (RUGBY) meta ♦ vt (LAW) giudicare; (test: also: ~ out) provare; (strain) mettere alla prova ♦ vi provare; **to have a ~** fare un tentativo; **to ~ to do** (seek) cercare di fare; **to ~ on** (clothes) provare; **~ing** adj (day, experience) logorante, pesante; (child) difficile, insopportabile

tsar [zɑː*] n zar m inv

T-shirt ['tiː-] n maglietta

T-square ['tiː-] n riga a T

tub [tʌb] n tinozza; mastello; (bath) bagno

tuba ['tjuːbə] n tuba

tubby ['tʌbɪ] adj grassoccio(a)

tube [tjuːb] n tubo; (BRIT: underground) metropolitana, metrò m inv; (for tyre) camera d'aria; **~ station** (BRIT) n stazione f della metropolitana

tubular ['tjuːbjʊlə*] adj tubolare

TUC (BRIT) n abbr (= Trades Union Congress) confederazione f dei sindacati britannici

tuck [tʌk] vt (put) mettere; **~ away** vt riporre; (building): **to be ~ed away** essere in un luogo isolato; **~ in** vt mettere dentro; (child) rimboccare ♦ vi (eat) mangiare di buon appetito; abbuffarsi; **~ up** vt (child) rimboccare le coperte a; **~ shop** n negozio di pasticceria (in una scuola)

Tuesday ['tjuːzdɪ] n martedì m inv

tuft [tʌft] n ciuffo

tug [tʌg] n (ship) rimorchiatore m ♦ vt tirare con forza; **~-of-war** n tiro alla fune

tuition [tjuː'ɪʃən] n (BRIT) lezioni fpl; (: private ~) lezioni fpl private; (US: school fees) tasse fpl scolastiche

tulip ['tjuːlɪp] n tulipano

tumble ['tʌmbl] n (fall) capitombolo ♦ vi capitombolare, ruzzolare; **to ~ to sth** (inf) realizzare qc; **~down** adj cadente, diroccato(a); **~ dryer** (BRIT) n asciugatrice f

tumbler ['tʌmblə*] n bicchiere m (senza

stelo)

tummy ['tʌmɪ] (inf) n pancia; ~ **upset** n mal m di pancia

tumour ['tjuːmə*] (US **tumor**) n tumore m

tuna ['tjuːnə] n inv (also: ~ fish) tonno

tune [tjuːn] n (melody) melodia, aria ♦ vt (MUS) accordare; (RADIO, TV, AUT) regolare, mettere a punto; **to be in/out of ~** (instrument) essere accordato(a)/scordato(a); (singer) essere intonato(a)/ stonato(a); ~ **in** vi: **to ~ in (to)** (RADIO, TV) sintonizzarsi (su); ~ **up** vi (musician) accordare lo strumento; **~ful** adj melodioso(a); **~r** n: **piano ~r** accordatore m

tunic ['tjuːnɪk] n tunica

Tunisia [tjuː'nɪzɪə] n Tunisia

tunnel ['tʌnl] n galleria ♦ vi scavare una galleria

turban ['təːbən] n turbante m

turbulence ['təːbjuləns] n (AVIAT) turbolenza

tureen [tə'riːn] n zuppiera

turf [təːf] n terreno erboso; (clod) zolla ♦ vt coprire di zolle erbose; ~ **out** (inf) vt buttar fuori

Turin [tjuə'rɪn] n Torino f

Turk [təːk] n turco/a

Turkey ['təːkɪ] n Turchia

turkey ['təːkɪ] n tacchino

Turkish ['təːkɪʃ] adj turco(a) ♦ n (LING) turco

turmoil ['təːmɔɪl] n confusione f, tumulto

turn [təːn] n giro; (change) cambiamento; (in road) curva; (tendency: of mind, events) tendenza; (performance) numero; (chance) turno; (MED) crisi f inv, attacco ♦ vt girare, voltare; (change): **to ~ sth into** trasformare qc in ♦ vi girare; (person: look back) girarsi, voltarsi; (reverse direction) girare; (change) cambiare; (milk) andare a male; (become) diventare; **a good ~** un buon servizio; **it gave me quite a ~** mi ha fatto prendere un bello spavento; "**no left ~**" (AUT) "divieto di svolta a sinistra"; **it's your ~** tocca a lei; **in ~** a sua volta; **a turno**; **to take ~s (at sth)** fare (qc) a turno; ~ **away** vi girarsi (dall'altra parte) ♦ vt mandare via; ~ **back** vi ritornare, tornare indietro ♦ vt far tornare indietro; (clock) spostare indietro; ~ **down** vt (refuse) rifiutare; (reduce) abbassare; (fold) ripiegare; ~ **in** vi (inf: go to bed) andare a letto ♦ vt (fold) voltare in dentro; ~ **off** vi (from road) girare, voltare ♦ vt (light, radio, engine etc) spegnere; ~ **on** vt (light, radio etc) accendere; ~ **out** vt (light, gas) chiudere; spegnere ♦ vi (voters) presentarsi; **to ~ out to be** ... rivelarsi ..., risultare ...; ~ **over** vi (person) girarsi ♦ vt girare; ~ **round** vi girare; (person) girarsi; ~ **up** vi (person) arrivare, presentarsi; (lost object) saltar fuori ♦ vt (collar, sound) alzare; **~ing** n (in road)

curva; **~ing point** n (fig) svolta decisiva

turnip ['təːnɪp] n rapa

turnout ['təːnaut] n presenza, affluenza

turnover ['təːnəuvə*] n (COMM) turnover m inv; (CULIN): **apple** etc ~ sfogliatella alle melle ecc

turnpike ['təːnpaɪk] (US) n autostrada a pedaggio

turnstile ['təːnstaɪl] n tornella

turntable ['təːnteɪbl] n (on record player) piatto

turn-up ['təːnʌp] (BRIT) n (on trousers) risvolto

turpentine ['təːpəntaɪn] n (also: **turps**) acqua ragia

turquoise ['təːkwɔɪz] n turchese m ♦ adj turchese

turret ['tʌrɪt] n torretta

turtle ['təːtl] n testuggine f; **~neck (sweater)** n maglione m con il collo alto

Tuscany ['tʌskənɪ] n Toscana

tusk [tʌsk] n zanna

tutor ['tjuːtə*] n (in college) docente m/f (responsabile di un gruppo di studenti); (private teacher) precettore m; **~ial** [-'tɔːrɪəl] n (SCOL) lezione f con discussione (a un gruppo limitato)

tuxedo [tʌk'siːdəu] (US) n smoking m inv

TV [tiː'viː] n abbr (= television) tivù f inv

twang [twæŋ] n (of instrument) suono vibrante; (of voice) accento nasale

tweed [twiːd] n tweed m inv

tweezers ['twiːzəz] npl pinzette fpl

twelfth [twelfθ] num dodicesimo(a)

twelve [twelv] num dodici; **at ~ (o'clock)** alle dodici, a mezzogiorno; (midnight) a mezzanotte

twentieth ['twentɪɪθ] num ventesimo(a)

twenty ['twentɪ] num venti

twice [twaɪs] adv due volte; ~ **as much** due volte tanto; ~ **a week** due volte alla settimana

twiddle ['twɪdl] vt, vi: **to ~ (with) sth** giocherellare con qc; **to ~ one's thumbs** (fig) girarsi i pollici

twig [twɪg] n ramoscello ♦ vt, vi (inf) capire

twilight ['twaɪlaɪt] n crepuscolo

twin [twɪn] adj, n gemello(a) ♦ vt: **to ~ one town with another** fare il gemellaggio di una città con un'altra; **~-bedded room** n stanza con letti gemelli; ~ **beds** npl letti mpl gemelli

twine [twaɪn] n spago, cordicella ♦ vi attorcigliarsi

twinge [twɪndʒ] n (of pain) fitta; **a ~ of conscience/regret** un rimorso/rimpianto

twinkle ['twɪŋkl] vi scintillare; (eyes) brillare

twirl [twəːl] vt far roteare ♦ vi roteare

twist [twɪst] n torsione f; (in wire, flex) piega; (in road) curva; (in story) colpo di scena ♦ vt attorcigliare; (ankle) slogare; (weave) intrecciare; (*roll around*) arrotolare; (*fig*) distorcere ♦ *vi* (*road*) serpeggiare

twit [twɪt] (*inf*) *n* cretino(a)

twitch [twɪtʃ] *n* tiratina; (*nervous*) tic *m inv* ♦ *vi* contrarsi

two [tuː] *num* due; **to put ~ and ~ together** (*fig*) fare uno più uno; **~-door** *adj* (*AUT*) a due porte; **~-faced** (*pej*) *adj* (*person*) falso(a); **~fold** *adv*: **to increase ~fold** aumentare del doppio; **~-piece** (*suit*) *n* due pezzi *m inv*; **~-piece** (*swimsuit*) *n* (costume *m* da bagno a) due pezzi *m inv*; **~some** *n* (*people*) coppia; **~-way** *adj* (*traffic*) a due sensi

tycoon [taɪˈkuːn] *n*: (**business**) ~ magnate *m*

type [taɪp] *n* (*category*) genere *m*; (*model*) modello; (*example*) tipo; (*TYP*) tipo, carattere *m* ♦ *vt* (*letter etc*) battere (a macchina), dattilografare; **~-cast** *adj* (*actor*) a ruolo fisso; **~face** *n* carattere *m* tipografico; **~script** *n* dattiloscritto; **~writer** *n* macchina da scrivere; **~written** *adj* dattiloscritto(a), battuto(a) a macchina

typhoid [ˈtaɪfɔɪd] *n* tifoidea

typhoon [taɪˈfuːn] *n* tifone *m*

typical [ˈtɪpɪkl] *adj* tipico(a)

typify [ˈtɪpɪfaɪ] *vt* caratterizzare; (*person*) impersonare

typing [ˈtaɪpɪŋ] *n* dattilografia

typist [ˈtaɪpɪst] *n* dattilografo/a

tyrant [ˈtaɪərnt] *n* tiranno

tyre [ˈtaɪə*] (*US* **tire**) *n* pneumatico, gomma; **~ pressure** *n* pressione *f* (delle gomme)

tzar [zɑː*] *n* = **tsar**

U, u

U-bend [ˈjuːˈ-] *n* (*in pipe*) sifone *m*

ubiquitous [juːˈbɪkwɪtəs] *adj* onnipresente

udder [ˈʌdə*] *n* mammella

UFO [ˈjuːfəu] *n abbr* (= *unidentified flying object*) UFO *m inv*

ugh [əːh] *excl* puah!

ugly [ˈʌɡlɪ] *adj* brutto(a)

UHT *abbr* (= *ultra heat treated*) UHT *inv*, a lunga conservazione

UK *n abbr* = **United Kingdom**

ulcer [ˈʌlsə*] *n* ulcera; (*also*: **mouth ~**) afta

Ulster [ˈʌlstə*] *n* Ulster *m*

ulterior [ʌlˈtɪərɪə*] *adj* ulteriore; **~ motive** *n* secondo fine *m*

ultimate [ˈʌltɪmət] *adj* ultimo(a), finale; (*authority*) massimo(a), supremo(a); **~ly** *adv* alla fine; in definitiva, in fin dei conti

ultrasound [ˈʌltrəˈsaund] *n* (*MED*) ultrasuono

umbilical cord [ʌmbɪˈlaɪkl-] *n* cordone *m* ombelicale

umbrella [ʌmˈbrelə] *n* ombrello

umpire [ˈʌmpaɪə*] *n* arbitro

umpteen [ʌmpˈtiːn] *adj* non so quanti(e); **for the ~th time** per l'ennesima volta

UN *n abbr* (= *United Nations*) ONU *f*

unable [ʌnˈeɪbl] *adj*: **to be ~ to** non potere, essere nell'impossibilità di; essere incapace di

unaccompanied [ʌnəˈkʌmpənɪd] *adj* (*child, lady*) non accompagnato(a)

unaccustomed [ʌnəˈkʌstəmd] *adj*: **to be ~ to sth** non essere abituato a qc

unanimous [juːˈnænɪməs] *adj* unanime; **~ly** *adv* all'unanimità

unarmed [ʌnˈɑːmd] *adj* (*without a weapon*) disarmato(a); (*combat*) senz'armi

unattached [ʌnəˈtætʃt] *adj* senza legami, libero(a)

unattended [ʌnəˈtendɪd] *adj* (*car, child, luggage*) incustodito(a)

unattractive [ʌnəˈtræktɪv] *adj* poco attraente

unauthorized [ʌnˈɔːθəraɪzd] *adj* non autorizzato(a)

unavoidable [ʌnəˈvɔɪdəbl] *adj* inevitabile

unaware [ʌnəˈwɛə*] *adj*: **to be ~ of** non sapere, ignorare; **~s** *adv* di sorpresa, alla sprovvista

unbalanced [ʌnˈbælənst] *adj* squilibrato(a)

unbearable [ʌnˈbɛərəbl] *adj* insopportabile

unbeknown(st) [ʌnbɪˈnəun(st)] *adv*: **~ to** all'insaputa di

unbelievable [ʌnbɪˈliːvəbl] *adj* incredibile

unbend [ʌnˈbend] (*irreg*: *like* **bend**) *vi* distendersi ♦ *vt* (*wire*) raddrizzare

unbias(s)ed [ʌnˈbaɪəst] *adj* (*person, report*) obiettivo(a), imparziale

unborn [ʌnˈbɔːn] *adj* non ancora nato(a)

unbreakable [ʌnˈbreɪkəbl] *adj* infrangibile

unbroken [ʌnˈbrəukən] *adj* intero(a); (*series*) continuo(a); (*record*) imbattuto(a)

unbutton [ʌnˈbʌtn] *vt* sbottonare

uncalled-for [ʌnˈkɔːld-] *adj* (*remark*) fuori luogo *inv*; (*action*) ingiustificato(a)

uncanny [ʌnˈkænɪ] *adj* misterioso(a), strano(a)

unceasing [ʌnˈsiːsɪŋ] *adj* incessante

unceremonious [ˈʌnserɪˈməunɪəs] *adj* (*abrupt, rude*) senza tante cerimonie

uncertain [ʌnˈsəːtn] *adj* incerto(a); dubbio(a); **~ty** *n* incertezza

unchanged [ʌnˈtʃeɪndʒd] *adj* invariato(a)

uncivilized [ʌnˈsɪvɪlaɪzd] *adj* (*gen*) selvaggio(a); (*fig*) incivile, barbaro(a)

uncle [ˈʌŋkl] *n* zio

uncomfortable [ʌnˈkʌmfətəbl] *adj* scomodo(a); (*uneasy*) a disagio, agitato(a); (*unpleasant*) fastidioso(a)

uncommon [ʌnˈkɔmən] *adj* raro(a), insolito(a), non comune

uncompromising [ʌnˈkɔmprəmaizɪŋ] *adj*

intransigente, inflessibile

unconcerned [ʌnkən'sə:nd] adj: **to be ~ (about)** non preoccuparsi (di or per)

unconditional [ʌnkən'dıʃənl] adj incondizionato(a), senza condizioni

unconscious [ʌn'kɔnʃəs] adj privo(a) di sensi, svenuto(a); (unaware) inconsapevole, inconscio(a) ♦ n: **the ~** l'inconscio; **~ly** adv inconsciamente

uncontrollable [ʌnkən'trəuləbl] adj incontrollabile, indisciplinato(a)

unconventional [ʌnkən'venʃənl] adj poco convenzionale

uncouth [ʌn'ku:θ] adj maleducato(a), grossolano(a)

uncover [ʌn'kʌvə*] vt scoprire

undecided [ʌndı'saıdıd] adj indeciso(a)

under ['ʌndə*] prep sotto; (less than) meno di; al disotto di; (according to) secondo, in conformità a ♦ adv (al) disotto; **~ there** là sotto; **~ repair** in riparazione

under... ['ʌndə*] prefix sotto..., sub...; **~-age** adj minorenne; **~carriage** (BRIT) n carrello (d'atterraggio); **~charge** vt far pagare di meno a; **~clothes** npl biancheria (intima); **~coat** n (paint) mano f di fondo; **~cover** adj segreto(a), clandestino(a); **~current** n corrente f sottomarina; **~cut** vt irreg vendere a prezzo minore di; **~developed** adj sottosviluppato(a); **~dog** n oppresso/a; **~done** adj (CULIN) al sangue; (pej) poco cotto(a); **~estimate** vt sottovalutare; **~fed** adj denutrito(a); **~foot** adv sotto i piedi; **~go** vt irreg subire; (treatment) sottoporsi a; **~graduate** n studente(essa) universitario(a); **~ground** n (BRIT: railway) metropolitana; (POL) movimento clandestino ♦ adj sotterraneo(a); (fig) clandestino(a) ♦ adv sottoterra; **to go ~ground** (fig) darsi alla macchia; **~growth** n sottobosco; **~hand(ed)** adj (fig) furtivo(a), subdolo(a); **~lie** vt irreg essere alla base di; **~line** vt sottolineare; **~mine** vt minare; **~neath** [ʌndə'ni:θ] adv sotto, disotto ♦ prep sotto, al di sotto di; **~paid** adj sottopagato(a); **~pants** npl mutande fpl, slip m inv; **~pass** (BRIT) n sottopassaggio; **~privileged** adj non abbiente; meno favorito(a); **~rate** vt sottovalutare; **~shirt** (US) n maglietta; **~shorts** (US) npl mutande fpl, slip m inv; **~side** n disotto; **~skirt** (BRIT) n sottoveste f

understand [ʌndə'stænd] (irreg: like stand) vt, vi capire, comprendere; **I ~ that ...** sento che ...; credo di capire che ...; **~able** adj comprensibile; **~ing** adj comprensivo(a) ♦ n comprensione f; (agreement) accordo

understatement [ʌndə'steıtmənt] n: **that's an ~!** a dire poco!

understood [ʌndə'stud] pt, pp of

understand ♦ adj inteso(a); (implied) sottinteso(a)

understudy ['ʌndəstʌdı] n sostituto/a, attore/trice supplente

undertake [ʌndə'teık] (irreg: like take) vt intraprendere; **to ~ to do sth** impegnarsi a fare qc

undertaker ['ʌndəteıkə*] n impresario di pompe funebri

undertaking [ʌndə'teıkıŋ] n impresa; (promise) promessa

undertone ['ʌndətəun] n: **in an ~** a mezza voce, a voce bassa

underwater [ʌndə'wɔ:tə*] adv sott'acqua ♦ adj subacqueo(a)

underwear ['ʌndəweə*] n biancheria (intima)

underworld ['ʌndəwə:ld] n (of crime) malavita

underwriter ['ʌndəraıtə*] n (INSURANCE) sottoscrittore/trice

undesirable [ʌndı'zaıərəbl] adj sgradevole

undies ['ʌndız] (inf) npl biancheria intima da donna

undo [ʌn'du:] vt irreg disfare; **~ing** n rovina, perdita

undoubted [ʌn'dautıd] adj sicuro(a), certo(a); **~ly** adv senza alcun dubbio

undress [ʌn'dres] vi spogliarsi

undue [ʌn'dju:] adj eccessivo(a)

undulating ['ʌndjuleıtıŋ] adj ondeggiante; ondulato(a)

unduly [ʌn'dju:lı] adv eccessivamente

unearth [ʌn'ə:θ] vt dissotterrare; (fig) scoprire

unearthly [ʌn'ə:θlı] adj (hour) impossibile

uneasy [ʌn'i:zı] adj a disagio; (worried) preoccupato(a); (peace) precario(a)

uneconomic(al) ['ʌni:kə'nɔmık(l)] adj antieconomico(a)

unemployed [ʌnım'plɔıd] adj disoccupato(a) ♦ npl: **the ~** i disoccupati

unemployment [ʌnım'plɔımənt] n disoccupazione f

unending [ʌn'endıŋ] adj senza fine

unerring [ʌn'ə:rıŋ] adj infallibile

uneven [ʌn'i:vn] adj ineguale; irregolare

unexpected [ʌnık'spektıd] adj inatteso(a), imprevisto(a); **~ly** adv inaspettatamente

unfailing [ʌn'feılıŋ] adj (supply, energy) inesauribile; (remedy) infallibile

unfair [ʌn'feə*] adj: **~ (to)** ingiusto(a) (nei confronti di)

unfaithful [ʌn'feıθful] adj infedele

unfamiliar [ʌnfə'mılıə*] adj sconosciuto(a), strano(a); **to be ~ with** non avere familiarità con

unfashionable [ʌn'fæʃnəbl] adj (clothes) fuori moda; (district) non alla moda

unfasten [ʌnˈfɑːsn] vt slacciare; sciogliere

unfavourable [ʌnˈfeɪvərəbl] (US **unfavorable**) adj sfavorevole

unfeeling [ʌnˈfiːlɪŋ] adj insensibile, duro(a)

unfinished [ʌnˈfɪnɪʃt] adj incompleto(a)

unfit [ʌnˈfɪt] adj (ill) malato(a), in cattiva salute; (incompetent): ~ (for) incompetente (in); (: work, MIL) inabile (a)

unfold [ʌnˈfəʊld] vt spiegare ♦ vi (story, plot) svelarsi

unforeseen [ˈʌnfɔːˈsiːn] adj imprevisto(a)

unforgettable [ʌnfəˈgetəbl] adj indimenticabile

unfortunate [ʌnˈfɔːtʃnət] adj sfortunato(a); (event, remark) infelice; **~ly** adv sfortunatamente, purtroppo

unfounded [ʌnˈfaʊndɪd] adj infondato(a)

unfriendly [ʌnˈfrɛndlɪ] adj poco amichevole, freddo(a)

ungainly [ʌnˈgeɪnlɪ] adj goffo(a), impacciato(a)

ungodly [ʌnˈgɒdlɪ] adj: **at an ~ hour** a un'ora impossibile

ungrateful [ʌnˈgreɪtful] adj ingrato(a)

unhappiness [ʌnˈhæpɪnɪs] n infelicità

unhappy [ʌnˈhæpɪ] adj infelice; **~ about/with** (arrangements etc) insoddisfatto(a) di

unharmed [ʌnˈhɑːmd] adj incolume, sano(a) e salvo(a)

unhealthy [ʌnˈhɛlθɪ] adj (gen) malsano(a); (person) malaticcio(a)

unheard-of [ʌnˈhɜːdɒv] adj inaudito(a), senza precedenti

unhurt [ʌnˈhɜːt] adj illeso(a)

uniform [ˈjuːnɪfɔːm] n uniforme f, divisa ♦ adj uniforme

uninhabited [ʌnɪnˈhæbɪtɪd] adj disabitato(a)

unintentional [ʌnɪnˈtɛnʃənəl] adj involontario(a)

union [ˈjuːnjən] n unione f; (also: trade ~) sindacato ♦ cpd sindacale, dei sindacati; **U~ Jack** n bandiera nazionale britannica

unique [juːˈniːk] adj unico(a)

unit [ˈjuːnɪt] n unità f inv; (section: of furniture etc) elemento; (team, squad) reparto, squadra

unite [juːˈnaɪt] vt unire ♦ vi unirsi; **~d** adj unito(a); unificato(a); (efforts) congiunto(a); **U~d Kingdom** n Regno Unito; **U~d Nations (Organization)** n (Organizzazione f delle) Nazioni Unite; **U~d States (of America)** n Stati mpl Uniti (d'America)

unit trust (BRIT) n fondo d'investimento

unity [ˈjuːnɪtɪ] n unità

universal [juːnɪˈvɜːsl] adj universale

universe [ˈjuːnɪvɜːs] n universo

university [juːnɪˈvɜːsɪtɪ] n università f inv

unjust [ʌnˈdʒʌst] adj ingiusto(a)

unkempt [ʌnˈkɛmpt] adj trasandato(a); spettinato(a)

unkind [ʌnˈkaɪnd] adj scortese; crudele

unknown [ʌnˈnəʊn] adj sconosciuto(a)

unlawful [ʌnˈlɔːful] adj illecito(a), illegale

unleaded [ʌnˈlɛdɪd] adj (petrol, fuel) verde, senza piombo

unleash [ʌnˈliːʃ] vt (fig) scatenare

unless [ʌnˈlɛs] conj a meno che (non) + sub

unlike [ʌnˈlaɪk] adj diverso(a) ♦ prep a differenza di, contrariamente a

unlikely [ʌnˈlaɪklɪ] adj improbabile

unlisted [ʌnˈlɪstɪd] (US) adj (TEL): **to be ~** non essere sull'elenco

unload [ʌnˈləʊd] vt scaricare

unlock [ʌnˈlɒk] vt aprire

unlucky [ʌnˈlʌkɪ] adj sfortunato(a); (object, number) che porta sfortuna

unmarried [ʌnˈmærɪd] adj non sposato(a); (man only) scapolo, celibe; (woman only) nubile

unmistak(e)able [ʌnmɪsˈteɪkəbl] adj inconfondibile

unmitigated [ʌnˈmɪtɪgeɪtɪd] adj non mitigato(a), assoluto(a), vero(a) e proprio(a)

unnatural [ʌnˈnætʃrəl] adj innaturale; contro natura

unnecessary [ʌnˈnɛsəsərɪ] adj inutile, superfluo(a)

unnoticed [ʌnˈnəʊtɪst] adj: **(to go) ~** (passare) inosservato(a)

UNO [ˈjuːnəʊ] n abbr (= United Nations Organization) ONU f

unobtainable [ʌnəbˈteɪnəbl] adj (TEL) non ottenibile

unobtrusive [ʌnəbˈtruːsɪv] adj discreto(a)

unofficial [ʌnəˈfɪʃl] adj non ufficiale; (strike) non dichiarato(a) dal sindacato

unpack [ʌnˈpæk] vi disfare la valigia (or le valigie) ♦ vt disfare

unpalatable [ʌnˈpælətəbl] adj sgradevole

unparalleled [ʌnˈpærəleld] adj incomparabile, impareggiabile

unpleasant [ʌnˈplɛznt] adj spiacevole

unplug [ʌnˈplʌg] vt staccare

unpopular [ʌnˈpɒpjʊləʳ] adj impopolare

unprecedented [ʌnˈprɛsɪdəntɪd] adj senza precedenti

unpredictable [ʌnprɪˈdɪktəbl] adj imprevedibile

unprofessional [ʌnprəˈfɛʃənl] adj poco professionale

unqualified [ʌnˈkwɒlɪfaɪd] adj (teacher) non abilitato(a); (success) assoluto(a), senza riserve

unquestionably [ʌnˈkwɛstʃənəblɪ] adv indiscutibilmente

unravel [ʌnˈrævl] vt dipanare, districare

unreal [ʌnˈrɪəl] adj irreale

unrealistic [ʌnrɪəˈlɪstɪk] adj non realistico(a)

unreasonable [ʌn'riːznəbl] *adj*
irragionevole

unrelated [ʌnrɪ'leɪtɪd] *adj*: ~ **(to)** senza
rapporto (con); non imparentato(a) (con)

unreliable [ʌnrɪ'laɪəbl] *adj* (*person, machine*)
che non dà affidamento; (*news, source of
information*) inattendibile

unremitting [ʌnrɪ'mɪtɪŋ] *adj* incessante

unreservedly [ʌnrɪ'zɜːvɪdlɪ] *adv* senza
riserve

unrest [ʌn'rɛst] *n* agitazione *f*

unroll [ʌn'rəul] *vt* srotolare

unruly [ʌn'ruːlɪ] *adj* indisciplinato(a)

unsafe [ʌn'seɪf] *adj* pericoloso(a), rischioso(a)

unsaid [ʌn'sɛd] *adj*: **to leave sth ~** passare qc
sotto silenzio

unsatisfactory ['ʌnsætɪs'fæktərɪ] *adj* che
lascia a desiderare, insufficiente

unsavoury [ʌn'seɪvərɪ] (*US* **unsavory**) *adj*
(*fig: person, place*) losco(a)

unscathed [ʌn'skeɪðd] *adj* incolume

unscrew [ʌn'skruː] *vt* svitare

unscrupulous [ʌn'skruːpjuləs] *adj* senza
scrupoli

unsettled [ʌn'sɛtld] *adj* (*person*) turbato(a),
indeciso(a); (*weather*) instabile

unshaven [ʌn'ʃeɪvn] *adj* non rasato(a)

unsightly [ʌn'saɪtlɪ] *adj* brutto(a), sgradevole
a vedersi

unskilled [ʌn'skɪld] *adj* non specializzato(a)

unspeakable [ʌn'spiːkəbl] *adj*
(*indescribable*) indicibile; (*awful*) abominevole

unstable [ʌn'steɪbl] *adj* (*gen*) instabile;
(*mentally*) squilibrato(a)

unsteady [ʌn'stɛdɪ] *adj* instabile,
malsicuro(a)

unstuck [ʌn'stʌk] *adj*: **to come ~** scollarsi;
(*fig*) fare fiasco

unsuccessful [ʌnsək'sɛsful] *adj* (*writer,
proposal*) che non ha successo; (*marriage,
attempt*) mal riuscito(a), fallito(a); **to be ~** (*in
attempting sth*) non avere successo

unsuitable [ʌn'suːtəbl] *adj* inadatto(a);
inopportuno(a); sconveniente

unsure [ʌn'ʃuə*] *adj* incerto(a); **to be ~ of
o.s.** essere insicuro(a)

unsuspecting [ʌnsə'spɛktɪŋ] *adj* che non
sospetta nulla

unsympathetic [ʌnsɪmpə'θɛtɪk] *adj*
(*person*) antipatico(a); (*attitude*) poco
incoraggiante

untapped [ʌn'tæpt] *adj* (*resources*) non
sfruttato(a)

unthinkable [ʌn'θɪŋkəbl] *adj* impensabile,
inconcepibile

untidy [ʌn'taɪdɪ] *adj* (*room*) in disordine;
(*appearance*) trascurato(a); (*person*)
disordinato(a)

untie [ʌn'taɪ] *vt* (*knot, parcel*) disfare;

(*prisoner, dog*) slegare

until [ʌn'tɪl] *prep* fino a; (*after negative*) prima
di ♦ *conj* finché, fino a quando; (*in past, after
negative*) prima che + *sub*, prima di
+ *infinitive*; ~ **he comes** finché *or* fino a
quando non arriva; ~ **now** finora, ~ **then** fino
ad allora

untimely [ʌn'taɪmlɪ] *adj* intempestivo(a),
inopportuno(a); (*death*) prematuro(a)

untold [ʌn'təuld] *adj* (*story*) mai rivelato(a);
(*wealth*) incalcolabile; (*joy, suffering*)
indescrivibile

untoward [ʌntə'wɔːd] *adj* sfortunato(a),
sconveniente

unused [ʌn'juːzd] *adj* nuovo(a)

unusual [ʌn'juːʒuəl] *adj* insolito(a),
eccezionale, raro(a)

unveil [ʌn'veɪl] *vt* scoprire; svelare

unwanted [ʌn'wɔntɪd] *adj* (*clothing*)
smesso(a); (*child*) non desiderato(a)

unwavering [ʌn'weɪvərɪŋ] *adj* fermo(a),
incrollabile

unwelcome [ʌn'wɛlkəm] *adj* non gradito(a)

unwell [ʌn'wɛl] *adj* indisposto(a); **to feel ~**
non sentirsi bene

unwieldy [ʌn'wiːldɪ] *adj* poco maneggevole

unwilling [ʌn'wɪlɪŋ] *adj*: **to be ~ to do** non
voler fare; **~ly** *adv* malvolentieri

unwind [ʌn'waɪnd] (*irreg: like* **wind**[1]) *vt*
svolgere, srotolare ♦ *vi* (*relax*) rilassarsi

unwise [ʌn'waɪz] *adj* poco saggio(a)

unwitting [ʌn'wɪtɪŋ] *adj* involontario(a)

unworkable [ʌn'wəːkəbl] *adj* (*plan*)
inattuabile

unworthy [ʌn'wəːðɪ] *adj* indegno(a)

unwrap [ʌn'ræp] *vt* disfare; aprire

unwritten [ʌn'rɪtn] *adj* (*agreement*)
tacito(a); (*law*) non scritto(a)

KEYWORD

up [ʌp] *prep*: **he went ~ the stairs/the hill** è
salito su per le scale/sulla collina; **the cat was
~ a tree** il gatto era su un albero; **they live
further ~ the street** vivono un po' più su nella
stessa strada

♦ *adv* **1** (*upwards, higher*) su, in alto; ~ **in the
sky/the mountains** su nel cielo/in montagna;
~ **there** lassù; ~ **above** su in alto

2: **to be ~** (*out of bed*) essere alzato(a);
(*prices, level*) essere salito(a)

3: ~ **to** (*as far as*) fino a; ~ **to now** finora

4: **to be ~ to** (*depending on*): **it's ~ to you** sta
a lei, dipende da lei; (*equal to*): **he's not ~ to
it** (*job, task etc*) non ne è all'altezza; (*inf: be
doing*): **what is he ~ to?** cosa sta
combinando?

♦ *n*: **~s and downs** alti e bassi *mpl*

---

upbringing ['ʌpbrɪŋɪŋ] *n* educazione *f*

update [ʌp'deɪt] vt aggiornare

upgrade [ʌp'greɪd] vt (house, job) migliorare; (employee) avanzare di grado

upheaval [ʌp'hi:vl] n sconvolgimento; tumulto

uphill [ʌp'hɪl] adj in salita; (fig: task) difficile
♦ adv: **to go ~** andare in salita, salire

uphold [ʌp'həuld] (irreg: like hold) vt approvare; sostenere

upholstery [ʌp'həulstəri] n tappezzeria

upkeep [ʌpki:p] n manutenzione f

upon [ə'pɔn] prep su

upper [ʌpə*] adj superiore ♦ n (of shoe) tomaia; **~-class** adj dell'alta borghesia; **~ hand** n: **to have the ~ hand** avere il coltello dalla parte del manico; **~most** adj il(la) più alto(a); predominante

upright [ʌpraɪt] adj diritto(a); verticale; (fig) diritto(a), onesto(a)

uprising [ʌpraɪzɪŋ] n insurrezione f, rivolta

uproar [ʌprɔ:*] n tumulto, clamore m

uproot [ʌpru:t] vt sradicare

upset [n ʌpset, vb, adj ʌp'set] (irreg: like set) n (to plan etc) contrattempo; (stomach ~) disturbo ♦ vt (glass etc) rovesciare; (plan, stomach) scombussolare; (person: offend) contrariare; (: grieve) addolorare; sconvolgere ♦ adj contrariato(a); addolorato(a); (stomach) scombussolato(a)

upshot [ʌpʃɔt] n risultato

upside down [ʌpsaɪd-] adv sottosopra

upstairs [ʌp'steəz] adv, adj di sopra, al piano superiore ♦ n piano di sopra

upstart [ʌpstɑ:t] n parvenu m inv

upstream [ʌp'stri:m] adv a monte

uptake [ʌpteɪk] n: **he is quick/slow on the ~** è pronto/lento di comprendonio

uptight [ʌp'taɪt] (inf) adj teso(a)

up-to-date adj moderno(a); aggiornato(a)

upturn [ʌptə:n] n (in luck) svolta favorevole; (COMM: in market) rialzo

upward [ʌpwəd] adj ascendente; verso l'alto; **~(s)** adv in su, verso l'alto

urban [ʌ:bən] adj urbano(a); **~ clearway** n strada di scorrimento (in cui è vietata la sosta)

urbane [ə:'beɪn] adj civile, urbano(a), educato(a)

urchin [ʌ:tʃɪn] n monello

urge [ə:dʒ] n impulso; stimolo; forte desiderio ♦ vt: **to ~ sb to do** esortare qn a fare, spingere qn a fare; raccomandare a qn di fare

urgency [ʌ:dʒənsɪ] n urgenza; (of tone) insistenza

urgent [ʌ:dʒənt] adj urgente; (voice) insistente

urinate [juərɪneɪt] vi orinare

urine [juərɪn] n orina

urn [ə:n] n urna; (also: tea ~) bollitore m per il tè

us [ʌs] pron ci; (stressed, after prep) noi; see also **me**

US(A) n abbr (= United States (of America)) USA mpl

usage [ju:zɪdʒ] n uso

use [n ju:s, vb ju:z] n uso; impiego, utilizzazione f ♦ vt usare, utilizzare, servirsi di; **in ~** in uso; **out of ~** fuori uso; **to be of ~** essere utile, servire; **it's no ~** non serve, è inutile; **she ~d to do it** lo faceva (una volta), era solita farlo; **to be ~d to** avere l'abitudine di; **~ up** vt consumare; esaurire; **~d** adj (object, car) usato(a); **~ful** adj utile; **~fulness** n utilità; **~less** adj inutile; (person) inetto(a); **~r** n utente m/f; **~r-friendly** adj (computer) di facile uso

usher [ʌʃə*] n usciere m; **~ette** [-'rɛt] n (in cinema) maschera

USSR n (HIST): **the ~** l'URSS f

usual [ju:ʒuəl] adj solito(a); **as ~** come al solito, come d'abitudine; **~ly** adv di solito

utensil [ju:'tɛnsl] n utensile m; **kitchen ~s** utensili da cucina

uterus [ju:tərəs] n utero

utility [ju:'tɪlɪtɪ] n utilità; (also: public ~) servizio pubblico; **~ room** n locale adibito alla stiratura dei panni etc

utmost [ʌtməust] adj estremo(a) ♦ n: **to do one's ~** fare il possibile or di tutto

utter [ʌtə*] adj assoluto(a), totale ♦ vt pronunciare, proferire; emettere; **~ance** n espressione f; parole fpl; **~ly** adv completamente, del tutto

U-turn [ju:'tə:n] n inversione f a U

V, v

v. abbr = **verse; versus; volt;** (= vide) vedi, vedere

vacancy [veɪkənsɪ] n (BRIT: job) posto libero; (room) stanza libera; **"no vacancies"** "completo"

vacant [veɪkənt] adj (job, seat etc) libero(a); (expression) assente

vacate [və'keɪt] vt lasciare libero(a)

vacation [və'keɪʃən] n (esp US) vacanze fpl

vaccinate [væksɪneɪt] vt vaccinare

vaccination [væksɪ'neɪʃən] n vaccinazione f

vacuum [vækjum] n vuoto; **~ cleaner** n aspirapolvere m inv; **~ flask** (BRIT) n Thermos ® m inv; **~-packed** adj confezionato(a) sottovuoto

vagina [və'dʒaɪnə] n vagina

vagrant [veɪgrnt] n vagabondo/a

vague [veɪg] adj vago(a); (blurred: photo, memory) sfocato(a); **~ly** adv vagamente

vain [veɪn] adj (useless) inutile, vano(a); (conceited) vanitoso(a); **in ~** inutilmente, invano

valentine ['væləntaɪn] n (also: ~ card)
cartolina or biglietto di San Valentino;
(person) innamorato/a

valet ['væleɪ] n cameriere m personale

valiant ['væliənt] adj valoroso(a),
coraggioso(a)

valid ['vælɪd] adj valido(a), valevole; (excuse)
valido(a)

valley ['vælɪ] n valle f

valour ['vælə*] (US **valor**) n valore m

valuable ['væljuəbl] adj (jewel) di (grande)
valore; (time, help) prezioso(a); **~s** npl
oggetti mpl di valore

valuation [vælju'eɪʃən] n valutazione f, stima

value ['vælju:] n valore m ♦ vt (fix price)
valutare, dare un prezzo a; (cherish)
apprezzare, tenere a; **~ added tax** (BRIT) n
imposta sul valore aggiunto; **~d** adj
(appreciated) stimato(a), apprezzato(a)

valve [vælv] n valvola

van [væn] n (AUT) furgone m; (BRIT: RAIL)
vagone m

vandal ['vændl] n vandalo/a; **~ism** n
vandalismo

vanilla [və'nɪlə] n vaniglia ♦ cpd (ice cream)
alla vaniglia

vanish ['vænɪʃ] vi svanire, scomparire

vanity ['vænɪtɪ] n vanità

vantage ['vɑ:ntɪdʒ] n: **~ point** posizione f or
punto di osservazione; (fig) posizione
vantaggiosa

vapour ['veɪpə*] (US **vapor**) n vapore m

variable ['vεərɪəbl] adj variabile; (mood)
mutevole

variance ['vεərɪəns] n: **to be at ~ (with)**
essere in disaccordo (con); (facts) essere in
contraddizione (con)

varicose ['værɪkəus] adj: **~ veins** vene fpl
varicose

varied ['vεərɪd] adj vario(a), diverso(a)

variety [və'raɪətɪ] n varietà f inv; (quantity)
quantità, numero; **~ show** n varietà m inv

various ['vεərɪəs] adj vario(a), diverso(a);
(several) parecchi(e), molti(e)

varnish ['vɑ:nɪʃ] n vernice f; (nail ~) smalto
♦ vt verniciare; mettere lo smalto su

vary ['vεərɪ] vt, vi variare, mutare

vase [vɑ:z] n vaso

Vaseline ® ['væsɪli:n] n vaselina

vast [vɑ:st] adj vasto(a); (amount, success)
enorme

VAT [væt] n abbr (= value added tax) I.V.A. f

vat [væt] n tino

Vatican ['vætɪkən] n: **the ~** il Vaticano

vault [vɔ:lt] n (of roof) volta; (tomb) tomba;
(in bank) camera blindata ♦ vt (also: ~ over)
saltare (d'un balzo)

vaunted ['vɔ:ntɪd] adj: **much-~** tanto

celebrato(a)

VCR n abbr = **video cassette recorder**

VD n abbr = **venereal disease**

VDU n abbr = **visual display unit**

veal [vi:l] n vitello

veer [vɪə*] vi girare; virare

vegan ['vi:gən] n vegetaliano(a)

vegeburger ['vedʒɪbɜ:gɜ*] n hamburger m
inv vegetariano

vegetable ['vedʒtəbl] n verdura, ortaggio
♦ adj vegetale

vegetarian [vedʒɪ'tεərɪən] adj, n
vegetariano(a)

vehement ['vi:ɪmənt] adj veemente,
violento(a)

vehicle ['vi:ɪkl] n veicolo

veil [veɪl] n velo; **~ed** adj (fig: threat)
velato(a)

vein [veɪn] n vena; (on leaf) nervatura

velvet ['vεlvɪt] n velluto ♦ adj di velluto

vending machine ['vendɪŋ-] n distributore
m automatico

vendor ['vendə*] n venditore/trice

veneer [və'nɪə*] n impiallacciatura; (fig)
vernice f

venereal [vɪ'nɪərɪəl] adj: **~ disease** malattia
venerea

Venetian [vɪ'ni:ʃən] adj veneziano(a);
~ blind n (tenda alla) veneziana

vengeance ['vendʒəns] n vendetta; **with a ~**
(fig) davvero; furiosamente

Venice ['venɪs] n Venezia

venison ['venɪsn] n carne f di cervo

venom ['venəm] n veleno

vent [vent] n foro, apertura; (in dress, jacket)
spacco ♦ vt (fig: one's feelings) sfogare, dare
sfogo a

ventilate ['ventɪleɪt] vt (room) dare aria a,
arieggiare; **ventilator** n ventilatore m

ventriloquist [ven'trɪləkwɪst] n ventriloquo/
a

venture ['ventʃə*] n impresa (rischiosa) ♦ vt
rischiare, azzardare ♦ vi avventurarsi; **business
~** iniziativa commerciale

venue ['venju:] n luogo (designato) per
l'incontro

verb [vɜ:b] n verbo; **~al** adj verbale;
(translation) orale

verbatim [vɜ:'beɪtɪm] adj, adv parola per
parola

verdict ['vɜ:dɪkt] n verdetto

verge [vɜ:dʒ] (BRIT) n bordo, orlo; **"soft ~s"**
(BRIT: AUT) banchine fpl cedevoli; **on the ~ of
doing** sul punto di fare; **~ on** vt fus rasentare

veritable ['verɪtəbl] adj vero(a)

vermin ['vɜ:mɪn] npl animali mpl nocivi;
(insects) insetti mpl parassiti

vermouth ['vɜ:məθ] n vermut m inv

versatile ['vɜ:sətaɪl] adj (person) versatile;

(*machine, tool etc*) (che si presta) a molti usi
verse [vəːs] *n* versi *mpl*; (*stanza*) stanza, strofa; (*in bible*) versetto
version ['vəːʃən] *n* versione *f*
versus ['vəːsəs] *prep* contro
vertical ['vəːtɪkl] *adj* verticale ♦ *n* verticale *m*; **~ly** *adv* verticalmente
vertigo ['vəːtɪɡəu] *n* vertigine *f*
verve [vəːv] *n* brio; entusiasmo
very ['vɛrɪ] *adv* molto ♦ *adj*: **the ~ book which** proprio il libro che; **the ~ last** proprio l'ultimo; **at the ~ least** almeno; **~ much** moltissimo
vessel ['vɛsl] *n* (*ANAT*) vaso; (*NAUT*) nave *f*; (*container*) recipiente *m*
vest [vɛst] *n* (*BRIT*) maglia; (: *sleeveless*) canottiera; (*US: waistcoat*) gilè *m inv*
vested interests ['vɛstɪd-] *npl* (*COMM*) diritti *mpl* acquisiti
vet [vɛt] *n abbr* (*BRIT*: = *veterinary surgeon*) veterinario ♦ *vt* esaminare minuziosamente
veteran ['vɛtərn] *n* (*also: war ~*) veterano
veterinary ['vɛtrɪnərɪ] *adj* veterinario(a); **~ surgeon** (*US* **veterinarian**) *n* veterinario
veto ['viːtəu] (*pl* **~es**) *n* veto ♦ *vt* opporre il veto a
vex [vɛks] *vt* irritare, contrariare; **~ed** *adj* (*question*) controverso(a), dibattuto(a)
via [vaɪə] *prep* (*by way of*) via; (*by means of*) tramite
viable ['vaɪəbl] *adj* attuabile; vitale
viaduct ['vaɪədʌkt] *n* viadotto
vibrant ['vaɪbrənt] *adj* (*lively, bright*) vivace; (*voice*) vibrante
vibrate [vaɪ'breɪt] *vi*: **to ~ (with)** vibrare (di); (*resound*) risonare (di)
vicar ['vɪkə*] *n* pastore *m*; **~age** *n* presbiterio
vicarious [vɪ'kɛərɪəs] *adj* indiretto(a)
vice [vaɪs] *n* (*evil*) vizio; (*TECH*) morsa
vice- [vaɪs] *prefix* vice...
vice squad *n* (squadra del) buon costume *f*
vice versa ['vaɪsɪ'vəːsə] *adv* viceversa
vicinity [vɪ'sɪnɪtɪ] *n* vicinanze *fpl*
vicious ['vɪʃəs] *adj* (*remark, dog*) cattivo(a); (*blow*) violento(a); **~ circle** *n* circolo vizioso
victim ['vɪktɪm] *n* vittima
victor ['vɪktə*] *n* vincitore *m*
Victorian [vɪk'tɔːrɪən] *adj* vittoriano(a)
victory ['vɪktərɪ] *n* vittoria
video ['vɪdɪəu] *cpd* video... ♦ *n* (~ *film*) video *m inv*; (*also*: ~ *cassette*) videocassetta; (*also*: ~ *cassette recorder*) videoregistratore *m*; **~ tape** *n* videotape *m inv*; **~ wall** *n* schermo *m* multivideo *inv*
vie [vaɪ] *vi*: **to ~ with** competere con, rivaleggiare con
Vienna [vɪ'ɛnə] *n* Vienna
Vietnam [vjɛt'næm] *n* Vietnam *m*; **~ese** *adj*, *n inv* vietnamita *m/f*

view [vjuː] *n* vista, veduta; (*opinion*) opinione *f* ♦ *vt* (*look at: also fig*) considerare; (*house*) visitare; **on ~** (*in museum etc*) esposto(a); **in full ~ of** sotto gli occhi di; **in ~ of the weather/the fact that** considerato il tempo/ che; **in my ~** a mio parere; **~er** *n* spettatore/ trice; **~finder** *n* mirino; **~point** *n* punto di vista; (*place*) posizione *f*
vigil ['vɪdʒɪl] *n* veglia
vigorous ['vɪɡərəs] *adj* vigoroso(a)
vile [vaɪl] *adj* (*action*) vile; (*smell*) disgustoso(a), nauseante; (*temper*) pessimo(a)
villa ['vɪlə] *n* villa
village ['vɪlɪdʒ] *n* villaggio; **~r** *n* abitante *m/f* di villaggio
villain ['vɪlən] *n* (*scoundrel*) canaglia; (*BRIT: criminal*) criminale *m*; (*in novel etc*) cattivo
vindicate ['vɪndɪkeɪt] *vt* comprovare; giustificare
vindictive [vɪn'dɪktɪv] *adj* vendicativo(a)
vine [vaɪn] *n* vite *f*; (*climbing plant*) rampicante *m*
vinegar ['vɪnɪɡə*] *n* aceto
vineyard ['vɪnjɑːd] *n* vigna, vigneto
vintage ['vɪntɪdʒ] *n* (*year*) annata, produzione *f* ♦ *cpd* d'annata; **~ car** *n* auto *f inv* d'epoca; **~ wine** *n* vino d'annata
vinyl ['vaɪnl] *n* vinile *m*
violate ['vaɪəleɪt] *vt* violare
violence ['vaɪələns] *n* violenza
violent ['vaɪələnt] *adj* violento(a)
violet ['vaɪələt] *adj* (*colour*) viola *inv*, violetto(a) ♦ *n* (*plant*) violetta; (*colour*) violetto
violin [vaɪə'lɪn] *n* violino; **~ist** *n* violinista *m/f*
VIP *n abbr* (= *very important person*) V.I.P. *m/f inv*
virgin ['vəːdʒɪn] *n* vergine *f* ♦ *adj* vergine *inv*
Virgo ['vəːɡəu] *n* (*sign*) Vergine *f*
virile ['vɪraɪl] *adj* virile
virtually ['vəːtjuəlɪ] *adv* (*almost*) praticamente
virtual reality ['vəːtʃuəl -] *n* (*COMPUT*) realtà virtuale
virtue ['vəːtjuː] *n* virtù *f inv*; (*advantage*) pregio, vantaggio; **by ~ of** grazie a
virtuous ['vəːtjuəs] *adj* virtuoso(a)
virus ['vaɪərəs] *n* (*also COMPUT*) virus *m inv*
visa ['viːzə] *n* visto
vis-à-vis [viːzə'viː] *prep* rispetto a, nei riguardi di
visibility [vɪzɪ'bɪlɪtɪ] *n* visibilità
visible ['vɪzəbl] *adj* visibile
vision ['vɪʒən] *n* (*sight*) vista; (*foresight, in dream*) visione *f*
visit ['vɪzɪt] *n* visita; (*stay*) soggiorno ♦ *vt* (*person: US also:* ~ *with*) andare a trovare; (*place*) visitare; **~ing hours** *npl* (*in hospital*

etc) orario delle visite; **~or** *n* visitatore/trice; (*guest*) ospite *m/f*; **~or centre** *n* centro informazioni per visitatori di museo, zoo, parco ecc

visor ['vaɪzə*] *n* visiera

visual ['vɪzjuəl] *adj* visivo(a); visuale; ottico(a); **~ aid** *n* sussidio visivo; **~ display unit** *n* visualizzatore *m*

visualize ['vɪzjuəlaɪz] *vt* immaginare, figurarsi, (*foresee*) prevedere

visually-impaired ['vɪzjuəlɪ-] *adj* videoleso(a)

vital ['vaɪtl] *adj* vitale; **~ly** *adv* estremamente; **~ statistics** *npl* (*fig*) misure *fpl*

vitamin ['vɪtəmɪn] *n* vitamina

vivacious [vɪ'veɪʃəs] *adj* vivace

vivid ['vɪvɪd] *adj* vivido(a); **~ly** *adv* (*describe*) vividamente; (*remember*) con precisione

V-neck ['viːnɛk] *n* maglione *m* con lo scollo a V

vocabulary [vəu'kæbjulərɪ] *n* vocabolario

vocal ['vəukl] *adj* (*MUS*) vocale; (*communication*) verbale; **~ cords** *npl* corde *fpl* vocali

vocation [vəu'keɪʃən] *n* vocazione *f*; **~al** *adj* professionale

vociferous [və'sɪfərəs] *adj* rumoroso(a)

vodka ['vɔdkə] *n* vodka *f inv*

vogue [vəug] *n* moda; (*popularity*) popolarità, voga

voice [vɔɪs] *n* voce *f* ♦ *vt* (*opinion*) esprimere; **~ mail** *n* servizio di segreteria telefonica

void [vɔɪd] *n* vuoto ♦ *adj* (*invalid*) nullo(a); (*empty*): **~ of** privo(a) di

volatile ['vɔlətaɪl] *adj* volatile; (*fig*) volubile

volcano [vɔl'keɪnəu] (*pl* **~es**) *n* vulcano

volition [və'lɪʃən] *n*: **of one's own ~** di sua volontà

volley ['vɔlɪ] *n* (*of gunfire*) salva; (*of stones, questions etc*) raffica; (*TENNIS etc*) volata; **~ball** *n* pallavolo *f*

volt [vəult] *n* volt *m inv*; **~age** *n* tensione *f*, voltaggio

voluble ['vɔljubl] *adj* loquace

volume ['vɔljuːm] *n* volume *m*

voluntarily ['vɔləntrɪlɪ] *adv* volontariamente; gratuitamente

voluntary ['vɔləntərɪ] *adj* volontario(a); (*unpaid*) gratuito(a), non retribuito(a)

volunteer [vɔlən'tɪə*] *n* volontario/a ♦ *vt* offrire volontariamente ♦ *vi* (*MIL*) arruolarsi volontario; **to ~ to do** offrire (volontariamente) di fare

voluptuous [və'lʌptjuəs] *adj* voluttuoso(a)

vomit ['vɔmɪt] *n* vomito ♦ *vt*, *vi* vomitare

vote [vəut] *n* voto, suffragio; (*cast*) voto; (*franchise*) diritto di voto ♦ *vt*: **to be ~d chairman** *etc* venir eletto presidente *etc*; (*propose*): **to ~ that** approvare la proposta

che ♦ *vi* votare; **~ of thanks** discorso di ringraziamento; **~r** *n* elettore/trice; **voting** *n* scrutinio

vouch [vautʃ]: **to ~ for** *vt fus* farsi garante di

voucher ['vautʃə*] *n* (*for meal, petrol etc*) buono

vow [vau] *n* voto, promessa solenne ♦ *vt*: **to ~ to do/that** giurare di fare/che

vowel ['vauəl] *n* vocale *f*

voyage ['vɔɪdʒ] *n* viaggio per mare, traversata

V-sign ['viː-] (*BRIT*) *n* gesto volgare con le dita

vulgar ['vʌlgə*] *adj* volgare

vulnerable ['vʌlnərəbl] *adj* vulnerabile

vulture ['vʌltʃə*] *n* avvoltoio

W, w

wad [wɔd] *n* (*of cotton wool, paper*) tampone *m*; (*of banknotes etc*) fascio

waddle ['wɔdl] *vi* camminare come una papera

wade [weɪd] *vi*: **to ~ through** camminare a stento in; (*fig: book*) leggere con fatica

wafer ['weɪfə*] *n* (*CULIN*) cialda

waffle ['wɔfl] *n* (*CULIN*) cialda; (*inf*) ciance *fpl* ♦ *vi* cianciare

waft [wɔft] *vt* portare ♦ *vi* diffondersi

wag [wæg] *vt* agitare, muovere ♦ *vi* agitarsi

wage [weɪdʒ] *n* (*also*: **~s**) salario, paga ♦ *vt*: **to ~ war** fare la guerra; **~ earner** *n* salariato/a; **~ packet** *n* busta *f* paga *inv*

wager ['weɪdʒə*] *n* scommessa

wag(g)on ['wægən] *n* (*horse-drawn*) carro; (*BRIT: RAIL*) vagone *m* (merci)

wail [weɪl] *n* gemito; (*of siren*) urlo ♦ *vi* gemere; urlare

waist [weɪst] *n* vita, cintola; **~coat** (*BRIT*) *n* panciotto, gilè *m inv*; **~line** *n* (giro di) vita

wait [weɪt] *n* attesa ♦ *vi* aspettare, attendere; **to lie in ~ for** stare in agguato a; **to ~ for** aspettare; **I can't ~ to** (*fig*) non vedo l'ora di; **~ behind** *vi* rimanere (ad aspettare); **~ on** *vt fus* servire; **~er** *n* cameriere *m*; **~ing** *n*: "**no ~ing**" (*BRIT: AUT*) "divieto di sosta"; **~ing list** *n* lista di attesa; **~ing room** *n* sala d'aspetto *or* d'attesa; **~ress** *n* cameriera

waive [weɪv] *vt* rinunciare a, abbandonare

wake [weɪk] (*pt* **woke**, **~d**, *pp* **woken**, **~d**) *vt* (*also*: **~ up**) svegliare ♦ *vi* (*also*: **~ up**) svegliarsi ♦ *n* (*for dead person*) veglia funebre; (*NAUT*) scia; **waken** *vt*, *vi* = **wake**

Wales [weɪlz] *n* Galles *m*

walk [wɔːk] *n* passeggiata; (*short*) giretto; (*gait*) passo, andatura; (*path*) sentiero; (*in park etc*) sentiero, vialetto ♦ *vi* camminare; (*for pleasure, exercise*) passeggiare ♦ *vt* (*distance*) fare *or* percorrere a piedi; (*dog*) accompagnare, portare a passeggiare; **10 minutes' ~ from** 10 minuti di cammino *or* a piedi da; **from all ~s of life** di tutte le condizioni sociali; **~ out** *vi* (*audience*) andarsene; (*workers*) scendere in sciopero; **~ out on** (*inf*) *vt fus* piantare in asso; **~er** *n* (*person*) camminatore/trice; **~ie-talkie** ['wɔːkɪ'tɔːkɪ] *n* walkie-talkie *m inv*; **~ing** *n* camminare *m*; **~ing shoes** *npl* pedule *fpl*; **~ing stick** *n* bastone *m* da passeggio; **W~man** ® ['wɔːkmən] *n* Walkman ® *m inv*; **~out** *n* (*of workers*) sciopero senza preavviso *or* a sorpresa; **~over** (*inf*) *n* vittoria facile, gioco da ragazzi; **~way** *n* passaggio pedonale

wall [wɔːl] *n* muro; (*internal, of tunnel, cave*) parete *f*; **~ed** *adj* (*city*) fortificato(a); (*garden*) cintato(a)

wallet ['wɔlɪt] *n* portafoglio

wallflower ['wɔːlflauə*] *n* violacciocca; **to be a ~** (*fig*) fare da tappezzeria

wallow ['wɔləu] *vi* sguazzare

wallpaper ['wɔːlpeɪpə*] *n* carta da parati ♦ *vt* (*room*) mettere la carta da parati in

wally ['wɔlɪ] (*inf*) *n* imbecille *m/f*

walnut ['wɔːlnʌt] *n* noce *f*; (*tree, wood*) noce *m*

walrus ['wɔːlrəs] (*pl ~ or ~es*) *n* tricheco

waltz [wɔːlts] *n* valzer *m inv* ♦ *vi* ballare il valzer

wand [wɔnd] *n* (*also: magic ~*) bacchetta (magica)

wander ['wɔndə*] *vi* (*person*) girare senza meta, girovagare; (*thoughts*) vagare ♦ *vt* girovagare per

wane [weɪn] *vi* calare

wangle ['wæŋgl] (*BRIT: inf*) *vt* procurare con l'astuzia

want [wɔnt] *vt* volere; (*need*) aver bisogno di ♦ *n*: **for ~ of** per mancanza di; **~s** *npl* (*needs*) bisogni *mpl*; **to ~ to do** volere fare; **to ~ sb to do** volere che qn faccia; **~ed** *adj* (*criminal*) ricercato(a); **"~ed"** (*in adverts*) "cercasi"; **~ing** *adj*: **to be found ~ing** non risultare all'altezza

war [wɔː*] *n* guerra; **to make ~ (on)** far guerra (a)

ward [wɔːd] *n* (*in hospital: room*) corsia; (: *section*) reparto; (*POL*) circoscrizione *f*; (*LAW: child: also: ~ of court*) pupillo/a; **~ off** *vt* parare, schivare

warden ['wɔːdn] *n* (*of park, game reserve, youth hostel*) guardiano/a; (*BRIT: of institution*) direttore/trice; (*BRIT: also: traffic ~*) addetto/a al controllo del traffico e del parcheggio

warder ['wɔːdə*] (*BRIT*) *n* guardia carceraria

wardrobe ['wɔːdrəub] *n* (*cupboard*) guardaroba *m inv*, armadio; (*clothes*) guardaroba; (*CINEMA, THEATRE*) costumi *mpl*

warehouse ['weəhaus] *n* magazzino

wares [weəz] *npl* merci *fpl*

warfare ['wɔːfeə*] *n* guerra

warhead ['wɔːhed] *n* (*MIL*) testata

warily ['weərɪlɪ] *adv* cautamente, con prudenza

warlike ['wɔːlaɪk] *adj* bellicoso(a)

warm [wɔːm] *adj* caldo(a); (*thanks, welcome, applause*) caloroso(a); (*person*) cordiale; **it's ~** fa caldo; **I'm ~** ho caldo; **~ up** *vi* scaldarsi, riscaldarsi ♦ *vt* scaldare, riscaldare; (*engine*) far scaldare; **~-hearted** *adj* affettuoso(a); **~ly** *adv* (*applaud, welcome*) calorosamente; (*dress*) con abiti pesanti; **~th** *n* calore *m*

warn [wɔːn] *vt*: **to ~ sb that/(not) to do/of** avvertire *or* avvisare qn che/di (non) fare/di; **~ing** *n* avvertimento; (*notice*) avviso; (*signal*) segnalazione *f*; **~ing light** *n* spia luminosa; **~ing triangle** *n* (*AUT*) triangolo

warp [wɔːp] *vi* deformarsi ♦ *vt* (*fig*) corrompere

warrant ['wɔrnt] *n* (*voucher*) buono; (*LAW: to arrest*) mandato di cattura; (: *to search*) mandato di perquisizione

warranty ['wɔrəntɪ] *n* garanzia

warren ['wɔrən] *n* (*of rabbits*) tana; (*fig: of streets etc*) dedalo

warrior ['wɔrɪə*] *n* guerriero/a

Warsaw ['wɔːsɔː] *n* Varsavia

warship ['wɔːʃɪp] *n* nave *f* da guerra

wart [wɔːt] *n* verruca

wartime ['wɔːtaɪm] *n*: **in ~** in tempo di guerra

wary ['weərɪ] *adj* prudente

was [wɔz] *pt of* **be**

wash [wɔʃ] *vt* lavare ♦ *vi* lavarsi; (*sea*): **to ~ over/against sth** infrangersi su/contro qc ♦ *n* lavaggio; (*of ship*) scia; **to give sth a ~** lavare qc, dare una lavata a qc; **to have a ~** lavarsi; **~ away** *vt* (*stain*) togliere lavando; (*subj: river*) trascinare via; **~ off** *vi* andare via con il lavaggio; **~ up** *vi* (*BRIT*) lavare i piatti; (*US*) darsi una lavata; **~able** *adj* lavabile; **~basin** (*US* **~bowl**) *n* lavabo; **~cloth** (*US*) *n* pezzuola (per lavarsi); **~er** *n* (*TECH*) rondella; **~ing** *n* (*linen etc*) bucato; **~ing machine** *n* lavatrice *f*; **~ing powder** (*BRIT*) *n* detersivo (in polvere)

Washington ['wɔʃɪŋtən] *n* Washington *f*

wash: ~ing up *n* rigovernatura, lavatura dei piatti; **~ing-up liquid** *n* detersivo liquido (per stoviglie); **~-out** (*inf*) *n* disastro; **~room** *n* gabinetto

wasn't ['wɔznt] = **was not**

wasp [wɔsp] *n* vespa

wastage ['weɪstɪdʒ] *n* spreco; (*in manufacturing*) scarti *mpl*; **natural ~** diminuzione *f* di manodopera (*per pensionamento, decesso etc*)

waste [weɪst] n spreco; (of time) perdita; (rubbish) rifiuti mpl; (also: household ~) immondizie fpl ♦ adj (material) di scarto; (food) avanzato(a); (land) incolto(a) ♦ vt sprecare; ~s npl (area of land) distesa desolata; ~ **away** vi deperire; ~ **disposal unit** (BRIT) n eliminatore m di rifiuti; ~ful adj sprecone(a); (process) dispendioso(a); ~ **ground** (BRIT) n terreno incolto or abbandonato; ~**paper basket** n cestino per la carta straccia; ~**pipe** n tubo di scarico

watch [wɔtʃ] n (also: wrist ~) orologio (da polso); (act of watching, vigilance) sorveglianza; (guard: MIL, NAUT) guardia; (NAUT: spell of duty) quarto ♦ vt (look at) osservare; (: match, programme) guardare; (spy on, guard) sorvegliare, tenere d'occhio; (be careful of) fare attenzione a ♦ vi osservare, guardare; (keep guard) fare or montare la guardia; ~ **out** vi fare attenzione; ~**dog** n (also fig) cane m da guardia; ~**ful** adj attento(a), vigile; ~**maker** n orologiaio/a; ~**man** (irreg) n see night; ~ **strap** n cinturino da orologio

water ['wɔːtə*] n acqua ♦ vt (plant) annaffiare ♦ vi (eyes) lacrimare; (mouth): **to make sb's mouth ~** far venire l'acquolina in bocca a qn; **in British ~s** nelle acque territoriali britanniche; ~ **down** vt (milk) diluire; (fig: story) edulcorare; ~ **cannon** n idrante m; ~ **closet** (BRIT) n water m inv; ~**colour** n acquerello; ~**cress** n crescione m; ~**fall** n cascata; ~ **heater** n scaldabagno; ~**ing can** n annaffiatoio; ~ **lily** n ninfea; ~**line** n (NAUT) linea di galleggiamento; ~**logged** adj saturo(a) d'acqua; imbevuto(a) d'acqua; (football pitch etc) allagato(a); ~ **main** n conduttura dell'acqua; ~**melon** n anguria, cocomero; ~**proof** adj impermeabile; ~**shed** n (GEO, fig) spartiacque m; ~-**skiing** n sci m acquatico; ~**tight** adj stagno(a); ~**way** n corso d'acqua navigabile; ~**works** npl impianto idrico; ~**y** adj (colour) slavato(a); (coffee) acquoso(a); (eyes) umido(a)

watt [wɔt] n watt m inv

wave [weɪv] n onda; (of hand) gesto, segno; (in hair) ondulazione f; (fig: surge) ondata ♦ vi fare un cenno con la mano; (branches, grass) ondeggiare; (flag) sventolare ♦ vt (hand) fare un gesto con; (handkerchief) sventolare; (stick) brandire; ~**length** n lunghezza d'onda

waver ['weɪvə*] vi esitare; (voice) tremolare

wavy ['weɪvɪ] adj ondulato(a); ondeggiante

wax [wæks] n cera ♦ vt dare la cera a; (car) lucidare ♦ vi (moon) crescere; ~**works** npl cere fpl ♦ n museo delle cere

way [weɪ] n via, strada; (path, access)

passaggio; (distance) distanza; (direction) parte f, direzione f; (manner) modo, stile m; (habit) abitudine f; **which ~? – this ~** da che parte or in quale direzione? – da questa parte or per di qua; **on the ~** (en route) per strada; **to be on one's ~** essere in cammino or sulla strada; **to be in the ~** bloccare il passaggio; (fig) essere tra i piedi or d'impiccio; **to go out of one's ~ to do** (fig) mettercela tutta or fare di tutto per fare; **under ~** (project) in corso; **to lose one's ~** perdere la strada; **in a ~** in un certo senso; **in some ~s** sotto certi aspetti; **no ~!** (inf) neanche per idea!; **by the ~ ...** a proposito ...; **"~ in"** (BRIT) "entrata", "ingresso"; **"~ out"** (BRIT) "uscita"; **the ~ back** la strada del ritorno; **"give ~"** (BRIT: AUT) "dare la precedenza"

waylay [weɪ'leɪ] (irreg: like lay) vt tendere un agguato a; attendere al passaggio

wayward ['weɪwəd] adj capriccioso(a); testardo(a)

W.C. ['dʌblju'siː] (BRIT) n W.C. m inv, gabinetto

we [wiː] pl pron noi

weak [wiːk] adj debole; (health) precario(a); (beam etc) fragile; (tea) leggero(a); ~**en** vi indebolirsi ♦ vt indebolire; ~**ling** ['wiːklɪŋ] n smidollato/a; debole m/f; ~**ness** n debolezza; (fault) punto debole, difetto; **to have a ~ness for** avere un debole per

wealth [welθ] n (money, resources) ricchezza, ricchezze fpl; (of details) abbondanza, profusione f; ~**y** adj ricco(a)

wean [wiːn] vt svezzare

weapon ['wepən] n arma

wear [weə*] (pt wore, pp worn) n (use) uso; (damage through use) logorio, usura; (clothing): **sports/baby ~** abbigliamento sportivo/per neonati ♦ vt (clothes) portare; (put on) mettersi; (damage: through use) consumare ♦ vi (last) durare; (rub etc through) consumarsi; **evening ~** abiti mpl or tenuta da sera; ~ **away** vt consumare; erodere ♦ vi consumarsi; essere eroso(a); ~ **down** vt consumare; (strength) esaurire; ~ **off** vi sparire lentamente; ~ **out** vt consumare; (person, strength) esaurire; ~ **and tear** n usura, consumo

weary ['wɪərɪ] adj stanco(a) ♦ vi: **to ~ of** stancarsi di

weasel ['wiːzl] n (ZOOL) donnola

weather ['weðə*] n tempo ♦ vt (storm, crisis) superare; **under the ~** (fig: ill) poco bene; ~-**beaten** adj (face, skin) segnato(a) dalle intemperie; (building) logorato(a) dalle intemperie; ~**cock** n banderuola; ~ **forecast** n previsioni fpl del tempo, bollettino meteorologico; ~**man** (irreg inf) n meteorologo; ~ **vane** n = ~**cock**

weave [wiːv] (pt **wove**, pp **woven**) vt (cloth) tessere; (basket) intrecciare; **~r** n tessitore/trice; **weaving** n tessitura

web [wɛb] n (of spider) ragnatela; (on foot) palma; (fabric, also fig) tessuto; **the (World Wide) W~** la Rete; **~site** n (COMPUT) sito (Internet)

wed [wɛd] (pt, pp **wedded**) vt sposare ♦ vi sposarsi

we'd [wiːd] = **we had**; **we would**

wedding ['wɛdɪŋ] n matrimonio; **silver/golden ~ (anniversary)** n nozze fpl d'argento/d'oro; **~ day** n giorno delle nozze or del matrimonio; **~ dress** n abito nuziale; **~ ring** n fede f

wedge [wɛdʒ] n (of wood etc) zeppa; (of cake) fetta ♦ vt (fix) fissare con zeppe; (pack tightly) incastrare

Wednesday ['wɛnzdɪ] n mercoledì m inv

wee [wiː] (SCOTTISH) adj piccolo(a)

weed [wiːd] n erbaccia ♦ vt diserbare; **~killer** n diserbante m; **~y** adj (person) allampanato(a)

week [wiːk] n settimana; **a ~ today/on Friday** oggi/venerdì a otto; **~day** n giorno feriale; (COMM) giornata lavorativa; **~end** n fine settimana m or f inv; **weekend** m inv; **~ly** adv ogni settimana, settimanalmente ♦ adj settimanale ♦ n settimanale m

weep [wiːp] (pt, pp **wept**) vi (person) piangere; **~ing willow** n salice m piangente

weigh [weɪ] vt, vi pesare; **to ~ anchor** salpare l'ancora; **~ down** vt (branch) piegare; (fig: with worry) opprimere, caricare; **~ up** vt valutare

weight [weɪt] n peso; **to lose/put on ~** dimagrire/ingrassare; **~ing** n (allowance) indennità; **~ lifter** n pesista m; **~y** adj pesante; (fig) importante, grave

weir [wɪə*] n diga

weird [wɪəd] adj strano(a), bizzarro(a); (eerie) soprannaturale

welcome ['wɛlkəm] adj benvenuto(a) ♦ n accoglienza, benvenuto ♦ vt dare il benvenuto a; (be glad of) rallegrarsi di; **thank you – you're ~!** grazie – prego!

weld [wɛld] n saldatura ♦ vt saldare

welfare ['wɛlfɛə*] n benessere m; **~ state** n stato assistenziale

well [wɛl] n pozzo ♦ adv bene ♦ adj: **to be ~** (person) stare bene ♦ excl allora!; ma!; ebbene!; **as ~** anche; **as ~ as** così come; oltre a; **~ done!** bravo(a)!; **get ~ soon!** guarisci presto!; **to do ~** andare bene; **~ up** vi sgorgare

we'll [wiːl] = **we will**; **we shall**

well: **~-behaved** adj ubbidiente; **~-being** n benessere m; **~-built** adj (person) ben fatto(a); **~-deserved** adj meritato(a); **~-**

dressed adj ben vestito(a), vestito(a) bene; **~-heeled** (inf) adj agiato(a), facoltoso(a)

wellingtons ['wɛlɪŋtənz] npl (also: wellington boots) stivali mpl di gomma

well: **~-known** adj noto(a), famoso(a); **~-mannered** adj ben educato(a); **~-meaning** adj ben intenzionato(a); **~-off** adj benestante, danaroso(a); **~-read** adj colto(a); **~-to-do** adj abbiente, benestante; **~-wisher** n ammiratore/trice

Welsh [wɛlʃ] adj gallese ♦ n (LING) gallese m; **the ~** npl i Gallesi; **~ Assembly** n Parlamento gallese; **~man/woman** (irreg) n gallese m/f; **~ rarebit** n crostino al formaggio

went [wɛnt] pt of go

wept [wɛpt] pt, pp of weep

were [wəː*] pt of be

we're [wɪə*] = **we are**

weren't [wəːnt] = **were not**

west [wɛst] n ovest m, occidente m, ponente m ♦ adj (a) ovest inv, occidentale ♦ adv verso ovest; **the W~** l'Occidente m; **the W~ Country** (BRIT) n il sud-ovest dell'Inghilterra; **~erly** adj (point) a ovest; (wind) occidentale, da ovest; **~ern** adj occidentale, dell'ovest ♦ n (CINEMA) western m inv; **W~ Germany** n Germania Occidentale; **W~ Indian** adj delle Indie Occidentali ♦ n abitante m/f delle Indie Occidentali; **W~ Indies** npl Indie fpl Occidentali; **~ward(s)** adv verso ovest

wet [wɛt] adj umido(a), bagnato(a); (soaked) fradicio(a); (rainy) piovoso(a) ♦ n (BRIT: POL) politico moderato; **to get ~** bagnarsi; **"~ paint"** "vernice fresca"; **~ suit** n tuta da sub

we've [wiːv] = **we have**

whack [wæk] vt picchiare, battere

whale [weɪl] n (ZOOL) balena

wharf [wɔːf] (pl **wharves**) n banchina

wharves [wɔːvz] npl of wharf

KEYWORD

---

what [wɔt] adj **1** (in direct/indirect questions) che; quale; **~ size is it?** che taglia è?; **~ colour is it?** di che colore è?; **~ books do you want?** quali or che libri vuole?

2 (in exclamations) che; **~ a mess!** che disordine!

♦ pron **1** (interrogative) che cosa, cosa, che; **~ are you doing?** che or (che) cosa fai?; **~ are you talking about?** di che cosa parli?; **~ is it called?** come si chiama?; **~ about me?** e io?; **~ about doing ...?** e se facessimo ...?

2 (relative) ciò che, quello che; **I saw ~ you did/was on the table** ho visto quello che hai fatto/quello che era sul tavolo

3 (indirect use) (che) cosa; **he asked me ~ she had said** mi ha chiesto che cosa avesse

detto; **tell me ~ you're thinking about** dimmi a cosa stai pensando
♦ *excl* (*disbelieving*) cosa!, come!

whatever [wɔt'ɛvə*] *adj*: ~ **book** qualunque *or* qualsiasi libro + *sub* ♦ *pron*: **do ~ is necessary/you want** faccia qualunque *or* qualsiasi cosa sia necessaria/lei voglia; ~ **happens** qualunque cosa accada; **no reason** *or* ~ **whatsoever** nessuna ragione affatto *or* al mondo; **nothing ~** proprio niente

whatsoever [wɔtsəu'ɛvə*] *adj* = **whatever**

wheat [wiːt] *n* grano, frumento

wheedle ['wiːdl] *vt*: **to ~ sb into doing sth** convincere qn a fare qc (con lusinghe); **to ~ sth out of sb** ottenere qc da qn (con lusinghe)

wheel [wiːl] *n* ruota; (*AUT*: *also*: steering ~) volante *m*; (*NAUT*) (ruota del) timone *m* ♦ *vt* spingere ♦ *vi* (*birds*) roteare; (*also*: ~ round) girare; **~barrow** *n* carriola; **~chair** *n* sedia a rotelle; **~ clamp** *n* (*AUT*) morsa che blocca la ruota di una vettura in sosta vietata

wheeze [wiːz] *vi* ansimare

KEYWORD

when [wɛn] *adv* quando, ~ **did it happen?** quando è successo?
♦ *conj* **1** (*at, during, after the time that*) quando; **she was reading ~ I came in** quando sono entrato lei leggeva; **that was ~ I needed you** era allora che avevo bisogno di te
2 (*on, at which*): **on the day ~ I met him** il giorno in cui l'ho incontrato; **one day ~ it was raining** un giorno che pioveva
3 (*whereas*) quando, mentre; **you said I was wrong ~ in fact I was right** mi hai detto che avevo torto, quando in realtà avevo ragione

---

whenever [wɛn'ɛvə*] *adv* quando mai ♦ *conj* quando; (*every time that*) ogni volta che

where [wɛə*] *adv, conj* dove; **this is ~** è qui che; **~abouts** *adv* dove ♦ *n*: **sb's ~abouts** luogo dove qn si trova; **~as** *conj* mentre; **~by** *pron* per cui; **wherever** [-'ɛvə*] *conj* dovunque + *sub*; (*interrogative*) dove mai; **~withal** *n* mezzi *mpl*

whet [wɛt] *vt* (*appetite etc*) stimolare

whether ['wɛðə*] *conj* se; **I don't know ~ to accept or not** non so se accettare o no; **it's doubtful ~** è poco probabile che; **~ you go or not** che lei vada o no

---

KEYWORD

which [wɪtʃ] *adj* **1** (*interrogative: direct, indirect*) quale; ~ **picture do you want?** quale quadro vuole?; ~ **one?** quale?; ~ **one of you did it?** chi di voi lo ha fatto?
2: **in ~ case** nel qual caso

♦ *pron* **1** (*interrogative*) quale; ~ (**of these**) **are yours?** quali di questi sono suoi?; ~ **of you are coming?** chi di voi viene?
2 (*relative*) che; (: *indirect*) cui, il (la) quale; **the apple ~ you ate/~ is on the table** la mela che hai mangiato/che è sul tavolo; **the chair on ~ you are sitting** la sedia sulla quale *or* su cui sei seduto; **he said he knew, ~ is true** ha detto che lo sapeva, il che è vero; **after ~** dopo di che

---

whichever [wɪtʃ'ɛvə*] *adj*: **take ~ book you prefer** prenda qualsiasi libro che preferisce; ~ **book you take** qualsiasi libro prenda

whiff [wɪf] *n* soffio; sbuffo; odore *m*

while [waɪl] *n* momento ♦ *conj* mentre; (*as long as*) finché; (*although*) sebbene + *sub*; per quanto + *sub*; **for a ~** per un po'; ~ **away** *vt* (*time*) far passare

whim [wɪm] *n* capriccio

whimper ['wɪmpə*] *n* piagnucolio ♦ *vi* piagnucolare

whimsical ['wɪmzɪkl] *adj* (*person*) capriccioso(a); (*look*) strano(a)

whine [waɪn] *n* gemito ♦ *vi* gemere; uggiolare; piagnucolare

whip [wɪp] *n* frusta; (*for riding*) frustino; (*POL: person*) capogruppo (*che sovrintende alla disciplina dei colleghi di partito*) ♦ *vt* frustare; (*cream, eggs*) sbattere; **~ped cream** *n* panna montata; **~-round** (*BRIT*) *n* colletta

whirl [wəːl] *vt* (far) girare rapidamente; (far) turbinare ♦ *vi* (*dancers*) volteggiare; (*leaves, water*) sollevarsi in vortice; **~pool** *n* mulinello; **~wind** *n* turbine *m*

whirr [wəː*] *vi* ronzare; rombare; frullare

whisk [wɪsk] *n* (*CULIN*) frusta; frullino ♦ *vt* sbattere, frullare; **to ~ sb away** *or* **off** portar via qn a tutta velocità

whiskers ['wɪskəz] *npl* (*of animal*) baffi *mpl*; (*of man*) favoriti *mpl*

whisky ['wɪskɪ] (*US, IRELAND* **whiskey**) *n* whisky *m inv*

whisper ['wɪspə*] *n* sussurro ♦ *vt, vi* sussurrare

whist [wɪst] *n* whist *m*

whistle ['wɪsl] *n* (*sound*) fischio; (*object*) fischietto ♦ *vi* fischiare

white [waɪt] *adj* bianco(a); (*with fear*) pallido(a) ♦ *n* bianco; (*person*) bianco/a; ~ **coffee** (*BRIT*) *n* caffellatte *m inv*; **~-collar worker** *n* impiegato; ~ **elephant** *n* (*fig*) oggetto (*or* progetto) costoso ma inutile; **W~ House** *n* Casa Bianca; ~ **lie** *n* bugia pietosa; **~ness** *n* bianchezza; ~ **paper** *n* (*POL*) libro bianco; **~wash** *n* (*paint*) bianco di calce ♦ *vt* imbiancare; (*fig*) coprire

whiting ['waɪtɪŋ] *n inv* (*fish*) merlango

Whitsun ['wɪtsn] *n* Pentecoste *f*

whittle ['wɪtl] vt: to ~ away, ~ down ridurre, tagliare

whizz [wɪz] vi: to ~ past or by passare sfrecciando; ~ kid (inf) n prodigio

who [hu:] pron 1 (interrogative) chi; ~ is it?, ~'s there? chi è?
2 (relative) che; the man ~ spoke to me l'uomo che ha parlato con me; those ~ can swim quelli che sanno nuotare

whodunit [hu:'dʌnɪt] (inf) n giallo

whoever [hu:'evə*] pron: ~ finds it chiunque lo trovi; ask ~ you like lo chieda a chiunque vuole; ~ she marries chiunque sposerà, non importa chi sposerà; ~ told you that? chi mai gliel'ha detto?

whole [həul] adj (complete) tutto(a), completo(a); (not broken) intero(a), intatto(a) ♦ n (all): the ~ of tutto(a) il(la); (entire unit) tutto; (not broken) tutto; the ~ of the town tutta la città, la città intera; on the ~, as a ~ nel complesso, nell'insieme; ~ food(s) n(pl) cibo integrale; ~hearted adj sincero(a); ~meal adj (bread, flour) integrale; ~sale n commercio or vendita all'ingrosso ♦ adj all'ingrosso; (destruction) totale; ~saler n grossista m/f; ~some adj sano(a); salutare; ~wheat adj = ~meal; wholly adv completamente, del tutto

whom [hu:m] pron 1 (interrogative) chi; ~ did you see? chi hai visto?; to ~ did you give it? a chi lo hai dato?
2 (relative) che, prep +il (la) quale (check syntax of Italian verb used); the man ~ I saw/ to ~ I spoke l'uomo che ho visto/al quale ho parlato

whooping cough ['hu:pɪŋ-] n pertosse f

whore [hɔ:*] (inf: pej) n puttana

whose [hu:z] adj 1 (possessive: interrogative) di chi; ~ book is this?, ~ is this book? di chi è questo libro?; ~ daughter are you? di chi sei figlia?
2 (possessive: relative): the man ~ son you rescued l'uomo il cui figlio hai salvato; the girl ~ sister you were speaking to la ragazza alla cui sorella stavi parlando
♦ pron di chi; ~ is this? di chi è questo?; I know ~ it is so di chi è

why [waɪ] adv, conj perché ♦ excl (surprise) ma guarda un po'!; (remonstrating) ma (via)!; (explaining) ebbene!; ~ not? perché

no?; ~ not do it now? perché non farlo adesso?; that's not ~ I'm here non è questo il motivo per cui sono qui; the reason ~ il motivo per cui; ~ever adv perché mai

wicked ['wɪkɪd] adj cattivo(a), malvagio(a); maligno(a); perfido(a)

wickerwork ['wɪkəwə:k] adj di vimini ♦ n articoli mpl di vimini

wicket ['wɪkɪt] n (CRICKET) porta; area tra le due porte

wide [waɪd] adj largo(a); (area, knowledge) vasto(a); (choice) ampio(a) ♦ adv: to open ~ spalancare; to shoot ~ tirare a vuoto or fuori bersaglio; ~-angle lens n grandangolare m; ~-awake adj completamente sveglio(a); ~ly adv (differing) molto, completamente; (travelled, spaced) molto; (believed) generalmente; ~n vt allargare, ampliare; ~ open adj spalancato(a); ~spread adj (belief etc) molto or assai diffuso(a)

widow ['wɪdəu] n vedova; ~ed adj: to be ~ed restare vedovo(a); ~er n vedovo

width [wɪdθ] n larghezza

wield [wi:ld] vt (sword) maneggiare; (power) esercitare

wife [waɪf] (pl wives) n moglie f

wig [wɪg] n parrucca

wiggle ['wɪgl] vt dimenare, agitare

wild [waɪld] adj selvatico(a); selvaggio(a); (sea, weather) tempestoso(a); (idea, life) folle; stravagante; (applause) frenetico(a); ~s npl regione f selvaggia; ~erness ['wɪldənɪs] n deserto; ~life n natura; ~ly adv selvaggiamente; (applaud) freneticamente; (hit, guess) a casaccio; (happy) follemente

wilful ['wɪlful] (US willful) adj (person) testardo(a), ostinato(a); (action) intenzionale; (crime) premeditato(a)

will [wɪl] (pt, pp ~ed) aux vb 1 (forming future tense): I ~ finish it tomorrow lo finirò domani; I ~ have finished it by tomorrow lo finirò entro domani; ~ you do it? – yes I ~/no I won't lo farai? – sì (lo farò)/no (non lo farò)
2 (in conjectures, predictions): he ~ or he'll be there by now dovrebbe essere arrivato ora; that ~ be the postman sarà il postino
3 (in commands, requests, offers): ~ you be quiet! vuoi stare zitto?; ~ you come? vieni anche tu?; ~ you help me? mi aiuti?, mi puoi aiutare?; ~ you have a cup of tea? vorrebbe una tazza di tè?; I won't put up with it! non lo accetterò!
♦ vt: to ~ sb to do volere che qn faccia; he ~ed himself to go on continuò grazie a un grande sforzo di volontà
♦ n volontà; testamento

willful ['wɪlful] (US) adj = wilful

willing ['wɪlɪŋ] adj volonteroso(a); ~ **to do**
disposto(a) a fare; **~ly** adv volentieri; **~ness**
n buona volontà

willow ['wɪləu] n salice m

will power n forza di volontà

willy-nilly ['wɪlɪ'nɪlɪ] adv volente o nolente

wilt [wɪlt] vi appassire

win [wɪn] (pt, pp **won**) n (in sports etc) vittoria
♦ vt (battle, prize, money) vincere; (popularity) conquistare ♦ vi vincere; ~ **over** vt
convincere; ~ **round** (BRIT) vt convincere

wince [wɪns] vi trasalire

winch [wɪntʃ] n verricello, argano

wind¹ [waɪnd] (pt, pp **wound**) vt attorcigliare;
(wrap) avvolgere; (clock, toy) caricare ♦ vi
(road, river) serpeggiare; ~ **up** vt (clock)
caricare; (debate) concludere

wind² [wɪnd] n vento; (MED) flatulenza;
(breath) respiro, fiato ♦ vt (take breath away)
far restare senza fiato; ~ **power** energia
eolica; **~fall** n (money) guadagno insperato

winding ['waɪndɪŋ] adj (road) serpeggiante;
(staircase) a chiocciola

wind instrument n (MUS) strumento a
fiato

windmill ['wɪndmɪl] n mulino a vento

window ['wɪndəu] n finestra; (in car, train)
finestrino; (in shop etc) vetrina; (also:
~ **pane**) vetro; ~ **box** n cassetta da fiori;
~ **cleaner** n (person) pulitore m di finestre;
~ **envelope** n busta a finestra; ~ **ledge** n
davanzale m; ~ **pane** n vetro; **~-shopping**
n: **to go ~-shopping** andare a vedere le
vetrine; **~sill** n davanzale m

windpipe ['wɪndpaɪp] n trachea

windscreen ['wɪndskriːn] n parabrezza m
inv; ~ **washer** n lavacristallo; ~ **wiper** n
tergicristallo

windshield ['wɪndʃiːld] (US) n = windscreen

windswept ['wɪndswɛpt] adj spazzato(a) dal
vento

windy ['wɪndɪ] adj ventoso(a); **it's ~** c'è vento

wine [waɪn] n vino; ~ **bar** n enoteca (per
degustazione); ~ **cellar** n cantina; ~ **glass** n
bicchiere m da vino; ~ **list** n lista dei vini;
~ **merchant** n commerciante m di vini;
~ **tasting** n degustazione f dei vini;
~ **waiter** n sommelier m inv

wing [wɪŋ] n ala; (AUT) fiancata; **~s** npl
(THEATRE) quinte fpl; **~er** n (SPORT) ala

wink [wɪŋk] n ammiccamento ♦ vi
ammiccare, fare l'occhiolino; (light)
baluginare

winner ['wɪnə*] n vincitore/trice

winning ['wɪnɪŋ] adj (team, goal) vincente;
(smile) affascinante; **~s** npl vincite fpl

winter ['wɪntə*] n inverno; ~ **sports** npl
sport mpl invernali

wintry ['wɪntrɪ] adj invernale

wipe [waɪp] n pulita, passata ♦ vt pulire
(strofinando); (erase: tape) cancellare; ~ **off**
vt cancellare; (stains) togliere strofinando;
~ **out** vt (debt) pagare, liquidare; (memory)
cancellare; (destroy) annientare; ~ **up** vt
asciugare

wire ['waɪə*] n filo; (ELEC) filo elettrico; (TEL)
telegramma m ♦ vt (house) fare l'impianto
elettrico di; (also: ~ **up**) collegare, allacciare;
(person) telegrafare a

wireless ['waɪəlɪs] (BRIT) n (set) (apparecchio
m) radio f inv

wiring ['waɪərɪŋ] n impianto elettrico

wiry ['waɪərɪ] adj magro(a) e nerboruto(a);
(hair) ispido(a)

wisdom ['wɪzdəm] n saggezza; (of action)
prudenza; ~ **tooth** n dente m del giudizio

wise [waɪz] adj saggio(a); prudente;
giudizioso(a)

...wise [waɪz] suffix: **time~** per quanto
riguarda il tempo, in termini di tempo

wish [wɪʃ] n (desire) desiderio; (specific desire)
richiesta ♦ vt desiderare, volere; **with best ~es**
(in letter) cordiali saluti, con i migliori saluti;
to ~ sb goodbye dire arrivederci a qn; **he ~ed
me well** mi augurò di riuscire; **to ~ to do/sb
to do** desiderare o volere fare/che qn faccia;
to ~ for desiderare; **~ful** adj: **it's ~ful thinking**
è prendere i desideri per realtà

wishy-washy ['wɪʃɪ'wɔʃɪ] (inf) adj (colour)
slavato(a); (ideas, argument) insulso(a)

wisp [wɪsp] n ciuffo, ciocca; (of smoke) filo

wistful ['wɪstful] adj malinconico(a)

wit [wɪt] n (also: **~s**) intelligenza; presenza di
spirito; (wittiness) spirito, arguzia; (person)
bello spirito

witch [wɪtʃ] n strega

KEYWORD

---

with [wɪð, wɪθ] prep **1** (in the company of)
con; **I was ~ him** ero con lui; **we stayed
~ friends** siamo stati da amici; **I'll be ~ you in
a minute** vengo subito

2 (descriptive) con; **a room ~ a view** una
stanza con vista sul mare (or sulle montagne
etc); **the man ~ the grey hat/blue eyes** l'uomo
con il cappello grigio/gli occhi blu

3 (indicating manner, means, cause): ~ **tears
in her eyes** con le lacrime agli occhi; **red
~ anger** rosso dalla rabbia; **to shake ~ fear**
tremare di paura

4: **I'm ~ you** (I understand) la seguo; **to be
~ it** (inf: up-to-date) essere alla moda; (: alert)
essere sveglio(a)

---

withdraw [wɪθ'drɔː] (irreg: like draw) vt
ritirare; (money from bank) ritirare; prelevare

♦ *vi* ritirarsi; **~al** *n* ritiro; prelievo; (*of army*) ritirata; **~al symptoms** (*MED*) crisi *f* di astinenza; **~n** *adj* (*person*) distaccato(a)

wither ['wɪðə*] *vi* appassire

withhold [wɪθ'həuld] (*irreg: like* **hold**) *vt* (*money*) trattenere; (*permission*): **to ~ (from)** rifiutare (a); (*information*): **to ~ (from)** nascondere (a)

within [wɪð'ɪn] *prep* all'interno, (*in time, distances*) entro ♦ *adv* all'interno, dentro; **~ reach (of)** alla portata (di); **~ sight (of)** in vista (di); **~ a mile of** entro un miglio da; **~ the week** prima della fine della settimana

without [wɪð'aut] *prep* senza; **to go ~ sth** fare a meno di qc

withstand [wɪθ'stænd] (*irreg: like* **stand**) *vt* resistere a

witness ['wɪtnɪs] *n* (*person, also LAW*) testimone *m/f* ♦ *vt* (*event*) essere testimone di; (*document*) attestare l'autenticità di; **~ box** (*US* **~ stand**) *n* banco dei testimoni

witticism ['wɪtɪsɪzm] *n* spiritosaggine *f*

witty ['wɪtɪ] *adj* spiritoso(a)

wives [waɪvz] *npl of* **wife**

wizard ['wɪzəd] *n* mago

wk *abbr* = **week**

wobble ['wɔbl] *vi* tremare; (*chair*) traballare

woe [wəu] *n* dolore *m*; disgrazia

woke [wəuk] *pt of* **wake**; **woken** *pp of* **wake**

wolf [wulf] (*pl* **wolves**) *n* lupo

wolves [wulvz] *npl of* **wolf**

woman ['wumən] (*pl* **women**) *n* donna; **~ doctor** *n* dottoressa; **women's lib** (*inf*) *n* movimento femminista

womb [wuːm] *n* (*ANAT*) utero

women ['wɪmɪn] *npl of* **woman**

won [wʌn] *pt, pp of* **win**

wonder ['wʌndə*] *n* meraviglia ♦ *vi*: **to ~ whether/why** domandarsi se/perché; **to ~ at** essere sorpreso(a) di; meravigliarsi di; **to ~ about** domandarsi di; pensare a; **it's no ~ that** c'è poco *or* non c'è da meravigliarsi che + *sub*; **~ful** *adj* meraviglioso(a)

won't [wəunt] = **will not**

wood [wud] *n* legno; (*timber*) legname *m*; (*forest*) bosco; **~ carving** *n* scultura in legno, intaglio; **~ed** *adj* boschivo(a); boscoso(a); **~en** *adj* di legno; (*fig*) rigido(a); inespressivo(a); **~pecker** *n* picchio; **~wind** *npl* (*MUS*): **the ~wind** i legni; **~work** *n* (*craft, subject*) falegnameria; **~worm** *n* tarlo del legno

wool [wul] *n* lana; **to pull the ~ over sb's eyes** (*fig*) imbrogliare qn; **~len** (*US* **~en**) *adj* di lana; (*industry*) laniero(a); **~lens** *npl* indumenti *mpl* di lana; **~ly** (*US* **~y**) *adj* di lana; (*fig: ideas*) confuso(a)

word [wəːd] *n* parola; (*news*) notizie *fpl* ♦ *vt* esprimere, formulare; **in other ~s** in altre parole; **to break/keep one's ~** non mantenere/mantenere la propria parola; **to have ~s with sb** avere un diverbio con qn; **~ing** *n* formulazione *f*; **~ processing** *n* elaborazione *f* di testi, word processing *m*; **~ processor** *n* word processor *m inv*

wore [wɔː*] *pt of* **wear**

work [wəːk] *n* lavoro; (*ART, LITERATURE*) opera ♦ *vi* lavorare; (*mechanism, plan etc*) funzionare; (*medicine*) essere efficace ♦ *vt* (*clay, wood etc*) lavorare; (*mine etc*) sfruttare; (*machine*) far funzionare; (*cause: effect, miracle*) fare; **to be out of ~** essere disoccupato(a); **~s** *n* (*BRIT: factory*) fabbrica ♦ *npl* (*of clock, machine*) meccanismo; **to ~ loose** allentarsi; **~ on** *vt fus* lavorare a; (*person*) lavorarsi; (*principle*) basarsi su; **~ out** *vi* (*plans etc*) riuscire, andare bene ♦ *vt* (*problem*) risolvere; (*plan*) elaborare; **it ~s out at £100** fa 100 sterline; **~ up** *vt*: **to get ~ed up** andare su tutte le furie; **~able** *adj* (*solution*) realizzabile; **~aholic** *n* maniaco/a del lavoro; **~er** *n* lavoratore/trice, operaio/a; **~force** *n* forza lavoro; **~ing class** *n* classe *f* operaia; **~ing-class** *adj* operaio(a); **~ing order** *n*: **in ~ing order** funzionante; **~man** (*irreg*) *n* operaio; **~manship** *n* abilità; **~sheet** *n* foglio col programma di lavoro; **~shop** *n* officina; (*practical session*) gruppo di lavoro; **~ station** *n* stazione *f* di lavoro; **~-to-rule** (*BRIT*) *n* sciopero bianco

world [wəːld] *n* mondo ♦ *cpd* (*champion*) del mondo; (*power, war*) mondiale; **to think the ~ of sb** (*fig*) pensare un gran bene di qn; **~ly** *adj* di questo mondo; (*knowledgeable*) di mondo; **~-wide** *adj* universale; **W~-Wide Web** *n* World Wide Web *m*

worm [wəːm] *n* (*also: earth~*) verme *m*

worn [wɔːn] *pp of* **wear** ♦ *adj* usato(a); **~-out** *adj* (*object*) consumato(a), logoro(a); (*person*) sfinito(a)

worried ['wʌrɪd] *adj* preoccupato(a)

worry ['wʌrɪ] *n* preoccupazione *f* ♦ *vt* preoccupare ♦ *vi* preoccuparsi

worse [wəːs] *adj* peggiore ♦ *adv*, *n* peggio; **a change for the ~** un peggioramento; **~n** *vt, vi* peggiorare; **~ off** *adj* in condizioni (economiche) peggiori

worship ['wəːʃɪp] *n* culto ♦ *vt* (*God*) adorare, venerare; (*person*) adorare; **Your W~** (*BRIT: to mayor*) signor sindaco; (: *to judge*) signor giudice

worst [wəːst] *adj* il(la) peggiore ♦ *adv*, *n* peggio; **at ~** al peggio, per male che vada

worth [wəːθ] *n* valore *m* ♦ *adj*: **to be ~** valere; **it's ~** it ne vale la pena; **it is ~ one's while (to do)** vale la pena (fare); **~less** *adj* di nessun valore; **~while** *adj* (*activity*) utile; (*cause*) lodevole

worthy ['wə:ði] adj (person) degno(a); (motive) lodevole; **~ of** degno di

---
KEYWORD
---

would [wud] aux vb 1 (conditional tense): **if you asked him he ~ do it** se glielo chiedesse lo farebbe; **if you had asked him he ~ have done it** se glielo avesse chiesto lo avrebbe fatto
2 (in offers, invitations, requests): **~ you like a biscuit?** vorrebbe or vuole un biscotto?; **~ you ask him to come in?** lo faccia entrare, per cortesia; **~ you open the window please?** apra la finestra, per favore
3 (in indirect speech): **I said I ~ do it** ho detto che l'avrei fatto
4 (emphatic): **it WOULD have to snow today!** doveva proprio nevicare oggi!
5 (insistence): **she ~n't do it** non ha voluto farlo
6 (conjecture): **it ~ have been midnight** sarà stato mezzanotte; **it ~ seem so** sembrerebbe proprio di sì
7 (indicating habit): **he ~ go there on Mondays** andava lì ogni lunedì

---

would-be ['wudbi:] (pej) adj sedicente
wouldn't ['wudnt] = would not
wound[1] [waund] pt, pp of **wind**[1]
wound[2] [wu:nd] n ferita ♦ vt ferire
wove [wəuv] pt of **weave**; **woven** pp of weave
wrangle ['ræŋgl] n litigio
wrap [ræp] vt avvolgere; (pack: also: ~ up) incartare; **~per** n (on chocolate) carta; (BRIT: of book) copertina; **~ping paper** n carta da pacchi; (for gift) carta da regali
wreak [ri:k] vt (havoc) portare, causare; **to ~ vengeance on** vendicarsi su
wreath [ri:θ, pl ri:ðz] n corona
wreck [rɛk] n (sea disaster) naufragio; (ship) relitto m (pej: person) rottame m ♦ vt demolire; (ship) far naufragare; (fig) rovinare; **~age** n rottami mpl; (of building) macerie fpl; (of ship) relitti mpl
wren [rɛn] n (ZOOL) scricciolo
wrench [rɛntʃ] n (TECH) chiave f; (tug) torsione f brusca; (fig) strazio ♦ vt strappare; storcere; **to ~ sth from** strappare qc a or da
wrestle ['rɛsl] vi: **to ~ (with sb)** lottare (con qn); **~r** n (pej) lottatore/trice; **wrestling** n lotta
wretched ['rɛtʃid] adj disgraziato(a); (inf: weather, holiday) orrendo(a), orribile; (: child, dog) pestifero(a)
wriggle ['rɪgl] vi (also: ~ about) dimenarsi; (: snake, worm) serpeggiare, muoversi serpeggiando
wring [rɪŋ] (pt, pp **wrung**) vt torcere; (wet clothes) strizzare; (fig): **to ~ sth out of** strappare qc a

wrinkle ['rɪŋkl] n (on skin) ruga; (on paper etc) grinza ♦ vt (nose) torcere; (forehead) corrugare ♦ vi (skin, paint) raggrinzirsi
wrist [rɪst] n polso; **~watch** n orologio da polso
writ [rɪt] n ordine m; mandato
write [raɪt] (pt **wrote**, pp **written**) vt, vi scrivere; **~ down** vt annotare; (put in writing) mettere per iscritto; **~ off** vt (debt, plan) cancellare; **~ out** vt mettere per iscritto; (cheque, receipt) scrivere; **~ up** vt redigere; **~-off** n perdita completa; **~r** n autore/trice, scrittore/trice
writhe [raɪð] vi contorcersi
writing ['raɪtɪŋ] n scrittura; (of author) scritto, opera; **in ~** per iscritto; **~ paper** n carta da lettere
written ['rɪtn] pp of **write**
wrong [rɔŋ] adj sbagliato(a); (not suitable) inadatto(a); (wicked) cattivo(a); (unfair) ingiusto(a) ♦ adv in modo sbagliato, erroneamente ♦ n (injustice) torto ♦ vt fare torto a; **you are ~ to do it** ha torto a farlo; **you are ~ about that, you've got it ~** si sbaglia; **to be in the ~** avere torto; **what's ~?** cosa c'è che non va?; **to go ~** (person) sbagliarsi; (plan) fallire, non riuscire; (machine) guastarsi; **~ful** adj illegittimo(a); ingiusto(a); **~ly** adv (incorrectly, by mistake) in modo sbagliato; **~ number** n (TEL): **you've got the ~ number** ha sbagliato numero
wrote [rəut] pt of **write**
wrought iron [rɔ:t-] n ferro battuto
wrung [rʌŋ] pt, pp of **wring**
WWW n abbr (= World Wide Web): **the ~** la Rete

X, x

Xmas ['ɛksməs] n abbr = **Christmas**
X-ray ['ɛksreɪ] n raggio X; (photograph) radiografia ♦ vt radiografare
xylophone ['zaɪləfəun] n xilofono

Y, y

yacht [jɔt] n panfilo, yacht m inv; **~ing** n yachting m, sport m della vela
Yank [jæŋk] (pej) n yankee m/f inv
Yankee ['jæŋkɪ] (pej) n = **Yank**
yap [jæp] vi (dog) guaire
yard [jɑ:d] n (of house etc) cortile m; (measure) iarda (= 914 mm; 3 feet); **~stick** n (fig) misura, criterio
yarn [jɑ:n] n filato; (tale) lunga storia
yawn [jɔ:n] n sbadiglio ♦ vi sbadigliare; **~ing** adj (gap) spalancato(a)

yd. abbr = **yard(s)**

yeah [jɛə] (inf) adv sì

year [jɪə*] n anno; (referring to harvest, wine etc) annata; **he is 8 ~s old** ha 8 anni; **an eight-~-old child** un(a) bambino(a) di otto anni; **~ly** adj annuale ♦ adv annualmente

yearn [jə:n] vi: **to ~ for sth/to do** desiderare ardentemente qc/di fare

yeast [ji:st] n lievito

yell [jɛl] n urlo ♦ vi urlare

yellow ['jɛləu] adj giallo(a)

yelp [jɛlp] vi guaire, uggiolare

yeoman ['jəumən] n: **~ of the guard** guardiano della Torre di Londra

yes [jɛs] adv sì ♦ n sì m inv; **to say/answer ~** dire/rispondere di sì

yesterday ['jɛstədɪ] adv ieri ♦ n ieri m inv; **~ morning/evening** ieri mattina/sera; **all day ~** ieri per tutta la giornata

yet [jɛt] adv ancora; già ♦ conj ma, tuttavia; **it is not finished ~** non è ancora finito; **the best ~** finora il migliore; **as ~** finora

yew [ju:] n tasso (albero)

yield [ji:ld] n produzione f, resa; reddito ♦ vt produrre, rendere; (surrender) cedere ♦ vi cedere; (US: AUT) dare la precedenza

YMCA n abbr (= Young Men's Christian Association) Y.M.C.A. m

yoga ['jəugə] n yoga m

yog(h)ourt ['jəugət] n = **yog(h)urt**

yog(h)urt ['jəugət] n iogurt m inv

yoke [jəuk] n (also fig) giogo

yolk [jəuk] n tuorlo, rosso d'uovo

KEYWORD

you [ju:] pron **1** (subject) tu; (: polite form) lei; (: pl) voi; (: very formal) loro; **~ Italians enjoy your food** a voi Italiani piace mangiare bene; **~ and I will go** tu ed io or lei ed io andiamo **2** (object: direct) ti; la; vi; loro (after vb); (: indirect) ti; le; vi; loro (after vb); **I know ~** ti or la or vi conosco; **I gave it to ~** te l'ho dato; gliel'ho dato; ve l'ho dato; l'ho dato loro **3** (stressed, after prep, in comparisons) te; lei; voi; loro; **I told YOU to do it** ho detto a TE (or a LEI etc) di farlo; **she's younger than ~** è più giovane di te (or lei etc) **4** (impers: one) sì; **fresh air does ~ good** l'aria fresca fa bene; **~ never know** non si sa mai

you'd [ju:d] = **you had**; **you would**

you'll [ju:l] = **you will**; **you shall**

young [jʌŋ] adj giovane ♦ npl (of animal) piccoli mpl; (people): **the ~** i giovani, la gioventù; **~er** adj più giovane; (brother)

minore, più giovane; **~ster** n giovanotto, ragazzo; (child) bambino/a

your [jɔ:*] adj il(la) tuo(a), pl i(le) tuoi(tue); il(la) suo(a), pl i(le) suoi(sue); il(la) vostro(a), pl i(le) vostri(e); il(la) loro, pl i(le) loro; see also **my**

you're [juə*] = **you are**

yours [jɔ:z] pron il(la) tuo(a), pl i(le) tuoi(tue); (polite form) il(la) suo(a), pl i(le) suoi(sue); (pl) il(la) vostro(a), pl i(le) vostri(e); (: very formal) il(la) loro, pl i(le) loro; see also **mine; faithfully; sincerely**

yourself [jɔ:'sɛlf] pron (reflexive) ti; si; (after prep) te; sé; (emphatic) tu stesso(a); lei stesso(a); **yourselves** pl pron (reflexive) vi; si; (after prep) voi; loro; (emphatic) voi stessi(e); loro stessi(e); see also **oneself**

youth [ju:θ, pl ju:ðz] n gioventù f; (young man) giovane m, ragazzo; **~ club** n centro giovanile; **~ful** adj giovane; da giovane; giovanile; **~ hostel** n ostello della gioventù

you've [ju:v] = **you have**

Yugoslav ['ju:gəu'slɑ:v] adj, n jugoslavo(a)

Yugoslavia ['ju:gəu'slɑ:vɪə] n Jugoslavia

yuppie ['jʌpɪ] (inf) n, adj yuppie m/f inv

YWCA n abbr (= Young Women's Christian Association) Y.W.C.A. m

---

Z, z

zany ['zeɪnɪ] adj un po' pazzo(a)

zap [zæp] vt (COMPUT) cancellare

zeal [zi:l] n zelo; entusiasmo

zebra ['zi:brə] n zebra; **~ crossing** (BRIT) n (passaggio pedonale a) strisce fpl, zebre fpl

zero ['zɪərəu] n zero

zest [zɛst] n gusto; (CULIN) buccia

zigzag ['zɪgzæg] n zigzag m inv ♦ vi zigzagare

Zimbabwe [zɪm'bɑ:bwɪ] n Zimbabwe m

zinc [zɪŋk] n zinco

zip [zɪp] n (also: ~ fastener, (US) ~per) chiusura f or cerniera f lampo inv ♦ vt (also: ~ up) chiudere con una cerniera lampo; **~ code** (US) n codice m di avviamento postale

zodiac ['zəudɪæk] n zodiaco

zombie ['zɔmbɪ] n (fig): **like a ~** come un morto che cammina

zone [zəun] n (also MIL) zona

zoo [zu:] n zoo m inv

zoology [zu:'ɔlədʒɪ] n zoologia

zoom [zu:m] vi: **to ~ past** sfrecciare; **~ lens** n zoom m inv, obiettivo a focale variabile

zucchini [zu:'ki:nɪ] (US) npl (courgettes) zucchine fpl

ITALIAN VERBS

1 Gerundio 2 Participio passato 3 Presente 4 Imperfetto 5 Passato remoto
6 Futuro 7 Condizionale 8 Congiuntivo presente 9 Congiuntivo passato
10 Imperativo

andare 3 vado, vai, va, andiamo, andate, vanno 6 andrò *etc* 8 vada 10 va'!, vada!, andate!, vadano!

apparire 2 apparso 3 appaio, appari *o* apparisci, appare *o* apparisce, appaiono *o* appariscono 5 apparvi *o* apparsi, apparisti, apparve *o* apparì *o* apparse, apparvero *o* apparirono *o* apparsero 8 appaia *o* apparisca

aprire 2 aperto 3 apro 5 aprii *o* apersi, apristi 8 apra

AVERE 3 ho, hai, ha, abbiamo, avete, hanno 5 ebbi, avesti, ebbe, avemmo, aveste, ebbero 6 avrò *etc* 8 abbia *etc* 10 abbi!, abbia!, abbiate!, abbiano!

bere 1 bevendo 2 bevuto 3 bevo *etc* 4 bevevo *etc* 8 beva *etc* 9 bevessi *etc*

cadere 5 caddi, cadesti 6 cadrò *etc*

cogliere 2 colto 3 colgo, colgono 5 colsi, cogliesti 8 colga

correre 2 corso 5 corsi, corresti

cuocere 2 cotto 3 cuocio, cociamo, cuociono 5 cossi, cocesti

dare 3 do, dai, dà, diamo, date, danno 5 diedi *o* detti, desti 6 darò *etc* 8 dia *etc* 9 dessi *etc* 10 da'!, dia!, date!, diano!

dire 1 dicendo 2 detto 3 dico, dici, dice, diciamo, dite, dicono 4 dicevo *etc* 5 dissi, dicesti 6 dirò *etc* 8 dica, diciamo, diciate, dicano 9 dicessi *etc* 10 di'!, dica!, dite!, dicano!

dolere 3 dolgo, duoli, duole, dolgono 5 dolsi, dolesti 6 dorrò *etc* 8 dolga

dovere 3 devo *o* debbo, devi, deve, dobbiamo, dovete, devono *o* debbono 6 dovrò *etc* 8 debba, dobbiamo, dobbiate, devano *o* debbano

ESSERE 2 stato 3 sono, sei, è, siamo, siete, sono 4 ero, eri, era, eravamo, eravate, erano 5 fui, fosti, fu, fummo, foste, furono 6 sarò *etc* 8 sia *etc* 9 fossi, fossi, fosse, fossimo, foste, fossero 10 sii!, sia!, siate!, siano!

fare 1 facendo 2 fatto 3 faccio, fai, fa, facciamo, fate, fanno 4 facevo *etc* 5 feci, facesti 6 farò *etc* 8 faccia *etc* 9 facessi *etc* 10 fa'!, faccia!, fate!, facciano!

FINIRE 1 finendo 2 finito 3 finisco, finisci, finisce, finiamo, finite, finiscono 4 finivo, finivi, finiva, finivamo, finivate, finivano 5 finii, finisti, finì, finimmo, finiste, finirono 6 finirò, finirai, finirà, finiremo, finirete, finiranno 7 finirei, finiresti, finirebbe, finiremmo, finireste, finirebbero 8 finisca, finisca, finisca, finiamo, finiate, finiscano 9 finissi, finissi, finisse, finissimo, finiste, finissero 10 finisci!, finisca!, finite!, finiscano!

giungere 2 giunto 5 giunsi, giungesti

leggere 2 letto 5 lessi, leggesti

mettere 2 messo 5 misi, mettesti

morire 2 morto 3 muoio, muori, muore, moriamo, morite, muoiono 6 morirò *o* morrò *etc* 8 muoia

muovere 2 mosso 5 mossi, movesti

nascere 2 nato 5 nacqui, nascesti

nuocere 2 nuociuto 3 nuoccio, nuoci, nuoce, nociamo *o* nuociamo, nuocete, nuocciono 4 nuocevo *etc* 5 nocqui, nuocesti 6 nuocerò *etc* 7 nuoccia

offrire 2 offerto 3 offro 5 offersi *o* offrii, offristi 8 offra

parere 2 parso 3 paio, paiamo, paiono 5 parvi *o* parsi, paresti 6 parrò *etc* 8 paia, paiamo, paiate, paiano

PARLARE 1 parlando 2 parlato 3

parlo, parli, parla, parliamo, parlate, parlano 4 parlavo, parlavi, parlava, parlavamo, parlavate, parlavano 5 parlai, parlasti, parlò, parlammo, parlaste, parlarono 6 parlerò, parlerai, parlerà, parleremo, parlerete, parleranno 7 parlerei, parleresti, parlerebbe, parleremmo, parlereste, parlerebbero 8 parli, parli, parli, parliamo, parliate, parlino 9 parlassi, parlassi, parlasse, parlassimo, parlaste, parlassero 10 parla!, parli!, parlate!, parlino!

piacere 2 piaciuto 3 piaccio, piacciamo, piacciono 5 piacqui, piacesti 8 piaccia *etc*

porre 1 ponendo 2 posto 3 pongo, poni, pone, poniamo, ponete, pongono 4 ponevo *etc* 5 posi, ponesti 6 porrò *etc* 8 ponga, poniamo, poniate, pongano 9 ponessi *etc*

potere 3 posso, puoi, può, possiamo, potete, possono 6 potrò *etc* 8 possa, possiamo, possiate, possano

prendere 2 preso 5 presi, prendesti

ridurre 1 riducendo 2 ridotto 3 riduco *etc* 4 riducevo *etc* 5 ridussi, riducesti 6 ridurrò *etc* 8 riduca *etc* 9 riducessi *etc*

riempire 1 riempiendo 3 riempio, riempi, riempie, riempiono

rimanere 2 rimasto 3 rimango, rimangono 5 rimasi, rimanesti 6 rimarrò *etc* 8 rimanga

rispondere 2 risposto 5 risposi, rispondesti

salire 3 salgo, sali, salgono 8 salga

sapere 3 so, sai, sa, sappiamo, sapete, sanno 5 seppi, sapesti 6 saprò *etc* 8 sappia *etc* 10 sappi!, sappia!, sappiate!, sappiano!

scrivere 2 scritto 5 scrissi, scrivesti

sedere 3 siedo, siedi, siede, siedono 8 sieda

spegnere 2 spento 3 spengo, spengono 5 spensi, spegnesti 8 spenga

stare 2 stato 3 sto, stai, sta, stiamo, state, stanno 5 stetti, stesti 6 starò *etc* 8 stia *etc* 9 stessi *etc* 10 sta'!, stia!, state!, stiano!

tacere 2 taciuto 3 taccio, tacciono 5 tacqui, tacesti 8 taccia

tenere 3 tengo, tieni, tiene, tengono 5 tenni, tenesti 6 terrò *etc* 8 tenga

trarre 1 traendo 2 tratto 3 traggo, trai, trae, traiamo, traete, traggono 4 traevo *etc* 5 trassi, traesti 6 trarrò *etc* 8 tragga 9 traessi *etc*

udire 3 odo, odi, ode, odono 8 oda

uscire 3 esco, esci, esce, escono 8 esca

valere 2 valso 3 valgo, valgono 5 valsi, valesti 6 varrò *etc* 8 valga

vedere 2 visto *o* veduto 5 vidi, vedesti 6 vedrò *etc*

VENDERE 1 vendendo 2 venduto 3 vendo, vendi, vende, vendiamo, vendete, vendono 4 vendevo, vendevi, vendeva, vendevamo, vendevate, vendevano 5 vendei *o* vendetti, vendesti, vendé *o* vendette, vendemmo, vendeste, venderono *o* vendettero 6 venderò, venderai, venderà, venderemo, venderete, venderanno 7 venderei, venderesti, venderebbe, venderemmo, vendereste, venderebbero 8 venda, venda, venda, vendiamo, vendiate, vendano 9 vendessi, vendessi, vendesse, vendessimo, vendeste, vendessero 10 vendi!, venda!, vendete!, vendano!

venire 2 venuto 3 vengo, vieni, viene, vengono 5 venni, venisti 6 verrò *etc* 8 venga

vivere 2 vissuto 5 vissi, vivesti

volere 3 voglio, vuoi, vuole, vogliamo, volete, vogliono 5 volli, volesti 6 vorrò *etc* 8 voglia *etc* 10 vogli!, voglia!, vogliate!, vogliano!

VERBI INGLESI

present	pt	pp	present	pt	pp
arise	arose	arisen	dream	dreamed,	dreamed,
awake	awoke	awaked		dreamt	dreamt
be (am,	was, were	been	drink	drank	drunk
is, are;			drive	drove	driven
being)			dwell	dwelt	dwelt
bear	bore	born(e)	eat	ate	eaten
beat	beat	beaten	fall	fell	fallen
become	became	become	feed	fed	fed
begin	began	begun	feel	felt	felt
behold	beheld	beheld	fight	fought	fought
bend	bent	bent	find	found	found
beset	beset	beset	flee	fled	fled
bet	bet,	bet,	fling	flung	flung
	betted	betted	fly (flies)	flew	flown
bid	bid, bade	bid,	forbid	forbade	forbidden
		bidden	forecast	forecast	forecast
bind	bound	bound	forget	forgot	forgotten
bite	bit	bitten	forgive	forgave	forgiven
bleed	bled	bled	forsake	forsook	forsaken
blow	blew	blown	freeze	froze	frozen
break	broke	broken	get	got	got, (US)
breed	bred	bred			gotten
bring	brought	brought	give	gave	given
build	built	built	go (goes)	went	gone
burn	burnt,	burnt,	grind	ground	ground
	burned	burned	grow	grew	grown
burst	burst	burst	hang	hung,	hung,
buy	bought	bought		hanged	hanged
can	could	(been	have	had	had
		able)	(has;		
cast	cast	cast	having)		
catch	caught	caught	hear	heard	heard
choose	chose	chosen	hide	hid	hidden
cling	clung	clung	hit	hit	hit
come	came	come	hold	held	held
cost	cost	cost	hurt	hurt	hurt
creep	crept	crept	keep	kept	kept
cut	cut	cut	kneel	knelt,	knelt,
deal	dealt	dealt		kneeled	kneeled
dig	dug	dug	know	knew	known
do (3rd	did	done	lay	laid	laid
person;			lead	led	led
he/she/			lean	leant,	leant,
it/ does)				leaned	leaned
draw	drew	drawn	leap	leapt,	leapt,

present	pt	pp	present	pt	pp
	leaped	leaped	sink	sank	sunk
learn	learnt, learned	learnt, learned	sit	sat	sat
			slay	slew	slain
leave	left	left	sleep	slept	slept
lend	lent	lent	slide	slid	slid
let	let	let	sling	slung	slung
lie (lying)	lay	lain	slit	slit	slit
			smell	smelt, smelled	smelt, smelled
light	lit, lighted	lit, lighted	sow	sowed	sown, sowed
lose	lost	lost			
make	made	made	speak	spoke	spoken
may	might	—	speed	sped, speeded	sped, speeded
mean	meant	meant			
meet	met	met	spell	spelt, spelled	spelt, spelled
mistake	mistook	mistaken			
mow	mowed	mown, mowed	spend	spent	spent
			spill	spilt, spilled	spilt, spilled
must	(had to)	(had to)			
pay	paid	paid	spin	spun	spun
put	put	put	spit	spat	spat
quit	quit, quitted	quit, quitted	split	split	split
			spoil	spoiled, spoilt	spoiled, spoilt
read	read	read			
rid	rid	rid	spread	spread	spread
ride	rode	ridden	spring	sprang	sprung
ring	rang	rung	stand	stood	stood
rise	rose	risen	steal	stole	stolen
run	ran	run	stick	stuck	stuck
saw	sawed	sawn	sting	stung	stung
say	said	said	stink	stank	stunk
see	saw	seen	stride	strode	stridden
seek	sought	sought	strike	struck	struck, stricken
sell	sold	sold			
send	sent	sent	strive	strove	striven
set	set	set	swear	swore	sworn
shake	shook	shaken	sweep	swept	swept
shall	should	—	swell	swelled	swollen, swelled
shear	sheared	shorn, sheared			
			swim	swam	swum
shed	shed	shed	swing	swung	swung
shine	shone	shone	take	took	taken
shoot	shot	shot	teach	taught	taught
show	showed	shown	tear	tore	torn
shrink	shrank	shrunk	tell	told	told
shut	shut	shut	think	thought	thought
sing	sang	sung	throw	threw	thrown

432

present	pt	pp	present	pt	pp
thrust	thrust	thrust	wed	wedded, wed	wedded, wed
tread	trod	trodden			
wake	woke, waked	woken, waked	weep	wept	wept
			win	won	won
wear	wore	worn	wind	wound	wound
weave	wove, weaved	woven, weaved	wring	wrung	wrung
			write	wrote	written